P9-DMX-841

ENCYCLOPEDIA OF HUMAN EVOLUTION AND PREHISTORY

Garland Reference Library of the Humanities
(Vol. 768)

ENCYCLOPEDIA OF HUMAN EVOLUTION AND PREHISTORY

Edited by

Ian Tattersall
American Museum of Natural History

Eric Delson
Lehman College, City University of New York
American Museum of Natural History

John Van Couvering
American Museum of Natural History

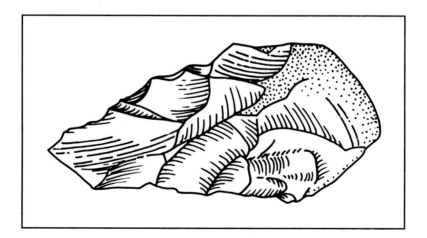

GARLAND PUBLISHING
NEW YORK & LONDON 1988

For

Andrea,
Bobbie,
and
Enid

and to the memory of

Nicholas Amorosi
who contributed so much to the
visual quality of this book

Library of Congress Cataloging-in-Publication Data

Encyclopedia of human evolution and prehistory.

(Garland reference library of the humanities ;
vol. 768)
1. Human evolution—Dictionaries.   2. Man,
Prehistoric—Dictionaries.   I. Tattersall, Ian.
II. Delson, Eric.   III. Van Couvering, John A.
IV. Series: Garland reference library of the
humanities ; v. 768.
GN281.E53   1988   573.2′03′21   87-23761
ISBN 0-8240-9375-5

Printed on acid-free, 250-year-life paper

MANUFACTURED IN THE UNITED STATES OF AMERICA

CONTENTS

PREFACE

The intense media coverage of new developments in human evolutionary studies testifies eloquently that to our egocentric species no subject is of greater interest than our own past. Yet up to now no comprehensive encyclopedia dealing with the evolution of humankind has been available. In the hope of providing such a source we have worked with our contributors and with Garland Publishing, Inc., to produce the present volume. We have defined human evolution in its broadest sense and so have covered such areas as systematics, evolutionary theory, genetics, primatology, primate paleontology, and Paleolithic archaeology in an attempt to provide the most complete context possible for the understanding of the human fossil record.

The contributions in this volume are written to be accessible to those with no prior knowledge of the subject, yet they contain sufficient detail to be of value as a resource to both students and professionals. The work should prove useful to the widest possible range of individuals interested in human evolution. Each entry has been prepared by a leading authority on its subject; and although every contributor was asked to represent all major points of view on the many topics that are the matter of dispute, each was left free to expound his or her preferred interpretation. The volume thus samples the heterogeneity of opinion that gives paleoanthropology so much of its liveliness, while remaining both authoritative and comprehensive.

We would like to thank our contributors for their efforts to ensure accuracy and comprehensiveness within the space limitations inevitable in a work of this kind. The project originated through the initiative of Gary Kuris, of Garland Publishing, whose enthusiasm and diligence were indispensable in seeing it through to completion. At Garland we would also like to thank Rita Quintas, Kennie Lyman, John M-Röblin, and Phyllis Korper. The late Nicholas Amorosi provided numerous clear renderings of fossils, artifacts, and prehistoric scenes and was responsible for a substantial part of the artwork in this volume. We are also indebted to the numerous other scientific illustrators who contributed to the visual qualities of the book. Jaymie Brauer helped with many editorial matters, as did David Dean; we are grateful to them both.

CONTRIBUTORS

Dr. Peter Andrews [P.A.]
Department of Palaeontology
British Museum (Natural History)

Dr. Raymond L. Bernor [R.L.B.]
Department of Anatomy
Howard University College of Medicine

Dr. Alison Brooks [A.S.B.]
Department of Anthropology
George Washington University

Dr. Frank H. Brown [F.H.B.]
Department of Geology
University of Utah

Dr. Bruce Byland [B.B.]
Department of Anthropology
Lehman College

Dr. Eric Delson [E.D.]
Department of Vertebrate Paleontology
American Museum of Natural History
and Department of Anthropology
Lehman College
and Graduate School
City University of New York

Dr. C. Jean de Rousseau [C.J.D.]
Department of Anthropology
New York University

Dr. Darryl P. Domning [D.P.D.]
Department of Anatomy
Howard University College of Medicine

Dr. Niles Eldredge [N.E.]
Department of Invertebrates
American Museum of Natural History

Dr. John G. Fleagle [J.G.F.]
Department of Anatomical Sciences
State University of New York at Stony Brook

Dr. Fred E. Grine [F.E.G.]
Department of Anthropology
State University of New York at Stony Brook

Dr. Andrew Hill [A.H.]
Department of Anthropology
Yale University

Dr. Ralph L. Holloway [R.L.H.]
Department of Anthropology
Columbia University

Dr. Richard F. Kay [R.F.K.]
Department of Anatomy
Duke University

Dr. Carol Kramer [C.K.]
Department of Anthropology
Lehman College

Dr. George Kukla [G.K.]
Lamont-Doherty Geological Observatory
of Columbia University

Dr. Jeffrey T. Laitman [J.T.L.]
Department of Anatomy
Mt. Sinai School of Medicine

Dr. Leslie Marcus [L.F.M.]
Department of Invertebrates
American Museum of Natural History
and Department of Biology
Queens College

Dr. Jon Marks [J.M.]
Department of Anthropology
Yale University

Mr. Alexander Marshack [A.M.]
New York City

Dr. John F. Oates [J.F.O.]
Department of Anthropology
Hunter College
and Anthropology Program
Graduate School
City University of New York

Dr. Todd R. Olson [T.R.O.]
Department of Anatomical Sciences
City University of New York Medical School
and Anthropology Program
Graduate School
City University of New York

Lorann S.A. Pendleton [L.S.A.P.]
Department of Anthropology
American Museum of Natural History

Dr. Geoffrey G. Pope [G.G.P.]
Department of Anthropology
University of Illinois

Dr. Richard Potts [R.P.]
Department of Anthropology
National Museum of Natural History

Dr. Philip Rightmire [G.P.R.]
Department of Anthropology
State University of New York at Binghamton

Dr. Alfred L. Rosenberger [A.L.R.]
Department of Anthropology
University of Illinois at Chicago

Dr. Kathy Schick [K.S.]
Department of Anthropology
Indiana University

Dr. Jeffrey H. Schwartz [J.H.S.]
Department of Anthropology
University of Pittsburgh

Dr. Brian T. Shea [B.T.S.]
Department of Anthropology
Northwestern University

Dr. Olga Soffer-Bobyshev [O.S.]
Department of Anthropology
University of Illinois

Dr. Frank Spencer [F.S.]
Department of Anthropology
Queens College

Dr. Christopher B. Stringer [C.B.S.]
Department of Palaeontology
British Museum (Natural History)

Dr. Frederick S. Szalay [F.S.S.]
Department of Anthropology
Hunter College
and Anthropology Program
Graduate School
City University of New York

Dr. Ian Tattersall [I.T.]
Department of Anthropology
American Museum of Natural History

Dr. David H. Thomas [D.H.T.]
Department of Anthropology
American Museum of Natural History

Dr. Nick Toth [N.T.]
Department of Anthropology
Indiana University

Dr. John A. Van Couvering [J.A.V.C.]
Micropaleontology Press
American Museum of Natural History

Dr. Frances J. White [F.J.W.]
Duke University Primate Center

Dr. Tim D. White [T.D.W.]
Department of Anthropology
University of California

HOW TO USE THIS BOOK

The *Encyclopedia of Human Evolution and Prehistory* is alphabetically arranged, with over 1,200 topic headings. About half of these are cross-references to articles that deal with the subject concerned and are provided to serve as an index. Referring to the entry for PROPLIOPITHECUS, for instance, will yield cross-references to FAYUM and PROPLIOPITHECIDAE, the entries in which this early catarrhine primate is discussed; looking up PUNCTUATED EQUILIBRIUM produces a cross-reference to EVOLUTION. To help readers locate topic headings relevant to a given area the "Subject List by Topic" cites headings by general subject, each following a major category heading. These major headings (e.g. EVOLUTIONARY BIOLOGY or HUMAN FOSSILS) are listed alphabetically; the order of the topic headings that follow may be either alphabetical or chronological, and in some cases such headings are listed both ways.

In addition each entry supplies cross-references to other articles in the volume that bear on the subject in question. Despite the unavoidable overlap among articles dealing with related subjects readers should consult all entries thus indicated to be certain of obtaining full information.

Paleoanthropology is a science in which there is unanimity of opinion on few areas, and we have not tried to impose a common view upon our contributors. There are thus cases in which articles by different contributors put forward different views of the same questions; such cases are not examples of editorial inconsistency but rather reflect the fact that paleoanthropology harbors a legitimate variety of interpretations in virtually every one of its subfields. It is this variety, indeed, that lends the study of human evolution its particular fascination.

The "Brief Introduction to Human Evolution and Prehistory" provides an alternative way of determining the headings under which information may be sought. This introduction briefly surveys paleoanthropology and related fields, making reference to articles dealing with each topic as it arises. It is not a substitute for reading any of the articles it cites but simply points to and places in context the major entries that comprise the bulk of the volume. The "Brief Introduction" does not attempt to refer to every short article; however, at the end of each main article cited in the introduction cross-references are given to other articles, long and short, that bear on the major subject involved. Additionally, all but the shortest entries are accompanied by suggestions for further reading. These reference lists are not exhaustive bibliographies but are pointers to (primarily) recent and easily accessible works to which readers can refer for more information. Each of these works contains a longer bibliography that serves as an entry point into the popular and technical literature on the subject.

SUBJECT LIST BY TOPIC

Summary of Major Subject Areas

Study Fields, Geographic Areas

GENERAL TERMINOLOGY, FIELDS OF STUDY
OVERVIEWS OF CONTINENTAL REGIONS

Evolutionary Biology

BASIC CONCEPTS
BEHAVIORAL BIOLOGY
GENETICS
NUMERICAL APPROACHES
SYSTEMATICS

Morphology

GENERAL AND ANTHROPOLOGICAL CONCEPTS
BODILY SYSTEMS AND FUNCTION

Primate Taxa

NONPRIMATES, GENERAL TERMS, GRADES
PRIMATES
  PAROMOMYIFORMES
  EUPRIMATES
    STREPSIRHINI
    HAPLORHINI
      ANTHROPOIDEA
      PLATYRRHINI
      CATARRHINI
        HOMINOIDEA

Human Fossils

*Geology, Paleontology,
Stratigraphy, Chronology*

GEOLOGICAL CONCEPTS
PALEONTOLOGICAL CONCEPTS
TIME INTERVALS

Fossil Localities (By Age)

PALEOGENE
MIOCENE
PLIOCENE
EARLY PLEISTOCENE
MIDDLE PLEISTOCENE
LATE PLEISTOCENE

*Fossil and Archaeological Localities
(By Continent)*

AFRICA
AMERICAS
ASIA
EUROPE

Archaeology

GENERAL TERMS AND CONCEPTS
TOOLS, USE AND MANUFACTURE
INDUSTRIES

*Archaeological Sites and Industries
(By Age)*

EARLY PALEOLITHIC
MIDDLE PALEOLITHIC
LATE PALEOLITHIC
EPIPALEOLITHIC
POSTPALEOLITHIC
PALEOINDIAN
DISPUTED OR REJECTED INDUSTRIES

Biographical Entries

Detailed List of All Articles by Topic

Study Fields, Geographic Areas

GENERAL TERMINOLOGY, FIELDS OF STUDY

Anthropology
Cultural Anthropology
Paleoanthropology
Paleobotany
Paleontology
Physical Anthropology

OVERVIEWS OF CONTINENTAL REGIONS

Africa
Americas
Asia
Australia
Europe

Evolutionary Biology

BASIC CONCEPTS

Adaptation
Adaptive Radiation
Cladistics
Cline
Evolution
Evolutionary Morphology
Evolutionary Systematics
Grade
Homology
Monophyly
Ontogeny
Phylogeny
Preadaptation
Scala Naturae
Speciation
Stratophenetic(s)
Transformation series

BEHAVIORAL BIOLOGY

Ecology
Ethology
Primate Ecology
Primate Societies
Sociobiology

GENETICS

Allele
Chromosome
DNA Hybridization
Gene
Genetics

Genotype
Immunological Distance
Molecular Anthropology
Molecular Clock
Non-Darwinian Evolution
Phenotype
Polytypic
Population
Race (Human)

NUMERICAL APPROACHES

Morphometrics
Multivariate Analysis
Numerical Taxonomy
Quantitative Methods
Phenetics

SYSTEMATICS

Cf.
Classification
Incertae Sedis
Nomenclature
Priority
Synonym(y)
Systematics
Taxon
Taxonomy
  Order
  Semiorder
  Suborder
  Infraorder
  Hyporder
  Superfamily
  Family
  Subfamily
  Tribe
  Genus
  Species
  Subspecies

Morphology

GENERAL AND ANTHROPOLOGICAL CONCEPTS

Bone Biology
Forensic Anthropology
"Laws": Pauwels's, Roux's, Wolf's
Morphology
Ontogeny
Paleopathology
"Rules": Allen's, Bergmann's, Glover's, Romer's
Speech (Origins of)

BODILY SYSTEMS AND FUNCTION
Allometry
Brain
Diet
Ischial callosities
Locomotion
Musculature
Sexual dimorphism
Skeleton
Skull
Tail
Teeth

Primate Taxa

NONPRIMATES, GENERAL TERMS, GRADES
Apatemyidae
Ape
Archonta
Higher Primates
Lower Primates
Microsyopidae
Monkey
Prosimian
Psychozoa
Tree Shrews

PRIMATES
Primates

PAROMOMYIFORMES
Plesiadapiformes
  Paromomyoidea
   Paromomyidae
   Picrodontidae
  Plesiadapoidea
   Plesiadapidae
   Saxonellidae
   Carpolestidae
  (genus incertae sedis:)
   Petrolemur

EUPRIMATES
Euprimates

STREPSIRHINI
Strepsirhini
 Adapiformes
  Adapidae
  Notharctidae
  Sivaladapidae
  (genera incertae sedis:)
   Amphipithecus
   Donrussellia
   Lushius

 Lemuriformes
  Lemuroidea
   Lemuridae
   Megaladapidae
  Indrioidea
   Indriidae
   Daubentoniidae
   Archaeolemuridae
   Palaeopropithecidae
  Lorisoidea
   Lorisidae
   Cheirogaleidae
   Galagidae

HAPLORHINI
Haplorhini
 Tarsiiformes
  Omomyidae
   Anaptomorphinae
   Omomyinae
    Ekgmowechashala
   Microchoerinae
  (genus incertae sedis:)
   Decoredon
  Tarsiidae
   Afrotarsius

ANTHROPOIDEA
Anthropoidea

PLATYRRHINI
Platyrrhini
 Ceboidea
  Cebidae
   Cebinae
   Branisellinae
   Callitrichinae
  Atelidae
   Atelinae
   Pitheciinae

CATARRHINI
Catarrhini
 (genera incertae sedis:)
  Pondaungia
  Oligopithecus
 Parapithecidae
 Cercopithecoidea
  Cercopithecidae
   Cercopithecinae
   Colobinae
   Victoriapithecinae
  Oreopithecidae
 Pliopithecoidea

Propliopithecidae
Pliopithecidae
HOMINOIDEA
Hominoidea
Proconsul
Afropithecus
Turkanapithecus
Hylobatidae
Hominidae
(genera incertae sedis:)
Dryopithecus
Kenyapithecus
Ponginae
Homininae
Australopithecus
Paranthropus
Homo

Human Fossils

Human
Human Paleontology (*see* Introduction)
Piltdown
Yeti
Australopithecus
Australopithecus afarensis
Australopithecus africanus
Australopithecus boisei
Australopithecus robustus
Paranthropus
Homo
Homo habilis
Homo erectus
Meganthropus
"*Hemanthropus*"
Homo sapiens
Archaic *Homo sapiens*
Neanderthals
Preneanderthal
Anteneanderthal
Archaic Moderns
Presapiens

Geology, Paleontology, Stratigraphy, Chronology

GEOLOGICAL CONCEPTS
Glaciation
Paleoenvironments
Breccia Cave Formation
Plate Tectonics
Pluvials

Sea-Level Change
Stratigraphy
Time Scale
"Golden Spike"
Geochronometry
Paleomagnetism
Taphonomy
PALEONTOLOGICAL CONCEPTS
Biochronology
Grande Coupure
Paleobiogeography
Paleobiology
Dwarfism
Extinction
Gigantism
Paleontology
Fossil
Dragon Bones (and Teeth)
TIME INTERVALS
Cenozoic
Tertiary
Paleogene
Paleocene
Eocene
Oligocene
Neogene
Miocene
Pliocene
Pleistocene
Holocene
Anthropogene

Fossil Localities (By Age)

PALEOGENE
Pondaung
Fayum
MIOCENE
Patagonia
Songhor
Koru
Rusinga
Muruarot
Buluk
La Venta
Maboko
Siwaliks
Fort Ternan
Baringo
Nachola

Samburu
St. Gaudens
Lufeng
Sahabi
Lothagam

PLIOCENE

Kanapoi
Laetoli
Hadar
Makapansgat
Omo
Sterkfontein
East Turkana
Kanam
West Turkana
Taung
KBS
Olduvai

EARLY PLEISTOCENE

Nariokotome
Peninj
Chesowanja
Swartkrans
Kromdraai
Melka Kontouré
Liucheng
Jian Shi
Kanjera
Modjokerto
Djetis
Sangiran Dome

MIDDLE PLEISTOCENE

Lantian
Yuanmou
Lainyamok
Tighenif
Yayo
Trinil
Kedung Brubus
Sambungmachan
Olorgesailie
Mauer
Vértesszöllös
Salé
Petralona
Arago
Ndutu
Kapthurin
Thomas Quarries
Bodo
Zhoukoudian

Montmaurin
Pontnewydd
Casablanca
Saldanha
Hexian
Ngandong
Jinniu Shan
Swanscombe
Steinheim
Atapuerca
Ehringsdorf
Bilzingsleben
Dali
Kabwe
Lazaret
Biache
Ngaloba
Zuttiyeh
Florisbad
Fontéchevade
La Chaise

LATE PLEISTOCENE

Narmada
Dingcun
Cave of Hearths
Gánovce
Ehringsdorf
Pech de l'Azé
Krapina
Klasies
Border Cave
Jebel Irhoud
Qafzeh
Eyasi
La Naulette
Spy
Shanidar
La Chapelle-aux-Saints
La Ferrassie
Neanderthal
Gibraltar
Haua Fteah
Kebara
Teshik-Tash
Tabūn
Le Moustier
La Quina
Skhūl
Amud
Saint-Césaire
Velica Pecina

Dyuktai
Kostenki
Malta
Mezhirich
Molodova
Sungir
Teshik-Tash
Vallonnet
Velica Pecina
Vértesszöllös

Archaeology

GENERAL TERMS AND CONCEPTS

Aggregation-Dispersal
Archaeological Sites
Archaeology
Complex Societies
Culture
Domestication
Economy, Prehistoric
Ethnoarchaeology
Exotics
Hunter-Gatherers
Jewelry
Lithic Use-Wear
Man-Land Relationships
Modes, Technological
Movius' Line
Musical Instruments
Paleolithic
Paleolithic Calendar
Paleolithic Image
Paleolithic Lifeways
Prehistory
Ritual
Site Types
Storage
Technology

TOOLS, USE AND MANUFACTURE

Awl
Baton de Commandement
Biface
Bipolar Technique
Blade
Bow and Arrow
Burin
Chopper-Chopping Tools
Cleaver
Clothing
Core
Fire

Flake
Flake-Blade
Handaxe
Harpoon
Lithic Use-Wear
Prepared-Core
Raw Materials
Retouch
Sagaie
Scraper
Spear
Split-Base Bone Point
Stone-Tool Making

INDUSTRIES

Abbevillian
Acheulean
Amudian
Antelian
Anyathian
Aterian
Athlitian
Aurignacian
Azilian
Badegoulian
Bambata
Baradostian
Bronze Age
Buda Industry
Chatelperronian
Clactonian
Clovis
Creswellian
Dabban
Early Paleolithic
Early Stone Age
Emiran
Epigravettian
Epipaleolithic
First Intermediate
Folsom
Gravettian
Hamburgian
Hoabinhian
Hope Fountain
Howieson's Poort
Ibero-Maurusian
Iron Age
Jabrudian
Kafuan
Karari
Kebaran

Howieson's Poort
Apollo-11
Rose Cottage
Pre-Aurignacian
Amudian
Aterian
Regourdou
Shanidar
La Ferrassie
Le Moustier
Haua Fteah
Kebarah
Tabūn
La Quina
Skhūl
Amud
Saint-Césaire
Drachenloch
Pietersburg
Orangian
Stillbay
Bambata
Second Intermediate
LATE PALEOLITHIC
Late Paleolithic
Later Stone Age
Dabban
Emiran
Upper Paleolithic
Istallöskö
Bacho Kiro
Laugerie Sites
bri Pataud
Chatelperronian
Aurignacian
Aurignac
Antelian
Baradostian
Gravettian
Szeletian
Perigordian
Předmosti
Dolni Věstonice
Dyuktai
Pavlov
Athlitian
Protomagdalenian
Protosolutrean
Solutrean
Solutré

Magdalenian
Badegoulian
Kebaran
Lascaux
Altamira
Cueva Morin
Mezhirich
Kostenki
Molodova
Sungir
Malta
Tshitolian
Ishango
EPIPALEOLITHIC
Epipaleolithic
Ibero-Maurusian
Azilian
Hamburgian
Sauveterrian
Tardenoisian
Wilton
Maglemosian
Creswellian
Romanellian
Epigravettian
Smithfield
Hoabinhian
Anyathian
POSTPALEOLITHIC
Mesolithic
Star Carr
Neolithic
Domestication
Jarmo
Jericho
Çatal Hüyük
Complex Societies
Iron Age
Bronze Age
PALEOINDIAN
Paleoindian
Meadowcroft Shelter
Tlapacoya
Guitarrero Cave
Fell's Cave
La Brea Tar Pits
Old Crow
Blackwater Draw
Clovis
Folsom

A BRIEF INTRODUCTION TO HUMAN EVOLUTION AND PREHISTORY

The study of human evolution embraces many subject areas that at first glance appear only tangentially related. Yet one cannot hope to understand our past without reference to the biotic and physical context out of which, and within which, our evolution has taken place. Thus the articles in this volume deal at least as much with questions of geology, primatology, systematics, evolutionary theory, and genetics as with the fossil and archaeological records themselves. This brief discussion is meant simply to provide a context for each of the longer entries in this encyclopedia (these are cited in CAPITAL letters), and no attempt is made to refer to every article. Readers will find references to relevant shorter entries at the end of each of the longer articles cited below.

Human beings are PRIMATES. The living primates are our closest relatives in nature, and their study enables us to breathe life into our interpretations of the rapidly improving fossil record of prehuman and early human species. The related questions as to exactly which mammals deserve to be classified as primates, and which are the closest relatives of primates, have been a matter of debate (see ARCHONTA; TREE SHREWS). Under current interpretation those extant primates that most closely resemble the early ancestors of our order are the "LOWER PRIMATES" of the Old World, including MADAGASCAR (see CHEIROGALEIDAE; DAUBENTONIIDAE; GALAGIDAE; INDRIIDAE; LEMURIFORMES; LEMURIDAE; LORISIDAE;

PROSIMIAN; STREPSIRHINI), to which are closely related several recently extinct forms from Madagascar (see ARCHAEOLEMURIDAE; MEGALADAPIDAE; PALAEOPROPITHECIDAE) and older forms from elsewhere (see GALAGIDAE; LORISIDAE; SIVALADAPIDAE). The enigmatic *Tarsius* (see HAPLORHINI; TARSIIDAE; TARSIIFORMES), uneasily straddles the divide between these forms and the "HIGHER PRIMATES," with which we ourselves are classified (see ANTHROPOIDEA; APE; HAPLORHINI; MONKEY; SKULL). These latter include the New World monkeys of South America (see ATELIDAE; ATELINAE; CALLITRICHINAE; CEBIDAE; PITHECIINAE; PLATYRRHINI) and the Old World higher primates, or CATARRHINI, of Africa and Asia. These embrace the Old World monkeys (see CERCOPITHECOIDEA; CERCOPITHECIDAE) as well as the greater and lesser apes (see APE; HOMINIDAE; HOMINOIDEA; HYLOBATIDAE; PONGINAE).

Extant forms can be studied in a variety of ways that are useful in widening the scope of our interpretation of the fossil record. Study of the morphology of modern primates (see BONE BIOLOGY; BRAIN; MUSCULATURE; SKELETON; SKULL; TEETH) provides a base for interpretation of fossil morphology (see also ALLOMETRY; SEXUAL DIMORPHISM), as do correlated aspects of behavior (see DIET; EVOLUTIONARY MORPHOLOGY; LOCOMOTION) and broader aspects of ecology and behavior in general (see PRIMATE ECOLOGY; PRIMATE SOCIETIES; SOCIOBIOLOGY). The traumas and developmental phenomena that occur to hard tissues during life (see

PALEOPATHOLOGY) can yield valuable information about health and dietary factors in vanished populations; comparative studies of proteins and the genetic material have formed the basis not simply for hypotheses of relationship among primate and other species but for calibrated phylogenies (see MOLECULAR ANTHROPOLOGY).

Interpretation of the fossil record clearly requires a grasp of the principles of EVOLUTION (see also EXTINCTION; GENETICS; PHYLOGENY; SPECIATION) and of the various approaches to the reconstruction of evolutionary histories and relationships (see CLADISTICS; EVOLUTIONARY SYSTEMATICS; PALEOBIOLOGY; QUANTITATIVE METHODS; STRATOPHENETICS; SYSTEMATICS). It also requires an understanding of the processes used to name and classify living organisms (see CLASSIFICATION; NOMENCLATURE) and of the nature of SPECIES (see also SPECIATION), the basic systematic unit. Further, it is important to comprehend the nature of the fossil record itself and the processes by which living organisms are transformed into fossils (see TAPHONOMY). This consideration brings us to the interface between paleoanthropology and geology.

No fossil can be properly interpreted without reference to the geological context in which it occurs, and various aspects of geology converge on the interpretation of fossilized remains. Next to its morphology the most important attribute of a fossil is its age. Traditionally fossils were dated according to their relative position in the sequence of geological events (see TIME SCALE and chart in the next section), as reflected in their locality of discovery in local sedimentary sequences (see STRATIGRAPHY). Particular sedimentary strata are confined to local areas, and rocks laid down in different regions could formerly be correlated with one another only by comparing the fossil faunas they contained (see BIOCHRONOLOGY). In the past few decades, however, methods have been developed of assigning chronometric dates, in years, to certain types of rocks and young organic remains (see GEOCHRONOMETRY). Additionally, the fact that the earth's magnetic field changes polarity from time to time has been used, in conjunction with measurements of the remanent magnetism of iron-containing rocks, to provide an additional relative, but datable, time scale independent of fossils (see PALEOMAGNETISM).

The movement of the continents relative to each other (see PLATE TECTONICS) over the period of primate evolution has significantly affected the course of that evolution (see PALEOBIOGEOGRAPHY). More recently the major geological process that has most profoundly affected human evolution has been the cyclical expansion of ice sheets in the higher latitudes (see GLACIATION; PLEISTOCENE) and the correlated fluctuation in sea levels worldwide (see SEA-LEVEL CHANGE).

We first find primates in the fossil record ca. 65 m.y. ago. A substantial radiation of primates of archaic aspect took place both in North America and Europe during the PALEOCENE epoch (see CARPOLESTIDAE; PAROMOMYIDAE; PLESIADAPIDAE; PRIMATES; SAXONELLIDAE; SKULL). In the succeeding EOCENE epoch these forms were replaced by primates more modern in aspect. Some of these, the ADAPIDAE and NOTHARCTIDAE, are considered to be related in a general way to the modern lorises and lemurs; the family OMOMYIDAE, which contains the subfamilies ANAPTOMORPHINAE, MICROCHOERINAE, and OMOMYINAE, is commonly classified within the infraorder TARSIIFORMES. Future studies may show this dichotomy among Eocene primates to be oversimplified.

The fossil record of New World monkeys goes back less far (to the latest OLIGOCENE, ca. 27 m.y.) than that of the Old World higher primates, but even quite early forms generally appear to be allocable, with few exceptions (see BRANISELLINAE) to extant subfamilies (see ANTHROPOIDEA; ATELINAE; CALLITRICHINAE; CEBINAE; PITHECIINAE; PLATYRRHINI). In contrast the earliest Old World higher primates are much more difficult to place in the context of living taxa. Some fragmentary jaws and teeth from the late EOCENE of Burma (ca. 40 m.y.) may represent an early anthropoid (see PONDAUNGIA, CATARRHINI), but the only good well-represented early catarrhine fauna comes from the FAYUM of Egypt, in the OLIGOCENE, dating to ca. 34–31 m.y. ago. Apart from the enigmatic OLIGOPITHECUS and the tarsioid AFROTARSIUS, the Fayum primates fall into two major groups. Of these PROPLIOPITHECIDAE may be close to the origin of the later Old World anthropoids; PARAPITHECIDAE, although perhaps "monkeylike" in a broad sense, bears no close relationship to any extant anthropoid taxon.

The MIOCENE epoch (see also NEOGENE) witnessed a substantial diversification of early

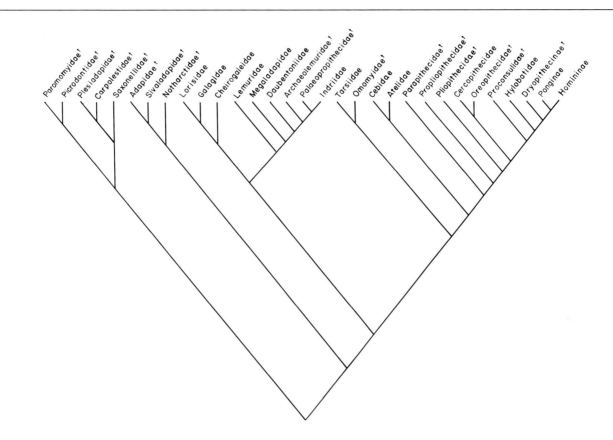

Cladogram showing possible relationships among the various primate families, living and extinct. This "consensus" cladogram is not intended to be a definitive statement but rather to provide a framework within which the various discussions in this volume can be understood; not all authors will agree with all the relationships hypothesized here, some of which are highly tentative. The three subfamilies of Hominidae are represented separately at the far right. Daggers indicate extinct taxa.

CATARRHINI. Probably most closely affined to the propliopithecids of the Fayum was the family PLIOPITHECIDAE, a paraphyletic grouping of small, conservative, but in some ways "apelike" forms, often considered in the past to be related to the gibbons but now regarded simply as generalized early catarrhines. The most puzzling of the Miocene catarrhines is *Oreopithecus*, known only from Italian sites dated to the late part of the epoch, although several earlier African species are also included in its family (*see* OREOPITHE-CIDAE). Opinions as to oreopithecid affinities have varied widely, but they are considered in this volume to be related to the cerocopithecid monkeys, representatives of which also first turn up in the Miocene (*see* CATARRHINI; CERCOPITHE-CIDAE; CERCOPITHECOIDEA; MONKEY; VICTORIAPITHE-CINAE). The cercopithecids diversified considerably during the Pliocene in Africa and Eurasia (*see* CERCOPITHECINAE; COLOBINAE).

The Miocene of East AFRICA was the scene of the first documented radiation of hominoid primates (*see* HOMINOIDEA; PROCONSUL), members of the superfamily containing apes and humans. In the period following ca. 20 m.y. the diversity of hominoid species reached its peak. The first surviving subgroup of Hominoidea to branch off in this period must have been the gibbons (*see* HYLOBATIDAE), but no known form can be considered a good candidate for gibbon ancestry. The first fossil hominoids that are clearly related to an extant form are assigned to the late Miocene (ca. 12–8 m.y.) genus SIVAPITHECUS and are already close in morphology to the modern orangutan, *Pongo* (*see* HOMINIDAE, in this volume interpreted to include both humans and the great apes; HOMINOIDEA; PONGINAE). This extinct genus also includes *Ramapithecus*, previously considered a potential ancestor of humans. Most authorities today consider that the two African-ape genera are more closely related to humans (*see* HOMININAE; MOLECULAR ANTHROPOLOGY) than are the orangutan and its fossil relatives, although the question is still debated. Despite the rich Miocene hominoid fossil record of East Africa, however, no convincing precursors of the chimpanzee or gorilla are known, with the possible exception of the gorillalike form recently reported from SAMBURU in KENYA.

A virtually complete hiatus occurs in the hominoid fossil record between ca. 8 and 4 m.y. ago, and subsequent to that gap the record consists almost entirely of early human relatives. The earliest forms that can clearly be admitted to the human lineage are allocated to the genus AUSTRALOPITHECUS. The first of these is AUSTRALOPITHECUS AFARENSIS, known from PLIOCENE sites in ETHIOPIA and TANZANIA in the 4–3-m.y. range (see also AFAR; HADAR; LAETOLI). Members of this species were small-bodied upright walkers (although the extent to which they had relinquished their ancestral climbing abilities is debated), as revealed not only by their anatomy but in the 3.5-m.y.-old trackways from the site of LAETOLI. The BRAIN remained small, but the chewing TEETH were relatively large compared with body size, and the face was rather projecting. No stone tools were made at this early stage of human evolution. *Australopithecus* was first discovered in SOUTH AFRICA in 1924, when R.A. DART described the juvenile type specimen of AUSTRALOPITHECUS AFRICANUS from the site of TAUNG. Later discoveries at the sites of STERKFONTEIN and MAKAPANSGAT provided more substantial samples of this species, which is represented between ca. 3 and 2 m.y. and which differed only in details from *A. afarensis* (e.g. in possessing a slightly shorter face, a slightly larger brain, and slightly smaller incisor teeth).

Usually, if not entirely accurately, characterized as "gracile," or lightly built, these two species of *Australopithecus* remain relatively generalized compared with the "robust" form AUSTRALOPITHECUS ROBUSTUS from the later South African sites of SWARTKRANS and KROMDRAAI (ca. 1.9–1.5 m.y.). This later form differs from the "graciles" in numerous details of cranial architecture functionally linked to the relative expansion of the chewing teeth and diminution of the front teeth. These differences are often considered to be great enough to warrant generic distinction, in which case the genus name PARANTHROPUS is used for the robust form. A related "hyper-robust" form is known from East Africa, AUSTRALOPITHECUS (or PARANTHROPUS) BOISEI. First discovered by M.D. and L.S.B. LEAKEY at Tanzania's OLDUVAI GORGE in 1959, this form, with its even larger chewing teeth and yet more diminished front teeth compared with *A. robustus*, is now well known from sites in KENYA (see also EAST TURKANA) and ETHIOPIA (see also OMO) ranging from ca. 2.2 to 1.3 m.y. in age. Recently a skull has been discovered in the Lomekwi Formation, west of Lake Turkana in northern Kenya, of an individual that most would consider represents yet a third species of robust australopith (see AUSTRALOPITHECUS). At ca. 2.6–2.2 m.y. old this individual and several less complete but similar fossils antedate known *A. boisei* specimens and have caused much recent rethinking of the early period of human phylogeny.

Although the earliest stone tools, between 2.5 and 2 m.y. old, are not definitely associated with any particular hominid species, it is widely believed that they were an innovation on the part of the earliest members of our own genus, HOMO. With this innovation the archaeological record begins. Understanding STONE-TOOL MAKING and the analysis of stone-tool assemblages in terms of the LITHIC USE-WEAR and the RAW MATERIALS from which they are made form only a small part of the concerns of PALEOLITHIC ("Old Stone Age") archaeologists. These specialists also study the nature of ARCHAEOLOGICAL SITES, which reflect the various SITE TYPES occupied by prehistoric people. These sites are located using a number of SAMPLING TECHNIQUES, and the information they contain is analyzed through the principles of TAPHONOMY. The goal is to reconstruct the PALEOLITHIC LIFEWAYS of vanished hominids.

The earliest species allocated to HOMO is HOMO HABILIS, first described from OLDUVAI GORGE in 1961, in levels slightly under 2 m.y. old. Fossils ascribed to *Homo habilis* have now been described from KENYA, SOUTH AFRICA, and ETHIOPIA as well, in the period between ca. 2 and 1.5 m.y., although it may well be that future workers will find cause to divide up the diverse assemblage of fossils involved. Distinctive features of *Homo habilis* appear to include a more modern body skeleton than that of *Australopithecus* (although a recent find at Olduvai Gorge is said to show archaic limb proportions), expansion of the BRAIN relative to body size, and reduction of the face. Accompanied by an OLDOWAN stone-tool kit (see also EARLY PALEOLITHIC; STONE-TOOL MAKING), *H. habilis* was clearly a HUNTER-GATHERER, actively hunting

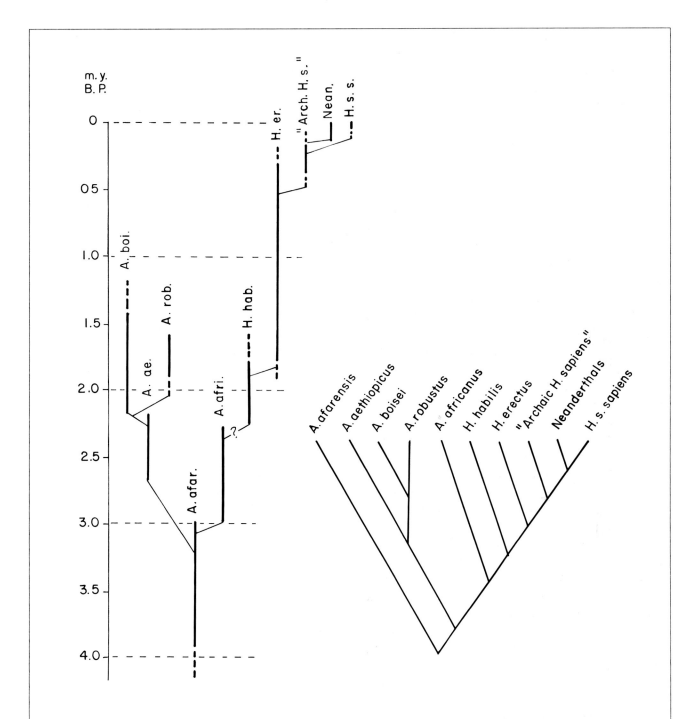

Two representations of relationships in the human fossil record. On the left, a family tree showing known ranges (solid vertical bars) and possible range extensions (broken bars) of the various species recognized; light oblique lines indicate *possible* paths of descent. On the right, a cladogram more formally expresses hypothesized relationships among the various species.

small or medium-sized animals as well as scavenging the carcasses of bigger ones and gathering plant foods. We have no evidence clearly demonstrating that these early humans used FIRE or constructed shelters.

The longest-lived species of our genus was HOMO ERECTUS (*see also* HOMO). First described from INDONESIA, *Homo erectus* is known from ca. 1.7 m.y. in East Africa, possibly from earlier in South Africa, and persists in CHINA up to ca. 250 k.y. ago. Typically this form is accompanied by a more evolved ACHEULEAN tool kit (*see also* EARLY PALEOLITHIC) based on large bifacially flaked utensils, such as handaxes and cleavers (*see*

STONE-TOOL MAKING), although in eastern ASIA this is only rarely the case. Robust but essentially modern in its body skeleton, *Homo erectus* nevertheless was highly distinctive in its cranial structure, although with a yet shorter face and larger BRAIN than *Homo habilis*. This was apparently the first form of human to learn to control FIRE, to spread beyond the confines of AFRICA (*see also* ASIA; CHINA; INDONESIA), and to live in caves as well as open sites (*see* ARCHAEOLOGICAL SITES). It is unclear whether *Homo erectus* ever occupied EUROPE; the earliest human remains (ca. 0.5 m.y. and younger) from that region of the world appear not to be identifiable as *Homo erectus*, but artifact sites are known that are considerably older.

The earliest Europeans are usually classified as belonging to an archaic form of our own species, despite strong physical differences in cranial form from ourselves (*see* ARCHAIC HOMO SAPIENS). Initially stone-tool-making techniques continued more or less the same as among *Homo erectus*, but eventually a refinement was developed, leading the way to the development of the later MIDDLE PALEOLITHIC stone industries. This was the PREPARED-CORE technique, whereby a core was shaped from which a more or less completed tool could be struck with a single blow. These early humans also provide us with the first definite evidence for the construction of shelters at open sites. These were constructed using a framework of branches embedded in postholes on the ground and tied together at the top. The same period has yielded evidence for similarly advanced humans, with BRAIN capacities larger than those of *Homo erectus* in other parts of the world, including AFRICA and ASIA. Their PALEOLITHIC LIFEWAYS depended on the hunting of herd animals.

Perhaps the most famous of all extinct forms of human are the NEANDERTHALS, a European and Near Eastern group known from ca. 150 to 32 k.y. ago. It is their western European representatives from the latest part of this period that show the morphological specializations of the Neanderthals in the most marked degree (*see also* EUROPE; NEAR EAST). These archaic people employed a sophisticated stone-working tradition known as the MOUSTERIAN, a variety of the MIDDLE PALEOLITHIC, and were the earliest humans to bury their dead with RITUAL practices. They were unquestionably replaced in Europe by invading waves of modern people (*see* HOMO SAPIENS; NEANDERTHALS), but the transition from archaic to modern human types in other parts of the world is less clear (*see* ARCHAIC MODERNS).

All modern HOMO SAPIENS share a distinctive skull anatomy, but the origin of this physical type remains a mystery. Sub-Saharan AFRICA provides the earliest hints of ARCHAIC MODERNS (over 100 k.y. ago), but in all cases either the fossils are fragmentary or the dating is insecure. More recently North Africa and the NEAR EAST have yielded remains in the 90–30 k.y. range of individuals who were reasonably modern in appearance yet distinct from any surviving group; fully modern humans appear to have been present in eastern ASIA by ca. 40 k.y. ago also. The earliest modern humans brought with them the highly sophisticated blade-based stone-working industries of the LATE PALEOLITHIC (*see also* STONE-TOOL MAKING). This phase is most clearly documented in EUROPE, where it is termed the UPPER PALEOLITHIC, and is accompanied by the earliest evidence for art, notation, music, and elaborate body ornamentation (*see* CLOTHING; PALEOLITHIC IMAGE; PALEOLITHIC LIFEWAYS; RITUAL). It was modern humans, too, who for the first time crossed into the New World (*see* AMERICAS; PALEOINDIAN) and traversed a substantial sea barrier to reach AUSTRALIA, where a series of highly interesting paleoanthropological finds has been made.

Following the end of the most recent glacial episode, ca. 10 k.y. ago, the big-game-hunting cultures of the European Upper Paleolithic waned, yielding to the differently adapted societies of the MESOLITHIC period. It was perhaps first in the "Fertile Crescent" of the NEAR EAST that the next major economic and social developments occurred, with the growth in the NEOLITHIC period ("New Stone Age") of settled village life and the DOMESTICATION of animals and plants. These developments paved the way toward COMPLEX SOCIETIES and the written word, and hence toward the end of the long period of human prehistory.

CLASSIFICATION OF THE PRIMATES

Primate classification is, and probably always will be, in a state of flux. This is because classifications, as the products of human minds rather than of nature itself, may legitimately reflect virtually any set of criteria, provided that those criteria are consistently applied (*see* CLASSIFICATION). Currently fashionable criteria range from the strict transliteration of phylogeny, as expressed in a cladogram (*see* CLADISTICS), to general expressions of overall resemblance. The first of these provides disputed and unstable classifications, because not all details (or in some cases major questions) of primate phylogeny have been definitively resolved. The second has much the same effect, because there exists no generally acceptable method of measuring such resemblance (but *see* EVOLUTIONARY SYSTEMATICS).

It was necessary, however, to settle upon a single classification for the purposes of organizing this volume. This is presented below. We wish to emphasize that we have not attempted to produce a "definitive" classification but rather the closest thing we could achieve to a "consensus" classification. No one, least of all the editors, will accept all of its details, and indeed some of our contributors take exception to parts of the classification in their articles; this was inevitable. Yet most of it will be acceptable to most students of the primates, and it certainly serves as a coherent framework upon which to arrange the systematic contributions in this encyclopedia. Our classification follows. († denotes an extinct genus.)

ORDER Primates
  SEMIORDER Paromomyiformes
    SUBORDER Plesiadapiformes
      SUPERFAMILY Paromomyoidea
        FAMILY Paromomyidae
          †*Purgatorius*
          †*Palaechthon*
          †*Plesiolestes*
          †*Palenochtha*
          †*Paromomys*
          †*Ignacius*
          †*Phenacolemur*
          †*Micromomys*
          †*Tinimomys*
          †*Navajovius*
          †*Berruvius*
        FAMILY Picrodontidae
          †*Picrodus*
          †*Zanycteris*
      SUPERFAMILY Plesiadapoidea
        FAMILY Plesiadapidae
          †*Pronothodectes*
          †*Plesiadapis*
          †*Chiromyoides*
          †*Platychoerops*
        FAMILY Saxonellidae
          †*Saxonella*
        FAMILY Carpolestidae
          †*Elphidotarsius*
          †*Carpodaptes*
  SEMIORDER Paromomyiformes, incertae sedis?
          †*Petrolemur*
  SEMIORDER Euprimates
    SUBORDER Strepsirhini
      INFRAORDER Adapiformes
        SUPERFAMILY Adapoidea
          FAMILY Adapidae
            †*Protoadapis*
            †*Agerinia*

†Europolemur
†Mahgarita
†Pronycticebus
†Anchomomys
†Huerzeleris
†Periconodon
†Microadapis
†Leptadapis
†Adapis
†Caenopithecus
†Simonsia
†Paradapis
†Hallelemur
†Alsatia
†Chasselasia
†Kohatius
FAMILY Notharctidae
†Pelycodus
†Notharctus
†Smilodectes
†Copelemur
FAMILY Sivaladapidae
†Sivaladapis
†Indraloris
FAMILY Adapidae, incertae sedis
†Donrussellia
†Lushius
INFRAORDER Adapiformes, incertae sedis?
†Amphipithecus
INFRAORDER Lemuriformes
SUPERFAMILY Lemuroidea
FAMILY Lemuridae
Lemur
Varecia
Hapalemur

SUPERFAMILY Indrioidea
FAMILY Indriidae
Indri
Propithecus
Avahi
†Mesopropithecus
FAMILY Daubentoniidae
Daubentonia
FAMILY Megaladapidae
†Megaladapis
Lepilemur
FAMILY Archaeolemuridae
†Archaeolemur
†Hadropithecus
FAMILY Palaeopropithecidae
†Palaeopropithecus
†Archaeoindris

SUPERFAMILY Lorisoidea
FAMILY Cheirogaleidae
Cheirogaleus
Microcebus
Mirza
Phaner
Allocebus
FAMILY Lorisidae
Loris

Nycticebus
Arctocebus
Perodicticus
†Mioeuoticus
†Nycticeboides
FAMILY Galagidae
Galago
G. (Euoticus)
Galagoides
G. (Sciurocheirus)
Otolemur
†Progalago
†Komba
SUBORDER Haplorhini
INFRAORDER Tarsiiformes
FAMILY Omomyidae
SUBFAMILY Omomyinae
†Omomys
†Chumachius
†Ourayia
†Macrotarsius
†Loveina
†Shoshonius
†Arapahovius
†Washakius
†Dyseolemur
†Hemiacodon
†Uintanius
†Utahia
†Stockia
†Rooneyia
†Ekgmowechashala
†Hoanghonius
SUBFAMILY Anaptomorphinae
†Teilhardina
†Chlororhysis
†Anaptomorphus
†Tetonius
†Absarokius
†Anemorhysis
†Altanius
†Mckennamorphus
†Trogolemur
SUBFAMILY Microchoerinae
†Nannopithex
†Necrolemur
†Microchoerus
†Pseudoloris
FAMILY Decoredontidae
†Decoredon
FAMILY Tarsiidae
†Tarsius
†Afrotarsius
INFRAORDER Platyrrhini
SUPERFAMILY Ceboidea
FAMILY Cebidae
SUBFAMILY Cebinae
Cebus
Saimiri
†"Saimiri"
†Neosaimiri
†Dolichocebus

SUBFAMILY Branisellinae
    †*Branisella*
SUBFAMILY Callitrichinae
    Callithrix (incl. *Cebuella*)
    Callimico
    Saguinus
    Leontopithecus
FAMILY Atelidae
SUBFAMILY Atelinae
TRIBE Atelini
    Ateles
    Brachyteles
    Lagothrix
TRIBE Alouattini
    Alouatta
    †*Stirtonia*
SUBFAMILY Pitheciinae
TRIBE Pitheciini
    Pithecia
    Chiropotes
    Cacajao
    †*Xenothrix*
    †*Cebupithecia*
    †*Mohanamico*
    †*Homunculus*
TRIBE Aotini
    Aotus
    Callicebus
    †*Tremacebus*
INFRAORDER Catarrhini
SUPERFAMILY Parapithecoidea
FAMILY Parapithecidae
    †*Parapithecus* (?incl.
      †*Simonsius*)
    †*Apidium*
    †*Qatrania*
SUPERFAMILY Cercopithecoidea
FAMILY Cercopithecidae
SUBFAMILY Cercopithecinae
TRIBE Cercopithecini
    Allenopithecus
    Cercopithecus
    Miopithecus
    Erythrocebus
TRIBE Papionini
    †*Parapapio*
    Papio
    P. (Mandrillus)
    †*P. (Dinopithecus)*
    Cercocebus (incl.
      Lophocebus)
    †*Gorgopithecus*
    Theropithecus
    Macaca
    †*Procynocephalus*
    †*Paradolichopithecus*
SUBFAMILY Colobinae
    Colobus
    Procolobus
    P. (Piliocolobus)
    †*Libypithecus*
    †*Cercopithecoides*

†*Paracolobus*
†*Rhinocolobus*
Presbytis
Semnopithecus
S. (Trachypithecus)
Pygathrix
P. (Rhinopithecus)
Nasalis
N. (Simias)
SUBFAMILY Colobinae, incertae sedis
    †*Mesopithecus*
    †*Dolichopithecus*
SUBFAMILY Victoriapithecinae
    †*Victoriapithecus*
    †*Prohylobates*
FAMILY Oreopithecidae
    †*Oreopithecus*
    †*Nyanzapithecus*
    ?†*Rangwapithecus*
SUPERFAMILY Pliopithecoidea
FAMILY Pliopithecidae
    †*Pliopithecus*
    †*Crouzelia*
FAMILY ?Pliopithecidae
    †*Dendropithecus*
    †*Simiolus*
    †*Laccopithecus*
    †*Limnopithecus*
    †*Dionysopithecus*
    †*Micropithecus*
    †*Platodontopithecus*
FAMILY Propliopithecidae
    †*Propliopithecus*
SUPERFAMILY Hominoidea
FAMILY Hylobatidae
    Hylobates
    H. (Symphalangus)
    H. (Nomascus)
FAMILY Proconsulidae
    †*Proconsul*
FAMILY Hominidae
SUBFAMILY Dryopithecinae
    †*Dryopithecus*
    †*Kenyapithecus*
    †*Heliopithecus*
    †*Afropithecus*
    ?†*Turkanapithecus*
SUBFAMILY Ponginae
    Pongo
    †*Sivapithecus* (incl.
      Ramapithecus)
    †*Graecopithecus*
    †*Gigantopithecus*
SUBFAMILY Homininae
    Pan
    Gorilla
    †*Australopithecus* (incl.
      Paranthropus)
    Homo
INFRAORDER Catarrhini, incertae sedis
    †*Pondaungia*
    †*Oligopithecus*

Standard time scale chart (mammalian faunal correlation chart).

M.Y.	EPOCHS	STANDARD STAGES	EUROPEAN STAGE STRATOTYPES	EUROPEAN MAMMALS (MN-ZONES)	EUROPEAN MAMMALS (AGES)	ASIAN MAMMALS (SITES)	ASIAN MAMMALS (INDOPAKISTAN "ZONES")	AFRICAN MAMMALS (AGES)	AFRICAN MAMMALS (SITES)	S. AMERICAN MAMMALS (AGES)	N. AMERICAN MAMMALS (AGES)
0	PLEIST. (E M L)	MILAZZIAN EMILIAN-SICILIAN CALABRIAN 1.6		20-21, 19, 18	CROMERIAN BIHARIAN ETC. 1.0	Maba, Zhoukoudian, Sangiran	NARMADA 1.5	NAIVASHAN 1.0 / NATRONIAN	Border Cave, Tighenif, Olduvai I	LUJANIAN 1.0 / ENSENADAN 2.0	RANCHOLABREAN / IRVINGTONIAN 1.5
	PLIOCENE (L)	PIACENZIAN 3.4	Piacenzian	17	VILLAFRANCHIAN		2.5 PINJOR	TURKANAN	Shungura C, Makapansgat	UQUIAN 3.0 / CHAPADMALALAN	
5	PLIOCENE (E)	ZANCLEAN 5.2	Zanclean	16 / 15 / 14	3.5 RUSCINIAN 5.2		3.4 TATROT / AFARIAN 4.0	AFARIAN 4.0	Hadar, Laetoli, Chemeron, Sahabi	MONTEHERMOSAN 5.0	BLANCAN 5.0
	MIOCENE (LATE)	MESSINIAN 6.5 / TORTONIAN 10.5	Messinian / Tortonian	13 / 12 / 11	TUROLIAN 9.5	Lufeng 7.8 / Maragheh Sinap	DHOK PATHAN / NAGRI 9.7	KERIAN 7.0 / SUGUTAN	Lothagam, Lukeino, Mpesida, Nakali, Samburu	HUAYQUERIAN 9.0 / CHASICOAN 10.5	HEMPHILLIAN 9.0 / CLARENDONIAN
10	MIOCENE (MIDDLE)	SERRAVALLIAN 15.0 / LANGHIAN 16.5	Serravallian / Langhian / Badenian	10 / 9 / 8 / 7 / 6	VALLESIAN 11.5 / 12.5 / ASTARACIAN 15.5	Pasalar 13.5 / Sihong / Ad Dabtiyah	CHINJI / KAMLIAL-MANCHAR 16.0	TUGENIAN 12.5 / TINDERETIAN 16.0	Ngorora, Ch'orora, Muruyur, Fort Ternan, Maboko	FRIASIAN / La Venta 15.0 / SANTACRUCIAN	BARSTOVIAN 16.0
20	MIOCENE (EARLY)	BURDIGALIAN 21.0 / AQUITANIAN 23.5 /24.0	Burdigalian / Aquitanian	5 / 4b / 4a / 3b / 3a / 2b / 2a / 1	ORLEANIAN 21.0 / AGENIAN 25.0		DERA BUGTI 18.0 ? ? ?	KISINGIRIAN 23.0	Kulu, Muruarot, Rusinga, Songhor, Koru	COLHUEHUAPIAN 19.0	HEMINGFORDIAN 20.0 / ARIKAREEAN
25	OLIGOCENE (LATE)	CHATTIAN 30.0	Chattian / Neo-chattian / Eo-chattian		ARVERNIAN 30.0					DESEADAN Salla	27.0
30	OLIGOCENE (EARLY)	RUPELIAN 36.6	Rupelian / Stampian		SUEVIAN 36.6 "Grande Coupure"			PHIOMIAN	Jebel Qatrani (upper) / Jebel Qatrani (lower)	DIVISADERAN 36.0	WHITNEYAN 30.8 / ORELLAN 32.3 / CHADRONIAN
40	EOCENE (LATE)	PRIABONIAN 40.0 / BARTONIAN 43.6	Priabonian / Lattorfian / Bartonian / Biarritzian		HEADONIAN 42.0 / BARTONIAN (Lattorfian)	Pondaung / ? ? ?	KOHAT / KULDANA ? ? ?		Qasr el-Sagha, Birket el-Qarun, Mokattam, Cabinda	MUSTERSAN	DUCHESNIAN 38.0 / UINTAN 42.0
45	EOCENE (MIDDLE)	LUTETIAN 52.0	Lutetian		LUTETIAN			MAGHREBIAN	Bir el-Atir	48.0	UINTAN 48.0 / BRIDGERIAN 51.0
50	EOCENE (EARLY)	YPRESIAN 57.8	Cuisian / Ypresian / Ilerdian		RHENANIAN				Gour Lazibe, El Kohol, Chambi	CASAMAYORAN 51.0 / 57.6	WASATCHIAN 56.0 /57.5
60	PALEOCENE (LATE)	SELANDIAN 62.4	Sparnacian / Thanetian / Selandian / Landenian		NEUSTRIAN				Ouarzazate	RIOCHICAN 61.0 / ITABORAIAN 63.6	CLARKFORKIAN 59.0 / TIFFANIAN 61.8
65	PALEOCENE (EARLY)	DANIAN 66.5	Danian / Montian / Cernaysian		66.5					66.5	TORREJONIAN 64.6 / PUERCAN 66.5

Standard time scale used in this encyclopedia. Standard stages refer to the major European divisions of epochs (often extrapolated worldwide) based on marine biostratigraphy; the ranges of the stratotypes of these and selected lesser stages are also shown. Zonations of mammalian faunas are shown for each continent, with the semiformal "Land Mammal Ages" or less formal equivalents shown in capital letters. In some cases, specific sites with primates are shown as well. For Europe, the set of numbered MN (Mammalian Neogene) zones subdivides the Neogene even more finely; vertically oriented terms refer to marine stage names used incorrectly (but often) in the literature as mammalian zones. Oblique broken lines represent uncertainty as to the boundary between successive time units. Parallel vertical lines indicate gaps in the local stratigraphic record. A more detailed subdivision of the Pleistocene is provided in the entry on that epoch.

TIME CHART

Recently published time scales differ widely from one another (*see* TIME SCALE), principally because of philosophical differences about the way dating is applied. We have thus felt it necessary to specify a standard scale in preparing this work. The pre-Pleistocene time scale we have adopted is that presented, with full documentation, in companion articles on the Paleogene by Berggren, Kent, and Flynn (1985) and on the Neogene by Berggren, Kent, and Van Couvering (1985), referenced below. In these works calibration to magnetostratigraphy and deep-sea microfossil zonations are the same as those in current use by the Deep Sea Drilling Program (*see* PALEOMAGNETISM), including the revised correlation of paleomagnetic Chron 11 rather than Chron 9 in stratigraphic sequences, to the extended normal polarity interval of seafloor Anomaly 5; this has the effect of changing the age of the basal Tortonian from ca. 8.5 to ca. 10.5 m.y. and extending the duration of the late Miocene at the expense of the middle Miocene, compared with earlier scales. It should also be noted that in this time scale the stratotypes of both the Lutetian and Bartonian stages are assigned to the middle Eocene, and the Priabonian represents the late Eocene. Correlation of the earliest African catarrhines (*see* FAYUM), in beds lying on Bartonian marine sediments, may thus be to the later Eocene rather than to the early and middle Oligocene, as was assumed when the Bartonian was thought to be late Eocene in age.

The Pleistocene time scale follows recent research on the newly designated boundary stratotype at Vrica in Calabria (Italy), as reported by Obradovich et al. (1982), and uses the conventions employed by most stratigraphers in subdividing this epoch (*see* PLEISTOCENE). In particular the boundaries are referred to marine strata as in all other epoch definitions and not to magnetostratigraphy or climate (*see* GLACIATION). The term *Holocene* conveys a misleading impression that the current postglacial, or interglacial, interval is of epochal rank. We see no outstanding difference between this interval and earlier parts of the Pleistocene, except perhaps for the alarming effects of human proliferation, and consider that such terms as *postglacial Pleistocene*, *modern*, or *recent* are preferable. However, some entries in this volume do employ the term "Holocene" as the most recent subdivision of the late Pleistocene.

In this work all year-ages are indicated by the abbreviation "m.y." or "k.y.," meaning "millions of years before present" and "thousands of years before present", respectively. Other conventions that mean the same, such as "Ma.," "Ka.," and "m.y.b.p.," are also used in other publications.

References Cited

Berggren, W.A., Kent, D.V., and Flynn, J.J. (1985) Jurassic to Paleogene, Part 2. In N.J. Snelling (ed.): The Geochronology of the Geological Record. London: Blackwell, pp. 141–195.

Berggren, W.A., Kent, D.V., and Van Couvering, J.A. (1985) Neogene, Part 2. In Snelling, pp. 211–260.

Obradovich, J.D., Naeser, C.W., Izett, G.A., Pasini, G., and Bigazzi, G. (1982) Age constraints on the proposed Plio-Pleistocene boundary section at Vrica, Italy. Nature 298:55–59.

THE ENCYCLOPEDIA

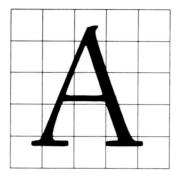

ABBEVILLIAN

Term once used to refer to early Acheulean stone-tool assemblages in Europe. This "stage" of tool technology was distinguished by crude, thick handaxes. It was named after Abbeville (France), where a middle Pleistocene site in the 45-m. terrace of the Somme River yielded roughly made handaxes.

See also ACHEULEAN; HANDAXE. [R.P.]

ABRI *see* ARCHAEOLOGICAL SITES

ABRI PATAUD

Rock shelter with archaeological and human remains located on the left bank of the Vézère River in Les Eyzies, Dordogne, in southwestern France, dated by radiocarbon determinations between 34,000 and 20,000 B.P. With 14 major archaeological horizons, from very early Aurignacian to Protomagdalenian and Solutrean, this site was excavated in the 1950s and 60s by H. L. Movius, with emphasis on paleoecological reconstruction, horizontal exposure of minimal stratigraphic units or occupation horizons, and quantitative analysis of archaeological materials. The excavations prompted significant revisions in the classic Upper Paleolithic sequence of southwestern France and also yielded a series of human remains from the Protomagdalenian level.

See also ARCHAEOLOGICAL SITES; AURIGNACIAN; PALEOENVIRONMENTS; PERIGORDIAN; PROTOMAGDALENIAN; SOLUTREAN; UPPER PALEOLITHIC. [A.S.B.]

ABSAROKIUS *see* ANAPTOMORPHINAE

ACHEULEAN

Early Paleolithic industry characterized by handaxes and similar types of modified stone tools. Acheulean artifact assemblages are known from ca. 1.5 to 0.2 m.y. and span Africa, Europe, and Asia. Based originally on numerous handaxes discovered at the site of St. Acheul (France), the term Acheulean is applied to stone assemblages with large bifacially flaked, ovoid tools. In an artifact assemblage such tools must be numerous and/or finely made in order for the term to apply. In Africa, where the oldest Acheulean occurrences are known, handaxes and similar tools, such as cleavers and picks, are grouped under the term *bifaces*. It has been suggested that Acheulean sites in Africa are those where 40 percent or more of the tools/cores are bifaces. However, sites where bifaces are fewer but are flaked carefully and symmetrically are also called Acheulean. In the view of some archaeologists these criteria distinguish the Acheulean from other industries containing rare and crudely flaked bifaces, such as the Developed Oldowan or Clactonian. Other researchers claim that since the Acheulean is a tradition of tool manufacture that involves the production of bifaces any assemblage with such tools represents the Acheulean.

Preceded by the Oldowan and related core-flake tool kits, the Acheulean may have originated by gradual transitions in the degree to which oval-shaped cobbles were flaked (chopper to protohandaxe to handaxe). Particularly in Europe the idea of gradual refinement in tool manufacture from pre-Acheulean to Acheulean and throughout the Early Paleolithic period has been thought to involve a shift from using hammerstones in tool manufacture to "soft"

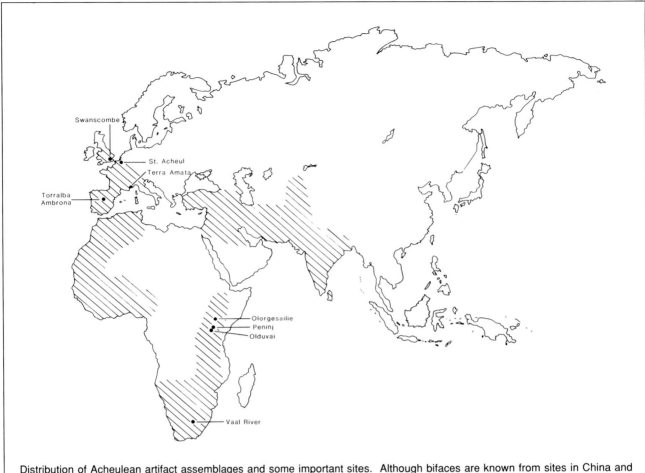

Distribution of Acheulean artifact assemblages and some important sites. Although bifaces are known from sites in China and Korea, it is not clear whether the term "Acheulean" is applicable to assemblages in eastern Asia.

hammers, such as bone or antler, which permit greater control over the transmission of force needed to remove a flake. It has been suggested by G.L. Isaac, however, that the ability to remove large flakes (greater than 10 cm. in length) was essential to the emergence of the Acheulean in Africa. This ability may have represented a threshold in tool manufacture, rapidly exploited as a starting point in the manufacture of bifaces. The rough oval shape of early bifaces is a natural extension of the original form of large flakes regardless of whether they had been further shaped intentionally into preconceived tools or simply used as cores for efficient production of numerous sharp flakes. In Acheulean assemblages, such as those at Olduvai, it is nonetheless true that bifaces were sometimes made on cobbles and also flakes smaller than 10 cm. Thus it is still unclear whether the manufacture of Acheulean bifaces came about by gradual refinement in the flaking of cobbles or by a technical innovation in the ability to produce large flakes.

Studies of sequences of sites from individual localities, such as Olorgesailie, have shown that handaxe manufacture and the overall make-up of Acheulean assemblages are marked by conservative, nonprogressive variation over hundreds of thousands of years. Moreover, examples of bifaces from Africa, Europe, and Asia are remarkably similar to one another, despite the great distances between sites. Acheulean bifaces represent the distinctive product of early human technology during a period exceeding 1 m.y. Yet biface forms did undergo refinement over the entire timespan of the Acheulean. Handaxes and related tools in the early Acheulean were chunky in section, with one face flatter than the other. The striking platforms of large flakes or parts of the cortex of handaxes made on cobbles often were not removed, and thus these handaxes were asymmetrical in shape. By the end of the Acheulean handaxes were extremely sophisticated, flat and symmetrical in shape, and required enormous skill to produce. Elaborate core preparation (e.g. Levallois) techniques, characteristic of Middle Paleolithic industries, were employed in producing highly refined bifaces in the latest Acheulean assemblages. Although many late Acheulean assemblages exhibit refined skills in tool making, others are characterized by crude bifaces and bold flaking typical of the early Acheulean. Indeed many factors may affect the degree of sophistication of bifaces, including the raw materials used. Overall change in the Acheulean is reflected by the fact that no early Acheulean assemblages are yet known to be as refined as some late Acheulean tool kits.

A set of lithic assemblages referred to as *chopper-chopping tool industries* are also known from the same time period throughout the Old World. These tool kits are characterized by basic core and flake technology and tend to lack handaxes. Examples include the Clactonian in northern Europe; the Buda industry represented at Vértesszöllös (Hungary); and the Zhoukoudian industry in China. It is unknown whether these assemblages represent a tradition of tool manufacture parallel to the Acheulean, geographical variants of the Acheulean, or in some cases an integral part of this industry. For example, it has been claimed that Clactonian assemblages reflect stages in the production of Acheulean tools. Other evidence suggests that biface and nonbiface assemblages are found in different habitats in the same area, as at Olorgesailie, and perhaps reflect different activities carried out by the same people. On the other hand it is clear that assemblages in certain geographic regions, especially in eastern Asia, simply are not characterized by bifaces.

It is widely assumed that most Acheulean assemblages were manufactured by populations of *Homo erectus*. Their first occurrences and ranges are nearly equivalent, although fossils of *Homo erectus* are only rarely associated with Acheulean tools (e.g. at Tighenif, Olduvai, and perhaps Swartkrans). Acheulean assemblages with bifaces first occur in Europe soon after 0.5 m.y. ago, about the same time that archaic *Homo sapiens* appears. Acheulean tools persist alongside early *Homo sapiens* populations in Europe (e.g. at Swanscombe) and Africa (e.g. at Saldanha) until they are succeeded by Middle Paleolithic tool kits ca. 200–150 k.y. ago. It is further assumed that these Acheulean toolmakers were hunter-gatherers who ranged widely for food. In fact little is really known about the specific behavior and ecology of these humans, for instance, whether they hunted big game or how they used their environments. Despite the prevalence of handaxes over an enormous timespan little is known about how they were used. One study of microscopic edge wear has shown that European handaxes were sometimes employed in butchery activities, and associated flakes also showed signs of working wood, hide, and bone. Experimental studies have indicated that bifaces are excellent all-purpose tools; their widespread distribution over much of the Paleolithic appears to bear this out.

See also **AFRICA; ARCHAIC HOMO SAPIENS; ASIA (EASTERN); CLACTONIAN; EARLY PALEOLITHIC; EUROPE; FRANCE; HOMO ERECTUS; HOMO SAPIENS; LITHIC USE-WEAR; MIDDLE PALEOLITHIC; MOVIUS' LINE; NEAR EAST; OLDOWAN; OLDUVAI; OLORGESAILIE; PALEOLITHIC LIFEWAYS; PREPARED-CORE; SALDANHA; SOLEILHAC; STONE-TOOL MAKING; SWANSCOMBE; SWARTKRANS; TIGHENIF; ZHOUKOUDIAN.** [R.P.]

Further Readings

Bordes, F. (1968) The Old Stone Age. London: World University Library.

Gowlett, J. (1986) Culture and conceptualisation: the Oldowan-Acheulean gradient. In G. Bailey and P. Callow (eds.): Stone Age Prehistory. Cambridge: Cambridge University Press, pp. 243-260.

Isaac, G.L. (1972) Chronology and the tempo of cultural change during the Pleistocene. In W. W. Bishop and J. A. Miller (eds.): Calibration of Hominoid Evolution. Edinburgh: Scottish Academic Press, pp. 381-430.

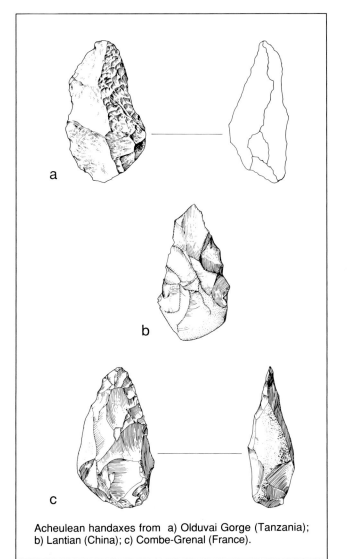

Acheulean handaxes from a) Olduvai Gorge (Tanzania); b) Lantian (China); c) Combe-Grenal (France).

Keeley, L. (1980) Experimental Determination of Stone Tool Uses: A Microwear Analysis. Chicago: University of Chicago Press.

ACTUALISTIC ARCHAEOLOGY *see*
ETHNOARCHAEOLOGY;
HUNTER-GATHERERS; LITHIC USE-WEAR;
STONE-TOOL MAKING; TAPHONOMY

ADAPIDAE

Extinct primate family that has come to include a plethora of European Eocene primates ranging in size from as small as a mouse (*Anchomomys*) to as big as a large cat (*Leptadapis*). Although Adapidae is associated here with Notharctidae and Sivaladapidae, it is only within the former group that the ancestry of modern strepsirhines has traditionally been sought.

History of Study

The genus *Adapis*, which gives its name to the family Adapidae and to taxa of other ranks, was described in 1821 by the French paleontologist Georges Cuvier, who thought it might be either a pachyderm or an artiodactyl. Despite this "false start" *Adapis* was the first fossil primate to be studied and has become one of the best known of all European fossil primates, being a particularly dominant mammal in collections from the limestone deposits of the Franco-Belgian basin. The genus *Leptadapis*, the largest of the adapids, used to be included as a species of *Adapis*, *A. magnus*, but the genus *Adapis* is now reserved for the original form, *A. parisiensis*, and perhaps one other species of comparable size.

In 1912 the Swiss paleontologist H.G. Stehlin published a monographic study of *Adapis* (including "*Adapis*" *magnus*). In comparing it especially with the North American *Notharctus*, he concluded that, while the Old and New World taxa may somehow be related, differences warranted distinction at the family level between the groups they represented. This mat-

ter was addressed by the American paleontologist W.K. Gregory in his 1920 work on *Notharctus*, in which he argued that differences between *Adapis* and *Notharctus* in skull shape and particularly in dental elaboration (more so in the latter taxon), while real, were no less profound than differences that existed among miacids, an assemblage of extinct but diverse carnivores that all paleontologists seemed to agree belonged in the same family. Thus Gregory concluded that it was appropriate to group the European taxa in the subfamily Adapinae and the North American forms in Notharctinae and to subsume both in the family Adapidae. The common ancestor of both adapid subfamilies was taken to be the early Eocene *Pelycodus* (then known only from North America but now also from Europe), from which Gregory felt the geologically younger *Adapis* and *Notharctus* could be derived.

This basic phylogenetic scheme has not changed in the ensuing decades, but largely through the studies of P. Robinson in 1957 and C.L. Gazin in 1958 Stehlin's suggestion that the European and North American taxa should be separated at the family level was revived. Thus two alternative classificatory schemes involve the family Adapidae: most recently E.L. Simons, and F.S. Szalay and E. Delson, have preferred Gregory's subfamily divisions, while in this volume, for example, the distinctiveness of the two groups is maintained at the family level.

Phylogenetic Relationships

In addition to their ancientness—mid-late Eocene—adapids have been sought as potential ancestors of modern strepsirhines because of features that have been presumed to be primitive. Adapids lack a tooth comb of the sort seen in modern lemurs and lorises; they typically have a greater number of premolars (four as opposed to three in each quadrant of the jaw); and they have a "lemurlike" bulla (which, because it is similar to that in *Lemur*, was seen, almost by definition, as primitive). Aside from the occasional inconsistency, such as having a fused mandibular symphysis, *Adapis* especially could fulfill the role of ancestor to the modern strepsirhines. Gregory even argued that dental similarities between the fossil form and the extant *Lepilemur* demonstrated the primitiveness among the living taxa of *Lepilemur* and thus demonstrated the descent from *Adapis* of other lemurs via *Lepilemur*. Just over 50 years later P.D. Gingerich thought the dental similarities were greater between *Adapis* and the extant *Hapalemur* and thus suggested that this lemur, not *Lepilemur*, was the link between the extinct taxon and the other modern strepsirhines. J.H. Schwartz and I. Tattersall turned the argument around and suggested that the distinc-

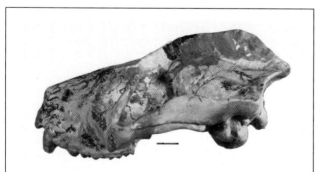

Lateral view of the cranium of *Leptadapis magnus*. Scale is 1 cm.

tiveness of the compressed cusps and shearing crests of the molars of *Adapis* as well as *Hapalemur* and *Lepilemur* indicated that these taxa were closely related and specialized members of Strepsirhini; these authors included the *Notharctus* group in Adapidae. Most recently Schwartz pointed out that there really are no features that would unite a *Notharctus* group with an *Adapis* group, and he and Tattersall have presented unexpected evidence suggesting a relationship between Adapidae, in the restricted sense of *Adapis* plus those few forms sharing derived characters with it, and a particular group of Malagasy primates, the indrioids.

During this latter review it also became apparent that past scholars placed taxa into a group with *Adapis* largely because these fossils were Eocene in age and European in location. An appraisal of the spectrum of so-called adapids revealed that some were actually related to *Notharctus* or *Pelycodus*, such as *Cercamonius* and *Protoadapis*, *Pronycticebus* and *Agerina*, respectively, others to extant taxa, such as the fossil genus *Huerzeleris* to the living *Phaner*, and yet others were lorisoids of uncertain affinity, such as *Anchomomys* and *Periconodon*. Adapidae seems therefore to be not only a group related to a small number of specialized extant primates, but a group of few members: *Adapis* and *Leptadapis* as well as the recently proposed genera *Simonsia* and *Paradapis*.

See also **INDRIOIDEA; LEMURIFORMES; LEMUROIDEA; LORISOIDEA; NOTHARCTIDAE.** [J.H.S.]

Further Readings

Gregory, W.K. (1920) On the structure and relations of *Notharctus*, an American Eocene primate. Mem. Am. Mus. Nat. Hist. 3:49–243.

Schwartz, J.H. (1986) Primate systematics and a classification of the order. In D.R. Swindler (ed.): Comparative Primate Biology, Vol. I: Systematics, Evolution and Anatomy. New York: Liss, pp. 1–41.

Schwartz, J.H., and Tattersall, I. (1985) Evolutionary relationships of living lemurs and lorises (Mammalia, Primates) and their potential affinities with European Eocene Adapidae. Anthropol. Pap. Am. Mus. Nat. Hist. 60:1–100.

Szalay, F.S., and Delson, E. (1979) Evolutionary History of the Primates. New York: Academic.

ADAPIFORMES

Primate infraorder erected by F.S. Szalay and E. Delson to distinguish a collection of primarily Eocene primates from more recent and supposedly descendant strepsirhines. Adapiformes here subsumes the superfamily Adapoidea, which in turn contains the families Notharctidae, Adapidae, and Sivaladapidae. Adapoidea, when used previously, had included only the Holarctic family Notharctidae and the European family Adapidae and had been grouped with extant taxa in the infraorder Lemuriformes. Recent discoveries in late Miocene deposits of India by P.D. Gingerich and A. Sahni of well-preserved jaws and teeth of *Sivaladapis* have convinced some paleontologists that this and other Indopakistan Miocene forms thought to be related to adapids should be distinguished as a group taxonomically; in the classification used here they are referred to the family Sivaladapidae.

As a group Adapiformes is distinguished from extant strepsirhines only by its members' greater antiquity. There are no morphological features peculiar to adapiforms that would attest to their monophyly. And aside from the possibility that at least some adapids possess a diminutive tooth comb, there are no features that indicate that adapiforms are phylogenetically strepsirhine. The association of adapiforms with extant taxa rests primarily on the sharing by various notharctids, adapids, and lemurs of the "lemurlike" bulla—i.e., an "inflated" auditory bulla whose lateral edge extends laterally beyond the inferior margin of the tympanic ring (the "free" tympanic ring).

See also **ADAPIDAE; NOTHARCTIDAE; SIVALADAPIDAE; STREPSIRHINI.** [J.H.S.]

Further Readings

Schwartz, J.H. (1986) Primate systematics and a classification of the order. In D.R. Swindler (ed.): Comparative Primate Biology, Vol. I: Systematics, Evolution and Anatomy. New York: Liss, pp. 1–41.

Schwartz, J.H., and Tattersall, I. (1985) Evolutionary relationships of living lemurs and lorises (Mammalia, Primates) and their potential affinities with European Eocene Adapidae. Anthropol. Pap. Am. Mus. Nat. Hist. 60:1–100.

ADAPINAE *see* ADAPIDAE

ADAPIS *see* ADAPIDAE

ADAPTATION(S)

States of organismic phenotypes (an item of behavior, physiological process, or anatomical property) shaped by natural selection to perform a specific role. The evolutionary process of natural selection acting to shape, maintain, or modify such properties is also known as *adaptation*. The theory of adaptation is the evolutionary biological explanation for the design apparent in nature, where organisms appear to display a close fit to their environments. Adaptation is the central focus of both Darwin's original formulation of evolutionary theory and modern formulations of the evolutionary process.

Much remains to be learned about the process of adaptation. On the one hand theorists since Darwin have argued that selection should constantly improve the quality of adaptations or modify adaptations to keep pace with changing environments. According to this view of adaptation constant, gradual change should be the norm. On the other hand many species remain stable in most of their characteristics for long periods of their history (the phenomenon of stasis), and thus it is assumed that natural selection lends stability and conserves adaptations for large portions of a species' history. According to this "punctuational" view adaptive change is relatively rare in evolution, is relatively rapid when it occurs, and is most often associated with speciation.

See also ADAPTIVE RADIATION; EVOLUTION; PHENOTYPE; PREADAPTATION. [N.E.]

Further Readings

Bock, W.J., and von Wahlert, G. (1965) Adaptation and the form-function complex. Evolution 19:269-299.

Futuyma, D.J. (1986) Evolutionary Biology, 2nd ed. Sunderland, Mass.: Sinauer.

Lewontin, R.C. (1978) Adaptation. Sci. Am. 239:212-230.

ADAPTIVE LANDSCAPE see ADAPTATION; EVOLUTION; GENETICS; SPECIATION

ADAPTIVE RADIATION

Evolutionary diversification of a monophyletic lineage, where descendant species occupy a variety of environments representing an array of ecological niches. Such evolutionary events are typically rapid and commonly follow mass extinctions or reflect the invasion of underexploited habitats. A classic example is the diversification of marsupials in Australia.

See also ADAPTATION; EVOLUTION; PHYLOGENY. [N.E.]

AD DABTIYAH see HELIOPITHECUS; HOMINIDAE; NEAR EAST

AEGYPTOPITHECUS see PROPLIOPITHECIDAE

AEOLOPITHECUS see PROPLIOPITHECIDAE

AETHIOPICUS, AUSTRALOPITHECUS see AUSTRALOPITHECUS

AFAR

The lowland area called the Afar Depression is located in Ethiopia at the triple junction of the continental East African Rift and the oceanic Red Sea and the Gulf of Aden rifts. It is bounded by the Red Sea and Gulf of Aden to the east, the Somalian Plateau to the south, and the Ethiopian Plateau to the west. The Afar is occupied by an equatorial desert stretching over nearly 200,000 sq. km., reaching over 100 m. below sea level in some areas.

Significant paleoanthropological discoveries have been made in the west-central Afar basin, a north-to-south trending structure adjacent and parallel to the Ethiopian Western Escarpment. The structural sink of the west-central Afar basin has seen rapid accumulation of thick fluvial, deltaic, and lacustrine sediments since Miocene time.

French geologist M. Taieb discovered the paleontological and archaeological potential of the Afar during geological reconaissance of the Awash River valley in the late 1960s. In 1971 and 1972 Taieb was joined by D.C. Johanson, Y. Coppens, and J. Kalb in an exploratory survey along the Awash River drainage, discovering dozens of fossil fields and archaeological localities. In 1973 the International Afar Research Expedition (IARE) began work at one particularly promising site, Hadar, continuing until 1977 with dramatic results. Kalb left the IARE in 1974 and continued Taieb's exploratory work along the Middle Awash area south of Hadar. His Rift Valley Research Mission in Ethiopia (RVRME) discontinued its efforts in 1978, but further survey in this area was accomplished in 1981 by a team led by J.D. Clark and T.D. White.

Although the Afar has not been worked as intensively or for as long as other regions of eastern Africa, it has already produced some of the most important early hominid remains from the continent. The most celebrated of these is a partial skeleton from Hadar nicknamed "Lucy." At the Hadar site the Hadar Formation is a series of sediments, ca. 280 m. thick, of middle Pliocene age, dating between ca. 2.8 and 3.7 m.y. Hominid remains are abundant and come from several units in the geological succession, including an important sample of 13 individuals from Locality 333. All of the Hadar hominids have been attributed to the species *Australopithecus afarensis*, whose name is derived from the Afar region. It is this region that has yielded the most numerous and complete specimens. *Australopithecus afarensis* is considered by many to be the ancestral species in hominid evolution. No stone tools are known from deposits containing the remains of this species, but sites in the Gona region of Hadar have yielded Oldowan tools that may date to 2.6 m.y.

The region south of Hadar along the central portion of the Awash River is known as the Middle Awash. The beds at Hadar are predominantly Pliocene in age, but the strata exposed in the Middle

Archaeologist J.D. Clark examines an Acheulean handaxe found eroding from middle Pleistocene deposits in the Middle Awash Valley of Ethiopia's Afar Depression. (Photograph by and courtesy of Tim D. White.)

Awash cover much of the last 6 m.y. Also unlike Hadar the Middle Awash geology is complex, with much faulting, but volcanic rocks are present and a radiometric dating program has begun.

In 1976 a partial hominid cranium was found in the Middle Awash at Bodo with large numbers of Acheulean tools and an abundant middle Pleistocene fauna. In 1981 a second hominid fossil was found at Bodo, a fragment of parietal. The older deposits at Bodo include beds with abundant late Pliocene fauna and a sequence of early Pleistocene strata with Oldowan tools. South of Bodo, at the sites of Belohdelie and Maka, portions of a hominid cranial vault and a proximal femur were found in 1981. Paleontological and archaeological localities occur on both sides of the Awash River between Gewane in the south and Hadar in the north. In addition to the fossil hominid discoveries all phases of the Acheulean and the Middle and Late Stone Age are represented by archaeological sites with stone tools and fauna. The earlier Pliocene and Miocene parts of the Middle Awash stratigraphy have also yielded mammalian remains.

Elsewhere in the Afar, near its southern edge at the town of Dire Dawa, excavations in the Porc Epic Cave have yielded a Middle Stone Age assemblage with a fragmentary hominid mandible.

See also **AUSTRALOPITHECUS AFARENSIS; BODO; HADAR; MIDDLE AWASH; RIFT VALLEY.** [T.D.W.]

Further Readings

Clark, J.D., Asfaw, B., Assefa, G., Harris, J.W.K., Kurashina, H., Walter, R.C., White, T.D., and Williams, M.A.J. (1984) Paleoanthropological discoveries in the Middle Awash Valley, Ethiopia. Nature 307:423–428.

Kalb, J.E., Oswald, E.B., Tebedge, S., Mebrate, A., Tola, E., and Peak, D. (1982) Geology and stratigraphy of Neogene deposits, Middle Awash Valley, Ethiopia. Nature 298:17–25.

Johanson, D.C., and Edey, M. (1981) Lucy: The Beginnings of Humankind. New York: Simon and Schuster.

Johanson, D.C., Taieb, M., and Coppens, Y. (1982) Pliocene hominids from the Hadar Formation, Ethiopia (1973–1977): stratigraphic, chronologic and paleoenvironmental contexts, with notes on hominid morphology. Am. J. Phys. Anthropol. 57:373–402.

AFARENSIS, AUSTRALOPITHECUS *see* AUSTRALOPITHECUS AFARENSIS

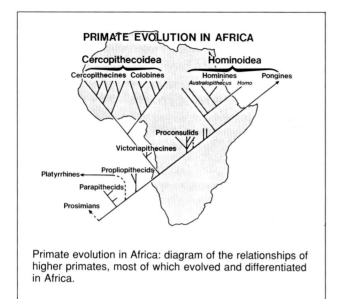

PRIMATE EVOLUTION IN AFRICA

Primate evolution in Africa: diagram of the relationships of higher primates, most of which evolved and differentiated in Africa.

AFRICA

No other continent rivals Africa for the richness of information it has provided about human evolution and prehistory. It offers both the earliest and the most continuous fossil record of the evolution of higher primates (monkeys, apes, and humans). Indeed, with the exception of the platyrrhine monkeys of South America, Africa has supplied most of our

evidence for the initial evolutionary divergence of every major group of anthropoid primates during the past 40 m.y.

Geology and Geography

The geology of Africa would seem to hold little promise for the study of human evolution and prehistory. Over roughly half the continent the only rocks exposed on the surface are remnants of the Precambrian shield that yield but minute traces of the earliest life forms. Another third of the continental surface is covered with unfossiliferous dune sands of Holocene age or Paleozoic and Mesozoic rocks containing fossils of fishes, reptiles, and some of the earliest mammals. Fossiliferous deposits from the Cenozoic comprise only a small portion of the exposed rocks on this continent, and many of these are in areas that are either covered by dense vegetation or virtually inaccessible by ground transportation. Due to a combination of geological, historical, and political coincidences the record of primate and human evolution in Africa comes primarily from three areas: North Africa, including the Mediterranean coast and the Nile Valley of Egypt; East African deposits associated with rifting and volcanic activity; and deposits in southern Africa associated with both rivers and limestone caves. Many equally promising areas in the western and central parts of this continent remain to be thoroughly explored and studied.

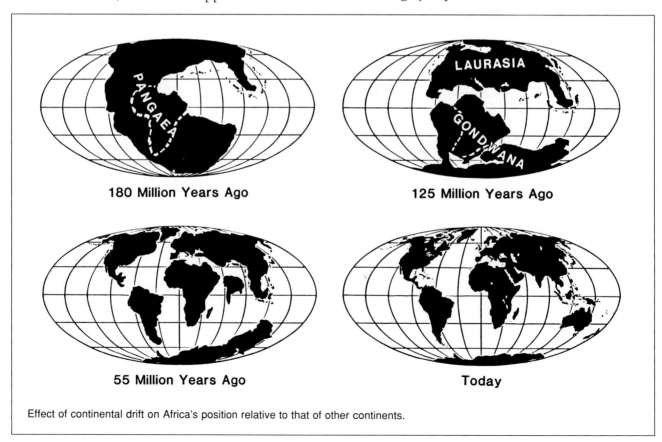

Effect of continental drift on Africa's position relative to that of other continents.

The geological and faunal connections between Africa and other continents have been a topic of speculation for centuries, and it was the apparent fit between the Atlantic coasts of Africa and South America that inspired early advocates of continental drift. We now know that Africa has held a central position in the collisions and separations of the continents over much of the Phanerozoic. At the end of the Permian (the time of the earliest dinosaurs), ca. 225 m.y. ago, Africa was joined with South America, Antarctica, Australia, and the Indian subcontinent in a supercontinent called Gondwanaland. During the Mesozoic the parts of Gondwanaland began to break apart and gradually form the continents and oceans as we know them. For much of the Cenozoic Africa has been an isolated continent, the site of the origin and radiation of many groups of mammals, including catarrhine primates. During the past 65 m.y., however, a long series of intermittent connections with Europe and Asia have allowed faunal interchange and hence played a major role in the evolution and dispersal of primates and other mammals.

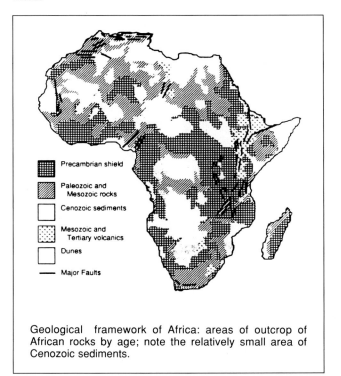

Precambrian shield

Paleozoic and Mesozoic rocks

Cenozoic sediments

Mesozoic and Tertiary volcanics

Dunes

Major Faults

Geological framework of Africa: areas of outcrop of African rocks by age; note the relatively small area of Cenozoic sediments.

Sitting astride the equator, Africa's climate is overall probably milder than that of any other continent except South America. Snow and frost are virtually unknown except on tall mountains. This climate certainly contributed to the abundance of primate and human ancestors in Africa. Although much of the continent is desert, other areas are well watered and support a variety of vegetation types that have played

a role in human evolution, as well as an abundant fauna that has long been exploited by hominids. Finally, the continent's mineral resources, including iron, gold, and precious gems, have featured in more recent periods of human evolution.

(*See also* CENOZOIC; GLACIATION; PALEOBIOGEOGRAPHY; PLATE TECTONICS.)

The Fossil Record

Oligocene   The fossil record of primate evolution in Africa begins in the latest Eocene or early Oligocene, between 35 and 40 m.y. ago. There is no significant African record of fossil mammals from either the Paleocene or Eocene, although some fragmentary Eocene specimens have been suggested as primate. Oligocene primates are known from the single rich site of the Fayum (Egypt), which was then a tropical rain forest near the Tethys Seaway. The Fayum has yielded some of the earliest fossils of many mammalian groups, including elephants and hyraxes as well as numerous primates, both prosimians and anthropoids. Among the prosimians is *Afrotarsius*, which shows similarities to the Eocene omomyids of Europe and the living *Tarsius* from Asia. A lorisid and an omomyid have recently been described, as well as the enigmatic *Oligopithecus*.

More significantly, from the perspective of human evolution, the Fayum provides the earliest evidence of higher primates, comprising two different families. The parapithecids are basal anthropoids. They were more advanced than any prosimians, including the adapids and omomyids from the Eocene of Europe and North America, but more primitive than any later higher primates, including the platyrrhines of South America. There were at least five species: the tiny, very primitive *Qatrania* (one species) from the lowest level; the generalized and well-known *Apidium* (two species); and the larger, very specialized *Parapithecus* (two species, of which one is sometimes placed in its own genus, *Simonsius*).

The other higher primates from the Fayum early Oligocene are the propliopithecids, primitive catarrhines ancestral to all later Old World anthropoids. The two genera, *Aegyptopithecus* and *Propliopithecus*, were medium-sized (3–6-kg.) arboreal frugivores, with sexually dimorphic canines.

The diversity of anthropoids and the presence of tarsiiform prosimians in the Fayum suggest that higher primates are African in origin. Similarly, the distinctiveness of the Fayum fauna compared with that of European and Asian localities similar in age indicates that Africa was separated from the northern continents during the Oligocene.

(*See also* ANTHROPOIDEA; CATARRHINI; FAYUM; LORISIDAE; OLIGOCENE; OLIGOPITHECUS; OMOMYIDAE; PARAPITHECIDAE; PLATYRRHINI; PLIOPITHECOIDEA; PROPLIOPITHECIDAE.)

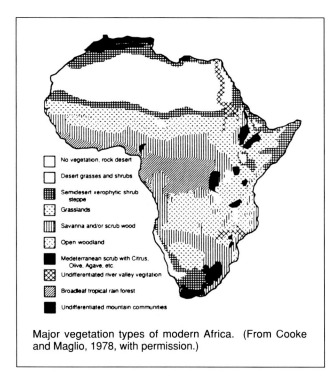

Major vegetation types of modern Africa. (From Cooke and Maglio, 1978, with permission.)

Legend:
- No vegetation, rock desert
- Desert grasses and shrubs
- Semidesert xerophytic shrub steppe
- Grasslands
- Savanna and/or scrub wood
- Open woodland
- Mediterranean scrub with Citrus, Olive, Agave, etc.
- Undifferentiated river valley vegetation
- Broadleaf tropical rain forest
- Undifferentiated mountain communities

Miocene   With the development of the major rift systems and associated volcanic activity, the Miocene was a time of dramatic geological activity in East Africa. The abundant Miocene fossils from many parts of Africa document numerous major events in higher primate and human evolution during this long epoch. The dozens of rich fossil sites from the early Miocene of East Africa bear many remains of apes, monkeys, and prosimians (lorises and galagos). The early Miocene sites seem to sample a range of paleoenvironments from rain forest (Napak, Songhor) to drier, more open woodland habitats (Rusinga, Muruarot). The composition of primate faunas at different sites is quite different over very small geographical and temporal distances, but recent research suggests that this is due in part to the greater age of the "forested" sites.

In the early Miocene of Kenya and Uganda we find evidence of a diverse radiation of apes more advanced than the propliopithecids from the Fayum but less advanced than the living great apes. In their size diversity (3–50 kg.), likely dietary habits (frugivores and some folivores), and habit preferences (arboreal and terrestrial species) they seem to have spanned the ecological niches occupied by both monkeys and apes of today. They had, however, different types of specializations in the dentition and the locomotor skeleton than those of modern catarrhines. Evolutionary relationships among the many genera (*Proconsul, Afropithecus, Turkanapithecus, Rangwapithecus, Nyanzapithecus, Dendropithecus, Lim-*

nopithecus, Simiolus, Xenopithecus, Micropithecus) of early Miocene fossil apes from East Africa are vague, and new species and genera are discovered every year. Yet it is likely that several later lineages can be traced back to this radiation, including oreopithecids (*Nyanzapithecus*) and great apes and humans (*Afropithecus*). There are also indications that parts of this radiation spread out of Africa into Asia, where fossils similar to *Micropithecus* and *Proconsul* are known from earlier Miocene sites in Pakistan and China, and from the early middle Miocene of Eurasia in general.

Contemporary with this extensive radiation of primitive apes we find the earliest Old World monkeys, *Victoriapithecus* and *Prohylobates*, in East Africa (Kenya and Uganda) and North Africa (Egypt and Libya). These early monkeys lie at the base of the Old World monkey radiation and are intermediate in many dental features between apes and later, more specialized colobines and cercopithecines. Fossil monkeys are known from only a few of the earlier Miocene localities (e.g. Napak, Buluk, and the slightly younger Maboko), and there are indications that these species inhabited more open woodland environments compared with many of their ape contemporaries.

Much less is known about primate evolution in Africa during the later Miocene. The few sites from this period (Fort Ternan, Nachola, Ngeringerowa) seem to indicate drier, more open habitats than those sampled by many of the earlier sites. The most common fossil ape is *Kenyapithecus*; a few remains of a small colobine (*Microcolobus*) have been found in Kenya and both a larger colobine and a cercopithecine at Marceau (Algeria). There is a large fossil ape from the Samburu Hills (10–8 m.y.), and two localities from the latest Miocene, Tabarin and Lothagam, have yielded remains of the earliest fossil hominid, *Australopithecus* cf. *afarensis*.

(*See also* AFROPITHECUS; BULUK; CATARRHINI; FORT TERNAN; GALAGIDAE; HOMINIDAE; HOMINOIDEA; KENYAPITHECUS; KORU; LORISIDAE; LOTHAGAM; MABOKO; MIOCENE; MURUAROT; NACHOLA; OREOPITHECIDAE; PLIOPITHECIDAE; PROCONSUL; RIFT VALLEY; RUSINGA; SAMBURU; SONGHOR; TIME SCALE; TURKANAPITHECUS; VICTORIAPITHECINAE.)

Pliocene   The African Pliocene is characterized by the evolutionary radiations of two major groups of higher primates, Old World monkeys and hominids. Fossil apes are unknown from either the Pliocene or the Pleistocene, and the only prosimians are a few remains of fossil galagos. Sites of this age in eastern Africa are especially well dated and correlated to each other on the bases of magnetic and radiometric geochronology.

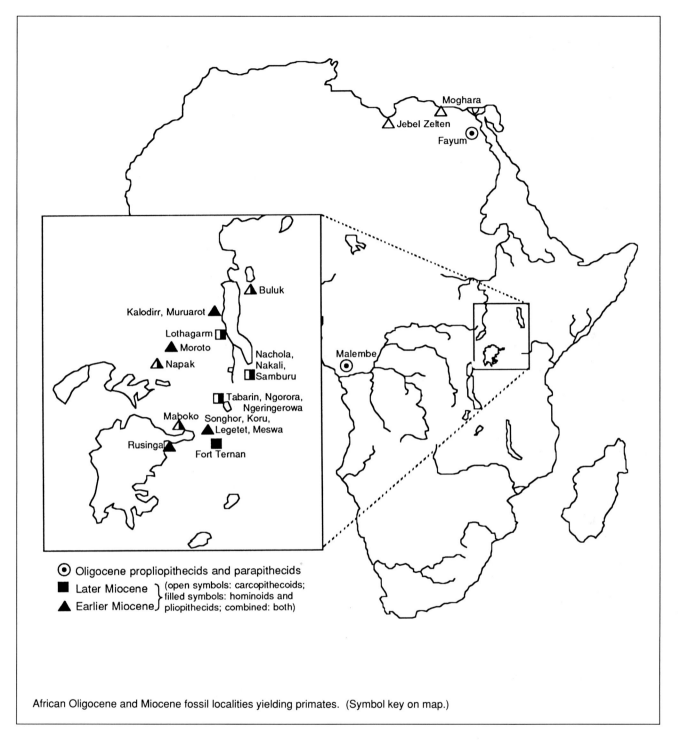

African Oligocene and Miocene fossil localities yielding primates. (Symbol key on map.)

The earliest Pliocene cercopithecids are fossil macaques and the long-faced colobine, *Libypithecus*, from Wadi Natrun and Sahabi in North Africa. The rich Pliocene sites in Ethiopia, Kenya, Tanzania, and South Africa document a diversity of both colobines and cercopithecines, many of which are considerably larger than their extant relatives. *Parapapio* is known from the southern sites of Sterkfontein and Makapansgat, as well as from Hadar and the Omo basin. In eastern and southern Africa fossil geladas (*Theropithecus*) were quite abundant, along with large colobines (*Cercopithecoides*, *Paracolobus*, and *Rhinopithecus*—the latter two as yet known only from eastern African localities). The genus *Cercopithecus*, which is so successful in Africa today, is known from only a handful of fossils, and *Papio* also is generally not common.

Early Pliocene hominid fossils, attributed to *Australopithecus afarensis*, have been recovered from the

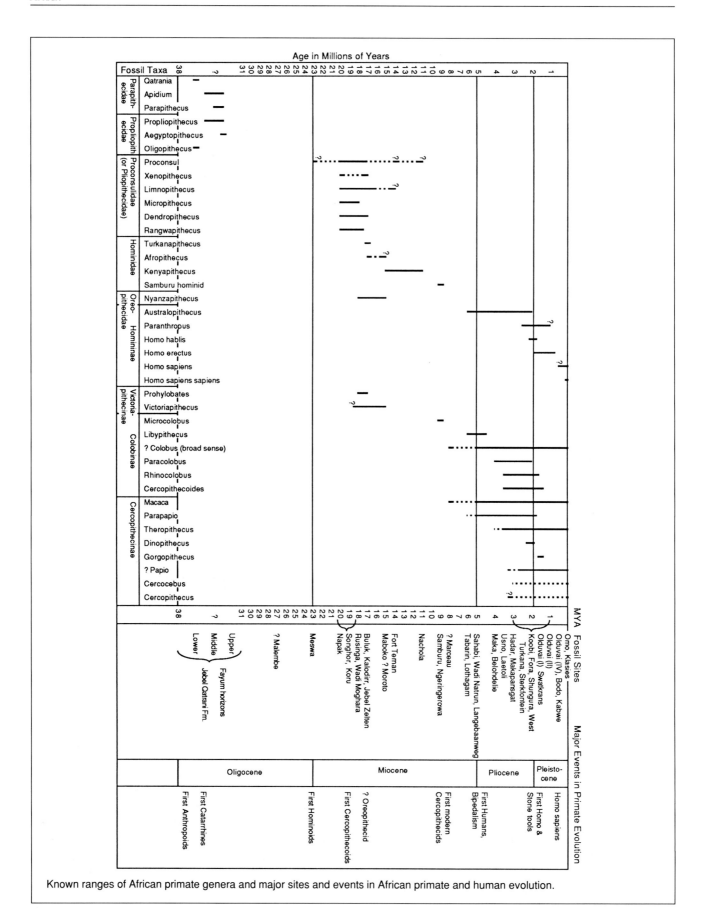

Known ranges of African primate genera and major sites and events in African primate and human evolution.

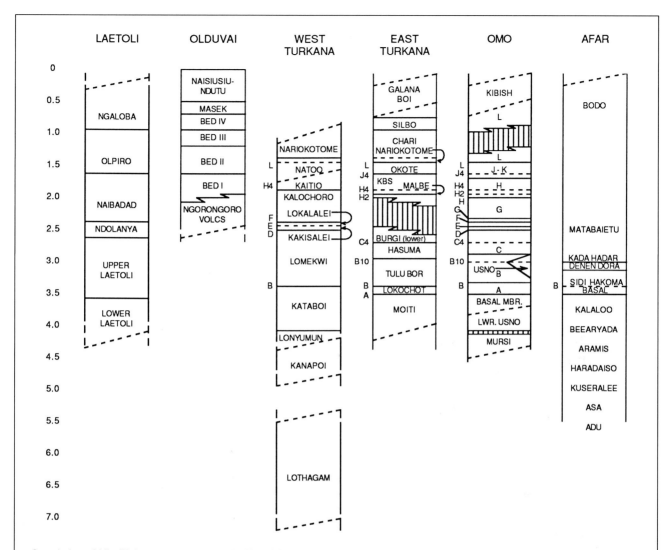

Correlation of Mio-Pleistocene sequences in East Africa. Tuff layers at the base are used to define units in the Turkana and Omo sequences; correlations are made by K-Ar ages on tuffs and lavas, chemical and mineralogical "fingerprinting" of tuff deposits, paleomagnetic reversals, and by paleontological comparisons. Some established ages are as follows: Moiti Tuff, 4.10 m.y.; Tulu Bor Tuff, 3.35 m.y.; Shungura D, 2.52 m.y.; Shungura G, 2.33 m.y.; KBS Tuff, 1.88 m.y.; and Chari Tuff, 1.39 m.y.

Hadar Formation, the sites of Belohdelie and Maka in the Middle Awash, the Usno Formation (Ethiopia), the Koobi Fora Formation (Kenya), and the Laetolil Beds (Tanzania). These fossils span the period between ca. 4 and 3 m.y., and *A. afarensis* appears to have occupied both closed forest and open savanna habitats. Its postcranial skeleton attests to both bipedal and climbing locomotor repertoires, and *A. afarensis* shows considerable sexual dimorphism.

The South African sites of Taung, Makapansgat, and Sterkfontein, which have been faunally dated to between ca. 3 and 2 m.y., contain fossils of *A. africanus*. There is as yet no convincing evidence for *A. africanus* in eastern Africa. Faunal evidence indicates a closed bush-cover environment for *A. africanus*.

This species is postcranially similar to *A. afarensis*, and it shows evidence of strong sexual dimorphism.

Two "robust" *Australopithecus* species are known from the Pliocene of eastern Africa. *A. aethiopicus* is represented by a cranium from the Lomekwi Formation (Kenya) and a mandible and probably some isolated teeth from the Shungura Formation (Ethiopia) that are dated to ca. 2.5 m.y. *A. boisei*, which is better known in Pleistocene-age sediments from eastern Africa, is also represented in Pliocene deposits from the Shungura Formation, the Koobi Fora Formation, and Bed I of Olduvai Gorge. The earliest fossils attributed to *A. boisei* date to ca. 2.2 m.y., and this species appears to have occupied both open and closed habitats.

The earliest evidence for the genus *Homo* derives

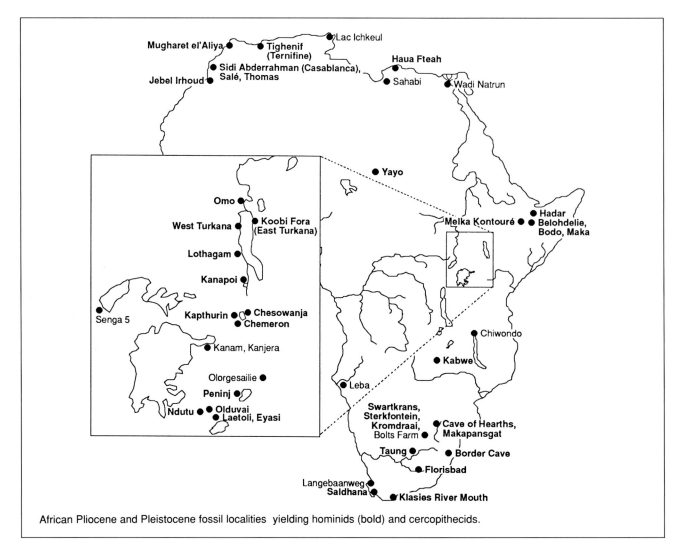

African Pliocene and Pleistocene fossil localities yielding hominids (bold) and cercopithecids.

from Pliocene deposits in eastern and southern Africa. The earliest representatives of this genus are commonly attributed to the species *H. habilis*, which is known from ca. 2.3 to 1.8 m.y. in the Omo Shungura Formation, the Koobi Fora Formation at East Turkana, Olduvai Gorge, and Sterkfontein. It is probably not coincidental that the earliest lithic artifacts date to ca. 2.4 or 2.3 m.y. at sites in the Omo and Afar regions of Ethiopia and possibly at Senga-5 in northern Zaire. These stone tools, like those from Olduvai Gorge and Koobi Fora (Karari), appear to represent the opportunistic flaking of small cobbles (Mode I), and a small proportion of animal bones that are associated with these Oldowan artifacts show evidence of stone-tool cutmarks.

(*See also* AFAR; AUSTRALOPITHECUS;
AUSTRALOPITHECUS AFARENSIS;
AUSTRALOPITHECUS AFRICANUS;
AUSTRALOPITHECUS BOISEI; BARINGO;
BRECCIA CAVE FORMATION; CERCOPITHECINAE; COLOBINAE;
EAST TURKANA; ETHIOPIA; GEOCHRONOMETRY; HADAR;
HOMO HABILIS; KANAPOI; KARARI; KENYA; LAETOLI;
MAKAPANSGAT; OLDOWAN; OMO; PALEOLITHIC;
PALEOMAGNETISM; PARANTHROPUS; PLIOCENE;
SAHABI; SENGA-5; SOUTH AFRICA; STERKFONTEIN;
STRATIGRAPHY; TAUNG; WEST TURKANA.)

Pleistocene   The fossil record during the Pleistocene shows further evolutionary radiations of Old World monkeys and hominids, the latter characterized by increasing reliance on technology, resulting in an abundant archaeological record. Although the global definition of the Plio-Pleistocene boundary is fixed at ca. 1.6 m.y., there is little significant change in Africa at that precise horizon.

Fossils of *Australopithecus boisei* are known from early Pleistocene deposits in the Shungura Formation, the Koobi Fora Formation, and Olduvai Gorge, as well as from the Humbu Formation at Peninj (Tanzania) and Chemoigut Formation at Chesowanja (Kenya). *A. boisei* is not represented in the fossil record after ca. 1.3 m.y. In South Africa the "robust" species *A. robustus* is known from the sites of Swartkrans and Kromdraai, dated to between ca. 1.8 and 1.5 m.y. *A. robustus* appears to have inhabited comparatively open environments.

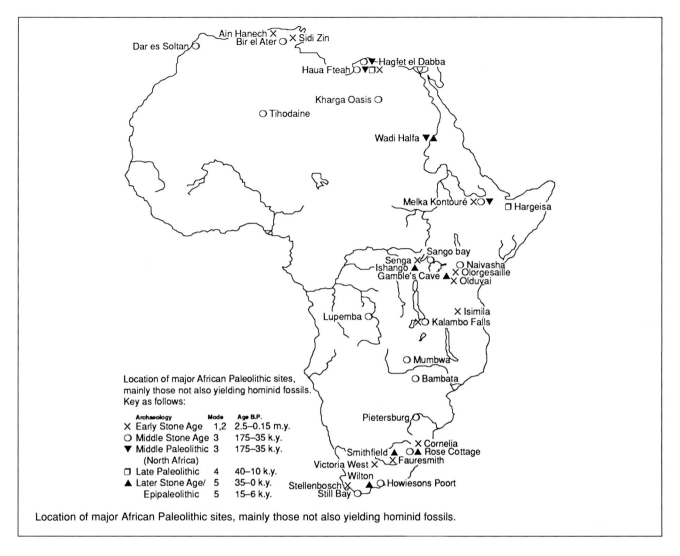

Dar es Soltan ○
Ain Hanech ✕
Bir el Ater ○ ✕ Sidi Zin
○▼ Hagfet el Dabba
Haua Fteah ○▼□✕ ▽
Kharga Oasis ○
○ Tihodaine
Wadi Halfa ▼▲
Melka Kontouré ✕○▼
□ Hargeisa
Sango bay
Senga ✕○ ○ Naivasha
Ishango ▲ ✕ Olorgesaille
Gamble's Cave ▲ ✕ Olduvai
✕ Isimila
Lupemba ○ ✕○ Kalambo Falls
○ Mumbwa
○ Bambata
Pietersburg ○
Location of major African Paleolithic sites, mainly those not also yielding hominid fossils. Key as follows:

Archaeology	Mode	Age B.P.
✕ Early Stone Age	1,2	2.5–0.15 m.y.
○ Middle Stone Age	3	175–35 k.y.
▼ Middle Paleolithic (North Africa)	3	175–35 k.y.
□ Late Paleolithic	4	40–10 k.y.
▲ Later Stone Age/ Epipaleolithic	5	35–0 k.y. 15–6 k.y.

✕ Cornelia
Smithfield ▲ ○▲ Rose Cottage
Victoria West ✕ ✕ Fauresmith
Wilton
Stellenbosch ✕ ▲ ○ Howiesons Poort
Still Bay ○

Location of major African Paleolithic sites, mainly those not also yielding hominid fossils.

Specimens of early *Homo erectus* are known from Swartkrans, the Koobi Fora Formation, and Nariokotome on the west side of Lake Turkana at ca. 1.8–1.5 m.y. Fossils from Olduvai Gorge, the Shungura Formation, Gomboré II at Melka Kontouré (Ethiopia), Yayo (Chad), and Tighenif (Algeria), and from Salé and the Sidi Abderrahman and Thomas Quarries (Morocco), are generally regarded as representing later *H. erectus*. African *H. erectus* fossils span a considerable period of time between ca. 1.8 and 0.7 m.y. Many of these fossils derive from deposits that contain lithic artifacts of the Acheulean tradition, and countless sites from this period throughout northern, eastern, and southern Africa preserve Acheulean artifacts but no hominid remains (e.g. Olorgesailie). In contrast to the opportunistic flaking that appears to have been a feature of the Oldowan tradition, the Acheulean assemblages (Mode II) are generally characterized by well-formed handaxes and cleavers, and there is evidence that a much wider landscape was being utilized by ca. 1.7 m.y. than had been the case before. In a number of instances the source rocks are located many kilometers from the Acheulean archaeological sites. Fire is documented by 1.4 m.y.

(*See also* ACHEULEAN; AUSTRALOPITHECUS ROBUSTUS; CASABLANCA; CHESOWANJA; EARLY PALEOLITHIC; ECONOMY, PREHISTORIC; FIRE; HOMO; HOMO ERECTUS; HOPE FOUNTAIN; KROMDRAAI; LAINYAMOK; LITHIC USE-WEAR; MAN-LAND RELATIONSHIPS; MELKA KONTOURÉ; NARIOKOTOME; OLDUVAI; OLORGESAILIE; PALEOLITHIC LIFEWAYS; PENINJ; PLEISTOCENE; RAW MATERIALS; SALÉ; STONE-TOOL MAKING; SWARTKRANS; TANZANIA; THOMAS QUARRIES; TIGHENIF; YAYO.)

Middle Pleistocene fossils of early (i.e. "archaic") *Homo sapiens* are known from such sites as Bodo (Ethiopia), Kabwe (Zambia), Ndutu (Tanzania), and Saldhana (South Africa). It has been argued that specimens from Rabat (Morocco), Lake Eyasi (Tanzania), the Kapthurin Beds at Baringo (Kenya), and possibly the Cave of Hearths (South Africa) are referable to early *Homo sapiens*. For the most part these fossils are associated with Acheulean artifacts, with some indications of the use of the Levallois technique of prepared-core flaking.

In sub-Saharan Africa industries of Acheulean or Mode II type are generally termed Early Stone Age, with local variants common in South and East Africa. Dates for the youngest such industries appear to span 200 and 150 k.y., as is also the case in Europe (although there the Micoquian may extend into the last interglacial).

By the Middle Paleolithic regional differentiation becomes important in African archaeology and human paleontology. South of the Sahara such specimens as those from Florisbad (South Africa) and Ngaloba, at Laetoli (Tanzania), probably date to between 175 and 125 k.y. They may represent examples of a transition from "archaic" to the earliest "anatomically modern" Homo sapiens. Archaeological tool kits of this age are mainly Mode III form and are broadly classed as Middle Stone Age (MSA). Such industries as the Pietersburg and Orangian typically include discoidal and Levallois cores, producing convergent flakes with faceted striking platforms, as well as flake-blades, points, and side-scrapers. Sangoan, Lupemban, and Fauresmith assemblages also incorporate large bifacial tools, such as handaxes and picks, in some cases perhaps related to a woodworking, forest-dwelling adaptation. MSA industries continue with little technological change until ca. 30 k.y., but they document a broader economic base (hunting of large game, shellfish, plant foods prepared with grindstones) than is common in the Eurasian Middle Paleolithic.

The earliest known representatives of "anatomically modern" Homo sapiens have been recovered from the Omo Kibish Formation (Ethiopia) and Klasies River Mouth Cave (South Africa). No tools are known from the former region, although a questionable date of 120 k.y. was reported from levels older than the human remains. At Klasies (and the nearby Nelsons Bay Cave), fragmentary human fossils are associated with MSA artifacts and dated to the Eemian (ca. 125–90 k.y.) by geological inference. The Border Cave site in southern Africa has yielded a partial cranium and other remains of apparently African (rather than Eurasian or indeterminate) morphology, but the suggested age of 90 k.y. has been questioned. Of similar age is the Howieson's Poort industry, an MSA variant that is superficially similar to the European Late Paleolithic and perhaps the Near Eastern pre-Aurignacian in the frequency of backed blades and other Mode IV tool forms, although it is still grouped with the MSA. As with the emergence of the genus Homo southern Africa probably saw the origin of modern humans and some contemporaneous technological and economic advancements.

In North Africa Middle Paleolithic (Mode III) Levallois-Mousterian and Aterian industries are known before, during, and after the Eemian interglacial. It does not appear that Neanderthals of European or Near Eastern type ever occurred south of the Mediterranean, but human fossils of pre-Weichsel age are rare. Archaic varieties of "anatomically modern" Homo sapiens occur in northern Africa during the Weichselian, at such sites as Jebel Irhoud, Temara, and Mugharet el 'Aliya (Morocco), Haua Fteah (Libya), Singa (Sudan), and Diré-Dawa (Ethiopia). They are morphologically less comparable with the Neanderthals than with Near Eastern "archaic moderns" from Skhūl and Jebel Qafzeh.

No true Mode IV (Late Paleolithic) industries are known well south of the Sahara, but they do appear after the Aterian in North Africa. At Haua Fteah the Dabban is comparable with European blade-based industries of 40–20 k.y., and similar assemblages are known in Kenya, Ethiopia, and Somalia. The Ibero-Maurusian (or Oranian) occurs in western North Africa between ca. 20 and 10 k.y., and the eastern Oranian of Libya is of similar age. Younger levels yield such industries as the Capsian in Tunisia. To the south Later Stone Age (LSA) industries are characterized by microlithic technology and greater emphasis on fishing and hunting of large plains ungulates. The LSA may begin as early as 30 k.y. and continue into the Holocene, in some areas into the historic present.

See also ACHEULEAN; ARCHAIC HOMO SAPIENS; ARCHAIC MODERNS; ATERIAN; BAMBATA; BODO; BORDER CAVE; BOW AND ARROW; CAVE OF HEARTHS; DABBAN; EARLY STONE AGE; EPIPALEOLITHIC; EYASI; FIRST INTERMEDIATE; FLORISBAD; HAUA FTEAH; HOMO SAPIENS; HOWIESON'S POORT; IBERO-MAURUSIAN; JEBEL IRHOUD; KABWE; KALAMBO FALLS; KAPTHURIN; KLASIES; LAETOLI; LATE PALEOLITHIC; LATER STONE AGE; LEVALLOIS; LUPEMBAN; MIDDLE PALEOLITHIC; MIDDLE STONE AGE; MOUSTERIAN; NDUTU; NGALOBA; OMO; ORANGIAN; PALEOLITHIC; PIETERSBURG; PRE-AURIGNACIAN; PREPARED-CORE; QAFZEH; ROSE COTTAGE; SALDANHA; SANGOAN; SECOND INTERMEDIATE; SKHŪL; SMITHFIELD; SPEAR; STILLBAY; TSHITOLIAN; WILTON. [J.G.F., F.E.G.]

Further Readings

Clark, J.D. (1970) The Prehistory of Africa. New York: Praeger.

Fleagle, J.G. (1986) The fossil record of early catarrhine evolution. In B.A. Wood, L.B. Martin, and P. Andrews (eds.): Major Topics in Primate and Human Evolution. Cambridge: Cambridge University Press, pp. 130–149.

Howell, F.C. (1978) Hominidae. In V.J. Maglio and H.B.S. Cooke (eds.): Evolution of African Mammals. Cambridge, Mass.: Harvard University Press, pp. 149–258.

Phillipson, D. W. (1985) African Archaeology. Cambridge: Cambridge University Press.

Pickford, M. (1986) The geochronology of Miocene higher primate faunas of East Africa. In J.G. Else and P.C. Lee (eds.): Primate Evolution. Cambridge: Cambridge University Press, pp. 19–33.

Szalay, F.S., and Delson, E. (1979) Evolutionary History of the Primates. New York: Academic.

AFRICANTHROPUS *see* ARCHAIC HOMO SAPIENS; ARCHAIC MODERNS

AFRICANUS, AUSTRALOPITHECUS *see* AUSTRALOPITHECUS AFRICANUS

AFROPITHECUS

Fossil hominoid represented by a skull, several jaws, and some elements of the postcranial skeleton. *Afropithecus turkanensis* comes from Kalodirr (near Muruarot), in northern Kenya, dated ca. 17 m.y. old. It is similar in many respects to *Kenyapithecus* from Fort Ternan and *Heliopithecus* from Ad Dabtiyah (Saudi Arabia). The skull and postcrania have many primitive characters.

See also FORT TERNAN; HELIOPITHECUS; HOMINOIDEA; KENYAPITHECUS; MURUAROT. [P.A.]

AFROTARSIUS

Discovered in 1984, the first and only tarsiiform fossil found in Africa, which harbors no living tarsiers. *Afrotarsius chatrathi* is represented by a single lower-jaw fragment from deposits in the Upper Fossil Wood Zone of the Fayum Depression (Egypt), older than 31 m.y. It demonstrates the important fact that forms quite closely related to modern tarsiers were once widespread geographically. This suggests the possibility that the ancestors of the living species arose far to the west of the Malay archipelago, where they are now confined. Because it shares similarities with both living tarsiers and the late Eocene microchoerine tarsiiform *Pseudoloris* of western Europe, *A. chatrathi* may clarify the affinities of the former. Resemblances to the molars of *Tarsius* in both size and occlusal function imply a similar diet of invertebrate and vertebrate prey.

See also FAYUM; MICROCHOERINAE; OMOMYIDAE; TARSIIDAE [A.L.R.]

Further Readings

Simons, E.L., and Bown, T.M. (1985) *Afrotarsius chatrathi*, first tarsiiform primate (?Tarsiidae) from Africa. Nature *313*:475–477.

AGE *see* BIOCHRONOLOGY; TIME SCALE

AGE, SKELETAL *see* FORENSIC ANTHROPOLOGY

AGERINIA *see* ADAPIDAE

AGGREGATION-DISPERSAL

Anthropological concept that refers to the differences in the number of people who live together in foraging societies in the course of a year. Ethnographic data on simple hunter-gatherer groups, those who directly forage for what nature provides and who do not store foods, indicate that their settlement systems feature seasonal pulsations in the size of the coresident groups. Information on such groups show that small numbers of people (ca. 25 to 30 individuals or five to six nuclear families) live together during one part of the year and that these groups join similar groups during other seasons. During these relatively short periods of aggregation population increases appreciably to 100 or more individuals (25 or more families). At these large gatherings various forms of group ritual behavior are a common feature, as is exchange of information and of mates. Such seasonal fluctuation in the size of the coresident units is considered to be a universal feature of simple hunter-gatherer adaptations.

Data on past settlement systems of hunter-gatherers suggest that such aggregation-dispersal pulsations in group size may have been a feature of some Upper Paleolithic settlement systems as well. Such sites as Altamira and Lascaux have been interpreted as seasonal aggregation camps at which a number of groups dispersed during the rest of the year gathered and engaged in groupwide rituals that may have involved painting figurative and nonfigurative designs on cave walls.

Evidence from other Late Paleolithic regions, most notably from the central Russian Plain, where no changes in group size have been found between the settlements occupied during different seasons, indicates that such changes in group size were not a universal feature of Late Paleolithic settlement systems.

See also ALTAMIRA; LASCAUX; RITUAL; SITE TYPES. [O.S.]

Further Readings

Conkey, M. (1980) The identification of prehistoric hunter-gatherer aggregation sites: the case of Altamira. Curr. Anthropol. 21:609–630.

Lee, R.B. (1979) The !Kung San. Cambridge: Cambridge University Press.

AGGRESSION *see* PRIMATE SOCIETIES; SOCIOBIOLOGY

AGRICULTURE *see* DOMESTICATION; NEAR EAST; NEOLITHIC

ALBUMIN *see* IMMUNOLOGICAL DISTANCE; MOLECULAR ANTHROPOLOGY

ALENGERR *see* FORT TERNAN

ALLELE

The ultimate source of genetic variation is *mutation*, the term applied to any alteration in a gene. Its effect is to create different kinds of genes in a population: genes responsible for identical functions but yielding slightly different products. Variant forms of a gene are *alleles*. Organisms with two identical alleles for the same gene are *homozygous*; organisms with two different alleles are *heterozygous*.

See also GENE; GENOTYPE. [J.M.]

ALLENOPITHECUS *see* CERCOPITHECINAE

ALLEN'S RULE *see* RULES

ALLERØD *see* GLACIATION; PLEISTOCENE

ALLOCEBUS *see* CHEIROGALEIDAE

ALLOMETRY

Living organisms exhibit tremendous variation in overall size, ranging from single-celled creatures to the 100-ton blue whale, the largest animal that has ever existed. Such variation in body size has major implications for the ways in which animals are constructed and function. The biological investigation of the morphological and physiological changes that are causally related to differences in body size is known as the study of *allometry* (from Greek roots meaning "of different measure or shape"). Allometric investigations are but one aspect of the broader study of *scaling* in biology, which focuses not merely on the morphological but also the ecological, life-historical, and even behavioral correlates of size change.

Early work in the field of allometry dates back at least to Galileo, who used physical principles to demonstrate the disproportionate changes in width or girth that long bones of larger animals must undergo if they are to function properly in their weight-bearing capacities. Just as in any physical body, when animals enlarge in size *geometric similarity* or *isometry* is maintained where lengths scale proportionately to lengths $^{1.0}$, areas $^{0.66}$, and volumes or weights $^{0.33}$. Since volumes in some real sense "outrace" surface areas and lengths, animals of roughly similar design but of significantly different overall size must frequently

change their shape (i.e. scale allometrically rather than isometrically) if they are to function equivalently. For example, it has been determined that the weight of the skeleton in mammals scales allometrically (with a log regression slope significantly greater than 1.0) relative to overall body weight in order to support the rapidly increasing total mass. Large mammals thus have *relatively* as well as absolutely heavier skeletons than smaller mammals. Another excellent example is provided by metabolic rate in birds and mammals, which scales with body weight to approximately the 0.75 power (see figure). As a

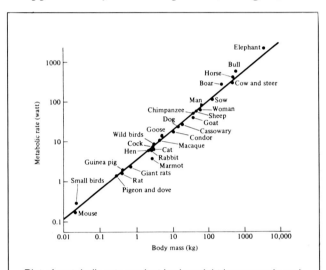

Plot of metabolic rate against body weight in mammals and birds, illustrating the strong correlation and exhibiting a slope of 0.74. (After Schmidt-Nielsen, 1984.)

result of this negatively allometric relationship (a regression slope value significantly less than 1.0) larger mammals have *relatively* lower metabolic rates, while smaller mammals have *relatively* higher rates. This negatively allometric pattern is presumably related at least in part to the progressively decreasing ratio of surface area to volume as mammals get larger. Without such an allometric scaling of metabolism, as Max Kleiber pointed out long ago, a steer with the relative metabolic rate of a mouse would have to maintain surface temperatures near the boiling point to dissipate heat adequately, while a mouse with the relative metabolic rate of a steer would require over 15 cm. of insulating fur to maintain sufficient body temperatures. Countless other examples from both biology and engineering could be given to support the claim that the maintenance of functional equivalence often requires a regular alteration of shape as size changes.

Allometric relationships are also frequently examined within particular species, either in ontogenetic sequences or among adults of different size. Here

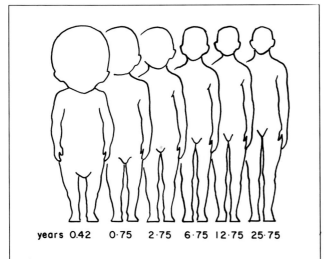

years 0.42 0.75 2.75 6.75 12.75 25.75

Graphic illustration of the progressive changes in shape during human ontogeny, made by scaling body shape at various growth stages to a common length. These shape changes reflect a positive allometry of hindlimb length and a negative allometry of skull size. (After McMahon and Bonner, 1983, and Medawar, 1945.)

brain or the relative lengthening of the hindlimbs during human ontogeny (see figure). These patterns of shape change result from shifts in the intrinsic and extrinsic controls of growth of various body regions, and we often discover a reasonable functional basis for these allometries as well.

Shape differences between adults of two or more species are thus determined to be allometric if they result either from the sharing and differential extension of common patterns of ontogenetic allometry (see figure), in which case we refer to the interspecific pattern as *ontogenetic scaling*; or from the need to maintain equivalence of some functional parameter or constraint as size changes (see figure), in which case we refer to the interspecific pattern as *biomechanical scaling*.

Allometric investigations are used in at least two important ways in studies of adaptation and phylogeny. Sometimes our focus is on the general scaling relationship itself, as reflected in the slope of the regression line relating the two variables under consideration; at other times our primary interest is in determining and explaining departures from such a best-fit line. Both of these related endeavors can be illustrated by classic analyses of brain/body allometry

progressive shape changes reflect differential growth, as in the general mammalian postnatal pattern of positively allometric growth of the face relative to the

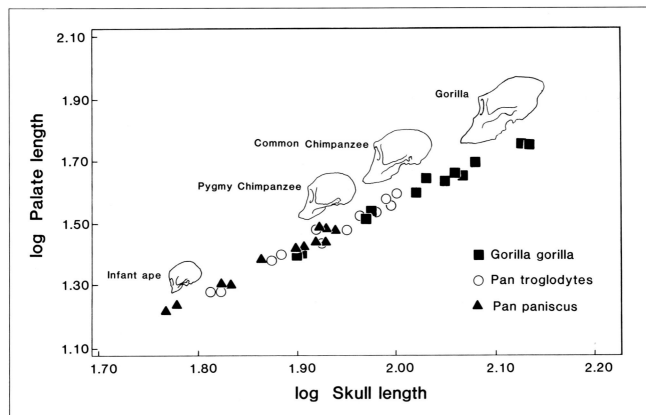

Plot of palate length against skull length in growth series of three species of African apes, illustrating a case of *ontogenetic scaling*. Shape differences in the skull (e.g. relatively longer palates) among adults of the three species result from the sharing and differential extension of common growth patterns of positive allometry.

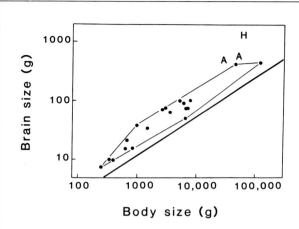

Plot of brain size against body size in haplorhine primates. The heavy solid line represents a regression line of $y=0.12 (x)^{3/4}$ fit to extant mammals. The polygon enclosing these primates lies above this line, reflecting their relatively high encephalization. Modern humans (H) and fossil hominids (A, for *Australopithecus africanus* and *boisei*) exhibit the strongest positive deviations from predicted values. (After H.J. Jerison, Evolution of the brain and intelligence. Academic Press, 1973.)

(see figure). Broad studies of interspecific scaling of the brain have demonstrated an allometric coefficient (regression slope) of somewhere between 0.66 and 0.75, or negative allometry. These empirical observations have led to important theoretical hypotheses concerning the physiological basis of such a pattern. Although these hypotheses are not fully tested at present, the scaling pattern suggests possible control of brain size by body-surface areas, metabolic rates, or certain other factors.

The placement of a particular species or group in relation to a general scaling pattern may also be informative, as, for example, when paleoneurologist H. Jerison demonstrated that the relatively "pea-brained" sauropod dinosaurs in fact had brain sizes in the range one would expect for such giant reptiles. In other words, their brain/body ratios fell along an extension of the general allometric relationship for extant reptiles.

Deviations from such allometric baselines therefore require examination as possible cases of "special adaptations" unrelated to simple body-size differences. The large size of our own brain is one such positive deviation from expected values for mammals of our overall body size (see figure). Another example is the relative length of our hindlimbs: in plots of hindlimb length against total size for higher primates humans are characterized by strong positive deviations from the general trend. This suggests a link to our peculiar pattern of bipedal locomotion and the fact that relatively long hindlimbs are functionally advantageous and not simply the result of our gener-

ally large size among primates. A third example from the human fossil record is the demonstration that the characteristic facial and dental proportions of robust australopithecines do not merely reflect shape changes expected to maintain functional equivalence at larger overall size, as some have previously suggested, but rather that they apparently indicate divergent dietary adaptations, as argued by many others.

It is intriguing and even ironic that something as obvious as variation in overall size has proven to be such a productive and exciting field of morphological investigation. Biologists will continue to probe questions of allometry and scaling in morphology, physiology, ecology, and behavior and in the process increase our understanding of the form, function, and evolution of organisms.

See also ADAPTATION; BONE BIOLOGY; DWARFISM; EVOLUTION; GIGANTISM; ONTOGENY. [B.T.S.]

Further Readings

Gould, S.J. (1966) Allometry and size in ontogeny and phylogeny. Biol. Rev. 41:587–640.

Huxley, J.S. (1932) Problems of Relative Growth. London: Mac-Veagh.

Jungers, W.L., ed. (1985) Size and Scaling in Primate Biology. New York: Plenum.

McMahon, T.A., and Bonner, J.T. (1983) On Size and Life. New York: Freeman.

Schmidt-Nielsen, K. (1984) Scaling: Why Is Animal Size So Important? Cambridge: Cambridge University Press.

Thompson, D.W. (1917) On Growth and Form. Cambridge: Cambridge University Press.

ALLOPATRY *see* SPECIATION

ALOUATTA *see* ATELINAE

ALPINE GLACIATIONS *see* GLACIATION; PLEISTOCENE

ALSATIA *see* ADAPIDAE

ALTAMIRA

Major Ice Age painted cave, located in northwestern Spain. Discovered in 1879, the famous painted ceiling of standing and lying bison was once considered a forgery. The polychrome red-and-black paintings were made in the middle Magdalenian phase of the Upper Paleolithic, ca. 13,500 B.P., although there are also earlier Aurignacian bone engravings and wall markings, as well as animal engravings from the Solutrean, ca. 22,000 B.P. Excavation in the cave has recovered the bones of bison, horse, boar, and deer, in addition to the engraved and painted signs, symbols, and animals on the walls and ceilings.

See also AURIGNACIAN; EUROPE; MAGDALENIAN; PALEOLITHIC IMAGE; SOLUTREAN; UPPER PALEOLITHIC. [A.M.]

ALTANIUS see ANAPTOMORPHINAE

ALTMÜHLIAN see MOUSTERIAN; UPPER PALEOLITHIC

ALTRUISM see SOCIOBIOLOGY

AMBRONA

Open-air archaeological site in northern Spain, faunally dated to later middle Pleistocene (late Elster to early Saale), ca. 0.4-0.25 m.y. Although briefly surveyed by a Spanish nobleman in the late 1800s, Ambrona was scientifically excavated in the 1950s and 60s by F.C. Howell and L. Freeman. A nearby "sister" site, Torralba, was further studied in the early 1980s. The two sites yielded an Acheulean industry with cleavers and a few possible bone and wood tools in association with scattered charcoal flecks. The partially articulated skeleton of an elephant (*Elephas antiquus*), and more fragmentary remains of other elephants, deer, horse, and aurochs, are often cited as evidence for cooperative hunting of big game by *Homo erectus* or more likely archaic *Homo sapiens* but could also represent some carnivore predation and/or natural accumulation. No human remains were recovered.

See also ACHEULEAN; ARCHAEOLOGICAL SITES; CLEAVER; EARLY PALEOLITHIC; ECONOMY, PREHISTORIC; EUROPE; FIRE; HANDAXE; MAN-LAND RELATIONSHIPS; PALEOLITHIC LIFEWAYS; SITE TYPES; TAPHONOMY. [A.S.B.]

AMERICAS

The New World landmass measures 15,000 km. from the Arctic to Cape Horn, both continents stretching 5,000 km. across at their widest points. This immense territory (42,081,000 sq. km.) covers more than one quarter of the world's habitable surface.

The most impressive physiographic feature in North America is the western cordillera, running the length of the continent like a gigantic backbone. A more ancient mountain chain flanks eastern North America, reaching only half the height of its western counterpart. The vast area between the Appalachians and the Rockies includes the glaciated Canadian Shield to the north, Great Plains in midcontinent,

and Mississippi basin to the south. East of the Appalachians is a coastal plain, relatively narrow in the north but widening significantly as it approaches the Gulf of Mexico.

An equally impressive range of mountains, the Andes, runs the full length of the South American continent. Although narrower than the North American cordillera, the Andes are much higher, reaching over 7,000 m. in places. Coastal lowlands, varying in width, border the Andes. The uplands of eastern South America are much older than the Andes, much more weathered, and considerably lower in elevation. The lowland plains of interior South America contain the Orinoco and Amazon drainage basins.

Primate History

North American Early Primates   The first well-documented faunal assemblages containing primates occur in the Paleogene of western North America. Although the order may have originated in eastern Asia, fossils are rare there throughout the Cenozoic. Numerous localities yielding diverse mammalian faunas are known throughout the Paleocene and Eocene of the Rocky Mountain region (then mainly lowland tropical forests), and primates are a common component of these faunas (see map). Plesiadapiform primates are the oldest widespread group, including a variety of archaic forms grouped into two superfamilies with five families.

Pugatorius, the oldest recognized primate, appears at the very end of the Mesozoic and continues into the earliest Cenozoic, at ca. 65 m.y. ago. It is usually included in the family Paromomyidae, which also includes a number of extremely small to small mainly Paleocene taxa that are among the least derived primates. Most of these are restricted to western North America, although two genera also occur in western Europe and the Arctic (Ellesmere Island). Most paromomyids were insectivorous, but larger forms, such as the speciose and widespread *Phenacolemur* (which persisted into the middle Eocene), were partly frugivorous. The dentally batlike picrodontids were rare nectar feeders restricted to western North America and perhaps derived from paromomyids. These two families are loosely grouped into the Paromomyoidea.

A larger range of sizes characterized the Plesiadapoidea, a group of three families linked by the development of mittenlike prongs on the enlarged central upper incisor. The Plesiadapidae and Carpolestidae range from early Paleocene into early Eocene in the American West, with some plesiadapids known also in Europe. Skulls and postcrania of plesiadapids are the best known among all the archaic primates, documenting a snouty face, lack of a postorbital bar

Selected North American fossil primate localities from early Paleocene to late Oligocene. Age and included taxa are indicated according to the following key.

Symbol	Age	Primate fossils
●	early Paleocene and latest Cretaceous (66–64 m.y.)	*Purgatorius*
○	middle-late Paleocene (63–55 m.y.)	Plesiadapiformes
■	early Eocene (55–49 m.y.)	Plesiadapiformes, Omomyidae, Notharctidae
×	middle Eocene (49–45 m.y.)	Omomyidae, Notharctidae
▢	late Eocene (45–36 m.y.)	(Plesiadapiformes), Omomyidae, (?)Notharctidae
✪	final Eocene (37-36 m.y.)	Adapidae
▼	early Oligocene (36–34 m.y.)	Omomyidae
▲	late Oligocene (25–24 m.y.)	Omomyidae

known in all other primates and a grasping foot (presumably related to primate arboreality). Plesiadapids are known that were as large as living marmots or woodchucks and ate a variety of vegetable materials. The generally smaller carpolestids are known from less-complete remains, but they are characterized by an enlarged, bladelike P_4 and enlarged flattened and multicusped P^{3-4}, which probably helped shearing of a fibrous diet.

(*See also* CARPOLESTIDAE; CENOZOIC; DIET; LOCOMOTION; PALEOCENE; PAROMOMYIDAE; PICRODONTIDAE; PLESIADAPIDAE.)

By the end of the Paleocene the first members of the modern primates, the euprimates, may have evolved in Asia, or perhaps in southern North Amer-

ica. Two groups of euprimates appear suddenly, through migration, in North America and Europe at the beginning of the Eocene (ca. 54 m.y. ago): the strepsirhine Adapiformes and the haplorhine Omomyidae. The archaic primates soon disappeared, competed into extinction not only by later primates but also by the rapidly diversifying rodents. In the American West the adapiforms are represented by the small-to-medium-sized Notharctidae, a mainly folivorous group similar in many ways to the living lemurs of Madagascar. Four genera of notharctids are known by a dozen species ranging into the middle Eocene, while one adapid of European affinity occurred in the late Eocene of Texas. The generally small omomyids were much more diverse and long-lived, with perhaps two dozen mainly monospecific genera, placed in the subfamilies Anaptomorphinae and Omomyinae, spanning from earliest Eocene to latest Oligocene. Species range from the size of the smallest marmosets up to that of medium-bodied monkeys, at least in toothrow length. Diets were similarly varied, with frugivores, folivores, and insectivores among the known species. Most taxa have enlarged lower incisors like those of less-derived archaic primates, but at least two species had incisors, and some foot bones, more like those of the ancestral anthropoids. It seems likely that the protoanthropoid stock was derived from an omomyid ancestry. With climatic cooling through the Eocene forested areas decreased in size, and most arboreal mammals were forced into competition for limited resources in the north or into the smaller geographic space of southern North America. Only two omomyids are known in the early Oligocene (ca. 35–32 m.y.) of Texas and Montana, and another from the late Oligocene (ca. 25 m.y.) of Oregon and South Dakota (possible forest refuges?).

(*See also* ADAPIFORMES; ANAPTOMORPHINAE; ANTHROPOIDEA; EOCENE; EXTINCTION; NOTHARCTIDAE; OLIGOCENE; OMOMYIDAE; OMOMYINAE; PALEOBIOGEOGRAPHY.)

South American Platyrrhines   Although the probable ancestry of the "higher" primates, or anthropoids, can be traced to the tarsiiform omomyids, the nature of their dispersal into the southern continents is less clear. Early anthropoids arrived in South America by the late Oligocene (27 m.y.), when *Branisella* is known from Bolivia. The living New World primates, the platyrrhine monkeys, are divided here into two families, Cebidae and Atelidae, each with a long fossil history. In fact *Branisella* can be included in the Cebidae, as can the early Miocene (ca. 22 m.y. old) Patagonian *Dolichocebus*, a close relative of the living squirrel monkey, *Saimiri*. Another early Miocene genus, *Tremacebus*, is apparently a phyletic relative of the living nocturnal owl monkey, *Aotus*; both forms show enlargement of the eye sockets typical of nocturnal mammals, especially anthropoids. The recently described *Soriacebus* is probably the oldest known pitheciin. In the middle Miocene (16–14 m.y. old) La Venta region of northern Colombia at least six genera continue to demonstrate the early diversification of the platyrrhines. *Micodon* is an early callitrichine, *Neosaimiri* is little different from *Saimiri*, while *Aotus* is represented by an extinct species. *Stirtonia* is a large form close to the modern howler monkey, while two other genera represent early members of the atelid subfamily Pitheciinae. At least two further distinctive genera are known from Holocene deposits on Caribbean islands, suggesting a dispersal through that region from a probable Central American source.

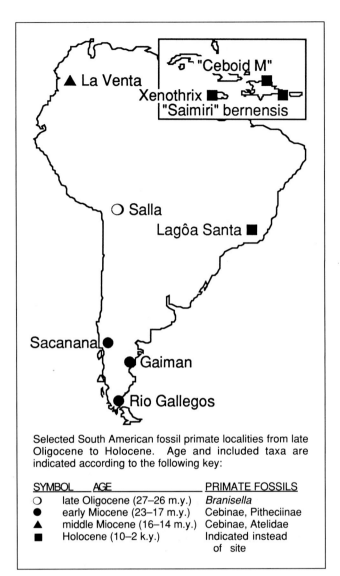

Selected South American fossil primate localities from late Oligocene to Holocene. Age and included taxa are indicated according to the following key:

SYMBOL	AGE	PRIMATE FOSSILS
○	late Oligocene (27–26 m.y.)	*Branisella*
●	early Miocene (23–17 m.y.)	Cebinae, Pitheciinae
▲	middle Miocene (16–14 m.y.)	Cebinae, Atelidae
■	Holocene (10–2 k.y.)	Indicated instead of site

The modern platyrrhines have a wide range of diets, social behavior, and locomotor adaptations. As in the early primates most genera can be distinguished by their dentitions. Yet despite the presence of a widespread plains fauna in South America during the Miocene no platyrrhine became terrestrial, in contrast to the multiple adaptations to ground life among Old World anthropoids. Instead all New World monkeys are restricted to forested environments, and the rapid encroachment of humans on their habitats is driving several species toward extinction.

(*See also* ANTHROPOIDEA; ATELIDAE; ATELINAE; BRANISELLINAE; CALLITRICHINAE; CEBIDAE; CEBINAE; MIOCENE; PITHECIINAE; PLATYRRHINI; PRIMATES.)

Humans in the New World

The New World was discovered at least three times. The most celebrated "discovery" is accorded Christopher Columbus, who landed on San Salvador in October 1492. But half a millennium earlier Norsemen from Greenland and Iceland had already fished the waters of North America, shipping its timber back to their families on tree-barren Greenland.

Although the New World adventures of Leif Eriksson were duly recorded in Norse epics, scholars debated the existence of a Norse New World settlement for nearly a millennium. The best archaeological evidence for their presence is at L'Anse aux Meadows (Newfoundland). Landing about A.D. 1020, the Vikings held onto their New World foothold for three decades before retreating. When the Vikings arrived at L'Anse aux Meadows, they encountered, and thoroughly alienated, the true first Americans, whom the Norse called *scraelings*.

The first human footprints on New World soil belonged to the American Indian and the closely related Eskimo. The Americas were "discovered" and then populated from northeastern Asia perhaps 30 k.y. ago. People migrated into this New World as fully evolved *Homo sapiens*. Human beings did not evolve in the Americas.

The first Americans brought certain basic cultural skills: fire making, flint chipping, and serviceable means of procuring food, shelter, and clothing. These early immigrants must also have brought with them the rudiments of kin-group social organization and beliefs about magic and the supernatural. They certainly possessed forms of human language. When Columbus arrived, Native Americans of Alaska, Canada, and the United States mainland spoke about 2,000 mutually unintelligible languages; the linguistic complexity in South America was comparable. Although some degree of linguistic diversity may have been imported with the earliest New World settlers, much of the linguistic evolution took place as Native Americans adapted to their new environment.

Paleoindian Occupations   The earliest well-defined archaeological complex in the Americas is termed *Paleoindian*, generally dated between 12,000 and 11,000 B.P. Whether the Paleoindians were actually the First Americans is not known, but many specialists believe that humans reached the Americas between 40,000 and 20,000 B.P., or even earlier.

Perhaps the best evidence for a pre-12,000 B.P. occupation in the New World comes from Meadowcroft Shelter in southwestern Pennsylvania. Evidence of human occupation at Meadowcroft accompanies the oldest cultural date, slightly over 19,000 B.P. Early radiocarbon dates are also available from South American sites. Hearths associated with pebble and flake tools in southern Chile and northeastern Brazil suggest to some that people entered South America sometime before 35,000 B.P. Additional controversial sites throughout the Americas have yielded simple stone and bone assemblages from less-definite cul-

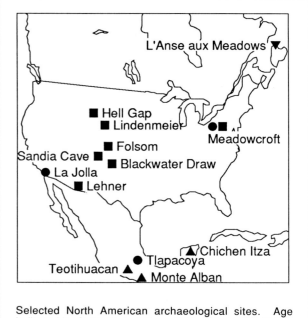

Selected North American archaeological sites. Age indicated by Symbols as follows: ● Pre-Clovis (35–13 k.y. B.P.); ■ Paleoindian (13–9 k.y. B.P.); ▼ Viking landing (ca. A.D. 1000); ▼ Postclassic.

tural contexts. Unfortunately the archaeology of each such site leaves many questions unanswered, and none of this evidence is universally accepted by New World archaeologists.

There is, however, no question that the Clovis culture was established in North America prior to 12,000 B.P. This widespread complex spans the width of North America and can be traced from northern Alaska to Guatemala. The Clovis (or Llano) complex comprises the oldest well-dated cultural material with clearly established association of humans and animals in North America. These sites, which lack established cultural antecedents, often contain choppers, cutting tools, a variety of bone tools, and (very rarely) milling stones, in addition to the diagnostic Clovis fluted points.

Despite technological similarities the Paleoindian lifeway in eastern North America differed from the big-game-hunting pattern evident on the Plains. By 12,000 B.P. the floral and faunal resources in the Ohio valley and far north into Wisconsin, Michigan, and Ontario were adequate to support scattered bands of hunters. Animal bones found in association with these Paleoindian sites are usually woodland caribou. Eastern Paleoindians concentrated their efforts on river-valley resources, in effect earning a head start toward the highly efficient gathering economies usually associated with later Archaic periods.

Similar early hunting adaptations can also be traced in South America. The diagnostic artifact of this tradition, fish-tail projectile points from El Inga

Selected South American archaeological sites. Age indicated by symbols as follows: ● Pre-Clovis (35–13 k.y. B.P.); ■ Paleoindian (13–9 k.y. B.P.); ▲ Postclassic.

stays. The regional density of seasonal hunting camps and more permanent settlements increased, migratory patterns involved smaller areas, and groups became increasingly sedentary. As a result technological capacities improved and intensified.

In South America the early hunting tradition gave rise to an Andean archaic pattern, a cultural tradition in which subsistence was provided by hunting deer and camelids and by collecting vegetable foods. A hallmark of this tradition was seasonal transhumance, shifting community residence as people pursued either highland hunting or coastal-lowland collecting. A distinctive tradition also developed along the Peruvian and Chilean coasts, where seasonal collecting camps began to be replaced by permanent villages whose inhabitants depended primarily upon marine foods, although in Peru plant gathering remained an important economic activity and provided the basis for the evolution of agriculture.

This full archaic stage of cultural development is evident throughout the New World, in general beginning with the climatic optimum, ca. 7000 B.P., and lasting until 4000 B.P. Pottery is found in a number of archaic-stage cultures, as among the Valdevia tradition in northwestern South America and the late archaic fiber-tempered ceramics in the southeastern United States. There are of course continuities of this stage into historic times in both North and South America, as for example in the later cultures of the California coast and the Northwest coast.

Throughout the archaic in Central and South America interrelated developments ultimately brought about the emergence of settled village life based on full-time farming. Native American population grew beyond the limits that could be supported by a hunting-gathering economy. Under human selection certainly plants, notably maize, became larger and more productive, and it became increasingly cost-effective to clear away the wild vegetation in order to plant crops. As crops contributed more to the human diet, communities became increasingly sedentary. Improved farming technology increased productivity still further, and settlement patterns began to select for agricultural needs rather than for hunting and foraging.

The term *Formative* commonly designates the threshold of subsistence agriculture in the traditions of Mesoamerica, the American Southwest, the Mississippian, the Great Plains, and Eastern Woodlands. In South America this stage includes similar traditions in Peru, the South Andes, the Caribbean, and Amazonia. Of these the latter two featured manioc cultivation; all others were primarily maize-based. In general the Formative stage dates from ca. 4000 B.P. into the historic period.

In Mesoamerica and Peru the criterion of settled

and elsewhere, resembles the Clovis-derived points of North America. Established largely in Andean South America, this early hunting tradition spread to the southern tip of the continent and eastward into the Argentine Plains. Between 13,000 and 12,000 B.P. people in central Colombia and southern Chile were collecting plants and hunting small game; there is no definite evidence that they hunted mastodons, as did contemporary El Jobo people in northern Venezuela. In southern Patagonia people hunted horses and ground sloths about 11,000 B.P., but there is no evidence that people in central and northern Brazil ever hunted such megamammals.

Later Developments　As the climate ameliorated, and an ever-thickening forest barrier formed between periglacial tundra and the temperate grasslands, different cultural orientations formed. In the far north this archaic stage is a generalized, primary response to forest conditions emerging during this period of flux. Although this tradition arose from a Paleoindian substratum of big-game hunting, a series of regional modifications emerged. Caribou hunting remained the primary economic activity on the northern fringes of the forest, but to the south other large species (elk, moose, and deer) became main-

urban life is used to define a *Classic* stage, beginning about the opening of the Christian era. Regional expressions of the Mesoamerican Classic include Teotihuacan (Valley of Mexico), the Zapotec culture (Oaxaca), and the Maya (Guatemalan highlands and Yucatan lowlands). Classic Andean cultures include the Mochica and Nazca kingdoms. How far the Classic can be extended into other areas is debatable, but it probably applies to the cultures of the Ecuadorian coast after 1000 B.P.

The *Postclassic* is an epiphenomenon of the Classic, characterized by developments in urban living, an increase in large-scale warfare and empire building, and secularization of political control, as opposed to previously religious leadership. In Mesoamerica the Postclassic began with the fall of the city of Teotihuacan and the rise of the militaristic Toltec empire and continued through the Aztec society encountered by Cortez. In Peru this chronology corresponds to the time when the Tiahuanaco-Huari empire overran the Moche and Nazca.

See also BLACKWATER DRAW; CLOVIS; FOLSOM; GLACIATION; LLANO; OLD CROW; PALEOINDIAN. [D.H.T., E.D.]

Further Readings

Bryan, A.L., ed. (1986) New Evidence for the Pleistocene Peopling of the Americas. Orono: University of Maine Center for Study of Early Man.

Dincauze, D. (1984) An archaeological evaluation of the case for pre-Clovis occupations. Adv. World Archaeol. 3:275–323.

Haynes, C.V. (1982) Were Clovis progenitors in Beringia? In D.M. Hopkins, F.J. Mathews, Jr., C.E. Schweger, and S.B. Young (eds.): Paleoecology of Beringia. New York: Academic, pp. 383–398.

Irving, W.N. (1985) Context and chronology of early man in the Americas. Ann. Rev. Anthropol. 14:529–555.

Jennings, J.D., ed. (1978) Ancient Native Americans. San Francisco: Freeman.

Owen, R. (1984) The Americas: the case against Ice-Age human population. In F.H. Smith and F. Spencer (eds.): The Origins of Modern Humans: A World Survey of the Fossil Evidence. New York: Liss, pp. 517–563.

Szalay, F.S., and Delson, E. (1979) Evolutionary History of the Primates. New York: Academic.

AMERSFOORT *see* GLACIATION; PLEISTOCENE

AMINO-ACID DATING *see* GEOCHRONOMETRY

AMIRIAN *see* PLEISTOCENE; SEA-LEVEL CHANGE

AMPHIPITHECUS

Fossil primate from the late Eocene of Burma, described in 1937 by E.H. Colbert. Although known for decades by only a mandibular fragment bearing two premolars and a first molar, *Amphipithecus* has played a central role in debates on the origins of anthropoid and even catarrhine primates. The depth of the mandible relative to molar crown height is the only anthropoidlike feature of this primate, but deep mandibles are not uncommon among fossil, subfossil, and extant strepsirhines. *Amphipithecus* apparently did have a centrally positioned hypoconulid on its M_1, which is otherwise characteristic of catarrhine primates, but the fossil lacks the derived premolar and other molar features necessary to support inclusion within Anthropoidea. Suggestions that *Amphipithecus* is related to omomyids or adapids are based largely on ancientness and primitive retentions, but intriguing comparisons with lorisoids in molar and especially premolar morphology may be instructive. *Amphipithecus* remains an enigmatic primate.

See also ANTHROPOIDEA; CATARRHINI; HAPLORHINI; LORISOIDEA; OMOMYIDAE. [J.H.S.]

Further Readings

Schwartz, J.H. (1986) Primate systematics and a classification of the order. In D.R. Swindler (ed.): Comparative Primate Biology, Vol. I: Systematics, Evolution and Anatomy. New York: Liss, pp. 1–41.

Szalay, F.S., and Delson, E. (1979) Evolutionary History of the Primates. New York: Academic.

AMUD

Israeli site excavated in 1961; it produced an important Neanderthal partial skeleton of an adult male. This Neanderthal had a large cranium and brain (size ca.

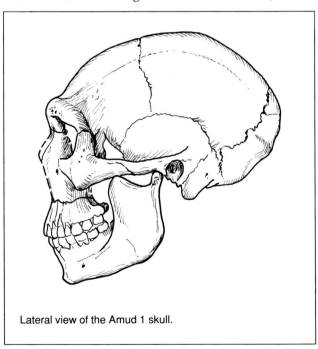

Lateral view of the Amud 1 skull.

1,740 ml.) but relatively small teeth and a mandible with a slight chin development. The individual was also particularly tall (estimated stature ca. 179 cm.). Although uncertainly dated, the Amud specimen may be one of the most recent Neanderthal finds from the area.

See also NEANDERTHALS. [C.B.S.]

AMUDIAN

Pre-Late Paleolithic blade industry of the Levant (Israel, Syria, Lebanon), comparable with the Pre-Aurignacian and dated to the end of the last interglacial (ca. 10,000 B.P.) on stratigraphic grounds. The Amudian was defined on the basis of Amud, Level B, but is better known from Tabūn and the Abri Zumoffen, where it is followed by a Jabrudian industry. Characteristic forms include blades with backing or "nibbled" retouch, burins, chamfered blades, and Levalloiso-Mousterian débitage, in contrast to the blade cores and Aurignacian-like carinate scrapers of the pre-Aurignacian.

See also AMUD; JABRUDIAN; LATE PALEOLITHIC; PRE-AURIGNACIAN; STONE-TOOL MAKING; TABŪN. [A.S.B.]

ANAPITHECUS *see* PLIOPITHECIDAE

ANAPTOMORPHINAE

Subfamily of omomyid primates known from Asia and Europe but primarily North America. Anaptomorphines are the oldest known representatives of their family, and the characters we know of the earliest species included in this taxon suggest that they may represent an earlier radiation of the tarsiiforms than the younger Omomyinae and Microchoerinae. It is also possible that equally ancient representatives of omomyines simply have not yet been recovered. Known stratigraphic precedence of one group by another does not automatically mean ancestor-descendant relationships, as some extreme practitioners of stratophenetics imply in their work. Anaptomorphines, which are less diverse than the omomyines, occur in the early to middle Eocene of North America and in the early Eocene of Europe and Asia. In general the diagnostic combination of dental characters present in the last common ancestor of this subfamily (and very likely of the family, too) appears to be a postprotocone fold on the upper molars coupled with a well-inflated base of the cusps of the trigonids on the lower molars.

Anaptomorphines are classified into two tribes,

the Anaptomorphini and Trogolemurini, and the former is further subdivided into the subtribes Teilhardinina, Anaptomorphina, and Tetoniina.

The best-known and only undoubted teilhardinan is *Teilhardina belgica* from the earliest Eocene of Europe, in many ways a good structural (not actual) ancestor for the known Euroamerican members of the whole family. These small anaptomorphines retain the primitive euprimate dental formula of two incisors and a full complement of teeth behind them.

The small incisors and sizable canines of *Teilhardina* are in sharp contrast to the earliest North American samples of *Anemorhysis* (which have been mistakenly called *Teilhardina*). *Anemorhysis* (including *Tetonoides* and *Uintalacus*), *Arapahovius*, *Tetonius* (including *Pseudotetonius* and *Mckennamorphus*), and *Absarokius* (including *Aycrossia* and *Strigorhysis*) share to varying degrees the enlargement of the lower central incisors, to form a kind of robust spoon, along with the reduction of the relative size of the canines. This combination of characters diagnoses the last common ancestor of the primarily early Eocene (Wasatchian) subtribe Tetoniina versus the earliest Eocene European Teilhardinina. Although *Anemorhysis* was probably primarily insectivorous, the enlarge-

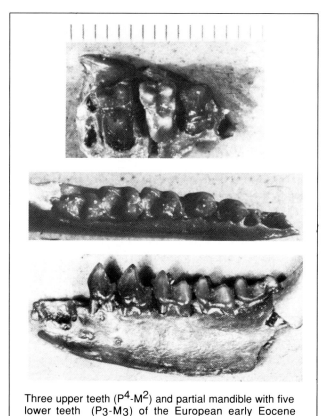

Three upper teeth (P^4-M^2) and partial mandible with five lower teeth (P3-M3) of the European early Eocene anaptomorphine *Teilhardina belgica*. Note large canine socket. Scale subdivisions represent 0.5 mm.

ment of incisors suggests possible exudate-scraping habits. The highly wrinkled molars of the small *Arapahovius* suggest a possible specialization for nectar and gum or other resins, with insects perhaps being the bulk of the diet. The remaining members of this subtribe, *Tetonius* and *Absarokius*, given their

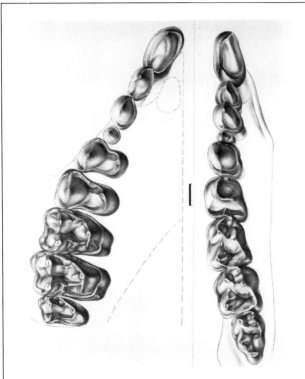

Upper and lower dentition of *Tetonius homunculus*. Scale is 1 mm.

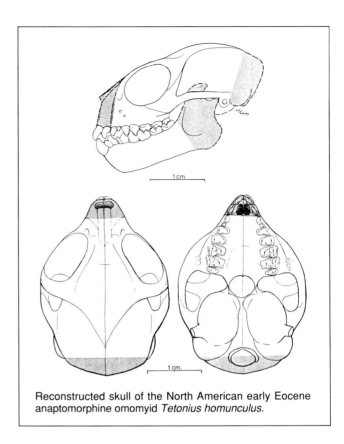

Reconstructed skull of the North American early Eocene anaptomorphine omomyid *Tetonius homunculus*.

primitive anaptomorphinan incisor enlargement coupled with their increasingly tall fourth premolars and relatively low and robust molars, may have been adapted to a particular form of frugivory that required an increasing reliance on crunching open hard fruits and nuts or some other unknown hard substances.

The third subtribe is the Anaptomorphina, with the middle Eocene (Bridgerian) genus *Anaptomorphus* (including *Gazinius*). This short-faced form lacked the enlarged incisors of the tetoniinans, yet this may well represent a phylogenetic reversal from a tetoniinan rather than from a teilhardinian, as the canine in the known jaws is relatively small. This genus was probably composed primarily of fruit eaters, although its species undoubtedly consumed their fair share of insects, as most small frugivores do.

The poorly known genera *Chlororhysis* from the early Eocene of North America, the late Paleocene–early Eocene Mongolian *Altanius*, and the early-to-middle Eocene Pakistani *Kohatius* are difficult to

place within the tribe Anaptomorphini. The genus *Kohatius*, known by three fragmentary specimens, is barely identifiable as a small euprimate.

The tribe Trogolemurini includes a single poorly known but fascinating primate. The small *Trogolemur*, known primarily from a deep and short lower jaw, was an animal whose estimated skull length (based on the jaw) was only ca. 2 cm. It had a relatively longer third lower molar than other anaptomorphines except *Altanius*, and it had an enormously enlarged central incisor, known unfortunately only from its root reaching under the molars. A mixed diet of gum and resins (scraped with the large incisors), nectar, and insects were the possible fare of this animal.

As far as we can tell from the isolated but allocable postcranial remains of anaptomorphines (mostly foot bones and some upper arm bones), these small primates were not particularly different from postcranially better known taxa like *Hemiacodon*. One important difference in the only good described skull of the anaptomorphine *Tetonius* from that of the omomyine *Rooneyia* lies in the construction of the region behind the ear, the petromastoid. In anaptomorphines and microchoerines this part of the skull is greatly inflated; the bone is a huge latticework of small air cells. This highly evolved condition is in sharp contrast to that seen in the omomyine *Rooneyia* and the living tarsiers, which have the less elaborate,

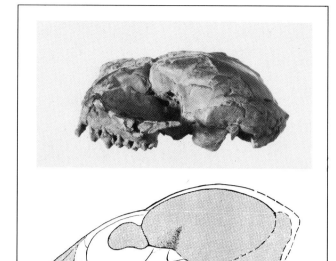

Side view of the skull (above) and reconstructed brain within the skull of *Tetonius homunculus* (below).

and perhaps therefore more primitive, uninflated petromastoid section of the petrosal bone.

See also MICROCHOERINAE; OMOMYIDAE; OMOMYINAE; STRATOPHENETIC. [F.S.S.]

Further Readings

Szalay, F.S., and Delson, E. (1979) Evolutionary History of the Primates. New York: Academic.

ANAPTOMORPHUS *see* ANAPTOMORPHINAE

ANATOMICALLY MODERN HOMO SAPIENS *see* ARCHAIC MODERNS; HOMO SAPIENS

ANATOMY *see* MORPHOLOGY

ANCESTRAL *see* CLADISTICS

ANCHOMOMYS *see* ADAPIDAE; LORISOIDEA

ANEMORHYSIS *see* ANAPTOMORPHINAE

ANGLES INTERSTADIAL *see* GLACIATION; PLEISTOCENE

ANKARAPITHECUS *see* HOMINOIDEA

ANTELIAN

Comprehensive term for Late Paleolithic industries of the Near East (Stages I–V), sometimes referred in part to the Aurignacian and represented at Ksar 'Akil (Wadi Antelias) in Lebanon, Jabrud Shelter III in Syria, and Mugharet el-Wad (Mount Carmel) in Israel. The industry may be separated into a lower phase, with more Mousterian forms and Emireh points, and an upper phase, with Font-Yves points, nose-ended scrapers, and busked burins but fewer Mousterian types.

See also AURIGNACIAN; EMIRAN; JABRUD; LATE PALEOLITHIC; MOUSTERIAN; NEAR EAST; STONE-TOOL MAKING; UPPER PALEOLITHIC. [A.S.B.]

ANTENEANDERTHAL

Term French workers use to identify European fossils that date from before the time by which true Neanderthals had appeared. The term is sometimes used distinctly from *preneanderthal*, which carries more connotations of direct ancestry. Nevertheless, many workers believe that anteneanderthals, such as the Mauer, Arago, and Atapuerca specimens, do represent probable ancestors for the Neanderthals.

See also ARCHAIC HOMO SAPIENS; NEANDERTHALS. [C.B.S.]

ANTHROPOGENE

Term used (rarely and not in this book) to refer to the last of the three periods of the Cenozoic, together with the Paleogene and Neogene. It is the time equivalent of the Pleistocene. The term, frequently used in the Russian literature, is derived from the assumption that man is the characteristic fossil of the "Anthropogene System."

See also CENOZOIC; PLEISTOCENE. [G.K.]

ANTHROPOIDEA

Higher primates, including platyrrhine monkeys of the New World and the catarrhine monkeys, apes, humans, and "prehumans" of the Old World. By any measure anthropoids are the most successful of the three major extant lineages of the primate order. The once-flourishing tarsiiform group is represented by a single genus, *Tarsius*, in the remote evolutionary outpost of the Malay archipelago, and the existing lemur-loris strepsirhines of the Malagasy Republic in Africa and the Indian subcontinent, are far less diverse than the higher primates, both taxonomically and adaptively.

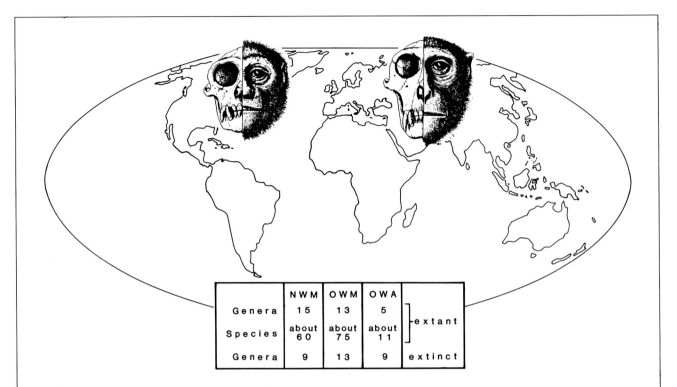

		NWM	OWM	OWA	
Genera		15	13	5	] extant
Species		about 60	about 75	about 11	
Genera		9	13	9	extinct

Faces of platyrrhine and catarrhine monkeys, suggesting the similarities and differences of their cranial and facial structures. The totals for genera and species of extinct and extant primates are estimates from Szalay and Delson, 1979. (Abbreviations: NWM, New World monkey; OWM, Old World monkey; OWA, Old World ape.)

Geographical Background

The success of the anthropoids has been influenced by geography in a number of ways, for their evolution has taken place in two distinct theaters, one in South America and the other in Afro-Eurasia, one large in area and the other relatively restricted. The occupation of four continents across two hemispheres makes their total areal distribution truly large. As a consequence there have been many and varied opportunities for differentiation within and between subregions, even to the extent of abandoning the tropical and subtropical habitats that have been fundamental to the history of the order Primates. Episodic mountain building, eustatic changes in sea level, continental collisions and climatic gradations, for example, have all had their effects on the evolutionary composition of the Old World fauna, which spans an enormous part of the globe, whereas isolation has perhaps been the primary macroevolutionary influence upon the history of platyrrhines in the New World.

The geographical disjunction between platyrrhines and catarrhines has been in effect for most of the Cenozoic, ever since the ancestral anthropoid stock split into two or more lineages. The timing of this separation is important, for after the original appearance of ceboids in South America the oceans blocked or strongly filtered all primate migrations into or out of the continent until the Panamanian isthmus arose ca. 3–2 m.y. ago. Thus the resident platyrrhines were permanently insulated from competition with nonplatyrrhine primates, at least for 27 m.y. and perhaps for as long as 40 m.y. The complexion and balance of the current platyrrhine fauna may therefore reflect a homogeneity, and perhaps a stability, achieved over many epochs. One of the pressing questions is whether the living forms are samples of the first and only platyrrhine radiation or of a successor to an earlier division that was replaced. Some fossil evidence suggests that a significant degree of taxonomic and morphological stasis occurred among the ceboids, and this may reflect a general macroevolutionary pattern related to continental insularity.

The Old World situation presents a contrasting geography. There continents were less isolated from one another. Faunal turnovers were probably more common, as Africa, Europe, and Asia shifted their respective positions and points of contact, mixing their occupants. Their paleodistribution maps of extinct genera cross today's continental boundaries for certain times during the Cenozoic, and the interruption of species ranges would have fostered speciation, differentiation, secondary contacts, competitive interactions, and replacement. Such conditions may have set an evolutionary premium on change rather than stasis, and upon adaptive improvement, or novelties. The fossil evidence suggests that there have been a number of successive catarrhine radiations, each with its own character. Apes, for example, are now at their nadir, having been displaced by quite a different type of primate, the cercopithecoid monkeys, which are fairly new on the scene.

The summation of these continental effects produced an anthropoid radiation of tremendous variety and success. One might even speculate that some of the evolutionary parallelisms between platyrrhines and hominoids have resulted indirectly from their geographical separation, for had they occurred together competition would surely have driven them farther apart anatomically and perhaps have pressured some forms into extinction. Geography, however, hardly explains the success of Anthropoidea or its real nature. Special adaptations set anthropoids apart from the other members of their order, and that foundation created the potential to exploit a broad spectrum of ecological niches, unsurpassed by any other group of primates during their 65-m.y. history.

Morphology and Adaptation

The skull, more than any other part of the skeleton, embodies novel anthropoid characteristics. In the simplest terms, the outward appearance of the anthropoid head is humanlike in aspect, having a relatively flat "face" with a vertical arrangement of eyes, nose, and mouth. Superficial structures, such as the external ears, lips, and nose, also tend to resemble us in shape and proportion. If there is a singular feature that sets humans apart typologically from the universal design of the anthropoid head, it is our recently evolved, vertical forehead, although squirrel monkeys and capuchins might even rival us there.

The major adaptive elements of this ensemble are the special senses of sight and smell, the cognitive

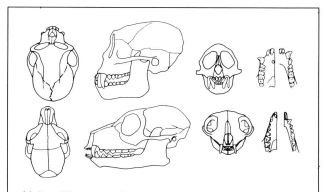

Main differences between the cranial and dental morphology of a euprimate, represented by *Cebus* (top), and *Lemur* (bottom). (From Rosenberger, 1986, with permission.)

functions of the brain and the design of the masticatory apparatus. The anthropoid braincase is large and rounded, accommodating as much volume as possible within a small space. As a consequence the foramen magnum is situated rather anteriorly within the skull base, which also makes head carriage more erect. The relatively small, close-set eye sockets face directly forward, maximizing stereoscopic vision. With the lower face tucked in beneath the eyes, facial bones tend to be short and deep, although snout length has increased secondarily in such forms as baboons and howler monkeys. The olfactory components, such as the size of the nasal cavity, the paper-thin scrolls inside it, and the endocranial space for the olfactory bulb, are all reduced, reflecting a diminished sense of smell. The mandible is fused solidly at the symphysis, and like the premaxilla it supports and stabilizes a battery of broad, vertical incisors. The lower jaw is also hinged well above the toothrows, giving the chewing muscles good leverage. The midline metopic suture between the frontal bones also fuses early in life. The premolars and molars vary in shape, but they tend to be blunt rather than penetratingly sharp. The petrosal bone covering the middle-ear region has a tendency to develop many small cells and/or partitions within it, contrasting with the balloonlike capsule common among nonanthropoids.

By comparison with strepsirhines olfactory cues are less important to an anthropoid than are visual ones. Apart from having a small main olfactory bulb, the secondary olfactory bulb and its receptor element, the Organ of Jacobson, are also reduced. Whereas the former structure is an all-purpose mediator of scent, the latter is important in sexual contexts. Its reduction indicates that anthropoids have shifted to a more direct, "personal" system of intersexual and social communication, involving more elaborate bodily coloration and adornment, facial gestures, postural signals, and close-up, interactive displays. Although scent-producing glands still play a role in communication, especially among the platyrrhines, sensory input from the environment comes chiefly via the eyes and ears. As J. Eisenberg points out, like other mammals who have come to capitalize upon sight, such as felid carnivores, both the eye and the brain have evolved specializations that make this possible, principally an enlargement in relative size in the case of the latter.

This reliance upon vision is predicated upon a critical adaptive shift and the emergence of a major primate stem group, the adoption of a diurnal lifestyle by the haplorhines, which included the ancestors of the anthropoids. From them anthropoids inherited not only a preadaptation to an advanced degree of stereoscopic vision but a rod-and-cone system of photoreceptor cells attuned to good color vision and a dense packing of cells near the retinal fovea, making the eye adept at pinpoint focusing. Within the anthropoid brain, the capacity to marshal these features and produce accurate stereoscopic images is elaborated by a complex network of crossover optical fibers that send nerve impulses to both sides of the brain for simultaneous processing. In other mammals without stereoscopy few such fibers cross between the cerebral hemispheres, whereas in anthropoids as many as 60 percent do. The higher visual centers in the occipital lobe are also correspondingly enlarged in anthropoids.

This pattern may have been of great selective advantage to ancestral anthropoids not because of its particular advantages but because of its generality. A visually precise image of the environment is one filled with the discriminants of size, shape, pattern, texture, color, and distance. Nothing could better serve an animal in the highly complex fabric of an arboreal environment. Sight is far richer in information than sound or taste. It also requires a complex system of memory storage, which in turn implies more storage space and higher cognitive functions to encode and decode the data. Thus the world of the anthropoid is a complex world of learning and subtleties, where the hue of a fruit reveals its ripeness, the texture of a branch suggests flexibility, and the glint of an eye spells trouble from a neighbor.

The bony anatomy that surrounds the eyeball represents another derived feature of anthropoids. They are the only mammals to have evolved a postorbital septum, essentially an eye socket. The septum is a thin sheet of bone that walls off the eyeball from behind, thereby becoming a bridge between the bones of the face and the braincase. This adaptation, however, may have nothing to do with good eyesight. While it may safeguard the delicate eyeball from injury or shield it from the masticatory actions of muscles lying behind it, these are probably tangential benefits. The structure of the postorbital septum suggests that it evolved as a mechanical brace to reinforce the connection between the face and the braincase, an interface known as the craniofacial junction. This role is an elaboration of the original function of the postorbital bar, the ancestral structure from which the septum evolved.

The postorbital bar is a vertical branch of the zygomatic arch, a horizontal bridge of bone with ends rooted in the facial skull and the braincase. It appeared first among the euprimates, ancestors of all the modern primates. There it served to stabilize the zygomatic arch and the toothrow against the pull of the masseter muscle, which inserts along the lower surface of the arch, and to minimize the shearing effect at the craniofacial junction, a reaction to the twisting of the face and palate that normally occurs during chewing. As anthropoids tear and grab at food with their large incisors, or chew tough foods with the cheek teeth, they are prone to generate relatively high levels of stress in the zygomatic arch and at the craniofacial junction. These loads may be acute in an anthropoid primate because the mandib-

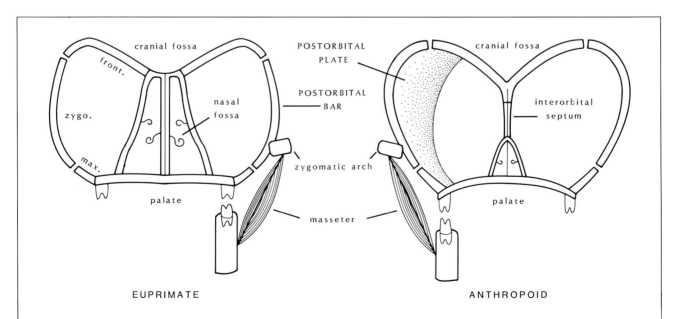

Mechanical model of the anthropoid postorbital plate (right), contrasted with the euprimate postorbital bar (left). The postorbital plate reinforces the connection between the facial and neurocranial parts of the skull in the absence of an enlarged nasal fossa and interorbital region, well developed in lower primates.

ular symphyseal joint is fused, rather than mobile as it is in most nonanthropoids. Hence the symphysis does not convert into motion the muscular forces delivered, say, from the right of the head as the animal chews on the left. Such internal stress is also difficult to balance or distribute within the head because of the shape of the anthropoid face. With their close-set eyes and reduced snouts there is less centralized bony mass to take up the forces of mastication. This is where the septum provides additional support. It compensates by acting as a lateral pillar. In this position the postorbital plate can also directly resist the tension of the powerful masseter muscle.

Thus one of the important innovations of the anthropoid head is associated with feeding. Whether this reflects a new dietary preference or merely a new mechanical approach to a preset feeding regime remains unclear. But since anthropoids also have a conspicuously enlarged set of incisor teeth, an obvious source for much of the mechanical stress the head is designed to endure, it is likely that the main dietary staple was originally fruit, perhaps species with resistant husks that had to be torn apart to access the nutritionally valuable meat. One other nagging question posed by the anatomy of the postorbital plate relates to its phylogenetic origin. Some maintain that the septum evolved in parallel among platyrrhines and catarrhines, for each tends to show different sutural mosaics at the location where the zygomatic contacts the braincase, the four pterion bones. Others argue that this is a labile feature, noting that the pterion pattern varies in large-bodied New World monkeys especially, where two different arrangements may appear on either side of the same head.

Among the other adaptations that make anthropoids unique those pertaining to life-history strategies are probably the most important. As relatively large primates, anthropoids tend to have relatively long gestation periods, lengthened phases of juvenile and adolescent dependency, and a long postreproductive life. Thus intelligence, learning, socialization, and many other factors are major features of the anthropoid life cycle. The production of an offspring with a relatively large brain at birth is also possibly related to a novel intrauterine physiology. The outer fetal membranes are attached to the wall of the uterus in an intimate way, so that fetal capillaries and maternal blood vessels exchange nutrients, immunogens, and waste materials very effectively. This haemochorial placenta is similar to the condition found in tarsiers. The anthropoid uterus is also an unusual bell-shaped chamber designed to accommodate one large fetus, whereas in other primates it tends to be Y-shaped, having a central cavity and two horns where multiple fetuses can attach.

Origins and Evolution: Geography

Although primatologists now are confident that the characteristics shared by the anthropoids indicate that they are monophyletically related, this issue has been a matter of serious doubt and discussion. Even until the 1970s some maintained that platyrrhines and catarrhines were products of parallel evolution, meaning that the anthropoid "grade" or stage of evolution was attained separately as each branch evolved from different lower primate ancestors. Geography figured importantly in this theory; the separation of the platyrrhines and catarrhines does imply a complex history. In fact the anthropoids were frequently cited by such great systematists as Alfred Russel Wallace and G.G. Simpson as a model case illustrating the principle of parallelism. Such a theory was comfortable to nineteenth-century zoologists especially who, influenced by the *scala naturae* doctrine and Victorian ideals of social progress, sought to epitomize adaptive improvement as the major driving force of the evolutionary machine. Then and thereafter prominent researchers claimed that the transition to a higher primate grade was a common phenomenon. All told, some reckoned it happened as many as four times during primate evolution, once among the platyrrhines, twice among the catarrhines, and once more among the Malagasy primates.

Although primatologists no longer accept this line of reasoning, we are still beset with the zoogeographic puzzle of platyrrhines and catarrhines. Three hypotheses have been advocated in recent years to explain it. When the geophysical principles of plate tectonics and continental drift were first applied to primates during the mid-1960s, it was argued that a pan–South America/Africa distribution of ancestral anthropoids was simply rifted apart as the South Atlantic Ocean inched northward to divide this huge southern landmass and its biota into two. This led to the idea that the parapithecid primates of the Fayum Oligocene were platyrrhine ancestors, a notion now generally rejected on anatomic grounds. In addition, since the dating of this event and the paleopositions of continents have become better known, it is clear that the opening of the South Atlantic Ocean began more than 30 m.y. before primates are known to have existed.

In the face of this evidence two modifications of this theory have been proposed. One postulates that tectonic mechanisms produced a system of east-west oceanic ridges within the Atlantic. Nearly all of these are now submerged, but they could have been footholds for primates dispersing across the ocean. Interestingly, this stepping-stone hypothesis was also popular a century before continental drift was an established fact. The second twist, championed by

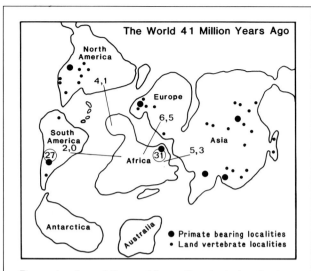

Reconstruction of the world's continents during the late Eocene. (After Savage and Russell, 1983.) (Abbreviations: 27 and 31, in millions of years, are minimal absolute ages of La Salla [Bolivia] and Fayum [Egypt], respectively. 4,1; 2,0; 6,5; 5,3 refer to mammalian families, genera shared in common by all continents and the Fayum.)

J.G. Fleagle, is a preference for the Fayum propliopithecids, rather than the parapithecids as the ancestral platyrrhine stock.

The third idea proposes that an ancestral stock of anthropoids occupied the northern continent, Laurasia, where early Cenozoic primates flourished in stunning variety. Spurred by a cooling effect and the expansion of grassland habitats, most Laurasian primates became extinct, but some shifted their range to the south, both in the eastern and western hemispheres. Among the latter were the protoanthropoids who found their way across the water barriers that separated South America and Africa from Laurasia during a global recession of sea level, which occurred in the late Eocene. The passage into South America probably went against the odds, for it seems to have involved only one other mammalian group, the hystricomorph rodents, relatives of the porcupines. Incidentally, it is the geographic and genealogical association of South American primates and rodents, each with their potentially closest relatives in Africa, that led such researchers as R.I. Hoffstetter to propose an African origin for platyrrhines in the first place. Perhaps the protoplatyrrhines and protohystricomorphs were filtered by an island arc, a large water gap, elevated mountain ranges, inhospitable habitat, or simply the narrow tail-shaped peninsula of southern Middle America. At any rate a concurrent, rich community of Old World mammals, including the tarsiiform primates that were ancestral to the anthropoids, was distributed about the proto-Mediterranean Sea, from western Europe to Northern Africa to Asia. As

sea level fluxed, populations of several orders realigned themselves across plate boundaries. Thus the entry of primates into Africa may have been uneventful in comparison with the sweepstakes conditions prevailing in the New World.

Unfortunately no good primate fossils support this last idea directly. The late Eocene Burmese genera, *Pondaungia* and *Amphipithecus*, occasionally touted as the earliest higher primates, are very dubious anthropoids. We need more and better fossils from that part of the world. The earliest definite anthropoids come from late Oligocene-early Miocene deposits of South America and early Oligocene of Africa, but even these give us few clues regarding the morphology of their predecessors. *Ourayia uintensis*, a form from the late Eocene of Utah, is currently classified as an omomyid tarsiiform, but its anatomy may be a good model for the protoanthropoid pattern, as E.L. Simons has pointed out. Nevertheless, *Ourayia* is known only from dental elements, and the significance of its anthropoidlike features are difficult to comprehend.

Origins and Evolution: Ancestry

To delve more deeply into the origins of anthropoids, without specific fossils revealing it to us literally, we must cast the question more broadly: which primates are anthropoid sister groups, their closest collateral relatives, if not the actual ancestors? The three best candidates are the adapids, omomyids, and tarsiids.

The hypothesis that anthropoids evolved from adapids is based largely upon jointly shared features of the anterior dentition and mandible. This notion was first proposed in the nineteenth century, but P.D. Gingerich has recently given it new force by laying out the details in a comprehensive way, including the identification of putative transitional fossil forms. For example, he argued that both adapids and anthropoids have fused mandibular symphyses, vertical spatulate incisors, and interlocking and sexually dimorphic canines with canine/premolar honing. However, by restudying the anatomy and introducing functional reasoning to assess possible linking homologies, it has been shown that this entire suite of adapid-anthropoid similarities resulted from convergent evolution. A second prominent objection is that these adapids were possibly already strepsirhines phylogenetically rather than a formative euprimate stock ancestral to all the modern groups. In their dentition, skull, and postcranial skeleton adapids frequently display derived characteristics that align them with modern strepsirhines.

Arguing that fossils are not highly informative here, M. Cartmill and co-workers have reasoned that tarsiids are the correct stem group. This, too, seems an unlikely proposition, because all we know of them is derived: tarsiers have always been too advanced anatomically to be the models of an anthropoid stock. But the features that seem to point in that direction are also difficult to interpret, for they are embedded in an extremely unusual anatomical pattern. Superficially, at least, the anatomies of the middle ear and postorbital septum of tarsiers and anthro-

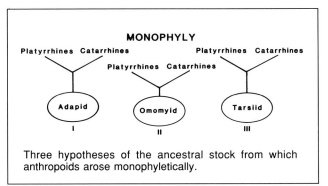

MONOPHYLY

Platyrrhines Catarrhines   Platyrrhines Catarrhines

Platyrrhines Catarrhines

Adapid   Omomyid   Tarsiid

I   II   III

Three hypotheses of the ancestral stock from which anthropoids arose monophyletically.

poids share some details. Researchers have also noted similarities in the position of the internal carotid artery's course through the petrosal bulla and its connection with the development of an unusual, dual-chambered bullar capsule. The anatomical particulars and the overall pattern, however, are strongly divergent in tarsiers and anthropoids, which suggests different genealogical origins and adaptations. For example, the incipiently developed postorbital septa of tarsiers is most likely related to the fact that they provide support for fantastically large eyeballs, which is not the case in anthropoids, with their relatively small eyes.

The most plausible hypothesis is that anthropoids arose during the Eocene from some group of omomyid tarsiiform primate that was widely distributed across North America and Eurasia, a position reviewed and endorsed by F.S. Szalay and A.L. Rosenberger. These animals are well represented in the fossil record by many species, but our current collections consist mostly of teeth and jaws. Given that the modern anthropoid head is so full of higher-primate novelties, the skulls of these fossils would be more telling, but they do at least indicate a significant morphological heterogeneity, including patterns that are much more primitive than the expected, tarsier-like departures. New evidence also demonstrates that some omomyids, known informally as "necrolemurs," were close relatives of living tarsiers, as early workers had thought. This makes it all the more likely that another omomyid stock, ancestral to both the platyrrhines and catarrhines, was widely distributed and sufficiently primitive to have evolved into the protoanthropoids.

Macroevolutionary Patterns

To comprehend and compare the evolutionary histories of the major divisions of the anthropoids we will need many more fossils that document changes in the taxonomic diversity, adaptations, and geographical distributions of the platyrrhines and catarrhines. For the crucial Paleogene phase in the Old World we have only the evidence from the Egyptian Fayum (35–31 m.y.); and from La Salla, Bolivia (27 m.y.) we have data at the Paleogene-Neogene boundary only, which means we know a bit about Africa and next to nothing about South America. Information on later epochs is even more biased in favor of the Old World. Therefore our reconstructions and comparisons must draw heavily upon the living forms for at least one side of the story. Nonetheless, as an entry to this area, E. Delson and A.L. Rosenberger began to examine the macroevolutionary histories of platyrrhines and catarrhines, concluding that each group experienced distinctly different patterns.

First, among the catarrhines both the fossil record and the extant forms indicate a dichotomization of adaptive zones into relatively nonoverlapping arboreal and terrestrial spheres. This is paralleled by an expansion out of the classical humid tropics into more xeric and even colder climates of the Old World. Terrestriality is also associated with the attainment of large body size in many catarrhines. Second, the terrestrial zone seems to be of recent vintage. The earliest catarrhines, ancestors of both the monkeys and apes, all appear to be arboreally adapted. The ancestral Old World monkey stock shifted to a terrestrial habit, as indicated by their many ground-related postcranial adaptations, and this probably explains a large part of their geographic success. Among the apes terrestriality seems to be superimposed upon an indelible arboreal heritage. Third, the morphology of the cercopithecoid radiation is fascinatingly simple; there is little variety other than in size and size-related features. The apes, on the other hand, are fairly diverse anatomically, given that they include a small number of taxa.

The New World monkeys present a contrasting picture. Abundant grasslands appeared in South America during the Cenozoic, but platyrrhines probably never evolved an open-country, terrestrial lineage. There is still no good explanation for this phenomenon, for these ancient savannas supported large populations of herbivores, as in Africa and Asia, where cercopithecoids eventually flourished. Perhaps the larger catarrhines were more formidable competitors than the platyrrhines, or maybe the grassland floras were quite different in the Old and New Worlds. Rather than invade such new ecological domains, platyrrhines capitalized upon their original adaptive zone by finely dividing up its microhabitats.

This is what makes for their great intergeneric diversity, each genus evolving distinctive adaptations to permit coexistence with its close relatives. A second factor that contributed to this pattern is that strict arboreality placed a cap on body-size evolution. Platyrrhines radiated at the small end of the anthropoid body-size spectrum. This enabled some of them to utilize two niches rarely exploited by the larger catarrhines. One is the hard-fruit/seed-eating niche, occupied by a whole subfamily, the pitheciines, and the second is a gum-eating niche, central to the adaptations of the small two-molared marmosets.

Another contrast between the radiations is their temporal patterning. Lineage stasis has been a more common occurrence among platyrrhines than among catarrhines. To properly evaluate this hypothesis we need good biostratigraphic information over geological time, which is severely lacking especially for the platyrrhines. The fossil record, however, suggests that generic lineages have a much longer duration in the New World. Among all of the Old World catarrhines the macaques and orangs show the greatest geologic longevity. Specimens of *Macaca* are known from deposits of 8 m.y. ago. Congeners of *Pongo* go back only as far as the Pleistocene, but the craniofacial morphology that marks it as a generic entity is well developed in late *Sivapithecus* at 8 m.y. These are preceded by dental remains of potential congeners back to ca. 14 m.y. In the Old World these examples are the only two cases of anagenetic/taxonomic stasis from a fossil record that is strikingly rich by comparison with the South American data.

Among the modern New World monkeys *Aotus* is closely related to, if not a descendant of, the fossil genus *Tremacebus*, 20–18 m.y. *Saimiri* is phylogenetically linked through *Neosaimiri*, at 15–14 m.y., to *Dolichocebus*, 20–18 m.y. Equivalent in age to *Neosaimiri* is *Aotus dindensis*, the first example of a living primate genus to occur deep in the fossil record. *Alouatta* is probably a descendant, and at least a sister genus of *Stirtonia*, at 15–14 m.y. In fact it is difficult to distinguish the latter two at the generic level. New fossil taxa, such as *Soriacebus ameghinorum*, 18–15 m.y., and *Micodon kiotensis*, 15–14 m.y., while still of uncertain phylogenetic status, indicate that prominent higher taxa, such as subfamilies and tribes of platyrrhines, also had remote origins.

See also ADAPIDAE; AMERICAS; ATELIDAE; BRANISELLINAE; CEBIDAE; CERCOPITHECIDAE; DIET; HOMINOIDEA; OMOMYIDAE; PALEOBIOGEOGRAPHY; PITHECIINAE; PLATE TECTONICS; SKULL; TEETH. [A.L.R.]

Further Readings

Cartmill, M., MacPhee, R.D.E., and Simons, E.L. (1981) Anatomy of the temporal bone in early anthropoids, with remarks on the problem of anthropoid origins. Am. J. Phys. Anthropol. 56:3–21.

Clark, W.E. Le Gros (1959) The Antecedents of Man. Edinburgh: Edinburgh University Press.

Delson, E., and Rosenberger, A.L. (1984) Are there any anthropoid primate "living fossils"? In N. Eldredge and S. Stanley (eds.): Living Fossils. New York: Springer-Verlag, pp. 50–61.

Eisenberg, J. (1984) The Mammalian Radiations. Chicago: University of Chicago Press.

Gingerich, P.D. (1981) Eocene Adapidae, paleobiogeography, and the origin of South American Platyrrhini. In R.L. Ciochon and A.B. Chiarelli (eds.): Evolutionary Biology of the New World Monkeys and Continental Drift. New York: Plenum, pp. 123–138.

Hoffstetter, R.I. (1981) Origin and deployment of New World monkeys emphasizing the southern continents route. In Ciochon and Chiarelli, pp. 103–122.

Rosenberger, A.L. (1986) Platyrrhines, catarrhines and the anthropoid transition. In B.A. Wood, L. Martin, and P. Andrews (eds.): Major Topics in Human and Primate Evolution. Cambridge: Cambridge University Press, pp. 66–88.

Rosenberger, A.L., and Szalay, F.S. (1980) On the tarsiiform origins of Anthropoidea. In Ciochon and Chiarelli, pp. 139–157.

Simons, E.L. (1972) Primate Evolution: An Introduction to Man's Place in Nature. New York: Macmillan.

Simpson, G.G. (1945) The principles of classification and a classification of mammals. Bull. Am. Mus. Nat. Hist. 85:1–350.

Szalay, F.S., and Delson, E. (1979) Evolutionary History of the Primates. New York: Academic.

ANTHROPOLOGICAL ARCHAEOLOGY *see* ARCHAEOLOGY

ANTHROPOLOGY

Academic discipline concerned with the study of aspects of human (and other primate) culture and biology, past and present. The subject matter of anthropology ranges widely; to make the breadth of information and the diversity of approaches employed more manageable, the field is often divided into four subdisciplines: physical anthropology, archaeology, cultural anthropology, and linguistics.

Physical anthropologists study the origins and evolution of primates (including humans), behavior of living primates, and human biology, which itself includes adaptation, variation, and genetics. Archaeologists study past human groups, focusing on the material evidence of behavior and adaptation, including both historical reconstructions of the past and processual studies of the mechanisms of change. Cultural anthropologists study all aspects of the community life of living human groups, encompassing social structure, political and economic relations, kinship and family life, religion and ideology, and even art and aesthetics. Anthropological linguists study human language and communication.

Taken together these diverse fields comprise an academic discipline with strong alliances to many other natural and social sciences as well as to the humanities and arts. In many ways anthropology is the great integrative discipline.

See also ARCHAEOLOGY; COMPLEX SOCIETIES; CULTURAL ANTHROPOLOGY; CULTURE; PHYSICAL ANTHROPOLOGY; PRIMATE ECOLOGY; PRIMATE SOCIETIES. [B.B.]

Further Readings

Harris, M. (1985) Culture, People, Nature: An Introduction to General Anthropology, 4th ed. New York: Harper and Row.

ANVIL see STONE-TOOL MAKING

ANYATHIAN

Paleolithic industry recognized in the 1930s from terraces of the Irrawaddy River (Burma). This industry consists of "chopper-chopping tools" manufactured from fossil wood, silicified tuff, quartzite, and quartz. Based on the stratigraphy of the terraces, the Anyathian was subdivided into Early and Late phases. The actual age of these artifacts can only be guessed at, since most of them (especially the Early Anyathian) are abraded and occur in secondary contexts. It also seems likely that at least some of these "tools" are in fact the result of natural fracturing.

See also ASIA (EASTERN); CHOPPER-CHOPPING TOOLS. [G.G.P.]

AOTUS see PITHECIINAE

APATEMYIDAE

Family of rare early Tertiary mammals related to insectivorans, not primates, that occurs in both Europe and North America. In North America its range is from the Paleocene well into the Oligocene; in Europe it spans the Eocene. These mammals are astonishingly similar in some of their adaptations to both the lemuriform primate *Daubentonia* (the aye-aye) and the phalangeriform marsupials *Dactylopsila* and *Dactylonax*. The robustness of the skull is related to the hypertrophied, rodentlike incisors, and new evidence from European middle Eocene specimens (from Messel) shows third- and fourth-hand ray elongation, somewhat similar to the elongated third finger in *Daubentonia*. All of the evidence suggests an insect- and grub-hunting, and possibly tree-gnawing, adaptive complex for apatemyids, one of the most striking of mammalian convergences of unrelated fossil mammals to living forms that themselves are convergent in their highly derived lifestyles. Paleocene dental evidence of apatemyids suggests their derivation from insectivorans unlike archaic primates.

[F.S.S.]

APE

Primates most closely related to humans. They consist of the African apes—the two species of chimpanzee and one of gorilla—and the Asian apes—the orangutan and six species of gibbon. Together with humans they make up the superfamily Hominoidea, which can be distinguished from other primates by a number of characters.

There is an important historical element in the ways in which apes are referred to in scientific and popular literature. The apes are seen as human "cousins," a group of closely related but distinct species. There is often an implication that humans are completely different from the brutish apes, and many attempts have been made to push back our evolutionary divergence from the apes into the remote past. None of this can be sustained, for in evolutionary terms there is no such thing as a group of nonhuman apes that is descended from a common ancestor not also ancestral to humans—in other words, the apes do not constitute a monophyletic group. It is thus an artificial, although still useful, group: artificial, because it has no evolutionary meaning, but useful because it is a convenient term encompassing all nonhuman hominoids. It can be further subdivided into the lesser apes—the gibbons, or Hylobatidae—and the great apes—the orangutan of Asia and the gorilla and chimpanzees of Africa—which together with humans make up the Hominidae, the other group of extant Hominoidea.

There are no defining characters of the apes. They can be described as having no tails, to distinguish them from the monkeys, but the lack of tails is a hominoid distinguishing mark shared also with humans, and the same goes for all the other characters that are described for the Hominoidea.

Gibbons

Six species of gibbon are included in a single genus, *Hylobates*. This is divided into three distinct groups, usually recognized by separate subgenera. The concolor group lives in Vietnam and Laos, the siamang group inhabits Malaysia and Sumatra, and the gibbons proper cover much of Southeast Asia. They are arboreal, highly active animals and are common wherever primary rain forest still exists. Their method of locomotion is extremely varied, including four-footed hanging, bipedal walking (on large branches), and bimanual swinging from below branches. The last of these behaviors is *brachiation*, and the gibbon version of brachiation is unique in the animal kingdom.

The gibbons have developed a monogamous family system, which is unusual in primates. The sexes have equal roles in defending territory, and one of the results of the sharing of roles by males and females is the lack of size distinction (sexual dimorphism) between them (body weights range from 4 to 13 kg. for all the species, but there is little difference between the sexes). They have also developed a complex system of vocalization that is related both to their social structure and to their environment: in the three-dimensional tree canopies of the forests, where visibility is poor but sound carries long distances, their wide range of vocalizations serves an important role in social interactions.

Orangutan

The orangutan is the only species of great ape in Asia. It is much larger than the gibbons, and its similarity in size to the African great apes has led in the past to all being included in the group called the Pongidae. Most of the similarities, however, are due only to size, and *Pongo*, the orangutan, is now put into its own subfamily, the Ponginae. The orangutan is today confined to the rain forests of Sumatra and Borneo, where two distinct subspecies live, one to each island. It is arboreal, despite its large size (ranges of body weight are from 40 kg. in females to 140 kg. in males), and locomotion in the trees is by slow, cautious, four-footed climbing. They eat mainly fruit, often from high in the tree canopy. They are solitary animals or live in small groups centered on

females, with male ranges overlapping those of females, and this has led to the marked sexual dimorphism so different from gibbons. Orangutans differ from gibbons also in being silent animals, with a low repertoire of calls.

Chimpanzees

Two species of chimpanzee are currently recognized, although the level of difference between them is actually less than that between the two subspecies of orangutan. As with the orangutan the two types of chimpanzee have allopatric distributions, the pygmy chimpanzee living south of the Congo (now Zaire) River and west of the Lualaba River and the common chimpanzee spanning West and Central Africa and into East Africa in a broad belt north of the Congo.

The pygmy chimpanzee lives in swamp forests and is more arboreal than its bigger relative. The common chimpanzee lives in a variety of habitats, spending much of its time on the ground, especially in more open or savanna habitats. All are fruit eating, and all move about on the ground in a unique form of quadrupedal locomotion called *knuckle-walking*. In this the weight of the body is taken on the middle parts of the extended fingers, thus lengthening the already elongated forearms. Social structure is complex, with large multimale groups occupying a large

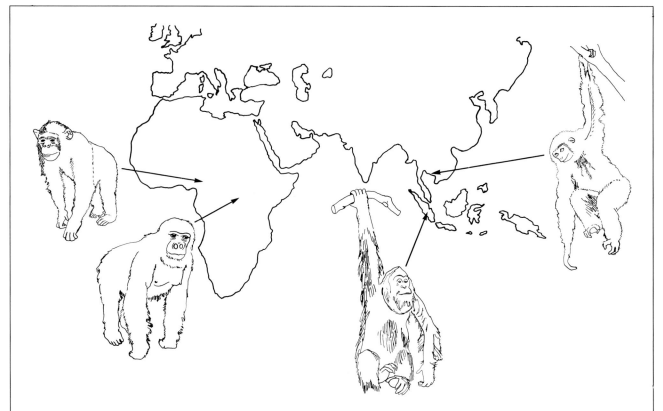

Outline of the world with the location of the chimpanzee (top left) and gorilla (bottom left) in Africa, the orangutan (bottom) in Borneo and Sumatra, and the gibbons in Southeast Asia (right). Drawings not to scale.

home range, but social structure can be varied according to need, and this fluidity is an important part of chimpanzee adaptation.

Gorilla

This is the last of the great apes to be considered here. Together with the chimpanzees and humans it is grouped in the subfamily Homininae, but the exact relationships within this grouping are far from clear at present. The gorillas are divided into three races or subspecies, a western form, an eastern form, and a rare subspecies found only on the mountains separating East from Central Africa. In all these diverse regions the gorilla is almost entirely terrestrial. It is restricted to forest habitats not so much because of the presence of trees as because these are the places where grows the lush ground vegetation on which gorillas depend. Its method of locomotion is knuckle-walking identical to that of the chimpanzees, although it differs from these other African apes in being much larger and more sexually dimorphic (body weights range from 75 to 180 kg., with almost no overlap between the sexes). The greater terrestriality and dependence on vegetable food as opposed to fruit are both related to this larger size. Gorillas live in multimale groups, as do the chimpanzees, but the groups are smaller and are age-graded. The oldest (and biggest) male is the dominant animal in the group, and in all three subspecies it develops a saddle of white hair on its back, commonly known as silver-back.

See also DIET; HOMINIDAE; HOMININAE; HYLOBATIDAE; LOCOMOTION; MONOPHYLY; PONGINAE; SEXUAL DIMORPHISM. [P.A.]

Further Readings

Chivers, D.J., Wood, B.A., and Bilsborough, A. (1984) Food Acquisition and Processing in Primates. New York: Plenum.

de Boer, L.E.M. (1982) The Orang Utan. The Hague: Junk.

Groves, C.P. (1970) Gorillas: The World of Animals. London: Barker.

Jolly, A. (1983) The Evolution of Primate Behavior, 2nd ed. New York: Macmillan.

Napier, J.R., and Napier, P.H. (1967) A Handbook of Living Primates. London: Academic.

APIDIUM *see* PARAPITHECIDAE

APOLLO-11

Rock-shelter site in the Orange River Valley of Namibia near the South African border. Excavated by W.E. Wendt in 1969 to 1972, the site is characterized by a long series of Middle Stone Age (Mode III, IV) and Later Stone Age (Mode V) industries, spanning the late Pleistocene and Holocene ca. 130-6 k.y. B.P. Industries include Middle Stone Age horizons based on both flake and blade technologies, possibly beginning as early as the last interglacial, ca. 130 k.y., and incorporating at least one layer of Howieson's Poort in association with pigments and incised ostrich-eggshell fragments. The uppermost Middle Stone Age horizon represents perhaps 20 k.y. of accumulation, dated between 46,400 and 25,500 B.P. by radiocarbon, and incorporates at the top the oldest "art" in Africa in the form of fragments of painted slabs. Unlike many sites in interior southern Africa the shelter was more or less continuously occupied or reoccupied between 20,000 and 6000 B.P., and preserves a long series first of nonmicrolithic Later Stone Age industries with ostrich-eggshell beads and then, by 10,420 B.P., of microlithic Wilton horizons.

See also HOWIESON'S POORT; KLASIES; LATER STONE AGE; MIDDLE STONE AGE; PALEOLITHIC IMAGE; STONE-TOOL MAKING; WILTON. [A.S.B.]

APOMORPHIC *see* CLADISTICS

AQUITANIAN *see* MIOCENE

ARAGO

Cave near Tautavel in the French Pyrenees that has been under excavation since 1964. Deep Pleistocene sediments contain faunal remains, Acheulean and "Tayacian" artifacts, and fossil hominids. The original dating of the main hominid finds was "Rissian" (i.e., late middle Pleistocene), but recently this dating has been revised, and faunal and absolute dating methods are now claimed to place them as "Mindelian" (ca. 450 k.y. old). The relevant small-mammal faunas and certain other absolute dates, however, point to a somewhat younger age. The first significant hominid remains from Arago were two mandibles, Arago 2 and 13. Both are robust and chinless, but they contrast strongly in overall size and dental dimensions. This difference is probably a reflection of sexual dimorphism, with the smaller Arago 2 mandible deriving from a female. This mandible also appears more Neanderthal-like in the forward positioning of the dentition. The most complete Arago fossil hominid is the partial skull represented by a face and frontal bone (Arago 21) and a right parietal (Arago 47), which probably derive from the same individual. Fragmentary postcranial bones have also been discovered, including a robust innominate bone (Arago 44). The classification of the Arago hominids has been a source of some dispute. The main describers of the material favor assignment to *Homo erectus*, while others regard them as fossils of "archaic *Homo sapiens*."

See also ARCHAIC HOMO SAPIENS. [C.B.S.]

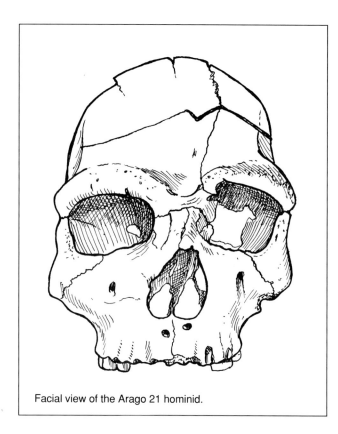

Facial view of the Arago 21 hominid.

ARAMBOURG, CAMILLE (1885–1969)

French paleontologist. Born in Algeria, Arambourg conducted the first geological and paleontological survey of the Omo region (Ethiopia) in 1933. Some 34 years later, in 1967, Arambourg led a French contingent that joined efforts with groups from the United States (led by F.C. Howell) and from Kenya (directed by L.S.B. Leakey) to inaugurate modern work in the region. This combined effort resulted in the discovery of the remains of several hundred fossil hominids, recovered between 1967 and 1974. The major focus of Arambourg's work, however, was the prehistory of North Africa. During the 1950s he discovered, with R.I. Hoffstetter, in a late middle Pleistocene deposit at Ternifine (now known as Tighenif), near Oran (Morocco), the remains of a hominid that he later dubbed *Atlanthropus mauritanicus*. He was also responsible for describing the mandibular fragments found by P. Biberson at Sidi Abderrahman (Casablanca) in 1954.

See also BIBERSON, PIERRE; CASABLANCA; OMO; TIGHENIF. [F.S.]

ARAPAHOVIUS *see* ANAPTOMORPHINAE

ARCHAEOINDRIS *see* PALAEOPROPITHECIDAE

ARCHAEOLEMUR *see* ARCHAEOLEMURIDAE

ARCHAEOLEMURIDAE

Recently extinct family of Lemuriformes, closely related to the extant indriids. The subfossil remains of archaeolemurids are known from marsh and cave deposits in south, southwestern, central, and northwestern Madagascar, and most recently a fragmentary specimen of *Archaeolemur* has been found in the far north of the island. The archaeolemurids gave rise to the idea that "monkeylike" primates once existed in Madagascar, but there is in fact no basis for this conclusion.

Two genera are attributed to Archaeolemuridae: *Archaeolemur* and *Hadropithecus*. At least two species of *Archaeolemur* are known: the relatively robust *A. edwardsi* from the center of the island and the more gracile *A. majori* from the south and southwest. Whether or not the two specimens of *Archaeolemur* known from the northwest and the far north represent one or two additional species will be shown only by further material. A single species of *Hadropithecus* has been described: *H. stenognathus*, from sites in both the center and the south and southwest of Madagascar.

In size the archaeolemurines are intermediate between their close relatives the living indriids and the extinct palaeopropithecids, cranial length in all three species falling between ca. 12 and 15 cm. *Archaeolemur* is the less specialized of the two archaeolemurid genera, retaining a general conformation of the skull that is close to the indriid condition, although of much heavier build due to greater size. Alone among the large-bodied extinct lemurs, for example, the archaeolemurids retain the primitive lemuriform inflated auditory bulla and the positioning of the eardrum at the outside of the skull. *Archaeolemur edwardsi* is slightly larger and considerably more robust than is *A. majori* and characteristically shows a well-developed sagittal crest and heavy nuchal ridging. In both species the mandible is robust, and the symphysis is fused and quite upright, in contrast to the oblique, unfused symphysis of the indriids.

The most striking skull specializations shown by the archaeolemurids lie in the dentition. The premolars are compressed laterally to form a continuous longitudinal, scissorlike, shearing blade, and the molars are small and squared-off, with a cusp at each corner. The front and rear cusp pairs are joined transversely by continuous crests, known as *lophs*, producing a "bilophodont" condition otherwise seen in primates only among Old World monkeys. The

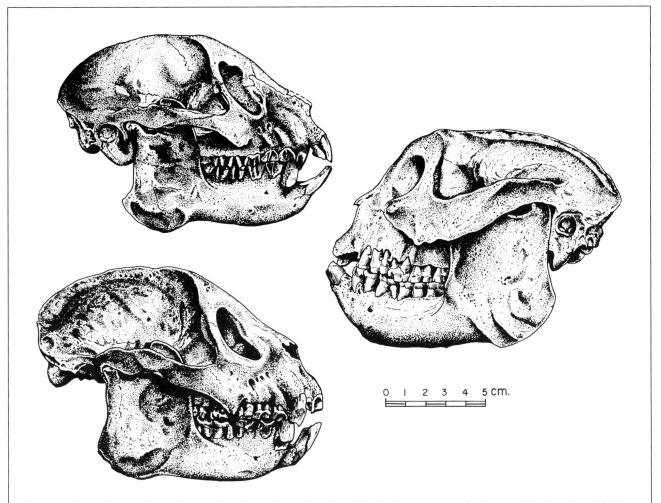

Crania, in lateral view, of the three archaeolemurid species. Top left: *Archaeolemur majori*; bottom left: *A. edwardsi*; right: *Hadropithecus stenognathus*.

central upper incisor is much enlarged, while the lower front teeth are relatively short and in contrast to those of other lemuriforms are not fully procumbent. The premolar *blade* represents an adaptation unmatched among extant primates, but the ensemble of dental characters suggests a diet preponderantly of fruit. The archaeolemurids retain a third premolar in each quadrant of the jaw that has been lost in the indriids and palaeopropithecids.

In its postcranial skeleton *Archaeolemur* shows a set of adaptations very different from those of the families just mentioned. This lemur appears to have been a short-legged and powerfully built quadruped, probably at least semiterrestrial in habit and with reduced abilities of arboreal leaping. An analogy has been made between *Archaeolemur* and baboons of the genus *Papio*, which are at home both on tree-savanna and in more forested environments.

Hadropithecus is yet more specialized in its dentition than is *Archaeolemur*. Its front teeth are greatly reduced and the lower ones are completely upright.

The molars, in contrast, are greatly expanded, with high, rounded enamel folds, and the last premolar is enlarged and incorporated into this grinding row, although the two anterior premolars are reduced and still show some vestiges of an *Archaeolemur*-like shearing edge. The grinding battery of cheek teeth rapidly wore flat to produce a surface of alternating shearing edges of enamel and shallow basins of dentine. The skull of *Hadropithecus* is modified to accommodate this powerful and unusual dentition; it is extremely short-faced, heavily built to absorb masticatory stresses, and it bears strong muscle markings, notably sagittal cresting. The postcranial skeleton of *Hadropithecus* is poorly known, but bones thought to belong to *H. stenognathus* are generally similar to those of *Archaeolemur* except in being more lightly built.

The contrasts between *Archaeolemur* and *Hadropithecus* have been likened to those between the close relatives *Papio*, the common baboon, and *Theropithecus*, the gelada. Like *Hadropithecus* the latter displays reduction of the anterior dentition and enlargement and elaboration of a rapidly wearing posterior grinding battery and for a baboon is short-faced. In contrast to *Papio*, essentially a woodland dweller, *Theropithecus* is adapted to an open, treeless habitat. Its sustenance comes entirely from terrestrial sources and consists largely of small, tough, and often gritty objects, such as the seeds, rhizomes, and blades of grasses, small bulbs, and arthropods. These objects are gathered by hand, obviating the necessity of cropping with the front teeth. In view of the detailed suite of dental similarities between the two we may conclude that *Hadropithecus* was adapted to an ecological role similar to the gelada's: that of an open-country "manual grazer."

The reconstruction of *Archaeolemur* as at least a semiterrestrial form, and of *Hadropithecus* as terrestrially specialized, raises the question of the environment in which these lemurs lived. Until recently the feeling generally was that upon the advent of humans, some 1,500 years ago, Madagascar was more or less completely forested. Over the past decade or so, however, it has become clear that great climatic fluctuations marked the tropics during the Pleistocene and that the tropical vegetation has been highly responsive to that fluctuation. Humid forests, for instance, would have contracted and grasslands expanded as the climate became cooler and drier, and the reverse would have taken place in warmer, wetter periods. It is not known precisely at what point in the cycle Madagascar, a huge island with many distinct vegetational zones, found itself when the first humans arrived; but it is unlikely that it was at the high point of forest expansion. Preliminary work at one rich subfossil site in the center of the island that has yielded remains of both *Archaeolemur* and *Hadropithecus* suggests that a mosaic of forests and grasslands existed around it while the fossiliferous deposits were accumulating in a lake. Under circumstances of this kind it is hardly surprising that the indroid radiation should have produced terrestrial forms as well as the highly arboreal ones we know today.

See also INDRIOIDEA; LEMURIFORMES; PALAEOPROPITHECIDAE; TEETH. [I.T.]

ARCHAEOLOGICAL SITES

Places that contain evidence of past human activity. This evidence consists of archaeological *inventories*— i.e. portable items like stone and bone tools or bones of animals hunted and eaten—and *features*—permanent objects like hearths, storage pits, burials, and dwellings.

Paleolithic sites vary in size from a handful of stone tools scattered over one or two square meters to huge villages that cover areas over 10,000 square meters and contain rich inventories and numerous features. The vast majority of the studied Pleistocene sites are found on land, although research indicates that some sites are today submerged under lakes and seas that expanded after the late Pleistocene deglaciation.

Archaeological sites contain information on an almost endless number of variables, including their location, the nature of the inventories and features they contain, and the geographic and geological context in which archaeological materials are found.

Archaeologists use these variables to classify sites. Since their research questions involve only a few variables—those that provide the most suitable data—the resulting site classifications are not all-inclusive, nor are they valid when other variables are considered. The following are some of the more common ways of classifying Paleolithic sites.

Classification of Sites
Classification by archaeological contents   The oldest classificatory scheme used in archaeology, one that gave rise to the term *Paleolithic*, or Old Stone Age, grouped sites according to the archaeological materials found in them. We still use this classification: for example, Pleistocene sites containing predominantly simple choppers and unmodified flakes are Oldowan; those with bifacially worked handaxes and cleavers are Acheulean; those containing tools made on flakes are Middle Paleolithic; those with a predominance of blade tools are Late Paleolithic. This way of grouping sites emphasizes the chronological relationship among stone-working technologies and is used when questions about the relative chronology of a site are being asked.

Classification by context   The geological context in which prehistoric features and inventories are found is often used for site classification as well. This variable separates *surface finds*, or *scatters*—which consist of stone tools and sometimes faunal remains found lying uncovered on present-day surfaces—from *stratified* ones found buried in geologic strata devoid of human-made items. *Stratified layers* or *sites* can consist of either *single levels*, which resulted from discrete occupational episodes in the past, or *multiple layers* superimposed on one another and separated by sterile geologic deposits. The latter came about because the same location was repeatedly used by prehistoric people.

Classification by condition of cultural remains   The condition in which features and inventories are discovered offers another way for classifying Paleolithic sites. If archaeological materials have remained where, and as, prehistoric groups left them, the sites are considered to be in *primary context* and are

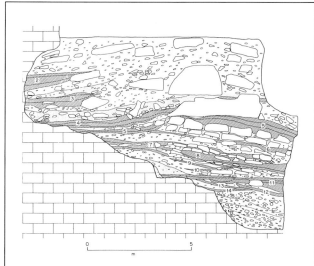

Stratified rock-shelter site of Abri Pataud in southwestern France. The numbers refer to levels with archaeological remains as follows:

level 1: lower Solutrean   level 4: Perigordian Vc
level 2: proto-Magdalenian level 5: Perigordian IV
level 3: Perigordian VI   level 6: evolved Aurignacian
       level 7: intermediate Aurignacian
       level 8,9,10: intermediate Aurignacian
       level 11, 12: early Aurignacian
       level 13, 14: basal Aurignacian.

(Modified after Champion, Gamble, Shennan, and Whittle, Prehistoric Europe, © 1984 by Academic Press, and after H.L. Movius.)

Yudinovo Late Paleolithic open-air site under excavation. (After Soffer, 1985.)

termed *in situ*. Often, however, postdepositional processes have severely affected the archaeological remains, redepositing them downslope, destroying some of them through erosion or weathering, and so on. Archaeological remains found in such a disturbed context are said to be in *secondary, disturbed,* or *redeposited* state.

Classification by site location   Another common

Masai Gorge rock-shelter site in Kenya. (Photograph courtesy of Dr. Stanley Ambrose.)

way of classifying sites is by their geographic context or location. This scheme produces such types as *cave* and *rock-shelter* (or *abri*) sites. The former usually refers to cases where cultural materials are found deep inside caverns; the latter two synonyms refer to materials found under rock overhangs. Human occupations that took place without the protection of such natural shelters are called *open-air* sites.

Since most human settlements took place in well-defined geographic locations, these are sometimes used to define site types as well. In this scheme archaeological remains found near present or past lakeshores are termed *lacustrine* sites, those near rivers or streams *fluviatile*, or *river valley*, sites, and so on.

Classification by duration of occupation   In some cases, especially when dealing with prehistoric settlement systems, the length of the time a site was occupied is used for classificatory purposes. This parameter separates *seasonal camps* or *occupations* from *sedentary* ones occupied year-round. Sites that show evidence for brief occupation, a few hours at most, by a single person or a small number of individuals, are sometimes termed *locations* to distinguish them from *sites*, which in this scheme show a greater intensity of occupation.

Classification by site function   Archaeological remains often indicate the kind of prehistoric behavior that took place at a site, and so sites can be grouped according to the behavior that went on in them. Such a classificatory scheme separates *habitation*, or *living, sites* from *special-purpose sites*, or *locations*, such as kill or butchery sites. Habitation sites occupied for relatively brief periods of time, say, one or two seasons, are called *base camps*; those inhabited year-round or nearly year-round are called *villages*. In later prehistory settled villages were occupied for hundreds of years. As time went on and structures became dilapidated, were abandoned, and ultimately collapsed, new ones were built on top of them. In time this produced huge mounds of old building debris, called *tells*, which are quite common in some parts of the Old World.

Lithic workshops, or *quarries*, are a type of task-specific site used by prehistoric groups to extract stone for tool making. *Middens*, found along seacoasts and rivers, contain sizable accumulations of shells, bones, and other cultural refuse. They occur where people routinely ate shellfish, snails, or goodly amounts of sea mammals and fish in prehistoric times. The resulting garbage dumps were sometimes used for burial of the dead but were rarely lived in.

A number of disparate sites where special types of nonutilitarian behavior took place in prehistory are known as *ceremonial sites*. When prehistoric burials took place outside of habitation sites, a special type of ceremonial site, the *burial site*, resulted. In other cases the painting of cave or rock-shelter walls during the Late Paleolithic and Mesolithic, possibly as a part of wider ritual practices, resulted in *cave-art* sites. Finally, some prehistoric groups, especially in the New World, constructed hillocks that they used for various purposes. Some of these earthen constructions, called *mounds*, were used as platforms for temples, others held burials, and still others were figurative in design and probably had some ritual or ideological significance for their builders.

See also RITUAL; SITE TYPES. [O.S.]

Further Readings

Fagan, B. (1985) In the Beginning, 5th ed. Boston: Little, Brown.

Hole, F., and Heizer, R.F. (1977) Prehistoric Archaeology. New York: Holt, Rinehart and Winston.

ARCHAEOLOGY

Recovery and study of material remains of past societies to gain insights into human history and prehistory. Modern archaeology also considers the association of these societies with one another (*man-man relationships*) and with the paleolandscape (*man-land relationships, archaeological context*). The goals of anthropological archaeology in particular include the reconstruction of cultural evolutionary sequences, the understanding of past lifeways, and the explanation of the natural and cultural processes that affect cultural systems and cause evolutionary shifts in human adaptations.

History of Archaeology

An interest in antiquities may be as old as *Homo sapiens*. Late Pleistocene fishing people at Ishango in eastern Zaire collected Pliocene fossils (e.g. *Stegodon kaisensis*), fossil shells were brought by early Aurignacian people to Abri Pataud in southern France, and some of the earliest historical records suggest that the ancient Babylonians treasured the artifacts of their vanished predecessors and even conducted excavations to recover them. (The first recorded field archaeologist *cum* museum curator appears to have been En-nigaldi-Nanna, the daughter of King Nabonidus.)

It was not until the eighteenth century, however, with the excavations at Pompeii and Herculaneum, that field archaeology was established as a valid approach to the history of past civilizations. In European regions that were peripheral to the classical civilizations, such as Denmark and England, excavations of megalithic monuments led to speculation about prehistoric and pagan antecedents, to the first study of Stonehenge (by John Aubrey), and to the first recorded use of stratigraphy, archaeological context, and association to establish the age of a buried monument (Edward Lhwydd). At the end of the eighteenth century John Frere identified handaxes from the Thames valley site of Hoxne as "weapons of war, fabricated and used by a people who had not the use of metals" and correctly ascribed them to "a very remote period indeed, even beyond that of the present world." By the nineteenth century archaeology was seen not only as a window into daily life in classical times but also as the only access to a long expanse of "prehistoric times," before written records.

In Denmark, during the late 1700s and early 1800s, the classification of Danish antiquities into three periods—Stone, Bronze, and Iron—provided the first relative chronology for archaeological sites. This "three-age system" was codified by Thomsen and Worsae in the exhibit halls and guidebook of the National Museum during the period 1829–1843. The study of classical antiquities also became more systematic, through the decipherment of hieroglyphic (1822) and cuneiform (1837–1846) scripts.

By 1860 the existence of a very ancient age of "chipped stone" (redefined as the "Paleolithic Epoch" by Lubbock in 1865) was established by excavations in both England and France, especially by the work of Boucher de Perthes in the Somme gravels and Lartet at Aurignac. By the end of the 1860s Paleolithic archaeology was firmly established by the excavation of ancient but recognizable *Homo sapiens* fossils in association with the bones of extinct animals in 1869 at Cro-Magnon in the Dordogne and by the beginnings of a biostratigraphic sequence for Paleolithic assemblages (Lartet and Christy, 1865–1875).

Important developments in twentieth-century archaeology include renewed emphasis in the period 1905–1920 on stratigraphy as the basis of relative chronologies; the development of regional sequences in most areas of the world between 1930 and 1970; a new focus beginning ca. 1940 on the reconstruction of paleoenvironments and paleoclimates; and a wide range of new techniques for the dating, recovery, and analysis of archaeological remains. Advances in data collection and analysis allowed later twentieth-century archaeologists to concentrate on questions concerning the processes of cultural evolution and the relationship between present and past cultures and the formation of the archaeological record.

Subfields of Archaeology

Since archaeology is simply a material approach to reconstructing the past, the questions asked by the archaeologist and the goals of archaeological investigations are determined by the particular historical discipline with which the archaeologist is affiliated.

Prehistorians study the archaeological remains of societies with no written records, and their training is often concentrated in geology and anthropology (ethnology). Depending on the prehistorian's training, the focus of inquiry varies from the reconstruction of cultural sequences through time, to paleoenvironmental reconstructions, to an understanding of past lifeways and the processes of change.

Classical archaeologists receive their primary training in art history, classics, or Near Eastern studies and have been concerned primarily with the documentation of art styles; the recovery and study of archives and inscriptions; the identification and description of particular monuments or sites of the ancient world, known from historical records; and, more recently, with the reconstruction of daily life in antiquity. *Biblical archaeologists* are classical archaeologists whose training may involve divinity school and whose interests include verification and amplification of biblical history.

Historic archaeologists study the material remains of the recent antecedents of modern societies to provide an alternative view to that given by written records. Of particular interest to historic archaeologists are the ordinary lives of common people (e.g.

workers, slaves, soldiers), who are often not well reflected in archival materials, as well as changing settlement patterns, trade networks, economic strategies, and symbolic systems. In England, for instance, *Anglo-Saxon*, *medieval*, and *industrial archaeologists* share some of the historical archaeologists' goals and training. *Salvage archaeologists* (or "cultural resource managers" in the United States), who may be trained in any archaeological speciality, conduct archaeological surveys and excavations for remains of any time period in areas threatened by construction or development.

Anthropological archaeologists, trained in anthropology, are the largest group of archaeologists, at least in the United States, where the connection between living Native Americans and the prehistoric past has led to greater expectations for the reconstruction of past lifeways. While early research in anthropological archaeology, as in other subfields, focused on the reconstruction of regional sequences, anthropological archaeologists since the 1960s have turned increasingly to questions concerning the processes responsible for cultural evolution as well as cultural adaptations to particular environments.

The new technologies of dating, data recovery, and analysis have interested individuals trained in the physical or natural sciences in archaeological research questions. These scientists are known variously as *archaeometrists* (dating techniques, human-bone biochemistry, physical and chemical analysis of artifacts, prospection techniques); *archaeozoologists*, who study archaeologically recovered faunal remains to determine diet, subsistence patterns, and other aspects of past cultures; and *archaeobotanists*, who study archaeologically recovered plant remains including fibers, phytoliths, pollen, seeds, and pottery or hardened mud impressions to determine human use of plants.

Formation of the Archaeological Record

Like the fossil record the archaeological record is created through natural taphonomic processes of concentration in the landscape, differential preservation and burial, and postdepositional disturbances. Formation of the archaeological record, however, is also strongly affected by cultural rules concerning such factors as technology and raw-material use; activity placement; storage, discard, or "dumping"; long-distance trade or transport; and burial and reoccupation. Archaeological sites, or concentrations of artifacts, may be created primarily by the culturally defined discard patterns of a group of prehistoric occupants (*primary context*) or may result from the transport and concentration of discarded artifacts and noncultural remains by natural processes, such as erosion or stream action (*secondary context*). Interpretation of archaeological data depends on understanding both natural and cultural formation processes, as well as the symbolic aspects of artifact styles, use of space, and human relationship to the environment.

Although knowledge of ethnographic data from present-day societies, particularly in regard to cultural formation processes, is essential to the understanding of archaeological data, it can also be misleading. Human societies of the past, particularly societies of non-*sapiens* humans, often have no close or even distant parallels in the present. While some scholars disparage the use of ethnographic data, particularly from hunter-gatherers living in marginal environments at the fringes of modern national economies, others have developed transformational models that use the limited variability of modern societies (and/or experimental reenactments or simulations of past behaviors) to predict (or retrodict) how past societies would have operated under specified conditions. The expected archaeological correlates of these predictions can then be tested against the data recovered from survey and excavation, though the use of *middle-range theory*, which specifies the relationship between the ethnographic pattern and the archaeological one.

Recovery of Archaeological Data

Archaeological data consist of three main classes: 1) the actual artifacts, structures, and land-surface modifications; 2) physiographic, sedimentological, faunal, and botanical evidence bearing on past landscapes and environments; and 3) the contextual relationships among artifacts and between artifacts and the reconstructed landscape, region, and environment of the past. In recovering archaeological data through survey, surface collection, or excavation, the archaeologist interested in past lifeways should attempt to gather an adequate and representative sample of artifacts and structures, rather than just the most beautiful pots, gold jewelry, and temples. Collection of pollen and sediment samples, and recovery of microfaunal and microbotanical remains through sieving and flotation procedures, will allow a more complete description of the environmental context and an estimation of chronological age independent of that suggested by the artifacts. Finally, careful measurement and recording of finds in their landscape and stratigraphic context, as well as in three-dimensional space, will permit the eventual study of interrelationships within and among different classes of recovered data.

Although the archaeologist's eye is naturally drawn to large concentrations of artifacts and structures that are visible on the surface, the research design should ensure that a data sample is representative of the buried archaeological record in a given area. The first task is to define a region to be sampled, either with reference to a present environmental feature, such as a river valley, or a past one, such as a paleolakeshore. Definition of the sampling region often requires the archaeologist to envision the territory or range utilized by a past society, which may combine a group of environmental features, such as a lake, a river valley, and a mountain area.

After setting the boundaries of the sampling universe, one chooses a sampling design. In rare cases the archaeologist attempts to walk over the entire region, recording all surface artifacts and features, with the assumption that this is an adequate sample of the buried remains. More commonly, he or she divides the region into grid squares, circles, or transects and surveys the surface of a given percentage of these, chosen either entirely at random or at even intervals across the region (e.g. every tenth unit). The entire region may be treated equally, or greater emphasis or coverage may be given to those natural environmental subdivisions of the region judged most likely to yield archaeological remains (*stratified random survey*).

Since archaeological remains on the present land-surface are often exposed through nonrandom processes of erosion and natural concentration (e.g. lag deposits, stream action, slopewash), the surface record may provide a poor picture of the buried record. There are several techniques for sampling the buried record, provided that the overburden is relatively shallow. These include deep plowing of selected grid units or transects, resistivity survey for magnetic anomalies in the soil, various forms of aerial remote sensing, and a posthole or auger sample at random or regular intervals. For more deeply buried remains the archaeologist may elect to excavate one-meter-square or -diameter units at random or regular intervals, although this technique is costly for the information gained.

Once the surface or subsurface concentration of archaeological remains has been determined or estimated, the archaeologist may select several locations for more intensive exploration through excavation. Since modern excavation is an expensive and time-consuming procedure, sites are often chosen so as to yield the maximum information about the widest range of past activities. Unfortunately this practice has resulted in a bias within regions toward areas in which certain past activities were concentrated (e.g. rock shelters, large towns) and away from loci where other activities may have been conducted in a more dispersed manner (homesteads, farms, gardens, low-density open-air patches of material). Strategies for correcting this bias through a deliberate emphasis on low-density sites are being developed in several archaeological research areas, from the Plio-Pleistocene of East Africa to the Upper Paleolithic of the Périgord region of France.

Analysis of Data

One of the archaeologist's first tasks is to reconstruct chronological sequences. The age of buried remains may be determined through a combination of techniques including geochronometry, biochronology, comparison with artifactual remains of known age (*cultural cross-dating*), or establishment of a putative regional sequence using site or assemblage similarity as a rough indicator of temporal proximity (*seriation*).

A second important task is the cataloguing, description, and analysis of the recovered artifacts from a technological, functional, and stylistic perspective. Bones are identified as to species and examined for evidence of butchery or deliberate shaping; stone tools may be analyzed for the existence of scars from use or manufacture, of chemical residues, or of micropolishes indicative of function; ceramics, glasses, and metals can be studied in terms of design elements, chemical traces of raw-material sources, or physical traces of technological processes. Other tasks are the reconstruction of the paleoenvironment and of the past diet and economy. Study of raw materials and their sources may provide information about trade routes, procurement practices, and economic organization; comparisons of technological practices, artifact styles, and differential access to materials may provide information about past social organizations. One question frequently asked of archaeological data, for example, concerns the relative abundance or poverty of grave or household goods for different segments of society (e.g. males versus females, adults versus children, leaders versus the majority, and central settlements versus outlying camps or villages) and the implications for the emergence of status or hierarchical differences. Finally, study of the symbolic aspects of the archaeological record can suggest clues to cognitive abilities, ritual practices, beliefs, and ideology.

See also AGGREGATION-DISPERSAL; ANTHROPOLOGY; ARCHAEOLOGICAL SITES; BIOCHRONOLOGY; BONE BIOLOGY; CLOTHING; COMPLEX SOCIETIES; CULTURAL ANTHROPOLOGY; CULTURE; DIET; DOMESTICATION; ECONOMY, PREHISTORIC; ETHNOARCHAEOLOGY; EXOTICS; FIRE; GEOCHRONOMETRY; HUNTER-GATHERERS; JEWELRY; LITHIC USE-WEAR; MAN-LAND RELATIONSHIPS; MUSICAL INSTRUMENTS; PALEOANTHROPOLOGY; PALEOBOTANY; PALEOENVIRONMENTS; PALEOLITHIC; PALEOLITHIC CALENDAR; PALEOLITHIC IMAGE; PALEOLITHIC LIFEWAYS; PALEOMAGNETISM; PALEONTOLOGY; PÉRIGORD; PHYSICAL ANTHROPOLOGY; PREHISTORY; RAW MATERIALS; RITUAL; SITE TYPES; STONE-TOOL MAKING; STORAGE; TAPHONOMY. [A.S.B.]

Further Readings

Binford, L.R. (1983) In Pursuit of the Past. London: Thames and Hudson.

Daniel, G. (1981) A Short History of Archaeology. London: Thames and Hudson.

Thomas, D.H. (1979) Archaeology. New York: Holt, Rinehart and Winston.

Willey, G.R., and Sabloff, J.A. (1980) A History of American Archaeology, 2nd ed. San Francisco: Freeman.

ARCHAEOZOOLOGY see DOMESTICATION

ARCHAIC HOMO SAPIENS

The usage of this species name has been extended over the last 25 years to include such fossil material as the European Neanderthals, the Broken Hill cranium, and the Ngandong (Solo) specimens, which many workers formerly regarded as representing species distinct from modern humans. Thus the species name *Homo sapiens*, when used in this wide way, consists of two main subgroups, "modern" *Homo sapiens* (living humans and closely related forms) and "archaic" *Homo sapiens* (Neanderthals and other nonmodern fossil forms). The Neanderthals are one type of archaic *Homo sapiens*, but since they have their own special characters they can be readily distinguished and are discussed separately. The Ngandong material has also been treated separately, as there is increasing evidence that these specimens in fact represent an evolved form of *Homo erectus* rather than archaic *Homo sapiens*.

Determining which specimens actually belong in archaic *Homo sapiens* rather than *Homo erectus* is not always straightforward, as many fossils from the middle Pleistocene display mosaic (mixed) features from the two species that may reflect the gradual nature of the evolutionary transition between the two groups. If a rapid punctuational evolutionary change had occurred between the two species *Homo erectus* and archaic *Homo sapiens*, fossils with such mixed and apparently intermediate characteristics would not be expected to have been preserved in the meager fossil sample so far available.

Characteristics of Archaic Homo sapiens

Broadly speaking, it is possible to list the following characteristics that typify (but do not occur universally or exclusively in) the fossil specimens from Europe, Asia, and Africa that are generally grouped in archaic *Homo sapiens* (excluding the Neanderthals). Endocranial capacity ranges between ca. 1,000 and 1,400 ml. with the minimum figure similar to the mean of *Homo erectus* and the maximum figure comparable with the means of Neanderthal and modern samples. The face shows a reduced total prognathism (i.e. it juts out less from the cranial vault) compared with *Homo erectus* specimens and approximates the form of Neanderthal and some modern skulls in this respect. The upper face itself tends to be relatively broad, as in *Homo erectus*, but with a more pronounced midfacial projection, similar to the mean level found in modern *Homo sapiens* and less than in Neanderthals. On the base of the skull the tympanic bone of the ear region is delicately built and nearly aligned with the adjoining petrous bone, both features being found in Neanderthal and modern humans but not in *Homo erectus*. As in the former groups also the temporal bone is relatively short with an evenly curved upper edge. This feature is probably correlated with the increase in brain size and cranial height over most *Homo erectus*, as are a number of other changes in the shape and proportions of the cranial vault in archaic *Homo sapiens* fossils. While the skull is still relatively long and low, the parietal bones tend to be longer and more curved, and the shape of the skull from behind does not show the upward narrowing found in *Homo erectus* specimens. Instead the parietal bones are usually vertical, with some expansion in their upper regions, where *Homo erectus* skulls are poorly filled. At the back of the cranium the occipital bone is higher and often less angled, and the occipital torus is reduced, especially at the sides. The nuchal (neck) musculature may still be strongly developed, but the nuchal area faces downward more.

Features of the skull of archaic *Homo sapiens* show a reduced robusticity compared with those of *Homo erectus*, and although the extent of this is variable the reduced occipital torus development, the generally less thickened vault, and the reduced degree of midline keeling and overall buttressing (e.g. the less common occurrence of the bony swelling at the back of the parietal known as the angular torus) all reflect this. In general the browridge is still strongly developed, but it may show a more curved form and internally may be lightened by the presence of large air spaces (sinuses), which are of uncertain significance. Little is known of the rest of the skeleton of archaic *Homo sapiens* specimens, although a number of isolated finds have been made. Until the Yinkou skeleton from China has been fully published, however, there is nothing to compare with the more complete material available for *Homo erectus*, Neanderthals, and modern *Homo sapiens*. Nevertheless, for the parts that are known, there is an overall robusticity like that found in *Homo erectus* and Neanderthals, and of the three pelvic specimens so far described that may represent archaic *Homo sapiens* two show the presence of the strong iliac pillar above the hip joint that is known from early *Homo* pelves. Despite this there are in some skeletal parts hints of a closer approximation to the modern morphology.

Fossil Material of Archaic Homo sapiens: *Europe*

Europe and Africa have the best records of archaic *Homo sapiens* material. The European specimens include incomplete fossils, such as those from Mauer, Vértesszöllös, and Bilzingsleben, which many workers would classify as actually representing *Homo erectus*, and it must be admitted that from their preserved parts it is difficult or impossible to resolve their taxonomic status. Yet where more complete material of comparable age is known from Europe it is apparent that it cannot readily be referred to *Homo erectus*. The skull from Petralona (Greece) is a particularly fine example of such a fossil, and it is a pity that dispute about its age has clouded its significance. The cranium does display *Homo erectus*-like characters in its laterally thick browridge, broad face, interorbital region, palate and base of the skull, centrally strong occipital torus, and thickened vault bones. Endocranial capacity is ca. 1,230 ml., overlapping the *Homo erectus* and advanced *Homo sapiens* ranges, and the endocranial cast is less flattened than in typical *Homo erectus* specimens. There are also, however, advanced (derived) characters that are shared with later Pleistocene (particularly Neanderthal) crania, and these include the reduced total facial prognathism but increased midfacial projection, the double curvature of the supraorbital torus, the prominent nasal bones, and the laterally reduced and lowered occipital torus. One particularly remarkable feature of the Petralona specimen is the degree of pneumatization of the maxillary, ethmoid, sphenoid, temporal, and frontal regions. While the maxillary sinuses are like those of Neanderthals, the frontal sinus development is even greater, since the pneumatization stretches right across the inside of the supraorbital torus. Such laterally developed sinuses are present also in the Broken Hill, Bodo, and Thomas 3 browridges, but variation is such that a specimen like Arago 21 seems to have a negligible development of the frontal sinus.

The Arago material has been classified as *Homo erectus* by some workers, mainly on the basis of primitive characteristics and the supposedly high antiquity of the specimens. When the material was thought to date from the "Riss" glaciation (ca. 200 k.y.?) of the late middle Pleistocene, it was usually considered to represent a hominid population comparable with those from Steinheim or Swanscombe (i.e. an archaic *Homo sapiens* or "anteneanderthal"). However, with the realization that the material was probably more ancient, perhaps dating from the "Mindel" glaciation (ca. 450–400 k.y.?), there was a

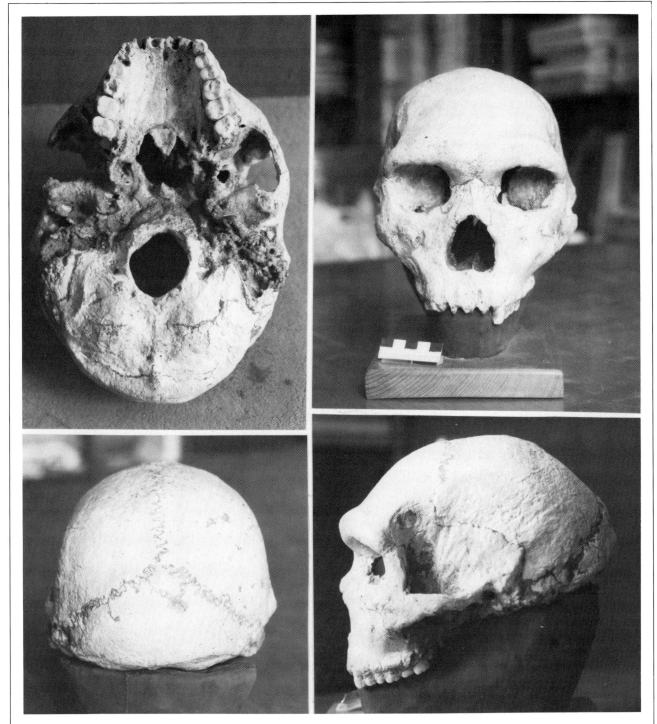

Four views of the Petralona cranium, the best-preserved example of "archaic *Homo sapiens*" yet discovered. The rear of the skull shows a number of *Homo erectus* characteristics, but the parietal bones, skull base, and face show features found in later hominids. In particular the supraorbital torus and cheek region are reminiscent of those of Neanderthals. Not to scale.

greater emphasis on the primitive *Homo erectus*-like characteristics present in the material, such as the robusticity of the postcranial specimens (including an iliac buttress on the Arago 44 pelvis), the large size and robusticity of the Arago 13 mandible, and the strong development of the supraorbital and angular tori of the Arago 21 face and Arago 47 parietal, respectively. The reconstruction of the Arago 21/47 skull also featured a high degree of facial prognathism, much greater than in the Petralona and Steinheim crania and comparable with that of true *Homo erectus* specimens. Yet it is not clear whether this prognathism is, partly at least, an artifact of remaining distortion in the reconstruction. In other respects the Arago specimens compare well with European fossils that are generally accepted as representing archaic *Homo sapiens*, such as the Petralona, Steinheim, and Atapuerca material. Like some of those specimens it is conceivable that the Arago sample derives from a population that was ancestral to the Neanderthals, and this is especially plausible in the case of the Arago 2 mandible.

Even more vexing than the classification of the Arago material is the assignment of the Bilzingsleben cranial fragments. These date from a middle Pleistocene interglacial that is certainly older than 200 k.y. and perhaps older than 350 k.y. These are the most *Homo erectus*-like of all the European cranial specimens in the strong supraorbital and occipital torus development and in occipital proportions and angulation. Yet the Bilzingsleben material lacks the areas that appear most *Homo sapiens*-like in the Petralona skull, and the absent areas of the parietal region may well have been more "advanced." Even considering the *Homo erectus*-like occipital region, one should note that it is less robust than that of any of the Zhoukoudian adults and is similar in proportions to that of the Saldanha skull, which is generally accepted as an African archaic *Homo sapiens*.

The Steinheim skull is a puzzling specimen that is small-brained and relatively large-browed yet in other respects shows advanced characteristics in its thin vault and occipital shape. In certain respects the occipital region resembles that of Swanscombe and the Neanderthals, yet the shape and proportions of the face seem distinctly primitive. This combination of a Neanderthal-like occiput and primitive face is exactly the opposite of the situation in the Petralona skull, and unless we can accept that this variation in expression of characters is related mainly to sexual dimorphism it is difficult to classify these fossils together or arrange them in an orderly morphological series from *Homo erectus*-like to Neanderthal-like specimens. It is apparent, however, that the Steinheim skull does not fit comfortably into the *Homo erectus* or Neanderthal groups, and by default it must be assigned to archaic *Homo sapiens* for the moment.

Several other middle Pleistocene fossil hominids are difficult to assign because of incomplete or conflicting data, and this is especially true of mandibular specimens, such as those from Mauer, Montmaurin, Arago, Atapuerca, and Azych (actually in the Asian Soviet Union). Some of these do appear to show Neanderthal characteristics, but it seems premature to assign them to the Neanderthal group proper at present. Yet by the later middle Pleistocene Europe was certainly populated by peoples who were closely related to the Neanderthals. The Swanscombe "skull"

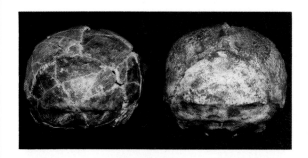

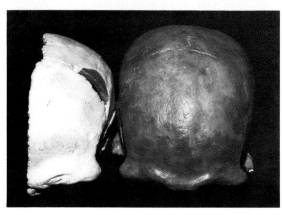

Above: rear (occipital) view comparing the specimens from Biache (left) and Swanscombe. The latter displays more primitive features, but both show Neanderthal characteristics. Below: comparison of the Irhoud 2 (left) and Pavlov 1 crania demonstrates the similarity in the region shown between a North African "archaic *sapiens*" specimen and a robust modern *Homo sapiens* fossil from Europe.

probably belongs in this group, along with the Biache, the Fontéchevade, and the more ancient of the La Chaise fossils. Such specimens may one day be referred to the species *Homo neanderthalensis* rather than to the archaic *Homo sapiens* grade (see below).

Africa

A number of North African fossil hominids from the middle Pleistocene have been referred to *Homo erectus* on the basis of primitive characteristics, such as the Salé skull, with its cranial capacity of only 900 ml. However, such specimens as the Salé and Thomas Quarries fossils do bear a general resemblance to European material discussed above under the category of archaic *Homo sapiens*, and further study may establish this relationship on firmer grounds. Certainly, from evidence elsewhere in Africa, there are strong grounds for linking African and European hominids of the middle Pleistocene in at least a general way to differentiate them from Asian *Homo erectus* fossils. In particular there are close resemblances in overall cranial form and in certain anatomical details among the Broken Hill, Bodo, and Petralona crania. The Bodo specimen, however, while probably having the largest endocranial capacity, was also the most *Homo erectus*-like in such features as cranial thickness, keeling, and facial prognathism. So there is a real problem involved in determining whether these fundamentally similar specimens should be grouped together as archaic *Homo sapiens* or whether the Bodo skull should be separated off as representing *Homo erectus*. One additional aspect of interest here is the postcranial material that may be associated with the Broken Hill skull. Although several individuals of both sexes are represented, it is apparent that the material combines archaic and modern features in a way that differs from that of *Homo erectus* and Neanderthal skeletons. While bone thickness in the tibia, femora, and at least one of the pelves is comparable with other nonmodern fossils, the inferred limb proportions indicate a relatively long tibia and a fairly tall stature, with femora of more "modern" shape than indicated from other early Pleistocene, middle Pleistocene, and Neanderthal specimens.

Other African middle Pleistocene specimens, such as Ndutu and Saldanha, involve fewer problems about assignment to archaic *Homo sapiens*, and in the absence of clear Neanderthal or modern synapomorphies this term is usually extended to include such fossils as those from Eliye Springs (Kenya), Florisbad, Jebel Irhoud 1, and Ngaloba. When we arrive at the terminal middle and early late Pleistocene, synapomorphies with modern *Homo sapiens* begin to appear in such specimens as Omo Kibish 2 and Jebel Irhoud 2, and this marks the point at which the term "archaic *Homo sapiens*" loses whatever validity it possesses.

Far East

The recently discovered skull from Narmada (India) is a candidate for assignment to archaic *Homo sapiens*, although it has been referred in preliminary reports to *Homo erectus*. While the specimen does appear to have a tented and keeled vault, it is also

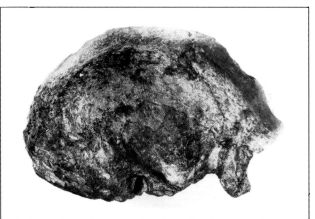

Lateral view of the cranium from the Narmada Valley (India).

very high, with a rounded occipital region. More definite examples of archaic *Homo sapiens* are known from farther east, in China, at sites like Maba, Dali, and Jinniu Shan (Yingkou). The latter two specimens are the most complete, although still not published in any detail, and the Yingkou specimen in fact consists of a partial skull and much of the postcranial skeleton. It is remarkable for its *Homo sapiens*-like characters, despite large brows and an absolute age determination of ca. 280 k.y., in that the vault is thin and well expanded (capacity ca. 1,390 ml.) and the face gracile. It might have been considered a female individual of the Dali group but for the fact that it is sexed as a male from the associated skeleton and has a considerably larger cranial capacity than the Dali skull. If the Yingkou skeleton is correctly dated, it has important implications for human evolution in the Far East, particularly in the difficulty involved in deriving it from the penecontemporaneous *Homo erectus* populations known from Zhoukoudian and Hexian.

In Southeast Asia the only plausible claimants for archaic *Homo sapiens* fossils are those from Ngan-

This cranium from Jebel Irhoud (Morocco) is a late Pleistocene example of "archaic *Homo sapiens*." Although displaying an archaic parietal and occipital region, the modeling of the face is more like that of archaic moderns. The Irhoud specimens have sometimes been regarded as North African Neanderthals, but they do not in fact display any Neanderthal derived characters.

dong (Solo) on the Indonesian island of Java. Many of the apparent *Homo sapiens*-like characteristics, however, may be reflections of endocranial expansion achieved in parallel with that of middle Pleistocene specimens in Europe and Africa, for in the majority of features the Ngandong crania closely resemble their *Homo erectus* antecedents, with whom they are most reasonably classified.

Status of archaic Homo sapiens

Although the characteristics of the group of extinct hominids usually referred to as archaic *Homo sapiens* were listed at the beginning of this article, the reality and utility of this term is not clear. Even under a conventional system of classification it is apparent that the specimens assigned to this group show great variation and are most easily typified by characteristics belonging to other groups, such as *Homo erectus* and Neanderthals, rather than by their own unique characteristics. Under a cladistic system of classification the meaning of the term archaic *Homo sapiens* becomes even less clear, since it is apparent that these specimens may have had different evolutionary origins and different evolutionary destinies. A separate, parallel transition may have occurred in different areas between local forms of *Homo erectus* and their archaic *Homo sapiens* descendants, and these distinct descendants could represent only an evolutionary grade rather than a clade. Furthermore, if the European archaic *Homo sapiens* specimens, such as Arago and Petralona, were in fact ancestral to Neanderthals, as many workers believe, and this could be demonstrated by the presence of synapomorphies, these specimens should be classified with the Neanderthals. Equally, if African archaic *Homo sapiens* uniquely gave rise to modern *Homo sapiens*, the African specimens should be classified with modern humans.

Another problem with the term "archaic *Homo sapiens*" is that most specimens in this group show more similarities to *Homo erectus* or Neanderthal fossils than to anatomically modern *Homo sapiens*, so the justification for assigning them to *Homo sapiens* at all is unclear. If the difference between Neanderthals and modern *Homo sapiens* were once again elevated to the level of a specific difference, as some workers are now suggesting, there would be more justification for extending the use of the taxon *Homo neanderthalensis* to include most of these specimens than for the current extended usage of the term *Homo sapiens*. Yet, given that the Neanderthals do display apomorphies not present in most archaic *Homo sapiens* fossils, it might be preferable for the moment to replace the term archaic *Homo sapiens* with a distinct species name, for which *Homo heidelbergensis* or *Homo rhodesiensis* are probably the most appropriate. This species would then be considered as the probable last common ancestor for the *Homo neanderthalensis* and *Homo sapiens* groups, and specimens that clearly postdated the divergence of the two clades would be allocated to one or the other group through synapomorphies. Thus, for example, while the Mauer and Baringo mandibles might represent *Homo heidelbergensis*, Swanscombe would be allocated to *Homo neanderthalensis* and the Jebel Irhoud fossils to *Homo sapiens*.

See also Archaic Moderns; Homo sapiens; Neanderthals. [C.B.S.]

Further Readings

Bräuer, G. (1984) A craniological approach to the origin of anatomically modern *Homo sapiens* in Africa and implications for the appearance of modern Europeans. In F.H. Smith and F. Spencer (eds.): The Origins of Modern Humans: A World Survey of the Fossil Evidence. New York: Liss, pp. 327–410.

Cook, J., Stringer, C.B., Currant, A.P., Schwarcz, H.P., and Wintle, A.G. (1982) A review of the chronology of the European middle Pleistocene hominid record. Yrbk. Phys. Anthropol. 25:19–65.

Howell, F.C. (1984) Introduction. In Smith and Spencer, pp. xiii–xxii.

Hublin, J.-J. (1985) Human fossils from the North African middle Pleistocene and the origin of *Homo sapiens*. In E. Delson (ed.): Ancestors: The Hard Evidence. New York: Liss, pp. 283–288.

Rightmire, G.P. (1984) *Homo sapiens* in sub-Saharan Africa. In Smith and Spencer, pp. 295–325.

Stringer, C.B. (1985) The definition of *Homo erectus* and the existence of the species in Africa and Europe. Cour. Forsch. Inst. Senckenberg 69:131–143.

Stringer, C.B. (1984) Middle Pleistocene hominid variability and the origin of late Pleistocene humans. In Delson, pp. 289–295.

Stringer, C.B., Hublin, J.-J., and Vandermeersch, B. (1984) The origin of anatomically modern humans in western Europe. In Smith and Spencer, pp. 51–135.

Tattersall, I. (1986) Species recognition in human paleontology. J. Hum. Evol. 15:165–175.

Wolpoff, M.H. (1980) Paleoanthropology. New York: Knopf.

Wolpoff, M.H., Wu, X.Z., and Thorne, A.G. (1984) Modern *Homo sapiens* origins: a general theory of hominid evolution involving the fossil evidence from East Asia. In Smith and Spencer, pp. 411–483.

ARCHAIC MODERNS

Various fossil hominids, while representing anatomically modern *Homo sapiens*, display certain archaic characteristics that appear to be primitive retentions. This is true even for some specimens of the terminal Pleistocene, such as the Kow Swamp material from Australia, but this discussion will restrict the use of the term "archaic moderns" to specimens that are probably more than 35 k.y. in age. Two geographical areas, Africa and Southwest Asia, contain fossils that fall into this category: there are only disputed examples from Europe or the Far East.

African Evidence

The African record of archaic moderns consists of specimens from the South African sites of Klasies River Mouth and Border Cave and the North African sites of Dar-es-Soltane and Omo Kibish. Florisbad (South Africa) and Jebel Irhoud (Morocco) also provide fossils that some workers include in the category, as well as other specimens whose age is uncertain, such as Kanjera (Kenya). Because several of the specimens are derived from dubious contexts or ones where absolute dating is not a practical proposition, some workers do not accept any of these specimens as representing genuinely early records of a modern morphology from Africa.

The material from the Klasies River Mouth complex of caves (South Africa) is fragmentary and shows clear morphological variation. The specimens are believed by their excavators to be more than 70 k.y. old, and they are all associated with Middle Stone Age (MSA) artifacts. Doubt has been expressed about the reliability of correlations used to date relatively the Klasies material to the early late Pleistocene, but the results of recent excavations by a different team of excavators have tended to support the proposed antiquity of the hominid specimens and have produced a new, robust hominid specimen that can be dated at more than 100 k.y.

The MSA-associated material from Klasies consists of cranial, maxillary, mandibular, dental, and postcranial fragments. The cranial pieces include one (adult?) frontal fragment that displays a small, modern type of supraorbital torus and other fragments that suggest a rounded but perhaps low cranial vault. The mandibular pieces are generally modern-looking, with small teeth, but there is variation in robusticity and chin development. The maxillary fragments are those found most recently at the site and are the oldest, and perhaps most robust, yet recovered. The few postcranial pieces appear to be gracile and modern in morphology. One must assess with caution the degree of modernity of the Klasies material when the specimens are so fragmentary, but they are at least bordering on a modern human morphology well before comparable evidence is available from such areas as Europe. It is certainly possible that the specimens document an increase in gracility and modernity through perhaps 30 k.y. of the early late Pleistocene.

While there may be doubts about the assignment of some of the Klasies material to modern *Homo sapiens*, the modernity of the MSA-associated fossil hominids from Border Cave (South Africa) is clear. The specimens consist of a partial skull, the partial skeleton of an infant, and two mandibles. All fall clearly into the overall range of modern humans, with only the moderately strong browridge development

of the skull indicating any possible archaic character. However, since the skull and one (unassociated) mandible were not excavated systematically, while the infant's skeleton and the other mandible may have been intentionally buried in the MSA levels from which they were excavated, doubt has been expressed about claims that they are all more than 70 k.y. in age. Further work at the site is clearly needed to resolve some of these questions, but, given the evidence from Klasies of modern-looking hominids associated with the MSA, the Border Cave evidence may yet prove to be important.

The site of Omo Kibish in southern Ethiopia has produced two fossil hominids that may represent archaic moderns (Omo 1 and 3), as well as a third skull of nonmodern type (Omo 2). The Omo 3 skull fragments show only a slight brow development but are probably younger than the more complete and informative Omo 1 partial skeleton. This was found in beds that considerably predate 40 k.y., based on radiocarbon dates from higher levels, and that may be as old as 130 k.y. according to uranium series dates on mollusk shells. The postcranial bones indicate a heavily built but anatomically modern individual, and the same can be said for the partial skull of Omo 1. It has a long and broad frontal bone with moderately strong brows, but the form of the rear of the skull and mandible appears entirely modern. If the specimen does derive from the oldest beds at Omo Kibish, it is a most important fossil hominid, one that documents the presence of essentially modern humans in northeastern Africa in the early late Pleistocene (although it would be premature to consider an age as much as 130 k.y. as accurate).

Elsewhere in Africa are specimens of fossil hominids that, while certainly more than 35 k.y. in age, are difficult to classify as archaic moderns because they show so many archaic characters and specimens that, while certainly representing modern humans, are not definitely more than 35 k.y. old. Examples of the former category are the fossils from Ngaloba (Laetoli hominid 18) and Jebel Irhoud, discussed elsewhere; examples of the latter category are the specimens from Kanjera (Kenya) and Springbok Flats (South Africa). There is, however, one more African sample that probably represents archaic modern *Homo sapiens*: the material from Dar-es-Soltane (Morocco). Mostly unpublished, this material includes a robust but modern partial skull and mandible associated with the Middle Paleolithic Aterian industry. It almost certainly dates from more than 40 k.y.

Western Asia

Western Asia has rich samples of archaic modern skeletons from the Israeli sites of Skhūl (Mount Carmel) and Qafzeh, many of which derive from intentional burials. The extensive material from the former site was at first united with the Neanderthal material from the adjacent cave of Tabūn, but it is now believed to date from the late Middle Paleolithic of the area (ca. 45–40 k.y.), thus probably postdating local Neanderthal populations. However, the dating of the even larger Qafzeh sample of partial skeletons is still unclear, since the Middle Paleolithic levels of Qafzeh may be of approximately the same age as the Skhūl fossils, or they could be considerably older (in the region of 70 k.y.). If the latter date is correct, the Qafzeh material would actually antedate many Neanderthal fossils, as well as most other unequivocally modern hominids so far known from any area.

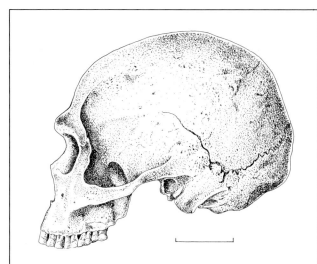

Skhul V cranium from Mount Carmel (Israel). Scale is 50 mm.

The fossil material from Skhūl and Qafzeh consists of partial skeletons of adult males and females, as well as several children and subadults. The adult crania have, by recent standards, large and prognathic faces with large teeth, well-developed supraorbital tori, and large cranial capacities. Yet these and other features that have been used to link the specimens to the Neanderthals are not in fact specifically Neanderthal-like, and details of facial morphology contrast strongly with those of Neanderthals. Similarly, in the rest of the skeleton, there is little of the robusticity and muscularity so typical of the Neanderthals (and of earlier humans generally), and details of pelvic structure are as in recent populations. Additionally, limb proportions for the Skhūl and Qafzeh skeletons are unlike those of Neanderthals and instead specifically resemble those of present-day tropical or subtropical populations. Overall the morphology of these Israeli archaic moderns can be characterized as modern, but with some primitive features retained from middle Pleistocene ancestors.

Those ancestors, to judge from certain details of the fossils, may have been African non-Neanderthals.

Archaic Moderns from Other Areas

Elsewhere claims for the occurrence of modern human skeletal materials that date from more than 35 k.y. are rare and always controversial. In western Asia archaic moderns possibly occur at such sites as Darra-i-Kur (Afghanistan) and Starosel'e (U.S.S.R.), while in Europe possible examples are found at such sites as Krapina (the child's skull labeled "A") and Bacho Kiro (Bulgaria). In the Far East there is the burial of the modern-looking skeleton of a youth from the Niah Cave (Borneo), which may be 40 k.y. in age, and beyond that is the very robust skull (WLH 50) from the Willandra Lakes in southern Australia, which may be of comparable age. Many of these finds, however, are isolated and have associated difficulties of dating or interpretation.

See also **Homo sapiens**. [C.B.S.]

Further Readings

Bräuer, G. (1984) The "Afro-European *sapiens* hypothesis" and hominid evolution in East Asia during the late Middle and Upper Pleistocene. Cour. Forsch. Inst. Senckenberg 69:145–165.

Bräuer, G. (1984) A craniological approach to the origin of anatomically modern *Homo sapiens* in Africa and implications for the appearance of modern Europeans. In F.H. Smith and F. Spencer (eds.): The Origins of Modern Humans: A World Survey of the Fossil Evidence. New York: Liss, pp. 327–410.

Rightmire, G.P. (1984) *Homo sapiens* in sub-Saharan Africa. In Smith and Spencer, pp. 295–325.

Trinkaus, E. (1984) Western Asia. In Smith and Spencer, pp. 251–293.

ARCHANTHROPUS   see   HOMO ERECTUS

ARCHONTA

Cohort (a taxonomic rank above the order) of mammals that includes four orders: Scandentia, Dermoptera, Primates, and Chiroptera. Tree shrews and fossil relatives like the Mixodectidae (scandentians), and the "flying lemurs" or colugos (dermopterans), were more widespread during the early Tertiary than they are today. Although their dental and cranial morphology marks them as distinct early in their history when compared with archaic primates or primitive bats (chiropterans), aspects of elbow morphology, and particularly the details of foot form and function, strongly indicate that archontans have a common ancestor exclusive of any other group of mammals. What is remarkable about the shared and derived character complex that unites the archontans is that the transformation series of the hind-foot characters and the special similarity between the gliding membrane of colugos and the wing of bats suggest a shared but differentially developed adaptation. It appears that the last archontan common ancestor was among the first placental mammals that took to a life fully committed to the trees, a way of life approximately retained by some of the tree shrews, such as *Ptilocercus*. Primates diversified for the most part in an arboreal environment. The colugos early became successful gliders and omnivores-herbivores, long before rodent gliders had a chance to displace them from that way of life. The earliest bats carried the ancestral archontan adaptation to the trees to an extreme in becoming the only known true flyers among the mammals.

See also PLESIADAPIFORMES. [F.S.S.]

ARCTOCEBUS *see* LORISIDAE

ARCY INTERSTADIAL *see* GLACIATION; PLEISTOCENE

ART *see* PALEOLITHIC IMAGE

ARTIFACT *see* STONE-TOOL MAKING

ASH-FALL *see* GEOCHRONOMETRY

ASIA (EASTERN)

Continent of ca. 27 million sq. km., whose regions have afforded most of the fossil record of hominid and hominoid evolution outside of Africa. The most important fossiliferous areas are South Asia, which has yielded an important collection of fossil hominoids from the Siwalik sediments of Pakistan and India, and East Asia (China), where both hominoids and hominids are known. In mainland Southeast Asia (Burma, Thailand, Laos, Vietnam, Malaysia, and Kampuchea) much archaeological evidence has been recovered. In island Southeast Asia Java has yielded early, middle, and late Pleistocene hominids. Western and southwestern Asia (Turkey, Israel, Iraq, and Iran) have also produced hominoid and middle and late Pleistocene hominid fossils (*see* NEAR EAST).

The geography and geomorphology of Asia are best understood in terms of a collision between the Indian plate and the mainland, which began over 35 m.y. ago after Turkey, Iran, and Indopakistan came into contact with the "underbelly" of the continent. This collision resulted in the uplift of the Taurides,

Elburz, Himalayas, and the Shan-Yunnan Massif that divides the tropical habitats from the more northerly temperate and subtropical regimes all across Asia, except for the Chinese Plain. The complex tectonics of northern China are probably also linked to this collision.

Eocene continental sediments are also found in northern India and Nepal, with faunas that suggest a biogeographic connection with both Africa and Eurasia shortly after Indopakistan and Iran collided with the northern continent, closing the Mesogean seaway. Interestingly, nothing in the Indian Eocene fauna appears to have survived from the endemic groups that populated the subcontinent during its passage across the Indian Ocean from much earlier contact with Africa. It may have been during this early Eocene time that prosimian primates were introduced into Africa from the north, although the group is an ancient one and may have a Paleocene record in Africa that has yet to be documented.

The earliest Asian primate is probably *Petrolemur*, a possible plesiadapiform of early to middle Paleocene age in South China. *Decoredon*, of comparable age, may be the earliest euprimate and suggests that omomyids, and perhaps adapoids, entered North America from eastern Asia. *Altanius*, from the early Eocene of Mongolia, supports this view of paleobiogeography; *Hoanghonius*, a possible omomyid from middle or late Eocene beds in China, has also been compared with the enigmatic *Oligopithecus* of Eo-Oligocene age in the Fayum beds of Egypt. Of similar or possibly younger age are *Pondaungia* and *Amphipithecus* from Pondaung (Burma), which have been given a late Eocene age based on insecure marine correlations of underlying strata. The first of these Burmese primates resembles those of the Fayum more than it does any of the abundant Eocene prosimians of western Europe.

For students of early hominoids the Indo-Asian collision has been a boon because of the uplift of the Potwar Plateau and the Salt Range in the foothills of the Himalayas, which exposed the famous Neogene fossil beds known as the Siwalik Series. The most fossiliferous exposures crop out in Pakistan and India, but the beds also extend into Nepal and Bangladesh. The oldest Siwalik faunas (Gaj series) and the equivalent levels at Dera Bugti (Baluchistan) and Perim Island document the immigration of proboscideans and bovids, among other African groups, via the newly formed Mesopotamian land bridge. In the middle Miocene Chinji fauna and at Paşalar (Turkey), ca. 14 m.y. ago, the earliest hominoids appear in Asia. These are pongines, apparently related to orangutans and *Gigantopithecus*. By late Miocene Nagri time, ca. 10 m.y., a diversity of *Sivapithecus*

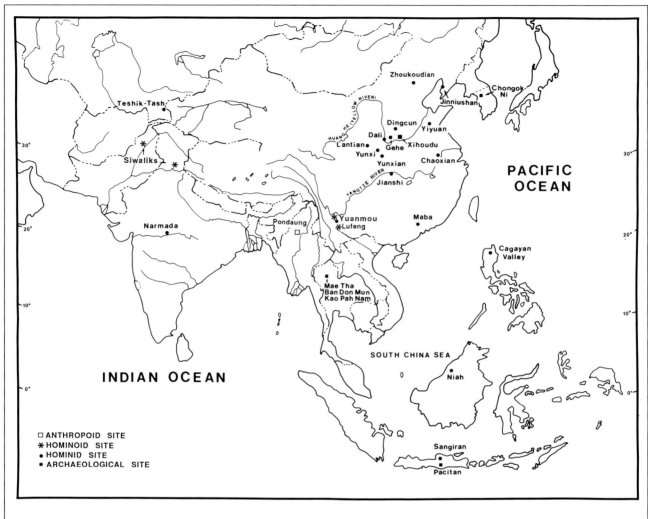

Map of Eastern Asia showing major fossil and archaeological localities mentioned in this and other articles.

species and related genera appears to have become established in the Siwaliks, China (Lufeng), the Near East, Greece, and possibly Malaysia (no known fossils); cercopithecoids are found throughout temperate Eurasia in drier and more open country, as at Pikermi (Greece) and Maragheh (Iran) and at relatively high latitudes (Tadzikistan, Mongolia).

Early hominids almost certainly reached the Far East from Africa by first passing through the Near East and then South Asia. What are perhaps the earliest fossil hominids in the region have been recovered from the island of Java. In the past Java and many other Indonesian islands were intermittently united with the mainland by exposure of the now-submerged Sunda Shelf, as the result of low sea levels during glacial periods, which provided dryland migration routes for hominids and other Pleistocene mammals.

Although there is still no consensus as to how many hominid species are represented in Java, it is

clear that the diversity of forms has been overestimated, as sometimes has been the early age of some of these specimens. There is now growing agreement that most of the adequately preserved specimens, representing more than 50 individuals, represent a form of *Homo erectus* that may have reached Java just over 1 m.y. ago. One form, "*Meganthropus*," has occasionally been hypothesized to represent an Asian form of australopithecine, but little evidence currently supports this conjecture. In general our interpretation of the Javanese forms has been hindered by the specimens' lack of accurate provenance, due in large part to the formerly common practice of purchasing fossils from local collectors.

An assemblage of younger forms that were excavated apparently *in situ* in the 1930s, the so-called Solo hominids (also known as the Ngandong hominids), have remained controversial both because of the claim that they show evidence of cannibalism and because they appear to be morphologically intermediate between *Homo erectus* and *Homo sapiens*. There has been much debate not only about which species they belong to but also about whether they were ancestral to Australian aborigines. It is safe to say that much of the controversy that began with Eugene Dubois's original hominid find in 1890 continues unabated today.

Although hominids probably reached mainland Southeast Asia before expanding into the northern latitudes, to date only one or two sites in Vietnam may afford direct fossil evidence of early hominids in the region. In northern Thailand a few sites (Kao Pah Nam, Ban Don Mun, and Mae Tha) offer archaeological evidence for hominids in mainland Southeast Asia during the late early Pleistocene. Almost all the other evidence for early humans in East Asia comes from China, with the earliest and best documented evidence of *Homo erectus* from Lantian in Shaanxi, north-central China. Here a partial cranium (Gongwangling) and mandible (Chenjiawo) may date to the late early Pleistocene (ca. 0.9–0.7 m.y.). The cranium may be slightly older than the mandible, but this is no longer certain. The cranium is small by comparison with later Chinese *Homo erectus*, and the low cranial capacity, 780 ml., has been explained by its presumably early date and by the interpretation of the specimen as a female.

A few other scattered finds also offer tantalizing evidence of early Chinese hominids. Three teeth found in a karst cave in Hupei (Jian Shi) were at first thought by Chinese workers to represent a form of *Australopithecus*. At least two of these teeth are aberrant, however, and Chinese and Western workers now place these specimens in the genus *Homo*. The early age of the finds is also perhaps indicated by the fact that they were found in association with *Gigantopithecus*. This is the only such association known in China, but a similar association may occur in Vietnam.

Although two incisors from Yuanmou, Yunnan, were once thought on the basis of associated fauna and paleomagnetic stratigraphy to be older than 1.67 m.y., recent geological work and reanalysis of the paleomagnetic stratigraphy now place these specimens at well under 0.6 m.y. Researchers have always recognized that the morphology of the shovel-shaped incisors bears a strong resemblance to that of the Zhoukoudian specimens. In 1987 at least 161 isolated teeth were reported from several levels at Yuanmou. Forty-one of these specimens have been assigned to *Australopithecus* and accorded a late Pliocene age on the basis of biostratigraphic associations. However, the specimens remain undescribed, and debate continues about the actual ages of this extensive and complex geological succession.

Zhoukoudian (formerly Chou-K'ou-Tien) Locality 1 is perhaps the most famous of the Chinese localities. This cave complex has yielded more than 40 individuals from the excavation of over 40 m. of brecciated sediments. The cave, located just southwest of Beijing, has been worked on and off since a few teeth were first recovered in 1927. Unfortunately the original collection was lost during the Japanese invasion at the beginning of the Second World War. The records of careful prewar excavation, the accurate casts made by F. Weidenreich, and postwar Chinese work have all helped to minimize the loss of information from the original excavations.

We are fairly confident that *Homo erectus* occupied the cave intermittently between ca. 0.6 and 0.2 m.y., because of the agreement of a variety of modern dating techniques. Much evidence bearing on the behavior of these hominids has also been forthcoming over the years. Layers of charcoal and ash interspersed throughout the middle and upper layers suggest that Zhoukoudian hominids used fire on a regular basis, even if it cannot be shown that they knew how to make it. Burned hackberry seeds and the charred remains of large mammals like deer and horses have also been put forward as evidence for the diet of "Peking man." Recently there has also been a renewed recognition of the role that carnivores, which also occupied the cave at times, must have played in the accumulation and modification of the bones that document the Zhoukoudian fauna. Nonetheless, some of the bones are indisputably worked by stone tools. There is much less evidence, however, for the existence of the bone-tool industry once postulated by early workers. The stone-tool industry from the cave consists mostly of crudely flaked vein quartz and other substances that are poor natural materials from which to construct more standardized artifacts.

The fossils of "Peking man" have at times been taken to show evidence of cannibalism, but again this is far from certain. Yet the cranial capacity of Peking hominids probably increased through time (from ca. 0.5 to ca. 0.2 m.y. ago), as did the complexity and standardizations of their tool kit. Further study of this unique locality will enlarge our knowledge of hominid adaptation in the Pleistocene. New, as yet inadequately reported, finds of *Homo erectus* have been announced from Hexian, Anhui, and Jinniu Shan, Liaoning. These probably document the latest phases of *Homo erectus* and the presence of "archaic *Homo sapiens*" in China.

In addition to China other portions of mainland Asia have provided evidence about the later phases of human evolution. Crania from India (Narmada), China, (Dali, Xujiayao, Mapa, Jinniu Shan), Teshik-

Tash (U.S.S.R.), and Shanidar (Iraq) testify to the presence of various forms of *Homo sapiens* morphologically intermediate between *Homo erectus* and anatomically modern *Homo sapiens*. Like the Ngandong hominids the Dali specimen has been of particular interest, since its morphology has been claimed to bridge the gap between *Homo erectus* and modern regional Asian populations while at the same time diverging from the morphology of the "archaic *Homo sapiens*" known from Africa and Europe.

The nature and antiquity of Asian archaeological assemblages continue to spark debate. The Early Paleolithic in central Asia is poorly known before late Pleistocene times. By far most of the research in Asia has centered in South Asia and the Far East. A major point of contention has been the distributions of Acheulean assemblages and the "chopper-chopping tool complex." In 1940 H.L. Movius recognized a difference in the geographical distribution of these assemblages, with Acheulean assemblages occurring in central and southern parts of the Indian subcontinent and more crudely manufactured nonbifacially worked assemblages occurring in the Far East. Local variations of the chopper-chopping tool complex have been given various names: the Pajitanian (Indonesia), Anyathian (Burma), Fingnoian (Thailand), Tampanian (Malaysia), and Hoabinhian (throughout Southeast Asia). Movius further suggested that a line, now known as "Movius' line," could be drawn between the "cultural backwater" of the Far East and the more "developed" cultures of Africa, India, and Europe. Others have suggested that this line may actually reflect different adaptations to contrasting environments, with the Far East assemblages reflecting the exploitation of decidedly more forested habitats. Debate has been further complicated by the fact that the vast majority of Asian archaeological assemblages, especially outside of China, cannot be shown to be earlier than ca. 60 k.y. ago. Some artifacts have in fact been recovered from middle Pleistocene contexts, but they tell us little about the nature and extent of variation of the Early Paleolithic in Asia.

As in Southeast Asia no Acheulean or handaxe assemblages have yet been recognized in China. Chinese workers recognize two "tool traditions" in what is probably a highly oversimplified interpretation of the archaeological record there: a large-tool tradition including "protobifaces" and "choppers" and a small-tool tradition composed largely of undifferentiated flakes. Some assemblages, like those from Dingcun, are said to be composed of both traditions. Clearly much remains to be done to clarify and define the Paleolithic in East Asia.

The origin and antiquity of the modern races of Asia are poorly understood. Early workers, such as Weidenreich, discerned contemporaneous racial "types" in samples drawn from the same cave (the Upper Cave at Zhoukoudian). He perceived Esquimoid, Mongoloid, and Polynesian types in northern China. Other authors, such as Coon, Wolpoff, and Thorne, have suggested that even middle Pleistocene Asian hominids show a "regional continuity" that allies them with recent and modern populations in the same areas of Asia. Most recently, on the basis of genetic data, it has been suggested that the anatomically modern *Homo sapiens* were the result of invading populations that "replaced" the descendants of *Homo erectus*. Of all the postulated models this one is most in conflict with the fossil evidence.

Early evidence of agriculture is known from southwestern Asia (the Near East) and northeastern Asia (Japan) as early as 11,000 B.P. Although dates as early as ca. 10,000 B.P. have been claimed for horticultural practices at Spirit Cave in northern Thailand, most workers feel that the evidence is equivocal and does not distinguish between food collecting and horticulture. At the Jomon site in Japan pottery is thought to antedate 12,500 B.P. and is followed by the introduction of cereal grains over 9000 B.P. By 5000 B.P. rice farming was established in several areas, including Thailand and coastal China.

See also ARCHAIC HOMO SAPIENS; CHINA; DECOREDON; HEXIAN; HOMO ERECTUS; HOMO SAPIENS; INDONESIA; LANTIAN; MEGANTHROPUS; NARMADA; NEAR EAST; PAKISTAN; PALEOLITHIC LIFEWAYS; PETROLEMUR; PONDAUNG; RAW MATERIALS; SIWALIKS; STONE-TOOL MAKING; TESHIK-TASH; THAILAND; YUANMOU; ZHOUKOUDIAN. [G.G.P.]

Further Readings

Andrews, P. and Franzen, J.L., eds. (1984) Courier Forschungs Institut. Senckenberg, no. 69.

Ikawa-Smith, F. (1978) Early Paleolithic in South and East Asia. The Hague: Mouton.

Wu, R., and Olsen, J.W., eds. (1985) Paleoanthropology and Paleolithic Archaeology in the People's Republic of China. New York: Academic.

ASIA, WESTERN *see* NEAR EAST

ASTARACIAN *see* TIME SCALE

ASTERION *see* SKULL

ASTIAN *see* TIME SCALE

ATAPUERCA

Complex of caves in Spain that has produced hominid fossils from stratified and unstratified contexts.

Believed to be of middle Pleistocene antiquity, the main specimens from the "Cueva Major" include a mandible with a thick body but small teeth, skull fragments, and isolated molars that show taurodontism. This condition was quite common in Neanderthals and is recognized by the presence of undivided tooth roots and expanded pulp cavities.

See also ARCHAIC HOMO SAPIENS; NEANDERTHALS. [C.B.S.]

ATELES *see* ATELINAE

ATELIDAE

Family of New World platyrrhine monkeys including the subfamilies Atelinae (*Ateles, Brachyteles, Lagothrix, Alouatta*) and Pitheciinae (*Pithecia, Chiropotes, Cacajao, Aotus, Callicebus*), with their fossil relatives. The atelid common ancestor was typified by a derived masticatory system, including moderate-to-large fourth cusps on the first and second upper molars, a posteriorly enlarged mandible, robust bony attachments on the zygomatic and pterygoid bones, and a deep temporomandibular joint surface, where the mandible articulates with the skull. This pattern implies powerful chewing and a specialized use of the pterygoid and masseter muscles, which are often well developed in mammalian herbivores. Apart from these traits atelids are highly varied morphologically, a reflection of the divergent ecological adaptations of the two descendant subfamilies. The term Atelidae was reintroduced recently to promote a taxonomically and conceptually balanced classification of the ceboids. It is meant to represent the unique common origins of the pitheciine and the ateline branches of the radiation and alleviate the adaptively diffuse and genealogically heterogeneous composition of the traditional cornerstone taxon of the platyrrhines, the Cebidae.

See also ATELINAE; CEBIDAE; PITHECIINAE. [A.L.R.]

Further Readings

Kinzey, W.G. (1986) New World primate field studies: what's in it for anthropology. Ann. Rev. Anthropol. *15*:121–148.

Rosenberger, A. L. (1981) Systematics: the higher taxa. In A.F. Coimbra-Filho and R.A. Mittermeier (eds.): Ecology and Behavior of Neotropical Primates, Vol. 1. Rio de Janeiro: Academia Brasiliera de Ciencias.

Szalay, F.S., and Delson, E. (1979) Evolutionary History of the Primates. New York: Academic.

ATELINAE

Subfamily of atelid platyrrhine monkeys including the tribes Alouattini (*Alouatta*), Atelini (*Ateles, Brachy-*

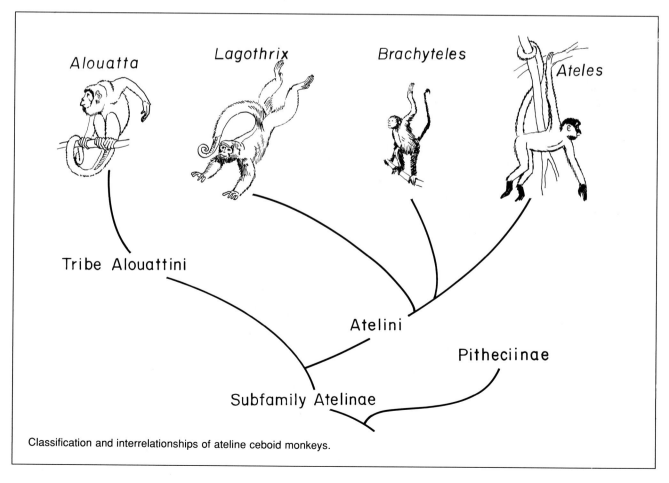

Classification and interrelationships of ateline ceboid monkeys.

teles, Lagothrix), and fossil allies. Physically the largest platyrrhines, atelines are noteworthy for their prehensile tails and suspensory positional behaviors, which many regard as apelike. During feeding they may hang by forelimb, hindlimb, and/or tail, and the more acrobatic spider (*Ateles*) and woolly spider (*Brachyteles*) monkeys can move swiftly through the forest canopy in a bimanual fashion analogous to brachiation. Howler (*Alouatta*) and woolly monkeys (*Lagothrix*), tend to move more cautiously, quadrupedally. The anatomical complex underlying the prehensile tail includes a specialized gripping pad near its tip and an enlargement of the areas of the brain that control tail function. These unique ateline attributes do not occur in the capuchin monkeys (*Cebus*) and squirrel monkeys (*Saimiri*), which have evolved "semiprehensile" tails in parallel.

Atelines are frugivore-folivores with a spectrum of dietary habits, ranging from *Alouatta*, the most highly folivorous of the platyrrhines, to *Ateles*, one of the most exclusive ripe-fruit specialists among the primates. They are represented in the fossil record by two species of *Stirtonia* of the La Venta middle Miocene (16–14 m.y.), an *Alouatta*-like form that may be more properly classified in the same genus as the howler.

Brachyteles is the largest, and one of the most interesting, New World monkeys. Although it is most closely related to *Ateles*, *Brachyteles* converges upon howlers in its dentition and reliance upon a leafy diet. In their skeleton and social organization, however, woolly monkeys resemble spiders. They are a monotypic form restricted to the southern portions of the Atlantic coastal forest of Brazil. This area has been severely disturbed by human population growth and industrialization during this century. Consequently the woolly spider monkey, which has become the conservation symbol for all of Brazil, survives in small numbers in a handful of remnant forests. It is one of the most severely threatened of all Neotropical mammals.

See also ATELIDAE; CEBINAE; DIET; LOCOMOTION; TAIL. [A.L.R.]

Further Readings

Erikson, G.E. (1963) Brachiation in New World monkeys and in anthropoids apes. Symp. Zool. Soc. Lond. *10*:135–164.

Rosenberger, A.L. (1980) Gradistic views and adaptive radiation of the platyrrhine primates. Z. Morph. Anthropol. *71*:157–163.

Rosenberger, A.L. (1983) Tale of tails: parallelism and prehensility. Am. J. Phys. Anthropol. *60*:103–107.

ATERIAN

Late Pleistocene industry of North Africa, named after the type site of Bir el Ater in southern Tunisia and dated from as early as ca. 100 k.y. on strati-graphic grounds to at least 30 k.y., with some radiocarbon ages as late as 21,000 B.P. Concentrated in the coastal regions from Mediterranean Morocco to Tunisia but extending over much of the Sahara and as far east as the western desert of Egypt, the industry is characterized by Levallois technology, discoidal and tortoise cores, flake scrapers with and without tangs, and small tanged bifacial ("Aterian") points. Associated human remains at such sites as Dar es Soltane (Morocco) are primarily of "Mechtoid" anatomically modern type. In western and central North Africa the Aterian succeeds a more generalized Levalloiso-Mousterian industry with small cordiform handaxes. Blades and blade tools appear in later Aterian sites, in a possible parallel to the development of the Dabban industry in Cyrenaica.

The maximum extent of the Aterian industry appears to have occurred during a wetter interval corresponding to the early phases of the Weichsel glaciation of higher latitudes. Associated faunal remains indicate that both sub-Saharan and Mediterranean faunas extended at this time into present-day desert areas. By 30 k.y. ago a period of increasing desiccation in the Sahara led to the abandonment of most Aterian sites.

See also DABBAN; HAUA FTEAH; IBERO-MAURUSIAN; LATE PALEOLITHIC; LEVALLOIS; MIDDLE STONE AGE; MOUSTERIAN; PREPARED-CORE; SEA-LEVEL CHANGE; STONE-TOOL MAKING. [A.S.B.]

Further Readings

Close, A., ed. (1987) Prehistory of Arid North Africa. New York: Academic.

ATHLITIAN

Late Paleolithic (Stage V) industry of the Levant, defined at Mugharet el-Wad (Mount Carmel) in Israel and characterized by polyhedric burins on tabular flint, steep and carinate scrapers, *lamelles Dufour*, and numerous backed points of Chatelperronian/Audi type. Retouch is much finer than in the preceding Aurignacian industry.

See also AURIGNACIAN; BLADE; BURIN; CHATELPERRONIAN; LATE PALEOLITHIC; SCRAPER; STONE-TOOL MAKING. [A.S.B.]

ATLANTHROPUS see HOMO ERECTUS; TIGHENIF

ATLATL see SPEAR

AURIGNAC

Cave in the Pyrenees (Haute Garonne) region of southwestern France, late Pleistocene, type site of

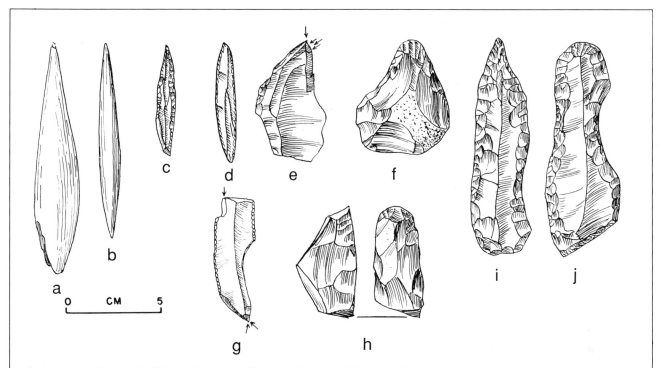

Aurignacian artifacts: a) split-base bone point (Early Aurignacian); b) biconical bone point (Evolved Aurignacian); c) Krems point (Eastern Aurignacian); d) Font-Yves point (?all stages); e) busked burin (Intermediate to Evolved Aurignacian); f) nose-ended scraper (all stages, but especially Intermediate); g) perforator on heavily retouched blade (Basal to Early Aurignacian); h) end-scraper on "strangled" blade (Basal to Early Aurignacian); i) double burin (Intermediate to Evolved Aurignacian); j) carinate scraper (all stages).

Aurignacian industry. E. Lartet's excavation of this site in 1860 formed the basis for his landmark 1861 paper establishing the coexistence of humans and extinct late Pleistocene mammals ("l'Age du Grand Ours des Cavernes"), although the human skeletal material later proved to be modern and intrusive.

See also AURIGNACIAN; UPPER PALEOLITHIC. [A.S.B.]

AURIGNACIAN

Early Upper Paleolithic industrial complex, ca. 34,000–29,000 B.P., extending over much of Europe although rare or absent in Russia, Greece, peninsular Italy, and western Iberia. A comparable industry often termed Aurignacian occurs in the Levant at many sites, such as Ksar 'Akil, Jabrud, Hayonim, and Mount Carmel. A few early Upper Paleolithic assemblages of Aurignacian type are found in Britain (e.g. Kent's Cavern and Ffynnon Beuno). The Aurignacian is the oldest Upper Paleolithic industry of Europe definitely associated with modern humans.

The Aurignacian is clearly distinguished from Middle Paleolithic industries by a strong emphasis on blade technology and on bone and antler working. This distinction, together with the large geographical area in which the Aurignacian is found, has been used to argue for an invasion of Europe at this time by modern humans with an advanced culture and technology. In the early stages blades are often large and irregular and bear heavy invasive marginal retouch on both sides. Lamellar removals are used to create carinate and nose-ended scrapers on thick flakes or chunks, as well as thick-edged carinate and busked burins or gouges, although the latter are rare in eastern Europe. Bladelets with semi-abrupt inverse-obverse retouch on one or both edges (Dufour bladelets) or narrow-pointed blades and bladelets with semiabrupt to abrupt retouch on both edges (Font-Yves/Krems Points) are associated with certain Aurignacian industries.

Named after the type site of Aurignac in the Haute Garonne (France), the Aurignacian as defined by Lartet and Christy and Breuil originally included all early Upper Paleolithic industries ("First epoch of the reindeer age") and was extended to encompass initial blade industries from as far away as Kenya. In 1933 Peyrony separated the Aurignacian *sensu stricto*, or Breuil's "middle" Aurignacian with bone points and lamellar retouch on thick blanks, from early Upper Paleolithic industries with backing or abrupt retouch (Breuil's "lower" and "upper" Aurignacian), which he termed Perigordian. These two complexes, each with five successive phases, were interpreted as expressions of two distinct ethnic groups or "phyla" who coexisted with little admixture over a period of ca. 15 k.y.

On the basis of four levels at La Ferrassie Peyrony distinguished four successive Aurignacian phases and added a fifth phase on the basis of a single assemblage from Laugerie Haute. The four stages were distinguished by changes in bone-point manufacture as follows: Aurignacian I, split-base bone points, heavily retouched blades (La Ferrassie F); Aurignacian II, lozengic points with flattened section, diminished marginal retouch, abundant nose-ended scrapers and busked burins (La Ferrassie H); Aurignacian III, lozengic points with oval section, fewer busked burins and nose-ended scrapers (La Ferrassie H'); and Aurignacian IV, biconical points, truncation burins, few pieces with heavy marginal or lamellar retouch (La Ferrassie H").

The Aurignacian V, stratified *above* the Perigordian III (now VI) at Laugerie Haute and known from few other sites, is much later (ca. 20,000 B.P.) and is characterized by thick, denticulate "carinate" scrapers, created by broader removals than in Stages I-IV, and biconical bone points. The relationship between this stage and the other four is poorly understood and probably does not reflect cultural or ethnic continuity.

In some French sites split-base bone points and marginal retouch, both possibly indicative of a simpler technology, may be associated with earlier Aurignacian horizons, while busked burins and nose-ended scrapers are more numerous in later assemblages. In general, however, the details of Peyrony's Aurignacian scheme have not been widely supported by evidence from most sites. In particular each "stage" is highly variable from site to site, with no exact counterparts to the Aurignacian III and IV at any site, apart from a generalized "evolved" Aurignacian. The overall synchrony of Aurignacian and Perigordian "traditions" is also disputed.

Aurignacian sites are associated initially with evidence of very cold, dry conditions and are dominated by remains of large, cold-adapted herd animals, such as reindeer, mammoth, woolly rhinoceros, steppe horse, and bison. Figurative carvings, especially in ivory, and including a male figure as well as a range of animals, are known from several very early German sites (e.g. Geissenklösterle, Vogelherd, Höhlenstein-Stadel). In addition a funerary complex at Cueva Morin (Spain), plaques with punctations interpreted by Marshack as calendars, an abundance of perforated objects, musical instruments (Istallösko), and widespread evidence of long-distance trade in stone, ivory, and fossil and marine shells attest to the social and cognitive complexity of Aurig-

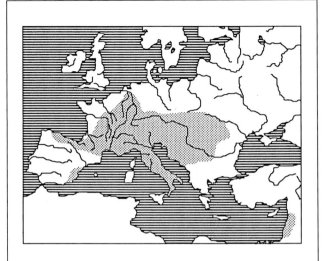

Distribution map of Aurignacian sites.

nacian adaptations to a much greater extent than in either the Mousterian or the Chatelperronian. Burials at Grimaldi and Cavillon on the Italian Riviera are robust but fully modern in physical type, comparable with the five individuals from Cro-Magnon (Les Eyzies) who are thought to be associated with Aurignacian industries. Other Aurignacian human remains from eastern Europe (e.g. Mladec, Vindija) preserve more archaic traits.

See also ABRI PATAUD; ANTELIAN; ATHLITIAN; AURIGNAC; BACHO KIRO; CHATELPERRONIAN; CRO-MAGNON; CUEVA MORIN; HOMO SAPIENS; ISTALLÖSKÖ; JABRUD; JEWELRY; LA FERRASSIE; LATE PALEOLITHIC; LAUGERIE SITES; MIDDLE PALEOLITHIC; MOUSTERIAN; MUSICAL INSTRUMENTS; PALEOLITHIC CALENDAR; PALEOLITHIC IMAGE; PALEOLITHIC LIFEWAYS; PERIGORDIAN; SKHŪL; STONE-TOOL MAKING; SZELETIAN; TABŪN; UPPER PALEOLITHIC. [A.S.B.]

Further Readings

Gamble, C. (1986) The Palaeolithic Settlement of Europe. Cambridge: Cambridge University Press.

Laville, H., Rigaud, J.P., and Sackett, J.R. (1980) Rock Shelters of the Périgord. New York: Academic.

Wymer, J. (1982) The Palaeolithic Age. New York: St. Martin's.

AUSTRALIA

Island-continent of ca. 8 million sq. km., with a history of human settlement stretching back at least 40 k.y. Recent studies have provided considerable insight into the prehistory of the Australian Aborigines, but many aspects of their past remain a mystery. When they first arrived, how they came, where they came from, or why they left their original homes are questions that remain at the heart of investigations on Australian prehistory.

Greater Australia

The island of Australia, together with those of New Guinea and Tasmania, constitute what is often referred to as "Greater Australia." This is an important relationship, which emphasizes that for most of their history these landmasses were united as part of a larger continent known as Sahul. Sahul has always been separate from the main landmass of Southeast Asia and most of Indonesia, an area known as Sunda Land. Between the two areas is a collection of smaller islands known as Wallacea, so named to honor the great biologist Alfred Russel Wallace, who in 1860 was the first to recognize the area as a faunal boundary line between the two larger landmasses.

The independent histories of the Sunda and Sahul landmasses have been a key element in determining the uniqueness of the fauna, particularly the mammals, of the present islands of New Guinea, Australia, and Tasmania. The water barrier between Sunda and Sahul enabled the marsupial mammals of Sahul to evolve largely independent of the placental forms on the Asian mainland. The sea also served to keep humans away from Greater Australia for almost 1 m.y. after their presence can first be identified in areas of Southeast Asia.

Earliest Inhabitants

The occupation of Greater Australia is a relatively recent event in human history. Paleogeographic data suggest that a possible date for the initial migration to the region may have been ca. 53 k.y. ago, a period when sea level was between 120 and 150 m. below what it is now. Archaeological and skeletal evidence indicates human presence by ca. 40 k.y. ago. Among the oldest findings has been a stone tool discovered at the Huon Peninsula on the northeastern coast of New Guinea, which is thought to be in excess of 40 k.y. old. Of roughly similar antiquity, and possibly the oldest remains on the island of Australia itself, are stone artifacts from a terrace of the upper Swan River in western Australia, although very recently stone tools have been reported from 47–43-k.y.-old deposits on the Nepean River.

Among the most important of all early occupation sites in Australia are those at Lake Mungo, located in the western part of the state of New South Wales in the southeastern part of the island. Lake Mungo is part of the Willandra Lakes region, a series of interconnected lake basins that have been dry for at least 15 k.y. Prior to this they were freshwater lakes. The sites at Lake Mungo come from erosion of the lake's lunette, a crescent-shaped dune formed on the shore of the lake when it was full. The sites have been dated at between 45 and 26 k.y. old.

Lake Mungo has yielded the oldest human skeletal remains from Australia. One specimen, known as Lake Mungo 1, is that of a slender young-adult female estimated by radiocarbon dating to be ca. 26 k.y. old. Heavily fragmented when discovered, the individual was possibly cremated. This is the earliest evidence of human cremation as yet found anywhere in the world.

Nearby another burial site was discovered containing the remains of an adult male dated at ca. 30 k.y. This individual, known as Lake Mungo 3, was not cremated but was placed in a shallow grave lying on his back with his hands folded together. Once placed in his grave, he was covered with powdered red ocher. The cremation of Mungo 1 and the postmortem red-ocher adornment of Mungo 3 illustrate the occurrence of complex ritual burials in Australia at least 30 k.y. before the present.

These specimens from Lake Mungo, along with some others, such as the largely complete skull from Keilor in Victoria (dated ca. 13 k.y.), show cranial features that have been described as being very modern. For example, these fossil specimens are generally lightly built with thin vault bones, well-rounded foreheads, weak or moderate browridge formation, and relatively small palates, mandibles, and teeth. Fossil Australian hominids that show these characteristics have often been categorized together as representing a "gracile" type of Australian ancestor.

Standing in contrast to the gracile Lake Mungo specimens are a group of individuals whose skeletal remains are much more "robust." These fossils are typified by remains from the shores of Kow Swamp in the northern portion of the state of Victoria. Fossil remains of over 40 individuals, including infants, juveniles, and adults, have been found at the site. These have been dated to between 14 and 9.5 k.y. ago, making them appreciably younger than the specimens from Lake Mungo. Although found at a different time, the cranium from Cohuna, near the northwestern edge of Kow Swamp, is usually considered part of the Kow Swamp population and is of similar age.

The Kow Swamp population, best exemplified by the partly intact crania of Kow Swamp (KS) 1 and KS 5, as well as by the Cohuna cranium, exhibit characteristics that contrast sharply with the gracile specimens from Lake Mungo or Keilor. Unlike these the robust Kow Swamp specimens are characterized by thicker bone; large, wide, often projecting faces; prominent browridges; flat, sloping foreheads; and large palates, mandibles, and teeth. Specimens exhibiting this morphology are frequently said to be more "archaic" in appearance. Often assigned to this group on the basis of these robust cranial characters are remains from Lake Nitchie (dating unclear, but

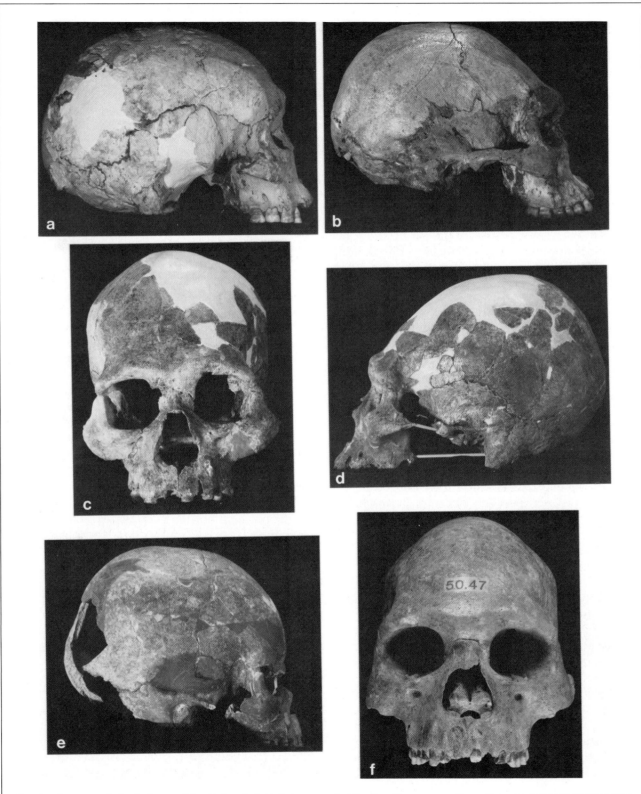

Crania of some early Australians: a) the Keilor skull; b) Cohuna, part of the Kow Swamp sample; c–d) an adult specimen from Kow Swamp (KS 5); e) a juvenile from Kow Swamp (KS 6); and f) one of the Coobool Crossing sample. Keilor has often been described as a "gracile" Australian hominid skull; the others have been spoken of as being representative of the "robust" type. (Photographs by J. Laitman.)

estimated ca. 7 k.y. ago), Mossgiel (ca. 6 k.y.), Cossack, (ca. 6.5 k.y.), and the heavily fragmented Talgai cranium (ca. 12 k.y.). A number of crania from a large and as yet undated sample (although thought to be of similar age to the Kow Swamp material) from Coobool Crossing near the Wakool River in southern New South Wales also exhibit a number of these robust traits.

Theories on the Peopling of Australia

Who were the first inhabitants of Greater Australia, the ancestors of the modern Aborigines? While many theories have been offered to answer this question, they fall into two basic groups: 1) Aboriginal origins are the result of two or more migrations to Australia that occurred at different times; and 2) the present population is descended largely from a single migration.

One of the "multiple-source" theories, based entirely upon aspects of contemporary morphological variation, has suggested that three waves of ancestors arrived in Australia. This explanation, advanced by anthropologist J.B. Birdsell, is known as the "trihybrid" theory. Birdsell theorized that an initial wave of Oceanic Negritos came to Australia first, followed by migrations of a group referred to as the Murrayians (the dominant group, who may be related to the Ainu people from northern Japan), and finally by a group known as the Carpentarians (whose geographic origins may be in India). The interbreeding of these three groups, according to this theory, has produced the extensive variability found among the present Aborigines.

A second multiple-origin theory, the "dual-source" hypothesis, has received considerable attention in recent years. This explanation is based upon the comparison of fossil hominid material from Asia with that of Australia. This theory holds that the extreme disparities found between the "gracile" and "robust" groups of ancestral Australians are too great to indicate a single lineage. The differences are deemed to be inherited from the respective parent populations. Proponents of this view suggest that the robust crania bear great similarities to some of the fossil hominids from the island of Java (such as the Sangiran or Ngandong specimens), while the gracile specimens show many resemblances to material from ancient China (such as those from Liujiang or the Upper Cave at Zhoukoudian). Accordingly, it is suggested that the ancestors of the gracile Australian hominids came originally from China, while the ancestors of the more robust Australians came from Java. The gracile and the robust groups would eventually have interbred, resulting in the variations currently found among modern Australian Aborigines.

The single-source theory, also known as the "homogeneity hypothesis," disagrees with the rigid categorization of Australian fossil hominids into discrete groups labeled gracile or robust. Proponents argue that the gracile and robust fossils merely represent morphological extremes of a highly variable population rather than evidence of two completely separate lineages. This theory suggests that present-day variability among modern Aborigines is due to both genetic and cultural influences having acted upon a small, founding population. This population came from a single homeland, most likely the Indonesian island of Java, and gradually spread out to colonize Australia.

While contrasting theories will undoubtedly remain for some time, recent finds are helping to clarify some potential relationships. For example, the discovery of a fully opalized calvaria from a site near Lake Mungo in the Willandra Lakes (WLH 50) shows features that are extremely "robust," more so than any previously discovered Australian hominid. This specimen shows many similarities to some of the Ngandong material from central Java that is thought to be ca. 200 k.y. old. While WLH 50 is currently undated, estimates of its age based upon its morphology suggest that it is over 30 k.y. old. If this proves to be the case, this robust hominid may tell us what the earliest Australians were like and provide a direct link with the earlier Indonesian material.

See also **ARCHAEOLOGY**; **ASIA** (**EASTERN**); **CHINA**; **HOMO SAPIENS**; **NGANDONG**; **SANGIRAN DOME**; **ZHOUKOUDIAN**.

[J.L.]

Further Readings

Birdsell, J.B. (1967) Preliminary data on the trihybrid origin of the Australian Aborigines. Arch. Phys. Anthropol. Oceania 2:100-155.

Flood, J. (1983) Archeology of the Dreamtime. Sydney: Collins.

Habgood, P.J. (1985) The origin of the Australians: an alternative approach and view. In P.V. Tobias (ed.): Hominid Evolution: Past, Present and Future. New York: Liss, pp. 367-380.

Habgood, P.J. (1986) The origin of the Australians: a multivariate approach. Arch. Oceania 21:130-137.

Kirk, R.L., and Thorne, A.G., eds. (1976) The Origin of the Australians. Canberra: Australian Institute of Aboriginal Studies.

Thorne, A.G., and Wolpoff, M.H. (1981) Regional continuity in Australasian Pleistocene hominid evolution. Am. J. Phys. Anthropol. 55:337-349.

White, J.P., and O'Connell, J.F. (1982) A Prehistory of Australia, New Guinea and Sahul. Sydney: Academic.

AUSTRALOPITHECUS

Genus name many paleoanthropologists use in reference to Pliocene and early Pleistocene hominid fossils from southern and eastern Africa that are not considered to belong to the genus *Homo*.

The name *Australopithecus*, literally "southern ape," was coined by R.A. Dart in 1925, when he described the juvenile hominid specimen from the site of Taung (South Africa) as belonging to the taxon *Australopithecus africanus*. In his analysis of the Taung skull Dart perceived several distinctly hominid, or "humanlike," features, such as the ventral position of the foramen magnum and relatively small canines, together with several more primitive, or "apelike," features, such as the small brain size and relatively large snout. Dart therefore recognized *Australopithecus* as a primitive human forebear whose small brain excluded it from being recognized as a member of the genus *Homo* but whose hominid features excluded it from the great-ape genera, proposing that it be accorded a separate "intermediate" familial rank between the Hominidae and "Pongidae."

In 1936 R. Broom recovered Pliocene fossils from the site of Sterkfontein that he recognized as being morphologically very similar to the Taung skull. He referred the Sterkfontein fossils to the genus *Australopithecus*, albeit to a separate species, *A. trans-vaalensis*. Subsequent discoveries of early hominid specimens by Broom from the sites of Kromdraai and Swartkrans he referred to a distinct genus, *Paranthropus*, because he considered them to be very distinct from the fossils found at Taung and Sterkfontein. In the late 1940s early hominid fossils from the site of Makapansgat were described by Dart, who attributed them to the genus *Australopithecus*, but to a separate species, *A. prometheus*.

In 1959 L.S.B. Leakey attributed the large-toothed and heavily crested hominid cranium discovered in Bed I of Olduvai Gorge to a novel taxon, *Zinjanthropus boisei*. J.T. Robinson was quick to recognize that this specimen had close affinities to the South African forms from Kromdraai and Swartkrans and proposed that *Zinjanthropus* was a junior synonym of *Paranthropus*. Robinson maintained, as had Broom, that *Australopithecus* and *Paranthropus* represented separate phyletic lines of evolution and that their generic separation was fully justified. Thus the hominid specimens from Taung, Sterkfontein, and Makapansgat (*Australopithecus*) and the fossils attributed to *Paranthropus* were viewed by Robinson as having comprised separate branches (clades) of evolution.

Subsequent studies, such as those by P.V. Tobias, C. Loring Brace, and M. Wolpoff, viewed all of these early hominid forms as comprising a single evolutionary grade of organization, characterized primarily by its comparatively small brain size. These studies, in which the differences between the fossils attributed to *Australopithecus* and *Paranthropus* were minimized, influenced opinion such that most students of, and all textbooks on, hominid evolution regard *Paranthropus* as a junior synonym of *Australopithecus*. The view that the Plio-Pleistocene hominid fossils of Africa that are not attributable to the genus *Homo* belong in the genus *Australopithecus* has had significant consequences, including the attribution by D.C. Johanson, T.D. White, and Y. Coppens of the Hadar and Laetoli fossils to the genus *Australopithecus*, with the name *A. afarensis*.

At present most workers recognize four species of *Australopithecus*: *A. afarensis*, *A. africanus*, *A. robustus*, and *A. boisei*. The latter two species are commonly regarded as having been of larger average body size than the former (although these estimates are all too often unduly influenced by cheek-tooth size rather than by postcranial element size), with the result that the term "gracile" has come to be generally applied to *A. afarensis* and *A. africanus* and the probably inappropriate sobriquet "robust" to *A. robustus* and *A. boisei*. The belief that all Plio-Pleistocene hominids

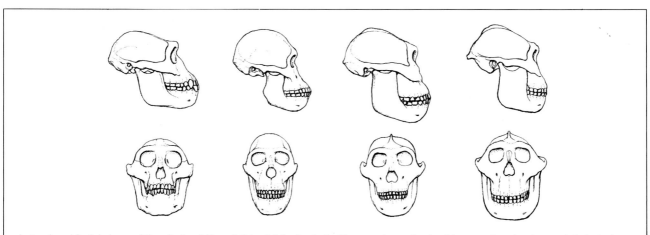

Lateral and facial views of the skulls of (from left to right): *Australopithecus afarensis, A. africanus, A. robustus,* and *A. boisei.*

that are not recognizable as belonging to an established species of *Homo* should be placed into the genus *Australopithecus* has also had the effect that the problematic term "australopithecine" has become firmly entrenched in the paleoanthropological literature.

In the 1950s both Broom and Robinson held that the genus *Australopithecus* (sensu stricto) was sufficiently distinct from *Homo* to warrant separate subfamilial rankings for the two, in the Australopithecinae and Homininae, respectively. This opinion was subsequently abandoned by Robinson, whose writings in the 1960s stressed that because *Australopithecus* (sensu stricto) was likely a part of the immediate human lineage, while *Paranthropus* represented a separate evolutionary lineage, the use of the genus *Australopithecus* (and thus the term "australopithecine") should be abandoned, since he considered *Australopithecus* a junior synonym of the genus name *Homo*.

The term "australopithecine" in fact represents a direct vernacular transliteration of the taxonomic subfamilial rank Australopithecinae, and its use denotes an implicit recognition that *Australopithecus* should be afforded separate subfamilial rank from *Homo*, although few if any of the workers who have had firsthand experience with the Plio-Pleistocene hominid fossil record would accept this level of distinction between *Australopithecus* (either sensu stricto or sensu lato) and *Homo*. Nevertheless, "australopithecine," despite its misleading connotation, has become so firmly entrenched in the vocabulary of early hominid studies that it is unlikely to fall into disuse in the near future. Suffice it to say that when "australopithecine" is used it is almost always taken to connote *Australopithecus* (sensu lato).

Although most workers, as mentioned above, recognize four distinct species of *Australopithecus*, recent discoveries in the Pliocene sediments west of Lake Turkana indicate that at least five distinct species will have to be recognized for hominid fossils that are not attributable to the genus *Homo*, and some authorities recognize as many as six.

A. afarensis

The hypodigm of this species consists of the specimens from the sites of Laetoli (Tanzania) and Hadar (Ethiopia), together with several referred specimens from the sites of Maka and Belohdelie (Ethiopia) and from the Tulu Bor Member (e.g. KNM-ER 2602) of the Koobi Fora Formation (Kenya). Fossils from the Usno Formation (Ethiopia) and from the sites of Lothagam and Tabarin (Kenya) also have been referred to this species, which appears to span the period between ca. 4 and 3 m.y. ago. This species is

characterized principally by its possession of a suite of primitive craniodental characters, including strong facial prognathism, a flat cranial base, a flat glenoid fossa without a discernible articular eminence, a postglenoid process that is situated anterior to the tympanic, a tubular tympanic, an anteriorly shallow (flat) palate, sharp lateral margins of the pyriform aperture, convex nasoalveolar clivus that is demarcated from the floor of the nose by a horizontal sill, maxillary lateral incisor roots that are lateral to the margins of the pyriform aperture, a strongly flared parietal mastoid angle together with an asterionic notch, large maxillary central incisors compared with lateral incisors, relatively large canines that wear primarily along the distal edge, and sectorial (unicuspid) to semisectorial (with small metaconid) mandibular P_3s.

A. africanus

This is the type species of the genus *Australopithecus*. The holotype derives from the site of Taung, and the hypodigm of this species is composed of specimens from Member 4 of the Sterkfontein Formation and from Members 3 and 4 of the Makapansgat Formation (South Africa). When the first Sterkfontein specimens were discovered in 1936, Broom designated them as *A. transvaalensis*, although two years later he proposed that they be placed in a separate genus, *Plesianthropus* (whence the name "Mrs. Ples" for the Sts 5 cranium). The hominid specimens recovered from Makapansgat were initially referred to the species *A. prometheus* by Dart in 1948. At present the names *Plesianthropus transvaalensis* and *A. prometheus* are universally regarded as being junior synonyms of *A. africanus*. This species is characterized principally by its possession of a more globular and less pneumatized cranium than that of *A. afarensis*, together with other derived features (such as the configuration of the glenoid region, the shape of the tympanic bone, bicuspid P_3s) that differ from the primitive conditions shown by *A. afarensis*. *A. africanus* is also characterized by craniofacial, mandibular, and dental features that differ from those displayed by specimens of *Homo*, *A. robustus*, and *A. boisei*. Indeed, *A. africanus* appears to lack any distinctive morphological characters that preclude it from being regarded as ancestral to *Homo* (see below). *A. africanus* specimens from Sterkfontein and Makapansgat likely date to between ca. 3 and 2.5 m.y.; the geochronological age of the Taung skull has long been a matter of dispute, but the most reliable faunal estimates place it between 2.3 and 2 m.y. at the latest.

A. robustus

The holotype of this species derives from the site of Kromdraai (South Africa), and it was described in

1938 by R. Broom, who referred it to the taxon *Paranthropus robustus*. To date only a handful of hominid fossils have been recovered from Kromdraai, and it is likely that all derive from Member 3 of the Kromdraai B East Formation. A decade after the recovery of the first Kromdraai specimen Broom discovered fossils at the site of Swartkrans; these he assigned to another species, *Paranthropus crassidens*. Most workers consider the Kromdraai and Swartkrans fossils to represent a single species of the genus *Australopithecus*, *A. robustus*, with the vast bulk of the hypodigm of this taxon deriving from Swartkrans. Specimens of *A. robustus* are known primarily from Member 1 of the Swartkrans Formation, although recent excavations by C.K. Brain have yielded *A. robustus* fossils from Members 2 and 3. While there is a consensus that the fossils from Kromdraai and Swartkrans are referable to a single species, both F.C. Howell and F.E. Grine have argued that morphological differences between these samples warrant the recognition of two species, *A. robustus* and *A. crassidens*. For present purposes, however, the Kromdraai and Swartkrans fossils will be treated as a single species, *A. robustus*, that is characterized principally by a flattened, "dished" face with the cheeks situated anterior to the margins of the pyriform aperture, large premolars and molars together with relatively small incisors and canines, a facial skeleton that is hafted high on the calvaria, a low forehead with a concave frontal trigone, a prominent glabella that is situated below the level of the supraorbital margin, a nasoalveolar clivus that passes smoothly into the floor of the nasal cavity, and a maxillary trigone. The Swartkrans specimens have a likely age of between 1.8 and 1.5 m.y.; the age of the Kromdraai fossils has been a matter of dispute, but faunal estimates indicate an age just slightly younger than that of Swartkrans.

A. boisei

The holotype of this species consists of a large cranium that was discovered in 1959 in Bed I of Olduvai Gorge and described that same year by L.S.B. Leakey, who attributed it to the taxon *Zinjanthropus boisei*. Robinson pointed out the similarities between this specimen and the fossils from Kromdraai and Swartkrans, and he proposed that the Olduvai cranium represented a novel species of the genus *Paranthropus*. Most workers presently refer to this and other similar specimens from eastern Africa as *Australopithecus boisei*. The hypodigm of this species comprises fossils from Beds I and II of Olduvai Gorge and from the Humbu Formation at Peninj, near Lake Natron (Tanzania), numerous fine specimens from Ileret and Koobi Fora (Kenya), a partial cranium from

the Chemoigut Formation (Kenya), and gnathodental remains from the Shungura Formation (Ethiopia). The majority of the fossils from Koobi Fora derive from sediments above the KBS Tuff, although several are known from below it; undoubted *A. boisei* fossils are known from Members E, F, G, and L of the Shungura Formation, and two isolated deciduous teeth that have been attributed to this taxon come from Member D. Thus specimens that have been attributed to *A. boisei* are known from ca. 2.2 to 1.4 m.y. Many of the principal features that characterize *A. boisei* are possessed also by *A. robustus* (e.g. the high hafting of the facial skeleton, the flattened, "dished" face, the large cheek teeth combined with relatively small anterior teeth, the smooth transition from the nasoalveolar clivus to the floor of the nasal cavity, the high petromedian angle), but *A. boisei* differs primarily in its greater maxillary depth, anteriorly shelved palate, laterally bowed zygomatic arches, and supraorbital configuration, as well as in the presence of sharply defined inferior and lateral orbital margins, absence of a maxillary trigone, and presence of a "heart-shaped" foramen magnum with a straight or posteriorly convex anterior margin. The cheek teeth of *A. boisei* also tend to be larger than those of *A. robustus*; dimensions for *A. boisei* premolars and molars are the largest recorded for any hominid taxon.

The question of the phylogenetic relationships among *Australopithecus* species, and the evolutionary relationship between *Australopithecus* and *Homo* has recently been brought into stark light by the discovery of a nearly complete, albeit almost edentulous cranium from Pliocene sediments (ca. 2.5 m.y.) on the west shore of Lake Turkana (known as the "black skull"). This male specimen from the Lomekwi Formation has been interpreted by A.C. Walker and colleagues as representing an early fossil of *A. boisei*, and they have argued that it indicates that *A. boisei* evolved from *A. afarensis*, while the southern African "robust" species, *A. robustus*, evolved independently from *A. africanus*. Thus two points are presently at issue: 1) Is the cranium from the Lomekwi Formation, KNM-WT 17000, attributable to *A. boisei*, and 2) Did the eastern and southern African "robust" australopithecines, *A. boisei* and *A. robustus*, evolve their remarkable craniodental similarities through functional convergence? The answers to both questions are likely in the negative.

While the cranium from the Lomekwi Formation displays similarities of a derived nature (*synapomorphies*) with *A. boisei*, these same features are shared also by *A. robustus*. Indeed, in not a few morphological characters this cranium is more similar to those of *A. robustus* than to *A. boisei* (e.g. in the form of the glenoid fossa, the presence of a maxillary trigone, an anteriorly shallow palate, straight zygomatic arches). The only feature in which it resembles *A. boisei* appears to be its "heart-shaped" foramen magnum. In addition to primarily facial similarities with *A. robustus* and *A. boisei* the Lomekwi cranium also presents primitive morphological features (*symplesiomorphies*) that are shared with crania of *A. afarensis* but not with other australopithecines. This unique combination of primitive features and derived characters shared with both *A. robustus* and *A. boisei* indicates that KNM-WT 17000 should be attributed to a separate species.

In their description and interpretation of the Lomekwi cranium Walker and colleagues suggested that, should this specimen be shown to be distinct from *A. boisei*, it might reasonably be accorded the taxonomic designation *A. aethiopicus*. In 1968 C. Arambourg and Y. Coppens described an edentulous mandible from Member C of the Shungura Formation, which they designated the type of a novel taxon, *Paraustralopithecus aethiopicus*, because they considered it to differ from the Natron mandible, the only mandible of *A. boisei* known at that time. The mandible described by Arambourg and Coppens and the KNM-WT 17000 cranium are of approximately the same geochronological age, and Walker and colleagues argued that if the cranium were to be shown to be different from *A. boisei* then it could be attributed to the same species as the similarly dated mandible from Member C of the Shungura Formation: thus the designation *A. aethiopicus*. Although the referral of the KNM-WT 17000 cranium to *A. aethiopicus* is based upon tenuous arguments, it is currently accepted by some workers.

Whether or not the name *A. aethiopicus* proves to be validly applied to the Lomekwi cranium, the name is at least available for this purpose, and there are good reasons to attribute this specimen to a separate species from *A. boisei* and *A. robustus*. *A. aethiopicus* will no doubt enjoy increased use as the name applied to a fifth recognized species of *Australopithecus*.

A. aethiopicus

This species is represented by the edentulous cranium KNM-WT 17000; several other specimens, principally isolated teeth and a few mandibles, from the lower Members of the Shungura Formation may also be attributable to this species, including the Omo 18-1967-18 mandible, the holotype of the taxon. This species may have a temporal range between ca. 2.8 and 2.2 m.y. It is characterized primarily by the presence of a "dished" midface with the anterior zygomatic surfaces anterior to the level of the pyriform aperture, sharp superior margins of the

pyriform aperture, coincident glabella and nasion, glabella situated below the level of the supraorbital margins, a maxillary trigone, marked alveolar prognathism, a nasoalveolar clivus that passes smoothly into the floor of the nose, marked ectocranial superstructures including a posteriorly prominent sagittal crest and compound temporonuchal crests (at least in males), extensive pneumatization of the temporal squama with strongly flared parietal mastoid angle, flat cranial base, anteriorly shallow palate, broad anterior palate with maxillary lateral incisor roots medial to margins of pyriform aperture, sharp inferior and smooth inferolateral orbital margins, glenoid fossa lacking a distinct articular eminence, postglenoid process anterior to tympanic plate, anterior tympanic surface vertical and concave, straight zygomatic arches, and a high petromedian angle.

Thus, at present, at least five distinct species of *Australopithecus* can be discerned among the Plio-Pleistocene fossils from southern and eastern Africa, and morphological differences between the "australopithecine" specimens from Kromdraai and Swartkrans strongly suggest that these samples also should be accorded separate specific status. Most authorities who have studied the fossils in question recognize *A. afarensis*, *A. africanus*, *A. robustus*, *A. boisei*, and *A. aethiopicus* as distinct species, and some have argued recently that *A. crassidens* should be added to this roster.

Evolutionary Relationships

There has been considerable controversy over the relationships among the "australopithecine" species and over the evolutionary relationships between these taxa and the genus *Homo*. The phylogenetic and taxonomic hypotheses put forward since the discovery and description of the Taung skull have all been either rejected outright or substantially altered by ongoing research and new discoveries. However, a brief review of some of the most recent theories will be useful.

Hypothesis 1 (advanced by T.D. White and D.C. Johanson in the late 1970s, and advocated until recently by them, W.H. Kimbel, and Y. Rak, among others): *A. afarensis* represents the stem hominid from which both the *Homo* and "robust australopithecine" lineages diverged. According to this hypothesis *A. africanus* is more closely related to the "robust" taxa *A. robustus* and *A. boisei* than to any other hominid taxon. The recent discovery of the "black skull" has led most workers to reject this hypothesis.

Hypothesis 2 (advanced by R. Skelton, H. McHenry, and G. Drawhorn, and advocated until recently by them, F.E. Grine, and M.C. Dean, among others): *A. afarensis* represents the stem hominid from which *A.*

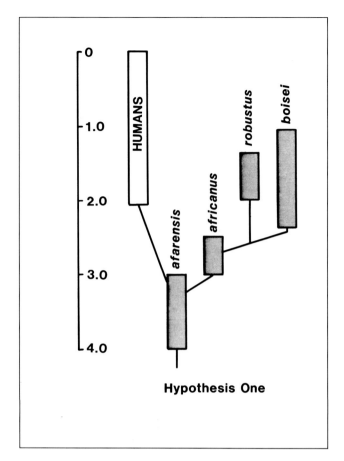

Hypothesis One

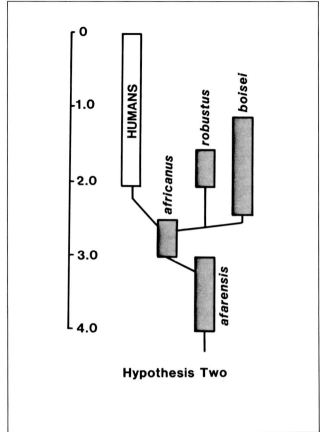

Hypothesis Two

africanus evolved, and *A. africanus* represents the last common ancestor of the *Homo* and "robust" (*A. robustus* and *A. boisei*) lineages. The discovery of the "black skull" has led most workers to reject this hypothesis.

Hypothesis 3 (advocated originally by J.T. Robinson in the late 1960s and early 70s): the "robust australopithecines" (*A. robustus* and *A. boisei*) represent a distinct evolutionary lineage that diverged very early from the human (*Homo*) line. According to this hypothesis, since *A. robustus* and *A. boisei* comprise a distinct evolutionary branch (clade), they should be accorded distinct generic separation (*Paranthropus*), as *P. robustus* and *P. boisei*, from those taxa on the *Homo* line. Robinson argued that since *A. africanus* comprised part of the latter lineage there was no longer any valid reason to recognize *Australopithecus* as a distinct genus: the specimens from Taung, Sterkfontein, and Makapansgat could be accorded membership in the genus *Homo* as the species *H. africanus*. This hypothesis, put forward by Robinson before the description of *A. afarensis*, was altered slightly by Olson, who argued that this latter taxon comprised two separate species, one of which was

related closely to the *Paranthropus* (i.e. "robust") lineage and the other being part of the *Homo* lineage. (Interestingly enough, while Robinson recognized the "Garusi," or Laetoli, fossils discovered in the 1930s to be part of the *Homo* line (*H. africanus*), Olson interpreted them as being part of the *Paranthropus* lineage.) The phylogenetic diagram published here represents Olson's alterations to the diagram originally proposed by Robinson. This hypothesis has been corroborated in large measure by the discovery of the "black skull," although there is now a consensus that the Laetoli and Hadar samples represent a single species, *A. afarensis*.

Hypothesis 4 (originally advocated by A. Walker and colleagues in their initial interpretation of the "black skull" and subsequently advocated by D.C. Johanson and a few others): *A. afarensis* represents the common stem from which the eastern African "robust" lineage (comprising *A. aethiopicus* and *A. boisei*) stemmed, together with another lineage that led ultimately to the southern African "robust" form (*A. robustus*) and to *Homo* via a common ancestor in *A. africanus*. This hypothesis states that the morphological resemblances between the southern and east-

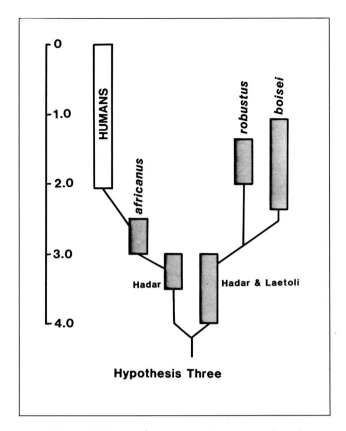

Hypothesis Three

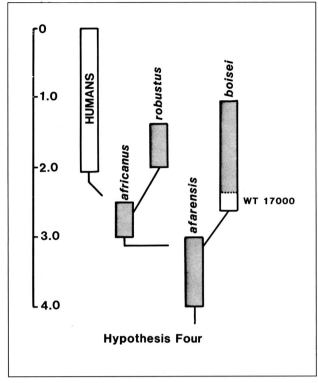

Hypothesis Four

ern African "robust" forms (*A. robustus* and *A. boisei*, respectively) arose through convergent evolution, that is, convergent functional adaptations to a heavily masticated diet.

Hypothesis 5 (advocated by E. Delson, F.E. Grine, T.R. Olson, and W.H. Kimbel, among others): this hypothesis is similar to Hypothesis 3 inasmuch as it recognizes the "robust" taxa from southern and eastern Africa, *A. robustus* and *A. boisei* together with *A. aethiopicus*, as representing a single evolutionary branch (clade). It differs from Hypothesis 3, however, in that a single species, *A. afarensis*, is recognized for the earlier fossils from Hadar and Laetoli. *A. afarensis* is postulated as the last common ancestor of the "robust australopithecine" line and the lineage leading to humans; *A. africanus* or an *A. africanus*-like form is held to represent the forebear of *Homo*.

This last hypothesis, which stems principally from the interpretation of the evolutionary relationships of the "black skull," largely corroborates Robinson's arguments than the "robust australopithecines" constitute a lineage distinct from that comprised by *A. africanus* and *Homo*, with the result that the genus name *Paranthropus* can be legitimately applied to members of the former clade. In a strictly cladistic interpretation of the taxonomy of this phylogenetic hypothesis not only would *Paranthropus* be the cor-

rect genus grouping for *P. aethiopicus, P. robustus*, and *P. boisei* but the species "*A.*" *afarensis* should properly be placed in a distinct genus; the name *Australopithecus* would pertain only to *A. africanus*. It is

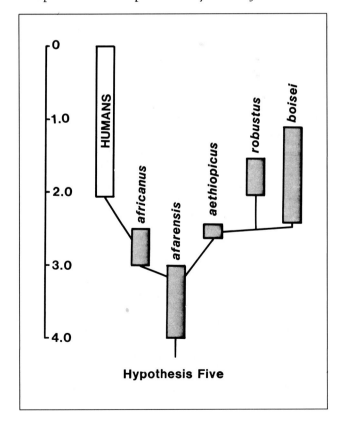

Hypothesis Five

not necessary to treat *Australopithecus* as a junior synonym of *Homo*, even under a strict cladistic application of taxonomy to the phylogenetic scheme proposed by this hypothesis. Certainly, however, the "robust" taxa appear to warrant identity as a separate genus, *Paranthropus*.

The name *Australopithecus* will likely find increased use only in reference to *A. africanus*. "Australopithecine" will therefore have little meaning, and it is hoped that the misleading sobriquets "gracile" and "robust" will fall into disuse.

See also AUSTRALOPITHECUS AFARENSIS; AUSTRALOPITHECUS AFRICANUS; AUSTRALOPITHECUS BOISEI; AUSTRALOPITHECUS ROBUSTUS; PARANTHROPUS. [F.E.G.]

Further Readings

Broom, R. (1950) The genera and species of the South African fossil ape-men. Am. J. Phys. Anthropol. 8:1–13.

Clarke, R.J. (1985) *Australopithecus* and early *Homo* in southern Africa. In E. Delson (ed.): Ancestors: The Hard Evidence. New York: Liss, pp. 171–177.

Delson, E. (1986) Human phylogeny revised again. Nature 322:496–497.

Grine, F.E. (1981) Trophic differences between "gracile" and "robust" australopithecines: a scanning electron microscope analysis of occlusal events. S. Afr. J. Sci. 77:203–230.

Howell, F.C. (1978) Hominidae. In V.J. Maglio and H.B.S. Cooke (eds.): Evolution of African Mammals. Cambridge, Mass.: Harvard University Press, pp. 154–248.

Olson, T.R. (1985) Cranial morphology and systematics of the Hadar Formation hominids and "*Australopithecus*" africanus. In E. Delson, pp. 102–119.

Robinson, J.T. (1954) The genera and species of the Australopithecinae. Am. J. Phys. Anthropol. 12:181–200.

Skelton, R.R., McHenry, H.M., and Drawhorn, G.M. (1986) Phylogenetic analysis of early hominids. Curr. Anthropol. 27:21–35, 38–39.

Walker, A.C., Leakey, R.E.F., Harris, J.M., and Brown, F.H. (1986) 2.5-Myr *Australopithecus boisei* from west of Lake Turkana, Kenya. Nature 322:517–522.

White, T.D., Johanson, D.C., and Kimbel, W.H. (1981) *Australopithecus africanus*: its phyletic position reconsidered. S. Afr. J. Sci. 77:445–470.

AUSTRALOPITHECUS AETHIOPICUS *see* AUSTRALOPITHECUS

AUSTRALOPITHECUS AFARENSIS

Species of *Australopithecus* named in 1978 to incorporate the early hominid fossil material from the Tanzanian site of Laetoli and the Ethiopian site of Hadar. This species is thought by many to be the common ancestor of all later hominid species in the genera *Homo* and *Australopithecus*.

The first specimens of *Australopithecus afarensis* were recovered from Laetoli during the 1930s. Because more abundant fossils of *Australopithecus afri-* *canus* were recovered during the 1920s through 40s in southern Africa most authorities attributed the Laetoli remains (a maxilla and molar; a canine and incisor recovered in the 1930s went unrecognized until the 1970s) to this taxon. In the 1950s, however, work by Weinert and Senyürek on primitive characters of the maxillary fragment led them to attribute the Laetoli fossils to *Meganthropus africanus* and *Praeanthropus africanus*, respectively. Few agreed with these workers, and the Garusi maxilla, as it was called, continued to be considered a northern representative of *Australopithecus africanus*.

Between 1973 and 1977 research by M. Taieb, D.C. Johanson, and Y. Coppens at the Hadar site in the Afar of Ethiopia led to the recovery of hundreds of hominid fossils dating to 4–3 m.y. These fossils included an intact knee joint, a partial skeleton nicknamed "Lucy," a sample of body parts from at least 13 individuals, and many isolated jaws and teeth. Almost simultaneously, between 1974 and 1978, M.D. Leakey and her colleagues recovered a smaller sample of hominid fossils dating to ca. 3.5 m.y. at the site of Laetoli. Also found at Laetoli were footprints left by hominids in freshly fallen volcanic ash.

The Laetoli hominids and part of the Hadar collection were at first considered to represent early *Homo* in eastern Africa. Other Hadar hominids, such as the partial skeleton of "Lucy," were attributed to *Australopithecus*. The recovery of more fossils from these sites, particularly from Hadar's 333 locality, led to a reassessment of these attributions. D.C. Johanson, who was studying the Afar material, joined T.D. White, who was studying the Laetoli material. Together they reached several conclusions. First, they found no evidence for multiple hominid species in the Hadar Formation or the Laetolil Beds. Instead they found a wide range of size and shape, which they attributed to individual and sexual dimorphism. Second, they found that the hominid fossils discovered at the two sites could be placed in a single hominid species. Third, they found that the combined sample from Tanzania and Ethiopia differed in many ways from the already recognized species *Australopithecus africanus* from southern Africa. Finally, they considered the more primitive hominid species from Laetoli and Hadar to be a suitable common ancestor for all later species of early hominids in both *Homo* and *Australopithecus*.

Johanson and White considered the Hadar and Laetoli hominids to belong to the genus *Australopithecus*, because they were bipedal but lacked the cranial expansion and facial reduction seen in the evolution of *Homo*. South African *A. africanus* differed from the more primitive remains from eastern Africa. The species name *africanus* applied by

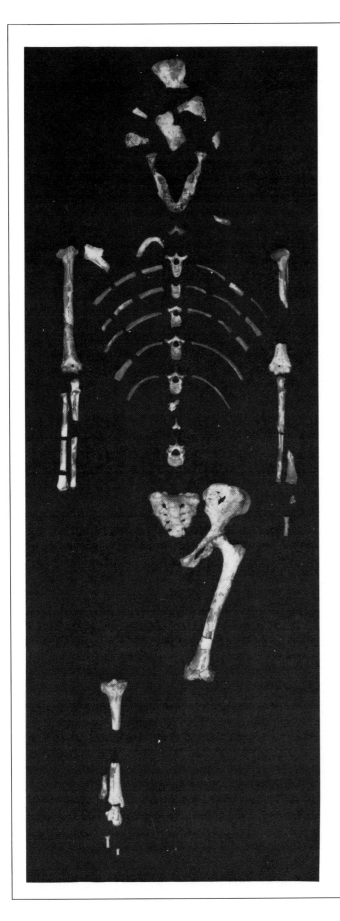

Specimens of *Australopithecus afarensis* from Hadar (Ethiopia). Left: Specimen A.L. 288-1, a partial adult skeleton nicknamed "Lucy." This is the most complete specimen known of *Australopithecus afarensis*. (Photograph courtesy of the Cleveland Museum of Natural History.) Upper right: A.L. 333-3, a distal femur attributed to a male individual of *Australopithecus afarensis*. Lower right: A.L. 129-1a, a distal femur attributed to a female individual of *Australopithecus afarensis*. (Photographs courtesy of the Institute of Human Origins.)

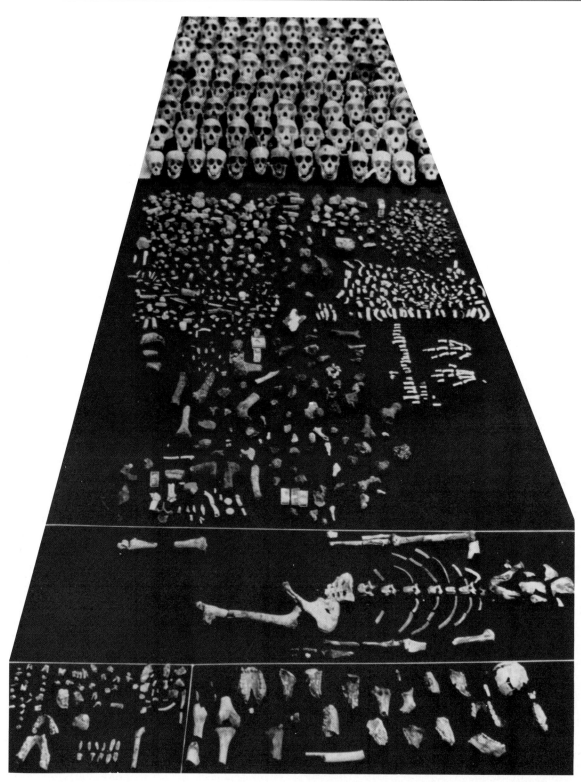

The 1978 collection of fossils comprising the taxon *Australopithecus afarensis*. In the lower-left corner is the collection from Laetoli. In the lower-right are remains from Hadar localities. The partial Hadar skeleton "Lucy" lies horizontally. The remains in the center of the photograph are all from locality 333 at Hadar, representing a minimum of thirteen individuals. The modern chimpanzee skulls in the background are part of the Hamman-Todd collection, which was used by Johanson and White for comparative purposes in establishing that the fossil material represented a single species. (Photograph by Don Johanson, courtesy of the Institute of Human Origins.)

Weinert and Senyürek to the original Laetoli fossils, however, already referred to the Taung child and other South African material. Therefore in 1978 Johanson, White, and Coppens named the material from Ethiopia and Tanzania *Australopithecus afarensis*, after the Afar region of Ethiopia, where most of the remains had been found. To emphasize the similarities between the Hadar and Laetoli material they chose the adult mandible from Laetoli as the holotype and emphasized variation in the new species by naming as paratypes all of the hominids then known from the two sites.

Australopithecus afarensis, according to Johanson and White, represents the only hominid species present between 4 and 3 m.y. ago. They hypothesize that *Australopithecus afarensis* gave rise to the "robust" *Australopithecus aethiopicus*, *Australopithecus robustus* and *Australopithecus boisei*, as well as to the genus *Homo* as first represented by *Homo habilis*.

Australopithecus afarensis is characterized by a distinctive suite of primitive cranial and postcranial characteristics. In the cranium the braincase is small, with a capacity of between 380 and 530 ml. for the few specimens available. The molars and premolars are large relative to body size but lack the molariza-

tion and extreme size seen in later *Australopithecus*. Palate and mandible shape is decidedly primitive, and incisors and canines are relatively large. The face is very prognathic. The base and posterior portions of the cranium are apelike in many features. Postcranially *Australopithecus afarensis* shows many anatomical characteristics indicating that it habitually practiced bipedalism. The curvature of the hand and foot phalanges and the extreme robusticity of these and other skeletal elements show that the species differed from the modern human condition. Female body size was much smaller than male body size, and this sexual dimorphism is also seen in the cranial and dental remains.

The description of *Australopithecus afarensis* in 1978 and the Johanson and White interpretation of this species's phylogenetic status have prompted considerable discussion and debate. Taxonomically some workers have suggested that the fossils be placed in the genus *Praeanthropus*, while others have advocated treating the fossils as northern representatives of a polytypic *Australopithecus africanus*. Several workers consider the Hadar and Lactoli fossils to be different and therefore question the choice of a Lactoli specimen as a holotype. Others continue to rec-

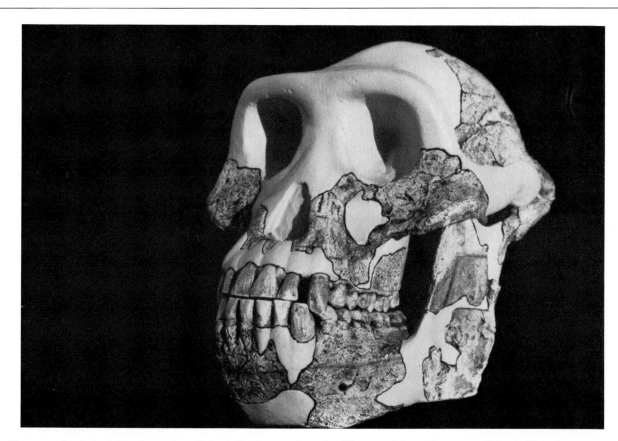

The reconstructed adult male cranium of *Australopithecus afarensis*. (Photograph by and courtesy of Tim D. White.)

ognize more than one species among the Hadar and Laetoli remains, but even among this group of workers there is no agreement about which specimens belong to which taxon. For example, some view Lucy as a relict *Ramapithecus*, some view her as an early representative of *Homo*, and others place her in *Australopithecus africanus*. The larger Hadar fossils are thought by different authors to represent *Sivapithecus*, robust *Australopithecus*, or early *Homo*.

Further debate has centered on the inferred locomotor activities and habitat of *Australopithecus afarensis*. Stern, Susman, and others have interpreted such postcranial characters as curved phalanges to indicate that the species spent large amounts of time in an arboreal substrate. For these workers *Australopithecus afarensis* is an intermediate between the pongid and hominid conditions. Lovejoy has consistently maintained that this species was fully committed and adapted to existence as a habitually terrestrial biped.

The primitive characters seen in the *Australopithecus afarensis* cranial and dental anatomy have been interpreted by some as evidence for a relatively recent divergence between the ape and human lines and therefore as support for biochemically derived divergence dates of less than 6 m.y. The presence of primitive characters in the relatively recent but definitely hominid fossils from Hadar and Laetoli has contributed to the climate of reassessment of the hominid status of the much earlier *Ramapithecus*, once heralded as a direct human ancestor.

The recovery of remains belonging to *Australopithecus afarensis* has given scientists a chance to study Pliocene hominids. This study has focused paleontological attention on the little-known periods between 8 and 4 m.y. ago and between 3 and 2 m.y. ago. As rocks of this age are investigated and further work is done at Hadar and other sites, the integrity and utility of the species *Australopithecus afarensis* will continue to be tested.

See also AFAR; AUSTRALOPITHECUS; HADAR; LAETOLI. [T.D.W.]

Further Readings

Ciochon, R.L., and Corruccini, R.S. (1983) New Interpretations of Ape and Human Ancestry. New York: Plenum.

Delson, E., ed. (1985) Ancestors: The Hard Evidence. New York: Liss.

Johanson, D.C., and Edey, M. (1981) Lucy: The Beginnings of Humankind. New York: Simon and Schuster.

Johanson, D.C., and others (1982) Special issue. Am. J. Phys. Anthropol. 57, 4.

Johanson, D.C., and White, T.D. (1979) A systematic assessment of early African hominids. Science 202:321–330.

White, T.D., and Suwa, G. (1987) Hominid footprints at Laetoli: facts and interpretations. Am. J. Phys. Anthropol. 72:485–514.

AUSTRALOPITHECUS AFRICANUS

Type species of the genus *Australopithecus*, and the taxonomic name that is commonly used in reference to the "gracile" australopithecine fossils from the South African sites of Taung, Sterkfontein, and Makapansgat.

The first of these specimens to be discovered was found at Taung in 1924. The fossil, consisting of a complete facial skeleton, a nearly complete mandible, and a hemiendocast of a juvenile individual with a complete deciduous dentition, was obtained by R.A. Dart, who described it in 1925. The name that Dart gave to the Taung skull, *Australopithecus africanus*, means literally "southern ape of Africa." The Taung skull was the first early hominid specimen to be recovered from ancient sediments in Africa, and Dart's pronouncement that *Australopithecus africanus* represented an intermediate between apes and humans was met with considerable resistance by the paleoanthropological community. The first adult specimen of *Australopithecus* was recovered some 11

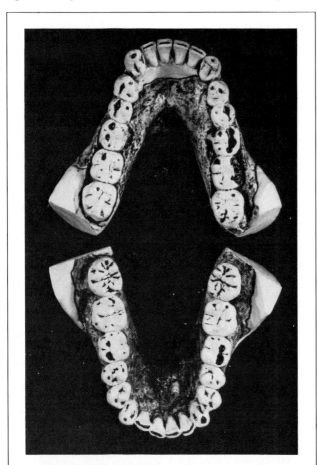

A comparison between casts of a lower jaw from Laetoli (top) and a lower jaw from Hadar (bottom). (Photograph by and courtesy of Tim D. White.)

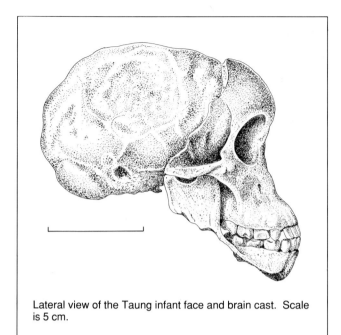

Lateral view of the Taung infant face and brain cast. Scale is 5 cm.

years later by R. Broom from the site of Sterkfontein. Broom described the Sterkfontein specimen in 1936, and because he was struck by the similarities between it and the Taung specimen he placed it into the same genus, albeit in a different species, *A. transvaalensis*. Further discoveries from Sterkfontein made in conjunction with the first hominid specimens to be recovered from Kromdraai caused Broom to refer the Sterkfontein fossils to a separate genus, *Plesianthropus*, whence the name "Mrs. Ples" for the supposedly female Sterkfontein cranium Sts 5. The first hominid specimen from Makapansgat was described in 1948 by Dart, who attributed it to a separate species of *Australopithecus*, *A. prometheus*.

Thus by the late 1940s three different taxonomic names had been applied to the fossils from Taung (*Australopithecus africanus*), Sterkfontein (*Plesianthropus transvaalensis*), and Makapansgat (*Australopithecus prometheus*). On the basis of detailed comparative studies of these and other fossil hominid samples J.T. Robinson proposed in 1954 that the specimens from these three sites were representative of a single species, *A. africanus*. This has received almost universal support by workers in the field, such that at present the hypodigm of *A. africanus* comprises the Taung skull (the type specimen) as well as the hominid fossils from Member 4 of the Sterkfontein Formation and those from Members 3 and 4 of the Makapansgat Formation.

The fossils from Makapansgat Member 3, representing the vast bulk of the sample from that site, appear to date close to 3 m.y., while the Sterkfontein Member 4 specimens are dated to ca. 2.5 m.y. based upon faunal comparisons with radiometrically dated samples from eastern Africa. The geochronological dating of the Taung fossil has been a matter of some dispute. An ill-founded attempt at geomorphological dating in the early 1970s suggested an age of less than 870 k.y., which prompted speculation that the skull may be that of a "robust" australopithecine, although analyses of the faunal remains from the site suggest a minimum age of 2 m.y. (between 2.3 and 2 m.y.). Moreover, the Taung specimen is morphologically similar to those from Makapansgat and Sterkfontein and quite distinctive from the younger "robust" specimens from Kromdraai and Swartkrans. Thus *A. africanus* appears to have existed in southern Africa between ca. 3 and 2 m.y. At present no fossil specimen from eastern Africa has been demonstrated convincingly to represent this taxon.

Initial studies of the faunal remains associated with *A. africanus* led Dart to postulate that this hominid was a hunter and that the faunal elements from the site of Makapansgat represented not only the food remains but also the implements of *A. africanus*. Dart referred to these purported bone, tooth, and horn tools as the Osteodontokeratic culture. Subsequent taphonomic studies by C.K. Brain, however, have demonstrated convincingly that far from representing the tools and food remains of *A. africanus* the associated faunal elements and indeed the hominids themselves probably represent the food remains of carnivores, such as leopards, and scavengers, such as hyenas. *A. africanus* appears to have been the hunted rather than the hunter!

Analyses of the teeth of *A. africanus* suggest a herbivorous diet, and the details of wear on these dentitions indicate subsistence upon fruits and foliage. The postcranial elements of *A. africanus*, including the structure of the shoulder girdle, the shape of the pelvis and structure of the femur, and the size and shape of the hand bones, are indicative of a creature that employed bipedal locomotion on the ground (although the mode of bipedality was likely somewhat different from that of modern humans), and of one that was well adapted to climbing. Estimates of body weight in *A. africanus* have varied quite widely, and many have been unduly influenced by tooth size, although recent estimates from postcranial element size indicate a likely average of between 45 and 46 kg., with considerable dimorphism in size between presumptive males and females.

Among the features that characterize *A. africanus*: cranial vault globular and lacking ectocranial superstructures in both males and females; calvaria hafted to facial skeleton at high level resulting in high supraorbital height index; slight forehead rise from glabella to bregma; cranium shows moderate pneumatization of mastoid region; lambda and inion moderately separated; glenoid fossa deep with

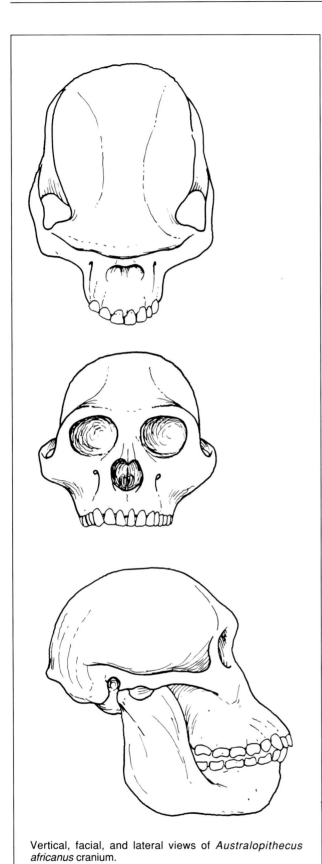

Vertical, facial, and lateral views of *Australopithecus africanus* cranium.

marked articular eminence; slight angulation of petrous to sagittal plane resulting in low petromedian angle; moderate to marked maxillary alveolar prognathism with nasoalveolar clivus delineated from floor of nasal cavity by distinct ridge; incisive canals open into inclined surface of nasal floor as a capacious incisive fossa; anterior palate shelved; alveolar margins of maxillary canine and incisor sockets arranged in an anteriorly convex line; pyriform aperture set anterior to level of anterior surfaces of zygomatics; lateral margins of pyriform aperture rounded with variable presence of canine pillars; glabella prominent and situated at level of supraorbital margin; nasion located below glabella as a result of high glabella; incisors and canines harmoniously proportioned to sizes of cheek teeth; P3 tends to possess two roots; dm$_1$ not "molarized" with anterior fovea lingually skewed and incompletely walled by mesial marginal ridge.

These traits, as well as other features, distinguish the skull and dentition of *A. africanus* from the generally more primitive *A. afarensis* and from the highly derived and specialized "robust" australopithecines. *A. africanus*, however, does not appear to possess any recognizable unique morphological features (autapomorphies) that would preclude it from being considered as the ancestor, or at least as the ancestral morph, from which *Homo* evolved. Indeed, a number of workers have argued that specimens that have been attributed to early members of the genus *Homo* (e.g. *H. habilis*) are virtually indistinguishable from *A. africanus*.

Endocranial capacity estimates for *A. africanus* are on the order of 410–450 ml. (with an average of ca. 440 ml.), which tend to be slightly larger than those for *A. afarensis* and slightly smaller than those for "robust" australopithecines, but noticeably smaller than those for most specimens of early *Homo*. To date no identifiable stone artifacts have been found in the cave breccias that contain *A. africanus* remains.

See also AUSTRALOPITHECUS; AUSTRALOPITHECUS AFARENSIS; AUSTRALOPITHECUS BOISEI; AUSTRALOPITHECUS ROBUSTUS; MAKAPANSGAT; PARANTHROPUS; STERKFONTEIN; TAUNG. [F.E.G.]

Further Readings

Clarke, R.J. (1985) *Australopithecus* and early *Homo* in southern Africa. In E. Delson (ed.): Ancestors: The Hard Evidence. New York: Liss, pp. 171–177.

Grine, F.E. (1981) Trophic differences between "gracile" and "robust" australopithecines; a scanning electron microscope analysis of occlusal events. S. Afr. J. Sci. 77:203–230.

Howell, F.C. (1978) Hominidae. In V.J. Maglio and H.B.S. Cooke (eds.): Evolution of African Mammals. Cambridge, Mass.: Harvard University Press, pp. 154–248.

Robinson, J.T. (1954) The genera and species of the Australopithecinae. Am. J. Phys. Anthropol. *12*:181–200.

Tobias, P.V. (1978) The place of *Australopithecus africanus* in hominid evolution. In D.J. Chivers and K.A. Joysey (eds.): Recent Advances in Primatology, Vol. 3: Evolution. New York: Academic, pp. 373–394.

White, T.D., Johanson, D.C., and Kimbel, W.H. (1981) *Australopithecus africanus*: its phyletic position reconsidered. S. Afr. J. Sci. *77*:445–470.

AUSTRALOPITHECUS BOISEI

Taxonomic name commonly used in reference to the "hyper-robust" australopithecine fossils from Plio-Pleistocene localities in Tanzania, Kenya, and Ethiopia.

The first of these fossils was discovered in 1959 by M.D. Leakey in the sediments of Bed I of Olduvai Gorge (Tanzania). The specimen, which consists of a nearly complete, massively built cranium and maxillary dentition, was described in 1959 by L.S.B. Leakey, who made it the type of a new taxon, *Zinjanthropus boisei*. J.T. Robinson considered that this specimen represented a novel species of the genus *Paranthropus*, as known from the sites of Kromdraai and Swartkrans (South Africa), whereas P.V. Tobias, in a thorough comparative study in which he sought to demonstrate the fundamentally similar structure of all australopithecines, referred it to a distinct species of the genus *Australopithecus*, *A. boisei*.

Following Tobias's study of the Olduvai Gorge cranium, there has been until recently a consensus that *A. boisei* is closely related to the southern African "robust" australopithecine, *A. robustus*. While most students of hominid evolution regard them as having been specifically distinct, some have argued that *A. boisei* and *A. robustus* represent subspecific, geographical variants of a single species. The "robust" australopithecine specimens from southern and eastern Africa do share a substantial suite of morphological features, and most workers have come to regard *A. boisei* as exhibiting further, extreme development of many of the features displayed by *A. robustus*.

Following the 1959 discovery by M.D. Leakey, further work at Olduvai Gorge resulted in the recovery of additional specimens of *A. boisei* from near the base of Bed I to near the top of Bed II. An isolated, well-preserved mandible of *A. boisei* from the Humba Formation at Peninj, near Lake Natron (Tanzania), is probably equivalent in age to the specimens from Bed II of Olduvai Gorge. An isolated, partial cranium of *A. boisei* is known from the Chemoigut Formation near Chesowanja (Kenya), and this specimen dates to ca. 1.5 m.y. Through the work of R. Leakey and his research team the largest number of *A. boisei* fossils

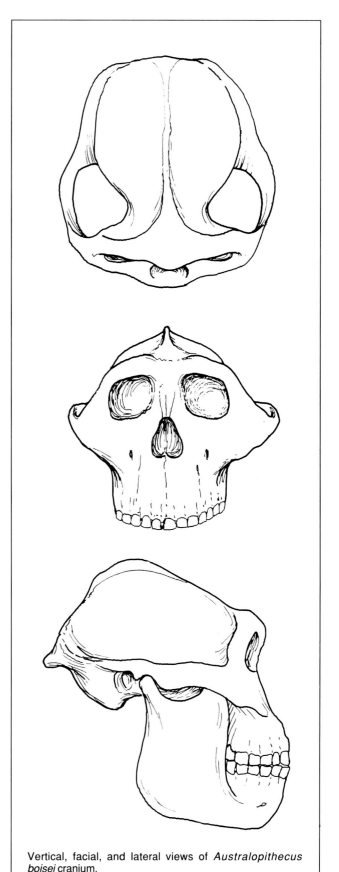

Vertical, facial, and lateral views of *Australopithecus boisei* cranium.

known at present have been recovered from the Plio-Pleistocene sediments of the Koobi Fora Formation, exposed on the eastern side of Lake Turkana (Kenya). Most of these fossils derive from the Upper and Ileret Members; only a comparatively few fossils recovered from below the KBS Tuff (the Lower Member) are definitely attributable to *A. boisei*.

Work by F.C. Howell and Y. Coppens has resulted in the discovery of numerous teeth, several massive mandibles, and some fragmentary cranial remains of *A. boisei* from the sediments of the Shungura Formation, which are exposed along the Omo River in southern Ethiopia. Within the Shungura Formation undoubted *A. boisei* fossils are known from Members E, F, G, and L, and two isolated deciduous teeth identified as belonging to *A. boisei* come from Member D. Thus specimens of *A. boisei* from the Shungura Formation span a considerable period, from ca. 2.4 m.y. to somewhat more than 1 m.y. This

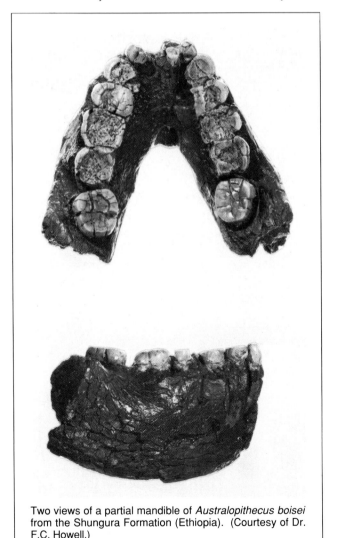

Two views of a partial mandible of *Australopithecus boisei* from the Shungura Formation (Ethiopia). (Courtesy of Dr. F.C. Howell.)

timespan also encompasses the *A. boisei* fossils from Olduvai Gorge, Peninj, Chesowanja, and the Koobi Fora Formation.

A substantial suite of morphological features characterize *A. boisei*, and while many of these are shown to some degree by *A. robustus* and some are possessed by other hominid taxa (e.g. *Homo*) *A. boisei* is unique in possessing these traits in combination.

Among the features that characterize *A. boisei*: cranium robustly constructed with ectocranial superstructures; cranium shows marked pneumatization with marked inflation of mastoid region; males with sagittal crest that is posteriorly divergent above lambda and with substantial nuchal crest that is simple medially and laterally but that may be compound (temporonuchal crest) intermediately; mastoid process not notably inflated and tip lies medial to lateral margin of elongate and concave tympanic; marked angulation of petrous axis to sagittal plane resulting in high petromedian angle; tendency for occipital-marginal sinus to be enlarged relative to transverse sinus; foramen magnum "heart"-shaped with straight or posteriorly convex anterior margin; calvaria hafted to facial skeleton at low level resulting in low supraorbital height index; forehead low and slightly concave with frontal trigone delimited laterally by posteriorly convergent temporal crests; strong postorbital constriction; temporal fossa capacious and mediolaterally expanded by laterally bowed zygomatic arch; presence of a broad gutter on the superior surface of the posterior root of the zygoma; supraorbital torus strong with flattened "rib" of bone across supraorbital margin but with twist between medial and lateral components; glabella prominent and situated below level of supraorbital margin; nasion and glabella nearly coincident as result of low glabella and internasal suture that projects higher than nasofrontale; superior portion of nasal bones tend to display a "diamond"-shaped expansion with "waisting" of nasals intermediately; bony face high and orthognathous; piriform aperture set in central facial hollow; deep nasoalveolar clivus passes smoothly into floor of nasal cavity without any demarcation; incisive canals open into horizontal surface of nasal floor without presence of capacious incisive fossa; alveolar margins of maxillary canine and incisor sockets tend to lie in same coronal plane; palate deep posteriorly and anteriorly and steeply shelved in front of incisive foramina; incisors and canines relatively small compared with large sizes of molars and especially premolars; P3 tends to possess three roots; dm_1 "molarized" with anterior fovea centrally situated and walled by complete mesial marginal ridge; mandibular corpus laterally inflated.

Many of these traits, as well as other features that

distinguish the skull and dentition of *A. boisei*, appear to be related to the generation and distribution of powerful masticatory forces.

Endocranial capacity estimates for several *A. boisei* specimens range between ca. 500 and 550 ml. Few postcranial bones that can be attributed with confidence to *A. boisei* are known; indeed, in only one instance have postcranial elements been found in reasonable association with *A. boisei* cranial remains. Those bones referred to *A. boisei*, however, suggest that its postcranial skeleton was robustly constructed and that the forelimb was relatively long compared with the hindlimb. Femora attributed to this species possess small heads and relatively long, anteroposteriorly flattened necks. *A. boisei* body size is generally held to have been greater than that of *A. robustus*, with estimates ranging from less than 30 to greater than 100 kg. Stature estimates have suggested values of ca. 148–168 cm. The body weight and stature estimates published to date, however, are tenuous, being based upon incomplete and referred long bones. Thus we still have little idea of how robust these "hyper-robust" australopithecines actually were.

See also AUSTRALOPITHECUS; AUSTRALOPITHECUS ROBUSTUS; CHESOWANJA; EAST TURKANA; ETHIOPIA; KENYA; LEAKEY, LOUIS; LEAKEY, MARY; OLDUVAI; OMO; PARANTHROPUS; PENINJ. [F.E.G.]

Further Readings

Howell, F.C. (1978) Hominidae. In V.J. Maglio and H.B.S. Cooke (eds.): Evolution of African Mammals. Cambridge, Mass.: Harvard University Press, pp. 154–248.

Rak, Y. (1983) The Australopithecine Face. New York: Academic.

Tobias, P.V. (1967) The cranium and maxillary dentition of *Australopithecus (Zinjanthropus) boisei*. In L.S.B. Leakey (ed.): Olduvai Gorge, Vol. 2. Cambridge: Cambridge University Press.

Walker, A.C., Leakey, R.E.F., Harris, J.M., and Brown, F.H. (1986) 2.5-Myr *Australopithecus boisei* from west of Lake Turkana, Kenya. Nature 322:517–522.

AUSTRALOPITHECUS ROBUSTUS

Taxonomic name commonly used in reference to the "robust" australopithecine fossils from the South African sites of Kromdraai and Swartkrans.

The first of these specimens was discovered at Kromdraai in 1938. The fossil, consisting of the left half of a cranium, a right mandibular corpus, and several teeth, was obtained by R. Broom and described by him that same year. Broom noted that the face of the Kromdraai hominid was flat, that the incisors and canines were small, and that the premolars and molars differed in their morphology and larger size from the Sterkfontein specimens of *Australopithecus*. He considered that the differences between the Kromdraai and Sterkfontein fossils war-

ranted their generic separation and made the Kromdraai specimen the type of a new taxon, *Paranthropus robustus*. A decade later the first australopithecine fossil was recovered from the site of Swartkrans, several kilometers from Kromdraai along the Blaubank River. Broom observed that the mandibular corpus of the Swartkrans specimen was similar in its robusticity to that from Kromdraai and that the teeth were morphologically similar to but larger than those known from Kromdraai. He considered that the Swartkrans and Kromdraai fossils were attributable to the same genus, *Paranthropus*, but that the subtle differences between them warranted their specific separation. Broom thus attributed the Swartkrans specimen to the novel species *P. crassidens*.

Several years later, on the basis of his study of larger samples of australopithecine fossils from the sites of Swartkrans, Kromdraai, and the other Plio-Pleistocene cave deposits in South Africa, J.T. Robinson argued that a single species, *Australopithecus africanus*, was represented by the specimens from Taung, Sterkfontein, and Makapansgat and that the Kromdraai and Swartkrans fossils could be accommodated in the hypodigm of a single species, *Paranthropus robustus*. Robinson noted, however, that the Kromdraai and Swartkrans fossils differed from one another in subtle dental features, and he suggested that these forms could be regarded as two subspecies (*P. robustus robustus* and *P. robustus crassidens*) that were "separated by a time interval."

Subsequent studies of the South African australopithecine remains by a number of workers who sought to demonstrate the fundamental similarities among these fossils have questioned the generic distinctiveness of *Paranthropus*. These studies have so influenced opinion that at present most students of hominid evolution regard *Paranthropus* as a junior synonym of *Australopithecus*. Nevertheless, there appears to be a general (although not universal) consensus that the Kromdraai and Swartkrans forms represent a distinct species, *A. robustus*. Some workers, like C. Loring Brace and M.H. Wolpoff, have even argued that all of the South African hominids are representative of a single species and that the differences between the samples attributed to *A. africanus* and *A. robustus* are related primarily to differences in body size or to sexual dimorphism.

An overwhelming body of evidence supplied by numerous workers, however, indicates that the specimens of *A. africanus* and *A. robustus* differ in a host of morphological and metrical features that probably reflect significant functional differences between them. A substantial suite of features characterize *A. robustus*, and although many of these are evinced also by *A. boisei*, and although some are shown by

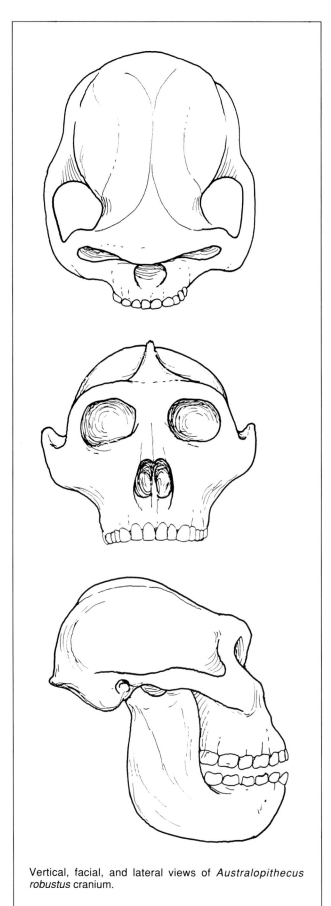

Vertical, facial, and lateral views of *Australopithecus robustus* cranium.

certain other early hominid taxa (e.g. *Homo*), *A. robustus* is unique among these other taxa in possessing these traits in combination.

Among the features that characterize *A. robustus*: cranium robustly constructed with ectocranial superstructures; cranium shows substantial pneumatization with marked lateral inflation of mastoid region; males with sagittal crest but lacking confluence of posteroinferior temporal and superior nuchal lines; temporal lines posteriorly divergent above lambda; mastoid process not notably inflected and tip lies medial to lateral margin of elongate and concave tympanic; marked angulation of petrous axis to sagittal plane resulting in high petromedian angle; tendency for occipital-marginal sinus to be enlarged relative to transverse sinus; calvaria hafted to facial skeleton at low level resulting in low supraorbital height index; forehead low and slightly concave with frontal trigone delimited laterally by posteriorly convergent temporal crests; strong postorbital constriction; supraorbital torus strong and horizontally disposed with flattened "rib" of bone across supraorbital margin and lacking twist between medial and lateral components; glabella prominent and situated below level of supraorbital margin; nasion and glabella nearly coincident as result of low glabella and tendency for internasal suture to project higher than nasofrontale; bony face of moderate height and orthognathous; piriform aperture set in central facial hollow; nasoalveolar clivus passes smoothly into floor of nasal cavity without strong demarcation; incisive canals open into horizontal surface of nasal floor without presence of capacious incisive fossa; alveolar margins of maxillary canine and incisor sockets tend to lie in same coronal plane; palate deep posteriorly and shallow anteriorly; incisors and canines relatively small compared with large sizes of premolars and molars; P3 tends to possess three roots; dm_1 "molarized" with anterior fovea centrally situated and walled by complete mesial marginal ridge; mandibular corpus laterally inflated.

Many of these traits, as well as other features that distinguish the skull and dentition of *A. robustus*, appear to be related to the generation and distribution of powerful masticatory forces. Analyses of gross and microscopic details of occlusal wear on the molar teeth indicate that the diets of *A. africanus* and *A. robustus* differed qualitatively and that the diet of *A. robustus* consisted of substantial amounts of hard items.

Endocranial capacity estimates for *A. robustus* are on the order of 450–550 ml., which tend to be slightly larger than those for *A. africanus*, but the paucity of *A. robustus* specimens leaves these estimates open to question. Few postcranial bones that can be reasonably attributed to *A. robustus* are known, and those elements that have been referred to *A. robustus* appear to be morphologically similar to *A. africanus* homologues. The femora of *A. robustus*, for example, possess small heads and relatively long, anteroposteriorly flattened necks. *Australopithecus robustus* body size is generally held to have been greater than that of *A. africanus*, with published estimates ranging from ca. 40 to more than 90 kg. These estimates, however, have been based upon questionable criteria, and, surprising as it may seem, we still have little idea of how robust these "robust" australopithecines actually were.

The specimens from Swartkrans probably date to between ca. 1.8 and 1.5 m.y.; while the geochronological age of the Kromdraai hominid fossils is wholly unresolved, the majority opinion would place them at somewhat less than 1.5 m.y. At the same time, however, the Kromdraai specimens appear to be more primitive than those from Swartkrans, and the differences between them have led some workers, like F.C. Howell and F.E. Grine, to suggest that they should be accorded separate specific status.

See also AUSTRALOPITHECUS; AUSTRALOPITHECUS AFRICANUS; AUSTRALOPITHECUS BOISEI; KROMDRAAI; PARANTHROPUS; SWARTKRANS. [F.E.G.]

Further Readings

Grine, F.E. (1981) Trophic differences between "gracile" and "robust" australopithecines: a scanning electron microscope analysis of occlusal events. S. Afr. J. Sci. 77:203–230.

Howell, F.C. (1978) Hominidae. In V.J. Maglio and H.B.S. Cooke (eds.): Evolution of African Mammals. Cambridge, Mass.: Harvard University Press, pp. 154–248.

Rak, Y. (1983) The Australopithecine Face. New York: Academic.

Robinson, J.T. (1954) The genera and species of the Australopithecinae. Am. J. Phys. Anthropol. 12:181–200.

Wofpoff, M.H. (1974) The evidence for two australopithecine lineages in South Africa. Yrbk. Phys. Anthropol. 17:113–139.

AUTAPOMORPHIC *see* CLADISTICS

AVAHI *see* INDRIIDAE

AVAILABLE *see* CLASSIFICATION; NOMENCLATURE

AVDEEVO *see* KOSTENKI; MOLODOVA

AWL

Pointed boring tool made out of stone (sometimes called a *perçoir*, perforator or borer) or bone, probably used for making holes in skins, wood, bone, antler, or other materials. Stone awls are found throughout

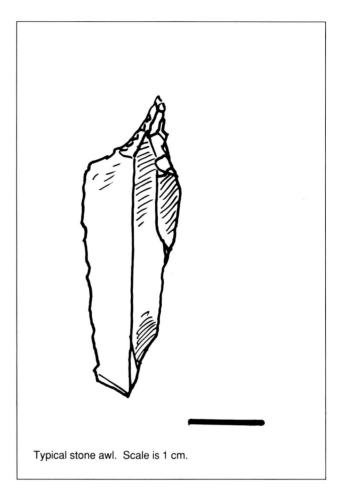

Typical stone awl. Scale is 1 cm.

the Stone Age, becoming more common and more standardized in shape in tool assemblages in the Mousterian and Late Paleolithic.

See also CLOTHING; LATE PALEOLITHIC; MOUSTERIAN. [N.T., K.S.]

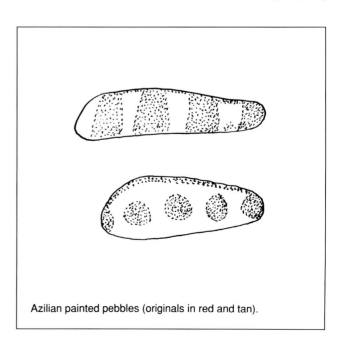

Azilian painted pebbles (originals in red and tan).

AZILIAN

First industrial stage in the classic Mesolithic/Epipaleolithic sequence of inland France, dated between 11,500 and 9500 B.P. Named after the type site of Mas d'Azil (Ariège) in the Pyrenees region, the industry is characterized by a large number of small, rounded thumbnail scrapers and "Azilian" points, created by an arc of semiabrupt retouch defining the margin of a medium- to small-sized blade. In contrast to the rich and varied aesthetic expressions associated with Upper Paleolithic industries of the region, schematic designs on pebbles are typical of Azilian sites.

See also ECONOMY, PREHISTORIC; EPIPALEOLITHIC; MESOLITHIC; PALEOLITHIC IMAGE; SAUVETERRIAN; STONE-TOOL MAKING; TARDENOISIAN. [A.S.B.]

AZYCH *see* ARCHAIC HOMO SAPIENS

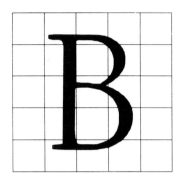

BABOON *see* MONKEY

BACHO KIRO

Stratified cave site in the Balkan Mountains of Bulgaria with three Mousterian and ten Upper Paleolithic layers. Layers 14 through 12 contained lithic inventories assigned to the Charentian and Typical Mousterian. Two fragments of bone from Layer 12 appear to have been intentionally engraved. The Late Paleolithic layers contain numerous faunal remains of both herbivores and carnivores; blade-tool assemblages predominantly fashioned of nonlocal flint, basalt, and quartzite; bone tools, including bone points; and bone jewelry. Remains of hearths have been found in these layers as well. A series of radiocarbon dates for the different layers indicate that Late Paleolithic inventories from Layer 11, dated to over 43,000 B.P. (and perhaps as old as 60–45 k.y. B.P.), represent the earliest Late Paleolithic remains in Europe. Assemblages from Layers 11 on have been classified as Bachokirian, a regional variant of the Aurignacian. Hominid remains from the Late Paleolithic layers, consisting of fragments of a neurocranium, two mandibles with teeth, and five single teeth, bear some primitive characteristics and may represent somewhat archaic modern humans or possibly forms transitional between the Neanderthals and fully modern *Homo sapiens*.

See also AURIGNACIAN; EUROPE; ISTALLÖSKÖ; LATE PALEOLITHIC; NEANDERTHALS; UPPER PALEOLITHIC. [O.S.]

BADEGOULIAN

Early Magdalenian-like industry of central France, ca. 16,000 B.P., with a distribution from the Perigord east to the Auvergne and north to the Paris basin. Sometimes referred to as Magdalenian "O" and "I," it differs from the classic Magdalenian in its emphasis on blades and burins, especially transverse burins on notches, presence of *raclettes*, rarity or absence of backed bladelets, and in the simplicity of its bone industry reflected in a small number of simple beveled bone spear points.

See also BLADE; BURIN; HARPOON; MAGDALENIAN; PÉRIGORD; SAGAIE; STONE-TOOL MAKING; UPPER PALEOLITHIC. [A.S.B.]

BAMBATA

African Middle Stone Age industry of Zimbabwe and Botswana (probable age ca. 100–40 k.y.), named after the Bambata Cave site in the Matopos Hills south of Bulawayo. The Bambata differs from the Stillbay, Pietersburg, Orangian, and other Middle Stone Age industries to the south in the relative rarity of blades, burins, perforators, end-scrapers, and backed knives. Characteristic forms include discoidal cores and small unifacial and bifacial points and side-scrapers. Other major sites, all near Bulawayo, include Pomongwe and Tshangula caves and the Khami waterworks open site. The industry appears to extend as far as ≠Gi in the northwestern Kalahari Desert of Botswana.

See also HOWIESON'S POORT; LEVALLOIS; MIDDLE STONE AGE; ORANGIAN; PIETERSBURG; STILLBAY; STONE-TOOL MAKING. [A.S.B.]

BAN DON MUN   see   ASIA

BARADOSTIAN

Late Paleolithic blade and burin industry defined by Solecki on the basis of Layer C at Shanidar Cave on Mount Baradost (Iraq), dated 34,000–29,000 B.P. by radiocarbon. Also found in western Iran, the industry differs from the Aurignacian in its high percentage of burins, some with a distinctive "nosed" profile, and in the lessened emphasis on carinate and nose-ended scrapers and "busked" burins.

See also AURIGNACIAN; BLADE; BURIN; LATE PALEOLITHIC; SHANIDAR; STONE-TOOL MAKING. [A.S.B.]

BARINGO

Lake, ca. 20 km. in length, situated in the Rift Valley of northern Kenya, just north of the equator. In the landscape around it are sedimentary rocks that contain fossils of plants and animals, including hominoids. The main importance of this area for human evolution lies in the age of these fossils. They range from older than 14 m.y. to the Holocene. Within this time range some of the sites document the period from 12 to 4 m.y., which is otherwise poorly represented in sub-Saharan Africa. It was during this time that the Ethiopian fauna evolved and became established and humans evolved from the line leading to the modern African apes.

The region has had a relatively long history of investigation. The type area of the Kamasian pluvial, it also was the source of the first pre–*Homo sapiens* hominid to be found in Kenya, at Lothagam. Some sites that can be regarded as falling in this region,

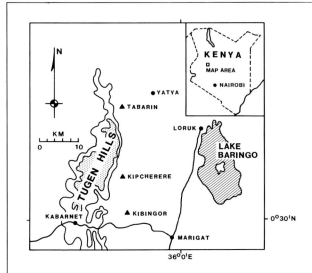

Map of the Baringo area showing the location of the Tugen Hills and the hominid-fossil locality of Tabarin.

such as Karmosit and Aterir, are isolated occurrences in the north. Others, like Alengerr and Chesowanja, are to the east. Chesowanja is important for having produced specimens of "robust" australopithecines, including a partial cranium, along with a related sequence of artifacts. Most of the Baringo sites, however, are found on the west of the lake as part of the succession of rocks forming the Tugen Hills.

Tugen Hills Stratigraphy and Dating

The Tugen Hills, sometimes known as the Kamasia Range, extend ca. 75 km. north-south along the rift on the west of Lake Baringo. This is a complicated region geologically, formed by a faulted horst block, tilted to the west and exposing ca. 3,000 m. of rock in the scarps and foothills facing toward the lake. The hills are diversified by both large-scale and small-scale faulting, which makes the elucidation of stratigraphy and correlation between separate areas difficult. Despite this the sediments can be placed in six main fossiliferous formations. From oldest to youngest these are the Muruyur Beds, Ngorora Formation, Mpesida Beds, and the Lukeino, Chemeron, and Kapthurin Formations. They are mostly separated from one another by volcanic rocks. This, along with the occurrence of tuffaceous horizons within the sedimentary units themselves, permits radiometric dating, which with paleomagnetic stratigraphy through the sedimentary sequence has led to fine-grained calibration.

The oldest fossiliferous unit is the Muruyur Beds. Older than 13 m.y., they are as yet little known, although a diverse fauna comes from a number of Muruyur sites. Above these is the more extensive Ngorora Formation, which has been shown to extend from 13 m.y. to younger than 9 m.y. in a fairly unbroken sequence. This is a long period for continental sediments in Africa. Most Ngorora fossil sites in this area are probably between 12.4 and 11 m.y., but some elsewhere in separate outcrops are most probably younger. Within a lava above the Ngorora Formation are some fossiliferous outcrops of the Mpesida Beds, dated at ca. 6.5 m.y. Above this is the more persistent Lukeino Formation, in which are a number of sites dated at ca. 6 m.y. Overlying the Lukeino is the Chemeron Formation. Many sites in this unit are about the same age, near 5 m.y. Some Chemeron sites in the type area, however, are certainly much younger than this, probably 3 m.y. younger. There is little evidence for sediments of intervening age. Above the Chemeron Formation are the Kapthurin Beds, an extensive blanket of sediments close to Lake Baringo that also contain important fossil sites.

In addition to fauna there is also botanical evidence from the succession. This includes an extensive macroflora indicating forest conditions at 12.2 m.y. Significant changes in fauna can be detected throughout the sequence. Change can be seen within the Ngorora Formation, but the most noticeable faunal shift comes between the top of the Ngorora and the Mpesida Beds, a suggestion reinforced by the overlying and better-sampled Lukeino Formation. This sees the establishment of an essentially modern Ethiopian fauna, a change from the Miocene character of the fauna from older sites. This change, however, need not have happened suddenly, nor synchronously in all lineages.

Tugen Hills Hominoids

Fossils of large hominoids have been found at several levels in the Tugen Hills sequence. The earliest is a fragmentary astragalus from the Muruyur Beds, older than 13 m.y. It is similar to those of *Proconsul major*. In the Ngorora Formation are a number of hominoid specimens, unfortunately all isolated teeth. One is a second premolar, also reminiscent of *Proconsul*.

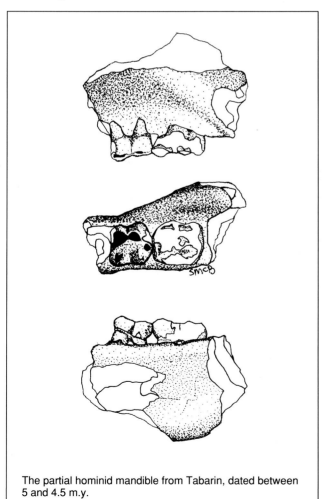

The partial hominid mandible from Tabarin, dated between 5 and 4.5 m.y.

Another specimen is an upper molar, difficult to assign to any known taxon. Neither of these specimens is as yet well dated, but both are probably ca. 11 m.y. old. Yet another isolated hominoid molar occurs at a site in the Lukeino Formation, at ca. 6 m.y. Again this does not unequivocally resemble any species so far known, but it could have belonged to a hominid. It is currently impossible to say, but if it is hominid then it would be the earliest so far known.

Three hominoid specimens come from the Chemeron Formation, all of them most probably hominids. Two of them derive from the older outcrops allocated to the Chemeron, and are no doubt about the same age, between 5 and 4.5 m.y. One of these, found at the site of Tabarin, is one of the earliest convincing hominids; only the specimen from Lothagam near Lake Turkana might be a little older. It is a piece of right mandible with first and second molars intact. In its dental features and details of subocclusal and mandibular morphology it closely resembles smaller specimens of *Australopithecus afarensis*, and it can be distinguished from all other known hominoid taxa. Another possible hominid fossil was found at a site some kilometers to the north of Tabarin. This is a proximal fragment of a humerus. Although it cannot be certainly distinguished morphologically as belonging to a hominid rather than to some other hominoid, it, too, closely resembles the humerus of *A. afarensis*. It is therefore possible, even likely, that it belongs to the same species as the Tabarin specimen. The third hominoid from the Chemeron Formation is much younger than these other occurrences, probably just in excess of 2 m.y. It is a temporal bone, showing some interesting features, that comes from a site in the Kapthurin River, not far from Lake Baringo itself. Additional sites in the Kapthurin River section, but in the younger Kapthurin Beds, have produced two hominid mandibles, and four postcranial bones.

See also AUSTRALOPITHECUS AFARENSIS; AUSTRALOPITHECUS BOISEI; CHESOWANJA; KAPTHURIN; KENYA; LOTHAGAM; MIOCENE; PALEOMAGNETISM; PLEISTOCENE; PLIOCENE; PROCONSUL; RADIOMETRIC DATING; RIFT VALLEY. [A.H.]

Further Readings

Hill, A., Curtis, G., and Drake, R. (1986) Sedimentary stratigraphy of the Tugen Hills, Baringo, Kenya. In L.E. Frostick et al. (eds.): Sedimentation in the African Rifts. Oxford: Blackwell, pp. 285–295.

Hill, A., Drake, R., Tauxe, L., Monaghan, M., Barry, J. C., Behrensmeyer, A.K., Curtis, G., Jacobs, B.F., Jacobs, L., Johnson, N., and Pilbeam, D. (1985) Neogene paleontology and geochronology of the Baringo Basin, Kenya. J. Hum. Evol. *14*:759–773.

Ward, S., and Hill, A. (1987) Pliocene hominid partial mandible from Tabarin, Baringo, Kenya. Am. J. Phys. Anthropol. 72:21–37.

BARRIERS *see* PALEOBIOGEOGRAPHY

BATON DE COMMANDEMENT

Characteristic artifact form of the Upper Paleolithic, especially the Magdalenian phase, made from antler (usually reindeer). It is usually perforated near the juncture of the main body and the two major branches of the antler. The function of these artifacts is not clear; suggestions have included spear-shaft straighteners, and thong softeners, as well as magical or symbolic devices (such as a sign of authority, thus the name).

See also MAGDALENIAN; SPEAR; UPPER PALEOLITHIC. [N.T., K.S]

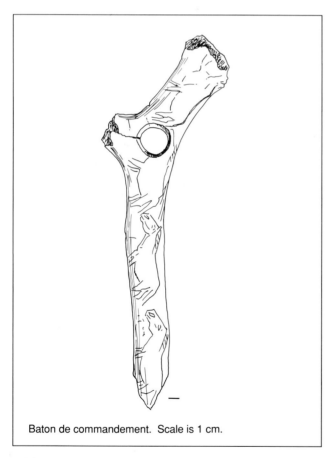

Baton de commandement. Scale is 1 cm.

BED *see* STRATIGRAPHY

BERGMANN'S RULE *see* RULES

BERINGIA *see* AMERICAS; PALEOBIOGEOGRAPHY; PALEOINDIAN

BERING LAND BRIDGE *see* AMERICAS; PALEOBIOGEOGRAPHY; PALEOINDIAN

BERRUVIUS *see* PAROMOMYIDAE

BIACHE

Site in northwestern France discovered during commercial excavations in a river terrace. Hominid occupation occurred during relatively warm phases at a time of climatic fluctuation, probably during the penultimate ("Saalian" or "Rissian") glaciation. Archaeological material from the site consists mainly of flint-flake tools rather than bifaces, and there are a number of Mousterian tool types. The Biache hominid consists of the back part of a skull and parts of the upper jaw and dentition; it is probable that the

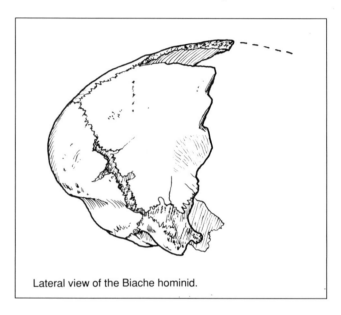

Lateral view of the Biache hominid.

whole skull was fossilized, but the remaining parts were not recovered. The partial vault is thin but is derived from a subadult individual. Brain size was quite small, with an indicated capacity of ca. 1,200 ml. The overall cranial form is decidedly Neanderthal-like, with a spherical shape when viewed from behind and an occipital chignon, very reminiscent of the form of the later La Quina Neanderthal skull. In addition there is a prominent occipitomastoid crest and a suprainiac fossa. There is little doubt that the specimen represents a member of an early Neanderthal population, and it also provides a morphological link between earlier specimens, such as Swanscombe, and the later Neanderthals.

See also ARCHAIC HOMO SAPIENS; NEANDERTHALS. [C.B.S]

BIBERSON, PIERRE (b. 1909)

French geologist and archaeologist. Biberson's main contribution was a long series of papers, published during the 1950s and 60s, relating stone-tool cultures to climate and sea-level changes in the North African

Pleistocene. In 1954, at Sidi Abderrahman, near Casablanca (Morocco), Biberson discovered fragments of an adult hominid mandible in a stratum dated as late middle Pleistocene. In 1955 these fragments were described by Arambourg, who concluded that they belonged to a form of hominid closely related to the Tighenif *Homo erectus*. Biberson also described the stone tools recovered from the quarry at Sidi Abderrahman, belonging to the so-called Moroccan Pebble Culture.

See also ARAMBOURG, CAMILLE; TIGHENIF. [F.S.]

BIBLICAL ARCHAEOLOGY *see* ARCHAEOLOGY

BIFACE

Strictly speaking, an artifact that is flaked on two different faces (surfaces) of a piece of stone, such as bifacial choppers, handaxes, or projectile points. The term is often used to describe the large Acheulean artifacts of the handaxe/pick/cleaver/knife variety. This can be something of a misnomer though, since in some typological systems unifacial picks or handaxes still go into the "biface" category; at present, however, there is no other generic term for describing these large Acheulean forms.

See also CLEAVER; HANDAXE; STONE-TOOL MAKING. [N.T., K.S]

BIGFOOT *see* YETI

BIHARIAN *see* TIME SCALE

BILZINGSLEBEN

Travertine site in East Germany, known as a paleontological site for many years. Only since 1973, however, has its importance been recognized through large-scale and productive excavations. Abundant faunal and archaeological remains have been recovered in hominid occupation levels that apparently include extensive butchery debris and remains of hut structures. The site certainly dates from a middle Pleistocene interglacial (Holsteinian?), but absolute dates vary from ca. 230 k.y. to more than 350 k.y. The only hominid specimens recovered to date probably derive from a single skull dispersed by water. The main pieces are a fragment of strongly built browridge and an occipital bone that is small, thick, and angled, with a developed occipital torus. Cranial capacity was probably less than 1,200 ml., and the hominid has been classified as a new form of *Homo erectus—Homo erectus bilzingslebenensis*. Yet it is apparent that the hominid fragments also resemble other middle Pleistocene specimens from Europe that many regard as representing archaic *Homo sapiens*.

See also ARCHAIC HOMO SAPIENS; HOMO ERECTUS. [C.B.S.]

BINOMEN *see* CLASSIFICATION; NOMENCLATURE

BIOCHRONOLOGY

Geological dating in terms of biological history. As in all geochronological methods, it depends on the evidence of irreversible change in a natural system. In radiometric dating the evidence is the steady accumulation of decay products from unstable isotopes. In biochronology it is the progressive modification of plant and animal species by speciation and natural selection that indicates, but only roughly measures, the passage of time. The difference in accuracy lies in the fact that rates of radioactive decay are fixed and predictable to a much closer degree than are rates of evolutionary change. As a result biochronological dating establishes chronological order but not "absolute" age. For reasons discussed below, the precision of biochronology exceeds that of radiochronology as the age increases.

The basic unit of evolutionary change is the species, but taxa recognized at the genus level are also widely used in biochronology. It is obvious, and well known, that with regard to fossils of extinct forms species must be recognized almost solely according to morphology, omitting many criteria (behavior, ornamentation, histology, genetics) used by zoologists and botanists for extant forms. Without these cross-checks morphological differences can be hard to interpret; in paleoanthropology controversies about sexual dimorphism versus species differentiation illuminate this problem. Preserved hard-part morphology, however, can be used to distinguish higher taxonomic categories with much greater reliability even in sparse and incomplete material. For this reason, as well as for considerations of geographical range, fossil genera are the usual criteria in pancontinental mammalian biochronology.

Biostratigraphy and Biochronology

Interpretations of the fossil record follow one of two systems of logic: the stratigraphic and the historic. Stratigraphic analysis makes use of the so-called "law of superposition," the simple but powerful geological rule that states that in any depositional sequence the higher stratum, and anything in it, is younger than the lower. Fossils, observed in this sense, are simply features of the rocks whose distribution pattern can be used to differentiate and organize stratigraphic units. Their age is known in terms of their relative stratigraphic position, and while post-hoc explanations of their distribution patterns are interesting they are basically irrelevant. Biostratigraphy, as such, was successfully practiced by William Smith and other geologists long before Darwin.

Biochronological units, on the other hand, are based on explanation of the pattern. They first of all express the sequence of real events that lies behind the accidental and fragmentary sample preserved in the paleontological record, and, second, they express the orientation of these events in time according to the irreversible processes of evolution. Biochronology is ideally probabilistic, which is to say less sensitive to accidents of observation or preservation than a deterministic procedure like biostratigraphy; at the same time, by proposing to go beyond direct observation and to construct explanatory scenarios, biochronology is more vulnerable to preconception, careless thinking, and other error.

Real Time and Rock Time

Geology grew as a science without a means to measure time, and in fact few modern stratigraphers use geochronology of any kind routinely in their work. Then, as now, correlation in detailed and regional studies is based on *chronostratigraphy*, or rock-time units. As an example, a biostratigraphic observation, such as the lowest and highest occurrence of a designated fossil in a given rock sequence, may be used to define a volume of rock termed a *zone* or *biozone*. This same interval is also considered to represent the beginning and end of a period of time, the *chronozone*. The chronostratigraphic units age, epoch, and era correspond in this same way to physical subdivisions of rock sequences: the stage, system, and series, respectively. In all such units the quantity of time involved is unknown, but the interval is precisely established by reference to the strata.

While stage, epoch, and era terms, as well as magnetozones and some marine chronozones, are applied globally, the stratigraphic facies on which they are based, whether lithological, paleontological, or paleomagnetic, are physically discontinuous. Correlation of deterministic models (i.e. pattern fitting) breaks down across wide gaps, and stratigraphic data are subject to iterative confusion. Without other options geologists originally developed a global correlation expressed in chronostratigraphic units, but one that necessarily involved tacit redefinitions in every region. As the synthesis improves, it becomes clear that most long-distance correlations are geochronologic rather than chronostratigraphic, no matter

what units may be specified. Biochronology then is of greatest use in interregional studies, and biostratigraphy is more exact in local studies.

Confusion and Resolution

Biochronology has here been distinguished from radiochronology as being more relativistic than absolute, and from biostratigraphy as being more probabilistic than deterministic. Although weaker on both counts for detailed correlation, biochronology grows in importance where the scope of time or distance makes absolute, or exact, correlation methods more difficult to apply. In addition historical reconstructions often provide useful tests for all but the most trivial stratigraphic syntheses.

In terms of time measurement precision in radiometric dating is a percentage error and thus becomes greater, in years, with greater age. In published biochronological studies it is fair to say that the relative age of two vertebrate faunas can be established from paleontological reasoning alone if they are not less than 0.5 m.y. different in actual age, and this discrimination remains constant with increasing age. Thus by ca. 10 m.y. ago, or the later Miocene, radiometric dating with an overall precision error of 5 percent has an inherent uncertainty approximately the same (without considering the accuracy of applying the date to the fauna) as that of a biochronological estimate.

In terms of stratigraphic correlation, as discussed above, a historical event can never be defined exactly in stratigraphy any more than a given stratigraphic horizon (save perhaps those resulting from unusual volcanic eruptions) can be historically remarkable. Events are the defining criteria in histories and can be said to be precise in this context only. Biochronological examples are the evolution, or immigration, of a taxon, or its extinction, either locally or absolutely. In some instances the biochronological events are related closely to geological or paleoclimatological events that affect the biological environment generally, such as climate change, sea-level change, or land-bridge exposure. Logically it is clear that the actuality of any such event is separate from the stratigraphic evidence that it happened, but it requires conscious effort when the evidence is sharp and obvious, such as the sudden abundance of *Hipparion* in mid-Miocene faunas of Eurasia, to keep this distinction in mind. In the above case most workers have considered that the "Hipparion datum" is both a stratigraphic level and an immigration event.

Terminology

The basic unit of biochronology, the *biochron*, is defined in terms of biological events like those noted above. Many of the "virtual biochrons" in use originated in biostratigraphic studies and continue to refer to type sections and type associations, such as the North American Regional Land-Mammal Ages. The term *datum*, or *datum event*, refers to the evidence in stratigraphy for the existence of a biochronological event. (In stratigraphic studies a well-defined datum should be called a *horizon* or *level*.) No terms of greater scope encompass the biochron, but originally the Neogene and Paleogene were used in a sense that would be called biochronological today.

Biochronological systems for land-mammal history are now well developed, with reasonably complete radiometric calibration, for the Cenozoic of North America, South America, central and western Eurasia, and Africa. Marine planktonic microfossil zonations are essentially biochronozones and not biochrons, although there is considerable reference to datum events and general historical scenarios.

See also CENOZOIC; RADIOMETRIC DATING; TIME SCALE. [J.A.V.C]

Further Readings

Berggren, W.A., and Van Couvering, J.A. (1978) Biochronology. In G.V. Cohee et al. (eds.): Contributions to the Geological Time Scale. Tulsa: American Association of Petroleum Geologists, Stud. Geol., pp. 39–56.

Berggren, W.A., Kent, D.V., and Van Couvering, J.A. (1985) Neogene, Part 2. In N.J. Snelling (ed.): The Chronology of the Geological Record. London: Blackwoods.

Russell, D.E., and Savage, D.E. (1983) Mammalian Paleofaunas of the World. Reading, Mass.: Addison-Wesley.

BIOGEOGRAPHY see
PALEOBIOGEOGRAPHY

BIOLOGICAL ANTHROPOLOGY see
PHYSICAL ANTHROPOLOGY

BIOSTRATIGRAPHY see
BIOCHRONOLOGY; STRATIGRAPHY

BIPEDALISM see LOCOMOTION

BIPOLAR TECHNIQUE

Technique of stone working in which the core is placed on an anvil stone and struck from above with a stone percussor. By this technique flakes can be detached from either end of the core. These flakes tend to have thin or punctiform platforms and a subtle, flattened, or sheared bulb of percussion. The resultant core, sometimes called an *outil écaillé*, tends to be barrel-shaped in planform and rather thin, with

flakes usually removed from either end. This Paleolithic technique can be found from the Early Stone Age to modern times.

See also STONE-TOOL MAKING. [N.T., K.S.]

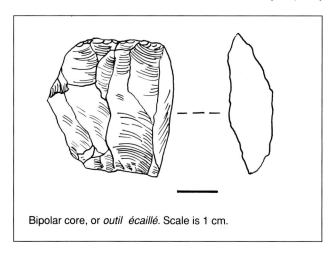

Bipolar core, or *outil écaillé*. Scale is 1 cm.

BISHOP, WILLIAM W. (1931–1977)

British geologist. Bishop was the leading authority on African Cenozoic geology, especially the fossil-bearing sediments of the East African Rift Valley. A member of the Uganda Geological Survey and director of both the Uganda Museum (1962–1965) and the Yale Peabody Museum (1976–1977), Bishop also held academic positions in British universities. From 1956 to 1971 he was co-organizer of the East African Geological Research Unit, which put British doctoral students in the field to work out the geology of Rift Valley strata. Bishop's students discovered many sites, including Chemeron, Chesowanja, Kapthurin, Lukeino, Ngorora, and Mpesida. His own work included valuable studies of fossils and stratigraphy at Kaiso, Moroto, Napak, Songhor, and Fort Ternan and the description of the Moroto "*Proconsul major*" (now allied with *Heliopithecus*).

[F.S.]

BLACK, DAVIDSON (1884–1934)

Canadian anatomist and paleoanthropologist. Black began his career as a lecturer at (Case) Western Reserve University in 1909. In 1918 he was appointed professor of anatomy at the Peking Union Medical College; later he was given added responsibility as director of the Cenozoic Laboratory, Geological Survey of China. While he long harbored an interest in paleoanthropology, as well as a conviction that Central Asia had been the homeland of the genus *Homo*, it was not until 1927 that Black's paleoanthropological career was finally launched. At this time a hominid lower molar was discovered at

Zhoukoudian, near Beijing. From this single tooth Black hypothesized the existence of a previously unknown hominid genus and species, which he thereupon called *Sinanthropus pekinensis*. Between 1929 and 1932 he supervised a spectacular series of fossil discoveries at this site that essentially confirmed his original diagnosis, although the material is no longer considered as a species separate from *Homo erectus*. Further discoveries at this site were made shortly after his death.

See also HOMO ERECTUS; WEIDENREICH, FRANZ; ZHOUKOUDIAN. [F.S.]

BLACK SKULL *see* AUSTRALOPITHECUS

BLACKWATER DRAW

Stratified Paleoindian locality on the Llano Estacado (New Mexico). The site contained a series of seep springs, which formed a large, deep pond. The sediments that ultimately filled the spring and associated channel have yielded a stratified, three-part succession of Paleoindian cultures. The basal grey-sand level contained elephant remains and Llano artifacts, including Clovis points, prismatic blades, and bone projectile point tips. A brown-sand level separated these Clovis materials from diagnostic Folsom artifacts contained in a diatomaceous earth zone. The overlying carbonaceous silts yielded Plano culture artifacts.

See also AMERICAS; CLOVIS; FOLSOM; LLANO COMPLEX; PALEOINDIAN; PLANO. [D.H.T.]

BLADE

Flake that is at least twice as long as it is wide, typically with straight, parallel sides and struck from a specially prepared blade core. Blade-tool (Mode IV) industries, especially characteristic of Late Paleolithic

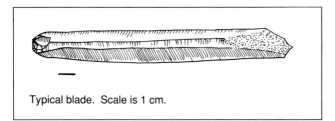

Typical blade. Scale is 1 cm.

and many later technologies, were often produced with a punch (indirect) percussion technique. Blades can be used without further modification or may serve as blanks for producing such tool forms as end-scrapers, burins, backed blades, and awls. In some areas, notably North America, the term *blade* has also been used for large, elongated bifacially flaked pro-

jectile points or knives, which has led to some confusion.

See also AWL; BURIN; LATE PALEOLITHIC; PREPARED-CORE; SCRAPER; STONE-TOOL MAKING. [N.T., K.S.]

BODO

Central Ethiopian stratified sequence dated from 4.5 to ca. 0.2 m.y. by K-Ar and fission-track dating combined with faunal analysis. Sediments of middle Pleistocene, early Pleistocene, and early Pliocene age exposed in the Middle Awash region of the Afar Depression have been named the Upper, Middle, and Lower Bodo Beds, respectively. Neither the Middle nor Lower Bodo Beds have yielded hominid remains. They have, however, both yielded abundant vertebrate fossils, and Oldowan tools have been recovered from the Middle Bodo Beds.

The Upper Bodo Beds contain abundant faunal remains in paleontological and archaeological contexts. The archaeological material belongs to the Acheulean industrial complex, but there are also small-tool occurrences that resemble the "Developed Oldowan." Possible traces of fire associated with some of the archaeological occurrences have also been reported.

In 1976 a massive, adult, presumably male specimen with large face and thick cranial vault was

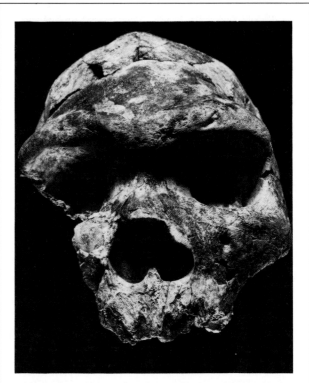

Facial view of the "Bodo man" fossil from middle Pleistocene deposits in the Middle Awash Valley (Ethiopia). (Photograph by and courtesy of Tim. D. White.)

recovered from the Upper Bodo Beds by a team headed by J. Kalb. It was a surface find, not clearly associated with the abundant Acheulean tools in the sandy gravel bed on which it lay. This find bears striking resemblances to the Kabwe (Broken Hill) specimen from Zambia and to the Petralona specimen from Greece. It has been attributed variously to advanced *Homo erectus* or to archaic *Homo sapiens*. Most agree that the specimen is a morphological intermediate between these two taxa. A second fossil, a fragment of parietal, was found in 1981 at Bodo, ca. 400 m. from the original find. This fossil represents a second adult individual.

The Bodo specimen bears fine striations on the face, on the vault, and within the orbit. These have been interpreted as cutmarks indicating an intentional defleshing by another hominid wielding a stone tool.

See also AFAR; ARCHAIC HOMO SAPIENS; MIDDLE AWASH. [T.D.W.]

Further Readings

Clark, J.D., Asfaw, B., Assefa, G., Harris, J.W.K., Kurashina, H., Walter, R.C., White, T.D., and Williams, M.A.J. (1984) Palaeoanthropological discoveries in the Middle Awash Valley, Ethiopia. Nature 307:423–428.

Conroy, G.C., Jolly, C.J., Cramer, D., and Kalb, J.E. (1978) Newly discovered fossil hominid skull from the Afar Depression, Ethiopia. Nature 275:67–70.

White, T.D. (1986) Cutmarks on the Bodo cranium: a case of prehistoric defleshing. Am. J. Phys. Anthropol. 69:503–509.

BOISEI, AUSTRALOPITHECUS *see* AUSTRALOPITHECUS BOISEI; PARANTHROPUS

BOLAS *see* STONE-TOOL MAKING

BØLLING *see* GLACIATION; PLEISTOCENE

BOLT'S FARM *see* SOUTH AFRICA

BONE *see* BONE BIOLOGY; FOSSIL; TAPHONOMY

BONE BIOLOGY

The study of human evolution depends heavily on comparisons of bones and teeth, the hard tissues most commonly preserved as fossils. Traditionally such comparisons have analyzed variation in the size and shape of anatomical structures in order to reconstruct past lifeways and evolutionary change.

Another approach to the study of hard tissues emphasizes the cellular processes by which a bone is formed and remodeled rather than the resultant form itself. The following discussion summarizes what is known about these processes in human bone.

Bone Behavior

Three types of cells are involved in the creation of a bone: osteoblasts, osteocytes, and osteoclasts. *Osteoblasts* secrete collagen around themselves, which is then hardened or mineralized with calcium salts to form bone tissue. When these cells become imprisoned by their own product, they are referred to as *osteocytes*. Although relative to osteoblastic activity, osteocytes are considered to be inactive; osteocytic processes are linked to form an intricate network of living tissue throughout the hard extracellular matrix. It is likely that these cells can tap the reservoir of calcium and phosphates stored as bone tissue, when levels in the bloodstream are deficient. When major amounts of bone must be broken down to accommodate other body functions, such as muscle and nerve activity, or to remodel existing structures, *osteoclasts* are called into action. These macrophagelike cells digest or reabsorb bone and return its constituent parts to the bloodstream for reuse or for excretion.

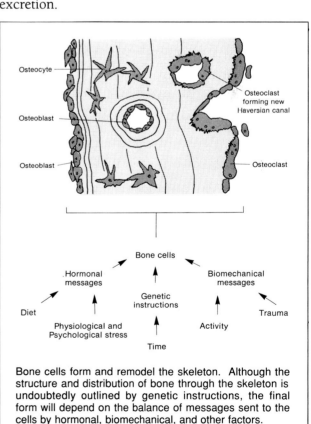

Bone cells form and remodel the skeleton. Although the structure and distribution of bone through the skeleton is undoubtedly outlined by genetic instructions, the final form will depend on the balance of messages sent to the cells by hormonal, biomechanical, and other factors.

The two processes, bone resorption and deposition, by their degree, distribution, and adequacy are responsible for the form and composition of the skeleton. It is clear from species-specific bony structures that these processes are guided by genetic instructions. It is equally clear from studies of bone physiology, however, that these processes respond quite readily to environmental conditions. Environmental circumstances are conveyed to the cell via at least two channels of communications: through hormonal messages that are themselves a response to circulating levels of calcium and phosphates in the bloodstream and through the generation and movement of the electrical charge that occurs when bone tissue is biomechanically deformed. In the presence of disease local immune and repair responses may also influence the behavior of bone cells.

Bone as a Record of Life History

After a certain stage of embryological development cells taken from a particular bone will assume the overall form of that bone even when grown in culture or transplanted to another part of the body. This canalization, as well as species-specific patterns of overall growth and aging, indicates that genetic factors guide bone behavior. Yet the final size of a bone may well depend on dietary and hormonal environments, while details of form, such as the angle at which a joint surface is placed relative to the shaft of a long bone, are probably responsive to biomechanical use of the skeleton during growth. Consider,for example, the dramatic increase in stature in second-generation American immigrants and the bowed legs characteristic of children who ride horses.

The potential impact of environment on bone form and size during adulthood may be considerably less than during the growth period, perhaps amounting to small adjustments in bone density and muscle attachments. A susceptibility to environment may return in later life, as when loss of estrogen production in postmenopausal females is associated with a reduced ability to maintain bone. At this time in the life cycle dietary or biomechanical insults may result in pathological conditions rather than in adjustments in form.

In summary, bone structure and adequacy can be seen as a record of previous life-history events. That record results from interactions between an underlying genetic program of development and aging and the environmental stresses that occur throughout the life cycle.

Two Applications of Skeletal Biology

Two fields in particular have explored the implications of bone behavior for human evolution and adaptation. One of these, bioarchaeology, concerns itself primarily with the study of prehistoric cemetery populations. It has used a largely statistical approach to document environmental perturbations in processes of growth and development and to describe the biological success and health of prehistoric populations. A few studies in this field have alternatively emphasized traits whose expression may be largely canalized and thus useful as measures of genetic distance. Combined with archaeological data, genetic distance measures, signs of growth disruption, disease, and dietary inadequacies have revealed much about recent human adaptations.

Another area of research that may be called "experimental biomechanics" is exploring the plasticity of primate bone subjected to biomechanical stresses. This research follows Washburn's early experiments, which showed that without muscle activity bone is resorbed. It often includes the use of bone-histology techniques to monitor bone behavior after experimentation (muscle removal, dietary manipulation, implants). Physical anthropologists have tended to focus their research in this area toward practical orthopedic and orthodontic problems, working closely with medical and dental experts.

Skeletal Biology and Paleoanthropology

The cellular and tissue properties of fossil bones and teeth have become an important focus in paleoanthropology. Differences in the timing of growth, development, and aging, as well as in the impact of environmental insults on these processes, have been confined largely to examinations of teeth, including various markers of incremental growth and hypoplasias. However, the fossilized record of bone-cell behavior combined with more traditional functional anatomy also offers the paleoanthropologist new insights into prehistoric lifeways.

See also ARCHAEOLOGY; FORENSIC ANTHROPOLOGY; ONTOGENY; PALEOPATHOLOGY; SKELETON.[C.J.D.]

Further Readings

Frankel, V.H., and Nordin, M. (1980) Basic Biomechanics of the Skeletal System. Philadelphia: Lea and Febiger.

Shipman, P., Walker, A., and Bichell, D. (1985) The Human Skeleton. Cambridge, Mass.: Harvard University Press.

Wilson, F.C., ed. (1983) The Musculoskeletal System: Basic Processes and Disorders. Philadelphia: Lippincott.

BONOBO *see* APE; HOMININAE

BORDER CAVE

South African cave site that has produced four important fossil hominid specimens, found between 1940 and 1974. The Border Cave 1 partial skull was not found during controlled excavations but from

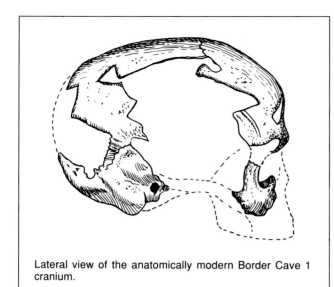

Lateral view of the anatomically modern Border Cave 1 cranium.

attached matrix is believed to derive from late Pleistocene deposits that also contained Border Cave 2 (a mandible), 3 (an infant burial), and 5 (a mandible). All the specimens are anatomically modern in morphology, and they do not display the robusticity found in other African early late Pleistocene fossils. The dating of the fossils is highly controversial, but the main researcher at the site believes that they all derive from levels below charcoal dated by radiocarbon at more than 49 k.y. Certainly the later discoveries were recovered from Middle Stone Age deposits, providing a parallel with the situation at the Klasies River Mouth caves, but some at least were burials that might have been intrusive from more recent levels, and this is supported by their relatively good preservation. Without better evidence of their exact age the significance of the Border Cave hominids remains uncertain. If they are more than 70 k.y. old, as claimed by some workers, they document the presence at that time in Africa of hominids indistinguishable in preserved parts from those alive today.

See also ARCHAIC MODERNS; HOMO SAPIENS. [C.B.S.]

BORDES, FRANÇOIS (1919–1981)

Noted French prehistorian who revolutionized European Early and Middle Paleolithic systematics in 1950 by creating a standard lithic typology consisting of 63 tool types. His excavations at the multilayered sites of Combe Grenal and Pech de l'Azé, Dordogne (France), revealed that some of these tool types regularly occur together. He interpreted these statistically patterned associations as reflecting the existence of four distinct tool kits (Denticulate, Typical, Mousterian of Acheulean Tradition, and Charentian with the Quina and Ferrassie subgroupings) and argued that they were made and used by different Mousterian tribes, each of whom had a distinct stone-tool-making tradition. This interpretation was subsequently challenged by scholars who argued that the variability that Bordes noted reflected not only stylistic differences but also functional and chronological ones and pointed out differences in the raw material used, as well as stages of the reduction sequences.

See also EUROPE; FRANCE; MIDDLE PALEOLITHIC; MOUSTERIAN; PÉRIGORD; DE SONNEVILLE-BORDES, DENISE. [O.S.]

BOREAL *see* GLACIATION; PLEISTOCENE

BORSCHEVO *see* KOSTENKI; MOLODOVA

BOULE, [PIERRE] MARCELLIN (1861–1942)

French paleontologist and geologist. For much of his career Boule occupied the chair of paleontology at the Muséum National d'Histoire Naturelle, Paris (1902–1936), and for many years was also director of the Institut de Paléontologie Humaine, Paris, established in 1914. He served as editor of *L'Anthropologie* from 1893 to 1940. Although he was originally trained as a geologist and paleontologist, and with important contributions to the geology of France to his credit, Boule's interest became increasingly focused on human paleontology. He is perhaps best remembered for his comprehensive study of the first complete Neanderthal skeleton, found at La Chapelle-aux-Saints (France) in 1908, and for his book *Les Hommes fossiles* (1912). Boule was an early supporter of the "presapiens theory," rejecting the proposition that the Neanderthals had been the precursors of modern humans.

See also LA CHAPELLE-AUX-SAINTS; NEANDERTHALS. [F.S.]

BOW AND ARROW

Important technological innovation characteristic of many Stone Age groups since the last glaciation, suggesting a shift from spear hunting to archery. The earliest direct evidence comes in the form of arrow shafts from Stellmoor (West Germany), ca. 10,500 B.P.; Mesolithic bows from Scandinavia; and a bowstave from Gwisho Springs (Zambia), ca. 3500 B.P., although small projectile points found in the Upper Paleolithic have been considered candidates for arrowheads by some prehistorians. Arrowheads could have been made of wood, bone, antler, or stone.

See also LATER STONE AGE; MESOLITHIC; STONE AGE; UPPER PALEOLITHIC. [N.T., K.S.]

BRACHIATION *see* LOCOMOTION

BRACHYTELES *see* ATELINAE

BRAIN

The human brain is the largest brain among primates but not the largest in either absolute or relative terms among the mammals. Accounting for ca. 2 percent of total body weight, the human brain consumes some 20 percent of our metabolic resources at any given time. By all estimates our brain is three times as large as would be expected for a primate of our body size, and that fact alone should suggest that our brain is an organ of exceptional importance related to our unique cultural and symbolic behavioral adaptations. The brain is not a homogeneous mass of jelly, however, but a composite of hundreds of nuclear masses and several more hundreds of interconnecting fiber tracts. Our uniqueness as a species depends on both the size of our brains and its organization. Trying to understand the evolutionary development of the human brain is a challenge, as we are left mostly with evidence regarding the size of our ancestors' brains but little about their organization or how they were used. Perhaps it is a tribute to our species that despite our grim problems of adapting to the world we alone in the animal kingdom can choose to study our own evolutionary development.

The brain is an extraordinarily complex organ. It has billions of parts, if one is simply talking about nerve cells, which are either basically firing or not and which can be excitatory or inhibitive. Thus there is a "digital" aspect to the functioning of so many components. Whether a nerve cell will fire, however, also depends on a summation process of thousands of inhibitory or facilitative connections with other nerve cells and the surrounding neuroglial cells. This is the "analogue" aspect to the brain. To make matters more complex the brain also has both "parallel" and "serial" organizations to its many components, so that information about the external and internal environments of the animal are evaluated both directly and indirectly. The brain is hierarchically organized, as between its most recent evolutionary-derived mantle, the grey cerebral cortex (*neopallium*), and the underlying basal ganglia, limbic system, and olfactory lobes that make up the *telencephalon*, or forebrain. This division surrounds the underlying *diencephalon*, the "between brain," which includes the thalamus, epithalamus, hypothalamus, and pineal gland or body. At a lower level there is the *mesencephalon*, or "midbrain," which is behaviorally a part of the brain stem, containing the *tectum* and *tegmentum*, consisting principally of the inferior and superior *colliculi*, which are auditory and visual in function, respectively. More ancient is the next level

of structures making up the *metencephalon* and *myelencephalon*, consisting of the cerebellum, pons, medulla, and third and fourth ventricles, which are integrated with the spinal cord.

While it is not strictly true that all parts of the brain are connected with each other, the combination of parallel and serial, crossed and uncrossed, fiber interconnections does mean that any complex volitional act involves most, if not all, of the brain working together. No one is certain how many "genes" control the development of the brain and its phenotypic expressions, but a rough estimate of 40,000 genes may in fact be conservative. This represents an enormous amount of potential genetic variability for natural selection to work upon. Many of these genes, however, must be very "conservative," for it is an awesome fact that despite all the variation in different animal species' behavioral repertoires (species-specific behavior) almost all mammals, if not vertebrates, have the same components in their brains. The human animal does not possess any "new" structures in its brain compared with most other mammals. What seems to have occurred during evolution is that certain parts of the brain have become enlarged relative to others; and in the mammals, particularly the higher primates, this has involved a dramatic increase in the cerebral cortex and the underlying thalamus, with which it has two-way connections. In the human animal the cerebral cortex accounts for roughly 76 percent of total brain weight, the highest ratio among primates.

Thus one of the major challenges facing any scientist trying to understand the evolution of the brain is how to account for a complex mixture of conservative and new genetic expression involved in all of the parts of the brain and how these relate to behavior, adaptation, and evolution. Much of our current scientific explanation focuses on brain size, as this is simple to measure. The more difficult task is to quantify the organization of the brain's components and relate this information to evolutionary histories and dynamics among species.

Lines of Evidence

Three lines of evidence exist for understanding the evolution of the human brain. The first is *direct*, derived from the study of endocasts, and is called *paleoneurology*. Data about the once-living brain are provided by either natural or human-made casts of the interiors of fossil crania. Such data include brain size (volume), convolutional details, traces of the meningeal vessels, and overall morphological patterns that include shape and asymmetries of the cerebral cortices. In life the brain is covered by three meningeal tissues that often prohibit the cortical gyri and sulci from being imprinted on the internal table of bone: the *pia mater*, the *arachnoid mater* (including cerebrospinal fluid), and the thick *dura mater*. It is extraordinarily rare, at least in higher primates, for the cortical convolutions to be fully preserved on endocasts, and thus the volume of the brain and possible asymmetries of the cortices constitute the most reliable evidence.

The second line of evidence is *indirect* and is provided by comparative *neuroanatomy*. This studies the brains of *living* animals, each an end product of its own line of evolutionary development. In this case quantitative studies are made of the brains of different primates, the neural nuclei and fibers of their brains as well as their brain sizes, and these data are correlated with variations in behavior. Within this line of study *allometry* is one of the most valuable tools of analysis.

A third line of evidence, even more indirect, is the study of the products once made by hominids, such as stone tools and different kinds of archaeological sites that preserve patterns of hominid behavior. In addition one can use the skeletal remains of hominids to understand their locomotor adaptations, such as bipedalism, or study bone fragments of the hands to appreciate manipulatory behavior. These provide only the most indirect clues, but major patterns of locomotor adaptation cannot evolve without some reorganization of the central nervous system controlling musculoskeletal patterns. All three lines of evidence should be used together in the attempt to enlarge our knowledge of human brain evolution, as none of them alone is sufficient for such understanding.

Paleoneurology, or the Study of Endocasts

The accompanying table provides a partial listing of the endocranial volumes determined for many of the earlier hominids and the methods used. The brain volume in our own modern species normally varies from ca. 1,000 to 2,000 ml., with an average volume of ca. 1,350 to 1,400 ml. No relationship has ever been shown between brain volume and behavior, aside from pathological cases, such as microcephaly or hydroencephaly, where behavior is often subnormal. Microcephaly is especially interesting, as there are recorded cases of human beings having brain volumes less than some pongids' but nevertheless using articulate language. This suggests that while brain size is important the organization of the brain's components is a significant contributing factor toward species-specific behavior.

This range of normal variation, without any known behavioral correlates, is about the same as the total evolutionary change in brain size from our earliest

hominid ancestors, *Australopithecus afarensis* (3 m.y. ago) to our own species, *Homo sapiens*. With the exception of the large-bodied robust australopithecines, which averaged ca. 525 ml. in brain volume, the earliest hominids, such as *A. afarensis* and *A. africanus*, had brain volumes ranging from 375 ml. to ca. 485 ml. When the genus *Homo* appears, currently dated at ca. 2–1.8 m.y. ago, the brain volume increases dramatically to ca. 750 ml., as represented by the KNM-ER 1470 *Homo habilis* specimen. At this time there is certain evidence for stone tools made to standardized patterns, hunting and scavaging behavioral activities, and archaeological sites suggesting complex social activities. The endocasts show three interesting developments: volume increase to ca. 750 ml. (and one supposes an increase in relative brain size), asymmetries of the cerebral cortex suggesting right-handedness, and a more complex humanlike pattern of the third inferior convolution, which includes the famous area of Broca, which helps to control the motor aspects of sound production. Unfortunately the posterior portion of the endocast, which contains Wernicke's region and is associated with receptive sound functions and intermodal associations, seldom if ever shows convolutional details that would permit one to conclude that these hominids possessed language. From the time of *Homo erectus* on (i.e. at least 1.6 m.y. ago), the endocasts of hominids do not show any primitive features, but rather a more or less constant growth in brain volume from ca. 800 ml. to our present average of ca. 1,400 ml. Neanderthals had slightly larger brains than modern humans, but this curious fact is perhaps explained as a part of an allometric relationship to lean body mass and perhaps cold-adaptation.

Evidence from Comparative Neuroanatomy

This line of indirect evidence is essential to our understanding of human brain evolution, a statement, incidentally, that could be made for any animal from aardvarks to zebras. While much is known about the naturalistic behavior of many species of animals, and each has a set of species-specific behavioral repertoires for adapting to its environment, the science of explaining species-specific behavior based on the structure and functioning of the brain is in its infancy. Consider the wide range of behavioral differences among the known primates, such as lemurs, tarsiers, New and Old World monkeys, the chimpanzee, gorilla, orangutan, and gibbon: none of these behavioral differences can yet be related to its respective brain organizations. Brain size, taken alone, has little explanatory power in this regard, yet it is obviously an important starting point. Indeed, considerable progress has been made through allo-

Table 1. Endocranial brain volumes of reconstructed hominids

Specimen	Taxon	Region	Endocranial Volume (ml.)	Method	Eval.
Taung	A. africanus	S.A.	440*	A	1
STS60	" "	"	428	A	1
STS71	" "	"	428	C	2–3
STS19/58	" "	"	436	B	2
STS5	" "	"	485	A	1
MLD37/38	" "	"	435	D	1
MLD1	" "	"	500–20	B	3
SK1585	A. robustus	"	530	A	1
OH5	"Z." boisei	E.A	530	A	1
ER406	" "	"	525	D	2
ER407	" "	"	510	A	1
ER732	" "	"	500	A	1
ER1805	Homo ?	"	582	A	1
ER1813	" "	"	510	A	1
ER1470	H. habilis	"	752	A	1
OH7	" "	"	687	B	2
OH13	" "	"	650	C	2
OH24	" "	"	590	A	2–3
OH9	H. erectus (?)	"	1067	A	1
ER3733	" " "	"	848	A	1
ER3883	" " "	"	804	A	1
HE1 (1892)	" "	Indo.	953	A	1
HE2 (1937)	" "	"	815	A	1
HE4 (1938)	" "	"	900	C	2–3
HE6 (1963)	" "	"	855	A	2
HE7 (1965)	" "	"	1059	C	1–2
HE8 (1969)	" "	"	1004	A	1
Solo I	" "	"	1172	A	1
Solo V	" "	"	1250	A	1
Solo VI	" "	"	1013	A	1
Solo X	" "	"	1231	A	1
Solo XI	" "	"	1090	A	1
Salé	" "	Moroc.	880	A	1
Spy I	H. sapiens (N)	Europ.	1553	A	1
Spy II	" " "	"	1305	A	1
La Chapelle	" " "	"	1625	X	1
La Ferassie I	" " "	"	1640	X	1
Neandertal	" " "	"	1525	X	2
La Quina	" " "	"	1350	X	1
Jebel Irhoud 1	" "	Moroc.	1305	A	1
AL 333-45	A. afarensis	Ethiop.	485**	C	2
AL 162-28	" "	"	375–400**	est.	2
AL 333-105	" "	"	310–320**	C	2

Some selected cranial capacities for different hominids. Method A) direct water displacement of either a full or hemi-endocast with minimal distortion and plasticene reconstruction; B) partial endocast determination as described by Tobias (1971); C) extensive plasticene reconstruction amounting to half of total endocast; D) determination from regression formulae. X refers to previously published values, confirmed by the author. Evaluation of 1 indicates highest reliability; 3 the lowest, depending on completeness of specimen, distortion, and author's techniques. An asterisk* refers to estimated adult volume from juvenile or child's endocast. A double**, confined to the Hadar (Ethiopia) *Australopithecus afarensis* materials, refers to provisional estimates based on current research of the author. The AL 333-105 endocast is severely distorted, mostly incomplete, and that of a young child.

Two additional endocasts, recently made by Dr. Alan Walker of the Johns Hopkins University, are not in the above table. Through personal communication Dr. Walker suggests that the cranial capacity of a newly discovered robust form of *Australopithecus*, dated at 2.6 m.y., from the western shore of Lake Turkana (Kenya), is 410 ml. (the specimen is a robust male). A recently discovered *Homo erectus* youth discovered at Lake Turkana has a cranial capacity of 900 ml., according to Dr. Walker.

metric studies that treat brain size as a dependent variable and in which relationships are then made to body weight, metabolism, gestation duration, longevity, and in some cases broad ecological domains relating to subsistence patterns, such as folivory, frugivory, omnivory, and predation. But the brain is a complex organ, consisting of many different neural cell masses and interconnecting fiber tracts, many of which are differentially susceptible to hormonal secretions and environmental stimuli. Within Mammalia it is a stark truism that all mammals have the same brain components: there are no "new" parts (nuclei or fiber systems) to distinguish among genera within orders, or among orders. Thus not only does brain size vary in animals, but so do the quantitative relationships among components of the brain and the

ontogenetic, developmental sequences of DNA-RNA interactions that specify the development of different brain regions and their underlying neurotransmitter substances. Humans are not the only animals that have asymmetrical brain regions: almost all animals have asymmetries to varying degrees, and some, like certain birds, have a seasonal sensitivity to increases and reductions of certain nuclei related to song patterns. In the human case, however, it is probably both the kind and the degree of cortical asymmetries that are distinctive.

As mentioned above, in our own species the brain accounts for approximately 2 percent of our total body weight but uses close to 20 percent of our metabolism at any given moment. It is a voracious organ. Thanks to more recent allometric studies it

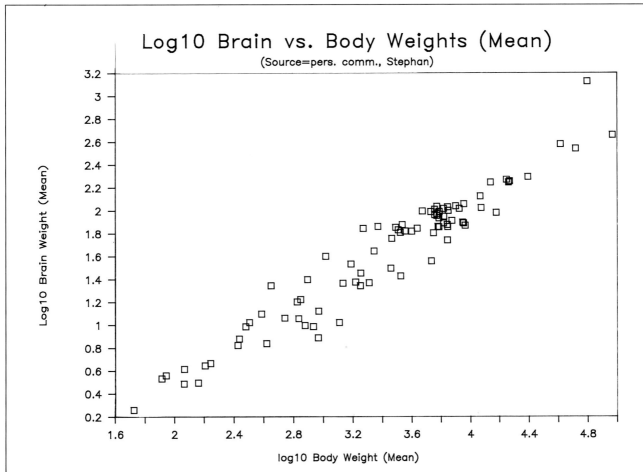

A log-log (base 10) plot of the mean brain and body weights for 85 species of primates, including our own species, *Homo sapiens*. The *Homo* value is in the extreme upper-right-hand corner of the figure. The closest three rectangles are the pongids, gorilla, chimpanzee, and orangutan. The correlation coefficient is about 0.97, without the *Homo* value, which is about three times higher than its predicted value based on body weight. The slope of the regression line, without the *Homo* value, is ca. 0.76, a number strongly suggestive of a metabolic constraint between body weight and the weight of the brain. It should be remembered that the points in this figure are for a large combination of prosimians, New and Old World monkeys, as well as the pongids and the human species. If the points are plotted *within* different taxonomic categories (i.e. prosimians alone, New World cebids alone, Old World monkeys, etc.), each group scales somewhat differently, with an average slope of ca. 0.66. This latter exponent suggests a geometric relationship between surface area and volume (i.e. the ratio 2/3). It is for this reason that encephalization quotients (E.Q.'s) are "relative," as each species value depends on the allometric equation used.

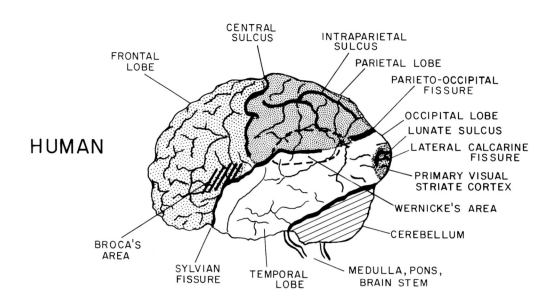

HUMAN

CENTRAL
SULCUS

INTRAPARIETAL
SULCUS

FRONTAL
LOBE

PARIETAL LOBE

PARIETO-OCCIPITAL
FISSURE

OCCIPITAL LOBE

LUNATE SULCUS

LATERAL CALCARINE
FISSURE

PRIMARY VISUAL
STRIATE CORTEX

WERNICKE'S AREA

CEREBELLUM

BROCA'S
AREA

SYLVIAN
FISSURE

TEMPORAL
LOBE

MEDULLA, PONS,
BRAIN STEM

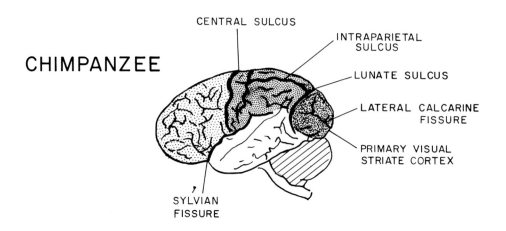

CHIMPANZEE

CENTRAL SULCUS

INTRAPARIETAL
SULCUS

LUNATE SULCUS

LATERAL CALCARINE
FISSURE

PRIMARY VISUAL
STRIATE CORTEX

SYLVIAN
FISSURE

The brains of chimpanzee (below) and human in lateral view. Although the human brain is some three to four times heavier than the chimpanzee brain, there is considerable similarity between the two species with regard to the convolutional details. The human brain has more convolutions and considerable variation of its gyri (hills) and sulci (valleys), particularly in the parietal and frontal lobes, but the primary and secondary gyri and sulci are the same between the two species. Of considerable interest to those studying the paleoneurology of our fossil ancestors are the sulci labeled the *lunate*, the *intraparietal*, the *sylvian*, and the *lateral calcarine*. In apes, such as the chimpanzee, the lunate sulcus is always present and is the anterior boundary of the primary visual striate cortex, which subserves visual functions. The intraparietal sulcus, in its posterior part, always terminates against the lunate sulcus and divides the parietal portion of the cerebral cortex into superior and inferior lobules. The calcarine fissure always runs medial to lateral but terminates before it reaches the lunate sulcus. When a lunate sulcus appears in the human brain, it is in a very posterior position relative to where it can be found in other apes. As the figures for the volume of visual striate cortex discussed in the text indicate, the human brain has relatively less of this cortex making up its cerebrum than does the ape brain. This means that the relative amount of parietal "association " cortex has increased in the human species. The challenge is to document when such change took place in hominid evolution. Unfortunately endocasts seldom show the convolutions that existed in the brain.

The central sulcus divides the frontal from the parietal lobe and functionally marks the separation between the mainly motor anterior gyrus and the posterior sensory gyrus. Both the inferior third frontal convolution (with Broca's area) and the posterior temporal and middle parietal lobes (containing Wernicke's area) appear more convoluted in the human species and have important relationships to both the motor and sensory (receptive) aspects of communication by language. These particular regions are seldom well preserved on fossil endocasts and are areas of considerable interpretative controversy among paleoneurologists.

appears that the relationship between brain and body size is constrained more strongly by metabolic factors than by surface-area/volume relationships, as once popularly believed. Thus, when the log (base 10) values of brain size and body weight are plotted together, the resulting slope is usually close to 0.75 rather than 0.66. This is for the order as a whole; in plotting the values for superfamilies or lower-level taxa (e.g. families), the slope is about 0.66.

Shown here is one such plot based on 85 species of primates from data kindly supplied by Dr. Heinz Stephan. The human value is clearly an "outlier" in this plot and has a brain volume (or weight) roughly three times that expected for a primate of this body size. The gorilla value is lower than expected, and indeed one can go through the list of primates and find differences between predicted and observed values of greater than 100 percent. The point here is that the slope of 0.75, reflecting metabolic factors, is not a *law*, but a *constraint*, around which species vary. The picture becomes more complex when individual parts of the brain are plotted against brain weight for different species of primates, and such data provide a basis for understanding differences in brain organization among primate species.

Usually brain components scale closely to total brain weight, and predicted and observed values differ under 10 percent. The cerebral cortex and the cerebellum are two good examples of this. The differences between expected and observed values are, for *Homo sapiens*, only 0.33 percent and 6.5 percent, respectively, when based on a sample of 44 primate species excluding *Homo*. There are, however, some extraordinary departures from predicted values for certain brain structures, and one of these in particular is important to a fuller understanding of human brain evolution and of the importance of certain key fossil hominid endocasts in showing *Homo*-like derived rather than pongidlike retained primitive characteristics.

The second figure shows a lateral view of pongid and human brains. In the posterior part of the cerebral cortex is found the *lunate sulcus*, which represents the most anterior boundary of purely sensory cortex: *primary visual striate cortex*. Anterior to this cortex is what we commonly call *association cortex* of the parietal and temporal lobes, a region of complex intermodality association and cognitive functioning, which happens to include, at least in humans, Wernicke's area. Based on the same sample of 45 primate species, the human primary visual striate cortex subserving vision is roughly -121 percent less than expected for a primate of this brain size. This fact does not mean that our visual sense is functionally reduced but rather that there has been a compensa-

tory increase in the relative amount of parietal and temporal lobe "association cortex." The ventricles of the brain, which in the fetal stages provide the neuroblasts that become part of the 10 billion neurons making up the adult cerebral cortex, are roughly 52 percent greater than expected on the basis of allometry. Some neural structures deviate from expected values by as much as 7,000 percent. These departures from allometric expectations could very well provide interesting clues about which structures in the human brain might have undergone significant evolutionary change.

Comparative studies of the brain provide other interesting clues about the evolution of our major organ of adaptation, of which three can be briefly mentioned: encephalization, asymmetries of cortical hemispheres, and sexual dimorphism of the brain.

Encephalization has two meanings in comparative neurology. First, it refers to evidence that in the course of evolution the cerebral cortex has taken on more functions and that the organization of the cortex is more susceptible to debilitating damage through injuries. A second more recent meaning of *encephalization* refers to a ratio where an animal's brain weight is divided by an allometric equation derived from a particular taxon. For example, the equation

$$\text{E.Q.} = \frac{\text{brain weight}}{.0991 \times (\text{body weight})^{.76237}}$$

provides an *encephalization quotient* (E.Q.), where the denominator is the allometric equation based on 88 species of primates. In this case, using an average brain weight for *Homo sapiens* of 1,300 gm., the E.Q. is 2.87. For chimpanzee and gorilla the E.Q.s are 1.14 and 0.75, respectively. If an allometric equation for insectivores were used, the human, chimpanzee, and gorilla E.Q.s would be 28.8, 11.3, and 6.67. The important points here are twofold: first, the human animal always has the highest E.Q. regardless of the denominator; second, the E.Q. values and their relative values among species can vary by as much as 20 percent. When these equations are applied to fossil hominids, their relative closeness to modern humans or to our pongid cousins, such as chimpanzees, will vary depending on the basal equation chosen. This is known as the "relativity of relative brain measures." Since the human animal apparently has the highest E.Q. value among mammals, we can use a "homocentric" equation, in which *Homo sapiens* has the highest value of 1.0, or 100 percent. This equation appears as follows:

$$\text{E.Q.} = \frac{\text{brain weight}}{\text{body weight}^{.64906}}$$

This equation is derived by drawing a line through the average log (base 10) values of modern *Homo* to the origin point of zero brain and body weights. The advantage of this equation is that all other animal e.q.s are expressed as a direct percentage of the human value. For example, the chimpanzee e.q. is 0.39 (39 percent) and the gorilla value 0.23 (23 percent). Unfortunately, it is a matter of taste as to which e.q. equation one selects, or which groups or taxa one wishes to compare and discuss.

Asymmetries of the cerebral cortex, while existing in animals other than humans, do not show the *pattern* that is most often expressed in our own species. Humans are mostly right-handed (numbering up to about 80 percent of most populations), and both the motor and sensory regions involved in symbolic language are dominant on the left side of the cerebral cortex. Evidence from the neurosciences shows that the left hemisphere controls symbolic parsing and cognitive tasks mediated by symbols. The right hemisphere appears to have more control over gestalt appreciation of visuospatial relationships, and emotions. While only sophisticated neurological examinations of the working brain show this, it is well known that the gross appearance of the cerebral hemispheres is highly correlated with handedness and thus cerebral dominance. *Petalias* are extensions of parts of the cerebral cortex extending beyond their counterparts on one side of the brain. For example, in most right-handers the classical *petalial* pattern is for a longer left occipital pole, a broader left parietal region, and a broader right frontal width. True left-handers and many mixed-handers show the opposite pattern. While other primates, particularly the gorilla, do show some asymmetries, they rarely show the combined torquelike petalial pattern described above for humans. There is also a lack of any clear-cut data demonstrating handedness (rather than preference) for other primates. It is thus an intriguing fact that fossil hominids show overwhelmingly the human petalial pattern, and Toth has discovered that many of the early stone tools were apparently made by right-handers. Some of the australopithecine fossil endocasts show a petalial pattern that suggests right-handedness, despite their pongidlike brain sizes. It is possible that the brain evolved some modernlike human patterns of organization early in hominid evolution before the great expansion of brain size, although it must be made clear that this is a controversial area.

Sexual dimorphism of the human brain can be found in the corpus callosum, through which pass most of the fiber tracts that interconnect the two cerebral hemispheres. Females show a larger splenial portion (which integrates the two occipital, parietal, and temporal regions of the cortices) than do males, when both are corrected for brain size. Given the cultural variability of most modern societies, this small anatomical difference probably does not have much significance in different cognitive-task abilities between our two sexes. It is more interesting to consider these differences (which are apparent by 26 weeks prenatal) as evolutionary *residua* from past selection pressures that may have favored a complementary behavioral adaptation between males and females for the increased period of social and maternal nurturance of longer-growing offspring.

Summary

Summarizing all of the changes that may have taken place over 3–4 m.y. of human brain evolution is a speculative matter. The earliest australopithecines (e.g. Taung and the Hadar 162-28 *A. afarensis*) already show evidence for cerebral reorganization in that the lunate sulcus is in a posterior position, suggesting that posterior parietal "association cortex" had increased beyond the ape level. Cerebral asymmetries are also present, but these are more strongly represented in early *Homo*, a period of time that coincides with a major expansion of brain size (to ca. 750 ml. from 450 ml.) at ca. 2 m.y. ago. Coincident with these patterns are stone tools and evidence for hunting and scavaging. The remaining doubling of size, to ca. 1,400 ml., is perhaps best explained through allometric processes where natural selection favored increased body size, longer periods of childhood growth, and, one assumes, more sophisticated brains. While this basic scenario fits well within our popular conceptions of mosaic evolution, it would be wise to remember that there were mosaics within the mosaic, and the brain has always been an important part of human adaptation whatever its size at various phases of hominid evolution. It is pointless to say that bipedalism evolved first, then brains. A complex musculoskeletal set of such adjustments as attend bipedalism could not evolve in a nervous vacuum, nor does the structural adaptation hold much meaning without reference to behavioral function. Thus the evolution of the brain can only be understood, not just in the context of its size, the reorganization of its components, and its asymmetries, but in the context of the total range of the ecological and behavioral record that is associated with the actual fossil hominid discoveries.

[R.L.H.]

Further Readings

Bryden, M.P. (1982) Laterality: Functional Asymmetry in the Intact Brain. New York: Academic.

Connolly, C.J. (1950) External Morphology of the Primate Brain. Springfield, Ill.: Thomas.

Damasio, A.R., and Geschwind, N. (1984) The neural basis for language. Ann. Rev. Neurosci. 7:127–147.

de Lacoste-Utamsing, M.C., and Holloway, R.L. (1982) Sexual dimorphism in the corpus callosum. Science 216:1431–1432.

Geschwind, N., and Galaburda, A.M., eds. (1984) Cerebral Dominance: The Biological Foundations. Cambridge, Mass.: Harvard University Press.

Holloway, R.L. (1975) The Role of Human Social Behavior in the Evolution of the Human Brain. 43rd James Arthur Lecture. New York: American Museum of Natural History.

Holloway, R.L. (1978) The relevance of endocasts for studying primate brain evolution. In C.R. Noback (ed.): Sensory Systems in Primates. New York: Plenum, pp. 181–200.

Holloway, R.L., and de Lacoste-Lareymondie, M.C. (1982) Brain endocast asymmetry in pongids and hominids: some preliminary findings on the paleontology of cerebral dominance. Am. J. Phys. Anthropol. 58:101–110.

Kinsbourne, M., ed. (1978) Asymmetrical Function of the Brain. Cambridge: Cambridge University Press.

LeMay, M. (1976) Morphological asymmetries of modern man, fossil man, and nonhuman primates. Annals N.Y. Acad. Sci. 280:349–366.

Martin, R.D. (1983) Human Evolution in an Ecological Context. 52nd James Arthur Lecture. New York: American Museum of Natural History.

Passingham, R.E. (1982) The Human Primate. Oxford: Freeman.

Radinsky, L.B. (1979) The Fossil Record of Primate Brain Evolution. 47th James Arthur Lecture. New York: American Museum of Natural History.

Stephan, H., Frahm, H., and Baron, G. (1981) New and revised data on volumes of brain structures in insectivores and primates. Folia Primatol. 35:1–29.

BRANISELLA *see* BRANISELLINAE; OLIGOCENE

BRANISELLINAE

Extinct subfamily of cebid platyrrhine monkeys including only *Branisella boliviana*. This form is the oldest and most archaic of the ceboid primates, known from a level of the late Oligocene Bolivian deposit at La Salla, which has been recently redated at ca. 27 m.y. *Branisella* upper molars are in part morphologically conservative, although they do resemble those of the cebid *Saimiri*. Its lower jaw is very shallow, as in the relatively primitive parapithecid catarrhines.

See also ANTHROPOIDEA; CEBIDAE; PARAPITHECIDAE; PLATYRRHINI. [A.L.R.]

Further Readings

Rosenberger, A.L. (1981) A mandible of *Branisella boliviana* (Platyrrhini, Primates) from the Oligocene of South America. Int. J. Primatol. 2:1–7.

BRECCIA CAVE FORMATION

Breccia refers to a type of sedimentary rock that consists of angular to subangular, freshly broken fragments that generally have not been transported far from their points of origin. Taking the five South African australopithecine-bearing deposits as an example, one sees that these fossiliferous breccias are composed principally of loose blocks in beds of sand, all cemented into a solid mass by the deposition of calcium carbonate within a subterranean solution cavity in limestone. The Transvaal sites of Kromdraai, Makapansgat, Sterkfontein, and Swartkrans represent the remains of breccia-filled solution chambers that formed in dolomitic limestone; the breccias at Taung, however, developed within a limestone tufa fan that extended outward from the dolomite of the Gaap (or Kaap) Escarpment along the southeastern margin of the Kalahari Desert.

Generally such breccia-filled caves begin with subterranean dissolution in limestone formations that are below the level of the water table. As the water table is lowered through time, these dissolution chambers remain as voids within the parent rock. Small openings from the chamber to the terrestrial surface form through progressive enlargement by rainwater of fissures and cracks in the parent rock. These small openings admit circulating air in the chamber, leading to the formation of stalactitic and/or stalagmitic travertines (dripstones) by the evaporation of calcareous waters that have percolated through the parent limestone. Through time, and the enlargement of these openings, the chamber may fill with sands and other surface debris, mixed with infalling blocks from walls and roof. The sand and debris, including bones and teeth, become cemented to form breccia by the deposition of waterborne carbonates that have continued to percolate through the parent limestone.

Eventually the talus cone of sediment that has formed in the chamber may become so extensive as to choke the opening through which it entered. With time a new solution channel may form a shaft through the sediment, resulting in the erosion of some of the original breccia together with the deposition and calcification of more recently derived sediments. By the same token other vertical avenues may open to the surface, and these may result in the deposition of "younger" material upon the original breccia mass. Erosion of the parent rock may eventually expose these breccia-filled chambers to the surface. A complex series of processes of dissolution, filling, cementation, secondary decalcification and erosion, and subsequent deposition and cementation are involved in the formation of cave breccias, making accurate stratigraphic interpretation of such sites extremely difficult.

See also KROMDRAAI; MAKAPANSGAT; STERKFONTEIN; SWARTKRANS; TAUNG. [F.E.G.]

Further Readings

Brain, C.K. (1958) The Transvaal ape-man-bearing cave deposits. Transvaal Mus. Mem. *11*:1-131.

Brain, C.K. (1976) A re-interpretation of the Swartkrans site and its remains. S. Afr. J. Sci. 72:141-146.

BREUIL, [ABBÉ] HENRI EDWARD PROSPER (1877-1961)

French archaeologist. Shortly after being ordained in 1897, Breuil became interested in Paleolithic art and prehistoric archaeology and rapidly established himself as a leading authority in both areas. Among his many contributions to the development of prehistoric archaeology was his seminal paper "Les Subdivisions du Paleolithique supérieur et leur signification" (1912). He was professor at the Muséum National d'Histoire Naturelle from 1910 and at the Collège de France from 1929 to 1947.

[F.S.]

BRIDGERIAN   see   EOCENE; TIME SCALE

BROCA, PIERRE PAUL (1824-1880)

French anatomist and physical anthropologist who made notable contributions to the fields of anatomy, pathology, surgery, and anthropology. Much of his anthropological research concerned the study of racial variations in crania and involved the invention of craniological techniques and instruments. He is also remembered for his comparative neuroanatomical studies. In 1861 he demonstrated the location of the speech center in the left frontal region of the brain, since known as "Broca's region." Broca also made a number of significant contributions to the institutional development of French anthropology, involving the founding of the Société d'Anthropologie de Paris (1859), the Laboratoire d'Anthropologie of the École Pratique des Hautes Études (1868), the École d'Anthropologie (Paris) in 1876, and the journal *Revue d'Anthropologie* (1872).

[F.S.]

BROKEN HILL   see   KABWE

BRONZE AGE

Second in the three-stage sequence of Stone Age, Bronze Age, Iron Age. This tripartite scheme was the first developmental framework widely adopted in the archaeology of Europe. It has since been extended to other regions where bronze metallurgy was developed. In any area the scheme is based on the mate-rial used to produce cutting tools. Despite this simple technological definition the Bronze Age has frequently been taken to refer to a period of broad-spectrum cultural advance.

The term first gained currency when employed by two early nineteenth-century Danish archaeologists, Christian Thomsen and Jens Worsae, in their efforts to order the prehistory of northern Europe. To these scholars the three-stage system reflected a unilinear development of human culture from simple origins to progressively more complex conditions. The Bronze Age was thought of as the period of time (in any given part of the world) when copper or bronze metallurgy began, when settled villages dependent on agriculture became the rule, and when disparate social ranking of members of society first developed. These developments are each products of long-term processes of change that are not necessarily linked to one another. Hence the simplistic unilineal development often implied in the term is not generally accepted today.

See also COMPLEX SOCIETIES; EUROPE; IRON AGE. [B.B.]

Further Readings

Coles, J., and Harding, A. (1979) The Bronze Age in Europe. New York: St. Martin's.

Redman, C. (1978) The Rise of Civilization. San Francisco: Freeman.

BROOM, ROBERT (1866-1951)

South African (b. Scotland) physician and paleontologist. On receiving his M.D. at the University of Glasgow in 1895, Broom moved to Cape Town (South Africa), where in 1903 he was appointed professor of geology at Victoria College, Stellenbosch, and became famous for his studies of mammal-like reptiles. Broom's interest in anthropology and more specifically paleoanthropology was heightened by the discovery of the Taung (infantile australopithecine) specimen in 1924, for which R.A. Dart had claimed hominid affinities—a conclusion Broom endorsed without reservation. In 1934 he joined the Transvaal Museum, Pretoria. This appointment coincided with his succession of spectacular finds of adult australopithecines at Sterkfontein and subsequently at the sites of Kromdraai and Swartkrans. These discoveries essentially vindicated his support of Dart's earlier claims for the Taung specimen. The remainder of Broom's career was devoted to exploration of these sites and the interpretation of the many early hominid remains discovered there.

See also AUSTRALOPITHECUS; DART, RAYMOND ARTHUR; KROMDRAAI; STERKFONTEIN; SWARTKRANS; TAUNG. [F.S.]

BRØRUP   see   GLACIATION; PLEISTOCENE

BROWN SANDS *see* OMO

BROWRIDGE *see* SKULL

BRUNHES *see* PALEOMAGNETISM

BUDA INDUSTRY

Diminutive-chopper-core industry of middle Pleistocene (Biharian) age in central Europe, probably ca. 0.6–0.4 m.y. First defined on the basis of a site at Budapest (Hungary), the industry is better known from Vértesszöllös. The small size of both flakes and cores is probably due to use of river cobbles as the raw-material source rather than natural stone outcrops or quarries.

See also CORE; EARLY PALEOLITHIC;
FLAKE; RAW MATERIALS. [A.S.B.]

BUKWA *see* UGANDA

BULBAR SCAR *see* FLAKE; STONE-TOOL MAKING

BULB OF PERCUSSION *see* FLAKE; STONE-TOOL MAKING

BULLA *see* SKULL

BULUK

Early Miocene site in northern Kenya where three species of hominoid and one ceropithecoid have been found. Originally assigned to *Sivapithecus*, the large hominoid has since been renamed *Afropithecus turkanensis* based on additional specimens from Kalodirr, a similar site.

See also CERCOPITHECOIDEA; HOMINOIDEA; MIOCENE;
SIVAPITHECUS. [P.A.]

BURDIGALIAN *see* MIOCENE

BURIAL *see* RITUAL

BURIN

Stone-tool class especially common during Late Paleolithic times (and after), with a sharp chisellike edge produced by removing one or more narrow flakes (burin spalls) along the thickness of a flake or

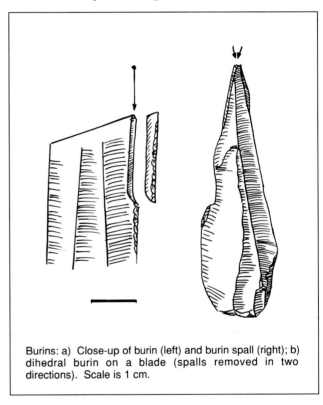

Burins: a) Close-up of burin (left) and burin spall (right); b) dihedral burin on a blade (spalls removed in two directions). Scale is 1 cm.

blake. Burins are thought to be primary tools for engraving and carving such materials as bone, antler, ivory, and probably wood.

See also LATE PALEOLITHIC;
STONE-TOOL MAKING; UPPER PALEOLITHIC. [N.T., K.S.]

BUXTON-NORLIM *see* TAUNG

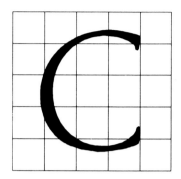

cf.

From Latin *confer*, compare. Used to indicate the probable affinities of systematic materials, most commonly fossil, that are insufficient to permit exact determination of species or genus. Thus a fragmentary middle Pleistocene hominid fossil that most closely compares with *Homo erectus* but cannot certainly be established as a member of that species might be classified as *Homo* cf. *erectus*.

See also CLASSIFICATION; TAXONOMY. [I.T.]

CACAJAO *see* PITHECIINAE

CAENOPITHECUS *see* ADAPIDAE

CALABRIAN *see* PLEISTOCENE; SEA-LEVEL CHANGE

CALENDAR, PALEOLITHIC *see* PALEOLITHIC CALENDAR

CALICO

Controversial archaeological site in an alluvial fan in San Bernardino County (California). Continuously excavated since 1964, it was given prominence by the involvement of L.S.B. Leakey. Although some claim that the earliest artifact-bearing deposits of the site are 200 k.y. old, the geomorphological context and the presence of human workmanship on the artifacts from Calico remain the subject of considerable debate.

See also PALEOINDIAN. [L.S.A.P., D.H.T]

CALLICEBUS *see* PITHECIINAE

CALLIMICO *see* CALLITRICHINAE

CALLITHRIX *see* CALLITRICHINAE

CALLITRICHINAE

Subfamily of cebid platyrrhine monkeys including the living tribes Callimiconini (*Callimico*) and Callitrichini (*Saguinus, Leontopithecus, Callithrix, Cebuella*) and the middle Miocene (16–14 m.y.) La Venta fossil *Micodon kiotensis*. Informally termed "marmosets" (and for some "tamarins," distinguished by low-crowned rather than high-crowned, marmosetlike incisors), there are more than 20 species, all of which exploit a canopy-subcanopy frugivorous-insectivorous feeding niche, where competition with the larger cebines is minimized. Callitrichines are on the whole the smallest living anthropoids, characterized also by reduced posterior dentitions, nonopposable thumbs and big toes and the occurrence of claws on all the fingers except for the large toe. The callimiconin tribe is a primitive branch. They produce a single offspring per litter and retain third molars, whereas the more derived callitrichins lack third molars, have reduced second molars, and produce dizygotic twins, an unusual strategy for an anthropoid. Their mating system and social organization, which involves extensive paternal and sibling care of young offspring and in some cases polyandrous mating, may relate to the heavy reproductive load that females experience.

Some species of *Callithrix*, and the monotypic *Cebuella*, are highly gumivorous, having evolved a modified dentition that permits them to gouge and scrape tree bark to promote the flow of secretions that the animals then harvest. Although they have rather unconvoluted brains, clawed fingertips and morphologically simple molars—all resemblances to "primitive" mammals—callitrichines evolved this adaptive pattern secondarily, at least partially as an allometric consequence of small size. The golden lion marmoset, *Leontopithecus*, literally on the brink of extinction in the 1980s, is the first mammal to have been capitively bred and then reintroduced successfully into a park preserve within its native geographical range. The recently discovered *Micodon* is the only known fossil marmoset. It is similar in size to the larger eastern Brazilian marmosets, but it does not have the highly reduced fourth hypocone cusp that typifies the callitrichin tribe. It indicates a fairly ancient origin for the group.

See also ALLOMETRY; BRAIN; CEBINAE; CEBOIDEA; DIET; DWARFISM. [A.L.R.]

Further Readings

Hershkovitz, P. (1977) New World Monkeys (Platyrrhini), Vol. 1: Callitrichidae. Chicago: University of Chicago Press.

Leutenegger, W. (1980) Monogamy in callitrichids: a consequence of phyletic dwarfism? Int. J. Primatol. 1:95–98.

Rosenberger, A.L. (1984) Aspects of the systematics and evolution of the marmosets. In M.T. de Mello (ed.): A Primatologia no Brasil. Belo Horizonte: University Federalas de Minas Gerais, pp. 160–180.

Sussman, R.W., and Kinzey, W.G. (1984) The ecological role of the Callitrichidae. Am. J. Phys. Anthropol. 64:419–449.

CALLOSITIES, ISCHIAL *see* ISCHIAL CALLOSITIES

ÇANDIR *see* NEAR EAST; PONGINAE

CANTIUS *see* NOTHARCTIDAE

CAPSIAN

Late Paleolithic industry of North Africa, named for the type site of el-Mekta near Gafsa in southern Tunisia, of early Holocene age, ca. 10,000–6,000 B.P. The Capsian is characterized by large backed points and blades, truncation burins, microburins, and microliths, especially lunates or segments and gravettes

in the early phase. In the more widespread "Upper" phase (actually contemporaneous or earlier) tools are smaller, and geometric microliths (especially trapezoids and triangles) along with bone awls, ostrich-eggshell beads, and polishing stones, more common. Sites are often associated with large piles of snail shells, leading to the theory that snails formed a large although seasonal part of the Capsian diet. An earlier and probably unrelated backed-bladelet industry in Kenya, the Eburran, was originally termed the Kenya Capsian.

See also ECONOMY, PREHISTORIC; LATE PALEOLITHIC; LATER STONE AGE; MESOLITHIC; STONE-TOOL MAKING. [A.S.B.]

CARBON-14 DATING *see* GEOCHRONOMETRY

CARNIVORY *see* DIET

CARPENTER, C.R. *see* PRIMATE ECOLOGY

CARPODAPTES *see* CARPOLESTIDAE

CARPOLESTIDAE

Family of primarily Paleocene archaic primates that are found in many North American localities but that, like the picrodontids, do not occur in Europe. There are two recognized genera, the middle Paleocene *Elphidotarsius* and the late Paleocene and locally earliest Eocene *Carpodaptes* (including *Carpolestes*).

Carpolestids display a specialization in their cheek teeth called *plagiaulacoidy*, a term coined for the similarity of some mammalian teeth to those of Jurassic multituberculate postcanine teeth. Plagiaulacoidy has been defined as a condition in which one or more of the cheek teeth are modified into compressed, bladelike structures with serrated cutting edges on the top. This specialization can be recognized in its incipient state in the oldest carpolestid genus. Both the older and more primitive and the later and more advanced species are characterized by a semicircular bladelike enlargement of the fourth lower premolar and the equally enlarged but flattened and expanded upper third and fourth premolars. In advanced carpolestids, upper premolars become polycuspate, and the cusps are arranged into three mesiodistally aligned parallel rows.

In addition to this premolar specialization carpolestids also display their heritage of enlarged incisors but seem to have independently evolved a reduced

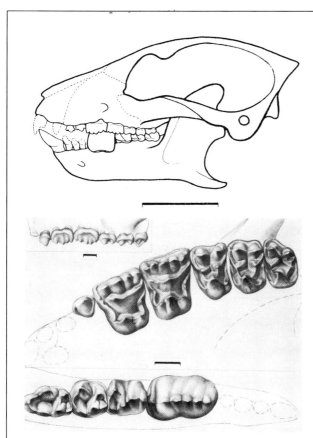

Reconstructed skull of the late Paleocene *Carpodaptes dubius* from North America (above), and the partial upper and lower dentition of the late Paleocene *Carpodaptes hazelae*. Scale for the skull is 1 cm, and scales for the teeth, 1 mm.

anterior dentition. The more advanced species of *Carpodaptes* drastically reduce the second incisors, the canines and the remaining second and third premolars above, and the third premolar below.

The incisors, the premolars, and the molars bear special similarity to the earliest well-known plesiadapid, *Pronothodectes*. This is why carpolestids are considered close relatives of plesiadapids and, along with the Saxonellidae, are included in the superfamily Plesiadapoidea.

The function and biological roles (we do not know the number of possible roles these teeth may have performed) of the plagiaulacoid dentition of carpolestids, along with those of the extinct multituberculates and the several lineages of plagiaulacoid marsupials, has been of great interest to many students. Although emphasis is clearly on some cutting-sawing function by these independently evolved dental structures, the nature of the selectional forces that molded this solution is not entirely clear. Carpolestids, with their plagiaulacoid lower blades moving food across the rasplike and unique upper premolars, probably consumed some vegetable diet of high

fiber content, such as fruits, nuts, or even succulent shoots. These mouse- to rat-sized primates might have exploited a relatively narrow adaptive zone due to the special abilities of their premolar dentitions. The great similarities between their molar teeth strongly suggest that the differences between *Elphidotarsius* and *Carpodaptes* species were not due to significantly different diets but rather to the steady improvement in design for the same biological roles through the latter half of the Paleocene.

Carpolestids are not known to have given rise to any other group of primates. Their fossils, along with those of the primate family Plesiadapidae, are of particular value to paleontologists for the dating of Paleocene rocks in North America. These species were rapidly evolving and widespread, with the consequence. that the individually recognized species were of short duration and therefore of great stratigraphic value.

[F.S.S.]

Further Readings

Szalay, F.S., and Delson, E. (1979) Evolutionary History of the Primates. New York: Academic.

CASABLANCA

Mandible fragments were discovered in association with handaxe tools in a gravel pit at Sidi Abderrahman, near Casablanca (Morocco), in 1954. This middle Pleistocene fossil may represent the same hominid population as that known from the Thomas Quarries and Salé, although the specimen has also been assigned to the same group as the earlier Tighenif specimens from Algeria.

See also **ARCHAIC HOMO SAPIENS; HOMO ERECTUS.** [C.B.S]

ÇATAL HÜYÜK

Neolithic site 40 km. southeast of Konya in central Turkey, occupied for at least 1,000 years, from ca. 8500 B.P. Excavations directed by J. Mellaart from 1961 to 1965 focused on the Neolithic 16-hectare eastern mound and largely ignored the later 13-hectare mound to the west. An unusually large site for its period, Çatal has yielded a wealth of organic materials, including baskets, textiles, and wooden objects; abundant ceramics and worked stone artifacts; unique and well-preserved architecture with elaborate paintings and plaster reliefs, both geometric and representational; and almost 500 intramural burials.

See also **COMPLEX SOCIETIES; NEAR EAST; NEOLITHIC.** [C.K.]

CATARRHINI

Old World infraorder of Anthropoidea, including the superfamilies Parapithecoidea, Pliopithecoidea, Cercopithecoidea, and Hominoidea. Of these four groups of Afro-Eurasian higher primates the first two are extinct and mainly or wholly African, while the latter two are extant in Africa and Asia, with extinct European representatives (other than the worldwide *Homo* and the relict or introduced Gibraltar macaque). Pliopithecoidea is a paraphyletic grade or "waste-basket" grouping of species linked mainly by possession of shared ancestral retentions, but the other three superfamilies appear to be monophyletic as they are understood here.

Catarrhine Characteristics

Defining the catarrhines by means of uniquely shared characters depends upon which taxa are considered when such a list is developed. If only the living forms are examined, the list of such characters is long and includes numerous features not determinable for any fossils, as well as others only known for a few extinct forms. Such a list, of course, can yield information only about the last common ancestor of the living forms, and still earlier catarrhines, or even earlier ancestors, might present a different mosaic of character states. Nonetheless, an abbreviated version of such a list does provide a starting point for a survey of catarrhine morphology and evolution.

Recent research suggests that the ancestor of living catarrhines would have been characterized by the

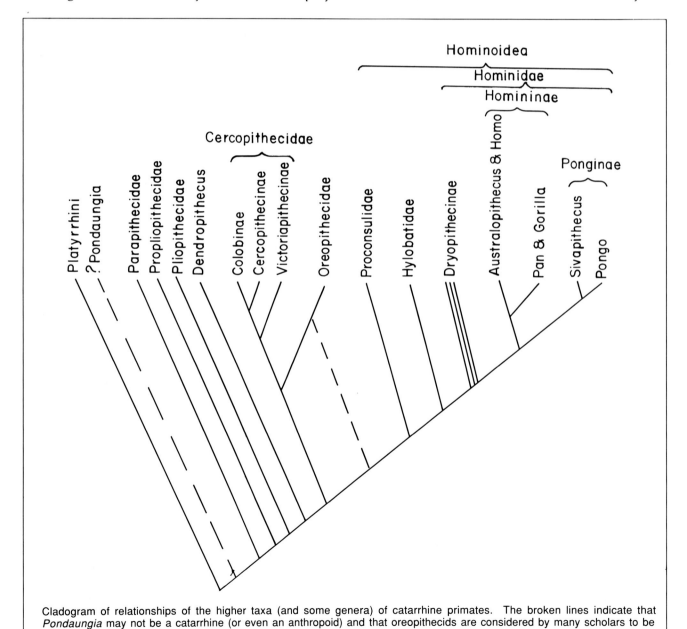

Cladogram of relationships of the higher taxa (and some genera) of catarrhine primates. The broken lines indicate that *Pondaungia* may not be a catarrhine (or even an anthropoid) and that oreopithecids are considered by many scholars to be hominoids.

following dental features, which are derived by comparison with those of an ancestral anthropoid and are not known to have evolved in parallel among platyrrhines: dental formula of 2-1-2-3; single-cusped, bilaterally compressed P_3, involved in honing C^1; and 5-cusped lower molars with no paraconid, midline distal hypoconulid (not very large on M_3), talonid and trigonid of roughly equal height, and M_2 rather larger than M_1 but only slightly smaller than M_3. The presence of a wear facet (termed x) caused by phase 2 contact between the distolingual surface of the protoconid and the mesiobucal aspect of the protocone has also been used as a diagnostic catarrhine feature, but it now appears that this may have been developed in parallel in several anthropoid lineages. Cranially such characters might include a prominent glabella, separate from the supraorbital tori; a tubular external auditory meatus; a moderately developed mandibular inferior transverse torus; long mandibular ramus with nearly vertical anterior margin; U-shaped mandibular arcade; and very reduced olfactory lobes of the brain. Postcranially characters of this type might include humerus with low deltopectoral and supinator crests, a narrow brachialis flange, and a deep olecranon fossa, but with no entepicondylar foramen or dorsal epitrochlear fossa; ulna with weak pronator crest and round head; ischium with expanded tuberosity (and callosities); and a synovial distal joint between the tibia and fibula.

Relationships of Major Catarrhine Subgroups

If we now examine a variety of fossils, it is possible to see which of these characters they share and thus how strongly they are linked to the modern catarrhines. Two ancient and poorly known species have been suggested as very early catarrhines. The Burmese late Eocene *Pondaungia cotteri* retains a paraconid and has subequal anterior molars, thus sharing no catarrhine synapomorphies; its damaged upper molars appear phenetically similar to those of *Propliopithecus*, but its position remains unclear. *Oligopithecus savagei*, from the early Oligocene lowest horizon in the Fayum sequence of Egypt, has a compressed P_3 with a large canine honing facet, but its small M_{1-2} hypoconulids are placed lingually near the entoconid, a paraconid is present, and the trigonids are somewhat higher than the talonids. Moreover, it has lingually open trigonid basins on P_4–M_2, a feature never seen in anthropoids. There is thus no evidence that *Oligopithecus* is a catarrhine, or even an anthropoid.

Parapithecidae The parapithecids include three or four genera from the Fayum Oligocene whose phyletic position has been the subject of much recent debate. Simons has long argued that they are the sister taxon to Cercopithecidae; Delson has considered them to be the sister of all other catarrhines and formally termed them Paracatarrhini as opposed to Eucatarrhini (which includes the other three superfamilies); Hoffstetter has proposed that they may be the African sister taxon of the platyrrhines; and recently Harrison, Fleagle, and Kay have suggested that parapithecids are the sister taxon to Platyrrhini plus Catarrhini, thus the most archaic anthropoids known. It is now widely agreed that parapithecids share no derived features with either cercopithecids or platyrrhines, the apparent similarities that do exist being best interpreted as parallelisms.

Of the list of catarrhine features noted above parapithecids share a prominent glabella, molar trigonids and talonids of nearly equal height, and a well-developed midline distal hypoconulid with a generally large distal fovea. They are clearly less derived than any other catarrhine in the following features (and conservative by comparison with platyrrhines in those marked with *): retention of P2 (which may show honing contact with the canine), molar paraconids (at least in some species), lingually open P_4 trigonid, small P_4 metaconid placed distolingual to protoconid*, a weak mandibular inferior torus, shallow corpus, short ramus with sloping anterior margin, narrow tibial shaft*, and a fibrous distal joint between the tibia and fibula. They share with the propliopithecids (see below) an annular auditory meatus, large olfactory bulb*, and numerous conservative postcranial features, such as humerus with prominent deltopectoral crest, high supinator crest, elongate capitulum, shallow olecranon fossa, moderate brachialis flange, entepicondylar foramen, and dorsal epitrochlear fossa; and ulna with prominent pronator crest. Two conservative parapithecid features cannot be determined in propliopithecids: ulna with narrow head* and ischium with narrow tuberosity* (and presumably no callosities). Unique derived features shared by at least several parapithecids are apparently restricted to a central conule on the upper premolars and a sulcus separating the metaconid from the protoconid on P_4.

The question now is whether one weights as more meaningful the derived characters parapithecids share with eucatarrhines or the conservative retentions found in a more derived state in platyrrhines. Either alternative leads to the presumption of parallel development of three to four derived features, either in eucatarrhines and platyrrhines or in eucatarrhines and parapithecids. At present this writer prefers to retain the parapithecids within Catarrhini as the least derived subunit, while recognizing that the question remains open.

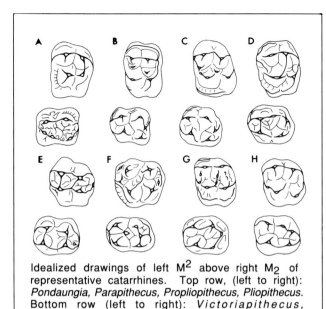

Idealized drawings of left M² above right M₂ of representative catarrhines. Top row, (left to right): *Pondaungia, Parapithecus, Propliopithecus, Pliopithecus.* Bottom row (left to right): *Victoriapithecus, Oreopithecus, Proconsul, Sivapithecus.*

Pliopithecoidea   The extinct superfamily Pliopithecoidea includes two fairly well known genera, each placed in a distinct family: Propliopithecidae and Pliopithecidae. Several less complete fossils are often referred to the latter family, but one of these, *Dendropithecus*, requires separate treatment. Most of these genera have at various times been allied with the Hylobatidae, but that was mainly on the basis of small size and relatively gracile limb bones, rather than by any sharing of the distinctive derived postcranial features of gibbons.

Propliopithecus of the Fayum mid-Oligocene is known by fragments of up to five species, but the most complete remains are those of *P. zeuxis*, sometimes placed in the genus *Aegyptopithecus*. This species, and presumably its congeners, is derived by comparison with the parapithecids in such features as having lost P2 and possessing a bilaterally compressed P_3 that hones C^1; P_4 with lingually closed trigonid and metaconid subequal in size to directly buccal protoconid; lower molars lacking paraconids but with facet x; inferior transverse torus of mandible moderately developed; long ramus with vertical anterior border; corpus deep under M_1; no contact between zygomatic and parietal bones in temporal fossa and clearly closed rear of orbit; and a moderately broad tibial shaft with synovial joint between tibia and fibula distally. It is as yet unknown whether propliopithecids are derived compared with parapithecids in the shape of the ulnar head, development of the ischial tuberosity, size of the femoral lesser trochanter, or depth of the femoral distal condyles. If not, the derived state(s) would have been evolved

independently in platyrrhines and later catarrhines; in turn this would strengthen the parapithecid link to catarrhines.

Pliopithecus, known from several European middle Miocene partial skeletons, is in turn further derived than *Propliopithecus* in having a P_4 somewhat longer than broad, a prominent glabellar region and a hallux with a modified saddle joint. Both genera retain such ancestral anthropoid conditions as a ringlike external auditory meatus (partly tubular in *Pliopithecus*); distinct prehallux bone in the foot; humerus with entepicondylar foramen, moderately broad brachialis flange, high supinator crest, shallow olecranon fossa, and elongate capitulum; ulna with prominent pronator crest and narrow head; and narrow ischial tuberosity (the latter two are unknown in propliopithecids).

A number of Miocene taxa have been described from mainly dental remains and often placed haphazardly into Pliopithecidae, although the lack of defining characters for this family makes such allocation tenuous at best. The European *Crouzelia* and various putative subgenera of *Pliopithecus*, the Chinese *Platodontopithecus*, and the Chinese and Siwalik *Dionysopithecus* are all known only by teeth from middle Miocene localities and cannot be readily linked to other forms. The East African early-to-middle Miocene *Micropithecus*, which may be congeneric with *Dionysopithecus*, is of equally indefinite position. *Laccopithecus* from the late Miocene site of Lufeng, southwestern China, preserves a damaged face that seems to ally it more with *Pliopithecus* than with *Hylobates*, as some have suggested. Of all these forms only the early-to-middle Miocene Kenyan *Dendropithecus*, and perhaps the newly described *Simiolus*, from Kalodirr, present postcranial elements that may place them closer to the last common ancestor of Hominoidea and Cercopithecoidea. The humerus of the former genus, for example, has low deltopectoral and supinator crests and a narrow bicipital groove, and it lacks an entepicondylar foramen, although the olecranon fossa is conservatively deep. While it may eventually be possible to array these taxa in a branching sequence or even ally them to one another, in light of current knowledge it appears most prudent to group them tentatively with the Pliopithecidae.

"Modern" catarrhines   The Hominoidea and Cercopithecoidea are discussed in detail elsewhere and need only be summarized here. In addition to the cercopithecid monkeys the extinct oreopithecids are included tentatively in the Cercopithecoidea. *Oreopithecus*, especially, presents a variety of derived postcranial and dental features sufficient to include it in the "modern" catarrhines, whatever its superfamil-

ial allocation. The hominoids comprise mainly the hylobatids and hominids, the latter including *Pongo* and its extinct allies, African apes plus humans, and a group of mostly fragmentary Miocene taxa that share with later hominids such derived features as thick molar enamel, elongated premolars, robust P_3 and canines, spatulate I^2, subparallel toothrows, deep mandibular symphysis with superior torus less pronounced than inferior, enlarged maxillary sinus, and/or prominent keels on humeral trochlea. The early Miocene *Proconsul* appears to fall between this latter group and the "advanced" pliopithecids like *Dendropithecus*, in that it presents such ancestral hominoid features as P_3 with low crown, upper premo-

lars with reduced cusp heteromorphy, development of the maxillary jugum, frontal bone wider at bregma than anteriorly, strong trochlear keels but without sulci bordering the lateral keel, humeral head medically oriented, rounded and larger than the femoral head, and scapula with elongated vertebral border and robust acromion (the last several not known for *Dendropithecus*). On this basis the family Proconsulidae is included in the Hominoidea.

Catarrhine Evolutionary History

Catarrhine origins depend greatly on alternative interpretations of the origins and deployment of the Anthropoidea. What is clear is that the earliest known catarrhines occur in Africa, which was an island continent until the later early Miocene. The Parapithecidae was the more abundant catarrhine family during Fayum time (ca. 33–31 m.y. ago), with the more "advanced" propliopithecids apparently lesser in number of both species and individuals. After a gap of 6–10 m.y. the East African early Miocene (23–16 m.y. ago) record of early catarrhines reveals that both parapithecids and propliopithecids had become extinct, but two new groups, related to the latter, were fairly common. Several genera of small-bodied ?pliopithecids are known, alongside several species of *Proconsul* ranging in body size from medium to large. In addition the first cercopithecoids are known, with teeth of victoriapithecine cercopithecids and jaws of the ?oreopithecid *Rangwapithecus*. Moreover, the fairly large *Afropithecus* and smaller *Turkanapithecus* probably represent early members of the Hominidae (great ape plus human clade).

In the middle Miocene (16–11 m.y. ago) there was a great flowering of catarrhine lineages. As a result of the plate tectonic contact between Africa and Eurasia after 19 m.y. it became possible for primates among other mammals to spread across the Old World. A variety of pliopithecids occurred in all three continental areas, with indications of greatest similarity between East Africa and China. *Heliopithecus* in Saudi Arabia, *Kenyapithecus* in Kenya, and *Dryopithecus* in Europe represent early, "unspecialized" hominids; the initial differentiation of the pongine lineage is documented by jaws of *Sivapithecus* from Pakistan as old as 12 m.y. An even earlier split is suggested by teeth from Turkey, and central Europe, referred to that genus that show the characteristic reduced I^2 but not the unambiguous derived features of the palate or face. *Nyanzapithecus* teeth clearly indicate its oreopithecid affinity. *Victoriapithecus* and *Prohylobates* document the earliest definite cercopithecids, albeit less completely bilophodont than later monkeys. Although there is no fossil record, it is likely that this

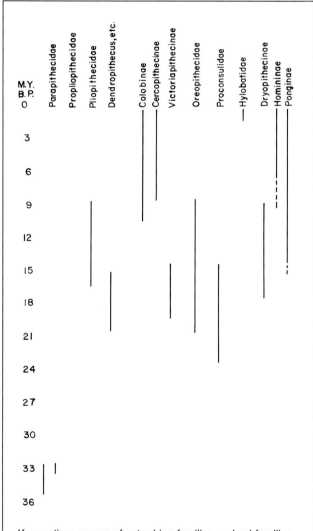

Known time ranges of catarrhine families and subfamilies. The broken lines indicate the existence of fossils uncertainly referred to the Homininae (especially the Samburu maxilla) and Ponginae (earliest ?*Sivapithecus*). The "*Dendropithecus*, etc." includes such taxa as *Dionysopithecus*, *Micropithecus*, and *Simiolus*, which may be more "modern" than the pliopithecids (see text).

time interval saw the divergence of the hylobatids from ancestral hominoids, perhaps in Eurasia.

Pliopithecids and hominoids decreased greatly in variety during the late Miocene (11–5 m.y. ago), especially compared with the cercopithecids. *Pliopithecus* is rare in western Europe at the outset of this interval, and the possibly related *Laccopithecus* is known from China ca. 8 m.y. ago. The last dryopithecines also appear in Europe, China, and perhaps Indopakistan between 11 and 8 m.y. *Sivapithecus* and relatives are widespread in eastern Europe, Turkey, the Siwaliks of Indopakistan, and southern China until ca. 8–7 m.y. *Oreopithecus* also has a brief flowering in Italy ca. 9–8 m.y. By contrast the cercopithecid fossil record documents the split into the two living subfamilies, with colobines the more successful: the small-bodied *Mesopithecus* reached Europe and the Near East by perhaps 10 m.y. and continued into the Pliocene; a similar form occurred ca. 7 m.y. in the Siwaliks; the very small *Microcolobus* is known in Kenya ca. 9 m.y., and a medium-sized species inhabited Algeria ca. 8 m.y. Generalized papionin cercopithecines are known from teeth in Algeria and Kenya between ca. 8 and 5 m.y. It is likely that the African-ape clade separated from human ancestors during the later Miocene, with the development of knuckle-walking versus bipedalism; the maxilla from Samburu might document part of this divergence.

During the Pliocene (5–1.6 m.y. ago) cercopithecids continued to diversify, especially in Africa, but the rise of the human lineage is the most exciting development. From an ancestral group similar to *Australopithecus afarensis* the "robust" australopith or *Paranthropus* lineage diverged in one direction, while a species like *A. africanus* may have given rise to *Homo*, which in turn dominated the Pleistocene as an environment-altering tool user.

See also AFRICA ANTHROPOIDEA; AUSTRALOPITHECUS; CERCOPITHECIDAE; CERCOPITHECOIDEA; DIET; EUROPE; FAYUM; HOMINIDAE; HOMINOIDEA; HOMO; LOCOMOTION; MIOCENE; OLIGOCENE; OREOPITHECIDAE; PARAPITHECIDAE; PLATYRRHINI; PLIOPITHECIDAE; PONGINAE; PROCONSUL; PROPLIOPITHECIDAE; SAMBURU; SKELETON; SKULL; TEETH. [E.D.]

Further Readings

Andrews, P. (1985) Family group systematics and evolution among catarrhine primates. In E. Delson (ed.): Ancestors: The Hard Evidence. New York: Liss, pp. 14–22.

Delson, E., and Andrews, P. (1975) Evolution and interrelationships of the catarrhine primates. In W.P. Luckett and F.S. Szalay (eds.): Phylogeny of the Primates: A Multidisciplinary Approach. New York: Plenum, pp. 405–446

Fleagle, J.G., and Kay, R.F. (1985) The paleobiology of catarrhines. In Delson, pp. 23–36.

Fleagle, J. G., and Kay, R.F. (1988) The phyletic position of the Parapithecidae. J. Hum. Evol. 16:483–531.

Harrison, T. (1987) The phylogenetic relationships of the early catarrhine primates: A review of the current evidence. J. Hum. Evol. 16:41–79.

Szalay, F.S., and Delson, E. (1979) Evolutionary History of the Primates. New York: Academic.

CATCHMENT ANALYSIS *see* ECONOMY, PREHISTORIC

CATEGORY *see* CLASSIFICATION; NOMENCLATURE

CAVE *see* ARCHAEOLOGICAL SITES

CAVE EARTH *see* GLACIATION; PLEISTOCENE

CAVE OF HEARTHS

South African site that produced a fragmentary mandible of a subadult individual, from an Acheulean context, in 1947. The mandible is robust and has a moderate development of a chin and three fairly large teeth. It is notable for the rare condition (in fossil hominids) of congenital absence of the third molar.

See also ARCHAIC HOMO SAPIENS. [C.B.S]

CAVE PAINTING *see* PALEOLITHIC IMAGE

CEBIDAE

Family of New World platyrrhine monkeys including the subfamilies Cebinae (*Cebus, Saimiri*) and Callitrichinae (*Callimico, Saguinus, Leontopithecus, Callithrix, Cebuella*), with their fossil allies, and the extinct subfamily Branisellinae. This taxonomic composition differs from most classifications. The traditional definition of the family dates back to the middle 1800s. It was a gradistic concept designed to accommodate taxa thought to be separated by a chasm of morphological difference. The cebid group distinguished nonmarmosets (i.e. all platyrrhines bearing nailed digits) from the marmosets, which have claws and were judged to be diverse enough to warrant their own family, Callitrichidae or Hapalidae (occasionally the Callimiconidae was recognized as well). It is now known, however, that this arrangement tends to confuse both the phylogenetic and adaptive relationships of various New World monkeys, particularly the cebines and callitrichines. The current concept of the Cebidae is based upon the hypothesis

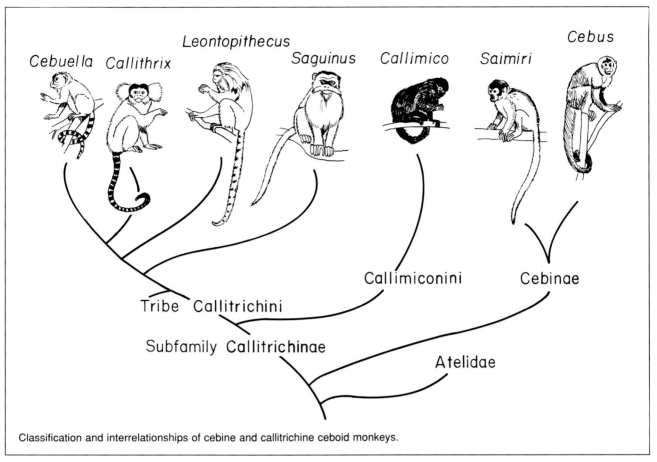

Classification and interrelationships of cebine and callitrichine ceboid monkeys.

that callitrichine marmosets and cebines form a monophyletic unit and that their morphological differences relate to alternative lifestyles within a common frugivorous-insectivorous adaptive zone. The derived traits that these cebids display in common include reduced third molars; broad, large premolars; relatively large canines; and short faces.

See also ATELIDAE; BRANISELLINAE; CALLITRICHINAE; CEBINAE. [A.L.R.]

Further Readings

Hershkovitz, P. (1977) Living New World Monkeys (Platyrrhini), Vol. 1: Callitrichidae. Chicago: University of Chicago Press.

Kinzey, W.G. (1986) New World primate field studies: what's in it for anthropology. Ann. Rev. Anthropol. 15:121–148.

Napier, P.H. (1976) Catalogue of Primates in the British Museum (Natural History), Part 1: Families Callitrichidae and Cebidae. London: British Museum.

Rosenberger, A.L. (1981) Systematics: the higher taxa. In A.F. Coimbra-Filho and R.A. Mittermeier (eds.): Ecology and Behavior of Neotropical Primates. Rio de Janeiro: Academia Brasiliera de Ciencias.

Szalay, F.S., and Delson, E. (1979) Evolutionary History of the Primates. New York: Academic.

CEBINAE

Subfamily of cebid platyrrhine monkeys including *Cebus* (capuchins), *Saimiri* (squirrel monkeys), and fossil allies. They comprise a predaceous-frugivorous,

large-brained radiation, which specializes in foraging concealed insects by gleaning them from foliage and crevices and sorting through dead leaf batches and infestations at broken branch ends. Extinct members include a Holocene form from the Dominican Republic, "*Saimiri*" *bernensis*; a Friasian Miocene (16–14 m.y.) species from Colombia's La Venta, *Neosaimiri fieldsi*; and a Colhuehuapian early Miocene (21–19 m.y.) form from Argentina, *Dolichocebus gaimanensis*. The latter two may have very close, potentially ancestral, phylogenetic ties with *Saimiri*. Cebines share only primitive platyrrhine resemblances with the atelid pitheciines and atelines, with whom they have been traditionally classified. *Cebus* and *Saimiri* share homologous derived traits, such as an enlarged brain, a rounded braincase, centrally placed foramen magnum, close-set orbits, abbreviated faces, large sexually dimorphic canines, broad premolars, robust mandibles, and a semiprehensile tail. These characteristics are all interrelated facets of their foraging strategy.

See also BRAIN; CEBIDAE; DIET; LA VENTA; LOCOMOTION; PATAGONIA; SKULL. [A.L.R.]

Further Readings

Biegert, J. (1963) The evaluation of characteristics of the skull, hands and feet for primate taxonomy. In S.L. Washburn (ed.): Classification and Human Evolution. Chicago: Aldine.

Delson, E., and Rosenberger, A.L. (1984) Are there any anthropoid primate "living fossils"? In N. Eldredge and S. Stanley (eds.): Living Fossils. New York: Springer-Verlag.

Kinzey, W.G. (1986) Primate field studies: what's in it for anthropology. Ann. Rev. Anthropol. 15:121–148.

Rosenberger, A.L. (1979) Cranial anatomy and implication of *Dolichocebus gaimanensis*. Nature 279:416–418.

Rosenberger, A.L. (1983) Tale of tails: parallelism and prehensility. Am. J. Phys. Anthropol. 60:103–107.

Szalay, F.S., and Delson, E. (1979) Evolutionary History of the Primates. New York: Academic.

CEBOIDEA

Primates of South and Central America, including Cebidae and Atelidae; also known as the New World monkeys, or platyrrhines, in reference to their pugnosed faces. Among the anatomical features that distinguish them from the living (but not all of the Oligocene) catarrhines are generally smaller size; 2.1.3.3 dental formula (except in derived callitrichines: 2.1.3.2); wall of eye socket completed by sutural contact of the zygomatic with the parietal bone of braincase; and eardrum supported by a ring-shaped ectotympanic bone fused to skull. The diversified, strictly arboreal ceboid radiation is represented by some 60 living species but by less than a dozen fossil forms. Although termed monkeys, ceboids tend to resemble living apes and their ancestors rather than the cercopithecoid monkeys of the Old World.

See also ATELIDAE; ATELINAE; CEBIDAE; CEBINAE; MONKEY. [A.L.R.]

CEBUELLA   *see*   CALLITRICHINAE

CEBUPITHECIA   *see*   PITHECIINAE

CEBUS   *see*   CEBINAE

CEMENTUM   *see*   TEETH

CENOZOIC

Youngest and shortest era in the geological time scale, encompassing the last 65 m.y. of earth history, from the last major extinction event at the end of the Cretaceous to the present. Traditionally the Cenozoic has been divided into two periods, the Tertiary and Quaternary, whose names echo primitive geological concepts of lithic succession (in which "Tertiary" meant sedimentary strata and "Quaternary" meant loose drift and alluvium). As a result the Tertiary comprises most of the Cenozoic and the Quaternary is restricted to the last 1.5 m.y., the period of glaciation and modern drainage systems. Recently the terms Paleogene and Neogene have grown in favor, especially in oceanographic studies, as approximately equal divisions of the Cenozoic that are based on less anachronistic criteria.

The Cenozoic is popularly known as the "Age of Mammals," more by inheritance than by conquest, as it now appears. Primates, together with monotremes and marsupials, are the only extant mammal group known to originate before the Cenozoic (the earliest primate, *Purgatorius*, is from the latest Cretaceous of Montana). All modern primates, however, apparently derive from a diverse stock that was isolated in Africa during the early Cenozoic, while the order was becoming extinct elsewhere.

From the Paleocene to the early Oligocene global climate was highly oceanic, with efficient transfer of equatorial heat to high latitudes and a well-developed circumtropical current via the Tethys Sea, which separated the southern and northern continents. Polar refrigeration was greatly reduced, although an ice cap was probably present on the Antarctic highlands, and as a result the deep seas were warm and relatively stagnant at depth. Seasons were relatively undifferentiated and aridity was rare.

Gradually, however, northward motion of "Gondwana" plates pinched off the Tethys while opening up the Antarctic. The Eocene closing of the Himalaya-Tien Shan-Elburz suture by the docking of the Indopakistan, Persian, and Anatolian landmasses, and the Oligocene closing of the Mesogean seaway in the Alpine-Carpathian suture, diverted but did not greatly impede the equatorial circumglobal circulation. Total blockage came first in the Miocene contact of Afro-Arabia against the Anatolian and Iranian borderland and subsequently by the Pliocene erection of the Isthmus of Panama. Simultaneously the Circum-Antarctic Current became influential in the later Oligocene and grew steadily more powerful as Australia and South America moved away from Antarctica. This was the main factor in the expansion of the Antarctic ice sheet and the change to the highly dynamic temperature-driven ocean circulation of the later Cenozoic. Under these circumstances the modern "continental" climate came into being. The seasonally variable, highly differentiated and unstable conditions intensified in a "stepwise" deterioration of conditions from the later Miocene onward, controlling the direction taken by hominoid and human evolution.

See also GLACIATION; GRANDE COUPURE; NEOGENE; PALEOGENE; PLATE TECTONICS; PLEISTOCENE; TIME SCALE. [J.A.V.C., R.L.B.]

Further Readings

Berger, W.H., and Crowell, J.C., eds. (1982) Climates in Earth History. Washington, D.C.: National Academic Press.

Briskin, M., ed. (1983) Paleoclimatology and chronology of the Cenozoic. Paleogeogr., Paleoclimatol., Paleoecol. 42:1–209.

CERCAMONIUS *see* ADAPIDAE

CERCOCEBUS *see* CERCOPITHECINAE

CERCOPITHECIDAE

Family of living and extinct anthropoid primates, commonly known as the Old World monkeys. Cercopithecidae as recognized here is classified in the superfamily Cercopithecoidea, along with the Oreopithecidae, and includes three subfamilies: Cercopithecinae, Colobinae, and the extinct Victoriapithecinae. The diagnostic derived characters of cercopithecids include loss of the hypoconulid on dP_4–M_2, elongation of the cheek teeth, and realignment of the cusps into a bilophodont pattern with occluding upper and lower molars becoming mirror images of each other, an adaptation mainly for folding and slicing leaves (incomplete in Victoriapithecinae); flare or widening of cheek teeth from the cusp apexes to the cervix; extension of the P_3 mesial flange below the alveolar plane and extension of the C^1 mesial sulcus onto the root, both especially in males (former unknown in Victoriapithecinae); shortened posterior calcaneal facet for the astragalus and divided anteromedial facet, which stabilizes the lower ankle joint (unknown in Victoriapithecinae); and restriction of the hallucal facet on the entocuneiform (also unknown in Victoriapithecinae), again to stabi-

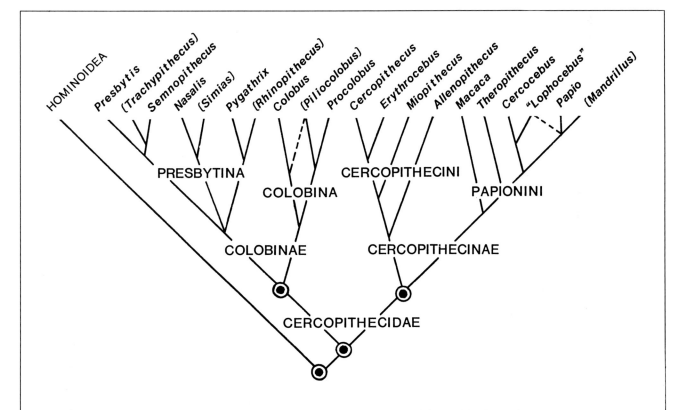

Cladogram of relationships among genera and subgenera (in parentheses) of Cercopithecidae, with subfamilies, tribes, and subtribes indicated. (From Strasser and Delson, 1987.)

lize the foot for terrestrial or cursorial locomotion. A high and narrow nasal aperture probably characterized the ancestral cercopithecid but is unknown in Victoriapithecinae and was secondarily modified in the cercopithecine tribe Papionini.

This combination of features, along with conservative retentions from a catarrhine ancestry, like a narrow thorax, long ulnar olecranon and styloid pro- cesses, narrow ilium, strong ischial tuberosity (and callosities), and long tail, allow some reconstruction of the mode of life of the common ancestor of the cercopithecids. One of the major adaptations of the family was a shift to greater use of a terrestrial substrate, either in open country or on the forest floor. The dentition is modified to include more leaves in the diet, a shift from the more purely frugivorous diet

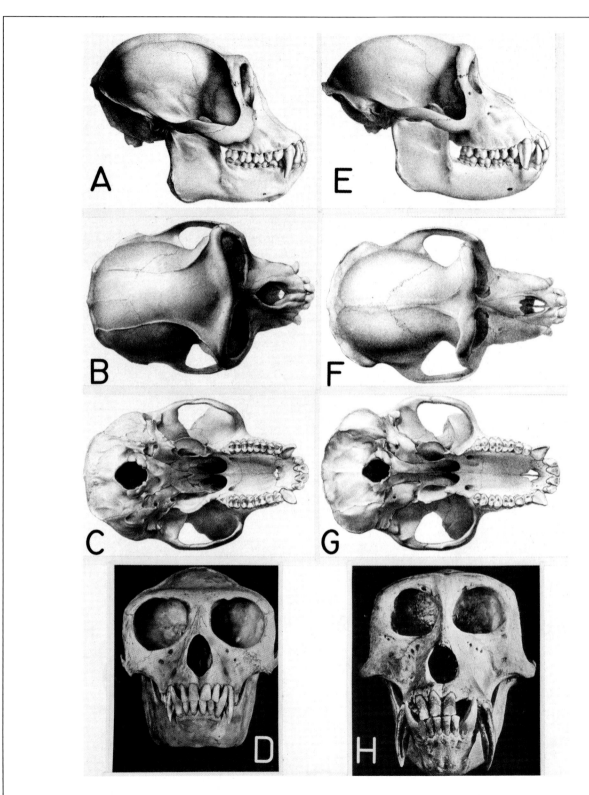

Crania of medium-sized male cercopithecids, illustrating the two major patterns seen in the family: on the left, *Pygathrix*, a colobine; and on the right, *Macaca*, a cercopithecine. Views, top to bottom: right lateral, dorsal, basal, frontal. (From Szalay and Delson, 1979.)

of early eucatarrhines. Perhaps this was to permit early monkeys to compete with contemporaneous pliopithecids and early hominoids in marginal or seasonally varying habitats, where fruits were sometimes scarce but leaves usually plentiful. This emphasis on lower-quality foods was increased in the colobines, where the dentition and digestive system were further modified to facilitate a diet that in some species consists mainly of young leaves. Cercopithecines, on the other hand, emphasized a more varied diet, often in at least partly open habitats in which a variety of foodstuffs were available.

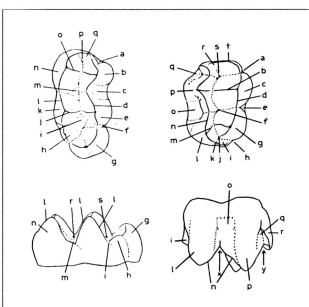

Upper and lower molar of *Theropithecus* to illustrate cercopithecid morphology and terminology used in descriptions. Left: M3 in lingual and occlusal views. Right: M3 in occlusal and buccal views. In all views, raised features indicated by solid line, depressed features by dotted line. For complete dentitions, see illustrations in articles CERCOPITHECINAE and COLOBINAE. Structures labelled on lower tooth: a) mesial buccal cleft; b) protoconid; c) median buccal cleft; d) buccal margin; e) hypoconid; f) distal buccal cleft; g) hypoconulid; h) 6th cusp (tuberculum sextum); i) distal fovea; j) hypolophid; k) entoconid; l) lingual margin; m) talonid basin; n) metaconid; o) protolophid; p) trigonid basin (mesial fovea); q) mesial shelf; r) median lingual notch; s) distal lingual notch. Structures labelled on upper tooth: a) mesial buccal cleft; b) paraloph; c) paracone; d) buccal margin; e) median buccal cleft; f) trigon basin; g) metacone; h) distal buccal cleft; i) distal shelf; j) distal fovea (talon basin); k) distal lingual cleft; l) hypocone; m) metaloph; n) lingual margin; o) median lingual cleft; p) protocone; q) mesial lingual cleft; r) mesial shelf; s) mesial fovea; t) mesial margin. From Szalay and Delson, 1979.

The early history of Cercopithecidae is entirely African, with the first entry to Eurasia probably in the earliest late Miocene (ca. 11 m.y. ago). The later early Miocene and early middle Miocene saw a variety of victoriapithecine species present in northern and eastern Africa, with the primate assemblage at the partly open woodland habitats of Maboko Island (Kenya) dominated by this group. Although the fossil record is scarce from 14 to 8 m.y., it is possible to suggest the following outline of cercopithecid diversification. The early colobines probably increased the proportion of leaves in their diet in a more arboreal habitat, as evidenced also by the beginning of thumb reduction even in the semiterrestrial *Mesopithecus*. This European late Miocene colobine represents a clade that may have exited Africa to Eurasia via a partly forested corridor, presumably through the Near East. At the same time early cercopithecines, with no fossil documentation at all, may have increased their adaptations to terrestriality, involving lengthened faces as well as postcranial changes; they appear also to have returned to a more frugivorous diet, perhaps as a result of competition with the colobines. In turn they may have competed successfully with the frugivorous hominoids, which were forced to alter their mode(s) of locomotion radically to obtain food unavailable to the cercopithecines. Probably later during the late Miocene the cercopithecins (tribe Cercopithecini) reentered the forest, undergoing dental changes in parallel with colobines (flare reduction and M$_3$ hypoconulid loss) and perhaps diversifying through chromosomal fissioning. The larger-bodied papionins appear to have been divided into three major units by the expansion of the Sahara desert barrier during the late Miocene, with the macaque group eventually spreading into Eurasia from North Africa, the geladas adapting to first edaphic and then drier grasslands and the baboon-mandrill-mangabey lineage entering a broad range of habitats in sub-Saharan Africa.

See also AFRICA; CATARRHINI; CERCOPITHECINAE; CERCOPITHECOIDEA; COLOBINAE; HOMINOIDEA; MONKEY; OREOPITHECIDAE; PRIMATE ECOLOGY; PRIMATE SOCIETIES; VICTORIAPITHECINAE. [E.D.]

Further Readings

Andrews, P. (1981) Species diversity and diet in monkeys and apes during the Miocene. In C.B. Stringer (ed.): Aspects of Human Evolution. London: Taylor and Francis, pp. 25-61.

Ripley, S. (1979) Environmental grain, niche diversification, and positional behavior in Neogene primates: an evolutionary hypothesis. In M.E. Morbeck, H. Preuschoft, and N. Gomberg (eds.): Environment, Behavior and Morphology: Dynamic Interactions in Primates. New York: Fischer, pp. 37-74.

Szalay, F.S., and Delson, E. (1979) Evolutionary History of the Primates. New York: Academic.

Temerin, L.A., and Cant, J.G. (1980) The evolutionary divergence of Old World monkeys and apes. Amer. Nat. *122*:335-351.

CERCOPITHECINAE

Subfamily of Old World monkeys including the cheek-pouched cercopithecids, such as guenons

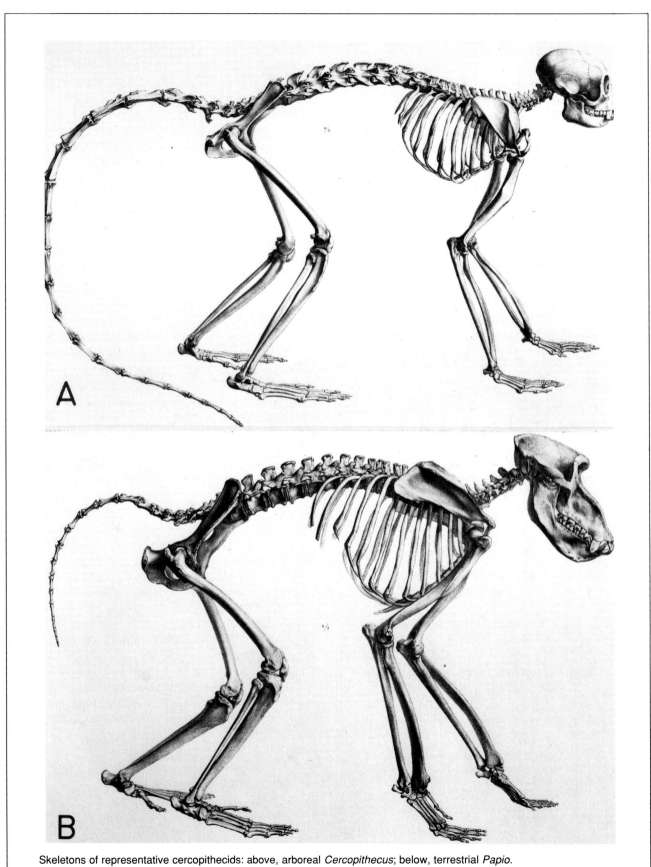

Skeletons of representative cercopithecids: above, arboreal *Cercopithecus*; below, terrestrial *Papio*.

(*Cercopithecus* and allies), baboons and mandrills (*Papio*), macaques (*Macaca*), and mangabeys (*Cercocebus*) and their extinct relatives. The underlying adaptation of the cercopithecines appears to be their increased reliance on the terrestrial environment for feeding and social activities, although some members of the subfamily are highly arboreal. As part of a general increase in terrestriality in comparison with ancestral cercopithecids the earliest cercopithecines apparently evolved several novel features that continue to characterize all of their descendants, whatever their current mode of life. The derived conditions of Cercopithecinae are essentially craniodental and include large pouches in the cheeks for temporary storage of food; relatively enlarged I²; loss of enamel on the lingual surfaces of both lower incisors; facial elongation, linked with narrow interorbital distance, long nasal bones, lacrimal bone extending beyond the anteroinferior border of the orbit with lacrimal fossa wholly enclosed within that bone, vomer expanded to form part of the medial wall of the orbit, and ethmoid apparently expanded anteriorly; low-vaulted and long neurocranium; mandibular corpus deepening mesially and symphysis with poorly developed inferior torus; brain modification involving rostral expansion of the occipital region and increase of association and visual cortex, documented on the surface by numerous sulcal modifications. Postcranially cercopithecines differ from colobines in several consistent ways, but the majority of these are conservative retentions from the common cercopithecid ancestor, while in others morphocline polarity is uncertain (e.g. robust and straight-shafted limbs, subequal supratrochlear and supracapitular fossae on the distal humerus, and doubled radial articular surface on the proximal ulna). Most of these locomotor-related features are probably retained from an increasingly terrestrial ancestral cercopithecine, which was also the interpretation offered for cheek pouches: filled with food while an animal was foraging terrestrially, then emptied if the animal fled to the security of upper branches. Carefully designed studies revealed to the contrary that terrestrial species have reduced pouches, implying less terrestriality at the origin of this feature. Cercopithecines have a varied diet including fruit as its usual central focus, and their generally large incisors and especially the reduction of enamel on the lowers are adaptations for scraping and cutting the outer covering of tough fruits prior to reduction of pieces by the molars. Cercopithecine cheek teeth appear to be broadly conservative, with low relief compared with those of colobines, as well as greater flare, or basal broadening, and longer trigonids; the last feature may in fact be derived. It appears that this dentition was originally evolved for a mixed leaf and fruit diet, by comparison with the more frugivorous ancestral catarrhine diet, and that cercopithecines, especially the baboon-macaque group, hardly modified it subsequently.

Within the Cercopithecinae there are two major subdivisions, or tribes, which can each be further divided into subtribes; for the sake of simplicity the latter level is not recognized here, but the characters of these groups can be reviewed. The tribe Cercopithecini includes the mainly arboreal guenons (*Cercopithecus*) and talapoins (*Miopithecus*), the perhaps semiterrestrial swamp monkey *Allenopithecus*, and the very terrestrial patas (*Erythrocebus*). All of these share loss of the hypoconulid on M₃ (lost on anterior cheek teeth in ancestral cercopithecids) and an increase in chromosome number above 42. *Allenopithecus* is conservative and the other three genera derived in having reduced molar flare and the male ischial callosities separated by a strip of hairy skin. *Cercopithecus* further presents greatly increased diploid chromosome number over the 48 of *Allenopithecus* and the 54 seen in *Miopithecus* and *Erythrocebus*, and it shares with *Erythrocebus* loss of a roughly monthly cycle in its female sexual swellings. This suggests that *Allenopithecus* is most similar to the common ancestor of all cercopithecins and its lineage diverged first, followed in turn by those of talapoins, patas, and the many guenons. The swamp-living adaptations of the first two of these clades may suggest this as the original environment to which the tribe was adapted.

Patas monkeys live in open woodlands with acacia trees between the Sahara and the rain forests of central Africa. Small troops led by a single adult male have large ranges. Different authorities recognize between one and two dozen species within *Cercopithecus*, but there are only about six to eight ecological-behavioral patterns. *C. aethiops* is quite terrestrial, living in gallery forests along watercourses, but most other species are highly arboreal. Members of four to six species may inhabit a single grove of trees, at different canopy levels or concentrating on complementary foods. Multispecies associations are common in generally unimale troops. The fossil record of this tribe is scarce, but characteristic teeth are known from Kenyan and Ethiopian localities as old as 3 m.y.

The second, far more diverse and widespread, cercopithecine tribe is Papionini, including the macaques of North Africa and eastern Asia and the baboons, mandrills, mangabeys, and geladas (*Theropithecus*) of sub-Saharan Africa. There may only be one distinct derived character of this tribe, a secondary increase in the maximum width of the nasal aperture, but papionins are characterized by further

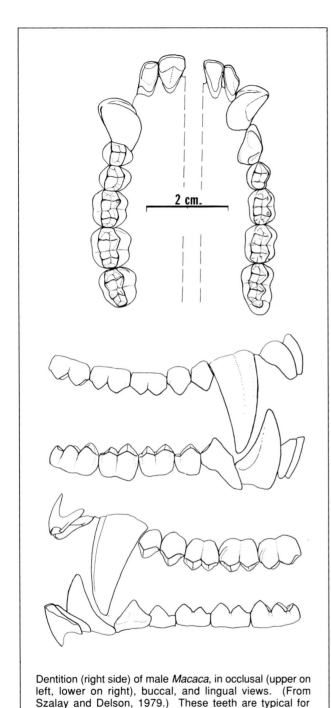

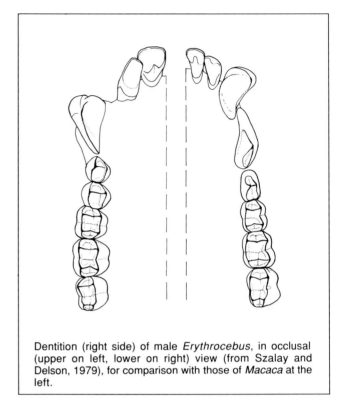

Dentition (right side) of male *Erythrocebus*, in occlusal (upper on left, lower on right) view (from Szalay and Delson, 1979), for comparison with those of *Macaca* at the left.

Dentition (right side) of male *Macaca*, in occlusal (upper on left, lower on right), buccal, and lingual views. (From Szalay and Delson, 1979.) These teeth are typical for Papionini.

development of such cercopithecine tendencies as increased molar flare, accessory cuspules in molar clefts, an elongated face, posterior inclination of the mandibular ramus, and a generally high degree of terrestriality. It has been suggested that the two geographic divisions of Papionini represent true clades, separated by the development of the Sahara Desert as an ecological barrier to continued north-south migration and gene flow during the late Miocene (ca. 10–7 m.y. ago). As yet no clear and consistent morphologi-

cal features characterize these two, but the African genera do share a steep drop in facial profile in front of the orbits and often hollows or fossae on the maxilla and the lateral surfaces of the mandible (facial fossae). Chromosome number is constant at 42 and the dentition of almost all papionins is identical, although some mangabeys have especially high flare, while geladas, which have at times been considered to represent a third subtribe, have uniquely derived dental and cranial form.

Macaques inhabit a wide range of environments, including rain forest, woodland, steppe, and snow-covered regions, and their diets are concomitantly varied. Some of the dozen or so recognized species are highly arboreal, others semiterrestrial, most live in multimale troops with female as well as male hierarchies and maternally inherited social status. Mangabeys are ecological equivalents of macaques in the African forests, with some species making much more use of the ground than others. Two groups are sometimes recognized as full genera, and some evidence suggests that they are not each other's closest relatives (i.e. that mangabeys as a group are paraphyletic). Savanna baboons form a single widespread species ranging from Guinea (West African coast) to Ethiopia and southern Saudi Arabia, down to South Africa and into Angola. Six subgroups may be recognized, which used to be thought full species but have since been observed to interbreed in overlap zones, confirming the genetic unity of the species. Multi-

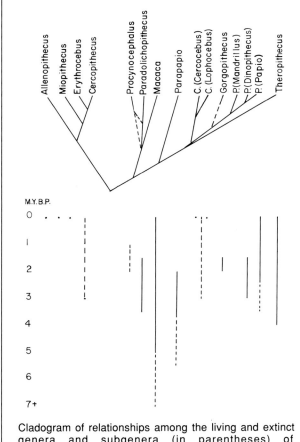

Cladogram of relationships among the living and extinct genera and subgenera (in parentheses) of Cercopithecinae. Dotted lines indicate uncertain links. Note that some molecular data contradict this morphological interpretation, suggesting instead that *Theropithecus* and *Lophocebus* are farther removed. Below the cladogram are indicated the known time ranges of these genera; solid lines indicate well-preserved fossils, dotted lines indicate fragmentary remains, less clear allocations or dating uncertainty.

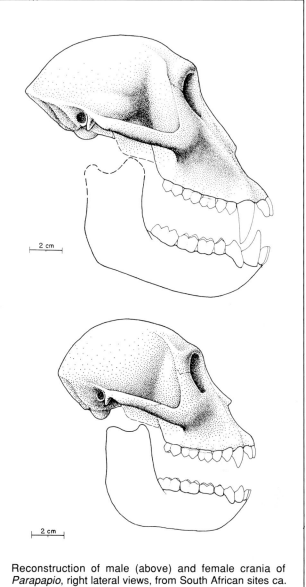

Reconstruction of male (above) and female crania of *Parapapio*, right lateral views, from South African sites ca. 3–2.5 m.y. old. The facial outline is close to that seen in some macaques (a conservative feature), and the postcranium suggests a semiterrestrial adaptation. (From Szalay and Delson, 1979.)

male troops are the rule, especially in open country, but in forest habitats the structured social hierarchies are less evident. Mandrills are deep-forest representatives of the same genus, with brightly colored faces in the male to serve as signals in unimale troops. The living gelada is the last remnant of a once widespread lineage, now restricted to the dry uplands of Ethiopia. There *Theropithecus* individuals live in unimale "harems," which may come together in associations of several hundred for sleeping on scattered cliffs and for feeding in certain seasons. They are the most terrestrially adapted of living monkeys, with short digits for better walking and for manipulation of the grass blades and stems that form their dietary staple. Their teeth have converged on those of colobines in having high relief (deep notches and elevated cusp tips), but they also have thick enamel and a characteristic wear pattern to prolong tooth life while grinding up this low-quality gritty diet.

The fossil record of Papionini is rich, especially in Africa. The earliest members of the tribe are known by teeth from North Africa and Kenya late in the Miocene (8–6 m.y.), perhaps, from geological evidence, after the Sahara had formed an ecological barrier. In the Pliocene (4–2 m.y.) of eastern and southern Africa the conservative *Parapapio* is fairly common. It has a similar facial conformation to macaques and mangabeys (but may share some anteorbital deepening with *Papio*), and rare postcranial elements suggest a semiterrestrial adaptation. *Para-*

papio may represent a form close to the common ancestor of later African papionins. At least three species of *Theropithecus* are frequent, especially at waterside sites. Two of these form a lineage known across Africa, from southern South Africa to Morocco, from the early Pliocene to the later middle Pleistocene. They are characterized by gradual size increase and anterior tooth reduction through time, and the late large forms probably were hunted by Acheulean peoples, perhaps to extinction. Several teeth suggest that this group also reached the Siwaliks of India ca. 2 m.y. ago! Another lineage is represented only in the Lake Turkana region, at Koobi Fora (Kenya) and Omo (Ethiopia) between ca. 3 and 2 m.y.; they had *Papio*-like large incisors and low, flat muzzle with typical gelada molars and flaring zygomatic arches.

The living *T. gelada* is more conservative than either of these clades and probably separated from them by 4–3 m.y. ago.

Cercocebus is poorly represented paleontologically, probably because forest soils are notoriously acid-rich (bone thus deteriorates quickly), but some East African Pleistocene specimens have diagnostic facial features of the genus. *Papio* is known by large-bodied populations probably referable to the living savanna baboon species in both eastern and southern Africa after 3 m.y., but they were almost always less common than *Theropithecus*. It has been suggested that they were then more forest-fringe dwellers, while geladas were more successful in open country, the pattern changing only recently. Small-bodied *Papio* is also known in South Africa between 2.5 and 1.5 m.y.

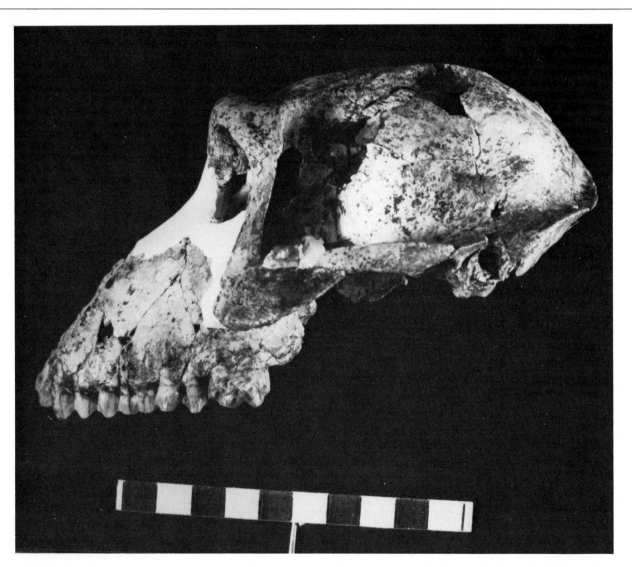

Female cranium of *Theropithecus oswaldi* in left lateral view, from Swartkrans (South Africa), ca. 1.8 m.y. (Photograph © Eric Delson.)

ago, and a very large form known as *P.* (*Dinopithecus*) is common at sites in South Africa, Angola, and Ethiopia from 3 to 1.5 m.y. Although this group has previously been given its own genus, it differs from *Papio* only in lacking facial fossae and is now considered a baboon subgenus, as are the mandrills. The large-bodied *Gorgopithecus* is represented only at one group of South African sites between 1.9 and 1.5 m.y. ago, but its distinctive facial conformation, deep fossae, and reduced dental sexual dimorphism justify its generic identity.

Macaque fossils are known in North Africa and across Europe from Britain to the Caucasus throughout the Pliocene and Pleistocene (5 m.y. onward). The living "Barbary ape" (*Macaca sylvanus*) of Algeria and Gibraltar probably represents the remaining relic of this far wider distribution. Living macaques have been divided into four to six subgroups, all of which show independent reduction in tail length and have overlapping distributions in eastern Asia. Fossil teeth document their arrival in India by ca. 2.5 m.y. ago, and a variety of populations are known from the Pleistocene of China and Indonesia. The extinct *Paradolichopithecus* was larger-bodied than any macaque, far more terrestrially adapted, and less cranially sex-dimorphic but had similar facial morphology. It is known from Spain through central Asia in

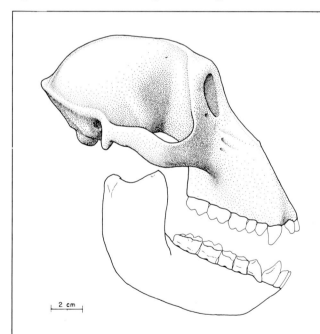

Reconstruction of female *Paradolichopithecus* cranium in right lateral view, from Senèze, France, ca. 2 m.y. B.P. Although cranially similar to macaques, this extinct genus was larger and more terrestrial and showed less sexual dimorphism in crania and teeth. (From Szalay and Delson, 1979.)

the later Pliocene (ca. 3–1.7 m.y.) and probably represents a baboonlike macaque derivative. A similar form, *Procynocephalus*, is represented by fragmentary remains from the later Pliocene of India and China; it is kept distinct until it is known to share the reduced dimorphism of its western "cousin."

See also AFRICA; CERCOPITHECIDAE; COLOBINAE; DIET; EUROPE; EXTINCTION; MIOCENE; MONKEY; PALEOBIOGEOGRAPHY; PLEISTOCENE; PLIOCENE; PRIMATE ECOLOGY; PRIMATE SOCIETIES; SIWALIKS; TEETH. [E.D.]

Further Readings

Delson, E. (1984) Cercopithecid biochronology of the African Plio-Pleistocene: correlation among eastern and southern hominid-bearing localities. Cour. Forsch. Inst. Senckenberg 69:199–218.

Lindburg, D.E., ed. (1980) The Macaques: Studies in Ecology, Behavior and Evolution. New York: Van Nostrand.

Maranto, G. (1986) Will guenons make a monkey of Darwin? Discover 10:87–101.

Murray, P. (1975) The role of cheek pouches in cercopithecine monkey adaptive strategy. In R. Tuttle (ed.): Primate Functional Morphology and Evolution. The Hague: Mouton, pp. 151–194.

Rowell, T.E. (1985) Guenons, macaques and baboons. In D. MacDonald (ed.): The Encyclopedia of Mammals. New York: Facts-on-File, pp. 370–381.

Shellis, R.P., and Hiiemae, K.M. (1986) Distribution of enamel on the incisors of Old World monkeys. Am. J. Phys. Anthropol. 71:103–113.

Strasser, E., and Delson, E. (1987) Cladistic analysis of cercopithecid relationships. J. Hum. Evol. 16:81–99.

Szalay, F.S., and Delson, E. (1979) Evolutionary History of the Primates. New York: Academic.

CERCOPITHECINI *see* CERCOPITHECINAE

CERCOPITHECOIDEA

One of the two extant superfamilies of Old World anthropoids (Catarrhini), including the families Cercopithecidae (Old World monkeys) and perhaps Oreopithecidae (extinct Italian "swamp monkeys"). Although cercopithecoids are termed *monkeys*, they are not closely related to the platyrrhine monkeys of the New World but instead are the sister taxon of the Hominoidea (apes and humans). Together the hominoids and cercopithecoids form a monophyletic subgroup of the catarrhines, but that grouping is not named here, to minimize proliferation of terminology. The common ancestor of hominoids and cercopithecoids was probably an animal comparable with the Oligocene Propliopithecidae or the Miocene Pliopithecidae.

The morphological distinctions of Cercopithecoidea are of necessity those that characterize both

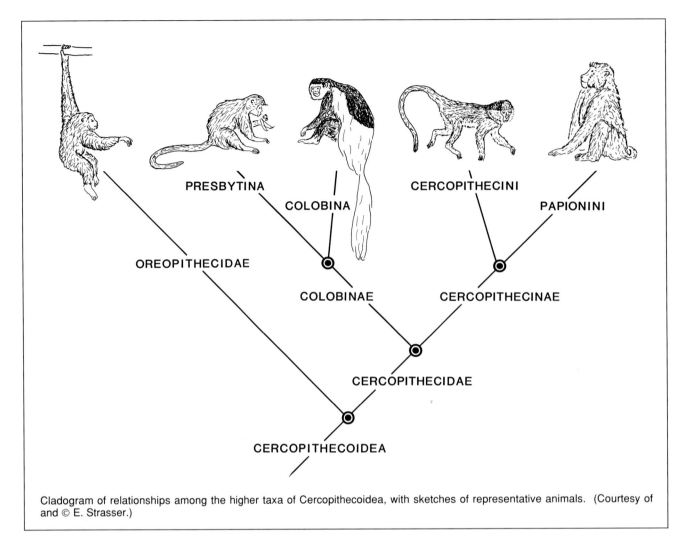

Cladogram of relationships among the higher taxa of Cercopithecoidea, with sketches of representative animals. (Courtesy of and © E. Strasser.)

cercopithecids and oreopithecids. These include increased relief of cheek teeth (between cusp tips and basin floors) and restriction of cingulum on both uppers and lowers mainly to intercusp clefts; elongation of upper molars; and perhaps some enlargement of lower molar trigonids and reduction of hypoconulids. Other researchers consider that the sharing of these features by oreopithecids and cercopithecids represents convergence, outweighed as an indicator of phylogeny by what they see as shared derived features of the postcranium. The conflict is not yet resolved, but here we assume common ancestry of Oreopithecidae and Cercopithecidae to the exclusion of the hominoids.

On that basis the origin of Cercopithecoidea may have occurred in the late Oligocene (ca. 30–25 m.y. ago), while Africa was still isolated from Eurasia. A shift toward the inclusion of more leafy material in a previously frugivorous diet would presumably have been at the root of the adaptive changes in morphology that we recognize as the differentiation of a distinct superfamily. Cercopithecoids are extremely rare until the later early Miocene (ca. 19 m.y.), when members of both families appear in eastern African localities. The first possible oreopithecid is *Rangwapithecus*, previously considered a variety of *Proconsul* but differing from that genus in the elongation of its upper molars and a greater development of shearing crests. A few younger African species provide a link to the only well-known oreopithecid, *Oreopithecus bambolii* of the later Miocene (9–8 m.y.) of Italy. That species presents a variety of postcranial features in common with hominoids, which indicate that it was a suspensory arborealist, but its feet are distinct from those of either cercopithecids or hominoids, based on the latest analysis.

The first cercopithecids are represented by teeth contemporaneous with *Rangwapithecus*, but jaws and postcranial specimens do not appear until the early middle Miocene (16–15 m.y.). At that time two genera assigned to the subfamily Victoriapithecinae occur in a number of eastern and northern African localities. The most complete information comes from the Kenyan site of Maboko Island, where hundreds of fragmentary fossils have been allocated to *Victoriapithecus macinnesi*. It has been suggested that more than one species is known in this collection, but that has recently been refuted. At least the great majority of specimens reveal an adaptation to partly terrestrial life and a diet probably combining leaves and fruits. Representatives of the two modern subfamilies, Colobinae and Cercopithecinae, first appear in the late Miocene (after 10 m.y.).

Early colobines in both Africa and Europe already demonstrate the further increased molar-crown relief indicative of a folivorous diet and, in Europe, the beginning of thumb reduction typical of the group today. The African branch of the subfamily diversified greatly during the Pliocene, with a number of species much larger than any now living, including one strongly adapted to terrestrial locomotion. This diversity decreased by the early Pleistocene, but two genera and perhaps six species survive today. The extinct European lineage, including three partly to fully terrestrial species, died out by the late Pliocene (ca. 3 m.y. ago), but was probably related to the numerous living species in Asia. The fossil record of the latter is scarce, but teeth first appear by 7 m.y., and at least one distinctive species, possibly belonging to the European genus *Dolichopithecus*, lived in Mongolia ca. 2.5 m.y. ago.

The Cercopithecinae is divided into two tribes, the mainly forest-living guenons and patas (Cercopithecini), with a poor fossil record, and the widespread Papionini (macaques, baboons, and relatives). The African Pliocene and Pleistocene document a succession of genera of partly to fully terrestrial baboons, as well as a variety of lesser-known taxa. Macaques are first known in the late Miocene of North Africa (ca. 8–5 m.y. ago), whence they spread into Europe, remaining until the end of the Pleistocene, and Asia, where numerous species persist today. Terrestrial offshoots of the macaques apparently evolved independently in Europe and eastern Asia during the Pliocene but disappeared by the earlier Pleistocene (before 1 m.y. ago).

See also ANTHROPOIDEA; APE; CATARRHINI; CERCOPITHECIDAE; HOMINOIDEA; MIOCENE; MONKEY; OREOPITHECIDAE; PLIOCENE; PLIOPITHECIDAE; PRIMATES; PROPLIOPITHECIDAE; TEETH; VICTORIAPITHECINAE. [E.D.]

Further Readings

Harrison, T. (1986) New fossil anthropoids from the Middle Miocene of East Africa and their bearing on the origin of the Oreopithecidae. Am. J. Phys. Anthropol. 71:265–284.

Szalay, F.S., and Delson, E. (1979) Evolutionary History of the Primates. New York: Academic.

CERCOPITHECOIDES see COLOBINAE

CERCOPITHECUS see CERCOPITHECINAE

CERNAYSIAN see EOCENE; TIME SCALE

CHAD see YAYO

CHADRONIAN see EOCENE; TIME SCALE

CHARACTER see CLADISTICS

CHARACTER ANALYSIS see CLADISTICS

CHARACTER STATE see CLADISTICS

CHARENTIAN MOUSTERIAN see MOUSTERIAN

CHASSELASIA see LORISOIDEA

CHATELPERRONIAN

Earliest Upper Paleolithic or final Middle Paleolithic industry of central and southwestern France, extending to northeastern Spain, and dated to 35–32 k.y. by radiocarbon, in association with sediments reflecting cold but fluctuating conditions at the end of a major Weichselian interstadial. Named after the Grotte des Fées at Châtelperron (Allier), the Chatelperronian is characterized by some of the earliest bone, antler, and ivory objects (especially tubular beads); by perforated teeth and shells and other pendants in stone and bone; by curved backed or abruptly retouched knives or points; and by the appearance of burins. Incised stone plaques have also been found at Chatelperronian sites. At the Grotte du Renne at Arcy-sur-Cure (Yonne), an arrangement of postholes, stone blocks, and artifacts was interpreted as a hut floor; traces of several smaller structures were reported from the open site of Les Tambourets (Haute-Garonne). Faunal remains at most sites are dominated by reindeer, with numerous examples of horse, bovines, and woolly rhinoceros.

Initially denoted by H. Breuil in 1906 as the earliest stage of the Aurignacian, the backing technique and dominance of burins led D. Peyrony in 1933 to classify the Chatelperronian industry, known from La Ferrassie E, as the first stage of the Perigordian tradition of southwestern France. Up to 50 percent of each Chatelperronian assemblage, however, is made up of Levallois flakes and cores, side-scrapers, and other tools of Mousterian type. The only clearly identifiable human skeletal material definitely associated with a Chatelperronian industry (excepting the material from Combe Capelle, which is of uncertain provenance) is that of a Neanderthal, discovered at Saint-Césaire (Charente-Maritime) in 1979. As in the early Upper Paleolithic leaf-shaped-point industries of central and eastern Europe the flake technology and skeletal associations of the Chatelperronian have been cited as evidence for an *in situ* development of Upper Paleolithic technology by humans of Neanderthal type.

At two sites in southwestern France, Roc de Combe (Lot) and Le Piage (Dordogne), the Chatelperronian is interstratified with the earliest Aurignacian industries, which are widespread in central and southern France by 32,000–30,000 B.P. This interstratification has been used to support Peyrony's "parallel phyla" hypothesis of contemporaneous Au-

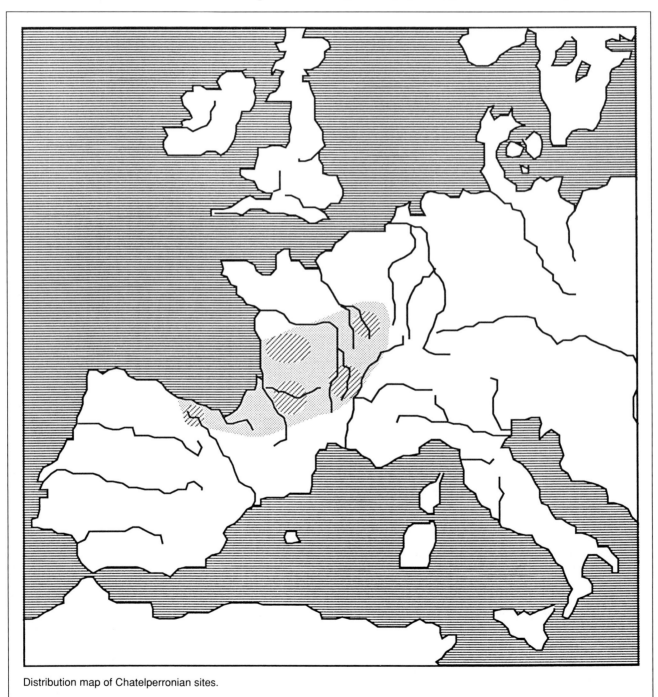

Distribution map of Chatelperronian sites.

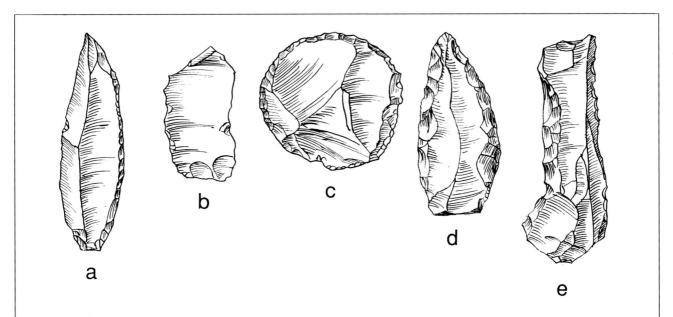

Chatelperronian lithic artifacts: a) Chatelperronian knife; b) burin; c) circular scraper; d) Mousterian point; e) denticulate on truncated blade.

rignacian and Perigordian cultural traditions repeatedly replacing each other at certain sites in southwestern France, with little admixture or mutual influence, over a period of ca. 15 k.y. Other scholars see little evidence for contemporaneity over large parts of the early Upper Paleolithic and do not recognize the similarities between Chatelperronian and later Perigordian assemblages as evidence of cultural continuity.

See also AURIGNACIAN; BREUIL, HENRI; JEWELRY; LA FERRASSIE; LATE PALEOLITHIC; MIDDLE PALEOLITHIC; MOUSTERIAN; NEANDERTHALS; PALEOLITHIC IMAGE; PALEOLITHIC LIFEWAYS; PERIGORDIAN; PEYRONY, DENIS; SAINT-CÉSAIRE; STONE-TOOL MAKING; SZELETIAN; UPPER PALEOLITHIC. [A.S.B.]

Further Readings

Wymer, J. (1982) The Palaeolithic Age. New York: St. Martin's.

CHEIROGALEIDAE

Family of Lorisoidea that contains the Malagasy members of the superfamily. Five genera, all extant, are recognized: *Cheirogaleus, Microcebus, Mirza, Allocebus,* and *Phaner.* All cheirogaleids are nocturnal in activity pattern and arboreal in habitat.

With body weights fluctuating seasonally around a mean of ca. 60 gm., the two species of *Microcebus,* the mouse lemur, are the smallest primates of Madagascar and among the smallest in the world, rivaled only by Demidoff's bushbaby and the pygmy marmoset. Although mouse lemurs are active individually at night, they generally sleep together in groups during the daylight hours, either in leaf nests or in tree hollows. "Population nuclei" of mouse lemurs, from which subordinate males appear to be peripheralized, contain a preponderance of females, the nightly ranges of several of which are overlapped by those of central males. These ranges are small, and *Microcebus* seems to be most successful in secondary forest formations. In correlation with their small body size mouse lemurs are the most insectivorous of the Malagasy primates, but fruit and flowers seem to provide a large proportion of their diet, which is essentially opportunistic.

Most closely related to *Microcebus,* but larger-bodied at ca. 280 gm., is *Mirza coquereli,* Coquerel's dwarf lemur. This lemur also constructs elaborate daytime sleeping nests and may exhibit a "loose pair bonding," although male and female nightly ranges, while overlapping, do not coincide. These ranges may be up to 25 acres in extent, but most time is spent in much smaller "core areas." During the wet season, when resources are abundant, Coquerel's dwarf lemurs feed opportunistically, primarily on fruit, flowers, and insects. In the dry season they subsist, at least regionally, mostly on larval secretions.

Allocebus, the hairy-eared dwarf lemur, and *Phaner,* the fork-marked lemur, form a group characterized by the presence of enlarged, caniniform anterior premolars; long, slender tooth combs; and strongly keeled nails. While *Phaner,* which weighs under a pound, has a widespread if patchy distribution in Madagascar, *Allocebus* is known only from a handful of museum specimens, and nothing is known of its

Two cheirogaleids: *Microcebus rufus* and *Cheirogaleus major.*

a mean of ca. 280 gm.) in the drier west. The latter, at least, is unusual in apparently undergoing a period of several weeks, or even months, of torpor during the dry season when resources are scarce. Storage of fat in the tail to help tide it over this dormant period has given this form its common name, the fat-tailed dwarf lemur. *Microcebus*, it should be noted, also has the ability to store some fat in its tail, but this appears not to be associated with seasonal torpor. Little is known about the species of *Cheirogaleus* in the wild, but olfactory marking is known to be an important component of their social behavior, a caudally displaced and protuberant anus emphasizing the significance of fecal marking in this genus. Dwarf lemurs forage alone; insects do not appear to be an important food resource, but fruit, nectar, and pollen have been reported as significant items in a seasonally varying diet.

See also LEMURIFORMES; LORISIDAE; LORISOIDEA; PRIMATES; STREPSIRHINI. [I.T.]

Further Readings

Tattersall, I. (1982) The Primates of Madagascar. New York: Columbia University Press.

CHEIROGALEUS *see* CHEIROGALEIDAE

CHEMERON *see* BARINGO

CHENJIAWO *see* LANTIAN

CHERT *see* RAW MATERIALS

CHESOWANJA

Central Kenyan stratified sequence of early Pleistocene age, ca. 1.4 m.y. by K-Ar dating of underlying basalt and faunal analysis. In this site west of Kenya's Lake Baringo a partial *Australopithecus boisei* cranium was found in 1970, and an additional, more fragmentary specimen from the same taxon was recovered 1 km. away in 1978. Systematic archaeological excavations began in 1978, and burnt clay lumps found *in situ* with Oldowan tools have been interpreted by some as evidence for early hominid control of fire.

[T.D.W.]

CHILHAC

Open-air site in the Auvergne region of south-central France, with early Pleistocene fauna including Villafranchian bovids and the best French specimen of

life in the wild—or even if it survives, the last known specimen having been obtained in 1965. *Phaner* often lives in pairs, which vocalize frequently during the night to maintain contact while foraging. The females are apparently dominant to the males, having priority of access to feeding sites. Feeding itself is highly specialized, being largely on gums exuded from the bark of certain tree species. The keeled nails and long tooth scraper seem to be adaptations related to a diet of this kind, facilitating movement on tree trunks and the prizing loose of gum deposits. Insects and, in the wet season, flowers and fruit also contribute to the fork-marked lemur's diet. Uniquely among cheirogaleids studied so far *Phaner* does not appear to employ urine or fecal marking. Males, however, possess throat glands with which they mark their partners as well as trees.

Two species exist of the dwarf lemur, *Cheirogaleus*: the larger *C. major* (weighing ca. 450 gm.) in the wetter eastern part of Madagascar and the smaller *C. medius* (whose weight fluctuates seasonally around

Anancus arvernensis, dated to 1.9 m.y. by K-Ar. The fauna is in questionable association with five irregular flaked pebbles, four in quartz, from a slope area.

See also EARLY PALEOLITHIC; EUROPE; FLAKE; FRANCE; RAW MATERIALS. [A.S.B.]

CHIMPANZEE *see* APE; HOMININAE

CHINA

Asian country covering ca. 6 million sq. km. Chinese topography and climate are varied and complex, with the west and southwest of the country dominated by highlands with a highly continental climatic regime. The country is also divided into northern and southern portions by the east-west-running Qinling Shan Mountains.

Both the extreme north and south, as well as the eastern coastal lowlands of China, were occupied by hominids by at least middle Pleistocene times. The fossils from Lantian in central Shaanxi may be the earliest known Chinese hominids, with a partial cranium dating to ca. 0.9–0.7 m.y. Other important finds include the famous fossils from Zhoukoudian (near Beijing), the recently discovered Hexian hominid from the coastal province of Anhui, and the well-preserved Jinniu Shan *Homo* cf. *erectus*. Other more fragmentary finds have also been recovered at scattered localities of various ages in both the north and south. No hominids of early antiquity have yet been recovered from the western highlands, but two incisors dated at perhaps 0.5 m.y. have been recovered from Yuanmou in the Yunnan highlands, in association with a varied Plio-Pleistocene mammalian fauna. The paleoanthropological and archaeological evidence from China suggests that early hominids in the region were exploiting a wide variety of habitats, which included the temperate as well as subtropical climatic regimes.

See also ASIA (EASTERN); DALI; DRAGON BONES; HEXIAN; HOMO ERECTUS; JINNIU SHAN; LANTIAN; LIUCHENG; NIHEWAN FORMATION; XIHOUDOU; YUANMOU; ZHOUKOUDIAN. [G.G.P.]

Further Readings

Wu, R., and Olsen, J.W., eds. (1985) Paleoanthropology and Paleolithic Archaeology in the People's Republic of China. New York: Academic.

CHINJI *see* SIWALIKS

CHIROMYOIDES *see* PLESIADAPIDAE

CHIROPOTES *see* PITHECIINAE

CHLORORHYSIS *see* ANAPTOMORPHINAE

CHOPPER *see* STONE-TOOL MAKING

CHOPPER-CHOPPING TOOLS

Numerous and often poorly defined Mode I archaeological assemblages from east of "Movius' line" in the Far East (East and Southeast Asia). This line seems to mark the boundary between Paleolithic assemblages in which handaxes and Levallois flakes are common and assemblages in which these components are rare or absent. Artifacts were separated into unifacial "choppers" and bifacially edged "chopping tools." Early workers interpreted this distribution as an indication of the "cultural retardation" of Far Eastern Paleolithic populations. More recent workers have sought ecological explanations that relate the geographic distribution of these assemblages to habitat types and the availability of raw materials. In spite of the implications of the term "chopper-chopping tools" many of these artifacts appear to be unutilized cores.

See also ACHEULEAN; ANYATHIAN; ASIA (EASTERN); MOVIUS' LINE; PACITANIAN; PALEOLITHIC; SOAN. [G.G.P.]

CHOPPING TOOL *see* STONE-TOOL MAKING

CHOROCLINE *see* CLINE

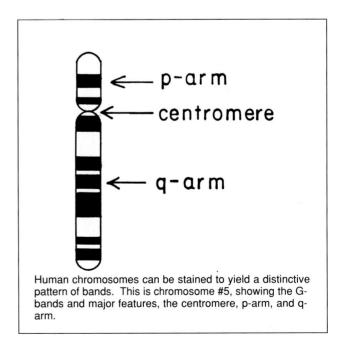

Human chromosomes can be stained to yield a distinctive pattern of bands. This is chromosome #5, showing the G-bands and major features, the centromere, p-arm, and q-arm.

CHOUKOUTIEN *see* ZHOUKOUDIAN

CHROMOSOME

Structure visible in the nucleus of a plant or animal cell during cell division. It is formed as a result of the coiling, folding, and condensation of the genetic material (DNA) with proteins. An individual has two sets of chromosomes in most cells, one set derived from each parent. A normal human cell has two sets of 23 chromosomes, for a total of 46 in the human karyotype; deviations usually result in congenital abnormalities. Any normal chromosome possesses a single constriction, the *centromere*, which divides the chromosome into a short arm (the p-arm) and a long arm (the q-arm).

See also GENETICS; MOLECULAR ANTHROPOLOGY. [J.M.]

CHRON *see* PALEOMAGNETISM

CHRONOCLINE *see* CLINE

CHRONOLOGY *see* BIOCHRONOLOGY; GEOCHRONOMETRY; TIME SCALE

CHRONOMETRIC DATING *see* GEOCHRONOMETRY

CHRONOSTRATIGRAPHY *see* BIOCHRONOLOGY; STRATIGRAPHY

CHUMASHIUS *see* OMOMYINAE

CITIES *see* COMPLEX SOCIETIES

CIVILIZATION *see* COMPLEX SOCIETIES

CLACTON *see* ACHEULEAN; CLACTONIAN

CLACTONIAN

Early Paleolithic industry without handaxes limited to Great Britain and northern France, with possible parallels in the pebble-tool industries of eastern Germany, Hungary (Buda industry), and Czechoslovakia (Přezletice, Stranská Skála) and dated to Zone II of the British Hoxnian (Holstein, Elster-Saale) intergla-

cial or earlier on stratigraphic and chronometric grounds (uranium-series date of 245 k.y. on bone). Named after an open-air site at Clacton-on-Sea, Essex, the industry is characterized by thick, heavy flakes with prominent bulbs of percussion due to the use of direct hard-hammer or hammer-and-anvil technique. Double bulbs of percussion or complete cones of percussion are also common, reflecting relatively poor control over the flaking technique. The corresponding cores are large and crude with deep negative flake scars and resemble crude chopping tools of East Africa. Pebble-chopper and flake industries of much smaller dimensions (Buda industry) are known from central Europe at this time or somewhat earlier (Elsterian glaciation, ca. 0.4 k.y.).

In situ Clactonian materials are associated exclusively with stream-channel deposits at a limited number of Thames Valley sites, especially Clacton and the lower loam at Swanscombe. Associated faunal remains indicate a predominance of *Elephas antiquus*, the straight-tusked forest elephant, and *Dama clactoniana* but include other large mammals, such as horse, bovids, red deer, and rhinocerotids.

Although the Clactonian has often been considered the earliest Paleolithic industry of Britain, faunal and stratigraphic evidence from Kent's Cavern in Devon and the earliest levels at Hoxne, Suffolk, may indicate that the Acheulean was as early or earlier here, on the basis of the presence of micromammals that are extinct elsewhere by Hoxnian times.

Like the Hope Fountain/Acheulean dichotomy in East Africa and the Tayacian/Acheulean dichotomy in France and elsewhere in Europe the existence of two somewhat contemporaneous but differing industries in England has been seen as reflecting two different cultural or taxonomic groups. In the British case the Clactonians were seen as indigenous Britons, the Acheuleans as invading from the south. As in explanations for variability in the Early Stone Age of Africa recent hypotheses have focused on functional, organizational, or taphonomic rather than cultural or taxonomic differences to explain the apparent coexistence of two distinct industries.

See also ACHEULEAN; BUDA INDUSTRY; EARLY PALEOLITHIC; EARLY STONE AGE; HOPE FOUNTAIN; HOXNE; PALEOLITHIC; PALEOLITHIC LIFEWAYS; PŘEZLETICE; STONE-TOOL MAKING; STRANSKÁ SKÁLA; SWANSCOMBE; TAPHONOMY; TAYACIAN; VALLONNET. [A.S.B.]

Further Readings

Ohel, M. (1979) The Clactonian: an independent complex or an integral part of the Acheulean? Curr. Anthropol. 20:685–726.
Wymer, J. (1982) The Palaeolithic Age. New York: St. Martin's.

CLADE *see* CLADISTICS; PHYLOGENY

CLADISTICS

Methodology for the reconstruction of phylogeny. First formulated explicitly by German entomologist Willi Hennig under the name *phylogenetic systematics*, cladistics is a branch of comparative biology in which taxa are defined and recognized exclusively by the possession of shared derived characteristics. Cladistics ranks with *numerical taxonomy* and *evolutionary systematics* as a methodology and school of thought in systematic biology. Since the 1970s cladistics has become the dominant approach to classification and phylogeny reconstruction.

Hennig's formulation is strongly rooted in evolutionary biology. The recognition of lineages by joint possession of all descendants of one or more evolutionary novelties inherited from a common ancestral species is based entirely on the pattern of "descent with modification" envisioned by Darwin as the fundamental result of the evolutionary process. Thus cladistics is the biological version of a more general methodology of genealogical reconstruction as developed in historical linguistics and in other fields.

The essence of reconstruction of any genealogical system is recognition of novelties introduced at a single point within a single lineage; descendant entities will inherit the novelty in its original, or a still further modified, form. Older known entities within the lineage of necessity lack the innovation, as do entities that are parts of collateral lineages. Joint possession of such novelties defines lineages from the point of origin of the novelty through the entire subsequent history of the lineage. For example, manuscripts copied by hand occasionally contain copying errors that themselves have been copied, thus forming a lineage of copies distinct from those not copied from the manuscript with the original introduced error.

As with manuscripts, so with organisms. Modifications introduced in due course as evolutionary novelties in one lineage but not in others automatically lead to a nested pattern of resemblance interlinking all members of the biota, past and present. This nested set of resemblances can be used to define and delineate taxa—one or more species—that belong to a genealogically coherent branch of the phylogenetic tree of life. Such taxa are monophyletic in the strictest cladistic sense: monophyletic taxa consist of all those species descended from a single ancestral species.

In cladistic analysis organismic characteristics are compared among a series of organisms of focal interest. Those characters that are invariant, and those that are unique to each specimen, or basic taxon (be it species, genera, or other taxon being compared) are of no further use in the analysis. The analysis instead examines patterns of shared similarity that appear to link up two or more entities within the sample under study. Typically, conflicting patterns of shared similarity emerge, and the task becomes one of determining which similarities represent joint possession of uniquely derived (i.e. evolutionary) similarities, which represent joint retention of evolutionary novelties inherited from some more remote ancestor (and are thus actually primitive similarities in the sample under study) and which are the result of parallel or convergent evolution (i.e. the similarities are not actually homologies).

Methods of Character Analysis in Cladistics

Because each specifiable attribute of any organism has a point in evolutionary history when it was introduced it follows that each such attribute has a finite distribution in the organic world. Some characteristics, such as fingerprint patterns, appear to be unique to a single organism; other characteristics, such as RNA, are common to all known forms of life. The vast majority of characters have a distribution somewhere between these two extremes. Mammary glands, placentation, and three middle-ear bones, for example, are some of the features shared by all placental mammals—and are thus interpreted as shared evolutionary novelties inherited from a common ancestral species. Such sets of characters define taxa and are termed *shared derived characters*, or, in Hennig's terminology, *synapomorphies*. Note that, within placental mammals, possession of a placenta becomes a primitive character: the placenta was present in the common ancestor, thus the simple character "placenta present" is of no further significance in recognizing separate lines of descent within the placental mammals. The placenta is a synapomorphy of placental mammals but is a *symplesiomorphy* (shared primitive character) when two mammalian groups (e.g. Rodentia and Primates) are being compared.

Thus the central analytic task of any cladistic analysis is the correct assessment of distribution of the characters observed to vary among the organisms or taxa under study. Two basic approaches are common to both the systematics of extant organisms and the study of fossils. The first is *outgroup comparison*. Most cladistic studies begin with some previously constructed hypothesis of affinity among the organisms under study—including a hypothesis of the next-most-closely-related taxon outside the group under direct examination, the *outgroup*. If a character that is observed to link two or more study taxa is also observed in the outgroup, the character is judged to be primitive for the study group and of no significance in linking any two or more taxa within the study group. Outgroup comparison is essentially a mapping exercise to determine the actual distribution of a given character. The second approach is *ontogeny*. The development of an organism from a fertilized zygote to an adult involves complexification as well as modification of structure. Often a character seems to be missing in adult form, only found to be present in early developmental stages—the classic example being pharyngeal gill slits of Vertebrata, present in adult form of various aquatic "fish" taxa but seen as well in developing embryos of tetrapods. Finally, because characters more widely distributed than the taxa within a particular study group are held to be "primitive" for that group, it is also commonly asserted that the order of appearance of characters in the fossil record also may serve as a direct form of inference in character analysis—a point that continues to be debated.

The results of a cladistic analysis are plotted on a *cladogram*, which depicts the relationships among the study taxa; the nodes joining the branches of such a diagram simply reflect joint possession of one or more synapomorphies. Evolutionary trees are more complex statements, specifying ancestral and descendant species in a reconstructed phylogeny. A single classification may be derived directly and unambiguously from a cladogram with a minimum of rules and conventions; however, a number of classifications may be consistent with any one evolutionary tree.

See also CLASSIFICATION; EVOLUTION; EVOLUTIONARY SYSTEMATICS; HOMOLOGY; PHYLOGENY; TAXONOMY. [N.E.]

Further Readings

Eldredge, N., and Cracraft, J. (1980) *Phylogenetic Patterns and the Evolutionary Process.* New York: Columbia University Press.

Platnick, N.I., and Cameron, H.D. (1977) Cladistic methods in textual, linguistic, and phylogenetic analysis. *Syst. Zool.* 26:380–385.

Wiley, E.O. (1981) *Phylogenetics.* New York: Wiley.

CLADOGRAM see CLADISTICS

CLARK, J. DESMOND (b.1916)

British-trained archaeologist. Professor emeritus at the University of California, Berkeley, Clark has been responsible for significant discoveries and has set directions and emphases in the study of African prehistory; he has also trained a large cohort of African archaeologists, both from the West and from Africa itself. His contributions, many in collaboration with international colleagues, include the initiation and leadership of the Pan-African Congress of Prehistory and Quaternary Studies; the definition of the basic Stone Age terminology for sub-Saharan Africa; an emphasis on behavioral and environmental reconstruction; the promotion of ethnoarchaeology as a tool for understanding the past; major excavations at Lunda (Angola), Kalambo Falls (Zambia), Mwanganda's Village (Malawi), and Latamne (Syria); and extensive surveys and excavations in Somalia, Ethiopia, and the Sudan, the latter relating to the origins of domestication.

See also AFRICA; EARLY STONE AGE; ETHNOARCHAEOLOGY; FIRST INTERMEDIATE; KALAMBO FALLS; LATER STONE AGE; MAGOSIAN; MIDDLE STONE AGE; SANGOAN; SECOND INTERMEDIATE. [A.S.B.]

CLARK, [SIR] WILFRED EDWARD LE GROS (1895-1971)

British anatomist. During the 1920s and 1930s Clark's work focused on primate evolution and the taxonomic status of tree shrews. After World War II his main interest shifted to the early stages of hominid evolution. Having examined Broom's australopithecine collection in Pretoria in 1946, Clark returned to England, where he began a zealous campaign supporting the hominid affinities of these fossils, a viewpoint that initially met with considerable opposition. In 1951, with L.S.B. Leakey, he made an important study of the Miocene hominid fossils recovered between 1949 and 1951 by the British Miocene Expedition to East Africa. Two years later he collaborated with J. Weiner and K. Oakley in the debunking of the celebrated Piltdown skull. From 1932 to 1962 Clark was professor of anatomy at Oxford University. Among his many papers and books perhaps the most popular and enduring are *History of the Primates* and *The Antecedents of Man*.

[F.S.]

CLARKFORKIAN see PALEOCENE; TIME SCALE

CLASSICAL ARCHAEOLOGY see ARCHAEOLOGY

CLASSIFICATION

In biology, the arrangement of organisms into sets. The world contains millions of kinds of living organisms. Many more existed in the past but are now extinct. For us to understand and to communicate with one another about this extraordinary variety of organisms it is essential that we classify them. But it is important to bear in mind that any classification we adopt is a product of our minds and not a property of nature. Rules exist for naming organisms, but organizing them in a classification is a less objective procedure.

Practice of Animal Classification

The system universally used today to classify animals and plants was devised by the eighteenth-century systematist Linnaeus. He expounded this system in his *Systema Naturae*, the definitive edition of which is taken to be the tenth, dated 1758. No names of organisms published before that date are recognized as valid, while all names of animals published subsequently must conform to the rules of the Linnaean system, codified today in the *International Code of Zoological Nomenclature* ("the Code").

The Linnaean approach to classification establishes an inclusive hierarchy of ranks, within which every living organism has its place. An inclusive hierarchy is one in which every rank includes all of those below it: all members of a subfamily, for example, belong also to a family. This contrasts with the exclusive, "military," type of hierarchy, where an individual can belong to only one rank. The basic unit of the Linnaean system is the species, which is denoted by a *binomen*, or a combination of two names, each of which is written in latinized form and italicized. We, for example, belong to the species *Homo sapiens*. Species are grouped into genera, and the first component (*Homo*) of the double name is the name of the genus. In combination with the first, the second (specific) name (*sapiens*) identifies the species. Species belonging to different genera can share a specific name (e.g. *Proconsul africanus, Australopithecus africanus*); it is thus the combination of the genus and species names that is unique. Sometimes one will see yet a third latinized, italicized name, as in *Lemur fulvus rufus*; the last name denotes a subspecies, a category within the species itself. The name that must be used in referring to any species is the one first applied to it in accordance with the international rules. This is the *valid* name; other names that may later have been given to the same organism are known as *junior synonyms*.

Categories in the Hierarchy of Classification

The vast number of living organisms necessitates having many categories in our classification, not all of which there is room to mention here. Continuing with *Homo sapiens* as an illustration, as animals we belong to the kingdom Animalia. This contains several phyla, ours being Chordata; within Chordata we belong to the subphylum Vertebrata, and within Vertebrata to the class Mammalia. Within Mammalia we are members of the order Primates, and within Pri-

mates we are classed as follows:

Order	Primates
Suborder	Anthropoidea
Infraorder	Catarrhini
Hyporder	Eucatarrhini
Superfamily	Hominoidea
Family	Hominidae
Subfamily	Homininae
Tribe	Hominini
Genus	*Homo*
Species	*Homo sapiens*

As we ascend the classification, we share our ranks with more and more relatives. Thus among living forms we share the order Primates with the lemurs, lorises, tarsiers, Old and New World monkeys, and the greater and lesser apes, whereas besides ourselves the superfamily Hominoidea includes only the apes. Each category, at whatever level, is known as a *taxon* (plural *taxa*): species are taxa, so are families, so are orders. From this we derive the term *taxonomy*, which is the study of the theory and practice of classification. Note that the family and subfamily names end in "-idae" and "-inae," respectively; this is required by the Code for taxa at those ranks. The Code also recommends the suffixes "-oidea" for superfamilies and "-ini" for tribes.

Principles of Classification

The only theoretical requirement of a classification is that it be consistent. We can use any criteria we like to construct the classification itself. Linnaeus's classification, in which he included *Homo* in Primates along with the apes, monkeys, and lemurs, predated the concept of evolution and was based purely on structural resemblance. Nowadays elements of both structure and evolutionary relationship are often included in arriving at zoological classifications. However, since the only information that can actually be retrieved from (as opposed to put into) a classification is the inclusive sets of animals represented, and the only attribute of nature to which this structuring corresponds is the branching of lineages in phylogeny, it has been strongly argued that classifications should strictly reflect evolutionary relationships. But while the point is well taken, such strict adherence to phylogeny makes classifications susceptible to constant change with advancing knowledge. Stability in classifications is essential if they are to serve as effective means of communication about groups of organisms, and their potential instability, together with the large number of categories they tend to require, makes strict phylogenetic classifications impractical. No classification will ever be satisfactory for all purposes, or remain useful forever, but those that are the most generally useful are likely to be based on phylogeny (and insisting on monophyly—i.e. that every group should contain all known descendants of the common ancestor of the group, and only them) but modified in the light of structural considerations to minimize the number of ranks. See the introduction to this volume for a classification of the primates.

See also CLADISTICS; INCERTAE SEDIS; NOMENCLATURE; PHYLOGENY; PRIORITY; SPECIES; SUBSPECIES; SYNONYM(Y); SYSTEMATICS; TAXONOMY. [I.T.]

Further Readings

Eldredge, N., and Cracraft, J. (1980) Phylogenetic Patterns and the Evolutionary Process. New York: Columbia University Press.

International Trust for Zoological Nomenclature (1985) International Code of Zoological Nomenclature, 3rd ed. Berkeley: University of California Press.

Mayr, E. (1969) Principles of Systematic Zoology. New York: McGraw-Hill.

Simpson, G.G. (1961) Principles of Animal Taxonomy. New York: Columbia University Press.

CLAW *see* SKELETON

CLAW CLIMBING *see* LOCOMOTION

CLEAVER

Large, usually bifacially flaked artifact with a straight, sharp-edged bit on one end, characteristic of the Acheulean technological stage and generally associated with handaxe industries (it can also be found in some Mousterian industries). Many cleavers, especially those in lava or quartzite, are made on large flakes with a natural flake-edge bit, while those of flint may also be shaped by bifacially flaking a straight-edged bit on the end of large biface, or by a tranchet blow to create a sharp, regular bit edge.

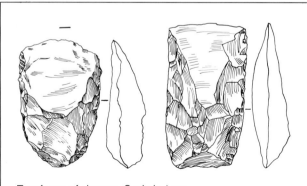

Two forms of cleaver. Scale is 1 cm.

Experiments indicate that these forms make excellent cutting tools in animal butchery and are also good woodworking tools.

See also ACHEULEAN; BIFACE; EARLY PALEOLITHIC; HANDAXE; RAW MATERIALS; STONE-TOOL MAKING. [N.T., K.S.]

CLINE

Linear pattern of variation in one or more phenotypic organismic features within a species. Generally such patterns adaptively match a linear range of variation of environmental features, such as altitude or mean annual temperature. Simpson termed such geographic clines *choroclines*, in contrast with *chronoclines*, which are linear, gradational patterns of phylogenetic change within a species through time. The two phenomena, however, are not strictly comparable, and use of these terms is to be discouraged.

See also ADAPTATION; EVOLUTION; PHYLOGENY. [N.E.]

CLOTHING

As hominids spread to cooler, more temperate zones, it is likely that the need for clothing became an adaptive necessity, especially during winter months. The earliest forms of clothing were probably simple garments of skin or beaten vegetable material, draped over or tied around the body, perhaps with the aid of skin thongs or other forms of cordage.

Although the materials from which early clothing might have been made are perishable and do not survive in the Paleolithic record, several lines of evidence suggest the use of garments—e.g. in later Acheulean and, especially, Mousterian times. The prevalence of well-made side-scrapers may suggest a reliance upon hide working, an activity corroborated by the detection of microscopic hide-polish development on some of these scraper edges. The presence of pointed *perçoirs* (awls) in some of these assemblages may also suggest the perforation of hides for lacing with leather thongs.

Bone and antler needles first appear in the Solutrean period of the Upper Paleolithic and suggest the sewing of hides with a thread made of sinew or vegetable material. The high frequency of end-scrapers found in Upper Paleolithic assemblages also suggests hide working, again corroborated by microwear analysis. Since many bone and antler needles may not have been strong enough to sew through hides by themselves, the use of *perçoirs* to initiate holes in material to be stitched is likely.

Artwork from the later phases of the Paleolithic may portray human figures with clothing: some of the figurines from the Upper Paleolithic appear to be wearing skirts, aprons, headdresses, or parkas.

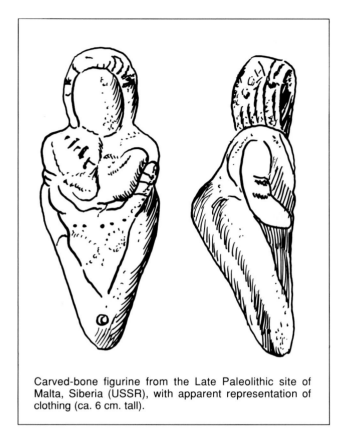

Carved-bone figurine from the Late Paleolithic site of Malta, Siberia (USSR), with apparent representation of clothing (ca. 6 cm. tall).

See also ACHEULEAN; AWL; MOUSTERIAN; PALEOLITHIC IMAGE; SCRAPER; STONE-TOOL MAKING; UPPER PALEOLITHIC. [N.T., K.S.]

Further Readings

Daumas, A., ed. (1969) *A History of Technology and Invention: Progress Through the Ages, Vol. I.* New York: Crown.

Hodges, H. (1976) *Artifacts: An Introduction to Early Materials and Technology.* London: Baker.

CLOVIS

Distinctive, large, bifacially flaked lanceolate point manufactured by percussion flaking. The base is thinned by one or more fluting flakes, and the edge is dulled, presumably to facilitate hafting. First discovered at Clovis (New Mexico), such points have since been found throughout much of North America. They date to 11,000 B.P. in the earliest layers of Blackwater Draw (New Mexico). Clovis points, typically associated with mammoth kills, belong to the earliest of the Paleoindian Traditions.

See also AMERICAS; LLANO COMPLEX; PALEOINDIAN. [L.S.A.P., D.H.T.]

COHUNA *see* AUSTRALIA; HOMO SAPIENS

COLOBINAE

Subfamily of Old World monkeys including the leaf-eating cercopithecids, such as langurs (*Presbytis* and *Semnopithecus*), doucs (*Pygathrix*), proboscis monkeys (*Nasalis*), guerezas (*Colobus*), and their extinct relatives. In adapting to the high proportion of leaves and other low-quality foods in their diet, colobines have evolved a number of derived conditions as compared with the cercopithecid morphotype. These include extra chambers in the stomach to enhance fermentation and digestion of cellulose; increased cheek-tooth crown relief (between cusp tips and notch bases), but reduced flare and short lower-molar trigonids (possibly conservative); mandible with expanded gonial region but shallowing mesially. As part of their adaptation to arboreal running and leaping colobines have relatively longer limbs, hands, and feet than do cercopithecines of similar weight. In addition the external thumb is reduced in length, in some cases lost entirely, as is the tarsal region; this is best seen in the cuboid-ectocuneiform contacts, where the distal facet is lengthened while the proximal is reduced or lost. Although in most catarrhines the major weight-bearing axis of the foot passes through the middle digit, which is longer than the fourth, in colobines these two are equal, signaling the shift of the axis of the foot to between these two rays. In concert with this a number of related muscle functions have been modified and a groove developed on the proximal astragalus. Colobines generally have retained the ancestral cercopithecid conditions of a short, broad face with wide interorbital distance, short nasal bones, and a lacrimal fossa extending onto the maxilla; relatively high-vaulted skull; fully enamel covered lower incisors; and simple cerebral sulcal pattern.

Within the Colobinae low-level taxa (subtribes) have been recognized for the Asian versus African genera, although the former may not be a natural (holophyletic) group. The African colobinans have completely lost the external thumb and the proximal cuboid-entocuneiform contact, while these features are reduced only in the presbytinians. Two living genera are recognized in Africa: *Colobus* (the guerezas or black-and-white colobus) with four species, characterized by the derived loss of female sexual swellings and the development of a large larynx and subhyoid sac; and *Procolobus* (for olive and red or bay colobus) with perhaps three to four species, typified by a four-chambered stomach (other colobines have only three chambers), a sagittal crest (perhaps implying relatively small brain), male perineal organ, and discontinuous male ischial callosities (also in Asian *Pygathrix*). The Asian colobines are more numerous and their interrelationships more complex. For the present four genera are recognized, most with subgeneric divisions. *Presbytis* may be the most conservative, *Semnopithecus* intermediate, and

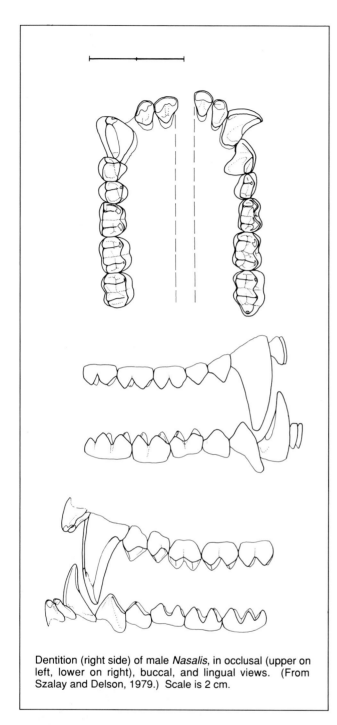

Dentition (right side) of male *Nasalis*, in occlusal (upper on left, lower on right), buccal, and lingual views. (From Szalay and Delson, 1979.) Scale is 2 cm.

ing much time on the ground; several fossil colobines have independently become terrestrial, however. Group composition is mainly multimale, with troop sizes up to 100 (e.g. *Procolobus badius*) but more commonly 20–40. Some species live in small groups with a single adult male (most *Colobus* and *Presbytis*, among others), and at least *Presbytis potenziani* is apparently monogamous. In *S. entellus*, among other species, coalitions of peripheral males may attack the primary male of a troop and kill or expel him, at which time they, or a new leader, may attack and kill juveniles. Among colobines juveniles are often carried by females other than the mother—known as "aunting" behavior, this may serve to speed independence of the infant from its mother and protect it from "infanticide" during male takeovers. Home-range size averages ca. 30 hectares but is variable both between species (e.g. 130 hectares in *Nasalis larvatus*) and even within species depending on environmental factors (e.g. from 5 to 1,300 hectares in *S. entellus*!) Numerous species are endangered, often as the result of human hunting and expansion of cultivated land.

The fossil record of the colobines is quite good in both Africa and Europe but poor in Asia. The earliest African colobine, *Microcolobus*, is known by a single mandible from Ngeringerowa (Kenya), estimated to date ca. 9 ± 1.5 m.y. This is the smallest known colobine, slightly smaller in tooth size than *Proco-*

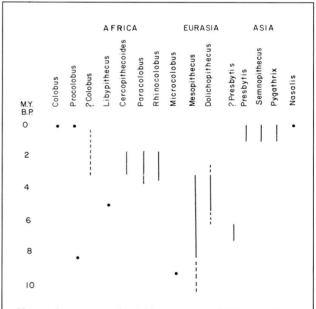

Known time ranges of colobine genera; solid lines indicate well-preserved fossils, dotted lines indicate fragmentary remains, less clear allocations, or dating uncertainty. The relationships among these taxa are still relatively unclear, and thus no attempt is made to present a cladogram, but see the diagram of living genera in the article CERCOPITHECIDAE.

Nasalis and *Pygathrix* the most derived, at least in terms of facial shape.

The colobine diet includes not only leaves but a variety of fruits, flowers, buds, shoots, seeds, insects, gums, and earth (for minerals). Their enlarged stomach permits the ingestion of foods high in toxic substances ("secondary compounds"), which can be detoxified through the action of the same bacteria that break down the cellulose in leaves. Most living colobines are active arboreal leapers and runners, with only one species, *Semnopithecus entellus*, spend-

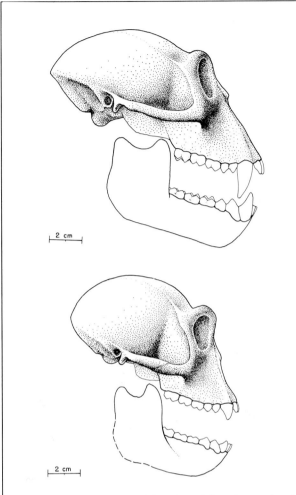

Reconstruction of male (above) and female crania of *Cercopithecoides*, right lateral views, from South African sites ca. 3–1.5 m.y. old. (From Szalay and Delson, 1979.) The postcranium shows strong adaptations to terrestrial life, and although the dentition is typically colobine, it is usually heavily worn, perhaps due to ingestion of gritty foods found on or under the ground.

lobus verus but rather larger than *Miopithecus talapoin*. Tooth relief is low for a colobine, and the inferior transverse torus of the symphysis is poorly developed, as in cercopithecines but no other colobine. A larger colobine is known by isolated teeth from the late Miocene (ca. 8 m.y.) of Marceau (Algeria). Originally identified as a macaque, then termed "*Colobus*" in the sense of an African colobine, these teeth show some similarities to the Pliocene *Cercopithecoides*. Early Pliocene sites in Libya and Egypt have yielded a nearly complete cranium, some teeth, and perhaps fragmentary limb bones of *Libypithecus*, a form broadly similar to the red colobus. The Pliocene of southern and especially eastern Africa saw a great flowering of colobine diversity. *Cercopithecoides* was long known by skulls and teeth in South African sites dating between 3 and 1.5 m.y. (e.g. Makapansgat,

Sterkfontein, Kromdraai), but an associated partial skeleton from Koobi Fora (Kenya) demonstrated that it was the most terrestrially adapted colobine known. Isolated limb bones can be mistaken for those of *Theropithecus* baboons. The teeth of *Cercopithecoides* are often heavily worn, suggesting that its diet included grit taken in with terrestrial foods but that enamel had not been thickened to prolong tooth life. Somewhat larger was *Paracolobus*, whose fossils span from 3.5 to 1.9 m.y. ago at such East African sites as Laetoli (Tanzania), Koobi Fora (Kenya), and Omo (Ethiopia). A nearly complete skeleton reveals a forelimb that looks like those of more terrestrial monkeys but a scapula and foot that indicate a relatively arboreal adaptation. A third genus, *Rhinocolobus*, from Koobi Fora, Omo, and Hadar (Ethiopia) localities between 3.5 and perhaps 1.3 m.y., was larger still, and fragmentary limb bones suggest a degree of arboreality comparable with that in living colobinans. This is unexpected for such a large-bodied species. A medium-sized colobine is known by a partial skull and skeleton from the Hadar region and from isolated teeth in other deposits, and small teeth of *Colobus* size have also been found at Laetoli, Omo, and Koobi Fora. Most of these species seem to have survived late Pliocene climatic cooling but had disappeared by the start of the Pleistocene.

The earliest Eurasian colobine, *Mesopithecus pentelici*, ranged over a wide area from Yugoslavian Macedonia to Afghanistan ca. 9–8 m.y., and a tooth from central Germany may be as old as 11–10 m.y. This species, known from dozens of skulls and numerous limb bones, was probably a semiterrestrial inhabitant of gallery forests bordering open steppe, comparable in its morphological features with the modern *Semnopithecus entellus*, the Hanuman langur. At the end of the Miocene, although southern Europe was rather arid, northern central Europe retained forested regions, which may have served as a refuge for a flora that spread rapidly from Spain to the Ukraine with the return of moist conditions at the start of the Pliocene. In one of these possible refugia is found an ulna of *Dolichopithecus*, which is quite common in early Pliocene sites over this wide range of "monsoon" forest. Larger than *Mesopithecus*, with a long face and numerous postcranial adaptations to life on the ground, *Dolichopithecus* was in some ways a colobine "mandrill" or forest baboon. It has been thought to be a direct descendant of *M. pentelici*, but that view is weakened because, while the latter species has the derived colobine loss of the proximal cuboid-entocuneiform contact, *Dolichopithecus* presents the less derived small facet. A second, less terrestrial, species of *Mesopithecus* coexisted with *Dolichopithecus* through most of the Pliocene. A major problem in colobine

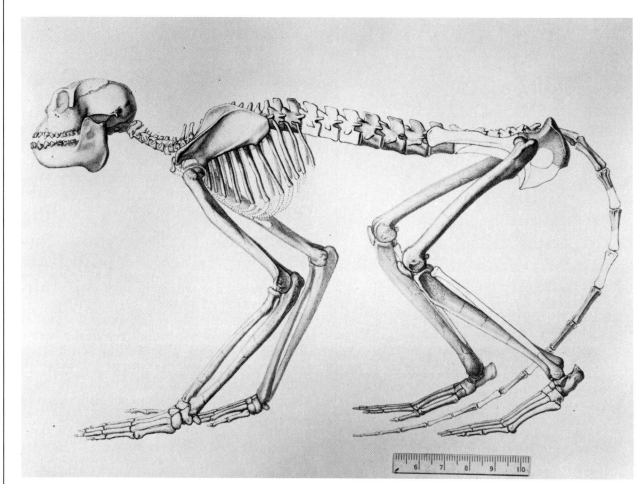

Reconstruction of female skeleton of *Mesopithecus*, from Pikermi (Greece), ca. 8 m.y. (From Gaudry, 1862.) A medium-sized, semi-terrestrial colobine, *Mesopithecus* is known from England through Afghanistan at times between 10 and 3 m.y. ago.

systematics is the relationship of this group (if indeed it is a unified clade) to the eastern Asian species.

Asian colobine fossils are quite rare, but a number of teeth have been recovered from levels in the Pakistan Siwaliks ca. 7–6 m.y. old. These might represent a late extension eastward of *Mesopithecus*, but as most colobine teeth are quite similar, it is difficult to make a comparison without cranial or postcranial material. Two mandibles and a partial elbow joint from Shamar (Mongolia), dated ca. 2.4 m.y., have been named "*Presbytis*" *eohanuman*, but they might represent an East Asian species of *Dolichopithecus* or an equally terrestrial parallel development. Fossils of the modern *Pygathrix* (*Rhinopithecus*) are known from several Pleistocene sites in China, while *Semnopithecus* and *Presbytis* species have been recovered in Java.

See also AFRICA; CERCOPITHECIDAE; CERCOPITHECINAE; DIET; EUROPE; MIOCENE; MONKEY; PLIOCENE; PRIMATE ECOLOGY; PRIMATE SOCIETIES; SIWALIKS; SOCIOBIOLOGY; TEETH. [E.D.]

Further Readings

Benefit, B., and Pickford, M. (1986) Miocene fossil cercopithecoids from Kenya. Am. J. Phys. Anthropol. 69:441–464.

Brandon-Jones, D. (1985) *Colobus* and leaf-monkeys. In D. MacDonald (ed.): The Encyclopedia of Mammals. New York: Facts-on-File, pp. 398–408.

Delson, E. (1984) Cercopithecid biochronology of the African Plio-Pleistocene: correlation among eastern and southern hominid-bearing localities. Cour. Forsch. Inst. Senckenberg 69:199–218.

Groves, C.P. (1970) The forgotten leaf-eaters, and the phylogeny of the Colobinae. In J.R. Napier and P.H. Napier (eds.): Old World Monkeys. London: Academic, pp. 555–587.

Leakey, M.G. (1982) Extinct large colobines from the Plio-Pleistocene of Africa. Am. J. Phys. Anthropol. 58:153–172.

Strasser, E., and Delson, E. (1987) Cladistic analysis of cercopithecid relationships. J. Hum. Evol. 16:81–99.

Szalay, F.S., and Delson, E. (1979) Evolutionary History of the Primates. New York: Academic.

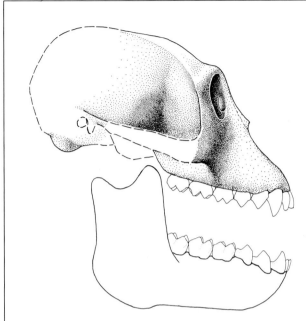

Reconstruction of female cranium of *Dolichopithecus*, in right lateral view, from Perpignan (France), ca. 2 m.y. B.P. (From Szalay and Delson, 1979.) *Dolichopithecus* was a terrestrial colobine known in mainly forested environments between Spain and the U.S.S.R. from 5 to 3 m.y., and perhaps from a slightly younger site in Mongolia.

COLOBUS *see* COLOBINAE

COMBE-CAPELLE *see* ARCHAIC MODERNS; HOMO SAPIENS

COMBE-GRENAL *see* HOMO SAPIENS; MOUSTERIAN

COMPARATIVE METHOD *see* EVOLUTIONARY SYSTEMATICS

COMPLEX SOCIETIES

Societies in which social stratification exists and access to real power is limited to members of the upper strata. The beginning of history is tied roughly to the emergence of complex societies in many parts of the world, a development that marks the close of the period of interest for this volume. Prehistory ends when writing begins, and this was often about the time that city-states appeared on the landscape.

An examination of complex societies requires, first, a broad understanding of what is meant by the term. Just how is "complex society" to be defined, and how is it to be distinguished from "noncomplex" or "simple society"? Second, we must ask how com-plex societies came into being: the eternal question of origins.

Definition

"Complex society" has often been taken to be synonymous with "state" or "stratified society," as those terms are used by such authors as E.R. Service and M. Fried. Service defined a state as a sociopolitical organization characterized by a centralized government with a ruling class. That class was clearly separated from the remainder of the community in that it was not bound by kinship ties to them, it had control of strategic goods and services, and it was able to enforce its will through the imposition of law and the force of sanction. Fried defined stratified societies by reference to their position on a scale of access to power. Stratified societies were those in which a class of people was defined in nonkinship terms to hold power over the other members of society. States in his view were political entities in which institutions had developed to hold and impose power. It is important to note that these views of complex society emphasize the relations of people within a society.

V.G. Childe had earlier tried to characterize the state in terms of a wide range of criteria. These have come to be seen as the traditional hallmarks of the state and civilization. His list included features like the aggregation of people into cities, the development of nonagricultural specialization of labor, the production and concentration of surpluses, the emergence of strictly defined class distinctions, and the creation of non–kin-based rules for membership in society. He also included the construction of monumental public works, such as temples or irrigation systems, the beginning of long-distance trade, the creation of an elite art style, and the development of writing and mathematics as abstract means of keeping records. Each of these characteristics might indeed be observable in a society that we might identify as complex, but they do not get at root variables that could define the abstract process of development of the complexity itself. Moreover, in some cases several appear well before complex societies. To understand the process we must appeal to more basic underlying ideas.

The definition of "complex society" requires a focus on the relations of people to the environment that supports them and of people to other people within that environment. The ability of individuals to influence the behavior of others rests on political and economic relationships, which Fried described in terms of *authority* and *power*. Authority is the ability to persuade others to comply with one's wishes. Power is the ability to require compliance under threat of sanction. He understood the source of power as control of the "basic resources" of society.

Any society can be characterized in these terms. Changes in those relations drive the development of complex societies. The origin of complexity in society can be reduced to the question "Why do the relationships of people and environment change in the first place?"

A definition that focuses on this level of understanding is necessarily a socioecological one. The recognition that interhuman relations have some external causes implies a materialist view of the nature of human relations. Society must be seen as the result of a complex system of interactions between several domains: people and groups of people, the productive capacity of the environment, and the physical characteristics of the environment that effect communication. This sort of approach was pioneered by J. Steward and has since been followed by many archaeologists, including R.M. Adams, C. Redman, and W. Sanders.

The outcome of this sort of view is one of gradation. When "complex society" is used as a term of relation, some societies are more complex than others because they have more marked development of institutions of power and authority and more structured control of the productive land. In more absolute terms we can say that when "complex society" refers to states, stratified society, civilization, or the like it must be defined in terms of the organization of relations between people, or political and social institutions, and the centralization of control over the subsistence base of the society and the actual products generated by farmers and other specialists.

Development of Complex Society

Understanding how simple societies become more complex requires an examination of both the stresses that drive change and the processes by which complexity arises. Traditionally archaeologists have tried to explain cultural evolution in terms of the response of a society to some single driving force for change, some "prime mover." Recently the various prime-mover explanations have come under heavy criticism for their oversimplification of a patently complex process. These explanations emphasize an initial stress without questioning the source of the initial condition that has been identified. When, for example, the rise of complex society is attributed to cultural responses to uncontrolled population growth, a host of effects of rising population may be identified but little attention is given to explaining why a population that has for many years been maintained at a relatively stable level has suddenly decided to grow. When warfare is seen as a prime mover, the question of why people fight is brushed aside in favor of a consideration of the consequences of conflict.

This sort of approach lacks rigor, and few active archaeologists still cling to such simple explanations. Instead most theorists today focus on a multiplicity of factors, combining several of the simpler explanatory frameworks generated over the past few decades. One can argue that such multiple-cause models are simply more tightly argued restatements and reorganizations of earlier constructions.

Unicausal Models   A broad range of simple, unicausal explanations have been put forward. Childe proposed that the development of craft specialists, especially in metallurgy, changed the social order because such people had to be fed with food produced by others. For the first time there were healthy, adult members of society who did not provide their own sustenance. The organization of the surplus production of farmers to support these specialists and the organization of means of redistributing their products led to a class of decision makers and hence to the state.

K. Wittfogel has argued that the development of intensive agricultural systems required the development of cooperative systems of planning and decision making. The creation of public utilities in the form of large-scale irrigation systems meant that some labor expended by members of society would benefit not only themselves but others. To regulate this cost and to ensure that the benefit from the utility was equitably apportioned a central decision-making apparatus was required. Progressively greater investment in the public utility led to more and more responsibility being vested in the central body and ultimately to the development of political integration based on the economic advantages of intensive agriculture.

Similar proposals have been made by W. Rathje and others concerning the advantages of a central administrative structure to regulate long-distance trade for the acquisition of important scarce commodities. Scarce goods that can measurably improve the quality of life in a region constitute a sort of universal objective. The trading expeditions required to gather these goods become a public utility, since not everyone can leave the agricultural system to trek off to trade for them. The administration of investment in the trading mission, support of the traders, and redistribution of the products would have the same consequence as the irrigation-regulating commission hypothesized by Wittfogel. Again the driving force of this formulation is the economic benefit derived from participation. Those who are party to the long-distance trade have an enhanced capacity to succeed; they have access to the products of the trade while nonparticipants do not.

Another broad set of unicausal proposals have

been made by theorists who focus on population growth and resultant competition as the engines of change. R. Carneiro, for example, points out that any environment is limited in size. Areas of high productive capacity are necessarily circumscribed by areas of lesser potential. This is the case whatever the cultural means of extracting energy might be. In other words the environment is patchy for any resource. Carneiro suggests that growing populations are faced with unreconcilable problems. The capacity of the land to support them is limited, but any nearby land to which they might emigrate is inferior and thus limited in its own way. Intensified use of the better land provides only a short-term solution. Ultimately conflict increases between groups of people who all want to have access to the most-productive land, leading to increased military organization; and military organization is seen as the root of political organization. The rise of military leaders represents the institutionalization of power within society, so the rise of complex society is a direct outgrowth of population growth in the context of circumscribed productive resources.

A model of the rise of complex societies based on competition between internal groups has been proposed by I. Diakonoff following Marx and Engels. He suggests that with the rise of intensive agriculture comes the ability of individuals to produce surplus energy, crops beyond the subsistence requirements of the producing families. The emergence of craft specialists is seen in this argument, as in Childe's, as the beginning of a class of people who do not directly provide for their own subsistence. Diakonoff's view is different from that of Childe in that he recognizes a divergence of self-interest between the agricultural producers and the craft producers. Craft producers are in a unique and novel position, because their sustenance depends on a system of exchange in which comparability of value is not evident. To the extent that they can overvalue their products they can concentrate wealth. Growing differences in economic status led to class consciousness and class conflict. Ultimately conflict among members of a single society led to the formation of the state as a means of protecting the self-interest of the new economic ruling class. In this view the growth of a market economy leads to the concentration of wealth, the emergence of classes, and the development of increasingly complex means of maintaining economic inequity.

Yet another approach to the question has been explored by R. Blanton for the particular case of Oaxaca (Mexico). Blanton's model is based on the same observations as Carneiro's. He suggests that in a compartmentalized, or circumscribed, environ-

ment some areas will be more productive than others. The division of the environment will lead to the development of separate self-identifying polities. The outcome is that less-productive areas, or polities, will compete with the polities in control of the more-productive areas. The model here diverges from Carneiro's. Blanton claims that the ultimate goal of the system is to reduce the costs of conflict rather than simply to dominate the entire social landscape. He suggests that one way to reduce these costs is for the wealthier groups to enter into an agreement for their mutual protection from the more hostile, poorer groups, the ones relegated to the least-productive parts of the environment.

The unicausal models of the rise of complex societies, although very different from one another, all seem to have structural similarities in terms of the stresses that initiate the cultural processes. Many of them skirt the question, but each appeals to a certain class of variables to explain why the system starts to change. Those variables are biological ones that have to do with the structure of the environment in which the cultural process takes place, or the capacity of the environment to produce accessible energy, or the capacity of human populations to grow (although they generally do not explain why a population grows but merely assume that it does). What these environmental characteristics have in common is simply that they are biological and ecological rather than cultural.

Multicausal Models   Most of these models are idiosyncratic, that is, they were created to help explain a particular case of the emergence of the state. K.V. Flannery, in 1972, made an important effort to generalize these and other theories through the application of systems theory. He suggested that the transition from simple to complex societies requires an explanation that identifies and explains the processes of cultural change, the mechanisms by which change occurs, and the stresses that motivate the change and select the mechanisms actually employed. These three aspects are requisite parts of an adequate systems explanation of any observed change. Flannery was striving for a single general explanation of the rise of the state in all cases. He identified two basic processes: *segregation*, the differentiation of subsystems within society, and *centralization*, the expansion of control by a central authority. The mechanisms that he identified were *promotion*, by which institutions expand their range of operation, and *linearization*, by which high-level authority takes direct control of low-level decisions. The systems approach has become almost universal among archaeologists studying the emergence of cultural complexity. Flannery's proposed processes and mechanisms have been far less widely adopted, because they seem to be more descriptive than explanatory. Segregation, centralization, promotion, and linearization each reflects aspects of the institutions of society rather than the relations of society that produce institutions.

All of the unicausal models can be described by two complementary cultural processes, in Flannery's terms. Each of these theories is based on one of two processes of social interaction, either *cooperation* or *competition* between people. These two interactions may take place either within a single community or society or between two or more communities.

The socioenvironmental stresses that drive the cultural processes of cooperation and competition and the institutional processes proposed by Flannery are the subjects of the various unicausal models enumerated above. Agreement on the efficacy of the stresses that motivate change in any particular case has long been elusive. The precise mechanisms in operation in any given case are certainly idiosyncratic and vary depending on historical and ecological conditions.

The kind of multicausal theories recently proposed by R.M. Adams, K.V. Flannery, C. Redman, W. Sanders, and others seems to be creating a new cultural ecology with a renewed emphasis on culture. If explanation of the stresses that drive change in cultural systems relies on human interaction with environmental conditions, like ecological variability and biological capacities, then cultural ecology is still alive and vigorous, although somewhat modified from its traditional form. The weakness of cultural ecology has been a perception that it had a one-sided view that explained change in relation only to environmental variability. It has long been hard to distinguish this approach from environmental determinism. The new cultural ecology takes into account the variability introduced by cultural tradition. Processes of cooperation and competition may be implemented in various ways depending on the physical circumstances and historical tradition of a given case. A single causal network must not be seen as the only avenue to complexity. External stresses can be responded to in an unlimited variety of ways; the adoption of mechanisms to alleviate stresses is an interactive outcome of culture, history, and ecology. Articulating the detailed relations that give rise to a particular historical case remains the challenge that it has always been.

Complex Societies Around the World

The operation of these stresses, mechanisms, and processes can be viewed archaeologically in many parts of the world. The emergence of complexity in society has followed many pathways, virtually as many as there are cases. In some areas pristine states have formed without benefit of communication with preexisting states; in others the development of complexity never yielded the special institutions that characterize the state, giving rise instead to organizations of lesser scope; in still others the state grew only in relation to earlier developments in neighboring areas as a secondary process.

Pristine, or largely pristine, states developed in only six regions: Mesopotamia, Egypt, the Indus Valley, China, Mesoamerica, and the Andes. The secondary development of the state occurred over a far wider range, including sub-Saharan Africa, India, central Asia, Southeast Asia, Japan, northern South America, and Europe. The institutions of these states grew in relation to nearby preexisting states. Communication between emerging elites at relatively similar levels of political integration allowed the less organized groups to emulate the characteristics of those that had already developed. This begs the question of just how the first states emerged, but articulating the mechanisms of cultural change in particular historical contexts is beyond the scope of this entry. Suffice it to say that a wide range of mechanisms, including those identified by Flannery, are available for selection.

In Mesoamerica, for example, the general pattern of development of complex society must be explained in these cultural and ecological terms. Within this region complexity arose in several areas: the Olmec civilization, the first influential group of chiefdoms, in the tropical lowlands of the Gulf Coast; the early Maya and ultimately Classic and Postclassic Maya civilization, in the eastern tropical forests of the Yucatan; the singularly important state at Teotihuacan and later the Aztec empire, in the semiarid basin of Mexico; and the Zapotec state at Monte Alban, in the semiarid valley of Oaxaca. In each case environmental and cultural factors interacted in a specific process of cultural evolution. The course of events varied widely and led to different outcomes. We are not yet in a position to explain why, but it is instructive that in such diverse circumstances channels existed that promoted the development of complex society. In some areas the course of change seems to have been almost continuously toward ever more complex organizations; in others change led at times to more complex organizations and at other times to their dissolution. These changes depended not solely on the environments but equally on the cultural and historical contexts of each case. In any study of process it is important to distinguish the underlying stresses from the operative mechanisms.

The Olmec rise to prominence in the coastal lowlands of the Gulf Coast likely coincided with the rise of maize agriculture as a locally important food crop. Their swift rise to the status of a dominant, although diverse, chiefly organization is well documented archaeologically. Excavations, particularly at San Lorenzo, have revealed a social and political order in which access to exotic goods and special positions of power were held in the hands of only a few Olmec leaders. Their ability to generate surpluses beyond their subsistence needs provided the energetic basis for these cultural developments. The richness of the fertile soils near the streams of the coastal plains would have given them an advantage over their highland neighbors, who lived in a riskier, less-productive environment. They used religion to reinforce their right to rule locally and both religion and economic interaction to extend their influence through much of the central highlands of Mexico. The great impact of the Olmec on the rising elites of the highlands has long been noted, but its nature is little understood. The cultural mechanisms are the most elusive part of the explanation of early Olmec ascendancy.

In the highlands the rise of the complex societies centered on Teotihuacan and Monte Alban are similarly difficult to explain. Much ink has been expended in efforts to discover the stresses that promoted the centralization of political control so inarguably observed at these two great cities. Most agree that in both cases the economic foundation of the state was the ability of the emerging elites to control the most productive land. The surplus was needed to support the members of society who produced goods and services other than food. Clearly there are complex interrelationships among environmental preconditions, human use of the landscape, and interactions of people within the environment, all of which effect the outcome of evolutionary processes. The operative mechanisms that produced the Pyramid of the Sun at Teotihuacan or Mound J at Monte Alban are hard to define. Just how Monte Alban extended its control over the valley of Oaxaca and surrounding areas or how Teotihuacan controlled the basin of Mexico and influenced so wide an area throughout highland Mesoamerica remain topics of inquiry.

Mesopotamia poses similar questions. In this region as well most explanations of the rise of complex societies appeal to changing relations between human populations and their environment. The

Pyramid of the Sun, "Avenue of the Dead," and neighboring structures in the Classic-phase city of Teotihuacan, Mexico. This city and its state were at their height ca. A.D. 500.

growth of early centers like Çatal Hüyük probably depended upon specially favored local resources, in the case of Çatal Hüyük perhaps the important nearby obsidian resource. Small centers like this one were the precursors of larger sites like Eridu and the later Ubaid-period cities of Uruk, Ur, and Umma. For these cities the important environmental feature may have been agricultural fields and the irrigation systems constructed to ensure their productivity. Intergroup conflict arising in the context of limited high-quality farmland or the administrative requirements of public utilities that promote production strike familiar chords in the realm of culture process.

The emergence of complex society and its institutions has fascinated archaeologists for decades and will undoubtedly continue to do so. In the near future the focus will likely be, as Flannery suggested, on the processes, mechanisms, and stresses by which change in cultural-environmental systems occurs. The recognition of the operative stresses as biological or ecological is rapidly emerging, even in the face of a resurgence in some quarters of a superorganic concept of culture divorced from the physical world. The processes themselves are coming to be seen as specifically cultural, whether one focuses on social processes like cooperation or competition or on institutional processes like promotion, linearization, segregation, and centralization. As a result the area that promises the most excitement is the analysis of the mechanisms that link ecological stress with cultural process.

See also AMERICAS; ARCHAEOLOGY; BRONZE AGE; ÇATAL HÜYÜK; CULTURE; DOMESTICATION; IRON AGE; NEAR EAST. [B.B.]

Further Readings

Adams, R.M. (1966) The Evolution of Urban Society. Chicago: Aldine.

Carneiro, R. (1970) A theory of the origin of the state. Science 169:733–738.

Flannery, K.V. (1972) The cultural evolution of civilizations. Ann. Rev. Ecol. and Syst. 3:399–426.

Fried, M. (1967) The Evolution of Political Society: An Essay in Political Anthropology. New York: Random House.

Redman, C. (1978) The Rise of Civilization. San Francisco: Freeman.

Sanders, W., Parsons, J., and Santley, R. (1979) The Basin of Mexico: Ecological processes in the Evolution of a Civilization. New York: Academic.

Sanders, W., and Webster, D. (1978) Unilinealism, multilinealism, and the evolution of complex societies. In C. Redman et al. (eds.): Social Archaeology. New York: Academic, pp. 249–302.

Service, E.R. (1962) Primitive Social Organization: An Evolutionary Perspective: New York: Random House.

Wright, H. (1977) Recent research on the origin of the state. Ann. Rev. Anthropol. 6:379–397.

Wright, H., and Johnson, G. (1978). Population, exchange, and early state formation in southwestern Iran. Am. Anthropol. 77:267–289.

CONSERVATIVE *see* CLADISTICS

CONTINENTAL DRIFT *see* PLATE TECTONICS

COPELEMUR *see* NOTHARCTIDAE

CORDILLERAN GLACIATIONS *see* GLACIATION; PLEISTOCENE

CORE

Block or nodule of stone from which flakes have been removed by deliberate flaking; also termed a *nucleus*. Many cores may simply be waste products of flake or blade manufacture, while others are thought to have been used after flaking (as in some choppers, handaxes, or picks), and the term *core-tool* is sometimes used. Cores with very small flakes removed, such as scrapers or projectile points, are sometimes called *retouched pieces* rather than cores.

See also BIFACE; PREPARED-CORE; STONE-TOOL MAKING. [N.T., K.S.]

CORRELATION *see* BIOCHRONOLOGY

CRANIAL LANDMARKS *see* SKULL

CRANIUM *see* SKULL

CRASSIDENS, AUSTRALOPITHECUS *see* AUSTRALOPITHECUS ROBUSTUS; PARANTHROPUS

CRESWELLIAN

Final Late Paleolithic industry of Britain, ca. 12,000–8000 B.P., with similarities to contemporary industries of northwestern France and Belgium (e.g. final Magdalenian, Hamburgian). Named for type sites, such as Mother Grundy's Parlor, in the Creswell Crag area of Derbyshire, the Creswellian contains medium- to large-sized angular backed blades, hooked perforators, or *zinken*, and shouldered points, together with uniserial and biserial harpoons of bone and antler. Faunas of Creswellian sites are dominated by horse remains but also include remains of reindeer, *Megaceros*, and other cold-adapted mammals as well as birds.

See also EPIPALEOLITHIC; HAMBURGIAN; LATE PALEOLITHIC; MAGDALENIAN; MAGLEMOSIAN; MESOLITHIC; PALEOLITHIC LIFEWAYS; STONE-TOOL MAKING. [A.S.B.]

CRO-MAGNON

Several Upper Paleolithic partial skeletons were recovered from the Cro-Magnon rock shelter, near Les Eyzies (France), in 1868. They probably represent late Aurignacian or Perigordian burials. Although strongly built and large-headed, the specimens contrast markedly with the Neanderthals in their morphology and body proportions.

See also HOMO SAPIENS. [C.B.S.]

CROMERIAN *see* TIME SCALE

CROUZELIA *see* PLIOPITHECIDAE

CRUSAFONT PAIRO, MIGUEL (1910–1983)

A lifelong resident of Sabadell, near Barcelona (Spain), Crusafont spent his early years as a passionate amateur paleontologist while making a successful career as a pharmacist. After publishing more than 40 papers on the Cenozoic mammals of the local Valles-Penedes basin, including descriptions of *Dryopithecus fontani*, he returned to university and obtained his doctorate at age 42. His later work expanded to include interregional and theoretical subjects, including studies of dryopithecines and adapids, but he continued to add to his enormous collection from the sub-Pyrenean basins. In the 1950s the Museo de Sabadell was constructed opposite his pharmacy, to house his work. Through interregional conferences, the famous "Cursillos Internacionales de Paleontología" at Sabadell, and the proposal of the Vallesian and Turolian mammal ages, based on his research in the Valles and Teruel basins, Crusafont was the founder of mammalian biochronology in Europe.

See also BIOCHRONOLOGY; EUROPE. [J.A.V.C.]

CSARNOTAN *see* TIME SCALE

CUEVA MORIN

Archaeologically important cave located near Santander in northeastern Spain, dated to the later late Pleistocene by faunal and archaeological correlations and radiocarbon ages. In the 1960s and 70s L. Freeman distinguished 16 archaeological levels at this site: nine Mousterian, one Chatelperronian, and six Aurignacian. One of the earliest levels in the latter group yielded a structural complex consisting of a rectangular subsurface depression interpreted as a hut floor, incorporating a hearth, a possible arrangement of small irregular elliptical holes interpreted as postholes, and four graves. Two graves had been destroyed in Aurignacian times; the other two contained *pseudomorphs*, or outlines of bodies with no associated skeletons.

See also AURIGNACIAN; CHATELPERRONIAN; MIDDLE PALEOLITHIC; MOUSTERIAN; RITUAL; UPPER PALEOLITHIC. [A.S.B.]

CUISIAN *see* EOCENE; TIME SCALE

CULTURAL ANTHROPOLOGY

Branch of anthropology that studies living human groups as cultural entities. It includes *ethnography*, or the effort to describe accurately the workings of human societies, and *ethnology*, the effort to explain those observations. The unifying concept of *culture*, the shared knowledge and patterns of behavior of human societies, is central to the practice of cultural anthropology.

See also ANTHROPOLOGY; ARCHAEOLOGY; CULTURE; PRIMATE SOCIETIES. [B.B.]

CULTURE

Term traditionally used in prehistoric archaeology to define a specific collection of portable material objects, most often stone and bone tools, that exhibit similarity in a number of variables and that are found within a delimited region and time period (e.g. the Magdalenian, Perigordian, or Solutrean cultures). This use of the term is widespread in the literature that deals with the culture history of regions.

Recent shifts in research focus, especially evident in North American anthropological archaeology, have brought with them an expansion of this concept, and the term has acquired a broader meaning, more like that used in sociocultural anthropology. Numerous definitions of culture exist in anthropology. Perhaps the most inclusive is Leslie White's, which sees culture as referring to all human extrasomatic means of adaptation, including ideas and beliefs, behavior, and material results of that behavior.

Applying this all-encompassing concept in archaeology raises many problems. The archaeological record contains direct information about only some materials used in the past—those, like lithics, that preserve the best. These remains, which constitute a small fraction of what was originally used, thus carry direct information about only a limited range of past behavior, and this information may be ambiguous. Finally, behavioral complexes without direct material expression are not preserved in the archaeological record and must be inferred indirectly through analogy.

See also ARCHAEOLOGY; CULTURAL ANTHROPOLOGY. [O.S.]

CULTURE PROCESS *see* COMPLEX SOCIETIES

CUSP *see* TEETH

CYPHANTHROPUS *see* ARCHAIC HOMO SAPIENS

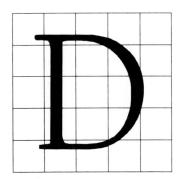

DNA *see* GENETICS; MOLECULAR ANTHROPOLOGY

DNA HYBRIDIZATION

DNA is a two-stranded molecule, built from pairs of *nucleotides*. A nucleotide consists of a sugar molecule (deoxyribose), a phosphate molecule, and one of four bases: adenine (A), guanine (G), cytosine (C), and thymine (T). The nucleotide pairs that are the building blocks of DNA consist of only two kinds: A-T and G-C. Thus, if the nucleotide sequence of one DNA strand is, say, AAGCTT, this determines that the other strand must be TTCGAA.

The bonds that hold the nucleotide pairs together, when summed over the entire DNA molecule, hold the two DNA strands together. Adding energy, in the form of heat, breaks these bonds and dissociates the two strands from one another. This is called *denaturing* the DNA. Controlled cooling allows a single DNA strand to "find" its complementary strand and regain its stable two-stranded conformation. Much of the cellular DNA, however, consists of short sequences repeated many times: these sequences are able to find a complementary stretch much more easily than is unique-sequence DNA. DNA hybridization can therefore be used to estimate the degree of complexity of the genome of a given species, by providing a measure of what proportion of the genome reanneals very rapidly, rapidly, or slowly.

Different species have accumulated unique point mutations during their separate histories. If we take the unique-sequence DNA from one species (the *tracer*), denature it, and mix it with a great excess of denatured DNA from a different species (the *driver*),

we make it unlikely that the tracer DNA will be able to "find" its own complementary strand. Instead it will bind imperfectly to the more abundant nearly complementary strand from the other species.

This *heteroduplex* DNA can be isolated and denatured again. This time, however, fewer bonds will be holding the DNA molecule together; less energy is required to break apart the two strands; and the molecule will therefore dissociate at a slightly lower

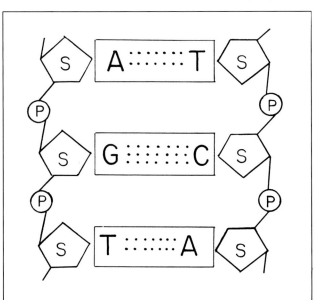

The two DNA strands are held together by weak bonds (dotted) joining the nucleotide pairs. S and P indicate the sugar and phosphate aspects, respectively, of the DNA molecule. Adenine (A) and Thymine (T) are joined by two bonds; Guanine (G) and Cytosine (C) are joined by three bonds. Heating breaks these bonds and leaves the DNA as two single strands.

temperature than the *homoduplex* DNA. As the dissociation of the DNA strands is a continuous process, the critical temperature is generally given as that at which 50 percent of the DNA being studied is single-stranded. The difference in dissociation temperature between homoduplex and heteroduplex DNA is proportional to the amount of genetic mutation that has accumulated between the two species. It can therefore be used as a measure of the *genetic distance* between the two species.

See also GENETICS; GENOME; MOLECULAR ANTHROPOLOGY. [J.M.]

Further Readings

Sibley, C., and Ahlquist, J. (1986) Reconstructing bird phylogeny by comparing DNA's. Sci. Am. 254:82–92.

DABBAN

Early Late Paleolithic backed-blade and burin industry of Cyrenaica (Libya), defined at Haua Fteah and Hagfet ed-Dabba (Cave of the Hyena) by McBurney. The first appearance of the industry at ca. 40,000–32,000 B.P., sometimes compared with the Emiran at Abu Halka, is marked by chamfered blades, end-scrapers, and a large component of backed blades. This is followed at Haua Fteah by a reappearance of Levalloiso-Mousterian, and then by a second Dabban phase with more burins and end-scrapers but no chamfered blades. The Dabban lasted until ca. 14,000 B.P., when it was replaced by an eastern Oranian industry with backed bladelets and microblade cores.

See also BLADE; BURIN; EMIRAN; HAUA FTEAH; IBERO-MAURUSIAN; LATE PALEOLITHIC; LEVALLOIS; MOUSTERIAN; STONE-TOOL MAKING. [A.S.B.]

DALI

Skull found in late middle Pleistocene loess (wind-blown) deposits in Shaanxi Province (China) in 1978. It is a well-preserved cranium with an endocranial capacity of less than 1,200 ml. and a large supraorbital torus but a gracile and flat face. It is usually classified as a Chinese archaic *Homo sapiens*, and several workers, particularly in China, regard it as morphologically intermediate between earlier *Homo erectus* and modern Chinese populations.

See also ARCHAIC HOMO SAPIENS; CHINA. [C.B.S.]

DAR-ES-SOLTANE

Cave site in Morocco that has produced hominid fossils in association with an Aterian industry that may be more than 45 k.y. old. Most of the fossils have not been described, but they include the robustly

built front of a skull and associated mandible. Although anatomically modern, this specimen is reminiscent of the earlier Jebel Irhoud crania from Morocco and perhaps indicates local continuity in this area between nonmodern and modern populations.

See also ARCHAIC MODERNS. [C.B.S.]

DART, RAYMOND ARTHUR (b. 1893)

South African (b. Australia) anatomist and paleontologist. Following completion of his medical training at the University of Sydney in 1917, Dart spent several years working with G.E. Smith (1871–1937) in England and R.J. Terry (1871–1966) in America before receiving the chair of anatomy at the University of Witwatersrand in 1922, a position he held until his retirement in 1958. In 1925 he was catapulted to international fame by his description and interpretation of the fossil hominid infant skull from Taung, which he named *Australopithecus africanus*. Dart claimed that this apelike creature stood on the threshold of humanity and as such warranted a new family name: "Homo-Simiiadae." While these pronouncements instantly embroiled him in controversy, his insights were later confirmed and represented a major milestone in the history of paleoanthropology. Following World War II Dart was responsible for the systematic excavation of the Makapansgat site, which yielded several dozen new australopithecine fossils along with an enormous accumulation of bone fragments from other animals. Dart concluded that the australopithecines inhabiting this site had been responsible for the bone accumulations and that they had fashioned and used some of these bones as primitive tools. To describe this tool making he coined the term *osteodontokeratic culture*. While the reaction to this hypothesis was largely negative, it had the positive effect of promoting the search for alternative explanations; a direct product of which was the incorporation of taphonomic research techniques in Paleolithic archaeological research. In addition to his paleoanthropological studies Dart also played an active role in developing studies on living subequatorial human populations and contributed to the development of nonhuman primate behavioral studies through his establishment in 1958 of the Witwatersrand University Uganda Gorilla Research Unit.

See also AUSTRALOPITHECUS; AUSTRALOPITHECUS AFRICANUS; MAKAPANSGAT; TAUNG. [F.S.]

DARWIN, CHARLES ROBERT (1809–1882)

British naturalist. Following a false start at Edinburgh as a medical student (1825–1827), Darwin went to

Cambridge, where he earned a Bachelor of Arts degree in 1831. At Cambridge Darwin's interest in natural history was fostered by the geologist Adam Sedgwick (1785–1873) and the botanist John S. Henslow (1796–1861). It was Henslow who subsequently recommended him for the position of companion to the captain of the H.M.S. *Beagle,* a vessel that had been commissioned to explore and survey the South American coastline and the islands of the South Pacific.

During the *Beagle's* voyage, from December 1831 to October 1836, Darwin gathered an immense body of scientific data on the flora, fauna, and geology of the lands and islands he visited. All of Darwin's later work stemmed directly from the observations and collections made during this voyage. The immediate result was the publication of a general account of the voyage, the *Journal of Researches into the Geology and Natural History of the Various Countries Visited by H.M.S. Beagle, 1832–36,* published in 1839, followed by three other books published in 1842, 1844, and 1846, respectively: *Structure and Distribution of Coral Reefs, Geological Observations on Volcanic Islands,* and *Geological Observations on South America.*

At this juncture Darwin's concerns shifted progressively from geology to biology. From 1846 to 1854 he devoted his attention primarily to the study of living and fossil barnacles, which did much to clarify his ideas on classification, variation, and the origination of species. It was not until 1858, when he received a manuscript from the young naturalist Alfred Russel Wallace (1823–1913) outlining similar ideas on natural selection and evolution, that Darwin was prompted to complete what he called an "abstract" of the full work he had been laboring on for years. This abstract was *On the Origin of Species,* which appeared on November 24, 1859. In this work he painstakingly documented the evidence supporting the view that the earth's diverse organic life had a common ancestry and presented a theory for the operation of the evolutionary process. The book was an immediate sensation and brought Darwin instant and enduring fame.

During the remaining years of his life Darwin published three more books that amplified and extended the principles presented in *Origin of Species.* These were *The Variation of Animals and Plants Under Domestication* (1868), *The Descent of Man and Selection in Relation to Sex* (1871), and *The Expression of the Emotions in Man and Animals* (1872). Although such honors as knighthood and the coveted Fellowship of the Royal Society eluded him in life, in death he received universal praise for having discovered the greatest general principle in biology. He died April 19, 1882, and was buried in Westminster Abbey.

See also EVOLUTION; HAECKEL, ERNST HEINRICH; HUXLEY, THOMAS HENRY; WALLACE, ALFRED RUSSEL. [F.S.]

Further Readings

Gillespie, N.C. (1979) Charles Darwin and the Problem of Creation. Chicago: University of Chicago Press.

Gruber, H. (1981) Darwin on Man: A Psychological Study of Scientific Creativity, 2nd ed. Chicago: University of Chicago Press.

Peckham, M. (1959) The Origin of Species by Charles Darwin: A Variorum Text. Philadelphia: University of Pennsylvania Press.

DARWINISM, SOCIAL *see* SOCIOBIOLOGY

DATING *see* BIOCHRONOLOGY; GEOCHRONOMETRY; TIME SCALE

DATUM *see* BIOCHRONOLOGY

DAUBENTONIA *see* DAUBENTONIIDAE

DAUBENTONIIDAE

Family of Lemuriformes that contains the aye-aye, *Daubentonia madagascariensis.* The only living member of its family, the aye-aye is a highly specialized form whose affinities appear to lie within Indrioidea but whose aspect is different from that of any other lemur. Subfossil bones some 15 percent larger than those of the living aye-aye have been assigned to a recently extinct species, *D. robusta,* but it is unclear whether the one good skeleton of this type that is known (which lacks the skull) indeed represents a separate species or merely a larger local variant of the living one.

Morphologically the aye-aye is unusual in a variety of ways. Perhaps the most marked peculiarity of this lemur lies in its anterior dentition, which has been reduced in the adult to a single pair of incisor teeth in each of the upper and lower jaws. These teeth are enlarged, laterally compressed, and continually growing, their open roots extending far back in the jaws above or below the roots of the molar teeth, which are greatly reduced in size and simplified in morphology. A single tiny permanent premolar is present in the upper jaw. The anterior teeth are thus reminiscent of those of rodents and are adapted to a similar gnawing function. This function has affected the entire structure of the skull, which is flexed to help absorb gnawing stresses, giving it a globular appearance in side view.

The most striking character of the postcranial skeleton of the aye-aye may be the great elongation of the digits of the hand, and particularly the middle one, which is thin and attentuated. When walking on a flat substrate, the aye-aye is obliged to hyperflex its wrist to clear the ground with these digits. This gives its terrestrial locomotion a stiff-armed appearance, even though the aye-aye is an animal of great agility in the trees. The digits of the aye-aye are tipped with highly compressed nails, or "pseudo-claws," except in the case of the hallux, which is equipped with a flat nail.

In the external characters of its soft anatomy the aye-aye is likewise unusual, especially in the large size of its external ears and in the quality of its fur, which has a layer of long and coarse guard hairs that overlie the softer fur beneath. Uniquely for a primate, female aye-ayes have a single pair of mammae situated far back on the abdomen.

Daubentonia madagascariensis. (From Owen, 1862.)

It is probable that the aye-aye was once distributed widely throughout the forests of Madagascar, but it is nowadays reported mainly from the humid forests of the east, and then but rarely. Recent observations have shown that of several individuals transferred in the 1960s from the mainland to the tiny island of Nosy-Mangabé, at the head of the Baie d'Antongil, some at least still survive and may be breeding, and other reports suggest that *Daubentonia* occurs more widely than previously thought. Nonetheless, the aye-aye is among the most critically endangered of all the lemurs, and its chances for survival are not helped by local beliefs that it is a harbinger of misfortune.

An arboreal quadruped, the aye-aye is nocturnal, and little is known about its behavior and ecology in the wild. Adults appear to range alone, adult females being accompanied by their immature offspring, but olfactory marking is an important part of the behavioral repertoire and presumably helps to maintain social relations between individuals with overlapping

ranges. Aye-ayes build elaborate nests that they sleep in during the daytime and during their nightly ranging may seek fruit as a substantial part of their diet. Their specialized front teeth allow them, for instance, to gnaw through the tough fibrous husk of coconuts to feed on the flesh within. One type of feeding behavior uses a combination of many of the aye-aye's specialized traits. An individual will listen, with its large sensitive ears, for the sounds of insect larvae burrowing inside dead branches. The front teeth are then used to gnaw a hole in the dead wood, exposing the larval tunnels. The thin middle finger, equipped with a claw, is used to spear larvae inside the tunnels and withdraw them. Body weight of an adult *D. madagascariensis* is ca. 2.7 kg.

Because certain very early primates possessed much-enlarged front teeth, albeit ones that did not continually grow, it has been suggested that a particular evolutionary relationship might exist between these forms and the aye-aye. Clearly, however, there is no basis for this conclusion, and the aye-aye has no known fossil record. The precise affinities of *Daubentonia* are hard to determine, because its anatomy is so highly modified in so many respects, but there is no question that it belongs in Lemuriformes, and various characters of the skull and dentition point toward a relationship with the indriids and their subfossil relatives.

See also INDRIOIDEA; LEMURIFORMES. [I.T.]

Further Readings

Tattersall, I. (1982) The Primates of Madagascar. New York: Columbia University Press.

DÉBITAGE   *see*   STONE-TOOL MAKING

DECIDUOUS   *see*   TEETH

DECOREDON

Small, middle Paleocene genus of euprimates from southern China. Until recently the two known specimens of the only known species, which belonged to the same individual animal, have been referred to two separate species of two genera, belonging to two different families of two orders. The poorly preserved teeth of the upper and lower dentition of this single species, however, show striking special similarities to the earliest euprimates. The great significance of *Decoredon* lies in its great antiquity in a region of the world that is just beginning to be explored paleontologically. *Decoredon*, along with the undoubted omomyid *Altanius*, suggests that the immense southern forests of the Asian Paleocene may have been an important theater for the evolution of the euprimates before they appear in Euroamerica in the early Eocene.

[F.S.S.]

DENDROCHRONOLOGY *see* GEOCHRONOMETRY

DENDROPITHECUS *see* CATARRHINI

DENEKAMP INTERSTADIAL *see* GLACIATION; PLEISTOCENE

DENEN DORA *see* HADAR

DENTICULATE *see* STONE-TOOL MAKING

DENTICULATE MOUSTERIAN *see* MOUSTERIAN

DENTINE *see* TEETH

DERIVED *see* CLADISTICS

DE SONNEVILLE-BORDES, DENISE (b.1919)
French prehistorian responsible, with Jean Perrot, for the most widely used typology of the European Upper Paleolithic, as well as for the application of descriptive statistics to Upper Paleolithic industries (with her late husband F. Bordes). In addition she has directed significant excavations at such Upper Paleolithic sites as Abri Caminade, has suggested important revisions to the Upper Paleolithic sequence of France, and has continued to stress stylistic and cultural (ethnic) distinctions among Upper Paleolithic industries.

See also BORDES, FRANÇOIS; UPPER PALEOLITHIC. [A.S.B.]

DEVELOPED OLDOWAN *see* ACHEULEAN; EARLY PALEOLITHIC; OLDOWAN

DEVIL'S TOWER *see* GIBRALTAR; NEANDERTHALS

DHOK PATHAN *see* SIWALIKS

DIET

Primate species exploit almost all the possible food sources they find in their environments. Arboreal species eat fruits, flowers, leaves, bark, pith, seeds, tree gum, and nuts. Animal foods include small vertebrates and invertebrates. Ground-living primates eat many of the same things as well as grasses, roots, and tubers. But primates do not simply eat anything that comes into their path that is tasty. Each species concentrates on a few kinds of foods, presumably to avoid competition with other species.

Categorizing Primate Foods
Primate adaptations for diet occur at two levels. First, food must be foraged for and, in the case of predation, captured and subdued. Behavioral adaptations for foraging are especially obvious among predators. Particularly important for nonhuman primates are specializations of the special senses and locomotor system for finding and capturing insects. Second, once the food is "in hand" it must be broken up in the mouth into suitable form for swallowing and then assimilated by the digestive tract. To understand dietary adaptations of the masticatory and digestive systems knowledge about the physical and chemical structure of food is most important. Keeping in mind food-acquiring, ingestive, and digestive aspects of dietary adaptation, primate dietary specializations will be discussed in three broad categories: animal foods (insects and other invertebrates as well as vertebrates); plant materials high in structural carbohydrates, such as cellulose, hemicellulose, and lignin (usually leaves, bark, and pith); and plant materials high in nonstructural carbohydrates, such as simple sugars or starches (some roots, fruits, nuts, gum, nectar). As a convenient shorthand these categories will be referred to by the most abundant food type within them: insects, leaves, and fruit, respectively.

A number of other aspects of potential foods are crucial for primate food choice. Primary considerations are physical location and availability. Some foods are preferred to others simply because they are more easily reached. Many foods are available only at certain times of the year, so their potential consumers must find other foods when the preferred ones are scarce. Also, some foods are clumped in space, whereas others are more uniformly dispersed, so consumers must make decisions about the energetic costs of obtaining the food versus the energetic or nutritive return for the effort.

To be successful a primate must also select a diet containing adequate amounts of protein, carbohydrate, fat, and trace nutrients in assimilable form. For example, although fruit is a particularly good source of carbohydrate, fruit is often protein-poor. Further, the consumer must be able to overcome various chemical defenses against being eaten. For example, many plants produce toxins in some of their parts to avoid or reduce predator activity; likewise many insect species have noxious tastes or smells, or mimic others that do have them, to discourage predation. Various physical properties of foods also constrain the potential consumer: some fruits have very hard exocarps that must be broken.

The table summarizes the physical and chemical properties of primate foods and some anatomical traits of the species that eat them.

Insect Eating

Animal foods are very good sources of energy and protein, so it is not surprising that most primate species eat at least some insects while some are strongly specialized for eating insects. Many prosimians are insectivorous. The roster of insectivores includes small nocturnal lemurs, lorises, and tarsiers like *Microcebus*, *Galago*, *Loris*, and *Tarsius*. Some of the small diurnal New World monkeys are also fairly insectivorous, especially *Saguinus* and *Saimiri*. Animals that eat other animals have special adaptations to capture and subdue prey. Methods of prey location and capture vary from species to species, but there are many similarities in feeding techniques of all primates as distinct from insectivorans. Consider the similarities and differences in the foraging techniques of two very different primate insectivores, tarsiers and slow lorises, and how this contrasts with nonprimate insectivores.

Tarsiers live close to trees that have ripe fruit lying on the ground beneath them. They apparently are attracted to the insects and other animals that are attracted to the fruit. They capture most of their prey on the ground. According to Fogden (1974): ". . . they would scan the forest floor from a perch a meter or more above the ground, and having located the prey (which is generally moving) leaped directly onto it, killing it by biting with tight shut eyes. Tarsiers

DIET	INSECTIVORY	FRUGIVORY	FOLIVORY
CHEMISTRY			
PROTEIN	high	low	high
LIPIDS	high	low (seeds high)	low
CARBOHYDRATE			
NONSTRUCTURAL	moderate	high	moderate
STRUCTURAL	low (chitin)	low to moderate	high
TOXINS,			
DIGESTIVE INHIBITORS	low	low to moderate	high
G-I TRACT			
DETOXIFICATION			
ABILITY	low	low	high
INTESTINAL VILLI,	many large villi		
FOLDING	few folds	many folds	few small villi
RELATIVE GUT			
DIMENSIONS	large	small	large
MECHANICAL PROPERTIES	brittle, hard (chitin)	deformable (except seeds,	tough, fibrous
OF FOOD		nuts)	
DENTAL STRUCTURE			
PUNCTURING	well developed	poorly developed	moderate
SHEARING	well developed	weak	well developed
CRUSHING, GRINDING	weak	well developed	variable
ENAMEL THICKNESS	thin	moderate (thick for nut eaters)	thin

Physical and chemical properties of primate diets and some dental and gastrointestinal characteristics of the species that eat them.

were seen to catch in this way with leaps up to 2 meters, but most leaps were considerably shorter. The scanning phase of hunting sometimes lasted up to 10 minutes at a single perch, with the tarsier remaining more or less immobile; but more usually a failure to locate the prey at one perch resulted in it moving on after only a minute or two. Some observations suggest that hearing as well as sight plays a part in locating prey."

Tarsiers also forage in the leaf litter with their hands. This hunting by touch also appears to be effective in causing cryptic insects to move so that they can be seen and pounced upon. This description accentuates the peculiarly primate hunting technique. Prey detection is generally a visual and to some extent auditory procedure, and prey capture involves precise hand-eye coordination; the mouth is rarely involved in actual prey capture; olfactory and snout-tactile senses are little used.

The highly insectivorous *Loris tardigradus* has a different prey-capture technique, but there are important similarities with tarsiers. Unlike tarsiers slender lorises are slow-moving and stalk their cryptic, slow-moving insect prey with deliberation. Like tarsiers, however, lorises catch their prey in both hands or in one hand. Only when securely caught is the prey taken into the mouth to be crushed to stop its struggle.

The special reliance on the eyes and stereoscopic vision in prey location and the enhanced importance of the hands for prey capture of both tarsiers and lorises are strikingly different from the way "primitive" mammalian insectivores locate and capture insects. In *Echinops*, a tenrec, prey is located with olfaction and by touch with the snout. Once located, "prey capture involves orientation to the prey object . . . sniffing and seizing it with the mouth. There is little involvement of the fore-paws in the capture of prey . . ." (Eisenberg and Gould, 1970). This distinction helps to explain the acquisition of stereoscopic-vision-reduced olfactory epthelium and snout-tactile sense along with augmentation of digital-tactile sense in the earliest primates, which were almost certainly insectivorous.

The different feeding approach of slow lorises compared with tarsiers and bushbabies highlights a reliance on different sorts of insect prey. Lorises eat mainly caterpillars and ants, which can be obtained readily with a slow deliberate form of prey stalking. Such slow-moving prey normally protect themselves by being cryptic or producing noxious smells or tastes, or by having stinging hairs. Tarsiers are active leapers and can capture and eat quick-moving insects: beetles, nocturnal moths, and grasshoppers, and the like.

Insect-eating species have a characteristic cheek-tooth structure reflecting common physical properties of the insects eaten. In their adult stages insects have tough exoskeletons composed in part of chitin. Chitin is essentially the animal equivalent of plant fiber in its physical and chemical properties. To puncture and cut chitin into the size and consistency required for swallowing, insect eaters have molars with tall, pointed cusps and sharp, trenchant crests. Cutting up of chitin has the added effect of increasing its surface area exposed to digestive action. Digestion of chitin is effected by special chitinolitic enzymes in the stomach.

Another important structural adaptation of insectivorous primates is small body size. The invertebrate prey of primates are small and often do not have communal habits; they have to be located one by one. This places an important upper body-size limit on primate insect predators above which it is difficult to capture enough insects to meet energy needs. It is rare to find a primarily insectivorous primate with a body weight over ca. 300–500 gm.

The aye-aye, *Daubentonia*, from Madagascar is insectivorous and weighs over 1,000 gm., an exception to this upper size limit. This animal probably feeds on wood-boring grubs or ants and termites. Once located, such food sources are quite abundant, so predators with larger body size and greater energy requirements can be supported.

Many larger primates occasionally eat insects, and these may contribute significantly to their protein requirements. For example, *Cebus* (the capuchin monkey) and some Old World monkeys forage on the ground for insect prey. Chimpanzees use tools, stripped twigs or grass blades, to poke into termite hills for grubs. Overall, however, insects do not amount to a particularly large proportion of the diet of these larger primates. Because of the small proportion of insects compared with fruits in the diets of these large species structural modifications for insectivory in the teeth or digestive tracts are not apparent.

Plant Eating

Plants are the essential food of most living primates, but all that is green is not edible. Many plant parts are composed principally of inedible woody materials. Other parts are protected from being eaten by poisonous secondary compounds or compounds like tannin that inhibit digestive processes. Thus the feeding strategy of primate plant eaters includes not just the ability to find and reach the food source but also the ability to prepare the foods adequately for rapid assimilation and to neutralize or avoid plant poisons. Prey capture is relatively unimportant, of course—you don't have to beat a banana over the head before eating it.

Leaf- and grass-eating primates Eating leaves and woody materials presents special challenges for the digestive tract, but the primates that have solved these problems have a high return in nutrients for their investment. Foliage commonly contains high percentages of energy-rich carbohydrates. Comparatively little of the carbohydrate, however, is in readily digestible forms like starch or sugar; the major part of this material is in structural carbohydrates: cellulose, hemicellulose, and pectin. Such substances are not directly available to primates, because these animals lack the enzymes needed to digest them. Foliage is also the major, superabundant, source of protein in plants, second in quality (digestibility) and quantity only to animal foods.

Feeding on leaves, bark, buds, and grasses is common among primates. Species of the strepsirhine family Indriidae appear to concentrate on arboreal leaves, as do several species of lemurids. Arboreal leaf eating is also commonly practiced by the platyrrhines *Alouatta* and *Brachyteles*. Among catarrhines the Colobinae, familiarly known as leaf monkeys, mainly eat tree leaves. Some of the terrestrial cercopithecines, especially *Papio*, *Erythrocebus*, and *Theropithecus*, eat considerable proportions of grasses in woodland-savanna environments.

Among the lesser apes *Symphalangus* eats a large amount of leaves, as do the great apes *Pongo* and especially *Gorilla*. The latter forages on the ground for many foods high in structural carbohydrates, such as bamboo, bark, pith, and buds.

Leaf-eating species have enlarged, elaborate digestive tracts. Often either the stomach or the caecum, a blind pocket at the end of the large intestine, is greatly enlarged. Species that have enlarged stomachs are said to practice *foregut* fermentation, whereas those that have an enlarged caecum are *hindgut* fermentors. Either of these parts of the digestive tract is home for symbiotic microorganisms that can digest cellulose and other structural carbohydrates. Without these microorganisms mammals would be unable to digest structural carbohydrates, because they cannot produce the digestive enzymes for this process. The by-products of this breakdown, together with the remains of the dead microorganisms themselves, satisfy an important part of the nutritional requirements of leaf eaters. Enlargement of certain parts of the gastrointestinal tract, and elongation of the tract as a whole, also slow the passage of food through the body. Since breakdown and assimilation of structural carbohydrate is a relatively slow process, such slowing enhances digestibility. One benefit for foregut fermentors is that many toxins

carried in leaves can be acted upon and neutralized by the microorganisms of the stomach before they reach a part of the gastrointestinal tract where they could be absorbed into the bloodstream. Another important adaptation to leaf eating may be a lowered basal metabolic rate.

Leaf-eating primates have elaborate cheek teeth with well-developed cutting edges that assist the digestive process. Carefully chewing these foods increases the surfaces exposed to digestive action and speeds the digestive process. Grass-eating species, such as some of the terrestrial Old World monkeys, have further specializations of the cheek teeth. Grass leaves contain large amounts of silica, making them extremely abrasive. A consequence of feeding on grasses is that the teeth wear down very fast. To counteract this grass eaters like *Theropithecus* have high-crowned teeth. In this way they can forestall the time when the teeth wear out.

Fruit-eating primates A number of different feeding strategies are subsumed under this general heading. Some species feed mainly on the pulp of ripe fruit, a particularly good source of readily metabolized simple sugars. These foods, however, are less nutritious in terms of protein, so often species that feed on ripe fruits will also eat either leaves or insects as a source of protein. Another specialization is for eating seeds. Many ripe-fruit eaters swallow the seeds of fruits whole, and the seeds pass through the gut in an undigested state. Others are seed "predators" that actually break open and chew up and digest seeds. For them seeds or nuts are extremely rich sources of lipids, a particularly high-energy nutrient.

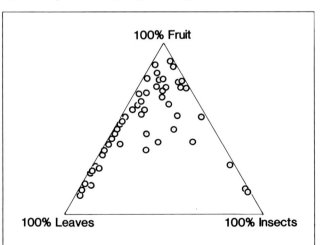

"Ternary" diagram illustrating the dietary behavior of some of the more fully studied primate species. Species that eat 100 percent leaves, insects, or fruit are plotted at the corners; a species that ate equal portions of all three would be in the middle. This highlights the fact that most primates concentrate on just a few or several dietary items. (After Kay and Covert, 1984.)

Feeding on fruit pulp is the commonest adaptive strategy among primates. Fruit eaters are found in practically all families of primates with the exception of the Indriidae. The digestive system of most fruit eaters is fairly simple and relatively much shorter than that of leaf eaters. Fruit eaters have comparatively little fiber in their diets, so there is not the need for slowed food-passage time as in folivores. The cheek teeth of frugivorous species have low, rounded cusps with smooth contours. The most important aspect of the fruit-eating dentition is the reliance on crushing and grinding surfaces, which often are enlarged. Special changes accompany reliance on breaking open seeds. Seed-eating primates, like the cercopithecine *Cercocebus* and the platyrrhines *Cebus* and members of the family Pitheciinae, have tusklike canines for cracking open hard exocarps or seed pods, and thick cheek-tooth enamel to resist the stresses engendered by crushing seeds.

A feeding pattern that does not fit very well in the above scheme is gum eating. *Galago* and some other small strepsirhines, as well as some cheirogaleines and marmosets, are gum eaters. *Galago* feeds especially on the gum of the acacia tree. Chemical analysis shows this to be an abundant source of carbohydrate and water and to contain small amounts of protein and minerals. One interesting point is the presence of large amounts of polymerized pentose and hexose sugar. It seems likely that *Galago* and other gum eaters may have symbiotic microorganisms in their digestive tracts (especially in the caecum) that enable them to use these complex carbohydrates. The front teeth of some gum eaters are specialized to allow them to cut into tree bark to promote gum flow and to allow them to scrape up the gum. *Phaner*, for example, has a sharp, projecting upper canine and upper front premolar, which it uses to dig into bark to accelerate gum flow. Gum is later collected from the damaged tree. The cheek teeth of gum eaters somewhat resemble those of frugivorous species.

See also PRIMATE ECOLOGY; TEETH. [R.F.K.]

Further Readings

Chivers, D.J., and Hladik, C.M. (1984) Diet and gut morphology in primates. In D.J. Chivers, B.A. Wood, and A. Bilsborough (eds.): Food Acquisition and Processing in Primates. London: Plenum, pp. 213–230.

Clutton-Brock, T.H., ed. (1977) Primate Ecology. London: Academic.

Eisenberg, J.F., and Gould, I. (1970) The tenrecs: a study in mammalian behavior and evolution. Smith. Contrib. Zool. 27:1–137.

Fogden, M. (1974) A preliminary field study of the western tarsier, *Tarsius bancanus* Horsefield. In R.D. Martin, G.A. Doyle, and A.C. Walker (eds.): Prosimian Biology. London: Duckworth, pp. 151–166.

Kay, R.F., and Covert, H.H. (1984) Anatomy and behaviour of extinct primates. In Chivers, Wood, and Bilsborough, pp. 467–508.

Parra, R. (1978) Comparison of foregut and hindgut fermentation in herbivores. In G.G. Montgomery (ed.): The Ecology of Arboreal Folivores. Washington, D.C.: Smithsonian Institution Press, pp. 205–230.

Waterhouse, P.G. (1984) Food acquisition and processing as a function of plant chemistry. In Chivers, Wood, and Bilsborough, pp. 177–212.

DIMORPHISM   *see*   SEXUAL DIMORPHISM

DINGCUN (TING-T'SUN)

Series of localities near Dingcun, Shanxi Province (China), that have yielded both hominid remains and archaeological assemblages. The sites are probably of late Pleistocene or latest middle Pleistocene age, based on faunal correlations. One adolescent hominid (represented by three teeth) and a separate parietal bone are known from Locality 54.100. In addition to hominid remains thousands of artifacts are also known from various localities at Dingcun. The Dingcun assemblage is unique in comparison with most other Chinese assemblages in exhibiting a relatively high percentage of bifacially flaked chopping tools as well as distinctive trihedral points, or "picks." Dingcun-like assemblages have apparently also been recovered from other nearby localities in Shanxi. Furthermore, it is possible that the Dingcun industries are somehow related to the distinctive Chongok-Ni "culture" of Korea.

See also ASIA (EASTERN); CHINA. [G.G.P.]

DINOPITHECUS   *see*   CERCOPITHECINAE

DIONYSOPITHECUS   *see*   PLIOPITHECIDAE

DIRECT PERCUSSION   *see*   STONE-TOOL MAKING

DISCOID   *see*   STONE-TOOL MAKING

DISCOIDAL CORE   *see*   STONE-TOOL MAKING

DJETIS (JETIS)

Fossil-collecting area in eastern Java, late Pliocene or early Pleistocene to middle Pleistocene stratified sequence, on the basis of biostratigraphy and radiometric dates. The name Djetis (Jetis), that of a village in the Sangiran area, was applied by von Koenigswald to vertebrate fossils supposedly derived from the "black clays" of the Putjangan (Pucangan) Formation of east-central Java. Originally he thought the presence of *Leptobos*, "primitive" proboscideans, and hippos indicated an early Pleistocene, Villafranchian-equivalent, age for the formation and for the hominid fossils, which he believed to have been derived from the marine and fluviatile clays. Furthermore, he argued that the fauna showed affinities with Siwalik faunas and characterized it as having a "Siva-Malayan" character. He distinguished the Djetis Fauna from the later middle Pleistocene Trinil Fauna, which he claimed showed "Sino-Malayan" affinities. Other workers argued that the vertebrates from the clays had been misidentified and really represented more "progressive" forms. Recent systematic recollections and excavations of the Pucangan area have indicated that this highly endemic and impoverished fauna may be of little utility for dating the hominids that supposedly derive from the Djetis Formation. The Djetis Fauna is thought to date from between ca. 2 m.y. and ca. 0.8 m.y. Fluorine studies have suggested that the majority of Djetis faunal elements and one or two of the hominid fossils from Java (Sangiran 5 and 6) may derive from the black clays of the uppermost portion of the formation.

See also ASIA (EASTERN); INDONESIA; KOENIGSWALD, G.H.R. VON; MEGANTHROPUS; TRINIL. [G.G.P.]

Further Readings

Hooijer, D.A. (1952) Fossil mammals and the Plio-Pleistocene boundary in Java. Kon. Nederl. Akad. van Weten. Amsterdam. Proceedings, Series B, 55:436–443.

Hooijer, D.A. (1983) Remarks on the Dubois collection of fossil mammals from Trinil and Kedungbrubrus in Java. Geol. Mijnbow 62:337–338.

DOBZHANSKY, THEODOSIUS (1900–1975)

American (b. Russia) geneticist. A former student of T.H. Morgan (1866–1945), Dobzhansky played a prominent role in the development of what Julian Huxley called the "evolutionary synthesis," which combined Darwinian evolution and Mendelian genetics. His book *Genetics and the Origin of Species* (1937) was the first major attempt at such a synthesis and marks the establishment of evolutionary genetics as an independent discipline. Among his many other notable and influential publications is *Mankind Evolving* (1962).

See also EVOLUTION; GENETICS. [F.S.]

DOLICHOCEBUS *see* CEBINAE

DOLICHOPITHECUS *see* COLOBINAE

DOLNI VĚSTONICE

Complex of at least six open-air Late Paleolithic sites and a huge accumulation of mammoth bones from over 100 individuals located on the slope of the Pavlov Hills some 35 km. south of Brno (Czechoslovakia). The features include hearths, small pits, surface bone accumulations, remains of round and oval dwellings, and a number of burials; several important new burials, one with three probable teenagers, were excavated in 1986–87. The rich lithic and bone inventories are assigned to the Pavlov industry and to the Eastern Gravettian technocomplex. A complete female "Venus" figurine, numerous small animals, and thousands of fragments of fired clay found at Dolni Věstonice together with remains of two rudimentary kilns are the earliest evidence for ceramic manufacturing. Chronometric estimates date the occupation to ca. 26,000 B.P.

See also EUROPE; PAVLOV; PŘEDMOSTI. [O.S.]

DOMESTICATION

Controlled breeding of animal and plant species for human use (including some exclusively for livestock fodder). Many of these domesticated species are primarily food for the humans who breed them, but some provide us with clothing, containers, companionship and protection, with raw energy for carrying heavy burdens or pulling carts, ploughs, or sleds, or with assistance in hunting, herding, and clean-up operations. Human beings have controlled plants and animals for only a tiny fraction of the 2–3 m.y. of their history and prehistory. Before domesticates were developed as the result of human interference in other species' reproduction, people relied entirely on whatever plant and animal products they could gather, hunt, and scavenge. Because writing was not invented until a little over 5,000 years ago, prehistoric hunter-gatherers' use of such resources has been reconstructed primarily from the remains of kills and meals found by archaeologists. These reconstructions are refined and augmented by observations made among the few surviving hunting and gathering societies, whose people use and interact with wild plants and animals. Such people are generally mobile, following their prey—but they can rarely predict whether it will be young or old, male or female. Domestication, in contrast, has introduced the crucial elements of choice and control over precisely such matters.

Plants and animals were domesticated in many parts of the world, but in all known cases, with the apparent exception of the dog, this process occurred within the past 10 k.y. The reasons for changing Holocene relationships between humans and other species were probably diverse, humans being interested in different species for different qualities, such as the camel's ability to survive on little water, the sheep's production of "harvestable" milk and wool, and the storability of cereal grains like corn, wheat, and rice, which generally yield abundant surpluses and which today are the staple foods for some three-quarters of the world's population.

The earliest animal domesticated was the dog (*Canis domesticus*), ca. 12 k.y. ago, in Iraqi Kurdistan. Sheep (*Ovis*) and goat (*Capra*) were also domesticated in the Near East by ca. 9000 B.P., and they were joined within a millennium by cattle (*Bos*, at Çatal Hüyük) and pig (*Sus*, in the Near East and southeastern Europe). Later Old World domesticates include camel (*Camelus* spp.), horse (*Equus caballus*), and donkey (*Equus asinus*), all domesticated by 4000 B.P. and perhaps substantially earlier. New World domesticates include turkey (*Meleagris gallopavo*), guinea pig (*Cavia porcellus*), and the meatier llama and alpaca (*Lama* spp.), valued for their strength and their wool,

respectively. Far fewer animal species were domesticated in the western hemisphere; perhaps there were fewer wild species of medium- and large-sized gregarious herbivores native to the New World.

The earliest known plant domesticates have been retrieved at Near Eastern sites; wheat (*Triticum*) and barley (*Hordeum*) dating to the ninth millennium B.P. are found in a number of areas and, at a few sites, in what appear to be even earlier contexts. Rice another major Old World cereal, was domesticated independently in West Africa (*Oryza glaberrima*) and East Asia (*O. sativa*); the earliest rice cultivation now appears to have been carried out in the lower Yangzi delta in east China in the seventh millennium B.P. Here archaeological deposits of rice are associated with bones of pig and water buffalo, both of which may have been domesticated in East Asia. Other species important in the tropics and subtropics of the Old World are millet, sorghum, and a variety of root crops, such as yam and taro. The history of the domestication of root crops is poorly known, partly because of preservation problems. Some plants, whose wild forms have a wide geographic distribution, may have been domesticated independently in

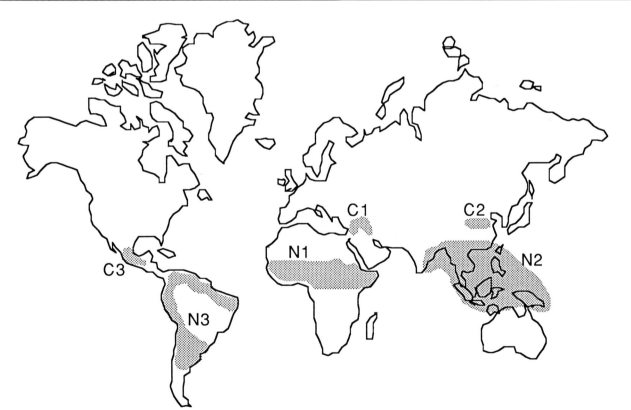

Possible centers and "noncenters" of plant domestication, as suggested by J.R. Harlan in 1971. In this model, each of three relatively restricted centers—C1) Near East; C2) North China; C3) Mesoamerica—was associated with a more diffuse noncenter—N1) central Africa; N2) south and southeast Asia; N3) coastal South America—where domestication took place over a broad area, in some cases perhaps, earlier than in the nearby center. (After J.R. Harlan, 1971. Science, *174*, © 1971 by the AAAS.)

both hemispheres; among these are the bottle gourd (*Lagenaria*) and cotton (*Gossypium*).

In general plant domestication in the New World is substantially later than it is in the eastern hemisphere. A triumvirate of plants used there today (corn, beans, and squash) frequently grows together in the wild and may have been domesticated as part of a mixed farming or intercropping strategy. The most important of these, corn (*Zea mays*), was domesticated in highland Mesoamerica some two millennia or more later than the earliest plant domestication in the Near East. Like *Zea, Triticum,* and *Hordeum* many plants domesticated in various geographic areas are annuals, growing in dense stands of single or few species, comparatively easily harvested on a predictable basis. The root crops, in contrast, have the advantage of serving as subsoil bank accounts from which capital can be extracted through much of the year. Of these the white potato (*Solanum*) and the yam (*Dioscorea*) are New and Old World domesticates, respectively.

Because humans were interested in each species for its own distinctive features, each underwent changes over time in morphology and behavior resulting from human selection for particular traits chosen for transmission to future generations. Many domesticated animal species, and their wild counterparts, are gregarious, and some tend to follow a leader. This animal behavior may have made it easier for prehistoric people to habituate herd animals to human companionship and the reproductive meddling that eventually accompanied it. A fundamental aspect of domestication is that humans decide which individuals in a particular population will transmit their genes to future generations. Thus, for example, if large pigs or bulls are particularly threatening or ferocious, they are more likely to be selected for the dinner table than left in the barnyard, and there will be fewer fierce piglets or calves in the next generation.

Benefits of Domestication

The appeal of many domesticated animals today, as it must have been in the early Holocene past, is that they are more useful alive than dead. Many people who raise livestock eat far less meat than the average urban North American; some, but by no means all, consume more milk, cheese, and yogurt. Animals provide resources that can be collected, or they have qualities that can be exploited on a predictable, repeated, and long-term basis; examples are eggs, milk, hair and wool, and labor. Dried animal manure is an essential fuel in many of the world's deforested regions; it is also good fertilizer for cultivated fields. Pigs are scavengers; eating, they convert garbage into

edible meat, and their value to humans increases. In some societies dogs play a comparable role. Domesticated animals are capital on the hoof.

Plants are equally appealing. Weather and technology permitting, surpluses surpassing the quantities sown are the rule rather than the exception; in extreme cases up to 40 or 50 times the quantity of seed planted can be harvested. Human selection of desirable and transmissible traits operates here, too, with humans playing an active role in deciding which plants to consume and which to store as seed grain. In sufficiently dry contexts many plants preserve well and can be consumed or sown for more than a year following their harvest. Harvested surpluses can also be used to support those not producing their own food, such as craftsmen or religious leaders or, like animals and their products, they can be offered in exchange for other goods.

Identification of Domesticates

The history and prehistory of domestication are reconstructed in greatest detail when nonperishable remains are recovered in archaeological contexts. For animals reconstructions are based on bones, horns, and teeth. The best direct evidence of prehistoric plants and their use comes from seeds, pits, pollen, and impressions in mud or pottery. The domestication of some species, such as potatoes, tomatoes, and various forms of poultry, is not well documented, either because conditions of preservation in their native habitats are less than optimal (e.g. they are buried in acid tropical soils) or because the elements routinely discarded by humans lack the hard parts that are generally most resistent to depredations of soil chemicals and bacteria. Circumstances of disposal and burial, and habitat ecology, affect the preservation of the botanical and zoological remains from which archaeologists reconstruct the history of human interaction with plants and animals. As a consequence our understanding of this history is still biased in favor of temperate and arid zones and of mammals and grain plants (in contrast, for example, to problematical reconstructions for avian fauna having cartilaginous bones and root crops lacking hard shells or pits).

The archaeological record for most animal species' domestication reflects a long-term selection for reduced overall body size, accompanied by increasingly shortened jaw and snout. Comparisons of wild and domestic members of the same genus can indicate which traits were subject to selective breeding. In the case of the pig, for example, tusks have been greatly reduced. The dog barks in a way that wild canids do not. Sheep generally have woolly fleece and reduced horns, and some subspecies also have economically useful fat tails.

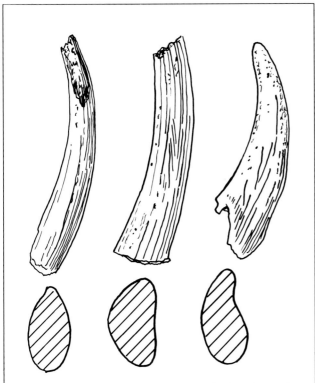

In the course of goat domestication in the Near East, the cross section of the horn changed, after many generations, from an oval shape (left), to flattened on one side, to indented on one side (right).

and domesticated forms. Before a given specimen can be characterized as either wild or domesticated, the zooarchaeologist must determine whether metric differences reflect intra- or interspecies variation.

Domesticated species also became increasingly tractable and dependent on humans. While some morphological changes occurred over a period of at least a millennium, the rate at which behavioral change associated with domestication occurred remains a matter for speculation; osteologically "wild" animals may have been behaviorally "domesticated." It has been suggested that taming and semidomestication may have involved the imprinting of juveniles caught and kept as pets, the use of salt as a lure, and/or the attracting of herd animals by altering vegetation communities through burning, which in some areas probably increased the grass cover so appealing to many herbivorous domesticates and their wild counterparts.

Comparable methodological problems exist for plants, whose domestication in many cases entailed size increases, as in cob corn, and/or increases in numbers of edible elements (as was the case in the change from two-row to six-row barley). In several plant species an important diagnostic nonmetric change involved selection for particular seed-dispersal and germ-protection mechanisms. For example, remains of wheat and barley reflect a shift from brittle to tough rachis and from tough to brittle glume. Humans evidently selected for plants that had stalks that neither snapped nor dropped grains immediately upon ripening (which a wild, brittle rachis allows) and for husks that could be crushed more readily than those that fell to the ground on ripening, protecting the enclosed seed until it could germinate months later (a nonshattering, tough glume, seen in wild forms). Plant domestication has also been reconstructed from representational art and from archaeological examples of distinctive technological items used today in processing domesticated plants (e.g. ceramic manioc graters in lowland South America). Some tools, such as sickles, identified from idiosyncratic damage to the edge of the tool, and such grinding implements as mortars and querns, are problematical, since they can also be used to process wild plants; indeed, in the Near East and elsewhere they are sometimes associated with food-collecting economies of the Mesolithic.

In addition to morphological change reflected in dentition and bones, domesticated animals and their transformations from wild forms have been reconstructed, in part, from other forms of evidence. These include representations (e.g. Neolithic clay figurines of domestic livestock at sites like Jarmo), as well as geographic distributions of bones. (Faunal remains found beyond the range of the current natural habitat zones of ancestral wild forms are potential candidates for identification as domesticates.) In gregarious species, such as sheep and goat, comparison of the demographic composition of wild herds may also reveal differences in age and sex ratios from those seen in domesticated flocks. It is also possible that the body parts of hunted wild animals found in archaeological sites will differ in kind and frequency from those of domesticated species killed and butchered nearer human habitations.

Where morphological changes involve metric rather than nonmetric attributes, or where bones revealing nonmetric features are not available archaeologically, it may be difficult to pinpoint where in the trajectory of domestication a particular specimen should be placed. Sample size can be critical: any species is characterized by a range of metric variability, and there may be overlaps between wild

Many plant species can be identified in prehistoric soil samples containing pollen. Datable pollen profiles are a vital source of information on the plant species in a particular area at a particular time, and hence on options available to humans. They may also be used to reconstruct the history of land use, since they may reveal changes in vegetative cover (such as

Corn cobs enlarged greatly in size and number of rows of kernels, as a result of domestication in Mexico from wild antecedents (7000 B.P.) to fully modern form (2000 B.P.). (Courtesy of and © by R.S. Peabody Foundation for Archaeology, Phillips Academy, Andover, Mass.)

a sharp decrease in arboreal species followed by an increase in grasses, perhaps including edible cereals) and may have associated charcoal flecks (which can reflect slash-and-burn cultivation). Even in the absence of direct evidence for plant domestication data on prehistoric pollen may be useful in developing hypotheses about the availability of ancestral wild forms and the transformation of the botanical landscape as plants were manipulated and domesticated. Finally, since some botanical species are consistently associated with one another, it is possible to use pollen profiles to pinpoint the presence or absence of wild ancestors at various times. In the late Pleistocene of the Near East, for example, oak pollen was absent in some areas where oak flourishes today; since wild wheat is often associated with oak, it is likely that when oak disappeared because of extreme cold during the latter part of the Pleistocene, cereal grasses were also unavailable to foraging human pop-

ulations using such areas on even a temporary basis. Palynology can suggest when and where some of the parameters permitting domestication might have existed. It might be an even more interesting and powerful tool if we were more secure in our reconstructions of the food preferences of wild ancestors of domesticated animals.

Origin of Domestication

Food collecting was the basic human subsistence adaptation for several million years preceding the beginning of agriculture and animal husbandry; domestication occurred comparatively rapidly, independently in many parts of the world, and in all known cases but one (the dog) in the ameliorating climate of the Holocene. Domesticates were imported into new areas (e.g. maize into North America) or, through processes of diffusion and imitation, were altered local species (e.g. rye in Europe). Several explanations of this fundamental and worldwide transformation in human lifeways have been offered. V.G. Childe noted that "post-Pleistocene" climatic change in the Near East, the setting for the earliest domestication, involved increasing desiccation and perhaps encouraged humans and other species to aggregate at oases. Such concentration in limited localities resulted, he suggested, both in animals' increasing habituation to humans and in humans' increasing knowledge of the behavior of both plants and animals. In this propinquity hypothesis familiarity bred appreciation rather than contempt. The degree to which Holocene climatic change affected spatial distribution and proximity of the key Near Eastern species remains a matter for investigation, but Childe's hypothesis has not been conclusively refuted. R.J. Braidwood was among the first to note that much of the Near East constitutes a "natural habitat zone" for the earliest domesticates: wheat, barley, dog, sheep, and goat. C. Sauer has noted that some of the domesticated plant species prefer disturbed soils (i.e. they are weedy "camp followers") and he suggested that wild ancestral forms left in the refuse at human camps might grow abundantly in the disturbed localities used repeatedly by nomadic hunter-gatherers, who would discover them during return visits.

L. Binford, K.V. Flannery, M. Cohen, and others have suggested that increasing population growth during the Pleistocene, resulting in population pressure by the Holocene, encouraged humans to experiment with new food sources. In such circumstances dense stands of such readily harvestable plants as wild wheat and such potentially tractable gregarious herbivores as sheep may have appeared increasingly attractive. (With climatic change they may also have been more available than they had been previously.) Where emigration was used as a solution to overpopulation, migrants to new regions may have taken familiar, wild, storable foods with them; such potential domesticates would thus have colonized new geographic areas. The seasonality and predictability of certain plants, and the seasonal movements of herd animals, may have provided an important basis for humans' increasing familiarity with and ultimate control over the ancestors of today's domesticates. "Capital on the hoof" and plant surpluses provide a potential hedge against uneven environments in which drought, insect pests, and flooding are frequent events, and they may have made the extra work involved in food production appear worthwhile to early Holocene hunter-gatherers.

Consequences of Domestication

Regardless of its causes in various world areas do-

mestication radically altered humans' relations to their environment and to one another. Food for stabled livestock must be grown and stored; fodder crops may compete with other plants for limited arable land. Where such animals as sheep, goats, and camels are able to forage freely, specialized forms of nomadic pastoralism have developed. Such nomads' livestock often graze on stubble in peasants' recently harvested fields, where their dung provides fertilizer for next season's crops. Complex economic, social, and political relations exist between pastoralists and the farmers with whom they exchange animal products for plant foods.

With domestication fields and animals became new forms of wealth, critical in marital alliances and inheritance disputes. Some plants or parts of plants, such as corn pollen in the American Southwest, play key roles in religious activities. Some domesticated animals have also acquired ritual status, such as the cat in ancient Egypt, the bull in ancient Greece, cattle in Hindu India, and the pig in the Near East (where it is abhorred equally by Muslims and Jews). In both farming and pastoralist societies larger families can be useful when livestock must be driven to distant pastures for weeks or months at a time, and when dispersed fields require tending at the same time; it is probable that domestication affected the size and composition of human families, perhaps encouraging larger households because of increased demands for labor.

In short, from its Neolithic origins domestication impinged upon and altered a range of existing social conventions concerning wealth, inheritance, and labor. It was associated with an increasingly sedentary way of life, in which the temporary camps of hunter-gatherers have been replaced by permanent communities—villages and towns—whose residents bring plants and animals to them rather than follow them through the landscape. Without domestication the complex urban life of the Bronze Age and subsequent periods could not have developed.

See also AMERICAS; BRONZE AGE; ÇATAL HÜYÜK; COMPLEX SOCIETIES; ECONOMY, PREHISTORIC; GENETICS; JARMO; MESOLITHIC; NEAR EAST; NEOLITHIC; PRIMATE SOCIETIES; TAPHONOMY. [C.K.]

Further Readings

Clutton-Brock, J. (1981) Domesticated Animals from Early Times. Austin: University of Texas Press.

Flannery, K.V. (1973) The origins of agriculture. Ann. Rev. Anthropol. 2:271–310.

Harris, D.R. (1977) Alternative pathways toward agriculture. In Reed, pp. 180–243.

Reed, Charles A., ed. (1977) Origins of Agriculture. The Hague: Mouton.

Renfrew, J. (1969) Palaeoethnobotany. New York: Columbia University Press.

Ucko, P.J., and Dimbleby, G.W., eds. (1969) The Domestication and Exploitation of Plants and Animals. London: Duckworth.

Zeuner, F.E. (1963) A History of Domesticated Animals. London: Hutchinson.

DONAU *see* GLACIATION; PLEISTOCENE

DONRUSSELLIA

Early Eocene European genus known from two species. The special significance of this group of primates lies in the fact that their known morphology, that of the teeth, shows the two species to be extremely similar to both adapids (particularly *Pelycodus*, in a broad sense) and omomyids (particularly *Teilhardina*). This "intermediacy" is a signal that *Donrussellia* is not much evolved from the last common ancestor of the known anaptomorphine omomyids and the adapids. Recent studies, however, indicate that in spite of overall similarities to both early groups of euprimates the most recent phylogenetic ties of *Donrussellia* are with the adapid radiation.

[F.S.S.]

DORDOGNE *see* PÉRIGORD

DRACHENLOCH

Cave in the Churfirsten Range in northeastern Switzerland where remains of more than ten cave bears (*Ursus spelaeus*) have been found in a 3-m.-thick deposit that also contained Mousterian stone tools. Dating of the bones indicates an age of ca. 49,000 B.P. The sorted distribution of the bear skeletal elements, the spatial association of the skulls with some sort of a stone cist, and the presence of Mousterian lithics led some researchers to associate all of the remains behaviorally and interpret them as evidence for Neanderthal bear cults. Recent taphonomic research suggests that both the death of the bears and the spatial sorting of their bones may have resulted from natural geomorphological processes and not from hominid ritual behavior.

See also MOUSTERIAN; NEANDERTHAL; RITUAL. [O.S.]

DRAGON BONES (AND TEETH)

These objects—called *lung gu* and *lung ya*, respectively, in Mandarin—are fossils that have traditionally been collected and sold in Chinese drugstores as ingredients for pharmaceuticals. Many of China's fossiliferous karst caves are referred to as Dragon Bone Caves. According to legend the land as well as earthquakes are associated with dragons that live in the earth. Thus many villagers have logically concluded that vertebrate fossils are the bones of dragons, and since the dragon is a revered and powerful entity it is not surprising that its bones are prized for their medicinal powers. One hominoid taxon, *Gigantopithecus blacki*, and two highly questionable hominid taxa, *Sinanthropus officinalis* and *Hemanthropus peii*, have been proposed solely on the basis of drugstore fossils.

See also GIGANTOPITHECUS; "HEMANTHROPUS." [G.G.P.]

DRENTHE *see* GLACIATION; PLEISTOCENE

DRUGSTORE FOSSILS *see* DRAGON BONES; FOSSIL

DRYAS *see* GLACIATION; PLEISTOCENE

DRYOPITHECUS

Extinct form of hominoid. The first specimen of *Dryopithecus* that was found predated Darwin's *On the Origin of Species* by three years. It was discovered near the village of St. Gaudens in southern France in 1856, and it was described the following year by E. Lartet as *Dryopithecus fontani* after its discoverer, M. Fontan. The material from this site consists of several mandibles and part of a humerus, and Lartet recognized its great-ape affinities, a view still accepted today.

More recent and much bigger collections of *Dryopithecus* have been made in Spain and Hungary. Unfortunately the fossils from these places have been given new names, but the Spanish specimens can be assigned to two species of *Dryopithecus*: *D. fontani* and *D. laietanus*. The Hungarian material from Rudabanya, which includes good cranial and postcranial specimens, all appears to fit within the species limits of *D. fontani*, and in fact it greatly enhances our knowledge of this taxon.

Dryopithecus species were small-to-moderate-sized hominoid primates. They had robust limb bones, similar to those of the living great apes, but in their teeth and skull characters they were little advanced over *Proconsul* from Africa. They lived during the middle Miocene, 12–10 m.y. ago.

See also APE; HOMINIDAE; HOMINOIDEA; MIOCENE; PROCONSUL. [P.A.]

DUBOIS, EUGENE (1858-1941)

Dutch physician and paleoanthropologist. In 1891, while serving as a military surgeon in the East Dutch

Indies, Dubois discovered at Trinil (Java) the calotte and femur of a fossil hominid. The fauna found in association with these remains indicated a relatively great age near the boundary of the Pliocene and Pleistocene as currently reckoned. According to Dubois the morphology of the skullcap suggested pithecoid features, while the femur was essentially modern, implying that the creature was bipedal. Initially he was convinced he had found the "missing link," and in deference to Haeckel (as whose assistant he had served at Jena University in 1880) Dubois fittingly dubbed the hominid *Pithecanthropus erectus.* Differences arose immediately in interpretation of the taxonomic status and phylogenetic significance of the fossil. In 1898 Dubois withdrew from the debate and remained silent on the issue until 1922. During this time his ideas changed. Where originally he had supported the view that the fossil represented a form that was transitional from hominoid to hominid, he now contended that it was nothing more than an extinct giant gibbon, a view that had been championed by Rudolph Virchow (1821–1902) during the mid-1890s. In 1922 he also published accounts of two late Pleistocene crania he had brought back from Java, namely the Wadjak I and II specimens, which he considered to have Australoid affinities.

See also HAECKEL, ERNST HEINRICH; HOMO ERECTUS; TRINIL; VIRCHOW, RUDOLPH. [F.S.]

DUCHESNEAN *see* EOCENE; TIME SCALE

DWARFISM

Selection for smaller body size in an evolutionary lineage is most commonly observed in large mammals isolated on islands, where resources sufficient to maintain a breeding population are limited. The limitations may be sensed in different ways depending on the species, and a variety of selective pressures are involved. In other instances isolation dwarfism may be nothing more than phenotypic response to poor nutrition. Anomalous dwarfism among individuals in a population is most often associated with achondroplasia.

See also GIGANTISM. [D.P.D., R.L.B.]

DWELLINGS *see* AGGREGATION-DISPERSAL; ARCHAEOLOGICAL SITES

DYSEOLEMUR *see* OMOMYINAE

DYUKTAI

Late Paleolithic archaeological industry of eastern Siberia (U.S.S.R.) characterized by bifacially worked stone projectile points and knives, wedge-shaped cores, and microblades. Inventories assigned to this industry have been found at the Dyuktai Cave type site, at Ikhine and Ust-Mil' in the vicinity of the Aldan River, and at Ushki on Kamchatka. Although no radiocarbon dates older than ca. 15,000 B.P. have been obtained for these sites, this industry may have existed from 30,000 to 11,000 B.P. The similarity of archaeological inventories from these Siberian sites, which are repeatedly found in association with bones of large herbivores, has led some researchers to see this industry as a part of the wider Paleoarctic Tradition and a possible precursor to the Paleoindian industries in the New World.

See also CLOVIS; PALEOINDIAN. [O.S.]

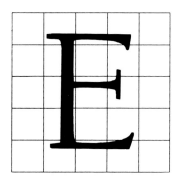

EARLY PALEOLITHIC

Term describing the archaeological sites, and the time interval of the Oldowan and Acheulean industries, as well as of the nonhandaxe traditions of the middle Pleistocene (e.g. the "chopper-chopping tool" complexes of Asia). Grouping all of these sites and industries under the same rubric is primarily a function of the history of archaeology, where divisions tended to be made in groups of three: lower, middle, and upper. In the nineteenth century handaxe industries were assigned to the Early Paleolithic and subdivided into the Chellean, Abbevillian, and Acheulean. The simple technologies of the Oldowan were subsequently also assigned to the Early Paleolithic (= African Early Stone Age) as research in Africa progressed.

There is probably no more similarity, in terms of technology, subsistence, and social behavior, between Oldowan and later Acheulean populations than there is between Acheulean and Mousterian (Middle Paleolithic) populations. At least 2 m.y. of biological evolution and cultural development are documented during the Early Paleolithic, and it is likely that there were many profound biological, cognitive, and cultural changes during this time.

East Africa

The earliest evidence for stone tools comes from Africa. Some Paleolithic sites in the Omo Valley (Ethiopia) are dated to ca. 2.4 m.y. ago, and tools from the Gona sites in the Hadar region of Ethiopia may be nearly as old. These early industries are normally assigned to the Oldowan, or "Mode I," industrial complex (the latter term proposed by British prehistorian J.G.D. Clark), characterized by simple core forms, casually retouched pieces, débitage, battered stones, and manuports (unmodified but transported pieces of stone). Other Oldowan sites from East Africa include Melka Kontouré and Gadeb (Ethiopia); Koobi Fora (Kenya); and Olduvai Gorge (Tanzania).

These sites all date to the early Pleistocene and vary enormously in the types of rock used for raw material, as well as the assemblage composition of the artifacts. At Olduvai Gorge such artifact classes as spheroids and a wide range of small retouched pieces tend to become more common through time and have been assigned to the "Developed Oldowan." Similar nomenclature has also been used in other parts of Africa.

Starting ca. 1.5 m.y. ago, new artifact forms make their first appearance in Africa: large picks, handaxes, and cleavers (collectively called *bifaces*), often shaped from large flakes struck from boulder cores. They are first documented from such sites as Peninj (Tanzania) and Olduvai Gorge. These new forms, which are characteristic elements of the early Acheulean, or Mode II, industrial complex, tend to become much more refined through time.

At some localities in the early and middle Pleistocene archaeological sites with handaxes are roughly contemporaneous with nonhandaxe sites; the latter are sometimes called "Hope Fountain" industries in Africa. The significance of these technological dichotomies is not yet understood; whether they represent contrasting functional activities, proximity to different types of raw material, distinct cultural norms, or other causes has not been adequately demonstrated.

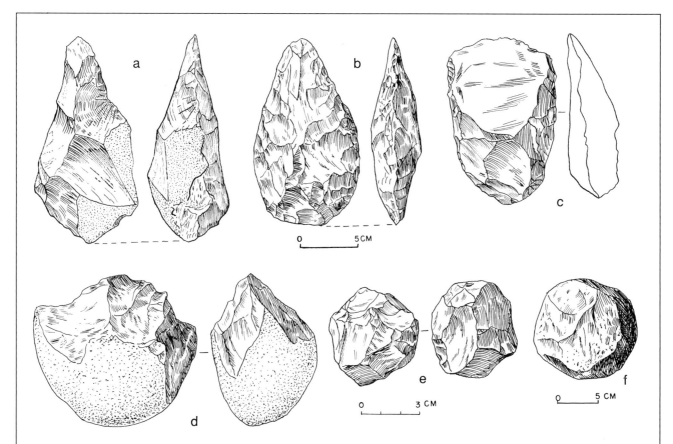

Representative Early Paleolithic lithic artifacts from Africa: a) pointed handaxe; b) ovate handaxe; c) cleaver; d) bifacial chopper; e) polyhedron; f) spheroid.

Important Acheulean sites from East Africa include Melka Kontouré, Gadeb, and the Middle Awash (Ethiopia); Kariandusi, Kilombe, Kapthurin, and Olorgesailie (Kenya); and Peninj, Olduvai Gorge, Chesowanja, and Isimila (Tanzania).

South and Central Africa

The earliest evidence for hominid tool making in south and central Africa is from the cave deposits of Sterkfontein and Swartkrans in the South African Transvaal. A range of simple artifact forms, primarily of Mode I, have been found in these deposits, believed to be ca. 2–1.5 m.y. old. Recently a few crude bifacial picks or handaxes have been discovered at Sterkfontein. The Sterkfontein artifacts are primarily from Member 5 breccias, which have also yielded the remains of hominid skull STW 53, identified as an early form of the genus *Homo*, but some may come from the older Member 4 (with only *Australopithecus*). At Swartkrans (Members 1–3) stone and bone implements are known in association with early *Homo* cf. *erectus* and also *Australopithecus robustus*. Recently some workers have suggested that hand bones identified as those of the latter species appear capable of making these tools, but this has not been widely

accepted. Stone artifacts recovered from Senga-5 in the Western Rift Valley of eastern Zaire are also believed to date to the early Pleistocene or late Pliocene.

Important middle Pleistocene Acheulean sites from south and central Africa include Victoria West, Cave of Hearths, and Saldanha (South Africa) and Kalambo Falls (Zambia). Kalambo is noteworthy in yielding the preserved remains of plant and wood materials.

North Africa

Several sites in North Africa have yielded materials that appear to be older than 1 m.y. These include possible Oldowan assemblages from the Casablanca marine-beach sequences in Morocco and the Tunesian site of Ain Hanech. Important middle Pleistocene Acheulean sites from North Africa include Tighenif (ex-Ternifine, Algeria); Rabat (Morocco); Sidi Zin (Tunisia); and Arkin and Kharga Oasis (Egypt).

Near East

The obvious route of hominid migrations out of Africa would have been via the Near East, since southwestern Asia was joined with that continent to

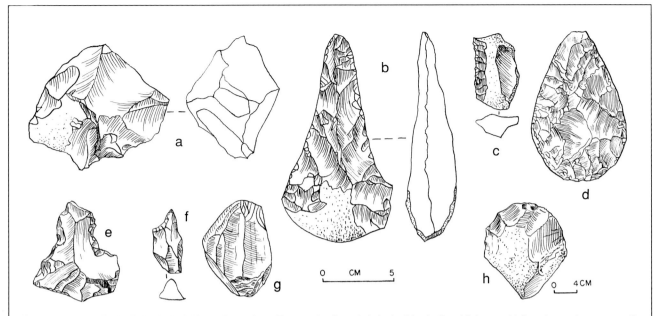

Representative Early Paleolithic lithic artifacts from Europe (a–f) and Asia (g–h): a) discoidal core; b) handaxe; c) scraper; d) handaxe; e) notch; f) Tayacian point; g) bipolar core; h) chopper.

an extent dictated by the size of the Red Sea. It is no surprise, then, that the earliest evidence of hominid groups outside of Africa comes from this area. The site of 'Ubeidiya west of the Sea of Galilee (Israel) is estimated to be ca. 1 m.y., based upon faunal correlations and paleomagnetism, and comprises superimposed cobble beaches from an ancient lakeshore containing fossil bones and stone artifacts. The industries consist of early Acheulean and Oldowan-like artifact forms.

Important middle (or early late) Pleistocene Acheulean sites from the Near East include Tabūn, Zuttiyeh, Benot Ya'aquov, and Ma'ayan Barukh (Israel); Latamne (Syria); Jabrud (Lebanon); and Lion's Spring (Jordan).

East and Central Asia

The earliest definitive evidence for hominid occupation of eastern Asia comes from sites yielding *Homo erectus* fossils and stone artifacts. Interestingly, handaxe industries are all but absent from the whole of eastern Asia, as pointed out by Hallam Movius several decades ago. "Movius' line," separating Acheulean industries in Africa and western Eurasia from "chopper-chopping tool" (Mode I) industries to the east shows an important technological dichotomy between these great geographical areas.

Exactly why there are no handaxe-cleaver industries to the east is not clear; certainly in these millions of square kilometers hominids must have frequented raw-material sources adequate for the large bifacial forms characteristic of the Acheulean. There are three commonly forwarded explanations. The

first theorizes that the cultural concepts of such handaxe-cleaver (Mode II) technologies never spread as far as eastern Asia (although very widespread from the tip of southern Africa all the way through western Europe and as far east as the Near East and parts of the Indian subcontinent); these eastern Asian populations thus were geographically "cut off" from the rest of the Old World and their technological innovations. The second claims that other raw materials, such as bamboo, were used in many parts of eastern Asia, so that there was much less emphasis on lithic materials for finished tools; stone served instead as a raw material for woodworking. The third view theorizes that the East Asian hominid populations had different, perhaps biologically determined, cognitive or cultural systems that were not shared by African or western Eurasian hominid groups. Another curious pattern that has emerged is that most of the earliest European Paleolithic sites do *not* appear to have handaxe-cleaver industries, but the more casual Mode I technologies similar to the East Asian material. None of the explanations for the lack of large bifacial forms in East Asia appears entirely satisfactory, however, and more fieldwork and refined chronological control will be necessary to explain this technological dichotomy.

On the island of Java stone tools (the "Pacitanian" industry) have been found in the Kabuh beds, thought to be ca. 0.8–0.4 m.y. old. Stone tools have not been found in direct association with the *Homo erectus* fossils of Java but rather in separate sedimentary contexts. These artifacts are typical of Mode I industries elsewhere in Southeast Asia, with simple

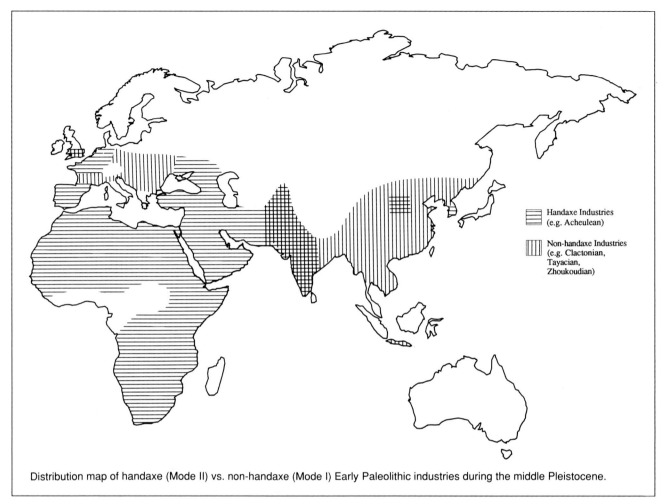

Distribution map of handaxe (Mode II) vs. non-handaxe (Mode I) Early Paleolithic industries during the middle Pleistocene.

chopper-cores and débitage being the most common forms, but other such assemblages usually come from fluvial contexts in which secure chronological placement is impossible. These include the "Soan" industry of India, the "Anyathian" of Burma, the "Tampanian" of Malaysia, and the "Fingnoian" of Thailand; some of these industries actually are of Holocene age. Most early Paleolithic industries in China—found at Zhoukoudian, Lantian, Yuanmou, and Xihoudu—are of characteristically simple Mode I type.

Europe

Establishing a chronology for the European Early Paleolithic is a formidable task, since most areas do not have volcanic rocks suitable for potassium-argon and fission-track dates, and much of the biostratigraphic work cannot be tied to a reliably dated sequence.

Although there are claims for very early occupation of Europe (e.g. the site of Chilhac in the French Massif Central, with a reported K-Ar date of 1.8 m.y.), the anthropological consensus sees little evidence of hominids in Eurasia prior to 1 m.y. ago. Hominid populations could have spread out of Africa and into

Europe by a number of routes: from northeastern Africa via the Near East; across the short expanse of water of the Straits of Gibraltar from northwestern Africa to Iberia; and by "island hopping" in the Mediterranean during low sea levels, from North Africa via Sardinia to the Italian mainland. The early dates suggested by 'Ubeidiya at present indicate a major hominid expansion through the Near East.

The first strong evidence for hominid groups in Europe comes from such sites as Isernia (Italy), which has yielded K-Ar dates of ca. 0.7 m.y. Other sites thought to be over 0.3 m.y. old include Vértesszöllös (Hungary) and Arago (France). All three of these candidates for early occupation of Europe are characterized by lithic assemblages best described as Mode I technologies: casual cores, numerous retouched flakes, and débitage. At some sites, like Vértesszöllös, the stone used for artifacts consisted primarily of small pebbles, so that morphological variability was further restricted by the raw material. Later assemblages without handaxes are termed "Clactonian" in northern Europe and "Tayacian" in the south, but their relationship to the biface-rich Acheulean is uncertain.

Handaxe industries are found throughout western Europe but tend to be less common in eastern Europe. Noteworthy middle Pleistocene sites of the Early Paleolithic include Clacton, Swanscombe, and Hoxne (Britain); Terra Amata, Abbeville, and St. Acheul (France); and Torralba and Ambrona (Spain). Middle Pleistocene hominids from this industrial stage have been assigned to archaic *Homo sapiens*, although some researchers have suggested identifying them as late *Homo erectus*.

See also ABBEVILLIAN; ACHEULEAN; AFRICA; AMBRONA; ARAGO; ARCHAEOLOGICAL SITES; ASIA (EASTERN); BIFACE; BODO; BUDA INDUSTRY; CHILHAC; CHINA; CHOPPER-CHOPPING TOOLS; CLACTONIAN; CLEAVER; CORE; EARLY STONE AGE; ECONOMY, PREHISTORIC; EUROPE; FIRE; FLAKE; FLORISBAD; HANDAXE; HOPE FOUNTAIN; HOXNE; HUNTER-GATHERERS; JABRUD; JABRUDIAN; KALAMBO FALLS; KANJERA; KAPTHURIN; KARARI; LAINYAMOK; LAZARET; LEVALLOIS; LITHIC USE-WEAR; MAN-LAND RELATIONSHIPS; MELKA KONTOURÉ; MICOQUIAN; MONTE PEGLIA; NIHEWAN FORMATION; OLDOWAN; OLDUVAI; OLORGESAILIE; PALEOLITHIC; PALEOLITHIC LIFEWAYS; PREPARED-CORE; PRIMATE SOCIETIES; PŘEZLETICE; RAW MATERIALS; RETOUCH; RITUAL; SALDANHA; SITE TYPES; SOAN; SOLEILHAC; SPEAR; SPEECH (ORIGINS OF); STONE-TOOL MAKING; STRANSKÁ SKÁLA; SWANSCOMBE; TABŪN; TABUNIAN; TATA; TAYACIAN; TIGHENIF; TORRE IN PIETRA; 'UBEIDIYA; VALLONNET; XIHOUDOU; ZHOUKOUDIAN. [N.T., K.S.]

Further Readings

Bordes, F. (1970) The Old Stone Age. New York: McGraw-Hill.

Gamble, C. (1986) The Settlement of Palaeolithic Europe. Cambridge: Cambridge University Press.

Phillipson, D.W. (1985) African Archaeology. Cambridge: Cambridge University Press.

Svoboda, J. (1987) Lithic industries of the Arago, Vértesszöllös, and Bilzingsleben hominids; comparison and evolutionary interpretation. Curr. Anthropol. 28:219-227.

Wu, R. and Olsen, J.W., eds. (1985) Paleoanthropology and Paleolithic Archeology in the People's Republic of China. New York: Academic Press.

Wymer, J. (1982) The Palaeolithic Age. New York: St. Martin's.

EARLY STONE AGE

First stage in a tripartite system for the African Stone Age (originally Earlier, Middle, and Later), formalized by Goodwin and Van Riet Lowe in 1929 for South Africa. The concept was later expanded to include Acheulean, Oldowan, and related early industries (Karari, Hope Fountain) from eastern, central, and northern Africa, and even from some areas of Asia, such as the Indian subcontinent. As originally defined, the Earlier Stone Age (ESA) referred to flake and core industries without prepared cores or "Mousterian" influences and included the Stellen-bosch (= Acheulean), Victoria West, and Fauresmith industries of South Africa. Later the three-stage scheme was modified to a five-stage scheme, with the transitional stages "First Intermediate" and "Second Intermediate" interposed between the Earlier and Middle, and Middle and Later Stone Ages, respectively.

Development of separate nomenclature for the African Stone Age reflected recognition of substantial differences between Africa and Europe in technological and economic development. Initially it was also thought that African development was retarded with respect to that of Europe; this is now known to be incorrect. Major differences between Africa and Europe during the Early Paleolithic/ESA include the over 2 m.y. of stone-tool manufacture in Africa, as opposed to less than 1 m.y. in Europe (e.g. Vallonnet); the greater elaboration of pebble-tool industries in Africa, now known from Europe as well (Buda industry); and the wider diversity of African tool forms (e.g. cleavers), technologies, and industries.

Since the 1960s new African archaeological data have made it difficult to sustain a single chronostratigraphic scheme for the entire continent. Recommendations include dropping the term "Early Stone Age," substituting the (equally vague) term "Early (or Lower) Paleolithic," using only specific industry terms (Oldowan, Karari, Acheulean), or instituting the Modes I and II of J.G.D. Clark's scheme, for simple pebble or flake industries (Oldowan) and biface industries (Acheulean), respectively.

The earliest stone-tool industries of Africa, consisting of split cobbles and simple flakes made largely of quartz, date to between 2.6 and 2.1 m.y., in the Omo and Hadar (Gona sites) regions of Ethiopia, and at Senga-5 in the Semliki Valley of Zaire. Except for a few possible handaxes from ca. 2 m.y. contexts at Sterkfontein (South Africa), the more formally shaped bifaces of the African Acheulean do not appear until 1.6-1.5 m.y. ago. After their initial appearance Acheulean tools continue in relatively unchanging form, along with industries consisting of simple Oldowan-type flakes, scrapers, backed knives, and pebble cores, well into the middle Pleistocene, but they are replaced by Middle Stone Age industries between 180 and 130 k.y.

Although different ESA industries have often been attributed to different "cultures," different ethnic groups, or even different hominids, more recent arguments suggest that ESA industries represent a stable, possibly biologically mediated, level of simple technological responses to the environment. Interassemblage differences are attributed to differing activities, social groupings, depositional histories, or other site-formation factors.

See also ACHEULEAN; BUDA INDUSTRY; CAVE OF HEARTHS; CHESOWANJA; EARLY PALEOLITHIC; EAST TURKANA; ECONOMY, PREHISTORIC; FIRST INTERMEDIATE; HANDAXE; HOPE FOUNTAIN; LATER STONE AGE; MELKA KONTOURÉ; MIDDLE STONE AGE; OLDOWAN; OLDUVAI; OLORGESAILIE; OMO; PALEOLITHIC; SECOND INTERMEDIATE; SENGA-5; STERKFONTEIN; STONE-TOOL MAKING; SWARTKRANS; TAPHONOMY; VALLONNET. [A.S.B.]

Further Readings

Phillipson, D. W. (1985) African Archaeology. Cambridge: Cambridge University Press.

EAST RUDOLF *see* EAST TURKANA

EAST TURKANA

Name now given, in place of "East Rudolf," to an extensive region of fossil-bearing exposures of Pliocene and Pleistocene age (4–0.7 m.y.) in northern Kenya. (Until 1975 Lake Turkana was known as Lake Rudolf, but with the change in name of the lake the region to the east became known as East Turkana, although the name Turkana refers specifically to the region west of the lake.)

Discontinuous exposures of Pliocene and Pleistocene strata extend ca. 25 km. inland from the lakeshore, from Ileret (4°20′N latitude) to Karsa (3°40′N latitude). The northern part of this area, for convenience often termed the Ileret region, extends from Ileret to the Kokoi, an uplifted block of basalts and sediments. The region from the Kokoi south to a junction of several major ephemeral streams that drain into Allia Bay is often called the Koobi Fora region, although this term is also employed for the entire area known as East Turkana. The area south of this is termed the Allia Bay region.

A single formation, the Koobi Fora Formation, encompasses most of the Pliocene and Pleistocene deposits of the region. In early publications the oldest deposits were referred to as the Kubi Algi Formation and the youngest as the Guomde Formation, but strata represented by these formations are now subsumed into the Koobi Fora Formation. The Koobi Fora Formation rests disconformably on, or is in fault contact with, Miocene volcanic rocks. Late Pleistocene deposits disconformably overlying the Koobi Fora Formation are referred to informally as the Galana Boi Beds.

The Koobi Fora Formation has an aggregate thickness of 565 m. in its composite type sections. It has been divided into eight members on the basis of widespread volcanic-ash layers that are recognized by their distinctive chemical compositions. The lowest is the Lonyumun Member, which is defined as all sediments between the underlying Miocene volcanic rocks and the base of the Moiti Tuff. Each member

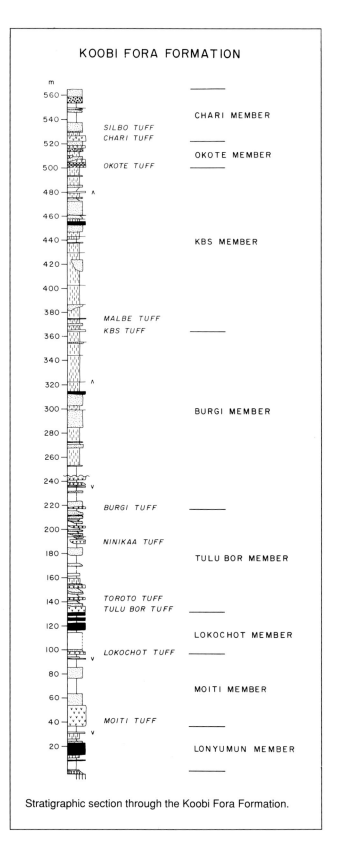

Stratigraphic section through the Koobi Fora Formation.

above the Lonyumun is named for its basal tuff and includes all strata above it to the base of the tuff for which the overlying member is named. In sequence from the base upward the members are Lonyumun,

Moiti, Lokochot, Tulu Bor, Burgi, KBS, Okote, and Chari.

The Lonyumun Member consists predominantly of claystones and siltstones reflecting deposition in a lacustrine environment. In its upper part, ca. 10 m. below the Moiti Tuff, there is a transition to fluvial environments, and strata of the Moiti Member and the lower part of the Lokochot Member were deposited in a fluvial setting. Following a brief lacustrine phase in the upper part of the Lokochot Member, the record is again one of fluvial deposition through the Tulu Bor Member and the lower part of the Burgi Member. It is believed that there is a hiatus within the Burgi Member lasting ca. 0.3 m.y. Following this hiatus, sedimentation resumes with siltstones and claystones representing deep-lake conditions. Deltaic sandstones and siltstones are encountered in the upper part of the Burgi member. Through the KBS and Okote Members conditions change frequently from deposition in shallow lakes to deposition by a large fluvial system. These are the best recorded in the Koobi Fora region. Within the Chari Member there is again a hiatus of ca. 0.5 m.y., after which sediments of the upper part of the Chari Member were deposited in the Ileret region.

Because of the discontinuous nature of the outcrops it is difficult to reconstruct lateral facies changes over the region for the lower part of the section. Within the KBS and Okote Members, however, strata along the eastern margin of outcrop are generally thinner and coarser than correlative strata near the lake. Channeling events and channel-fill deposits are also much more apparent in the eastern exposures of these members. The local paleogeography appears to have been somewhat more subdued than at present, with small, largely ephemeral streams draining westward into a broad plain dominated by the ancestral Omo River or occupied by a shallow lake.

Many of the strata of the Koobi Fora Formation are still nearly flat-lying. Near Koobi Fora spit is a broad zone of small faults, and there the strata dip several degrees to the west. Several of the larger structures of the region are demonstrably younger than 0.7 m.y., such as a large fault that bounds the Kokoi along its northwestern slope.

Age control on the Koobi Fora Formation is based mainly on potassium-argon dating of feldspars derived from pumice clasts of nine volcanic-ash layers. The Moiti Tuff is dated at 4.10 ± 0.07 m.y. The Toroto and Ninikaa Tuffs, within the Tulu Bor Member, are dated at 3.32 ± 0.02 m.y. and 3.06 ± 0.06 m.y., respectively. In the KBS Member the KBS Tuff is securely dated at 1.88 ± 0.02 m.y., and the Malbe Tuff at 1.87 ± 0.02 m.y. Pumices from

the lower Okote Tuff yield ages of 1.65 ± 0.05 m.y. The Chari Tuff, 1.39 ± 0.01 m.y. old, underlies an unnamed tuff in the Chari Member dated at 1.25 ± 0.02 m.y. The youngest tuff in the sequence is the Silbo Tuff, dated at 0.74 ± 0.01 m.y. These data are supplemented by, and consistent with, the paleomagnetic polarity zonation of the formation.

The Koobi Fora Formation contains 58 distinct tuffs for which chemical analyses are available. Secure correlations from the Koobi Fora Formation to the Shungura Formation have been established at nine levels by analysis of glass separates from tuffs in the two regions. Similarly, 13 correlations have been established between the Koobi Fora Formation and strata exposed west of Lake Turkana. Correlations have been established to the Hadar Formation at one level (the Tulu Bor Tuff) and to the deep sea of the Western Indian Ocean at five levels.

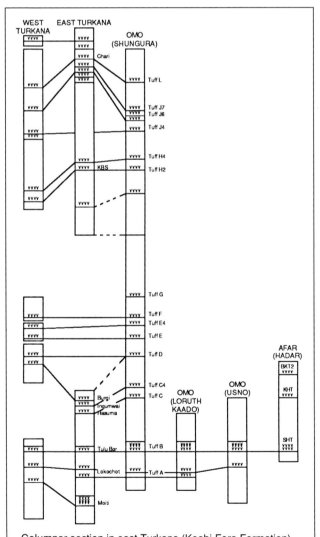

Columnar section in east Turkana (Koobi Fora Formation). Dated tuffs are correlated to tuffs in the Omo basin, West Turkana, and the Afar (Ethiopia) by chemical and mineralogical "fingerprinting." For dating, see AFRICA.

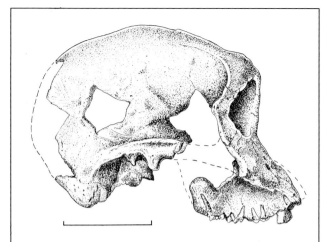

The robust female cranium KNM-ER 732, from the Koobi Fora Formation, East Turkana. Scale is 5 cm.

Fossil remains from the Koobi Fora Formation are highly diverse. Fossil pollen has provided useful information concerning ancient floras of the region, and remarkable changes in molluskan faunas have provided evidence on the mode and rate of evolutionary transformations, but the region is best known for its mammalian fossil record. Several well-represented mammalian groups, like the suids, bovids, equids, and proboscideans, help establish the age of other Plio-Pleistocene fossil sites where radiometric dating is not possible.

Hominid fossils from the Koobi Fora Formation are known from all members except the Lokochot and the Chari. They thus range in age from slightly over 4 m.y. to ca. 1.4 m.y. All good cranial specimens, however, derive from levels between the upper part of the Burgi Member and the Chari Tuff and therefore lie between ca. 2 and 1.4 m.y. in age. The hominids have been assigned both to *Australopithecus* and to *Homo*.

Artifact sites are restricted largely to the eastern part of the area. The oldest are associated with the KBS Tuff, and the youngest slightly postdate the Chari Tuff, having a probable age near 1.3 m.y. Late Pleistocene archaeological and faunal sites have also been investigated in the region.

See also OMO; WEST TURKANA. [F.H.B.]

Further Readings

Brown, F.H., and Feibel, C.S. (1986) Revision of lithostratigraphic nomenclature in the Koobi Fora region, Kenya. J. Geol. Soc. London *143*:297–310.

Coppens, Y., Howell, F.C., Isaac, G.L., and Leakey, R.E.F., eds. (1976) Earliest Man and Environments in the Lake Rudolf Basin. Chicago: University of Chicago Press.

Harris, J.M., ed. (1983) Koobi Fora Research Project, Vol. 2: The Fossil Ungulates: Proboscidea, Perissodactyla and Suidae. Oxford: Clarendon.

Leakey, M.G., and Leakey, R.E.F., eds. (1978) Koobi Fora Research Project, Vol. 1: The Fossil Hominids and an Introduction to Their Context, 1968–1974. Oxford: Clarendon.

McDougall, I. (1985) K-Ar and 40Ar/39Ar dating of the hominid-bearing Plio-Pleistocene sequence at Koobi Fora, Lake Turkana, northern Kenya. Bull. Geol. Soc. Am. *96*:159–175.

EBOULIS   *see*   GLACIATION; PLEISTOCENE

EBURON   *see*   GLACIATION; PLEISTOCENE

ECOLOGY

Adaptation and evolution through natural selection result from the interactions of living organisms with their surroundings, or *environment*. Ecology (from the Greek *oikos*, a house or household) is the science that studies such interactions. To an ecologist the environment is all those living and nonliving things that impinge upon an organism or group of organisms and that may influence their growth, survival, and reproductive success.

Population ecology studies the interactions between the environment and members of a single species. It usually pays special attention to the dynamics of population growth and decline and the influence on these processes of such factors as food supply, predation, and disease. Community ecology concerns itself with multispecies interactions and especially with questions of coexistence and competition between species. The plant and animal communities of any given area, together with their inanimate surroundings, form an *ecosystem*, in which solar energy is captured by green plants (primary producers) and transferred along food chains to several levels of animal consumers (from herbivores to top carnivores). Ecosystems are dynamic and highly complex, and their study frequently involves mathematical modeling techniques.

An important concept in ecology is that of the *niche*, the functional position of an organism (or population) within an ecosystem. It is not so much the physical location of an organism but rather a description of its pattern of interactions with the rest of the system. The ecological niche (or econiche) of an extinct organism can be reconstructed from fossil assemblages and a knowledge of present-day ecosystems. Such paleoecology can provide crucial insights on the causes of events in human evolution.

See also ADAPTATION; DIET; MAN-LAND RELATIONSHIPS; PALEOENVIRONMENTS; POPULATION; PALEOBIOGEOGRAPHY; PRIMATE ECOLOGY; ZOOGEOGRAPHY. [J.F.O.]

ECOLOGICAL NICHE *see* ECOLOGY; SPECIATION; SPECIES

ECONOMY, PREHISTORIC

Economic behavior can be defined as the subset of general cultural practices that involves the acquisition and transformation of matter and energy from nature, the distribution of these products among people, and the use or consumption of these products. Economic practices of both prehistoric and present-day groups are multidimensional entities shaped by the interaction of the perception of the environment by the group, the ideas people have about their needs and how to satisfy them, the knowledge available to exploit the resources, the technology used to do so, and the social relationships that govern acquisition, production, and distribution. Some of these variables can be observed directly in the archaeological record; others can only be inferred by analogy with ethnographically observed behavior.

Reconstructing the nature of the environment in which a prehistoric group lived, including the climate and the distribution of organic and inorganic resources, is usually the first step in investigations of prehistoric economies. Information for this comes from such disciplines as botany, climatology, geology, and zoology. *Site-catchment analysis*, a particularly fine-tuned application, is directed to reconstructing what resources were available within a reasonable distance from sites under study (usually a two-hour walk or a 10-km. radius around a site). This research strategy is most effective where local environments have changed little since the sites were occupied. Data on reconstructed paleoenvironments, including such variables as the availability, abundance, and predictability of key resources, have also been used recently to model human economic behavior. *Optimal foraging* and *linear programming* models delimit the most effective mix of resources that would have been harvested in a given region through different seasons and isolate suitable locations for

Storage pit under excavation at the Gontsy Late Paleolithic site in the U.S.S.R. (After Soffer, 1985.)

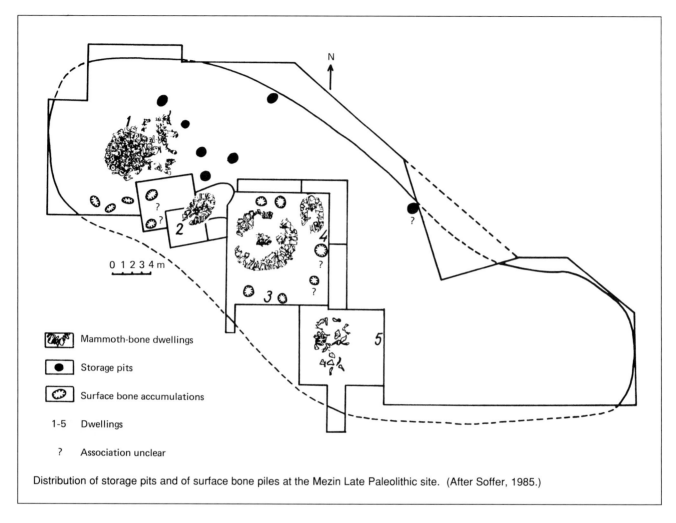

Mammoth-bone dwellings

● Storage pits

Surface bone accumulations

1-5 Dwellings

? Association unclear

Distribution of storage pits and of surface bone piles at the Mezin Late Paleolithic site. (After Soffer, 1985.)

doing so. Although such studies give clues about why particular locations may have been selected for occupation, they basically indicate what was *available* but not what was *used*. Evidence for the latter comes from the archaeological remains left behind at the sites. This information is used in both site-catchment analyses and predictive models for insights into actual versus optimal economic decision making in the past.

Past subsistence practices—what food people ate, what materials they used, and how they obtained both—are reflected in the kinds of inventories and features and in their distribution at sites. Remains of plants and animals consumed provide information about prehistoric diets. Since morphological differences exist between domesticated plants and animals and their wild progenitors, organic remains indicate whether a particular group depended on wild products gathered from nature or grew their own food. The study of animal bones by archaeozoologists (or zooarchaeologists) indicates not only what animals were hunted but at what age they were killed and often in what season the hunting took

place. Furthermore, the kinds of animals hunted and the age-sex profiles of different species indicate what hunting methods were used and whether wild or domesticated taxa were harvested. The prevalence of herd animals at a particular site, for example, suggests hunting by mass drives; solitary species suggest stalking and individual kills. Plant remains, which in general preserve poorly and are the most difficult to recover archaeologically, yield information about what species were harvested and about the season or seasons when this harvesting took place. Direct evidence for past diets is also obtained from coprolites (human feces) and from bone-chemistry analysis of human remains.

Tools and implements, too, help reveal economic practices. For instance, sickle blades with wear polish resulting from harvesting of cereals imply plant collecting, as do grinding stones and pestles; bows and arrows indirectly attest to hunting; nets and fish hooks are evidence for fishing; and fire-cracked rocks in hearths point to cooking of food.

Other aspects of technology provide valuable clues about both the organization of production and social and economic relationships. High levels of standardization, for example, suggest that artifacts were produced by a small group of specialists and imply a more complex division of labor than that found in simple societies where all members are capable of making, and do make, everything they use. The presence of exotic materials and the use to which they were put often indicate exchange with distant groups and give clues to social networks.

Features found at sites similarly can yield information about past economies. First, the elaborateness of the structures (e.g. houses, storage facilities) reflects the degree of permanence of occupation. Ephemeral features in general suggest short-term occupations and imply group mobility; an increased investment of labor in dwellings and other facilities is associated with more sedentary lifeways. Such features as drying racks or smudge pits used in large-scale processing and preservation of food, as well as the presence and content of storage bins, pits, or rooms, indicate that the economy in question involved logistical organization and delayed consumption rather than simple "feed as you go" foraging.

The distribution of inventories and features at sites is also important. Equal distribution of food and other remains among households at a site, for example, suggests an open and equal access to goods and resources. Finding most storage facilities associated with one or two households, on the other hand, suggests that the resources were controlled by a small group of individuals. Similar inferences can be drawn from the distribution of valuable nonlocal materials and from the comparison of size and contents of the dwellings. Exotics consistently concentrated in large-sized households suggest the existence of unequal access to resources, as do differences in size and elaborateness of dwellings for same-sized social units.

Finally, settlement patterns within a region also can yield information. For example, finding early agricultural villages clustered exclusively in river valleys suggests the use of simple floodplain irrigation, while a more scattered pattern across the landscape suggests dry farming.

See also ARCHAEOLOGICAL SITES; HUNTER-GATHERERS; MAN-LAND RELATIONSHIPS; PALEOLITHIC LIFEWAYS; SITE TYPES; STORAGE. [O.S.]

Further Readings

Fagan, B. (1985) In the Beginning, 5th ed. Boston: Little, Brown.

Hole, F., and Heizer, R.F. (1977) Prehistoric Archaeology. New York: Holt, Rinehart and Winston.

Jochim, M.A. (1981) Strategies for Survival: Cultural Behavior in an Ecological Context. New York: Academic.

Soffer, O. (1985) The Upper Paleolithic of the Central Russian Plain. Orlando, Fla.: Academic.

EEM see GLACIATION; PLEISTOCENE

EHRINGSDORF

During commercial and controlled excavations between 1908 and 1925 fossil hominids were recovered from travertine deposits at this site in East Germany. The most significant specimens are an adult cranial vault, an adult mandible, a child's mandible, and postcranial remains. Found in association with artifacts of Mousterian type, the fossils appear to represent early Neanderthals, although it is not clear whether they date from ca. 120 k.y. or from more than 200 k.y. ago.

See also NEANDERTHALS. [C.B.S.]

EKGMOWECHASHALA

Latest Oligocene omomyid primate from North America. This highly modified tarsiiform is not only the youngest known member of the omomyids, but it also displays the most frugivorous cheek dentition in this family. It has small incisors and large canines, attributes it shares with the middle Eocene genus *Washakius*. The special details of its teeth (metastylids, hypocone construction) suggest that this group originated near the middle Eocene Washakiini.

See also AMERICAS; OLIGOCENE; OMOMYINAE. [F.S.S.]

ELANDSFONTEIN see SALDANHA

ELPHIDOTARSIUS see CARPOLESTIDAE

ELSTER see GLACIATION; PLEISTOCENE

EMILIAN see PLEISTOCENE, SEA-LEVEL CHANGE

EMIRAN

Initial Late Paleolithic (Stage I) or transitional (from Mousterian) industry of the Levant, with type site Mugharet el-Emireh but best known from Mugharet el-Wad at Mount Carmel (Israel). Although burins, backed blades, and chamfered blades indicate a Late Paleolithic technology in some ways similar to the Dabban of Libya, the characteristic triangular points with thinned bases ("Emireh points") and blade cores with large striking platforms and evidence of direct percussion suggest Mousterian affinities.

See also DABBAN; LATE PALEOLITHIC; MIDDLE PALEOLITHIC; MOUSTERIAN; STONE-TOOL MAKING. [A.S.B.]

ENAMEL *see* TEETH

END-SCRAPER *see* SCRAPER; STONE-TOOL MAKING

ENGIS

Cave near Liège (Belgium) that is famous as one of the first sites where the great antiquity of Paleolithic humans was demonstrated by systematic excavations, around 1830. Fossil mammals, stone tools, and fossil hominids were discovered, and one of the latter specimens, the skull of a child, was the first Neanderthal fossil ever found (although unrecognized as such at the time).

See also HOMO SAPIENS; NEANDERTHALS. [C.B.S.]

ENGRAVING *see* PALEOLITHIC IMAGE; STONE-TOOL MAKING

ENVIRONMENT *see* ECOLOGY; PALEOENVIRONMENTS; PRIMATE ECOLOGY

EOCENE

Epoch spanning the time between the Paleocene and the Oligocene. In his original use of the concept Charles Lyell included both Paleocene and Oligocene time in the Eocene. Eocene rocks, both marine and continental, are well represented on most of the continents, and therefore this epoch has been much studied. The Eocene rocks were typified in the Paris and London basins, where marine rocks, containing the mollusks Lyell used in 1833 for his definition, interfinger with mammal-bearing rocks laid down on land. At least in Europe, therefore, the original stages and substages based on invertebrates need not be replaced by Land Mammal Ages. The exceptions are areas that yielded animals from different ecologies and of which the determination of the biostratigraphy is difficult.

Eocene time lies between ca. 54 and 35 m.y. ago, and its subdivisions are well understood in North America, Europe, South America, and increasingly in Asia. The African Eocene, although better explored than the Paleocene, is still largely unknown. For the study of primates the Eocene is of great interest, since the earliest time of the North American and European Eocene (essentially the same faunal realm at this period) is marked not only by the sudden appearance of rodents, horses, artiodactylis, and other mammals, but also by the simultaneous presence of the euprimate (or modern primate) families Adapidae and Omomyidae.

The distribution of land and seas during the immense span of the Eocene slowly changed from that in the Paleocene. A North American and European connection during the early Eocene is strongly supported by the astonishingly similar mammal faunas in the two areas. The land or the ecology was severed by later early Eocene times, and the Euroamerican faunal province came to an end. The Tethys Sea was still present throughout the Eocene, and the Atlantic was slowly widening. The exact nature of the Turgai Straits between Europe and Asia is not known but it is likely that the southern reaches of Europe and Asia were continuous land. During the Eocene India collided with and became attached to the Asian plate, and Australia broke away from Antarctica. South America continued, to paraphrase G.G. Simpson, its splendid isolation. Although the first known rodents and the first reported primate in South America, *Branisella*, were supposed to have been late Eocene arrivals, new studies place these events ca. 28–26 m.y. ago, well within the Oligocene.

The plant remains of the Eocene suggest a continuation of the warm, moist climate of the Paleocene, and there are indications that the beginning of the Eocene was a period of climatic warming. This period of warming may be correlated with the great faunal turnover of Euroamerica at the beginning of the Eocene. This climate extended as far as the present-day Arctic. Ellesmere Island, with a paleolatitude of at least 76°N (78°N today) had a rich primate and colugo (Dermoptera) fauna during the early and middle Eocene, in spite of the puzzling problem of the Arctic winter darkness. To appreciate the climate we can contemplate the fact that a ca. 22°C mean annual temperature of southern Alaska made that area similar in climate to the southern reaches of Mexico today. Although the Eocene was the warmest period during the Cenozoic, the great climatic deterioration of the later Cenozoic began at the end of the Eocene, leading into the Oligocene. At the end of the Eocene, based on floras of temperate broad-leaved deciduous and coniferous forests at high latitudes, the climate could be characterized as having a high mean annual range (greater than 30°C) and a low mean annual temperature (less than 10°C). Even during this cool part of the Eocene the North Pole would have been not less than 25°C warmer than today. During the warmer phase of the Eocene the Pole may have been 30–35°C warmer than today.

Adapid and omomyid primates largely disappear by the end of the Eocene from most areas in Europe and North America, although they remain known from selected younger localities, even as far north as Oregon and South Dakota in the latest Oligocene.

There are indications that during the Eocene stocks ancestral to the famous Fayum catarrhines occurred in North Africa. Enigmatic late Eocene primates, *Amphipithecus* and *Poundaungia*, from Southeast Asia compound the mystery of anthropoid origins. The African and Asian history of primates during the Eocene is the key to most questions of primate diversification; this history still largely eludes us.

See also OLIGOCENE; PALEOCENE. [F.S.S.]

Further Readings

Savage, D.E., and Russell, D.E. (1983) Mammalian Paleofaunas of the World. Reading, Mass.: Addison-Wesley.

Szalay, F.S., and Delson, E. (1979) Evolutionary History of the Primates. New York: Academic.

EON *see* TIME SCALE

EPIGRAVETTIAN

Upper Paleolithic industries of Mediterranean Europe characterized by backed microblades but lacking geometric microliths or microburins. In Italy Epigravettian industries with leaf-shaped points begin shortly after 20,000 B.P., contemporary with the Solutrean and Magdalenian of southwestern Europe. The final phases, with short end-scrapers, thumbnail scrapers, and some geometric microliths, at around 9000 B.P., are equivalent in some areas to the Romanellian. *Epigravettian* implies a continuity, expressed in the backed microblades, with the earlier Gravettian industries of western and central Europe.

See also EPIPALEOLITHIC; GRAVETTIAN; LATE PALEOLITHIC; MAGDALENIAN; ROMANELLIAN; SOLUTREAN; STONE-TOOL MAKING; UPPER PALEOLITHIC. [A.S.B.]

EPIPALEOLITHIC

Term used in place of "Mesolithic" to describe final late Pleistocene and Holocene assemblages that reflect a continuation of a Paleolithic way of life, based on hunting of large herbivores, from ca. 12,000 B.P. to as late as 3000 B.P., in northern Europe. Tool kits are highly variable but often include small tanged or backed points, scrapers and burins, a wide range of bone and antler tools including barbed harpoons, and some geometric microliths reflecting the development of composite tools. Specific industries may include the reindeer-hunting cultures of the North European plain (Hamburgian, Ahrensburgian); the Maglemosian of the North European plain; the Azilian, Sauveterrian, and Tardenoisian of France and Belgium; the Asturian of Spain; Romanellian of Italy; and Creswellian of England; together with comparable industries from Provence, Portugal, and other

areas of Europe. Some authors limit the use of "Epipaleolithic" to industries of southern and southeastern Europe, as well as Africa, where greater continuity exists between late Pleistocene and early Holocene adaptations, due to greater environmental continuity over the period involved.

Other users of the term Epipaleolithic reserve the designation Mesolithic for industries that reflect economic intensification in the direction of domestication, sedentism, or environmental modification. The Natufian culture of the Levant would thus be a clear example of Mesolithic; the Kebaran of the Levant and later Iberomaurusian of North Africa, as well as much of the Later Stone Age of sub-Saharan Africa, would be Epipaleolithic. Economic intensification is characteristic of the Epipaleolithic but tends to be reflected in specialized procurement of single resources (reindeer, red deer) or of new kinds of resources that require advanced technologies (birds, fish, seals, and marine/lacustrine resources generally). Either of these economic strategies requires considerable scheduling of resource use, according to limited seasonal availability.

One major difference between Late Paleolithic and Epipaleolithic cultures in Europe is the apparent disappearance of widespread imaging traditions based on animals. The few images associated with these sites are either abstract (Azilian) or represent schematic human figures (Asturian).

See also AZILIAN; CRESWELLIAN; DOMESTICATION; ECONOMY, PREHISTORIC; HAMBURGIAN; HUNTER-GATHERERS; IBERO-MAURUSIAN; KEBARAN; LATE PALEOLITHIC; LATER STONE AGE; MAGLEMOSIAN; MAN-LAND RELATIONSHIPS; MESOLITHIC; PALEOLITHIC LIFEWAYS; ROMANELLIAN; SAUVETERRIAN; STONE-TOOL MAKING; TARDENOISIAN; UPPER PALEOLITHIC. [A.S.B.]

Further Readings

Champion, T., Gamble, C., Shennan, S., and Whittle, A. (1984) Prehistoric Europe. New York: Academic.

Koslowski, S.K., ed. (1973) The Mesolithic in Europe. Warsaw: Warsaw University Press.

Mellars, P., ed. (1978) The Early Postglacial Settlement of Northern Europe. London: Duckworth.

Phillips, P. (1975) Early Farmers of West Mediterranean Europe. London: Hutchinson.

EPIPLIOPITHECUS *see* PLIOPITHECIDAE

EPOCH *see* TIME SCALE

ERA *see* TIME SCALE

ERECTUS, HOMO *see* HOMO ERECTUS

ERYTHROCEBUS *see* CERCOPITHECINAE

ESTRUS *see* PRIMATE SOCIETIES

ETHIOPIA

Nation comprising much of the horn of Africa, bordered on the southeast by Somalia, on the northeast by the Red Sea, on the west by Sudan, and on the south by Kenya. At the intersection of three active

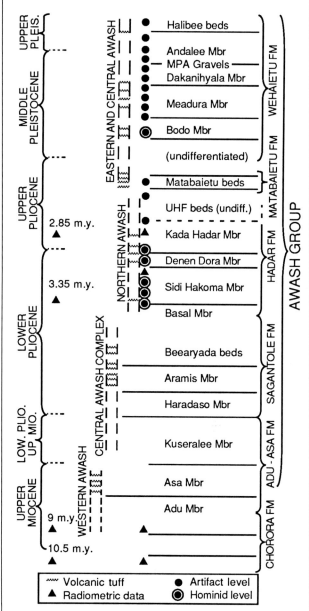

Stratigraphy of the Awash Group, Afar Depression, Ethiopia. The Sidi Hakoma tuff, indicted by the s symbol, has been correlated to the Tulu Bor tuff, 3.35 m.y., of the East Turkana sequence in Kenya and tuff B of the Shungura sequence in southwestern Ethiopia.

rifting systems—the Red Sea, the Gulf of Aden, and the Great Rift Valley of Africa—the volcanic plateaus and deep valleys of Ethiopia contain many sites of archaeological and paleontological significance.

One of the most important of these sites is found in the valley of the Omo River, where it drains southward toward Kenya into Lake Turkana. Deposits here contain artifacts and fossils interbedded with radiometrically dated volcanic ashes covering a timespan of 4 to ca. 0.5 m.y. During the 1970s, after the Omo region had been established as the best-dated and most complete record of Pliocene and Pleistocene faunal evolution on the continent, work began farther north, in the Afar Depression of Ethiopia. This large triangular area bounded by the Red Sea yielded impressive collections of hominid remains and artifacts that rival those of Kenya and Tanzania to the south. The central Ethiopian sites of Melka Kontouré and Gadeb constitute additional important Early Paleolithic occurrences. The Middle Stone Age of Ethiopia is also well known.

Paleoanthropological exploration in Ethiopia is as yet in an early stage, but results already suggest that Ethiopia may well rival or surpass Kenya and Tanzania as a source of data for understanding human origins.

See also **AFAR**; **AFRICA**; **HADAR**; **OMO**. [T.D.W.]

Further Readings

Johanson, D.C., and Edey, M. (1981) Lucy: The Beginnings of Humankind. New York: Simon and Schuster.

ETHNOARCHAEOLOGY

Collection and use of ethnographic data by archaeologists interested in behavior relating to material culture. The term was first used in the American Southwest, where archaeologists are fortunate in being able to draw on a rich ethnohistoric record, itself complementing robust and longstanding indigenous cultural traditions, some of which are thought to be traceable into the prehistoric past. More recently this and comparable terms, such as *action archaeology, living archaeology, archaeoethnography,* and *archaeological ethnography,* have been applied to research among groups as diverse as hunter-gatherers in Australia, Alaska, and Africa; tribal agriculturalists in the Philippines and nontribal farmers in Central America; villagers and pastoral nomads in Africa, Europe, and the Near East; and potters in India, Peru, and elsewhere. Observations made among ethnographically documented groups considered analogous in specific ways to societies known archaeologically are used to support inferences based on analysis of prehistoric materials, as well as to suggest ways in which

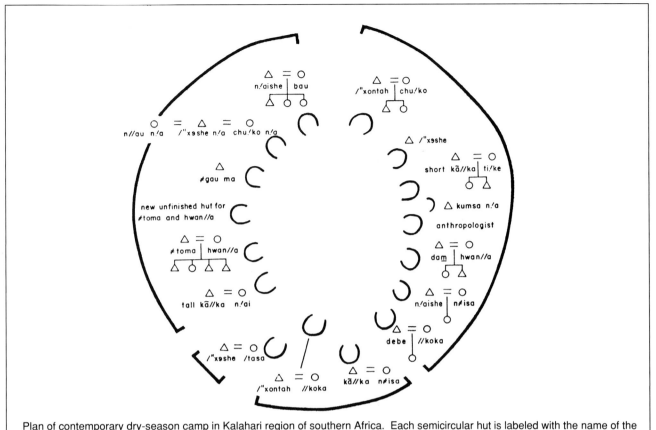

Plan of contemporary dry-season camp in Kalahari region of southern Africa. Each semicircular hut is labeled with the name of the occupants: a married couple (triangle male, circle female, = marriage symbol) and children, or single individual (note anthropologist's hut at center right). (From Yellen, 1977.)

archaeological data may be collected and analyzed (e.g. how sites and regions might be more effectively sampled and how archaeologists' typologies might be reevaluated or refined in light of native systems of classification).

Recent ethnoarchaeological research has illuminated a variety of subjects traditionally of interest to archaeologists. These include the manufacture, use, curation, and disposal of tools and ceramics; subsistence strategies, butchering, modification, and redistribution of animal parts; identification of activity areas and objects associated with them; internal organization of houses and villages and the relationship of differences among rooms to differences in activities, social relations, and economic status; interaction among ethnic groups and material markers of ethnicity and of boundaries among groups; and symbolic and ideological contexts for the creation and use of objects and structures.

Not all forms of human behavior observable today existed in the past, nor is it likely that all past adaptations have survived to the present. For example, the validity of applying studies of present-day hunter-gatherers to archaeological remains predating *Homo sapiens sapiens* has been questioned. This chal-

lenge has heightened some researchers' appreciation of the potential applications of research in primate and carnivore ethology to investigations of the behavior of the earlier hominids, particularly with respect to subsistence, settlement, and social organization. General ecological principles relating to responses to resource distributions, travel costs, predation threats, and other environmental variables have considerable potential for suggesting constraints within which "presapiens" groups may have operated and possible ranges of variation that may have characterized their adaptive strategies; such hypotheses can be tested in the archaeological record. A growing body of information about hunter-gatherers in diverse habitats is beginning not only to reveal points of difference but also to suggest some shared features that may have relevance to understanding "presapiens" time ranges as well as more recent periods.

Ethnoarchaeological research projects with agrarian groups and with pastoralists do not face quite the same challenge, since these adaptations were developed by members of our own subspecies, in the comparatively recent past. Even in such research, however, it is important to specify why one has

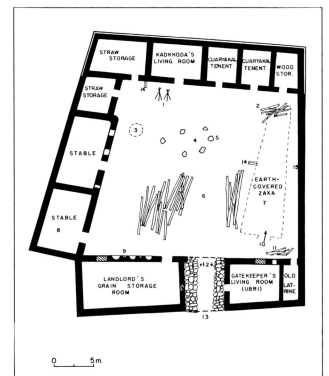

Floor plan of contemporary house in Hasanabad village (Iran). Key: 1) yogurt-churn; 2) wood; 3) grain storage pit; 4) rock salt for animals; 5) salt; 6) poplar poles; 7) sloping cover of zaxa; 8) wooden threshing machine storage area; 9) animal mangers and hitches; 10) entrance to covered zaxa; 11) wood; 12) stone platforms; 13) entryway; 14) wooden drain spout; 15) wall, 2.7 m. high. Special terms: Kadkhoda=headman; zaxa=underground stable. (Reprinted from Archaeological Ethnography in Western Iran, by P.J. Watson, © 1979 by the Wenner-Gren Foundation for Anthropological Research, New York.)

selected a particular locality and how one is applying analogical models to archaeological remains. A research bias favoring contemporary hunter-gatherers, work designed in some cases to answer questions about our Paleolithic ancestors, is gradually being balanced by ethnoarchaeological work among farmers and herders. A related geographic bias toward the "marginal" areas occupied by most modern food-collecting peoples is increasingly complemented by research in more temperate zones in other parts of the world, some of it by archaeologists interested in Neolithic and later periods.

See also ARCHAEOLOGY; CULTURE; PRIMATE SOCIETIES. [C.K.]

Further Readings

Binford, L.R. (1978) Nunamiut Ethnoarchaeology. New York: Academic.

Hodder, I. (1982) Symbols in Action. New York: Cambridge University Press.

Kramer, C., ed. (1979) Ethnoarchaeology: Implications of Ethnography for Archaeology. New York: Columbia University Press.

Yellen, J. (1977) Archaeological Approaches to the Present. New York: Academic.

ETHNOGRAPHY *see* CULTURAL ANTHROPOLOGY; CULTURE

ETHNOLOGY *see* CULTURAL ANTHROPOLOGY; CULTURE

ETHOLOGY

Study of animal behavior from an evolutionary perspective (from the Greek *ethos*, meaning custom or habit). Its roots lie in Charles Darwin's ideas on the evolution of "instincts" as developed in the 1930s by the European zoologists K. Lorenz and N. Tinbergen. Ethology uses observation, experimentation, and the comparative method to investigate the proximate causes of behavioral acts, the relative contributions of inheritance and learning to these acts, and the adaptive significance and evolutionary history of different patterns of behavior within and across species.

See also PRIMATE SOCIETIES; SOCIOBIOLOGY. [J.F.O.]

EUCATARRHINI *see* CATARRHINI

EUOTICUS *see* GALAGIDAE

EUPRIMATES

Taxonomic concept, formally named by Hoffstetter in 1977, that encompasses all primates except the archaic forms. In contrast to the classification used in this encyclopedia some students classify the primates into the semiorder Paromomyiformes and semiorder Euprimates. The following derived features, which are the diagnostic characteristics of the latter taxon, occurred in the given combination in the last common ancestor of the semiorder Euprimates: continuous postorbital rings; orbital convergence; enlarged brain compared with archaic primates, suggested by the increased neural skull in proportion to the facial one, and an increased height of the occiput in early representatives compared with archaic primates like *Plesiadapis*; stapedial and promontory arteries, like the carotid in archaic primates, enclosed in a bony canal; on all digits of the hand and foot, except for the specially and secondarily modified toilet claws on the foot, the claws (falculae) are replaced by nails; general elongation of the tarsal bones compared with the archaic forms; the ilium bone of the hip flattened and elongated for the origin of the gluteus medius muscle, which is greatly enlarged for leaping during locomotion; the groove for the kneecap (patella) on the distal end of the femur is deep and elongated, also indicating a habitual leaping component in the locomotion.

Additional detailed and consistent characteristics in the dentition, hand, foot, and other areas of the postcranium all support the hypothesis that the first euprimates were distinct from their archaic ancestors in the way they adapted to the arboreal environment. Euprimates is a monophyletic taxon within Primates.

See also ANTHROPOIDEA; PLESIADAPIFORMES; PRIMATES.

[F.S.S.]

EUROPE

Continental area with the longest, most nearly continuous record of primate (including human) evolution. Europe does not have the most ancient primates (as does North America), nor a good series of *Homo erectus* fossils and very early primates (as in Asia), and its fossil record lacks the broad representation of almost all primate groups and most major events in catarrhine and human history (Africa). Yet Europe is distinguished by good representation of both early and later primates and many human types combined with the longest history of the study of paleoanthropology. As a consequence the definitions of Cenozoic, and most other, time-scale subdivisions (epochs and stages), as well as of many types of lithic industries, technologies, and artifacts, are based on European type sections, especially from the Mediterranean and Paris-London basins and from southwestern France.

Europe is the smallest mainland continent, with an area of 10 million sq. km., of which only the southern two-thirds is potentially habitable by nonhuman primates. Western Europe was faunally connected to North America but not to Asia in the early Cenozoic; Africa was isolated; a seaway divided central Asia from most of eastern Europe. By the mid-Cenozoic Asia and Europe were in contact, and faunal interchange with Africa via the Near East became possible early in the Miocene. Late in that epoch intermittent contact was probably feasible across the Mediterranean basin, both in the center (ca. 11–9 m.y.) and in the far west (ca. 6 m.y.). At this time the mainly forested environments present since the Mesozoic were increasingly restricted northward, so that steppes dominated most of southern Europe from 8 to 5 m.y. ago. The Mediterranean basin became desiccated at the end of the Miocene, as the result of tectonic contact with Africa in the west, preventing sufficient inflow of Atlantic water to keep the basin filled. After massive downcutting of river channels emptying into the basin the "Gibraltar Falls"

cut through to the ocean, and the Mediterranean refilled, marking the beginning of the Pliocene ca. 5.2 m.y. ago. Humid monsoon-type forest spread through southern Europe, but then global climatic cooling led to more open conditions in the later Pliocene and early Pleistocene (ca. 3–1 m.y.). A number of local mountain ranges that had risen mostly during the later Cenozoic were the centers of regional glaciation through the Pleistocene, as was the Scandinavian sector to the north. Latitudinal zonation of climatic belts typifies Europe today and probably did so through much of the Cenozoic.

(*See also* AFRICA; AMERICAS; ASIA (EASTERN); CENOZOIC; GLACIATION; PALEOBIOGEOGRAPHY; PLATE TECTONICS; SEA-LEVEL CHANGE; TIME SCALE.)

Rise of Primates

Primates first appeared in the European fossil record in the late Paleocene. *Plesiadapis* occurred in France at Cernay (and similar sites) and in Germany at the Walbeck fissure-fill, which also yielded the unique specimens of *Saxonella*. Plesiadapids continued into the early Eocene in England, France, and Belgium (the important locality of Dormaal), alongside *Phenacolemur* and the first euprimates: the notharctid *Pelycodus* (=*Cantius*) and the anaptomorphine omomyid *Teilhardina*. Over a dozen genera here included in the Adapidae ranged through the Eocene of Europe, from Portugal to England to northern Germany. The greatest number of localities are in southern France, especially the group of fissure-fillings and stratified sites in the Quercy region. Microchoerine omomyids coexisted with adapids at many if not all of the localities in the middle and late Eocene. In general they were small, while adapids ranged in size from tiny to that of a cat, filling the niches taken by both adapids and omomyids in North America. At the end of the Eocene a major faunal turnover known as the *Grande Coupure*, or "Great Cutoff," took place, and all primates disappeared from the European fossil record throughout the Oligocene and early Miocene.

(*See also* ADAPIDAE; ANAPTOMORPHINAE; CATARRHINI; EOCENE; LORISOIDEA; MICROCHOERINAE; NOTHARCTIDAE; OMOMYIDAE; OMOMYINAE; PALEOCENE; PAROMOMYIDAE; PLESIADAPIDAE; SAXONELLIDAE.)

Only in the early middle Miocene do primates again appear in Europe, as a result of immigration from Africa. Pliopithecids were apparently the first to arrive, probably via the "sub-Alpine" route along the northern shore of the Mediterranean from the Near East. At this time a major inland sea extended roughly east-west in the center of Europe and down to meet the Mediterranean in the Adriatic region. *Pliopithecus* and allies were essentially restricted to the west and north of this seaway, from Spain

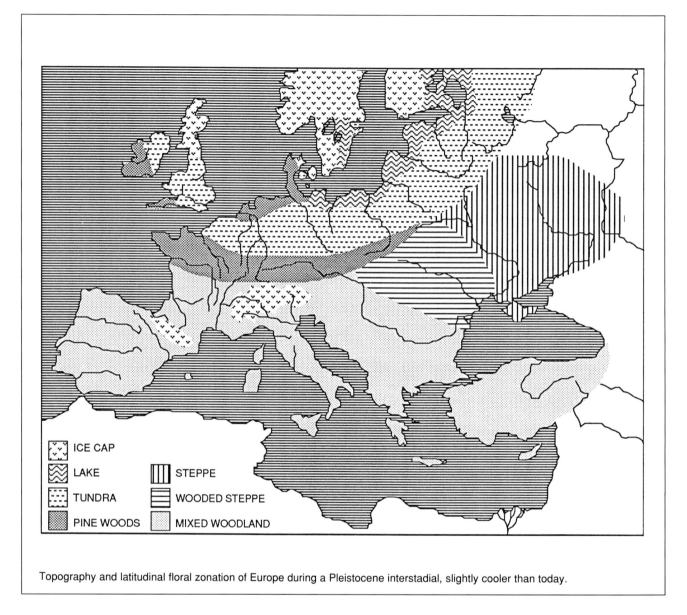

ICE CAP

LAKE   STEPPE

TUNDRA   WOODED STEPPE

PINE WOODS   MIXED WOODLAND

Topography and latitudinal floral zonation of Europe during a Pleistocene interstadial, slightly cooler than today.

through to Poland and Hungary, between 16 and 11 m.y. *Dryopithecus* arrived slightly later, perhaps by ca. 14 m.y., and sometimes occurred alongside the pliopithecids. At least two species are known, *D. fontani* and *D. laietanus* (=?*D. brancoi*), and a third may occur in Spain; teeth from Udabno (Georgian S.S.R., ca. 12 m.y.) might be *D. fontani* or a distinct species comparable with eastern Asian forms. Although *Dryopithecus* appears to have conservatively thin molar enamel, its humerus displays several features more like those of "modern" hominoids than is known for the African *Kenyapithecus*. At present both these genera may be included in the probably paraphyletic hominid subfamily Dryopithecinae, but the relative position of these forms within the Hominidae is still ambiguous. Material from the site of Rudabányá (early late Miocene of Hungary, ca. 11 m.y.) has not been fully described but includes a partial

skull and upper facial fragments assigned to *D. fontani*, as well as pliopithecid jaws and a large mandible that may have thicker enamel and derived premolar morphology. That specimen may be referable to the Ponginae, as part of a complex of species (and genera) related to *Sivapithecus*. A few teeth from Neudorf (Czechoslovakia, ca. 14 m.y.) may represent the earliest entry of that group into Europe, but the best material comes from Greece: Ravin de la Pluie (near Saloniki, ca. 11 m.y.) and Pyrgos (Athens, ca. 11–8 m.y.). These specimens have been termed *Dryopithecus* and *Ouranopithecus*, but *Graecopithecus* seems the correct name; the specimens show great sexual dimorphism and are morphologically close to *Sivapithecus* in having thick, fast-formed molar enamel and reduced I^2 but present a more conservative (rather *Gorilla*-like) incisive foramen complex.

Cercopithecoids appeared in Europe in the late

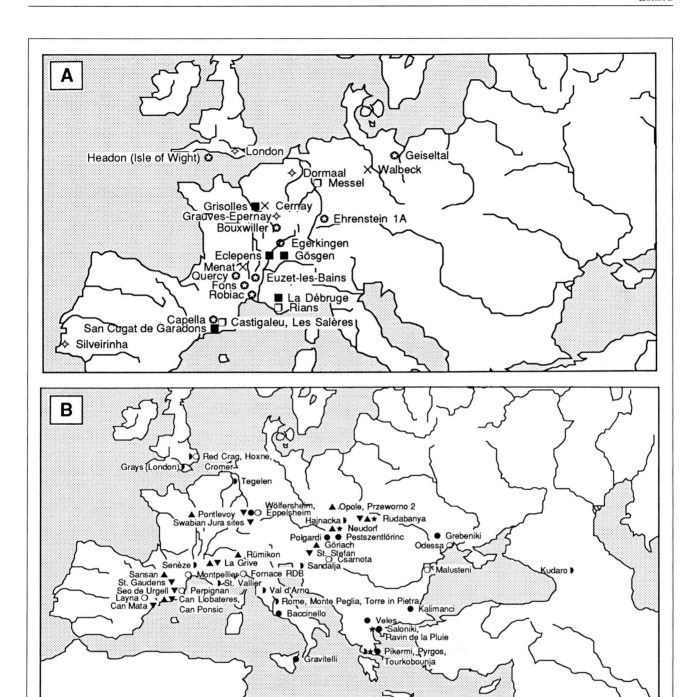

Selected European fossil primate localities A) late Paleocene to late Eocene; and B) middle Miocene to later Pleistocene. Age and included taxa are indicated according to the following key:

Symbol	Age	Primate fossils
×	late Paleocene (58–55 m.y.)	Plesiadapiformes
▢	Eocene (55–36 m.y.)	Adapoidea
◇	Eocene (55–36 m.y.)	Adapoidea and Plesiadapiformes
✪	Eocene (55–36 m.y.)	Adapoidea and Omomyidae
■	Eocene (55–36 m.y.)	Microchoerinae only
▲	Miocene (16–5 m.y.)	Pliopithecidae
▼	Miocene (16–5 m.y.)	Dryopithecinae
★	Miocene (16–5 m.y.)	?Ponginae
●	Miocene (16–5 m.y.)	Cercopithecoidea
○	early Pliocene (5–3 m.y.)	Cercopithecoidea
◗	late Pliocene and Pleistocene (3–0.1 m.y.)	Cercopithecoidea

Miocene, when *Mesopithecus pentelici*, a semiterrestrial colobine, was common in the southeastern part of the continent: Pikermi and Saloniki (Greece), Titov Veles (Yugoslavia), Kalimanci (Bulgaria), and Grebeniki (Ukrainian S.S.R.), all 9–8 m.y. old. The range of this species continued eastward at least into Afghanistan. One premolar tooth from Wissberg, in the Eppelsheim-area "*Deinotherium*-Sands" of Germany, may be 11 m.y. or older. *Oreopithecus bambolii* is known only from five neighboring localities in central Italy also dated to ca. 9–8 m.y. Although it has been reported from the Ukraine and Moldavia, no specimens are now known. This suspensory folivore is placed in its own family, Oreopithecidae, but there is some discussion as to whether it was a cercopithecoid (as here accepted) or a hominoid. It may have entered Europe from northern Africa by a tectonic land bridge across the Mediterranean early in the late Miocene.

With the aridification of southern Europe all primates disappeared except a few poorly dated colobines known from forested localities in Hungary. The return of humid forests saw the spread of macaques (presumably from North Africa) and two new colobines: a smaller and more arboreal species of *Mesopithecus* and the moderately large-bodied, terrestrial *Dolichopithecus ruscinensis*. Between 5 and 3 m.y. these species are often found together at localities between Spain and the Ukraine and as far north as Germany (Wölfersheim) and southern England (Red Crag). Later Pliocene and Pleistocene cooling probably led to the extinction of the colobines, but macaques indistinguishable from the living *M. sylvanus* of Gibraltar and North Africa persisted into the latest middle Pleistocene across all of Europe from England and Spain to the Caucasus. The large-bodied terrestrial baboonlike *Paradolichopithecus* was apparently a local macaque derivative that converged on the savanna baboon niche. It is known from only a few sites in the later Pliocene of Spain, France, Romania, and Tadzhikistan (Soviet central Asia).

(*See also* CERCOPITHECINAE; CERCOPITHECOIDEA; COLOBINAE; DRYOPITHECUS; HOMINIDAE; HOMINOIDEA; KENYAPITHECUS; MIOCENE; OREOPITHECIDAE; PLEISTOCENE; PLIOCENE; PLIOPITHECIDAE; PONGINAE.)

Earliest Humans

The earliest evidence of human occupation in Europe is controversial. *Homo erectus* fossils and associated Acheulean artifacts are known in Africa by 1.6 m.y., and hominid remains appear in Asia between 1.6 and 1 m.y. Most workers do not expect to see human fossils or stone tools in Europe before 1 m.y., and in fact all occurrences older than 500 k.y. are subject to question. Many such early finds consist of small assemblages of often rolled, weathered, and possibly natural pebbles, as in the Roussillon region of south-central France. In the past archaeologists mistakenly recognized as "eoliths" similar sets of stones selected from larger natural assemblages, and thus caution has been instilled. But several sites in France, Italy, and Czechoslovakia are especially worthy of careful consideration. Vallonnet Cave (west of Monaco) has yielded choppers and flakes alongside fauna dating to ca. 1 m.y., and paleomagnetic studies suggest a date around 900 k.y. (Jaramillo) or perhaps 700 k.y. (earliest Brunhes). Soleilhac, farther northwest, is an open site with flakes, choppers, and broken animal bones of comparable age, as well as roughly aligned basalt blocks, perhaps documenting a structure. Stranská Skála and Přezletice (Czechoslovakia) also yield small assemblages of rough artifacts associated with fauna, paleomagnetically dated to the late Matuyama (over 730 k.y.). Isernia, in central Italy, is a recently excavated open site of comparable antiquity but with a greater concentration of better-made artifacts. Chilhac and St. Estève (France) and Monte Peglia (Italy) are other potential early assemblages, perhaps of less clearly human origin.

It is important to note that none of these possibly ancient sites has produced a rich industry with bifaces, such as those known far earlier in Africa, nor have any sites older than at most 500 k.y. yielded human fossils. A variety of explanations has been offered for the absence of these expected features of the European archaeological record, some of which might apply to Asia as well, although human fossils and lithic industries lacking bifaces are well established in China by ca. 1. m.y. Clearly the difference in climate between (sub-) tropical Africa and temperate Eurasia, with particular emphasis on the long and cloudy winters of mid-latitude Europe, was a significant factor in the delay in human entry. In southern Africa a comparable situation is reflected in the apparent absence of human and archaeological remains from the temperate regions south of the Vaal River prior to ca. 1 m.y., despite evidence of several species of hominines as old as ca. 3 m.y. in the Transvaal. An additional factor is the steady increase in the tempo and scale of glaciation-related climatic fluctuation in Eurasia. From the late Pliocene to the early middle Pleistocene glacial cycles lasted ca. 40 k.y., with slow cooling and warming phases. After ca. 900 k.y. the cycles spanned ca. 100 k.y. and were characterized by long cooling trends, followed by rapid warming and short interglacial intervals (warm phases always seem to have lasted only 10–20 k.y. from 2.5 m.y. onward). Fire is known in eastern Africa by ca. 1.5 m.y. ago but is rare both there and in the early European record, so it may not yet have been fully controlled.

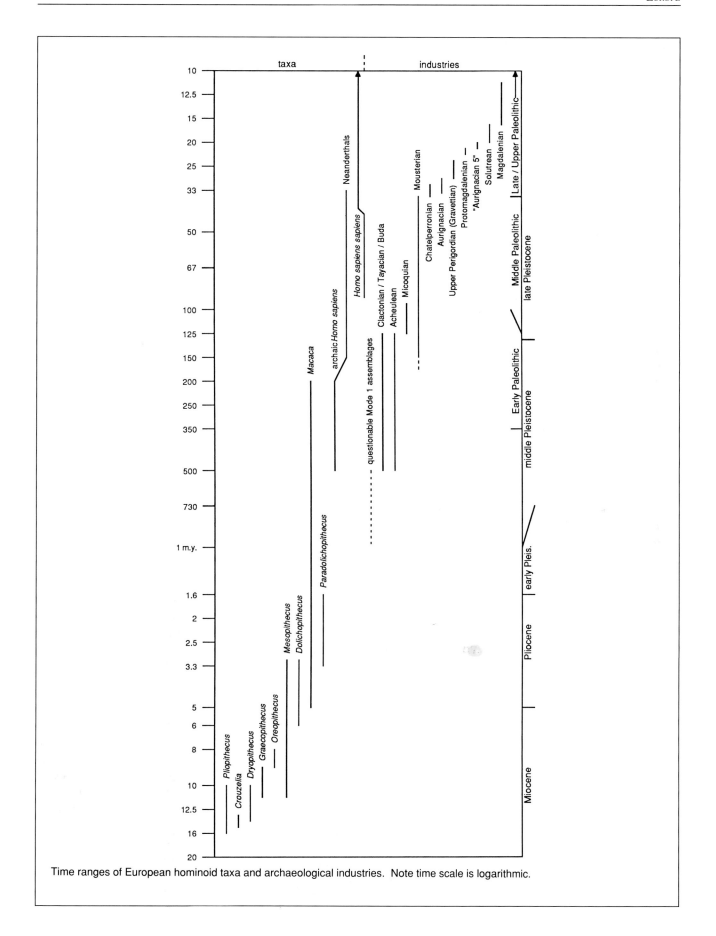

Time ranges of European hominoid taxa and archaeological industries. Note time scale is logarithmic.

Other differences between the African record and the Eurasian relate to the mode of life of the hominids involved. Dennell has suggested that hunting patterns had to change in order for early humans to cope with the shorter growing season of the European landmass. A greater need for meat would have required small hunting bands traveling away from perhaps more than one base camp to hunt cooperatively for single large animals like elephant or rhinoceros, then returning with meat for all group members to last a long period. In Africa G. Isaac and M.D. Leakey have argued for the existence of base camps in the early Pleistocene archaeological record, but current interpretations of that record do not support this, despite evidence that both meat-bearing bones and raw materials for stone tools were transported over the landscape. Similarly, the early European record is concentrated in stream-channel and lakeshore deposits, possibly representing secondarily altered butchery or ambush locations, and does not suggest the existence of repeatedly occupied base camps. On this basis humans may well have been rare in early middle Pleistocene Europe, perhaps migrating in and retreating out again to occupy colder areas only during the interglacial phases.

But two problems have not yet been answered: why are there no bifaces, and what happened to change the pattern? A similar lack of finely made artifacts characterizes the earliest sites in the New World, leading to comparable controversy over the age of the earliest Americans, although there the absence is more often attributed to the corresponding lack of blade-and-burin industries in East and Southeast Asia prior to 20,000 B.P. Is it possible that the activities of early Europeans did not include those requiring handaxes, as in many early African industries without bifaces? Or could the known sites just be short-term butchery camps, where crude flake tools and choppers were expediently manufactured and discarded? Perhaps formally shaped tools either were group signatures or represented raw-material conservation strategies and in either case developed only at higher levels of human population density. The lack of human remains must also reflect low densities, as several of the ancient (pre-0.5 m.y.) European sites are surely of human origin.

After 500 k.y. human fossils begin to occur in greater number, and they do not seem to be the same morphological type as those known contemporaneously in Africa or Asia, nor are the associated industries entirely comparable with African ones. The discontinuities and regional variability of the European record, and its marked differences from the records of contiguous continental landmasses, may be explained by the repeated isolation of peripheral human populations in Europe due to fluctuating geographical barriers: especially montane glaciers but also deserts and high sea levels. Around 500 k.y. ago, possibly during an especially severe and relatively rapid onset of glacial conditions, some populations of the *Homo erectus* variety that had occupied Europe on and off since the late early Pleistocene were not able to retreat to warmer climes. Some individuals in these populations may have survived by virtue of genetically controlled features that permitted them to better withstand the climate and perhaps to be more culturally flexible in their adaptation to the environment. Over time these populations grew in numbers and diverged genetically from their ancestors. In succeeding interglacial intervals their descendants left fossils that we term "archaic *Homo sapiens*," the first members of our own species. It is at least equally likely that *Homo sapiens* arose from *Homo erectus* in Africa and moved into Europe during a succeeding interglacial interval, displacing the few *Homo erectus* populations that remained there. Although either hypothesis provides an explanation for the sudden appearance of more "modern" humans in south-central Europe, the former one uses an allopatric model of speciation, rather than merely gradual anagenesis. As usual more fossils, sites, and better dating may test the model.

(*See also* AFRICA; AMERICAS; ARCHAEOLOGICAL SITES; ASIA (EASTERN); CHILHAC; CHOPPER-CHOPPING TOOLS; EARLY PALEOLITHIC; ECONOMY, PREHISTORIC; FIRE; FRANCE; HOMO ERECTUS; MONTE PEGLIA; PALEOLITHIC LIFEWAYS; PŘEZLETICE; RAW MATERIALS; SITE TYPES; SOLEILHAC; STRANSKÁ SKÁLA; VALLONNET.)

Archaic *Homo sapiens*

Several localities thought to be younger than 500 and older than 300 k.y. have yielded hominid fossils attributed to archaic *Homo sapiens*, but few have also produced artifacts, and those are generally without bifaces. The most important are Mauer (near Heidelberg, Germany), Vértesszöllös (Hungary), Petralona (Greece), and Arago (France), in an approximate chronological order based mainly on rough estimates. These fossils are similar to African forms, such those from Ndutu, Saldanha and Kabwe, but differ from Asian and African *Homo erectus* in reorientation of the occipital area, perhaps slightly larger brain size, and the development of facial pneumatization and reorientation. Several researchers consider some or all of these specimens as belonging to a more broadly defined *Homo erectus*, and others would place them in a separate species, but because the listed features are shared with later members of *Homo sapiens*, including Neanderthals and "moderns," it appears best to include these fossils in *Homo sapiens* as well. The artifacts associated with the Arago and

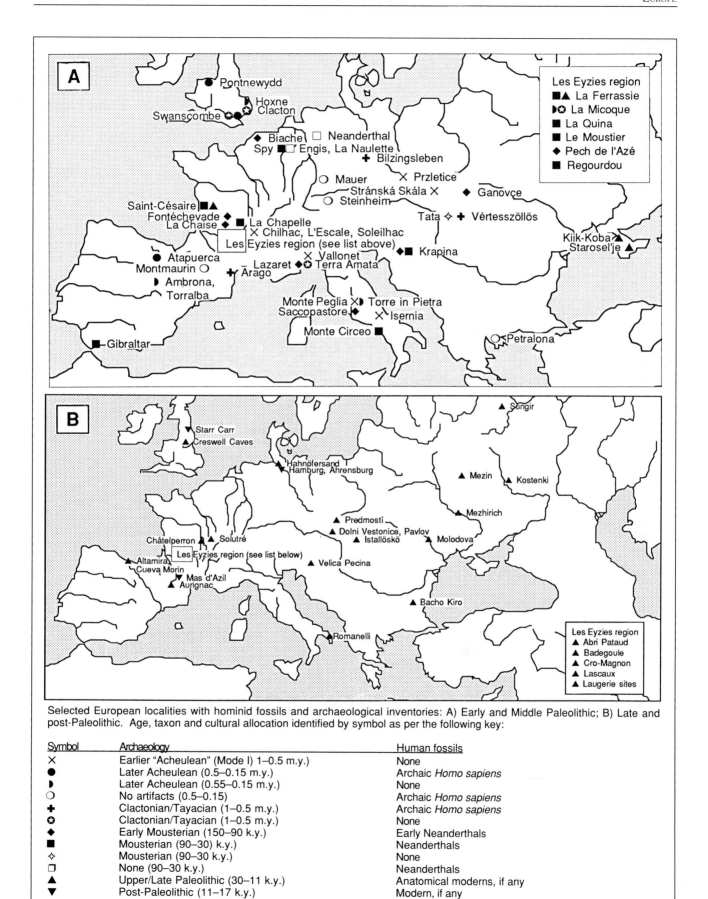

Selected European localities with hominid fossils and archaeological inventories: A) Early and Middle Paleolithic; B) Late and post-Paleolithic. Age, taxon and cultural allocation identified by symbol as per the following key:

Symbol	Archaeology	Human fossils
✕	Earlier "Acheulean" (Mode I) 1–0.5 m.y.)	None
●	Later Acheulean (0.5–0.15 m.y.)	Archaic *Homo sapiens*
◗	Later Acheulean (0.55–0.15 m.y.)	None
○	No artifacts (0.5–0.15)	Archaic *Homo sapiens*
✚	Clactonian/Tayacian (1–0.5 m.y.)	Archaic *Homo sapiens*
✪	Clactonian/Tayacian (1–0.5 m.y.)	None
◆	Early Mousterian (150–90 k.y.)	Early Neanderthals
■	Mousterian (90–30) k.y.)	Neanderthals
◇	Mousterian (90–30 k.y.)	None
▢	None (90–30 k.y.)	Neanderthals
▲	Upper/Late Paleolithic (30–11 k.y.)	Anatomical moderns, if any
▼	Post-Paleolithic (11–17 k.y.)	Modern, if any

Vértesszöllös hominids are generally small flakes and cores, with no larger bifacial pieces.

The pace of both morphological and technological change increased in the European record between 300 and 150 k.y. and continued to accelerate thereafter. Dating is still quite uncertain in this time range, with age estimates based on climatostratigraphy calibrated by deep-sea core studies and those derived by chronometric methods often in disagreement. Nonetheless, hominids that may be characterized as "later archaics" are known from sites apparently of this age, including Steinheim, Bilzingsleben, and perhaps Ehringsdorf (Germany), Montmaurin and Lazaret (France), Pontnewydd (Wales), Swanscombe (England), and Atapuerca (Spain). They all present a mosaic of features combining conservative *Homo erectus* or early *Homo sapiens* characters with derived conditions found elsewhere only in younger Neanderthals; on that basis these hominids may be considered broadly as the ancestors of the Neanderthals. Finely worked Acheulean bifaces appear at least by the beginning of this interval and continue to the Eemian, at such sites as Torre in Pietra (Italy), Hoxne and Swanscombe (England), and the Torralba and Ambrona pair in Spain. At the latter site several elephants and smaller mammals may have been butchered at the edge of a lake, where they were perhaps driven and ambushed by hominids. Toward the end of this interval the use of Levallois prepared cores becomes frequent in some sites. Local variability may increase also, with the terms Clactonian (in the north) and Tayacian (in the south of Europe) being used to describe assemblages lacking bifaces. It is unclear whether these assemblages reflect distinct cultural patterns (and different human groups?), the uses to which different sets of tools were put, or even stages in the manufacture of a single tool kit.

Neanderthals

By ca. 150 k.y. ago, probably in the waning stages of the glacial interval before the last (late Saale or "Riss"), hominid fossils are known that appear to be identifiable as early Neanderthals. Fossils from Biache, Fontéchevade, La Chaise, and Pech de l'Azé (all France) fall into this category. Later Neanderthals are almost always associated with a Middle Paleolithic industry broadly termed Mousterian, but there is much uncertainty as to whether the tool kits found with these earliest Neanderthals can be identified as early Mousterian or should be considered as late variants of the Early Paleolithic, under such names as late Acheulean, Tayacian, or "pre-Mousterian." During the succeeding Eemian interglacial (ca. 130–115 k.y. ago) it appears that the Neanderthals spread widely across Europe and into the Near East, with

representative sites including Saccopastore (Italy), Krapina (Yugoslavia), and Gánovce (Czechoslovakia). Fewer sites of this age are known, in part because of the scouring of caves during an interglacial with the increase in glacial meltwater and precipitation, in part because of the absence of sedimentation of cold-fractured detritus in rock shelters, and of wind-blown loess in open-air sites.

During almost all of the last, or Weichselian, glaciation (ca. 110–30 k.y.) Neanderthals were the only hominids in Europe. The western forms, known as the "classic" group, were somewhat more derived than eastern European and Near Eastern varieties, which seem to have changed little from the interglacial populations. This is presumably a result of greater adaptation to cold climate in the west, where the Neanderthals were closer to the effects of the ice front and harsher climate. Also especially in western Europe the Mousterian industrial complex most often associated with Neanderthals has been subdivided into several recognized variants, which are for the most part regionally and chronologically widespread. In France these include the Charentian (Quina and Ferrassie) variants with high percentages of scrapers, the Typical variant with moderate percentages of scrapers, and the Denticulate Mousterian, with low percentages of scrapers and many denticulates, as well as the Mousterian of Acheulean tradition, with handaxes or backed knives in addition to low-to-moderate numbers of scrapers. Central and eastern European Middle Paleolithic assemblages include industries assigned to the Typical, Denticulate, and Quina Mousterian, as well as industries with bifacial leaf-shaped points ("Altmuhlian") or handaxes ("Micoquian"), the latter term reserved in France for transitional industries with pointed handaxes dating to very early in the last glacial period. There is some evidence that the Mousterian begins to give way to the Late Paleolithic earlier in eastern Europe than is the case farther west.

The underlying determinants of variation in European Middle Paleolithic industries are unclear; ethnic signatures or "styles" do not explain the alternation of industries with very little internal change over a long period in the same region; "functional," or activity-based, explanations fail to account for the lack of association between types of sites, faunas, and Mousterian variants. This period also displays a significant increase in rock-shelter and cave as opposed to open-air occupation sites, in constructions at both open-air sites and rock shelters, in the density of remains at particular sites, in hunting skills as reflected in single-species faunal concentrations, and in occupation of the cold steppe and periglacial regions of northeastern Europe. In addition evidence of symbolic and ritual behavior is provided by scarce pendants (La Quina, Pech de l'Azé) and carved objects (Tata), by coloring material including "crayons" (Pech de l'Azé), and by evidence of deliberate burial of the dead with associated grave goods.

(*See also* ABBEVILLIAN; ACHEULEAN; AMBRONA; ARAGO; ARCHAIC HOMO SAPIENS; ATAPUERCA; BIACHE; BILZINGSLEBEN; CLACTONIAN; DRACHENLOCH; FONTÉCHEVADE; HOMO SAPIENS; HOXNE; LA CHAISE; LA FERRASSIE; LA QUINA; LAZARET; LE MOUSTIER; LEVALLOIS; MAUER; MICOQUIAN; MONTMAURIN; MOUSTERIAN; NEANDERTHALS; PECH DE L'AZÉ; PETRALONA; PONTNEWYDD; PREPARED-CORE; REGOURDOU; SAINT-CÉSAIRE; STEINHEIM; SWANSCOMBE; TAYACIAN; TORRE IN PIETRA.)

Modern Humans and the Upper Paleolithic

In Europe the term Upper Paleolithic is widely used to refer to blade-and-burin–based industries that show the social and economic intensification typical of the Late Paleolithic as understood in this book. At such sites as Istallöskö (Hungary) and Bacho Kiro (Bulgaria) assemblages similar to the Upper Paleolithic have been radiocarbon dated to greater than 40 k.y., but some researchers doubt the validity of dates that old. Some of the earliest industries exhibit close similarities to Mousterian antecedents. The Szeletian industries of eastern Europe have been considered either as Middle or Late Paleolithic by different authors. In western Europe the youngest dated Neanderthals are ca. 35 k.y. old, but at Saint-Césaire (France) a partial skeleton of a female classic Neanderthal has been recovered in association with a Chatelperronian assemblage, dated elsewhere to ca. 32 k.y. For decades there has been controversy as to whether the Chatelperronian was a local outgrowth of the Mousterian or a "true" Upper Paleolithic industry, derived from new populations reaching Europe from the east and south. The Saint-Césaire find has been used to support both views: either late Neanderthals developed Upper Paleolithic tools, or, if Upper Paleolithic industries are necessarily the product of *Homo sapiens sapiens*, the Chatelperronian was the last phase of the European Middle Paleolithic.

Whatever the decision, after 30 k.y. ago there are no more Neanderthals or Mousterian assemblages in Europe. It now appears that anatomically modern humans probably arose in Africa and migrated into eastern Europe via the Near East, possibly interbreeding with Neanderthals on a small scale and replacing them regionally. The European Upper Paleolithic industries have no clear African sources, but some Near Eastern and North African assemblages found interstratified with Mousterian (or late Acheulean) contain broadly similar blade and burin forms. In western Europe the widespread Aurignacian industry is characterized by abundant bone, antler, and ivory artifacts, including beads, pendants, pierced batons, carved animal figurines, points, and awls. The earliest sites are dated to 34 k.y., although there is evidence of initial overlap with the Chatelperronian in France, with the Uluzzan in Italy, and with the Szeletian in eastern Europe. All are succeeded by the Gravettian, characterized by backed points, ca. 28 k.y. ago. In western Europe Gravettian and Chatelperronian have been considered part of a Perigordian complex, paralleling the Aurignacian in both time and space, but some of the evidence for long-term overlap is based on sedimentologically based chronological equivalences among different sites and is hence suspect. Although Gravettian sites are linked by backed-tool technology and female figurines, the degree of regional variation across the vast area involved suggests the presence of ethnic signatures in the archaeological materials. The eastern variant of the Gravettian is particularly rich in carved female and animal figurines and in burials and exhibits evidence both for effective hunting and storage of meat from large herbivores and for elaborate control of fire (Dolni Věstonice) by 27 k.y.

During the last glacial maximum northern Europe was either abandoned or sparsely populated; in southern Europe, especially Spain and southern France, the Solutrean industries (22–18 k.y.) reflect greatly improved hunting specializations as well as the most refined stone technology of the Paleolithic. Magdalenian (18–11 k.y.) industries, with increasingly specialized economies, microlithic technologies, and elaborate bone working, complete the Upper Paleolithic sequence in western Europe and represent the high point of large-scale ritual and symbolic activity, documented in deep painted cave sites, such as Lascaux, Font-de-Gaume, and Altamira. The Upper Paleolithic succession as a whole is based on deeply stratified sites (e.g. Laugerie Haute and Abri Pataud), with long successions of horizons spanning large portions of the Upper Paleolithic. Outside of France, particularly in eastern Europe, the Solutrean is absent, and the period following the glacial maximum is characterized by a continuation of the Gravettian with the addition of microliths (evolved Gravettian); in Mediterranean Europe microlithic tools of Gravettian type ("Epigravettian") typify the final Paleolithic industries.

Throughout the Upper Paleolithic in central and eastern Europe, except during the glacial maximum when the area was sparsely populated or abandoned, sites in Czechoslovakia (such as Předmosti, Dolni Věstonice, and Pavlov) and the U.S.S.R. (e.g. Kostenki, Mezhirich, Molodova, and Sungir) document somewhat different and more complex adaptations to life on the open loess steppes and in Russian river valleys. Elaborate dwellings made of dozens of already fossilized elephant jaws, skulls, and tusks, burials with thousands of carefully drilled bone beads, and exotic raw materials from hundreds of miles away imply the existence of trade routes, social stratification patterns, and interrelationships among various hunting bands far beyond what was once expected for Late Paleolithic peoples.

The last great glaciers began to melt after 20 k.y., and by 11 k.y. the climate had ameliorated to the point where herds of game animals no longer foraged in open country. Instead forests spread over Europe, and human groups adapted to hunting smaller, solitary game and to fishing, except on the recently deglaciated northern European plain, where the first human occupants (Hamburgian, Ahrensburgian) were reindeer hunters. Final Paleolithic and Mesolithic industries, such as the Azilian, Sauveterrian, Tardenoisian, Maglemosian, Creswellian, and Romanellian, occur across western and central Europe between 12 and 8 k.y. ago. Typical features of these societies include the use of microlithic tools, presumably many small blades hafted to a holder, and the beginnings of animal (canine) domestication. In the succeeding millennia additional species were domesticated, sedentary village life replaced migrational hunting, and Europe entered the Neolithic.

See also ABRI PATAUD; AGGREGATION-DISPERSAL; ALTAMIRA; AURIGNACIAN; AZILIAN; BACHO KIRO; CHATELPERRONIAN; CRESWELLIAN; CUEVA MORIN; DOLNI VĚSTONICE; DOMESTICATION; EXOTICS; GRAVETTIAN; HAMBURGIAN; ISTALLÖSKÖ; KOSTENKI; LASCAUX; LAUGERIE SITES; MAGDALENIAN; MAGLEMOSIAN; MESOLITHIC; MEZHIRICH; MOLODOVA; NEOLITHIC; PALEOLITHIC CALENDAR; PALEOLITHIC IMAGE; PAVLOV; PERIGORDIAN; PŘEDMOSTI; ROMANELLIAN; SAUVETERRIAN; SOLUTREAN; SUNGIR; SZELETIAN; TARDENOISIAN; UPPER PALEOLITHIC. [E.D., A.S.B.]

Further Readings

Bordes, F., and Thibault, C. (1977) Thoughts on the initial adaptation of hominids to European glacial climates. Quat. Res. 8:115–127.

Dennell, R. (1983) European Economic Prehistory: A New Approach. London: Academic.

Gamble, C. (1986) The Palaeolithic Settlement of Europe. Cambridge: Cambridge University Press.

Savage, D.E., and Russell, D.E. (1983) Mammalian Paleofaunas of the World. Reading, Mass.: Addison-Wesley.

Smith, F.H., and Spencer, F., eds. (1984) The Origins of Modern Humans: A World Survey of the Fossil Evidence. New York: Liss.

Soffer, O. (1985) The Upper Paleolithic of the Central Russian Plain. Orlando, Fla.: Academic.

Szalay, F.S., and Delson, E. (1979) Evolutionary History of the Primates. New York: Academic.

White, R. (1986) Dark Caves, Bright Visions: Life in Ice Age Europe. New York: Norton.

EUROPOLEMUR *see* ADAPIDAE

EVENT *see* PALEOMAGNETISM

EVOLUTION

Hypothesis that all organisms are descended from a single ancestor by a process that Charles Darwin termed, aptly and simply, "descent with modification." More generally *evolution* has been applied to change within any historical system—including the physical universe and its component parts, especially the solar system, the earth itself, and its climate. Within biology evolution or its equivalent (e.g. *evolution* in French, *Entwicklung* in German) has meant ontogenetic as well as phylogenetic (i.e. true evolutionary) "development." As applied to hominids, evolution is taken in the usual biological (phylogenetic) sense insofar as anatomical and physiological features are concerned; behavioral evolution within hominids is generally termed *cultural evolution*. This article considers only biological evolution.

The two fundamental aspects of biological evolution are both implicit in Darwin's concept of descent with modification. The first is the simple precept that life has had a history, that organisms alive today are interrelated by virtue of descent from a remote common ancestor. Evolutionary history is termed *phylogeny*. The second basic sense of evolution forms the focus of this article: the processes, or patterns of causation, that underlie patterns of evolutionary change through time.

The Russian-born geneticist and naturalist Theodosius Dobzhansky once remarked that "nothing in biology makes sense except in the light of evolution." And indeed the intricate patterns of similarity and difference among all living organisms can be explained scientifically in no way other than by a notion of genealogical interrelatedness. Although the writings of Greek and Roman savants provide suggestive hints that they entertained notions of the interrelatedness of living beings, it was not until naturalists of the seventeenth and eighteenth centuries began a serious and systematic study of living plants and animals that early versions of modern evolutionary conceptions began to take shape. The great Swedish naturalist Carolus Linnaeus (Carl von Linné), whose *Systema Naturae* proved to be the forerunner of our modern system of classification, sensed variation around basic anatomical themes, although he later rescinded his doctrine that new species could arise from ancestral species. Most early naturalists were content to arrange living forms in order from the more simple to the more complex, deviating little from the ancient concept of the Scale of Nature. Similarly, the overall trend of the fossil record, where more complex ("higher") forms of life appear in younger rocks lying above the older rocks containing simpler forms of life, was interpreted as a form of simple progressivism, often seen as loosely equivalent to the order of Creation as given in Genesis. Alternatively, some paleontologists, like Baron Georges Cuvier, noting the many instances of extinction and subsequent proliferation of newer, different faunas and floras, attributed the changing complexion of the fossil record to a series of multiple catastrophes and creation events.

Yet despite the prevalent attempt to reconcile observations on the fossil record and living plants and animals with received biblical interpretation early scientists like Buffon, Geoffroy St. Hilaire, and Lamarck held definitely evolutionary views. Lamarck in particular is noteworthy in that he put forward a coherent theory on how life might have changed through time. Lamarck agreed with other biologists who postulated that features acquired during the lifetime of an organism may be passed on to descendants—the "inheritance of acquired characteristics" discredited by August Weismann in the late nineteenth century. (It is not generally appreciated that Charles Darwin also accepted the inheritance of acquired characteristics as a legitimate means of evolutionary change, emphasizing this process especially in later editions of his *Origin of Species*—notably the sixth, the one most often reproduced today—after his own theory of natural selection had been so strongly attacked).

It was Charles Darwin who brought respectability to evolution as a legitimate scientific notion. Darwin's epochal *On the Origin of Species* was first published in 1859; the initial edition of 2,000 copies sold out on the first day, testimony indeed that evolution was an idea whose time had come. Although earlier authors had articulated the notion of natural selection, and although Alfred Russel Wallace had produced a manuscript that so nearly coincided with Darwin's own formulations that Darwin was shocked by the similarity of the very phrases both used, nonetheless it was Darwin's exposition, long awaited by his colleagues throughout the western world, that transformed evolution from a daring, heretical, and even irrational notion into a hypothesis of undoubted respectability. Because of Darwin's efforts evolution became the theory of life's history, a conjecture whose overall truth was so evident—supported as it was by facts and arguments from paleontology, embryology, comparative anatomy, and geographic distribution of plants and animals—that overnight most scientists and a large segment of the educated public embraced the notion that evolution

has occurred. Yet for all the evidence that Darwin adduced in the *Origin* his main argument, that life has evolved, sprang from his promulgation of the process of natural selection, a notion that still lies at the center of modern evolutionary theory. It is both ironic and instructive that whereas the basic idea of evolution was accepted in most quarters immediately upon publication of the *Origin* Darwin's notion of natural selection sustained withering criticism from the outset and continues to attract critics to the present day. Thus it is something of an oversimplification to conclude that Darwin succeeded when all others failed to convince the world that life had evolved because he, and he alone (save Wallace) had come up with a convincing mechanism to explain how life evolves.

But for all its critics the simple, direct idea of natural selection remains an accurate description of a common dynamic process in nature, based on sound premises and their logical consequences. Selection has been modeled mathematically, mimicked in the laboratory, and analyzed in the wild to such an extent that there can be no doubt of its status as the main source of deterministic change in the evolutionary process.

Natural Selection

Both Darwin and Wallace experienced a sort of "Eureka!" when the concept of natural selection fell into place for each of them. Darwin said that he well remembered the spot in the road where he was riding in his carriage when all became clear. That was in 1838. Wallace saw much the same in a malaria-induced feverish dream on the Spice Island of Ternate in 1858. Both men had read a pamphlet by Thomas Malthus, published in 1798—a tract dealing with the perils of overpopulation in humans. From Malthus they learned of the natural tendency for geometric increase of sexually reproducing organisms, unless breeding was checked by some factor, most obviously food supply. Both men realized that Malthus's analysis of the human condition applied equally well to any sexually reproducing species. Darwin, writing in the *Origin*, calculated that a single fertile pair of elephants would leave 15 million elephants within 500 years, assuming a generation time of one offspring every ten years, which he reckoned was a conservative estimate. The conclusion is obvious: elephants have not overrun the earth; hence there must be some natural check on their potentially geometric increase. Of all the offspring born each generation only some are destined to survive and reproduce. Presumably those individuals best suited to the demands of life that are faced by all organisms of any given species will, on average, be the ones that manage to survive and to reproduce.

Nothing was known about the mechanics of heredity in the mid-nineteenth century. Yet, as Darwin soon discovered, every animal breeder realized two cardinal facts. In each generation there is variation in a breeding population; not all organisms are alike. It was also known that, in general, organisms tend to resemble their parents; some factor of heredity ensures that particular traits of parents are inherited by at least some of their offspring. These two observations had immediate practical consequences in animal husbandry. Darwin begins his *Origin* with an account of variation under domestication, reflecting his apprenticeship at the hands of pigeon fanciers, who were selecting only those organisms that carried the traits they desired to see passed along and even enhanced. Pigeons lacking the desired traits were not allowed to breed. This artificial selection is an exact analogue of natural selection, the only difference lying in the actual agent of selection. In nature, instead of a Master Breeder, there is the competition engendered by a world of finite resources and harsh physical realities, such that only a limited few, those best suited to the exigencies of the day, will manage to reproduce. Their offspring will tend to inherit the characteristics of the parents that led to their success. Yet the variation present in each generation has the effect that, should conditions change and a different spectrum of features prove advantageous, the mindless force of selection will shift gears and begin to favor organisms with a different set of characteristics. It will be they who will tend to out-survive and out-reproduce their conspecifics, and thus it will be their traits that will be passed on to the next generation—not exclusively, but preferentially. Natural selection is deterministic: organisms that do better in coping with life's exigencies produce more offspring, hence, in today's understanding, leave more genes. But natural selection is also stochastic, or probabilistic: only on the average will organisms best suited to the exigencies of life tend to survive and reproduce with greater frequency than those less well matched to their environmental conditions.

Adaptation

The theory Darwin developed offered an alternative, noncreationist explanation of the apparent design in nature: the often remarkably close fit exhibited by an organism's physical make-up, or morphology (*phenotype* in modern terms), and behavior, and the roles played by the organism in extracting energy, surviving, growing, and reproducing in its environment. For the will of a supernatural Creator Darwin substituted the mindless mechanism of natural selection. Change in organic form through time reflects changing adaptations wrought by natural selection working on a groundmass of variation. Evolution to Darwin essentially was adaptation, and the theory of evolution to the present day remains strongly centered on the notion of adaptive origin, maintenance, and modification of organismic phenotypes—the morphologies, behaviors, and physiologies of organisms.

Darwin's ideas on why organisms tend to resemble their parents differed widely from modern concepts of genetics; nor was anything known of the ultimate source of phenotypic variation when Darwin was writing the *Origin*. Beginning around 1900 with the simultaneous rediscovery (by three different geneticists) of the nineteenth-century experiments of the Austrian monk Gregor Mendel, the science of genetics began to develop, quickly bringing a realization that factors of heredity (genes) were located on chromosomes within the nucleus of eukaryotic organisms. Many of the early discoveries of genetics seemed at odds with Darwinian formulations. For example, H. DeVries, a Dutch botanist and cytologist, thought that the conspicuous mutations of the evening primrose *Oenothera* implied that new species could arise by sudden disruptions of the hereditary material of a single organism and that natural selection was consequently an unnecessary construct. Later geneticists argued that mutations were mostly deleterious and large-scale in their effects (these being the easiest to detect in the laboratory), and thus the spectrum of finely intergradational variation required by Darwin, and observed in the wild in many populations of organisms, seemed not to be based on mutation. These and similar apparent incongruities were resolved in the 1920s and 30s, particularly through the efforts of three mathematically inclined geneticists, R. Fisher and J.B.S. Haldane in England and S. Wright in the United States. The way had been paved for a full rapprochement between the traditional Darwinian visualization of the evolutionary process and the understanding of heredity as of the mid-1930s, an understanding that while remaining in outline form in modern genetics has been greatly augmented and partly supplanted by the revolution in molecular biology begun in the 1950s with the analysis of the structure of DNA and the later understanding of the nature of the genetic code itself. Discovery of certain self-organizing aspects of DNA has altered our picture of genetic change to some degree; but it is remarkable that Darwin's basic formulation of natural selection still stands as the major force for maintenance and change of organismic adaptations. Despite great inroads of discovery into the contents of Darwin's "black box" of heredity the essentials of the Darwinian position on adaptation through natural selection remain; his was a genuine discovery of a dynamic process in nature.

The Modern Synthesis

It was T. Dobzhansky who effected the fusion between the new genetics and the Darwinian view, in his book *Genetics and the Origin of Species* (1937). The systematist E. Mayr followed shortly thereafter, in 1942, with his *Systematics and the Origin of Species*. Both zoologists emphasized the essentially adaptive nature of geographic variation within species; Dobzhansky in particular was concerned to link patterns of variation in organismic phenotypes to the principles of genetics. But both zoologists were also concerned to explain patterns of discontinuity in nature—the existence of species and their mode of origin. Their discussions of isolating mechanisms—features of the environment and of organisms themselves that initiate or act to strengthen a separation between two species—added a novel element to evolutionary theory. Both concluded that reproductive isolation is the factor underlying phenotypic gaps between species.

Soon thereafter paleontologist G.G. Simpson attempted a reconciliation between the data of the fossil record and the emerging science of genetics (*Tempo and Mode in Evolution*, 1944). Arguing that gaps between species in the fossil record are for the most part the products of poor preservation, Simpson nonetheless took the gaps between large-scale biological entities, such as families and orders, as reflecting something real about the evolutionary process. In his concept of *quantum evolution* Simpson explained gaps as reflecting the relatively sudden shift in adaptations of a population from one "peak" in the "adaptive landscape" to another, a shift relatively so rapid that most events were not likely to be preserved in the fossil record. Simpson was addressing large-scale features of the evolution of life; earlier, following Darwin's lead, Dobzhansky had written that, however reluctantly, it was necessary to put "a sign of equality" between "microevolution" and "macroevolution." Microevolution—small scale, generation-by-generation change in gene content and frequency within natural populations—reflects the interface between the mechanics of heredity and the principles of population genetics, where the dynamics of natural selection (and the essentially chance effects of "genetic drift") enter in. Macroevolution is generally understood to be large-scale changes in organismic form. The essential ingredient of the Modern Synthesis insofar as macroevolution is concerned was to return to the Darwinian position that macroevolution is nothing but microevolution summed up over geological lengths of time: what small change can be effected within a few generations turns to large-scale change over millions of years. This view essentially reduces the question of evolutionary mechanics to the manageably observable processes of generation-by-generation genetic change. The grand simplicity of this view is one of the strengths, as well as the potential major weakness, of both Darwin's original view and modern evolutionary theory.

Competing macroevolutionary theories, still very much focused on organismic phenotypes, came especially from the paleontologist Otto Schindewolf and the geneticist Richard Goldschmidt, both of whom formulated notions of sudden "jumps" ("saltations") to explain gaps between species, genera, families, orders, and so on. The founders of the Modern Synthesis were concerned to refute saltationist claims and to uphold the Darwinian notion of gradual adaptive modification as the dominant theme in the evolution of life.

Soon after Simpson's work was published, the Modern Synthesis was complete, and evolutionary biology entered a long period of essential agreement based on the original Darwinian formulation of adaptation through natural selection. There have, however, been important advances in the study of selection and adaptation, and there has been, as well, some extension of the important work of Dobzhansky and Mayr on the nature of species and the general problem of discontinuity among biological entities.

Modern Evolutionary Theory

By the 1960s, with the advent of biochemical methods to assay genetic variation, it became apparent that organisms are a good deal more genetically variable than had been expected. In particular for many enzymes there seem to be a number of variations, so many that it has been assumed that many must be "selectively neutral" (i.e. the variants are equally viable, all performing the particular role of the enzyme equally well). Thus the variation can accumulate without the mediation of natural selection, a model of evolutionary change that some have called "non-Darwinian." The existence of variants that are equally functional in a given environment, however, is not on the face of it counter to a Darwinian world view—only, perhaps, to an "ultra-selectionist" perspective that assumes that selection is constantly winnowing all but the very "best" from the environment, a hypermechanized view of biological nature hardly in accord with the experiences of most biologists.

Perhaps more important has been the strengthening of the very notion of natural selection within the mainstream of evolutionary theory. In response to the suggestion that natural selection may work on entire groups of organisms ("group selection") biologist G. Williams presented a careful analysis of the nature of selection and adaptation in his influential book *Adaptation and Natural Selection* (1966). Pointing out that selection can act only on variations that exhibit a spectrum of success at any given moment, Williams attacked the notion that selection can be "for the good of the species," hence cast doubt on the very idea of group selection, claiming that the evidence for such was in any case slight, and the few *bona fide* examples seemed not in any case to be important. Selection operates to maximize the reproductive success of individuals at any moment. Williams's formulation led directly to the "selfish gene" concept of Richard Dawkins, who saw selection acting not so much on phenotypic properties of organisms (which would convey differential reproductive success to the organisms carrying the features) but rather on the underlying "immortal" genes themselves. This view represents a sort of "ultra-Darwinism."

Such formulations of selection theory, when coupled with the analyses of William D. Hamilton (who formulated the theory of kin selection), has led directly to the discipline of sociobiology. The tendency of organisms in social systems to behave cooperatively, and to varying degrees altruistically, is an apparent enigma, particularly from the standpoint of selection acting to benefit organisms, specifically by maximizing the spread of their genes over those of other, conspecific organisms. Hamilton's analyses showed that cooperative, altruistic behavior should be greatest among close relatives (i.e. organisms that share proportionately more genes than would be the case if two organisms were randomly sampled from the population at large). Thus modern trends in selection theory were reconciled with observations of the social structure of a variety of organisms, and sociobiology has become an important empirical and theoretical aspect of modern evolutionary biology. The relationship of sociobiological principles to human sociocultural evolution is highly contentious and beyond the scope of this article.

Another important theme in contemporary evolutionary theory stems from the move by Dobzhansky, Mayr, and others to incorporate the notion of *discontinuity* (between species), especially the idea that species are reproductive communities separate from other such communities and that new species arise from old by a process of speciation. The theory of *punctuated equilibria* represents an application of speciation theory to the fossil record and is based on the observation, known to Darwin and contemporary paleontologists, that most species exhibit little or no change throughout the vast bulk of their histories. Thus adaptive change, rather than being continual, gradual, and progressive, is actually a rare event—and considered, under punctuated equilibria, to

occur generally during speciation—when new reproductive communities form from old ones. The fossil record seems to support the notion that species are discrete entities in time as well as space. Recognition that species may be spatiotemporally bounded, discrete entities has led to a revival of interest in theories of differential species originations and extinctions, thus contributing to patterns of stability and cumulative change of organismic phenotypic attributes through time. For example, trends (linear change through long periods of time, such as increase in brain size in hominid evolution over the past 4 m.y.) are always considered to be the direct result of long-term directional natural selection under Darwinian and synthesis-based evolutionary theory. Yet such trends may well reflect differential survival (and/or origination) of species whose component organisms differ with respect to the phenotypic feature undergoing directional change. Thus natural selection may not be inexorably changing the frequency of the trait on a generation-by-generation basis, but rather only during speciation events, with the bulk of a species's subsequent history marked by little or no change at all. The accumulation of numerous speciation events may lead to the sort of long-term protracted macroevolutionary change we can identify as a trend. The recognition that species are real, spatiotemporally bounded entities increases the number of entities seen to play a role in the evolutionary process. Recent work in molecular biology indicates that the complex organization of the genome contains elements, such as transposons, that are capable of biasing the replication of genetic information and thus of influencing the course of evolution. Several lines of inquiry have been expanding the scope of evolutionary theory beyond the strict, traditional domain of explanation of the maintenance and modification of the phenotypic traits of organisms through time.

See also ADAPTATION; ADAPTIVE RADIATION; GENETICS; GENOTYPE; NON-DARWINIAN EVOLUTION; PHENOTYPE; PHYLOGENY; SOCIOBIOLOGY; SPECIATION; SPECIES. [N.E.]

Further Readings

Darwin, C. (1859) On the Origin of Species. . . . London: Murray.

Dawkins, R. (1976) The Selfish Gene. Oxford: Oxford University Press.

Dobzhansky, T. (1951) Genetics and the Origin of Species, 3rd ed. New York: Columbia University Press.

Eldredge, N. (1985) Time Frames. New York: Simon and Schuster.

Eldredge, N. (1985) Unfinished Synthesis. New York: Oxford University Press.

Futuyma, D.J. (1979) Evolutionary Biology. Sunderland, Mass.: Sinauer.

Mayr, E. (1942) Systematics and the Origin of Species. New York: Columbia University Press.

Simpson, G.G. (1944) Tempo and Mode in Evolution. New York: Columbia University Press.

Simpson, G.C. (1953) The Major Features of Evolution. New York: Columbia University Press.

Williams, G.C. (1966) Adaptation and Natural Selection: A Critique of Some Current Evolutionary Thought. Princeton: Princeton University Press.

EVOLUTIONARY MORPHOLOGY

Study of the morphology of organisms in a comparative biological perspective and in accordance with evolutionary theory. All systematic studies are based on descriptive morphology, but creating accurate descriptions for taxa often depends on a comparative framework. Successful endeavors in this field must be a blend of traditional comparative and descriptive morphology and the newest concepts of functional and ecological morphology, and they must be handled within the framework of the theoretical principles of evolution and phylogeny.

For a balanced perspective on any morphological characteristic one must take into account three distinct yet interrelated constraints: 1) the morphogenetic constraints that manifest themselves through the biochemical programs of growth patterns and that represent also the constraints of physical organizations; 2) the functional-adaptive constraints that result from organism-environment interactions; and 3) the phylogenetic constraints (the history-related morphogenetic constraints) that exert a profound influence on all characters of organisms. All of these are completely compatible with the neoDarwinian synthesis of population evolution by various genetic mechanisms and natural selection.

The foundations of evolutionary morphology are descriptive and comparative morphology, ideally undertaken within the context of definite questions of function, ecological or behavioral adaptation, and phylogeny or of some hypothesis relating to principles of evolutionary change. "Pure" descriptions, or descriptions from the old comparative anatomical literature, lack this conceptual orientation and therefore are usually of little use. Comparisons and new descriptions often yield not only new basic information but also new insights into unsolved problems. Clearly definite questions, and attempts to solve them, are not possible in all descriptive studies. Yet this problem-oriented framework can make a description of scientific value. The success of a descriptive and comparative study thus is often dependent more on the characters chosen and the questions posed than on the descriptive details it may provide.

Functional anatomy within evolutionary morphology is concerned primarily with understanding the mechanical properties of morphology, and it interdigitates with physiological studies. Separating the concepts of form and function is difficult. Form is usually understood as the material shape and structure of parts of organisms, function as all the chemical and physical properties of a specified form.

Ecological and behavioral morphology, within evolutionary morphology, concerns itself with an organism's form-function in the natural environment and the selectional forces that may be responsible, among other factors, for the nature of its characters. For example, reasons for the existence of an enlarged hyoid bone in the throat of howler monkeys become clear only when territorial interactions, through intimidating howling, are observed in nature. Thus the environmentally related aspect of a character, its relation to specific selectional forces, is referred to as its *biological role* or *biorole*, a concept distinct from physiological or mechanical function. Students of evolution must have some ideas of the bioroles of features before they can begin to understand their evolutionary history.

A concept of fundamental importance in evolutionary morphology is that of *homology*. Because equivalent parts or areas of organisms are studied, one must understand what those equivalencies are. Given the fact of organic evolution, organisms possess attributes that have remained relatively unchanged, or that at least can be identified as equivalents, from their common ancestor. We term these attributes *homologies* or *homologues*. A theoretical definition of a homologous feature in two or more organisms would specify that homologues are features hypothesized to have been present in the last common ancestor of the specified organisms. The operational, or practical, testing of such hypotheses is a complex biological research undertaking that in the final analysis is based on the recognition and evaluation of various kinds of similarities between the proposed homologues. Rejecting a set of observed similarities as a homology turns this hypothesis into a hypothesis of independent evolution of those features—in other words, *convergence*. It is important to realize that homology is not an intrinsic property of an aspect of an animal. It is a specified relationship that depends on corresponding aspects (parts, behaviors, biochemistry, etc.) of other species. Students of morphology, therefore, must clearly specify the conditions of homology. Nails at the end of the digits are *euprimate* homologies, the conditional statement telling us that it was the last common ancestor of euprimates in which this feature appeared.

The essence of evolutionary morphology is the

intimate interplay of accurate descriptive, comparative, and functional anatomy, all within the conceptual discipline of systematic biology. A close feedback exists between these activities and the observation of bioroles in free living organisms.

See also **PALEOBIOLOGY**. [F.S.S.]

Further Readings

Bock, W.J. (1977) Adaptation and the comparative method. In M. Hecht, P. Goody, and E. Hecht (eds.): Major Patterns in Vertebrate Evolution. New York: Plenum.

EVOLUTIONARY SYSTEMATICS

Study of the biological diversity of organisms and all kinds of relationships among them. This is sometimes considered distinct from *taxonomy*, the theoretical study of classification, its foundations, procedures, and rules. Taxonomy, however, is clearly dependent on the results of systematic studies. Lines of distinction are sometimes difficult to draw between students who practice Hennigian, or "cladistic," systematics and those who adhere to what has been dubbed the Simpsonian, or "evolutionary," school. The issues are much more complicated than these labels imply, since both cladistic and evolutionary systematists are interested in unraveling the one and only history of organisms. The theoretical perspectives on which they base their analyses are different, and they also have distinct preferences about how to translate a phylogeny into a practical classification.

Phylogeneticists (both the cladists and evolutionists believe that the core aim of systematics should be the understanding of phylogeny) base their hypotheses on the understanding of homologous characters. Yet the word *phylogeny* means different things to cladistic and evolutionary systematists. For evolutionists phylogeny means the history of organisms—their "descent with modification," as Darwin called it—or the path of this history. This view of genealogy includes both the ancestor-descendant and the sister-group relationships that result from a split lineage. Evolutionists concentrate their research efforts on character analysis, in order to understand or explain the most probable path of transformation of homologous characters.

Before the analytical aspect of character analysis can really begin, systematists must ascertain the distribution of the characters studied, their pattern, in all taxa. But rather than rely only on simple rules to make sense of character evolution—i.e. which characters were primitive (ancestral or plesiomorph) and which advanced (derived or apomorph)—various approaches are used to establish a degree of confidence in a proposed phylogeny of homologous char-

acters. These research programs attempt to understand not only *what* characters are available but also *how* they function, *why* they survived in nature, and (as the fossil record permits) *when* they appeared. All these studies have important bearing on the interpretation of the evolution of characters.

Evolutionary systematists believe that the evolutionary process results in either stasis or evolution and that the result of the process is ultimately the modification of descendants relative to their ancestors. The path of descent—i.e. how species are related to one another given that the relationships can be of either the ancestor-descendant or sister-group kind—which is a consequence of evolution, results in the enormous variety of organisms that lived in the past and are extant today. To understand this history evolutionary systematists interpret the known samples of living and fossil organisms in the light of what we know of all available and relevant biological and evolutionary processes. The pattern, as evolutionists understand it, is only the evidence (data) retrieved from the study of the organisms themselves. The *interpretation* of this pattern, even the identification of what is or is not a species different from others, is completely process-dependent, or at least based on process-dependent assumptions. In other words, assumptions based on biological and evolutionary processes are used to make interpretations in all aspects of systematic activity. The demonstration of the "pattern" of phylogeny is the result of a process-steeped analytical procedure and not something that can be credibly accomplished with the use of a simple assumption that evolution is a fact.

Evolutionary systematists believe that because much evolutionary change is adaptive understanding the functional-adaptive aspect of the characters of organisms helps in understanding the evolution of many different but homologous characters. Ancestral conditions often leave unmistakable influence in altered features, particularly if the features are complicated ones.

Phylogeneticists who lean more toward an evolutionary process-steeped systematics, and who do not believe that a meaningful separation of systematics from evolutionary theory is desirable or possible, concentrate on understanding character transformation (evolution) of the organisms they study. Any information from biological and paleontological studies that bears on the extinct and extant samples may hold significant clues for the probability of one as opposed to another transformation. With the knowledge of as many character transformations (i.e. character phylogenies) as possible, using shared and derived features weighted in a biologically *a priori* manner (complex features being most valuable and simple or "loss" characters the least useful), the systematist constructs a taxon phylogeny, using both sister-group and ancestor-descendant concepts for the taxa themselves.

The classifications constructed by evolutionists (phylogeneticists, some "evolutionary cladists," etc.) attempt to reflect evolutionary history, both the history of branching and descent as well as the extent of divergence (from a measure of dissimilarity) and relative size of the adaptive radiation, as much as this is possible in a classification. Evolutionists understand that they are aiming to discover phylogeny and not to construct a classification that singlemindedly reflects the latest branching hypothesis. This latter goal, while arguably impossible to achieve on a piece of paper, is shunned primarily because it simply attempts to duplicate in words a cladogram or a phylogenetic tree.

Only groups that comprise the last common ancestor of included species are constructed (*monophyletic groups*). Whenever information permits and traditional channels of communications justify this, all the descendants of a common ancestor are included in a group (*holophyletic groups*). Groups that represent the initial radiation of the close relatives of some successful descendants (e.g. the primate family Omomyidae), but of which the exact affinities of its various subgroups to later descendants are not clear, are contained in monophyletic taxa that do not include all the descendants (*paraphyletic groups*) of the last common ancestor. Paraphyletic groups (sometimes called *horizontal taxa*) can also be justified by their utility in allowing future readjustments of group relationships without the necessity for an entirely new classification, which a cladistic system would dictate. Paraphyletic taxa are often well diagnosed by their derived attributes compared with their ancestry and by the primitive characters that are shared by their varied descendants that diversified from one another. Although paraphyletic taxa are often a practical necessity, their use along with holophyletic taxa allows compatibility with traditional systems of classifications, while permitting steady refinements to incorporate new understanding of both the extinct and extant record, without attempting to treat fossils as some peculiar manifestations of life as some cladistic classifications have done.

See also CLADISTICS; CLASSIFICATION; EVOLUTIONARY MORPHOLOGY; MONOPHYLY; PHYLOGENY; STRATOPHENETICS; SYSTEMATICS. [F.S.S.]

Further Readings

Bock, W.J. (1977) Foundations and methods of evolutionary classification. In M. Hecht, P. Goody, and E. Hecht (eds.): Major Patterns in Vertebrate Evolution. New York: Plenum.

Bock, W.J. (1981) Functional-adaptive analysis in evolutionary classification. Am. Zool. 21:5–20.

EXOTICS

Archaeological materials, especially lithics, originating at distances of more than 30 km. from the site where they are found. While rare exotic stones are present even in the oldest Paleolithic sites, such as Olduvai Gorge, their scarcity at Early and Middle Paleolithic sites and the lack of patterning in either the use of these materials or in the directionality of the sources suggest that their presence at the sites resulted from the mobility of groups occupying the sites. The voluminous presence of different kinds of exotics (lithics, marine shells, amber) found at many Late Paleolithic sites, the special use made of these nonlocal materials, and the disparate but patterned sources of origin for these materials all suggest that these exotics were transported via exchange networks and that their distribution at the sites reflects past social relationships rather than mobility of the groups themselves.

See also JEWELRY; LATE PALEOLITHIC. [O.S.]

EXPERIMENTAL ARCHAEOLOGY *see* LITHIC-USE-WEAR; STONE-TOOL MAKING

EXTINCTION

In biology, the cessation of existence of taxa. Extinction of species, like the appearance of new species, is a natural process reflecting changes in the environment, biotic and abiotic.

In simple terms extinction follows after all breeding populations in a group are reduced to levels from which they cannot recover. This may occur in a *catastrophic extinction*, when mortality rates are so extreme, due to some unusual circumstance, that death overtakes all viable members of an otherwise flourishing species in a few generations. On the other hand extinction may occur periodically, even without major change in environmental conditions. This is *background extinction*, which (without begging the question) is primarily associated with a reduction in individual numbers. With reduced numbers inbreeding makes the genetic pool less stable. Runaway genetic drift may spread lethal or inhibiting variations throughout the population faster than selection can compensate, leading to a final crash. A second factor in background extinctions is the obvious fact that, all considerations being equal, a small population is also inherently less likely to survive any given environmental crisis than a larger population. The distinction between catastrophic and background extinction, aside from a perhaps illusory perception that they involve different rates of population decline, is that catastrophic extinctions involve many species, and thus higher taxonomic categories, more or less simultaneously. Analysis of background extinctions generally involves a search for specific causative factors in ecology and interspecific adaptations, whereas the study of catastrophic extinctions tends to focus on geologic and even planetary factors.

Competition and Extinction

Since favorable as well as unfavorable variations are fixed more rapidly in smaller groups, crises that isolate parts of a population or reduce its numbers overall tend to stimulate evolution as well as background extinctions. In other words extinction is often accompanied by origination as part of the same wider process. The reduction in numbers that precedes extinction is most often due to other environmental factors, such as disease, community disruption, or climatic change. The concept of *competitive extinction* is greatly overdrawn from dramatic examples (e.g. the replacement of the native red squirrel by the imported grey in northwestern Europe). The special case in competitive extinction known as *evolutionary replacement*, or competitive exclusion of an ancestral species by a daughter species, is even less common and seems to be mainly a projection of the Victorian world view upon the face of nature.

In the case of catastrophic extinctions the empty niche may not be immediately filled, if ever. The fossil record shows, for instance, that the disappearance of the predaceous dinosaurs left a world without carnivores in the earliest Tertiary, a niche that was filled first by giant flightless raptors, the phororacids, and only after several million years by mammalian carnivores. In less drastic catastrophes and in background extinction it is often the case that a new species will arise from a declining species, which then moves into the abandoned niche. While this looks like competitive replacement, it may in fact be simple opportunism by a species preadapted by its inheritance. As evidence for opportunistic rather than competitive replacement in the fossil record several instances have been documented in which an extinct species, or group, is replaced by a species that is demonstrably less fit than its immediate precursor.

Living Fossils and Extinction Rates

Some species, in particular the various "living fossils," have a remarkable amount of redundancy in their genetic code, such that inbreeding has less effect and relatively few individuals can make up a viable population. This confers upon the species a degree of immunity from extinction. In such lineages genetic variability gradually decreases through feedback from reiterated selection for a highly successful phenotype. The potential for adaptation is sup-

pressed for the sake of stabilizing a successful model that is able to survive almost any disaster. In the opposite strategy some long-lived groups are unusually labile, replacing one species with another at every minor opportunity.

Extinction rates may be measured in *macarthurs*, or taxonomic units per million years. (These are not named after the general whose most famous words were "Old soldiers never die, they just fade away," but in honor of R.H. MacArthur, whose 1972 book *Geographical Ecology* described modern extinction dynamics as expounded here.) When averaged over large groupings, such as the mollusks or mammals, or (using higher categories, such as families) over all life forms, extinction rates have been cited as an indication of changes in global environment. Since a family or order survives in the fossil record if a single one of its species survives, analysis at higher taxonomic levels is most sensitive to catastrophic extinction, with its attendant geological implications.

Mass Extinctions

Major catastrophic extinctions, in which over 20 percent of animal families (meaning over 50 percent of species and nearly all individuals) disappear from the face of the globe, have always been interesting subjects of debate. The best known of these in the fossil record is at the end of the Cretaceous, marked by the extinction of the "dinosaurs" (a set of large vertebrates whose only common characteristic is that they did not survive into the Cenozoic) and diverse marine invertebrate groups. Other groups, such as the planktonic foraminifera, survived this event with just one species. The evidence now supports a massive bolide impact as the proximal cause, but it is also clear that this final blow came during a period of lowered sea level, greatly reduced diversity among many groups (the pterosaurs, for instance, had declined to just a few giant, highly specialized species), and high environmental stress.

Three other mass extinctions of this magnitude are recorded: at the end of the Ordovician, within the later Devonian, and near the end of the Triassic; but even these pale in comparison with the great mass extinction at the end of the Permian, in which more than 50 percent of families and perhaps as many as 96 percent of all marine animal species were eliminated. A lesser, but very noticeable, wave of extinctions marked the end of the Eocene, known as the "Grand Coupure" in land-mammal faunas. The beginning of the Cambrian, when shelled life-forms appeared in abundance in a number of unrelated phyla, may also have followed an extinction event. These catastrophic extinctions occurred, as in the end-Cretaceous, during periods of lowered sea level and worldwide environmental stress, and in some there is again evidence of massive bolide strikes. It may be that collisions with large meteorites are not rare, on the geological scale, but that only those impacting during periods of ecological disruption can synchronize a wave of extinctions among groups that are struggling to survive.

Evidence has been cited for periodicity in mass extinctions at ca. 29 m.y., which may, moreover, coincide with the near approach of a normally undetectable dwarf companion of the sun aptly termed Nemesis. As with many other periodicities, however, the data have been criticized as being selected from a nonrandom context.

Pleistocene Overkill

The extinction of many groups of large mammals at the end of the Pleistocene has engendered spirited debate among anthropologists. Many view this wave of extinctions as the result of human predation. Others, citing the need for scientific caution, have objected to drawing such conclusions from the available, mainly circumstantial, evidence. Behind scientific caution, however, many in the second camp have expressed a reluctance to convict preagricultural peoples of such wanton environmental vandalism, considering the fact that in existing hunting-gathering cultures, such as the Inuit and !Kung, there is a functional equilibrium between large-prey species and hunting pressure.

In the most recent instances of preindustrial human colonization of large unspoiled territories, the case against unsophisticated humankind, armed with nothing more than the Neolithic hunting kit, appears to be irrefutable. In Madagascar, New Zealand, and Hawaii, the most recently colonized lands, subfossil remains and local survivors give unequivocal testimony of far-reaching extermination of diverse endemic faunas beginning with the first few generations of human settlement. In some instances these depredations are further documented in oral histories, as in clear descriptions of the extinct flightless moa in Maori legend. The remains of highly diverse and specialized faunas, no longer with us, have also been found in prehistoric kitchen middens on New Caledonia, Hispaniola, Sardinia, and Taiwan.

Objectors have pointed to the large regions with hunter cultures, such as Australia, New Guinea, and the "jungle" regions of Southeast Asia and Africa, as areas where the late Pleistocene extinction rates among large vertebrates have not been extraordinary, and humans live in harmony with nature. The last two are regions with a long period of human habitation, however, and the hunted fauna may be adapted to preindustrial human predation so that harmony is more "could not" than "would not." In the case of Australia it happens that recent discoveries in Kow Swamp and elsewhere document a remarkable Pleistocene fauna of much greater variety than the present, dominated not by the lean and speedy kangaroo but by giant, slow-moving marsupials and a "komodo dragon" top predator, which vanished in the past 20 k.y.

P.S. Martin, a leading student of Pleistocene extinctions, has pointed out that the sudden decline in large-mammal species that followed human immigration into North America, from 79 to 22, was not only catastrophic in the definition given above but was also unaccompanied by significant extinctions in parts of the ecology (perching birds, plants, small mammals, fish) that are less affected by human predation. Worldwide the timing of large-mammal extinctions during the last glacial and postglacial, down to the colonization of outlying islands noted above, also can be shown to follow the expansion of human populations. Martin has noted that "overkill" may be associated with the abundance and innocence of prey species and the absence of real or cultural limits on human population and behavior in the first phase of colonization. The "harmony" seen in existing hunting cultures comes later, like the new sense of ecological management in industrial societies, as the remaining prey becomes more difficult to secure.

The most dramatic evidence of late Pleistocene overkill may be the sudden wave of extinction in the Proboscidea, an extremely diverse and successful group with a pan-global distribution. At the beginning of the late Wisconsinian, ca. 25 k.y., proboscidean species in four distinct families—elephantids (mammoths and forest elephants), mammutids, mastodonts, and stegodonts—were dominant elements in the megafauna of all continents but Australasia. By the time the Wisconsinian expansion of humans was over, ca. 10 k.y. ago, the proboscidean fauna of the "new lands" in North America, South America, and northern Eurasia was gone, and just two reclusive species of forest elephants survived in southern Asia and Africa. In many areas from which proboscideans suddenly vanished—the Ukraine, Siberia, and North America—the archaeological record of Neolithic hunters begins with evidence of predation on these "walking meat lockers," as they have been called. Neolithic innovations in weapons, technology, and social structure may have launched an "elephant rush" that carried humankind across the Bering Straits in pursuit of a dwindling resource.

Modern Extinctions

Studies of global mass extinctions indicate a possible variety of causes. Dramatically sudden catastrophes appeal to the imagination, but in most instances detailed study of the fossils and strata suggests that mass extinctions actually represent an increase in extinction rates over an appreciable, if geologically short, interval of several million years, punctuated (as it may be) by a few years of Armageddon resulting from a bolide impact. To give a sense of scale to the word "short" in this context, the changes in land and marine biota from 25 to 5 k.y., as the result of Pleistocene climate change and Neolithic predation, would seem catastrophically rapid and extensive in the Cretaceous context. These 20 k.y. of rapid change are recorded in ca. 20 cm. of seafloor sediments, or ca. 5 m. of alluvial terrace deposits, at average deposition rates. By comparison the geometric increase in preemptively farmed acreage over the past 500 years, let alone the impact of industrialization and urbanization in the last 100 years, has wrought a global transformation of environment and biota that would be recorded as the greatest dislocation ever seen, in less than a centimeter of strata in the deep-sea record. Since change at this pace must soon end, one may wonder what new balance will be recorded in the meters of deep-ocean sediment that will overlie this final single stratum.

See also GRAND COUPURE; PLEISTOCENE; SPECIATION. [J.A.V.C.]

Further Readings

Elliott, D.K., ed. (1986) The Dynamics of Extinction. New York: Wiley.

Hallam, A. (1984) The causes of mass extinctions. Nature 308:686–687.

Martin, P.S., and Klein, R.G., eds. (1984) Quaternary Extinctions. Tucson: University of Arizona Press.

Unwin, D.K. (1986) Extinction—back to basics. Mod. Geol. 10:261–270.

EXUDATIVORY *see* DIET

EYASI

Hominid remains recovered in Tanzania between 1935 and 1938. Parts of at least two crania were found, and there has recently been dispute about their age and significance. They appear to represent late middle or early late Pleistocene nonmodern hominids, with a long, low skull and large brows but an occipital torus morphology with some modern characteristics. Discoveries from Ngaloba (Tanzania) and Eliye Springs (Kenya) may represent the same East African hominid population.

See also ARCHAIC HOMO SAPIENS. [C.B.S.]

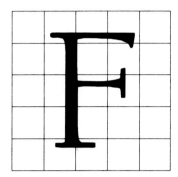

FAMILY

Principal family-group category of the classificatory hierarchy, falling immediately below the superfamily and above the subfamily. The *International Code of Zoological Nomenclature* requires that all family names end in the suffix "-idae."

See also CLASSIFICATION; NOMENCLATURE. [I.T.]

FAR EAST *see* ASIA (EASTERN)

FAYUM

Eocene to Oligocene stratified sequence in northern Egypt. The fossil beds crop out in an escarpment over 500 m. high on the northwest side of the Fayum Depression, a gigantic wind-excavated bowl on the west side of the Nile Valley just south of Cairo. The Fayum sequence is exposed in a series of bluffs and broad benches rising from the shore of Birket Qarun, a below-sea-level lake that is the largest in North Africa. The lowest of the benches marks the top of the Qasr el Sagha Formation, a deltaic near-shore facies of middle or late Eocene age that succeeds the marine middle Eocene Mokattam Beds. Whale bones from these beds were the first vertebrate fossils found in Africa, reported in the 1870s by the botanist Georg Schweinfurth. The formation has also yielded remains of sea cows, proboscideans, barytheres, and some smaller terrestrial animals, such as creodont carnivores, but no primates. Correlative beds, with a similar vertebrate fauna, are also exposed in eastern Libya at Zella and Dor el-Talha.

Resting on the deltaic beds are the continental, coastal plain deposits of the Jebel Qatrani Formation (named after the "Hill of Tar," an inlier with a capping of black basalt). Serious collecting in these beds was begun by the British Museum (Natural History) at the turn of the century and continued with major expeditions from the American Museum of Natural History. After 1960 work resumed under the direction of E.L. Simons, first at Yale and later at Duke University. The formation has yielded thousands of specimens in a magnificent representation of large and small African land mammals, including a wide diversity of tethytheres (sirenians, hyraxes, proboscideans, barytheres, moeritheres): the unique rhinoceroslike *Arsinoitherium*; anthracotheres, southern rodents, bats, pantolestids, elephant shrews, and primates; together with late Eocene immigrants from western Eurasia, such as creodonts, didelphid marsupials, and a pangolin. (Conceivably the omomyidlike primate in this fauna was also an immigrant from the Eurasian side.) Unconformably capping the uppermost bench of the Jebel Qatrani Formation is the Widan al-Faras Basalt, most recently dated at 31 m.y., and above that the barren, unfossiliferous plain underlain by sandy beds of the Miocene Kashab Formation.

The Fayum environment was that of a shallow sea bordered by moist tropical coastal forest growing on a sandy substrate. Fossil plants are extremely abundant and together with the inferred habitats of the fossil mammals and lower vertebrates indicate estuarine river-gallery forests, with large vine-draped trees and mangroves, in an area of sharply seasonal rainfall drained by slow-moving tidal rivers. The Nile River system did not then exist and local drainage was westward into a proto-Sirtean Gulf.

Fossil primates from the Fayum come from three

View of the Jebel Qatrani Formation (early Oligocene) in Fayum Province (Egypt). The line of cliffs in the background is capped by a basalt layer dated at ca. 31 m.y. (Photography courtesy of J.G. Fleagle.)

distinct levels in the Jebel Qatrani Formation. Faunal turnover from the lowest level to the middle is high, indicating significant elapsed time, but there is little difference between the middle and upper level faunas. In the lowest levels ca. 100 m. above the deltaic Eocene beds occur remains of a possible omomyid, as well as the parapithecid *Qatrania* and *Oligopithecus*, a primate of undetermined affinities. This level is generally called the "lower fossil wood zone" because of the abundance of large silicified tree trunks.

In the middle levels of the Jebel Qatrani Formation are found remains of the parapithecid *Apidium* as well as *Propliopithecus*, with dental characteristics that place it near the ancestry of all later catarrhines. More advanced species of *Apidium* and the parapithecid *Parapithecus* (?including *Simonsius*) occur in the upper level together with *Propliopithecus* and *Aegyptopithecus*. Also from the upper level are sparse remains of a possible lorisid and a very small primate, *Afrotarsius*, which may quite possibly be a little-modified survivor of the protoanthropoid stock.

See also Catarrhini; Lorisoidea; Oligocene; Oligopithecus; Omomyidae; Parapithecidae; Propliopithecidae; Tarsiidae. [R.F.K., J.A.V.C.]

Further Readings

Bown, T.M., Krause, M.J., Fleagle, J.T., Tiffany, B., and Simons, E.L. (1982) The Fayum primate forest revisited. J. Hum. Evol. *11*:603–632.

Fleagle, J.G., Bown, T.M., Obradovich, J.D., and Simons, E.L. (1986) How old are the Fayum primates? In J.G. Else and P.C. Lee (eds.): Primate Evolution. Cambridge: Cambridge University Press, pp. 3–17.

FELLS CAVE

Stratified Paleoindian archaeological site in the Straits of Magellan (Chile). Excavated by J. Bird in the 1930s, Fells Cave contained the bones of horse and guanaco, as well as distinctive Fells Cave fishtailed projectile points and ground-stone disks. The site suggests that humans had reached the tip of South America between 11,000 and 10,000 B.P.

See also Americas; Paleoindian. [L.S.A.P., D.H.T.]

FENDANTIA   *see*   LORISOIDEA

FENNOSCANDIAN GLACIATIONS   *see* GLACIATION; PLEISTOCENE

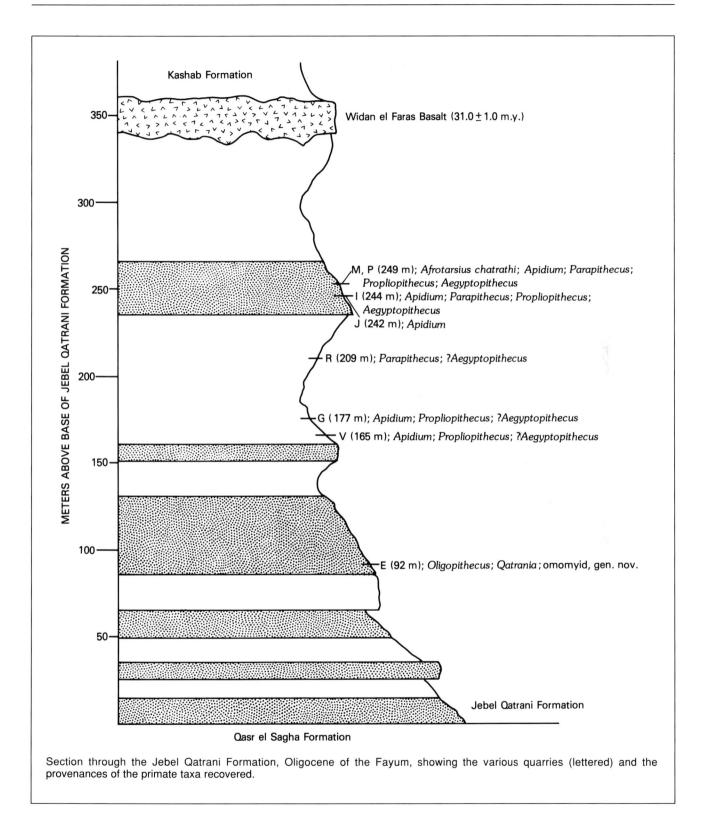

Section through the Jebel Qatrani Formation, Oligocene of the Fayum, showing the various quarries (lettered) and the provenances of the primate taxa recovered.

FERRASSIE MOUSTERIAN *see*
MOUSTERIAN

FERTILE CRESCENT *see*
DOMESTICATION; NEAR EAST; NEOLITHIC

FIRE

One of the most important technological innovations during the course of human evolution was the controlled use of fire, which played a critical role in the spread of hominid populations out of Africa and into colder climates.

The benefits of fire production were enormous. It could be used to provide warmth; to produce light; to cook foods to increase digestibility, kill parasites, or detoxify; to keep away dangerous animals and pests; to drive game; to work wood and other materials; and to rejuvenate stands of plants. Many anthropologists have also stressed the strong socialization pressures on a group of hominids clustered around a fire. Finally, the control of fire was a prerequisite for two critical technological innovations: pottery and metallurgy.

The earliest evidence of the hominid use of fire is controversial. One major problem is finding distinctive features in the archaeological record that can serve as certain evidence of deliberate fires. Even in the modern and recent ethnographic record fireplaces used for warmth or cooking are not always elaborate affairs that would leave a lasting record over time. Human-made fires may be large or quite small; often they are casual affairs burned on the surface of the ground, perhaps used very briefly; or they may be made in shallow pits dug in the ground. The stone-lined hearth commonly associated with camp fires is by no means universal and may be a relatively recent phenomenon in prehistory.

Proposed evidence for hominid use of fire includes charcoal; baked (hardened and usually discolored) sediment; thermally altered bones and/or stones; and a feature like a hearth structure (usually a concentrated area of ash and charcoal, sometimes bordered by rocks).

By the Middle Paleolithic there is fairly widespread evidence for controlled use of fire by human groups, but prior to 150 k.y. ago this evidence is controversial. The ash and charcoal produced by fires do not survive well in the early prehistoric record, particularly in tropical regions where organic materials are in general highly perishable. In the case of fires used for long or successive periods of time, especially with very hot fires, there may be localized baking and discoloration, particularly reddening, of the underlying earth. In the absence of deliberate hearth structures, though, it can be difficult to distinguish the results of natural brushfires from evidence of fire produced by human agency. Nevertheless, prehistoric investigators have found several intriguing indications of the possible control of fire in the Early Paleolithic.

The claims for the earliest evidence come from Africa. Localized areas of apparently baked sediment have been discovered at Koobi Fora and Chesowanja (Kenya), ca. 1.5 m.y. old. Paleomagnetic studies of realignment of iron-oxide minerals suggest baking of these patches of sediment but remain inconclusive and await further testing. Paleomagnetic evidence from the Acheulean site of Gadeb (Ethiopia) is also equivocal but could point toward baking of discolored stones in a fire. However, distinguishing these from baked areas that could be produced by natural brushfires in such deposits may prove difficult. Paleomagnetic analysis of some cone-shaped baked patches of earth near sites in the Middle Awash Valley (Ethiopia) does indicate burning, but their shape may indicate natural burning of tree stumps.

During the middle Pleistocene several sites in Africa, Asia, and Europe appear to show signs of more habitual use of fire. Some of the best known are Zhoukoudian (China), Vértesszöllös (Hungary), Vallonnet Cave, Lazaret, and Terra Amata (France), and Kalambo Falls (Zambia), although some researchers are skeptical that all of these represent solid evidence of hominid-controlled fire. At Zhoukoudian the evidence has been recently thrown into question. Many levels with ash deposits have been identified, not in localized hearths but in layers, some of them quite extensive and several meters deep. Binford has suggested that these layers may represent spontaneous combustion of deposits of organic material or guano left in the cave by owls or other raptors. The burned bones reported from the cave could then be coincidental casualties of smoldering fires engulfing bone brought in by hominids, carnivores, or other agencies and not represent refuse of cooked food. The problem needs further investigation, including analysis of the probable temperature of the fires and a critical investigation of whether spontaneously combusted fires would be likely to account for the repeated, extensive ash deposits in the cave. The lack of structured hearths and the possible use of living space in a way unlike that in later periods of time are problematic here, but unfortunately we do not know what the cultural remains associated with the early use of fire should look like.

There are other early sites with reported evidence for fire in Asia, including Xihoudu, Lantian, and Yuanmou. At Xihoudu the evidence is in the form of discolored mammalian ribs, antlers, and cracked horse teeth. These black, grey, and grey-green specimens have been analyzed and interpreted as charred bone. At Lantian a wood ash and bits of charcoal have been reported in a layer slightly above one yielding a fossil hominid cranium, and the site of Yuanmou has yielded apparent charcoal and burned bone. While such finds remain problematic in view of the questions being raised about the hominid origins of all fires, the prevalence of such evidence is interesting and suggestive.

In Europe two small hearths situated in an apparent hut structure have been reported at Lazaret (France). Likewise, the nearby site of Terra Amata in

Nice has features apparently involving charcoal and burned bone in depressions partially lined with rocks that have been interpreted as hearth structures. At the site of Vértesszöllös (Hungary) fragments of burned bone have suggested the use of fire.

The evidence for relatively early hominid control of fire during the Early Paleolithic is suggestive, although not overwhelming as yet. A traditional view has been that the hominids' spread out of tropical Africa into the colder, temperate regions of the Old World was hindered until they gained mastery over the use and making of fire. As yet we do not have enough evidence to support or refute this hypothesis. It is likely—although again there is no definite evidence—that the earliest hominid populations to use fires first experimented with maintaining those produced by such natural phenomena as lightning strikes, spontaneous combustion, and volcanic events, before they actually understood the logistics of producing fire.

Ethnographically the most common form of fire making is by the drill technique of twirling one piece of wood into another to produce enough friction to make the wood dust or kindling smolder. This is usually enhanced by blowing until the material flames up. More elaborate forms of fire making by friction include the bow-drill, pump-drill, saw, and plow techniques. Striking a flint against an iron-rich rock, such as a pyrite, can also produce a spark that can be used to light kindling. Such pyrites are known from the Late Paleolithic.

See also ACHEULEAN; ASIA (EASTERN); CHESOWANJA; EAST TURKANA; KALAMBO FALLS; LANTIAN; LAZARET; PALEOMAGNETISM; VALLONNET; XIHOUDOU; YUANMOU; ZHOUKOUDIAN. [N.T., K.S.]

Further Readings

Barbetti, M. (1987) Traces of fire in the archaeological record, before one million years ago. J. Hum. Evol. 15:771–781.

Binford, L.R. and Ho, C.K. (1985) Taphonomy at a distance: Zhoukoudian, "The Cave Home of Beijing Man"? Curr. Anthropol. 26:413–442.

Clark, J.D. and Harris, J.W.K. (1985) Fire and its roles in early hominid lifeways. Afr. Archaeol. Rev. 3:3–27.

Gowlett, J.A.J. (1984) Ascent to Civilization: The Archaeology of Early Man. New York: Random House.

Harrison, H.S. (1967) Fire-making, fuel, and lighting. In C. Singer, E.J. Holmyard, and A.R. Hall (eds.): A History of Technology, Vol. 1. Oxford: Clarendon, pp. 216–237.

Jia, L. (1980) Early Man in China. Beijing: Foreign Languages Press.

Oakley, K.P. (1956) Fire as a palaeolithic tool and weapon. Proceed. Prehistoric Soc. 21:36–48.

Perlès, C. (1981) Hearth and home in the Old Stone Age. Nat. Hist. 90:38–41.

Shipman, P., Foster, G., and Schoeninger, M. (1984) Burnt bones and teeth: an experimental study of color, morphology, crystal structure and shrinkage. J. Archaeol. Sci. 11:307–325.

FIRST INTERMEDIATE

Term proposed at the Third Pan-African Congress in 1955 to refer to a group of African Paleolithic industries intermediate between the Acheulean or Early Stone Age, and the Middle Stone Age industries, such as Lupemban and Stillbay. The term includes the Sangoan, Fauresmith, and Acheuleo-Levalloisian industries with evolved bifaces, picks, and Levallois or other prepared-core technologies. Since the contemporaneity of these industries is no longer accepted, it has been recommended that the term be dropped.

See also ACHEULEAN; EARLY PALEOLITHIC; EARLY STONE AGE; LEVALLOIS; LUPEMBAN; MIDDLE PALEOLITHIC; MIDDLE STONE AGE; SANGOAN; SECOND INTERMEDIATE; STILLBAY. [A.S.B.]

FISSION-TRACK DATING *see* GEOCHRONOMETRY

FITNESS, INCLUSIVE *see* SOCIOBIOLOGY

FLAKE

Characteristic spall removed from a stone core during artifact manufacture. A flake is characterized by a striking platform or butt; a dorsal surface that may exhibit scars of previous flake removals from a core; and a ventral (release) surface with a bulb (semicone) of percussion, bulbar scar (*éraillure*), ripples or waves curving away from the point of percussion, and fissures or hackle marks radiating out from the point of percussion (see illustration in STONE-TOOL MAKING). Flakes may represent by-products of tool manufacture, may be tools in their own right, or may serve as blanks for production of flake tools.

See also CORE; STONE-TOOL MAKING. [N.T., K.S.]

FLAKE-BLADE

Flake nearly twice as long as wide. Flake-blades are characteristic of certain tool industries, such as the late Mousterian, which are probable precursors to the early Upper Paleolithic of France (the Chatelperronian). Normally Mousterian flake-blade industries do not have the standardization and carefully prepared blade-core techniques of true blade industries of the Upper Paleolithic. Some Middle Stone Age industries from South Africa are also characterized by flake-blades.

See also BLADE; CHATELPERRONIAN; FLAKE; MIDDLE STONE AGE; MOUSTERIAN; PREPARED-CORE; STONE-TOOL MAKING; UPPER PALEOLITHIC. [N.T., K.S.]

FLINT *see* RAW MATERIALS

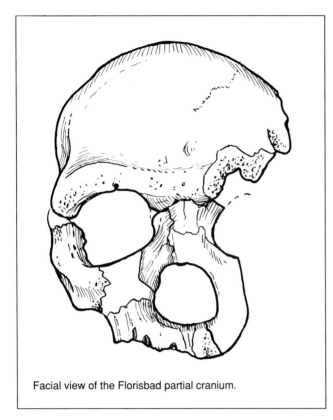

Facial view of the Florisbad partial cranium.

FLORISBAD

South African site near Bloemfontein, where a partial skull was discovered in 1932 from the lowest peat level. The skull has recently been reconstructed more accurately, and its broad frontal bone is now accompanied by a broad face and palate. The cranial vault is thick, the frontal is moderately low, and supraorbital development is strong by modern standards, although less than in such crania as Saldanha and Broken Hill. Radiocarbon dates from a Middle Stone Age occupation site higher in the stratigraphy suggest an age for this level of more than 43 k.y., and new absolute dates for the skull layer suggest an antiquity of more than 100 k.y. The Florisbad hominid is thus probably of late middle or early late Pleistocene age and may provide a morphological link between the archaic southern African hominids associated with the Acheulean (e.g. Saldanha) and early modern hominids associated with the Middle Stone Age (e.g. Klasies River Mouth).

See also ARCHAIC HOMO SAPIENS;
ARCHAIC MODERNS. [C.B.S.]

FLUORINE DATING   see
GEOCHRONOMETRY

FOLSOM

Projectile-point style dating to 10,400 B.P. at Blackwater Draw and representing the middle range of the Paleoindian Tradition. Folsom points are relatively small and lanceolate, made by pressure flaking, and thinned by a single channel flute detached from each face. First discovered at the Folsom site (New Mexico), they are best known from Lindenmeier (Colorado), where they occur with unfluted points, various scrapers, choppers, and bones of *Bison occidentalis*.

See also AMERICAS; PALEOINDIAN. [L.S.A.P., D.H.T.]

FONTÉCHEVADE

The two fragmentary fossil hominids from the late middle Pleistocene levels of the Fontéchevade Cave in France have received an inordinate amount of attention because of the significance accorded them in the "presapiens" scheme proposed by Boule and developed by Vallois. Fontéchevade 1 is a small fragment of frontal bone from around the center of the browridge area, yet it lacks any development of a supraorbital torus. Vallois argued that it was an adult specimen and hence of fundamentally modern type, despite its antiquity, but other workers have suggested that it may derive from an immature skull or is intrusive from later levels. Fontéchevade 2 consists of a larger part of the cranial vault but does not preserve the browridge area. Nevertheless, Vallois postulated that the forehead and torus development would have been of modern type. Other workers studying the specimen have noted its Neanderthal-like shape. Statistical tests on cranial measurements also align the specimen with early and late Neanderthals rather than with modern humans, and few workers now support Vallois's interpretations.

See also NEANDERTHALS; PRESAPIENS;
VALLOIS, HENRI VICTOR. [C.B.S.]

FORBES' QUARRY   see   NEANDERTHALS

FORENSIC ANTHROPOLOGY

Branch of anthropology that deals with the identification of, and the causes of mortality in, individual remains. In many ways the skeleton records the life history of an individual. It shows not only characteristics due to phylogenetic position and population affinity but also variations due to trauma, diet, and disease. Forensic anthropologists commonly use this record to identify unknown skeletal remains, in conjunction with information gathered by the medical examiner, the police, the court system, and other forensic specialists.

The same strategy and skills help in the analysis of prehistoric skeletons. Anthropologists first of all carefully note the context in which bones are found, their stratigraphy and positioning, in order to address the

Life-History Variation Used to Identify Skeletal Remains

Women bear children; men do not.

Sex Determination from the Pelvis

	Female	**Male**
	Evidence of enlarged pelvic dimensions:	No evidence of enlarged pelvic dimensions:
Inlet	Elevated sacroiliac articulation Preauricular sulcus present	No elevation of articulation Sulcus not present
Cavity	Quadrangular pubis shape Pubis long relative to ischium	Triangular pubis shape Ischium as long as pubis
Outlet	Obtuse subpubic angle Wide greater sciatic notch	Acute subpubic angle Narrow greater sciatic notch

Men are generally larger and more muscular than women.

Sex Determination from the Skull and Long Bones

	Female	**Male**
	Evidence for small size with unremarkable muscle development:	Evidence for large size with pronounced muscle development:
Long bones	Small joints Muscle markings not pronounced	Large joints Muscle markings pronounced
Cranium	Small supraorbital tori Small mastoid process Minor nuchal crests	Pronounced supraorbital tori Large mastoid process Pronounced nuchal crests
Mandible	Pointed chin Obtuse gonial angle	Square chin Square gonial angle

Processes of growth and aging proceed through fairly predictable stages.

Age Determination

	Child	**Adolescent**	**Young adult**	**Older adult**
Teeth	1st permanent molars erupt	2nd permanent molars erupt	3rd permanent molars erupt	Cusps show wear
Limb bones	Secondary ossification centers appear	Arm/leg epiphyses fuse	Medial clavicle fuses	Joints show arthritis
Cranium	Metopic suture closes	— — —	Spheno-occipital suture closes	All vault sutures close
Pelvis	Pubis and ischium fuse	Ilium fuses to pubis/ischium	Secondary growth centers fuse	Pubic symphysis shows remodeling

manner and cause of death and the antiquity of the remains. Knowledge of skeletal variation helps determine whether the remains are human, represent more than one individual, are male or female, young or old, or show racial affinities. These identifications depend on fairly predictable life-history changes but are best stated cautiously. A useful rule of thumb: to reach the most likely identification consider all possible observations together. An individual's age, sex, and race are not really separate questions. For example, the cranium of an adolescent male may look like that of a female because it is not yet fully developed. An individual's skeleton may look younger or older than his or her chronological age depending on the pattern of growth characteristic of the population or ethnic group.

In addition to generalized population parameters, such as sex, age, and race, indicators of more specific or individualistic life events may be seen in the skeleton. For example, a healed fracture of the forearm indicates that the individual broke an arm and was able to survive the episode. In the case of contemporary material such traumas and other disease conditions (e.g. a pattern of arthritis or a dental abscess) may create a profile of specific insults that can be matched against medical or dental records. Toward this end some forensic anthropologists also reconstruct facial parts from the skull itself, estimating the thickness of fat, muscle, and skin over various portions of the face.

The American Association of Forensic Anthropologists has been growing considerably as more and more physical anthropologists participate in this kind of investigative research. Involvement of anthropologists in the identification of war dead has greatly increased the precision of skeletal identification through the detailed study of large numbers of identified remains. New techniques using the microstructure of bone for "aging," and multivariate discriminant functions for "sexing," have resulted from initial forensic work on such remains.

See also BONE BIOLOGY; ONTOGENY; PALEOPATHOLOGY; RACE; SEXUAL DIMORPHISM; SKELETON. [C.J.D.]

Further Readings

Krogman, W.M., and Iscan, M. (1986) The Human Skeleton in Forensic Medicine. Springfield, Ill.: Thomas.

Stewart, T.D. (1979) Essentials of Forensic Anthropology. Springfield, Ill.: Thomas.

FORMATION *see* STRATIGRAPHY

FORT TERNAN

Western Kenyan stratified site of middle Miocene age, 14 m.y. by numerous K-Ar ages on included tuffs, and other dates on enclosing lavas. Discovered on Wicker's Farm on the north shoulder of Timboroa (Tinderet) volcano by the owner in 1959 and excavated largely by L.S.B. and M.D. Leakey in the 1960s, the main site has provided a large collection indicating more open habitat than Maboko. The sites of Alengerr in the Baringo sequence and Nachola in the Samburu Hills have similar fauna, including many hominoid specimens, and are probably of the same general age. Fort Ternan is the type site of *Kenyapithecus wickeri* and also yields remains of other, uncertainly identified proconsuline forms.

See also KENYA; KENYAPITHECUS; MABOKO; PALEOENVIRONMENTS. [J.A.V.C.]

Further Readings

Shipman, P., Walker, A., Van Couvering, J.A., Hooker, P.J., and Miller, J.A. (1981) The Fort Ternan hominoid site, Kenya: geology, age, taphonomy, and paleoecology. J. Hum. Evol. 10:49–72.

FOSSIL

Our most important means of learning about extinct life. In its original sense a *fossil* meant anything curious that was dug up and included such things as minerals. With the development of paleontological sciences the meaning became more restricted, to denote actual remains or other indications of past organisms. Any definition remains slightly vague, however, in terms of both the materials referred to and their context. Fossils normally carry with them some sense of antiquity. Therefore bones or shells of animals buried quite recently, geologically speaking, or found in late archaeological situations, are sometimes designated as "subfossil" to indicate this distinction. There are also implications of chemical change. The term *fossilized* reflects this, although the actual ways in which something can become fossilized are various. These in part depend upon the environment of burial, some circumstances being more favorable to the preservation of fossils than others. A fossil can be an actual part of an organism, in which case it is usually some hard part, such as a piece of the skeleton of a vertebrate or wood from the trunk of a tree, that is suited to resist mechanical and chemical destruction. Most hominid fossils are of this kind, being parts of the skeleton of the creatures concerned. Another category comprises *trace fossils*. These are indications of the life or behavior of organisms that do not involve remains of the organisms themselves, such as the feeding burrows of invertebrate animals. There can be problems in relating a particular kind of trace fossil to the species of organism responsible for it. A hominid example of a trace fossil is the sets of footprints preserved in volcanic ash at Laetoli (Tanzania), believed to have been produced by *Australopithecus afarensis* 3.6 m.y. ago.

See also AUSTRALOPITHECUS AFARENSIS; LAETOLI; TAPHONOMY. [A.H.]

Further Readings

Rudwick, M.J.S. (1985) The Meaning of Fossils: Episodes in the History of Palaeontology, 2nd ed. Chicago: University of Chicago Press.

FOSSILIZATION *see* FOSSIL; TAPHONOMY

FRANCE

Country in western Europe with one of the longest and most complete records of human and primate evolution in that continent. During the Paleocene *Plesiadapis* flourished in France, which has yielded the best cranial and postcranial samples of the genus in the world. Archaic primates, such as *Phenacolemur*, persisted into the Eocene, alongside early euprimates, such as the adapids *Pelycodus* (or *Cantius*) and *Adapis*, the microchoerine *Necrolemur*, the anaptomorphine *Teilhardina* (in neighboring Belgium), and the enigmatic *Donrussellia*. The major faunal change at the beginning of the Oligocene saw the end of European primates for nearly 20 m.y., but by the middle Miocene France began to receive anthropoid emigrants from Africa. The pliopithecids *Pliopithecus* and *Crouzelia* first arrived ca. 16 m.y. ago, are well represented at Sansan, and persisted until ca. 13 m.y. *Dryopithecus* was a slightly younger form, known especially from St. Gaudens (ca. 13–12 m.y.). A variety of cercopithecid monkeys characterized the Pliocene and early Pleistocene, such as the colobines *Dolichopithecus* and *Mesopithecus* (5–3 m.y.) and the cercopithecines *Paradolichopithecus* (3.5–1.5 m.y.) and *Macaca*, which arrived at the start of the Pliocene (5 m.y.) and persisted into the later middle Pleistocene less than 0.25 m.y. ago. Many of these primates were first described from French localities, some in the last century.

France has a long history of prehistoric studies, including such famous names as Boucher de Perthes, Lartet, Boule, Breuil, Peyrony, Bordes, and Leroi-Gourhan. These workers led France to be recognized as the cradle of prehistoric research, with a wide variety of human fossils and archaeological assemblages known over nearly 1 m.y. Unlike many other Paleolithic areas with gaps in their prehistoric record France shows an uninterrupted increase in the number of archaeological sites from the early middle Pleistocene through to the Holocene.

The earliest evidence for human occupation comes from the southern part of the country. Numerous finds of rolled and weathered quartz pebbles and cobbles possibly flaked by early humans have been found together with bones of Villafranchian (early Pleistocene) mammals (including *Elephas meridionalis*, which became extinct ca. 900 k.y. ago), especially in the gravels of Chilhac on the Massif Central and at a number of localities along the Roussillon terraces near the Spanish border. France's oldest well-documented site, Vallonnet, is a small cave located on the Mediterranean coast near the town of Menton, west of Monaco. Its ten-piece lithic inventory of choppers and utilized flakes is associated with remains of Villafranchian fauna. Paleomagnetic and paleoenvironmental data suggest that Vallonnet was occupied ca. 900 (or perhaps 700) k.y. ago during a warm and dry interval. Soleilhac, on the Massif Central, is the earliest open-air site, documenting a camp on a lakeshore beach at the side of an extinct volcanic crater. The archaeological inventory here consists of small retouched flakes and fragmented bones of Villafranchian mammals, scattered over a 100–150-sq.-m. area. There is also a 6-by-1.5-m. alignment of basalt blocks, which may represent the oldest evidence for habitation structure in Europe.

Later in the middle Pleistocene, perhaps ca. 400,000 B.P., humans occupied a beach area at Nice called Terra Amata over successive summers. No human fossils have been found there, but a large number of archaic *Homo sapiens* remains were recovered from the Arago Cave near the eastern Pyrenees, close to where both *Dolichopithecus* and earlier artifacts are known. Generally similar hominid fossils are known from Montmaurin, and Acheulean archaeological assemblages of comparable age (0.4–0.2 m.y.) include those from the type site of St. Acheul, the Abbeville gravels, and the Atelier Commont, on the Somme River. The Neanderthal lineage is especially well represented in France, beginning with the Biache skull of ca. 150,000 B.P., and the probably slightly younger Fontéchevade, Lazaret, and La Chaise fragments, all of which are early members of this group, mainly associated with an early Mousterian industry. Other famous Neanderthal fossils from the Weichselian (ca. 90,000–30,000 B.P.) include La Chapelle-aux-Saints, La Ferrassie, Le Moustier, La Quina, and Saint-Césaire, the youngest of all. These sites and many others have yielded a vast inventory of Mousterian artifacts, burials, and paleoenvironmental data.

The western European Upper Paleolithic is also best typified and defined in France, with a sequence of Chatelperronian, Aurignacian, Gravettian (Perigordian), Solutrean, Magdalenian, and Azilian industries. These are often found superposed in caves, rock shelters and open-air encampments, associated with burials of anatomically modern humans (the "Cro-Magnons," named after an early French discovery), mobile and parietal art, calendrical and numerical notation devices, and grave goods.

See also ACHEULEAN; ADAPIDAE; ANAPTOMORPHINAE; ARCHAIC HOMO SAPIENS; CERCOPITHECINAE; COLOBINAE; DRYOPITHECUS; EARLY PALEOLITHIC; EUROPE; HOMO SAPIENS; MICROCHOERINAE; NEANDERTHALS; PALEOLITHIC IMAGE; PAROMOMYOIDEA; PLESIADAPOIDEA; PLIOPITHECIDAE; UPPER PALEOLITHIC. [E.D., O.S.]

Further Readings

Gamble, C. (1986) The Palaeolithic Settlement of Europe. Cambrige: Cambridge University Press.

Stringer, C.B., Hublin, J.-J., and Vandermeersch, B. (1984) The origin of anatomically modern humans in western Europe. In F.H. Smith and F. Spencer (eds.): The Origins of Modern Humans: A World Survey of the Fossil Evidence. New York: Liss, pp. 51–135.

Szalay, F.S., and Delson, E. (1979) Evolutionary History of the Primates. New York: Academic.

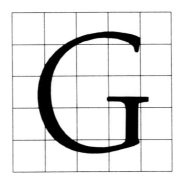

GAIMAN *see* CEBINAE

GALAGIDAE

The galagos—or, less appropriately, bushbabies—are a much more ecologically, behaviorally, and morphologically diverse group than previously recognized. They constitute the family Galagidae, which is classified, together with the families Lorisidae and Cheirogalidae, in the strepsirhine superfamily Lorisoidea. The family includes 11 extant species that are restricted to sub-Saharan Africa, where they occupy a variety of habitats ranging from dense tropical forest to open-woodland savanna. The extant species can be classified into three genera:

Genus *Galago*
    Subgenus *Galago* (the lesser galagos)
      Species *Galago senegalensis*
            Galago moholi
            Galago gallarum
    Subgenus *Euoticus* (the needle-nailed galagos)
      Species *Galago elegantulus*
            Galago matschiei

Genus *Galagoides*
    Subgenus *Galagoides* (the dwarf galagos)
      Species *Galagoides demidoff*
            Galagoides thomasi
            Galagoides zanzibaricus
    Subgenus *Sciurocheirus* (the squirrellike galagos)
      Species *Galagoides alleni*

Genus *Otolemur* (the greater galagos)
      Species *Otolemur crassicaudatus*
            Otolemur garnettii

Galagos are small-to-moderate-sized animals with adult body weights ranging from a mean of 100 gm. in the smallest species of dwarf galago, *Galagoides demidoff*, to 1,800 gm. in the largest greater galago, *Otolemur crassicaudatus*. Males typically are solitary, while females frequently live in small groups. Galagos feed primarily on exudates, fruits, and insects. All are nocturnal and use vocalizations and scent-marking behaviors in social situations. During the day, they usually sleep in groups in semipermanent nests of leaves or inside trees. Galagos have never been observed to eat leaves. Although predominantly arboreal, galagos occupy a wide variety of habitats from the ground to the upper canopy. All species in the family are active quadrupedal runners and leapers.

All galagos have an adult dental formula of 2.1.3.3. The lower incisors and canines are procumbent and together with the caniniform P_3 are arranged in a tooth comb, which is homologous to the condition seen in most extant lemuroids. The premolars and molars are brachydont and bunodont, lacking primitive crests, cingula, or high pointed cusps. M^1 and M^2 both possess a hypocone. The pinna of the ear is prominent and mobile. The eyes are large, the rostrum typically reduced, and the petromastoid region inflated. The galagids differ from cheirogaleids in having an ectotympanic outside of the auditory bulla.

The most distinct specializations of the living galagos are found in their postcranial anatomy and are associated with their active running, vertical-clinging-and-leaping mode of locomotion. All galagids possess long hindlimbs with greatly elongated calcanea and navicula. Members of the genus *Galago* have the longest hindlimbs relative to forelimbs of any living primate and can easily perform vertical leaps

Small and large bushbaby: *Galagoides demidoff*, the smallest species (above) and *Otolemur* (or *Galago*) *crassicaudatus*, the largest (below).

in excess of 2 m. The tail is long and hairy, usually exceeding the length of the head plus body. Unlike the tarsier, which uses a similar form of posture and locomotion, the galagos do not use their tails for support while in a vertical-clinging position. All digits have flat nails except the second digit of the pes, which is a clawlike grooming nail. The grasp is greatly enhanced by the presence of broad flat pads at the tips of the digits.

The species in the genus *Galago* are the most specialized and highly evolved members of the family and live in the widest range of habitats. Populations in each of the three species of the subgenus *Galago* occupy dry woodland savanna, while species in the subgenus *Euoticus* are found in dense tropical forests. The galagos in this genus are the most agile and active vertical-clingers and leapers. They feed extensively upon gums, which they obtain by scraping the bark of trees with their tooth comb. All digits

of the needle-nailed galagos, except for the second pedal, which retains the grooming nail, have nails with a raised central ridge, which gives the nail a sharp pointed or needlelike tip.

Species in the genus *Galagoides* are the most generalized of the galagos. They have long pointed snouts and rely more extensively upon the primitive quadrupedal running, rather than leaping, mode of locomotion. Their diet consists primarily of fruits and animal prey. Both subgenera prefer dense undergrowth to more open upper canopy.

The greater galagos in the genus *Otolemur* are the largest and most terrestrial of the galagos. Like *Galago* they occupy a wide variety of habitats, although they are not found in the tropical rain forests of central Africa. These galagos are not fully adapted to vertical clinging and leaping, but they are active quadrupedal leapers and use a form of bipedal hopping when crossing open country. *Otolemur crassicaudatus* has been reported to travel up to 3 km. across open acacia savanna in southern Africa.

The geological antiquity of the family and the three extant genera goes back minimally to the late Pliocene in Africa. Fossil galago specimens described by Wesselman from 3-to-2-m.y.-old Omo deposits in the Turkana basin (Ethiopia) demonstrate the existence of three species of galago, which can be referred to each of the extant genus groups. *Otolemur howelli*, an extinct species ancestral to the greater galagos, and two contemporary species, *Galago senegalensis* and *Galagoides demidoff*, have been recovered from these deposits. Specimens indistinguishable from *Galago senegalensis* have also been reported from the 1.75-m.y.-old FLK I site in Bed I at Olduvai Gorge (Tanzania). The status and relationships of the early Miocene lorisoid genera *Komba*, *Progalago*, and *Mioeuoticus* from East Africa to living lineages of galagos are unclear.

See also CHEIROGALEIDAE; LEMURIFORMES; LOCOMOTION; LORISIDAE; LORISOIDEA; OMO; STREPSIRHINI. [T.R.O.]

Further Readings

Bearder, S.K. (1987) Lorises, bushbabies, and tarsiers: diverse societies in solitary foragers. In B. Smuts, D. Cheney, R. Seyfarth, R. Wrangham, and T. Struhsaker (eds.): Primate Societies. Chicago: University of Chicago Press, pp. 11–24.

Kingdon, J. (1971) East African Mammals, Vol. 1. New York: Academic.

Wesselman, H.B. (1984) The Omo Micromammals. In M.K. Hecht and F.S. Szalay (eds.): Contributions to Vertebrate Evolution, Vol. 7. Basel: Karger, pp. 1–219.

GALAGO *see* GALAGIDAE

GALAGOIDES *see* GALAGIDAE

GALILEE *see* ZUTTIYEH

GAMBLIAN *see* PLUVIALS

GAME DRIVES *see* PALEOLITHIC LIFEWAYS

GÁNOVCE

Czechoslovakian hominid remains recovered from travertine deposits in 1926 and 1955. They comprise a natural endocranial cast with a capacity of ca. 1,320 ml., some cranial fragments, and natural molds of postcranial bones. The site also contained Mousterian ("Taubachian") artifacts and is usually attributed to the last interglacial age.

See also NEANDERTHALS. [C.B.S.]

GARROD, DOROTHY ANNE ELIZABETH (1892–1968)

British archaeologist responsible for important excavations in Europe and the Middle East. In 1925–1926 she directed work at the Devil's Tower (Neanderthal) site at Gibraltar, which was followed in 1928 by research in southern Kurdistan. Shortly thereafter she excavated the Shukbah Cave, near Jerusalem, and between 1929 and 1934 she was director of excavations at the Mount Carmel site in Israel (then Palestine), which led to the discovery of skeletal and cultural remains of primary importance to the understanding of hominid evolution during the Middle Stone Age. In 1939 she became the first woman to receive a professorship at Cambridge University, where she was professor of archaeology until 1952.

See also KEITH, ARTHUR; MCCOWN, THEODORE D.; NEANDERTHALS; SKHŪL; TABŪN. [F.S.]

GEBEL ZELTEN *see* AFRICA; VICTORIAPITHECINAE

GENE

Segment of DNA responsible for the production of a specific functional macromolecule. Its direct product is called RNA, which may itself perform a cellular function or which may simply bear the instructions for the production of a specific protein, which in turn performs the function. The production of RNA from a DNA molecule is *transcription*; the production of protein from an RNA molecule is *translation*. Use of the term *gene* is occasionally extended to refer to DNA stretches that are not themselves transcribed but that may have significant structural properties or affect the transcription of neighboring genes.

See also ALLELE; GENETICS; GENOME; GENOTYPE; MOLECULAR ANTHROPOLOGY. [J.M.]

GENE FLOW *see* GENETICS

GENE POOL *see* GENETICS

GENERALIZED *see* CLADISTICS

GENETIC DRIFT *see* GENETICS

GENETICS

Name given by William Bateson in 1906 to the study of "the physiology of heredity and variation." The laws of heredity and variation were unknown to Charles Darwin, who nevertheless recognized them as the major unanswered questions in his own nineteenth-century theory of evolution. The field of genetics is thus essentially a twentieth-century endeavor, and we now acknowledge that evolution is in its fundamentals the genetic divergence of populations across time (*phyletic change*) and space (*allopatric change*). The nature of those changes and how they result in what we recognize as evolution are studied by the numerous subdisciplines of genetics.

Genetics has traditionally been a sister discipline to physical anthropology, of great interest to students of human origins and prehistory. To an earlier scientific generation genetics formed a basis for racial classifications of humanity; but modern interests focus upon the causes of individual differences within human populations, mechanisms of microevolutionary change, and the primary basis of relationships among the primates.

Classical Genetics

Gregor Mendel derived the basic tenets of heredity in the mid-1860s, but his work was not appreciated until the turn of the century. His Law of Segregation states that inheritance is packaged into units (later called *genes*) that ordinarily occur in pairs but separate from one another at some stage of the reproductive cycle. The expression of a gene may depend upon the constitution of its partner: if they differ, one may conceal the effects of the other. A pair of genes that differ from one another are now called *alleles*; the allele whose effect is masked is *recessive*; the expressed allele is *dominant*.

Mendel's Law of Independent Assortment states that the separation of any pair of alleles during the reproductive cycle is random with respect to the separation of any other pair (i.e. combinations of alleles do not travel together). We now know this to be true only for genes that are unlinked or located on different chromosomes.

While Mendel's laws lay the foundation for our understanding of heredity, we now know their direct applicability to be rather limited. To observe Mendel's laws operating it is necessary that the genetic constitution (*genotype*) be directly translated into an observable character (*phenotype*) that can be assessed in the organism and that a sufficient number of offspring from each mating be available for the investigator to establish the pattern of inheritance. As the development of an organism is an extraordinarily complicated process, it follows that most characters directly attributable to single-gene variations manifest themselves as pathologies. It is no surprise, therefore, that much of our knowledge of classical genetics comes from the fruitfly, *Drosophila*, rather than from our own species. Indeed, simple Mendelian inheritance is usually demonstrable for humans only in the case of familial genetic diseases or in biochemical variants, such as the blood type.

covery of Mendel's laws it became apparent that these microscopically observable structures were themselves the bearers of the genes, which were shown to be arranged linearly along the length of the chromosomes. Chromosomes were also seen to be the structures that actually do segregate during the reproductive cycle, physically following the letter of Mendel's law.

Chromosome sizes and shapes are generally constant for each cell of the body and characteristic as well of the species from which they come. Rearrangements of the chromosomes may occur in some individuals, however. When such a rearrangement does not alter the amount of genetic material but merely shuffles it around, it is said to be *balanced* and is accompanied by few or no clinical manifestations. When the rearrangement does involve a change in the quantity of material, it is *unbalanced*, and many syndromes are known to be the result of such rearrangements—Cri-du-chat syndrome is due to a deletion in chromosome 5, and Down's syndrome is due to a duplication of at least part of chromosome 21.

Since balanced rearrangements usually have no effect upon the phenotype, we find that closely related species may frequently vary in the numbers,

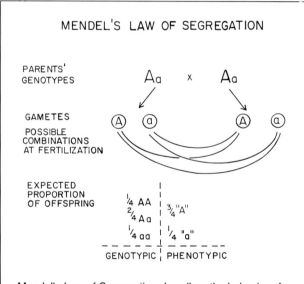

Mendel's Law of Segregation describes the behavior of a trait determined by a single gene. Here two heterozygotes (genotype Aa) produce two classes of gametes (A and a). Since, presumably, fertilization occurs at random, we expect three classes of genotypes (AA, Aa, and aa) approximately in the ratio of 1:2:1. Since the heterozygote has the same phenotype as the dominant homozygote, we expect two phenotypic classes in the ratio 3:1. Thus a couple each heterozygous for Tay-Sachs disease (caused by a recessive allele) has a 25 percent chance of producing an offspring afflicted with the disease.

Cytogenetics

Cytogenetics is the study of the cellular components of heredity, the chromosomes. Shortly after the redis-

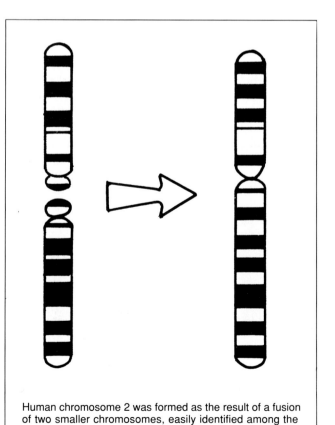

Human chromosome 2 was formed as the result of a fusion of two smaller chromosomes, easily identified among the chromosomes of the great apes and Old World monkeys. The pattern of bands observable are Giemsa, or G-bands.

shapes, and sizes of their chromosomes, and variation in chromosome form may be useful as phylogenetic characters. The chromosomes of the great apes, for example, differ but little from those of humans. The most noteworthy difference is the fusion of two chromosome pairs in a human ancestor, creating the human state of 23 chromosome pairs per cell, as opposed to the 24 chromosome pairs in the cells of the great apes.

Quantitative Genetics

While the followers of Mendel's work developed a particulate theory of inheritance, a different school of thought developed to study the inheritance of *quantitative characters*. Quantitative characters are those that are continuously distributed, such as weight or height, rather than discretely distributed, such as albinism or sickle-cell anemia. Discrete traits could often be shown to follow Mendel's rules of particulate inheritance, but continuous traits could not. Indeed, these traits (e.g. skin color) often appeared to blend in offspring. Genetic studies of continuous traits were initiated by Galton and refined by K. Pearson and R. Fisher, in terms of the correlations between relatives for values of the trait under study. The modern science of statistics was born in the study of quantitative genetics.

A schism between the "Mendelian" and "Biometric" approaches soon developed over the role of heredity in Darwinian evolution. If heredity were primarily Mendelian, then evolution must proceed by the substitution of a "tall" allele for a "short" allele, or a "black" allele for a "white" allele. This is a saltational view of evolution, in which populations "jump" across character states. If, on the other hand, evolution is gradual, as Darwin conceived it, then the discrete characters and Mendelian rules that govern their inheritance are interesting but irrelevant, because those rules do not describe the changes in mean values of phenotypic distributions that are the main foci of Darwinian evolution.

The rivalry between the two schools was effectively resolved by R. Fisher, who showed in 1918 that if several genes contribute additively to a single character then the biometric data are accountable under Mendelian inheritance. For example, it has been proposed that the difference between the skin color of African and European aboriginals is due to the cumulative effects of five to seven genes.

While the rivalry between classical and quantitative genetics no longer exists, the difference in emphasis remains. Classical genetics concerns itself with the material foundations of biological diversity and the hereditary mechanisms; quantitative genetics is more abstract and more statistically refined, and it studies only phenotypic products.

Population Genetics

The field of population genetics dates to shortly after the rediscovery of Mendel's laws, when Hardy, Weinberg, and Castle independently showed that the operation of these laws could be mathematically extrapolated from a single individual to an entire population. Now colloquially called the "Hardy-Weinberg Law," this extension of Mendelian laws shows that the relative frequencies of two alleles in a population will remain unaltered if the only forces operating upon them are those of Mendelian segregation and assortment.

By 1932 four mathematically oriented biologists, Chetverikov, Fisher, Wright, and Haldane, had published major works describing the perturbations that would occur to the genetic composition of populations under various circumstances. These circumstances, which represent deviations from the conditions of the Hardy-Weinberg equilibrium, include preferential matings between relatives, whose genotypes are more likely to be identical than mates drawn at random (*inbreeding*); the generation of new alleles (*mutation*); constrained population size (*genetic drift*); migration (*gene flow*); preferential mating based on phenotypic similarity (*assortative mating*); and the differential average reproduction of individuals with unlike genotypes (*natural selection*). The powerful mathematical model that combines these factors into a single theory is S. Wright's "shifting balance" or "adaptive landscape," which emphasizes the interaction of deterministic forces (natural selection) and stochastic forces (genetic drift) in producing evolutionary novelties.

The fundamental construct of population genetics is the *gene pool*, a summation of all possible gametes in a population. The gene pool is partitioned every generation into groups of pairwise combinations, or *genotypes*. The gene pool can change through time or can be split geographically: this is the formal basis for the study of microevolution.

The major drawback of population genetics is that while the perturbations in the gene pool can be modeled with a high degree of sophistication relatively little is known about either the translation of genetic differences into anatomical characters or the generation of reproductive incompatibilities among different parts of a population.

Molecular Genetics

Molecular genetics studies the transmission, function, and variation of the hereditary material, DNA. The structure of DNA is the famous double helix, deduced by Watson and Crick in 1953. The inner part of the molecule contains the sequence of nucleotides (adenine, guanine, cytosine, thymine) that regulates the form and production of proteins and most cellular processes. A gene is therefore an informational segment of DNA; and the total DNA contribution of one parent is the genome. It is now known, however, that very little of the DNA actually is genic in nature. The vast bulk of genomic DNA lies between genes, is not expressed phenotypically, and is either functionless or has at best a very cryptic function.

The fundamentals of gene function were elucidated in the 1960s. The nucleotide sequence of genic DNA is informational when read in groups of three, or *codons*. In the nucleus DNA is used as a template for the production of a molecule of messenger RNA (mRNA), whose structure conveys the information encoded by the DNA into the cytoplasm. After certain modifications to the mRNA molecule, the codons are translated into a precise sequence of amino acids, which constitutes a protein. This process of translation is mediated by a different class of RNA molecules, transfer RNAs (tRNA).

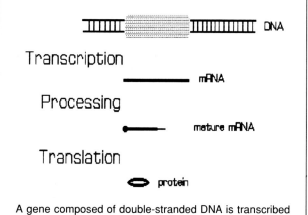

A gene composed of double-stranded DNA is transcribed in the cell nucleus, yielding a single-stranded mRNA molecule. The mRNA is processed by removing some stretches, "capping" one end, and adding a "tail" of adenines to the other end. The instruction in the processed or "mature" mRNA is then translated outside the nucleus to yield a specific protein.

Variation is produced at the molecular level by several processes, most of which are only sketchily understood. First and foremost are random point mutations, the substitution of one nucleotide for another (or insertion or deletion) at a specific site. Sickle-cell anemia, for example, is traceable to a single point mutation in the beta-globin gene. Next there are processes that produce duplications or deletions of DNA segments and often lead to tandemly repeated DNA sequences, or families of genes lying adjacent to one another. These gene families are often coordinated in their regulation and evolution. Finally there are processes in which a foreign piece of DNA is inserted or deleted. An example is the interpolation of the estimated 910,000 *Alu* sequen-

ces, each about 300 nucleotides long, throughout the human genome.

The early breakthroughs in the study of molecular evolution in the 1960s produced expectations that molecular studies would solve all, or at least many, of the existing questions of evolutionary biology. Unfortunately this has not turned out to be the case. While some questions have been resolved, others have remained unanswered, and still other questions have been generated by the study of the evolution of macromolecules.

Developmental Genetics

This subfield is concerned with the translation of the organism's genotypic instructions into its phenotypic characters. This is still largely unexplored terrain, with nearly all of the data coming from very few organisms: fruitfly, frog, sea urchin, nematode worm, and mouse.

The two most important current research areas are *genetic regulation* (the processes by which genes are turned on and off) and *cell differentiation* (the processes by which the cells of a growing embryo become progressively more specialized). These are related by the fact that cell differentiation apparently results from the selective expression of genes.

Genetic regulation is poorly understood and involves molecular controls over the rate and efficiency of both transcription and translation. These controls are known to include the chemical modification of nucleotides, such as methylation; altered DNA conformations, such as the "left-handed" Z-DNA structure; folding of the DNA or mRNA molecule, changing its accessibility to transcription or translation; interactions of genes with other macromolecules, such as regulators or repressors; posttranscriptional changes in the mRNA, such as intron removal; posttranslational modifications in proteins; and even the frequencies of certain codons in the gene, which may limit the rate of translation via the availability of certain tRNA molecules.

In the fruitfly *Drosophila* mutations that affect the most primary aspects of development are now being carefully analyzed: determination of polarity in the embryo (dorsal/ventral; anterior/posterior; etc.) and laying down of the body segments. Some of these genes are expressed within hours of fertilization of the egg and contain a DNA sequence that codes for a protein domain of about 180 amino acids, the *homeo box*. The homeo-box domain appears to have the property of binding to DNA and has been found virtually intact in mammals as well. In humans the homeo-box mRNA has been found in neural cells of the very early embryo. Its function is still unclear.

See also ALLELE; CHROMOSOME; DNA HYBRIDIZATION;

GENE; GENOME; GENOTYPE;
MOLECULAR ANTHROPOLOGY. [J.M.]

Further Readings

Cavalli-Sforza, L., and Bodmer, W. (1970) The Genetics of Human Populations. San Francisco: Freeman.

Crow, J.F. (1986) Basic Concepts in Population, Quantitative, and Evolutionary Genetics. New York: Freeman.

de Pomerai, D. (1985) From Gene to Animal. Cambridge: Cambridge University Press.

Falconer, D.S. (1981) Introduction to Quantitative Genetics, 2nd ed. New York: Longman.

MacIntyre, R., ed. (1985) Molecular Evolutionary Genetics. New York: Plenum.

McKusick, V.A. (1986) Mendelian Inheritance in Man, 7th ed. Baltimore: Johns Hopkins University Press.

Wright, S. (1970) Random drift and the shifting balance theory of evolution. In K. Kojima (ed.): Mathematical Topics in Population Genetics. New York: Springer-Verlag, pp. 1–31.

GENOME

Totality of genetic material, or DNA, contained in a gamete, or reproductive cell. It was once thought that the genome simply consisted of protein-coding sequences, linked end-to-end. We now know that the human genome contains ca. 3 billion nucleotide pairs; this figure varies little among extant reptile, bird, and mammal species. Some lungfish are known, however, with 50 times more DNA per cell. Among amphibians alone genomes are known to range from about one third to 25 times the size of the human. There is thus no clear relationship between organismal evolution and genome size.

About 90 percent of the human genome consists of intergenic DNA (i.e. DNA that lies between genes). On the average only about 10 percent of any gene is actually informational. Protein-coding sequences are now known to be interrupted by noncoding stretches, often quite lengthy, and are also flanked by noncoding sequences. Thus only about 1 percent of the genome appears to be functional or informational and hence important in organismal evolution.

The genome is often arbitrarily divided into two components, *repetitive* and *unique-sequence*, which are of roughly equal proportion in humans. Repetitive DNA actually forms a continuum of sequences that vary both in length and in frequency of repetition. The most highly repetitive and simplest genomic DNA is called *satellite* DNA; this constitutes 4 percent of the human genome and is scattered across all the chromosomes, generally localized in the region around the centromere. Unique-sequence DNA also forms a continuum of sequences, which, while often not literally unique, are at least not highly redundant. This DNA component contains the genes,

as well as other elements as yet to be well characterized.

Genes are located in clusters that form as the result of tandem duplications of an ancestral primordial gene. A derivative copied gene is superfluous and therefore may accumulate mutations that either enable it to take on a new, related function or shut it down because of incapacitating mutations. In the latter case it becomes a *pseudogene*. Sometimes, by processes not yet understood, the duplicate gene can be corrected against the original, so that the two (or more) appear to evolve in concert. Often the new function is similar to the old but is specialized for a different developmental stage.

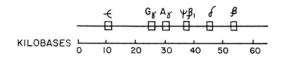

A minuscule segment of the human genome is the betaglobin gene cluster, located on chromosome 11. The actual protein-coding sequence of each gene is 438 nucleotides, but the five functional genes occupy nearly 70,000 nucleotides in the genome.

The human beta-globin cluster, for example, is responsible for producing part of the hemoglobin molecule, which transports oxygen in the bloodstream. It is located on chromosome 11, and spans ca. 70,000 nucleotides. It consists of an embryonic gene (ϵ), two fetal genes ($^G\gamma$ and $^A\gamma$, which are corrected against one another), a pseudogene ($\psi\beta1$), and two different adult genes (δ and β), but all bear profound similarities to one another.

In a microevolutionary context we may note that a single nucleotide change in the β gene is the cause of sickle-cell anemia, a genetic syndrome afflicting many human populations. In a macroevolutionary context we find that the fetal-embryonic genes duplicated from the adult group ca. 200 m.y. ago in an early eutherian mammal; the subsequent duplications occurred in a later mammal, ca. 120 m.y. ago. The fetal genes duplicated in the catarrhine lineage, ca. 40 m.y. ago.

The alpha-globin gene cluster is located on human chromosome 16, and its genes code for the other hemoglobin subunit. The alphas and betas diverged from one another ca. 400 m.y. ago. The frog *Xenopus* still retains the close physical linkage between the alpha and beta genes, while the jawless fishes retain but a single globin gene.

See also GENE; GENETICS;
MOLECULAR ANTHROPOLOGY. [J.M.]

Further Readings

MacIntyre, R., ed. (1985) Molecular Evolutionary Genetics. New York: Plenum.

GENOTYPE

Genetic constitution of an individual. As any human has two copies of each gene, the genotype is often represented by a pair of letters. Different genotypes can have identical expressions, as occurs when one allele is dominant (A) to another (a) for a particular trait. Here the heterozygote (Aa) is phenotypically identical to one of the homozygotes (AA), despite the difference in genotype.

See also ALLELE; GENETICS; PHENOTYPE. [J.M.]

GENUS

Rank in the hierarchy of classification that lies below the family group (including tribes and subtribes) and above the subgenus. The first component of the italicized and latinized species name (e.g. *Homo sapiens*) is the name of the genus (in this case, *Homo*). Genera are in essence monophyletic groupings of species, each species included within the genus bearing a different second (specific) name. No absolute rules determine how many related species should be included within a given genus, but as with any inclusive taxon monophyly is essential. Remarkably, given the fact that genera may contain widely differing numbers of species, and hence of branching events, genera do tend to possess an individual "Gestalt" reality; it is rarer than one might expect that in the living biota one has to puzzle over the allocation of "intermediate" species to one genus or another.

Each genus must be defined by a *type species*, with which all other species placed in the genus must be compared. The valid name for a genus is the first half of the binomen first applied to its type species according to the provisions of the *International Code of Zoological Nomenclature*.

See also CLASSIFICATION; NOMENCLATURE; SPECIES; SUBGENUS; SYSTEMATICS; TAXONOMY. [I.T.]

Further Readings

Eldredge, N., and Cracraft, J. (1980) Phylogenetic Patterns and the Evolutionary Process. New York: Columbia University Press.

International Trust for Zoological Nomenclature. (1985) International Code of Zoological Nomenclature. Berkeley: University of California Press.

GEOCHRONOMETRY

Branch of geology that deals with the quantitative measurement of geologic time. The discipline known as *geochronology* is broader, including relative methods of dating, such as biochronology, to determine the order of events in earth history as well as quantitative measures of geologic time. Most geochronometric methods are based on the decay of radioactive isotopes that leave a record of their initial abundance in one way or another. This record may be the presence of daughter isotopes, physical damage to a material, electrons trapped in energy wells, or deviation of the isotopic composition of a sample from similar samples being formed at the present time. Aside from radioactive decay few processes occur with sufficient regularity to be useful for geochronometric purposes, but astronomical variations in orbital parameters of the earth may prove to be of value. Some chemical changes in geological and fossil materials, such as racemization, fluorine uptake, and hydration, have promise for use in dating where other more reliable methods fail, but these changes are strong functions of the temperature history of the materials and of their local chemical environment, as well as of elapsed time.

A distinction must be made between placement of an event in time and establishment of the time interval over which a process has operated. In varved (annually or otherwise periodically layered) sedimentary sequences it may be possible to state quite accurately the duration of accumulation of the sequence and the amount of time that separates two biologic events without being able to state the age of the sequence itself with much accuracy. For some purposes this is sufficient, but more commonly the age of the strata is desired as well.

Some methods, although useful in geochronology, do not yield quantitative measures of geologic time by themselves. Once calibrated, however, these may yield additional chronological information about a stratigraphic sequence that cannot be gained in any other way. While biostratigraphy, paleomagnetic polarity zonation, and tephrochronology are clearly of geochronologic value, they are not geochronometric methods, depending as they do on other more basic techniques for their calibration.

The radiometric dating methods that provide reasonably precise ages for Tertiary and Quaternary strata are of greatest interest here. Other methods, such as uranium-lead isotope dating, do not provide sufficiently precise ages in young strata to be of much use and are not discussed here. Still other methods— e.g. ^{210}Pb dating and some of the uranium-disequilibrium methods—are applicable over too short a time period to be of use to hominid studies, although they may be of value to archaeology. The methods of greatest importance to hominid studies are potassium-argon (K-Ar) and its variants; fission-track dat ing; and uranium-disequilibrium dating. Radiocarbon dating is of interest for late Pleistocene materials. In general these methods cannot be applied to fossil materials themselves, so ascription of an age to a fossil requires thorough understanding of the stratigraphic relation between the dated materials and the fossils.

Potassium-Argon Dating

Most of the age control on fossil hominids comes from potassium-argon dating. It provides the primary control on the age of most East African and many European fossil sites.

Potassium, a common element in the earth's crust, is the dominant cation in micas, many alkali feldspars, and leucite. It occurs in high concentration in nepheline and many volcanic glasses and in lower concentration in amphiboles, plagioclase, and basic volcanic rocks, such as basalts. The isotopic composition of potassium is constant in natural materials, and one isotope, ^{40}K, is radioactive. ^{40}K decays either to ^{40}Ca by beta emission or to ^{40}Ar by electron capture or positron emission. As a result the ratios of $^{40}Ar/^{40}K$ and $^{40}Ca/^{40}K$ increase with time in potassium-bearing phases. Measurement of these ratios provides a measure of time.

Argon is a gas that at high temperatures diffuses rapidly through solid materials but at low temperatures is quantitatively retained by many substances. The event that is dated is the time of cooling of a mineral or a glass to temperatures at which argon is effectively trapped or the time at which low-temperature minerals, such as glauconite, crystallize. As a result the isotopic composition of argon differs from sample to sample, as the gas accumulates over time at a rate dependent on its potassium content. In its application to fossils volcanic rocks and minerals are the most common materials dated. Since the time interval over which cooling occurs in such materials is brief, from a few minutes to a few years, it can be assumed to be instantaneous.

What is required for a potassium-argon date is measurement of the ^{40}K and radiogenic ^{40}Ar in a sample, together with knowledge of the rates of decay of ^{40}K to ^{40}Ar and ^{40}Ca (λ and $\lambda\beta$, respectively). Many materials have been used, and the principal ones are listed above. Dates are computed from the equation

$$t = \frac{1}{\lambda} \ln \left[\left(\frac{\lambda}{\lambda\epsilon}\right) \left(\frac{^{40}Ar^*}{^{40}K}\right) + 1 \right],$$

where λ = total decay constant for ^{40}K, λ_t = constant for decay of ^{40}K to ^{40}Ar, and $^{40}Ar^*$ is the amount of radiogenic argon in the sample.

Most laboratories adopted new values of the decay

constants and the abundance of ^{40}K in 1975, so ages computed after that date from the same $^{40}Ar/^{40}K$ ratio are ca. 2.7 percent older than those using old constants. Constants are generally stated in the initial paper reporting the dates and should be noted, especially for data published in the mid-1970s.

The precision with which potassium can be determined is a function largely of the amount of potassium present in a sample, but in general the potassium determination does not limit the precision of the age. The determination of radiogenic argon is less straightforward, because ^{40}Ar is present in the atmosphere, and some atmospheric argon is always present in the gas extracted from a sample. Correction for the atmospheric component is made by measuring ^{36}Ar (which is not a radiogenic isotope), assuming that its ratio to ^{40}Ar is the same as that in the atmosphere, and subtracting the computed amount of ^{40}Ar from the total amount measured. The ratio of ^{36}Ar to ^{40}Ar in the atmosphere is 1:295.5, so that small errors in determining the ^{36}Ar content lead to large errors in estimation of the amount of radiogenic ^{40}Ar. Errors stated on a K/Ar age refer mainly to the estimated analytical precision of this determination.

In conventional K-Ar dating two assumptions are made that are critical to the interpretation of an age: first, that the material has remained closed with respect to potassium and argon since the time of cooling; second, that there was no ^{40}Ar initially present in the sample. In many cases these assumptions are justified, but some samples have been shown to contain initial argon and thus yield conventional potassium-argon ages that are too old (regardless of how replicable they are). Many other samples have been shown to have lost argon, and they yield ages that are younger than they should be.

Argon-40/Argon-39 dating is an outgrowth of the conventional potassium-argon method. In this method the sample is first irradiated to produce ^{39}Ar from ^{39}K in the sample. The ^{39}Ar content then becomes a measure of the potassium content of the sample. One advantage of this method is that the entire analysis is done on a single sample and not with separate aliquots for K and Ar analysis. The age may be measured by extracting all of the gas at once, which produces an age comparable with that of a conventional K-Ar determination; ages measured in this way are called *total fusion*, or *total release*, ages. It is also possible to extract the gas in a series of steps at higher and higher temperatures and to compute an age for each fraction of the gas; this method is referred to as *step heating*, or *incremental release*. Ages are commonly plotted against temperature of release, or the fraction of ^{39}Ar released, to show a spectrum of ages. In this method it is expected that the first gas released at low temperature will have come from poorly retentive sites within the material but that as gas is extracted at higher and higher temperatures it will come from more retentive sites and therefore yield ages nearer the time of initial cooling. Experience has borne this out, and commonly the successive higher temperature fractions of gas yield reach a plateau of indistinguishable ages, whereas the lowest temperature fractions often have lower apparent ages. In such a case the higher temperature fractions are said to form an *age plateau*, usually interpreted to mean that the source is largely undisturbed. Some ages are reported only for those fractions of the gas that lie in the plateau region, and these are referred to as *plateau ages*. In other cases the ages from individual gas fractions form a pattern that is not readily interpretable.

If isotopic data from incremental release experiments are plotted on an isochron diagram ($^{40}Ar/^{36}Ar$ vs. $^{39}Ar/^{36}Ar$), the slope of a line plotted through the points is proportional to age. If only atmospheric argon is present as a contaminant, the intercept on the $^{40}Ar/^{36}Ar$ axis (which represents argon not associated with potassium) will be that of the atmosphere (295.5). If initial argon is present, the intercept will be greater than atmospheric, but a valid age can still be computed from the slope. Ages calculated in this way are called *isochron ages* and may utilize all data, or only the data from the plateau region.

Fission-Track Dating

Many natural materials contain small amounts of uranium, which decays, through a series of elements by emission of alpha and beta particles, to lead. This has been exploited for dating since the inception of radiometric methods. ^{238}U decays not only by alpha-particle emission but also by spontaneous fission. The high mass and energies of the fission products disrupt the physical structure of the host material and leave trails of damage that can be enlarged by etching. The density of these *fission tracks* (number/unit area) is dependent on the age of the specimen and the uranium concentration, hence an age can be calculated by measurement of the track density and uranium content. If materials containing fission tracks are heated, the tracks are found to fade as the damaged parts are annealed. Thus the event being dated is the time of cooling of the material below a temperature at which fading is important.

Fission tracks are small and are not visible without enlarging the damaged area. This is done by etching with strong reagents, such as hydrofluoric acid or anhydrous sodium hydroxide. A polished surface is prepared, the sample is etched, and the fission tracks counted over a determined area. The uranium content of the material is measured by counting new tracks generated by irradiating the sample with a closely monitored dose of thermal neutrons. The neutrons induce a calculable fraction of ^{235}U atoms to fission, and, as the $^{238}U/^{235}U$ ratio is known, the amount of ^{238}U may be calculated from the resulting new tracks.

By far the most important mineral for fission-track dating is zircon (zirconium silicate). Zircon is a minor phase associated with many volcanic rocks. It crystallizes at very high temperatures but is resistant to weathering and can often be recognized as a primary magmatic constituent by its sharp crystal faces. Containing relatively high concentrations of uranium, it is very resistant to track fading, making it nearly ideal for production and retention of tracks. Aside from zircon, sphene (calcium titanium oxide) is probably the most useful mineral for fission-track dating. Micas have also been used but have relatively low uranium contents and thus have low track densities in young rocks. Apatite (calcium hydroxy-phosphorate) contains enough uranium, but its tracks anneal at low temperatures, and track fading is often a problem. Volcanic glass differs widely in its ability to retain tracks but has been used for dating as well.

Uranium-Disequilibrium Dating

Many elements are formed as uranium decays by alpha and beta emission to lead. If a mineral containing uranium is closed to all of the elements in the decay series, each element will eventually be present in an amount related to its half-life, a condition known as *radioactive equilibrium*. When this condition obtains, the activities of each of the intermediate daughter products in the series is equal. Because they are different elements the intermediate daughter products may be separated from each other by weathering, differential adsorption, crystallization of minerals that favor one element or another, and various biological processes. This leads to new geochemical systems that are out of equilibrium, and the quantitative departure of the activities from equality can be used as a measure of the time the series was disrupted. Several different isotopic pairs in the uranium decay series have been used for dating in the range from a few years to ca. 1 m.y.

Although the principal use of some uranium-disequilibrium dating systems has been the study of deep-sea sediments, others, notably $^{234}U/^{238}U$, have also been applied with reasonable success to nonmarine carbonates. In water and minerals on continents the $^{234}U/^{238}U$ ratio is greater than unity, because ^{234}U is preferentially leached from minerals after they are damaged by previous decays in the chain leading to it. Uranium is incorporated into calcium carbonate and other secondary minerals, and thereafter the excess ^{234}U decays more rapidly than it is formed until the activity ratio reaches the equilibrium value of unity. The half-life for this process is 248 k.y., and consequently the method is useful over a period of ca. 1 m.y. Another method for dating terrestrial carbonates is based on the ratio ^{230}Th/^{234}U. The basis of the method is that calcium carbonate excludes thorium from its structure during crystallization but includes significant quantities of uranium. As time passes, the amount of ^{230}Th increases because of the decay of both ^{234}U and ^{238}U in the sample. This method is useful over time periods of ca. 300 k.y.

These methods have been applied to carbonates deposited in caves and have helped date fossils of genus *Homo* from southern Europe. These fall mainly in the time interval between 100 and 300 k.y., where other methods are not applicable.

Radiocarbon Dating

Radiocarbon dating is based on the decay of ^{14}C to ^{14}N by beta emission. The method is useful only over the past 70 k.y. or so and therefore finds its principal application in dating the final stages of hominid evolution and in archaeology. Nonetheless, it is useful in some contexts, most of all in archaeology. ^{14}C is produced in the upper atmosphere by cosmic-ray bombardment, oxidized to CO_2, and enters biological systems through the photosynthetic reaction and metabolic reactions of herbivores. Living organisms therefore become radioactive. Inorganic carbonate minerals precipitated from water are also radioactive, because radiocarbon in the atmosphere exchanges with carbonate in solution in lakes and in the ocean. When an organism dies, or when carbonate minerals form, they are removed from the active carbon cycle, and the ^{14}C within them begins to decay. To calculate an age an initial activity of radiocarbon is assumed, the activity of the sample is measured, and ages are computed from

$$t = 1/\lambda \ \ln(A_o/A),$$

where t = time, A = initial activity, A_o = initial activity, and λ is the decay constant. Uncertainties in the age arise from analytical error on the determination of activity and from variations in the assumed initial activity. The latter can be corrected for by using curves calibrated against tree rings and by measuring the ^{13}C content to correct for isotopic fractionation. Radiocarbon dating is the only method that can be applied to fossil materials themselves, although "bone" dates are often not reliable.

See also BIOCHRONOLOGY; STRATIGRAPHY; TIME SCALE. [F.H.B.]

Further Readings

Cook, J., Stringer, C.B., Currant, A.P., Schwarcz, H.P., and Wintle, A.G. (1982) A review of the chronology of the European middle Pleistocene hominid record. Yrbk. Phys. Anthropol. 25:19–65.

Dalrymple, G.B., and Lanphere, M.A. (1969) Potassium-Argon Dating. San Francisco: Freeman.

Faure, G. (1977) Principles of Isotope Geology. New York: Wiley.

Fleischer, R.L., and Hart, Jr., H.R. (1972) Fission track dating: techniques and problems. In W.W. Bishop and J.A. Miller (eds.): Calibration of Hominoid Evolution. Edinburgh: Scottish Academic Press, pp. 135–170.

Ku, T.L. (1976) The uranium-series methods of age determination. Ann. Rev. Earth and Planetary Sci. 4:347–379.

York, D., and Farquhar, R.M. (1972) The Earth's Age and Geochronology. Oxford: Pergamon.

GEOMETRIC MICROLITH *see* STONE-TOOL MAKING

GIBBON *see* APE; HOMINOIDEA; HYLOBATIDAE

GIBRALTAR

The Rock of Gibraltar contains many caves, and two of these have produced Neanderthal remains. An adult (female?) skull was blasted from Forbes' Quarry in 1848, and a child's skull was excavated from the Devil's Tower rock shelter in 1926. Both show typical Neanderthal features, although the adult specimen is small and gracile and cannot be dated accurately. The child is remarkable for its large brain size (ca. 1,450 ml.) for an individual of less than five years of age.

See also NEANDERTHALS. [C.B.S.]

GIGANTISM

The development of radically larger body size is common in small mammals isolated in islands, apparently because the inevitable impoverishment of the island fauna selects for more generalism in the surviving species. "Cope's Rule," the tendency of successive species to become larger in the course of evolution, generally if not always holds true. Many groups originate with a small body size relative to the adaptively optimal size. Also, in herbivores, increased body size in itself is advantageous in that reduced heat loss permits the use of less nutritive and more widely available food; above ca. 15 kg., for instance, mammalian herbivores can subsist entirely on grass and leaves. Individuals may also show phenotypic size increase in response to improved food supply, but abnormally large body size in an individual is usually pathological, especially when caused by hyperpituitarism.

See also DWARFISM; RULES. [D.P.D., R.L.B.]

GIGANTOPITHECUS

Extinct giant hominoid genus first recognized by von Koenigswald on the basis of a single M_3 purchased in a Hong Kong drugstore in 1935. Since then more than 1,000 other specimens, including three massive mandibles, have been recovered from the Siwalik Hills and from the karst caves of southern China and Vietnam. The Chinese species, *Gigantopithecus blacki*, is thought to span the early Pleistocene and at least part of the middle Pleistocene. The earlier

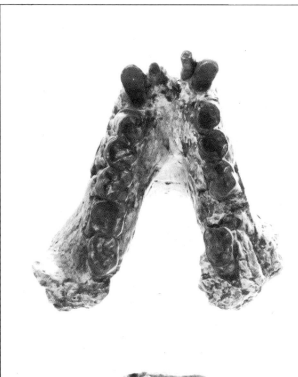

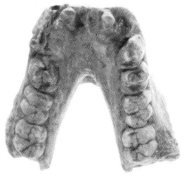

Two of the three mandibles of *Gigantopithecus blacki* from Liucheng, southern China. Photographs of casts. (From Tattersall, 1970.)

Gigantopithecus giganteus (= *G. bilaspurensis*) dates to ca. 9–6 m.y. ago in the Siwalik sequences of Indopakistan. This species is smaller than the Pleistocene Chinese species, and it thus appears that *Gigantopithecus* increased in size throughout the Pliocene and Pleistocene. There has been much discussion concerning the taxonomy and ecology of *Gigantopithecus*. A few workers have argued that this genus should be classified as a hominid. Most workers, however, feel that the supposed hominid traits of *Gigantopithecus* actually represent convergences brought about by a diet necessitating heavy mastication.

See also ASIA (EASTERN); CHINA; DRAGON BONES; HOMINIDAE; HOMINOIDEA; KOENIGSWALD, G.H.R. VON; PONGINAE; SIWALIKS. [G.G.P.]

Further Readings

Koenigswald, G.H.R. von (1952) *Gigantopithecus blacki* von Koenigswald, a giant fossil hominoid from the Pleistocene of southern China. Anthropol. Pap. Am. Mus. Nat. Hist. 43:293–325.

Koenigswald, G.H.R. von (1957) Remarks on *Gigantopithecus* and other hominoid remains from southern China. Proc. Kon. Nederl. Akad. West. 60:153–159.

GILBERT *see* PALEOMAGNETISM

GILSA *see* PALEOMAGNETISM

GLABELLA *see* SKULL

GLACIAL *see* GLACIATION; PLEISTOCENE

GLACIATION

In a narrow sense the formation of glaciers, or glacierization. However, the term is also used in a broader sense to mean a variety of processes related not just to the formation of glaciers but also to their effect on the landscape and their action as an agent of transport and deposition of rock debris. Regions currently or formerly covered by ice are termed "glaciated."

Models of glacial buildup are complicated in detail, but, in simple terms, ice will accumulate wherever snow is not completely melted before more snow falls. In Antarctica it is so cold that melting rates are very low, and ice builds up even though the total annual precipitation compares with that of the Mojave Desert. In many temperate-climate mountain ranges the summer temperatures are quite warm, but glacierization occurs because the winter snowfall still exceeds the summer melt. The Antarctic conditions of constant dry cold also occur in the rest of the world at high altitudes; thus even in the tropics great mountains, such as Kilimanjaro, Ruwenzori, Mount Carstensz in New Guinea, and Aconcagua and other Andean volcanos, are glaciated even though most "snow" occurs only in the form of nightly frost.

Ice is a crystalline mineral that yields readily to pressure. Thus glaciers flow under the force of gravity, partly through internal deformation and partly by sliding on films of water where the ice presses against its bed. This is because water expands on freezing, and (by the same token) shrinks on melting; pressure can "squeeze" ice down into a liquid. The warmer the ice, the more easily it liquefies under pressure; by the end of the summer the slow rise in the body temperature of the ice at the lower end of a mountain glacier can cause its base to turn suddenly to water and send a mass of ice several miles long skating ponderously downhill in a *jokul-laup*, or "ice-run." Normally, however, the lower margins—end and sides—of glaciers are more or less stationary even though the ice within the glacier is constantly moving forward. This is because the edge of the glacier is at the point where the rate of melting and the rate of inflow of more ice are at a zero balance. Under stable climate conditions the ice edge may remain in one well-defined zone for many years, while rocks, sand, and clay brought by the ever-flowing ice keep piling up.

Evidence of Glaciation

The former presence of glaciers can be reconstructed from the sediments, landforms, and fossils that remain after the ice has melted. The sedimentary evidence is in the form of *drift*, or ice-deposited sediments, and in the secondary effects of glaciation on ocean waters and climate, which can be seen in nonglacial strata. Drift includes *till* or stony clays deposited directly from glacial melting; stratified till or *outwash* laid down under the influence of currents in lakes and estuaries; deep-ocean tills or *diamictite* composed of fine clays and scattered pebbles and boulders deposited from the melting of glacial ice at sea; and *loess* formed of windblown glacial dust.

Till is laid down in characteristic ways that are identified by the shape and extent of the resulting deposit. These include *moraines*, ridges of loose till built up from the material riding on the ice, or in it, which mark the melting zones along the margins and bottom of the glacier; *kames*, *eskers*, and *drumlins*, mounds or sinuous ridges of till deposited beneath the ice in meltwater channels or in fissures; *kettles*, depressions in the moraines left by the melting of solitary blocks of ice under the debris; and *erratics*, solitary rocks that were carried by glaciers (or by

icebergs floating in the ocean) to resting places far outside their expected occurrence.

Outwash and diamictite build up in layers, and in protected basins the glacial clays may settle out such that each summer's melting is reflected by a thin layer. Such annual layers are termed *varves*, and varved deposits have been used to construct prehistoric time scales in the same way that tree rings have been used in the southwestern United States. Annual accumulation layers have also been detected in glacial ice itself, and cores taken in Greenland and Antarctica have been analyzed to show year-by-year variations in atmospheric carbon dioxide, carbon-14 production, and other conditions back to the middle Pleistocene. Varve chronology, on the other hand, has not been extended much past the end of the last glacial, but it has yielded important information about changes to vegetation and human occupation in northern lands.

Loess is deposited as blankets of yellow-brown, highly porous silt downwind from the continental ice sheets in the central United States, in central Europe and the Ukraine, and above all in the North China plains, where total thickness locally exceeds 100 m. The fine, often limy dust, known as "rock flour," is produced by the grinding of the boulder-studded glacial ice against bedrock. "Rock flour" is carried in suspension by meltwater (causing the flat powder-blue color of glacial lakes) to mudflats, where it is exposed to the cold, dry winds that blow constantly off the glaciers. Late summer near the glacial fronts must have been a time of repeated, choking dust storms, and the loess plains of the United States and China have proven to be very subject to renewed wind erosion when droughts reduce the soil moisture.

The effects of glaciation on landscape, when adequately preserved, are unmistakable. On relatively low-relief terrain, the entire ice sheet passes over the land like giant's sandpaper, removing soil and loose rock and grinding the bedrock down to gently rolling swells and hollows. Where the ice covers the entire landscape, its base can "flow" uphill over obstacles and out of depressions, grinding down the land with regard more to its variations in hardness than to slope or preexisting drainage. The result of this random excavation, and the irregular dumping of glacial debris, is that glaciated flatlands are very poorly drained. Stream patterns are incoherent, and the land is dotted with swamps, ponds, and gouged-out lakes. Some glacial lakes, such as the Great Lakes of the central United States, Lake Winnipeg, and Great Slave Lake, are among the largest in the world. Glacial excavation was also responsible for the beautiful lochs of Scotland, the Swiss lakes, and the Baltic Sea.

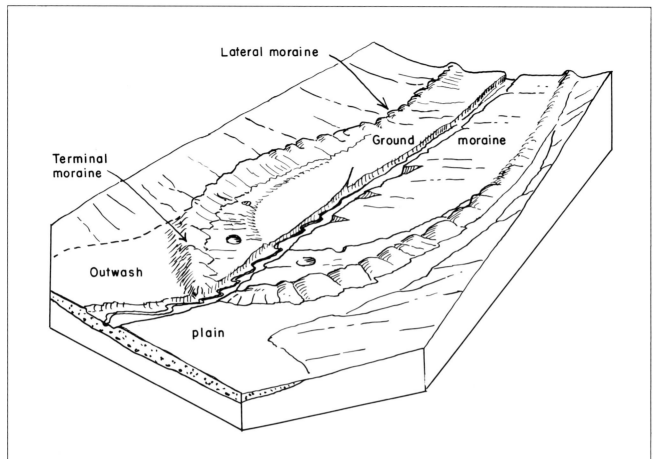

Moraines. Debris brought by flowing ice accumulates in terminal, lateral, and ground moraines and is redeposited as outwash terraces by meltwater. As the glacier retreats, successive outwash plains are developed upstream. (After Flint, 1971, Glacial and Quaternary Geology. Redrawn by permission of John Wiley & Sons.)

Where mountains protrude above the surface of the moving ice, their sides are hollowed out into steep cliffs with knifelike junctures quite different from those resulting from normal erosion; the Matterhorn, Jungfrau, and other toothlike peaks in the Alps owe their odd shape to this effect. Some ranges are sliced away until only isolated pegs, called *monadnocks* (after Mount Monadnock in New Hampshire) or *nunataks*, remain. Mountain valleys, like Yosemite, through which glacial ice has passed are scooped out to a distinctive U-shaped profile, unlike the V-shaped profile of nonglaciated valleys. In northern regions where such valleys were carved far below modern sea levels during the glacials, their drowned lower reaches are seen as the deep, winding inlets known as *fjords*. The most durable and conclusive evidence of glaciation, however, is the unmistakable polish given to hard bedrock by the scouring and scraping of rock-laden ice. Such rounded, glossy surfaces covered with parallel grooves, called *striated pavements*, are evidence for glaciations 300 m.y. ago in the Sahara Desert, and for

the presence of the final ice sheets of the Pleistocene some 15 k.y. ago in New York's Central Park.

Glaciation also has an effect on sea level because of the vast amounts of water that can be trapped as glacial ice on land. The coastal landscapes of today, with broad, shallow continental shelves extending out to a dramatic shelf-break at ca. 300-m. depth, and stair-step alternations of cliffs and terraces going inland, are a product of sudden drops in sea level and equally abrupt returns to near present levels during Pleistocene glacial cycles. "Normal" landscapes, when sea-level changes were much more gradual, consisted of very gently sloping coastal plains that extended for hundreds or even thousands of kilometers inland, and an offshore apron of sediment with a slope that gradually grew steeper with depth.

Fossil evidence of glaciation is partly negative— snakes have not yet repopulated the island of Ireland since it was last covered by ice—and partly positive. For instance, the fossil remains of cold-adapted life forms are found embedded in glacially influenced deposits (e.g. with glacial erratics, loess, or glacial

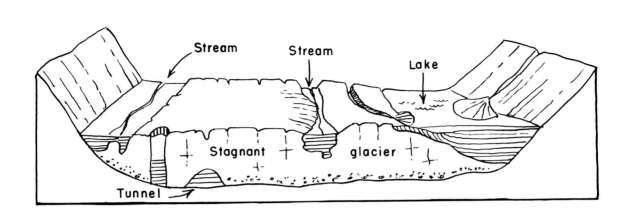

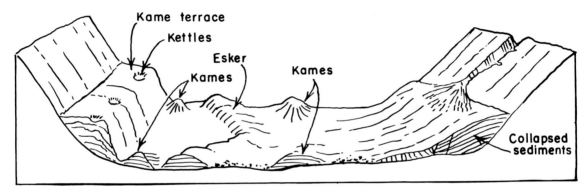

Kames and eskers. As stagnant ice (above) melts, bodies of sediment under the ice are exposed and those on the ice are left unsupported. (After Flint, 1971, Glacial and Quaternary Geology. Redrawn by permission of John Wiley & Sons.)

outwash debris), while nonglacial beds interstratified with the glacial beds contain fossils of distinctly more warm-climate types. The fossil record also contains clear indications of interisland and intercontinental migrations stimulated by lowered sea level, which in turn has been ascribed to the build-up of ice during glacial periods.

Glaciation in the Pleistocene

Some 20 k.y. ago most of Canada and the north-central United States was covered by a dome of ice ca. 3 km. thick centered not on the North Pole but on the west side of Hudson Bay. Similarly, northern Europe (including the north of Russia and western Siberia) was covered by another mass with its thickest part in central Sweden. The North American ice, termed the Laurentide Ice Sheet, bulged outward under its own weight as far as New York, Cincinnati, and Kansas City; in central Alberta it met mountain glaciers flowing eastward onto the plains from the Cordilleran (Rocky Mountains) Ice Sheet. In Europe the Scandinavian Ice Sheet buried all of Ireland and most of England and extended past the future sites of Berlin, Warsaw, and Moscow, to join with ice flowing down from the mountains of the northern Urals and

the Tamyr peninsula. In addition, in all the mountainous regions of the earth—not only the Cascades, Alps, Elburz, Tien Shan, and Himalayas but also on the high mountains of the tropics and in southern regions, such as Tierra del Fuego, the Falklands, and New Zealand—the small glaciers and ice caps of today were greatly enlarged and extended more than two kilometers in elevation below their present melting limits.

This was the last "Ice Age," which ended suddenly only 13.5 k.y. ago. Until very recently textbooks presented a relatively simple picture of a Pleistocene with four such "Ice Ages." Deep-sea studies, however, have provided cores from relatively undisturbed and complete sequences that show a variety of climatic oscillations superimposed on one another. In the current view continental drift has caused the oceans to grow progressively colder and climate patterns more and more unstable because of changes in ocean circulation. Sea-level changes of several hundred meters during the Cenozoic are evidence for periodic waxing and waning of polar ice caps as the trend toward colder climates proceeded in a stepwise fashion. Not until the Pleistocene, though, did ice sheets also begin to appear on the plains around the Arctic

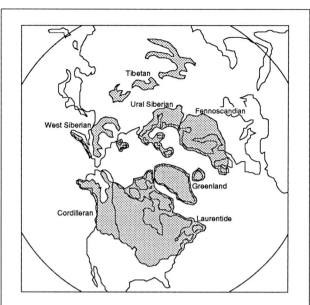

Pleistocene glaciers of the northern hemisphere. Shaded areas are the regions usually covered by glacial ice during a glacial maximum; lines broken by X's are the zones of coalescence between major ice sheets. Note that Beringia is normally ice-free even during a glacial advance but that the way south is blocked by the Cordilleran ice sheet. Actual shorelines (during glacial regression of sea level) not shown. (After Flint, 1971, Glacial and Quaternary Geology. Redrawn by permission of John Wiley & Sons.)

Ocean, as the climate changes became sharply stronger. The second half of the Pleistocene, in some sets of evidence, shows even wider and more uneven swings in climate than the first part, so the trend may be continuing.

Also as a result (probably) of continuing change in ocean circulation during the Pleistocene, it has been observed that the center of accumulation of the great North American ice sheets in each of the four periods of maximum advances—the classic Nebraskan, Kansan, Illinoisan, and Wisconsinian—was to the east of the previous one, as their names (based on deposits at the margins) would indicate.

Europeans also counted four glacial periods, first recognized as Günz, Mindel, Riss, and Würm (from oldest to youngest) in the river terraces of the upper Danube valley, but now more widely known from the more accurate stratigraphy in the North Sea basin by the names of Menap, Elster, Saale, and Weichsel. Many correlations to the North American sequence have been argued, but it now seems clear that in Europe the first continental glaciers (Menap) did not appear until the time of the Kansan. The Saale glacial phase is not considered as a separate ice age in North America and is identified as an early phase of the Wisconsinian. According to the area covered by ice sheets, and by estimates of average temperature,

the Illinoisan or Elster glacial episode was the most severe of the Pleistocene, and the interglacial that followed was the mildest.

Glacial Climate Cycles

It has become apparent that in the Pleistocene normally inconsequential impulses from several different sources, such as variations in the earth's orbit and in the carbon dioxide content of the atmosphere, have triggered catastrophic swings from glacial to interglacial conditions. The Pleistocene record shows that there were about 15 major cold periods and 50 minor advances during its 1.5-m.y. duration, or one major cold period every 100 k.y. These major glacial advances are termed *glacials*, and are separated by periods of warmer climate termed *interglacials*. Some stratigraphers refer to the minor glacial extremes as *stadials*, and periods of retreat as *interstadials*. In addition the record shows that glacials were most intense at ca. 0.5-m.y. intervals, and it is the broad but diffuse imprint of these four groups of cold-climate cycles that gave rise to the four-glacials hypothesis in North America. The 0.5-m.y. periods are first seen clearly in the middle Pliocene when a distinct cold-climate spell at ca. 2.5 m.y., known as the Pinedale or in Europe the Pretiglian, caused a marked expansion of mountain glaciers, changes in continental ecology, and an expansion of colder surface waters in the oceans. A few geologists have argued that this should mark the beginning of the Pleistocene. The shorter periods are not conspicuous until about 1.5 m.y. Even broader glacio-eustatic cycles with an irregular (probably multiplex) period of ca. 5 m.y. seem to have affected world climate and sea level during the entire Cenozoic; the last minimum in this cycle occurred in the early Pliocene at ca. 4.5 m.y., so it is possible that Pleistocene conditions owe something to this effect as well.

Orbital Effects (Milankovitch Cycles)   It has long been known that the earth's attitude and orbit exhibit long-term variations. The tilt of the earth's axis rocks back and forth between 22 and 25 degrees at periods close to 41 k.y. (it is presently at about 23½ degrees). Precession of the axis (such that the tilted poles wobble in a circle) and precession of the orbit (such that the apex of the orbital ellipse rotates slowly around the sun) have a combined effect that results in a shift of summer and winter times with respect to the apex of the orbit every 22 k.y. At one extreme, summers in the northern hemisphere occur when the earth is closest to the sun in its elliptical orbit, which makes the summers very hot, and northern winters occur when the earth is farthest away, making them abnormally cold. In the southern hemisphere, of course, the opposite effect is felt at the

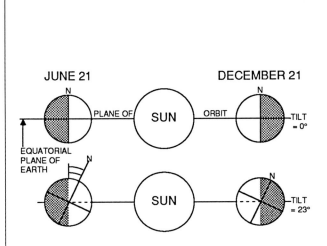

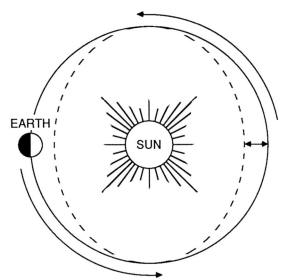

Changing Shape of the Ellipse

Axial tilt. When tilt is increased, polar regions receive more sunlight, since the summer sun is higher in the sky, while intensity of winter light is little changed. When tilt is low, regions close to the pole receive practically no sunlight the year round.

Orbital eccentricity. The shape of the earth's orbit changes from nearly circular to more elliptical, in cycles that repeat at irregular intervals concentrating around 100,000 and 400,000 years.

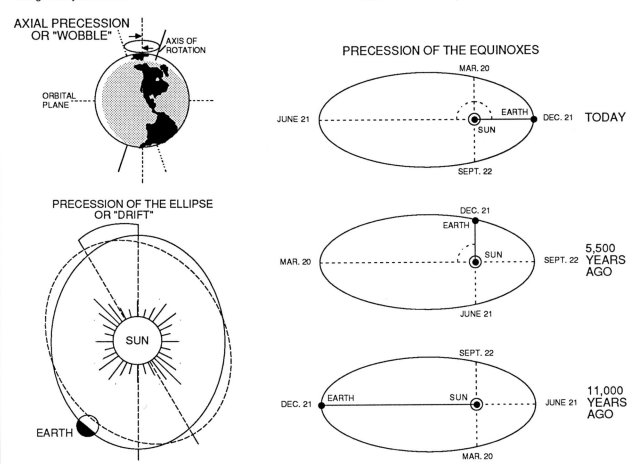

Precession of axial tilt and orbit. "Wobble" and "drift" together result in a cycle of 22,000 years in the timing of the seasons with regard to the orbit. Today the winter solstice in the northern hemisphere occurs when the earth is near the sun; 11,000 years ago it occurred when the earth was far from the sun.

same time, with cool summers and mild winters. Some 11 k.y. later the situation is reversed.

Finally, the shape of the orbit itself changes from an almost perfect circle to a slight ellipse (eccentricity of 0.06) in complex variations that work out to two principal frequencies grouped about 100 k.y. and 450 k.y. When the orbit is most elliptical the 22-k.y. seasonality cycle has maximum effect. At such times the abnormally cold winters appear to lead to maximum glacial advances in the northern hemisphere, while coincidental mild summers and winters in the southern hemisphere have little impact on the Antarctic, which is thermally isolated by the circum-Antarctic Current. In sum, the unstable climate of the northern hemisphere is where the Pleistocene is happening, while the Antarctic cools the world oceans to make the Pleistocene possible but does not enter into short-term glacial cycles in any significant way.

That orbital variations would affect climate was first hypothesized by the Scots geologist James Croll in the 1860s, and with much more mathematical precision by the Serbian geographer M. Milankovitch in the late 1930s. It was not until deep-sea cores,

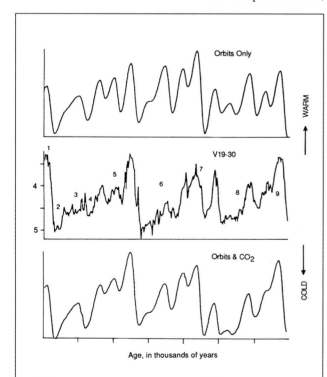

Pleistocene temperature changes. With present day on the left, the top figure expresses the calculated effect on global temperatures due to Milankovitch cycles back to about 350,000 years ago and the middle figure is the change in ice volume estimated from oxygen isotope ratios during the same time. The "fit" of these two curves is improved when the probable effect of carbon dioxide change due to temperature change is added to the orbital curve (bottom figure).

with their long undisturbed record, became available in the 1960s, however, that the Milankovitch periodicities could be shown to have actually influenced global climate. The 100-k.y. cycles and the 22-k.y. cycles are both much more strongly expressed during the past 1 m.y. than in the earlier Pleistocene, while the 41-k.y. cycles seem to have about the same amplitude in terms of temperature change from the beginning of the Pleistocene. These trends cannot be due to marked differences in precession or eccentricity variations in such a short time and must be because plate tectonics continue to change ocean circulation and make northern-hemisphere climate ever more sensitive to such influences.

Isotopic Temperature Measurements

Individual atoms of chemical elements (such as carbon, oxygen, potassium, or uranium) are not uniform in weight, due to variations in the number of neutrons in the nucleus. The atoms of different weight are the *isotopes* of an element. Some isotopes (e.g. carbon with 14 neutrons, potassium with 40 neutrons, or uranium with 236 neutrons) are radioactive because the number of neutrons causes an awkward or unstable nuclear geometry, but most are stable in any of the common elements. Isotopes cannot be distinguished by chemical activity, but the differences in mass make a slight difference in the speed at which they make and break chemical bonds. "Speed" at this level of reality is the same as temperature, and changes in temperature therefore affect the behavior of isotopes. With the development of the mass spectrometer, which accurately measures isotopic abundances in very small samples, it has become possible to interpret isotope percentages in the geologic record in terms of past temperatures.

Of these paleothermometers the isotopes of oxygen are the system most widely used to interpret glacial climates. The most common isotope of oxygen is ^{16}O (oxygen with 16 neutrons), but ^{18}O is also relatively abundant. Because ^{18}O is fully 12.5 percent heavier and consequently harder to excite, molecules of water made with this isotope are more difficult to evaporate from the ocean surface than those made with ^{16}O. As a result the water condensing from atmospheric water vapor, including the water in continental ice sheets, is isotopically "lighter" than sea water. When considerable amounts of fresh water are temporarily trapped in ice, the percentage of ^{18}O in sea water and in the bodies of marine life forms increases. With some other factors accounted for it is possible to derive a fairly accurate picture of global ice volume changes by monitoring changes in the relative abundance of ^{18}O and ^{16}O in fossil shells found in successive layers of deep-sea sediments.

Carbon isotopes in marine fossils also provide a measure of climate change. Increases in ocean temperature are associated with increases in atmospheric carbon dioxide: present data indicate a 40-percent increase in atmospheric carbon dioxide since the end of the last glacial. Lighter ^{12}C is preferentially moved out of the ocean and into the air, compared with ^{13}C, in a way similar to the trapping of light oxygen in ice. When carbon and oxygen data are combined, the glacial climate history measured by isotopic ratios becomes almost precisely similar to the climate changes predicted by orbital mathematics.

The isotopic climate curve is now relatively well dated back to ca. 360 k.y. Preliminary observations, as well as other estimates based on interpretations of chemistry and paleontology in deep-sea cores, extend glacial climate curves with less certainty back to the beginning of the Pleistocene at 1.5 m.y. A particular point of notice is the "spike" or ice-volume minimum known as 5e, at ca. 127 k.y., which appears to mark a time of considerably greater glacial regression and probably warmer climate than the present postglacial interlude. This is known to be the level of the Eemian interglacial, at which most stratigraphers place the beginning of the late Pleistocene.

See also MILANKOVITCH, MILUTIN; PLEISTOCENE; SEA-LEVEL CHANGE. [J.A.V.C., G.K.]

Further Readings

Berger, W., Imbrie, J., Hays, J., Kukla, G., and Salzman, B., eds. (1984) Milankovitch and Climate Change. Hingham, Mass.: Riedel.
Bowen, D.Q. (1978) Quaternary Geology. Oxford: Pergamon.
Denton, G.H., and Hughes, T.J., eds. (1981) The Last Great Ice Sheets. New York: Wiley.
Flint, R.F. (1971) Glacial and Quaternary Geology. New York: Wiley.

GLOVER'S RULE   *see*   RULES

"GOLDEN SPIKE"

In stratigraphy, a physical reference point. This concept, following the work of the Stratigraphic Committee of the London Geological Society, has been used to pick apart several durable tangles. In the 1950s and 1960s, with improved correlation techniques like radiometric dating and planktonic microfossil zonations, it became obvious that the boundaries of geological ages and epochs, as defined in separate type sections, left significant gaps and overlaps. Also, many of the ages and epochs were tacitly redefined in each region, not to mention in each discipline, according to special or locally appropriate criteria. This was particularly true in the later Cenozoic, and

especially in the Pleistocene, due to the differing criteria used by anthropologists and glaciologists as well as marine and vertebrate paleontologists.

In resolving the conflict of definitions the Committee first proposed the principle that "base defines boundary," which sets the rule that each successive unit extends up to, and no further than, the base of the next. The Committee further proposed that each unit have as its sole definition a physical reference point at the base, located in an appropriate geological exposure. From this "golden spike" (in actual fact, often an iron bar) the recognition of the unit in other areas is a matter of correlation rather than redefinition. The location, or relocation, of a "golden spike" is a matter of international agreement. The principles of the Committee have been fully adopted in modern stratigraphical codes.

See also BIOCHRONOLOGY; CENOZOIC; MIOCENE. [J.A.V.C.]

Further Readings

Ager, D.V. (1984) The stratigraphic code and what it implies. In W.A. Berggren and J.A. Van Couvering (eds.): Catastrophes in Earth History. Princeton: Princeton University Press, pp. 91–99.

GOMBORÉ   *see*   MELKA KONTOURÉ

GONGWANGLING   *see*   LANTIAN

GORGOPITHECUS   *see* CERCOPITHECINAE

GORILLA   *see*   APE; HOMININAE

GORJANOVIĆ-KRAMBERGER, DRAGUTIN KARL (1856–1936)

Croatian paleoanthropologist. Between 1899 and 1905 Gorjanović-Kramberger initiated excavations at Krapina, a Paleolithic rock shelter ca. 40 km. west of Zagreb (Yugoslavia). This work yielded some 800 fragments of fossil hominids, a large collection of faunal remains, and several thousand stone tools. Gorjanović-Kramberger concluded that these Mousterian remains represented a population of Neanderthals, which he considered to have been directly ancestral to anatomically modern *Homo sapiens*.

See also KRAPINA; NEANDERTHALS. [F.S.]

GRADE

Ill-defined term, derived from the archaic idea of the *scala nature*, loosely denoting a "level of organization." The epithet *monkey*, for example, applies both to members of the Ceboidea and to the Cercopithecoidea, although together these do not represent a monophyletic grouping. In this case the grade *monkey* denotes those living primates that are in some intuitive way "more evolved" than the strepsirhine primates but "less evolved" than the apes and humans. Within the human lineage the notion of grades has been used to obscure the necessity for the precise delineation of species; as long as forms of more or less similar brain size or archaeological context could be grouped together as a grade, there was no need to inquire as to whether the grouping actually corresponded to an identifiable biological reality. Thus, while the notion of the grade may occasionally be useful in a vague, vernacular sort of way, it should never be employed when species or monophyletic taxa are under discussion.

See also MONKEY; MONOPHYLY; SCALA NATURAE. [I.T.]

GRADUALISM see EVOLUTION

GRAECOPITHECUS see NEAR EAST; PONGINAE

GRANDE COUPURE

Originally proposed in 1909 by H.G. Stehlin to denote a "first order" event in mammalian history, the "Grande Coupure" denotes the wholesale replacement of archaic lineages in central and western Europe by modern ungulate and carnivore groups from North America, and by cricetids, murids, and other advanced rodents from Southeast Asia, during the early Oligocene. Stehlin saw this change as a single event that coincided with the end of the Eocene and as the greatest revolution in mammalian faunas during the entire Tertiary. Although Stehlin's idea of perfect sychronicity has not survived, modern stratigraphers still recognize a massive turnover beginning in the basal Oligocene (Stampian). This was in fact coincident with an episode of global cooling, sea-level regression, and very high extinction rates in marine invertebrates, including mollusks and microfauna, which has been termed the "End-Eocene Event." The length of time involved in the mammalian turnover, however, is a subject of debate, since many of the immigrant taxa do not appear in Europe until after the great mid-Oligocene sea-level regression.

The African mammal fauna was also revolutionized in the Grande Coupure, although the evidence is found only in the Eo-Oligocene "before" of the Fayum and the early Miocene "after" of Songhor and Rusinga and does not provide more than a broad estimate of early to mid-Oligocene age for this momentous transition. Equids did not enter Africa at this time, and some of the rodent lineages that did invade were of European origin, but with these exceptions the immigrants into Africa were from groups that were also part of the Grande Coupure in Europe: rhinoceroses, chalicotheres, primitive hornless ruminants (tragulids, gelocids, moschids), suids, fissiped carnivores (mustelids, viverrids, arctocyonids, felids), ochotonids, and Asian-origin rodents. The introduction of this diversity of new mammals and their explosive adaptation (most notably in the ruminants, which rapidly gave rise to giraffids and bovids) had a predictably strong effect on the indigenous African groups. By the early Miocene some, such as the tenrecs, hyraxes, African hyaenodonts, and southern-hemisphere rodents, were greatly reduced, while others, such as barytheres, embrithopods, African lorises and marsupials, and possibly the last mainland lemurs, had become extinct. On the other hand the advanced proboscideans and above all the catarrhine primates adapted to the new conditions and entered the Miocene with a wide diversity of successful new lineages.

Recent redating of middle Cenozoic faunas in South America suggests that ancestral platyrrhines (not far removed from Fayum anthropoids) and southern-hemisphere rodents first appeared there in the early or middle Oligocene and not in the middle Eocene. Evidence for a South Atlantic crossing between Africa and South America at about this time is also apparent in the present disjunct distribution and fossil record of other terrestrial animals, from constrictors and iguanas to cichlid fishes and various insects. Apparently the Grande Coupure was a time of unusual opportunities for intercontinental migration as a result of extreme sea-level regression.

See also CENOZOIC; FAYUM; RUSINGA; SEA-LEVEL CHANGE.
[J.A.V.C.]

Further Readings

Savage, D.E., and Russell, D.S. (1983) Mammalian Paleofaunas of the World. Reading, Mass.: Addison-Wesley.

Van Couvering, J.A., Aubry, M.-P., Berggren, W.A., Bujak, J.P., Naeser, C.W., and Wieser, T. (1981) The Terminal Eocene Event and the Polish connection. Palaeogeogr. Palaeoclimatol. Palaeoecol. 36:321–362.

GRAVE GOODS see RITUAL

GRAVETTIAN

Early Upper Paleolithic industrial complex of Europe, ca. 28,000–19,000 B.P., characterized by straight-backed points and burins. While the broad-

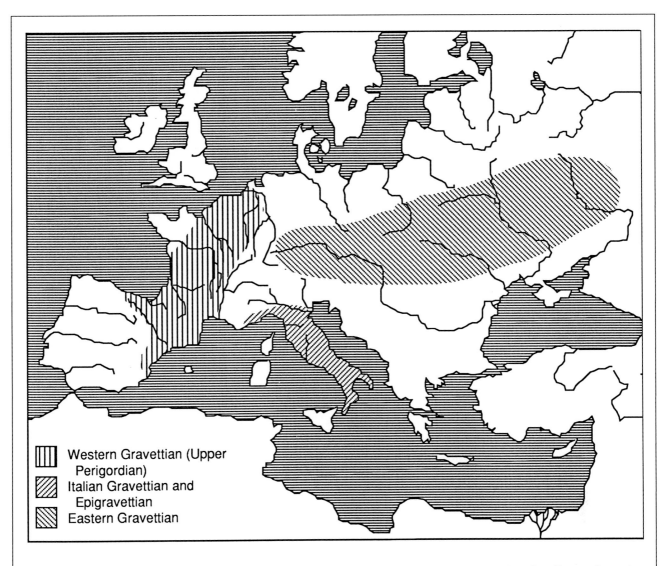

Distribution map of Gravettian and Upper Perigordian sites, separated into Franco-Belgian Upper Perigordian, Eastern Gravettian of central and eastern Europe, and Italian Gravettian and Epigravettian.

est use of this term sometimes includes the Upper Perigordian complex of southwestern France, the Gravettian is more often restricted to industries from eastern France, southern Germany, Austria, Czechoslovakia, southern Poland, Russia, the Ukraine, Romania, Yugoslavia, Greece, and Italy, as well as from Mediterranean Spain. These industries are distinguished by regionally specific forms but lack the specific tool types that mark the various stages of the Upper Perigordian (with the exception of Font-Robert tanged points and Noailles burins). Early Upper Paleolithic industries with backed *and* Font-Robert points from Belgium and northern France are most often grouped with the Upper Perigordian.

In eastern Europe local variants of the Gravettian, such as the Pavlovian, Molodovan, and Streletskayan, each with distinctive point forms (e.g. Kostenki

shouldered points, bifacial tanged points, triangular concave-based points with bifacial pressure flaking), are grouped as the Eastern Gravettian. Eastern Gravettian sites suggest greater economic specialization, technological skills, and social complexity than are currently known from other contemporaneous regions. Exploitation of large herd animals, especially mammoth, formed the basis for this adaptation, which included large-scale meat storage, use of bone for fuel in deep pit-hearths, construction of huts or tents using mammoth bone for support when wood was unavailable (Pavlov, Dolni Věstonice, Dömös, Kostenki I-1), baked-clay animal figurines fired to temperatures of ca. 800° C (Dolni Věstonice), elaborate burials with numerous ornaments and tools (Sungir), and large numbers of female or "Venus" figurines in bone, stone, and ivory (Kostenki I,1,

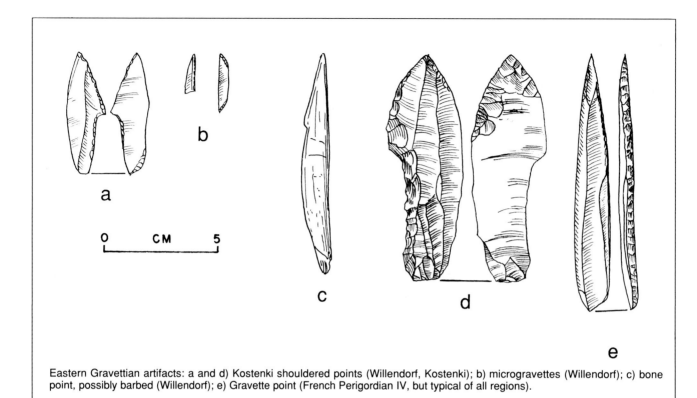

Eastern Gravettian artifacts: a and d) Kostenki shouldered points (Willendorf, Kostenki); b) microgravettes (Willendorf); c) bone point, possibly barbed (Willendorf); e) Gravette point (French Perigordian IV, but typical of all regions).

Dolni Věstonice, Willendorf, Pavlov, Předmosti). Long-distance trade is attested to by the appearance of shells at inland sites and by the presence of "foreign" stone. A mammoth tusk with elaborate incised patterns from Předmosti and other carved pieces in bone and ivory hint at symbolic and ritual complexity. Human remains associated with Gravettian sites in this region are essentially of modern type, although some (e.g. Předmosti) exhibit extremely robust brow- and nuchal-ridges, which have been used to suggest local retention of "Neanderthal" characteristics.

In the Mediterranean area Gravettian industries are associated with fewer details of cultural elaboration, although female figurines are known from several sites (Savignano, Grimaldi). In Italy Noailles burins are numerous and are associated with gravettes and backed bladelets as early as 27,000 B.P.; other Gravettian assemblages contain Font-Robert points and/or truncated pieces, all hallmarks of Perigordian V substages in southwestern France. The latest Gravettian levels, at ca. 20,000 B.P., contain geometric elements that presage the subsequent development of Epigravettian industries in this area. Engraved and painted slabs are rare or absent in the southern facies of the Gravettian, although an engraved ibex on bone was recovered from Paglicci (Italy), in addition to a human burial with elaborate grave goods from an underlying Gravettian level at the same site.

The Gravettian occurs during a major cold phase of the last glaciation. Although brief warmer fluctua-tions are represented at some sites (e.g. Dolni Věstonice), glacial conditions appear to have prevented the occupation of the North European plain during the entire interval.

See also AURIGNACIAN; BACHO KIRO; DOLNI VĚSTONICE; ECONOMY, PREHISTORIC; EPIGRAVETTIAN; EXOTICS; JEWELRY; KOSTENKI; LATE PALEOLITHIC; MAN-LAND RELATIONSHIPS; MOLODOVA; PALEOLITHIC IMAGE; PALEOLITHIC LIFEWAYS; PAVLOV; PERIGORDIAN; PŘEDMOSTI; STORAGE; SUNGIR; UPPER PALEOLITHIC. [A.S.B.]

Further Readings

Gamble, C. (1986) The Palaeolithic Settlement of Europe. Cambridge: Cambridge University Press.

Valoch, K. (1968) Evolution of the Palaeolithic in central and eastern Europe. Curr. Anthropol. 9:351–368.

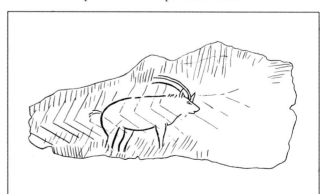

Engraved bone with ibex and chevrons (Italy), outline emphasized.

GREGORY, WILLIAM KING (1876-1970)

American paleontologist. While a student at Columbia University (1899-1910) Gregory became assistant to H.F. Osborn (1857-1935) at the American Museum of Natural History in New York City. In 1921, 11 years after joining the museum full-time, he founded the Department of Comparative Anatomy (later incorporated into the Department of Vertebrate Paleontology). Although his interests in vertebrate paleontology ranged from fish to reptiles and mammals, he had a particular interest in paleoprimatology. During his highly productive career he published a number of influential works in this area, such as his 1920 paper on *Notharctus*. He also published extensively on the evolution of mammalian dentition, with particular reference to human origins. It is worth noting that Gregory was the first American to endorse Dart's view that *Australopithecus* was a hominid. Among the several books he wrote was *Evolution Emerging* (1951), which summarizes his lifework.

[F.S.]

GROUP SELECTION *see* EVOLUTION; SOCIOBIOLOGY

GUITARRERO CAVE

Paleoindian cave site in the Andean foothills of central Peru. Excavated by T. Lynch, the cave contained a series of lozenge-shaped or tanged projectile points dating between 11,000 and 10,000 B.P. and also preserved a wide range of perishable artifacts—fragments of textiles, baskets, wooden and bone tools—previously unknown from this early period. The more recent deposits contained abundant plant remains, including cultivated beans.

See also PALEOINDIAN. [L.S.A.P., D.H.T.]

GUMBA *see* RUSINGA

GÜNZ *see* GLACIATION; PLEISTOCENE

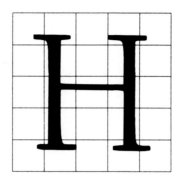

HABILIS, HOMO   see   HOMO HABILIS

HADAR

Central Ethiopian (see map in MIDDLE AWASH entry) stratified series of middle Pliocene age, 3.6–2.9 m.y. by K-Ar, volcanic tephra correlation, faunal analysis, and paleomagnetic dating. The area of fossiliferous exposures in the Afar site of Hadar thus far explored measures ca. 16 by 6 km. The Pliocene sediments are mostly horizontal, exposed in desert-badland topography, and contain abundant, well-preserved mammalian fossils including the remains of early hominids.

Hadar's paleontological and anthropological significance was discovered in 1968 by M. Taieb, a French geologist working on the Awash River system. Taieb organized a brief geological and paleontological survey of the Afar in 1971, in which he was joined by D.C. Johanson, Y. Coppens, and J. Kalb. These workers formed the International Afar Research Expedition (IARE). They chose Hadar from the many other available sites to begin intensive investigation because of its estimated age, the potential for dating, and the excellent preservation of faunal remains.

During the initial field season in 1973 the first early hominid fossils were recovered from Hadar, a knee joint with fragmentary proximal femora and a partial temporal. Nearly 6,000 fossils of artiodactyls, perissodactyls, proboscideans, nonhuman primates, carnivores, birds, reptiles, rodents, and other mammals, a total of 87 species, were recovered in 1973 and in subsequent seasons. In the fall of 1974 a larger team returned to continue the search and soon recovered hominid teeth, maxillae, and mandibles.

At the end of November D.C. Johanson discovered at Locality 288 the partial skeleton of a tiny female hominid, which was nicknamed "Lucy." The 1975 field season brought even more hominid remains, this time at Locality 333. This locality has been interpreted as evidence for the catastrophic death of a group of hominids. The 333 site yielded, by the close of excavations during the 1976–1977 field season, hundreds of hominid fossil fragments derived from at least 13 individuals representing all ages. All of the Hadar fossils were returned after study to the National Museum of Ethiopia in Addis Ababa, where they are permanently housed.

The Hadar Formation consists of at least 280 m. of sediment. Over 100 stratigraphic sections have been studied thus far, and it has been possible to subdivide the sedimentary sequence into four stratigraphic members. The majority of fossil vertebrates and all of the hominid fossils are derived from the Sidi Hakoma, Denen Dora, and lower Kada Hadar members. The Sidi Hakoma member (SH) yielded the 1973 hominid knee joint, several hominid mandibles, and the hominid palates. The Denen Dora member (DD) contained the hominid sample from the 333 locality, while the Kada Hadar member (KH) produced the "Lucy" specimen.

Radiometric dating has established the top of the Hadar hominid-bearing succession at ca. 2.9 m.y. ago. Dating for the lower units has been more controversial, with estimates from radiometric, biochronologic, and trace-element composition analysis ranging between 3.6 and 3.3 m.y. ago. Thus it can be stated confidently that the "Lucy" specimen is ca. 3 m.y. old, while some of the other, stratigraphically lower Hadar hominids are at least 3.3 and possibly as

Outcrops of Pliocene sediments at the site of Hadar (Ethiopia). (Photograph by Don Johanson, courtesy of the Institute of Human Origins.)

much as 3.6 m.y. old.

The wealth of paleontological material at Hadar is partly due to the low-energy depositional context in the Hadar basin during Pliocene times. The sediments are fluvio-lacustrine in nature, with interbedded, alternating sand units and silty clay units. The relatively regular interbedding combines with the lateral continuity seen in the Hadar units to give the impression of rhythmic sedimentation in and around a lake. The taphonomic setting is unusual, in that the bones are remarkably intact and unweathered, indicating little postmortem transport. Partial and even intact skeletons are relatively common, and the bones show little evidence of weathering, which suggests rapid burial.

The focal element of Hadar environment during Pliocene times was a freshwater lake surrounded by marshes and fed by rivers from the Ethiopian Escarpment. Microfauna and pollen indicate that the entire site occupied an elevation much higher than it does today. The local environment was far more humid and wooded than the barren badlands that characterize the area today. Fossil remains of such megafauna as hippopotamus and crocodile are also consistent with these paleoenvironmental recon-

structions for Hadar. The Hadar fauna and environment, therefore, were dramatically distinct from those encountered at the Pliocene site of Laetoli (Tanzania), a site that has also yielded early hominid remains.

During the investigations at Hadar interpretations of the hominid fossils changed as new discoveries made more material available. At first thought to represent up to three species, the Hadar hominids were later grouped into a single, sexually dimorphic species, Australopithecus afarensis, by D.C. Johanson, T.D. White, and Y. Coppens in 1978. Some workers continue to consider the Hadar hominid fossils as more than one early hominid species.

Analysis of the locomotor skeleton among the Hadar hominids has shown that they were fully bipedal. The bony pelvis and the knee-joint anatomy are commensurate with an upright, striding locomotion. This finding has been confirmed by the discovery of the slightly older hominid footprints at Laetoli. The Hadar hominids, however, display a host of features that differ from the modern human condition. Most evident of these is the tendency for skeletal robusticity and for strong curvature of the hand and foot phalanges. Such features have been interpreted as evidence that the early hominids of Hadar were adapted to a semiarboreal existence.

Although the Hadar deposits have been searched for archaeological remains, no stone tools have yet been found in the area. In 1976–1977, however, Oldowan tools were recovered from an excavation in the Gona area, east of the main hominid-bearing Hadar succession. These tools are stratigraphically above and therefore younger than the youngest of the Hadar hominids, "Lucy." Nevertheless, it is thought that the tools could date to 2.6 m.y., making them among the oldest in Africa.

See also AFAR; AUSTRALOPITHECUS AFARENSIS; ETHIOPIA; RIFT VALLEY. [T.D.W.]

Further Readings

Aronson, J.L., and Taieb, M. (1981) Geology and paleogeography of the Hadar hominid site, Ethiopia. In G. Rapp and C. Vondra (eds.): Hominid Sites: Their Paleoenvironmental Settings. Washington, D.C.: American Association for the Advancement of Science, pp. 165–195.

Johanson, D.C., and Edey, M. (1982) Lucy: The Beginnings of Humankind. New York: Simon and Schuster.

Johanson, D.C., Taieb, M., and Coppens, Y. (1982) Pliocene hominids from the Hadar Formation, Ethiopia (1973–1977): stratigraphic, chronologic and paleoenvironmental contexts, with notes on hominid morphology. Am. J. Phys. Anthropol. 57:373–402.

Johanson, D.C., and White, T.D. (1979) A systematic assessment of early African hominids. Science 202:321–330.

HADROPITHECUS see ARCHAEOLEMURIDAE

HAECKEL, ERNST HEINRICH (1834–1919)

German zoologist and philosopher. Haeckel was an early proponent of the Darwinian evolutionary synthesis in Germany. His Generelle Morphologie der Organismen, published in 1866, contains the first formal phylogenetic tree purporting to depict the course of human evolutionary history. In this regard Haeckel predicted the existence of a phylogenetic link between humans and the apes, namely the "missing link," with a blend of pongid and hominid traits. To this hypothetical construct he gave the name Pithecanthropus, the term later employed by Dubois to describe the fossil hominid remains he discovered in Java. Besides being the originator of the famous dictum "ontogeny recapitulates phylogeny," Haeckel was also a leading exponent of monistic philosophy. Haeckel's entire academic career was spent at the University of Jena (East Germany), where he was appointed full professor in 1865.

[F.S.]

HAHNÖFERSAND

Isolated frontal bone that was recovered without any associated material from river deposits near Hamburg (West Germany). The frontal is interesting because of its thickness and flatness, suggesting archaic affinities, although the browridge is of robust but modern type. Because of radiocarbon and amino-acid dates of ca. 36 k.y. the specimen has been claimed to represent a transitional or hybrid type between a Neanderthal and early modern population, but both morphological and chronological interpretations of this fossil remain problematic.

See also HOMO SAPIENS. [C.B.S.]

HALLELEMUR see ADAPIDAE

HAMBURGIAN

Late Paleolithic industry of northwestern Europe associated with late glacial Zone I and II pollen diagrams, ca. 10,500 B.P., defined by A. Rust on the basis of such open sites as Meiendorf, Stellmoor, and Ahrensburg, near Hamburg (West Germany). At these sites a Paleolithic way of life based on reindeer hunting, using tanged flint and barbed bone points, continued after it had disappeared from southern Europe. Piles of reindeer bones at these sites have been interpreted as supports for skin tents or remains of processing stations.

See also ECONOMY, PREHISTORIC; EPIPALEOLITHIC; HARPOON; HOLOCENE; LATE PALEOLITHIC; MAN-LAND RELATIONSHIPS. [A.S.B.]

HAMMERSTONE see STONE-TOOL MAKING

HANDAXE

Characteristic artifact of the Acheulean technological stage (also found in some Mousterian industries), normally a large bifacial implement of either pointed or ovate planform. Along with cleavers this artifact type represents the first definite, deliberately stylized form of artifact in prehistory. These artifacts, made from either large flakes, large cobbles, or nodules are found in many parts of Africa, Europe, and the Middle East, as far east as India. Microwear analysis suggests that some of these forms were butchery knives, but a range of other functions is possible as well.

See also ACHEULEAN; BIFACE; CLEAVER; EARLY PALEOLITHIC; MOUSTERIAN; STONE-TOOL MAKING. [N.T., K.S.]

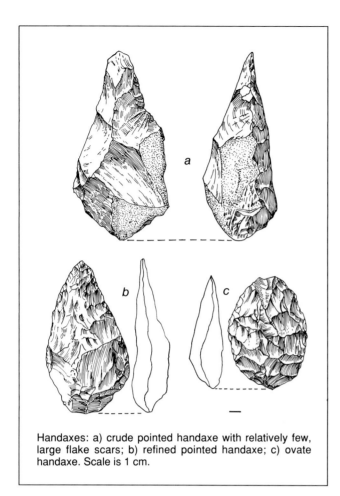

Handaxes: a) crude pointed handaxe with relatively few, large flake scars; b) refined pointed handaxe; c) ovate handaxe. Scale is 1 cm.

HAPALEMUR *see* LEMURIDAE

HAPLORHINI

Suborder within Primates, based in 1918 by Pocock (and students before him without formally naming the taxon), on the special derived attributes shared between the Southeast Asian tarsiers and the anthropoid primates. Among the first to notice these shared advanced similarities was Hubrecht. In 1897, after examining series of embryos of *Tarsius*, Hubrecht noted that features of the placenta and fetal membranes were not like those of other lemurs, with which the tarsiers were supposed to belong, but rather like those of anthropoid primates. Hubrecht knew of the Eocene tarsiiform fossils discovered earlier from North America and concluded that the tarsiiforms were an ancient and distinct lineage derived from the lemuriforms. Hubrecht's studies on this important problem have been recently corroborated and developed by W.P. Luckett. The development of the placenta and various fetal membranes (body stalk, allantois, yolk sac, etc.) consists of an intricate series of steps, and the very complexity of these features provides a character complex of great systematic significance.

In addition to these studies on the placenta and fetal membranes Pocock's initial observations on the special similarity of the external nose of tarsiers (in spite of some primitive primate retentions) to that of anthropoids have been elaborated upon and fully confirmed. Unlike strepsirhine primates (living lemuriforms and lorisiforms), which have an outer nose structure quite similar to what is considered the ancestral condition for both placental and marsupial mammals (a condition broadly understood as strepsirhine—a term not restricted to a description of the shape of the nostrils), the living tarsiers have lost the naked rhinarium (wet and hairless nose skin), the cleft in the upper lip, and the philtrum (the median part of the rhinarium that is connected to the gum, after passing through between the two halves of the upper lip) and have greatly reduced the vibrissae ("whiskers"; also called "sinus hairs" because of the well-developed venous sinuses around their follicles) into short and stiff structures. Their nasal area is instead covered with hairy skin, although the nasal opening is similar to the crescent-shaped, primitive mammalian condition retained in lemuriforms and in the platyrrhine anthropoid *Aotus*. Tarsiers, like anthropoids, have the derived mammalian condition of a relatively free upper lip that is continuous from side to side; unlike that of any living strepsirhine primate this is mobile.

The third important area of special similarity between tarsiers and anthropoids is the construction of the retina at the back of the eyes. Like the previous two character complexes this cannot be assessed in fossils. In strepsirhine primates, as in many other mammals, there is a layer of tissue behind the retina called the tapetum lucidum, which somehow plays a role in light gathering and reflection. Tarsiers and anthropoids, however, not only lack this primitive mammalian condition but have a retina that contains, within an area called the macula (the yellow spot), a special area of great visual acuity, marked by a depression and called the fovea centralis. It is probable that the eyes of tarsiers, like those of the nocturnal platyrrhine *Aotus*, have become relatively large when compared with the enlarged eyes of other nocturnal mammals because the common ancestor of anthropoids and tarsiers lost the tapetum lucidum, probably as an early adaptation to diurnality. All subsequent nocturnal haplorhines, however, had to compensate for the absence of this tapetum lucidum if they pursued a nocturnal way of life.

The fourth area of special similarity shared by the living haplorhines (and by the fossils where its hard components are preserved) is the nature of the arterial circulation in the middle ear. The vessel that embryonically courses through the stapes is not functional in adult haplorhines. The emphasis in these living primates is on another branch of the carotid artery, the promontory artery, in the blood supply of the brain. In lemuriforms the primitively large stapedial and vertebral arteries fulfill this role, and the lorisiforms capture a newly recruited vessel for this purpose.

The fifth area of special similarity shared by living (and fossil) haplorhines is a character of exceptional importance relating to the construction of the skull. The olfactory process of the brain passes below the interorbital septum in strepsirhine primates but above the persistent fetal septum formed by the orbitosphenoid bone in all living haplorhines and in the known fossil omomyid skulls. This fact is a strong indicator that the ancestral haplorhine species fundamentally reorganized the development of the skull due to some adaptive shift involving the visual and olfactory, and maybe even the feeding, mechanisms. Any argument to the effect that shortening of the face will result in similar and independent developmental constraints is weakened by the fact that short-faced strepsirhines like the living lorisids did not develop along the haplorhine lines.

It is important to realize that the taxonomic concepts Strepsirhini and Haplorhini are not simply descriptive of nasal conditions in primates. The two terms are formal names, which are not affected by what we know or do not know of the nose or fetal membrane evolution of living or fossil primates. It is equally important to understand that the fossil groups included within the Haplorhini, the subfamilies of the Omomyidae, are allocated to this suborder because they share osteological features with living haplorhines or with the deduced common ancestor of the living species. Omomyids are not considered haplorhine primates because we assume their nasal area (not only the nostrils) to have been of the haplorhine type. Similarly, linking of such fossil groups as the Adapidae with the Strepsirhini, or the Omomyidae with the Tarsiiformes within the Haplorhini, does not depend on the assumption of the presence of particular soft anatomical features in the fossils. On the contrary, the sharing of derived osteological attributes between the fossil forms and the respective living groups makes it probable that the former possessed the appropriate soft anatomical characters.

See also OMOMYIDAE; TARSIIDAE; TARSIIFORMES. [F.S.S.]

Further Readings

Hill, W.C.O. (1955) Primates. Comparative Anatomy and Taxonomy, Vol. VII: Haplorhini: Tarsioidea. Edinburgh: Edinburgh University Press.

Szalay, F.S., and Delson, E. (1979) Evolutionary History of the Primates. New York: Academic.

HARD HAMMER see STONE-TOOL MAKING

HAROUNIAN see PLEISTOCENE; SEA-LEVEL CHANGE

HARPOON

Barbed spear point that appears in the Upper Paleolithic, especially typical of the Magdalenian phase (ca. 17,000–11,000 B.P.), and is also seen in later technologies. The harpoon, barbed on one or both sides, is normally made of a piece of antler removed by the groove-and-splinter technique. These points

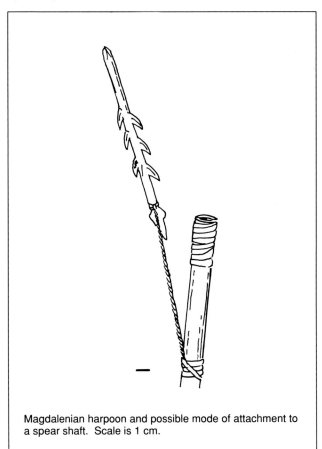

Magdalenian harpoon and possible mode of attachment to a spear shaft. Scale is 1 cm.

could have been attached to a main shaft with a line and could have become detached from the shaft upon penetration. Harpoons could have been used for hunting or for spear fishing.

See also MAGDALENIAN; RAW MATERIALS; SPEAR; STONE-TOOL MAKING; UPPER PALEOLITHIC. [N.T., K.S.]

HAUA FTEAH

Large cave in Cyrenaica (Libya); excavated by McBurney in the 1950s. An extensive series of archaeological deposits was sampled, producing mainly tools of Levalloiso-Mousterian affinities. A distinctive blade-based industry, the pre-Aurignacian, was excavated in levels within the Mousterian sequence dated by radiocarbon at more than 47 k.y. Later horizons produced the best evidence for the Dabban and eastern Oranian (Ibero-Maurusian), as well as Neolithic. Two posterior mandible fragments from an adult and subadult were recovered in 1952 and 1955 from levels dated at ca. 47 k.y. They have low and broad ascending rami but lack the retromolar space characteristic of Neanderthals.

See also ARCHAIC HOMO SAPIENS; DABBAN; IBERO-MAURUSIAN; LATE PALEOLITHIC; MOUSTERIAN; PRE-AURIGNACIAN. [C.B.S., A.S.B.]

HEADONIAN   *see*   EOCENE; TIME SCALE

HEARTH   *see*   FIRE

HEIDELBERG   *see*   MAUER

HELIOPITHECUS

Some fragmentary remains of a fossil hominoid from Ad Dabtiyah (Saudi Arabia), including a maxilla and some isolated teeth, have been described as *Heliopithecus leakeyi*. The morphology is similar to that of *Kenyapithecus* and *Afropithecus*, and it is likely that they are related.

See also AFROPITHECUS; KENYAPITHECUS; NEAR EAST. [P.A.]

HELVETIAN   *see*   MIOCENE

"HEMANTHROPUS" ("HEMIANTHROPUS")

Taxon based on drugstore teeth collected by von Koenigswald in Asia. Although he referred these teeth to the Hominidae, this assignment is far from certain for all the specimens. Since no specimens have been recovered *in situ*, dating is impossible. Some of the hypodigm may represent hominids, but at least part of it may be referrable to some form of Miocene hominoid. Von Koenigswald originally referred the specimens to "*Hemianthropus*" *peii* but later changed this nomen because it was already taken.

See also ASIA (EASTERN); CHINA; DRAGON BONES; KOENIGSWALD, G.H.R. VON. [G.G.P.]

HEMIACODON   *see*   OMOMYINAE

HENGELO INTERSTADIAL   *see* GLACIATION; PLEISTOCENE

HERBIVORY   *see*   DIET; PRIMATE ECOLOGY

HEXIAN

Cave deposit in Anhui Province (China); late middle Pleistocene, ca. 0.2 m.y. on the basis of hominid morphology and associated fauna. In 1980 this karst cave locality yielded a partial cranium of *Homo erectus*. The specimen has been classified as a "progressive" form, which apparently shows affinities to the hominids recovered from the upper part of Locality 1 at Zhoukoudian. The Hexian specimen has an estimated cranial capacity of ca. 1,025 ml. The associated fauna is also interesting, because it seems to represent a mixture of cold-adapted northern mammals and more tropical southern elements.

See also ASIA (EASTERN); CHINA; HOMO ERECTUS; ZHOUKOUDIAN. [G.G.P.]

Further Readings

Huang, W., Dusheng, F., and Yongxiang, Y. (1982) Preliminary study of the fossil skull and fauna from Hexian, Anhui. Vert. Palasiatica 20:248–256.

Wu, R. (1982) Preliminary study of *Homo erectus* remains from Hexian, Anhui. Acta Anthropol. Sin. 1:2–13.

HIGHER PRIMATES

Anthropoid primates (monkeys, apes, humans, and their extinct relatives), as distinguished from the lower or prosimian members of the order. This term originally dates to a *scala naturae* view of evolution, with "lower" evolving into "higher" forms of life. It has come back into use recently as a way of referring to anthropoids as opposed to the paraphyletic group of lower primates. Anthropoids may be considered "higher" in terms of their greater relative brain size, social complexity, and other features, all of which link them to humans.

See also ANTHROPOIDEA; BRAIN; LOWER PRIMATES; PRIMATE SOCIETIES; PRIMATES; PROSIMIAN; SCALA NATURAE. [E.D., I.T.]

HISTORICAL ARCHAEOLOGY see ARCHAEOLOGY

HIWEGI see RUSINGA

HOABINHIAN

Broadly and often nebulously defined archaeological technocomplex found throughout mainland Southeast Asia. Originally proposed by Colani in the 1930s on the basis of assemblages from Vietnam, the Hoabinhian seems to span the last 10 k.y. This industry includes unifacially worked flakes, cores, polished flakes, and cord-marked pottery in what are presumably its later phases. There is a great deal of variation in Hoabinhian assemblages. It may well be that the Hoabinhian as it is recognized today does not constitute a single archaeological entity (i.e. culture, tradition, industry, or facies).

See also ASIA (EASTERN); PACITANIAN. [G.G.P.]

HOLOCENE

Last division of the Pleistocene epoch, which started ca. 10 k.y. ago and continues at present time. It runs concurrent with the present interglacial.

Its approximate time equivalents, used in the earlier literature, are the Postglacial, Alluvium, and Recent. *Holocene* refers to the "entirely modern" aspect of the embedded fossils, contrasting with the "mostly new" aspects of the fossils in Pleistocene strata. Thus the underlying concept of the Holocene is evolutionary and follows the biostratigraphic classification of geologic time proposed by Charles Lyell in 1833. However, the internal subdivision of the Holocene and its lower boundary are based on climatostratigraphic criteria. The Holocene begins with the rapid retreat from the Salpausselka moraine line in northern Europe, formed during the Younger Dryas and with immigration of birch and pine into the arctic tundras. Elsewhere in the world the beginning of the current interglacial and of the Holocene is proposed at ca. 13.5, 12, 6, or 5 k.y.

The Holocene can be divided into three substages

with differing air-temperature and precipitation regimes: the early, or *anathermal*, stage, cooler but mostly wetter than today; the *hypsithermal*, or *altithermal*, stage, the so-called climatic optimum, warmer and mostly drier than today; and the late *medithermal* stage, marked by progressive cooling and return to present-day precipitation regimes.

The frequently used subdivision of the Holocene is based on the pollen stratigraphy of Denmark and Sweden.

See also PALEOBIOGEOGRAPHY; PLEISTOCENE. [G.K.]

HOLOPHYLY see MONOPHYLY

HOLOTYPE see NOMENCLATURE

HOLSTEIN see GLACIATION; PLEISTOCENE

HOMA BAY see KANJERA

HOMINIDAE

As used in the present work, the family comprising the great apes and humans. It is linked with the Hylobatidae in the superfamily Hominoidea.

A word of explanation is needed before going on to describe the subfamilies and genera contained in the Hominidae. In the past—when it was thought that there was a broad distinction between apes and humans, with the apes put in one family, the Pongidae, and humans in another, the Hominidae—Hominidae was generally used to contain humans and their immediate ancestors. With the recognition that some apes are more closely related to humans than they are to other apes this convention starts to break down, for if the concept of Pongidae can no longer be applied to the apes the taxonomic level of difference between the apes must be matched by a similar level of taxonomic difference between humans and apes.

One way of matching taxonomic levels would be to recognize all groups of hominoid at the same, family level. This would allow the retention of Hominidae for just humans, but it would also require Pongidae for the orangutan, Gorillidae for gorillas and chimpanzees (or Panidae also for the chimpanzees), and Hylobatidae for the gibbons. This is taxonomically valid, but it creates an imbalance with the other major catarrhine group, the Cercopithecoidea. In this superfamily only one family is recognized, and the diversity of species and genera, which is much greater than that of the hominoids, is divided between two subfamilies. It is more consistent and logical, therefore, to divide the hominoids at a similarly lower taxonomic level, and this is what is done here.

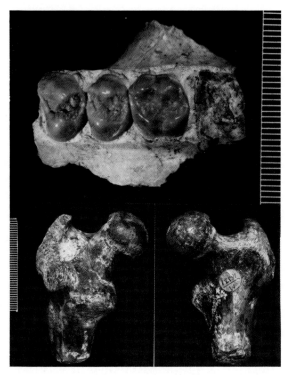

Upper jaw (top) and anterior and posterior views of a left femur of *Kenyapithecus africanus* from middle Miocene deposits on Maboko Island (Kenya).

The major divisions of the Hominidae are the two subfamilies, Ponginae and Homininae. Among living forms Ponginae includes just the orangutan (generic name *Pongo*), and the Homininae includes the African apes and humans (*Homo, Pan,* and *Gorilla*). It would have been equally possible, in parallel to the discussion above, to have recognized more than these two families in order to emphasize the distinctiveness of humans—for instance, by restricting Homininae to humans and having Gorillinae (and possibly Paninae as well) for the African apes. This also lacks consistency with other catarrhine groups, and for this reason is not used here.

The hominids include the largest of all primates. Other primates in the past have matched them in size (such as *Gigantopithecus*, a derivative of the

Sivapithecus group in eastern Asia, and *Archaeoindris*, a subfossil lemur from Madagascar), but no living group comes close to them in body size. Probably linked with this in some way, the degree of sexual dimorphism (the differences in size and morphology between males and females of the same species) is generally high, certainly much higher than in the gibbons. Gorillas and orangutans show the greatest amount of sexual dimorphism, humans and chimpanzees the least, but a number of fossil genera appear to have been at least as sexually dimorphic as any of the living hominids. *Sivapithecus*, which is related to the orangutan, had levels of sexual dimorphism similar to that of the living ape, and the largest species were only slightly smaller in overall size. Indeed, *Gigantopithecus* has already been mentioned as being even larger and was probably a member of this clade; thus increased body size and sexual dimorphism appear to be ancient characteristics of this part of the hominid lineage.

The African apes and humans, which form the other part of the hominid clade, are more variable in size. The gorilla is the largest hominid species and the chimpanzee the smallest, and sexual dimor-

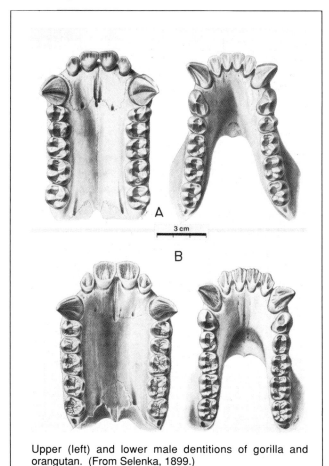

Upper (left) and lower male dentitions of gorilla and orangutan. (From Selenka, 1899.)

phism matches these size differences. None of the fossil species known in the Miocene is as large or as dimorphic as the gorilla, but some later taxa belonging to the human lineage appear to have been extremely variable. In the Miocene the fossil genera *Dryopithecus* and *Kenyapithecus* are grouped in the hominid clade, and the way these genera are divided into species makes it appear that they were not variable at all. If, however, some of these species are combined, as the lack of morphological differences between them seems to indicate, the new combinations would have as great a degree of sexual dimorphism as that of gorillas. Much needs to be done to resolve this problem.

Based on fossil evidence and the molecular clock, the time of origin of the hominids was ca. 17 m.y. ago. The early fossil evidence is restricted to Africa, so the origin of the group was almost certainly African. The hominids subsequently diverged into two groups, of which one, Ponginae, left Africa and migrated early in its history to Asia, where it is now represented by the orangutan. The other group, Homininae, remained in Africa until less than 1 m.y. ago. The history of the African apes is not known, although a recently discovered fossil from Samburu in Kenya may throw some light on their origin. The human lineage is well documented by fossils covering almost the last 4 m.y., and the early human fossils have all come from Africa.

See also APE; CATARRHINI; DRYOPITHECUS; FAMILY; HOMININAE; HOMINOIDEA; HYLOBATIDAE; KENYAPITHECUS; MIOCENE; PONGINAE; SAMBURU; SEXUAL DIMORPHISM; SUPERFAMILY. [P.A.]

Further Readings

Ciochon, R.L., and Corruccini, R.S. (1983) New Interpretations of Ape and Human Ancestry. New York: Plenum.

Szalay, F.S., and Delson, E. (1979) Evolutionary History of the Primates. New York: Academic.

Wood, B.A., Martin, L., and Andrews, P. (1986) Major Topics in Primate and Human Evolution. Cambridge: Cambridge University Press.

HOMININAE

Subdivision of Hominidae containing humans, chimpanzees, and gorillas. This subfamily category is not always used in this sense, of course, and more commonly it signifies just humans and their ancestors. This view was acceptable while humans and apes were still considered to make up the major subdivisions of the Hominoidea, but if one believes that the African apes are more closely related to humans than are the orangutan and gibbons it becomes necessary to denote this grouping with a name. The name that has priority is Homininae.

The relationships of the species within the Homi-

ninae are ambiguous. Some evidence indicates that humans and chimpanzees share a common ancestor after the divergence of gorillas, while other evidence indicates that gorillas and chimpanzees share a common ancestor after the divergence of humans. This is an important issue from the point of view of human evolution, for the correct interpretation of character change during the evolution of our species depends on knowing what the starting point was, and this in turn depends on correctly identifying our closest living relative.

The main evidence supporting relationship between chimpanzees and gorillas (i.e. for an African-ape clade) comes from their shared morphology. There are many characters, but most of these relate to two complexes of the dentition and the limb bones. The teeth of chimpanzees and gorillas are alike in the distinctive structure of the enamel, which is thin and is formed with 40 percent pattern 1 prisms. The ancestral hominid pattern is thought to be thick pattern 3 enamel, which is the condition in human teeth. Linked with these differences are related characters of enamel accretion rate and other structures developed in the enamel, and the complexity of the changes makes it unlikely that the derived condition in the African apes could have been achieved independently. Another way of putting this is that the characters are so complicated that they must have been present in this form in the common ancestor for them to show such close correspondence in the descendant species.

The same argument applies even more to the complex of characters related to knuckle-walking. This is an unusual form of locomotion by which the African apes use the knuckles of their hands to take their weight when walking. This both extends the lengths of their arms and enables them to hold objects in their bent fingers even when walking and running. This form of locomotion is not practiced by orangutans, even though they live in similar habitats, are of similar size, and have many similarities in posture and gait; and this makes the identical adaptations in the chimpanzees and gorillas all the more significant. They share numerous characters of the elbow, wrist, and hand that are concerned mainly with stabilizing the joints when they are fully extended by deepening fossae, enlarging guiding ridges, and shortening tendons. The complexity of these changes, which are completely shared by chimpanzees and gorillas, makes it unlikely that they could have been developed independently but suggests rather that they were already present in their common ancestor. Since humans share none of these characters, it would appear that the African apes shared a common ancestor after the divergence of humans.

In addition to the characters just described are other morphological characters that support an African-ape clade. There is also evidence from the chromosomes and molecular data, but much of this is ambiguous. Some interpretations of the chromosomes, for instance, are taken to provide support for a relationship between humans and chimpanzees, and much of the evidence from molecular anthropology also supports this view. Certain amino-acid substitutions are shared uniquely by humans and chimpanzees, and since these are not present in any other hominoid they are strong evidence for the human-chimpanzee relationship. There are many DNA substitutions similarly shared, and these also indicate that humans and chimpanzees had a common ancestor after the divergence of the gorilla and that chimpanzees are therefore our closest living relatives.

There is no immediate solution to this conflict in evidence over the relationships within the Homininae. It is unfortunate that for this stage of hominoid evolution the fossil evidence is almost nonexistent. Two groups of fossils can be assigned to this subfamily: the australopithecines, and other related fossils that are on or near the direct ancestry to humans, and a single fossil from Samburu Hills (Kenya) that has not yet been named. The australopithecines were clearly bipedal and had already developed many characters of the teeth and skull that are otherwise unique to humans. Their fossil record is good back to nearly 4 m.y., with direct evidence of bipedalism at 3.7 m.y., and some fragmentary fossils are known back to 5 m.y. Before that, however, nothing is known until the single fossil from Samburu Hills in the Kenyan Rift Valley, and the interpretation of this specimen is difficult. It comes from poorly dated deposits, bracketed between dates of 6 and 9 m.y., and it is remarkably gorillalike in its morphology. Whether this resemblance to gorillas is significant is hard to say, but in its molar proportions, premolar morphology, and the cusp development on the molars it shares characters with the gorilla and with nothing else. In other words, these characters are otherwise unique to the gorilla, and their presence on the Samburu fossil could indicate relationship. If this is so, it could indicate that the gorilla had diverged from chimpanzees and humans by this 9–6-m.y. time period, and that therefore the latter two species are related more closely to each other than either is to the gorilla, thus supporting the evidence from molecular anthropology.

See also APE; AUSTRALOPITHECUS; HOMINIDAE; HOMINOIDEA; LOCOMOTION; MOLECULAR ANTHROPOLOGY; SAMBURU; SUBFAMILY. [P.A.]

Further Readings

Goodman, M., and Tashian, R.E. (1976) Molecular Anthropology. New York: Plenum.

Ishida, H. (1984) Study of the Tertiary hominoids and their palaeoenvironments in East Africa. African Study Monographs, Supplementary Issue 2, Kyoto University.

Patterson, C. (1987) Molecules and Morphology in Evolution: Conflict or Compromise. Cambridge: Cambridge University Press.

Wood, B.A., Martin, L., and Andrews, P. (1986) Major Topics in Primate and Human Evolution. Cambridge: Cambridge University Press.

HOMINOIDEA

Superfamily to which apes and humans belong. It can conveniently be divided into the lesser apes, Hylobatidae, and the great apes and humans, Hominidae. Little is known about the evolution of the hylobatids, but the divisions within the hominids are better documented. Within this group the orangutan was the first to branch off from the others, leaving a group comprising the African apes and humans, called here the Homininae. Thus the nearest living relatives to humans are either or both of the African apes, but it is not clear yet whether chimpanzees and gorillas are more closely related to each other or whether one of them is more closely related to humans.

Hominoid Origins

By comparing all the living species of hominoid we can make inferences about the morphology of their common ancestor. These inferences are based on the likelihood that if all or most of the living species possess the same character that character was probably also present in their common ancestor. The alternative is to suppose that the character evolved independently in each of the living hominoids, and while this might have occurred in some instances it is not likely. The majority of characters present in every animal are inherited from more or less remote ancestors, ranging from basic characters like a backbone (in all vertebrates), warm-bloodedness (in all mammals), nails instead of claws on the hands and feet (in all euprimates), or a reduced number of premolars in the jaw (in all catarrhines).

All of these characters are present in the hominoids, but they are not diagnostic of them, since they are present in other animals as well. What we want is to identify those characters present only in hominoids, and the following abbreviated description includes just such characters. These are the defining characters for the superfamily that were present in its common ancestor. The middle part of the skull is expanded, although overall size is no greater than in other catarrhines; the palate is deep and the sinuses are enlarged; the teeth have broader incisors and molars and the differences between the premolars is reduced; the clavicle is elongated; the trapezius mus-

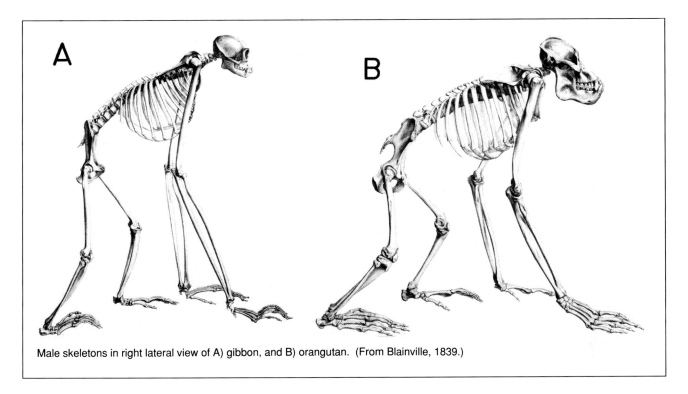

Male skeletons in right lateral view of A) gibbon, and B) orangutan. (From Blainville, 1839.)

cle inserts on to the clavicle; the humeral head is rounded, more medially oriented and larger than the femoral head; the deltoid insertion is low on the humerus; the elbow joint is adapted for stability and for mobility in the differential articular surfaces for the ulna and radius; the wrist joint is adapted for mobility; the femur has asymmetrical condyles; the iliac blade of the pelvis is expanded; the talus neck and calcaneus are short and broad; the metacarpals have broad distal ends; numbers of vertebrae are lumbar—5, sacral—4-5, caudal—6 (tail is lost); a vermiform appendix is developed.

Having established the probable morphology of the ancestral hominoid on the basis of the comparative method, we can now look at the fossil record to see if any fossils fit this pattern. In the early Miocene of East Africa is a group of fossil species with the generic name *Proconsul*. Several species are known from partial skulls and limb bones, and these show that *Proconsul* had acquired a number of the defining hominoid characters listed above. For instance, they have expanded skulls, reduced heteromorphy of the premolars, rounded and enlarged humeral heads, and the adaptations for stability of the joints (although not the ones for mobility). These lead to the conclusion that *Proconsul* was a hominoid, and we can now say a little about hominoid origins on the basis of what we know about these species.

Proconsul species lived in Africa in the early Miocene. The earliest record is 22 m.y. ago, and so the origin of the hominoids was earlier than that. There are no earlier fossils to pinpoint this date any more

accurately, but one of the features of the early Miocene fossil record provides a clue. At between 20 and 17 m.y. the diversity of hominoid species in Africa reached its greatest extent, much greater than comparable levels of hominoid diversity anywhere today, and this is something that would have taken several millions of years to achieve. If they were already well established by 22 m.y., it would therefore seem likely that the time of origin of the hominoids must have been at least 28-25 m.y. ago, a date that closely corresponds to estimates of hominoid divergence based on the molecular clock.

The place of origin of the hominoids is difficult to determine based on the comparative method alone, because living hominoids are divided equally between Africa and Asia. The fossil evidence, however, is exclusively African for about the first 10 m.y. of hominoid history, with no reliable evidence for fossil hominoids in Europe or Asia until ca. 13 m.y. ago.

Gibbon Divergence

The earliest branching point within the living hominoids is that dividing the gibbons from the rest of the apes and humans. The fossil species of *Proconsul* just discussed branched off earlier than the divergence of the gibbons, so provide no information on gibbon origins. The gibbons themselves are a highly derived group, with many distinctive features, but despite this no fossil taxon has yet been found that shares any of these distinctive characters. They include characters of the forelimb related to the brachiating mode of locomotion (characters not present in the

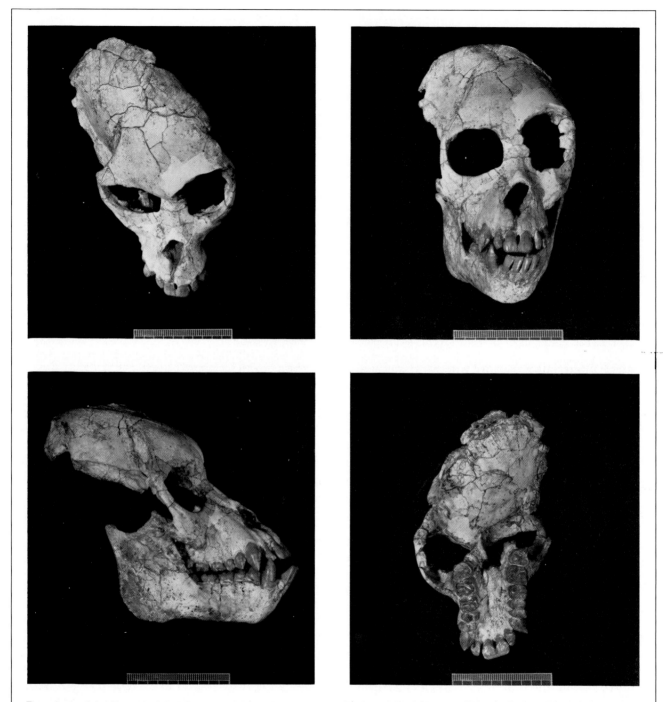

Four views of the *Proconsul* skull found by M.D. Leakey in 1948 on Rusinga Island (Kenya). This is still one of the most complete specimens of a fossil hominoid ever found.

great apes), the lack of sexual dimorphism in both body size and in such aspects of its skull and jaws that are related to this (e.g. equal-sized and large canine teeth), and social structure and complex vocalizations.

The branching event that gave rise to the gibbons also produced the great apes and humans—or hominids, as defined here—and evidence for this will also provide some indirect evidence for gibbon origins. The ancestral morphotype for the hominid clade can be defined as follows: skull with distinct mastoid processes, large medial pterygoids, lengthened premaxilla and increased alveolar prognathism, reduced incisive foramen; the dentition has spatulate lateral incisors, robust canines, elongated premolars, and molars with thick enamel; the tooth rows are wide apart, the maxillary and mandibular bodies deep; the elbow joint has increased adaptations for stability in the trochlear region; the ulnar styloid process does not contact carpal bones; the hindlimb is reduced in length, so that intermembral index (the relationship of forelimbs to hindlimbs) is high; the deltoid muscle is greatly developed and the pectoralis abdominis is missing.

Several fossil groups must be considered as potential hominids in relation to this list of characters. First of all there are some early Miocene hominoids from Buluk and Kalakol (Kenya). Recently named *Afropithecus turkanensis*, they have at least one hominid character in the very deep mandibular body and symphysis. The material is relatively complete, with parts of a skull, several jaws, and postcrania, but the descriptions published so far do not allow any further conclusions to be drawn. Another recently described fossil comes from the Ad Dabtiyah site (Saudi Arabia). (At this stage of the Miocene the Arabian peninsula was connected with Africa and separate from Eurasia.) This is about the same age as Buluk, and the fossil hominoid from there has been named *Heliopithecus leakeyi*. It again has at least one hominid character in its premolar elongation; it also has incipient thickening of molar enamel. Two intermediate stages can be recognized in enamel thickness between thin and thick, and the enamel of the Ad Dabtiyah hominid falls into the higher of these, so that enamel thickness is greater than in the ancestral hominoid state but has not reached the full thickness seen in hominids.

Two other groups belonging to the hominid clade are later in time. These are *Kenyapithecus* from middle Miocene deposits in Kenya and *Dryopithecus* from younger but still middle Miocene sites in Europe. Both of these have hominid characters of the skull and postcranium, so they provide corroborative evidence for this interpretation of character change, although not in the same way. *Dryopithecus* fossils from Rudabanya show adaptations of the elbow joint very close to those of the living hominid species. *Kenyapithecus*, on the other hand, has less-advanced postcrania but has developed thick enamel on its teeth, the earliest occurrence of this character in the fossil record.

The evidence from these fossils indicates that the divergence of the hylobatid and hominid clades occurred at least 17 m.y. ago, probably in Africa. The initial changes leading to the hominid clade included enlargement of the premolars, deepening of the jaws, thickening of molar enamel, and stabilizing of the elbow joint. It is likely that in all of these characters the ancestral gibbons, which by definition must have been present alongside the hominids,

would have retained the ancestral condition. It is in fact possible that the early gibbon ancestors retained ancestral characters in most respects, making them difficult to identify in the fossil record, for they would have been little different from the ancestral hominoids. Generalized hominoids that have been identified under a variety of names are known from middle and late Miocene sites as far apart as Kenya and China (e.g. *Micropithecus* from Africa and *Dionysopithecus* from eastern Asia). Since these lack either hylobatid or hominid characters, they are impossible to place on present evidence within the framework of hominoid evolution, but some of them may be shown with further evidence to be part one or other of these two clades.

Dates from the molecular clock are in general accord with the dates from the fossil evidence. DNA-DNA hybridization data give an age range of 22–18 m.y. for gibbon divergence, based on assumed divergence dates for the orangutan of 16–13 m.y. A similar, if slightly younger date, is given by the clock from nuclear DNA-sequencing data, whereas sequencing of mtDNA indicates a younger divergence date still.

Orangutan Divergence

Probably the most solid evidence for any of the branching points within the Hominoidea is available for the orangutan lineage. The orangutan is highly derived, both in its morphology and in its molecules. For these characters the African apes and humans (the Homininae) share the same character states as gibbons, and often with cercopithecoid monkeys as well, so that they retain the ancestral condition for hominoids or catarrhines, respectively. In fact within Hominoidea the hominines are characterized mostly by retention of ancestral characters, and this makes them a difficult clade to define. Some of the defining characters of the pongine clade are as follows. The skull has an expanded and flattened zygomatic region, giving the face a concave aspect, no glabellar thickening, narrow distance between the eyes, no browridges, and a rotated premaxilla giving a smooth floor to the nose and an extremely reduced incisive fossa; in the dentition the upper lateral incisors are very small relative to the central, the molar enamel is of intermediate thickness as a result of some secondary reduction in thickness, and the molars have a flattened dentine surface and deeply wrinkled enamel; and the articular surfaces of the limb bones are adapted for extreme mobility at the elbow, wrist, and hip joints.

None of the fossils so far discussed shares any of these pongine characters. They all retain the ancestral condition, where it is known, in these characters and therefore have nothing to do with the pongine

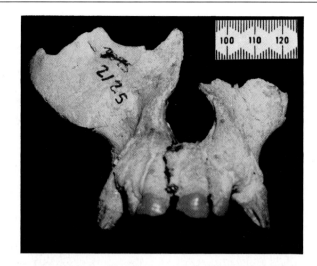

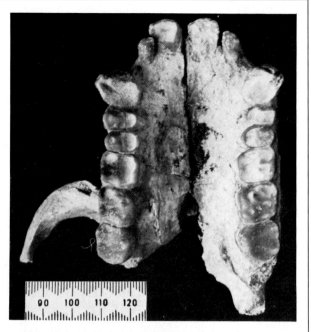

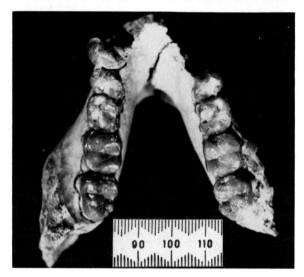

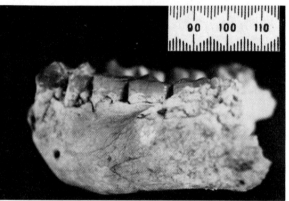

Fossil hominoids from Turkey. Top left: facial view of *Sivapithecus meteai* from late Miocene deposits at Sinap, showing the nasal aperture and the lower outline of the right orbit and zygomatic process. Top right: the same specimen in occlusal view, showing the full dentition. Bottom left: occlusal view of the mandible from middle Miocene deposits at Candir originally attributed to *Sivapithecus alpani*, later referred to *Ramapithecus*. Right: the same specimen seen in side (buccal) view.

clade. Some of the characters are present in a widespread group of fossils generally included in the genus *Sivapithecus*, which is thus grouped with the orangutan clade. Included in *Sivapithecus* are a number of other genera that have formerly been separated, including particularly *Ramapithecus*, which was at one time thought to be directly ancestral to humans. Other fossil genera from Greece and Turkey—*Graecopithecus*, *Ouranopithecus*, and *Ankarapithecus*—may also be grouped with *Sivapithecus*. For some of these fossils the body parts are not known to provide evidence for or against links with the orangutan, but *Ankarapithecus* is certainly part of the pongine clade even if it is not congeneric with *Sivapithecus*. Both share all of the facial characters

detailed above for the pongine clade, and where they differ they retain the ancestral hominoid condition. They can thus be interpreted as within the pongine clade but as less advanced than the living orangutan.

All of the taxa linked to the pongine clade come from the middle and late Miocene of Europe and Asia, stretching from Greece in the west to India in the east. Their age range is from 12 to 8 m.y., with the earliest good evidence for pongine affinities coming from Pakistan. Earlier (ca. 13 m.y.) deposits at Paşalar (Turkey) have yielded a large collection of what has been described as *Sivapithecus*; these specimens share two of the pongine characters described above, the flattened enamel-dentine junction and the small lateral incisors. Neither of these characters is particu-

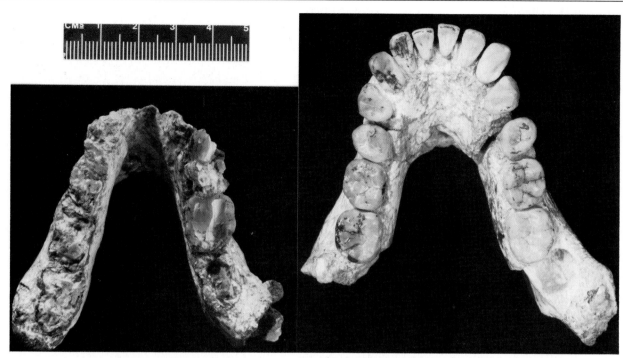

Two specimens from Greece. Left: *Graecopithecus freybergi*; right: *Ouranopithecus macedoniensis*. In both cases the type specimen is shown, lined up so that the second molars are alongside each other. Both taxa have been referred to *Sivapithecus*, which may be valid; if not, the name that has priority for the genus including these specimens is *Graecopithecus*.

larly strong, but if they do correctly indicate relationship with the pongines then the time of divergence of this clade is put back by at least another million years to at least 13 m.y.

Workers have assigned a number of other fossils to *Sivapithecus*. This genus, or taxa said to be similar to it, has been described from Lufeng (China) and Rudabanya (Hungary), but there appears to be no justification for this. Even if this were correct, however, these specimens would add little beyond extending the geographical range of this hominoid. *Sivapithecus* has also been recently described from Kenya, but the original authors have withdrawn that identification.

The conclusion from the fossils, therefore, is that the branching point of the pongine clade was at least 12 m.y. ago and maybe more than 13 m.y. if the Turkish evidence is proved correct. No specimen currently known from Africa can be grouped in this clade, but since *Sivapithecus* is the earliest hominoid known outside Africa it appears likely that it originated from a presently unknown group somewhere in Africa. The age range for the divergence of the orangutan from molecular data is 16.4–12.7 m.y. based on sequencing of nuclear DNA, and a younger date of 12.1–9.7 m.y. is given by sequencing of mtDNA.

Hominines

The last group of hominoids, and the sister group to the pongines, is that containing the African apes and humans. This is a hard group to define, because it

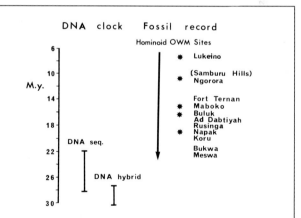

Divergence dates for the origin of the hominoids. On the right are shown the fossil sites from which specimens that can fairly certainly be considered hominoid have been recovered. The earliest of these is Meswa (Kenya), 22 m.y. The Old World monkey (OWM) fossil record is not as complete. On the left of the figure are shown the divergence dates of hominoids and monkeys based on estimations from the molecular clock: DNA sequencing on the left and DNA-DNA hybridization on the right. These appear to indicate hominoid origins at ca. 27–25 m.y.

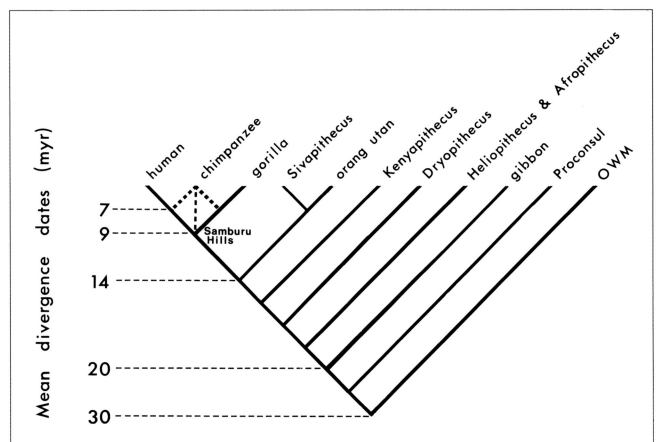

Relationships of the hominoids. Both recent and fossil hominoid taxa are included on this cladogram, and maximum ages are assigned to several of the major branching points based on the oldest record of the fossils contained within the respective clades.

has so few shared derived characters, particularly of features likely to be preserved as fossils. Chimpanzees, gorillas, and humans share the following list of characters, which are taken to define the node. The skull has a true frontal sinus developed and the browridges form a continuous bar across glabella, and a postorbital sulcus is developed; middle-ear depth is increased; two of the wrist bones are fused (os centrale and scaphoid); the prostate is subdivided; apocrine glands are scarce and eccrine glands abundant; there is a large axillary organ; and the aorta type is different. At the molecular level several amino-acid residue substitutions are uniquely shared in this clade, and large numbers of DNA substitutions.

Weak as this evidence is, it is still much stronger than that linking any other hominoid species with humans. The evidence put forward recently suggesting that orangutans and humans are more closely related is poor, and the same applies to the evidence, or lack of it, linking the three great apes together.

The situation is not made any easier by the lack of any fossils that can be assigned to this clade. A frontal sinus has been reported for some of the genera mentioned earlier, but it is not certain if these structures

are homologous with the hominine frontal sinus, and there are no other characters to go on. One fossil that is of interest to this branching event is the unnamed hominoid from Samburu Hills (Kenya), but this raises the question of the relationships within the hominine clade. The Samburu fossil is dated at between 10 and 6 m.y., and it has a morphology very close to that of gorillas. Only a single upper jaw is known, but the molar and premolar proportions and shape, and the cusp morphology of the molars, are all similar to the condition in gorillas. The polarity of these characters is hard to determine, but it is possible that they are gorilla synapomorphies.

Evidence from comparative morphology strongly supports the existence of an African-ape clade distinct from humans. Chimpanzees and gorillas share two major complexes of characters relating to knuckle-walking on the one hand (with ten characters of the elbow, wrist, and hand) and to enamel structure on the other (with enamel thickness, accretion rate, and prism type all combining to give an interrelated whole). They also share some characters of the chromosomes and DNA at the molecular level. In contrast to this is the evidence, this time only from the molecules, indicating a closer link between humans and chimpanzees. This evidence, though strong, is supported by no morphological evidence at all. As far as it goes, the single fossil from Samburu Hills supports the latter view, if its gorilla affinities are correct, for it might imply the early separation of the gorilla clade from that linking humans and chimpanzees.

The lack of fossils makes it hard to say anything about the time and place of the origin of the hominine clade. Since humans and African apes have Africa as the only common geographical factor, that seems the likely place of origin, and this fits with the only fossil known. Early human ancestors of the genus *Australopithecus* are known only from Africa, but their fossil record starts long after the branching times indicated by the molecular clock. These are 10-6 m.y. (DNA-DNA hybridization) and 8.1-6.3 m.y. (DNA sequencing), and since these dates have been shown to be concordant with fossil evidence, where available, it seems reasonable to accept them where fossil evidence is lacking.

See also APE; BULUK; CATARRHINI; DRYOPITHECUS; KENYAPITHECUS; LUFENG; MOLECULAR CLOCK; PROCONSUL; SAMBURU; SUPERFAMILY. [P.A.]

Further Readings

Ciochon, R.L., and Corruccini, R.S. (1983) New Interpretations of Ape and Human Ancestry. New York: Plenum.

Ciochon, R.L., and Fleagle, J.G. (1985) Primate Evolution and Human Origins. Menlo Park, Calif.: Benjamin.

Delson, E., ed. (1985) Ancestors: The Hard Evidence. New York: Liss.

Goodman, M., and Tashian, R.E. (1976) Molecular Anthropology. New York: Plenum.

Patterson, C. (1987) Molecules and Morphology in Evolution: Conflict or Compromise? Cambridge: Cambridge University Press.

Stringer, C.B. (1981) Aspects of Human Evolution. London: Taylor and Francis.

Szalay, F.S., and Delson, E. (1979) Evolutionary History of the Primates. New York: Academic.

Wood, B.A., Martin, L., and Andrews, P. (1986) Major Topics in Primate and Human Evolution. Cambridge: Cambridge University Press.

HOMO

Genus to which modern humans belong, named in 1758 by the Swedish naturalist Linnaeus. In the eighteenth century genera and species were regarded as fixed entities, and no possibility of change through evolution was entertained. As described by Linnaeus, *Homo* was made up only of living humans belonging to one species, *Homo sapiens*. Fossil representatives of the genus were not uncovered until the middle of the next century. The first Neanderthal to excite real debate was found in Germany in 1856 and named as a new species in 1864. Still more archaic humans were excavated in Java in 1890 and 1891. *Homo* is now considered to contain two extinct species in addition to living people. *Homo habilis* was present in eastern Africa at least 2 m.y. ago and probably earlier. This form was followed by *Homo erectus*. *Homo erectus* seems also to have evolved in Africa and then to have spread into other parts of the Old World tropics. By the middle Pleistocene populations of this species had reached such areas as northern China, where they were able to adapt to harsh environmental circumstances. These archaic people were eventually supplanted by early members of our own species, including the Neanderthals, but fully modern *Homo sapiens* did not appear until after 100 k.y. ago. Since that time humans have developed elaborate technologies that allow exploitation of the humid forests, arid deserts, and even some arctic regions. Virtually no part of the planet is now closed to habitation. *Homo sapiens* has become the most dominant of mammalian species and is just becoming aware of its responsibilities to preserve the earth's resources and maintain the many fragile ecosystems on which all life depends.

Definitions of the Genus

Modern descriptions of *Homo* emphasize features that set this genus apart from other extinct or living groups of the family Hominidae, including the large apes. One often-cited definition was provided by W.E. Le Gros Clark in 1964. Clark suggested that *Homo* can be distinguished primarily on the basis of brain size, along with morphology of the skull and teeth. Since he recognized only the two species *Homo erectus* and *Homo sapiens*, he stipulated a relatively large cranial capacity (900 to ca. 2,000 ml.). The description makes note of the strong supraorbital development in earlier representatives of *Homo*. The facial profile is said to be straight rather than projecting, and the temporal muscles never reach to the top of the braincase to produce a sagittal (midline) crest. The dental arcade is rounded in form, the canine teeth are small, and the last molar is reduced in size. Clark makes little mention of the postcranial skeleton, suggesting only that the limbs are adapted to a fully upright posture and gait.

In the same year (1964) important new discoveries from Olduvai Gorge in East Africa were announced by L.S.B. Leakey and his colleagues. These fossils consisted of several small skulls as well as postcranial material, and they prompted some reassessment of Clark's definition. Leakey, together with P.V. Tobias and J. Napier, argued that the Olduvai finds should be included within *Homo*, as a new species called *Homo habilis*. This could be done only if the description of the genus were revised. These authors characterize *Homo* as having a brain variable in size but larger on average than the brain of *Australopithecus*. Other aspects of cranial and dental anatomy are treated in much the same manner as by Clark, although several points concerning tooth size and proportions are elaborated. The pelvis and hindlimb are again said to be adapted to upright posture and a bipedal gait, and the hand is described as capable of fine manipulation.

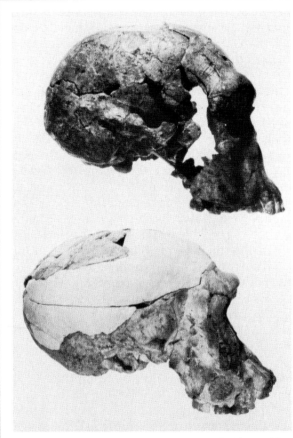

Side views of two crania described as early *Homo*. The individual above, numbered ER-1813 from the Koobi Fora region, has a brain volume of only ca. 500 ml. but shows some anatomical resemblances to later *Homo erectus*. The cranium pictured below, hominid 24 from Olduvai Gorge, is slightly larger but shares facial characters with *Australopithecus*. Although both specimens are often referred to *Homo habilis*, there is continuing doubt as to how they should be classified.

Homo habilis was greeted by substantial controversy, but many paleontologists now accept the species as valid. Current definitions of *Homo* reflect this consensus, by emphasizing other characters or complexes in addition to brain size, which varies considerably among species. C. Howell, for example, has

tried to describe in broad terms the structural adaptations of the genus. He does list changes in the proportions of the brain, which are reflected in the enlarged side walls and frontal portion of the cranium. In *Homo* there is generally some reduction of the area at the back of the braincase occupied by the nuchal (neck) muscles. The size of the facial skeleton is also decreased, and there are changes in the architecture of the nose and cheek. Howell comments further on tooth size and patterns of dental wear. Like earlier workers he notes that *Homo* species are built to walk erect and use the hands skillfully. To this anatomical description he adds one more important characteristic. *Homo* may be recognized as the (first) hominid dependent on culturally patterned behavior. Even *Homo habilis* made stone tools, and these artifacts tell us about the lifeways of the ancient hominids.

Species of Homo

The earliest recognized representatives of *Homo* are referred to the species *Homo habilis*. Skulls and postcranial parts of this creature were recovered first at Olduvai Gorge (Tanzania). Since the Olduvai fossils were named in 1964, more material has been found elsewhere in eastern Africa, particularly in the Koobi Fora region east of Lake Turkana (Kenya). At Koobi Fora the fossils are scattered through a lengthy sequence of ancient lake deposits. One of the best-preserved crania of early *Homo* comes from a layer now dated quite securely as ca. 2 m.y. Other specimens are not quite this old, but none of the East African finds is younger than ca. 1.5 m.y. During this time period *Homo habilis* may have ranged into southern Africa as well. Evidence from the caves at Swartkrans and Sterkfontein in the Transvaal suggests this, although the bones are broken and are therefore hard to interpret with certainty.

While there is still doubt about just which fossils should be placed in this species, most paleoanthropologists agree that *Homo habilis* differs from *Australopithecus* in important ways. The first cranium from Olduvai is far from complete, but brain size can still be estimated. This volume may approach 680 ml. or even 700 ml. Such a figure is larger than expected for *Australopithecus*. Several more skulls have confirmed that early *Homo* had an enlarged brain, and some of the East African jaws contain teeth that are smaller than those of most *Australopithecus* specimens. If *Homo habilis* was a lightly built creature of small body size, as has been claimed, then these trends toward brain expansion and dental reduction are even more significant. It can be argued that such traits link the Olduvai and Koobi Fora populations with later members of the *Homo* lineage.

Homo erectus is known to have lived at the same East African localities. This species is represented by several incomplete crania, lower jaws, and other bones recovered at Olduvai Gorge. More material, including nearly complete skeletons, has been collected near Lake Turkana. Some of the Turkana fossils are ca. 1.6 m.y. old, while specimens from Olduvai are younger. During the early Pleistocene populations of *Homo erectus* seem to have been distributed widely across Africa. By 1 m.y. ago the species had reached the southeastern parts of Asia. The first Asian discoveries were made in Java, late in the last century. These early finds at Trinil have been followed by many later ones, and it is now clear that *Homo erectus* lived in China as well as Java during the middle Pleistocene.

This species differs from *Homo habilis* in both size and shape of the skull. Even the oldest *Homo erectus* crania from East Africa have internal capacities of 800–900 ml., and one large braincase from Olduvai Gorge has a volume well in excess of 1,000 ml. Some of the younger specimens from Asia show a slight increase over this figure. The skull itself is long and low in outline. Individual bones tend to be thicker than is usual for *Homo habilis*, and buttresses or crests are prominent. Brows over the orbits are especially thick and projecting. The rear of the cranium is strongly angled, and a transverse shelf of bone is present on the occiput. The face and jaws are large relative to overall size of the braincase, but the cheek teeth especially are much reduced compared with those of *Australopithecus*. Parts of the postcranial skeleton recovered from the East African sites suggest that *Homo erectus* weighed nearly as much as more recent humans.

Sometime in the later middle Pleistocene *Homo erectus* was followed by *Homo sapiens*. Early representatives of our own species have been found in Europe as well as Africa and Asia. The skulls of these people are still archaic in general appearance but exhibit features that set them apart from *Homo erectus*. An example is provided by the well-preserved individual from Petralona Cave in northern Greece. This cranium is low in outline, with a strong brow. The rear of the braincase is not sharply curved, however, and several small but important details of cranial base anatomy are modern. Endocranial volume for Petralona is expanded well beyond the average for *Homo erectus*. Another useful assemblage has been excavated at Arago Cave in France, and additional remains of archaic *Homo sapiens* have been recovered at such sites as Lake Ndutu and Kabwe in sub-Saharan Africa and Dali in China. All of these fossils show advances in their morphology relative to the *Homo erectus* condition. None of them has been dated very accurately, but some may be 300 k.y. or more in age.

Neanderthals make their appearance in Europe and southwestern Asia by the beginning of the late Pleistocene. These populations possess a suite of distinctive anatomical characters, by which they can easily be recognized. Since many Neanderthal sites have been investigated, we know quite a lot about how these people lived. Their Mousterian flake tools

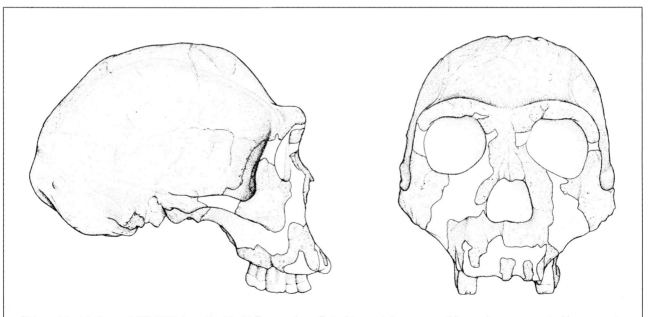

Side and facial views of ER-3733 from the Koobi Fora region. Dated to ca. 1.6 m.y. ago, this cranium represents *Homo erectus* from East Africa. Populations of this species probably evolved first in Africa and spread only after ca. 1 m.y. ago into Asia and Europe. Most paleontologists believe that *Homo erectus* evolved into *Homo sapiens* sometime in the later middle Pleistocene.

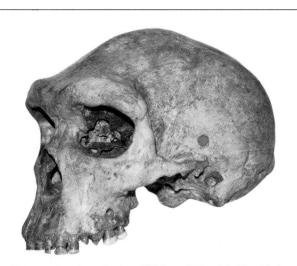

This cranium from Broken Hill (now Kabwe) in Zambia is usually described as early *Homo sapiens*. Although the brows are thick and the low vault is rather archaic in appearance, this individual had a brain larger than expected for *Homo erectus*. Other characteristics of the occiput and cranial base also align Broken Hill with more modern humans.

are quite sophisticated, and their caves contain abundant indications that fire was used regularly for cooking and for warmth. Simple graves show that the dead were buried intentionally, perhaps for the first time in human history. The Neanderthals continued to inhabit parts of Europe until ca. 35 k.y. ago. After this date they disappear from the record. The populations that succeed them in Europe and the Near East have fully modern skeletons and must have resembled people of today. Just where these anatomically modern groups originated, and whether such people may have existed for a considerable time in Africa or elsewhere as contemporaries of the Neanderthals, are important questions. Firm answers are not available, but it is clear that 35 k.y. ago or earlier modern *Homo sapiens* occupied nearly all regions of the Old World.

Evidence for Early Cultural Activities

Stone artifacts have been recovered from a number of the sites yielding early *Homo*. These tools and waste materials provide clues concerning human behavior. One especially informative locality is Olduvai Gorge. Crude chopping tools and sharp flakes of the Oldowan industry are common at several levels in Bed I, where they often occur with animal remains. Until recently this association of artifacts with bones has been taken as evidence that the hominids hunted animals, brought them to their living sites, and butchered the carcasses with the Oldowan implements. The situation at Olduvai and other early Pleistocene sites is now known to be more complicated than this. Taphonomic studies have demonstrated

that such assemblages may be formed by various agencies, not all related to hominid activities.

Continuing research on the Olduvai material does suggest that early humans used animal products. That cutmarks on some of the Bed I bones must have been produced by stone tools has been shown with the aid of scanning electron microscopy. This finding, however, does not prove that all of the animals were hunted. SEM analysis makes it clear that the Olduvai bones carry signs of rodent or carnivore tooth damage as well as definite evidence of cutting. It is quite likely that some of the game was killed by large cats or other carnivores. Probably the Olduvai hominids were able to obtain such carcasses only after these had been fed upon by other animals. The people may well have hunted small antelopes and other prey, but they functioned as scavengers as well.

The supposition that hominids used the Olduvai sites as home bases can also be questioned. There is little indication that people actually lived at the spots where the animal bones accumulated, and such areas must have been attractive to a variety of dangerous predators. Perhaps these sites were treated simply as convenient caches of stone artifacts and raw materials, to which animal parts could be transported for rapid processing. If this is the case, then we do not know where the hominids were living or whether their social patterns resembled those of later hunter-gatherers. Certainly *Homo habilis* engaged in cultural activities, but these early people probably behaved quite differently from *Homo sapiens*.

There is evidence that *Homo erectus* possessed more sophisticated technological skills. Stone industries associated with these populations in Africa and Asia show more diversity. There is still little indication that *Homo erectus* hunted large animals systematically, however. At many of the middle Pleistocene sites where Acheulean tools and bones are concentrated it is difficult to be sure whether the game was killed or scavenged by humans or by other carnivores. Some of the animal remains may represent natural deaths and may not document the activity of predators at all. Given these uncertainties, it can be argued that advanced hunting techniques were not developed until late Pleistocene times.

Another question concerns the acquisition of language by early members of the *Homo* lineage. Evidence bearing on this issue is indirect and subject to several interpretations. Some anatomists have claimed that brain casts of *Homo habilis* show enlargement of the regions associated with spoken communication. Others disagree, and in fact the number of well-preserved braincases from which detailed casts can be prepared is small. Anthropologists approach this question from the perspective offered by the archaeological record. Some suggest that even crude Oldowan artifacts imply a capacity for language. Alternatively, it may be argued that the Oldowan represents only opportunistic stone working, while Acheulean tools are more carefully formed and often display impressive symmetry. Perhaps *Homo erectus* was the first hominid to use symbols and speak effectively. Critics point out that the link between technological and linguistic behavior has not been firmly established and note that simple tools could have been made by hominids lacking language. Just when *Homo* developed the linguistic skills that characterize modern humans is therefore not clear.

Evolution of the Homo Lineage

Many workers think that the evolution of *Homo* was a process of gradual, progressive change. *Homo habilis* is widely presumed to have evolved from an australopithecine ancestor. This first species of *Homo* resembles gracile australopithecines in a number of features, although there are signs of increased encephalization and reduction in tooth size. Near the beginning of the Pleistocene *Homo habilis* was transformed into *Homo erectus*. Trends begun early in the history of the genus were continued, to produce a larger brain and cheek teeth still more reduced in comparison with *Australopithecus*. Paleontologists favoring this view regard the two *Homo* species as successive segments of a single lineage. Such species must be defined arbitrarily. It is assumed that if the fossil record were complete late representatives of *Homo habilis* would closely resemble early *Homo erectus*. Middle Pleistocene populations of *Homo erectus* are said in turn to show steady evolution toward the anatomy characteristic of *Homo sapiens*, and all three species are linked in an unbroken progression of slowly changing forms.

This interpretation of the fossils can be challenged. Some paleontologists see indications that the evolution of *Homo* proceeded less smoothly, with substantial variations in the rate at which morphological change occurred. *Homo habilis* is still too poorly known to provide much information in this regard, but many more specimens of *Homo erectus* have been collected. The older skulls from eastern Africa look much like the later ones from Java and China, and it can be argued that evolution slowed during the middle of the Pleistocene. The pace quickened again with the origin of *Homo sapiens*. Precisely when and where our own species emerged is not known, but this event may have taken place in a restricted geographic area. Some (perhaps many) *Homo erectus* populations became extinct during this time. The people living only a relatively short time afterward are distinctly more modern in appearance. Read in this way, the record of *Homo* is more complex. It is not obvious why the tempo of evolution varied during the Pleistocene or why some groups became extinct while others flourished. Gaining a better understanding of these processes is an important item on the agenda of modern paleoanthropology.

See also ACHEULEAN; CLARK, W.E. LE GROS; DALI; EAST TURKANA; GENUS; HOMO ERECTUS; HOMO HABILIS; HOMO SAPIENS; KABWE; MOUSTERIAN; NEANDERTHALS; OLDOWAN; OLDUVAI; PETRALONA; PLEISTOCENE; SPECIATION; SPECIES; SPEECH (ORIGINS OF); TRINIL. [G.P.R.]

Further Readings

Clark, W.E. Le Gros (1978) The Fossil Evidence for Human Evolution, 3rd ed. Chicago: University of Chicago Press.

Cronin, J.E., Boaz, N.T., Stringer, C.B., and Rak, Y. (1981) Tempo and mode in hominid evolution. Nature 292:113-122.

Delson, E., ed. (1985) Ancestors: The Hard Evidence. New York: Liss.

Howell, F.C. (1978) Hominidae. In V.J. Maglio and H.B.S. Cooke (eds.): Evolution of African Mammals. Cambridge, Mass.: Harvard University Press, pp. 154-248.

Isaac, G. (1978) The food-sharing behavior of protohuman hominids. Sci. Am. 238:90-108.

Königsson, L.-K., ed. (1980) Current Argument on Early Man. Oxford: Pergamon.

Potts, R. (1984) Hominid hunters? Problems of identifying the earliest hunter-gatherers. In R. Foley (ed.): Hominid Evolution and Community Ecology. London: Academic, pp. 129-166.

Smith, F.H., and Spencer, F., eds. (1984) The Origins of Modern Humans: A World Survey of the Fossil Evidence. New York: Liss.

Walker, A., and Leakey, R.E.F. (1978) The hominids of East Turkana. Sci. Am. 239:44-56.

HOMO ERECTUS

Extinct form of human known to have inhabited the Old World. This species probably originated in Africa, where it may have evolved nearly 2 m.y. ago from another species called *Homo habilis*. Populations of *Homo erectus* seem to have been confined to Africa for several hundred thousand years, before spreading slowly into Asia and probably into parts of Europe. Fossil remains of these people have been recovered from many sites. At numerous other localities stone tools and animal bones suggest the presence of *Homo erectus*, even though traces of the tool makers themselves are not present. This evidence has been accumulating since the end of the last century. Some particularly important discoveries have been made recently, and we now know a great deal about where and when *Homo erectus* lived, what these people looked like, and how they adapted to the Pleistocene environment. As a species *Homo erectus* flourished until later middle Pleistocene times. It is likely that at

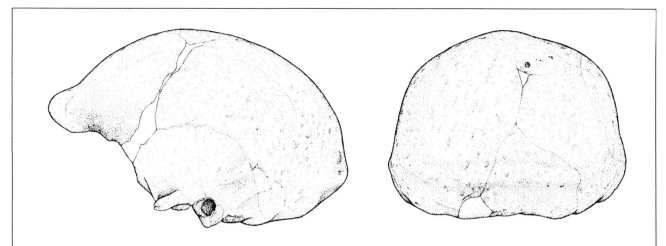

Side and rear views of the Sangiran 2 braincase. This small cranium from Java has a (brain) volume of just over 800 ml. and may be female. The low, broad vault and flexed occiput are characteristic of *Homo erectus*.

least some populations then evolved further, to become *Homo sapiens*.

First Discoveries in Asia

The first fossils were brought to light by E. Dubois. Dubois, a young Dutch physician, traveled to Indonesia to search for the missing link, and he was tremendously lucky. His first specimen turned up in 1890, and in 1891 a skullcap was excavated from the bank of the Solo River at Trinil in central Java. Several years later, after a remarkably complete and modern-looking femur had also been recovered at Trinil, Dubois named the Java hominid *Pithecanthropus erectus*, or upright ape-man. Apart from a few limb fragments no further discoveries were made at this time. More substantial traces of these archaic humans did not appear until the 1920s, when fossils were found far to the north, near Beijing (China). This site at Zhoukoudian proved to be very rich, and well-preserved parts of many individuals were dug out of different levels in the cave. It is most fortunate that this material was described without delay and in meticulous detail by the anatomist F. Weidenreich, as nearly all of it was lost during World War II. None of the bones has ever been relocated. Since the war continuing work at Zhoukoudian has produced a few new fossils, along with stone tools, animal bones, and evidence of fire. Accumulations of ash and charcoal have been interpreted as hearths by the excavators, who suggest that the cave was occupied by middle Pleistocene hunters and foragers seeking shelter.

Since 1938 other sites in Indonesia have yielded additional relics. In the Sangiran area of Java early discoveries were made by the paleontologist G.H.R. von Koenigswald, who followed Dubois in referring most of his material to *Pithecanthropus*. Von Koenigs-wald's collecting activities were interrupted during World War II, but Sangiran has become the most important of the Javanese localities. Altogether remains representing more than 40 human individuals have been found in these ancient lake and stream deposits. Several more fossils, mostly incomplete crania, have been collected at other sites in central and eastern Java. Most workers now refer these assemblages to *Homo erectus*, and the name *Pithecanthropus* has been dropped. One intriguing question is whether *Homo erectus* in southeastern Asia possessed a stone technology similar to that which was so well developed farther north in China. Few stone artifacts have been recovered at Sangiran or elsewhere on Java. This has prompted some anthropologists to argue that the hominids fashioned implements from less durable materials, such as bamboo, instead.

Geographic Distribution

For more than 50 years following Dubois's initial discoveries virtually all of the fossils attributable to *Homo erectus* were found in the Far East. It was not until 1954 and 1955 that three lower jaws and a single parietal bone from Ternifine (Algeria) made it clear that the species had lived in northwestern Africa as well. The site at Ternifine (now Tighenif) consists of sands and clays stratified in a small Pleistocene lake. Stone artifacts occurring with the fossils include bifaces and cleavers, and this industry is best described as Acheulean. Evidence of *Homo erectus* has come also from the Atlantic coast of Morocco. Fragmentary lower jaws and other specimens are known from Sidi Abderrahman, near Casablanca, and from the Thomas Quarries located nearby. The only more complete cranium from northwestern Africa was picked up near Salé in 1971. This Salé braincase is small, and it is possible that the rear of the skull has been deformed. Nevertheless, the speci-

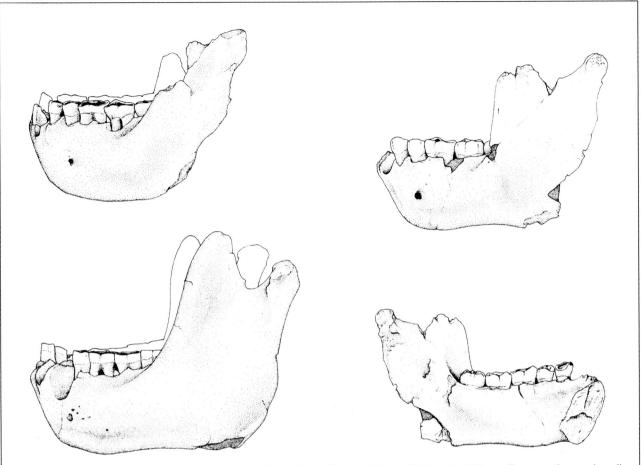

Three lower jaws from Tighenif in northwestern Africa. Tighenif 1 and Tighenif 3 (on the left) are larger and more heavily constructed than Tighenif 2 (shown in lateral and medial views on the right), which may be female. All three jaws are robust, lack a bony chin, and show substantial buttressing internally, at the symphysis.

men resembles *Homo erectus* in a number of respects.

Many more fossils have been discovered in eastern Africa. Two of the most important and best-studied localities are Olduvai Gorge (Tanzania) and the Turkana basin in northern Kenya. Olduvai is one of the most famous of prehistoric sites, and it has provided a great deal of information about the living habits, food preferences, and cultural activities of earlier hominids. *Australopithecus* and *Homo habilis* are both documented in the lower levels of the gorge, while traces of *Homo erectus* occur in Bed II as well as in more recent deposits. A partial cranium of a large (probably male) *Homo erectus* was found in the upper part of Bed II by L.S.B. Leakey in 1960. More material, including several lower jaws, another broken braincase, and a hip bone together with part of the lower limb, shows that *Homo erectus* lived at Olduvai for a substantial period of time. Stone tools associated with some of the fossil assemblages are of Acheulean manufacture.

Koobi Fora lies on the eastern shore of Lake Turkana. R. Leakey has directed fieldwork in this area since 1968. Vast quantities of animal bones have been collected and a number of excavations carried out. As at Olduvai Gorge it is clear that several forms of extinct human lived in the basin, and one of the species represented by many fossils is *Homo erectus*. Several of the crania are especially well preserved and rival the best of the specimens from the Far East. A skeleton that is nearly complete has also been recovered. Unfortunately the bones of this Koobi Fora individual are severely affected by disease, but a second skeleton, free of pathology, has recently been excavated at Nariokotome, on the western side of Lake Turkana. Investigations of this adolescent boy from Nariokotome are continuing and promise to yield valuable details about the growth process in earlier humans.

Hominids must also have been present in Europe at an early date. Signs of their occupation are preserved in caves and at open sites, often located near the Mediterranean Sea. Assemblages of chopping

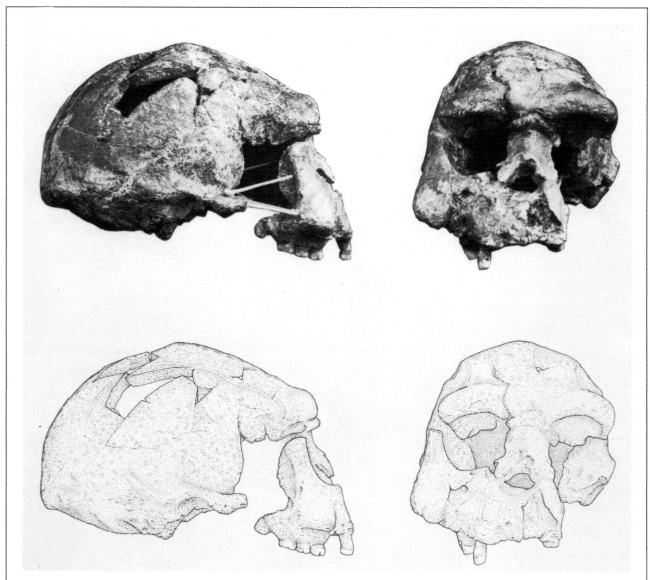

Side and facial views of Sangiran 17. This braincase is larger than that of Sangiran 2. Thicker brows, stronger supramastoid crests and the more prominent transverse torus of the occiput suggest that this individual is male.

tools and faunal remains have been uncovered at the oldest localities, which are thought to be of late early Pleistocene age. We have no good indication of what these people looked like, but it is probable that they resembled *Homo erectus*. The middle Pleistocene populations that followed them are better known and are certainly archaic in appearance. Particularly fine crania and jaws have been excavated from a long sequence of deposits at Arago Cave (France) and Petralona Cave (Greece). There are numerous less-complete fossils from other European sites. Specialists disagree about the classification of these finds, but it can be argued that they show some similarities to modern humans. If this view is correct, then many of the middle Pleistocene hominids are best grouped with *Homo sapiens*. Remains more definitely attribut-able to *Homo erectus* may still come to light, but for now the history of this species in Europe is obscure.

Dating

Populations of *Homo erectus* were widely dispersed, and there is much evidence suggesting that these fossils differ in absolute age. The remains from the Turkana basin are certainly among the oldest recovered so far. One of the most complete crania from Koobi Fora was located in deposits ca. 1.6 m.y. old, and the boy from Nariokotome on the west side of Lake Turkana is of the same geological age. The Olduvai hominids are somewhat younger. The large braincase from the upper part of Bed II is ca. 1.2 m.y. old. Ages of another incomplete cranium and the hip and limb bones from Bed IV cannot be obtained so easily, as the rocks from this part of the Olduvai sequence cannot be dated radiometrically. Sediment thickness and paleomagnetic measurements indicate that Bed IV must have been deposited between ca. 0.8 and 0.6 m.y. ago.

Nearly all of these East African fossils are more ancient than any from Algeria or the Atlantic coast of Morocco. The site at Tighenif may be of earliest middle Pleistocene date, while the materials from Moroccan quarries are probably younger by several hundred thousand years. The latter may be close in age to the assemblage from Zhoukoudian. At Zhoukoudian several methods have been used to gauge the antiquity of the many levels in the cave. Results suggest that the site was first occupied ca. 500 k.y. ago, and that *Homo erectus* continued to make use of this shelter for at least 200 k.y.

Dates for the Indonesian hominids are less certain. In some instances exact locations where finds were made are no longer known, and these specimens may never be placed securely in a chronological framework. Other fossils, particularly those collected more recently at Sangiran, can be given provisional dates, subject to confirmation as more work is done. At Sangiran *Homo erectus* is present mainly in the Kabuh sediments. These levels were deposited during the middle Pleistocene and (probably) during the latest early Pleistocene as well. A few of the hominids may also have come from the uppermost Pucangan sediments, which underlie the Kabuh horizons. Such individuals may be ca. 1 m.y. old, but it is not likely that any of the Indonesian specimens are as ancient as the first *Homo erectus* from East Africa. Given this evidence, it is reasonable to believe that *Homo erectus* evolved in Africa and spread only later into other regions of the Old World.

Anatomical Characters of Homo erectus

Many of the fossils from Southeast Asia and China are cranial bones, lower jaws, and teeth. A few limb bones have been recovered from the Javanese sites and from Zhoukoudian, but these fragments are not very informative. The one complete femur excavated at Trinil by Dubois may be of more recent geological age than the other fossils and not in fact representative of *Homo erectus* at all. As a consequence it is not surprising that descriptions of the species have emphasized the shape of the skull rather than the limbs or hands and feet. Discoveries in Africa are helping to fill out this picture. Postcranial parts as well as more skulls and teeth have turned up both at Olduvai Gorge and at the Turkana localities, and it is now possible to discuss the anatomy of *Homo erectus* in detail.

The cranium is distinctly different from that of other humans. It is low in profile and encloses a brain averaging a little less than 1,000 ml. in volume. The browridges are prominent and thickened, even in smaller individuals that may be females. Just behind the face the frontal bone is narrowed or constricted to an extent not seen in modern people. The forehead is flattened, but there may be a low ridge or keel of bone extending from the frontal onto the parietals in the midline. The parietal or side wall of the cranium is relatively short. On its surface the line marking the upper border of the temporal muscle curves downward toward the back, to produce a torus or bulge at the (mastoid) angle. Other crests in the mastoid region tend to be strongly developed. The skull is relatively broad at the base. The occipital bone, making up the rear of the braincase, is sharply curved. The division between its upper and lower parts is marked by a transverse torus or shelf, below which the neck muscles are attached. This area of muscle attachment is more extensive in *Homo erectus* than in *Homo sapiens*. Other features that distinguish *Homo erectus* are apparent on the underside of the cranium, particularly in the region of the joint for the lower jaw. The anatomy of the joint and its surrounding structures is a little different from that of living humans. The lower jaw itself is deep, very robust, and lacking any noticeable development of a chin eminence.

The part of the postcranial skeleton that has been most frequently preserved is the femur. Several of these thigh bones were recovered at Zhoukoudian and described by Weidenreich. More have been found in Africa, and it is clear that the *Homo erectus* femur exhibits several interesting characters. The shaft is flattened from front to back and the compact bone layer is thick, narrowing the (internal) medullary cavity. This robusticity is also seen in other parts of the skeleton, such as the pelvic bone found at Olduvai Gorge. Such a pattern may reflect a high level of biomechanical stress, and it suggests that *Homo erectus* probably had a physically demanding lifestyle.

Limb bones also provide information about body size. Size is an important attribute of any primate species, as it has a bearing on behavior and influences various aspects of anatomy, including the proportions of one body part to another. One measure of size is stature, or height. A good estimate of stature cannot be obtained from the incomplete femora collected at Zhoukoudian or other sites, but dimensions of the skeleton from Nariokotome in West Turkana suggest that this individual was large. Although he was not fully grown, the Nariokotome boy was ca. 1.6 m. tall. This figure is close to that expected for modern adult males.

Another measure of size is body weight. Weight can be estimated from skeletal fragments, such as the

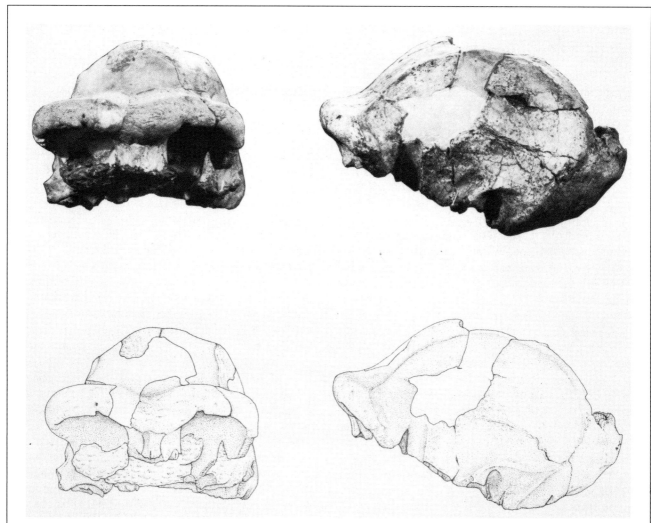

Facial and side views of hominid 9 from Olduvai Gorge in East Africa. This large cranium, with a volume of over 1,000 ml., is similar to the braincases from Java and China. The supraorbital torus is very thick, and many other characters of the vault and cranial base suggest that this individual represents *Homo erectus*.

shaft of the femur, although results are subject to some error. Figures for a number of *Homo erectus* individuals are available. Four lower limb bones from Zhoukoudian give an average size of ca. 47 kg., while the femora from Olduvai and East Turkana suggest a body weight of close to 50 kg. These estimates must be regarded as approximations only. They do indicate that body sizes for *Homo erectus* fall toward the lower end of the range recorded for living people. This information can be put to further use, to provide a measure of relative brain size for the extinct species. Brain volume as determined from the fossil skulls can be compared with the size expected for modern humans of comparable body bulk, to give a ratio of encephalization. When this is done treating all of the Asian and African specimens together, one can conclude that *Homo erectus* had a brain about 87 percent as large as that of recent *Homo sapiens*.

Role of Homo erectus *in Human Evolution*
Skulls identified as *Homo erectus* are quite different from those of other humans. The low, heavily constructed braincase is not like that of *Homo habilis* or *Australopithecus*. The cranium and jaws can also be distinguished from those of *Homo sapiens*, even if some of the early representatives of our own species are still archaic in appearance. In other parts of the skeleton that have been studied closely *Homo erectus* again shows distinctive features. This complex of anatomical characters was well established in Africa at least 1.6 m.y. ago. Remains from the Turkana basin attest to this, and several of the individuals from Koobi Fora are remarkably like Asian *Homo erectus*. Similar people were present at Olduvai Gorge a few hundred thousand years later. Populations of this species roamed over Asia as well as Africa during much of the middle Pleistocene, and *Homo erectus*

seems to have flourished for well over a million years. During at least part of this long span of time *Homo erectus* is the only form of human known to have inhabited the Old World. Therefore it is very likely that this species gave rise to more modern people, sometime in the later middle Pleistocene.

Just how this process took place is not clear. One line of reasoning holds that *Homo erectus* changed gradually, throughout its long history. Advocates of this view argue that the early African individuals have small brains coupled with relatively large jaws and teeth, so that they appear more primitive than later finds. By contrast the middle Pleistocene skulls from Zhoukoudian exhibit some increase in brain volume and seem generally to be more appropriate ancestors for recent humans. Continuing evolution has carried not only the Zhoukoudian population but also other late *Homo erectus* in the direction of *Homo sapiens*. In this scenario many groups of the archaic species contributed to the genetic make-up of modern humans. Few if any bands of *Homo erectus* became extinct, in the sense of leaving no descendants, and *Homo sapiens* must have emerged in several different geographic areas.

If evolution proceeded in this fashion, through the slow and steady transformation of primitive peoples across the entire range of territory inhabited by *Homo erectus*, then claims for regional continuity are plausible. Several anatomists and anthropologists, including F. Weidenreich, have suggested that there are discernible links between *Homo erectus* assemblages and the humans who today occupy the same geographic regions. An example is provided by Zhoukoudian. Weidenreich and other scholars have argued that fossils from the cave exhibit morphological resemblances to living Chinese. These similarities are apparent in cranial anatomy and also in the dentition. They are taken as evidence for biological continuity of populations extending from the early middle Pleistocene to the present. Local cultural progress accompanying this genetic change is also read from the record in the cave, where stone artifacts are preserved along with the fossils.

Comparable scenarios may be sketched for other regions. It has been claimed that *Homo erectus* from Java is related, albeit distantly, to the recent indigenous populations of Australia. Fossils from Europe are said to fall into a progression beginning with archaic, *erectus*-like forms and ending with modern people, and the hominids from northwestern Africa have been interpreted in the same way. The evidence for regional continuity, however, is often not convincing. In Asia there are large gaps in the record. Few fossils seem actually to document the transition from *Homo erectus* to *Homo sapiens*. Even where the

bones are more plentiful, their significance is questionable. It is difficult to identify anatomical characters that unequivocally link the middle Pleistocene assemblages to later humans.

Such doubts prompt other authorities to suggest a different evolutionary story. When all of the early and late *Homo erectus* fossils are measured, there are in fact not many indications of steady change. It is true that brain size does increase in Asian populations like that at Zhoukoudian, but in other features the later middle Pleistocene specimens are not different from the Koobi Fora or Olduvai material. One can propose that little change took place during more than a million years. Perhaps *Homo erectus* should be characterized as a stable species, within which trends are not readily apparent. If this is the case, then it is not surprising that evidence for regional continuity is hard to find. Populations within the species do, as expected, show a good deal of variation, but all are more similar to one another than to later representatives of *Homo sapiens*. Here we are left with little indication of the path actually followed when *Homo erectus* did evolve abruptly into our own species. This transition may have occurred in a hundred thousand years or less, and it probably took place in a restricted geographic area. Confirming this hypothesis, or compiling solid evidence to support another view, is a major challenge to students of human evolution in the later Pleistocene.

See also ACHEULEAN; ARAGO; EAST TURKANA; FIRE; NARIOKOTOME; OLDUVAI; PETRALONA; PLEISTOCENE; SALÉ; SANGIRAN DOME; SPECIES; THOMAS QUARRIES; TIGHENIF; TRINIL; WEIDENREICH, FRANZ; ZHOUKOUDIAN. [G.P.R.]

Further Readings

Andrews, P., and Franzen, J.L., eds. (1984) The early evolution of man with special emphasis on Southeast Asia and Africa. Cour. Forsch. Inst. Senckenberg 69:1–277.

Delson, E., ed. (1985) Ancestors: The Hard Evidence. New York: Liss.

Howells, W.W. (1980) *Homo erectus*—who, when and where: a survey. Yrbk. Phys. Anthropol. 23:1–23.

Sigmon, B.A., and Cybulski, J.S., eds. (1981) *Homo erectus*: Papers in Honor of Davidson Black. Toronto: University of Toronto Press.

Wu, R., and Lin, S. (1983) Peking Man. Sci. Am. 248:86–94.

HOMO HABILIS

Extinct species of the genus *Homo* that inhabited sub-Saharan Africa at the end of the Pliocene. Fossils representing this taxon were discovered first at Olduvai Gorge in northern Tanzania. A lower jaw, along with pieces of a cranium and hand bones, were picked up in the lower part of the gorge in 1960. More specimens followed, and it was soon recognized that these hominids differed anatomically

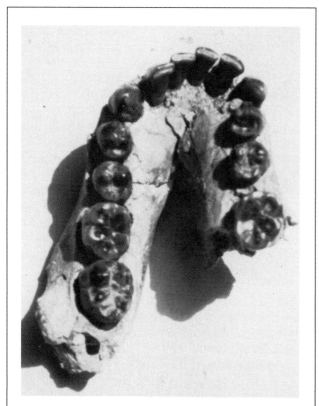

This mandible of hominid 7 from Olduvai Gorge was designated as *Homo habilis* in 1964. Although the jaw itself is thick, the premolar and molar teeth are a little smaller than expected for *Australopithecus*. Two parietal bones found with the mandible suggest that OH 7 has a brain close to 700 ml. in volume.

Anatomical Characteristics

Crania, jaws, and teeth recovered in eastern Africa provide a fair amount of information about the anatomy of *Homo habilis*. The braincase is clearly expanded in size relative to that of *Australopithecus*. The original Olduvai parietal bones can be reconstructed to form a partial vault, and the endocranial capacity estimated for this individual is close to 700 ml. The more complete cranium numbered ER-1470 from Koobi Fora has a volume of ca. 780 ml., and one or two additional fragmentary skulls from this locality may be about the same size. Other individuals are considerably smaller. A range for brain size extending from somewhat less than 600 ml. to ca. 800 ml. seems to be characteristic of the species.

The cranium is thin-walled and lacks the heavy crests and buttresses that distinguish later *Homo erectus*. Browridges are not strongly projecting, and the contour of the vault is rounded rather than low and flattened. The occipital bone is flexed as in other archaic *Homo* but does not carry a transverse torus. The lower part of the occiput covered by the neck muscles is short, compared with the nuchal area of *Homo erectus*. Faces are partly preserved for several individuals. There is substantial variation in facial proportions, and at least one of the Olduvai hominids is really more similar anatomically to *Australopithecus* than to later *Homo*. The nasal region of OH 24 is flattened, while the cheek bones are prominent. The facial skeleton of ER-1470 also shows resemb-

from *Australopithecus*. In 1964 L.S.B. Leakey and his colleagues named the new species *Homo habilis*. In their description Leakey, P.V. Tobias, and J. Napier emphasized an increase in volume of the brain and a reduction in size of the premolar and molar teeth as important features. In these respects the new species seemed to foreshadow the condition seen in later *Homo*.

Although the validity of *Homo habilis* has been questioned, P.V. Tobias has continued to defend his view that the Olduvai fossils are among the earliest members of the Homo lineage. More material has since come to light, not only at Olduvai but also at other African localities. Several skulls recovered at Koobi Fora on the eastern shore of Lake Turkana in Kenya are especially well preserved, while more fragmentary remains are known from cave deposits in South Africa. Dating of some of these assemblages is still uncertain, but *Homo habilis* was present in the Turkana basin at least 2 m.y. ago. Apparently this species was relatively short-lived, as none of the fossils seems to be less than ca. 1.5 m.y. old. Many anthropologists now agree that these early hominids are the ancestors of *Homo erectus*.

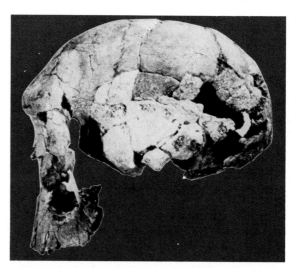

Side view of ER-1470 from the Koobi Fora region. This cranium, with a volume of ca. 780 ml., is one of the largest referred to early *Homo*. It may be a male of *Homo habilis*. Several smaller individuals from Koobi Fora and from Olduvai are often described as females of the same species, although they differ from ER-1470 in ways that are not clearly related to sex (see figure accompanying the HOMO article).

lances to *Australopithecus*, although another of the Koobi Fora individuals has been described as more *Homo*-like. In general the anterior teeth of *Homo habilis* are not reduced in size relative to those of *Australopithecus*. The premolar and molar crowns, however, do exhibit narrowing, especially in the lower jaw.

Few limb bones have been discovered. Parts of the postcranial skeleton that can be attributed to *Homo habilis* suggest that this species was as fully adapted to upright, bipedal locomotion as later humans. Pieces of an immature hand associated with the Olduvai parietals have been studied extensively. This hand retains some features that are apelike, but there seems to be no reason to deny that this individual was able to manipulate objects in a precise fashion. Stone artifacts occur in the same levels at Olduvai Gorge and also at other localities where early *Homo* has been found. These Oldowan tools are crude but do constitute further evidence that *Homo habilis* was capable of shaping stone.

Evolutionary Role Played by Homo habilis

Anatomical evidence is usually interpreted to mean not only that *Homo habilis* differs from *Australopithecus* but also that this species is the first to exhibit trends that continue during the history of the *Homo* lineage. The expansion of the brain that sets (some of) the Olduvai and Koobi Fora individuals apart from *Australopithecus* becomes more apparent in *Homo erectus*. Brain size is still larger in our own species, and increasing encephalization is a hallmark of human evolution. Other trends toward reduction in tooth size and restructuring particularly of the nasal region of the face are said to begin with *Homo habilis*. It has also been argued that this species was able to make a variety of simple tools and to use language. Oldowan artifacts do attest to the technological skills of early hominids, but this ability to work with stone may not by itself imply a capacity for spoken communication. The extent to which *Homo habilis* spoke or behaved like later humans is difficult to ascertain, given the very limited archaeological record.

This view of early *Homo* must be generally accurate, but some questions remain. *Homo habilis* is after all a poorly known species, as compared with *Homo erectus* or *Homo sapiens*. Only a few individuals have been recovered, and most are not well preserved. One question concerns the significance of anatomical differences that occur within the assemblages of fossils from eastern Africa. Some of the crania are quite large, for example, while others are much smaller. It is often suggested that this variation is due to sex. Individuals like ER-1470 are regarded as

males, while smaller crania, such as OH 24, are taken to be those of females. Differences, however, extend to shape as well as size. The facial skeleton of OH 24 shows similarities to *Australopithecus*, as noted previously. This Olduvai hominid differs from other large-brained *Homo habilis* in ways that are not obviously related to sex. The fossils may in fact represent two taxa rather than one sexually dimorphic group.

If the specimens can most reasonably be assigned to two lineages, then both must be fit into a scheme of hominid phylogeny. One reading of the evidence places the smaller crania including OH 24 and perhaps other individuals from Olduvai and Koobi Fora in a gracile species of *Australopithecus*. In this case only the larger skulls can be regarded as representing an early stage in the evolution of *Homo*. Other workers who surmise that two species are present prefer to lump both of them in the genus *Homo*. According to this scenario there is more diversity among early human populations than has previously been recognized, and the idea that all *Homo* species fall in a simple unilinear progression will have to be questioned. If two taxa lived between 2 and 1.5 m.y. ago, only one can be the direct antecedent of *Homo erectus*. Which of two such contemporary species may be the more closely related to later humans is not entirely clear. Problems of this sort surrounding early *Homo* will be solved only as new fossils are recovered.

See also Australopithecus; East Turkana; Homo; Homo erectus; Leakey, Louis; Oldowan; Olduvai; Species. [G.P.R.]

Further Readings

Delson, E., ed. (1985) Ancestors: The Hard Evidence. New York: Liss.

Howell, F.C. (1978) Hominidae. In V.J. Maglio and H.B.S. Cooke (eds.): Evolution of African Mammals. Cambridge, Mass.: Harvard University Press, pp. 154-248.

Leakey, L.S.B., Tobias, P.V., and Napier, J.R. (1964) A new species of the genus *Homo* from Olduvai Gorge. Nature 202:7-9.

HOMO SAPIENS

Species to which modern humans belong. In the last century and the earlier years of this century it was common for workers who studied newly discovered fossil hominids to erect new species or even genus names for virtually every new find, even where the specimen was clearly closely related to previous finds. Thus after the Neanderthal skeleton was discovered it was made the type of a new species of the genus *Homo*, called *Homo neanderthalensis*, and this practice was repeated by some workers for various other Neanderthal finds, such as those from Spy ("*Homo spyensis*"), Le Moustier ("*Homo transprimigenius mousteriensis*"), and La Chapelle-aux-Saints ("Homo chapellensis"). Similarly, the Broken Hill cranium was assigned to *Homo rhodesiensis* and later to "*Cyphanthropus rhodesiensis*," the Skhūl remains to "*Palaeanthropus palestinus*," and the Steinheim skull to "*Homo steinheimensis*."

During the period 1943–1964, however, a number of influential papers reexamined the basic concepts of hominid classification from the perspectives of more general paleontology and from the developing field of population genetics. It was argued that, as living *Homo sapiens* represented a polytypic species, so did fossil humans at any one time level in the past. Particularly important to these discussions was the status of the Zhoukoudian remains (then commonly attributed to "*Sinanthropus pekinensis*"), and the Mount Carmel (Skhūl and Tabūn) remains (then commonly attributed to a single nonmodern population). Weidenreich, who described the Zhoukoudian fossils, actually regarded them as representing only a distinct race of early humans, despite his persistent use of a separate generic name for the material. This led several workers to suggest that the Zhoukoudian remains in fact represented merely a subspecies of an early human species, *Homo erectus*. McCown and Keith's interpretation of the Mount Carmel fossils as representing a highly variable single population led them to suggest that the taxonomic boundary between Neanderthals and modern *Homo sapiens* had been broken down. The Mount Carmel "population" could be interpreted as either a group in the process of evolving from a Neanderthal to a modern morphology or as a hybrid population between two (closely related) forms.

Thus reassessments of the fossil material suggested that no more than a single hominid species had existed at any one time in the Pleistocene, and that *Homo erectus* (including such geographical variants as "Java man" and "Peking man") and *Homo sapiens* (including such variants as Neanderthals and modern humans) were polytypic species. This viewpoint was formalized by Campbell in the 1960s, when he proposed that *Homo sapiens* Linnaeus 1758 should be subdivided into the following living or fossil subspecies: *sapiens* (modern humans), *neanderthalensis*, *steinheimensis*, *rhodesiensis*, and *soloensis* (for the Ngandong remains). This scheme has been widely adopted in the period since 1964, and a number of previous and new fossil discoveries have been incorporated into it under one or other subspecific categories. Subsequently it has become common to differentiate the anatomically modern form of *Homo sapiens* (*Homo sapiens sapiens*) from the other forms of the species by

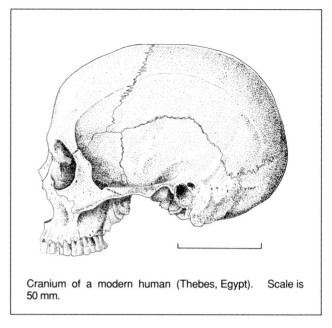

Cranium of a modern human (Thebes, Egypt).   Scale is 50 mm.

the additional epithets "modern" or "archaic" *Homo sapiens*, and thus archaic *Homo sapiens* includes middle or late Pleistocene hominids that are distinct from, but supposedly closely related to, modern humans.

Modern Homo sapiens

Anatomically modern *Homo sapiens* can be characterized by a number of anatomical features found in all living human populations, and many of these features are related to an overall gracility of the skeleton compared with archaic humans. Although living *Homo sapiens* around the world display a remarkable variation in stature, physique, and weight (much of which can be attributed to environmental adaptations and nutritional factors), most modern humans are quite large-bodied but have slenderly constructed bones and a less heavy musculature than was the case in archaic humans. This may well be an indication of the extent to which sophisticated behaviors found in all living humans have taken the selective weight off the skeleton (almost literally) through an emphasis on economy of effort rather than high activity and muscle power as the basic behavioral adaptation of the species.

Compared with archaic humans, modern *Homo sapiens* have large brains (also found in Neanderthals), with an average volume exceeding 1,300 ml. (but varying somewhat according to sex and body size). To house this large brain there is a highly distinctive and derived cranial shape in modern humans. The vault is relatively short (front to back) and high, with a domed forehead and well-arched (rather than flattened) parietals. The base of the skull is narrow, as is the occipital bone, and this bone is rounded in profile, lacking the transverse torus and heavy neck musculature of many archaic forms, as well as the distinctive torus shape and suprainiac fossa found in Neanderthals. As in Neanderthals, but to an even greater extent, the skull walls are relatively thin, and this lack of robusticity is also reflected in the small or nonexistent browridge and the gracile face and jaws with small teeth. The mandible itself is not thickened and has a bony chin on its outside. The degree of flatness of the face and the shape of the nose vary in different populations, but in none of them is there the large and projecting nasal region found in Neanderthals. The whole skeleton is slenderly built with thin walls to the limb bones and only moderate muscularity. The scapula (shoulder blade) has less muscle attachment on the back edge, and the pelvis is not robustly constructed, while also lacking the extended pubic ramus found in Neanderthals.

There are also distinctive features of growth and development in modern humans when compared with our closest primate relatives, since humans have a long period of childhood growth and dependency, mature later, and complete growth much later than the apes. In addition the lifespan of humans is such that there is often a long period of postreproductive survival, which is undocumented in the apes. The slow development of humans and the presence of postreproductive survival into old age may both be linked to the importance of intergenerational transmission of cultural information. Thus old individuals may be provisioned for since they have a wealth of experience useful to younger, less-experienced individuals. Similarly, the slow development of children allows them ample time to develop linguistic skills, which are of use in absorbing the complexities of the culture into which they have been born. Although this developmental pattern is found in all living human populations, there is little evidence (but much speculation) about when this distinctive pattern emerged.

Until recently it was generally believed that the human pattern of slow development was present in early hominids, such as the australopithecines, *Homo habilis*, and *Homo erectus*. However, new techniques of determining more accurately the age at death of fossil remains of young individuals have suggested that the modern human growth pattern was not present in these early hominids. If this is so, the modern *Homo sapiens* pattern may have originated quite recently and without further proof cannot even be assumed to have been fully developed in archaic *sapiens* populations (including the Neanderthals). This area will no doubt become a focus of research over the next few years.

Origin of Modern Homo sapiens

Two extreme models have been proposed to account for the origin of modern people, with workers adopting various intermediate positions. One extreme view postulates that modern humans evolved locally in different parts of the world from dissimilar archaic ancestors. This model of local continuity is sometimes termed the "Neanderthal phase" model, since it envisages hominids of comparable evolutionary grade to the European Neanderthals giving rise to local descendant "modern" populations by parallel or polyphyletic evolution. Thus in Europe a direct unilinear evolutionary sequence might exist between the oldest European populations, represented by the Mauer mandible, and modern Europeans, via such intermediates as the Neanderthals and Cro-Magnons. Similarly, in the Far East the Lantian and Zhoukoudian *Homo erectus* specimens could represent ancient ancestors for modern Asian peoples, via such intermediates as the Maba, Yingkou, and Dali material. And in Indonesia Javanese *Homo erectus* fossils could represent populations that eventually gave rise to modern Australasian peoples, via such intermediates as the Ngandong (Solo) and Kow Swamp fossils.

In this model "racial" variation is very ancient, with "local" features traceable between ancient and modern populations over periods longer than half a million years. Variants of this model allow for significant gene flow to have occurred between the local lineages, so that speciation did not occur and so that the fundamentally similar anatomy of all modern peoples can be explained. In the "center and edge" model, for example, the great variation found in recent and Pleistocene Australians is explained as a result of local evolution (from Indonesian *Homo erectus*) combined with migration or gene flow from the Asian mainland (e.g. as represented by the Mungo fossils).

In contrast with the local continuity model the "Noah's Ark" model proposes that all modern humans derived from a single fairly recent common ancestral population. From this model it follows that population movement or expansion was the primary determinant of the spread of modern human characteristics during the last 50 k.y., rather than local evolution. Local "racial" features evolved *after* the anatomical features that are shared by all living *Homo sapiens*, whereas in the local continuity model, "racial" or "local" features were much more ancient.

The geographical location of such a source population for all living humans is still uncertain, but most proponents of the "Noah's Ark" model favor southern Africa as the critical area, with a minority case also presented for Southwest Asia. The evidence for the earliest occurrence of anatomically modern fossils in these areas is discussed elsewhere (*see* ARCHAIC MODERNS), but there is support for the model that is independent of the fossil evidence, from considerations of modern human skeletal variation and recently published genetic analyses. Different human populations show a fundamental similarity in anatomy, and it is difficult to believe that such a large number of characters in common could have evolved independently under very different environmental or cultural conditions in various parts of the world. Those features that distinguish modern humans from each other are relatively minor and could easily have been superimposed on a fundamentally modern anatomy inherited from a recent common ancestor.

The genetic data that support a recent African origin for all modern *Homo sapiens* come from several distinct kinds of analyses. When data from many different biochemical systems are combined to compare different human populations with each other, the results show a stronger similarity between European and Asian populations than between either of these and African populations. By assuming a constancy of molecular mutation, it has been estimated from these data that European and Asian populations shared a last common ancestor ca. 40 k.y. ago and in turn that they had a last common ancestor with African populations ca. 110 k.y. ago. Similar results have been obtained from a detailed analysis of the DNA of beta-globins, in that there are many shared similarities among the non-African populations, suggesting they are more closely related, while sub-Saharan populations are more distinct.

But the most powerful genetic evidence for an African origin for modern *Homo sapiens* comes from the entirely separate system of mitochondrial DNA (mtDNA). The degree of variation shown by samples of human mtDNA from all over the world is remarkably small compared with those so far obtained from our closest relatives, the apes and monkeys, suggesting a recent origin for the human types involved. Computer-derived trees have been constructed to link up the 150 or so mtDNA types so far identified in modern humans, and the tree constructed shows once again a basic dichotomy between southern African and other mtDNA types. By applying a "molecular clock" to the data, we obtain results suggesting that the most ancient mtDNA material was African in origin, perhaps 200 k.y. in age, and that mtDNA types in Europe, Australia, and the Americas are much younger. This would not be expected from the local-continuity model, since, for example, Asian and Australasian populations should contain genetic material from ancient local *Homo erectus* ancestors rather than from more recent African ancestors. Equally, given

the long period of Neanderthal evolution in Europe, it would be expected that more ancient genetic lines should exist in recent Europeans if they were even partly derived from Neanderthals, but these have not so far been found.

Thus the most probable scenario for the origin of modern *Homo sapiens* has a southern African origin for modern morphological and genetic variation, and this origin was probably during the timespan of the African Middle Stone Age (MSA), which lasted from ca. 120 to 40 k.y. ago. Ancestral populations probably resembled such specimens as Ngaloba or Omo Kibish 2, while fossils approaching the modern condition in more respects occur at Florisbad (South Africa) and Jebel Irhoud (Morocco). Specimens within the modern anatomical range can be recognized from such sites as Klasies River Mouth, Border Cave, and Omo Kibish (1), all of which are likely to be older than 50 k.y., with MSA associations. The extent to which modern behavioral patterns were already present in MSA populations is still unclear, with some workers suggesting that there is a precocious appearance of "Upper Paleolithic" aspects in some MSA industries, while others argue that such changes do not occur until the end of the MSA. So it is also still uncertain whether there was a linkage or decoupling between the morphological and behavioral changes that heralded the advent of modern *Homo sapiens* in Africa.

Following an early late Pleistocene establishment of modern features in Africa, the modern anatomical pattern probably radiated by population expansion, migration, or gene flow into Southwest Asia, where it can be recognized as present by at least 40 k.y. (Skhūl) and perhaps much earlier (70 k.y.?) if the more ancient dates for Qafzeh are favored. Modern humans may also have been present in the Soviet Union (Starosel'e) and eastern Europe (Krapina A and Bacho Kiro?) by 40 k.y. ago and were probably widespread in Europe by 35 k.y. to judge by the appearance of Aurignacian industries as far west as Spain and France by that time.

In all cases where a hominid association with the Aurignacian is unequivocal, that hominid is always anatomically modern *Homo sapiens*, and the European populations of these early modern people are collectively known as "Cro-Magnons." The term was formerly considered to be virtually synonomous with the term "Upper Paleolithic humans," covering the period from ca. 35 to 10 k.y. in Europe, but the discovery of a genuine Neanderthal associated with the early "Upper Paleolithic" Chatelperronian industry at Saint-Césaire (France) necessitates a revision of this usage. The term Cro-Magnon now covers a wide range of fossil material associated with different

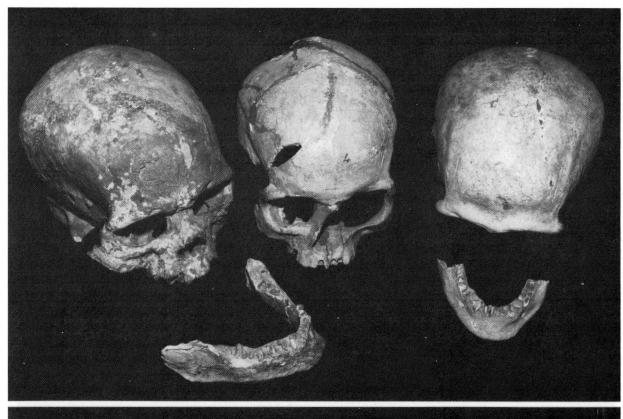

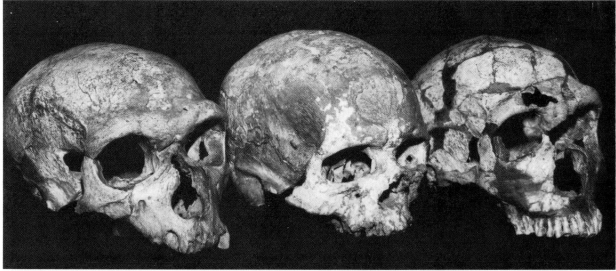

Above: the most famous early modern fossils from Europe: three of the Cro-Magnon specimens found in France in 1868. The crania on the left (Cro-Magnon 1) and right (Cro-Magnon 3) are probably male, and the other (Cro-Magnon 2), female. These crania probably date from 30–28 k.y. ago. Below: the Cro-Magnon 1 skull (center) positioned between the Neanderthal specimens from La Chapelle-aux-Saints (left) and La Ferrassie. The Neanderthal specimens actually appear to be more derived in facial form, while some of the early modern specimens from Europe and southwestern Asia retain more of the middle Pleistocene facial shape and proportions.

"cultures," such as the Aurignacian, Gravettian, Solutrean, and Magdalenian, and the extent to which it is legitimate to group this range of material is debatable.

While no one doubts that the Cro-Magnons do represent anatomically modern humans, they were undoubtedly distinct in a number of respects from modern Europeans. In some of these aspects it is possible to see retained primitive characters, such as relatively large teeth and brows, but attempts to recognize these aspects as specifically derived from

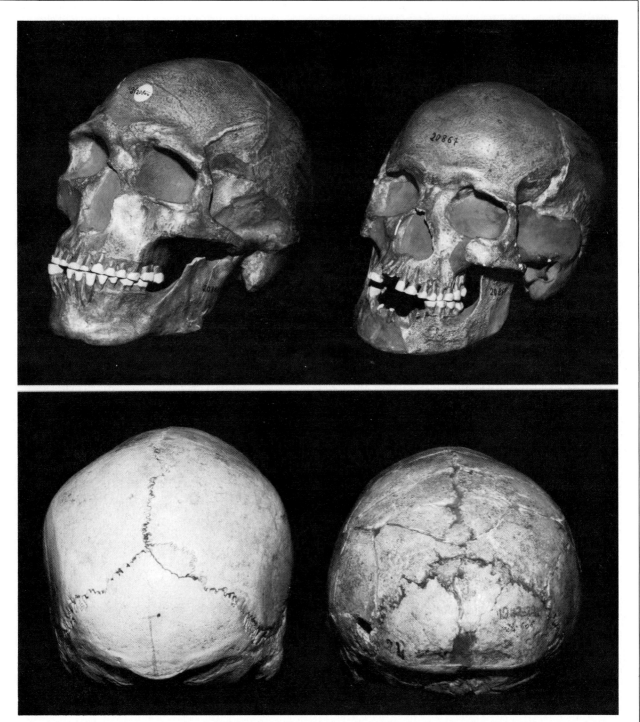

Above: these two crania from Predmosti (Czechoslovakia) represent some of the most robust early modern specimens from Europe. They probably date from ca. 26 k.y. ago. Predmosti 3 (left) even shows Neanderthal-like characteristics in the face, suggesting the possibility of gene flow from late Neanderthal populations. Below: an occipital comparison of an early modern skull from Europe (Abri Pataud, left) and a Neanderthal (La Quina 5). Both specimens may be of female individuals, but they contrast markedly in a number of respects, typifying the differences between Neanderthals and *Homo sapiens* in general.

ancestral Neanderthals are generally unconvincing, and in some respects it is the Neanderthals who seem more derived in their characters. For example, the body proportions of the Cro-Magnons were quite distinct from those of Neanderthals, since the lower portions of their arms and legs were elongated compared with the upper parts, whereas in the Neanderthals they were relatively shortened. In modern humans this elongation is a pattern characteristic of warm-adapted populations, and this physique may be a Cro-Magnon retention from African ancestors. Similar retentions may be observed in certain indices of facial shape (such as in possessing a shorter, flatter, and relatively broader face, with low orbits and short nose), and these features were present in middle and early late Pleistocene African specimens but not in Neanderthals.

Another feature that distinguished Neanderthals and Cro-Magnons was the greater stature of the latter, despite their overall similarity in a relatively heavy body build, probably comparable with that of modern Europeans. The Cro-Magnons probably averaged a stature of more than 180 cm. (over 6 ft.) in males and ca. 167 cm. (5½ ft.) in females, a significant increase over typical European Neanderthals (males ca. 167 cm. and females ca. 160 cm.). This tall, slender physique of the Cro-Magnons certainly more closely resembled that of the Skhūl and Qafzeh specimens than that of the Neanderthals, since average stature in the European and Israeli early moderns was virtually identical. There is uncertainty about the ancestral African pattern, but it may also have been more similar to that found in Eurasian early modern, rather than Neanderthal, skeletons.

However, certain early Cro-Magnon specimens from eastern Europe do not fit so neatly into this distinct Neanderthal/Cro-Magnon dichotomy, such as Předmosti 3, a specimen with some Neanderthal-like features in facial shape. This indicates the possibility that some gene flow did occur between late Neanderthal and early modern humans in Europe during a probable period of coexistence between at least 35 and 30 k.y., and a possible hybrid fossil between the two groups has even been claimed from the site of Hahnöfersand (West Germany). This specimen is not adequately dated, however, and can be interpreted in a variety of ways. If such hybridization did occur, it must have been on a limited scale, and even then there is no certainty that such hybrids gave rise to later Europeans.

Modern Homo sapiens Fossils from Outside Europe

Early modern fossils have been discovered in Africa and Southwest Asia, but those so far discussed are probably all older than 35 k.y. Unfortunately there is a dearth of late Pleistocene human material from many of these areas, with the notable exception of the large North African collections from such sites as Afalou and Taforalt. What material there is suggests that even at the end of the Pleistocene there were still rather robust modern humans represented at such sites as Iwo Eleru (Nigeria), East Turkana (Kenya),

and Springbok Flats and Cape Flats (South Africa). At the same time there were other populations that already closely resembled the modern Khoisan ("Bushman") peoples of southern Africa.

From the slender evidence available from Central Asia certain populations of the late Pleistocene seem to have been physically and culturally related to those of the European Upper Paleolithic. Farther east, however, there is evidence of populations that may be related to modern aboriginal populations of the Far East and the Americas. Several partial skeletons from the Upper Cave at Zhoukoudian (China) may have represented a population ancestral to Amerindians (the past tense is used because these specimens were lost at the same time as the main Zhoukoudian collection of Homo erectus fossils). An isolated skull from Liujiang, however, seems more similar in its facial form to modern "Mongoloids" of Asia, which suggests that such "racial" differences were evolving by 20 k.y. ago.

In Southeast Asia there is evidence from the cave site of Niah (Borneo) that modern humans were present there by 40 k.y., but this controversial date will soon be tested by the application of direct accelerator radiocarbon dating. Farther south there is archaeological evidence that modern humans had reached Australasia by 40 k.y. ago, but the nature of the original colonists, and whether they represented a single population or multiple migrations from different source areas is still unclear. The Mungo skeletons from southern Australia are dated at 30–24 k.y., and the most complete specimens (1 and 3) seem remarkably gracile by the standards of many early modern humans from elsewhere in the world, or even in comparison with some peoples alive today. The contrast is all the more marked because the same region of Australia was populated by much more robust peoples at the end of the Pleistocene, as represented by the Cohuna and Kow Swamp samples. Publications concerning this latter group have tended to emphasize the robusticity of the specimens (which is certainly very evident), but the sample also includes Mungo-like cranial and postcranial material.

One scenario postulates that two founder populations originally entered Australia, the first derived from Indonesian ancestors (such as Javanese Homo erectus and the Ngandong material) and represented by the Kow Swamp, Cohuna, and Talgai specimens, while another migrated into the region from the Asian mainland, as represented by the Mungo and Keilor fossils. These two groups coexisted through the later Pleistocene and eventually gave rise to modern Australian aboriginal populations by hybridization. It is also possible to propose that there was only *one* founding population from either Indonesia or farther afield and that much variation was created within Australia as the huge unpopulated continent became colonized. This variation may also have been compounded by pathological factors and the practice of head binding, which was certainly responsible for some of the peculiarities in cranial shape amongst the Kow Swamp sample. What is probably the most archaic-looking specimen from Australia, however, may also be the most ancient, providing possible evidence of an Indonesian origin for at least some Pleistocene Australians. This skull (WLH 50) is still unpublished, but if it can be accurately dated, it should throw further light on the mysterious origins of modern *Homo sapiens* in Australia.

Editors' note: Since this article was written, the sites of Jebel Qafzeh (Israel) and Jebel Irhoud (Morocco) have been dated at ca. 90 k.y. These are the earliest firm dates for undoubted anatomically modern *Homo sapiens*, and approximately double the well-documented span of this form, especially north of the Sahara. They provide further support for the "Noah's Ark" theory discussed in this article.

See also ARCHAIC HOMO SAPIENS; ARCHAIC MODERNS; NEANDERTHALS. [C.B.S.]

Further Readings

Bräuer, G. (1984) The Afro-European *sapiens* hypothesis, and hominid evolution in Asia during the late Middle and early Upper Pleistocene. Cour. Forsch. Inst. Senckenberg 69:145–165.

Delson, E. (1985) Late Pleistocene human fossils and evolutionary relationships. In E. Delson (ed.): Ancestors: The Hard Evidence. New York: Liss, pp. 296–300.

Howell, F.C. (1984) Introduction. In F.H. Smith and F. Spencer (eds.): The Origins of Modern Humans: A World Survey of the Fossil Evidence. New York: Liss, pp. xiii–xxii.

Howells, W.W. (1976) Explaining modern man: evolutionists versus migrationists. J. Hum. Evol. 5:477–495.

Smith, F.H. (1985) Continuity and change in the origin of modern *Homo sapiens*. Z. Morph. Anthropol. 75:197–222.

Stringer, C.B., Hublin, J.-J., and Vandermeersch, B. (1984) The origin of anatomically modern humans in western Europe. In Smith and Spencer, pp. 51–135.

Tattersall, I. (1986) Species recognition in human paleontology. J. Hum. Evol. 15:165–175.

Wolpoff, M.H. (1986) Describing anatomically modern *Homo sapiens*: A distinction without a definable difference. Anthropos (Brno) 23:41–53.

Wolpoff, M.H., Wu, X.Z., and Thorne, A. (1984) Modern *Homo sapiens* origins: a general theory of hominid evolution involving the fossil evidence from east Asia. In Smith and Spencer, pp. 411–483.

HOMOLOGY

Features of organisms that by virtue of position, structure, or function seem to be comparable are held to be homologous. Under the notion of evolution, homologies are organismic attributes derived from a single ancestral condition. Thus homologies may consist of very similar attributes (the eyes of all vertebrates) or those that differ widely (hair of mammals, feathers of birds, scales of reptiles). The term *homology* is usually contrasted with *analogy*, where attributes appear to be similar but have separate evolutionary origins (the wings of birds, bats, and pterosaurs are homologous as vertebrate forelimbs but analogous as wings; the wings of insects are analogous only with the wings of any vertebrate).

Evolution necessarily produces a complex nesting of adaptations (modified structures); these are homologies. In the reconstruction of evolutionary (phylogenetic) history taxa (groups of species) are defined and recognized on the basis of features held in common, thus possibly derived from a single ancestral condition as homologies. Such restricted sets of homologous features are *synapomorphies*. Homology is a more general term (hair is a synapomorphy linking all mammals; hair is homologous with the dermal structures—feathers and scales—of birds and reptiles, respectively).

See also ADAPTATION; CLADISTICS; EVOLUTION; PHYLOGENY. [N.E.]

Further Readings

Eldredge, N., and Cracraft, J. (1980) Phylogenetic Patterns and the Evolutionary Process. New York: Columbia University Press.

HOMOPLASY *see* HOMOLOGY

HOMUNCULUS *see* PITHECIINAE

HOOTON, EARNEST ALBERT (1887–1954)

American physical anthropologist. When Hooton left the University of Wisconsin in 1910 for Oxford as a Rhodes Scholar, he had every intention of continuing his studies in the classics. But at Oxford he came under the influence of the archaeologist R.R. Marett (1866–1943) and of the anatomist A. Keith (1866–1955) at the Royal College of Surgeons, London. Hooton returned to America in 1913 to begin a career in physical anthropology at Harvard University (1914–1954), where he was an influential teacher and responsible for supervising some two dozen doctoral students in physical anthropology, including the first generation of professionally trained physical anthropologists in the United States.

[F.S.]

HOPEFIELD *see* SALDANHA

HOPE FOUNTAIN

Early Paleolithic industry from southern and eastern Africa, characterized by crudely worked flakes struck by direct percussion and exhibiting a variety of edge shapes, together with choppers, and bearing a superficial resemblance in technology and absence of handaxes to the Tayacian and Clactonian industries of Europe. Often interpreted by L.S.B. Leakey as evidence along with the Acheulean industry for two separate lineages of earlier Pleistocene hominids, the Hope Fountain can also be interpreted as a functional or behavioral variant of a general Early Stone Age tradition that includes industries with and without handaxes. The industry occurs at Olduvai Bed III (Tanzania) and at Olorgesailie (Kenya) and is probably early middle Pleistocene in age, ca. 0.9–0.6 m.y.

See also ACHEULEAN; CHOPPER-CHOPPING TOOLS; CLACTONIAN; EARLY PALEOLITHIC; EARLY STONE AGE; HANDAXE; LEAKEY, LOUIS; OLDUVAI; OLORGESAILIE; STONE-TOOL MAKING; TAYACIAN. [A.S.B.]

HOPWOOD, ARTHUR TINDELL (1897–1969)

British paleontologist. On graduating from the University of Manchester in 1924, Hopwood joined the Department of Geology of the British Museum (Natural History), where he remained until his retirement in 1957. In addition to establishing himself as an authority in the field of fossil mollusks Hopwood also developed an interest in mammals, particularly fossil primates, and was a pioneer researcher with H. Reck and L.S.B. Leakey at Olduvai in the 1930s. He was responsible for describing *Proconsul africanus* from Koru, the first fossil hominoid found in Africa, during the mid-1920s. After his retirement from the museum Hopwood became professor at the Lycée Français, where he taught zoology.

See also KORU. [F.S.]

HORIZON   see   BIOCHRONOLOGY

HOSHANGABAD   see   NARMADA

HOWELLS, WILLIAM WHITE (b. 1908)

American physical anthropologist. On completing his doctoral dissertation (under the direction of E.A. Hooton) at Harvard, and following a short spell at the American Museum of Natural History, Howells received an academic appointment at the University of Wisconsin (1939–1954). In 1954 he returned to his alma mater, where he remained until his retirement in 1974. His interests are wide, ranging over the entire anthropological spectrum, as indicated by his highly popular book *The Heathens*, published in 1948. In physical anthropology he has researched problems ranging from craniometry to paleoanthropology—e.g. the use of factor analysis in anthropometry, the role of Neanderthals in the evolution of *Homo sapiens*, and the application of discriminant function equations to determine racial affiliation of human crania and range of variation within such types. He is also an authority on the anthropology of Oceania.

[F.S.]

HOWIESON'S POORT

Southern African Middle Stone Age industry, named for a site near Grahamstown, Cape Province (South Africa), and characterized by discoidal, Levallois, and blade technologies, backed and retouched blades, backed segments, and bifacial and unifacial leaf-shaped points. Originally grouped with transitional Second Intermediate industries, such as the "Magosian," the industry has been shown to underlie classic Middle Stone Age levels at several sites, such as Klasies River Mouth. The Howieson's Poort is also sometimes associated with a shift to smaller prey animals along with evidence of a possible increase in rainfall. Other names for related industries in southern Africa include epi-Pietersburg, Umguzan, Tshangula (earlier variant), and South African Magosian. Its probable age is greater than 40 k.y., possibly as old as 100 k.y.

See also KLASIES; MAGOSIAN; MIDDLE PALEOLITHIC; MIDDLE STONE AGE; SECOND INTERMEDIATE; STONE-TOOL MAKING. [A.S.B.]

HOXNE

Open-air archaeological site in Suffolk (England), dated to late middle Pleistocene (Hoxnian interglacial), ca. 400–300 k.y., by stratigraphic and faunal correlation, with middle Acheulean industry *in situ* in lake sediments. In 1797 Hoxne was the first site where Paleolithic stone tools were recognized as such, by John Frere.

See also ACHEULEAN; EARLY PALEOLITHIC; EUROPE. [A.S.B.]

HOXNIAN   see   GLACIATION; PLEISTOCENE

HRDLIČKA, ALEŠ (1869–1943)

American (b. Bohemia) physical anthropologist. On completing his medical training in New York City in the mid-1890s, Hrdlička became increasingly involved with anthropological expeditions from the American Museum of Natural History. This work ultimately led to his appointment in 1903 as curator of the newly created Division of Physical Anthropology in the National Museum of Natural History (Smithsonian Institution), where he remained until his retirement in 1942. Today he is perhaps best remembered for his classic paper *The Neanderthal Phase of Man*, which was delivered as the Huxley Memorial Lecture of 1927. Prior to this paper his researches had been directed largely to understanding events leading to the emergence, dispersion, and differentiation of modern *Homo sapiens* in the Old World. After 1927 Hrdlička collected evidence in Beringia to support the hypothesis of the Asian origin of the American aborigines. Hrdlička also founded the *American Journal of Physical Anthropology* (1918) and the American Association of Physical Anthropologists (1928).

[F.S.]

HUERFANIUS *see* OMOMYINAE

HUERZELERIS *see* ADAPIDAE; LORISOIDEA

HUMAN

According to one dictionary, "Of, pertaining to, or resembling man in his essential nature as distinguished from the nonhuman." But while the idea of "human," as opposed to "nonhuman," is relatively (although hardly totally) straightforward when only organisms now existing are under consideration, the concept loses all clarity when it is applied to the fossil record. Some paleoanthropologists apply the term "human" solely to anatomically modern *Homo sapiens*; others use it to describe all members of the genus *Homo*; yet others extend its use to *Homo* + *Australopithecus*. The term "human," and the concept it was intended to convey, originated at a time when our own kind was believed to have been specially created, and thus to be separated from the rest of the natural world by an unbridgeable gulf; there can thus be no hard and fast definition of it in terms of the world view resulting from modern scientific knowledge. Given this origin, however, there is perhaps merit in limiting the term to the description of extinct people (and their inferred behaviors) who can be fully understood in the terms of modern ethnology—and hence, effectively, to anatomically modern forms. In this sense one could characterize as "human evolution" the long sequence of events leading to the emergence of modern people, without implying that remote members or collaterals of our

own lineage are properly describable as themselves "human." On the other hand there may be utility in retaining a certain degree of ambiguity in the term, provided that this ambiguity is fully recognized.

[I.T.]

HUNTER-GATHERERS

A small number of people in the world today, probably fewer than 5,000, do not grow their food but obtain it by collecting plants, fishing, and hunting animals found in the area that they occupy. The !Kung of the Kalahari Desert (Botswana), the Pygmies of the Ituri Forest (Zaire), and the Inuit (Eskimos) of northwestern Canada and Alaska are some of the better-known groups. This way of obtaining food by harvesting what nature provides—the hunting-gathering subsistence strategy—is the oldest known to us, and has been practiced in one form or another for at least the last 2 m.y. In fact it was the only way of obtaining food until the beginning of plant and animal domestication ca. 10 k.y. ago. Hunter-gatherers have not done well in competition with food-producing societies in the last ten millennia. Their numbers have steadily dwindled, and they have been forced into occupying the least productive regions of the world. While modern-day groups are found in marginal environments, such as deserts, tropical forests, or arctic barrens, their predecessors in the Paleolithic occupied the most productive habitats of both the Old and New Worlds.

The hunter-gatherers of today can help us understand human adaptations in the past. It has to be underscored, however, that ethnographically known groups are in no way fossil relics of ancestral lifeways. Contemporary hunter-gatherers, like their historically known equivalents, are as much a product of their histories as are other people. Furthermore, they are not a particular type of people predisposed for this way of life. On the other hand, of all subsistence strategies practiced today, such as extensive and intensive agriculture, pastoralism, and industrialism, theirs is the closest to the way of life that prevailed throughout the Pleistocene. Hunting-gathering, then, is the simplest and the most stable way of making a living that is still effective for some people in their particular habitats. Understanding the organization of this way of life provides us with a route for approaching the study of the past.

Subsistence Practices

Since hunter-gatherers use nature itself as a storehouse, their survival most directly depends on what, when, and where their habitats produce. Needed resources, be they food, water, or other vital raw materials, are neither evenly nor predictably distributed across the landscape. Ripe plants and game animals that these resources attract are found in scattered patches. In most parts of the world seasonality is an important temporal variable that greatly affects the availability of food. In higher latitudes, for example, the shortness of the growing season restricts the availability of vegetal resources to the brief warm period. In lower latitudes seasonal differences in rainfall affect the availability and distribution of food resources as well. Because of these and many other environmental differences the mix of foods harvested by hunter-gatherers can take many forms, depending on the nature, availability, and predictability of the resources in their habitat. While fishing and harvesting of shellfish may play major roles in food-procurement strategies of groups living along seacoasts, groups occupying the continental interiors obtain the dominant portion of their calories from gathering wild plants and hunting animals. Overall it is the plant resources that play the dominant role in hunter-gatherer diets worldwide. Since in general many more plants are found in tropical than in temperate to polar regions, and because the productivity of terrestrial environments decreases with increasing latitude, plants play a much greater role in diets of lower-latitude hunter-gatherers.

The structure of the resource base of a region (the abundance, availability, distribution, and predictability of food resources) profoundly affects both the size of the coresident group as well as the degree of mobility among hunter-gatherers. While adaptations based on harvesting food from nature in general require a good deal of mobility and a small group size, these aspects of adaptation exhibit a good deal of variability. Ethnographic research suggests that hunter-gatherer food-management strategies can best be understood when viewed as a continuum. Simple foragers, occupying one end of this continuum, employ strategies that involve moving the entire coresidential group to the available resources. While the group is camped in one location, food search parties go out daily to harvest what is available within a reasonable distance from the camp. Such groups remain in an area until foods are depleted in the vicinity of their settlements and then move off to exploit other areas. Occasionally, when the productivity of local resources permits it, these small groups may be joined by other like-sized ones for brief periods of time. In the course of their annual rounds people employing this food-management strategy occupy a number of short-term residential sites within a region. The regional archaeological record of such groups includes widely scattered, like-sized, briefly occupied base camps together with a number of nearby special-purpose locations used in the course of resource procurement.

Logistically organized hunter-gatherers occupy the other end of the continuum. They use small special task groups to procure the food and bring it back to the group at large. In this strategy, most often encountered in regions with temporally or spatially clumped resources, such as herds of migratory animals or large seasonal runs of fish, food is harvested in quantities considerably beyond the daily requirements of the whole group. Much of this food is stored or cached for future consumption. Hunter-gatherers employing this strategy generally live in larger settlements that are moved less frequently than those of foragers. Among them special food-procurement groups exploit larger territories and travel to greater distances from residential locations. These travels usually involve overnight stays away from the main residential locales. The archaeological record of such groups include at least two types of residential camps: large ones occupied by the whole group and small overnight camps occupied by food-procurement task groups. In addition it may include special-purpose food-harvesting locations, as well as evidence for food storage either in the settlements themselves or as food caches scattered across the hunting territory.

Technology

All hunter-gatherers know much about the location of resources in their regions, as well as how and when best to exploit them, but their technology to do so is quite simple. They invest little energy in their tools and shelters yet are able to extract a sufficient return on their labor to support fairly leisurely lifeways. Since the hunter-gatherer adaptation necessitates residential mobility, the number of tools and possessions is kept to a minimum. Multipurpose tools and implements are favored over special purpose ones. Environmental conditions are far harsher in higher latitudes, and survival in these regions requires the use of more items of material culture (e.g. more clothing, more substantial shelters), so the elaboration of technology among hunter-gatherers shows a latitudinal gradation. Likewise, more mobile foragers possess simpler and fewer tools than do more permanently settled logistically organized groups. These facts have numerous archaeological implications. First, other things being equal, we can anticipate finding more diversified inventories and more complex features among groups who occupied higher latitudes in the past than among groups who lived closer to the equator. Second, we can also anticipate richer and more elaborate archaeological records for groups that were logistically organized in their procuring of food.

Artist's rendering of a base camp of foraging hunter-gatherers like the !Kung. (After Jelinek, 1986.)

Social Organization

Since the success of a hunting-gathering way of life depends on a close fit between the available resources and the number of people who can be supported, there are a few regularities in group size and in social organization of hunter-gatherers. In general coresident group size among present-day groups is small and consists of five to six nuclear families related to each other by ties of descent and marriage. Such a group of 25–30 people is called a *minimal band*. Membership in such bands is quite fluid, and families living in one band often move to join their relatives in another. When food supplies in the home territory of a band are particularly low, the minimal band itself may temporarily break up into even smaller coresidential units, such as a single family. Conversely, when food supplies are abundant, a few minimal bands may camp together in an area. This fluidity and flexibility in group size and membership is more in evidence among foraging hunter-gatherers. Logistically organized groups that rely on stored resources exhibit more permanent group affiliation and residence, as well as larger-sized coresidential units.

While food procurement in band societies is a family or household undertaking, a number of important limiting mechanisms bring about a relatively equal distribution of goods and resources among the families. Perhaps the most important of these are strong reciprocal obligations among people that ensure that foods and other goods are shared with others in the band. Obligations to share extend well beyond the household and entail all other members of the minimal band. This rule of reciprocity in effect makes the whole coresident group a minimal subsistence unit and ensures a relatively equal distribution of goods between households in band societies. The prestige obtained by sharing one's possessions, and the reality that frequent residential mobility itself imposes limits on acquisition of goods beyond one's immediate needs, result in both a paucity of material possessions and their equal distribution. Since residential mobility is a powerful factor limiting the amount of personal possessions owned by individuals, groups with reduced residential mobility exhibit a greater accumulation of possessions and invest more energy in their technologies and material culture.

The relatively egalitarian economic and social relationships characteristic of band societies have implications for the archaeological records of similar groups in the past. First, archaeological inventories left behind by prehistoric hunter-gatherers in general are sparse and simple. Furthermore, the nature and quantity of the inventories differs little among households. Thus remains of all past residential structures are similar in size and contain almost identical kinds and amounts of features and inventories. Similarly, we can anticipate few qualitative or quantitative differences in either features or inventories among like settlements on a regional level. All archaeological sites in a given region identified as the same type of occupations will be quite alike and differ from each other only by season of occupation.

Political Relationships

Political relationships among hunter-gatherers are egalitarian, and there are seldom any permanent leaders in band societies. While differences in status do exist, positions of higher status are generally earned and limited in scope, and there are as many positions of status as individuals within an appropriate age-sex category capable of filling them. These positions, however, are not institutionalized into offices. Individuals with high status neither have special say in matters outside their particular area of competence nor do they enjoy economic advantages. Decision making among hunter-gatherers is fairly evenly spread among the entire coresident group, and decisions are reached by consensus rather than by the say of an individual who specializes in making decisions.

Research into group decision making indicates a strong positive relationship among egalitarian sociopolitical relationships, residential mobility, and group size. Specifically it appears that specialization in decision making by part-time or full-time leaders is tied to large groups of individuals interacting on a permanent basis. While decisions by consensus, a hallmark of egalitarian sociopolitical relationships, are possible when groups are small and residential mobility a viable option for individuals or families who do not agree, this form of decision making breaks down as the size of the group exceeds some five to six households. The group then either disintegrates, as some families leave, or there is hierarchization of decision making. Thus, among logistically organized hunter-gatherers where groups exceed the minimal band size of foragers (some 25–30 individu-

als), larger basal social units, such as extended or multifamily units or various kin-based descent groups (e.g. clans), become minimal social and subsistence units. This horizontal hierarchization is often accompanied by vertical hierarchization, where a few permanent, or often part-time, leaders specialize in making significant decisions. Thus, although hunter-gatherer societies are broadly characterized as egalitarian in political relationships, in reality we find that these relationships grade from purely egalitarian to simple hierarchical ones.

Since differences in status are usually marked by specific items of material culture (e.g. pieces of personal adornment often made of hard-to-obtain or exotic materials), the existence of such differences in prehistory can often be inferred from the presence and distribution of such items at archaeological sites. Burials with differential grave goods offer one clue to past differences in status. A differential distribution of exotic jewelry or other nonutilitarian items among the households at a site offers another clue. In general we can anticipate finding more evidence for sociopolitical differentiation among past groups who were logistically organized in their food-procurement pursuits than among foragers who employed group mobility in their subsistence strategies.

Origins of Hunter-Gatherer Adaptations

While we know that hominids harvested food from nature from the very beginning of their existence ca. 5 m.y. ago, the origins of hunter-gatherer adaptations as we know them from ethnography are more difficult to pinpoint in time. Both the nature and wealth of archaeological data from Late Paleolithic sites, dating in some parts of the Old World to before 80 k.y., indicate hunter-gatherer adaptations like those known from the ethnographic record, but how similar Neanderthal adaptations were to these lifeways is at present a moot question. Some scholars argue that the basic elements of foraging hunter-gatherer lifeways (i.e. division of labor between the sexes, food sharing, and seasonal mobility) can be traced all the way back to *Australopithecus*. Others insist that even inventories left behind by the Neanderthals differ significantly from those generated by present-day band societies. Although these differences of opinion cannot be securely resolved at present, we can state with some degree of certainty that hunter-gatherer adaptations similar to those we know today have been around for at least the last 50 k.y. Furthermore, it is quite likely that ethnographically known lifeways represent a mosaic of behavioral complexes that did not evolve in unison and were in part responses to historic factors. This suggests that as we move back in time we should anticipate finding a more patchy and incomplete record of hominid behavior that will be less analogous to present-day cases. Some parts of this record, especially those from more recent times (e.g. evidence for food sharing among the Neanderthals), will be easier to comprehend. Other parts, however, will be quite unlike what we know, and we shall have a difficult time interpreting them if we only use present-day hunter-gatherer behavior as our baseline for reconstructing the past.

See also AGGREGATION-DISPERSAL; ECONOMY, PREHISTORIC; SITE TYPES. [O.S.]

Further Readings

Binford, L.R. (1980) Willow smoke and dog's tails: hunter-gatherer settlement systems and archaeological site formation. Am. Antiquity 45:4–20.

Kelly, R.L. (1983) Hunter-gatherer mobility strategies. J. Anthropol. Res. 39:277–306.

Lee, R.B., and DeVore, I., eds. (1986) Man the Hunter. Chicago: Aldine-Atherton.

Pfeiffer, J.E. (1985) The Emergence of Humankind, 4th ed. New York: Harper and Row.

Testart, A. (1982) The significance of food storage among hunter-gatherers: residence patterns, population densities, and social inequalities. Curr. Anthropol. 23:523–537.

Winterhalder, B., and Smith, E.A., eds. (1981) Hunter-Gatherer Foraging Strategies. Chicago: University of Chicago Press.

Woodburn, J. (1980) Hunters and gatherers today and reconstruction of the past. In E. Gellner (ed.): Soviet and Western Anthropology. New York: Columbia University Press, pp. 95–118.

HUNTING *see* DIET; PALEOLITHIC LIFEWAYS

HUXLEY, THOMAS HENRY (1825–1895)

British anatomist and physical anthropologist. Huxley was one of the first scientists to be converted to Darwin's views on evolution and became the foremost advocate of the Darwinian theory and its underlying materialist and mechanistic principles. Huxley's most influential and enduring book, *Evidences as to Man's Place in Nature*, published in 1863, contains the essential elements of his structural-functional argument for accepting Darwin's thesis of natural selection and the demonstration that, zoologically, the genus *Homo* is a primate. Huxley held that the presumed chasm between human beings and the apes had been greatly exaggerated by such anatomists as Richard Owen (1771–1858), with whom Huxley had clashed earlier over this very issue. During the course of his influential career Huxley held a number of prestigious positions ranging from Hunterian Professor of the Royal College of Surgeons, London (1863–1869), to president of the Royal Society (1883–1885).

[F.S.]

HYLOBATES *see* APE; HYLOBATIDAE

HYLOBATIDAE

The gibbons, or lesser apes, are the smallest and in many respects the most primitive of the living apes. Both morphological and biochemical studies indicate that the gibbons are the earliest branch of apes to evolve and are closest to the divergence of monkeys and apes. There is a single genus of living gibbons (*Hylobates*), with ten species ranging in size from ca. 5 kg. to over 10 kg. All are from the rain forests of Southeast Asia, where they are very abundant. In both numbers of species and numbers of individuals they are the most successful of the living apes.

Like all catarrhines gibbons have a dental formula of 2.1.2.3., and their molar teeth are simple with broad basins and small rounded cusps. There is no sexual dimorphism in the teeth of gibbons; both sexes have long, daggerlike canines. Gibbon skulls have short snouts, large orbits, and rounded, globular braincases that generally lack either sagittal or nuchal crests. The gibbon's most distinctive skeletal features are the long slender limbs. They have relatively long hindlimbs, extremely long forelimbs, and long curved fingers and toes. Like all apes they have no tail. They are unusual among apes and resemble Old World monkeys in having ischial callosities, or sitting pads.

In external appearance gibbons are characterized by dense fur and coat colors ranging from black through gold and brown to silvery grey. While there is no size difference between male and female gibbons, in many species there are marked differences in pelage coloration.

All gibbons are totally arboreal. They are the most suspensory of all living primates and move primarily by brachiation and climbing, but they also run bipedally along branches. Gibbons are all primarily frugivorous, but various species supplement their diet to a greater or lesser degree with foliage or invertebrates. All gibbons (with one possible exception) live in monogamous social groups consisting of a single male, a single female, and their offspring. They advertise their territories with loud vocal duets and actively defend them from other families with fights and chases. In contrast with other apes gibbons do not build nests for sleeping. Rather, when they sleep, they either sit hunched over on branches or recline at the end of tree limbs among the small twigs.

Authorities disagree over the exact number of gibbon species found on the islands of Southeast Asia; however, most believe that there are three main groups of lesser apes, often placed in separate subgenera.

The siamang (*H. syndactylus*) from Malaysia and

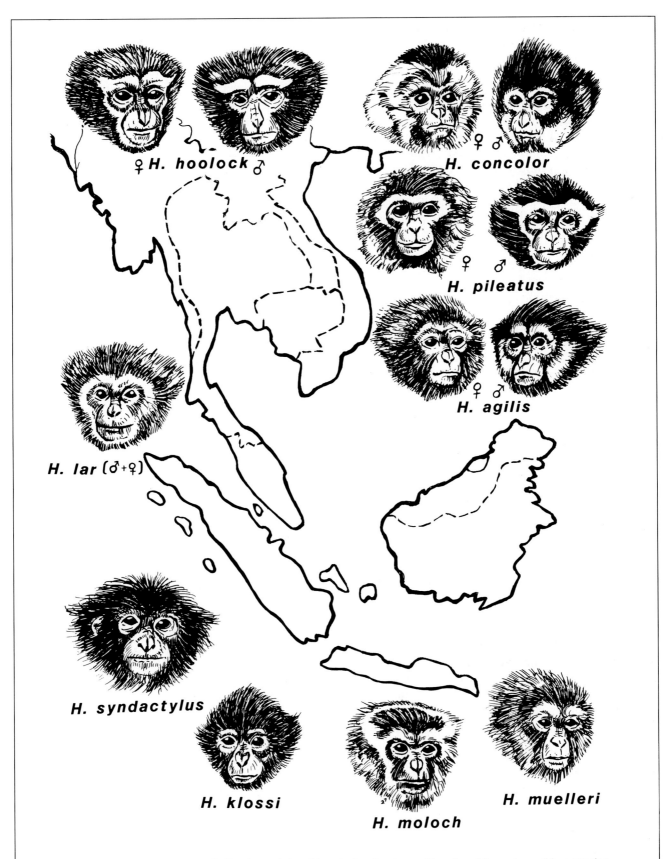

Map of the area of gibbon distribution in Southeast Asia, with portraits of males and females of the various gibbon species.

Sumatra is the largest gibbon. It is a solid-black species with a large throat pouch and webbing between the third and fourth digits of its hands and feet. Siamangs are the most folivorous of the gibbons. Their social behavior is unusual in that the father transports the offspring and cares for it during the second year after birth.

The crested gibbon (*H. concolor*) from China and Indochina is slightly smaller than the siamang. Males and females are strikingly different in pelage coloration. The ecology of this species is poorly known, but recent reports from China indicate that this gibbon may live in larger social groups than other species.

The remaining species of gibbons are more closely related to one another than to the siamang or the crested gibbon. The hoolock gibbon (*H. hoolock*) is a large species from Burma, Bangladesh, and eastern India. Kloss's gibbon (*H. klossi*) is a gracile species from the Mentawai Islands off the western coast of Sumatra. Kloss's gibbon has an unusual diet of fruits and a large percentage of invertebrates, with no foliage.

The white-handed gibbon (*H. lar*) from Thailand, Malaysia, and Sumatra is the best-known species. Its diet consists predominantly of fruits, and it seems to specialize on fruit species that are found in small patches widely dispersed throughout the forest. As a result white-handed gibbons travel over long distances each day in search of food. The other lesser apes, the agile gibbon (*H. agilis*), the pileated gibbon (*H. pileatus*), the silvery gibbon (*H. moloch*), and Mueller's gibbon (*H. muelleri*) are similar to white-handed gibbons, and some authorities consider them geographical variants of the same species.

Paleontologists have identified many small fossil apes from the Miocene (23-6 m.y. ago) as fossil gibbons. These include *Pliopithecus* from Europe, *Dendropithecus* and *Micropithecus* from Africa, and *Dionysopithecus* and *Laccopithecus* from China. All of these have dental and cranial similarities to living gibbons. None, however, shows the unique skeletal adaptations that characterize the living hylobatids, and it is questionable whether any is directly ancestral to modern gibbons. It seems equally likely that small frugivorous apes have evolved many times during the past and that the living hylobatids are the most recent radiation of small apes and the only one that has survived to the present day. Their species diversity seems to be the result of the fluctuating land connections in the islands of Southeast Asia that resulted from sea-level changes during the Pleistocene.

See also APE; HOMINOIDEA; PLIOPITHECIDAE; PLIOPITHECOIDEA. [J.G.F., F.J.W.]

Further Readings

Chivers, D.J. (1980) Malayan Forest Primates. New York: Plenum.

Preuschoft, H., Chivers, D., Brockelman, W., and Creel, N. (1985) The Lesser Apes: Evolutionary and Behavioral Biology. Edinburgh: Edinburgh University Press.

HYPORDER

Category in the classificatory hierarchy that falls between the infraorder and the superfamily. This rank has been recently devised in light of an awareness that a larger number of categories than traditionally recognized is necessary to accommodate the phylogenetic diversity of mammalian groups. For example, in Primates the hyporders Paracatarrhini and Eucatarrhini have been used within the infraorder Catarrhini to reflect the phylogenetic distinctness of the Oligocene parapithecoids (the paracatarrhines) from the cercopithecoids and hominoids, which together form a monophyletic group, Eucatarrhini.

See also CLASSIFICATION. [I.T.]

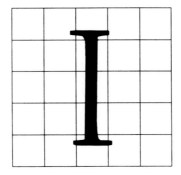

IBERO-MAURUSIAN

North African Epipaleolithic industry, also called Oranian, superimposed above Aterian at several sites from Atlantic Morocco to Cyrenaica, from ca. 20,000 to 10,000 B.P., in association with cooler climates of the Mediterranean coast and desiccation of the Sahara. The Ibero-Maurusian is characterized by microblade core technology, backed bladelets, and grinding and polishing stones. The type site of el Mouillah, near Lala Marnia in the Oran district of Algeria also contained ostrich-eggshell fragments and pierced pebbles and shells. Human remains of mechtoid type are associated with several sites in Morocco and Algeria, such as Taforalt. The Ibero-Maurusian is distinguished from the partly contemporaneous eastern Oranian industry of Haua Fteah by the relative scarcity or absence of burins, geometric microliths, or large backed blades. The "Ibero" refers to a supposed typological connection with Epipaleolithic industries in Spain.

See also EPIPALEOLITHIC; HAUA FTEAH; LATER STONE AGE; MESOLITHIC; STONE-TOOL MAKING. [A.S.B.]

ICE AGES *see* GLACIATION; PLEISTOCENE

ICE-FREE AREAS *see* GLACIATION; PLEISTOCENE

IGNACIUS *see* PAROMOMYIDAE

ILERET *see* EAST TURKANA

ILLINOISAN *see* GLACIATION; PLEISTOCENE

IMMUNOLOGICAL DISTANCE

The surface of a cell contains specific marker molecules (*antigens*) that identify the cell. Vertebrates, and mammals to an extreme degree, have evolved an immune system as a defense mechanism against infection by foreign cells. This sensitive system is stimulated by foreign antigens to produce highly specific molecules (*antibodies*), whose function is to destroy the foreign cell. In addition to cell-surface antigens any substance that can elicit the production of antibodies is considered an antigen. Examples of the function of the immune system are the familiar blood-transfusion incompatibilities in which, for example, blood with type A antigens is rejected by a patient with type O blood. An organism that has been exposed to a specific antigen can then produce copious specific antibodies on subsequent exposure and is said to be *immunized* against the antigen; this is the basis for vaccinations.

The immune system possesses a property that makes it useful in primate systematics: *cross-reactivity*. A rabbit immunized against a specific human antigen (e.g. the protein albumin) will react also to the homologous antigen from a rhesus macaque. But its antibody production will not be as strong, because the antigen is not quite identical. Since the antigenic difference between the human and rhesus macaque is genetic in its basis, the amount of difference detectable in the immunological reaction is a rough estimate of a genetic "distance" between the two. Various methods, notably agar-gel diffusion and microcomplement fixation, were developed and refined in the 1960s for measuring such "immunological distances" among the primates.

See also MOLECULAR ANTHROPOLOGY; MOLECULAR CLOCK. [J.M.]

Further Readings

Goodman, M. (1963) Serological analysis of the systematics of recent hominoids. Hum. Biol. 35:377-436.

Sarich, V., and Wilson, A. (1967) Immunological time scale for hominid evolution. Science 158:1200-1202.

INCERTAE SEDIS

Of uncertain taxonomic position. Placed after the name of a taxon at any level of the classificatory hierarchy to indicate that the affinities of that taxon are not precisely determinable. The rank at which a taxon is placed as incertae sedis indicates the level at which the uncertainty exists. Thus a large family well classified within itself, but of uncertain placement within an order, would be classified within that order, incertae sedis, and not allocated to any intermediate rank.

See also CLASSIFICATION; SYSTEMATICS; TAXONOMY. [I.T.]

INCEST see PRIMATE SOCIETIES; SOCIOBIOLOGY

INCLUSIVE FITNESS see SOCIOBIOLOGY

INDIA

Asian subcontinent covering ca. 3.4 million sq. km. For a large area in the Old World, India is relatively deficient in material evidence of human evolution. Miocene hominoids have been collected from sites in the north, where the Siwalik Group of rocks forms part of the Himalayan foothills. The earliest indications of hominid habitation in the region is in the form of Early Paleolithic stone tools, but so far only one relevant hominid fossil has been found. A cranium from the site of Hathnora in the central Narmada Valley is claimed to have features more in common with late Homo erectus than with archaic Homo sapiens and has been named Homo erectus narmadensis.

See also ACHEULEAN; HOMO ERECTUS; NARMADA; SIWALIKS. [A.H.]

INDIRECT PERCUSSION see STONE-TOOL MAKING

INDOADAPIS see SIVALADAPIDAE

INDONESIA

Nation comprising most of the longest island archipelago in the world, stretching along the equator for more than 5,800 km. between Sumatra and New Guinea, and encompassing over 14,000 islands. Many of the Indonesian islands are volcanically active and rise from the now-submerged Sunda Shelf. This shelf was exposed several times during the Pleistocene by glacial-eustatic lowering of world sea level. These periods of exposure provided periodic opportunities for the migration of hominids and other animals to and from Java.

In spite of intensive research efforts throughout Indonesia only Java has yielded fossils of early hominids. The principal collections have come from central and eastern Java, at Sangiran, Trinil, and Ngandong (Solo). Paleoanthropologists generally agree that most of the early specimens are attributable to Homo erectus (Trinil and Sangiran hominids), an archaic form of Homo sapiens or a late form of Homo erectus (Ngandong hominids), and Homo sapiens sapiens (Wadjak hominids).

Because Java is an island characterized by a spine of active volcanoes there have been ample opportunities to date radiometrically the earliest hominids from Java, but there is still little consensus about when hominids first reached the island. The main difficulty is that most of the Javanese hominids have not been recovered in situ. Thus it has been extremely difficult to place the hominids within a reliable chronological framework. On the basis of the most recent excavations and radiometric studies many scientists feel that the earliest colonizers of the island did not arrive before about 1.3 m.y. ago.

See also ASIA (EASTERN); DJETIS; DUBOIS, EUGENE; HOMO ERECTUS; KOENIGSWALD, G.H.R. VON; MEGANTHROPUS; NGANDONG; SANGIRAN DOME; TRINIL. [G.G.P.]

Further Readings

Bemmelen, R.W. van (1949) The Geology of Indonesia, Vol. 1A: General Geology of Indonesia and Adjacent Archipelagos. The Hague: Government Printing Office.

Pope, G.G. (1985) Taxonomy, dating, and paleoenvironment: the paleoecology of the early Far Eastern hominids. Mod. Quat. Res. Southeast Asia 9:65-81.

INDRALORIS see LORISIDAE; LORISOIDEA; SIVALADAPIDAE

INDRI see INDRIIDAE

INDRIIDAE

Family of Lemuriformes that includes the extant genera Indri, Avahi, and Propithecus. Traditionally it has

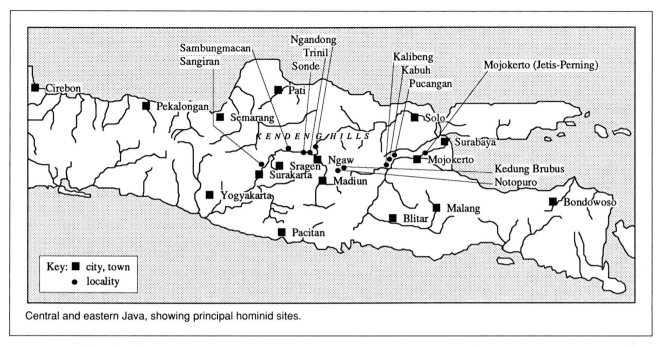

Central and eastern Java, showing principal hominid sites.

been considered also to contain the extinct *Mesopropithecus*, but reappraisal may suggest that this is a plesiomorph sister of the palaeopropithecids, although it is discussed here. All indriids occur exclusively on the island of Madagascar; the living forms are all vertical clingers and leapers, with greatly elongated hindlimbs.

At a weight of ca. 6 kg. *Indri*, the babakoto, is the largest of the surviving lemurs and is particularly unusual in possessing only a vestigial tail. Although pelage coloration is quite variable, only one species, *Indri indri*, is recognized; this lives in the northern half of the eastern humid forest belt of Madagascar. Diurnal, the babakoto is pair-bonding and subsists on a diet largely of leaves and fruit. Two recorded group home ranges were ca. 18 hectares; there is little overlap between the ranges of different groups, which appear to space themselves by means of their loud, haunting vocalizations.

Avahi laniger, at ca. 1 kg. the smallest indriid, is found throughout the eastern rain-forest strip and also in the northwest of Madagascar. Little is known of the behavior and ecology of this nocturnal and pair-bonding form, but separate eastern and western subspecies are generally reckoned to exist.

The most ubiquitous of the indriids is the sifaka, *Propithecus*. Two species are recognized: *Propithecus diadema*, of the eastern rain forest, and the slightly smaller (ca. 4 kg.) *P. verreauxi* from the drier forests of the west and south of Madagascar. Each species contains local color variants recognized as separate subspecies. Some subspecies, at least, of *P. diadema* are probably pair-bonding, whereas *P. verreauxi* is generally seen in groups of from three to ten individ-

uals, most commonly five. Most such groups contain more than one adult male, but it may be outsiders who mate with the resident females during the extremely brief breeding season. Home ranges are variable in size but appear often to be ca. 8 hectares. The diet may be predominantly of leaves but is highly variable seasonally, fruit predominating at certain times of the year.

From subrecent marsh and cave sites in the center, south, and southwest of Madagascar are known the remains of another indriid, *Mesopropithecus*. In cranial and dental morphology this form is very similar to *Propithecus*, especially in the case of the gracile species *Mesopropithecus globiceps* from localities in the south and southwest of the island. *Mesopropithecus pithecoides*, known from central Madagascar, is very robustly built, with pronounced sagittal and nuchal cresting on the cranium. Postcranial fragments that have been assigned to *Mesopropithecus* are, on the other hand, quite distinct from the corresponding bones in *Propithecus* and perhaps suggestive of a more quadrupedal habit. Associations are poor, however, and the question of which subfossil postcranials are indeed attributable to *Mesopropithecus* needs reassessment.

See also INDRIOIDEA; LEMURIFORMES. [I.T.]

Further Readings

Tattersall, I. (1982) The Primates of Madagascar. New York: Columbia University Press.

INDRIOIDEA

Superfamily of Lemuriformes that includes the families Indriidae, Daubentoniidae, Megaladapidae, Ar-

Two indriids: *Indri indri*, in midleap (left); and *Propithecus verreauxi verreauxi* (right).

chaeolemuridae, and Palaeopropithecidae. The last two of these consist of large-bodied genera (*Archaeolemur* and *Hadropithecus*, and *Palaeopropithecus* and *Archaeoindris*, respectively) that are recently extinct and known only as subfossils but that can be considered as part of the modern Malagasy primate fauna. Megaladapidae consists of the extant "sportive" lemur, *Lepilemur*, and of the large-bodied subfossil form *Megaladapis*. Daubentoniidae contains only the highly specialized, and surviving, aye-aye, *Daubentonia*. Of the three living indriids two, *Indri* and *Propithecus*, are diurnal; the third, *Avahi*, is nocturnal. An extinct genus, *Mesopropithecus*, has traditionally been considered closely related to *Propithecus* but may in fact prove to be classifiable as a palaeopropithecid.

All indrioids are unique to the island of Madagascar, and the superfamily is by far the most diverse component of Lemuriformes. Until recently the megaladapids were considered more closely related to the lemuroids than to the indrioids; characters of the dentition, however, suggest that phylogeny dictates the inclusion of Megaladapidae in Indrioidea.

See also ARCHAEOLEMURIDAE; DAUBENTONIIDAE; INDRIIDAE; LEMURIFORMES; MEGALADAPIDAE; PALAEOPROPITHECIDAE. [I.T.]

Further Readings

Schwartz, J.H., and Tattersall, I. (1985) Evolutionary relationships of living lemurs and lorises (Mammalia, Primates), and their potential affinities with European Eocene Adapidae. Anthropol. Pap. Am. Mus. Nat. Hist. 60:1–100.

Tattersall, I. (1982) The Primates of Madagascar. New York: Columbia University Press.

INFRAORDER

Category in the classificatory hierarchy lying below the suborder and above the hyporder. Until the addition of the rank of hyporder the infraorder was the rank intermediate between the superfamily and the suborder.

See also CLASSIFICATION. [I.T.]

INSECTIVORY *see* DIET

IRON AGE

Final step in the three-stage sequence of cultural development introduced in European archaeology during the early nineteenth century by Christian Thomsen and Jens Worsae. These Danish archaeologists arranged European prehistory into three successive developmental levels: Stone Age, Bronze Age, and Iron Age. These levels were seen as a unilineal developmental sequence from simple to complex cultures, as defined by the material employed to produce cutting tools, but the terms generally imply much more than technology.

The Iron Age is taken to mean a period of time roughly between 3000 and 2000 B.P., when in various parts of the world the complicated technology of iron production and working was developed, highly centralized states emerged, warfare and imperial expansion were commonplace, and craft specialization and market economies developed. These cultural developments are not necessarily linked, and the use of the term in the context of unilineal schemes of cultural evolution is unwarranted. "Iron Age" remains as a term of reference for those parts of the world in which iron working was developed and is best used to identify the early periods of development and use of the metal.

See also BRONZE AGE; COMPLEX SOCIETIES; EUROPE. [B.B.]

Further Readings

Wells, P. (1984) Farms, Villages, and Cities: Commerce and Urban Origins in Late Prehistoric Europe. Ithaca, N.Y.: Cornell University Press.

ISAAC, GLYNN LLYWELYN (1937–1985)

South African archaeologist. Isaac received his doctorate from Cambridge University in 1961 as a protégé of L.S.B. Leakey. He quickly established himself as a leader in African archaeology at the University of California, Berkeley, and in 1983 went to Harvard University. While his name is linked with the careful excavation of a number of East African archaeological sites, primarily Olorgesailie, Naivasha, and Peninj, he will probably be best remembered for his association with the East Turkana Research Project, of which he was co-leader with R. Leakey from 1970 until his untimely death.

[F.S.]

ISCHIAL CALLOSITIES

Sitting pads found in all Old World monkeys and gibbons. They are cushions of fatty-fibrous tissue covered with a specialized skin, attached to an expanded ischial tuberosity. They enable monkeys and small apes to sit on branches during feeding and sleeping without either sliding off the branch or damaging other structures in the perineum. Whether they evolved independently in cercopithecids and

hylobatids or were a feature of early eucatarrhines later lost in Homindae is an intriguing problem in catarrhine systemetics.

See also CATARRHINI; MONKEY. [J.G.F.]

ISERNIA see EUROPE

ISHANGO

Late Pleistocene open-air stratified site in eastern Zaire at the exit of the Semliki River from Lake ex-Amin (ex-Edward, Rutanzige). Excavated by de Heinzelin in the 1950s, the site shows a sequence of three strata of beach deposits with successive types double-, single-barbed) of bone harpoons, small crude quartz tools, and abundant fish and mammal remains. These strata are capped by levels of aceramic microlithic and ceramic Iron Age materials, also associated with fishing debris, but not directly with beach deposits. Scattered human remains from the middle stage of the culture, along with bone harpoons (Ishangian), have been attributed to robust but entirely modern and long-limbed people of negroid type. Radiocarbon and amino-acid racemization determinations have suggested an age of ca. 18,000 B.P. for the bone-harpoon horizons and ca. 7000 B.P. for the microlithic horizon.

See also AFRICA; ECONOMY, PREHISTORIC; LATE PALEOLITHIC; LATER STONE AGE; MESOLITHIC; PALEOLITHIC LIFEWAYS. [A.S.B.]

ISTALLÖSKÖ

Stratified Upper Paleolithic cave site in northeastern Hungary, some 15 km. south of the Szeleta Cave. The two cultural layers found at the bottom of the deposit held faunal remains of large-sized gregarious herbivores as well as numerous carnivores. Stone- and bone-tool assemblages containing diagnostic Mladeč-type bone points have been assigned to the eastern variant of the Aurignacian. A fragment of an unerrupted second molar found at Istallösko belonged to an early anatomically modern Homo sapiens. Radiocarbon dating of bone found in the lower cultural layer gave dates between 44,000 and 40,000 B.P. A number of scholars have questioned the association of the dated bone with other cultural remains and suggest that the much younger dates of ca. 30,000 B.P. for the upper and 31,500 B.P. for the lower layers are probably more correct.

See also AURIGNACIAN; EUROPE; LATE PALEOLITHIC; UPPER PALEOLITHIC. [O.S.]

INTERGLACIAL *see* GLACIATION; PLEISTOCENE

INTERSTADIAL *see* GLACIATION; PLEISTOCENE

IRVINGTONIAN *see* TIME SCALE

ISOTOPE *see* GEOCHRONOMETRY; TIME SCALE

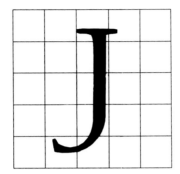

JABRUD (YABROUD)

Archaeological site complex in the Anti-Lebanon Mountains of Syria near Nebek, consisting of four rock shelters, ranging in age from late middle Pleistocene (Shelter IV) with a "Tayacian" industry to Neolithic (Shelter III). A long sequence in Shelter I contains a pre-Aurignacian blade industry in the midst of Early and Middle Paleolithic levels, Shelter II materials were grouped as Aurignacian or Upper Paleolithic, while Shelter III preserves traces of the transition from Late Paleolithic to Mesolithic.

See also ANTELIAN; EARLY PALEOLITHIC; JABRUDIAN; LATE PALEOLITHIC; MESOLITHIC; MIDDLE PALEOLITHIC; PRE-AURIGNACIAN; TAYACIAN. [A.S.B.]

JABRUDIAN

Early Paleolithic industry (probable age, end of last interglacial and beginning of Weichselian, ca. 100-80 k.y.). The Jabrudian, first defined by Rust at Jabrud Shelter I in Syria, is characterized by large numbers of side-scrapers, especially asymmetrical forms, and and by few or no handaxes. The term has also been applied, probably erroneously, at Tabūn (Israel), where a Tayacian-like industry, also called Tabunian, is associated with Levallois technology and occurs both above and below the pre-Aurignacian industry.

See also EARLY PALEOLITHIC; LEVALLOIS; PRE-AURIGNACIAN; STONE-TOOL MAKING; TABŪN; TABUNIAN; TAYACIAN. [A.S.B.]

JARAMILLO   *see*   PALEOMAGNETISM

JARMO

Early Neolithic village site 11 km. east of Chemchemal in Iraqi Kurdistan, occupied for several centuries during the period ca. 9000-8000 B.P. Innovative multidisciplinary fieldwork at this 1.3-hectare site, including three seasons of excavations (1948-1954) directed by R.J. Braidwood, produced abundant artifactual, botanical, and osteological evidence of the transition from a hunting-gathering adaptation to food production, the development of ceramic technology, early village architecture, and long-distance trade in obsidian. Jarmo provided samples for radiocarbon dating during the developmental stages of this important archaeological tool; dates for Jarmo and Jericho were debated by their excavators.

See also DOMESTICATION; JERICHO; NEAR EAST; NEOLITHIC. [C.K.]

JAVA   *see*   INDONESIA

JAVANTHROPUS   *see*   HOMO ERECTUS

JEBEL IRHOUD

Moroccan cave that has produced at least three hominid fossils, two adult skulls (1 and 2) and a child's mandible (3). All three probably date from between 80 and 100 k.y. ago and show interesting combinations of archaic and modern characters. Irhoud 1 has an archaic vault shape, while its face is broad and flat with modern-looking cheek bones. Irhoud 2 has a modern frontal bone, while the parietal and occipital regions remain archaic in form. The child's mandible has large teeth but shows some chin development. Some workers consider the fossils to represent the local precursors of early modern hominids from such sites as Dar-es-Soltane and Afalou.

See also ARCHAIC HOMO SAPIENS. [C.B.S.]

JERICHO

Multilevel archaeological site at Tell es-Sultan, situated in Israel between Jerusalem and the Jordan River. It was excavated for six seasons (1930–1936) by J. Garstang and for seven seasons (1952–1958) by K. Kenyon, who identified it with the biblical town, although not all researchers agree. The deposits are, in places, ca. 20 m. thick and represent occupations ranging from aceramic ("Pre-Pottery") Neolithic (PPN) through Chalcolithic, Bronze Age, and Iron Age periods. The PPNA and PPNB occupations (ca. 10,300–8000 B.P.) are now estimated to have been ca. 2.4 hectares in extent. These strata yielded complex structural remains (including retaining walls and a tower), evidence for long-distance trade in obsidian

and other exotic raw materials, human skulls with faces of modeled plaster, and large plaster human figures.

See also JARMO; NEAR EAST; NEOLITHIC. [C.K.]

JERMANOVICIAN see SZELETIAN; UPPER PALEOLITHIC

JETIS see DJETIS

JEWELRY

Ostrich-eggshell beads from an early Later Stone Age stratum in Border Cave (South Africa), dating between 45,000 and 33,000 B.P., are the earliest recognized examples of jewelry in the archaeological record. Items of personal adornment, including diadems, beads, pins, pendants, bracelets, rings, and pectorals made of stone, bone, animal teeth, ivory, shell, and amber, are found in increasing numbers at

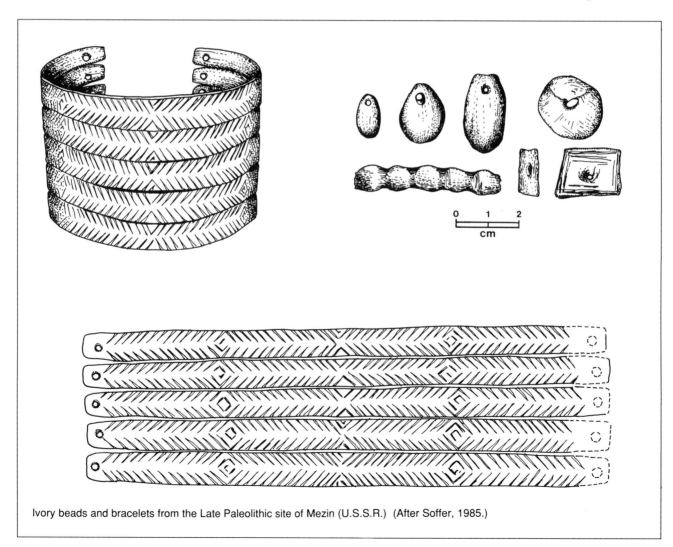

Ivory beads and bracelets from the Late Paleolithic site of Mezin (U.S.S.R.) (After Soffer, 1985.)

Late Paleolithic sites in Eurasia after 40,000 B.P. Their relative sparseness at sites in southern latitudes suggests a direct association of jewelry with fur or hide clothing. The presence of jewelry in both burial and living contexts after 40,000 B.P. is interpreted as indicating a newly emergent personal and social awareness. While items of jewelry found at the early Late Paleolithic sites are predominantly made of locally available materials, those found at sites dating after the glacial maximum (20,000–18,000 B.P.) show greater percentages made of such exotic materials as fossil marine shells and amber.

See also Exotics; Late Paleolithic. [O.S.]

Further Readings

Wymer, J. (1982) The Palaeolithic Age. New York: St. Martin's.

JIAN SHI (GAO PING)

Hubei Province (China) cave deposit, dated to later early or early middle Pleistocene (ca. 1 m.y.) by faunal correlation. This karst cave in Hubei Province has yielded the first known association of hominids and *Gigantopithecus*. Three hominid molars recovered from the site were first attributed to *Australopithecus* cf. *africanus*, but most Chinese scientists now agree that two of them (belonging to one individual) are clearly aberrant and that all are best assigned to a species of *Homo*.

See also Asia (Eastern); China. [G.G.P.]

JINNIU SHAN (YINGKOU)

Middle Pleistocene hominid and Paleolithic locality in Yingkou County, Liaoning Province (China), dated to late middle Pleistocene, ca. 0.2 m.y. by faunal correlation and hominid morphology.

Jinniu Shan (Golden Ox Mountain) is the site of a recent find of an unusually complete hominid specimen, which includes a cranium (capacity 1,390 ml.) and substantial postcranial material. Jinniu Shan actually encompasses a number of fissure-infilling localities that have yielded artifacts and the fossils of at least 76 mammalian species. Evidence of fire in the form of burned animal bones and a hearth have also been reported. A uranium-series date of 0.31 m.y. has been attributed to the fissure locality that yielded the hominid. Although the hominid has been referred informally to *Homo erectus*, judging from preliminary photographs it may in fact show affinities with more "progressive" members of the genus.

See also Archaic Homo sapiens; Asia (Eastern); Homo erectus; Zhoukoudian. [G.G.P.]

Further Readings

Lu, Z. (1987) Cracking the evolutionary puzzle—Jinniushan Man. China Pictorial 1987(4), 34-35.

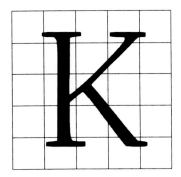

K-AR DATING *see* GEOCHRONOMETRY

KBS

Acronym for an artifact site (FxJj1) in the Koobi Fora region (Kenya), named for its discoverer, K. Behrensmeyer. The acronym was subsequently applied to a volcanic-ash layer exposed at the site, the KBS Tuff, which became well known because stone tools were found in direct association. This tuff was initially dated at ca. 2.6 m.y., and thus it appeared that the artifacts were the earliest well-documented stone tools in the world. Later work, however, established that the age of the KBS Tuff is 1.88 ± 0.02 m.y. and that the stone tools are about the same age as those in Bed I, Olduvai Gorge.

The KBS Tuff is a widespread volcanic-ash layer 0.1–1 m. thick exposed over much of the northern half of the Koobi Fora region. In many localities it consists of both light-grey and dark-brown glass shards, giving it a distinctive salt-and-pepper appearance and making it a useful marker bed in the field. It commonly contains large pumice clasts chemically identical to the composition of the light and dark glass shards (which are also compositionally identical). These clasts are the source of the alkali feldspars used for age determination. The KBS Tuff has been correlated with Tuff H2 of the Shungura Formation in Ethiopia on the basis of its chemical composition and age, and it has also been identified at Kaitio west of Lake Turkana. The source of the tuff is not known, but it is believed to lie in the Ethiopian highlands.

See also EAST TURKANA. [F.H.B.]

Further Readings

Cerling, T.E., and Brown, F.H. (1982) Tuffaceous marker horizons in the Koobi Fora region and the Lower Omo Valley. Nature 299:216–221.

KABUH *see* SANGIRAN DOME

KABWE

Site in Zambia, also known as Broken Hill, that produced fossil hominid specimens in the period 1921–1925. Discovered during mining operations, they were derived from a cave that was subsequently destroyed. The main discovery was the well-preserved cranium of an adult, which became the holotype of *Homo rhodesiensis* Woodward 1921 and *Cyphanthropus rhodesiensis* Pycraft 1928 and which is often now assigned to *Homo sapiens rhodesiensis*. It shows evidence of disease, such as dental caries and abscessing, and perhaps also a tumor in the temporal bone. The cranium shows a mosaic of characteristics, with a moderately large cranial capacity of ca. 1,280 ml.; a moderately thick, long, and flattened vault; and a massive and pneumatized supraorbital torus. There is a centrally strong occipital torus like those of *Homo erectus* skulls, but the cranium is high with parallel-sided walls. The remainder of the Broken Hill hominid material cannot be directly related to the cranium because of the uncontrolled manner in which it was excavated, but a modern-looking tibia was closely associated. The only additional cranial material recovered was a maxillary fragment like that from Ngaloba and a small vault fragment. Postcranial remains of at least three individuals appear to be pres-

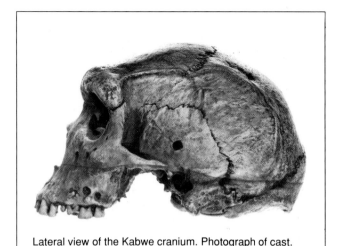

Lateral view of the Kabwe cranium. Photograph of cast.

ent, however, represented by femoral, humeral, and pelvic fragments as well as the tibia. In general the postcranial bones, although robust, appear somewhat more "modern" than those of the Neanderthals, despite the presence of a strong *erectus*-like buttress on one of the pelvic bones.

See also ARCHAIC HOMO SAPIENS;
WOODWARD, ARTHUR SMITH. [C.B.S.]

KADA HADAR   *see*   HADAR

KAENA   *see*   PALEOMAGNETISM

KAFUAN

Purported ancient split-pebble industry of sub-Saharan Africa defined by Wayland on the basis of rolled material from the Kafu River in western Uganda. It was extended by van Riet Lowe to include materials from the Kagera Valley and the lower ferricrete horizon at Nsongezi, both in Uganda, as well as to a supposed "pluvial" interval represented by the gravels incorporating these tools. The Kafuan has been shown to be invalid, due to the prevalence of natural fracturing in these water-lain deposits.

See also EARLY PALEOLITHIC; EARLY STONE AGE;
GLACIATION; OLDOWAN. [A.S.B.]

KAFZA   *see*   QAFZEH

KAGERAN   *see*   PLUVIALS

KAISO   *see*   UGANDA

KALAMBO FALLS

Open-air stratified Pleistocene site in Zambia near the border with Tanzania close to the southeastern shore of Lake Tanganyika, with archaeological materials ranging in age, on comparative typological and faunal grounds, from probable middle Pleistocene to recent. The site, excavated by J.D. Clark between 1953 and 1966, yielded an unusually complete sequence of African Paleolithic industries, beginning with the Acheulean and continuing through industries with Sangoan (Chipeta), Lupemban, and Lupembo-Tshitolian (Polungu) affinities to a local microlithic Epipaleolithic culture (Kaposwa, ca. 4000 B.P.), followed by Iron Age horizons. At Kalambo Falls the Sangoan and Lupemban horizons, which are among the very few stratifed *in situ* occurrences of these industries, are both characterized by a wide range of small- and medium-sized scrapers, as well as by the core-axes typical of these industries. Exceptional preservation of organic materials resulted in the recovery of roughly modified and fire-hardened wooden implements from the earliest Acheulean horizons. Radiocarbon dates on wood and charcoal of greater than 60,000 B.P. for the Acheulean and 46,000–36,000 B.P. for the Sangoan probably indicate ages for these industries that are beyond the range of this technique, rather than cultural conservatism.

See also ACHEULEAN; AFRICA; CLARK, J. DESMOND;
EARLY STONE AGE; LATER STONE AGE;
LUPEMBAN; MIDDLE STONE AGE; SANGOAN;
SECOND INTERMEDIATE. [A.S.B.]

KALODIRR   *see*   MURUAROT

KALOKOL   *see*   MURUAROT

KALOMA   *see*   MABOKO

KAMASIAN   *see*   PLUVIALS

KAMLIAL   *see*   SIWALIKS

KANAM

Western Kenyan stratified sequence with lower level of late Miocene age, ca. 6 m.y. and upper level of middle Pliocene age, ca. 4 m.y. by K-Ar dating. Kanam is a site on the shore of Lake Victoria at Homa Bay, where L.S.B. Leakey's 1932 expedition to eastern Africa discovered a fragment of fossil hominid mandible. Leakey maintained that the specimen had been found *in situ* in the Mio-Pliocene sediments. Coupled with the discovery of human cranial remains thought to be of middle Pleistocene age at the nearby Kanjera site, the Kanam mandible was used by Leakey to support his belief that the human line had an extremely ancient beginning and that such forms as *Australopithecus* and *Homo erectus* were merely side branches in human evolution.

Announced by Leakey in 1932 and named "*Homo kanamensis*" in 1935, the Kanam find became the object of controversy because of its modern appearance and ancient date. Even though the geologist Boswell visited the site in 1934–1935 and reported that the context of the jaw was in doubt, Leakey clung to Kanam throughout his career. Subsequent work by M. Pickford in the 1980s has shown that the Kanam stratigraphy is indeed complex, with faunal elements correlative to Lothagam, and that the original Kanam mandible probably was not in a primary context but rather represents a late Pleistocene specimen washed in with some of the other fossil fauna.

Thus the significance of the Kanam hominid fossil relates to the major influence it had on the beliefs of its discoverer, L.S.B. Leakey, rather than any insights it gives into human evolution.

See also LEAKEY, LOUIS; LOTHAGAM. [T.D.W.]

Further Readings

Reader, J. (1981) Missing Links. Boston: Little, Brown.

Pickford, M. (1987) The geology and palaeontology of the Kanam Erosion Gullies (Kenya). Mainzer Geowiss. Mitt. *16*:209–226.

KANAPOI

Northern Kenyan stratified sequence of early Pliocene age, between 5 and 4 m.y. according to K-Ar dating of associated basalts and faunal analysis. Discovered in the 1960s by a Harvard team led by B. Patterson, the site is southwest of Lake Turkana and ca. 70 km. south of Lothagam. About 70 m. of clastic sediments have yielded a Pliocene fauna decidedly more evolved than that of Lothagam. Included in the surface collection from the site is an adult hominid distal humerus.

See also LOTHAGAM. [T.D.W.]

KANJERA

Group of hominid and mammal fossil sites, from early Pleistocene to Holocene in age, located on Winam Gulf, Lake Victoria (Kenya). This open-site group consists of a set of shallow erosion gullies that cut through clays, silts, and sands related to ancient Lake Victoria. Surface collection from 1932 to 1935 by L.S.B. Leakey yielded mostly cranial remains of at least four hominid individuals, associated on the surface with early Pleistocene mammals. Although

several fragments of Kanjera hominid 3 were believed to be *in situ*, stratigraphic provenance of the finds is not certain. More cranial and postcranial pieces of hominids were found during surface survey in 1974 and 1981. Anatomical, chemical, and geological evidence suggests that the hominid fossils are considerably later than the early Pleistocene fauna. The hominid remains cannot be distinguished from anatomically modern humans, and they contain a considerably lower concentration of uranium (^{238}U) than do the other mammal fossils. The site is also known for slumping of sediments, whereby materials on the surface or in overlying beds may become incorporated into underlying beds. The presence of surface artifacts ranging from Acheulean bifaces and Middle Stone Age flake tools to pottery implies mixing of materials from early Pleistocene to Holocene. Fossils of extinct gelada monkey (*Theropithecus oswaldi*), probably from an early Pleistocene horizon, are similar to those from Beds I and II at Olduvai, smaller than those from Olorgesailie.

See also CERCOPITHECINAE; KANAM; LEAKEY, LOUIS. [R.P.]

KANJERAN *see* PLUVIALS

KANSAN *see* GLACIATION; PLEISTOCENE

"KANSUPITHECUS" *see* PLIOPITHECIDAE

KAO PAH NAM *see* ASIA (EASTERN)

KAPSIBOR *see* FORT TERNAN

KAPTHURIN

Geological formation west of Lake Baringo (Kenya), of early to middle Pleistocene age. Kapthurin yielded two hominid mandibles, one referred to *Homo erectus*, and Oldowan and Acheulean tools (including early prepared cores) associated with fauna.

See also BARINGO; HOMO ERECTUS; KENYA. [R.P.]

KARARI

Early Pleistocene stone industry (ca. 1.6–1.3 m.y.) known from the Karari escarpment, east of Lake Turkana (Kenya). Characterized by large core scrapers but otherwise similar to the Oldowan stone assemblages of East Africa.

See also OLDOWAN; SCRAPER. [R.P.]

KARUNGU *see* RUSINGA

KASWANGA *see* RUSINGA

KAZINGA CHANNEL *see* UGANDA

KEBARA

Israeli cave that first produced fossil hominid specimens in 1931 and has recently been further excavated. Earlier excavations produced the remains of a child from Middle Paleolithic levels, but the more extensive recent work has already recovered the most complete trunk skeleton of a Neanderthal yet found. This presumed burial has no cranium but a massive mandible and a large-bodied skeleton of the entire upper part of the body of an adult male. The well-preserved scapulae and pelvis show the characteristic Neanderthal morphology.

See also NEANDERTHALS. [C.B.S.]

KEBARAN

Late Paleolithic industry (Stage VI) of the Near East, defined at Mugharet el-Kebarah on the Mount Carmel ridge in Israel and characterized by microblades and backed bladelets. Sometimes seen as transitional to the mesolithic Natufian industry, the Kebaran coincides with the "terminal" Pleistocene, ca. 15,000–10,000 B.P. At Jabrud (Syria) variants of this industry, the "Skiftian" and "Nebekian," were recovered from Shelter III.

See also JABRUD; KEBARA; LATE PALEOLITHIC; MESOLITHIC; STONE-TOOL MAKING. [A.S.B.]

KEDUNG BRUBUS

Eastern Java fossil-collecting area of middle Pleistocene age, ca. 0.5 m.y. One of E. Dubois's earliest discoveries was a *Homo erectus* partial mandible at a site ca. 30 km. from Nawi in the Kendeng Hills. As with most other fossils from eastern Java the exact provenance of the specimen is unknown. On the basis of mammalian fossils recovered from the exposure assumed to have yielded the mandible a Kabuh equivalent age has been attributed to the specimen. Recently it has also been pointed out that the mandible is that of a juvenile.

See also ASIA (EASTERN); INDONESIA. [G.G.P.]

KEITH, [SIR] ARTHUR (1866–1955)

British anatomist and paleoanthropologist. For much of his career Keith was conservator of the Museum of the Royal College of Surgeons, London (1907–1933). Prior to his appointment he had been a demonstrator and lecturer in anatomy at the London Hospital Medical School (1895–1907). Although an earlier sojourn in Thailand (then Siam) in 1889–1892 had awakened his interest in the subject of human evolution, it was only after 1908 that he was able to devote himself exclusively to such matters. Largely as a result of his increasing commitment to the notion of the great antiquity of the modern human form, Keith withdrew from his earlier position that the Neanderthals had been the progenitors of modern *Homo sapiens*. Likewise, while accepting the Piltdown skull as a genuine fossil, he did not accept it as a precursor of the human lineage. In his general thinking on evolution, particularly in his later years, Keith emphasized the competition factor in human history and considered racial and national prejudice as inborn. In 1933, because of ill-health, Keith gave up his post as conservator and became master of Buckston Browne Farm, the experimental research station of the College of Surgeons at Down in Kent. He held this post until his death in January 1955.

See also HOOTON, ERNEST ALBERT; McCOWN, THEODORE D. [F.S.]

KENYA

Nation on the Indian Ocean coast of Africa, bordered by Ethiopia, Uganda, and Tanzania. Kenya is one of the world's most prolific sources of archaeological, paleontological, and contextual data bearing on human evolution, ranging from the early Miocene to the Iron Age. In geological terms Kenya owes this abundance of sites to the fossilizing conditions created by rifting along the crest of the great Kenya Dome uplift in the west-central part of the country. The two main zones of subsidence extend northward and south-southeastward to form the Kenya segments of the eastern Rift Valley, but a shallower "failed" arm also extends westward as the Nyanza Rift into the Winam Gulf of Lake Victoria. In these zones are found nearly all of the fossil sites in Kenya.

The Miocene fossil beds, deposited during the earliest stages of vulcanism and rifting, provide nearly all of the world's knowledge of the earliest hominoids and cercopithecoids. On the slopes of the Kenya Dome paravolcanic "moats" around great early Miocene volcanoes accumulated thick deposits of sediment mixed with ash and lava. These now are exposed in very rich sites at Koru and Songhor at the base of Timboroa (Tinderet); Rusinga, Mfwangano, and Karungu in the Kisingiri (Rangwa) complex, all in the Nyanza Rift; and Bukwa on the west flank of Elgon. The highland appears to have been covered by a tropical closed-canopy forest, but local alkali-flats were created by poor drainage of the hyperalkaline ash-falls in the subsiding basins. These were ideal fossilizing sites and sampled a full range of forest and forest-edge biota, even fruits and soft-bodied insects. The primate fauna included a diversity of prosimians and at least six genera of primitive catarrhines, mostly proconsuls but also the earliest oreopithecid, *Nyanzapithecus*, dated to 17.8 m.y. at Rusinga. Farther north, in the older Ethiopian Rift, the early Miocene sites of Muruarot, Loperot, Mwiti, Buluk, and others, dated between 18 and 16 m.y., lay near sea level and represent a different ecology. The catarrhines (e.g. *Afropithecus*, *Turkanapithecus*, and *Simiolus*), proboscideans, bovids, and suids in this regional fauna are clearly different from those in the forest-adapted faunas of Rusinga and Songhor to the south and show a much stronger resemblance to early Miocene coastal faunas from Libya, Israel, and Saudi Arabia.

The middle Miocene, beginning at ca. 15 m.y., was a time of global climate change, as forests gave way to woodlands on the Kenya Dome. Sites in the Nyanza Rift, at Maboko and Fort Ternan, contain the earliest known cercopithecoids and the first thick-enameled "ramapithecine," *Kenyapithecus*, which also occurs in abundance at Nachola in the main Rift Valley. In the later Miocene, from ca. 12 to 5 m.y., few hominoid remains are known despite numerous mammal localities of this age: Kanam on Lake Victoria (the "Kanam skull" comes from a much younger level), the Ngorora sites of the Baringo basin, and Namurungule and Nakali south of Lake Turkana. This interval is generally unfossiliferous elsewhere in Africa, and thus material that might demonstrate the adaptations leading toward *Australopithecus* is virtually unknown.

As it happens, the earliest evidence of what some would identify as direct human ancestors is also found in Kenya, in the latest Miocene. These are postcranial fragments and isolated teeth dated to ca. 6 m.y. in the lower levels of Lothagam, south of Lake Turkana. Other specimens dubiously referred to *Australopithecus* come from the slightly younger, earliest Pliocene sites of Kanapoi, near Lothagam, and Tabarin (Chemeron), northwest of Lake Baringo. The oldest undoubted member of this genus in Kenya, referred by some to *A. aethiopicus* and by others to *A. boisei*, is the "black skull" from the West Turkana site of Nariokotome, found in 1985 and dated to ca. 2.5 m.y., or middle Pliocene age. The famous Plio-Pleistocene beds of East Turkana, which are comparable with Olduvai (Tanzania) and to the Omo and Hadar sequences (Ethiopia), have yielded important fossils of *Australopithecus*, *Homo habilis*, and *Homo erectus*, and new discoveries of this age have also been made near Nariokotome in the West Turkana district. Oldowan tool cultures are found in stratigraphic context in the Turkana basin, and Acheulean sites, some with thousands of handaxes, have been

uncovered throughout the Kenya Rift, most notably at sites developed by L.S.B. and M.D. Leakey at Kariandusi and Olorgesailie. The Leakeys were also pioneers of mid-Pleistocene and younger archaeology in Kenya, with important excavations at Gamble's Cave (Elmenteita), Hyrax Hill (Nakuru), Njoro River, and the Naivasha Railway rock shelter.

See also BARINGO; BULUK; EAST TURKANA; FORT TERNAN; KANAM; KANAPOI; LEAKEY, LOUIS; LEAKEY, MARY; LOTHAGAM; MABOKO; NACHOLA; RIFT VALLEY; RUSINGA; WEST TURKANA. [J.A.V.C., T.D.W.]

Further Readings

Andrews, P.J., and Van Couvering, J.A.H. (1975) Paleoenvironments in the East African Miocene. In F. Szalay (ed.): Approaches to Primate Paleobiology. Basel: Karger, pp. 62–103.

Cole, S. (1975) Leakey's Luck. London: Collins.

Reader, J. (1981) Missing Links. Boston: Little, Brown.

KENYAPITHECUS

During the early part of the middle Miocene there appeared in Africa for the first time a type of hominoid with a radically different adaptation of its teeth. Up to this time all hominoids had thin dental enamel; but with *Kenyapithecus* thick enamel appeared, and this was to have far-reaching consequences for hominoid evolution.

Kenyapithecus is best known from two sites in Kenya, Fort Ternan and Maboko, but more recently an important collection has been made from Nachola in northern Kenya. The genus was originally discovered and named by L.S.B. Leakey, who named the specimens from Fort Ternan *Kenyapithecus wickeri*. A previously described fossil from Maboko was later assigned by Leakey to this genus as a separate species, *K. africanus*. There is some doubt now as to whether these two species are really distinct: they are very similar, but if only one actually exists it shows considerable size dimorphism.

Kenyapithecus was a small-to-medium-sized hominoid primate, related to the great apes and postdating the divergence of the gibbons. It had robust jaws, which together with the thick enamel of its teeth suggest a specialized diet. Its limb bones were more lightly built than those of *Dryopithecus*.

See also APE; DRYOPITHECUS; FORT TERNAN; HOMINOIDEA; MABOKO; MIOCENE; NACHOLA; SEXUAL DIMORPHISM. [P.A.]

KERIAN *see* TIME SCALE

KIAHERA *see* RUSINGA

KIBISH

Three sites in the area of the Kibish tributary of the Omo River (Ethiopia) produced hominid fossils in

1967. The most important specimens are an archaic and robustly built skull, lacking the face (Omo 2), and a more fragmentary anatomically modern skull with associated partial skeleton (Omo 1). These specimens are both claimed to date from the late middle or early late Pleistocene (ca. 130 k.y. ago), but the morphological differences between them suggest that they cannot represent a single population.

See also ARCHAIC MODERNS. [C.B.S.]

KIBOKO ISLAND   *see*   MABOKO

KIN SELECTION   *see*   SOCIOBIOLOGY

KIRIMUN   *see*   MURUAROT

KISINGIRI   *see*   RUSINGA; KENYA

KISINGIRIAN   *see*   TIME SCALE

KLASIES

The complex of caves at Klasies River Mouth (South Africa) contains important archaeological and fossil hominid remains that appear to show the presence of modern humans and the manufacture of sophisticated stone tools more than 70 k.y. ago, although the dating of the sites remains controversial. The hominid specimens are fragmentary and show clear variation, but some are indistinguishable in the form of the supraorbital torus and mandible from those of living humans.

See also ARCHAIC MODERNS. [C.B.S.]

KNUCKLE-WALKING   *see*   LOCOMOTION, HOMININAE

KOENIGSWALD, GUSTAV H. RALPH VON (1902–1982)

Dutch (b. Germany) paleoanthropologist. From 1928 to 1930 von Koenigswald was an assistant curator at the Munich Geological Museum. After joining the Geological Survey of the Dutch Indies, he discovered the remains of a number of fossil hominids in Java, including some of the Ngandong calvariae in 1933, the first Sangiran calvaria in 1937 (Pithecanthropus II=*Homo erectus*), and the *"Meganthropus"* mandibular fragments (also from Sangiran) in 1939. He also described four molars, attributed to *Gigantopithecus*, which he purchased between 1935 and 1939 in

Hong Kong and Canton. When the Japanese occupied Java during World War II, von Koenigswald was imprisoned. After the war he remained in Java until 1948, when he was appointed professor at the State University of Utrecht. He concluded his career as curator of paleoanthropology at the Senckenberg Museum, Frankfurt am Main.

See also DRAGON BONES; GIGANTOPITHECUS; HOMO ERECTUS; MEGANTHROPUS; NGANDONG; SANGIRAN DOME; WEIDENREICH, FRANZ. [F.S.]

KOHATIUS   *see*   ANAPTOMORPHINAE

KOMBA   *see*   GALAGIDAE

KOMBEWA   *see*   PREPARED-CORE

KOOBI FORA   *see*   EAST TURKANA

KORO-TORO   *see*   YAYO

KORU

Western Kenyan stratified exposures of early Miocene age, ca. 20 m.y. according to K-Ar dating of pyroclastic biotite. Discovered in 1909 by a gold prospector, Koru was the first Miocene site known in sub-Saharan Africa. Rich concentrations of fossils occur in red clays and silts sandwiched between carbonatite and nephelinite flows in Koru and Legetet formations. Early finds were natural exposures on Legetet Hill (Koru Red Beds, Maize Crib, Gordon's Farm), but others have developed as a result of quarrying in the carbonatites (Koru Lime sites). The lowest level is at Meswa Bridge near Muhoroni, ca. 5 km. from Legetet. Koru is the type site of *Proconsul africanus*, *Xenopithecus koruensis*, and *Limnopithecus legetet* and also has yielded numerous important specimens of *Proconsul major*, *Micropithecus clarki*, and *Dendropithecus macinnesi*.

See also KENYA; LEAKEY, LOUIS; RUSINGA; SONGHOR. [J.A.V.C.]

Further Readings

Harrison, T.E. (1981) New finds of small fossil apes from the Miocene locality at Koru in Kenya. J. Hum. Evol. *10:* 129–137.

Pickford, M.H., and Andrews, P.J. (1981) The Tinderet Miocene sequence in Kenya. J. Hum. Evol. *10:*13–33.

KOSTENKI

Rich Late Paleolithic culture region on the River Don some 35 km. south of the city of Voronezh (U.S.S.R.).

Some 25 single and multilayered open-air sites assigned to the related Gorodtsovskaya, Kostenki-Avdeevo, Kostenki-Borschevo, and Streletskaya industries are found in loesslike loam, humic beds, and colluvium (slope wash) along a 10-km. stretch of the Don. They are situated at the river's edge, on two old river terraces, as well as at the edge of the interfluve plateau up to 2 km. away from the river.

The sites have produced rich and diverse inventories of stone and bone tools, portable figurative art including ivory "Venus" figurines, animal figurines carved of bone and stone, and fragmentary remains of fired clay. Numerous complex features at the sites include pits and hearths. The alignment of these at some sites (e.g. Kostenki I-1, I-2, and IV) was in the past interpreted as evidence for remains of rectangular long houses measuring up to 35 m. by 15 m. Current research suggests that all these features were not a part of a single dwelling but represent a number of occupational sequences at the sites. Other sites (Kostenki II, XI) contain remains of small round or oval mammoth-bone dwellings. Human burials have been found at Kostenki II, XIV, XV, and XVII. Occupation of the sites spans a period from ca. 35,000 to 11,000 B.P.

See also EUROPE; GRAVETTIAN; LATE PALEOLITHIC; MEZHIRICH; ROGACHEV; SUNGIR; UPPER PALEOLITHIC. [O.S.]

Further Readings

Klein, R.G. (1969) Man and Culture in the Late Pleistocene: A Case Study. San Francisco: Chandler.

Praslov, N.D., and Rogachev, A.N. (1982) Paleolit Kostenkovsko-Borchevskogo raiona na Donu. Moscow: Nauka.

KOW SWAMP *see* ARCHAIC MODERNS; AUSTRALIA; HOMO SAPIENS

KRAPINA

Cave in Yugoslavia, excavated between 1899 and 1905 by Gorjanović-Kramberger, that produced a large number of fragmentary hominid remains derived from adults and children. The main hominid levels at the site probably date from the early part of the last glaciation, and the sample represents an early Neanderthal population characterized by the particular prevalence of taurodontism in the molar teeth (roots are undivided, with expanded pulp cavities). The material includes several partial skulls, one of which has an associated facial skeleton, and many postcranial bones of robust morphology. The condition of the Krapina hominid material has fueled speculation about cannibalism at the site, and some workers even believed that the Krapina Neanderthals had fallen victim to early modern people. The distribu-

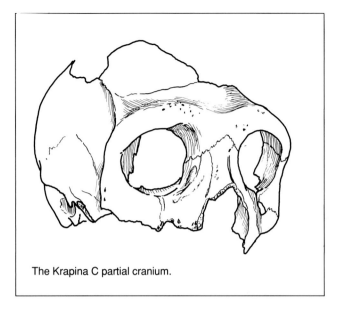

The Krapina C partial cranium.

tion of skeletal parts represented, however, is reminiscent of bones from disturbed burials, which has led to recent suggestions that the Krapina bones were defleshed and secondarily interred at the site.

See also GORJANOVIĆ-KRAMBERGER, DRAGUTIN; NEANDERTHALS. [C.B.S.]

KROMDRAAI

South African stratified cave breccias of late Pliocene or early Pleistocene age. Fossiliferous deposits in dolomitic limestone are located south of the Bloubank River some 3.6 km. east-northeast of the site of Sterkfontein at 25°59′ S and 27°47′ E in the Transvaal Province. The site consists of two elongate and narrow surface exposures of breccia that are separated by some 9 or 10 m. at their closest. These two deposits are known as Kromdraai A (the "Faunal Site") and Kromdraai B. (the "Hominid Site"). Kromdraai B comprises eastern (KBE) and western (KBW) breccia deposits that are separated by a rib of dolomite bedrock. Five sedimentary members are discernible in Kromdraai B East (KBE). All of the hominid fossils thus far recovered from Kromdraai come from KBE, and all appear to have derived from Member 3. Three breccia units are recognizable at KBW, and it is uncertain as to how these relate to the KBE members, if at all.

The first hominid specimen from this site was found in 1938 and described by R. Broom, who attributed it to a novel genus and species, *Paranthropus robustus*. Excavations by Broom (1938–1941), C.K. Brain (1955–1956), and E.S. Vrba (1977–1985) have yielded 13 hominid specimens, all of which are attributable to this "robust" australopithecine species. At least one unquestionable lithic artifact, a chert flake, has been recovered from Kromdraai B. Paleo-ecological indications suggest that the KBE breccias were accumulated under higher average rainfall with a greater prevalence of dense woodland than in historical times.

The faunal assemblages from Kromdraai A and B are not contemporaneous, and the age of the KBE hominid specimens is difficult to ascertain, since most of the diagnostic faunal elements from KBE do not derive from Member 3. While there seems to be universal agreement that KBE Member 3 postdates Sterkfontein Member 4 (i.e. it is younger than ca. 2.5 m.y.), its chronological relationship to the Swartkrans australopithecine-bearing breccias (ca. 1.8–1 m.y.) is the subject of debate.

See also **Australopithecus robustus; Breccia Cave Formation; Paranthropus; Sterkfontein; Swartkrans.** [F.E.G.]

Further Readings

Grine, F.E. (1982) A new juvenile hominid (Mammalia; Primates) from Member 3, Kromdraai Formation, Transvaal, South Africa. Ann. Tvl. Mus. 33:165–239.

Vrba, E.S. (1981) The Kromdraai australopithecine site revisited in 1980: recent investigations and results. Ann. Tvl. Mus. 33:17–60.

KUBI ALGI   *see*   EAST TURKANA

KULU   *see*   RUSINGA

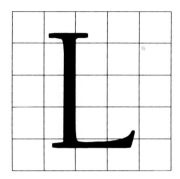

LA BREA TAR PITS

In Los Angeles (California) lies one of the richest deposits of "Ice Age" fossils at Rancho La Brea, popularly called "La Brea Tar Pits." An incredible record of plants and animals has been excavated from the asphalt-rich sediments. Pollen, birds, humans, saber-toothed cats, and mammoths are represented among the 565 species that inhabited the area at intervals between 40,000 and 4,000 years ago.

[L.M.]

LA CHAISE

The La Chaise sites of Abri Bourgeois-Delaunay and Suard (France) have produced a number of hominid specimens of early Neanderthal affinities. Absolute dates suggest that those from Bourgeois-Delaunay are late middle Pleistocene in age, while those from Suard date from the early late Pleistocene.

See also NEANDERTHALS. [C.B.S.]

LA CHAPELLE-AUX-SAINTS

Cave in France that in 1908 produced one of the most famous Neanderthal fossils, that of the "Old Man" of La Chapelle-aux-Saints. This fairly complete skeleton was studied by M. Boule in a series of monographs that greatly influenced paleoanthropological opinion about the Neanderthals for many years. Recent dating places the site at ca. 60 k.y. ago.

See also NEANDERTHALS. [C.B.S.]

LA FERRASSIE

Cave in southwestern France that produced a sample of two adult and six immature Neanderthals from 1909 to 1972. The specimens may derive from a cemetery complex. The adults are represented by partial skeletons and show clear evidence of sexual dimorphism. The adult male (La Ferrassie 1) has a particularly well preserved cranium with a capacity of more than 1,600 ml. Recent dating suggests that the Neanderthal sample from La Ferrassie may be as much as ca. 70 k.y. old.

See also NEANDERTHALS. [C.B.S.]

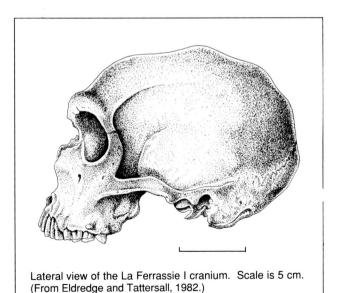

Lateral view of the La Ferrassie I cranium. Scale is 5 cm. (From Eldredge and Tattersall, 1982.)

LA MADELEINE see MAGDALENIAN; PÉRIGORD

LA NAULETTE

The Trou de la Naulette, a huge cave in Belgium, produced a human mandible and postcranial fragments in 1866. The specimen is of great historical importance, as it was the first mandible of Neanderthal type ever discovered and was found in association with such cold-adapted mammals as reindeer and such extinct forms as mammoth and woolly rhinoceros.

See also NEANDERTHALS. [C.B.S.]

LA QUINA

French cave site that has produced a large sample of Neanderthal fossils over years of excavation, the most important being an adult partial skeleton (specimen 5), an adult mandible (9), and the skull of a child (18). La Quina 5 has a long, relatively narrow cranial vault with a small endocranial volume but large brows, jaws, and teeth. It is not certain whether it represents a male or female. Mandible 9 is one of the more modern-looking Neanderthal jaws, while the La Quina 18 child, aged ca. six years at death, shows a number of Neanderthal characteristics but a brain size of only ca. 1,200 ml. Recent dating suggests an age of ca. 65 k.y. for these fossils.

See also NEANDERTHALS. [C.B.S.]

LA VENTA

Area in western Colombia, including middle Miocene Honda Formation fossil localities of early Friasian (15–14 m.y.) or perhaps latest Santacrucian (16–15 m.y.) age. Situated in a desertic depression of the Andean mountain range near the Magdalena River, the La Venta badlands were once a subtropical-tropical forest floodplain and part of the greater Amazonian ecosystem. The area has yielded the richest series of fossil vertebrates in northern South America, and the most primates. One of the significant features of the La Venta primate fauna is that many of its forms are barely distinct from modern genera, suggesting an important degree of lineage stasis among New World monkeys.

See also ATELINAE; CALLITRICHINAE; CEBINAE; PATAGONIA; PITHECIINAE. [A.L.R.]

LACCOPITHECUS *see* PLIOPITHECIDAE

LAETOLI

Northern Tanzanian stratified sequence of middle and late Pliocene, early Pleistocene, and late Pleistocene age, ca. 4.3–0.1 m.y. by K-Ar and faunal analysis.

Pliocene hominid footprint excavated at the site of Laetoli in northern Tanzania. (Photograph by and courtesy of Tim D. White.)

On the edge of the Serengeti Plains near Lake Eyasi, Laetoli lies ca. 50 km. south of Olduvai Gorge. It was discovered by the Leakeys in 1935, but the lone hominid tooth recovered then went unrecognized until 1979. L. Kohl-Larsen worked at Laetoli in the 1930s and recovered a small portion of hominid maxilla with two premolars, an isolated molar, and an isolated incisor. These specimens were known as the Garusi hominids, for the Garusi River, which drains the Laetoli area.

During the 1970s a team led by M.D. Leakey explored the Garusi River valley more completely, recovering additional hominid remains and abundant vertebrates from the Pliocene Laetolil Beds, which are dated to ca. 3.7–3.5 m.y. ago. The hominid fossils include adult and juvenile mandibles, an adult maxilla, a partial juvenile skeleton, and many isolated teeth. All of these remains have since been assigned to *Australopithecus afarensis.*

The Laetolil Beds are volcanic in origin and were deposited in a dry, relatively open environment. The unique paleoecology at Laetoli indicates a dramatic difference from the habitat in the slightly younger site of Hadar in Ethiopia.

In the late 1970s volcanic-ash layers bearing mammalian footprints were found at Laetoli, and in 1978–1979 trails left by hominids were found by P. Abell. Excavation and analysis of these trails confirmed the early hominid acquisition of bipedal locomotion. No stone tools have been recovered from the Laetolil Beds.

The late Pleistocene Ngaloba Beds at Laetoli yielded Middle Stone Age tools and the cranium of an archaic *Homo sapiens*, LH 18, the "Ngaloba cranium."

See also Australopithecus afarensis; Ngaloba; Tanzania.
[T.D.W.]

Further Readings

Hay, R.L., and Leakey, M.D. (1982) The fossil footprints of Laetoli. Sci. Am. 246:50–57.

Leakey, M.D., and Harris, J.M. (1987) Laetoli: A Pliocene Site in Northern Tanzania. Oxford: Oxford University Press.

LAGOTHRIX   *see*   ATELINAE

LAINYAMOK

Middle Pleistocene locality in southern Kenya, 8 km. west of Lake Magadi. Surface bones and artifacts originally suggested that Lainyamok represented a hominid butchery area. Excavations showed that animal bones were gnawed by carnivores and were not associated with stone tools. A hominid maxilla and femoral shaft were found *in situ.*

See also Kenya; Olorgesailie. [R.P.]

LAKE MUNGO   *see*   ARCHAIC MODERNS; AUSTRALIA; HOMO SAPIENS

LAKE RUDOLF   *see*   EAST TURKANA; KENYA

LAMBDA   *see*   SKULL

LAND BRIDGES   *see* PALEOBIOGEOGRAPHY

LANGEBAANIAN   *see*   TIME SCALE

LANGHIAN   *see*   MIOCENE; TIME SCALE

LANGUAGE   *see*   SPEECH (ORIGINS OF)

LANTIAN

Fossil site in Shaanxi Province (China), dated to the middle or late early Pleistocene on paleomagnetic and faunal correlation. "Lantian man" actually consists of two specimens from two different localities: the Gongwangling cranium and the Chenjiawo mandible. The cranium occurs in paleomagnetically reversed sediments that have been assigned to the terminal part of the Matuyama Chron. The Chenjiawo mandible reportedly came from a slightly higher level, in sediments of normal polarity, and thus has been assigned to the lower portion of the Brunhes Normal. It has been recently suggested, however, that the two specimens occurred in stratigraphically equivalent sediments. It has also been suggested on the basis of oxygen-isotope chronology and biostratigraphy that the two specimens are from an interval that straddles the Jaramillo reversal at ca. 0.9 m.y. ago. In either case the Gongwangling cranium probably represents the earliest known hominid fossil from mainland East Asia. The cranium is low and robust, with thick bones and an estimated endocranial volume of ca. 780 ml. It has been considered to be a female of ca. 30 years of age. The mandible has also been classified as female but probably belongs to an older individual; it exhibits agenesis of the third molars. Stone tools and indications of fire have also been recovered from stratigraphically equivalent deposits in the same area.

See also Asia (Eastern); China; Homo erectus. [G.G.P.]

Further Readings

Aigner, J.S., and Laughlin, W.S. (1973) The dating of Lantian Man and his significance for analyzing trends in human evolution. Am. J. Phys. Anthropol. 39:97–110.

LARYNX   *see*   SPEECH (ORIGINS OF)

LASCAUX

Most important Ice Age painted cave in France, with ceilings and walls painted in an early Magdalenian style, ca. 17,000–16,000 B.P. In addition to images of aurochs (wild cattle), bison, ibex, and deer Lascaux has one imaginary animal (the "unicorn"), a bear, a rhinoceros, and a scene with a wounded bison and a supine, ithyphallic man. The cave is also rich in engravings and signs. Although only one reindeer image appears, a large number of reindeer bones was excavated from the cave, indicating that the animals eaten were not necessarily those most represented in the art. Discovered in 1942, Lascaux was seen by thousands of visitors, but algae contamination appeared on the paintings, and the cave was closed to tourists. A copy of a major portion of the cave, "Lascaux II," was built nearby and is open to the public.

See also EUROPE; MAGDALENIAN; PALEOLITHIC IMAGE; UPPER PALEOLITHIC. [A.M.]

LASCAUX INTERSTADIAL *see*
GLACIATION; PLEISTOCENE

LATE PALEOLITHIC

As broadly defined here, a stage in human cultural development characterized by diversified blade-tool (Mode IV) technology, mainly occurring at the end of the late Pleistocene between ca. 40,000 and 10,000 B.P.

This stage was first recognized in southwestern France, where it was called the *Upper Paleolithic*. The similarity of cultural remains dating to this period from adjacent areas of Europe, and eventually all of the Mediterranean basin, led to the adoption of this designation there as well. Archaeological inventories outside of Europe, however, are different enough to be distinguished as Late Paleolithic. In sub-Saharan Africa Mode IV technologies are rare, although they may appear during the Middle Stone Age, ca. 90–40 k.y. B.P. The Later Stone Age, first appearing between 40 and 20 k.y. in different regions, is mainly Mode V. Thus a true Late Paleolithic is uncommon south of the Sahara (except for some industries in Kenya and Ethiopia). Some scholars, especially those working in the Near East, call industries between 40,000 and 20,000 B.P. Late Paleolithic and those after 20,000 B.P. Epipaleolithic. Paleoindian industries of the New World are also Late Paleolithic in this broad conception of the term.

Important worldwide developments during this period included a deterioration of climatic conditions; the emergence of anatomically modern humans (*Homo sapiens sapiens*) and new technologies; an explosion in the arts and other forms of symboling behavior; significant changes in subsistence practices and economic and social relationships; and the colonization of Australia and the Americas.

Climates and Environments

Climatic conditions during the Late Paleolithic were significantly different from those of today. Late Pleistocene glaciers expanded to their greatest extent in both hemispheres, and mile-high sheets of ice covered all of northern Europe, Alaska, and Canada.

This expansion of the ice, which peaked between 20,000 and 18,000 B.P., brought about much colder climates and a significant reduction in annual precipitation.

In higher latitudes advancing ice sheets caused a profound change in the distribution of biotic communities and resulted in a southward displacement of forest belts. In Europe forests were found only around the Mediterranean, and much of Eurasia was covered by a unique periglacial steppe, which while cold and extremely continental in climate was able to support large herds of such gregarious herbivores as bison, horse, mammoth, and reindeer.

Environmental data from lower latitudes suggest that this period saw increasing aridity, shrinkage of forests, and expansion of deserts onto former grasslands. Late Paleolithic climates and environments were in general considerably harsher than those of today.

Late Paleolithic People

Although Late Paleolithic industries succeeded those of the Middle Paleolithic at about the same time that Neanderthals were replaced by anatomically modern humans in much of Europe and the Near East, the relationship between the tool makers and tool industries was not simple and straightforward. The discovery of fully modern humans with Middle Paleolithic tools in the Near East and of Neanderthals with Upper Paleolithic ones in France indicates that both kinds of hominid used both kinds of industries. In southern Africa the earliest Mode IV (within the Middle Stone Age) tool kits and the earliest anatomically modern humans may be even older, but their association is unclear and most dates are questionable.

Technology

Archaeological inventories at Late Paleolithic sites are extremely varied in raw materials and the tools fashioned from them. Advances in stone-tool making include a new way of preparing cores to produce long, thin, parallel-sided blades. Blades allowed a more economical use of nodules and permitted tool makers to obtain far more working edge per unit of stone. The blades were then retouched into tools by a variety of techniques, among them finely controlled pressure flaking. We can see a decrease in the size of some tools made on blades during this period as well. The growing production of microblades in Africa and Eurasia after 20,000 B.P. is probably related to the rise of hafting technologies and composite tools. These tools included stone-tipped spears, lances, spear throwers, and probably bows and arrows. These weapons permitted the killing of animals at far greater distances. Finally, techniques of grind-

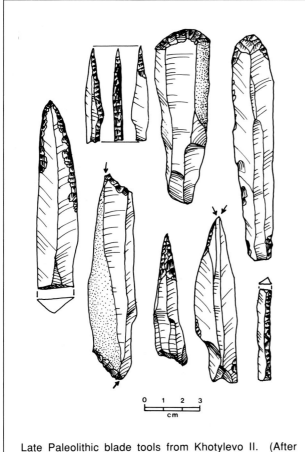

Late Paleolithic blade tools from Khotylevo II. (After Soffer, 1985.)

making traditions remained more conservative and changed little through time.

In some regions of the Old World Late Paleolithic industries overlie transitional ones that contain both Middle Paleolithic tools made on flakes and Late Paleolithic tools on blades. Such sequences, found, for example, in parts of central and eastern Europe, North Africa, and Siberia, suggest that Late Paleolithic industries may have evolved slowly from preceding Middle Paleolithic ones. In other regions Late Paleolithic industries make a sudden appearance, indicating that their makers may have moved into these regions from elsewhere. This is clearly the case in Australia and the New World, which were colonized only after ca. 40,000 B.P., but is also evident in less dramatic fashion in areas like Japan.

Among other Late Paleolithic technological innovations was the systematic use of a much wider spectrum of materials for tools, including antler, bone, ivory, and wood. Bone working became especially elaborate; tools and implements ranging from spear throwers and shaft straighteners to harpoons, fish hooks, and eyed needles are repeatedly found at Late Paleolithic sites. Bone, especially in the higher latitudes of Eurasia, was burned as fuel in hearths and used as a construction material for dwellings. Another innovation was kiln-fired ceramics. Remains of fired-clay animal and female figurines have been found in central and eastern Europe and Siberia.

ing and polishing were also used to fashion stone into beads and pendants.

Late Paleolithic stone-tool makers were much more selective than their predecessors in the raw materials they used, often preferring superior materials from some distance. High-quality chocolate-colored flint from the Holy Cross Mountains in central Poland, for example, has been found at sites up to 400 km. away.

Late Paleolithic tool kits contain many more standardized tool types than those of the Middle Paleolithic. Two of these tools, end-scrapers and burins, are often found in great quantities. Late Paleolithic tool inventories also show increased variation from region to region and change more quickly through time. This patterned interregional and chronological variability, however, is not universal, being more prevalent in Europe and Africa than in parts of Asia and of Australia. Thus for many areas around the Mediterranean we can outline regional sequences of Late Paleolithic industries that replace each other through time in a manner similar to those in western Europe. Yet archaeological records from much of Asia and Australia, although less studied, overall do not exhibit similar patterns of variability. Here tool-

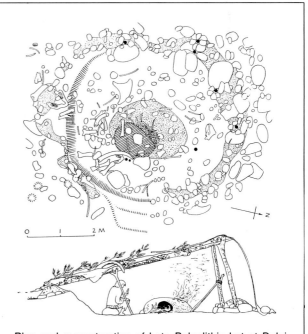

Plan and reconstruction of Late Paleolithic hut at Dolni Vestonice with a clay oven used to fire ceramic figurines. (After Wymer, 1982.)

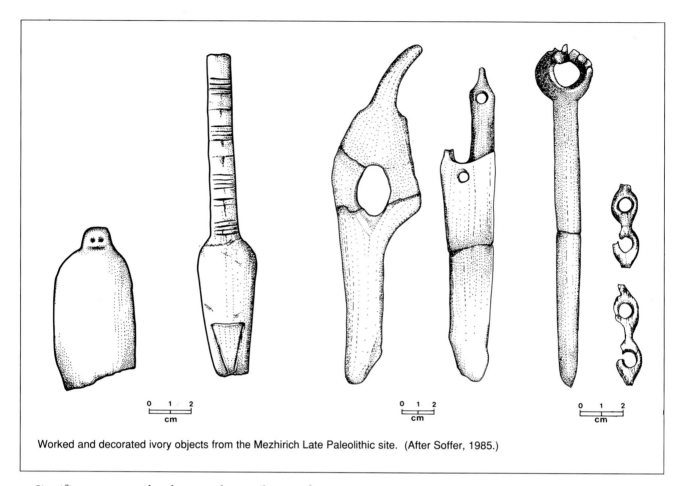

Worked and decorated ivory objects from the Mezhirich Late Paleolithic site. (After Soffer, 1985.)

Significant new technology is also evident in features at Late Paleolithic sites. Carefully prepared hearths bordered with stones for heat retention and constructed with tangential air-flow channels for fire control have been found at sites in higher latitudes. Other hearths were surrounded by clay walls and served as kilns for ceramic production and possibly as baking ovens. Pits that measured up to 2 m. in diameter and up to 1.5 m. in depth were dug into permafrost and used first to store food and then to store bone and ivory for future use. In colder climates large, elaborate dwellings measuring from 20 to 30 sq. m. were constructed from bones of large-sized species like mammoths. Careful selection of skeletal parts for specific dwellings noted at sites with mammoth-bone dwellings on the central Russian Plain suggests that the construction of dwellings occurred on a planned site-wide basis.

Finally, the increase in both the size of residential sites (in some cases exceeding 10,000 sq. m.) and the number of dwellings at sites indicate that people lived together on a permanent basis in greater numbers than during the preceding Middle Paleolithic period.

Cultural Explosion

The most distinctive feature of the Late Paleolithic is the appearance and proliferation of nonutilitarian symbolic behavior revealed in the production of art, decorative objects, jewelry, and musical instruments. Although a handful of Middle Paleolithic sites contain remains of coloring materials and one or two pieces etched with unpatterned lines, Late Paleolithic sites in many parts of Eurasia and Africa consistently feature decorative and decorated objects.

Art and Engravings   Art dating to this period comes in two forms, *parietal* and *mobiliary*. The first includes paintings on cave and rock-shelter walls and in general is relatively scarce outside of the Franco-Cantabrian region of western Europe, although examples have been found in South Africa, Bulgaria, and in the Ural Mountains (U.S.S.R.). Some sites in the European U.S.S.R. have also yielded painted mammoth bones, which because of their weight do not qualify as portable art objects but fit more closely the permanent mode represented by parietal cave art.

Late Paleolithic sites from Czechoslovakia and Poland all the way to Siberia have yielded an abundance of mobiliary art carved out of stone, bone, and amber as well as modeled out of clay and subsequently fired in kilns. These human and animal figurines span a variety of styles, from the classic "Venus"

Artist's rendering of dwelling 1, made of 95 mammoth mandibles at the Mezhirich Late Paleolithic site. (After Jelinek, 1986.)

figures to more abstract representations.

The sites also contain great quantities and varieties of engraved and otherwise decorated objects, some of which were used for utilitarian tasks, like snow shovels, shaft straighteners, piercers, and awls. The function of other engraved pieces remains unclear, and scholars have interpreted them as early calendars, schematic maps, or other types of mnemonic devices. Engraving was done on bone, ivory, antler, and various types of stone.

Personal Adornment   Jewelry and other items of personal adornment, such as beads and pendants, bracelets and rings, and pectorals and diadems, are also regularly found in Late Paleolithic sites, especially in higher latitudes. They were made from polished stone, ostrich-eggshells, ivory, bone, antler, amber, fossil marine shells, and drilled animal teeth. Their presence at the sites strongly suggests an emerged sense of personal and social identity, which may have been absent during the preceding period.

Musical Instruments   Finally, sites in northern Africa and Eurasia include whistles and flutes made of animal and bird long bones. Soviet scholars have also argued that some of the painted mammoth bones found at Late Paleolithic sites on the Russian Plain were used as percussion instruments.

Burial

Planned disposal of the deceased in prepared graves began during the Middle Paleolithic, but the Late Paleolithic witnessed a dramatic increase in the amount of grave goods buried with the dead. Both single and multiple interments are known, and there is no clear pattern favoring either sex or any age category. The most spectacular of these burials, found in Sungir at the outskirts of the city of Vladimir in the European U.S.S.R., contained a joint grave of two adolescents who were buried head to head, their clothing covered with ca. 3,000 sewn-on ivory beads each, and who had rich burial inventories. The nearby grave of a mature male was equally rich and elaborate. At Předmosti, a Late Paleolithic site in Czechoslovakia excavated at the beginning of this century, a mass grave covered by mammoth scapulae contained skeletal remains of over 29 men and women.

During the Late Paleolithic, as today, burial of the dead was not a universal phenomenon but one practiced from time to time primarily in Eurasia, the Near East, and Australia.

Subsistence Strategies

Like those who came before them Late Paleolithic people made their living by hunting and gathering,

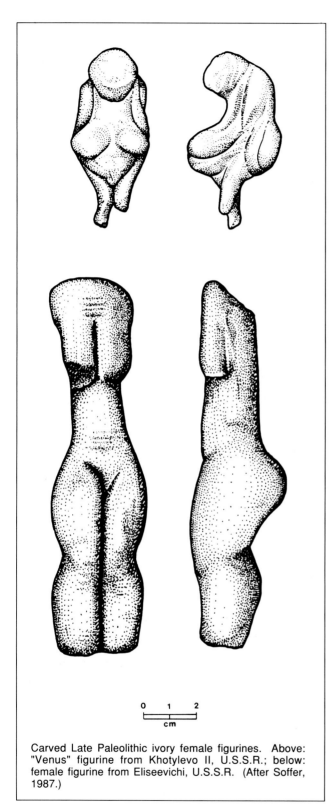

Carved Late Paleolithic ivory female figurines. Above: "Venus" figurine from Khotylevo II, U.S.S.R.; below: female figurine from Eliseevichi, U.S.S.R. (After Soffer, 1987.)

basis. This resulted in a good deal of regional differentiation in paleoeconomies and in the habitual use of such effective mass-harvesting techniques as drives, stampedes, and jump kills.

The increasing presence in the inventories of such dangerous species as wild boars is witness that the invention of long-distance weapons, like bows and arrows and spear throwers, allowed hunters to go after animals more difficult to hunt. Remains of fur-bearing animals and aquatic and terrestrial birds suggest that trapping and snaring were practiced as well.

Groups living in lower latitudes harvested a wide variety of plant and animal resources. Coastal groups, such as those living around the Mediterranean and in southern Africa, harvested fish and shellfish, took birds, and hunted medium- to large-sized bovids as well as collected wild cereal grasses. Groups in Australia also fed on wild cereals, small mammals, lizards, fish, shellfish, birds, and bird eggs. The types of sites occupied in these regions indicate that people here were foragers who migrated to be near ripening resources.

Groups living in higher latitudes, especially on the huge Eurasian periglacial steppe, were confronted by far less predictable resources. These areas were characterized by a relative scarcity of vegetation but an abundance of animals. The latter, however, were available in huge numbers only during the short warm seasons and were sparse during the long, cold winter months. Food management here meant mass-harvesting animals during the seasons of peak abundance and storing surplus food for use during the lean months. These storage economies, which involved both delayed consumption and greater planning, organization, and cooperation on a permanent basis, indicate a more complex organization of subsistence pursuits than found among simple foragers.

A site-by-site comparison of organic assemblages recovered from Middle and Late Paleolithic sites in all latitudes at first glance shows that Late Paleolithic sites contain concentrations of one or two species while Middle Paleolithic ones show a greater range. A regional perspective, however, one that looks at all the sites in a particular area, indicates not so much a narrowing of the resource base during the Late Paleolithic as an organizational change in subsistence behavior from "feed as you go" to planned food harvesting. Groups that lived in areas with diverse but predictable resources, which were generally found in lower latitudes, migrated to position themselves near the available resources and selectively harvested those that were most abundant in a given location. Groups in higher latitudes practiced logistically organized storage economies, harvesting and

but their food-procurement strategies were considerably more planned and effective. Organic remains at Late Paleolithic sites show that people had become finely tuned to local environmental conditions and organized their food procurement on a regional

storing the most abundant animal species.

Finally, the discovery of valued exotics at Late Paleolithic sites—both lithics and decorative items like fossil marine shells—suggests that many groups during this period participated in long-distance exchange networks that linked them socially with groups living at considerable distances from them.

Sociopolitical Organization and Settlement Patterns

The elaboration and regionalization in Late Paleolithic technologies, the emergence of storage economies in parts of the Old World, the explosion in the production of art and jewelry, the use of exotic materials, the growing elaboration and differentiation in funerary inventories, and the increase both in size of sites and in the permanence of their features—taken together, all these indicate changes in sociopolitical relationships.

These changes were not universal but regional. The ephemeral nature of archaeological remains generated by groups in lower latitudes (few artifacts, insubstantial features) and the relative sparseness of such status goods as jewelry and art at these sites suggest that people probably lived in fairly egalitarian, small social units like those known ethnographically for band societies. Like their modern-day equivalents these coresidential groups may have joined other like-sized groups at aggregation sites, where ceremonial behavior took place, including possibly the painting of cave and rock-shelter walls.

Late Paleolithic groups in higher latitudes, especially those whose subsistence was based on storage economies, lived in larger groups and occupied residential locales for much longer periods of time. They did not undertake long-distance seasonal moves, nor did they break up into smaller social units during some seasons. Data on the distribution of stored resources and exotic and status goods, as well as on the differences in burial inventories, indicate that groups like those that occupied the central Russian Plain lived in larger and more complex, hierarchically organized social units, where positions of status and authority were restricted to just some members of the groups.

Colonization

Late Paleolithic people were able to adapt successfully to a wide variety of environments and to colonize both Australia and the Americas. People from Southeast Asia may have arrived in Australia by ca. 40,000 B.P. and soon afterward reached Melanesia (New Ireland). Since they would have had to cross a large body of open water, they must have possessed seaworthy boats and considerable navigational skills. Those who peopled the Americas came from Siberia and crossed Beringia, a land bridge that connected Siberia with Alaska during the stadial periods of the last ice age but today lies submerged under the shallow Bering Straits. Although they may have come on foot, their technological skills and knowledge were sophisticated enough to permit them to survive in the cold and harsh tundra environments of Siberia and Alaska. There is much debate about the date of arrival of these first Americans, with some scholars arguing that it took place before 30,000 B.P. and others dating the event sometime after 20,000 B.P.

See also AFRICA; AGGREGATION-DISPERSAL; ARCHAEOLOGICAL SITES; ASIA (EASTERN); AUSTRALIA; ECONOMY, PREHISTORIC; EUROPE; EXOTICS; HUNTER-GATHERERS; JEWELRY; MIDDLE PALEOLITHIC; MUSICAL INSTRUMENTS; PALEOINDIAN; PALEOLITHIC; PALEOLITHIC IMAGE; PŘEDMOSTI; RITUAL; SITE TYPES; STORAGE; UPPER PALEOLITHIC. [O.S.]

Further Readings

Fagan, B.M. (1985) People of the Earth, 5th ed. Boston: Little, Brown.

Gowlett, J. (1984) Ascent to Civilization. New York: Knopf.

Pfeiffer, J.E. (1982) The Creative Explosion. New York: Harper and Row.

Soffer, O. (1985) The Upper Paleolithic of the Central Russian Plain. Orlando, Fla.: Academic.

Wymer, J. (1982) The Palaeolithic Age. New York: St. Martin's.

LATER STONE AGE

Third stage in a tripartite system of nomenclature for the African Stone Age (Early, Middle, and Later), formalized in 1929 by Goodwin and Van Riet Lowe for South Africa and later expanded to microblade and other epipaleolithic industries throughout Africa and on the Indian subcontinent. Original South African industries assigned to the Later Stone Age (LSA) included the microlithic Wilton industry and three phases of the Smithfield industry (A, B, and C), differentiated from the Wilton by its exclusively interior (noncoastal) distribution, abundance of scrapers, and relative lack of microlithic segments and backed bladelets.

Small tool size, bladelet technology, and hafting of arrows and other tools are among the most distinctive aspects of LSA industries across the continent; other features are widespread use of ostrich-eggshell and shell beads, bored stones that may have served as digging-stick weights, engraved and painted plaques, and an elaborate series of bone and wood tools, including hafts, points, linkshafts, net sinkers, fish gorgets, and barbed harpoons. Faunal remains indicate intensification of resource use through greater utilization of lacustrine and marine resources as well as more consistent hunting of large plains game (giant buffalo, giant zebra, giant haartebeest,

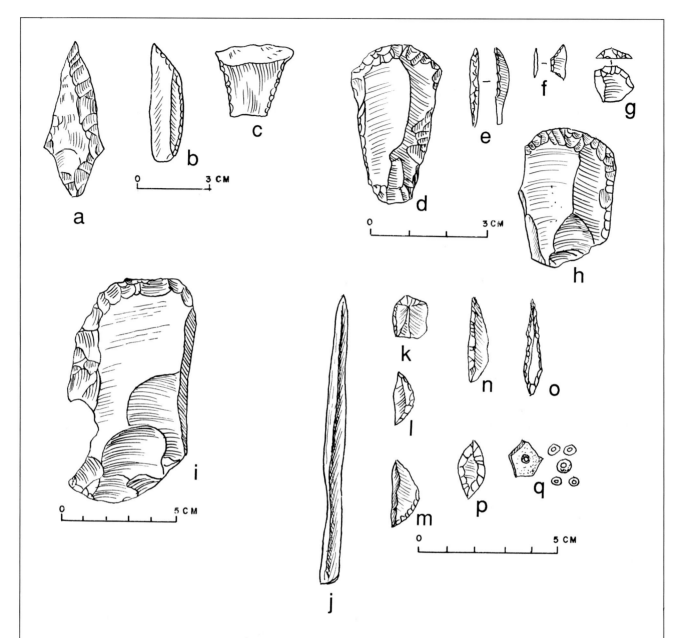

Later Stone Age artifacts from sub-Saharan Africa. Tshitolian industry (Zaire and Angola): a) bifacial tanged point; b) backed blade; c) tranchet. Smithfield industry (South Africa): d) end-scraper (late phase); e) backed blade; f) lunate; g) small convex scraper; h) side- and end-scraper; l–m) lunates; n) straight-backed microlith; o) awl; p) double crescent; q) ostrich-eggshell beads. (After J.D. Clark, The Prehistory of Africa, 1970.)

large warthog) toward the end of the late Pleistocene, possibly contributing to the extinction of several giant species at this time.

The earliest microblade technology is found in central Africa by ca. 20 k.y. at sites in Zaire (Matupi), Uganda (Buvuma Island), Tanzania (Kisese), Kenya (Lukenya Hill), and Zambia (Kalemba). In eastern Zaire, where microlithic technology may date back to 40,000 B.P. at Matupi Cave, sites in the Semliki Valley near Ishango indicate reliance on fishing technology in the form of bone harpoons by the final late Pleisto-

cene, ca. 18,000–12,000 B.P. Intensification of resource use is also reflected in faunal remains from Kalemba and other early sites of the Nachikufan industry. Microliths may be present as early as 25,000 B.P. at Rose Cottage Cave in the Orange Free State (South Africa) but do not become widespread in this area until after 10,000 B.P. Southern African industries that follow the Middle Stone Age dating to between 30,000 and 10,000 B.P. are largely nonmicrolithic (Apollo-11, Border Cave) and are characterized by few formal tools, other than medium- to large-

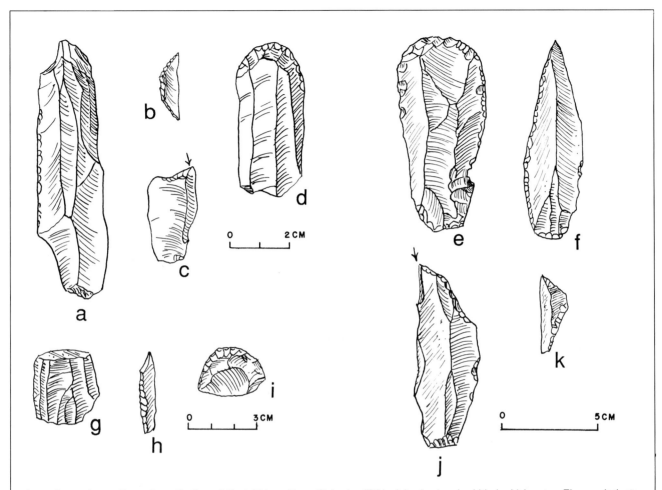

Later Stone Age artifacts from North and East Africa. From Gobedra (Ethiopia): a) retouched blade; b) lunate. Eburran industry (Kenya): c) burin; d) end-scraper. Ibero-Maurusian industry (Morocco): e) alternate-ended microblade core; f) backed bladelet; g) short end-scraper. Capsian industry (Tunisia): h) end-scraper; i) backed blade; j) burin; k) microlith. (After Clark, 1970; and Phillipson, © 1985 by Cambridge University Press. Reprinted with permission.)

sized scrapers and an abundance of bone tools at some sites. In North Africa Iberomaurusian industries are widespread by 14 k.y. and may appear as early as 20–18 k.y.

Later Stone Age technologies lasted into historic times in some areas, with the addition of small quantities of iron, indigenous pottery, and occasional herding of small stock. Interactions between hunters, fishers, and herders of the Later Stone Age and Iron Age agriculturalists and pastoralists were varied and complex and may have ranged from occasional contact through long-distance trade networks to intensive economic interactions and mutual dependency, as typified by ongoing pygmy-villager interactions in the Ituri Forest of Zaire.

Originally the Later Stone Age was seen as parallel in age to the European Mesolithic but was distinguished from it by continued dependence on large herd animals. As in the other stages of Goodwin and Van Riet Lowe's scheme the technological innova-

tions of the Later Stone Age are now known to occur as early in Africa as anywhere in the world. As part of a general move to discard pan-African chronostratigraphic schemes, in view of the richness and diversity of Paleolithic adaptations throughout the continent, the term "Later Stone Age" is increasingly discarded in favor of J.G.D. Clark's use of Mode V to refer to industries with microlithic technology and composite tools.

In most areas Mode V (LSA) industries directly succeed Mode III (MSA) industries, with no intervening stage of widespread large-blade-tool and burin technology comparable with the European Upper Paleolithic (Mode IV). Only in Kenya (the Eburran, previously the Kenya Capsian), Ethiopia (Gobedra shelter), Somalia (Hargesian), and northeastern Africa generally (Dabban, Khormusan) are large-blade industries widespread between 40,000 and 10,000 B.P. Other aspects of the European Upper Paleolithic, however, such as images, body decoration, economic intensification, trade, and social complexity, have contemporary or earlier parallels throughout Africa in association with MSA and LSA industries.

See also APOLLO-11; BORDER CAVE; CAPSIAN; DABBAN; EARLY STONE AGE; ECONOMY, PREHISTORIC; EPIPALEOLITHIC; FIRST INTERMEDIATE; IBERO-MAURUSIAN; LATE PALEOLITHIC; MESOLITHIC; MIDDLE STONE AGE; PALEOLITHIC; PALEOLITHIC IMAGES; PALEOLITHIC LIFEWAYS; ROSE COTTAGE; SECOND INTERMEDIATE; SMITHFIELD; STONE-TOOL MAKING; UPPER PALEOLITHIC; WILTON. [A.S.B.]

Further Readings

Deacon, J. (1984) Later Stone Age people in southern Africa. In R.G. Klein (ed.): Southern African Prehistory and Paleoenvironments. Rotterdam: Balkema.

Phillipson, D.W. (1985) African Archaeology. Cambridge: Cambridge University Press.

LAUGERIE INTERSTADIAL *see* GLACIATION; PLEISTOCENE

LAUGERIE SITES

Two adjacent rock shelters on the right bank of the Vézère River just upstream from Les Eyzies, Dordogne (France), with important Upper Paleolithic remains. Laugerie Haute is one of several deeply stratified rock shelters on which the classic succession of Upper Paleolithic industries in southwestern France is based. First excavated in 1868, the Laugerie Haute sequence industries include Perigordian "III" (now VI), Protomagdalenian, Aurignacian "V," Solutrean, and early Magdalenian (to Stage III). The site is divided by a rock fall into eastern (Est) and western (Ouest) parts and dated by radiocarbon to 22,000–19,500 B.P. The younger nearby shelter, Laugerie Basse, is a middle-to-late (Stages III–VI) Magdalenian site that also yielded the cranial remains of several individuals and a possible burial of an adult male.

See also AURIGNACIAN; MAGDALENIAN; PÉRIGORD; PERIGORDIAN; PEYRONY, DENIS; PROTOMAGDALENIAN; SOLUTREAN; UPPER PALEOLITHIC. [A.S.B.]

LAURENTIDE GLACIATIONS *see* GLACIATION; PLEISTOCENE

LAWS

It has long been recognized that the shape and the internal structure of a given bone are well suited to the mechanical demands placed on it. This recognition has led to the search for "laws" that define the relationship between a bony structure and its function. One of the earliest statements of this kind, popularized as Wolff's Law, suggested that the trabeculi, or the internal struts within a bone, are oriented along the major pathways of stress acting on that bone. More generally this principle has been stated as the tendency for bone to be laid down where it is needed mechanically and resorbed where it is not. This "trajectory theory" was supported by Roux's biomechanical analysis of a pathological knee, in which he showed that the observed pattern of trabeculi coincided with the amounts and distribution of abnormal stress caused by the pathology. Such theories of functional adaptation have been criticized for their failure to recognize the soft-tissue context of a bone and the dynamic nature of both bone and positional behavior.

More recently Pauwels has used photoelastic techniques to test the trajectory theory. His work suggests that, overall, anatomical structures, including muscles and ligaments as well as the bones, themselves function to reduce bending stresses within bones. Furthermore, experimental work by Lanyon and others suggests that bone-cell behavior may be guided by several biomechanical characteristics, including not only stress distribution and magnitude but also the history of previous remodeling and the rates at which stresses change.

See also BONE BIOLOGY; SKELETON. [C.J.D.]

Further Readings

Murray, P.D.F. (1936, 1985) Bones: A Study of the Development and Structure of the Vertebrate Skeleton. New York and London: Cambridge University Press.

Pauwels, F. (1980) Biomechanics of the Locomotor Apparatus. (Translated by P. Maquet and R. Furlong.) Berlin and New York: Springer-Verlag.

LAZARET

Cave near Nice (France) that has been excavated extensively over a long period of time and has produced hominid teeth and the parietal of a child. The latter specimen may represent an early Neanderthal and shows an extensive internal lesion that may have been caused by a meningeal tumor.

See also NEANDERTHALS. [C.B.S.]

LE MOUSTIER

French cave site where the partial skeleton of a Neanderthal youth was excavated in dubious circumstances in 1909; much of the skeleton was destroyed by bombing in 1945. Stone tools from the Middle Paleolithic sequence of the cave gave the name Mousterian to the whole Eurasian cultural complex of the time, although it is not certain with which level the hominid itself was associated. Recent dating work suggests that Neanderthal occupation of the site was quite recent (less than 45 k.y. ago).

See also MOUSTERIAN; NEANDERTHALS. [C.B.S.]

LEAKEY, LOUIS SEYMOUR BAZETT (1903-1972)

Louis Leakey was born in Kenya, the son of British missionary parents, and spent his youth with the Kikuyu people of Kenya before going up to Cambridge to read archaeology and anthropology (1922-1926). During his career he held a variety of visiting academic appointments in British and American universities and was from 1945 to 1951 curator of the Coryndon Memorial Museum, Nairobi.

Primarily, however, Louis Leakey was a fieldworker. After an initial introduction to field techniques at the Tendaguru dinosaur site in southern Tanzania in the early 1930s he began his pioneering work on Rift Valley prehistory, summarized in his book *The Stone Age Races of Kenya*, published in 1935. It was in this same period that he began work on the Miocene faunas of western Kenya, where he uncovered new early hominoids at such sites as Rusinga, Songhor, and Fort Ternan. After his marriage to Mary Nicoll Leakey's attention focused increasingly during the 1940s and 50s on the search for hominid fossils at Olduvai Gorge. Finally, in 1959, there came to light a fossil hominid cranium, which Louis named *Zinjanthropus boisei* (now generally regarded as a species of *Australopithecus*). As a result of this discovery Louis and Mary Leakey embarked on an intensive study of the Gorge that yielded a succession of fossil hominid remains, among them those of a second, more gracile form, promptly named *Homo habilis*. Leakey considered that *Homo habilis* was a tool maker that lived contemporaneously with the robust, noncultural *"Zinjanthropus"* and that the former species represented a hominid on the direct line to modern *Homo sapiens*. Summaries of his particular view and interpretation of human history can be found in several of his books, among them *Adam's Ancestors* and *Unveiling Man's Origins*.

See also AFRICA; FORT TERNAN; OLDUVAI; RUSINGA. [F.S.]

LEAKEY, MARY DOUGLAS (B. 1913)

Kenyan (b. England) archaeologist. Began working with Louis Leakey in East Africa in the mid-1930s. Although she published extensively on a variety of paleontological subjects including fossil primates, she was and is by inclination and training an archaeologist. In this regard it is worth noting that she is the great-great-great granddaughter of John Frere (1740-1807), the pioneer of British archaeology. She was responsible for the systematic archaeological excavation of numerous sites at Olduvai Gorge and in 1959 discovered there the cranium of "Zinjanthropus." After the death of her husband she reinitiated excavations at the Pliocene site of Laetoli and continued to work at Olduvai until 1982. Besides her long-range work on the lithic industries of East Africa she has also conducted major studies of rock art in Zambia.

See also AFRICA; LAETOLI; OLDUVAI. [F.S.]

LEGETET see KORU

LEHM see GLACIATION; PLEISTOCENE

LEHNER see PALEOINDIAN

LEMUR see LEMURIDAE

LEMURIDAE

Family of Lemuriformes that includes the genera *Lemur*, *Varecia*, and *Hapalemur*. The two former genera are closely related and fall into the subfamily Lemurinae; *Hapalemur*, a more distant relative, occupies its own subfamily, Hapalemurinae. The entire family is unique to the large island of Madagascar, off the southeastern African coast.

Members of genus *Lemur*, the "true lemurs," are for the most part arboreal quadrupeds with a body weight of ca. 3 kg. Six species are recognized within the genus. *Lemur catta*, the ringtailed lemur of the south and southwest of the island, is the only semiterrestrial form, living in multimale groups of ca. 15 members and traveling mainly on the ground over home ranges of ca. 5-20 hectares. The diet is primarily of fruit. Coloration is similar in both sexes, in contrast to the other species of *Lemur*, among which sexual dichromatism ranges from the subtle to the pronounced.

Lemur mongoz, the mongoose lemur of northwestern Madagascar and the Comoro Islands, usually lives in monogamous pairs in small home ranges. Unlike the other species of its genus (which may, however, be active at night as well as during the day) the mongoose lemur is entirely nocturnal, at least seasonally. *Lemur macaco*, the black lemur of northwestern Madagascar, consists of two contiguous but subtly distinct subspecies, about neither of which a great deal is known. Both appear, however, to live in multimale groups averaging ca. ten individuals. *Lemur coronatus*, in the north of the island, probably lives in groups of similar size and composition but

Three lemurids: *Lemur fulvus mayottensis*, grooming (above); *Hapalemur griseus griseus* (lower left); *Varecia variegata variegata* (lower right).

may spend more time on the ground. *Lemur rubriventer*, of the eastern humid forests, is highly arboreal and probably pair-forming, but is very little known.

The widely distributed species *Lemur fulvus* contains seven subspecies, of which two have been well studied. *L. f. rufus* of western and southwestern Madagascar lives in multimale groups averaging ca. ten individuals; where studied, its home ranges are only of ca. 1 hectare, overlap considerably, and are undefended. Leaves compose the bulk of the diet. *L. f. mayottensis* is an offshoot of *L. f. fulvus* that is confined to the island of Mayotte, the most southerly of the Comoro group. Its diet varies greatly between seasons but overall consists primarily of fruit. These lemurs are seen in fluid, temporary "associations" of an average size of ca. ten individuals; they are opportunistic feeders but are primarily frugivorous at most times of year. Activity is evenly divided between the day and the night, with long rest periods at both times.

The ruffed lemur, *Varecia variegata*, is represented by a red-and-black and a black-and-white subspecies, neither of which has been adequately studied. With a body weight of ca. 4 kg., these primates are agile arboreal quadrupeds that live in the humid forests of eastern Madagascar. It seems likely that they are pair-bonding and primarily frugivorous.

The gentle lemurs, genus *Hapalemur*, occur primarily in eastern Madagascar, with a small isolate on the west coast. The smaller species, *H. griseus*, contains three subspecies of which one, *H. g. griseus*, is found more or less throughout the eastern rain forest and is specialized for feeding on the young shoots of bamboo. Weighing ca. 1 kg., these lemurs are diurnal and crepuscular semierect arboreal quadrupeds and are found in groups averaging about three individuals, although up to six have been observed together. *Hapalemur g. alaotrensis* is slightly larger-bodied and lives only in the reed beds fringing Lake Alaotra in eastern Madagascar. In locomotion combining some of the characteristics of both quadrupeds and vertical clingers, these diurnal and crepuscular lemurs leap between vertical reed stems and are ready swimmers. Their diet is largely if not entirely composed of the leaves and shoots of *Phragmites* reeds, and the buds and pith of papyrus; group sizes seem to vary seasonally. In the drier, seasonal forests of the west-central and northwestern coasts are found two isolates of the little-known and relatively small-bodied *H. g. occidentalis*, which apparently depends on the shoots of bamboo vines for much of its diet, although it has also been observed to eat fruit.

The largest gentle lemur is *Hapalemur simus*, today known only from one locality in the central part of the eastern rain forest but apparently much more widespread formerly; indeed, the species is known in subfossil form from the site of 'Ampasambazimba, in the center-west of the island. Probably diurnal, this lemur lives in small multimale groups and has been observed to feed on bamboo shoots and fruit.

In common with all of the other Malagasy primates members of Lemuridae are severely threatened by hunting and by the destruction of the forests in which they live. All species are officially classified as endangered, and the populations of some, such as *Hapalemur simus*, have probably already fallen below the minimum necessary for long-term survival. A slightly larger close relative of the ruffed lemur is already known from subfossil evidence to have become recently extinct, probably since the arrival of humans on Madagascar.

See also LEMURIFORMES; LEMUROIDEA. [I.T.]

Further Readings

Tattersall, I. (1982) The Primates of Madagascar. New York: Columbia University Press.

LEMURIFORMES

Infraorder of Primates that contains the "lower primates" of Madagascar, Africa, and Asia. These include the lemurs of Madagascar (families Lemuridae, Megaladapidae, Cheirogaleidae, Indriidae, Daubentoniidae, Archaeolemuridae, and Palaeopropithecidae, the last two extinct), the bushbabies of Africa (family Galagidae), and the lorises and pottos of Africa and Asia (family Lorisidae). It is possible that the enigmatic tarsier of insular Southeast Asia will also prove to belong with this group (*see* STREPSIRHINI), but discussion here is limited to the other taxa mentioned. These are classified into three superfamilies: Lemuroidea (Lemuridae), Indrioidea (Indriidae, Archaeolemuridae, Palaeopropithecidae, Megaladapidae, and Daubentoniidae), and Lorisoidea (Lorisidae, Galagidae, and Cheirogaleidae).

The accompanying cladogram shows a recently proposed scheme of relationships among all living genera of Lemuriformes. In testimony of their common ancestry all members of this group possess in common two striking attributes: a dental comb and a "toilet" claw. The dental comb, or "tooth scraper," is formed by the "procumbent" front teeth of the lower jaw. Elongated and closely approximated to each other, these teeth lie horizontally forward and are used both in grooming of the fur, an important individual and social activity, and in feeding. The tooth comb is particularly elongate in species that use it for gouging resins from the bark of trees, but although there has been much discussion about which function, grooming or dietary, is the primary one for

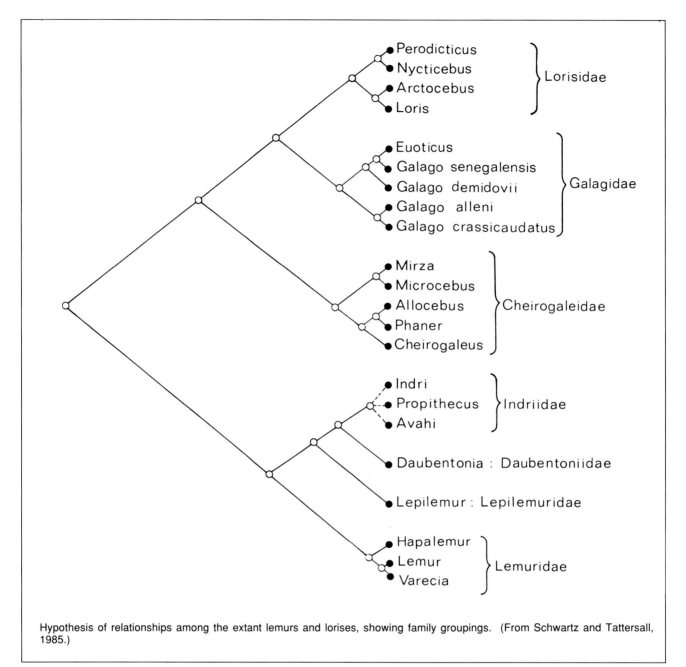

Hypothesis of relationships among the extant lemurs and lorises, showing family groupings. (From Schwartz and Tattersall, 1985.)

which this specialized structure evolved there has been no clear resolution of the question. In the indrioids (except for *Daubentonia*, in which a single pair of continuously growing front teeth is found in each jaw), only two pairs of teeth, usually identified as the central and lateral incisors but alternatively interpreted as one pair of canines and one of incisors, are present in the tooth comb; in almost all other lemuriforms six teeth are represented, two incisors and a canine bilaterally.

Like all other extant primates the lemuriforms possess flat nails in place of claws. These back sensitive pads on the ends of all the digits, with one exception: the second digit of the foot terminates in a

"toilet" (or "grooming") claw. This structure is not found elsewhere among primates, although the callitrichines are secondarily clawed on all digits except the hallux, and among the lemuriforms *Daubentonia* shows very compressed and clawlike nails on the same digits. The replacement of claws by nails among primates reflects an increasing reliance on grasping (and hence potentially manipulative) hands and feet and the related enhancement of tactile sensitivity in these organs. Lemuriforms, however, use "whole-hand prehension" when manipulating objects, in contrast to the more precise forms of prehension characteristic of most "higher" primates.

The balance between the senses of vision and

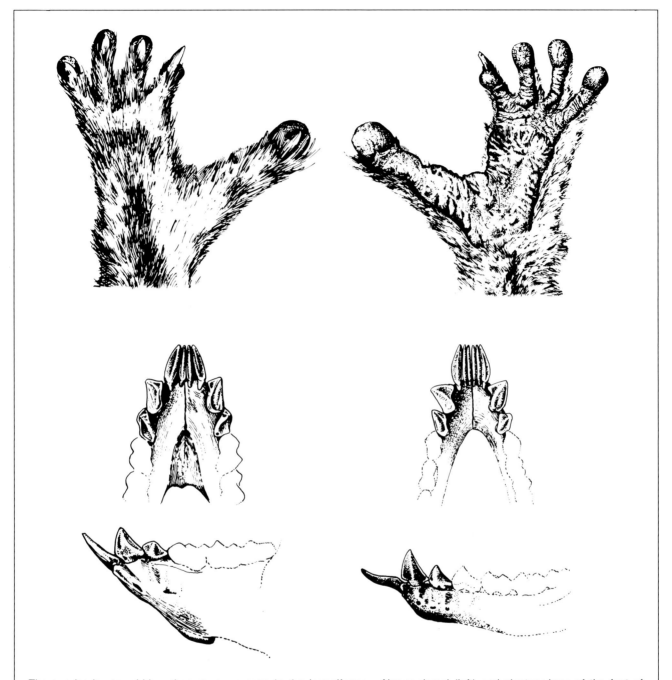

The two basic strepsirhine characters, as seen in the lemuriforms. Above: dorsal (left) and plantar views of the foot of *Propithecus verreauxi*, showing the toilet claw. Middle and bottom: occlusal and lateral views of the dental scraper/combs of *Propithecus verreauxi* (left) and *Lemur fulvus*.

smell is less heavily tilted in favor of vision among lemuriforms than it is among the "higher" primates. Olfactory marking, and thus communication via smell, is of considerable importance to most lemuriforms, while color vision is less developed than in monkeys and apes in the diurnal forms and is understandably absent in most of the nocturnal ones. The visual fields of the left and right eyes of lemuriforms overlap sufficiently to provide a good field of stereo-

scopic vision; but although the orbits are completely ringed by bone they are not completely walled off in the rear as they are in other extant primates. Compared with body size, the brains of lemuriforms tend to be smaller than those of other primates, so that in the lemuriform skull the largest component tends to be the facial skeleton, which houses an elaborate olfactory apparatus, rather than the braincase. In nearly all lemuriforms the middle-ear cavity is housed in a protruding and inflated "bulla" rather than within the structure of the skull base as in ourselves and our closer relatives, and the eardrum is located at the external surface of the skull rather than at the end of a bony tube. In the brain itself lemuriforms tend to show less enlargement than do anthropoids of the "association areas," the structures devoted to the integration of sensory inputs.

In body plan and in locomotion the lemuriforms show great variety, although virtually all living forms are arboreal. Quadrupedalism takes many forms, from the deliberate "slow-climbing" of the lorisids, apparently related to manual predation, through the "scrambling" of the smaller cheirogaleids, to the agile bounding and leaping of the lemurids. Many lemuriforms, including the indriids, the galagids, and *Lepilemur*, the surviving megaladapid, prefer to hold their trunks erect and to leap between vertical supports, landing on as well as pushing off with their elongated hindlimbs. These forms also tend to use more suspensory behaviors when foraging in the trees. Most lemuriforms subsist primarily on leaves, fruits, and/or flowers; insects form a large part of the diet of some of the smaller lorisoids, in particular, while other members of this group feed heavily on resins, at least seasonally.

Behaviorally the lemuriforms have often been considered rather stereotyped. Recent studies, however, have shown that among the lemuriforms can be found almost the entire variety of types of social organization known among primates: male ranges overlapping those of more than one female; monogamous pairs with immature offspring; small groupings with a few adults of each sex, plus immature offspring; larger multimale-multifemale groupings with numerous immature offspring at various stages of development; even fluid and constantly reforming associations of individuals. Types of social organization are not grouped along systematic lines, however. Within-group social behaviors appear to be generally less complex among lemuriforms than are those exhibited among, say, Old World monkeys; but this kind of thing is hard to pin down precisely, and a recent study has concluded that there is no quantum distinction between "lower" and "higher" primates in problem solving.

The primates of Madagascar are often referred to collectively as the "lemurs" and have generally been considered as descended from a single ancestor isolated on the island for many millions of years. This is not the case, however; the cheirogaleid lemurs are more closely related to the mainland lorisoids than to the other Malagasy forms. The term "lemur," then, means simply "Malagasy primate" and has no strict systematic significance.

See also ARCHAEOLEMURIDAE; CHEIROGALEIDAE; DAUBENTONIIDAE; GALAGIDAE; INDRIIDAE; INDRIOIDEA; LEMURIDAE; LEMUROIDEA; LORISIDAE; LORISOIDEA; LOWER PRIMATES; MEGALADAPIDAE; PALAEOPROPITHECIDAE; PRIMATES; PROSIMIAN; STREPSIRHINI. [I.T.]

Further Readings

Doyle, G.A., and Martin, R.D., eds. (1979) The Study of Prosimian Behavior. New York: Academic.

Napier, J.R., and Napier, P.H. (1986) The Natural History of the Primates. Cambridge, Mass.: MIT Press.

Schwartz, J.H., and Tattersall, I. (1985) Evolutionary relationships of living lemurs and lorises (Mammalia, Primates) and their potential affinities with European Eocene Adapidae. Anthropol. Pap. Am. Mus. Nat. Hist. 60:1–100.

Tattersall, I. (1982) The Primates of Madagascar. New York: Columbia University Press.

LEMUROIDEA

Superfamily of Lemuriformes that contains the family Lemuridae. All of the lemuroids occur uniquely on the large island of Madagascar, ca. 450 km. off the southeastern African coast. Lemuridae includes the three extant genera *Lemur, Varecia,* and *Hapalemur. Lemur* and *Varecia* are classified together in the subfamily Lemurinae, while *Hapalemur* is placed in the separate subfamily Hapalemurinae. Genus *Lemur*, the "true" lemurs, consists of six species, of which one, *Lemur fulvus*, contains seven subspecies and another, *L. macaco*, contains two. *Varecia variegata*, the ruffed lemur, also has two subspecies. *Hapalemur*, the gentle lemur, includes the two species *H. griseus* and *H. simus*; the former contains three distinct subspecies.

See also LEMURIDAE; LEMURIFORMES. [I.T.]

LEONTOPITHECUS   *see*   CALLITRICHINAE

LEPILEMUR   *see*   MEGALADAPIDAE

LEPTADAPIS   *see*   ADAPIDAE

LEPTOLITHIC   *see*   UPPER PALEOLITHIC

LEROI-GOURHAN, ANDRÉ (1911–1986)

French prehistorian, a noted investigator who pioneered both the systematic study of Paleolithic cave art and sophisticated data-recovery and recording techniques in the excavation of Upper Paleolithic sites. His work at Arcy-sur-Cure and Pincevent elicited a great deal of paleoethnological information about human behavior during the Paleolithic.

See also PALEOLITHIC IMAGE. [O.S.]

L'ESCALE

Cave in the Durance Valley of southeastern France (also known as St. Estève Janson), with mid-middle Pleistocene ("Upper Biharian") fauna. The absence of *Equus stenonis* and *Elephas meridionalis* suggests a probable age of ca. 0.6–0.4 m.y. Although no archaeological industry was recovered, a thick ash layer was originally interpreted as the earliest evidence of anthropogenic fire in Europe but could well represent remains of naturally caused fires.

See also Europe; Fire. [A.S.B.]

LES TROIS FRÈRES *see* PALEOLITHIC IMAGE

LEVALLOIS

Prepared-core technology named after a suburb of Paris where flakes and cores of this type were first recovered and defined. Levallois technology is most characteristic of Middle Paleolithic industries but begins to appear before 200,000 B.P., in some cases in association with Early Paleolithic industries.

Levallois cores were carefully preshaped, or "prepared," for the striking of flakes of a controlled shape and thickness. Centrally directed removals were generally used to create a square, ovoid, or other regularly shaped block of stone, which was more or less flat on the upper surface and markedly convex on the lower surface (planoconvex). A striking platform, at an acute angle to the upper or flatter surface, was prepared at one end of the core by roughening or faceting. The Levallois flake was then removed by bringing the striking platform down sharply at an angle on an anvil. The large flake that often resulted was extremely thin for its size, conformed closely to the outline of the prepared core, and retained the pattern of centrally directed removals on its upper surface as well as the facets of the striking platform.

Although not all of these features characterize every Levallois flake or core, the distinctive thinness of Levallois flakes, together with their regular shape, are evidence for the use of the technology in a particular assemblage. Industries made on Levallois flakes are often characterized by a lesser amount of secondary retouch than contemporaneous non-Levallois industries, as in the case of Ferrassie Mousterian (Levallois) as opposed to Quina Mousterian (non-Levallois) assemblages. Levallois "points" are pointed forms created entirely by preshaping on the core, with no secondary retouch.

Levallois technology produces large numbers of trimming flakes but relatively few Levallois flakes per core; it is used to flake both flint and coarser rocks, such as quartzite. It is particularly common in the Mousterian of the Near East and North Africa. The Victoria West, a related technology that results in an elongated core, preshaped for striking repeated flakes from one end, is found in the final Early Stone Age of southern Africa.

Prepared-core technology like the Levallois is thought to have been an important development in human cultural evolution, both because the mental imagery needed to preshape a flake on the core required considerable cognitive ability and because it presaged the invention of blade technology. Indeed, Levalloiso-Mousterian industries often contain a substantial number of flake-blades struck from Levallois cores.

See also Blade; Core; Early Paleolithic; Early Stone Age; Flake; Middle Paleolithic; Mousterian; Prepared-Core; Stone-Tool Making. [A.S.B.]

Further Readings

Bordaz, J. (1970) Tools of the Old and New Stone Age. New York: Natural History Press.

LEVALLOIS MOUSTERIAN *see* MOUSTERIAN

LEVANT *see* NEAR EAST

LEVEL *see* STRATIGRAPHY

LIAONING *see* JINNIU SHAN

LIBYPITHECUS *see* COLOBINAE

LIMNOPITHECUS *see* PLIOPITHECIDAE

LINDENMEIER *see* PALEOINDIAN

LINEAGE *see* CLADISTICS

LINNAEUS, C. *see* CLASSIFICATION; EVOLUTION

LITHIC USE-WEAR

Modification of stone tools caused by their utilization. The adaptive role of stone tools is one of the most important questions in the study of human evolution, and for over a century prehistorians have attempted the difficult task of trying to infer the function of Paleolithic artifacts. Early attempts tended to be based on simplistic morphological comparisons with ethnographic materials of known function or on "common sense": that is, asking the question, based on intuition, of what a likely activity was for a given artifact type. Contextual evidence, such as a Paleoindian Folsom point found between the ribs of an extinct form of bison, can also yield critical functional information, although dramatic evidence of this sort is relatively rare in the Stone Age record. Experimental archaeology is useful in showing the feasibility of whether a certain artifact form can in fact be used in a prescribed way, as well as the relative suitability of a particular tool for different tasks or of different tools for a given function.

At our present state of knowledge, however, the most reliable indications of stone-tool use are from use-wear studies—the examination of modification of stone-artifact surfaces that may indicate the activity for which they were used. These studies have their roots in the late nineteenth century, such as the observation that Neolithic flint sickle blades tended to have a bright, glossy appearance along their edge ("corn/sickle/silica gloss") that could be replicated experimentally by cutting cereal grasses with hafted versions of similar artifacts.

The major pioneer in use-wear studies in this century was the Russian prehistorian Sergei Semenov, whose landmark *Prehistoric Technology* laid the foundation for most subsequent research. Semenov stressed the microscopic examination of prehistoric stone artifacts for traces of use-wear and proposed a number of types of modification still deemed important by researchers today: *edge damage* (breaking or chipping of an artifact edge); *polish* (modification of the surface of a stone artifact); and *striations* or *scratches* on an artifact.

Three major schools of use-wear study have developed since Semenov's publication, although none of them is incompatible with the others and some researchers have combined elements of all three in recent years. All of them use experimentation to discern patterns of wear from known functional activities and then apply these observations to prehistoric materials.

Low-power optical microscopy: Using low-power magnification (normally less than 100X), and concentrating on edge damage, this approach is exemplified by the work of Tringham and colleagues and of Odell. It appears to be especially useful in separating major wear categories, such as damage produced by cutting relatively soft materials versus scraping relatively harder materials.

High-power optical microscopy: Using a higher powered, bright field magnification (usually 100–500X),

and concentrating on polish as well as edge damage, this approach is exemplified by the work of Keeley, Moss, and Vaughan. It attempts to make fine distinctions among wear patterns produced by diverse functions (e.g. slicing, scraping, or sawing) and also to specify the particular type of material to which a tool was applied (e.g. wood, soft plant, meat, bone, fresh hide, dry hide, antler). The principal criteria used in this technique are polish (a combination of brightness, luster, and texture), striations, pitting, and edge damage. At present this technique is primarily restricted to fine-grained siliceous materials, such as flint, chert, and chalcedony, of an unweathered and unabraded nature, in which optical polishes develop through tool use. Pieces must also be carefully cleaned to remove any adhering surface material.

Scanning electron microscopy: Using much higher magnifications, researchers can examine topographic features of stone for surface modification or inclusions. This approach is exemplified by the research of Anderson.

Close-up view (x 100) of working edge of chert flake fragment from Koobi Fora, Kenya (ca. 1.5 m.y. old) showing polish caused by use on soft plant materials. (Courtesy of L. Keeley.)

At present an approach that incorporates both low-powered and high-powered optical microscopy appears to be the most reliable, as it maximizes the amount of information regarding damage or alteration incurred during stone-tool use. Expertise in microwear analysis is to a large extent a function of experience in analyzing experimental and prehistoric specimens. Since functional interpretations are subjective, and criteria difficult to quantify, there are potential problems in assessing the reliability of an individual researcher's conclusions. To demonstrate proficiency a set of blind tests using experimental, or ethnographic, materials of known function should be carried out in order to demonstrate the range of reliability of the particular technique and the practitioner. Recent studies by Loy suggest that organic residues on stone artifacts, especially blood residues, are diagnostic of the species that had been butchered with stone tools. Such organic residue studies, once refined, should provide critical evidence of stone-tool function in the future and will greatly augment inferences made from use-wear analysis.

See also PALEOINDIAN; PALEOLITHIC LIFEWAYS; RAW MATERIALS; STONE-TOOL MAKING. [N.T., K.S.]

Further Readings

Anderson, P. (1980) A testimony of prehistoric tasks: diagnostic residues on stone tool working edges. World Archaeol. 12:181-194.

Coles, J. (1973) Archaeology by Experiment. London: Hutchinson.

Hayden, B., ed. (1979) Lithic Use-Wear Analysis. New York: Academic.

Keeley, L.H. (1980) Experimental Determination of Stone Tool Uses: A Microwear Analysis. Chicago: University of Chicago Press.

Loy, T.H. (1983) Prehistoric blood residues: detection on tool surfaces and identification of species of origin. Science 220:1269-1270.

Moss, E. (1983) The Functional Analysis of Flint Implements—Pincevent and Pont d'Ambon: Two Case Studies from the French Final Paleolithic. Oxford: British Archaeological Reports.

Odell, G. (1979) A new improved system for the retrieval of functional information from microscopic observation of chipped stone tools. In B. Hayden (ed.): Lithic Use-Wear Analysis. New York: Academic, pp. 239-244.

Semenov, S. (1964) Prehistoric Technology. Bath: Adams and Dart.

Tringham, R., Cooper, G., Odell, G., and Voytek, B. (1974) Experimentation in the formation of edge damage: a new approach to lithic analysis. J. Field Archaeol. 1:171-196.

Vaughan, P.C. (1985) Use-Wear Analysis of Flaked Stone Tools. Tucson: University of Arizona Press.

LITHICS *see* RAW MATERIALS; STONE-TOOL MAKING

LIUCHENG

Chinese fossil locality of latest Pliocene–early Pleistocene, ca. 2 m.y. based on faunal correlation. This cave (Juyuandong) in Guangxi has yielded three *Gigantopithecus* mandibles, together with over 1,000 isolated teeth of *Gigantopithecus* and the remains of several other mammalian taxa. The Liucheng fauna is the unofficial type site for the "*Gigantopithecus* Fauna," which is thought to present a more archaic aspect than the "*Stegodon-Ailuropoda* Fauna" of southern China. In fact these two faunas are distinguished largely on the basis of the size of a few taxa.

See also GIGANTOPITHECUS; STEGODON-AILUROPODA FAUNA. [G.G.P.]

Further Readings

Pei, W.C. (1957) Discovery of *Gigantopithecus* mandibles and other materials in Liucheng of central Kwangsi in south China. Vert. Palasiatica 1:65-72.

LLANO COMPLEX

Clovis-period (ca. 12,000-11,000 B.P.) material culture centered on the High Plains of New Mexico, best known from the Blackwater Draw site. The assemblage is characterized by lanceolate, bifacially flaked projectile points, thinned by one or more fluting flakes. These points likewise exhibit basal and end grinding. Burins, scrapers, knives, and gravers accompany the stone (and occasional bone) points in the Llano assemblage. The name derives from the *Llano Estacado* (Texas and New Mexico), where the Clovis type site is located.

See also AMERICAS; CLOVIS; PALEOINDIAN. [L.S.A.P., D.H.T.]

LOCOMOTION

Animals are distinguished by their ability to move around in search of food, mates, and shelter. Primates in particular have evolved many types of locomotion in conjunction with their ability to exploit many habitats. Each of these methods is associated with anatomical specializations of the skeleton and musculature. The locomotor habits of most primates can be divided into five categories.

The most common type of primate locomotion is *arboreal quadrupedalism*, walking and running along branches. This is the most generalized type of locomotion among mammals and is probably the way in which the earliest primates moved. Most other locomotor specializations have evolved from this type of movement. The skeletal proportions of arboreal quadrupeds and many aspects of their musculature and limb joints indicate that the greatest mechanical difficulties presented by this type of locomotion are maintaining balance upon the irregular, unstable supports provided by tree branches. Thus arboreal quadrupeds are characterized by grasping hands and feet. Their forelimbs and hindlimbs are similar in length and relatively short so that their center of gravity is close to the branch for stability, and many have a long tail for balance.

A few primates regularly walk and run across the ground, a type of locomotion that is called *terrestrial quadrupedalism*. Like arboreal quadrupeds these species have forelimbs and hindlimbs that are similar in length. Because the ground is flat and stable, however, balance is less of a problem for them. Thus they

Arboreal   Quadruped

Terrestrial   Quadruped

Leaper

Knuckle   Walker

Climber

Biped

Representatives of various primate locomotion categories. Skeletons of similar forms are illustrated in the article SKELETON.

have shorter fingers and toes and longer limbs. Many also have short tails.

The African apes use a special type of quadrupedal locomotion called *knuckle-walking*, in which they rest their hands on the knuckles of the third and fourth digits rather than on their palms or the tips of their fingers. This special hand posture enables them to walk quadrupedally on the ground using the long curved fingers they also need for climbing.

Many primates move by leaping to cross gaps between trees. In leaping, the propulsive forces come almost totally from the hindlimbs and back. Leaping primates have long hindlimbs, a relatively long, flexible back, and often a long tail. In many small primates the ankle region is also elongated to aid in leaping.

Larger primates often move by *suspensory locomotion*, such as swinging by their arms (*brachiation*) or climbing. In this type of locomotion they usually hang below arboreal supports, and their limbs seem to function primarily in tension rather than compression. Suspensory locomotion enables a large species to spread its body mass over many slender supports and thus to forage in parts of a forest that it might not otherwise be able to reach. Suspensory primates are often characterized by long hindlimbs, very long forelimbs, and joints that permit a wide range of motion in many directions. They also have long hands and feet for grasping arboreal supports. They usually have a short, stiff backbone, and many have lost their tail.

The bipedalism that characterizes humans is one of the most unusual forms of locomotion that has evolved in the entire animal kingdom. The mechanical problems of balancing and moving our body atop two limbs have led to many of the distinctive anatomical specializations of our species. Our hindlimbs are long to provide a long stride. The human foot lacks the grasping abilities found in the feet of other primates and instead is a stiff propulsive lever with a long heel, short toes, and a hallux (great toe) aligned with the other digits.

During part of each stride in bipedal progression our entire body weight is balanced over a single limb as the opposite limb swings forward for the next step. We have evolved many structural features to deal with this precarious situation. The human ilium (the largest bone in the pelvis) is short and broad to provide a large base for the attachment of the hip muscles that keep the trunk balanced over the lower limb. Humans are naturally knock-kneed, so that the lower part of our hindlimb is lined up close to the center of body mass. In addition the curvature of our back helps keep the center of gravity lower for balance.

The first hints of human bipedalism appear in the fossil record over 4 m.y. ago, but many of the more subtle anatomical features we associate with this form of locomotion apparently came much later. There is considerable debate over the ecological factors that predisposed human ancestors to become bipeds. Early theorists linked the evolution of bipedalism with the evolution of stone tools. This theory, however, seems to be contradicted by the paleontological record showing bipedal hominids well before the first stone artifacts. Some have argued that the selective advantage of bipedalism lay more generally in the freeing of the hands for transporting food or water from distant foraging sites in order to provision offspring or other family members. Others have linked the evolution of bipedalism with foraging in an open woodland environment in which food resources were widely scattered and required long-distance travel over flat terrain.

Although it is not possible to reconstruct the ecological conditions surrounding the origin of human bipedalism, the paleontological record clearly indicates that this locomotor adaptation was probably the first adaptive breakthrough that characterized the origin of hominids. The ability to walk on two legs preceded the later hallmarks of human evolution, such as the manufacture of tools and enlargement of the brain.

See also **HOMINIDAE; SKELETON.** [J.G.F.]

Further Readings

Jenkins, F.A., Jr. (1974) Primate Locomotion. New York: Academic.

Jolly, A. (1985) The Evolution of Primate Behavior, 2nd ed. New York: Macmillan.

Jungers, W.L. (1985) Size and Scaling in Primate Biology. New York: Plenum.

Lovejoy, C.O. (1981) The origin of man. Science 211:341–350.

LOESS *see* GLACIATION; PLEISTOCENE

LOPHOCEBUS *see* CERCOPITHECINAE

LORIS *see* LORISIDAE

LORISIDAE

Family of lower primates that includes both fossil and extant taxa. The extant lorisids are distributed throughout sub-Saharan Africa (*Perodicticus* and *Arctocebus*) and Asia (*Loris* in Sri Lanka and *Nycticebus* in southern China and the large islands of the Southeast Asian archipelago.) All extant lorisids are nocturnal and essentially proteinivorous and are characterized by their extremely slow, cautious locomotion. To enhance the range of sizes of branches they can grasp with their hands lorisids develop rudimentary second digits (one of the features that typifies the group), thereby permitting prehension between the first and third digits. There is also evidence that, in order to sustain the metabolic demands of maintaining muscular contraction while locomoting as slowly but as continually as they do, lorisids have developed a collateral vascular supply to the limbs that aids in the elimination of accumulating lactic acid.

As a group extant lorisids are also characterized by such features as lack of a tail; expansion of the angular or gonial region of the mandible; marked frontation of the bony orbits, whose margins are elevated or "lipped"; in the auditory region a stout but short lateral tubular extension of the ectotympanic; and compression dorsoventrally of the distal femur. In their teeth lorisids are distinguished by having lower premolars that are expanded lingually; but more striking is the configuration of the lower molars, which appear "pinched" into two components due to the centrally emplaced cristid obliqua, which isolates the protoconid and creates a deep hypoflexid notch.

Lorisids can also be described as differing from lemuroids and indrioids in aspects of the arterial circulation of the auditory region. Lorisids lack one of the branches within the auditory bulla of the internal carotid artery (the stapedial), thus retaining the promontory artery as the major internal artery, but they develop another artery, the ascending pharyngeal ("anterior carotid"), which branches off the internal carotid artery and courses medially around the bulla to anastomose or network with the promontory artery. These two features are indeed striking, but they are not unique to lorisids. Cheirogaleids (mouse and dwarf lemurs) and galagids (bushbabies) also develop an ascending pharyngeal artery—and this is one of the major characteristics that points to the close relationship of these two groups with lorisids. With regard to the lack of a stapedial artery, this feature is noted in some cheirogaleids, but it is more consistent in galagids and along with a suite of dental features serves to join the latter group closely with the lorisids. Lorisids and galagids are also distinguished in their bony auditory region: the tympanic ring fuses in its entirety to the edge of the auditory bulla. Given the apparent relatedness of lorisids to galagids and, more broadly, to cheirogaleids, we might suggest that the last common ancestor of the extant lorisids had undergone secondary reduction of the calcaneus and navicular bones, which are otherwise typically more elongate in the other two groups of lorisoids.

Among the extant lorisids close relationships are not between biogeographic neighbors. Rather, as G.G. Simpson and later J.H. Schwartz and I. Tattersall

The two African lorisids. *Arctocebus calabarensis*, the angwantibo (left), and *Perodicticus potto*, the potto (right).

pointed out, it appears that the Asian *Loris* is most closely related to the African *Arctocebus*, while the Asian *Nycticebus* is most closely allied with the African *Perodicticus*. The former sister group is united, for example, by the development of an anterior prolongation of the premaxilla (into a little "snout") and such dental features as a large submolariform posterior upper premolar that bears a small hypocone, an anteriorly placed upper canine that is transversely rotated, buccal cingulids on the lower molars, and a large M³. *Nycticebus* and *Perodicticus* both possess a distinctive, "puffy" anterior maxillary region (created in part by the large root of the upper canine swelling out the bone of the maxilla) as well as relatively lower and broader upper and lower cheek-tooth cusps, which become so inflated (in fact "puffy") in *Perodicticus* that shearing crests and tooth basins are virtually obliterated. *Perodicticus* and *Nycticebus* are also the two extant strepsirhines with the most robust (and thus least slender and elongate) tooth combs, which are also the least procumbent of strepsirhine tooth combs. These two primates are further distinguished among lorisoids in general by their possession of very stout and enlarged upper central incisors. In *Nycticebus* emphasis on these teeth is evidenced in some individuals by the diminution of the lateral incisors to very slender structures and, in others, to the loss entirely of the lateral incisors.

Fossils whose affinities appear to lie with extant lorisids include *Mioeuoticus*, from the Miocene of East Africa, and *Nycticeboides*, from the Miocene of the Siwaliks of Indopakistan. *Mioeuoticus* is broadly related to *Arctocebus* and *Loris*, whereas *Nycticeboides* appears to be closely related to *Nycticebus*. A third possible fossil lorisid is *Indraloris*, from the Miocene of Indopakistan, which, although classified by some paleontologists as an adapidlike sivaladapid, shares with *Loris* specific and seemingly phylogenetically significant details of M₁ morphology, including a well-developed protostylid.

See also CHEIROGALEIDAE; GALAGIDAE; LORISOIDEA; SIVALADAPIDAE; STREPSIRHINI. [J.H.S.]

Further Readings

Martin, R.D., Doyle, G.A., and Walker, A.C., eds. (1974) Prosimian Biology. London: Duckworth.

Napier, J.R., and Napier, P. (1967) A Handbook of Living Primates, 3rd ed. London: Academic.

Schwartz, J.H. (1986) Primate systematics and a classification of the order. In D.R. Swindler (ed.): Comparative Primate Biology, Vol. I: Systematics, Evolution and Anatomy. New York: Liss, pp. 1–41.

Schwartz, J.H., and Tattersall, I. (1986) Evolutionary relationships of living lemurs and lorises (Mammalia, Primates) and their potential affinities with European Eocene Adapidae. Anthropol. Pap. Am. Mus. Nat. Hist. 60:1–100.

Simpson, G.G. (1967) The Tertiary lorisiform primates of Africa. Bull. Mus. Comp. Zool. 136:39–62.

LORISOIDEA

In this volume this superfamily is included with the primates of Madagascar in the strepsirhine infraorder Lemuriformes rather than in its own infraorder, Lorisiformes, as has been common practice over the past decades. While Lorisoidea here contains the expected groups of lorises (family Lorisidae) and bushbabies (family Galagidae), it also subsumes the mouse and dwarf lemurs of Madagascar (family Cheirogaleidae), which have traditionally been classified and thought of as closely related to the other, larger primates of that island. Biogeography, however, does not phylogenetic relationships make, and thus features of the hard- and soft-tissue anatomy of the auditory region and details of dental morphology present compelling reasons for associating the cheirogaleids with lorisids and galagids. Within Lorisoidea the lorisids and galagids are the most closely related.

Fossils from Miocene deposits of East Africa and Indopakistan are readily noted as having affinities with various lorisoids (*Komba* and *Progalago* with galagids and *Mioeuoticus*, *Nycticeboides*, and *Indraloris* with lorisids), but J.H. Schwartz and I. Tattersall have recently suggested that certain Eocene taxa may also be related to lorisoids, either broadly (*Fendantia*, *Anchomomys*, *Periconodon*) or specifically (*Huerzeleris* with cheirogaleids and *Chasselasia* with galagids). Schwartz has even offered evidence that fossil "tarsioids" in general may be the sister group of Lorisoidea and that *Tarsius* is the primitive sister of this large clade.

See also CHEIROGALEIDAE; GALAGIDAE; LORISIDAE; OMOMYIDAE; SIVALADAPIDAE; STREPSIRHINI; TARSIIFORMES. [J.H.S.]

Further Readings

Schwartz, J.H. (1986) Primate systematics and a classification of the order. In D.R. Swindler (ed.): Comparative Primate Biology, Vol. I: Systematics, Evolution and Anatomy. New York: Liss, pp. 1–41.

LOSODOK *see* MURUAROT

LOTHAGAM

Northern Kenyan stratified sequence of late Miocene to middle Pliocene age by K-Ar dating of underlying basalt and by faunal correlation. Discovered in the late 1960s by a team led by B. Patterson of Harvard University, the site lies southwest of Lake Turkana. Sediments exposed here yielded a rich and diverse, 6–5 m.y.-old vertebrate assemblage from a succession of levels, including an adult hominoid mandible fragment with first molar from the lower levels. This specimen displays several primitive features, and various workers have assigned it to *Ramapithecus, A. africanus, A. afarensis, Australopithecus* sp., and Hominoidea indet. The last attribution seems the most appropriate pending recovery of more substantial material of this age.

[T.D.W.]

LOTHAGAMIAN *see* TIME SCALE

LOVEINA *see* OMOMYINAE

LOWER PALEOLITHIC *see* EARLY PALEOLITHIC; EARLY STONE AGE

LOWER PRIMATES

Prosimian primates, including the lemurs, lorises, galagos, tarsiers, their extinct relatives, and all early primates, as distinguished from the higher, or anthropoid, members of the order. This term originally dates to a *scala naturae* view of evolution, with "lower" evolving into "higher" forms of life. It has come back into use recently as a way of referring to this paraphyletic, or "wastebasket," group. Although tarsiers are widely recognized as the closest living relatives of the anthropoids, and the extinct Plesiadapiformes are not closely related to any specific living primates, many authors prefer to refer to all members of this assemblage as if they were a natural group. The prosimians may be considered "lower" in terms of their lesser relative brain size and other features that separate them from the anthropoids.

See also ADAPIDAE; ANTHROPOIDEA; BRAIN; EUPRIMATES; HAPLORHINI; HIGHER PRIMATES; PRIMATE SOCIETIES; PRIMATES; PROSIMIAN; SCALA NATURAE; STREPSIRHINI; TARSIIDAE.[E.D., I.T.]

LUFENG

Stratified lignite (brown coal) exposures ca. 90 km. northwest of Kunming, Yunnan Province (China), dated to late Miocene between 10 and 8 m.y. by faunal correlation. Biostratigraphic studies suggest that the Lufeng fauna is roughly equivalent to the Nagri fauna of the Siwaliks. The deposits have yielded several partial crania, gnathic and dental remains of hominoids, and some postcranial remains. The specimens have been grouped by some researchers according to size, with the larger hominoids supposedly representing a species of *Sivapithecus* and the smaller representing a species of *Ramapithecus*. Other workers have suggested that the large and small forms may actually represent a single

sexually dimorphic species, as may be the case for the Nagri hominoids. Most recently a new genus *Lufengpithecus* has been proposed for this species.

See also ASIA (EASTERN); CHINA. [G.G.P.]

LUKEINO *see* BARINGO

LUPEMBAN

Central African Middle Paleolithic (Middle Stone Age) industry named for exposures on Lupemba Stream near Tshikapa in Kasai Occidental Province (Zaire) and defined by Breuil on the basis of Levallois or discoidal prepared-core technology, and backed or bifacially worked leaf-shaped points, many small enough to have been arrowheads. Core axes, particularly lanceolate forms, and discoidal cores are significantly smaller and thinner than in the Sangoan industry. The Upper Lupemban is further distinguished by occasional tanged points and by finer lanceolate and leaf-shaped points, similar to the younger Tshitolian. Usually assumed to be a woodworking industry associated with densely wooded areas, the Lupemban also occurs in a small-tool facies at Mwanganda's Village (Malawi) and at Peperkorrel (Namibia) in association with evidence of more open environments. The probable age is early late Pleistocene, with some Zairian sites falling within the range of radiocarbon dating.

See also MIDDLE STONE AGE; SANGOAN; STONE-TOOL MAKING; TSHITOLIAN. [A.S.B.]

LUSHIUS

The type specimen of this genus, from the late Eocene of China, is a right maxillary fragment that retains the last premolar and M^1. It was described in 1961 by M.-C. Chow, who suggested that its affinities might lie with tarsioid primates. F.S. Szalay and E. Delson, however, thought that this cat-sized primate possessed more of a primitive adapid "Gestalt" in its dental morphology. Most recently J.H. Schwartz argued that a comparison with *Omomys* was the most compelling.

See also OMOMYIDAE. [J.H.S.]

Further Readings

Schwartz, J.H. (1986) Primate systematics and a classification of the order. In D.R. Swindler (ed.): Comparative Primate Biology, Vol. I: Systematics, Evolution and Anatomy. New York: Liss, pp. 1–41.

Szalay, F.S., and Delson, E. (1979) Evolutionary History of the Primates. New York: Academic.

LUTETIAN *see* EOCENE; TIME SCALE

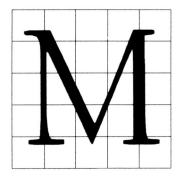

MABOKO

Middle Miocene site in western Kenya, dated to ca. 15 m.y. by interpolation. Fossil-bearing clays and silts beneath phonolite lava on Maboko (Kiboko) Island and on the nearby mainland at Majiwa Bluff and Kaloma were first excavated by W.E. Owen in the early 1930s. Over 600 primate specimens have been found (mostly by sieving Owen's dumps) in a fauna that overall indicates a radical modernization from the 17-m.y. upper Rusinga (Kulu) fauna. Correlative sites occur not far to the west at Ombo-Mariwa and on the opposite shoulder of the Nyanza Rift at Nyakach near Sondu. Maboko is the type site of the earliest thick-enameled hominoid, *Kenyapithecus africanus*, the oreopithecid *Nyanzapithecus pickfordi*, and the earliest well-documented cercopithecid, *Victoriapithecus macinnesi*.

See also CERCOPITHECOIDEA; FORT TERNAN; KENYA; KENYAPITHECUS. [J.A.V.C.]

Further Readings

Andrews, P.J., Meyer, G.E., Pilbeam, D.R., Van Couvering, J.A., and Van Couvering, J.A.H. (1981) The Miocene fossil beds of Maboko Island, Kenya: geology, age, taphonomy, and palaeontology. J. Hum. Evol. 10:35-48.

Pickford, M. (1982) New higher primate fossils from the middle Miocene deposits at Majiwa and Kaloma, western Kenya. Am. J. Phys. Anthropol. 58:1-19.

MACACA see CERCOPITHECINAE

MACROEVOLUTION see EVOLUTION

MACROTARSIUS see OMOMYINAE

MADAGASCAR

One of the world's largest islands, ca. 1,600 km. long, and lying ca. 450 km. off the southeastern coast of Africa. Madagascar has been approximately at this remove from the African continent for 100 m.y., that is, since well before primates are known to have evolved; thus the primate inhabitants of the island, known as the *lemurs*, as well as any later invaders, must have crossed a substantial water gap to get there. The fact that only such "lower" primates have successfully established themselves on Madagascar may thus say something about their ecological competitiveness, even though the relatives of these animals in Africa and Asia are supposed to have been crowded into nocturnal "refuge" niches by the later-appearing anthropoid primates.

As almost a microcontinent Madagascar offers a wide spectrum of ecological zones, from semidesert to lush rain forest, and it is in this variety of settings that the most diverse surviving fauna of lower (strepsirhine, prosimian) primates has established itself, the ancestral forms having most probably, on present evidence, reached the island at some time during the Eocene. Around 20 species of lemur, many with diverse subspecies, are found on the island today, and before the arrival of humans only ca. 1,500 years ago at least a dozen more species existed, most of them much larger than the largest living lemur, which weighs ca. 5-6 kg. Surviving lemurs are grouped into five families: Lemuridae, Indriidae, Daubentoniidae, Megaladapidae (*Lepilemur*), and Cheirogaleidae; major extinct forms are grouped into Archaeolemuridae, Palaeopropithecidae, Megaladapidae (*Megaladapis*), and, possibly, Indriidae (*Mesopropithecus*). No primate fossil record is known in Madagascar prior to ca. 10–5 k.y. ago.

See also ARCHAEOLEMURIDAE; CHEIROGALEIDAE; DAUBENTONIIDAE; INDRIIDAE; INDRIOIDEA; LEMURIDAE; LEMURIFORMES; LEMUROIDEA; LOWER PRIMATES; MEGALADAPIDAE; PALAEOPROPITHECIDAE; PROSIMIAN; STREPSIRHINI. [I.T.]

MAE THA *see* ASIA (EASTERN)

MAGDALENIAN

Late Upper Paleolithic European industry characterized by an extensive use of unretouched blades as well as increasing production and use of microlithic blades, burins, scrapers, and borers. A distinctive feature of this industry, dated between 17,000 and 11,500 B.P., is fine bone and antler technology including the production of first single- and then double-rowed barbed harpoons and of bone points, awls, needles, polishers, shaft straighteners, and spear throwers. Sites assigned to the Magdalenian have repeatedly yielded numerous remains of figurative engravings on antler, ivory, bone, and slate of both animals and somewhat abstracted female forms. Jewelry and other items of personal adornment are often found at Magdalenian sites and are included in

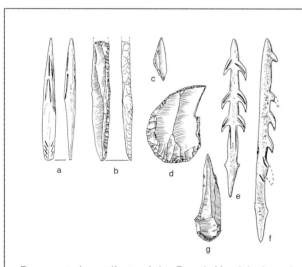

Representative artifacts of the French Magdalenian: a) decorated bone point with beveled base (*sagaie*); b) backed bladelet; c) triangular microlith; d) parrot-beaked burin; e) bone harpoon with two rows of barbs; f) antler harpoon with single row of barbs. The much earlier "Protomagdalenian" industry is placed by some authors at the end of the Upper Perigordian sequence but by others as an antecedent of the Magdalenian: g) end-scraper and double burin. Not to scale.

elaborate burials, such as that found at Duruthy (France). Finally, the most spectacular Upper Paleolithic cave paintings, such as those at Altamira and Lascaux, also date to this period and are associated with this archaeological industry.

This Upper Paleolithic industry is named after discoveries made at the La Madeleine rock shelter at the outskirts of Les Eyzies in southwestern France. Its distribution, however, went far outside this classic Paleolithic region and includes both cave and open-air sites in northern France, Spain, Belgium, Switzerland, Germany, Czechoslovakia, and southern Poland.

See also ALTAMIRA; EUROPE; LASCAUX; PALEOLITHIC IMAGE; UPPER PALEOLITHIC. [O.S.]

Further Readings

Bordes, F. (1968) The Old Stone Age. London: Weidenfeld and Nicolson.

Gamble, C. (1986) The Paleolithic Settlement of Europe. Cambridge: Cambridge University Press.

Wymer, J. (1982) The Palaeolithic Age. New York: St. Martin's.

MAGLEMOSIAN

Hunting and fishing Mesolithic culture of late pre-Boreal and Boreal times, ca. 9500–7700 B.P. on the North European plain from the east Baltic to Britain. Most Maglemosian sites represent summer and fall lakeshore settlements, some with small individual or nuclear family hut-floors, where both hunting of forest species (aurochs, elk, red deer, roe deer) and the consumption of marine or lacustrine resources (fish, shellfish, seals) are reflected in the faunal remains as well as in the artifacts. In addition to a stone industry with chipped-core axes and microliths, such as lunates and backed bladelets, Maglemosian sites have yielded wooden paddles, netweights, nets, floats, canoes, fishhooks, barbed and notched points and harpoons, and even nutshells, due to the excellent organic preservation of wet sites.

See also BOW AND ARROW; ECONOMY, PREHISTORIC; EPIPALEOLITHIC; MESOLITHIC; STAR CARR; STONE-TOOL MAKING. [A.S.B.]

MAGOSIAN

Purported African Paleolithic industry supposedly intermediate between Middle and Late Stone Age at Magosi rock shelter in northeastern Uganda, and by extension to other African industries combining bifacial points, Levallois and discoidal cores, and microliths or backed pieces. Later reinvestigation of the type site showed that the "Magosian" resulted from admixture between an earlier classic Middle Stone Age horizon with bifacial points and Levallois tech-

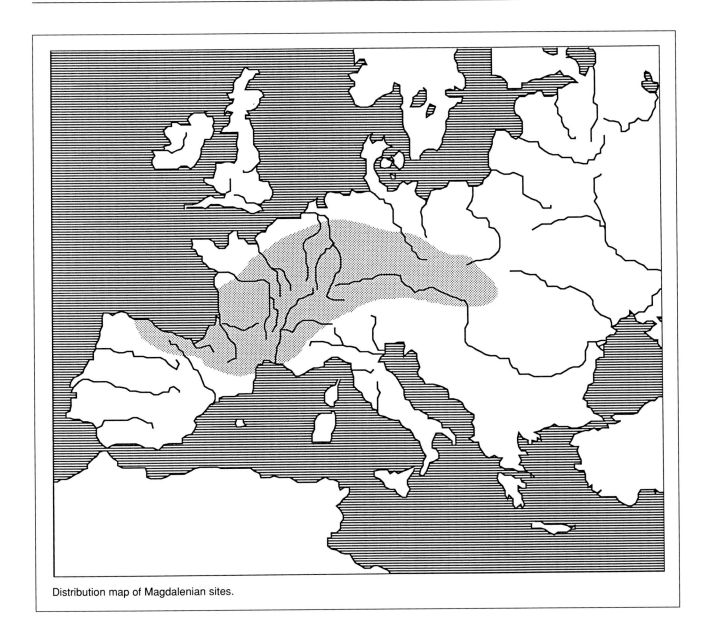

Distribution map of Magdalenian sites.

nology, and a later microlithic horizon associated with a radiocarbon age of ca. 14,000 B.P.

See also LATER STONE AGE; MIDDLE STONE AGE; SECOND INTERMEDIATE. [A.S.B.]

MAHGARITA *see* ADAPIDAE

MAJIWA *see* MABOKO

MAKAPANSGAT

South African stratified cave breccias of late Pliocene age; main fossil level between 3 and 2.6 m.y. by faunal correlation. These extensive deposits are lo-

cated some 16 km. east-northeast of the town of Potgietersrus in the northern Transvaal Province, at 24°12′S and 28°57′E. The largest of the South African early hominid-bearing sites, Makapansgat comprises the remains of a system of karstic solution chambers of ca. 1.5 hectare in extent. The deposits were heavily mined for lime between 1925 and 1935, during which time fossil bones were recovered. The first hominid specimen, discovered by J.W. Kitching in 1947, was described the following year by R.A. Dart, who attributed it to a new species of *Australopithecus, A. prometheus*. Work by Kitching and A.R. Hughes since then has resulted in the recovery of several dozen hominid specimens from the Limeworks rubble dumps. All of the hominid specimens thus far recovered from the site are attributable to the hypodigm of *Australopithecus africanus*.

Five sedimentary (breccia) members have been recognized by Partridge, although the basis for this lithostratigraphic division has been brought into question. All but one of the hominid specimens derives from Member 3 (the "Grey Breccia"). A single

Occlusal view of a partial hominid mandible from Makapansgat. Photograph of cast. (From Tattersall, 1970.)

hominid specimen derives from Member 4. Dart originally interpreted the faunal remains from Makapansgat as comprising the food remains and "osteodontokeratic" artifacts of *Australopithecus*, but these faunal elements are now regarded as carnivore and/or scavenger assemblages. No undisputed artifacts have been recovered from the *Australopithecus*-bearing breccias.

The geochronological age of the site is a matter of dispute, with faunal estimates ranging between ca. 3 and 2.6 m.y. for the hominid-bearing units. Interpretations of the paleomagnetic data for Makapansgat Limeworks should be treated with extreme circumspection in view of the numerous problems associated with the lithostratigraphy of the site.

See also AUSTRALOPITHECUS; AUSTRALOPITHECUS AFRICANUS; BRECCIA CAVE FORMATION; DART, RAYMOND ARTHUR.
[F.E.G.]

Further Readings

Dart, R.A. (1954) The minimal bone-breccia content of Makapansgat and the australopithecine predatory habit. Am. Anthropol. 60:923–931.

Delson, E. (1984) Cercopithecid biochronology of the African Plio-Pleistocene: correlation among eastern and southern hominid-bearing localities. Cour. Forsch. Inst. Senckenberg 69:199–218.

Maguire, J.M. (1985) Recent geological, stratigraphic and palaeontological studies at Makapansgat Limeworks. In P.V. Tobias (ed.): Hominid Evolution. New York: Liss, pp. 151–164.

MALTA

Late Paleolithic open-air site on the banks of the Belaya River, a tributary of the Angara River in Siberia (U.S.S.R.). Archaeological inventories include bone and stone tools and portable art of bone and mammoth ivory, depicting birds and females in a manner distinct from that found in European sites. Features at Malta include remains of 15 stone-slab and bone-curbed dwellings, some of which probably represent summer and others winter occupation. Other features include a child's burial, with ocher, jewelry, and grave goods, and a number of small cache pits. Malta, like the nearby site Buret, dates to ca. 15,000 B.P. Stone-tool inventories from both sites are assigned to the Malta-Buret industry.

See also DYUKTAI. [O.S.]

MAMMAL AGES *see* BIOCHRONOLOGY

MAMMOTH *see* PALEOMAGNETISM

MAMMOTH HUNTING *see* PALEOLITHIC LIFEWAYS

MAN *see* HUMAN

MANDIBLE *see* SKULL

MANDRILLUS *see* CERCOPITHECINAE

MAN-LAND RELATIONSHIPS

Interactions between human groups and their environment, a concept developed by K.W. Butzer. Human adaptations, past and present, are specific cultural solutions to problems of survival posed by the natural and social environments. Thus to understand these adaptations at any point in time, as well as to explain changes observed in cultures through time, one must consider both the man-land relationships (the natural environment and human utilization of that environment) and man-man relationships (social arrangements both among individuals within a group and among different groups). In studying past adaptations in a specific region, prehistoric archaeologists most often begin by considering such variables as climate; the availability, distribution, and predictability of the biotic resources; and the environmental limiting factors that created specific problems for groups in the area. Archaeological data obtained from the sites are then used to understand how people who occupied the area perceived their natural environment and which strategies they chose to use to exploit the available resources.

See also ARCHAEOLOGY. [O.S.]

Further Readings

Butzer, K.W. (1982) Archaeology as Human Ecology. Cambridge: Cambridge University Press.

Jochim, M.A. (1981) Strategies for Survival: Cultural Behavior in an Ecological Context. New York: Academic.

MANUPORT   see   STONE-TOOL MAKING

MARIWA   see   MABOKO

MARTIN, RUDOLF (1862-1925)

German physical anthropologist. Martin's primary research interest was anthropometry, and he was responsible for producing a highly influential manual, *Lehrbuch der Anthropologie* (1914, 1928). This was subsequently updated by K. Saller (in three volumes) between 1956 and 1962.

[F.S.]

MASEK BEDS   see   OLDUVAI

MATOPAN   see   WILTON

MATUPI   see   WILTON

MATUYAMA   see   PALEOMAGNETISM

MAUER

A mandible was discovered accidentally in a sand and gravel pit at Mauer near Heidelberg (West Germany) in 1907. The associated fossil mammals suggest a middle Pleistocene age somewhat later than the Cromerian interglacial but older than the Holsteinian (perhaps 0.5 m.y.). The Mauer jaw is in fact

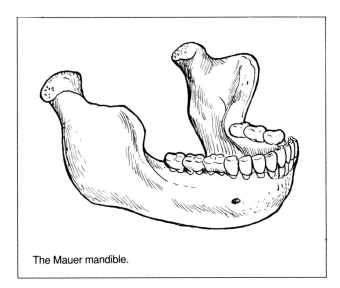

The Mauer mandible.

probably the oldest European fossil hominid yet discovered. Although it has been claimed that stone and bone artifacts have also been found at Mauer, in some cases there is doubt about their age and in other cases doubt about their identification as artifacts. The mandible has a thick body and a very broad ascending ramus. There is no chin development, but the teeth are quite small, leading to the suggestion that this might even represent a female. Although there is no development of the retromolar space found in Neanderthal jaws, the specimen is long, indicating that the associated face was probably projecting. Originally classified as the holotype of a new species, *Homo heidelbergensis*, most workers now regard the jaw as representing a European form of *Homo erectus* or an archaic form of *Homo sapiens* similar to that known from sites like Arago and Petralona.

See also ARCHAIC HOMO SAPIENS; HOMO ERECTUS. [C.B.S.]

MAYR, ERNST (b. 1904)

American (b. Germany) ornithologist and systematist. Mayr was a prominent figure in the movement responsible for the "new evolutionary synthesis" that emerged between 1937 and 1947. Following a stint at the University Museum, Berlin (1926-1931), and the American Museum of Natural History, New York (1932-1946), Mayr moved to Harvard University, where he spent the remainder of his career. Influenced by Dobzhansky's work, Mayr presented his own ideas in a 1940 paper, which led ultimately to the publication in 1942 of his influential book *Systematics and the Origin of Species*.

See also EVOLUTION. [F.S.]

McCOWN, THEODORE D. (1908-1969)

American paleoanthropologist perhaps best remembered for his collaborative work with A. Keith in the mid-1930s on the preparation and description of the fossil hominids from Skhūl and Tabūn in Israel (then Palestine). Their 1939 report raised important questions about the biological affinity of Neanderthals to anatomically modern *Homo sapiens*. McCown later became professor of anthropology at the University of California, Berkeley.

[F.S.]

MCKENNAMORPHUS *see* ANAPTOMORPHINAE

MEADOWCROFT SHELTER

Stratified archaeological site near Avella, in southwestern Pennsylvania, dating back nearly to 20,000 B.P. J. Adovasio and colleagues have documented a sequence of more than 40 radiocarbon dates, in perfect stratigraphic order. The oldest cultural date is slightly over 19,000 B.P.; the oldest stone artifacts appear to date between 15,000 and 14,000 B.P. Evidence for human occupation (in lower stratum IIa) consists of "occupation floors" containing firepits, prismatic blades, biface-thinning flakes, flake knives, two bifaces, a wooden foreshaft, a piece of plaited basketry, and two human bone fragments.

The archaeology of Meadowcroft Shelter leaves many questions unanswered. The stone implements are few, small, and uninformative; they are surprisingly similar to much later artifacts. No diagnostic Early Archaic or Paleoindian artifacts occur. Pleistocene megafauna is likewise absent from stratum IIa, and this is surprising for deposits so old. The temperate character of the vegetation throughout the Meadowcroft stratigraphy (and particularly the presence of hardwood forest macrofossils in stratum IIa) also seems anomalous, since during a part of this time the ice front was less than 75 km. to the north. There is no stratigraphic unconformity to match the gaps in the radiocarbon dates in stratum IIa. These difficulties notwithstanding, Meadowcroft Shelter remains the only site providing solid support for human occupation of North America prior to 12,000 B.P.

See also AMERICAS; CLOVIS; FOLSOM; PALEOINDIAN.

[D.H.T.]

Further Readings

Adovasio, J.M., and Carlisle, R.C. (1986) The first Americans. Nat. Hist. 95:20–27.

Adovasio, J.M., Gunn, J.D., Donahue, J., and Stuckenrath, R. (1978) Meadowcroft Rockshelter, 1977: an overview. Am. Antiquity 43:632–651.

Dincauze, D.F. (1981) The Meadowcroft papers. Quart. Rev. Archaeol. 2:3–4.

Lepilemur mustelinus, the surviving megaladapid.

MEGALADAPIDAE

Family of Indriiformes that contains the extant weasel or sportive lemurs, genus *Lepilemur*, and the extinct genus *Megaladapis*. The latter is a highly specialized form, but both genera share several distinctive features of the dentition, including the lack of upper permanent incisor teeth and certain characteristics of the lower molars.

Lepilemur is a genus of nocturnal lemurs widespread throughout the forested areas of Madagascar. Examination of such characters as pelage coloration, ear size, and certain cranial features reveal several distinctive populations of *Lepilemur*, along with some others that are less well defined. What is less certain, however, is at what taxonomic level these forms can be distinguished. They are karyotypically variable and on that basis have been characterized as different species; but since variability in chromosome number can be found even within the same forest, it is unclear whether the karyotypic evidence is conclusive. It seems a reasonably good bet, however, that when we know more about variation within the genus and about the precise distributions of the populations involved, we will conclude that several separate species exist among the more or less continuous *Lepilemur* populations in the forests that fringe

Madagascar.

Although *Lepilemur* populations are found in a wide variety of forested environments, ranging from rain forest through seasonal gallery formations to arid-adapted scrub forests, this lemur has been studied in detail in only one of these environments. *Lepilemur mustelinus leucopus* (perhaps better viewed as a separate species, *L. leucopus*) has been the subject of two studies in the arid south of Madagascar. Nocturnal in its activity but often observed awake during the day, the white-footed sportive lemur, as

this form is cumbersomely known, is a specialized feeder on leaves. Small ranges of males (under 0.4 hectare) extensively overlap even smaller ranges of females, and male-female pairs of "range-mates" may associate for part of the night's activity. Weighing between ca. 0.5 and 1 kg., sportive lemurs are long-hindlimbed vertical clingers and leapers.

The large-bodied *Megaladapis* is perhaps the best known of the "subfossil" lemurs that became extinct subsequent to the arrival of human beings on Madagascar, perhaps 1,500 years ago. Remains of three

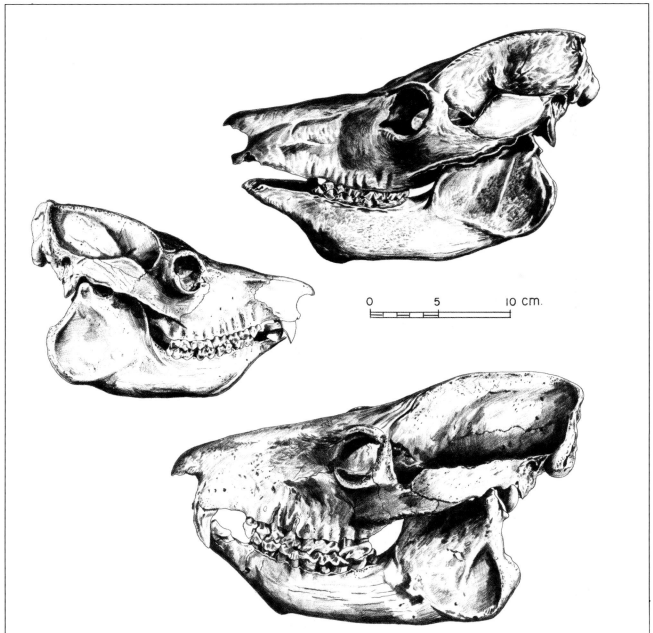

Crania in lateral view of the three species of *Megaladapis*: *M. grandidieri* (above); *M. madagascariensis* (center); and *M. edwardsi* (below). (Drawn by Nicholas Amorosi.)

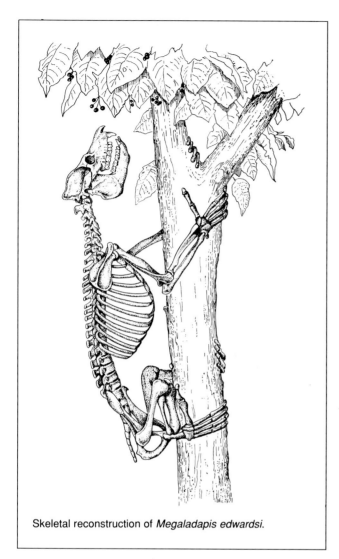

Skeletal reconstruction of *Megaladapis edwardsi*.

permanent upper incisor teeth, which were presumably replaced by a horny pad, as in some ruminants. With highly vascularized nasal bones overhanging the nasal aperture, it is even possible that in life *Megaladapis* possessed a small mobile snout. Unusually for a lemur, the ear cavity is entirely accommodated within the cranial base and communicates with the exterior via a bony tube.

Despite its great body size *Megaladapis* was certainly arboreal, as its long grasping extremities, among other features, attest. In its locomotion *Megaladapis* was probably a modified vertical clinger and leaper of limited agility. Its closest living locomotor analogue is said to be the koala of Australia, which progresses up tree trunks in a series of hops and makes short leaps between vertical supports. Taken together, the characteristics of the skull and postcranium of *Megaladapis* suggest the lifestyle of an arboreal browser, probably specialized for leaf eating like its living relative *Lepilemur*.

See also **INDRIOIDEA; LEMURIFORMES**. [I.T.]

Further Readings

Tattersall, I. (1982) The Primates of Madagascar. New York: Columbia University Press.

MEGAFAUNA   *see*   EXTINCTION

MEGALADAPIS   *see*   MEGALADAPIDAE

MEGANTHROPUS

Form of hominoid recognized from two partial mandibles recovered by G.H.R. von Koenigswald in 1939 and 1941 in Java. The mandibles were described in 1945 by F. Weidenreich from casts. Von Koenigswald felt that the 1939 fragment (Sangiran 5) and the 1941 fragment (Sangiran 6) represented a female and male, respectively. Weidenreich disagreed and published Sangiran 5 under the nomen "*Pithecanthropus dubius*" because he doubted that the specimen was a hominid. He did, however, agree that Sangiran 6 was a hominid and published it under the generic name that von Koenigswald had suggested in a letter that accompanied the casts.

Both specimens were described only from casts that von Koenigswald made and sent to Beijing prior to his internment in a Japanese concentration camp. Because of its large teeth and robust mandible Weidenreich carefully considered the possibility that *Meganthropus* was pathological. In the end he decided it was not, because the teeth, although extremely large, were proportionate to the large mandible. He also rejected the possibility of acromegaly, because the mandible did not exhibit the exagger-

distinct species are known from marsh and cave deposits in central, southern, and southwestern Madagascar. The largest-bodied of these, *Megaladapis edwardsi*, is found in sites of the south and southwest and is distinguished by its large dentition. This species attained the size of a St. Bernard dog, but the skull is disproportionately large, about a foot long. In sites of the same region occur also the subfossil remains of a smaller species, *M. madagascariensis*, with a skull ca. 20 percent shorter. Sites in the center of Madagascar have yielded bones of *M. grandidieri*. This species has a skull almost as long as that of *M. edwardsi*, but its molar teeth are hardly larger than those of *M. madagascariensis*.

The morphology of all three species is quite similar. As the illustration shows, the skull is greatly elongated in the braincase as well as in the facial portion, even though brain size was relatively small. This elongation, together with an unusual upward flexion of the cranial base, is probably related to an adaptation for cropping food with the front teeth. Also related to this dietary adaptation is the lack of

Lateral view of the "Meganthropus" mandibular fragment discovered by G.H.R. von Koenigswald in 1941. Photograph of cast. (From Tattersall, 1970.)

ated chin of modern acromegalics. Thus the type of *Meganthropus* entered the literature as an Asian hominid that was less advanced than "*Sinanthropus.*"

Subsequently other fragmentary finds were also included in this taxon. Of particular interest are cranial and facial fragments that are claimed to document the presence of an Asian form of australopithecine. Actually the speculation that *Meganthropus* was an Asian australopithecine was introduced almost inadvertently as the result of J.T. Robinson's initial arguments for the inclusion of australopithecines in the Hominidae. He reasoned that the African australopithecines were just as hominid in their morphology as *Meganthropus*. Subsequently Robinson's arguments were augmented by speculations that australopithecines were present in Asia. To date, however, no convincing body of evidence supports these hypotheses.

Relative to other specimens that have been included in *Homo erectus* it is clear that previously known and recently reported *Meganthropus* specimens exhibit robust and extremely thick cranial bones. Nevertheless, nothing about the morphology of the specimens suggests a taxon other than *Homo erectus*. The possibility that the specimens are aberrant should also be borne in mind, since the taxon was actually named on the basis of a cast and newer cranial material has yet to be adequately described. It is also possible that the robusticity of *Meganthropus* reflects an insularized hominid population isolated on Java for hundreds of thousands of years. In any case no consensus has yet been reached on the taxonomic and phylogenetic status of *Meganthropus*.

See also INDONESIA; KOENIGSWALD, G.H.R. VON. [G.G.P.]

Further Readings

Sartono, S. (1982) Sagittal cresting in *Meganthropus paleojavanicus* (V. Koenigswald). Mod. Quat. Res. Southeast Asia 7:201–210.

Weidenreich, F. (1945) Giant early man from Java and south China. Anthropol. Pap. Am. Mus. Nat. Hist. 40:1–143.

MELKA KONTOURÉ

Central Ethiopian stratified sequence of Plio-Pleistocene age ca. 1.7–0.1 m.y. by K-Ar, paleomagnetic, and faunal correlations.

Located ca. 50 km. south of Addis Ababa, the composite Melka Kontouré stratigraphic column comprises 30 m. of successive formations spanning the latest Pliocene and much of Pleistocene time. Stretching for ca. 5–6 km. along both banks of the Awash River, the Melka Kontouré outcrops are mostly fluvial deposits, interspersed with volcanic layers that have permitted dating. The deposits contain abundant artifacts and faunal remains. More than 50 archaeological sites have been identified, and ca. 30 "living floors" have been excavated here by J. Chavaillon and co-workers.

The most important localities and their archaeological content are Garba (Oldowan through Middle Stone Age); Gomboré (Oldowan through middle Acheulean); Simbirro (middle Acheulean); and Karre (Oldowan). Hominid fossils have been recovered from both the Garba and Gomboré localities.

From an Oldowan level at Garba IV comes a partial child's mandible attributed to early *Homo*. From another Oldowan level at Gomboré IB comes a partial hominid humerus. From a middle Acheulean level at Gomboré II there is a parietal fragment attributed to *Homo erectus*, and from the Terminal Acheulean unit of Garba III comes a frontal of what may be a late *Homo erectus*.

See also ACHEULEAN; ETHIOPIA; OLDOWAN. [T.D.W.]

Further Readings

Chavaillon, J., Chavaillon, N., Hours, F., and Piperno, M. (1979) From the Oldowan to the Middle Stone Age at Melka-Kunturé (Ethiopia). Quaternaria 21:87–114.

MEMBER *see* STRATIGRAPHY

MENAPIAN *see* GLACIATION; PLEISTOCENE

MESOLITHIC

Period or group of industries that falls between Paleolithic and Neolithic in time, technology, and economic development. In Lubbock's original (1865) division of the Stone Age into two epochs the Paleolithic and Neolithic were thought to have been separated by a hiatus, representing a time when mid-latitude Europe was abandoned after the retreat of the reindeer and their hunters to the extreme north. Subsequent excavations at Mas d'Azil and other sites documented the existence of early Holocene hunting and gathering cultures in mid-latitude regions. By the last quarter of the nineteenth century several authors (e.g. A. Brown) independently suggested the use of the term "Mesolithic" for these industries, although the first synthetic studies of European Mesolithic industries, compiled by J.G.D. Clark, were not published until the 1930s.

Definitions

The meaning of Mesolithic and the list of industries assigned to this interval are far from uniform. Like other subdivisions of the Stone Age the term carries technological (microliths, composite tools), chronological (early Holocene), and socioeconomic (broad-spectrum resource use, economic intensification, semisedentism) connotations. Some scholars reserve the designation Mesolithic for northern and western Europe, where societies adapted to forest-based subsistence, practicing hunting, gathering, and fishing, and using composite tools, succeeded one another over perhaps 6,000 years before the advent of domesticated stock and agriculture. In this view societies that continued a "Paleolithic" way of life, characterized by nomadic hunting of large herbivores, or whose tool traditions continue relatively unchanged from late Pleistocene to Holocene times, are referred to the *Epipaleolithic*, a term originally suggested by Obermaier as a synonym for Mesolithic. Such societies are found in the extreme north of Europe, where reindeer hunting continued to form the subsistence base, and in the Mediterranean basin, where red deer and other forest species dominated both late Pleistocene and Holocene assemblages and where Epigravettian industries continue with no abrupt shifts from the glacial maximum at ca. 20,000–18,000 B.P. into the Holocene. *Epipaleolithic* also refers to final late Pleistocene and Holocene industries of North Africa.

In contrast to the use of Mesolithic to refer to specialized Holocene hunter-fishers of Europe, V.G. Childe and others reserved the Mesolithic (or *Protoneolithic*) designation for contemporaneous societies of the Near East that were experimenting with food production. The Mesolithic stage encompassed only those societies actually in transition between Paleolithic and Neolithic. In this view it is the European Holocene industries that are relegated to the Epipaleolithic and whose adaptations are seen as a specialized "dead end" in human cultural evolution.

To resolve these conflicting uses of the term, several authors (e.g. Price) have emphasized the chronological aspects of the Mesolithic and suggested that this phase incorporates *all* post–late Pleistocene hunter-gatherers, whatever their location, dietary or technological specializations, or experimentation with domesticates (provided that most of the diet is still derived from wild resources). In such a definition the Mesolithic industries of northwestern Europe constitute a large part of the universe under discussion, since domestication of food resources was not established in this area until relatively late, after 6000 B.P. Paradoxically, the term "Mesolithic" is rarely used to refer to African late-Pleistocene and Holocene hunter-gatherers, although archaeological sites in southern Africa dominated by stone and bone tools and remains of wild animals are dated to the last 200 years!

In the New World Holocene hunter-fisher-gatherers with a diversified subsistence base are referred to as *Archaic*, in an attempt to avoid the multiple connotations of the Old World terminology. American terminology is based primarily on stages of economic, rather than technological, development, so that specialized hunter-fisher-gatherer societies that experimented with metals are still classed as Archaic, while early agricultural societies without pottery fall into the *Formative* period.

Broad-Spectrum Revolution

In 1965 K.V. Flannery introduced the concept of the broad-spectrum revolution to emphasize the shift in man-land relationships that took place in the final late Pleistocene to early Holocene. Even in such areas as the Levant, which experienced minimal environmental shifts, early Holocene adaptations were often different from their late Pleistocene antecedents. Despite the argument over specific terminologies there is now general agreement that the Mesolithic or its equivalent represented a level of more intensive exploitation of the natural environment. Small-scale resources like fish, shellfish, nuts, snails, birds, and tortoises were increasingly important in the diet of Holocene hunters, who developed new strategies and technologies for taking large nonmigratory forest and marine species. At Franchthi Cave in Greece, for example, tuna comprise 50 percent of the faunal remains by the Late Mesolithic. Shellfish mounds from Hoabinhian sites in Southeast Asia, and abundant fish remains from other East and Southeast Asian early Holocene sites, demonstrate the worldwide extent of Mesolithic adaptations.

The scheduling of resource use was particularly important. Although the site of Star Carr in Yorkshire (England) was occupied by red-deer hunters in win-

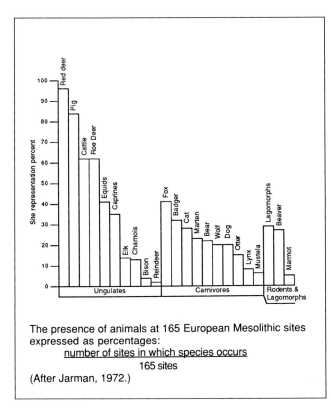

The presence of animals at 165 European Mesolithic sites expressed as percentages:

number of sites in which species occurs
165 sites

(After Jarman, 1972.)

Technologies

The most definitive and widespread, although not universal, characteristic of Mesolithic technology is the use of small, often geometric forms called *microliths*. Whether derived from small blade core (microbladelet technology) or from regular-sized blades that were divided into two or more often triangular or trapezoidal pieces (geometric microliths, microburin technique), microliths formed the basis for a wide range of composite tools, including arrows, barbed fish spears, and sickles. Since the stone elements of composite tools could be easily replaced in a haft of worked bone, antler, or wood, composite tools may have represented a more efficient technology, as well as a way to create long, curved stone cutting edges with multiple blades set in a sickle haft, and detachable arrowheads. The widespread use of very small (less than 2.5 cm.) projectile points in the Mesolithic suggests that arrow points may have been designed to remain in the animal, possibly to dissolve a poison into its bloodstream, rather than to kill the animal on contact. In Europe the sequential forms of microliths, from tanged/shouldered points to triangles to trapezes are often used to establish chronological and even "cultural" relationships (e.g. Azilian, Sauveterrian, Tardenoisian), although the regional distribution of these

ter and early spring, Maglemosian lake-side sites of northern Europe reflect largely summer and fall occupations, when both nut-harvesting and fishing opportunities were at a maximum. Seasonal movement from lowland winter camps to upland hunting settlements is documented for the Late Paleolithic and Mesolithic of Greece. In the Archaic of the mid-Atlantic region of North America occupation sites along rivers are concentrated in the spring and fall, when anadromous fish were running. North African Mesolithic populations exploited snails on a seasonal basis, and in southern Africa a possible seasonal round may have included coastal shellfish harvesting in one season and inland hunting and collecting in another, an adaptation that may also be reflected in the spatial separation and differing faunal inventories of Asturian and late Azilian sites of Cantabria. In such widely separated areas as the Levant, Yorkshire, Kyushu (Japan), and Idaho domesticated dogs appear in early Holocene contexts, presumably as an aid to the tracking and killing of solitary forest prey.

The broadening of the subsistence base to include more species and a greater proportion of small-scale (low-trophic-level) resources did not occur suddenly, nor did it necessarily coincide with the major climatic shifts ca. 10,000 B.P. An increased use of marine resources, birds, and small game is evident in the later Upper Paleolithic (e.g. Magdalenian) of Europe, as well as in the Later Stone Age of Africa, which is well underway by 20,000 B.P. in central Africa.

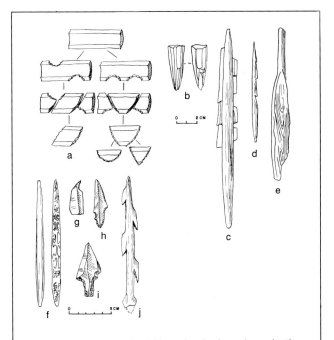

Mesolithic and Epipaleolithic technologies: a) production of geometric microliths from segmented blades; b) microblade core; c) antler spear with hafted stone barbs; d) barbed antler point (Star Carr); e) antler mattock (Star Carr); f) carved half-round bone wand (Ahrensburgian); g) "zinken" or perforator; h) tanged point (Ahrensburgian); i) tanged point (Lyngby culture); j) biserial barbed antler point (Ahrensburgian).

forms is extensive, and different forms coexist or overlap in time. *Lunates* (also called *segments* or *crescents*) are particularly common in the Near East (Natufian) and Africa (Capsian, Wilton).

Other innovations in stone technology are an increase in the use of ground stone (present in Africa from the Middle Stone Age on) for bowls, mortars, and pestles, in both the Old and New Worlds, reflecting an increased use of tubers and wild grains. In African Later Stone Age sites bored stones, which may have served as digging-stick weights, also reflect an intensification of plant harvesting and possibly incipient cultivation. Chipped-stone axes were common in northern European Mesolithic contexts, and stone for axes was mined and transported over longer distances than before.

The development of Mesolithic bone-and-antler technology is equally distinctive. Bone, antler, and wood formed the hafts of such composite tools as sickles, as well as the points, barbed or smooth, of arrows, harpoons, fishhooks, and leisters. The detachable point, which may first appear in the Late Paleolithic of several areas, from Europe to central Africa, was as important an innovation in fishing as in hunting, as it enabled the fisher to tire the prey and to land a greater proportion of the larger species. Other accoutrements of fishing, including the nets themselves recovered from sites in northern Germany and Scandinavia, demonstrate the use of various fishing strategies (nets, traps, weirs, harpoons, lines) by Mesolithic peoples. Dugout canoes and paddles indicate the widespread use of boats, whose presence is implied at an earlier date by the importation of obsidian from Melos to the Greek mainland during the final late Pleistocene (18,000–12,000 B.P.) as well as by the early peopling of Australia and Melanesia by ca. 32,000 B.P.

In a few places entirely new materials were worked by Mesolithic peoples: cold-hammered metals, especially native copper, in Anatolia and parts of North America; basketry matting in the North American Great Basin, northern Europe, and southern Africa; and ceramics in Japan, where pottery was in use as early as 12,000 B.P., as well as in the final Mesolithic (Ertebølle) of southern Scandinavia, 6600–5300 B.P.

Settlement and Social Organization

The economic and technological developments of the Mesolithic also made possible a greater degree of sedentism, often based on fishing. At Eynan on Lake Huleh (Israel) and Vlasac in the Iron Gates region of the Danube stone foundations dating to 8000 B.P. or before attest to the permanence of dwellings; elsewhere in Europe and the Near East small lake-shore huts may have been seasonally reoccupied in alterna-

tion with rock shelters or forest camps. Within-settlement differentiation of activities and public versus family areas is more marked than previously. Large Mesolithic cemeteries in southern Scandinavia and in the Sudan also argue for increased sedentism. Finally, the sizes of social territories, whose boundaries are reflected in trade networks, microlith styles, bone-point forms, and decorative motifs, are correspondingly reduced from Paleolithic times, from ca. 100,000 to 15,000–20,000 sq. km. in northern Europe.

In certain areas (e.g. upland regions of the Near East, Tehuacan Valley of Mexico, Peruvian uplands, Greece, Mississippi Valley, Southeast Asia) Mesolithic adaptations, especially semisedentism and scheduling of resource use within a defined territory, provided an economic, social, and technological milieu that favored experimentation with more intensive forms of procurement, leading ultimately to domestication of plants and animals.

See also ASIA (EASTERN); AUSTRALIA; AZILIAN; BOW AND ARROW; CAPSIAN; ÇATAL HÜYÜK; CRESWELLIAN; CULTURE; DIET; DOMESTICATION; ECONOMY, PREHISTORIC; EPIGRAVETTIAN; EPIPALEOLITHIC; ETHNOARCHAEOLOGY; HAMBURGIAN; HAUA FTEAH; HOABINHIAN; HOLOCENE; HUNTER-GATHERERS; IBERO-MAURUSIAN; JARMO; JERICHO; JEWELRY; KEBARA; KEBARAN; LATE PALEOLITHIC; LATER STONE AGE; MAGDALENIAN; MAGLEMOSIAN; MAN-LAND RELATIONSHIPS; NEAR EAST; NEOLITHIC; NIAH; PALEOINDIAN; PALEOLITHIC; RAW MATERIALS; ROMANELLIAN; SAUVETERRIAN; SEA-LEVEL CHANGE; SMITHFIELD; STAR CARR; STONE-TOOL MAKING; TARDENOISIAN; TSHITOLIAN; UPPER PALEOLITHIC; WILTON. [A.S.B.]

Further Readings

Clark, J.D., and Brandt, S., ed. (1984) From Hunters to Farmers: The Causes and Consequences of Food Production in Africa. Berkeley: University of California Press.

Clark, J.G.D. (1980) Mesolithic Prelude: The Palaeolithic-Neolithic Transition in Old World Prehistory. Edinburgh: Edinburgh University Press.

Deacon, J. (1984) Later Stone Age people and their descendants in southern Africa. In R.G. Klein (ed.): Southern African Prehistory and Paleoenvironments. Rotterdam: Balkema.

Kosłowski, S.K., ed. (1973) The Mesolithic in Europe. Warsaw: Warsaw University Press.

Megaw, J.V.S., ed. (1977) Hunters, Gatherers and First Farmers Beyond Europe. Leicester: Leicester University Press.

Mellars, P., ed. (1978) The Early Postglacial Settlement of Northern Europe. London: Duckworth.

Price, T. D. (1983) The European Mesolithic. Am. Antiquity 48: 761-774.

MESOPITHECUS *see* COLOBINAE

MESOPROPITHECUS *see* INDRIIDAE

MESSAOUDIAN *see* PLEISTOCENE; SEA-LEVEL CHANGE

MESSINIAN *see* MIOCENE; TIME SCALE

MESWA *see* KORU

MEZHIRICH

Major open-air Late Paleolithic site at the interfluve of two minor tributaries of the Dnepr in the Ukraine, some 160 km. south of Kiev (U.S.S.R.). Excavations through 1986 have revealed four round or oval surface dwellings, ranging in area from 12 sq. m. to 24 sq. m., that are made of mammoth bones. Other features include in-ground storage pits, hearths, and surface bone piles. The clear selective patterning of specific bones evident in the construction of the dwellings suggests that they were constructed to conform to a particular village design plan. Radiocarbon dates assign the occupation of this cold-weather base camp at Mezhirich to ca. 15,000 B.P.

See also EUROPE; KOSTENKI; LATE PALEOLITHIC; MALTA; SUNGIR. [O.S.]

MFWANGANO *see* RUSINGA

MICODON *see* CALLITRICHINAE

MICOQUIAN

Final Early Paleolithic (Acheulean) industry found in western Europe during the Eemian and Weichsel I, ca. 130–70 k.y. ago. Named after the type site of La Micoque near Les Eyzies, Dordogne, in southwestern France, the industry is characterized by fine, thin lanceolate or foliate handaxes with concavo-convex outlines and by numerous side-scrapers and denticulates, including the convergent denticulate Tayac point. Levallois technology may be present to varying degrees.

See also ACHEULEAN; EARLY PALEOLITHIC; HANDAXE; LEVALLOIS; STONE-TOOL MAKING; TAYACIAN. [A.S.B.]

MICROADAPIS *see* ADAPIDAE

MICROCEBUS *see* CHEIROGALEIDAE

MICROCHOERINAE

Subfamily of omomyid primates that occurs in Europe from the middle Eocene to early Oligocene. The following four recognized genera easily accommodate the modest known diversity of ca. 15 species: *Nannopithex, Necrolemur, Pseudoloris* (including *Pivetonia*), and *Microchoerus*.

The diagnostic characteristics of the last common ancestor of the subfamily from the other omomyids are not easily definable, yet there is no doubt about the monophyly of these primates. The dental formula, although debated in the literature, was different from other known omomyids in that there was one pair of teeth fewer in the lower dentition than in the upper one. The formula in the ancestral microchoerines was probably two incisors, one canine, three premolars above and two below, and three molars. This peculiarity may have been the result of the probably adaptive enlargement of the lower central incisors. The molar teeth of the most primitive and oldest genus, *Nannopithex*, are reminiscent of the primitive omomyines with its relatively large last molars and somewhat buccally displaced paraconids on the lower molars. The greatly enlarged central incisors, however, as in some anaptomorphines and in the known skulls of both *Nannopithex* (crushed) and *Necrolemur*, show the same extreme inflation of the petromastoid portion of the petrosal bone as does the skull of the anaptomorphine *Tetonius*. Postcranial

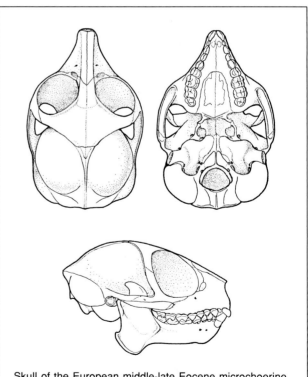

Skull of the European middle-late Eocene microchoerine omomyid *Necrolemur antiquus*. Note the bulging area behind the auditory bulla, shared also with the anaptomorphine *Tetonius*. This advanced character does not occur in tarsiids or in known skulls of omomyines.

morphology is poorly known for the microchoerines. Information from the hindleg of *Necrolemur* suggests that tarsal elongation and distal fusion of the tibia and fibula, convergently tarsierlike in some adaptive respects, was more advanced than the homologous areas in the other omomyids.

Although there are differences from the North American omomyids, the phylogenetic ties of microchoerines to one of the subgroups of the former make it unnecessary to elevate the European forms to family status.

In spite of their relative morphological uniformity the dental differences suggest different adaptive strategies for the two most derived genera, *Pseudoloris* and *Microchoerus*. The former was undoubtedly a predatory, or at least fully insectivorous, genus, whereas the latter displays the molar attributes associated with a diet including a greater portion of plants than insects. The large incisors of the last common ancestor of the subfamily certainly suggest an initial adaptation to some form of exudativory in addition to feeding on animal (including insect) prey.

The well-preserved crania of *Necrolemur* are one of the important bases for our knowledge of the family Omomyidae. The circulatory pattern of the ear region in this genus has been instrumental in the understanding of the evolutionary history of the family in relation to other primates.

See also ANAPTOMORPHINAE; OMOMYIDAE; OMOMYINAE. [F.S.S.]

Further Readings

Szalay, F.S., and Delson, E. (1979) Evolutionary History of the Primates. New York: Academic.

MICROCHOERUS *see* MICROCHOERINAE

MICROCOLOBUS *see* COLOBINAE

MICROCOMPLEMENT FIXATION *see* IMMUNOLOGICAL DISTANCE; MOLECULAR ANTHROPOLOGY

MICROEVOLUTION *see* EVOLUTION

MICROFAUNA *see* PALEONTOLOGY

MICROLITH *see* STONE-TOOL MAKING

MICROMOMYS *see* PAROMOMYIDAE

MICROPITHECUS *see* **CATARRHINI**

MICROSYOPIDAE

Family of Eocene mammals known from North America and considered by some paleontologists to be archaic primates. They range from tiny, mouse-sized forms in the early Eocene to almost cat-sized ones in the middle Eocene. Microsyopid cheek teeth are primatelike, but only convergently, and they have a pair of enlarged anterior incisors. That this dental morphology is convergently primatelike can be ascertained without recourse to any other characters. Known skulls show a relatively small brain, like many archaic forms, and a related large sagittal crest in the larger species. The basicranial morphology, particularly the ear region, much valued by mammalian systematists, shows them to lack a petrosal bulla, which is present in all known primates identified by either dental or postcranial features. Microsyopid ear-region morphology also displays some striking and probably derived similarities shared with the living colugos ("flying lemurs") of the order Dermoptera. Remains of the hind foot, particularly the tarsus, attributed to microsyopids, show unequivocally that these animals shared the derived specializations of colugos to pedal hanging on branches. The living colugos are gliders and have a membrane stretched between their limbs, so they roost upside down like bats. The structure of the tarsus, the best-known postcranial area so far, shows a complex of special similarities to tupaiids, archaic primates, and bats. The microsyopids, then, in spite of their enlarged incisor specialization, are most probably an early family of the order of gliding mammals, the Dermoptera. This order, along with the Scandentia (tree shrews or tupaiids and fossil relatives), the Primates, and the Chiroptera (bats) make up a monophyletic higher category, the cohort Archonta.

See also ARCHONTA. [F.S.S.]

MIDDLE AWASH

Central Ethiopian stratified series of late Miocene to late Pleistocene age, according to K-Ar, fission-track, and faunal analysis.

This study area includes sites located along both eastern and western sides of the Awash River as it flows northward from the town of Gewane toward the hominid site of Hadar, over a distance of ca. 100 km. Discovered by M. Taieb in the late 1960s, the Middle Awash region was surveyed by J. Kalb in the mid-1970s and by J.D. Clark and T.D. White in 1981. These surveys established a long and complex geological succession in the region that stretches back ca. 6 m.y. Thus late Miocene, Pliocene, and Pleisto-

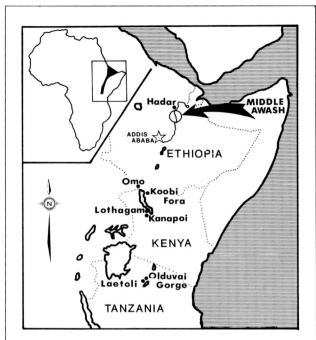

Map showing the location of the Middle Awash region, Hadar, and other hominid sites associated with the East African Rift Valley.

cene strata all crop out in the study area. Oldowan, Acheulean, Middle Stone Age, and Later Stone Age archaeological sites have been discovered here, the most important ones at Andalee, Bodo, Hargufia, and Meadura. Paleontological occurrences are abundant in this region, and a wide variety of mammalian fossils are found in datable geological context.

The Bodo cranium was found in Middle Awash strata containing Acheulean artifacts in 1976. Later, in 1981, a second middle Pleistocene hominid parietal was found ca. 400 m. south of the original Bodo find. Archaeological excavations were undertaken in 1981 to study Acheulean occurrences at Hargufia and Bodo and Oldowan occurrences at Bodo.

Pliocene strata crop out discontinuously along the eastern side of the Awash. About 15 km. south of Bodo a series of lacustrine beds is overlain by the Cindery Tuff, a volcanic layer dated to 3.9 m.y. Below this tuff, in the Belohdelie drainage, portions of a Pliocene hominid cranium including frontal and parietal were found in 1981. In the same year the adjacent Maka drainage yielded a proximal hominid femur from above the Cindery Tuff.

See also AFAR; BODO; RIFT VALLEY. [T.D.W.]

Further Readings

Clark, J.D., Asfaw, B., Assefa, G., Harris, J.W.K., Kurashina, H., Walter, R.C., White, T.D., and Williams, M.A.J. (1984) Paleoanthropological discoveries in the Middle Awash Valley, Ethiopia. Nature 307:423–428.

Kalb, J.E., Oswald, E.B., Tebedge, S., Mebrate, A., Tola, E., and Peak, D. (1982) Geology and stratigraphy of Neogene deposits, Middle Awash Valley, Ethiopia. Nature 298:17–25.

MIDDLE PALEOLITHIC

Stage of the Paleolithic characterized by the predominance of prepared-core flake technologies and flake tools (Mode III); by improved hunting technologies reflected both in the tools themselves and in their frequent association with large, cold-adapted herbivores; by repeated occupations of rock shelters and of constructed features at open-air sites; and by the initial emergence of many forms of symbolic expression, including use of coloring material (rare) pendants and incised or painted pieces, and human burial. The first mid-nineteenth-century formulations of European Paleolithic development divided the Paleolithic into two phases, an age of. the caves, or Upper Paleolithic, and a pre-cave age, or Lower Paleolithic. Originally included with the Upper Paleolithic as the first epoch of the caves, the Middle Paleolithic, or "Cave Bear and Mammoth Age," was quickly recognized as a separate entity by Lartet, based on the material from the site of Le Moustier, in the Dordogne (France). The Mousterian industries of Europe and the Near East and the MSA (Middle Stone Age) industries of Africa and India are now recognized as regional equivalents within a Middle Paleolithic stage that extended over most of the Old World. Middle Paleolithic industries are widespread during the early part of the last glacial stage (ca. 110–40 k.y.) but may begin well before the last interglacial (more than 130 k.y.), particularly in Africa, and may last until 20,000 B.P. in some areas.

Chronology and Geographical Boundaries

In Europe most Middle Paleolithic industries are grouped in the Mousterian complex, although flake industries with leaf-shaped points (*Blattspitzen*) localized in southern Germany are often referred to a separate tradition, the "Altmuhlian," and assemblages from most of western and central Europe with small sharply pointed handaxes are known as "Micoquian." Although no European Middle Paleolithic sites are unequivocally assigned to the last interglacial or before, a few (e.g. Tata and possibly also Pech de l'Azé) have been radiometrically dated by thermoluminescence to the end of oxygen-isotope stage 5 (ca. 100 k.y.), in association with faunal and sedimentological evidence of cool temperate conditions. Older assemblages, such as that from Biache, are accepted as Mousterian by a growing minority of researchers. The bulk of the European Middle Paleolithic material, however, is correlated with oxygen-

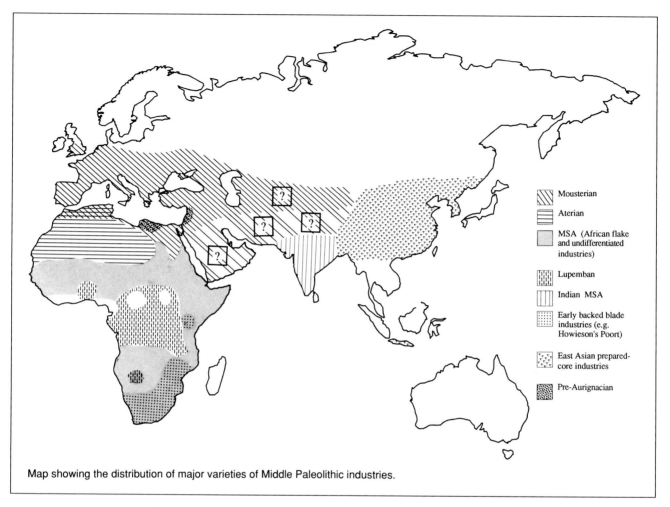

Map showing the distribution of major varieties of Middle Paleolithic industries.

isotope stages 4 and 3, from 75 k.y. to ca. 34 k.y. at the youngest. While several Mousterian variants have been recognized, these are not regionally or chronologically distinctive, with the exception of the Mousterian of Acheulean Tradition.

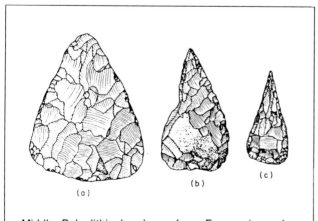

Middle Paleolithic handaxes from Europe (see also MOUSTERIAN): a) Mousterian of Acheulean tradition; b–c) Micoquian (Germany, France). (After Champion, Gamble, Shennan, and Whittle, Prehistoric Europe, © 1984 by Academic Press.)

The Middle Paleolithic of Asia is particularly diverse. In the Near East and extending into central Asia Mousterian levels have been described from cave sites in the Levant (e.g. Jabrud, Tabūn, Ksar 'Akil), Iraq (Shanidar), and Uzbekistan (Teshik-Tash) in association with Neanderthal fossil remains, possibly representing burials. This area, together with the northeastern corner of Africa, shares population and culture traits most clearly with Europe. As in Europe these industries are correlated on sedimentological grounds primarily with the early part of the last glacial stage (ca. 110–40 k.y.). One significant difference between the Levantine and northeastern African Middle Paleolithic industries and those of Europe is the appearance of blade-and-burin (Mode IV) industries within or just prior to the former group.

On the Indian subcontinent the Middle Paleolithic is poorly dated and is associated primarily with fluviatile depositional contexts. Typologically the discoidal prepared cores and trimmed points from many areas are unlike those associated with Mousterian industries and are referred to as "Middle Stone Age," suggesting a comparison with African materials. East

—342—

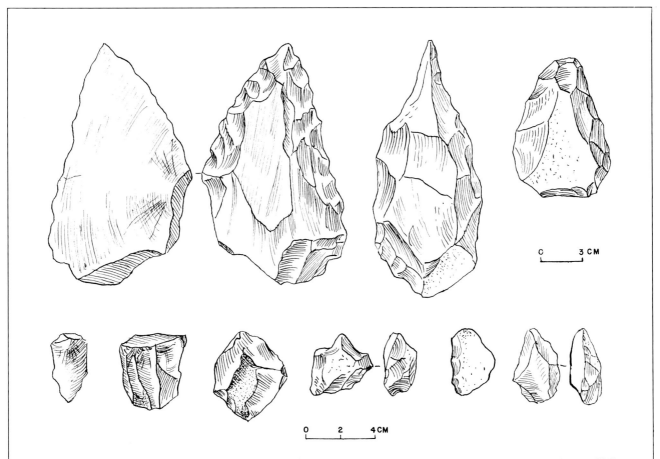

Middle Paleolithic lithic artifacts from China: large pointed flakes from Dingcun (top); small retouched flakes and cores, Xujiayao (bottom). (After Qiu, in Wu and Olsen, eds., © 1985 by Academic Press.)

Asian Middle Paleolithic industries, associated in China with early last glacial faunas, continue the bipolar cores (e.g. Xujiayao), pebble tools (e.g. Zhoukoudian), and large, crude flake tools (e.g. Dingcun) of the Early Paleolithic in that area, with the addition of prepared cores and trimmed points. Regional differences between large- and small-tool traditions present in the Early Paleolithic continue into the Middle phase, and no clear shifts in economic strategy or cognitive behavior are evident. Associated fossils (e.g. Dali, Dingcun, Jinniu Shan, Maba, Xujiayao, Changyang) are described as early *Homo sapiens*, with significant differences from Neanderthals. The Chinese data thus suggest a considerable degree of regional isolation and internal development during the middle and late Pleistocene. Although some early New World industries have been described as Middle or even Early Paleolithic in character (i.e. as lacking in blade technology), none has been dated to the comparable time interval (100–35 k.y.), nor is there clear evidence of human occupation in Japan, Siberia, or Australia prior to 40,000 B.P.

African Middle Paleolithic industries are similarly distinct from the classic European Mousterian, with the exception of northeastern African Levalloiso-Mousterian industries at such sites as Haua Fteah, with a possible outlier on the Moroccan coast (Jebel Irhoud). Even in this area, however, the presence of leaf-shaped and tanged points at some sites and elongated foliate points at others suggests affinities with purely African industries, such as the Aterian tanged-point tradition of the northwest and the Sahara and the Lupemban tradition of central Africa. In general African as opposed to European Middle Paleolithic industries are characterized by a greater degree of regional distinctiveness, more consistent chronological trends, different prepared-core technologies (discoidal, Victoria West), greater elaboration of points and core-axe forms (many of which were probably hafted as spears or arrows), and the relatively widespread use of blade (Mode IV) technologies, either interspersed with flake-technology levels in stratified sites (e.g. Howieson's Poort) or as a consistent element in a regionally distinctive sequence (e.g. Pietersburg). Other distinctions between African and European Middle Paleolithic societies

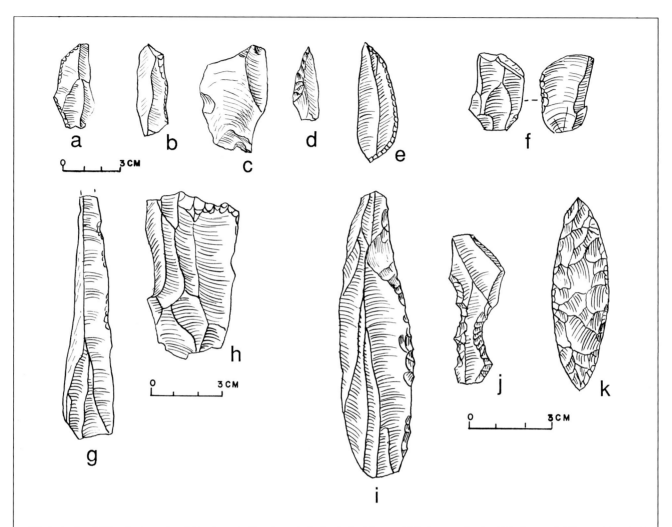

Blade tools of "Pre-Aurignacian," Howieson's Poort, and similar industries: a–b) Lebanon: backed blades; c–f) Libya: c) backed blade; d) burin; e) blade; f) blade-core. g–k) South Africa: g) backed crescent; h) burin; i) borer; j) strangled blade or double concave scraper; k) bifacial point. (After C.B.M. McBurney, The Haua Fteah [Cyrienaica] and the Stone Age of the South-East Mediterranean, © 1967 by Cambridge University Press, reprinted with permission; and C.G. Sampson, The Stone Age Archaeology of Southern Africa, © 1974 by Academic Press.)

are described below.

African Middle Paleolithic sites are also associated with rather older initial dates than corresponding industries of Europe. In Ethiopia and central Kenya potassium-argon dates ranging from 150 to ca. 400 k.y. have been obtained for industries with side-scrapers and shaped points; at sites in southern Africa (Klasies River Mouth, Border Cave) the earliest Middle Paleolithic industries have been dated to between 120 and 200 k.y., based on stratigraphic evidence, sea-level correlations, and oxygen-isotope determinations on shells from the deposits.

Middle Paleolithic (Mode III) industries with blade (Mode IV) elements but without microliths or backed elements may also continue to ca. 20,000 B.P. in some areas (e.g. Lupemban of central Africa, possibly some Aterian sites), while being replaced by blade-tool (e.g.

Khormusan) or microblade (e.g. Matupi, Zaire) industries as early as 40,000 B.P. in other areas. The transition period to Late Paleolithic in Africa is poorly understood and does *not* appear to correspond with the appearance of modern Homo sapiens. Indeed, African Middle Paleolithic industries are associated with both archaic (Ndutu, Florisbad, Diré Dawa) and fully modern (Border Cave, Klasies River Mouth) fossil representatives of Homo sapiens.

Middle Paleolithic Sites

Despite the intercontinental and interregional diversity in Middle Paleolithic industries, sites, technologies, and economies of this period shared several features across the vast area under consideration. On each continent new subsistence strategies and technologies, reflected in leaf points prepared for hafting (eastern Europe) and fine lanceolate points and core axes (Lupemban), allowed humans to utilize areas that had been too marginal for extensive human occupation. These included the steppes and open plains of Russia and central Asia, as well as much of the tropical-forest region of central and western Africa. As Lartet recognized in 1865, the Middle Paleolithic represents a significant shift to rock-shelter and cave occupations from the predominantly open-air, stream-channel, and lakeshore contexts of Early Paleolithic sites. While Early Paleolithic horizons do occur in a limited number of cave and rock-shelter sites throughout the Old World, Middle Paleolithic rock-shelter occupations are both denser and more numerous, possibly indicating a more systematic use and reuse of specific locations, greater need for shelter and vantage points in the harsher winters and reduced growing seasons of the early last glacial, and more successful challenging of resident carnivores. As suggested by the original designation of the "Cave Bear and Mammoth Age" (which included the early Upper Paleolithic Aurignacian and Perigordian industries as well), large-carnivore remains indicative of "time sharing" by humans and carnivores are still abundant at many cave and rock-shelter sites until ca. 20,000 B.P. Middle Paleolithic sites are also increasingly associated with remains of

open-air structures, such as the ones from Molodova and Cracow, as well as of stone walls delimiting or perhaps protecting the occupation area within rock-shelters, as at Pech de l'Azé and Cueva Morin.

Economy and Technology

Middle Paleolithic subsistence depended on the hunting of large herbivores, which dominate the faunal assemblages of both rock-shelter/cave and open-air sites. Hunting implements included hafted stone-tipped and wooden spears, actually recovered in association with mammoth remains in England (Hounslow) and Germany (Lehringen), as well as smaller projectiles, possibly arrows, suggested by micro-mousterian points, small *Blattspitzen*, and bifacial MSA points. Passive strategies are indicated by structures and types of faunal remains at lake and river margins and by "catastrophic" faunal profiles near cliff sites (Hortus). At many sites one or two species, such as ibex at Hortus (France), mammoth at Molodova, warthog and zebra at ≠Gi (Botswana), are responsible for 50–80 percent of the recovered remains, suggesting that hunting strategies at these locations were nonopportunistic but designed to take either a large portion of a single herd or repeated members of a single species over time. Several open-air localities in southern Africa (≠Gi, Kalkbank, Orangia) may represent Middle Paleolithic ambush stations.

At Khor Musa, in the Nile Valley, and at other river-margin sites, Middle Stone Age people exploited primarily fish. Shellfish were also eaten by MSA coastal dwellers, as at Klasies River Mouth, although to a lesser extent than in the succeeding Later Stone Age. Seals and penguins were important in the southern African MSA diet. Bird remains elsewhere are relatively rare, except for ostrich-eggshells, which were probably used as canteens after the egg had been consumed. Grindstones, presumably used for vegetable-food preparation, are common at several MSA sites and may have been cached there for repeated use.

In sum, Middle Paleolithic people were more specialized in their subsistence pursuits and employed more elaborate subsistence technologies than their predecessors, and they may have also developed a well-defined annual subsistence round that included specific stations in their territory or range. Long-distance transport of raw materials over 80–100 km., particularly seashells (Apollo-11, Border Cave) but more rarely imported stone (Krakow, ≠Gi, Bacho Kiro), is present but much more limited in both distance and extent than in the succeeding Later Paleolithic and may have been effected by the occupants themselves during their annual round.

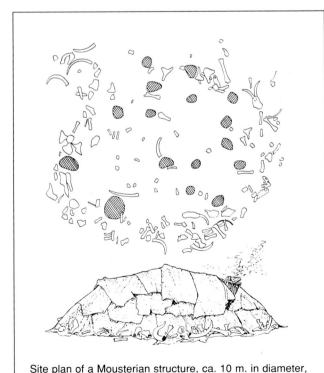

Site plan of a Mousterian structure, ca. 10 m. in diameter, at Molodova (Ukrainian S.S.R.), showing hearth areas (shaded) and faunal remains. A hypothetical reconstruction of a skin, bone, and brush "hut" is shown below. (From Wymer, 1982.)

Cognitive, Symbolic, Ritual Behavior

The best-documented evidence for symbolic and ritual behavior is the complex of Neanderthal burial sites from Europe, the Levant, and North Africa. Features of these burials, of which Regourdou is one of the best and most recently excavated examples, include careful interment of the body in a flexed position, often within an artificial pit or cairn; the provision of minimal grave goods (tools, meat-bearing bones); and association with cranial elements of specific animals, including bears (Regourdou) and ibex (Teshik-Tash). Some type of belief in the afterlife, as well as in the ritual significance of animal spirits, may be indicated by these sites. What is *not* evident is a pan-Mousterian reverence for cave bears; those sites with extensive cave-bear remains (e.g. Drachenloch), while excavated in the nineteenth century with relatively crude techniques, are probably lairs rather than ritual locations.

Although the evidence for ritual behavior is concentrated in the Mousterian area in the form of Neanderthal burial sites, areas, such as southern Africa, that lack evidence for burial traditions (except for the Border Cave infant) were equally rich in evidence for other symbolic behaviors. Ocher lumps and "crayons" are found at many MSA sites (Apollo-11, Howieson's Poort), as in the Mousterian (Pech de l'Azé), and a hematite-mining operation has been described from the Swaziland MSA. Perforated objects are also rare but present, both in Europe (Pech de l'Azé, La Quina, Bocksteinschmeide) and in Africa (Border Cave); occasional painted, incised, and carved objects have been recovered from both continents in Middle Paleolithic contexts (Tata, Apollo-11).

Summary

Middle Paleolithic industries characterized by prepared-flake core technologies are known from Europe, the Near East, East and South Asia, and Africa. While all regions appear to share the development of more specialized technologies, subsistence strategies, social interactions, and symbolic behavior, significant interregional differences exist, particularly between Africa and other regions. The African MSA industries not only begin considerably earlier but also include more consistent evidence of technological sophistication (blades, geometric forms, fishing, ambush hunting) and equivalent evidence for long-distance trade and symbolic behavior. In addition regionally specific tool traditions predominate in the African record, in contrast to the more monotonous character of the European Mousterian.

See also ATERIAN; EARLY PALEOLITHIC; ECONOMY, PREHISTORIC; LATE PALEOLITHIC; LEVALLOIS; LITHIC USE-WEAR; MIDDLE STONE AGE; MOUSTERIAN; PALEOLITHIC IMAGE; PALEOLITHIC LIFEWAYS; STONE-TOOL MAKING; UPPER PALEOLITHIC. [A.S.B]

Further Readings

Bordes, F. (1972) A Tale of Two Caves. New York: Harper and Row.

Gamble, C. (1986) The Palaeolithic Settlement of Europe. Cambridge: Cambridge University Press.

Phillipson, D.W. (1985) African Archaeology. Cambridge: Cambridge University Press.

Qiu Zhonglang. (1985) The Middle Palaeolithic of China. In Wu Rukang and J. Olsen (eds.): Palaeoanthropology and Palaeolithic Archaeology in the People's Republic of China. New York: Academic, pp. 187–210.

Volman, T. (1984) Early prehistory of southern Africa. In R.G. Klein (ed.): Southern African Prehistory and Paleoenvironments. Rotterdam: Balkema, pp. 169–220.

Wymer, J. (1982) The Palaeolithic Age. New York: St. Martin's.

MIDDLE STONE AGE

Second stage in a tripartite system for the African Stone Age, formalized by Goodwin and Van Riet Lowe in 1929 for South Africa and later expanded to include prepared-core (e.g. Stillbay, Bambata) and core-axe (Lupemban) industries from the entire continent, as well as from the Indian subcontinent. Originally included within the Later Stone Age as the "Eastern Variant," the Middle Stone Age was separated from the Later, due to both stratigraphic evidence and the absence of microblade technology. Characteristic Middle Stone Age forms include discoidal and Levallois-type cores, convergent flakes with faceted striking platforms, flake-blades and a variety of tools, such as side-scrapers and bifacial and unifacial points. Industries that combine prepared flake cores and microblade technologies were later placed in a separate transitional stage ("Second Intermediate"), while handaxe industries with prepared flake-core technology, such as the Fauresmith, were referred to the transitional "First Intermediate" stage.

Even within southern Africa the term "Middle Stone Age" (MSA) includes a large number of regionally specific industries, such as the Pietersburg, Orangian, Stillbay, and Bambata industries, each with several phases of development, which differ in the forms and percentages of retouched points, knives, and scrapers and in the technology of blank manufacture. In the Cape Province of South Africa a chronological variant, the Howieson's Poort, bears a superficial resemblance to Upper Paleolithic industries in its preponderance of backed blades and is probably somewhat comparable in time with the earliest blade industries of the Levant, such as the Pre-Aurignacian and Amudian.

Middle Stone Age peoples were accomplished

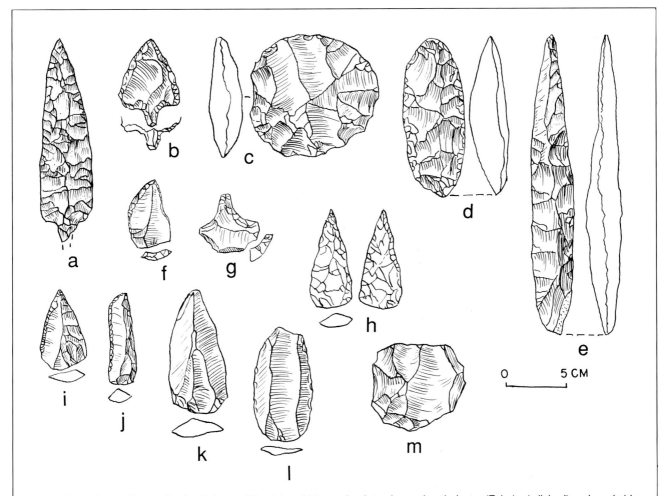

Middle Stone Age artifacts. Aterian industry (Algeria): a–b) tanged points. Lupemban industry (Zaire): c) disk; d) end- and side-scraper; e) bifacial lanceolate. Bambata industry (Zimbabwe): f) backed flake with concave marginal retouch on working edge; g) borer; h) bifacial point. Pietersburg industry (South Africa): i) unifacial point; j) double side-scraper; k) triangular flake from prepared core; l) Levallois-type flake; m) disk core. (After J.D. Clark, The Prehistory of Africa, 1970; and Phillipson, © 1985 by Cambridge University Press. Reprinted with permission.)

hunters, who regularly captured large antelope, zebra, and warthog at probable ambush locations, as well as a wide range of smaller game. Plant foods, reflected indirectly by large numbers of grindstones at some sites (e.g. Kalkbank, ≠Gi), shellfish, and ostrich eggs contributed to the MSA diet.

The technological sophistication of MSA industries, particularly in blade manufacture and possible hafting of projectile points, and the degree of regional and chronological specificity were widely interpreted as derivative "Upper Paleolithic" elements in a relatively "backward" context, at a time when the MSA was thought to coincide with the Upper Paleolithic of Europe. Recent K-Ar dates for initial MSA occupations prior to the late Pleistocene (greater than 130 k.y.) in Ethiopia and evidence from Tanzania (Laetoli) and southern Africa suggest instead that MSA industries may represent technoeconomic and social advances lacking in the Middle Paleolithic of Eurasia but pre-saging later developments there. These advances, which now include decorated stone slabs and incised ostrich-eggshell from Apollo-11 Cave, may be associated with what are possibly the earliest examples of modern humans (Homo sapiens sapiens) at such sites as Border Cave, Cape Flats (Skildergat), and Klasies River Mouth, as well as with more archaic populations of Homo sapiens, as at Florisbad. Final dates for Middle Stone Age industries of southern Africa seem to predate 30,000 B.P.

Middle Stone Age core-axe industries of central Africa, such as the Lupemban and Kalinian, are poorly known from excavated contexts, with a few exceptions (e.g. Kalambo Falls) but are thought to predate considerably a widespread recession of the tropical forest at ca. 20,000 B.P. In North Africa the Aterian industry with its tanged bifacial points and scrapers is the local counterpart of the Middle Stone Age, between the last interglacial (ca. 100 k.y.) and

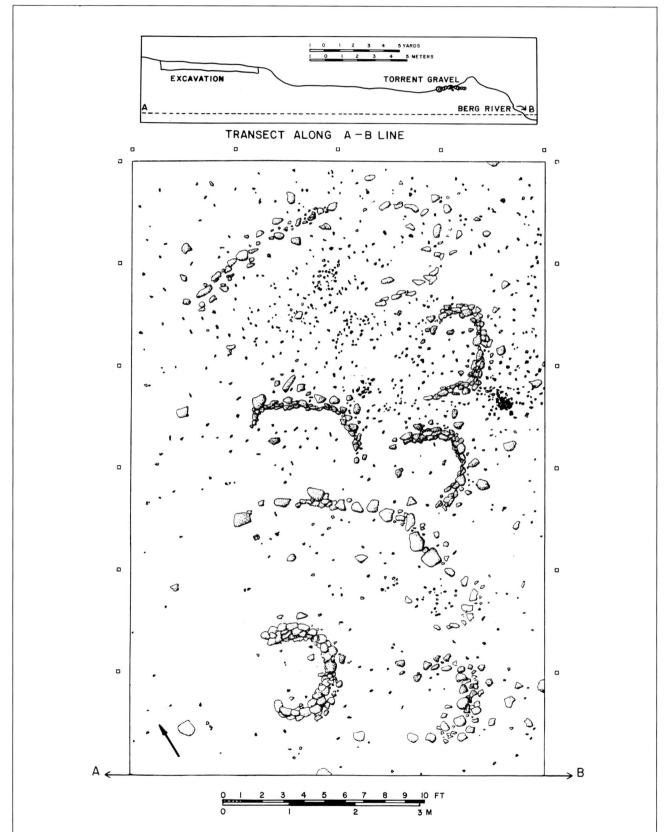

TRANSECT ALONG A—B LINE

Stone structures on the Middle Stone Age floor at Orangia 1, Orange Free State (South Africa). Below: site plan; above: section along bottom of plan view, showing that semicircular arrangements of stone "face" toward old river channel represented by gravel.

ca. 30 to 20 k.y.

Since the term "Middle Stone Age" has been used as a general category for any industry with prepared cores lacking both handaxes and microliths, its use has been formally discontinued by the Pan African Congress of Prehistory and Quaternary Studies. Until the definition and chronology of regional industries of the late middle and early late Pleistocene have been worked out, the Congress has recommended the use of regionally specific industry names, combined with the Mode III designation of J.G.D. Clark, for flake industries with prepared cores, to avoid implications of chronological, stratigraphic, and cultural uniformity across the African continent.

See also AMUDIAN; APOLLO-11; ATERIAN; BAMBATA; BORDER CAVE; CAVE OF HEARTHS; EARLY STONE AGE; FIRST INTERMEDIATE; FLORISBAD; HANDAXE; *HOMO SAPIENS*; HOWIESON'S POORT; KALAMBO FALLS; KLASIES; LATE PALEOLITHIC; LATER STONE AGE; LEVALLOIS; LUPEMBAN; MIDDLE PALEOLITHIC; ORANGIAN; PALEOLITHIC; PIETERSBURG; PRE-AURIGNACIAN; ROSE COTTAGE; SECOND INTERMEDIATE; STILLBAY; STONE-TOOL MAKING; UPPER PALEOLITHIC. [A.S.B.]

Further Readings

Phillipson, D.W. (1985) African Archaeology. Cambridge: Cambridge University Press.
Volman, T.P. (1984) Early prehistory of southern Africa. In R.G. Klein (ed.): Southern African Prehistory and Paleoenvironments. Rotterdam: Balkema.

MIGRATION *see* PALEOBIOGEOGRAPHY

MILANKOVITCH, MILUTIN (1879–1945)

As the professor of physics and celestial mechanics at the University of Belgrade, Milankovitch published his seminal work, *Canon of Insolation of the Earth and Its Application to the Problem of Ice Ages* (in English), in 1941. The essence of the Milankovitch theory, or "Milankovitch cycles," is that the major fluctuations in global climate are caused by variations in the pattern of incoming solar radiation, which are in turn caused by combinations of slow changes in orbital geometry, axial tilt, and axial wobble of the earth. Superimposed cycles of warm and cold climate with periodicities of ca. 24 k.y., ca. 90 k.y., and ca. 450 k.y., among others predicted by Milankovitch, have been clearly identified in Pleistocene deep-sea and continental sequences. Orbitally forced climate fluctuations are seen in cyclic layering of evaporite formations at least as far back as the Permian.

See also GLACIATION; PLEISTOCENE; SEA-LEVEL CHANGE. [J.A.V.C.]

Further Readings

Berger, W., et al., eds. (1984) Milankovitch and Climate Change. Hingham, Mass: Reidel.

MILAZZIAN *see* PLEISTOCENE; SEA-LEVEL CHANGE

MINDEL *see* GLACIATION; PLEISTOCENE

MIOCENE

Epoch spanning the interval between 23.5 and 5.3 m.y. in the later Cenozoic. "Miocene," from the Greek meaning "moderately recent," was introduced in 1833 by Charles Lyell for the marine strata in which 40–60 percent of the fossil species were extinct. Lyell later felt compelled to remind his readers—as in the sixth edition of *Elements of Geology* (1865), pp. 187–188—that notwithstanding the inclusion of freshwater and volcanic rocks, " . . . the terms Eocene, Miocene and Pliocene were originally invented with reference purely to [marine] conchological data, and in that sense have always been and are still used by me." These data initially came from fossils found in Cenozoic basins in western Europe (the North Sea basin, the London-Paris basin, the Bordeaux basin, and the upper reaches of the Po basin), and it is to these classical marine sequences that the modern definitions and subdivisions of this epoch have also been related.

The Miocene is conventionally, if not formally, divided into three parts, based on the marine record of the classical sequences. The early Miocene is held by most modern stratigraphers to be time-equivalent to the Aquitanian and Burdigalian stages, both of which are typified in beds specifically included in the Miocene by Lyell in the vicinity of Bordeaux. The base of the Aquitanian thus defines the base of the Miocene, and a "golden spike" (physical reference point) in the Aquitanian stratotype at Moulin de Bernachon, near Saucats, has been recognized as the unique criterion for this definition. Micropaleontological correlations indicate that this level is equivalent to paleomagnetic Chron C6CN, as seen in deep-sea cores, and to marine deposits in California that are interbedded with radiometrically dated lavas. The dating from both lines of evidence agrees on an age of 23.7 m.y., but since this may not relate precisely to the stratotype the age of the boundary is rounded off to 23.5 m.y.

The middle (or medial) Miocene is equivalent to the Langhian and Serravallian stages, founded on exposures in the northern Apennine foothills that were among those most closely studied by Lyell. (The underlying Bormidian Stage in this area also includes strata noted by Lyell, and has been proposed as an alternative definition for the early Miocene.) The base of the Langhian, a period of rising global sea level, is correlated to radiometrically dated magnetostratigraphy and microfossil zones, as in the Vienna basin, New Guinea, Japan, and California, at 16.5 m.y.

The late Miocene is conventionally represented by the Tortonian and Messinian stages, also typified in the marine rocks of Italy. The base of the Tortonian, recently recorrelated to the worldwide time scale, is dated at 10.4 m.y., and the base of the Messinian, marking the beginning of a worldwide drop in sea level and the temporary desiccation of the Mediterranean basin, is at 6.5 m.y.

Strata of Messinian age were not included in Lyell's discussion, being mostly absent from the sections he studied due to late Miocene erosion, and it has been argued that they could be considered as belonging to the Pliocene. Under modern stratigraphic principles the top of the Miocene, however, is defined not by the highest known Miocene but by the base of the known Pliocene. The Pliocene is clearly identified in Lyell's work as the deposits laid down in the post-Messinian transgression, and modern dating puts the beginning of this episode at 5.3 m.y. ago.

Miocene Environments

The Miocene saw major changes in global climate, as the world ocean continued to shift toward the unstable, thermally stratified "cold ocean" of today and away from the stable, salinity-stratified "warm ocean" of the Cretaceous and earlier Paleogene. Thus the early Miocene, between 19.5 and 16.5 m.y., was warmer and had less seasonal variation than at any time since, as indicated by oxygen-isotope studies. During this interval "subtropical" conditions extended well into higher latitudes, even though upwelling cold currents had already begun to generate onshore aridity in Namibia, North Africa, the Arabian and Iranian regions, and the western United States.

By the end of the middle Miocene the collapse of the Tethys Sea had closed the connection between the Mediterranean and the Indian Ocean at the head of the Persian Gulf, and free flow between the Indian Ocean and the Pacific had also been disrupted. At the same time old and new suture zones developed into a continuous east-west mountain wall, all across the Gondwana-Laurasia contact zone from the Alps and Carpathians through the Elburz, Tien Shan, and Himalayas. This further impeded heat exchange between temperate and tropical weather regimes and introduced the monsoon cycle in the Indopakistan region. Conditions changed noticeably to become more seasonal, and at higher latitudes with colder and colder winters. By 11 m.y., as Miocene seas withdrew to their lowest point, great tracts of evergreen broadleaf forest in the temperate zones were replaced by communities better adapted to seasonal

aridity and temperature change. The Canary Islands are the last refuge of many members of the Miocene temperate woodland, since in these isles the requisite warm, stable conditions are perpetuated. After a slight warming trend and sea-level advance in the later Tortonian, at ca. 8 m.y., the Miocene ended with a sharp drop in ocean levels and a new low in average global temperatures, which seems to be well correlated with a major expansion of the Antarctic ice sheet.

Miocene Faunas

The open-country habitats that developed in response to increased seasonality in the later Miocene have been termed "savanna," "steppe," and even "grasslands," but they appear to have no real contemporary analogue, being a mosaic of closed-canopy forest, open woodlands, and grassy bush. In southeastern South America and in Mongolia, open-country (e.g. semiarid and possibly seasonal) habitats with precociously developed "steppe faunas" appeared as early as the middle Oligocene, probably in response to continental exposure during the great mid-Tertiary regression, combined with orographic effects of the Andean and Himalayan mountain zones. Yet in most of the world's temperate and subtropical regions open conditions did not develop until after global circulation changes in the middle Miocene.

The tropical and subtropical forests were refuges for the more conservative animal groups, among which should be included the great apes and most monkeys and prosimians. The groups that colonized the open country, however, displayed conspicuous adaptations. In dental morphology many herbivores (e.g. murid and cricetid rodents, rabbits, warthogs, antelopes, giraffes, rhinos, horses, hyraxes, and elephants) exhibited parallel trends toward ever-growing or continuously renewed teeth to cope with heavy wear, while others (bush pigs, bears, and hominoids), perhaps more omnivorous or more root-oriented, adopted radically thickened enamel as an alternative way to deal with a more abrasive diet. Behaviorally, seasonal food and water shortages in the open were met with strategies not usually found in forest animals, including fossorial colonies, herding, synchronized reproduction, food caches, and (among carnivores) cooperative hunting, food transport, and den minding. The fossil record contains evidence of most of these trends beginning in the middle Miocene, and the others may be inferred from the fact that many modern lineages that show such behavior are first recognized at this time.

The carrying capacity of the open environment, with more sunlight reaching ground level and faster-growing and more diverse vegetation available, greatly exceeds that of the forest. Both abundance and seasonality are attested in the great bone-pile sites found in middle and late Miocene open-habitat localities, such as Valentine, Pikermi, Maragheh, and Nihowan. Aside from rare *Mesopithecus* remains no primates are found in the mass-mortality sites, however, and for the most part Miocene primates appear to have favored the more closed and well-watered habitats even in "savanna" mosaic.

Miocene Events

In the later early Miocene, at ca. 18 m.y., sea-level decline exposed dry-land connections between Africa and Eurasia, via key "bridges" at the Bab el Mandab and in the shoaling contact between Mesopotamia and northern Iran. The African fauna, specifically that of the coastal plains of East Africa and Arabia, found Eurasia much to its liking. Many of the endemic African lineages (tragulids, primitive antelopes and giraffids, proboscideans, creodonts, nimravine felids, and true chalicotheres, among others) appear at this time in Orleanian ("Burdigalian") faunas of western Europe at the MN4b level, dated to ca. 17.5 m.y.

However, it was not until 16 m.y. (early middle Miocene), by which time the proboscideans had already reached North America and sea levels had begun to rise, that the higher primates began to spread out of Afro-Arabia. *Dryopithecus* and *Pliopithecus* appear at this time in western and central Europe, and the sivapithecines (*Sivapithecus* and related or synonymous genera, such as *Ouranopithecus* and *Austriacopithecus*) colonized a wide area from the Vienna basin and Turkey to Indopakistan. Ancestral *Oreopithecus* reached the Italian peninsula only to be marooned by the middle Miocene highstand. The sivapithecines are specialized, presumably seasonally adapted taxa closely related to *Heliopithecus* and *Kenyapithecus* from tropical lowland environments in Kenya and Arabia, but the others were more like the early Miocene proconsulines and oreopithecines of the equatorial highlands. Cercopithecoids, the only higher primates found in North African early and middle Miocene faunas, did not emerge from Africa until late Miocene time at ca. 12 m.y., concurrently with the expansion of more open habitats in temperate Eurasia and also with the first exposure of the Suez isthmus.

In North America the last of the aboriginal Laurasian prosimians, *Ekgmowechashala*, became extinct in the early Miocene. The isolated South American platyrrhines, already well diversified in the late Oligocene, are known principally from the middle Miocene La Venta fauna of Colombia.

See also CENOZOIC; EUROPE; PLIOCENE; SEA-LEVEL CHANGE. [J.A.V.C., R.L.B.]

Further Readings

Berggren, W.A., Kent, D.V., and Van Couvering, J.A. (1985) Neogene, Part 2. In N.J. Snelling (ed.): The Chronology of the Geological Record. London: Blackwoods.

Haq, B.U., Hardenbol, J., and Vail, P.R. (1987) A chronology of fluctuating sea-levels since the Triassic. Science 235:1156-1165.

Russell, D.E., and Savage, D.E. (1983) Mammalian Paleofaunas of the World. Reading, Mass.: Addison-Wesley.

MIOEUOTICUS   *see*   LORISIDAE

MIOPITHECUS   *see*   CERCOPITHECINAE

MIRZA   *see*   CHEIROGALEIDAE

MLADEC

The Mladec (Lautsch) caves in Czechoslovakia have provided some of the earliest anatomically modern fossils from Europe. Skeletal remains of several adults and a child were recovered from choked chimney deposits, which also contained Aurignacian stone and bone tools. Several of the hominid crania are very robust and have even been regarded as Neanderthal-like. Unfortunately most of the material was destroyed in a fire in 1945, but casts of the best crania have survived as well as the most complete cranium (1), stored in Vienna.

See also HOMO SAPIENS. [C.B.S.]

MODERN HOMO SAPIENS   *see*   ARCHAIC MODERNS; HOMO SAPIENS

MODERN HUMANS   *see*   ARCHAIC MODERNS; HOMO SAPIENS; HUMAN

MODES, TECHNOLOGICAL

Scheme or sequence of mainly Paleolithic technological stages devised by J.G.D. Clark in 1968 to get away from the use of local industrial terminology outside the area of its definition. For example, rather than discussing Oldowan-like or chopper-chopping tool assemblages in Europe, the less "loaded" term "Mode I" could be applied to the Buda industry. Mode I implies simple flakes and cores; Mode II, direct-percussion flaking of more formally shaped pieces; Mode III, the wide use of prepared cores to yield flake variety; Mode IV, dominance of blades and burins; and Mode V, microliths.

See also PALEOLITHIC; STONE-TOOL MAKING. [E.D.]

MODJOKERTO

Eastern Java fossil-collecting area, of early or middle Pleistocene age by stratigraphic correlation. The Modjokerto infant hominid calvaria was supposedly excavated from a site north of Perning in East Java, and its provenance and taxonomic affinities have been a constant source of debate. Von Koenigswald originally referred to the specimen as "*Homo modjokertensis*" but subsequently referred it to "*Pithecanthropus modjokertensis*" and "*Pithecanthropus robustus*." His arguments as to its taxonomic affinities appear to have been strictly stratigraphic. The date of 1.9 m.y. ± 0.4 m.y. often quoted for the specimen probably has little or nothing to do with its actual age. No fauna is associated with the specimen, and there is even doubt as to whether the actual excavation site has been reidentified. Although current estimates of its antiquity range from latest early Pleistocene to late Pleistocene, the absence of a reliable provenance for this specimen makes such estimates moot.

See also ASIA (EASTERN); INDONESIA; KOENIGSWALD, G.H.R. VON. [G.G.P.]

Further Readings

Sartono, S., Semah, F., Astadiredja, K.A.S., Sukedarmono, M., and Djubantono, T. (1981) The age of *Homo mojokertensis*. Mod. Quat. Res. Southeast Asia 6:91–101.

MOERIPITHECUS see PROPLIOPITHECIDAE

MOGHARA see AFRICA; VICTORIAPITHECINAE

MOGHREBIAN see PLEISTOCENE; SEA-LEVEL CHANGE

MOHANAMICO see PITHECIINAE

MOLECULAR ANTHROPOLOGY

Systematic study of primate taxa using comparative genetic methods. Since evolutionary change involves change in the genes, a study of the genetic systems of primates should reveal the relationships of species. The subfield dates to Nuttall's (1902) pioneering work on the immunological cross-reactions between the bloods of different species. Little progress was made in this area, however, until the studies of Goodman in the 1960s.

As immunological distances are a rough measure of protein (and therefore genetic) similarity, the first use of these data involved primate phylogeny and

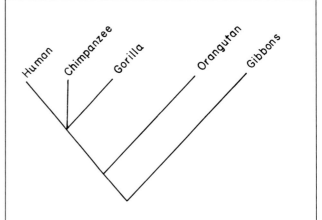

Molecular data are unable to resolve a phylogenetic trichotomy of human, chimpanzee, and gorilla but place the orangutan clearly apart from the African apes and humans.

established that the African apes (chimpanzee and gorilla) are more closely related to humans than to orangutans. Another method that became available in the 1960s was the direct sequencing of the amino acids composing specific proteins, a more direct reflection of the genetic material. Protein-sequence data not only confirmed the immunological results but showed that humans, chimpanzees, and gorillas were genetically more similar to one another than had previously been imagined.

Concurrently empirical data and theoretical advances pointed to the conclusion that most evolutionary changes in proteins are nonadaptive and not subject to the operation of natural selection. The spread of these "neutral" changes is governed by *genetic drift*, a statistical process. Consequently any neutral mutation has a (low) probability of spreading through a population over time; and the spread of these mutations is simply a function of how often neutral mutations arise. Natural selection is here relegated to a primarily constraining role, limiting the rate at which a given protein can change but not affecting its evolution in a constructive, directional way.

Thus, although the vast majority of neutral mutations are lost shortly after arising, the laws of probability admit a few to spread through a population. They do so at a rate that fluctuates in the short run but approximates a constant rate in the long run. The amount of genetic difference between two species, therefore, could be taken as a measure of how long two species have been separated from one another.

Molecular Clock

The findings that molecular evolution proceeds at a roughly constant rate and that humans, chimpanzees, and gorillas are unexpectedly similar genetically could be reconciled in two ways, which represent the poles of a long-unresolved controversy.

Goodman and co-workers inferred that since humans and the African apes are so similar genetically the rate of molecular evolution in these species has been slowing down. Alternatively, Wilson, Sarich, and co-workers inferred that since molecular evolution is constant humans and the African apes must have diverged more recently than 4 m.y. ago.

Sarich and Wilson argued that the prevailing opinion in 1967, that humans and African apes had diverged from each other by 15 m.y. ago because the fossil *Ramapithecus* was a uniquely human ancestor, was flawed. Time has borne out their conclusion, but it also appears that the divergence dates calculated by Sarich and Wilson are somewhat underestimated and that there was indeed a slowdown in the rate of molecular evolution among the great apes and humans.

Cytogenetic Data

Techniques were developed in the 1970s for distinguishing the 23 chromosome pairs in the human karyotype, and while these techniques have been most useful in clinical applications they have generated evolutionary data as well.

Chimpanzees and gorillas share several chromosomal inversions, inherited from a recent common ancestor, as well as a unique distribution of C-bands. In humans these bands, which distinguish areas where the DNA is more tightly condensed than elsewhere, appear only at the centromere of each chro-

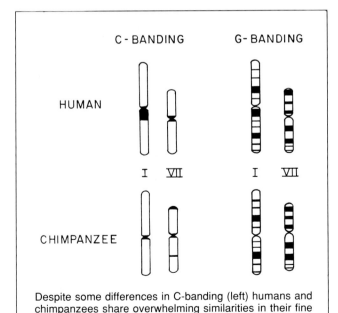

Despite some differences in C-banding (left) humans and chimpanzees share overwhelming similarities in their fine structure, as revealed by G-banding (right). Pictured are two chromosomes (1 and 7) from the human and their counterparts in the chimpanzee.

mosome; below the centromere of chromosomes 1, 9, and 16; and on the long arm of the Y-chromosome. In the African apes, however, they appear at the tips of most chromosomes.

In general the chromosomes of humans and the African apes are highly similar, when prepared by the common procedure of G-banding. The most significant difference seems to be a recent fusion of two chromosomes in the human lineage, reducing the number of chromosome pairs from 24 (retained in the great apes) to 23 and creating what we now recognize as chromosome #2 in the human karyotype.

Rates of chromosomal change vary widely across primate taxa. We find rapid rates of chromosomal evolution in the gibbons and the most arboreal cercopithecine monkeys, slow chromosomal evolution in the baboons, and a moderate rate in the great apes and humans.

DNA Studies

The development of molecular genetics in the late 1970s brought studies of molecular evolution away from phenotypes—even a protein or antibody reaction is, properly speaking, a phenotype—and down directly to the genotype. These studies examine direct aspects of the DNA nucleotide sequence itself or indirect measures of DNA divergence. As phylogenetic data the results obtained from DNA studies support those obtained from protein analyses. For example, the specific relations among human, chimpanzee, and gorilla are as unclear in their DNA as in their proteins, yet these species all still cluster apart from the orangutan.

Mitochondria are organelles that exist in the cytoplasm of each bodily cell. Although subcellular structures, they contain their own genetic machinery and information encoded in a circular piece of DNA ca. 16,500 nucleotides long in humans. While the evolutionary rules that govern change in mitochondrial DNA are still unclear, in primates their rate of change seems to be about tenfold higher than that of nuclear DNA. Moreover, mitochondria are inherited exclusively through the mother, in contrast to nuclear DNA. These facts have already been used to study the genetic splitting of the human races, using mitochrondrial DNA as genetic markers. It has recently been proposed, based on the rate of change in this DNA, that the principal human groups diverged from one another about 200 k.y. ago, a considerably more ancient date than is usually thought.

Studies of DNA sequences across species have established that the neutral theory of molecular evolution is more applicable to DNA than to proteins. This is because the genome is now known to be very complex. Although a gene codes for a protein, only a portion of the gene actually consists of coding instructions. These regions (*exons*) are interrupted by DNA segments (*introns*) that do not become translated into part of the protein molecule. Untranslated regions are also found at the beginning and end of each gene. Further, most of the DNA in the genome consists of intergenic DNA (i.e. DNA that lies between genes).

It is now clear that between any two species intergenic DNA is most different, intron DNA is slightly more similar, and exon DNA is least different. Further, differences in exon DNA fall into two categories: those that direct a different amino acid to become part of the protein (*replacement mutations*) and those that do not change the protein (*silent mutations*). Silent mutations far outnumber replacement mutations in any gene compared across two species.

What this means is that the neutral theory proposed to explain protein evolution is really only a first approximation, since the mutations that actually are detectable in protein evolution represent the slowest-evolving part of the genome. These replacement mutations are affected by the constraints of natural selection to a greater degree than silent mutations, intron and untranslated mutations, or intergenic mutations.

Levels of Evolution

While evolutionary change is genetic change, and ultimately molecular change, it is impossible at present to associate any adaptive anatomical specialization of humans with any particular DNA change. We may analogize to what is known about phenotypic evolution in other organisms, such as the fruitfly, but we have never located a gene for bipedalism or cranial expansion, and it is likely that there are no genes "for" these traits in the sense that there is a gene "for" cytochrome C or beta-hemoglobin.

Thus, while it is certain that the processes of bone growth and remodeling are under genetic control, as are the processes that govern the development of facultative responses to stresses on bone growth, such genes have not been located. Further, it is difficult to envision at this point how such genes work, or what their primary product might be, much less how to isolate such a product.

Consequently we are not able to explain at present how the primarily nonadaptive changes we find in the DNA account for the primarily adaptive morphological changes we find in the anatomy of the animal. This seems attributable less to any flaws in contemporary evolutionary theory than to our ignorance of how one gets phenotypic expressions out of genotypic information. It is therefore useful to conceive of evolution as a multilevel system: first, a level of the

genome, where changes are clocklike over the long run and primarily unexpressed and nonadaptive; second, a level of the karyotype, where chromosomal rearrangements are primarily unexpressed and nonadaptive but may generate reproductive incompatibilities that facilitate the process of speciation; and third, a level of morphology, where changes usually track the environment and individuals with certain anatomical characters out-reproduce those with other similar anatomies, on the average.

See also DNA HYBRIDIZATION; GENETICS; GENOME; IMMUNOLOGICAL DISTANCE; NON-DARWINIAN EVOLUTION. [J.M.]

Further Readings

Buettner-Janusch, J., and Hill, R.L. (1965) Molecules and monkeys. Science *147*:836–842.

Gillespie, J. (1986) Variability in evolutionary rates of DNA. Ann. Rev. Ecol. Syst. *17*:637–665.

Goodman, M., Tashian, R., and Tashian, J., eds. (1976) Molecular Anthropology. New York: Plenum.

King, M.-C., and Wilson, A.C. (1975) Evolution at two levels in humans and chimpanzees. Science *188*:107–116.

Marks, J. (1983) Hominoid cytogenetics and evolution. Yrbk. Phys. Anthropol. *25*:125–153.

Wilson, A.C., Cann, R.L., Carr, S.M., George, M., Gyllensten, U.B., Helm-Bychowski, K.M., Higuchi, R., Palumbi, S.R., Prager, E.M., Sage, R.D., and Stoneking, M. (1985) Mitochondrial DNA and two perspectives on evolutionary genetics. Bio. J. Linn. Soc. *26*:375–400.

MOLECULAR CLOCK

Comparative studies of protein structure suggested the "molecular clock hypothesis" to Zuckerkandl and Pauling in 1962: that proteins evolve at statistically constant rates and that a simple algorithm relates amount of protein difference between two species and the time since divergence of those species from their last common ancestor. It presents a sharp contrast to anatomical evolution, in which rates of evolution are usually related to environmental exigencies and may fluctuate widely. The concept of a molecular clock was used by Sarich and Wilson to modify earlier assumptions about the remoteness of common ancestry between humans and the African apes.

Kimura, a theoretical population geneticist, showed mathematically in the late 1960s that if most genetic changes had no adaptive effect on the organism then the evolution of these "neutral" mutations would be essentially constant over the long run. While predictions of the neutral theory accord well with the empirical data of protein evolution, it is also possible that models based on natural selection can account for these data.

It is now clear that each protein has its own characteristic rate of change. The most fundamental proteins (e.g. histones, which package cellular DNA) evolve slowly, while globins (which transport oxygen) evolve more rapidly. Further, this rate may fluctuate in the short run, but averages to a constant rate over the long run.

DNA evolution can be modeled along the same lines as protein evolution. The discovery that most of the genomic DNA is not transcribed or expressed makes it likely that most DNA evolution is more nearly neutral than protein evolution. This makes noncoding DNA a good candidate for the mathematical models of the neutral theory.

See also IMMUNOLOGICAL DISTANCE; MOLECULAR ANTHROPOLOGY; NON-DARWINIAN EVOLUTION. [J.M.]

Further Readings

Wilson, A.C., Carlson, S.S., and White, T.J. (1977) Biochemical evolution. Ann. Rev. Biochem. 46:573-639.

MOLODOVA

Geographic region with three major stratified Paleolithic sites (Molodova I and V and Korman IV), located along the middle course of the Dnestr River in the western Ukraine (U.S.S.R.). The sites, which have received extensive attention from a multidisciplinary team of scholars, are found on the second terrace of the river; cultural remains lay in both buried soils and colluvial deposits. Molodova I and V contain eight and 13 superimposed cultural layers, respectively. A sequence of radiocarbon dates indicates that they were occupied from at least 50,000 B.P. to the close of the glacial Pleistocene, ca. 11,000 B.P. At both sites a sequence of layers with Middle Paleolithic tools underlies those assigned to the Late Paleolithic. Extensive archaeological inventories of stone tools and faunal remains have been found in all the layers. The Mousterian layer IV at Molodova I contained bones of at least 13 mammoths arranged in a 10-by-7-m. oval pattern that contained 15 hearths within it as well as over 44,000 pieces of lithics. This feature, dating older than 44,000 B.P., has been interpreted as remains of the oldest mammoth-bone dwelling. A similar patterning of mammoth bone was also found in level 11 of Molodova V. The consistency in stone- and bone-tool inventories from these sites has led Soviet and East European researchers to assign the Late Paleolithic archaeological remains found here to a single uniform evolving Molodova industry, a local variant of the Eastern Gravettian technocomplex.

See also EUROPE; GRAVETTIAN; LATE PALEOLITHIC; SITE TYPES. [O.S.]

Further Readings

Klein, R.G. (1973) Ice-age Hunters of the Ukraine. Chicago: University of Chicago Press.

MONKEY

Grade or level of primate evolution characterized by moderate body and brain size, usually with a long tail, frugivorous or folivorous diet, above-branch quadrupedal locomotion, and multimale social organization. There are two main groups of monkeys in the modern primate fauna, the ceboids, or platyrrhines, of the Neotropics and the cercopithecids of Asia and Africa. At least one distinct group of fossil primates is also termed monkey, the Oligocene parapithecids of the Fayum. The most important evolutionary aspect of the concept *monkey* is that it is not a phyletic term: those animals called monkeys are not each other's closest relatives. Instead it represents an informal grade of organization, such as those denoted by *ape, human,* or *prosimian.* Among the monkeys the platyrrhines are the sister taxon of all the Old World anthropoids or catarrhines. Similarly, the closest living relatives of the cercopithecids are the hominoids (apes plus humans), while the extinct parapithecids, once thought to be specially related to cercopithecids, are now thought to be the sister taxon of all other catarrhines, or even all other anthropoids. This confusing concept of monkey, having no real evolutionary meaning, arose before evolution was understood, as an outgrowth of the *scala naturae* thinking of the time. Nonetheless, we can use this concept to compare the two main types of living monkeys.

Platyrrhine Monkeys

The New World monkeys, or superfamily Ceboidea, include two families whose arrangement differs somewhat among authors. Here we recognize Cebi-

Brazilian *Callithrix jacchus*, the common marmoset, clinging to a tree trunk which it has gouged for sap feeding. (Courtesy of and © W.G. Kinzey.)

Yellow-handed titi (*Callicebus torquatus*) feeding on fruit, Amazonian Peru. (Courtesy of and © Warren Kinzey.)

in length from long to very short. Within the ceboids the cebids are characterized by lightly built jaws and teeth, with the third molars reduced (in Cebinae) or lacking (in Callitrichinae); the thumb is often reduced as well, and the nails are clawlike in the callitrichines. Atelids have more robust jaws and zygomatic arches, deep mandibles, and large posterior teeth; one subfamily, the Atelinae, is characterized by a unique prehensile (grasping) tail—an independently evolved and less-complex version of this organ is found in one cebine.

All platyrrhines inhabit rain forests or other densely wooded environments, none being at all terrestrial. Diets vary greatly among gums, insects, leaves, and fruits, both soft- and hard-skinned. In turn the teeth of ceboids are varied and often distinguishable at the genus level. Social organization varies as well, with monogamy and a range of multimale patterns known. It is also interesting to note that ceboids are characterized by the early occurrence of extinct members of several modern lineages, either generic or subfamilial.

Catarrhine Monkeys

Two groups of catarrhines may be called monkeys: the living Cercopithecidae and the extinct Parapithecidae. In addition to their features discussed by contrast to ceboids cercopithecids retain ischial callosities, tough sitting pads that are probably an ancestral character of catarrhines. Their molars are uniformly bilophodont, with two parallel crests that interlock with those of opposing teeth.

The family Cercopithecidae comprises two subfamilies, Cercopithecinae and Colobinae. The former have cheek pouches for the temporary storage of food and a mainly frugivorous-to-omnivorous diet, while the latter have a diet comprising large quanti-

dae and Atelidae. Ceboids are characterized by external noses with wide side-facing nostrils, three premolar teeth in both upper and lower jaws, mainly curved nails on fingers and toes, and generally long tails. By contrast the cercopithecids have a narrower nasal septum with nostrils opening downward, only two premolar teeth, flattened nails, and tails varying

Savanna baboons (*Papio hamadryas cynocephalus*) in Kenya. The male in the center is grooming a female. Note the size difference between the sexes and the open nature of the terrain. (Courtesy of and © J.F. Oates.)

Wanderoo macaque (*Macaca silenus*) in tree in South India. The two white rump patches are the ischial callosities. (Courtesy of and © J.F. Oates.)

ties of mainly young leaves and buds and are characterized by a complex stomach to process this hard-to-digest food. Colobine teeth are also taller and sharper than those of cercopithecines, for better shearing of leaves, and their thumbs are reduced and sometimes completely absent externally.

Cercopithecines are quite variable in their environmental tolerance and locomotor adaptations, with terrestrial quadrupedalism having evolved independently several times, and at least twice more among the usually arboreal colobines. They range from desert margins in Arabia and North Africa through savanna, woodland, and rain forest to snowy regions of India and Japan. Most species have some form of multimale social organization, but unimale groups are common among the Cercopithecini. The baboons of sub-Saharan Africa (genus *Papio*) epitomize the terrestrial, omnivorous cercopithecine, with multimale troops involving intermale coalitions. One species ranges over most of the more open regions of the continent, while two species of forest baboons (mandrills and drills) inhabit small areas of western coastal forest. Their Asian equivalents are the macaques (*Macaca*), of which numerous species divide up variable habitats more finely. Colobines are generally restricted to tropical forest habitats, but at least one living species, and several extinct forms, inhabited more open woodland or savanna. Unimale groups are common, but multimale troops, often with male takeovers, and even monogamous units are known. The fossil record of the cercopithecids is well documented, with a variety of African species and several extinct European genera.

South Indian rain-forest habitat of wanderoo and Nilgiri langur, typical of that of most arboreal cercopithecids. (Courtesy of and © J.F. Oates.)

Nilgiri langur (*Semnopithecus [Trachypithecus] johnii*) in South Indian rain forest, sitting on tree branch on its ischial callosities. (Courtesy of and © J.F. Oates.)

See also APE; ATELIDAE; CATARRHINI; CEBIDAE; CERCOPITHECIDAE; CLADISTICS; DIET; EVOLUTION; LOCOMOTION; PARAPITHECIDAE; PHYLOGENY; PLATYRRHINI; PRIMATES; PROSIMIAN; SCALA NATURAE; TEETH. [E.D.]

Further Readings

Napier, J.R., and Napier, P.H. (1985) Natural History of the Primates. Cambridge, Mass.: MIT Press.

Szalay, F.S., and Delson, E. (1979) Evolutionary History of the Primates. New York: Academic.

MONOPHYLY

A set of organisms, or taxon, is said to be *monophyletic* if it includes all (and only) those species hypothesized to be descended from a common ancestral species. Noting that other, more liberal definitions have been adopted in the past, some biologists have used the term *holophyletic* for this strict conception of monophyly, but the definition given above has become pervasive in contemporary systematic biology. Thus *holophyletic* is simply a synonym of *monophyletic*.

Taxa are *nonmonophyletic* if they fail to meet the definitional specifications of monophyly. Two types of nonmonophyly are sometimes distinguished. *Paraphyly* results when species are included in a taxon on the basis of shared possession of primitive (*symplesiomorphous*) characters; if a family of great apes (Pongidae) is recognized that excludes the genus *Homo* (placed in its own family, Hominidae), Pongidae is in all probability a paraphyletic taxon. *Polyphyly* generally refers to taxa thought to share derived states evolved independently. Thus paraphyletic taxa tend to exclude species that should be included, while polyphyletic taxa include species that should be excluded. In practice the two forms of nonmonophyly are often difficult to distinguish.

See also CLADISTICS; HOMINIDAE; HOMOLOGY; PHYLOGENY. [N.E.]

MONTE CIRCEO   see   NEANDERTHALS

MONTE PEGLIA

Bone breccia deposit containing numerous remains of early Biharian or latest Villafranchian fauna, found near the city of Orvieto in central Italy. A few heavily patinated limestone and quartzite implements with fresh fracture planes and no evidence for rolling or transport were also found in the breccia. The three considered as human-made include a chopper and two modified flakes; all bear extensive manganese concretions like those found on the nearby bones in the breccia. The remains are tentatively dated older than the Cromerian period, making this one of the earliest possible occurrences of artifacts in Europe.

See also EARLY PALEOLITHIC; PŘEZLETICE; STRANSKÁ SKÁLA; VALLONNET. [O.S.]

MONTMAURIN

Mandible from a French site, found in 1949. It is probably of middle Pleistocene antiquity and is thick and chinless, with large teeth. Some workers regard it as Neanderthal-like in morphology, but it is distinct in a number of respects from "anteneanderthal" mandibles from such sites as Arago and Atapuerca.

See also ARCHAIC HOMO SAPIENS. [C.B.S.]

MORAINE   see   GLACIATION; PLEISTOCENE

MOROTO   see   UGANDA

MORPHOCLINE   see   CLADISTICS; CLINE; TRANSFORMATION SERIES

MORPHOLOGY

Quite simply, "shape." In the context of living organisms the term is essentially synonymous with *anatomy*, which in fossil forms is effectively restricted to teeth and bones. The morphology of a human fossil, then, includes all of its inherited attributes that can be detected by the eye, with or without the aid of a microscope.

See also MORPHOMETRICS; SKELETON; SKULL; TEETH. [I.T.]

MORPHOMETRICS

Study of measurement of the shape of organisms. It is concerned with change in shape and size in development and evolution and with the description and comparison of forms or shapes. Statistical methods are used to summarize and compare shapes of samples of living or fossil organisms.

See also MORPHOLOGY; MULTIVARIATE ANALYSIS; QUANTITATIVE METHODS. [L.M.]

MORPHOTYPE   see   CLADISTICS; TRANSFORMATION SERIES

MORTILLET, GABRIEL DE (1821–1898)

French prehistorian. During the late 1860s and early 1870s Mortillet proposed a scheme for dealing with Pleistocene chronology in western Europe based on

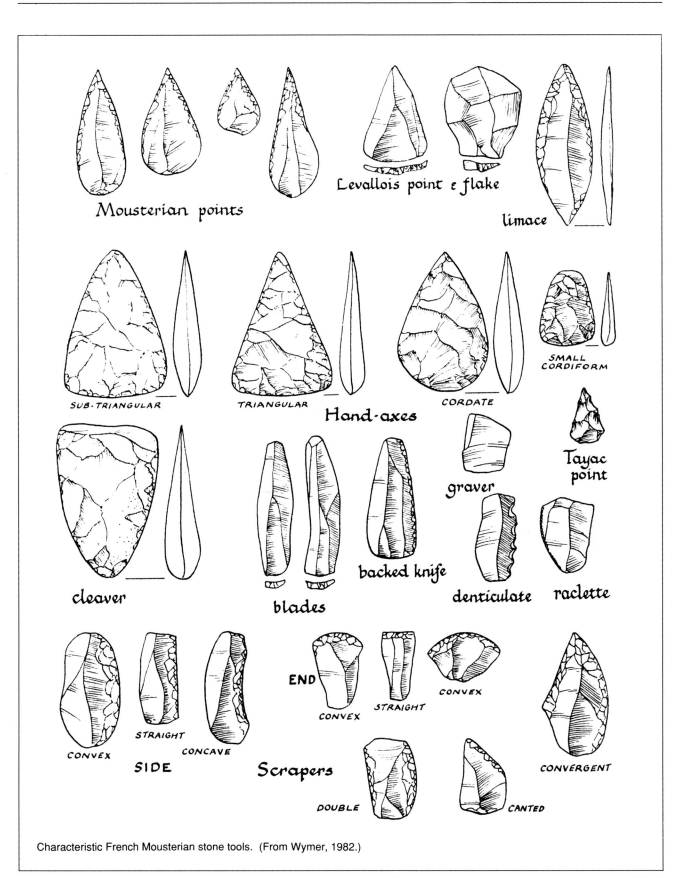

Characteristic French Mousterian stone tools. (From Wymer, 1982.)

the prevailing types of artifacts. As an advocate of Darwin's evolutionary synthesis Mortillet was an eager supporter of the view that the genus *Homo* had originated somewhere in the Tertiary period. This Tertiary precursor he called "Homo-simius," and to characterize its primitive tool industry he coined the term *eoliths*. He was also responsible for founding, in 1864, the journal *Materiaux pour l'Histoire Primitive de l'Homme*, which he edited until 1870.

[F.S.]

MOSSEL BAY *see* PIETERSBURG

MOUNT CARMEL *see* SKHŪL; TABŪN

MOUSTERIAN

Middle Paleolithic flake industries of Europe, the Near East and central Asia, and northeastern Africa, named for the type site of Le Moustier, Dordogne (France). The Mousterian is characterized by Levallois and discoidal-core technologies, as well as by variable proportions of side-scrapers, backed knives, handaxes, denticulates, and points. Mousterian industries may begin as early as the late Saale glacial (e.g. at Biache), ca. 150,000 B.P., but are predominantly dated, mostly on stratigraphic grounds, to early last glacial times, 80,000–35,000 B.P., during cooling but fluctuating climates. While most human fossils associated with Mousterian industries are Neanderthals, several Neanderthals occur in association with non-Mousterian industries at some sites (e.g. Saint-Césaire with Chatelperronian industry). Moreover, "archaic modern" humans are associated with Mousterian industries from Morocco to Israel.

The geographical limits of the Mousterian, however, are roughly coincident with the geographical limits of Neanderthals, suggesting that the two are associated and reflect a physical and cultural adaptation to particular (cold) conditions. The meaning of variability in Mousterian assemblages, together with the degree to which Mousterian sites reflect fully "human" behavior, particularly symbolic and cognitive capacities, are much debated.

Southwestern France

On the basis of the presence or absence of Levallois technology, and varying percentages of 63 flake-tool types and 21 handaxe types, F. Bordes distinguished four major variants of the French Mousterian:

The *Charentian* group, especially prevalent in the Charente district just to the north of the Dordogne, is characterized by high numbers of scrapers and the absence or rarity of backed knives and handaxes. This in turn is subdivided into two variants: the *Quina* type, with a low Levallois index and large numbers of Quina scrapers (thick, with stepped-retouch) and transverse scrapers (scraping edge is opposite striking platform), and the *Ferrassie* type, with a high Levallois index and few Quina or transverse scrapers.

The *Typical* group shows a medium but variable percentage of scrapers, variable proportions of Levallois débitage, and low percentage or absence of Quina scrapers, transverse scrapers, backed knives, and handaxes. Points are most common in this variant.

The Mousterian of Acheulean Tradition is characterized by variable Levallois index, medium to low percentages of scrapers, Quina scrapers rare or absent, Upper Paleolithic types (burins, end-scrapers) pre-

---

Major assemblage variants in the Mousterian of south-west France

Variant	Percentages of: Levallois types	Side scrapers	Upper Paleolithic types (Group III)	Denticulates Group IV	Quina retouch	Handaxes
Charentian		50–80		low		absent / rare
(a) Quina subtype	< 10				14–30	
(b) Ferrassie subtype	14–30				6–14	
Typical	very variable	> 50		moderate	0–3	absent / rare
Denticulate	very variable	4–20		60	0	low
Mousterian of Acheulean Tradition (MTA)	very variable				very low	
subtype A		25–45	seldom > 4	common		8–40
subtype B		4–40	strong	60		absent / rare

Chart showing differences among major Mousterian variants.

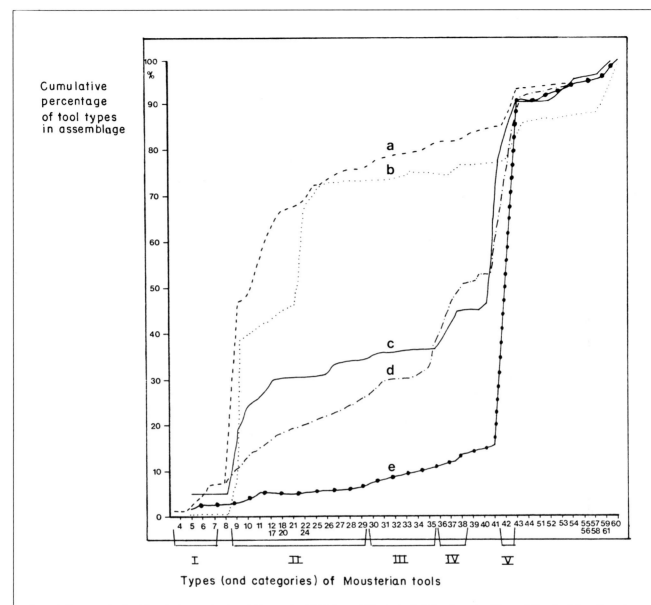

Cumulative percentage of tool types in assemblage

a
b
c
d
e

Types (and categories) of Mousterian tools

Cumulative graphs for Mousterian variants: a) Ferrassie; b) Quina; c) Typical; d) Acheulean tradition; e) Denticulate. Based on Bordes type-list: I, points; II, side-scrapers; III, Upper Paleolithic tools; IV, backed knives; V, notched and denticulate pieces. (After Gamble, © 1986 by Cambridge University Press. Reprinted with permission.)

sent, numerous denticulates, and, most characteristically, backed knives and/or handaxes. Two subdivisions of this type exist, one (Type A) with triangular handaxes, the other (Type B) with few, poorly made handaxes but numerous backed knives. Type B is always later than Type A.

Denticulate Mousterian shows a high percentage of denticulate and notched pieces, variable Levallois index, and all other types (scrapers, Quina scrapers, backed knives, handaxes) rare or absent.

With the exception of the Mousterian of Acheulean Tradition which is also the only variant that changes consistently through time, much of the variability between the Bordesian facies is due to two factors: changes in the percentage of scrapers from high to medium to low and changes in the Levallois index. Bordes attributed the variants to different ethnic groups whose technology changed little through time but who replaced one another in space with little admixture over a period of ca. 50 k.y. In response L. and S. Binford argued that the patterning of variability in Mousterian assemblages did not suggest "stylistic" or "ethnic" variables but rather the underlying patterning of different activities or combinations of activities. In this view the different Mousterian variants represent special-purpose sites or base camps within a relatively unchanging pattern of activities. This "functional" argument has also been challenged, both by Bordes and de Sonneville-Bordes and by others (e.g. Mellars), on the grounds that regional differentiation and directional change through time do characterize some aspects of the Mousterian pattern, particularly with regard to the Mousterian of Acheulean Tradition. In addition the expected correlates of functional differentiation in stone-tool assemblages and faunal and/or locational differences have not been demonstrated.

Europe

Although most of the variants occur throughout Europe, the Mousterian of Acheulean Tradition is rare in the Charente and absent in Provence, although present in northern France, Belgium, and England. In Iberia and the Pyrenees region of France Typical, Denticulate, and Charentian variants are recognized, together with a Vasconian variant distinguished by the addition of cleavers. Typical Mousterian assemblages are widespread in central and eastern Europe, at both rock-shelter/cave (e.g. Bacho Kiro, Bulgaria), and open-air sites, such as Molodova on the Dneistr River; Quina Mousterian assemblages are described from Erd, Tata, Krapina, and Vindija; and Denticulate Mousterian from several areas including the Alpine foothills of northeastern Italy. At many sites leaf-shaped, bifacially worked points (*Blattspitzen*) are found in later Mousterian contexts, sometimes referred to as Altmühlian (after a river valley in southern Germany) rather than Mousterian assemblages. These forms continue into the earliest Upper Paleolithic of central and eastern Europe (Szeletian, Jermanowician) and form the basis for theories of Middle to Upper Paleolithic continuities.

The "witness section" in the lower shelter at Le Moustier (Périgord, France), type site of the Mousterian, with François Bordes. Recently this sequence was dated to between 60 and 40 k.y . B.P. (Photograph © Eric Delson.)

In Mediterranean Europe (e.g. Greece, Italy, and Yugoslavia) Mousterian assemblages often consist of very small implements (Micromousterian), of the Typical or Quina types. Denticulate Mousterian is also known from this area, and multilevel stratified sites with an alternation of different Mousterian facies are common (e.g. Torre in Pietra).

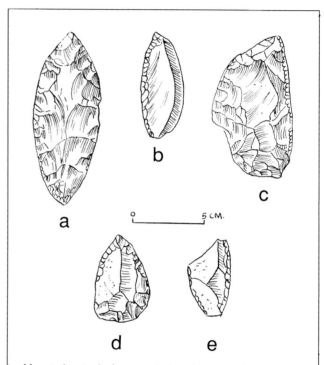

Mousterian tools from central and eastern Europe and North Africa: a) leaf-shaped point (Germany); b) side-scraper (Germany); c) leaf-shaped point (U.S.S.R.); d) Mousterian point (Morocco); e) double side-scraper (Morocco). (In part after J.D. Clark, The Prehistory of Africa, 1970.)

Outside Europe

Mousterian industries of the Near East and North Africa are distinguished by a relatively consistent use of Levallois technology, as well as by the appearance of blade industries (e.g. Amudian, pre-Aurignacian) within or just prior to Mousterian sequences at Tabūn, Jabrud, Haua Fteah, and other sites. The alternation of Mousterian industries displays a non-directional pattern strongly influenced by variations in technology and scraper abundance, similar to that observed in France. The industry extends to central Asia, where a Neanderthal burial was recovered in association with a Mousterian industry containing blades from Teshik-Tash. Farther to the east and south, although flake industries with prepared cores are present, they are not generally attributed to the Mousterian, since the specific technology and scraper or point types are absent. In western North Africa the Mousterian is rare (e.g. Jebel Irhoud), and the Middle Paleolithic is dominated by flake/blade industries with bifacial tanged points known as Aterian.

Mousterian Lifeways

Mousterian sites are associated with evidence of significant development in economic, social, and cognitive development compared with the preceding Early Paleolithic stage. Not only are Mousterian sites more numerous in Europe, they are also associated, although not exclusively, with cold faunas and with the first occupation of the plains and river valleys of Russia and the Ukraine. Also in contrast to the Early Paleolithic of Europe repeated occupation of rock shelters is a common feature of the settlement pattern. Mousterians hunted a wider range of species than did their predecessors, from the first evidence of mollusk exploitation at Haua Fteah and Gorham's Cave (Gibraltar) to a wide range of cold-adapted herbivores, although the number of carnivore remains in Mousterian sites suggests that not all of the faunal remains are due to human agency. Evidence of hut construction and sophisticated hearths are known from the Ukrainian site of Molodova, among others. Clearly the Mousterian adaptation represents a successful attempt to cope with glacial and near-glacial conditions.

Of particular interest is the meaning of the scanty evidence for symbolic behavior at Mousterian sites, in the form of ocher and manganese "crayons," occasional perforated teeth and bones, and rare incised bones, as well as in the practice of burial. One of the most elaborate burials associated with a Mousterian industry is at the site of Regourdou in the Dordogne; of the other known sites (e.g. La Ferrassie, Le Moustier, Monte Circeo, Saccopastore) many were excavated in the nineteenth or early twentieth century and are disputed as burials. The existence of purposeful burial with flowers at Shanidar (Iraq) is also disputed, although the long-term survival of a Neanderthal with a damaged right arm carries implications about the cognitive and moral qualities of Mousterians at this site.

See also ACHEULEAN; AFRICA; AMUD; AMUDIAN; ARCHAIC MODERNS; ASIA (EASTERN); ATERIAN; BACHO KIRO; BIACHE; CLEAVER; CULTURE; DRACHENLOCH; ECONOMY, PREHISTORIC; EMIRAN; EUROPE; FIRE; FLAKE; FLAKE-BLADE; HAHNÖFERSAND; HANDAXE; HAUA FTEAH; HOMO SAPIENS; JABRUD; JABRUDIAN; JEBEL IRHOUD; JEWELRY; KRAPINA; LA CHAPELLE-AUX-SAINTS; LA FERRASSIE; LA QUINA; LE MOUSTIER; LEVALLOIS; MAN-LAND RELATIONSHIPS; MICOQUIAN; MIDDLE PALEOLITHIC; MIDDLE STONE AGE; MOLODOVA; NEANDERTHAL; NEANDERTHALS; NEAR EAST; PALEOLITHIC; PALEOLITHIC IMAGE; PALEOLITHIC LIFEWAYS; PECH DE L'AZÉ; PLEISTOCENE; PRE-AURIGNACIAN; PREPARED-CORE; REGOURDOU; RITUAL; SAINT-CÉSAIRE; SCRAPER; SHANIDAR; SITE TYPES; SKHŪL; SPEECH (ORIGINS OF); STONE-TOOL MAKING; SZELETIAN; TABŪN; TATA; TESHIK-TASH; TORRE IN PIETRA; UPPER PALEOLITHIC. [A.S.B.]

Further Readings

Binford, L.R. (1973) Interassemblage variability—the Mousterian and the "functional" argument. In C. Renfrew (ed.): The Explanation of Culture Change: Models in Prehistory. London: Duckworth.

Bordes, F. (1972) A Tale of Two Caves. New York: Harper and Row.

Bordes, F., and de Sonneville-Bordes, D. (1970) The significance of variability in Palaeolithic assemblages. World Archaeol. 2:61–73.

Gamble, C. (1986) The Palaeolithic Settlement of Europe. Cambridge: Cambridge University Press.

Mellars, P. (1970) Some comments on the notion of "functional variability" in stone-tool assemblages. World Archaeol. 2:74–89.

Mellars, P. (1986) A new chronology for the French Mousterian period. Nature 322:410–411.

Ronen, A., ed. (1983) The Transition from Lower to Middle Palaeolithic and the Origin of Modern Man. Oxford: British Archaeology Reports, International Series No. 151.

Trinkaus, E., ed. (1983) The Mousterian Legacy. Oxford: British Archaeology Reports, International Series No. 164.

Wymer, J. (1982) The Palaeolithic Age. New York: St. Martin's.

MOUSTERIAN OF ACHEULEAN TRADITION see MOUSTERIAN

MOVIUS' LINE

Imaginary line that seems to separate so-called hand-axe from chopper-chopping tool assemblages in Asia. The term "Movius' line" came into use among archaeologists working in Asia after Hallam Movius pointed out in the 1940s that the Paleolithic assemblages of East and Southeast Asia and India south of the Punjab differed from other Old World areas in the absence of "handaxes" and other Acheulean elements. Specifically he suggested that the "chopper-chopping tool complex" of the Far East reflected its position as a largely isolated cultural backwater. Although Movius' line does seem to be "real" in that it demarcates the Far East from other parts of Eurasia and Africa, many workers have suggested alternative explanations for the low frequency of bifacially worked tools in these areas, from the lack of suitable materials to a reliance on a largely nonlithic technology east of the line. The real significance of this differential distribution and frequency of artifact "types" is still the subject of much debate.

See also ACHEULEAN; ASIA (EASTERN); CHINA; CHOPPER-CHOPPING TOOLS; INDIA; INDONESIA. [G.G.P.]

MTETEI see SONGHOR

MUGHARA see SKHŪL; TABŪN

MUGHARET *see* SKHŪL; TABŪN

MULTIVARIATE ANALYSIS

Statistical techniques for analyzing simultaneously many variables or characters measured on each individual unit. This is in contrast to *univariate* statistical analysis, which considers one measured variable (t test, analysis of variance, etc.). Some common methods are principal components, discriminant analysis, and factor analysis.

See also MORPHOMETRICS; QUANTITATIVE METHODS. [L.M.]

MURUAROT

Northern Kenyan stratified exposures of early Miocene age in Tiati Grits, between 18 and 16 m.y. by K-Ar dating of enclosing lavas and by faunal correlation. Fossiliferous sediments on the southwestern side of Lake Turkana, inland from Kalokol (formerly called Ferguson's Gulf) were first described by C. Arambourg in 1933, after their discovery by V. Fuchs. The west-dipping, strongly faulted section crops out for ca. 15 km. between the Muruarot and Losidok (Lothodok) Hill sites and Kalodirr, where most of the hominoid specimens have been found. Loperot to the south is also in Tiati Grits, and similar mammals are found at Mwiti (Kajong, Loengalani sites) southwest of Lake Turkana; at Buluk on Lake Stephanie, dated to between 18 and 17.2 m.y.; and at Kirimun and Palagalagi near Maralal. The Muruarot sites yield the types of *Xenopithecus hamiltoni, Turkanapithecus kalokolensis, Afropithecus turkanensis,* and *Simiolus njiessi,* plus remains of other hominoid species.

See also AFRICA; BULUK; KENYA. [J.A.V.C.]

Further Readings

Leakey, R.E., and Leakey, M.G. (1986) Two new Miocene hominoids from Kenya. Nature 324:143–148.

Savage, R.J.G., and Williamson, P.G. (1978) The early history of the Turkana depression. In W.W. Bishop (ed.): Geological Background to Fossil Man. Edinburgh: Scottish Academic Press, pp. 375–394.

Van Couvering, J.A.H., and Van Couvering, J.A. (1976) Early Miocene mammal fossils from East Africa: aspects of geology, faunistics, and paleoecology. In G.L. Isaac and E.R. McCown (eds.): Human Origins: Louis Leakey and the East African Evidence. Menlo Park, Calif.: Benjamin, pp. 155–207.

MUSCULATURE

Muscles are the organs that make movement possible by humans, primates, and most other animals. Although the individual muscles in a human body come in many sizes and shapes and attach to many parts of the skeleton, each muscle is capable of only a single movement; it is able to contract and bring its attachments closer together. Obviously most human movements involved in locomotion and manipulation involve coordinated action of many muscles or parts of muscles. The experimental technique of electromyography permits scientists to study which muscles are active during particular movements.

In general human musculature is more similar to that of the living African apes, chimpanzees, and gorillas than to that of any other mammals. Indeed, as comparative anatomists have observed for over 100 years, humans are more similar to the great apes than apes are to other primates. The unique aspects of human musculature are those of the hindlimb associated with our bipedal gait and some features of the hand associated with human manipulative abilities. In most instances these unique features of human musculature are extreme developments of variations found in chimpanzees and gorillas.

See also LOCOMOTION; SKELETON. [J.G.F.]

MUSICAL INSTRUMENTS

The oldest unequivocal musical instruments in archaeological context date to the Late Paleolithic period. Beginning with 30,000 B.P., remains of flutes and whistles made of perforated bird and bear bones and reindeer antler are found across Europe from France (Isturitz) to Hungary (Istallöskö), Czechoslovakia (Pekarna), and the Russian Plain (Molodova V, Kostenki I). An ambiguous claim has also been made that the painted mammoth bones found at the Late Paleolithic site of Mezin (U.S.S.R.) represent the earliest percussion instruments. Moreover, a perforated fragment of a bovid phalanx discovered in the pre-Aurignacian layer (possibly dating to the last interglacial) in the Haua Fteah Cave (Mediterranean Libya) is claimed by some to be the remains of the earliest whistle on record.

See also EUROPE; HAUA FTEAH; PALEOLITHIC IMAGE; RITUAL. [O.S.]

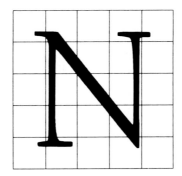

NACHIKUFAN *see* WILTON

NACHOLA
Locality in the Nachola Formation in the Kenya rift valley north of Lake Baringo that has recently yielded teeth and jaw fragments of *Kenyapithecus africanus*. This site is provisionally dated at 11 m.y. ago, which is several million years later than Fort Ternan and Maboko, whence this species was first described.

See also FORT TERNAN; KENYAPITHECUS; MABOKO. [P.A.]

NAGRI *see* SIWALIKS

NAILS, ON DIGITS *see* SKELETON

NAKALI *see* KENYA

NAMURUNGULE *see* SAMBURU

NANNOPITHEX *see* MICROCHOERINAE

NAPAK *see* UGANDA

NARIOKOTOME
Large ephemeral stream west of Lake Turkana in northern Kenya, at about 4°10′N latitude, which drains from the Morua Erith and Labur Ranges into the lake. This name has been applied to a fossil site

on the south bank of the stream where a nearly complete *Homo erectus* skeleton 1.6 m.y. old was discovered in 1984.

See also WEST TURKANA. [F.H.B.]

NARMADA
Valley in central India where more than 50 m. of alluvial sediments have yielded an extensive late or latest middle Pleistocene mammalian fauna and numerous artifacts. Recently the cranium of a fossil hominid has also been reported from this sequence; although this has been assigned to *Homo erectus*, it possesses a cranial capacity of 1,260 ml., and most workers feel that it is best referred to an archaic form of *Homo sapiens*.

See also ARCHAIC HOMO SAPIENS; HOMO ERECTUS. [G.G.P.]

Further Readings

Sonakia, A. (1985) Early *Homo* from the Narmada Valley, India. In E. Delson (ed.): Ancestors: The Hard Evidence. New York: Liss, pp. 334–338.

NASALIS *see* COLOBINAE

NATRONIAN *see* TIME SCALE

NATURAL SELECTION *see* ADAPTATION; EVOLUTION

NAVAJOVIUS *see* PAROMOMYIDAE

NDUTU

Middle Pleistocene site west of Lake Ndutu in the Serengeti Plains (Tanzania). A partial hominid cranium, stone artifacts, and faunal remains were recovered from clays that underlie a volcanic tuff associated with the Masek Beds, or possibly the Lower Ndutu Beds, of Olduvai Gorge (ca. 0.4–0.2 m.y.). The thickness of the cranial vault bones and small cranial capacity (ca. 1,100 ml.) resemble middle Pleistocene specimens of *Homo erectus*, but the shape of the occipital and parietal regions suggests an association with later skulls attributed to archaic *Homo sapiens*.

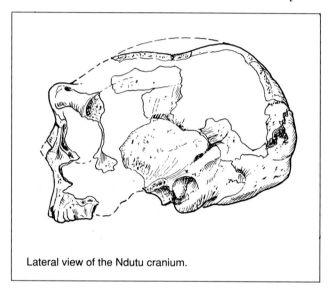

Lateral view of the Ndutu cranium.

The artifacts consist of cores (especially spheroids), hammerstones, and flakes, but few handaxes. This collection may represent a variant of the Acheulean or a middle Pleistocene non-Acheulean assemblage.

See also ARCHAIC HOMO SAPIENS; HOMO ERECTUS; TANZANIA. [R.P.]

NDUTU BEDS *see* OLDUVAI

NEANDERTAL *see* NEANDERTHALS

NEANDERTHAL

The 1856 discovery of a skullcap and partial skeleton in the Feldhofer Cave in the Neander Valley near Dusseldorf (West Germany) was a momentous event. Although it was subsequently recognized that humans of this kind had already been found at Engis (Belgium) and Forbes' Quarry (Gibraltar), the Neanderthal skeleton was the first to be described in any detail and recognized as a distinct human type. King in 1864 actually named a new human species, *Homo neanderthalensis*, for the remains, the first time this had been done. Unfortunately associated faunal or

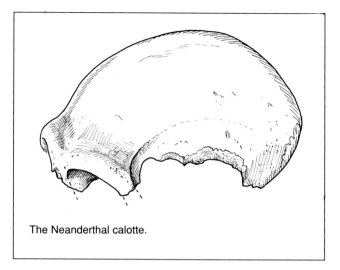

The Neanderthal calotte.

archaeological materials were not recovered, so the precise age of the specimen remains uncertain. The morphological features displayed by the skeleton, however, are consistent with those known in other last glaciation Neanderthals, and the skullcap particularly resembles one found at Spy (Belgium) in 1886. The skull has a strongly developed and curved browridge, is flattened and elongated, and has a projecting occipital region. Brain size is ca. 1,400 ml., which is low for a Neanderthal individual sexed as male from the pelvis. The postcranial skeleton is robustly constructed with long bones that are thick-walled and bowed (which led to erroneous suggestions that rickets was responsible). The Neanderthal humerus, however, does show a pathology of the elbow joint probably caused by a fracture.

See also NEANDERTHALS. [C.B.S.]

NEANDERTHALENSIS *see* NEANDERTHALS

NEANDERTHALS

Group of archaic humans known predominantly as late Pleistocene European hominids of the early part of the last glaciation (ca. 100–35 k.y.). However, our lack of knowledge of their middle Pleistocene antecedents and of their Asian representatives limits our perception of the Neanderthals, since they undoubtedly had a much wider distribution in time and space than this. The term *Neanderthal* is sometimes also used in a wide sense to indicate fossils that are considered to represent their grade equivalents in various parts of the world (including the Far East and Africa), although this unsatisfactory usage has declined recently, as the special characters of the European specimens have been increasingly appreciated. As yet there is no evidence that true Neanderthals

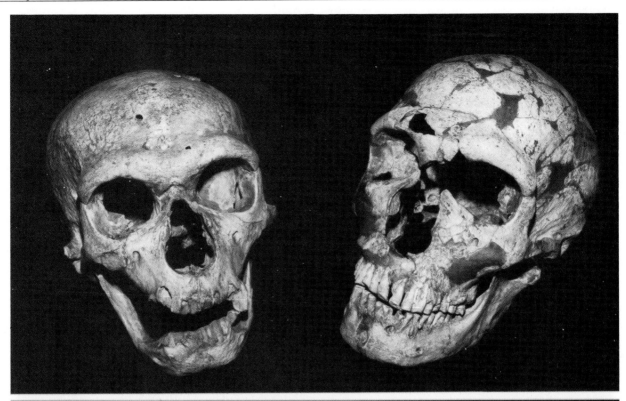

Above: two Neanderthal crania from France. On the left, from La Chapelle-aux-Saints, and, on the right, from La Ferrassie. Both specimens show the characteristically large nasal region and midfacial projection of Neanderthal crania, and the La Ferrassie cranium exhibits the rounded wear of the front teeth. Below: two Neanderthal crania, probably from female individuals. On the left, the Krapina C specimen from Yugoslavia, which may be ca. 70 k.y. in age, and on the right, the Gibraltar (Forbes' Quarry) skull, which is probably of comparable early late Pleistocene age.

ever extended into Africa, but they were certainly present in western Asia from known occurrences in Israel, Iraq, and the Soviet Union (including as far east as Uzbekistan, almost in Afghanistan), and their western limits reached as far as the Iberian peninsula and the British Isles. To the north they extended at least as far as northern Germany and Poland. It is usually considered that the Neanderthals were cold-adapted, as is indicated by their body proportions, and perhaps also by their facial shape, although in fact they never extended into real Arctic environments. They did, however, exist in a variety of temperate and boreal environments, including Mediterranean interglacial and northern glacial conditions. The first recognized Neanderthal discovery was made at the Feldhofer Cave in the Neander Valley (West Germany) in 1856. Earlier unrecognized finds of Neanderthal type had been made at the Engis Cave (Belgium), between 1829 and 1830 and at a cave in Forbes' Quarry (Gibraltar) in 1848. Initial dispute about the significance of the unusual morphology of the Neander Valley partial skeleton was eventually settled by further fossil discoveries during the next 60 years that showed a comparable morphology, such as the Belgian finds from La Naulette and Spy and, in particular, the French finds from La Chapelle-aux-Saints, La Ferrassie, and La Quina. Important material of numerous but fragmentary Neanderthals from Krapina (Yugoslavia) received less attention at the turn of the century but in fact represented an equally informative and far larger source of data about the group. By this time also two different interpretations of the evolutionary significance of the Neanderthals were emerging. Some workers believed that the Neanderthals were the direct ancestors of living Europeans, while others believed that they represented a lineage of primitive hominids that had become extinct. As the sample increased and morphological variation was recognized in the fossils, further intermediate viewpoints were to develop between these extreme positions.

Neanderthal Characters

Many observations made on the relatively small sample of Neanderthals known by the early years of this century have been confirmed, while others have been shown to be misconceptions based on incomplete knowledge or preconceived ideas about the course of human evolution. Some Neanderthal features regarded as primitive are now known to be present in at least some modern populations; others appear to be rather specialized. Some supposedly aberrant features are in fact primitive for hominids and can be recognized in recent discoveries representing more archaic groups. Primitive features

found in the Neanderthals include the long, low cranial vault, with a flattened top to the skull, and a short parietal arch. There is a primitive (for humans in general), well-developed supraorbital torus that is especially strong centrally, a large face with a broad nasal opening, a fairly large dentition (especially incisors), and a mandible that in most cases lacks a bony chin. The cranial base is broad and in some specimens, at least, is flattened rather than well flexed. The postcranial skeleton shares a whole suite of characters with those of earlier archaic humans, through an emphasis on strong musculature and thickened shafts to the bones.

Advanced (derived) characters that the Neanderthals appear to share with living humans include lateral reduction of the browridge, reduced development of the occipital torus, relatively rounder occipital profile and longer occipital plane, large brain, reduced facial prognathism, and unthickened ilium of the pelvis, above the hip joint (acetabulum).

The Neanderthals also show their own special characters, present in most or all specimens, but rarely found outside the group. These specialized features include the spherical shape of the cranial vault in rear view and the posterior position of the (usually very large) maximum breadth of the skull. On the occipital bone is a central depression at the upper limit of the neck musculature (a suprainiac fossa), and a prominent juxtamastoid crest along the lower margins of the bone. In the face are a number of special features associated with the phenomenon of midfacial projection, where the enormous nose stands out from the swept-back and inflated cheek bones, and the teeth are similarly positioned far forward. This positioning of the teeth leads to the occurrence of a space behind the third molars (retromolar space). On the internal surface of the ascending ramus of the lower jaw there is often an unusual shape (called horizontal-oval or H-O) to the mandibular foramen or hole, which may be related to the strong musculature of the jaws in Neanderthals.

The rest of the skeleton shows other features that may be specialized in Neanderthals, although because of limited information about these areas in earlier hominids we cannot be sure. One aspect concerns the body proportions of Neanderthals, which may have been the result of cold-adaptation. Another concerns the shoulder blade (scapula), which has on its back edge a well-developed groove for a muscle that runs to the upper arm. And at the front of the pelvis is a long and flattened pubic ramus in all Neanderthals (male and female) where this part has been preserved. This latter feature has been linked with the birth of large-headed infants in Neanderthal women. The length of fetal development in

Neanderthals may have been closer to 12 months rather than the nine of modern humans, since an enlarged birth canal could have allowed a larger baby to develop. Alternatively, early brain growth and general development may have been faster in Nean-derthal babies compared with their modern counter-parts, or their unusual pelvic shape could simply be an effect of their peculiar large-brained, large-headed but short and stocky physiques.

Neanderthals were certainly large-bodied by the

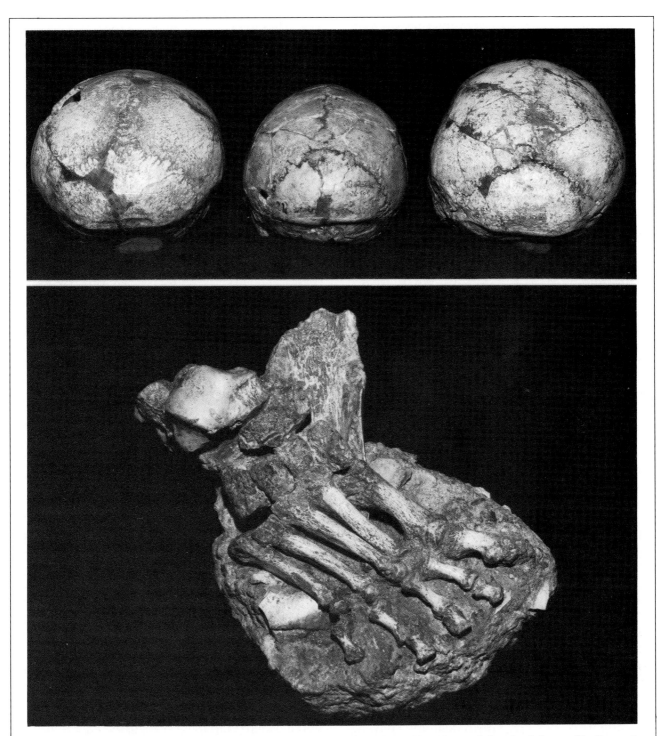

Above: rear (occipital) views of three French Neanderthals. From left to right: La Chapelle-aux-Saints, La Quina, and La Ferrassie. This view shows the characteristic rounded profile of Neanderthal skulls, together with the typical morphology of the occipital region. Below: the beautifully preserved foot bones of the La Ferrassie Neanderthal woman.

standards of modern hunter-gatherers, and by various means it is possible to estimate their body weight as ca. 65 kg. (over 140 lb.) in males and perhaps 50 kg. (110 lb.) in females. This weight would have been for lean and heavily muscled bodies. Since many Neanderthals lived in relatively cold environments, it is not surprising, considering Bergmann's biological "rule," that they were heavily built. Similarly, following Allen's "rule," it would be expected that body extremities would be shortened if Neanderthals were cold-adapted, and this also appears to be the case. As in present-day cold-adapted peoples, such as the Lapps and Eskimos, the forearms (radius and ulna) and shinbones (tibia and fibula) of European Neanderthals were proportionately shortened compared with the upper-arm and leg bones. This effect was less marked in the Neanderthals of Iraq and Israel. As well as being stockily built, the Neanderthals were fairly short in stature. Estimates from the long bones of their skeletons suggest males averaged ca. 169 cm. (5'6"), while females averaged ca. 160 cm. (5'3") tall. The Neanderthals were large-brained, and their known average cranial capacity is larger than the modern average (over 1,450 ml.). In common with earlier humans, however, the brains of Neanderthals were low and broadest near the base, with small frontal lobes and large, bulging occipital lobes at the back. The significance for Neanderthal intellectual capabilities of the large size and unusual shape of their brains is still unclear.

Neanderthal Behavior

Behaviorally the Neanderthals certainly showed traits found in living humans, such as burial of the dead, care of disabled individuals (such as the Shanidar 1 man), and at least a limited ability to communicate and to hunt large mammals. However, just as earlier workers may have overemphasized the potential differences between Neanderthals and living humans, so more recent workers may have overemphasized their possible similarities to us in behavior. Current reassessments of Neanderthal behavior may well lead to indications of a significant inferiority in their cultural adaptations when compared with those of any modern hunter-gatherers. Thus the Neanderthals may well turn out to have more in common with the behavior of primitive hominids than with people alive today. Their Mousterian stone-tool industries show a degree of specialization in the presence of tool kits for particular activities, yet many of the features of these "cultures" are invariant through long periods of time and large geographical areas, suggesting a lack of response to environmental parameters. Compared with the tool kits of anatomically modern hominids, such as the Upper Paleolithic peoples who produced the Aurignacian industry, Neanderthals made little use of bone, antler, or ivory and probably did not manufacture composite tools, such as hafted spears or harpoons.

Origin of the Neanderthals

The ancestors of the Neanderthals are thought to be the middle Pleistocene hominids of Europe (and perhaps also of western Asia, although little is known of them). The extent and significance of supposed Neanderthal characters in such fossils, however, are matters of dispute. Early European fossils, such as those from Mauer and Bilzingsleben, are not complete enough to be conclusively classified but are primitive in the characters they do display. A number of Neanderthal features are present in such fossils as those from Arago, Petralona, Vértesszöllös, and Atapuerca, which are more usually classified as representing *Homo erectus*, archaic *Homo sapiens*, or "ante-neanderthals." Yet it is difficult to justify assigning any of these specimens to the Neanderthal group proper, and it is not until we reach the later middle Pleistocene that Neanderthal derived characters begin to predominate over more primitive ones.

The Swanscombe "skull" displays a number of primitive features, such as its thickened, parallel-sided vault, but in details of the occipital torus morphology, presence of a suprainiac fossa, and probable development of juxtamastoid crests are clear Neanderthal affinities. Such affinities are even more obvious in the Biache partial cranium, since the spherical (in rear view), thin-walled vault and bulging occipital profile bear a particular resemblance to the form of the La Quina 5 Neanderthal. The Steinheim skull, which is probably also of later middle Pleistocene age, is more enigmatic and perhaps more primitive, but its occipital region is reminiscent of that of Swanscombe, and hence that of Neanderthals. The younger Fontéchevade specimens, like Swanscombe, were once directly linked in an evolutionary scheme with modern humans, via the "presapiens" lineage, but the more complete Fontéchevade 2, at least, is most plausibly regarded as an early Neanderthal.

Further probable early Neanderthals from the period between 200 and 100 k.y. ago include the specimens from La Chaise (Abri Suard and Bourgeois-Delaunay), Ehringsdorf, and Saccopastore. The last site produced an interesting association of two early Neanderthal crania with such fauna as elephant and hippopotamus, and these specimens differ from later specimens primarily in their smaller size and less-developed midfacial projection and basicranial flattening. The Ehringsdorf site also produced Neanderthal-like cranial, mandibular, and postcranial bones from an interglacial environment, but it is unclear whether they date from the same last interglacial period as the Saccopastore specimens (ca. 120 k.y. in age) or whether they derive from the previous interglacial (ca. 220 k.y.). The La Chaise fossils, which include very Neanderthal-like mandibular and occipital specimens, mostly date from the period 150–100 k.y.

The large sample of early Neanderthals from the Yugoslavian site of Krapina has been the subject of many interpretations since its discovery at the turn of the century. Some workers, noting the fragmentary condition and apparent variation displayed by the Krapina fossils, believed that they resulted from a battle between Neanderthal and early modern populations that was followed by a cannibalistic feast. Other workers thought the specimens were related to the "generalized Neanderthals" from western Asia (the Zuttiyeh, Tabūn, and Skhūl fossils, at a time when these were regarded as representing a single early late Pleistocene "progressive" population). Further study of the Krapina specimens, however, has confirmed that they in fact represent rather robust early Neanderthals, with large teeth and strong brows in some specimens. Where shoulder blades, pelves, and hand and limb bones are preserved, these seem to display the typical Neanderthal pattern described earlier. The large dental sample is especially important, since it derives from at least 15 individuals, many of whom were children, and the condition of taurodontism (unseparated roots in the molars with expanded pulp cavities) is especially developed. The real reasons for the fragmentary condition of the Krapina sample are still uncertain, but ancient human interference seems to be at least partly responsible. Actual cannibalism by Neanderthals may have occurred, or skeletons may have been defleshed and broken up for ritual reburial.

Typical Neanderthals

The best-known Neanderthals are those from the period ca. 70–50 k.y. in western Asia and 70–35 k.y. in Europe. The western European specimens in this time range probably include the original Neander Valley partial skeleton (although its date cannot now be established accurately), the Spy Neanderthals from Belgium; the Devil's Tower and (perhaps) the Forbes' Quarry crania from Gibraltar; the Guattari Cave (Monte Circeo) skull and mandibles from Italy; and the La Quina, La Chapelle-aux-Saints, La Ferrassie, and Saint-Césaire partial skeletons from France. The latter specimens are particularly important, as the La Ferrassie assemblage is a group of late Neanderthal skeletons that may have comprised a family

cemetery of an adult male, female, and young children, while the Saint-Césaire material is the youngest in age (associated with the early Upper Paleolithic Chatelperronian industry) and establishes with a fair degree of certainty the contemporaneity of late Neanderthals and early modern populations in Europe.

The eastern European material consists of less-complete specimens but includes a lower jaw and other specimens from Subalyuk (Hungary), an upper jaw and other fragments from Kulna (Czechoslovakia), and the fragments from Vindija (Yugoslavia). Some workers believe that the eastern European specimens show evolutionary trends that indicate a gradual progression toward a modern morphology, and the Vindija specimens certainly appear more gracile than the earlier Krapina hominids. No European specimens have yet been discovered, however, that display a clear transitional morphology between Neanderthals and early modern humans.

The Asian Neanderthals differed in certain respects from their European counterparts. Variation in size, robusticity, and morphology is evident when comparing the Shanidar Neanderthals from Iraq with each other, or the male and female Neanderthals from the Israeli sites of Amud, Kebara, and Tabūn. Yet these fossils and others from such sites as Kiik-Koba and Teshik-Tash (U.S.S.R.) have major similarities in derived characteristics with European Neanderthals. The large Shanidar sample is especially important, probably spanning more than 15 k.y. and consisting of nine individuals of both sexes and various ages. The specimens include an adult man who had suffered extensive injuries sometime before he died (Shanidar 1) and one of the most massive but characteristic Neanderthal faces ever discovered (Shanidar 5). The Amud, Kebara, and Tabūn skeletons contrast markedly in lying at the extremes of size variation in Neanderthals. The Kebara man had the most massive jaw and skeleton, while the Amud man was the largest-brained and tallest Neanderthal yet found. The Tabūn woman, however, was one of the smallest and most gracile of all Neanderthals. As with the eastern European specimens some scientists perceive signs of evolution toward a modern morphology in the Neanderthals of Asia, but the dating of the specimens is not precise enough to construct valid evolutionary trends for the whole sample. Nevertheless, the Asian Neanderthals are less extreme than their European relatives when both are compared with modern humans. There may well have been as abrupt a transition between the Asian Neanderthals and the first modern humans as there was between the European Neanderthals and the first Cro-Magnons. This is indicated by the non-

Neanderthal morphology of the Qafzeh and Skhūl hominids, which more than anything argues against a direct evolutionary connection with Neanderthal ancestors.

Evolutionary Significance of the Neanderthals

The role of the Neanderthals in human evolution has been a subject of dispute for over a century. In some respects they seem to fill an intermediate position between earlier archaic hominids and modern humans. Yet they also display unique characteristics, which seem to have developed over hundreds of thousands of years in Europe. These special characteristics are rare or nonexistent in the succeeding anatomically modern peoples of Europe and western Asia, and the lack of morphological intermediates at the appropriate time between late Neanderthals and early moderns speaks against any direct evolutionary connection between the two groups. Additionally, it seems that in western Europe, and possibly elsewhere, there may have been a coexistence between Neanderthals and early modern peoples that lasted several thousand years. However, before it can be stated with confidence that the Neanderthals were not ancestors of any modern peoples, there are still some tantalizing pieces of evidence that suggest otherwise. This evidence includes, as we have seen, the fossil material from eastern and central Europe, where some Neanderthal specimens are less extreme in their characteristics and some early modern specimens appear particularly robust, and the evidence from Saint-Césaire that some Neanderthals were capable of producing Upper Paleolithic-style industries that were formerly thought to be exclusively the province of the European Cro-Magnons. Perhaps there was some cultural or genetic contact between these two very different peoples before the last Neanderthals disappeared, about 30 k.y. ago.

See also ARCHAIC HOMO SAPIENS; HOMO SAPIENS. [C.B.S.]

Further Readings

Delson, E. (1985) Late Pleistocene human fossils and evolutionary relationships. In E. Delson (ed.): Ancestors: The Hard Evidence. New York: Liss, pp. 296–300.

Howell, F.C. (1984) Introduction. In F.H. Smith and F. Spencer (eds.): The Origins of Modern Humans: A World Survey of the Fossil Evidence. New York: Liss, pp. xiii–xxii.

Smith, F.H. (1984) Fossil hominids from the Upper Pleistocene of Central Europe and the origin of modern Europeans. In Smith and Spencer, pp. 137–209.

Spencer, F. (1984) The Neanderthals and their evolutionary significance: a brief historical survey. In Smith and Spencer, pp. 1–49.

Stringer, C.B. (1982) Towards a solution to the Neanderthal problem. J. Hum. Evol. 11:431–438.

Stringer, C.B., Hublin, J.-J., and Vandermeersch, B. (1984) The origin of anatomically modern humans in western Europe. In Smith and Spencer, pp. 51–135.

Trinkaus, E. (1983) The Shanidar Neanderthals. New York: Academic.

Trinkaus, E. (1984) Western Asia. In Smith and Spencer, pp. 251–293.

Trinkaus, E. (1986) The Neanderthals and modern human origins. Ann. Rev. Anthropol. 15:193–218.

Wolpoff, M.H. (1980). Paleoanthropology. New York: Knopf.

NEANTHROPUS see HOMO SAPIENS

NEAR EAST

Geographic region extending from western Turkey to eastern Afghanistan and to the Persian/Arabian Gulf; sometimes referred to as the Middle East or Southwest Asia. Bounded on the south and west by the Mediterranean and on the east by Pakistan, it shares many cultural and ecological features with North Africa (including Egypt), South Asia (Pakistan, India, and Sri Lanka), and the U.S.S.R. (particularly the Caucasian and Central Asian republics). Despite long and complex cultural and historical interactions among these areas, however, the Near East is sufficiently distinctive in its ecology and culture to be treated as a separate entity by historians, geographers, and social scientists. The rest of Asia is considered in the article ASIA (EASTERN).

The Near East encompasses a wide range of habitats—temperate, hyperarid, humid, desert, steppe, mountains—but it is generally characterized by long, hot, rainless summers and cooler, wetter winters. Linguistically and culturally diverse in the earliest historic periods five millennia ago, the area is dominated today by Muslims of various sects but is also home to Christians, Jews, Yazidis, and other religious minorities distributed among a range of ethnic groups. The region was the setting for the first successful experiments in plant cultivation and stock breeding, as well as the earliest civilizations, and current adaptations are marked by complex interactions among sedentary village agriculturalists, mobile pastoralists, and city dwellers.

Our current understanding of prehistoric settlement pattern is distorted both by the history of archaeological investigation and by the burial of sites by late- and postglacial geomorphological processes. Some areas, like the Arabian desert and Anatolia, are poorly known; others, especially the Levantine border of the eastern Mediterranean and the Zagros Mountains of Iraq and Iran, have been comparatively well explored. As further research is carried out in the Near East, our understanding of various prehistoric periods there, and of the area's place in the prehistoric world, will continue to improve. The archaeology of the Near East is best and most extensively

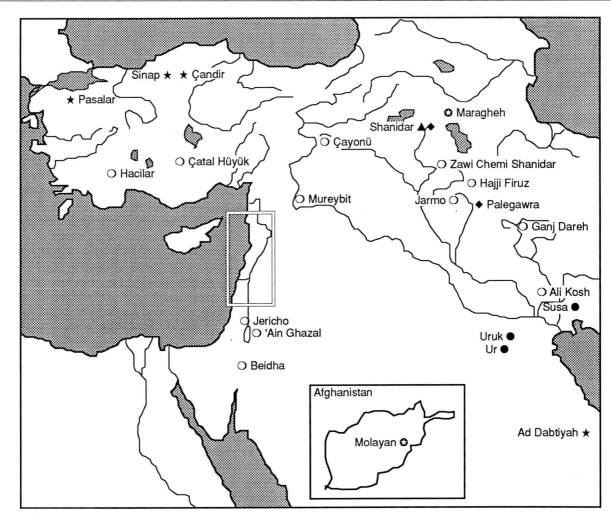

Near Eastern localities yielding fossil primates, hominids, and archaeological remains. Box shows Levant area enlarged in illustration on page 374. Symbols indicate age and site contents as per following key:

Symbol	Archaeology	Fossils	Symbol	Archaeology
★	None	*Heliopithecus* or *Sivapithecus*	○	"Mesolithic" and Neolithic
✪	None	*Mesopithecus*	●	Post-Neoliothic
❑	Acheulean (1–0.13 m.y.)	None		
■	Pre–Aurignacian (130–90 k.y.)	Archaic *Homo sapiens* if any		
△	Mousterian (90–30 k.y.)	Early anatomical moderns		
▲	Mousterian (90–30 k.y.)	Neanderthals or none		
◆	Late Paleolithic (30–11 k.y.)	Anatomical moderns		

documented for the Holocene, but there is scattered evidence of occupation earlier in the Pleistocene. Palynological analysis suggests that climatic regimes and vegetational successions during the later Pleistocene differed from one region to the next, but through much of the past 2 m.y. the greater part of Southwest Asia was colder and drier than it is at present.

Primate Fossils

During the Paleogene the Near East was effectively part of the Eurasian landmass and thus separated from the island continent of Africa, although it was broken up into a number of small tectonic plates. By ca. 18 m.y. ago the Afro-Arabian plate made contact with Eurasia in the northeast, allowing the passage of terrestrial mammals, including primates, between the two areas. Central to this interchange was the western part of the Near East, with important early fossils in both Saudi Arabia and Turkey in the Miocene. A hominoid jaw fragment and several teeth from Ad Dabtiyah (Saudi Arabia), named *Heliopithecus* and dated to ca. 17 m.y., document the continuity of the African catarrhine fauna across the Red Sea rift at this time. *Heliopithecus* is very similar to the contemporaneous *Afropithecus* from northern Kenya, and together these forms represent the earliest members of Hominidae. This is determined by the presence of thick, pattern 3 molar enamel, not found in either the *Proconsul* group or the Hylobatidae, as well as relatively large upper premolars.

The importance of this region as a migration corridor for higher primates during the Miocene is documented by the presence of several species of monkeys and *Sivapithecus*, as well as one usually placed in *Dryopithecus*. The latter form, consisting of two teeth originally named *Udabnopithecus*, is known only from the Georgian S.S.R., on the northern margin of the Near East. From Paşalar and Candir, western Turkish sites dated at ca. 14–12 m.y., come a partial mandible and hundreds of isolated teeth that can be tentatively identified as *Sivapithecus* on the basis of reduction of the upper lateral incisor. Two younger specimens from the Sinap Beds (western Turkey, 10–8 m.y.) were once termed *Ankarapithecus* but are now recognized as *Sivapithecus meteai*. A palate and lower face presenting the typical I² reduction, narrow interorbital region, and small incisive canal of the genus was among the first specimens demonstrating the close link between *Sivapithecus* and *Pongo*, the orangutan. This species has been said to include contemporaneous fossils from northern Greece, but the latter present a more conservative palatal region and may be best considered a distinct genus, *Graecopithecus*.

In the later Miocene the southern European colobine monkey *Mesopithecus* is known from Maragheh (northwestern Iran) and Molayan, near Kabul (Afghanistan), and may extend eastward into the Siwaliks. Macaque monkeys probably also spread through the region in the Pliocene, but the earliest fossils are from the possibly early Pleistocene archaeological site of 'Ubeidiya (Israel). No human remains are known until the later middle Pleistocene, as previously reported older finds are today considered intrusive.

Paleolithic Hunters

Largely on the basis of lithic typology several sites in the Near East have been assigned to the Early Paleolithic, and rather more to subsequent periods. Among the sites classified as Early Paleolithic are 'Ubeidiya and Jisr Banat Yaqub (Israel), Latamne and Jabrud (Syria), and Barda Balka (Iraq). A number of Early Paleolithic sites in the Orontes and Euphrates valleys (Syria) are associated with Saale and Eemian deposits. Pebble choppers, handaxes, cleavers, and a variety of flake tools have been reported from other localities throughout the Near East, at various elevations, but many are in undatable and/or secondary deposits. Most of the Paleolithic cultural material that has been found in caves and rock shelters is, typologically, Late Paleolithic; for the most part earlier material derives from open-air localities, some of

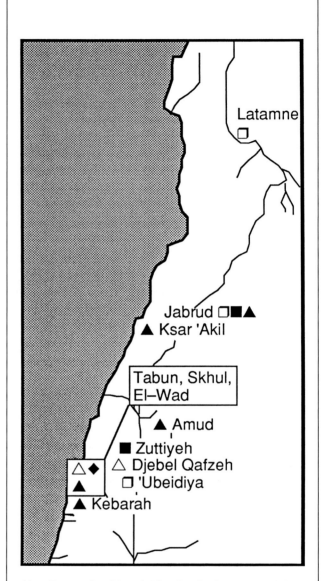

Near Eastern localities yielding fossil primates, hominids, and archaeological remains from Levant region. Symbols as on preceding page.

them badly eroded and deflated by wind and water. One important exception is the Israeli cave of Zuttiyeh, which has yielded a hominid frontal bone ("Galilee man") and late Acheulean artifacts. The fossil is now considered to represent an archaic *Homo sapiens* population of late Saale or Eemian age that cannot be related directly either to the Neanderthals or to modern humans. Of similar age are the enigmatic Jabrudian and pre-Aurignacian industries recovered at several Levantine sites, presaging the Late Paleolithic but interstratified in Early to Middle Paleolithic sequences.

Most sites attributed to the Middle Paleolithic are

also undated or undatable, but they are typologically comparable with European assemblages. They contain chipped lithic artifacts of various Mousterian types, sometimes produced with Levallois technique and often termed Levalloiso-Mousterian. In the Levant some of the most important sites of this time range (Eemian and earlier Weichselian) are in Israel (Tabūn, Skhūl, Kebara, and Qafzeh), in the Syrian desert (El Kowm, Jerf ʿAjla), in Iraq (Shanidar Cave in the northern Zagros and the al-Tar caves on the lower Euphrates), and in Iran (Kunji and Warwasi caves, in the central Zagros). Shanidar (level D) yielded nine Neanderthal skeletons, one of which was apparently buried with flowers and another evidently cared for following the amputation of an arm. Skhūl and Qafzeh produced a number of comparatively robust skeletons, classified as *Homo sapiens sapiens*, associated with Mousterian artifacts. The latest skeletal material at Shanidar dates to ca. 44,000 B.P., and the uppermost Middle Paleolithic deposits at Jerf ʿAjla and Ksar ʿAkil (Lebanon) date to ca. 43,000 and 44,000 B.P., respectively (radiocarbon dating); early Late Paleolithic deposits at Qafzeh (E-D) and Ksar ʿAkil produced dates of 39–32,000 and 34–28,000 B.P., respectively (amino-acid dating). A number of Levantine and Zagrosian sites, and others elsewhere in the Near East, are deeply stratified, and at several of them Late Paleolithic materials overlie those of Mousterian type, perhaps suggesting the reuse of optimal areas over considerable periods. During portions of the early Weichsel some parts of the Near East did not support the vegetation communities seen today (including oak, pistachio, wheat, and barley), but the mammals hunted (including gazelle, onager, red deer, cattle, sheep, and goat) continued to occupy the area into the Holocene, and some of them were ancestral to species domesticated subsequently.

Late Paleolithic assemblages in the Near East are by and large restricted to chipped stone tools. As in Europe increasing numbers of tools were made on blades punched from prismatic cores. While the two best-investigated areas (the Levant and the Zagros) reveal generic similarities to the blade-dominated assemblages of Europe and North Africa, they are sufficiently different from one another that terminological distinctions, relating in part to historical differences in research programs in the two areas, have been retained in the literature. Thus the Levant has an "Aurignacian" industry, followed by the "Epipaleolithic" Kebaran (ca 19–14,000 B.P.); the Zagrosian Baradostian is followed by the Zarzian. Radiocarbon dates from Shanidar (level C) and Yafteh Cave (western Iran) indicate that the Baradostian falls in the range ca. 38–35,000 B.P.; it probably extended sub-

stantially beyond this in at least some areas. Some high-altitude areas, such as the high Zagros and the Iranian and Anatolian plateaus, may have been abandoned during the coldest and driest part of the Weichsel (ca. 28–14,000 B.P.); there seem to be gaps in the occupational histories of parts of the Zagros, in northern Afghanistan, and in Soviet Central Asia during this period. In both the Levant and the Zagros, however, the number of sites and the diversity of ecological niches they occupied increased throughout the late Weichsel, and faunal analyses suggest increasing local specializations involving the hunting of particular species. Regional and interregional movement, and perhaps long-distance exchange, are suggested by finds of ocher, marine shells, and obsidian in areas where they do not occur naturally.

Several changes during the latter part of the Late Paleolithic suggest the development of increasingly diversified subsistence strategies. Some Near Eastern sites have produced remains of mollusks, fish, and turtles; a few have abundant remains of land snails. The sample of avifauna is larger for this time range, although this may be partly a function of better preservation in more recent deposits. The earliest domesticate, the dog, is reported from a Zarzian site, Palegawra (Iraq), where it is dated to ca. 14,000 B.P. Oak wood suggests that acorns (and the often-associated pistachios) had become available for fall harvesting; wild cereal grasses, such as wheat and barley, may have accompanied oak as it recolonized the area after 11,000 B.P. Both in the Levant and the Zagros a number of sites have grinding stones, which may have been multipurpose implements used to crush nuts, hard-husked grasses, and pigments.

No Near Eastern area has yet produced the variety and number of complexly constructed shelters, worked-bone artifacts, personal ornaments, or the representational parietal or mobiliary art known in Europe and parts of Africa and India during the late Pleistocene. Despite these differences—which may well reflect the comparatively small size of the sample—Near Eastern Late Paleolithic hunter-gatherers were similar to their counterparts in several important ways. Aside from anatomical similarities (they, too, were fully modern *H. sapiens sapiens*), they relied on tool kits centered on blade tools of ever-diminishing size and reflecting increasingly localized or regionalized typological distinctiveness. These tools, whose increasingly regional aspect may reflect greater boundary marking between social units, were used largely to exploit an increasingly diverse number of small animal species and a few species of large mammals. As in Europe there is some evidence for one or two species being the key resource at a

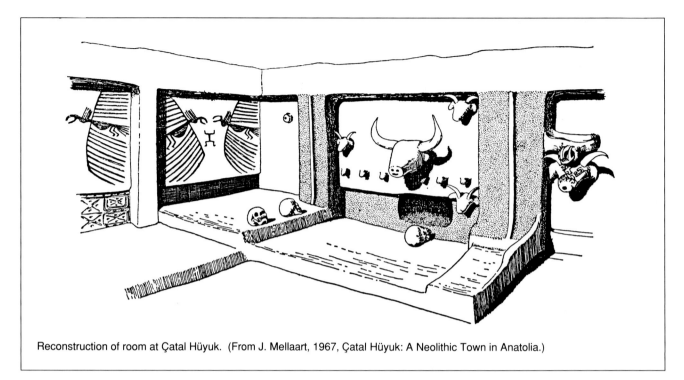

Reconstruction of room at Çatal Hüyuk. (From J. Mellaart, 1967, Çatal Hüyuk: A Neolithic Town in Anatolia.)

given site. Perhaps it is significant that few ancestors of domesticated mammals known today are abundantly represented in the art and faunal debris of the European Upper Paleolithic (exceptions include the horse, the aurochs, and possibly also the pig), whereas several of the species represented in the domestic refuse at Late Paleolithic Near Eastern sites went on to be domesticated as climate ameliorated at the close of the late Pleistocene.

Neolithic Villages and Domestication

This climatic change was accompanied by changes in botanical and faunal distributions and in human settlement and technology. For the first time there is substantial evidence of construction—in the Levantine Natufian (ca. 12–10,500 B.P.) such sites as 'Ain Mallaha, Mureybit, and Abu Hureyra revealed round structures; similar structures may have served as dwellings at Zawi Chemi, near Shanidar Cave. The tool kit includes grinding implements, increasing numbers of bone tools (harpoons, fish hooks, projectile points, awls, needles, scrapers) and microliths, some embedded in bone or antler handles to create sickles, some of which display the edge sheen that accompanies grass harvesting. Anatolian obsidian is rare, but it does occur at some Zagros sites; this, as well as marine shells, ocher, and bitumen (with which stone tools were sometimes hafted), reflect on interregional exchange. Ground-stone objects include celts, palettes, beads, pendants, and bangles. Experimentation with pyrotechnology and with clay is suggested by the existence of lightly baked figu-

rines and other objects at Karim Shahir, Ganj Dareh (E); and elsewhere; some lumps of clay carry impressions of matting and basketry, more perishable items of technology.

Plant and animal remains from the Natufian and from such Zagros sites as Zawi Chemi Shanidar and Karim Shahir reveal the existence of an economy still based on hunting and collecting. There is, however, evidence of a growing interest in protein sources that come in small packages and large numbers, such as land snails, mussels, clams, and nuts. Humans were possibly beginning to exercise some degree of control over sheep (at Zawi Chemi, ca. 10,500 B.P., there is a disproportionately large number of juveniles' bones), but better-dated evidence from such slightly later sites as Çayönü (Turkey) and Ganj Dareh (Iran) suggests that in some areas plants were domesticated before animals. In any case evidence from several stratified sites demonstrates that prehistoric Near Easterners lived in villages with solid structures while still eating (mostly, if not exclusively) wild foods. These early Neolithic people may have been semi-sedentary, but their built habitats reflect substantial energy investments, considerable durability, and numerous renovations; these, and the succession of floors, imply prolonged if sometimes seasonally discontinuous occupation. These structures have also yielded more human remains than were found in earlier periods. Many are juveniles, some are decapitated adults, others are simply adult skulls. It has been suggested that because some individuals at Natufian sites were interred beneath large stone slabs, with comparatively elaborate personal ornaments, this period was marked by developing rank or status hierarchy.

The so-called "Pre-Pottery" Neolithic (PPN) witnessed an increase in the number and diversity of sites, some of considerable size and duration. Sites in this time range (ca. 10,500–8500 B.P.) include Abu Hureyra, Mureybit, and Bouqras (Syria), 'Ain Ghazal and Beidha (Jordan), and Jericho (Israel). North of the Taurus Mountains and east of the Euphrates River lithic technology and food resources were somewhat different; sites of the same period include Çayönü and Çatal Hüyük (Turkey), Ganj Dareh, Asiab, Sarab, Guran, and Ali Kosh (Iran), and Jarmo and M'lefaat (Iraq). Gazelle, deer, ox, onager, boar, sheep, and goat were hunted in the tenth and ninth millennia, but domesticated forms had appeared at a number of sites throughout the Neat East by 8500 B.P. The earliest domesticated plants, evident in the late tenth and ninth millennia, were wheat and barley,

accompanied by lentil, chickpea, vetch, and others. Several sites dating to the ninth millennium B.P. have yielded pottery, and many have substantial architecture—rectilinear, multiroomed structures with hearths, ovens, and in a few cases painted walls and other internal ornamentation. Çatal Hüyük produced a large assemblage of sculpted figures, wall paintings, and combinations of cattle horns and plaster arranged in benches, platforms, and on walls. Elsewhere representational figures were carved on bone, and small figures of animals and humans were molded in clay, as was a wide range of geometric shapes considered by some to have served as counting devices or gaming pieces. A few late ninth-millennium sites, including Jericho, 'Ain Ghazal, and Tell Ramad, have produced human skulls covered with molded plaster, and some of these also yielded large anthropomorphic statues of clay and plaster molded over reed cores. As in earlier times interregional exchange in Red Sea cowries and Anatolian

Aerial view of excavation in progress at Jarmo. (Courtesy of the Oriental Institute, University of Chicago.)

obsidian was carried out; such exchange is best monitored by analyzing raw materials whose origins can be traced, because their chemical or mineralogical composition is idiosyncratic (they are "fingerprinted" by such techniques as X-ray spectroscopy and neutron activation).

The period 12–8000 B.P. saw increasing sedentarization, with the development of villages as a settlement type, increasing interregional interaction in the form of exchange for exotic materials (evidently including, in a few cases, plants and animals), and increasing regionalism, as well as growing diversification in the subsistence base and control over an ever-widening range of domesticates. The dead, often buried intramurally, provide some evidence for social differentiation; burials were not "standardized," and some were accompanied by comparatively elaborate, exotic, and therefore presumably costly grave goods. Many sites were occupied for several generations and some for centuries; the absence of large burial populations at some sites suggests the early use of specialized disposal grounds, but there are no substantial cemeteries yet known from this early time range.

Throughout the Near East the eighth and seventh millennia B.P. represent a period of "consolidation" and growing regional differentiation. Villages like Hajji Firuz and Guran (Iran), Yarim Tepe, Umm Dabaghiyah, Hassuna, Halaf, and Eridu (Iraq), Hacılar and Mersin (Turkey), Ghassoul (Jordan), Munhata (Israel), and Byblos (Syria) were based largely on plant cultivation and stock breeding; their inhabitants lived in agglutinated multiroomed rectilinear structures, some with courtyards and upper stories; they made ceramics, textiles, basketry, metal objects, and personal ornaments, as well as a range of stone, bone, and wooden utilitarian objects. It was on this broad foundation that increasing social differentiation and occupational specialization developed. Pottery, whose manufacture was presumably at first a cottage industry, varied stylistically from one region to another; eventually the ceramic craft, which requires special clays and abundant fuel, came to be controlled by a small number of specialists whose wares were needed by and distributed among a larger population. Other early specialties may have included copper metallurgy, with which early experiments had been undertaken at Çayönü; the carving of stone and bone seals, possibly used as signets or as stamps for painting textiles; and the sculpting of stone in amulets, ornaments, and representational figures. A few settlements, such as Hacılar and Tell es-Sawwan (Iraq), were surrounded by large walls, perhaps defensive in nature. Others had structures provisionally identified as shrines. At a few sites of the seventh-

millennium Ubaid period of Mesopotamia there is some evidence pointing to the development of irrigation canals, suggesting the concomitant rise of organizational principles by which decisions governing allocation of scarce water might be made, conflicts resolved, and canal digging and cleaning tasks assigned; at the same time these modifications in the landscape imply the growing need to intensify agrarian technology, although whether to meet the needs of an expanding population, the whims of a burgeoning elite, or the need for a surplus to exchange for skills, labor, or exotic materials is unclear. During this period settlements became increasingly diverse in location, size, and function. Some sites, such as Tepe Tula'i (Iran), may be the ephemeral remains of early specialized pastoral nomads; others may have served as regional centers of trade, transport, production, and administration.

By the sixth millennium B.P. some centers had become quite large, with areas of ten or more hectares implying populations exceeding 1,000 and more. A number of these sites, such as Godin Tepe and Susa (Iran) and Fara, Jemdet Nasr, Ur, and Uruk (Iraq), have yielded clear evidence of the world's earliest writing: clay tablets inscribed in cuneiform in the unrelated languages Sumerian, Elamite, and Akkadian. The decipherment of these languages has added immeasurably to our understanding of the ancient Near East, since it permits us to read letters, poems, marriage and divorce contracts, ledgers, schoolboys' exercises, myths, religious and omen texts, pharmaceutical recipes, legal codes, historical narratives, city archives, travel itineraries, trade documents, accounts of sales of land, slaves, and animals, and bilingual dictionaries left by the thousands at scores of sites over a period exceeding 3,000 years. From such texts king-lists have been compiled, relations between cities and between nations have been reconstructed, and many aspects of daily life in this earliest civilization have been fleshed out. There is rich evidence for complex division of labor, marked status differentiation (with social groups ranging from royalty to slaves), a polytheistic religion associated with specialist officials and elaborate temples and ritual, sprawling and internally differentiated cities, abundant and representational art that sometimes depicts military activities, and hierarchical bureaucracies. *Civilization*, a term much used and abused, is not discussed here, but it is fair to say that it would not have been possible without the developments of the late Pleistocene and early Holocene.

See also ACHEULEAN; ARCHAIC MODERNS; COMPLEX SOCIETIES; DOMESTICATION; ETHNOARCHAEOLOGY; EXOTICS; GEOCHRONOMETRY; HELIOPITHECUS; HOMINIDAE; HOMO SAPIENS; LATE PALEOLITHIC; MOUSTERIAN;

NEANDERTHALS; NEOLITHIC; PONGINAE; PROCONSUL; QAFZEH; SKHŪL; ZUTTIYEH. [C.K., E.D.]

Further Readings

Bar-Yosef, O. (1980) Prehistory of the Levant. Ann. Rev. Anthropol. 9:101–133.

Bintliff, J.L., and Van Zeist, W., eds. (1982) Palaeoclimates, Palaeoenvironments and Human Communities in the Eastern Mediterranean Region in Later Prehistory. Oxford: BAR International Series 133 (i and ii).

Braidwood, L.S., Braidwood, R.J., Howe, B., Reed, C.A., and Watson, P.J. (1983) Prehistoric Archeology Along the Zagros Flanks. Oriental Institute Publication 105. Chicago: University of Chicago Press (The Oriental Institute).

Braidwood, R.J., and Howe, B., eds. (1960) Prehistoric Investigations in Iraqi Kurdistan. Studies in Ancient Oriental Culture 31.Chicago: University of Chicago Press (The Oriental Institute).

Brice, W.C., ed. (1978) The Environmental History of the Near and Middle East Since the Last Ice Age. New York: Academic.

Curtis, J. ed. (1982) Fifty Years of Mesopotamian Discovery. London: British School of Archaeology in Iraq.

Flannery, K.V. (1969) Origins and ecological effects of early domestication in Iran and the Near East. In P.J. Ucko and G.W. Dimbleby (eds.): The Domestication and Exploitation of Plants and Animals, London: Duckworth, p. 73–100.

Lloyd, S. (1978) The Archaeology of Mesopotamia. London: Thames and Hudson.

Smith, P.E.L. (1986) Palaeolithic Archaeology in Iran. American Institute of Iranian Studies Monograph 1. Philadelphia: University Museum, University of Pennsylvania.

NEBRASKAN *see* GLACIATION; PLEISTOCENE

NECROLEMUR *see* MICROCHOERINAE; TARSIIDAE

NEEDLE *see* AWL; CLOTHING; STONE-TOOL MAKING

NEOGENE

Biochronological term introduced by M. Hoernes (as "Neogen") in 1856 to denote the younger faunas of the Cenozoic, as opposed to the "Palaeogen," or earlier Cenozoic faunas. Hoernes divided the Cenozoic fossil record at a marked transition to post-Eocene assemblages, which was well displayed in the Vienna basin. This wholesale overturn in Eocene marine groups, and also in Eocene mammal and floral communities, is widely recognized today at the base of the Oligocene, ca. 37 m.y. However, when Hoernes's coinage was revived by Gignoux in the early 1900s as a chronostratigraphic term, it was applied to the Miocene and Pliocene only. The trend among modern researchers is to follow Hoernes's original intent in including the Pleistocene, but the consensus is to retain the base of the Miocene as the beginning of the Neogene.

See also BIOCHRONOLOGY, CENOZOIC; GRANDE COUPURE; SEA-LEVEL CHANGE. [J.A.V.C., R.L.B.]

NEOLITHIC

Phase of human cultural development marked mainly by village settlement, domestication, and new implement types. In its earliest widespread usage among archaeologists Neolithic (New Stone Age) referred to particular assemblages of chipped and ground stone tools known from prehistoric sites in the Old World. In stratified contexts these tools reflected changes in technology of manufacture, tool morphology, and frequencies of types made in earlier periods. Increases in smaller tools, often made on snapped and retouched fragments of larger blades punched off prismatic cores, and blades with edge sheen acquired in plant harvesting, along with an increasing number and variety of pecked and ground-stone objects (querns, mortars, pestles, knives, axes, adzes, hoes, net sinkers and other weights, and the like), combine to identify as Neolithic the assemblages at sites like Jarmo in the Near East, Lepenski Vir in Europe, and P'an-po in China. By the beginning of this century it was generally recognized that tools termed Neolithic had been used not by hunter-gatherers but by farmers and herders. Thus, while relating initially to stone-tool typology, the term Neolithic has taken on important derivative connotations.

During the first half of the twentieth century archaeologists' efforts shifted from the necessary empirical description of cultural assemblages and, later, of their chronometric parameters, to improving understanding of the internal workings of societies earlier thought of somewhat simplistically as ethnic groups (such as Europe's Neolithic Linearbandkeramik folk—i.e. those who had made and used a particular ceramic assemblage). Among the archaeologists responsible for this important change in focus were J.G.D. Clark and V.G. Childe. In his influential work at the Holocene (Mesolithic) site of Star Carr in Yorkshire (England) Clark demonstrated that archaeologists could reconstruct many aspects of prehistoric economic organization, particularly in relation to subsistence and seasonality of settlement. Childe, whose familiarity with several European languages gave him access to a large body of archaeological literature, suggested that there had been two crucial transformations in the course of the human career: a change from a food-collecting way of life to one based on plant cultivation and stock breeding, and the subsequent founding of cities and the development of complexly stratified societies. Childe referred to these as the Neolithic and Urban Revolutions, respectively, and he formulated a hypothesis accounting for the change to reliance on produced rather than collected food on which later developments were based. This process, now referred to as *domestication*, was seen as intimately related to major climatic changes in the Near East at the end of the Pleistocene. Childe suggested that increasing desiccation caused aggregation of animals and people at oases and that this propinquity resulted in increasingly habituated and tamable—domesticable—animals. Childe's work also explicitly links technological change to changes in environment, subsistence, and sociopolitical organization.

Immediately following World War II Childe's hypothesis was examined in fieldwork designed and directed by R.J. Braidwood. In an ambitious multidisciplinary program Braidwood coordinated experts in prehistoric archaeology, zoology, botany, geology, and ceramic technology. This fieldwork, carried out in northeastern Iraq, was designed, among other things, to document the process of domestication, with concomitant changes in settlement organization and technology, and also to establish whether or not these transformations had occurred in tandem with significant early Holocene climatic change in the "hilly flanks" of the so-called Fertile Crescent (an arc-shaped area extending from the Nile to the mouths of the Tigris and Euphrates Rivers). The team concluded that while environmental change at the late Pleistocene/Holocene boundary had occurred in this region, it had not been sufficiently drastic to have caused altering relationships among plants, animals, and people. More recently, however, H.E. Wright has used palynological evidence to show that the nature of early Holocene climatic change varied locally within the Near East but that in a number of areas it involved increasing moisture rather than increasing aridity, as had been suggested by Childe. Wright now argues that climatic change at the end of the glacial Pleistocene was significant, affecting the geographic distribution of domesticable plants available to people. It now appears that the precise nature of late Pleistocene climatic change may differ from what was initially suggested by Childe; however, while it was certainly far more complex and regionally varied, it did, in some parts of the world (if not equally in all), affect distributions and associations of both plants and animals and hence transformed the stage upon which humans acted and from which they selected a few species for domestication.

Continuing disagreement about the precise timing and nature of the events of the Neolithic is due in large part to inadequate samples from representative sites and regions and to imprecision, despite ongoing improvements and refinements, in chronometric techniques. Nonetheless, research in a variety of geographic areas continues to demonstrate that Holocene changes in settlement pattern, food-procurement strategies, and technology were complex and highly varied and also that the rates at which changes occurred differed from one part of the world to another. In several world areas people radically modified their relationships with plants and animals, and these altered relationships led in turn to other important cultural changes.

Even when such wild ancestors of domesticates invaded new areas with ameliorating Holocene climate, not all took advantage of their presence. Some societies "invented" the complex of behaviors now identified as Neolithic; others failed to do so but were comparatively quick to imitate and modify such activities once exposed to them, using local species or importing foreign domesticates; yet others continued to rely on the collection of wild plants and animals, as do a few groups even in the present day. Where domestication was autochthonous, as in Mesoamerica and the Near East, cultural complexes associated with plant and animal domestication were distinctive, and rates of change varied considerably. Of particular interest is the association of settled village life, and the radical alteration in land use that it implies, with an increasing reliance on domesticated species. In the Near East sedentary life appears to have predated domestication, while in Mesoamerica, where the domestication of maize and other vegetable species was a comparatively slower process, village life seems to have followed plant domestication by several millennia.

"Neolithic," then, may be considered the complex of changes that, at the start of the Holocene and in many parts of the world, involved radically altered relationships between humans and the plants and animals on which they relied in many ways, associated changes in land use (including settlement pattern), and the technology by means of which humans adapted to their altered niches. The earliest manifestation of this complex of changes occurred in the Near East, in the tenth millennium B.P. (and perhaps slightly earlier). In the ninth and eighth millennia domestic plants and animals and changed technocomplexes appeared in Europe, and by the seventh millennium, in China (in the Yang-shao assemblage), where they were also associated with villages occupied for much if not all of the year. The idea of domestication and village life, along with some of the particular domesticated species, may have been introduced from the Near East into Europe and East Asia—but tighter chronological controls

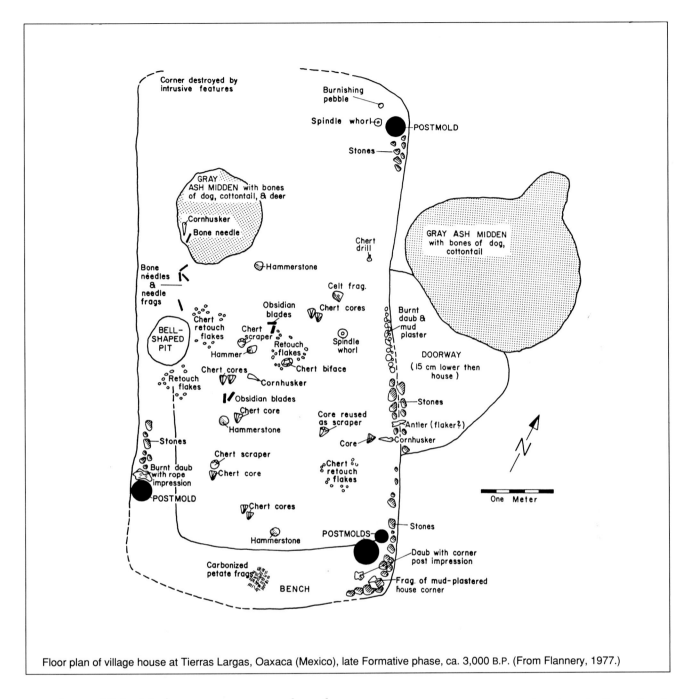

Floor plan of village house at Tierras Largas, Oaxaca (Mexico), late Formative phase, ca. 3,000 B.P. (From Flannery, 1977.)

must be established before routes, rates, and mechanisms of diffusion can be firmly identified.

See also ARCHAEOLOGICAL SITES;
COMPLEX SOCIETIES; DOMESTICATION;
NEAR EAST; PALEOLITHIC; SITE TYPES. [C.K.]

Further Readings

Binford, L.R. (1968) Post-Pleistocene adaptations. In S.R. Binford and L.R. Binford (eds.): New Perspectives in Archeology. Chicago: Aldine, pp. 313–341.

Childe, V.G. (1941) Man Makes Himself. London: Watts.

Clark, J.D., and Brandt, S.A., eds. (1984) From Hunters to Farmers: The Causes and Consequences of Food Production in Africa. Berkeley: University of California Press.

Flannery, K.V. (1969) Origins and ecological effects of early domestication in Iran and the Near East. In P.J. Ucko and G.W. Dimbleby (eds.): The Domestication and Exploitation of Plants and Animals. London: Duckworth, pp. 73–100.

Flannery, K.V., ed. (1976) The Early Mesoamerican Village. New York: Academic.

Ford, R.I., ed. (1985) Prehistoric Food Production in North America. Ann Arbor: University of Michigan Press.

Megaw, J.V.S., ed. (1977) Hunters, Gatherers and First Farmers Beyond Europe. Leicester: Leicester University Press.

Reed, C.A., ed. (1977) Origins of Agriculture. The Hague: Mouton.

Young, T.C., Jr., Smith, P.E.L., and Mortensen, P., eds. (1983) The Hilly Flanks and Beyond: Essays on the Prehistory of Southwestern Asia Presented to Robert J. Braidwood. Chicago: University of Chicago, The Oriental Institute.

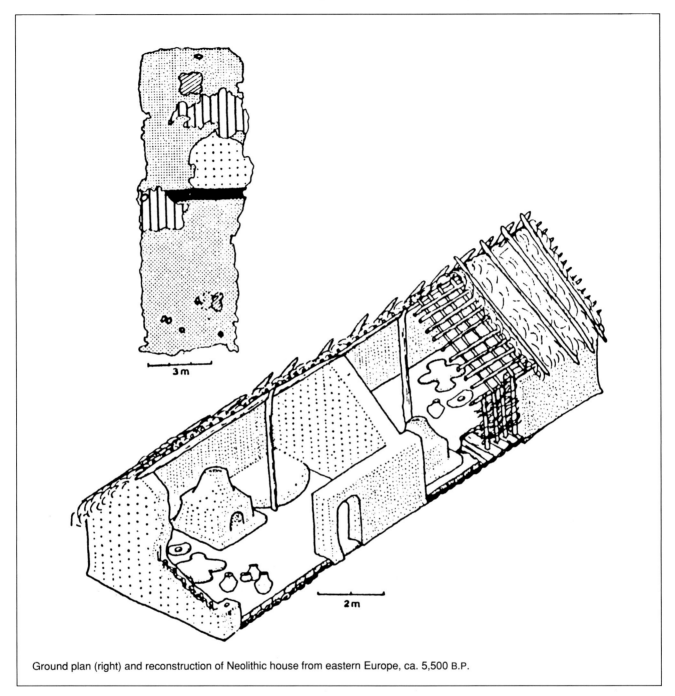

Ground plan (right) and reconstruction of Neolithic house from eastern Europe, ca. 5,500 B.P.

NEOSAIMIRI *see* CEBINAE

NGALOBA

The hominid skull from Ngaloba (Laetoli hominid 18) was discovered in late middle early late Pleistocene deposits in Tanzania in 1976. Middle Stone Age artifacts were reportedly associated with the discovery, which can be dated to ca. 120 k.y. ago by correlation with a dated volcanic deposit at nearby Olduvai Gorge. The skull comprises most of the cranial vault and the lower part of the face, which unfortunately cannot be directly fitted together because of damage. Brow-ridge development is archaic although not strong and the frontal bone is long, low, and receding, but the occipital region is rounded. In this respect and in occipitomastoid crest development the specimen is Neanderthal-like. Cranial capacity was originally quoted as only ca. 1,200 ml., but a higher figure (ca. 1,350 ml.) has also been measured. The Ngaloba skull is generally regarded as an archaic *Homo sapiens* fossil, but some workers believe that it is close to a modern human morphology.

See also ARCHAIC HOMO SAPIENS. [C.B.S.]

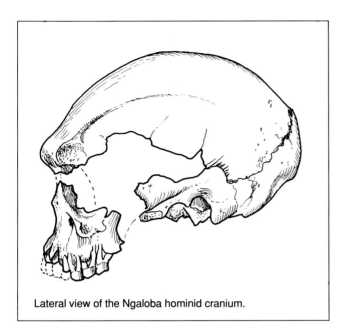

Lateral view of the Ngaloba hominid cranium.

NGANDONG (SOLO RIVER)

Middle Pleistocene surface exposure in eastern Java, dated at ca. 1–ca. 0.2 m.y. by faunal correlation. Between 1931 and 1933 the calvaria, calottes, and tibiae of at least 12 individuals were excavated from the banks of the Solo River near Ngandong. The reconstructed cranial capacities range from 1,035 to 1,225 ml. (n = 6). The phylogenetic and taxonomic status of these specimens has been debated ever since their discovery. Early workers felt that they might represent "neanderthaloid" forms. Few now accept this interpretation, but there is still much debate about whether to classify the Ngandong hominids as an early form of archaic *Homo sapiens* or a late form of *Homo erectus*. The total morphological pattern includes characteristics of both. Some have also suggested that the Ngandong specimens make a good morphological ancestor for Australian aborigines.

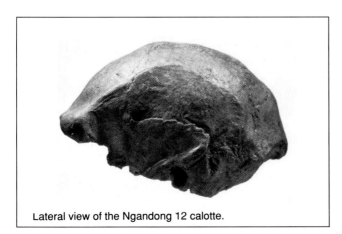

Lateral view of the Ngandong 12 calotte.

The dating and taphonomic context of the Ngandong finds have also been a source of speculation. The hominids have generally been assigned a late Pleistocene or latest middle Pleistocene age. It has also been suggested, however, that the Ngandong vertebrate assemblage is a mixed time-transgressive assemblage, some components of which may have been transported and redeposited. Taphonomic considerations have also entered into longstanding contentions that some of the Ngandong crania bear evidence of cannibalism in the form of damaged or missing basicrania and facial regions. On the basis of current evidence most workers attribute the preservation of the Ngandong crania to nonhominid taphonomic agencies.

See also ASIA (EASTERN); INDONESIA; SANGIRAN DOME. [G.G.P.]

Further Readings

Santa Luca, A.P. (1980) The Ngandong Fossil Hominids: A Comparative Study of a Far Eastern *Homo erectus* Group. New Haven, Conn.: Yale University Publications in Anthropology, No. 78.

Thorne, A., and Wolpoff, M.H. (1981) Regional continuity in Australian Pleistocene hominid evolution. Am. J. Phys. Anthropol. 55:337–349.

Weidenreich, F. (1951) Morphology of Solo Man. Anthropol. Pap. Am. Mus. Nat. Hist. 43:201–290.

NGERINGOROWA *see* BARINGO

NGORORA *see* BARINGO

NIAH

Hominid that may represent the oldest anatomically modern remains yet discovered in eastern Asia. The skull and partial skeleton of an adolescent were excavated from the Niah Cave (Borneo) in 1958 and certainly represent a specimen of modern type. Doubts have been raised, however, about whether the burial could have been wrongly associated with charcoal dated by radiocarbon at ca. 40 k.y. ago.

See also ARCHAIC MODERNS. [C.B.S.]

NIAUX *see* PALEOLITHIC IMAGE

NICHE *see* ECOLOGY; SPECIATION; SPECIES

NIHEWAN (NIHOWAN) FORMATION

Stratified exposures of late Pliocene to middle Pleistocene age, in Hebei Province, northern China; lower level (Red Beds) ca. 2.5 m.y.; upper level (White Beds) ca. 0.7 m.y by faunal correlation. The Nihewan Formation crops out over a wide area in the Sanggan He Valley and has long been considered the type site of the "Chinese Villafranchian." The formation was said to have yielded associations of *Equus* and *Hipparion*, but there is doubt as to whether these horse genera actually derive from the same stratigraphic levels. It is possible that *Hipparion*, which may have become extinct in the early Pleistocene, derives from the "Red Beds" and that the *Equus* fossils came from the unconformably overlying "White Beds." On the basis of current evidence it seems that the Nihewan Formation spans the late Pliocene and at least part of the early Pleistocene and middle Pleistocene. One artifact has been recovered in association with the skeleton of *Elephas namadicus*, a typically middle Pleistocene form in China.

See also ASIA (EASTERN); CHINA. [G.G.P.]

Further Readings

Teilhard de Chardin, P., and Piveteau, J. (1930) Les mammifères fossiles de Nihowan (Chine). Ann. Paléontol. *19*:1–134.

Xu, Q., and You, Y. (1982) Four post-Nihewan Pleistocene mammalian faunas of North China: correlation with deep-sea sediments. Acta Anthropol. Sin. *1*:180–187.

NOAILLIAN *see* GRAVETTIAN; PERIGORDIAN

NOMASCUS *see* APE; HYLOBATIDAE

NOMENCLATURE

Zoological nomenclature is the process of naming the animal groups that one recognizes in nature. The rules by which names are applied are laid down in the *International Code of Zoological Nomenclature*, a publication issued and revised at intervals by the International Trust for Zoological Nomenclature. In its periodical the *Bulletin of Zoological Nomenclature* this independent international body also publishes comments and issues rulings by its Commission, a committee composed of taxonomists from several countries, on the many problems of nomenclature that arise. The Trust also maintains official lists of names and publications that the Commission has accepted or rejected.

The system of nomenclature laid down in the *Code* is often referred to as the *binominal* (not *binomial*) system. This is because the species, the basic unit of the system, is identified by two names, both of which are italicized and either of Latin derivation or latinized (given a Latin ending). Our species, for example, is *Homo sapiens*. The first name (*Homo*) is the

name of the genus; the second (*sapiens*) is the specific name, and the combination of the two names is unique. Each species must be identified on the basis of a *type specimen*, or *holotype*, with which all other individuals allocated to the same species must be compared. The provisions of the *Code* apply only to taxa of the family-group or below and among other things prescribe endings for the names of families ("-idae," as in "Hominidae") and subfamilies ("-inae," as in "Homininae"). The endings "-oidea" and "-ini," respectively, are recommended for superfamilies and tribes.

See also CLASSIFICATION; TAXONOMY. [I.T.]

Further Readings

International Trust for Zoological Nomenclature. (1985) International Code of Zoological Nomenclature, 3rd ed. Berkeley: University of California Press.

Mayr, E. (1969) Principles of Systematic Zoology. New York: McGraw-Hill.

NON-DARWINIAN EVOLUTION

Darwinian natural selection operates on physical or phenotypic variations of varying degrees of survival and reproductive value. Since, however, only a tiny portion of the genome is actually expressed in the phenotype, it follows that natural selection cannot be the major force guiding the evolution of the genome. It appears that most genetic change is adaptively neutral and simply indifferent to natural selection. Mathematically the evolutionary rate of such genetic change is governed by the rate of mutation.

See also EVOLUTION; GENOME; MOLECULAR ANTHROPOLOGY. [J.M.]

NOTHARCTIDAE

Family traditionally regarded as a group of Eocene, primarily North American, primates, related to the European adapids via the Holarctic genus *Pelycodus*. As had happened with *Adapis*, *Notharctus* and *Pelycodus*, described in 1870 and 1875 by R. Leidy and E.D. Cope, respectively, were not recognized at first as being primate. By the turn of the century these errors were corrected, and in 1902 H.F. Osborn suggested that the early Eocene *Pelycodus* might be related to the middle Eocene *Notharctus*. In his monographic study of *Notharctus* W.K. Gregory argued that the European *Adapis* and its kin were also descended from *Pelycodus*. (Gregory also suggested that New World monkeys had evolved from *Notharctus*, but this scheme received no support from other systematists.) Although specimens had been known since Osborn's study, it was not until 1958 that C.L. Gazin pointed out that the species known as "*Notharctus gracilis*" could be distinguished easily

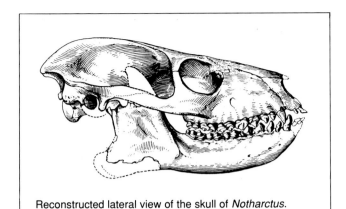

Reconstructed lateral view of the skull of *Notharctus*.

from *Notharctus*; this species he referred to J.L. Wortman's 1903 genus *Smilodectes*, which Gazin suggested had also evolved from *Pelycodus*. Most recently E.L. Simon's *Cantius* (very close to *Pelycodus*) and P.D. Gingerich's *Copelemur* (enigmatic, to say the least) have been added to the array of notharctids, as have various European taxa that had been lumped with *Adapis*. Breaking with tradition, J.H. Schwartz has recently argued that if notharctids do indeed constitute a monophyletic group they are probably the sister group of all proper strepsirhines, the whole being united by the possession of the "lemurlike" bulla.

See also ADAPIDAE; SIVALADAPIDAE. [J.H.S.]

Further Readings

Gazin, C.L. (1958) A review of the middle and upper Eocene primates of North America. Smith. Misc. Coll. *136*:1–112.

Schwartz, J.H. (1986) Primate systematics and a classification of the order. In D.R. Swindler (ed.): Comparative Primate Biology, Vol. 1: Systematics, Evolution and Anatomy. New York: Liss, pp. 1–41.

NOTHARCTUS *see* NOTHARCTIDAE

NUCLEUS *see* CORE; STONE-TOOL MAKING

NUMERICAL TAXONOMY

Grouping of taxonomic units based on a numerical measure of relationship. Character states are coded numerically as presence or absence (coded 0 or 1), in rank orders or as measurements on a continuous scale. Relationships are frequently presented in the form of a tree diagram, or *dendrogram*.

See also CLADISTICS; PHENETICS; QUANTITATIVE METHODS. [L.M.]

NYAKACH *see* MABOKO

NYANZAPITHECUS *see* OREOPITHECIDAE

NYANZA *see* KENYA; RIFT VALLEY; RUSINGA

NYCTICEBOIDES *see* LORISIDAE, LORISOIDEA

NYCTICEBUS *see* LORISIDAE

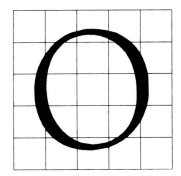

OAKLEY, KENNETH PAGE (1911-1981)

British geologist and paleontologist. On graduating from University College, London, in 1933, Oakley went to work as a geologist with the British Geological Survey. Two years later he joined the Department of Palaeontology of the British Museum (Natural History), where he spent the rest of his career. As a result of his former connection with the Geological Survey Oakley had developed a consuming interest in vertebrate paleontology, especially paleoanthropology. He later acquired an international reputation for his work on analytical methods of dating bones, particularly the technique of fluorine dating. The application of this technique to bones in the Piltdown faunal assemblage contributed to the eventual exposure of the forgery, and it was also used to demonstrate that the Galley Hill and Bury St. Edmunds crania were not of middle Pleistocene age, as previously contended. Oakley produced a number of popular books, including *Man the Toolmaker* (1949) and *Frameworks for Dating Fossil Man* (1964).

[F.S.]

OBSIDIAN *see* RAW MATERIALS

OCHER *see* RAW MATERIALS; RITUAL

OHE INTERSTADIAL *see* GLACIATION; PLEISTOCENE

OLD CROW

Archaeological locality in the northern Yukon (Canada) that has yielded a series of bone tools thought to predate Clovis in antiquity. A bone apatite radiocarbon determination on a distinctive flesher provided an age of 27,000 B.P. But bone collagen from this artifact, recently redated by the accelerator-based radiocarbon method, provides a fairly modern age estimate (1350 B.P.). Significant questions linger regarding both the age of this artifact and the Old Crow bone assemblages in general.

See also **AMERICAS; PALEOINDIAN.** [L.S.A.P., D.H.T.]

OLDENBURGIAN *see* TIME SCALE

OLDOWAN

Oldest formally recognized set of stone-artifact assemblages of Early Paleolithic. This lithic industry, or industrial complex, was defined on the basis of artifact assemblages from Bed I and lower Bed II, Olduvai Gorge, ca. 1.9–1.6 m.y. old. It is characterized by pieces of stone (e.g. choppers, scrapers) modified by simple stone-on-stone chipping and the flakes detached by this process. As originally defined, the Oldowan is confined possibly to eastern Africa, although similar industries of simply modified stone cores and flakes dated to over 1 m.y. occur from northern to southern Africa. The term Oldowan has generally not been applied to stone assemblages outside of Africa. Assemblages of simple tools/cores and flakes, however, are found at archaeological sites from the early and middle Pleistocene in Asia and Europe. Some Oldowan-type artifacts, especially choppers, also occur in stone-tool assemblages up to the present. Because several hominid species occur at sites yielding Oldowan assemblages (or of similar age), there is some question as to who made these tools. Most paleoanthropologists consider that *Homo habilis*, which first appears in the fossil record at about the same time as the earliest Oldowan tools or slightly later, was probably the toolmaker.

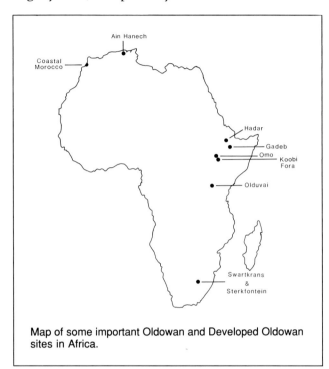

Map of some important Oldowan and Developed Oldowan sites in Africa.

Rocks modified by deliberate flaking, referred to as *tools* or *cores*, which characterize the Oldowan, are classified into several types: choppers, discoids, polyhedrons, scrapers, spheroids and subspheroids, burins, and protobifaces. Oldowan choppers are further divided into subtypes based on the relationship of the chipped edge to the original shape of the stone. Modification is often simple enough to identify the size and shape of the original stone as well. The Oldowan is also characterized by "utilized material," such as battered hammerstones and anvils, and flakes with chipped edges thought to connote use; unmodified flakes, or débitage, which represent sharp-edged products detached from the large, chipped pieces; and manuports, or unmodified cobbles and other rocks that have been brought to a site by early humans. Based on spatially confined assemblages of these chipped rocks and related utilized and unutilized pieces, Oldowan archaeological sites are distinguished from natural occurrences of broken rocks by 1) patterns of repeated flaking, and conchoidal fracture, evidenced by the tools/cores, and 2) geologic contexts where naturally transported and broken rocks do not occur.

Although defined on the basis of entire assemblages of artifacts, the usual predominance of choppers, in particular, and the absence of certain other types of chipped rock, like bifaces, distinguish the

Oldowan from related stone industries. At Olduvai choppers represent from 28 to 79 percent of the tools/cores in Oldowan assemblages. Choppers made from rounded cobbles also typify the "Pebble Culture" assemblages of Morocco and Tunisia; however, choppers and other tool/core types of the Oldowan are made from varied shapes of raw material—angular lumps (e.g. quartzite) and irregular nodules (e.g. chert) in addition to water-worn cobbles. The KBS industry from Koobi Fora, ca. 1.9 m.y., is similar to the Oldowan in that it contains simply chipped pieces and flakes. Although some characteristic tool/core forms of the Oldowan, such as small scrapers, spheroids, and subspheroids, are rare in the KBS industry, the latter is considered to be part of the Oldowan. The younger Karari industry at Koobi Fora is also similar to the Oldowan, but the presence of large core scrapers distinguish it from the Oldowan and other early stone industries. Bifaces are rare in the Karari artifact assemblages; yet their presence suggests an affinity with the Developed Oldowan. Stone assemblages known from Ethiopia, Zaire, and Malawi are older than 2 m.y. and may also be covered by the term Oldowan.

The Developed Oldowan is an industry also defined at Olduvai. It is characterized by a poorer representation of choppers (less than 28 percent of all tools/cores) and a greater abundance of spheroids, subspheroids, and small scrapers. Bifaces also appear for the first time in the Olduvai sequence in the Developed Oldowan assemblages, which are prevalent from middle Bed II (ca. 1.6 m.y.) through Beds III/IV (ca. 0.7 m.y.). According to some researchers, bifaces, like handaxes and cleavers, indicate that the Developed Oldowan is part of the Acheulean industrial complex. M.D. Leakey maintains, however, that the Developed Oldowan is a tradition of tool manufacture continuous with the Oldowan and that both are characterized by the production of small flakes (less than 10 cm.), in contrast with the Acheulean.

All pieces modified by flaking in the Oldowan, as defined by Leakey, are referred to as *tools*, and the unmodified flakes are considered to be waste products. Nevertheless, other researchers have suggested that the flaked stones may represent mainly *cores* (i.e. by-products of manufacturing sharp flakes useful as implements). Indeed studies of microscopic wear on the edges of siliceous stone tools from Koobi Fora (KBS and Karari industries) show that unretouched flakes were used for cutting plant and animal material. Oldowan assemblages at Olduvai are all associated with fossil animal bones, some of which bear cutmarks made by stone tools. Oldowan technology largely entailed making sharp-edged flakes and flaked pieces, many of which exhibit slight damage

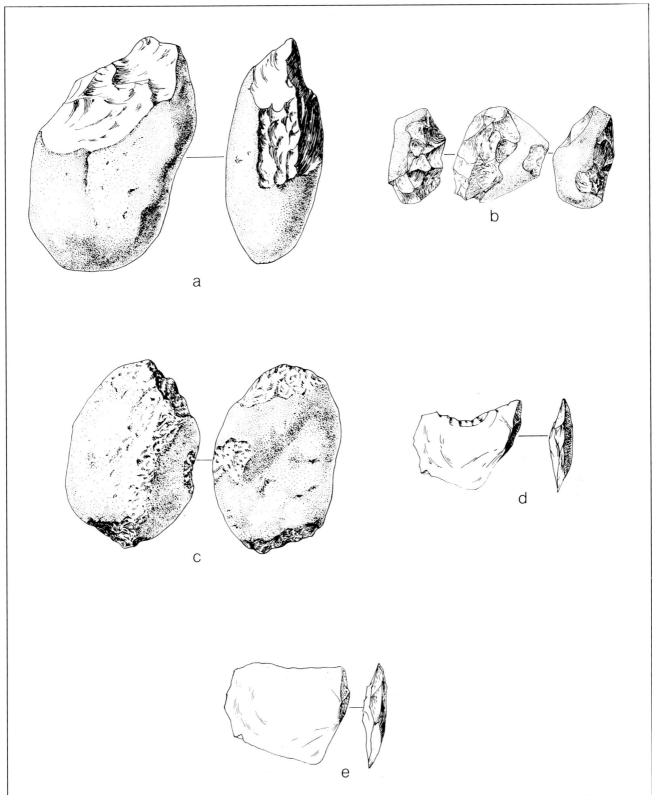

Typical artifacts from Oldowan assemblages at Olduvai Gorge: a) chopper; b) polyhedron; c) hammerstone; d) utilized flake; e)*débitage* flake.

to the edges visible by eye. Thus Oldowan stone technology was devoted largely to production of cutting implements. The presence of subspheroids, hammerstones, and anvils, though, also implies that implements were available for smashing or crushing functions. In fact many of the major limb bones of animals on Oldowan sites show signs that the diaphyses were broken open, as people today do by pounding such bones in the middle to obtain marrow.

The Oldowan in East Africa persisted for at least 0.5 m.y. with little evidence of change in artifact morphology or techniques of manufacture. This long stability in technology contrasts with heterogeneity in technology and artifact assemblages in time and space over the past 30 k.y. Interpretations of "culture" implied by Oldowan tool making must incorporate ideas about conservatism and stability in behavior that are not evident over such long periods of time in the cultural behavior of modern humans.

See also ACHEULEAN; AFRICA; EARLY PALEOLITHIC; HOMO HABILIS; KARARI; OLDUVAI; PALEOLITHIC LIFEWAYS; STONE-TOOL MAKING. [R.P.]

Further Readings

Isaac, G.L. (1984) The archaeology of human origins. Adv. World Archaeol. 3:1-87.

Keeley, L., and Toth, N. (1981) Microwear polishes on early stone tools from Koobi Fora, Kenya. Nature 293:464-465.

Leakey, M.D. (1966) A review of the Oldowan culture from Olduvai Gorge, Tanzania. Nature 210:462-466.

Leakey, M.D., ed. (1971) Olduvai Gorge, Vol. 3. Cambridge: University of Cambridge Press.

Potts, R., and Shipman, P. (1981) Cutmarks made by stone tools on bones from Olduvai Gorge, Tanzania. Nature 291:577-580.

OLDUVAI

Northern Tanzanian stratified series of late Pliocene to late Pleistocene age, between 1.9 and ca. 0.1 m.y. according to radiometric, paleomagnetic, and faunal analyses. This famous site on the edge of the Serengeti Plains is a small canyon that stretches from east to west for ca. 25 km. and drains eastward into a depression at the foot of the Ngorongoro caldera. Shaped in the form of the letter Y, Olduvai Gorge, found in 1911 by Kattwinkel, consists of a main canyon and a tributary called the Side Gorge. The most important geological, paleontological, and archaeological localities are found near the junction of these two canyons.

Serious geological and paleontological research at Olduvai began in 1913 under H. Reck. Reck developed the basic stratigraphic nomenclature of Olduvai Gorge, which divides the ca. 100 m. of Olduvai strata into Beds I, II, III, and IV, from bottom to top. Reck's first expedition to Olduvai discovered a human skeleton, numbered Olduvai Hominid One (OH 1) in Bed II with many extinct mammals. Exploration resumed in 1931, when L.S.B. Leakey organized an expedition and invited Reck to accompany him. Leakey recognized stone tools in the Olduvai sediments and initially accepted Reck's claims about the antiquity of the human skeleton. Subsequent work, however, showed that the skeleton was a relatively recent, intrusive burial and hence unassociated with the stone tools or extinct fauna.

In 1935 Leakey led another expedition to Olduvai, which recovered two hominid parietal fragments among large numbers of faunal remains and artifacts. This and subsequent expeditions were devoted to surface survey of the gorge. Individual sites were identified according to the korongo, or gully, in which they were found. Thus FLK sites refer to "Frida Leakey Korongo" named after Leakey's first wife. Layers in that gully and others, such as BK, SHK, DK, and HWK, have yielded many artifacts and fossils.

Excavations began in the 1950s in the Side Gorge. Again, thousands of artifacts and fossils were recovered, but hominid remains were elusive and only isolated teeth were found. Finally, in 1959, M.D. Leakey discovered the cranium of a fossil hominid eroding from the surface of Bed I at FLK. This specimen featured enormous molars, molarized premolars, a small braincase, a flat face, and a large, anteriorly placed sagittal crest. In these and other regards it resembled robust Australopithecus specimens from southern Africa. L.S.B. Leakey, however, was convinced that he had found Olduvai's toolmaker, a direct human ancestor. He first informally suggested the name "Titanohomo mirabilis" for the specimen but later described it as Zinjanthropus boisei. Today this specimen, OH 5, is often referred to as "Zinj," but most recognize it as the holotype of Australopithecus boisei.

The discovery of the "Zinj" cranium heralded the beginning of modern paleoanthropological research in eastern Africa. Interest centered on Olduvai during the 1960s. Volcanic rocks interbedded with the fossils and artifacts at the base of the Olduvai Gorge were dated at the University of California by G. Curtis and J. Evernden to nearly 2 m.y. With the discovery of "Zinj" came substantial financial support, and many important archaeological sites were opened. One of these, at FLKNN, yielded the remains (OH 7) of a second type of Bed I hominid, which Leakey and his colleagues P.V. Tobias and J. Napier named Homo habilis in 1964. With the recovery of H. habilis Leakey changed his mind about the contemporary "Zinjanthropus," relegating it to a side branch of human evolution. Homo habilis was based on fragmentary, partly immature material, and the species distinction was questioned by many anthropologists.

View of the Olduvai Gorge with the Lemagrut volcano in the background. (Photograph by and courtesy of Tim D. White.)

Work by the Leakeys and geologist R.L. Hay has made Olduvai Gorge one of the most important localities in the world for the study of human evolution. During the deposition of sediments in Bed I the Olduvai region was characterized by a shallow, alkaline lake ca. 25 km. across. Along the southeastern lakeshore streams that arose from nearby volcanic highlands brought fresh water into the lake. The Bed I sediments were laid down in this lake and in the stream valleys that contributed to it between 2.1 and 1.7 m.y. ago. This deposition continued into the lower part of the Bed II but was disrupted ca. 1.6 m.y. ago when faulting altered the topography of the basin, reducing the size of the lake. During Bed I and Lower Bed II times hominid occupation sites were clustered along the southeastern lake margin. These sites are recognized by an abundance of broken stones and bones, sometimes associated with the remains of hominids themselves. These concentrations were at first thought to represent "living floors"—"home bases" or campsites of early hominids—by the Leakeys and G. Isaac. Interpretation of these "sites" has become a controversial question for archaeologists in the 1980s. *Australopithecus boisei* and *Homo habilis* are both represented at these loca-

The Olduvai Hominid 9 skullcap. Photograph of cast. (From Tattersall, 1970.)

tions. The tools themselves belong to the Oldowan industrial complex, a stone-tool industry dominated by crude cores, battered hammerstones, and many flakes. The presence of foreign stone clasts and tools made of fine-grained lavas, quartzite, and quartz in the clays and silts of lake-margin environments at Olduvai shows that hominids carried stone to these environments. Which hominids were involved, the functions of these stone tools, and the nature of the behaviors represented by these assemblages are all questions that remain to be answered at Olduvai and other early Pleistocene archaeological sites.

Hominid remains in upper Bed II, Bed III, and Bed IV have been attributed to *Homo erectus*. They include postcranial remains as well as the important OH 9 specimen, first called "Chellean man" because of the abundant Acheulean artifacts in the upper part of the Olduvai geological succession. Hominid activity in Bed III and Bed IV times was confined largely to a main river system and tributary streams that flowed from the west into the basin. Therefore much of the Acheulean and "developed Oldowan" material is in a disturbed archaeological context, unlike the well-preserved sites in Bed I.

When M.D. Leakey retired from work at Olduvai in 1983, a total of 60 hominid specimens had been recovered from the gorge. About 30 percent of these came from excavations; the others were found by surface survey. In addition thousands of paleontological and archaeological specimens have come from work in the gorge. Work at Olduvai continues. In 1986 a joint Institute of Human Origins, University of California, and Tanzania National Museum team discovered OH 62, parts of a tiny *Homo* skeleton, in Bed I. The Olduvai succession records biological and cultural change over nearly 2 m.y. of human history. It has yielded the type specimens for two hominid species, *Australopithecus boisei* and *Homo habilis* and important specimens of *Homo erectus* as well. Because the soft sedimentary rocks of Olduvai Gorge contain many more fossils and artifacts the erosion from each new rainstorm has the potential to enrich our knowledge of human evolution.

See also AUSTRALOPITHECUS BOISEI; HOMO ERECTUS; HOMO HABILIS; LEAKEY, LOUIS; LEAKEY, MARY; OLDOWAN; TANZANIA. [T.D.W.]

Further Readings

Binford, L.R. (1981) Bones: Ancient Men and Modern Myths. New York: Academic.

Hay, R.L. (1976) Geology of the Olduvai Gorge. Berkeley: University of California Press.

Johanson, D.C., et al. (1987) New partial skeleton of *Homo habilis* from Olduvai Gorge, Tanzania. Nature 327:205–209.

Leakey, M.D. (1971) Olduvai Gorge, Vol. 3. Cambridge: Cambridge University Press.

Leakey, M.D. (1984) Disclosing the Past. Garden City, N.Y.: Doubleday.

Reader, J. (1981) Missing Links. Boston: Little, Brown.

OLDUVAI EVENT   *see*   PALEOMAGNETISM

OLIGOCENE

Epoch spanning 13 m.y. in the middle Cenozoic. Its base, which marks the end of the Eocene, is dated to ca. 37–36 m.y., and its top is marked by the base of the Miocene at 23.5 m.y. The Oligocene series is divided into two parts, with the Lower Oligocene taking its definition from the Rupelian Stage and the Upper Oligocene, beginning at ca. 32 m.y., equivalent to the Chattian Stage. Both stages are typified in the North German Plain, an area not studied or referred to by Charles Lyell in formulating the Eocene and Miocene (1838); in fact Lyell objected that the new epoch was redundant when Beyrich proposed the name in 1854. The identification of the Oligocene remained a problem because of the poor correlation between the northern molluscan faunas of the Oligocene stages and the subtropical species that characterized the Eocene and Miocene type sections in France and Italy. The controversy was only recently put to rest with the determination, based on planktonic microfossils, that the Lattorfian Stage, underlying the Rupelian, is time-equivalent to the Priabonian Stage of the Mediterranean region. The Priabonian in turn has been determined to be Upper Eocene in the classic sense. This has the effect of shortening the Oligocene, a loss for Beyrich's side, and of relocating the underlying Bartonian, formerly held to be of late Eocene age, to the middle Eocene.

The earliest fossil remains of the Old World Anthropoidea (catarrhine monkeys, apes, and humans) are found in the southern continents at two sites loosely dated to the Eocene-Oligocene transition; the earliest South American monkeys date from the late Oligocene. The decline and extinction of prosimians in the northern continents also took place during the Oligocene. These events together mark a shift in the locale of primate evolution from the northern to the southern hemisphere.

The earliest examples of the southern primate faunas are known from Burma and Egypt. The most important of these is the Fayum Depression south of Cairo, where the Jebel Qatrani Formation yields a diverse primate fauna representing at least two families of lower primates (Omomyidae and ?Lorisidae), two of higher primates (Parapithecidae and Propliopithecidae), and two taxa of uncertain affinities (*Oligopithecus* and *Afrotarsius*).

The Jebel Qatrani levels are in the upper part of a sequence that rests on middle Eocene (basal Bartonian) marine beds and is unconformably overlain by basalts dated to the middle Oligocene, at 31 m.y. The fossil beds are widely considerd to be of Oligocene age, but this is mainly because the Bartonian has until recently been dated to the Upper Eocene. With revision of the Eocene time scale this interpolation is no longer certain. The Pondaung locality in Burma, with problematic anthropoids *Pondaungia* and *Parapithecus*, is commonly considered to be of late Eocene age, but here again the stratigraphy of associated marine beds, on which the age assessment depends, needs to be reviewed in the light of modern time scales.

In South America the earliest known primate is the ceboid *Branisella*, from Salla (Bolivia), dated to ca. 26 m.y. in the late Oligocene. The next oldest are *Tremacebus* and *Dolichocebus* from the Colhehuapian of Argentina, formerly thought to be of later Oligocene age but recently redated to early Miocene.

North America was the last refuge of the omomyids in the Oligocene. *Rooneyia* comes from the Chambers Tuff of west Texas, dated to the basal Oligocene at 36 m.y., and *Macrotarsius* is found in a Chadronian horizon in Montana with an age between 34 and 32 m.y. The last North American nonhuman primate, *Ekgmowechashala*, has been found in latest Oligocene (Lower Arikareean) beds, dated to ca. 25 m.y., in South Dakota (thus the Siouxian etymology) and in Oregon.

No primates of unambiguously Oligocene age are known from either Asia or Europe. The early Miocene prosimians *Sivaladapis* and *Indraloris* of northern Indopakistan are probably the last descendants of Eurasian Eocene adapids but may have been derived from Indo-Malaysia or Africa, the only known refuges of prosimians after the Oligocene.

Oligocene Environments

The Oligocene saw a sharp, steplike decline in world climate toward modern conditions. The Eocene epoch was the heyday of the prosimians, with abundant remains known from all northern continents. Eocene environments were marked by broadleaf forest and vertebrate faunas adapted to year-round frost-free conditions from Baffin Island to Antarctica. Toward the end of the Eocene, however, climate began to deteriorate, and at the end of the epoch a sharp drop in sea level coincided with a decrease in winter minima of at least 11 degrees C in middle latitudes. The broadleaf evergreen forests of this region began to be replaced by deciduous elements, and there was a concomitant wave of replacement in marine and continental faunas, known as the *Grande Coupure* or, more generally, as the "Terminal Eocene Event." The northern prosimians were nearly exterminated during this event and lingered on only in North America.

On the southern continents the patterns was reversed. The primate fossil record of this entire hemisphere up to the latest Eocene is virtually blank, if we discount the problematical "adapid," *Azibius*, from the early(?) Eocene of Morocco, the affinities of which have been questioned. The earliest undoubted primate fauna, however, shows an endemic diversity indicating a long period of radiation and evolution separate from the northern hemisphere.

Oligocene Paleogeography

Continental drift sheds some light on primate faunal evolution. Prior to the Miocene Eurasia was isolated by the Tethys Sea from Africa and Southeast Asia, and faunal interchange from north to south was restricted. In the late Eocene creodont carnivores, didelphid marsupials, and pangolins reached Africa from Europe; primitive tethytheres (the group of modern proboscideans, sirenians, and hyraxes), anthracotheres, and protoanthropoids (i.e. the Pondaung primates) occur on both southern and northern shores of the eastern Tethys, but only the anthracotheres in the western part. More information on Eocene history of the East Asian and African faunas may soon be available from new sites in China and the inner Atlas basins of Morocco, Algeria, and Tunisia, but it may be that the primates of the southern continents (and perhaps eastern Asia) were mostly separate from those of western Eurasia since the early Eocene or even earlier.

The source of South American Oligocene primates is also uncertain. The early mammalian faunas of South America, unlike those of Africa, are well known, and it can be confirmed that both primates and rodents were absent before the late Oligocene. South America was an island continent, like Australia, from the earliest Cenozoic to the Pliocene. This helps to explain why the diverse primate faunas of the North American Eocene have no South American counterpart. Sea-level lowering at the end of the Eocene may have made it possible for (as yet unknown) North American protoanthropoids to reach South America and to evolve into the anthropoids first found in the later Oligocene. This would, however, require either that the Anthropoidea be polyphyletic or that a circum-Pacific protoanthropoid fauna evidenced by *Hoanghonius* of China and *Pondaungia* of Burma also connected North America to the Fayum at this critical juncture. This seems unlikely; hystricomorph rodents and cichlid fishes, two other groups that appeared in South America at the same time as the primates, have fossil records that indicate a strictly Afro-Arabian history in the Old World going back well before their South American debut. Many other vertebrate and invertebrate groups found today in South America and Africa are so closey related that a mid-Cenozoic common ancestor is indicated, although the fossil record is less clear in these cases.

Thus it seems most probable that the South American anthropoids originated as the result of a transatlantic migration from Africa. The terminal Eocene fall of sea level, or more likely the great regression of the middle Oligocene, may have allowed elements of the African fauna, with assistance from favorable currents, to filter across island chains in the south Atlantic. The discovery of mid-Cenozoic coral reefs buried under deep-sea sediments on the Pernambuco-Benin transform ridge lends credence to this scenario. By the end of the Oligocene rising sea level and further widening of the south Atlantic prohibited further interchange. Once in South America the anthropoids radiated during the late Oligocene into new adaptive forms, such that both modern subfamilies can be recognized already in the early Miocene.

See also ANTHROPOIDEA; ASIA (EASTERN); CATARRHINI; CEBOIDEA; CENOZOIC; FAYUM; GRANDE COUPURE; PALEOBIOGEOGRAPHY; SEA-LEVEL CHANGE. [R.F.K., J.A.V.C.]

Further Readings

Berggren, W.A., Kent, D.V., Flynn, J.J., and Van Couvering, J.A. (1985) Cenozoic geochronology. Geol. Soc. Am. Bull. 96:1407–1418.

Ciochon, R.L., and Chiarelli, A.B., eds. (1980) Evolutionary Biology of the New World Monkeys and Continental Drift. New York: Plenum.

McFadden, B.J. (1985) Drifting continents, mammals, and time scales: current developments in South America. J. Vert. Paleontol. 5:169–174.

Savage, D.E., and Russell, D.E. (1983) Mammalian paleofaunas of the world. Reading, Mass.: Addison-Wesley.

Van Couvering, J.A., Aubry, M.-P., Berggren, W.A., Bujak, J.P., Naeser, C.W., and Wieser, T. (1981) The terminal Eocene event and the Polish connection. Palaeogeogr. Palaeoclimat. Palaeoecol. 36:222–260.

OLIGOPITHECUS

Poorly known fossil primate from the lowest Oligocene level of the Fayum deposits (ca. 35 m.y.). A partial lower jaw of *Oligopithecus savagei* was described in 1961 by E.L. Simons and considered to represent an early eucatarrhine. Several later authors have questioned this interpretation and place *Oligopithecus* only hesitantly within the catarrhines. The type mandible preserves only the C_1-M_2, but the presence of just two premolars has suggested a relationship to the "modern" catarrhines rather than to the parapithecids. On the other hand the mesiobuccal face of the P_3 bears a honing flange, which has been worn through to dentine, presumably by contact with the C^1, a condition otherwise unknown among anthropoids and indicative of an "imperfect" adaptation to canine honing. Moreover, the molar trigonids are higher and narrower than the talonids, as is common among "lower" primates but not among anthropoids; the entoconid is close to the hypoconulid, as in sivaladapids and *Hoanghonius* but not anthropoids; and the talonid wear facet typical of catarrhines is lacking. Pending further discoveries, *Oligopithecus* is best regarded as only doubtfully a catarrhine.

See also ANTHROPOIDEA; CATARRHINI; FAYUM; PARAPITHECIDAE; PONDAUNGIA; SIVALADAPIDAE; TEETH. [E.D.]

Further Readings

Szalay, F.S., and Delson, E. (1979) Evolutionary History of the Primates. New York: Academic.

OLORGESAILIE

Early middle Pleistocene locality (ca. 0.8 m.y.) in southern Kenya known for concentrations of Acheulean handaxes. Some handaxe sites, including one associated with numerous *Theropithecus* (gelada) remains, have been viewed as butchery and camp sites. The sandy-stream-channel contexts of these sites, however, have caused doubt about such interpretations.

See also ACHEULEAN; ISAAC, GLYNN; KENYA. [R.P.]

OMBO-MARIWA see MABOKO

OMNIVORY see DIET

OMO

River in southwestern Ethiopia that is the principal source of water for Lake Turkana. The term *Omo Group* refers to richly fossiliferous Pliocene and Pleistocene sedimentary deposits exposed in the lower part of the Omo Valley and has been extended to all Pliocene and Pleistocene strata of the Lake Turkana basin.

The importance of the Omo Valley region lies in the superb exposures of abundantly fossiliferous strata ranging in age from somewhat older than 4 m.y. to ca. 1 m.y.; closely spaced controls provided by potassium-argon dates on numerous interbedded volcanic-ash layers; and paleomagnetic study of the sediments. Faunal remains from these stratigraphic intervals have been used to estimate the age of other African fossil sites where radiometric ages cannot be obtained.

Three principal formations are exposed in the lower Omo Valley: the Mursi, Usno, and Shungura Formations. These formations were studied by French, Kenyan, and American scientists of the International Omo Research Expedition between 1966 and 1974.

The Mursi Formation consists of 110 m. of fluvial and lacustrine sediments capped by a basalt flow that has been dated at 4 ± 0.1 m.y. It is exposed over a small area east of the Omo River at latitude 5°30′N. The fauna consists of only 12 taxa and includes no primates.

The Usno Formation is exposed in a series of small outcrops west of the Omo River at ca. 5°20′N latitude and 36°10′E longitude. It consists dominantly of fluvial sediments ca. 170 m. thick, which have been correlated with Members A and B of the Shungura Formation. Two of the outcrops, White Sands and Brown Sands, are exceptionally fossiliferous, having yielded several thousand mammalian specimens. The fossiliferous levels correlate with strata in the lower part of Member B of the Shungura Formation. At the base the Usno Formation is dated by a thin basalt with an age of 4.05 ± 0.04 m.y. The fossiliferous levels, though, lie above a vitric tuff 10 m. thick (Tuff U-10) in the middle of the formation that correlates with Tuff B of the Shungura Formation and with the Sidi Hakoma Tuff of the Hadar Formation and is thus ca. 3.3 m.y. in age. The fauna is reasonably diverse and consists of some 45 mammalian taxa in addition to reptiles and fish. Fossil primates include colobines, papionines, and *Theropithecus*. All hominid fossils from the formation have been attributed to *Australopithecus*. Most of the primate fossils consist of isolated teeth.

The Shungura Formation is exceptionally well exposed along the west side of the Omo River southward from ca. 5°10′N latitude to the Ethiopian border. The formation consists of ca. 760 m. of fluvial and lacustrine sediments deposited between 3.6 and ca. 0.9 m.y. ago. It has been divided into 12 members on the basis of widespread volcanic-ash layers (tuffs) designated Tuffs A through H, and J through L from the base upward. Each member begins at the basal tuff and includes all overlying sediments up to the base of the next major tuff. Thus Member F consists of all strata from the base of Tuff F to the base of Tuff G. Sediments that lie below Tuff A are assigned to the Basal Member of the formation. Each member is subdivided into submembers on the basis of fining-upward sedimentary cycles, minor tuffs, or other breaks in deposition; these are numbered sequentially from the base upward within each member. There are two main areas of outcrop of roughly equal dimensions. The northern area, called the Type Area, includes sediments from the base of the formation to Member J. The southern, or Kalam Area, includes sediments from Member C to the top of Member L.

Volcanic-ash layers are numerous in the Shungura Formation, and many of them contain pumice clasts that have been dated by the potassium-argon method. This has resulted in a reasonably well defined chronology for the formation, especially when taken in conjunction with the paleomagnetic polarity zonation.

The Shungura Formation preserves a clear record of the order of deposition of ca. 120 tuffs. Chemical

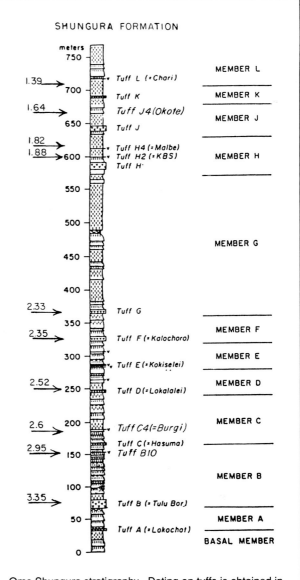

Omo Shungura stratigraphy. Dating on tuffs is obtained in part from exposures at Koobi Fora (East Turkana). Names in parentheses refer to field names in the Turkana sequence (Tuffs D, E, F are found only in West Turkana).

analysis has shown that most are readily distinguishable on the basis of their major and trace-element content. Although these ash layers are widespread in the Turkana basin, they are not confined to it, some having been recognized in the Suguta Valley south of Lake Turkana, in the Afar region nearly 1,000 km. to the northeast, and in deep-sea cores raised from the Gulf of Aden and off the coast of Kenya more than 1,500 km. to the northeast and southeast, respectively. Identification of these volcanic ashes in widely separated places has provided important stratigraphic links between fossil sites on land and the marine paleoclimatic record.

The Shungura Formation has yielded fossil plants (wood and pollen), invertebrates (ostracods and mollusks), and ca. 50,000 vertebrate fossils. Together with geologic features indicative of particular depositional environments these remains show that in a general way the history of the region can be divided into three parts. The first is a period of fluvial deposition from ca. 3.5 to 2 m.y. ago; the second, a brief period between ca. 2 and 1.9 m.y., when the region was occupied by a lake. The third period, from 1.9 to 0.9 m.y., records conditions in which a large river was again dominant, although short-lived lakes also occupied the area from time to time. Following deposition of Member L, the region was tectonically deformed; strata were faulted along roughly north-south lines and tilted to the west. Late Pleistocene sediments of the Kibish Formation disconformably overlie the older formations of the region.

Among the vertebrate fossils the rapidly evolving and abundant suids (pigs) and elephants (*E. recki* lineage) have proven especially useful for correlation to other localities where radiometric dates cannot be obtained.

The record of fossil primates comes mainly from the interval between Member B and the lower part of Member G, corresponding to the time from ca. 3.3 to 2.1 m.y. Many of the specimens were retrieved from channel deposits, and consequently the record is biased toward teeth, but excellent cranial and postcranial primate material also exists. The Shungura hominids have been assigned to *Australopithecus* and *Homo*. Artifact sites are known from the middle part of the Shungura Formation in Members E and F. These seem to be securely dated between 2.3 and 2.4 m.y., making them among the most ancient yet documented. Three partial calvaria of archaic *Homo sapiens* have been collected from the Kibish Formation in the northern part of the region, and these are putatively dated at ca. 0.1 m.y., but this date should be considered only as an order-of-magnitude estimate.

See also AUSTRALOPITHECUS; EAST TURKANA; HOMO; PALEOMAGNETISM; WEST TURKANA. [F.H.B.]

Further Readings

Brown, F.H., McDougall, I., Davies, T., and Maier, R. (1985) An integrated Plio-Pleistocene chronology for the Turkana basin. In E. Delson (ed.): Ancestors: The Hard Evidence. New York: Liss, pp. 82–90.

Heinzelin, J. de (1983) The Omo Group: Stratigraphic and Related Earth Science Studies in the Lower Omo Basin, Southern Ethiopia. Tervuren: Musée Royal de l'Afrique Centrale.

Howell, F.C., and Coppens, Y. (1974) Inventory of remains of Hominidae from Pliocene/Pleistocene formations of the lower Omo basin, Ethiopia (1967–1972). Am. J. Phys. Anthropol. 40:1–16.

OMOMYIDAE

Group of fossil tarsiiform primates. The family makes its appearance in Europe and North America during the earliest Eocene (Wasatchian and Sparnacian) and survives into the late Oligocene (Arikareean) in the genus *Ekgmowechashala*. The early Eocene record of the Omomyidae in the northern hemisphere coincides with the appearance of the Adapidae, the other major group of euprimates of the Eocene. The late Paleocene–early Eocene occurrence of a Mongolian genus of omomyid (*Altanius*) and the middle Paleocene presence of a southern Chinese euprimate, *Decoredon*, a possible omomyid, suggest an Asian origin of both the Euprimates and the Omomyidae.

Although there is no serious doubt that the omomyids are haplorhine tarsiiforms, the known cranial features of the family can be easily distinguished from the tarsiid type, and the postcranial attributes are much less advanced in most omomyid genera than in *Tarsius*. The astonishing variety of dentitions known for such a relatively size-restricted group, particularly diversified during the Eocene, is certain testimony that omomyids were an important component of the subtropical and tropical forest ecology of their day.

In a brief appraisal of the family the following aspects of their paleobiology will be discussed: diversity, cranium and brain, dentition, and postcranium.

Diversity

The Omomyidae are grouped into three subfamilies: Anaptomorphinae, Omomyinae, and Microchoerinae. The size range of species, as estimated not from individual teeth (which are notoriously unreliable in predicting body side when it comes to specific taxa) but from the length of the tooth row, was from tiny forms like the living pygmy marmosets to medium-sized platyrrhines like the pithecines (sakis and ouakaris). There was probably no "typical" omomyid, and many of them were quite dissimilar to *Tarsius* in their way of life. Some of the species, however—of the Anaptomorphinae, Omomyinae, and Microchoerinae—were probably more representative of the primitive omomyid, the last common ancestor, than such modified forms as the highly frugivorous *Ekgmowechashala* or the small folivorous *Macrotarsius*.

Cranium and Brain

The known skulls of omomyids are limited to those of the early Eocene North American *Tetonius*, the late Eocene European *Necrolemur* (whose skull is exceedingly similar to that of *Microchoerus*, a somewhat younger descendant), and the early Oligocene North American *Rooneyia*. A crushed skull is known for *Nannopithex* from the middle Eocene of Europe, and facial fragments and palates of sundry genera reveal important information confirming the interpretations from the more complete specimens.

Although the dentally primitive omomyid *Teilhardina* from the earliest Eocene of Europe is unknown cranially, all other omomyids known from either maxilla fragments or skulls clearly indicate the presence of orbital rings as in adapids. Omomyids had relatively large eyes and had orbital orientation indicating highly stereoscopic eyes. Perhaps as a causal consequence of the large convergent orbits they had the relatively short and pinched snouts like those in present-day lorisids and tarsiers. The problem of large eyes is not an easy one. Relatively large eyes do not necessarily mean a nocturnal way of life in a small primate, as the smaller a large brained primate is, the larger are its eyes compared with its cranium. In larger forms like *Rooneyia* the size of the eyes compared with the skull is relatively slightly larger than that of an ordinary diurnal platyrrhine primate. A genus like *Necrolemur* probably represents a nocturnal radiation independent of tarsiids. It is also important to remember that tarsiers have enormously hypertrophied eyes, because their retina seems to be constructed on the same plan as the diurnally adapted anthropoids (*see* HAPLORHINI).

A few natural casts of the inside of the neurocranium supply important information about the brain in omomyids. In spite of statements in the literature members of this family had relatively much larger brains than other Eocene mammals of similar body size, and they had relatively larger brains than the adapids. The Eocene adapids also had significantly larger brains than other mammals of their time, although they were much less encephalized than the living lemuriforms, conflicting interpretations in the literature notwithstanding. In the small *Tetonius* and the larger *Necrolemur* the olfactory bulb and the frontal lobe were relatively small compared with the enlarged occipital and temporal regions of the neocortex. The geologically younger *Rooneyia* further reduced the olfactory bulbs and enlarged the frontal lobe and attained a relatively larger brain size compared with (estimated) body size than other known omomyids.

Dentition

This, the most abundant evidence available, allows important inferences of relationships within the family as well as a good approximation of feeding behavior of the known species, which surely represent a mere fraction of the actual diversity and taxonomic abundance of the Omomyidae.

There is little doubt that the last good structural (but not necessarily actual) common ancestor of the known omomyids, like the genus *Teilhardina*, had two smallish incisors, a canine larger than either tooth preceding it or following it, and the full primitive eutherian complement of four premolars and three molars. As in other groups of primates, however, there is widespread tooth reduction and modification of the dental formula in subsequent omomyids. Any generalization in the literature about "the" omomyid incisor morphology must be viewed with some skepticism, because this area is relatively poorly known. Yet there is clear evidence that when the lower incisors become enlarged the central pair usually forms a spoonlike device rather than anything sharply pointed, like the anterior dentition of *Tarsius*. Some of the characteristic details of specific taxa are discussed under the subfamilies.

Postcranium

Although some recent authors have considered the omomyids poorly known postcranially, they were in fact well enough known a half-century ago to indicate, based on postcranial attributes, their unequivocal euprimate ties. The characteristically modified pelvis with its flattened iliac blade, the morphological details of the foot (all of these in *Hemiacodon*), and the local abundance in mammal quarries where omomyids occur of diagnostic flattened terminal phalanges (almost certainly nail bearing) are ample testimony that omomyids are more recently related to adapids than to archaic primates.

What is being learned of omomyid postcranial morphology suggests that the various species were fast and agile jumpers and branch runners, which employed a firm and powerful grasp in most aspects of their locomotor behavior. Some of these graspleapers such as *Necrolemur*, were undoubtedly fully capable of being habitual vertical clingers and leapers in the manner of tarsiers.

As the postcranial diversity of omomyids is slowly becoming appreciated, it is obvious that although they share common ancestral attributes they were not any more stereotyped in their locomotor strategies than are the living lemuriforms. For most of the species we lack even the more common (compared with the other elements of the skeleton usually found) tarsal bones like astragali and calcanea.

See also ANAPTOMORPHINAE; HAPLORHINI; MICROCHOERINAE; OMOMYINAE; TARSIIFORMES. [F.S.S.]

Further Readings

Szalay, F.S., and Delson, E. (1979) Evolutionary History of the Primates. New York: Academic.

OMOMYINAE

Subfamily of omomyid primates known mostly from North America. The Asian genus *Hoanghonius* is pos-

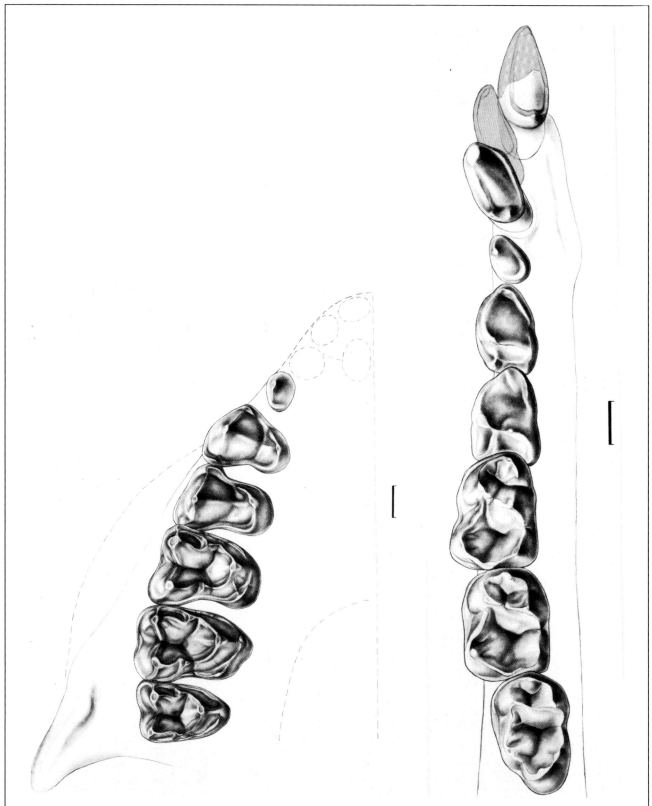

Upper and lower teeth in a reconstructed palate (left) and mandible (right) of the middle Eocene omomyine omomyid *Omomys carteri*. Note reconstruction of the anterior sockets of the palate. Scale is 1 mm.

sibly a representative. This diverse and adaptively complex, long-lasting subfamily ranges from the early Eocene into the late Oligocene, a timespan of over 25 m.y. We can subdivide these primates into six tribes in order to express what we know of both their phylogeny, diversification, and adaptive history: Omomyini, Uintaniini, Utahiini, Washakiini, Ekgmowechashalini, and Rooneyiini.

The tribe Omomyini consists of three subtribes, the Omomyina, with the genera *Omomys* and *Chumashius*; the Mytoniina, containing *Ourayia* and *Macrotarsius*; and the Asiatic late Eocene Hoangho-niina, which includes *Hoanghonius*. All the genera included in this taxon appear to share an interesting combination of a small hypocone (more a shelf in *Chumashius*) coupled with a lack of postprotocone fold. Although the first premolars have been lost from the omomyinans, they appear to have retained, particularly the Californian *Chumashius*, relatively large canines and modest-sized incisors. Both *Omomys* and *Chumashius* were in the size range of living marmosets and appear to have been highly insectivorous, judged from their shearing molars and sharp premolars. The subtribe Mytoniina contains the larg-

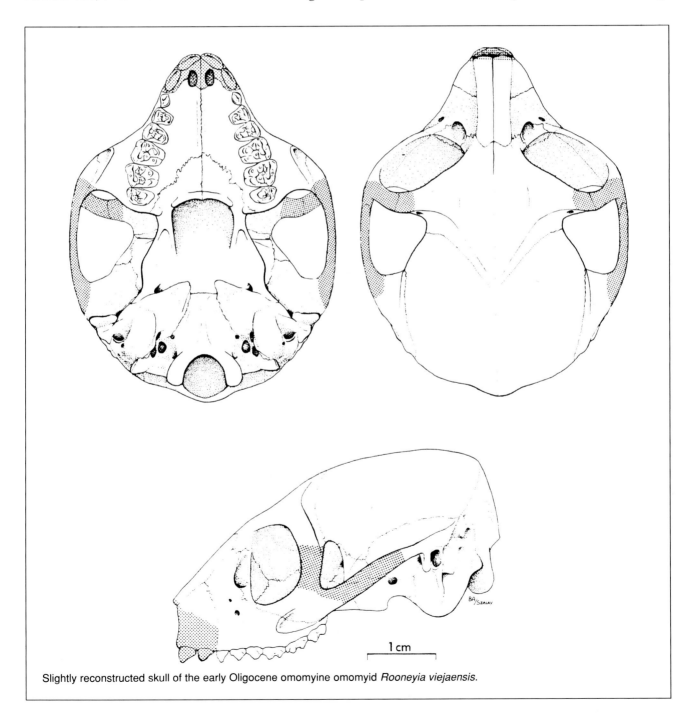

Slightly reconstructed skull of the early Oligocene omomyine omomyid *Rooneyia viejaensis*.

est omomyids, and the included genera have molarized fourth premolars and molars suited primarily for a vegetarian diet. Whereas *Ourayia* may have been frugivorous, *Macrotarsius*, with its upper-molar mesostyles and lingual crests on the lower molars (both are extra cutting edges), was probably inclined toward a folivorous diet like the equally small living lemurid *Lepilemur*.

The tribe Uintaniini, containing the small genus *Uintanius* (including *Huerfanius*), has transformed its third and fourth premolars into tall, trenchant blades, an adaptive theme that recurs independently among both primates and marsupials and also in other small mammals. In combination with the premolar specialization this group retains the more open lower-molar trigonid construction of the Omomyinae. A similar premolar adaptation had evolved independently in the closely related subfamily Anaptomorphinae, in the genus *Absarokius*, but it is difficult to determine whether the biological roles of the two genera were similar. It is likely that in *Uintanius* the premolars were primarily a device for slicing insects, whereas the wider-based premolars in *Absarokius* were serving some fruit- or seed-related masticatory activity. The poorly known genus *Steinius* may be a primitive member of this tribe.

The tribe Utahiini contains two poorly known genera, *Utahia* and *Stockia*. Both of these are characterized by the derived and extreme constriction of the trigonids on the lower molars and the concomitant enlargement of the talonid basins. Although upper molars are not known, this type of trigonid construction is closely correlated in platyrrhines and other primates with an enlarged hypocone. Whatever their dietary adaptation, utahiinins clearly placed an evolutionary premium on a large talonid and probably a hypocone as well.

The tribe Washakiini is a varied group that inherited from its last common ancestor a combination of a postprotocone fold and at least an incipient hypocone, or a strong postcingulum where the hypocone develops. This appears to be a decidedly herbivorous (at least more so than the Omomyini) radiation within the subfamily. The somewhat more primitive, or perhaps differently advanced, subgroup, the Hemiacodonina, contains the primitive but poorly known genus *Loveina* and the more advanced *Hemiacodon*, known not only from many jaws but also from various postcranial remains. Judged from uniquely derived dental attributes and a robust jaw, this genus had more of a plant (?frugivorous) than insectivorous diet. The subtribe Washakiina includes the genera *Shoshonius*, *Washakius*, and *Dyseolemur*. All of these have an additional extra cutting edge on their lower molars, a metastylid, and some have another cutting edge on the upper molars, a mesostyle or an

additional conule. Small as these animals were, they probably had a significant plant component in their diet. Small size, in spite of some claims in the primatological literature, is not a good predictor of diet in all small mammals. Large groups within the immense rodent radiation are an ample testimony to the fact that small mammals can exploit high-energy resources, such as seeds of various plants, without recourse to significant insectivory.

The tribe Ekgmowechashalini consists of a single genus, the highly modified, at least dentally, late Oligocene *Ekgmowechashala*. This genus, like *Washakius*, has incisors distinctly smaller than the canines and has the derived combination of upper-molar mesostyle and lower-molar mesostylid. It is likely to have been derived from the vicinity of *Washakius* and not from a form like *Rooneyia*. The extreme adaptive similarity of the teeth of *Ekgmowechashala* to fruit-eating relatives of raccoons suggests a habitual diet of soft fruits in the remnant warm forests of the late Oligocene of the Rocky Mountain states.

The tribe Rooneyiini contains only the genus *Rooneyia* from the early Oligocene of Texas, and the genus is known from a single, albeit magnificent and justly famous, fossil skull. No lower teeth are known.

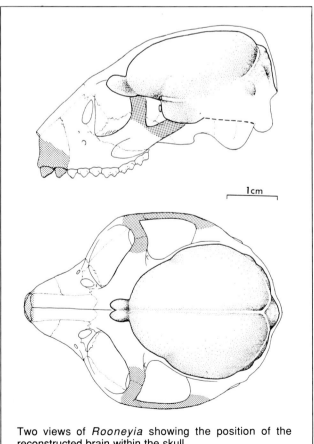

Two views of *Rooneyia* showing the position of the reconstructed brain within the skull.

The small canine of this genus makes it highly improbable that it gave rise to the younger *Ekgmowechashala*, as some earlier literature suggested. The unique low-crowned and bunodont cusps of the teeth of the genus strongly suggest a primarily frugivorous diet.

There are no explanations why the omomyines dominated the middle Eocene small-primate faunas of North America or why they managed to survive almost to the Miocene. No biological information is available to us that would explain the apparent competitive advantage of omomyines in contrast to the anaptomorphines, if there was any such group-related attribute. Postcranially the two North American subfamilies appear to have been similar to one another, and the cranial differences have been noted under the treatment of the family.

See also ANAPTOMORPHINAE; MICROCHOERINAE; OMOMYIDAE. [F.S.S.]

Further Readings

Szalay, F.S., and Delson, E. (1979) Evolutionary History of the Primates. New York: Academic.

OMOMYS *see* OMOMYINAE

ONTOGENY

Total life history of an individual organism, from roots meaning the "development of being." Ontogeny begins with conception and proceeds through embryonic development, when the formation of various structures and organ systems occurs, to fetal development, when these systems undergo further elaboration and growth. Following birth, overall growth of these structures, and the appearance of certain new features (such as teeth and secondary sexual characteristics), characterize the periods of infancy, childhood, and adolescence. The later stages of ontogeny are adulthood and, ultimately, death. Humans can be distinguished from other primates by their markedly prolonged life-history periods, from infant to adult.

Human growth and development form a complex process influenced by interacting genetic, hormonal, and environmental factors. Different tissues and body regions exhibit considerable variations in the timing and rate of their growth during ontogeny. These variations are of particular significance to evolutionary biologists, since phylogenetic transformations result from modifications of ontogenetic histories.

See also ALLOMETRY; HAECKEL, ERNST HEINRICH; SEXUAL DIMORPHISM. [B.T.S.]

Further Readings

Gould, S.J. (1977) Ontogeny and Phylogeny. Cambridge, Mass.: Harvard University Press.

Tanner, J.M. (1978) Foetus into Man: Physical Growth from Conception to Maturity. London: Open Books.

OPEN-AIR SITE *see* ARCHAEOLOGICAL SITES

ORANGIAN

South African Middle Stone Age industry closely related to the Pietersburg but largely restricted to the Orange Free State and differing from the Pietersburg in greater emphasis on blades and rare occurrence of true burins and trimmed points. These differences may also relate to the exclusive association of the Orangian with open sites and with the availability of abundant fine-grained isotropic raw material. The industry is best known from the open site of Orangia, where semicircular stone structures may represent shelters or hunting blinds. The Orange Free State site of Rose Cottage may represent a rock-shelter variant of this industry or a southwestern extension of the Pietersburg industry. The probable age of the Orangian is greater than 40 k.y., possibly as great as 130 k.y.

See also BORDER CAVE; FLORISBAD; HOWIESON'S POORT; MIDDLE STONE AGE; PIETERSBURG; ROSE COTTAGE; SECOND INTERMEDIATE; SITE TYPES; STONE-TOOL MAKING. [A.S.B.]

ORANGUTAN *see* APE; HOMINOIDEA; PONGINAE

ORANIAN *see* IBERO-IMAURUSIAN

ORDER

Principal major unit of classification within the Class. Human beings belong to the order Primates, together with the lemurs, lorises, tarsiers, Old and New World monkeys, and the lesser and great apes. Other mammalian orders include such familiar major groupings as the Carnivora, Rodentia, and Cetacea.

See also CLASSIFICATION; PRIMATES. [I.T.]

OREOPITHECIDAE

Family of enigmatic Miocene catarrhines, including the European *Oreopithecus* and several African species. There is currently some controversy as to whether the Oreopithecidae is more closely related to the living hominoids or to the Old World monkeys. In this volume the latter, minority opinion is followed.

Oreopithecus bambolii was first reported in 1872, on

the basis of a juvenile mandible. The original describer, P. Gervais, considered that it was most similar dentally to the gorilla but that it also had features in common with cercopithecids. Over the next 70 years a variety of authors offered their opinions, mostly based on incomplete studies of poor replicas (casts). Some argued that *O. bambolii* was a hominoid, others that it was a cercopithecoid, still others that it was somehow intermediate between these major groups. In 1915 G. Schwalbe placed *Oreopithecus* in its own family, which most authors continued to include in the Hominoidea. An additional dozen jaws and a few postcranial fragments were described from a cluster of five localities in the Tuscan region of north-central Italy. The age of these fossils was also uncertain but generally estimated at ca. 12 m.y.

In the late 1940s and through the 1950s J. Hürzeler, of Basel, reawakened scientific and popular interest in *Oreopithecus* through his restudy of known specimens and collection of new fossils. He argued that *Oreopithecus* was a close human relative, if not an ancestor (at that time *Australopithecus* was poorly known and thought by many European scholars to be a distinctive ape). Hürzeler thought that *Oreopithecus* had a small canine and tooth proportions most similar to those of *Homo erectus*. He recognized that in some ways (e.g. a large central cusp on lower molars) *O. bambolii* was unique, but for him the majority of observed features were shared with human ancestors as he interpreted them. In 1958, with the aid of local Tuscan miners, Hürzeler recovered a partial skeleton of a young adult male. It was badly flattened like most of the *Oreopithecus* fossils (which are found in a lignite, or soft brown coal deposit laid down in a swampy forest). Hürzeler made a partial reconstruction of the skull, which indicated a large brain, supporting his view that *Oreopithecus* was a human forebear.

More recently several researchers have studied parts of this skeleton, coming to quite different conclusions. The supposedly large brain has been shown to be based on the misinterpretation of large sagittal and nuchal crests as being the top of the skull and of crushed vertebrae as the rear; in fact the brain is only about the size of those of monkeys of similar body weight. Male canines are quite large, and sexual dimorphism is high, as in most Miocene catarrhines. The gonial region of the mandible (where the corpus meets the ramus) is expanded, as in colobines and other leaf-eating mammals, and the molar teeth emphasize crests, for slicing leafy food items. The face is short and rather wide, admittedly as in humans, but also as in gibbons, colobines, and conservative catarrhines generally. Thus almost all current students think that *Oreopithecus* resembles humans only convergently, in a few characters, while they see closer phyletic links to either hominoids or cercopithecids.

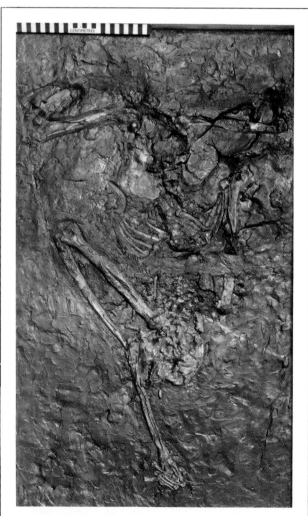

Oreopithecus bambolii skeleton as originally recovered in 1958. (Photograph of replica courtesy of the British Museum [Natural History].)

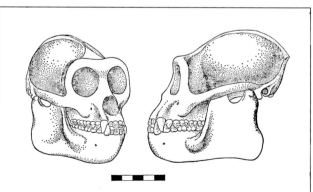

Reconstruction of the cranium of *Oreopithecus bambolii* in oblique and lateral views. Divisions of scale are 1 cm. (From F. Szalay and A. Berzi, 1973. *Science*, *180*, © 1973 by the AAAS.)

A. Rosenberger and E. Delson have suggested that in a number of dental features, *Oreopithecus* is intermediate in a homologous way between ancestral cercopithecids (e.g. victoriapithecines or the inferred common ancestor of all cercopithecids) and early catarrhines. For example, *O. bambolii* has elongate upper molars (while those of most hominoids are square or wide); reduced hypoconulids on dP_4-M_2; reduced cingulum on upper and lower molars, with remnants in the same places as seen (further reduced) in cercopithecids; molar cusps placed in transverse pairs (protoconid opposite metaconid, paracone opposite protocone, etc.), rather than offset as in hominoids, and with some development of transverse cresting; increased relief of molar teeth (tall cusps and deep clefts); and a partial approach to the mirror-image pattern of occluding uppers and lowers seen in Old World monkeys. It is clear that *Oreopithecus* is not bilophodont, as are modern cercopithecids, but neither was the earliest ancestor of monkeys. The suggestion here is that a common ancestor of cercopithecids and oreopithecids had already experienced selection for a number of shared trends before the two groups diverged in different directions.

T. Harrison has recently shown that two or three African Miocene species are probably oreopithecids, in addition to *Oreopithecus* itself. The middle Miocene site of Maboko has yielded a few isolated teeth named *Nyanzapithecus pickfordi*, which are quite similar to those of *O. bambolii* in form and elongation. *N. vancouveringi* of the early Miocene is only slightly better known. Previously the latter species was placed in the genus *Rangwapithecus*, and the remaining species of that genus, *R. gordoni*, also presents some dental features similar to *Oreopithecus*, especially molar elongation and slight cresting, so it may belong in the family as well. The morphocline in molar shape seen from these African species to the more derived *Oreopithecus* appears to support a link to cercopithecids.

Harrison, E. Sarmiento, and many previous workers (such as W.L. Straus) have based much of their interpretation on the postcranial skeleton. They consider that the above-noted dental features were evolved convergently by oreopithecids and cercopithecids, due to similar dietary adaptations. They argue that the detailed similarities in the shapes of the thorax (chest), and shoulder, elbow, and knee joints, must reflect a long period of shared ancestry between *Oreopithecus* and hominoids, especially hominids (great apes and humans). Other workers, such as F.S. Szalay, consider that the foot of *Oreopithecus* is uniquely evolved, sharing no derived features with either hominids or cercopithecids. It is difficult to argue that the shared postcranial features are all convergences due to similar locomotor adaptation, but some of them may be so, and while it is possible that the dental features could also be convergent, that seems less likely. For the present, oreopithecids are placed here with cercopithecids phyletically and classified within the Cercopithecoidea.

There is less argument about the paleobiology of *Oreopithecus bambolii*, the only well-known oreopithecid. The skeleton demonstrates that this species had longer forelimb than hindlimb; well-developed potentials for raising the forelimb above the head, for a variety of movements at the elbow joint and for flexibility of the wrist and mobility of the hindlimb; relatively erect posture during feeding and locomotion; and a flexible ankle with powerful grasping foot. Taken together, these functional interpretations allow reconstruction of *O. bambolii* as a powerful climber of vertical tree-trunks and a suspensory arm-swinger and arm-hanger. There are similarities in this interpretation to both modern orangutans and chimpanzees, although not precisely to either ape. The body weight of *Oreopithecus* was probably ca. 32 kg. for a male, as estimated both by statistical analysis of weight-bearing joint surfaces (by W.L. Jungers) and by general comparisons of long bone lengths (Szalay). This is nearly twice the weight estimated by several authors from anthropoid tooth size/body size ratios, implying that the dentition of *O. bambolii* was

Comparison of the left P_4–M_2 (above) and right M^2 of *Oreopithecus bambolii* (O) and *Rangwapithecus gordoni* (R), in occlusal view. (From P.M. Butler, in Major Topics in Primate and Human Evolution, ed. by B.A. Wood, L.Martin, and P. Andrews, © 1986, by Cambridge University Press. Reprinted with permission.)

quite small for its probable body size. The dentition itself was apparently adapted to a folivorous diet, which fits well with the swampy forest habitat in which the species probably lived.

See also CATARRHINI; CERCOPITHECOIDEA; HOMINOIDEA; LOCOMOTION; MIOCENE.[E.D.]

Further Readings

Azzaroli, A., Boccaletti, M., Delson, E., Moratti, G., and Torre, D. (1987) Chronological and paleogeographical background to the study of *Oreopithecus bambolii*. J. Hum. Evol. *15*:533–540.

Delson, E. (1987) An anthropoid enigma: historical introduction to the study of *Oreopithecus bambolii*. J. Hum. Evol. *15*:523–531.

Harrison, T. (1986) New fossil anthropoids from the middle Miocene of East Africa and their bearing on the origin of the Oreopithecidae. Am. J. Phys. Anthropol. *71*:265–284.

Harrison, T. (1987) A re-assessment of the phyletic position of *Oreopithecus bambolii* Gervais, 1872. J. Hum. Evol. *15*:541–583.

Hürzeler, J. (1958) *Oreopithecus bambolii* Gervais, a preliminary report. Verh. naturforschenden Gesellschaft Basel. *69*:1–47.

Sarmiento, E. (1987) The phylogenetic position of *Oreopithecus* and its significance in the origin of the Hominoidea. Amer. Mus. Novitates *2881*:1–44.

Szalay, F.S., and Delson, E. (1979) Evolutionary History of the Primates. New York: Academic.

OREOPITHECUS *see* OREOPITHECIDAE

OSTEODONTOKERATIC *see* DART, R.A.

OSTEOLOGY *see* BONE BIOLOGY; SKELETON

OTOLEMUR *see* GALAGIDAE

OULJIAN *see* PLEISTOCENE; SEA-LEVEL CHANGE

OURANOPITHECUS *see* NEAR EAST; PONGINAE

OURAYIA *see* OMOMYINAE

OUTWASH *see* GLACIATION; PLEISTOCENE

OVERKILL HYPOTHESIS *see* EXTINCTION

OWEN, W.E. *see* MABOKO

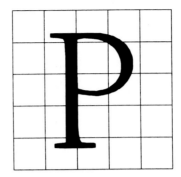

PACITANIAN (PAJITANIAN)

Supposedly Early Paleolithic industry from Indonesia recognized by von Koenigswald in the mid-1930s. The Pacitanian is represented by flake implements and so-called core choppers. The original designation refers to surface finds from terraces of the Baksoka Valley (Java). Recently the Pacitanian has been shown on geomorphological grounds to be less than 60 k.y. old. Furthermore, some now view it as a Javanese local variant of the broadly defined Hoabinhian of Southeast Asia. It now seems likely that a great many Pacitanian "artifacts" are in fact the result of natural nonhuman processes.

See also Hoabinhian. [G.G.P.]

PAINTING, CAVE *see* PALEOLITHIC IMAGE

PAJITANIAN *see* PACITANIAN

PAKISTAN

Country comprising the northwestern part of the Indopakistan subcontinent. Pakistan's main contribution to our knowledge of hominoid evolution comes from the vast thicknesses of fossiliferous Siwalik sediments in the north of the country. Ranging in age from 18 m.y. to the Pleistocene, they provide the most extensive samples in the world of Miocene hominoids and associated fauna. There is no trace of hominoids in Pakistan after 7.4 m.y. until Paleolithic artifacts belonging to the Soan industry, deriving from the Pleistocene Potwar Silts. No human fossils have yet been found with these archaeological occurrences.

See also Paleolithic; Siwaliks; Soan. [A.H.]

Further Readings

Shah, S.M.I., and Raza, S.M. (1985) Problems of paleoanthropological research in Pakistan. In E. Delson (ed.): Ancestors: The Hard Evidence. New York: Liss, pp. 339–345.

PALAEANTHROPUS *see* NEANDERTHALS

PALAECHTHON *see* PAROMOMYIDAE

PALAEOANTHROPUS *see* NEANDERTHALS

PALAEOPROPITHECIDAE

Extinct family of large-bodied lemuriforms closely related to the indriids. Two genera are known from marsh and cave sites in the center, south, southwest, and northwest of Madagascar: *Palaeopropithecus* and *Archaeoindris*. These sites probably fall in age between ca. 1000 and 3000 B.P., and the "subfossil" forms they contain may be regarded as members of the modern fauna of Madagascar; they probably became extinct subsequent to the arrival of humans on the island, and their extinction seems to have been at least in major part a result of human activity. A skeleton of *Palaeopropithecus* discovered recently in the cave of Anjohibé in northwestern Madagascar assumes particular importance because its elements were associated. Most subfossil specimens known from Madagascar were excavated a considerable time ago from marsh sites that were insufficiently drained and not systematically excavated. Positive association of different parts of the skeleton is thus rare; this has led on occasion to profound disagreements over which postcranial elements should be matched with which skulls, and even now uncertainty persists in some cases. It now seems likely that the subfossil genus *Mesopropithecus*, traditionally viewed as an indriid, also belongs in this family, but in this volume it is discussed under Indriidae.

Two species of *Palaeopropithecus* have generally been recognized: *P. ingens*, from the coastal regions, and *P. maximus* from the center of the island. While what we know of the distribution in Madagascar of different species of living genera suggests that they may indeed be distinct, these two species are closely similar. The skull of *Palaeopropithecus* is massively built and ca. 20 cm. long. The face is elongated, and the overall proportions of the skull are like those of the long-faced *Indri*, although the braincase is relatively smaller and bears nuchal and sometimes sagittal crests. The orbits are heavily ringed by bone, the nasal bones overhang the nasal aperture in a curious manner, and the gonial region of the mandible is vastly expanded. The middle-ear cavity is housed entirely within the base of the skull, without bulla formation, and a bony tube leads to the outside. The dentition of *Palaeopropithecus* is close in morphology

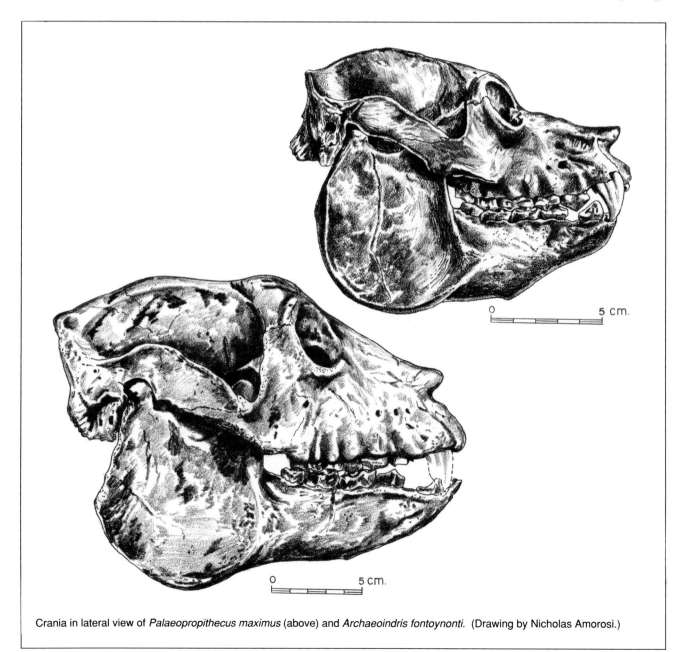

Crania in lateral view of *Palaeopropithecus maximus* (above) and *Archaeoindris fontoynonti*. (Drawing by Nicholas Amorosi.)

to those of the much smaller indriids, especially to that of *Propithecus*. It also shows the reduction of the premolars to two in each quadrant of the dentition characteristic of the indriids, but the tooth comb is reduced and stubby.

The hands and feet of *Palaeopropithecus* are long and curved and attest eloquently to an arboreal way of life. The feet and ankles are not well adapted to weight bearing, and indeed the emphasis of mobility over stability in many of the joints of the skeleton points to a primarily suspensory form of locomotion. Further, *Palaeopropithecus* was large-bodied enough to have needed to adopt suspensory postures in most areas of the forest canopy. The nearest locomotor analogue to *Palaeopropithecus* in the living primate fauna appears to be the quadrumanous orangutan, in which only the large males, much larger than *Palaeopropithecus*, spend a considerable amount of time on the ground.

Archaeoindris is much less well known than its close relative *Palaeopropithecus*, only a single skull and a few other elements having been recovered in the center of the island. The one skull known is somewhat over 25 cm. long, is massively built, and is greatly deepened compared with that of *Palaeopropithecus*. This last feature gives it overall proportions reminiscent of *Propithecus*. Like *Palaeopropithecus*, *Archaeoindris* exhibits curious paired swellings of the nasal bones above the nasal aperture, lacks prominent auditory bullae, and has a bony tube connecting the eardrum with the exterior. Similarly, its cheek dentition closely recalls in its morphology that of the indriines, albeit as in *Palaeopropithecus* a little more elongated, particularly in the lower jaw. Postcranial bones are uncertainly associated with the skull of *Archaeoindris* and are in any case few; it has been provisionally suggested that in its locomotion this lemur may have resembled *Megaladapis* in being a heavy-bodied modified vertical clinger and leaper.

It is uncertain whether the palaeopropithecids or the archaeolemurids among the subfossil lemurs are the closest known relatives of the living indriids; the palaeopropithecids closely resemble the indriids in their dentition but show modified characters of the skull, while in the case of the archaeolemurids the reverse applies. However, the fact that the archaeolemurids retain the primitive premolar number of three, while the palaeopropithecids share with the indriids the derived reduced number of two, points in the direction of a more recent common ancestry between Palaeopropithecidae and Indriidae.

See also ARCHAEOLEMURIDAE; INDRIIDAE; LEMURIFORMES. [I.T.]

Further Readings

Tattersall, I. (1982) The Primates of Madagascar. New York: Columbia University Press.

PALAEOPROPITHECUS *see* PALAEOPROPITHECIDAE

PALAGALAGI *see* MURUAROT

PALENOCHTHA *see* PAROMOMYIDAE

PALEOANTHROPOLOGY

As broadly defined here, the branch of anthropology including studies of primate and human evolution, prehistory, and the biological and geological backgrounds essential to the study of these topics. This volume is essentially an encyclopedia of paleoanthropology (*see* "Introduction"), but that term is not as widely known as *human evolution* and *prehistory*, and some scholars still restrict its meaning to either its paleontological or archaeological aspects. The unified nature of this concept owes much to the pioneering fieldwork of L.S.B. and M.D. Leakey at Olduvai Gorge (Tanzania), where a team of specialists was brought together to investigate fully all the natural phenomena forming the background to the early fossil humans and their artifacts recovered there. F.C. Howell extended this approach at his excavations at Isimila, Torralba, and Ambrona and especially at the Omo deposits, and his work more than anything else probably brought the term paleoanthropology into broader use to refer to this multidisciplinary approach rather than merely as a synonym for prehistoric archaeology (or human paleontology).

See also ANTHROPOLOGY; ARCHAEOLOGY; LEAKEY, LOUIS; LEAKEY, MARY; PALEONTOLOGY; PREHISTORY; PRIMATES. [E.D.]

Further Readings

Howell, F.C. (1965) Early Man. New York: Time-Life.

PALEOBIOGEOGRAPHY

Scientific field that uses biological species records (paleobotany, invertebrate and vertebrate paleontology) and geological earth-history records (stratigraphy, geochronology, plate tectonics) to reconstruct the history of biotic distributions. The primary biological data base is species recognition, or alpha taxonomy; the second is the interpretation of interspecific evolutionary relationships, or phylogeny, of all related species across all of their composite geographical ranges. The primary geological data base is the stratigraphic distribution of species in single series of mappable geological strata (this is termed *biostratigraphy*); the second is the chronological relationship of individual species and the geological strata that contain them. This can be determined by direct correlation or by recognition that species identity in two separate series of geological strata roughly equates those strata as being isochronous (of equivalent age). Yet another means of recognizing chronological equivalency between species in two or more geological units is by invoking the use of an independent "absolute" dating tool, such as potassium-argon dating (K-Ar), magnetostratigraphy, or carbon-14 (C-14) dating. A third geological data base is information gained from the study of plate tectonics and the change of land-sea relationships. Paleobiogeographical studies of higher taxonomic categories, such as the primates, are best made when the phylogenetic relationships of the group have been rigorously detailed and compared with independently developed geological, chronological, and tectonic records. Obviously these kinds of work proceed simultaneously, but the most detailed resolution is achieved when they are strictly adhered to.

Paleobiogeographical methods have recently been a major area of scientific debate, at the core of which has been the issue of how one reconstructs a paleobiogeographical record. The traditional approach has been highly empirical and mostly inductive. Using the traditional approach, one gains an understanding of a lineage's biogeographical relationships by studying the chronological and biogeographical ranges of all the relevant species. Having done this, the traditional biogeographer is set to infer the center-of-origin of the lineage, based on the oldest known occurrence of the (presumably) most primitive form, and interpret its areas of subsequent dispersal.

A more recent school of cladistic, or *vicariance*, biogeography claims that the traditional approach embraces a philosophical position of *extreme* empiricism, viewing science as nothing more than ordered observation. Cladistic biogeographers embrace the view that all scientific knowledge is hypothetical, conjectural, and speculative and can never be confirmed, only falsified. Cladistic paleobiogeographers believe that ancestors cannot be found, but rather that it is the level of phylogenetic relationship, or cladistic relationship, that can and should be found. Therefore these advocates believe that the primary basis for paleobiogeographic reconstruction is the development of cladograms, showing relative recency of ancestry and secondarily searching the geological record of the earth for clues to explain the geographical relationships of related *sister taxa*.

As with most constructive scientific debates this one has provoked considerable thought on how paleobiogeographers should interpret complex data sets on species evolutionary relationships and geographical distribution. First, it has refocused attention on the need to develop accurate evolutionary histories of organisms prior to making higher-order interpretations of biogeographical relationships. Second, it has focused the need to marshall a broad array of geological data in reconstructing paleobiogeographical histories. Both the more traditional and new cladistic or vicariance paleobiographical approaches would view as important the development of an independent empirical geological framework including stratigraphy, biochronology, absolute dating, and magnetochronology. While the traditional approach would merely integrate this extensive data set, the cladistic approach would use it to test a vicariance hypothesis. Dispersal hypotheses would only be erected when a vicariance hypothesis was rejected by relevant geological data. The failure to delineate species relationships precisely (in a cladistic fashion) risks an errant reconstruction of the evolutionary pattern, which is in turn vital to the paleobiological interpretation. Clearly both the traditional "empirical" approach and the cladistic approach benefit by demanding an explicit phylogeny prior to paleobiogeographical reconstruction.

Studies of primate phylogeny and paleobiogeography are not static but dynamic. The collection of more fossil material, rigorous analysis of its phylogenetic relationships, and increasingly broad geological and paleogeographical contexts will change and refine our current understanding of primate evolutionary history.

See also CLADISTICS; PALEONTOLOGY. [R.L.B., D.P.D.]

Further Readings

Bernor, R.L. (1983) Geochronology and zoogeographic relationships of Miocene Hominoidea. In R.L. Ciochon and R.S. Corruccini (eds.): New Interpretations of Ape and Human Ancestry. New York: Plenum, pp. 21–64.

Nelson, G., and Platnick, N. (1981) Systematics and Biogeography: Cladistics and Vicariance. New York: Columbia University Press.

PALEOBIOLOGY

Integrated part of biological and geological studies dealing with extinct life. The number of kinds of organisms that lived in the past is vastly greater than the number alive today. The numerous ways these organisms survived, and the communities and biotas they formed, are the primary subject matter of paleobiology.

The single most important activity of paleobiologists is the description of both the organisms and the sediments in which they are found and the distributional and functional analysis of fossil animals and plants. Following descriptions and recognition of taxa, perhaps the most fundamental undertaking involving the documentation of fossils and their spatial and temporal occurrence is the reconstruction of the path of evolution. Although this is an area of controversy as well as an arena where opposing views of both theory and empirical interpretation meet head on, it is the aspect of paleobiology most visible in the scientific and popular literature. The evolutionary relationships of animals and plants can also be tied to their relationship with the environment in which they lived and evolved. This activity, commonly referred to as the reconstruction of the way of life of fossil species (literally, their paleobiology), makes up the second major area of this complex activity. Although the study of both the relationships of fossil species and of the understanding of their behavior and ecology are not quite separable from one another, and neither is completely independent from the developmental, historical, and functional-adaptive analysis of living species, these activities are usually pursued independently.

Systematic Paleobiology

Paleontology supplies us with the raw material for much of paleobiology: new organisms and the description of the sediments in which they were buried or better and more specimens of known ones. In addition to the systematic treatment of these forms the diversity described becomes the data base of a variety of paleobiological activities that are systematic in nature. The science of systematics deals both with the delineation of species and with all relationships among them, and therefore also with the nature of evolutionary change between succeeding species. This inquiry leads to the evaluation of hypotheses concerning the mode of life of past species, and information generated in this process of analysis becomes critical also in phylogeny reconstruction. Paleobiology, like all sciences, attempts to answer questions not only of "what" and "how" but also of "why," and—a particular contribution of this science —the question of "when" as well.

The questions of why and when, applied to whole ecosystems of the past, involve studies of stratigraphy, paleontology, plate tectonics, climatic changes and their causes, and virtually all aspects of the earth sciences. When we question why a fossil species is a particular way, we begin a complex series of analytical procedures that attempts to relate the lifestyle and subsequent adaptations, or at least known modifications, of that species to its hypothesized ancestral condition. The theoretical issues that relate to the biological roles of various parts of extinct species (as distinct from the function or mechanics of these components) are formidable. One has to

make convincing connections between the morphology and mechanics (function) of fossil forms before the even more difficult association between form-function and postulated behavior can be established with any degree of probability. The major method of accomplishing this for fossils is first to establish causal relationships between form and function in living forms. The well-established causal relationships in living taxa are then used as analogies when applied to the fossils. There is considerable constructive disagreement over the specific logic and rules of applying such analogies, but ultimately it is some form of rigorous analogy argument that often supplies the best behavioral explanation in paleobiology. This should not be confused with using fossil morphology and morphology in living forms as simple analogies. Nevertheless, paleobiologists must forever contend with the reality that no matter how convincing is the analogy applied to some fossil species biological roles often cannot be predicted with any degree of certainty from the form and function of parts of fossils. Similarly, morphologically based fossil species can never be matched with certainty with the concept embodied in the dimensionless biological-species concept.

Clearly, however, there is a spectrum from near certainty to plain ignorance. The power of "predicting" paleobiological roles for taxa is increased if the focus is on more recently acquired (derived) characters. These characters, from a theoretical point of view, are more likely to reflect the mode of life of a species than are traits that this animal shares with many other distinct species and that are thus inherited from a more remote common ancestry. The analogy applied is even more powerful when one uses a feature that is independently derived (convergent) in two or more living species, and these features are causally explicable and exclusively correlated with the same biological roles. Such a feature in a fossil is likely to have performed the same bioroles.

Ecological Paleobiology

Reconstruction of fossil communities is an activity based equally on our understanding of living assemblages of organisms and on the wealth and reliability of the fossil record of a locality or localities judged to be contemporaneous in the same area. Ancient environments are best explained when the animal and plant life and the geological evidence can be accounted for by the same hypothesis. Vertebrates, primates included, are often used in the understanding of sediments of various ages. While fishes and whales will certainly indicate extensive aquatic habitats, remains of primates with arboreal adaptations just as certainly suggest a forest environment. Thus, when all the remains of animals and plants are carefully analyzed and special relationships between their adaptations and habitats can be shown with some degree of confidence, we arrive at a highly probable description of past ecosystems.

Macroevolution and Paleobiology

The way science solidifies its gains has a lot to do with the view that new and more complex theories, concepts, or even perceptions of the world are not accepted until the views they oppose have been shown to be inadequate. This pragmatic and reductionist view of science maintains that as long as existing hypotheses of science appear to account for observed patterns the need for new theories must be demonstrated by showing that the older theories cannot in fact account for the known patterns of nature. This does not mean that nature can be explained at only one level of reality. The problem in paleobiology (and evolutionary theory) is whether the processes that account for the evolution of individual species can also account for other patterns of life that we recognize (e.g. higher categories).

Some paleontologists have suggested that various patterns seen in the fossil record suggest evolutionary mechanisms other than those involved in the processes of phyletic evolution and speciation. The original definition of species selection is only an expression of natural selection acting on individuals viewed in a larger context. Species selection as a causal process of evolution is an interesting and proper model, but so far not a single substantiated example is agreed upon by all. The same appears to hold true for the *species drift*, or *effect macroevolution*, hypothesis: no validated examples are universally accepted.

The most powerful candidate for such a "macro" mechanism (or, more properly, phenomenon), one not reduceable to microevolutionary processes, originates from the well-documented extinction events that cut across taxonomic boundaries. Wholesale dying out, without regard to the adaptations of various organisms, creates a new spectrum of opportunities for the surviving lineages and therefore temporarily alters previously existing competitive relationships. But both diversification and extinction in evolution ultimately result in so-called megaevolutionary patterns that may have their roots in microevolutionary mechanisms. So the question remains whether such a historical cataclysm as an extinction event independent of biotic factors should be called an evolutionary process.

See also ECOLOGY; EVOLUTIONARY MORPHOLOGY; EVOLUTIONARY SYSTEMATICS; SPECIES; SYSTEMATICS. [F.S.S.]

Further Readings

Behrensmeyer, A.K., and Hill, A., eds. (1980) Fossils in the Making. Chicago: University of Chicago Press.

Szalay, F.S., ed. (1975) Approaches to Primate Paleobiology. Basel: Karger.

PALEOBOTANY

Study of fossil plants. A major subdiscipline is *palynology*, which is concerned with fossil pollen and spores. *Dendrochronology*, the construction of regional chronologic frameworks by correlation of tree rings, is a related field with direct bearing on archaeology.

[D.P.D., R.L.B.]

PALEOCENE

Earliest epoch of the Tertiary period within the Cenozoic era, a time that ushered in the Age of Mammals after the disappearance of the dinosaurs. The Paleocene was originally recognized not as distinct but merely as an equivalent of the basal part of the Eocene. Lyell's original proposal, made in 1833, recognized strata as Eocene in age if 1–5 percent of their mollusk species were also present in the Recent fauna.

Paleocene-age rocks in North America, Europe, and Asia are the earliest ones to yield fossil primates. The beginning of the Paleocene immediately follows the end of the Mesozoic era. In North America land-mammal faunas are divided into "mammal ages" called the Puercan, Torrejonian, Tiffanian, and Clarkforkian. The Paleocene primates and other mammals are not known as well in Europe as in North America. In Europe the Dano-Montian Age (based on foraminifera) is roughly equivalent to the North American Paleocene up to the younger half of the Tiffanian, whereas the Thanetian Age is the equivalent of the rest of the North American Paleocene. Dating of the rocks and faunas is difficult, although the Paleocene probably spans the time between 64 and 54 m.y. ago. The Asian Paleocene is just beginning to yield primates (*Petrolemur, Decoredon, Altanius*), but the dating of the faunas, due to their unique composition in comparison with the better-known Euroamerican ones, is as yet imprecise. The terrestrial Paleocene faunas of Africa, presumably with primate remains, await discovery. Although the South American Paleocene is reasonably well known, it has yielded no primates.

In Paleocene times the geography, climate, and vegetation of the world were quite different from what we know today. Euroamerica was a continuous landmass across Greenland and northern Europe, and most of present-day Europe was separated from Asia by a major seaway, the Turgai Straits, where the Ural Mountains stand today. North America (more properly Euroamerica at that time) was intermittently connected to Asia at the Bering Straits. The seaway separating Africa from the land north of it was the Tethys Sea, which went from the narrow Atlantic Ocean to the Indian Ocean. South America had only a possible island-arc connection with the southern reaches of Euroamerica, and India did not have full contact with the landmass of Asia. Australia was still connected to Antarctica, which may, in turn, have been still barely in contact with South America.

This was a world with a climate and vegetation distribution drastically different from our own or that of the later Cenozoic. A change from the Cretaceous equable subtropical climates to a warm, but perhaps warm-temperate and less equable, climate appears to have occurred in the Paleocene. The Paleocene was characterized by broad-leaved evergreen forests almost as far north as 60°, and toward the equator south of these evergreen forests were broad-leaved deciduous forests. It is likely that coniferous forests occupied the northernmost latitudes. Judged from paleobotanical evidence, the Paleocene was quite wet, in contrast to the Eocene to come. In the midlands of North America the Cannonball Sea, a remnant of the Cretaceous seaway, which cut the continent into western and eastern halves during the end of the Age of Reptiles, still persisted as far north as Montana. In North America, and presumably in the remaining northern land areas, were extensive forests and woodlands with a subtropical and wet climate. This pleasant climate was warm, with no pronounced seasonality, as the palms, ferns, angiosperms, turtles, lizards, and crocodilians that occur together with the land mammals suggest.

At least in North America the archaic Paleocene primate fauna was an extensive one. Judged from the poorly known postcranial remains of these ancient relatives, they were arboreal, capable tree dwellers much like some of the present-day tree shrews (tupaiids).

The remarkable aspect of the Paleocene radiation of the archaic primates, as far as we can understand it from the relatively scanty remains from North America, Europe, and Asia, is that they display an astonishing dental diversity. This clearly indicates that several major radiations were well established in the world during this time and that adaptive solutions in the ancestral species of these families played a key role in the further radiation of these groups, some of which made it into the Eocene. The paromo-

myids represented the group most similar to the ancestral primates, and they display teeth that suggest that they were feeding on fruits, seeds, and insects. Some of these paromomyids are the smallest primates known, but they do not show the purely insectivorous adaptations of equally small insectivorans. The picrodontids were tiny, probably gum- or pollen-feeding forms, whereas the carpolestids and saxonellids may have specialized on fibrous vegetation. The widespread plesiadapids, while clearly arboreal, were primarily fruit and perhaps to some degree leaf eaters. The Paleocene holds many mysteries for the formative beginnings of the Primates.

See also CARPOLESTIDAE; EOCENE; PAROMOMYIDAE; PICRODONTIDAE; PLESIADAPIDAE; PLESIADAPIFORMES; SAXONELLIDAE. [F.S.S.]

Further Readings

Savage, D.E., and Russell, D.E. (1983) Mammalian Paleofaunas of the World. Reading, Mass.: Addison-Wesley.

Szalay, F.S., and Delson, E. (1979) Evolutionary History of the Primates. New York: Academic.

PALEOCLIMATE *see* CENOZOIC; PALEOENVIRONMENTS

PALEOECOLOGY *see* ECOLOGY; PALEOENVIRONMENTS; PRIMATE ECOLOGY

PALEOENVIRONMENTS

In reconstructing human evolution the actual fossil remains of hominids form the primary evidence. They make it possible to define fossil species and their arrangement in phylogenies reflecting the course that evolution may have taken. In addition comparative anatomical work on fossils reveals behavioral aspects of these species, such as locomotion and feeding. Scientists, however, have increasingly come to realize that they cannot properly understand the subject except in a broader context of the paleoecology and paleoenvironments pertaining at a given time. Human evolution has witnessed many radical alterations in anatomy and in human ecology. At certain periods, for example, more than one species of hominid existed at the same time. Conventional evolutionary theory holds that such changes come about in response to changes in the environment, factors external to the organisms concerned. This is why a knowledge of paleoenvironments is important; it is not simply cosmetic information to adorn the anatomical and taxonomic data of the fossils themselves. To a degree it is possible to understand how evolution has occurred by just looking at the fossils. To explain why evolution has occurred in a specific way at a particular time paleoenvironmental data are fundamental.

Environments in the past, *paleoenvironments*, were different than they are now. There is good evidence that world environments have varied considerably since the origins of humans ca. 10–6 m.y. ago. We know, for instance, that at different times during the last 2 m.y. much of the northern hemisphere was covered by ice; ca. 5.6. m.y. ago the Mediterranean more or less dried up; and many of the animal species of which past faunas were composed are now extinct.

The study of paleoenvironments involves the analysis of a whole range of matters, some of them biotic, others concerned with the physical environment; it is partly the nature of the subject that has given rise to the multidisciplinary approach prevalent in paleoanthropological work. Only a few indications of the range of approaches can be given here. Many of the methods used in paleoenvironmental investigations focus on hominid sites or other localities contemporary with them, where the fossils have actually been found. Other sources of information are deep-sea cores and Antarctic ice, which have recorded temperature fluctuations in the past. Deep-sea cores have been of considerable value in documenting environments over the last few million years; scientists examine the distribution of fossil marine microorganisms, such as foraminifera, and the isotopic composition of their shells and other materials. Oxygen isotope ratios, for example, reveal the amount of water bound up in ice, and this can be related to fluctuation in world temperature. Glaciations are also reflected in sea-level changes, which can be investigated in littoral regions by geological and geomorphological means.

All studies except those based upon the actual stratigraphical levels at sites from which hominids derive have the problem of assessing contemporaneity. When examining interrelationships and causality it is essential to know the order in time of events recorded in the fossil record. Here basic data come from geological work. *Lithostratigraphy*, along with some means of calibrating and comparing sections, such as radiometric dating and paleomagnetic stratigraphy, is vital to understanding paleoenvironmental information. More directly, the disposition of different kinds of rock bodies permits the reconstruction of ancient geography, the location of lakes, volcanoes, and other features. Detailed sedimentological investigations, as well as mineralogical and isotopic analyses of suitable sedimentary minerals, plays a large role in determining climatic conditions at the time when such sediments were laid down.

Evidence of past vegetation is provided for the most part by *palynology*, the study of pollen and spores. For temperate regions such evidence is good, and much is known from this source about the fluctuations of vegetation and climate for the Pleistocene of Europe and North America. In Africa, particularly for the earlier periods of human evolution, relatively less is known, in part because the circumstances for the preservation of pollen are less favorable.

Fauna associated with hominids gives a good idea of contemporary communities of animals living in the area. Inferences about environments can be made by assuming that past species lived in situations similar to those of their closest living counterparts. Anatomical features may also be used to deduce the habits and habitats of past species.

When trying to understand human evolution, and the faunas with which humans have been associated, it is tempting to imagine that their environments were direct analogues of situations seen at the present day. But it is important to realize that environments and ecology in the past could have been different in significant ways from anything we know of now. Much of the current work on paleoenvironments in the context of human evolution is directed explicitly to explaining the controls on speciation, change, and extinction. This is one of its most exciting contributions: increasing understanding of major human evolutionary shifts in terms of adaptation.

See also ECOLOGY; GLACIATION; PALEOBIOLOGY; PALEOBOTANY; SEA-LEVEL CHANGE. [A.H.]

Further Readings

Butzer, K.W. (1971) Environment and Archeology. Chicago: Aldine.

Coppens, Y., Howell, F.C., Isaac, G.L., and Leakey, R.E.F. (1976) Earliest Man and Environments in the Lake Rudolf Basin. Chicago: University of Chicago Press.

Hay, R.L. (1976) Geology of the Olduvai Gorge. Berkeley: University of California Press.

PALEOETHNOBOTANY see ETHNOARCHAEOLOGY; PALEOBOTANY

PALEOGENE

Subdivision (period or, for some, subperiod) of the Cenozoic era. Division into Paleogene and Neogene replaces the previous division of the Cenozoic into Tertiary and Quaternary periods. The Paleogene contains the Paleocene, Eocene, and Oligocene epochs, covering the time period from ca. 64 to 22 m.y. The term also refers to the system of strata deposited during this time.

See also CENOZOIC; EOCENE; NEOGENE; OLIGOCENE; PALEOCENE. [F.S.S.]

PALEOGEOGRAPHY *see* PALEOBIOGEOGRAPHY

PALEOINDIAN

First well-defined and widely recognized archaeological phase in the Americas, from the most ancient sites through those dating to 11,000 B.P.

Surely the most important, if least dramatic, event in the history of the Americas was the passage of that first human from Asia into the New World. Nobody knows exactly when this happened—perhaps 30 k.y. ago or more—or even where. We do not know what these Paleoindians wore, spoke, looked like, or thought. We do not know why they left their Asian homeland or what conditions they encountered on their journey.

And yet there is no reasonable doubt that the first Americans did indeed travel from Asia during the late Pleistocene. Biology, language, and archaeology all point to an Asian homeland; it is the timing and conditions surrounding their arrival that remain unknown.

But something is known about the environmental conditions that permitted this migration. The Pleistocene ice advanced and retreated according to a global pulse. As the glaciers grew, at times covering Canada to a depth of perhaps 3 km., sea levels simultaneously dropped, as much as 100 m. Depressed sea levels radically changed the earth's appearance; the Bering and Chukchi seas retreated, leaving a land bridge over 2,000 km. wide at its maximum. This vast bridge was available to East Asians, some of whom crossed into a New World.

Clovis Culture

There is no question that Paleoindians were established in the New World prior to 12,000 B.P. The Clovis culture, named for an archaeological site in New Mexico, can be traced from northern Alaska to Guatemala, from the west to east coasts of the United States.

Clovis spear points, among America's most distinctive artifacts, measure up to 15 cm. in length, (although some are as short as 4 cm.), bases are concave, and a distinctive *fluting*, or channeling, extends from the base upward to half the length of the artifact. The Clovis (or Llano) complex documents the earliest well-dated association of human cultural (and skeletal) remains with extinct animals in North America. There are no established cultural antecedents for this culture anywhere in the New World. Clovis sites are mainly mammoth kills, mostly dating between ca. 11,500 and 11,000 B.P. Archaeological remains usually include choppers, cutting tools, a variety of bone tools, and (very rarely) milling stones,

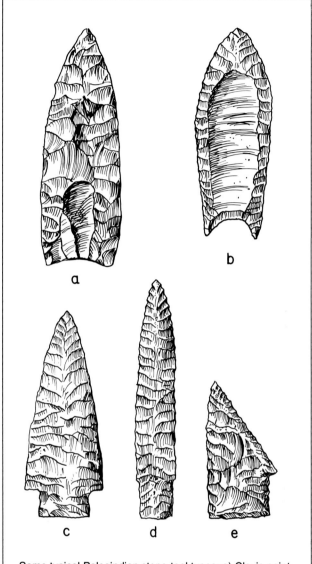

Some typical Paleoindian stone-tool types: a) Clovis point; b) Folsom point; c) Scottsbluff point; d) Eden point; e) Cody knife. Not to scale.

as well as the characteristic Clovis fluted points. In many localities the Folsom and Plano cultures succeed Clovis occupations.

At the end of the last glacial interval the North American boreal forest was gradually replaced by deciduous forests; between 10,000 and 8000 B.P. much forest was being replaced by grasslands. By this time large portions of the Great Plains had thus become suited for occupation by large, gregarious herbivores. The bison began providing both material and spiritual focus for aboriginal lifeways on the Great Plains. These Paleoindians hunted a variety of big game, some now extinct: mammoth, caribou, musk-ox, and long-horned bison. Some think that changing climates and rapid shifts in vegetation so altered regional ecology that it no longer favored several of these species. Less water meant, among other things, fewer coarse grasses and reeds available for elephant herds. But many feel that humans, the world's most efficient predators, literally hunted these great beasts into extinction.

A different pattern emerged in the eastern United States. Despite similarities in technology the Paleoindian mode of life in this area differed from the pattern of big-game hunting found in the western plains. By 12,000 B.P. the floral and faunal resources available between the Ohio Valley and Ontario were sufficient to support scattered bands of hunters. The considerable homogeneity of tool forms in the Northeast suggested a single technological complex, adaptable to a wide variety of environments, from coastal plain to upland, from river valley to northern lakes. Animal bones found in association with these Paleoindian sites are usually woodland caribou.

There are many mastodon and mammoth finds in the eastern United States but no evidence that humans either slew or butchered these animals. Other foods, such as nuts, seeds, berries, fish, and fowl, were available and not beyond the procurement capabilities of these early populations. Eastern Paleoindians emphasized the exploitation of river-valley resources, thus beginning to adapt in the direction of later, more efficient gathering economies.

Hunting adaptations similar to Clovis can also be seen in early South American cultures. The diagnostic artifacts of this tradition are fish-tail projectile points from El Inga and other sites, which resemble Clovis points of North America. Established largely in Andean South America, this early hunting tradition seems to have begun in the Andean region, from where it spread eastward into the plains of Argentina and south to the tip of South America. Between 13,000 and 12,000 B.P. Paleoindians hunted mastodons at El Jobo in northern Venezuela. Their contemporaries in central Colombia and southern Chile seem to have concentrated on collecting plants and hunting smaller game. In southern Patagonia people hunted horses and ground sloths ca. 11,000 B.P., but we have no evidence that Paleoindians in central and northern Brazil ever hunted such big game.

The human fossil record for Paleoindians remains skimpy. Perhaps the earliest readily acceptable specimen is a complete cranium recovered from Cerro Sota Cave in Patagonia (Chile) by J. Bird in 1936. The skull is small, showing modest browridges and little facial projection; but in all respects the morphology of the Cerro Soto material is fully modern and consistent with the variability seen in native Americans from South America.

The oldest Paleoindian human remains in North America date from the Clovis period: Midland

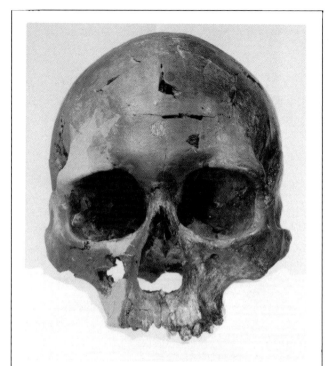

Facial view of the Cerro Sota 2 cranium from southern Chile. (Courtesy of Ian Tattersall.)

(Texas), Marmes Shelter (Washington), Gordon Creek (Colorado), and Anzick (Montana). Although claims for a more extreme antiquity have been made, the evidence remains clouded. Aspartic acid racemization reactions suggested, for instance, that skeletons found near La Jolla, Del Mar, and Sunnyvale (California) ranged from 70,000 to 26,000 B.P. in age. But more recent research, employing the accelerator mass spectrometry method of radiocarbon dating, now places the age of these skeletons between 6300 and 3600 radiocarbon years B.P. Similar empirical problems exist for other reputedly pre-Holocene-age human fossils in the New World.

Pre-Clovis Cultures

Clovis is the earliest well-documented human population known in the Western Hemisphere. Decades of concerted research have provided no undisputed proof of a pre-Clovis human presence in North America. Perhaps the best evidence for a pre-12,000 B.P. occupation comes from Meadowcroft Shelter in southwestern Pennsylvania. Accompanying a ladder of more than 40 radiocarbon dates is evidence of human occupation: firepits, stone tools, a piece of basketry, and two human bone fragments. The oldest cultural date at Meadowcroft is slightly over 19,000 B.P. Yet the evidence at Meadowcroft Shelter remains controversial; early stone tools are rare and identical to later artifacts; diagnostic Paleoindian artifacts are absent, as is Pleistocene megafauna. The temperate vegetation evidence throughout the Meadowcroft sequence seems anomalous, since the ice front was less than 75 km. to the north.

Early radiocarbon dates are also available from South American sites. Hearths associated with pebble and flake tools in southern Chile and northeastern Brazil suggest to some that people entered South America sometime before 35,000 B.P. Additional controversial sites throughout the Americas have yielded simple stone and bone assemblages from less definite cultural contexts. Unfortunately the archaeology of each such site leaves many questions unanswered, and none of this evidence is universally accepted by New World archaeologists.

Despite such empirical difficulties many specialists believe that humans reached North America long before Clovis—sometime prior to 40,000–30,000 B.P. Scholars favoring a pre-Clovis occupation of North America argue, among other things, that the great diversity in projectile points manufactured 12,000–10,000 B.P. precludes the possibility of first migration from Asia only a couple of millennia before. The variety of ecological adaptations already evident by this date, ranging from interior subarctic to coastal/tropical, can be used to argue similarly. Moreover, there is no convincing demonstration that the precursors of Clovis came from Asia.

See also AMERICAS; BLACKWATER DRAW; CALICO; CLOVIS; FOLSOM; GLACIATION; LLANO; MEADOWCROFT SHELTER; OLD CROW; PLEISTOCENE. [D.H.T.]

Further Readings

Bryan, A.L., ed. (1986) New Evidence for the Pleistocene Peopling of the Americas. Orono: University of Maine Center for Study of Early Man.

Dincauze, D. (1984) An archaeological evaluation of the case for pre-Clovis occupations. Adv. World Archaeol. 3:275–323.

Haynes, C.V. (1982) Were Clovis progenitors in Beringia? In D.M. Hopkins, F.J. Mathews, Jr., C.E. Schweger, and S.B. Young (eds.): Paleoecology of Beringia. New York: Academic, pp. 383–398.

Irving, W.N. (1985) Context and chronology of early man in the Americas. Ann. Rev. Anthropol. 14:529–555.

Owen, R. (1984) The Americas: the case against Ice-Age human population. In F.H. Smith and F. Spencer (eds.): The Origins of Modern Humans: A World Survey of the Fossil Evidence. New York: Liss, pp. 517–563.

PALEOLITHIC

Earliest division of the Stone Age, first defined by Lubbock in 1865 as the epoch of "the Drift [=Ice Age] when man shared the possession of Europe with the Mammoth, the Cave Bear, the Woolly-haired Rhinoceros, and other extinct animals." Today the term refers to late Pliocene and Pleistocene archaeological sites worldwide that reflect the human coexistence with and dependence on extinct (and extant) large herbivores. Lubbock's definition succeeded those based on paleontology and biostratigraphy (e.g. those by Lartet and Christy) rather than on the characteristics of stone tools or human adaptations.

As the first stage of Thomsen's three-age system (Stone, Bronze, Iron) the Stone Age was initially divided by Lubbock into two epochs, Paleolithic and Neolithic, in accordance with a French division into "chipped stone" and "polished stone" ages. Since early definitions of the Paleolithic combined chronological (biostratigraphic), technological (chipped stone), and economic (big-game hunters) criteria, subsequent use of the term has been inconsistent, particularly at the chronological and geographic boundaries of the original definitions, which were based on middle and late Pleistocene European contexts. For example, African Paleolithic industries are often referred to a different system: Early, Middle, and Later Stone Age. These do not coincide in time with the "Ice Age," and they include industries with ground-stone and occasionally metal objects, as well as evidence of economic intensification (e.g. fishing).

Boundaries and Divisions of the Paleolithic

Even the earliest chipped-stone industries, of which three are known between 2.6 and 2.1 m.y., are generally included in the study of Paleolithic archaeology. The inclusion within the Paleolithic of industries made by specialized hunter-fisher-gatherers of the late Pleistocene and early Holocene is more problematic, but where these industries appear prior to 20,000 B.P., as in Zambia, their attribution to the Paleolithic is widely accepted. Thus, although the Paleolithic is intended to represent a stage of *cultural* evolution, it is often defined chronologically, particularly in Europe, and limited to industries occurring before the late Pleistocene/Holocene boundary at ca. 10,000 B.P.

The Paleolithic is usually divided (especially in Europe) into three stages: Lower, Middle, and Upper, or, as in this volume worldwide, Early, Middle, and Late. The Early Paleolithic includes industries with handaxes and/or cleavers (Acheulean, Abbevillian, Micoquian), choppers and flakes (Oldowan, Buda), and unspecialized flakes (Clactonian, Tayacian, Hope Fountain). Prepared-core technologies (Levallois, Victoria West) develop only toward the end of this stage. In Africa the Early Paleolithic (or Early Stone Age) lasts over 2 m.y., with only limited introductions of new tool forms (handaxes and cleavers at 1.6 m.y.) or economic strategies (shift to rock-shelter use, increased dependence on hunting of large her-

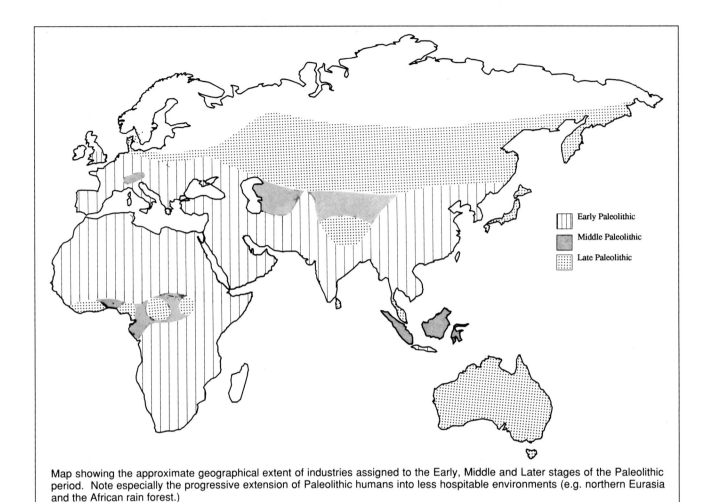

Map showing the approximate geographical extent of industries assigned to the Early, Middle and Later stages of the Paleolithic period. Note especially the progressive extension of Paleolithic humans into less hospitable environments (e.g. northern Eurasia and the African rain forest.)

bivores by later middle Pleistocene, as at Cave of Hearths). Control of fire may have been present from 1.5 m.y. on or may have developed only later. In Europe and Asia the earliest Paleolithic industries are dated to ca. 1 m.y. or less (Vallonnet, Isernia, Nihowan, Xihoudu). Handaxes do not appear until after 350 k.y. in Europe and are entirely absent from East Asia, with the possible exception of South Korea (Chongok-Ni).

The Middle Paleolithic stage reflects increasing sophistication of stone-tool technology, economic patterns, and cognitive development. In both Europe and Africa tools are frequently made on small thin flakes of regular shape and are often preshaped on the core by a Levallois-like technology. European sites, usually rock shelters rather than stream channels, show evidence of considerable hunting skill and some degree of specialization on large herbivore prey species, as well as some of the earliest evidence for symbolic, aesthetic, and advanced cognitive behavior, in the form of "crayons" of coloring material, human burials with occasional "grave goods," and rare examples of incised and perforated bones or teeth.

In Africa and the Near East Middle Paleolithic industries are interspersed with horizons in which true blades are present. In addition African Middle Paleolithic industries begin earlier than in Europe (by 180 k.y., according to dates from Ethiopia), have more evidence of complex technologies (backing, hafting), and are occasionally associated with colored, engraved, or incised objects of stone and ostrich-eggshell. Unlike industries of the Early Paleolithic those of the Middle Paleolithic exhibit a degree of regional specificity on a smaller-than-subcontinental scale, especially in southern Africa. Increasing interregional diversity suggests that Middle Paleolithic humans may have begun to be organized into discrete societies with different groups reflected in their styles of artifact manufacture or alternatively that patterns of economic exploitation were more tightly adapted to regionally specific resources.

Without question the greatest shift in Paleolithic adaptations is that between the Middle and Late Paleolithic at ca. 35,000 B.P. or slightly earlier. In its strictest sense the Upper Paleolithic is limited to Europe, and perhaps the Near East and northeastern Africa, where the most characteristic innovations are

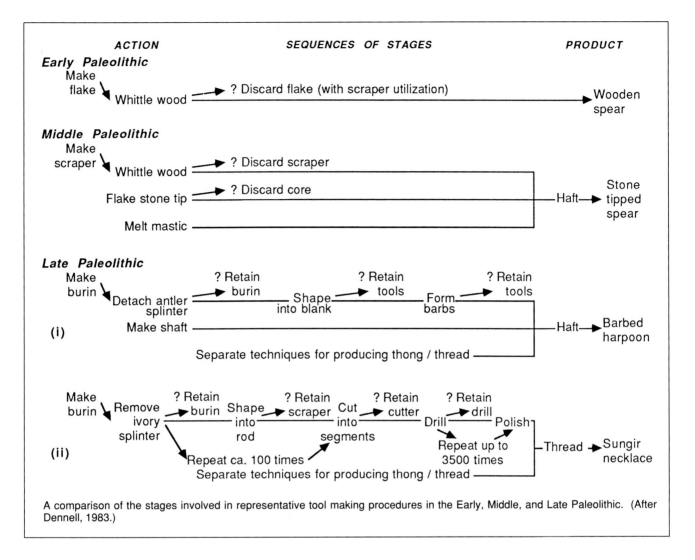

A comparison of the stages involved in representative tool making procedures in the Early, Middle, and Late Paleolithic. (After Dennell, 1983.)

the appearance of blade technology and the use of burins and other tools to work bone, antler, ivory, tooth, and shell. Faunal remains at particular sites are increasingly dominated by a single species (e.g. reindeer, horse, mammoth, red deer, ibex), indicating increased technological skill, scheduling of resource use, and possibly processing of meat for storage. Decorative beads and pendants were manufactured and raw materials, such as stone, ivory, and shell, traded over long distances, suggesting greater complexity of social organization. Finally, a profusion of carved, painted, modeled, or engraved images (whether on cave walls or on small pieces of bone, antler, ivory, or baked clay), together with rare but elaborate burials, as at Sungir, attest to an elaboration of symbolic behavior, possibly in response to the increased complexity and risk of economic strategies and/or to the greater requirements of expanded social interactions.

Although microlithic tools were made in many areas of Europe after 20,000 B.P., and economic specialization increases after this time, with greater em-

phasis on small-scale resources, it is customary to place the limit of the Upper Paleolithic at the end of the last Ice Age, ca. 10,000 B.P., when large gregarious herbivores disappear from much of the area covered by Upper Paleolithic adaptations.

To avoid the Eurocentric Early, Middle, and Late/Upper Paleolithic divisions, and to separate the technological, economic, and social implications of the terms, J.G.D. Clark proposed five technological modes to describe the changes in Paleolithic industries; Mode I, industries with simple flakes and cores/choppers (Oldowan, Clactonian); Mode II, industries with some formally shaped tools and simple direct-percussion flaking techniques (Acheulean); Mode III, industries with flakes struck from prepared cores (Mousterian, Bambata, Stillbay); Mode IV, blade and burin industries; and Mode V, industries with microliths. In this scheme the fact that Upper Paleolithic technology (Mode IV) is lacking over most of Africa would not obscure the fact that many of the same social, economic, and cognitive shifts, such as creation of images, long-distance trade, body orna-

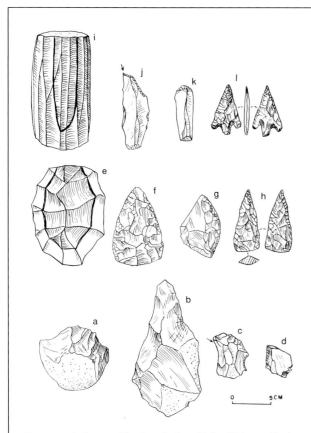

Representative artifacts of the Paleolithic. Early Paleolithic: a) Oldowan chopper (Africa); b) early Acheulean handaxe (Africa); c) Clactonian flake tool (Europe); d) flake tool (China). Middle Paleolithic: e) Levallois core and flake removed from it (Europe); f) Mousterian handaxe (France); g) Quina convex scraper (Europe); h) Pietersburg bifacial point (South Africa). Late Paleolithic: i) prismatic blade core (Old World); j) Capsian burin on blade (Tunisia); k) Perigordian end scraper (France); l) Solutrean tanged point (Spain).

second, to explain the variability in the archaeological record, so as to shed light on Paleolithic lifeways (including particularly the technological, economic, social, ritual, and ideological aspects of Paleolithic societies at various times in the past) and their relationship to the formation of archaeological sites. Although both goals are inherent in most Paleolithic research, prehistorians trained in geology tend to emphasize sequences and culture-historical reconstruction, while those trained in anthropology (or ethnology) emphasize the reconstruction of past lifeways.

Recent syntheses have tended to combine the two approaches. The need to order assemblages from different sites in a chronological sequence has led to new approaches to age determination, particularly at sites beyond the range of radiocarbon (40 k.y.), including microfaunal biostratigraphy, geochemical dating (e.g. thermoluminescence, electron-spin resonance, oxygen-isotope ratios, uranium series, amino-acid racemization), and microstratigraphy. In addition to chronology these techniques have yielded an improved understanding of paleoenvironments. Attention to formation processes and taphonomy has resulted in a consensus that most Paleolithic sites are palimpsests of repeated activities in a given location; that different sites within a group's annual range may have been used for different activities; and that the energy invested in objects, together with cultural rules of disposal and "curation" (retention for future use) are as important as technological capabilities, stylistic norms, and localized activities in determining the content of archaeological assemblages. The result is a shift to regionally based interpretive frameworks.

mentation, diversification, and/or economic specialization, take place as early or earlier in Africa than the Middle/Upper Paleolithic boundary of Europe. The separation of technological from socioeconomic development also allows the discussion of Paleolithic stages to be extended to Australia, the Pacific, and the New World. These areas all appear to have been colonized from Asia between ca. 40 and 15 k.y. ago by fully modern (if somewhat robust) humans, who do not appear to have practiced a Mode IV or V technology at the time of their arrival. Mode IV industries, called Lithic or Paleoindian, are widespread in North America by 12,000 B.P.

Aims of Paleolithic Archaeology

Paleolithic archaeology aims, first, to provide an inventory of the Paleolithic record so as to allow reconstruction of "culture history" through the definition and dating of regional industrial sequences, and,

Human Evolution and Cultural Development

One of the major questions in Paleolithic research concerns the relationship between morphological and cultural change in the fossil and archaeological records, respectively. For example, is the *Homo habilis* to *Homo erectus* "boundary" correlated with the appearance of the Acheulean and other innovations, or the *neanderthalensis* to *sapiens* boundary with the shift from Middle to Upper Paleolithic? Recent evidence has suggested that morphological and cultural evolution are less clearly associated than previously supposed, particularly at the Middle to Upper Paleolithic boundary, where Neanderthals have been associated with Upper Paleolithic industries (Saint-Césaire, ?Vindija), and fully modern humans in Africa with flake industries grouped with the Middle Paleolithic (Klasies River Mouth, Border Cave). In the Early Paleolithic the correlation between human biology and culture is even less clear, with increasing speculation that some of the relatively similar, early stone-tool assemblages may have been produced by different hominid species, including *Australopithecus robustus*.

Other ways in which morphological concerns impinge on Paleolithic studies concern the capacity for culture of pre-*sapiens* hominids. Particularly in the early stages of the Paleolithic the relatively unchanging simple technology and spatial distribution of tool types and sites suggest that if entities comparable with human societies or "cultures" existed they either did not recognize intergroup differences or did not symbolize them in the manufacture and use of implements. The extent to which Plio-Pleistocene hominids exhibited fully "human" behavior, such as food sharing, division of labor by sex, home bases, nuclear-family organization, provisioning of juveniles, hunting, or control of fire, has been much debated, as the earliest Paleolithic record provides little evidence for the existence of any of these behaviors. The record does show, however, that early Pleistocene humans were unlike groups of chimpanzees in that they made, used, and discarded stone tools repeatedly at the *same* landscape points and also transported stone and carcass parts to these locations.

Another focus of this debate concerns the degree and interrelationship of language capabilities reflected in the Neanderthal skeleton and symbolic activities, including communication, reflected in the Middle Paleolithic archaeological record. In this case some morphologists and archaeologists have advocated minimal symbolic and cognitive capabilities for Neanderthals, while certain of their colleagues have argued otherwise. The comparisons between the two kinds of data have led each side to reexamine their conceptions and pose new questions.

Regional Differences in Paleolithic Adaptations

Although study of the Paleolithic is still somewhat Eurocentric, investigators have realized that the continents and subcontinental regions of the Old World have profoundly different histories and patterns of human development. During the last million years of the Pleistocene East Asian industries changed little from the Mode I forms recovered from the earliest sites, although there are a few irregular bifacial forms (e.g. in Korea), and prepared cores appear in later late Pleistocene contexts. Human morphological shifts, however, parallel those observed in Africa, although possibly at later time periods throughout. In sub-Saharan Africa Mode IV industries (e.g. Howieson's Poort) appear only intermittently within Mode III sequences (Middle Stone Age). A stage comparable with the European Upper Paleolithic in both tech-

nology and other aspects of economic and social intensification is lacking over much of the continent. On the other hand fully modern humans appear earlier in sub-Saharan Africa than in Europe. Within Europe itself the Mediterranean region has a different history of settlement and technological development, particularly at the end of the Paleolithic. Whether these regional differences were due to differing adaptations, ethnic groups, raw materials, or histories of human evolution and migration remains to be determined, but the shift in focus from a site-oriented perspective to a regional one is the most important step in a comprehensive understanding of the Paleolithic age.

See also ABBEVILLIAN; ACHEULEAN; AFRICA; AMERICAS; ASIA (EASTERN); AUSTRALIA; BIOCHRONOLOGY; BRAIN; CLACTONIAN; EARLY PALEOLITHIC; EARLY STONE AGE; ECONOMY, PREHISTORIC; EPIPALEOLITHIC; EUROPE; EVOLUTION; FIRE; GEOCHRONOMETRY; GLACIATION; HANDAXE; HOMININAE; HOMO; HOMO ERECTUS; HOMO HABILIS; HOMO SAPIENS; HOPE FOUNTAIN; HOWIESON'S POORT; HUNTER-GATHERERS; LATE PALEOLITHIC; LATER STONE AGE; LEVALLOIS; MESOLITHIC; MICOQUIAN; MIDDLE PALEOLITHIC; MIDDLE STONE AGE; MOUSTERIAN; NEANDERTHALS; NEAR EAST; NEOLITHIC; OLDOWAN; PALEOENVIRONMENTS; PALEOINDIAN; PALEOLITHIC IMAGE; PALEOLITHIC LIFEWAYS; PLEISTOCENE; PREHISTORY; PREPARED-CORE; RAW MATERIALS; RITUAL; SAINT-CÉSAIRE; SITE TYPES; SPEECH (ORIGINS OF); STONE-TOOL MAKING; STORAGE; STRATIGRAPHY; TAPHONOMY; TAYACIAN; UPPER PALEOLITHIC. [A.S.B.]

Further Readings

Gamble, C. (1986) The Palaeolithic Settlement of Europe. Cambridge: Cambridge University Press.

Klein, R.G., ed. (1984) Southern African Prehistory and Paleoenvironments. Rotterdam and Boston: Balkema.

Phillipson, D.W. (1985) African Archaeology. Cambridge: Cambridge University Press.

Wu, R., and Olsen, J. (1985) Palaeoanthropology and Palaeolithic Archaeology in the People's Republic of China. New York: Academic.

Wymer, J. (1982) The Palaeolithic Age. New York: St. Martin's.

PALEOLITHIC CALENDAR

The first book to describe the carved and engraved images and the bone and stone tools of the "Reindeer Age" in France (as the Upper Paleolithic, or Late Ice Age, was called at first) was published by E. Lartet and H. Christy in 1875. In that volume the British anthropologist E.R. Jones described a number of bones incised with accumulated sets of tiny marks, which he considered to be "tallies," implying that they may have been hunting or gaming tallies. Jones documented the presence of comparable items made by hunters and farmers from many parts of the world

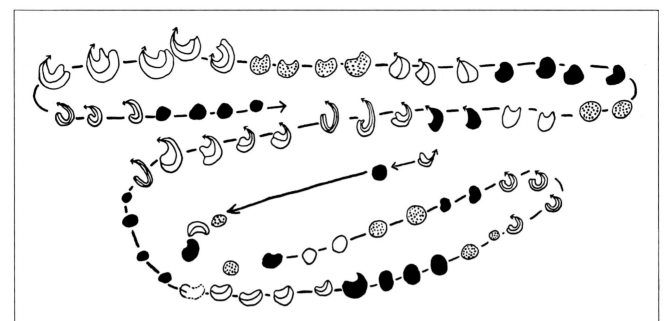

The serpentine notation engraved on a piece of bone from the early Upper Paleolithic (Aurignacian period, ca. 30,000 B.P.), rock shelter of Abri Blanchard, France. Sixty-nine marks were accumulated with 26 changes of point and style or pressure of marking. The notation images the waxing and waning of the moon and encompasses 2 1/4 lunar months, with the full moon periods at the left, the crescents and days of invisibility at the right.

in the historic period. Almost a century later these Ice Age objects, which had begun to be found in both West and East Europe, were subjected to microscopic analysis to determine how they were made and accumulated. A. Marshack published several analyses that indicated that these "tallies" had often been accumulated over a considerable period of time, one set of marks being added sequentially to the next. The analyses indicated that the sets of marks were usually made by different engraving points and that they were often incised with different pressures, rhythms, and direction of marking, suggesting that they were in fact some form of record keeping or notation. Historic tallies made by hunters or by farmers of goods borrowed or lent did not show this form of continuous, sequential linear accumulation. The Upper Paleolithic notations sometimes had hundreds of marks, broken down into sets. An internal analysis of these sets indicated that they were nonarithmetic, that they were not broken down into fives or tens. They provided no indication of an arithmetical counting system.

The sequences of shorter sets, however, tallied almost perfectly with an observation of the phases of the moon and the longer sets with an observation of passing lunar months. They therefore seemed to be records of the passage of time, marking off the phases of the moon and the passage of lunar months, or "moons," and the seasons. Since these analyses were published, it has become common among ar-

chaeologists to describe the hunting and gathering cultures and economies of the Ice Age as highly mobile and seasonally organized, with hunting groups often moving long distances to follow the migrating herds of reindeer, bison, horse, or mammoth, culling different species at different times for their antlers, meat, or skins.

The Upper Paleolithic notations, which were probably kept by tribal specialists, would have helped in planning and scheduling the complex sequence of social, cultural, and economic activity. Archaeologists have begun to acknowledge that there were probably seasonal periods for group dispersal and aggregation, with the latter periods involving barter and exchange and probably group rituals and ceremonies. True arithmetical and astronomical calendars, in which the year was established as an arithmetical sum, began to appear only with the political and religious temple organization that developed in the farming civilizations that rose some thousands of years after the Ice Age ended.

See also PALEOLITHIC IMAGE; UPPER PALEOLITHIC. [A.M.]

Further Readings

Marshack, A. (1972) The Roots of Civilization. New York: McGraw-Hill.

Marshack, A. (1984) Hierarchical Evolution of the Human Capacity: The Paleolithic Evidence. 54th James Arthur Lecture. New York: American Museum of Natural History.

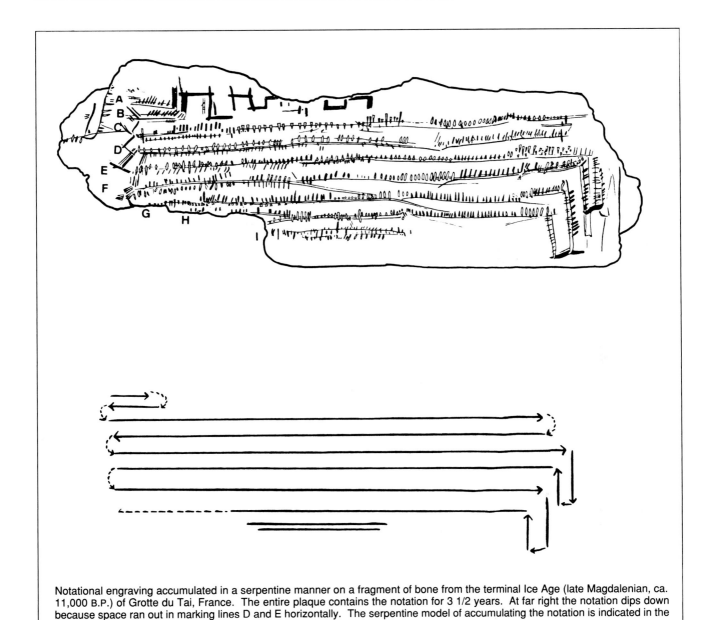

Notational engraving accumulated in a serpentine manner on a fragment of bone from the terminal Ice Age (late Magdalenian, ca. 11,000 B.P.) of Grotte du Tai, France. The entire plaque contains the notation for 3 1/2 years. At far right the notation dips down because space ran out in marking lines D and E horizontally. The serpentine model of accumulating the notation is indicated in the schematic model below.

PALEOLITHIC IMAGE

The first widespread body of imagery and symbol, or "art," to appear in the archaeological record is from the Upper Paleolithic, or Later Stone Age period, of Europe, popularly known as the last Ice Age, ca. 35,000–11,000 B.P. These images were made by the hunters of such extinct animals as the woolly mammoth, woolly rhinoceros, and large-antlered elk (*Megaceros*), as well as reindeer, bison, horse, aurochs (wild cattle), ibex (wild goat), and deer. All of these species, along with lion, bear, wolf, fox, fish, seal, serpent, amphibians, migratory water birds, regional birds, insects, and plants, were depicted in the art of the European Ice Age. These images, incised or carved on antler, bone, ivory, and stone, began to be found in the habitation sites of the Ice Age hunter-gatherers more than a century ago, not long after Charles Darwin published *On the Origin of Species* (1859) with its suggestion of a long evolutionary history for humans and other species. Darwin theorized that forms of humans must have lived on earth long before the beginnings of written history and civilization. A few years after publication of the *Origin* the validation of human-made stone tools or hand-axes found in the soil with the bones of extinct animals began to document the ancient ancestry of modern humans.

Discovery of Ice Age Art

In 1865 the engraved outline of a woolly mammoth

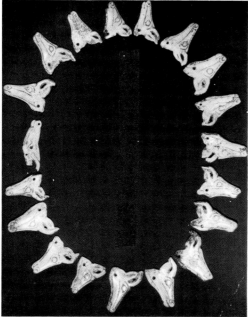 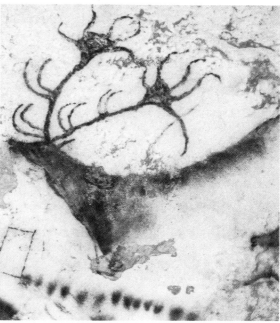

Top: three "Venus" figurines made in the same style, from the early Upper Paleolithic of Europe (Gravettian, ca. 27,000–23,000 B.P.) Left: figure in mammoth ivory, from Kostenki (Ukrainian S.S.R.); center: figure carved in limestone and covered with red ocher, from Willendorf (Austria); right: figure carved of mammoth ivory, from Lespugue (France). Bottom left: necklace of 18 ibex heads and one bison head, carved from bone and incised, from Labastide (France), dating to the late Magdalenian. Bottom right: painting of a stag with full antlers, head up and mouth open, baying in the time of the autumn rut. A set of painted dots and a geometric sign accompany this work from Lascaux (France), dated ca. 16,500 B.P.

on a shaped piece of mammoth ivory was excavated at La Madeleine, a limestone rock shelter on the shore of the Vézère River in the Dordogne area of southwestern France. The engraving proved that humans capable of representational art had lived in Europe in a cold period when mammoth roamed the continent. In 1868 the skeletons of four Ice Age adults, including one woman, were found a few kilometers downstream on the Vézère, in a tiny cliffside burial cave called Cro-Magnon, within the farming village of Les Eyzies. The skeletons were of anatomically modern humans. It slowly became clear that the Cro-Magnons, as they came to be called, had displaced the Neanderthals, who had occupied Europe for the previous 100 k.y. Found with the Cro-Magnon skeletons were beads of seashells that came from the Atlantic to the west and the Mediterranean to the southeast, indicating that these early humans not only made images but had walked or traded at great distances to secure symbolic materials. They were, then, modern humans in both their morphology and ways of thinking, even though they were relatively ancient, prehistoric hunter-gatherers.

In the century that followed hundreds of images were excavated from Ice Age habitation sites and burials across Europe, within those areas that lay below the great ice sheets that had blanketed northern Europe and the central region of the Alps. These habitation sites lay along the network of rivers that flowed to the Atlantic or to the Mediterranean and Black Seas, within the area that today contains France, Spain, Italy, Germany, Austria, Czechoslovakia, and the Ukraine. During the last Ice Age maximum cold phase large portions of this area consisted of open steppe, some woodland along the rivers, and areas of permafrost tundra toward the north. Ice Age culture also dispersed into Siberia. The remains of a homesite—including tents or huts constructed of poles, antler, and skins, with fireplaces, stone and bone tools, a burial, and a rich collection of carved and engraved images and costume pieces made of mammoth ivory—has been found at Malta, on the Angara River in central Siberia, dated at ca. 16,500 B.P., or near the end of the Ice Age.

The seemingly sudden "explosion" of art that developed across this vast area included many forms: a wide range of personal decoration, like necklaces, rings, bracelets, headbands, anklets, and pendants, as well as elaborately beaded clothes, along with a variety of nonutilitarian symbolic artifacts, such as carved ritual batons, wands, and strangely shaped objects. Bone tools began to be decorated with the images of animals, humans, signs, and motifs. There are engraved and painted images of shamans in ritual costume. The library of imagery includes imaginary or fantastic creatures. There are different types of human imagery: the best known are the human females from the early Upper Paleolithic or Gravettian period, ca. 28,000–23,000 B.P., the naked, so-called "Venus" figurines carved in ivory and stone. Even earlier, in the Aurignacian period of France, ca. 30,000 B.P., one finds carved and engraved vulva images and occasional phalluses.

In the late Upper Paleolithic of western Europe a different style of representing the human female appears. It is usually the abstracted, headless image of a female body, known as the "buttocks" image because of a flat or concave front and an exaggerated, protruding rear. Musical instruments, including whistles, flutes, and percussion instruments, appear early. With these recognizable products there begins to appear a number of prewriting, nonrepresentational symbol systems consisting of geometric signs and motifs and accumulations of sets of marks. Found in the homesites and the caves, these are among the major puzzles of the late Ice Age cultures. An internal analysis of the accumulated sets of marks, once thought to be "hunting tallies," suggests that they may have been a form of notation or record keeping, perhaps marking the passage of months and seasons, an activity that would have been useful for scheduling both economic and ritual activity in the sharply delineated seasons of mid-latitude Europe. Within this huge and diverse body of symbolic materials are exquisite masterpieces of "art," clearly made by trained specialists, although the majority of examples are artistically unexceptional, except for their early presence and extraordinary variety.

Sanctuary Caves: A Regional Development

In 1879 Altamira, a painted and engraved Ice Age cave, was discovered in the foothills of the Cantabrian Mountains of northwestern Spain. The depicted animals, including the bison painted in red and black on the ceiling, were so startling that they were declared to be fake, until comparable images of bison, horse, ibex, and aurochs were discovered some years later in the small cave of La Mouthe in France, a short walk from the burial of Cro-Magnon and not far from the site of La Madeleine. Since then almost 200 painted and engraved caves have been found among the limestone hills of southern France and northwestern Spain, the "Franco-Cantabrian" area. Rare examples of Ice Age cave art have been found elsewhere: along the southern Mediterranean coast of Spain (La Pileta, Nerja), in the cave of Cucialat in Romania, and in the cave of Kapova in the Ural Mountains of the U.S.S.R. Upper Paleolithic cave engravings have been found in Italy and Sicily, and some Late Paleolithic engravings on rock walls have apparently been found in Siberia.

It was the powerful imagery in the Franco-Cantabrian "sanctuary" caves, however, and the dramatic stories of their discovery and validation, that for almost half a century turned the attention of archaeologists and the public away from the complexity and variety of the symbol systems that were being continuously found in Ice Age homesites across Europe. Most popular books on Ice Age art have focused on the caves, often providing highly imaginative descriptions of the rituals that were supposed to occur there. A few caves do provide evidence of group rites, but they are rare and never suggest large groups. On the clay wall of the cave of Montespan (France) the headless carving of a clay bear and the incised image of a horse were repeatedly stabbed with spears, perhaps in a ritual involving a few persons. In the cave of Tuc d'Audoubert (France) two carved clay bison were accompanied by a few heel prints of adolescents in the clay floor, suggesting a short hooflike ritual dance. In the Santander region of northwestern Spain the cave of El Juyo has revealed a complex ritual altar that would have required the time and effort of a number of persons to construct, but it may have been a specialized sanctuary used by a few persons at special times. At Lascaux, the most important decorated cave in France, a scaffolding had been built to paint the high walls and ceiling, but whether the complex cave was a public "sanctuary" or a specialized place to be used at particular times is not known.

Many of the painted and engraved caves are too small or narrow for group rituals. A large proportion of the more complex compositions, signs, and images, even in the major caves, are in hard-to-reach, hidden, and narrow recesses where only one person at a time can enter. The evidence suggests that the caves were by and large used by few persons, sometimes by small specialized groups, often by individuals who did no more than add a single sign or motif to a larger composition or wall. At Gargas (France), among almost 150 negative hand prints in red and black paint, some with "missing" finger joints, an adult held an infant hand to the wall and blew paint over both hands. Such private usage does not indicate the overdramatized activity of supposed shamanistic performances as imagined by popular writers. Besides, there are engraved depictions on bone and stone of rituals being conducted outside of the caves.

Analysis of the homesite imagery and their modes of use suggests that different symbolic or ritual activities were conducted at the living site. These modes of homesite ritual activity were perhaps more common than the rituals performed in the caves. The evidence is found throughout Europe. At the homesite of Dolni Věstonice (Czechoslovakia), in an area without sanc-

tuary caves, a kiln was found in which clay "Venus" figurines and animals had been fired, apparently to be used in homesite rituals. The presence of burials, often with stone and bone tools, symbolic artifacts, and elaborate costumes, also suggests a rich symbolic and ritual culture, within which the sanctuary caves were a specialized, regional development.

For almost a century it was common to write about the animal and female images of the Ice Age and merely to note with some perplexity the rich and varied library of nonrepresentational signs, symbols, and notations found, for instance, at Altamira, Lascaux, and the other Franco-Cantabrian caves. Many of these were at first interpreted as "hunting magic" and were even described as traps, snares, corrals, pitfalls, or weapons. Some of the structured images were thought to be huts or even dancing costumes.

Only slowly have researchers begun to realize that in the late Ice Age, as in modern human cultures, there were dozens of symbol systems, each with its own iconography or set of images and its own modes of use. In the second half of the twentieth century it has become apparent that the Ice Age images were more than just "art," or the expression of primitive magic and the evidence of a simple, "primitive" philosophy. These images represented different, often complex concepts and mythologized referential systems. They were often the product of highly evolved specialized skills and technologies. Realization of this complexity, made possible in large part by the accumulation of thousands of symbolic images and artifacts as well as the discovery of dozens of major sanctuary caves, led to new, sophisticated methods for studying the categories of image and symbol and their manufacture and use. It became possible to begin both internal and comparative analyses of widely dispersed images and traditions. These differed from the purely visual studies and tracings initiated by the Abbé H. Breuil, the foremost illustrator and interpreter of Ice Age art in the first half of the century. The new studies differ also from early efforts to explain the images and the supposed beginnings of art by reference to the images of historic "primitive" cultures or to changing anthropological theories about what images and symbols in a "primitive" culture should do and mean. A major step in the study of Ice Age art was initiated by the effort of French researchers to clarify the "organization" among the hundreds of images accumulated in the Franco-Cantabrian caves.

Mapping the Caves

Early in the second half of the twentieth century the French archaeologists A. Laming-Emperaire and A. Leroi-Gourhan began to study the apparent relationships among the animal species depicted in the caves. They came to the conclusion that major species, such as the horse and bovids (bison and aurochs), were associated, or "paired." To test this insight Leroi-Gourhan began to catalogue all the images in a cave, charting the position of the animals, as well as the signs and motifs. These were visual studies, without internal analysis of any of the images or compositions. Leroi-Gourhan suggested that the apparent relationship between horse and bison in central areas of a cave represented an "opposition," a suggestion concerning the supposed polar thinking among "primitive" peoples largely derived from structuralist theories that were then common in France among such anthropologists as Lévi-Strauss. According to this hypothesis the horse, even if it was a mare, was "male" and a bison, even if it was a bull, was "female." Long, thin signs were considered male, while wide and round signs were female. This argument, which contained elements of Freudianism, has not been accepted by other archaeologists, particularly those working with the Ice Age images. For one thing, the "oppositional" associations that Leroi-Gourhan attributed to Ice Age art and thought do not occur in the homesite imagery, either in Leroi-Gourhan's Franco-Cantabrian area or in Ice Age homesites dispersed across Europe.

Leroi-Gourhan's visual and statistical studies did, however, provide the first systematic charts of where the major images and compositions in a cave were usually located. From these studies he proposed what he assumed to be an ideal model of a sanctuary cave, with "opposed" major animals in a central position and subsidiary animals and signs in the periphery. He also provided a catalogue of the signs found in the caves, and he revised the chronology of developing styles for depicting animals within the Franco-Cantabrian region. He listed four major styles covering the 25 k.y. of animal art in his region, beginning with simple animal outlines and developing toward images of great realism, animation, and detail. Unfortunately the scheme did not hold for the rest of Europe. The earliest animal images known, the Vogelherd carvings from the early Aurignacian of Germany, ca. 32,000 B.P., are not in Leroi-Gourhan's Style I. They are instead highly sophisticated three-dimensional carvings of lion, horse, bison, and mammoth, with detailed rendering of the eyes, nose, mouth, ears, and hair. The Vogelherd lioness and horse have a grace and animation that would not be found in the Franco-Cantabrian area until thousands of years later, in the Magdalenian period.

Leroi-Gourhan's work nevertheless marked a major change in the systematic study of Ice Age art. His structural, topographic, cataloguing, and stylistic studies made it possible for others, including many of his students, to begin the next stage of intensive, internal analytical inquiry.

Internal Analyses and Comparisons: New Questions and Methods of Study

It became evident through the work of the researchers who followed Leroi-Gourhan that the animal images in the homesites and the caves, particularly during the Magdalenian period of the Franco-Cantabrian area, 16,000–12,000 B.P., were more than mere images of species. A. Marshack stressed the fact that as the Magdalenian tradition developed the art increasingly depicted animals in terms of their dimorphic sexual and seasonal characteristics and behaviors: a horse in its summer coat (Lascaux) or winter coat (Niaux); a bison in summer molt (Lascaux, Altamira, Niaux) or its fall-winter coat (Lascaux); stags carrying mature antlers and baying during the autumn rut (Lascaux); hinds with fawns, cows with calves, juvenile ibex and deer with their springtime antler and horn buds; male salmon with the hook on the lower jaw that only the males acquire during the spawning season. The referential detail in these Magdalenian images of the Franco-Cantabrian area clearly did not represent an "oppositional" philosophy but were derived instead from the Ice Age hunters' observations of the diversity in animal behavior and appearance and the sequence of seasonal changes occurring in the Franco-Cantabrian ecology. This tradition of depicting the seasonal and sexual characteristics of different species did not occur in other areas of Ice Age Europe where animals were always depicted as generalized species, without an indication of sexual, seasonal, behavioral, or age differences. The exception to this rule concerning animal depiction occurred in those neighboring areas into which the Magdalenian traditions temporarily intruded.

As a result of comparative studies of the Ice Age images throughout Europe Marshack has suggested that the unique ecological and geographic conditions within the Franco-Cantabrian area may have contributed to the development of the referential mode of animal depiction. These conditions included wide areas of flatland steppe, cut by a tight network of rivers, that served as a human conceptual frame and a temporal-spatial organizational structure. These rivers ran through deeply cut, steep valleys in the interior region of limestone hills that provided abrupt altitudinal, microecological differences and gradations. These conditions supported a diversity of species during the Ice Age, including subarctic, temperate, steppe, and alpine fauna; they produced sharp seasonal changes in the fauna and flora and

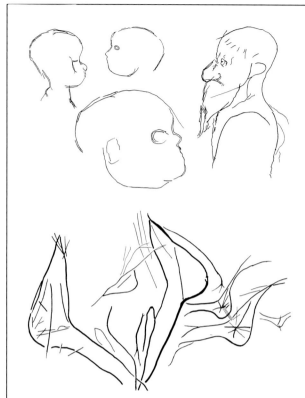

Top: incised heads of children, an infant, and an old man with a beard, all drawn on heavily overengraved limestone blocks found in the habitation site of La Marche (France), dating from the middle Magdalenian (ca. 16,500 B.P.). Other stones here contain portraits of women, dancers, and animals and are overmarked as though used in rituals. The images were unscrambled from the heavy overengraving by L. Pales and T. de Saint Pereuse. Bottom: six abstracted and schematic female images, without heads, arms, or feet, incised on a limestone block found on the floor of the habitation site of La Roche (Lalinde, France), dated to the late Magdalenian. The large female in the center, apparently the first to be engraved, has two breasts; the figure at right has one breast; the other figurines are increasingly abstracted and schematized. Each of these "buttocks" images has been struck through by engraved lines as though they had been used in rituals.

kia and on the Russian Plain, together with the tradition of carving naked, full-figure "Venus" statuettes. Vulva images were carved and painted on cave walls of the Franco-Cantabrian area during the Magdalenian period. Marshack has suggested that the early use of the vulva image in the homesite may have been a "folk" form of ritual activity, perhaps involving women concerned with the processes of menstruation, pregnancy, and birth, while the early masterpieces of carving known as the "Venus" figurines were the product of skilled artisans making a more generalized, long-term image, with perhaps a wider range of meanings and uses. Female imagery in the Ice Age is complex. It includes slim, young females; buxom, mature, or older females; and pregnant and nonpregnant females. A Magdalenian image from Gönnersdorf (Germany) shows an infant being carried on a woman's back; abstracted images of the breasts and vulva symbolize the nurturant aspect of the female. Female images are sometimes associated with animals, plants, the phallus, the bison horn, and geometric signs, suggesting that it was often a generic symbol of the "feminine." Just as the Ice Age animal images represented more than a meal or "hunting magic," the female images apparently represented a recognition of periodicity and process in nature and were more than mere images of "fertility magic" or the erotic.

The prewriting, prearithmetic forms of notation that first appear in the Dordogne area of France, ca. 30,000 B.P., and the other sign and symbol systems throughout Ice Age Europe document a range of nonrepresentational symboling modes, many of which may have been developed by a specialized elite, perhaps the "shamans." The simultaneous growth of "folk" images and ritual modes of using motifs, and the development over time of highly skilled artistic productions in carving, engraving, and painting, perhaps by persons trained and specialized in these skills, suggest that a cultural and symbolic complexity arose among these early hunter-gatherers of the European late Ice Age that would not be reached again until the historic period.

The recognition of various types of symbol systems and modes of symbol use poses a set of questions about these early cultures different from those posed by previous efforts to find a single, unitary explanation for the "origins" of art and the seemingly "sudden" explosion of Ice Age art and creativity. These earlier attempts began with anthropological theories concerning "primitive" forms of thinking and involved concepts of "animism" and hunting and fertility "magic." Leroi-Gourhan, when cataloguing and classifying the Ice Age images, sought a simple, unitary explanation and as a result claimed that many of

fostered the arrival and departure of riverine, aerial, and steppic migratory species. It was the richness and diversity of this regional ecology, and the human cultural tapestry that was woven upon this frame, that was apparently the basis for the realistic referential animal art that developed in this area.

Other equally important symboling traditions developed during the Ice Age and were dispersed more broadly across Europe, reaching into Siberia. Female vulvas began to be carved and engraved on stones in rock shelters of the Dordogne region of France around Les Eyzies during the Aurignacian period, ca. 30,000 B.P. Abstracted vulvas of this type, carved in bone and stone, are found in Czechoslova-

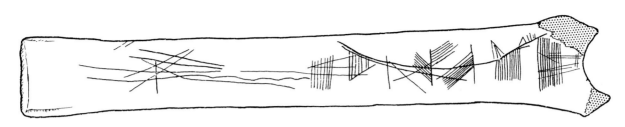

Engraved sets of marks, connected one to the other and accumulated sequentially on a fragmented piece of mammoth ivory. These markings were found with other forms of symbolic marking and accumulation in the later Late Paleolithic habitation huts of Mezhirich, on the Russian Plain. Such notational sequences and symbolic accumulations are found in habitation sites across Ice Age Europe, as well as in the Upper Paleolithic caves in western Europe.

the images in the caves were "male" or "female," within a closed conceptual system of "oppositions." Subsequent analysis of how the images in the caves were made and used has indicated the presence of different symbol systems, each of which had its own iconography and mode of use or accumulation. Animal and female images could be used in a range of ways for different symbolic purposes. Many of the geometric signs and motifs found in the caves were periodically altered by additions that changed their original shape or form. Animal images were often used and reused, at times being "killed" by darts; at times being renewed by the addition of extra eyes, ears, muzzles, legs, tails, or backs; at times being used in association with a library of signs and symbols. Painted or engraved serpentine motifs were accumulated in the caves and on bone and stone in the homesites, at times so thickly as to give the appearance of "macaroni." A study of these "macaroni" accumulations has suggested that they represented a system of periodic ritual marking, using a motif that may have been related to the symbolism of water.

A new generation of researchers have instituted systematic, methodological studies of the Ice Age images that go beyond what was possible with earlier visual studies of style and chronology and that are not dependent on *a priori* anthropological theory. L. Pales and M.T. Saint Péreuse performed a careful internal analysis of hundreds of intricately overengraved limestone tablets from the Magdalenian site of La Marche (France), unscrambling human portraits and animal images. Significantly, both the images and the stones were heavily overengraved as though by a ritual marking. B. and G. Delluc studied the carved and incised images on stone from the early Ice Age in the Dordogne area and found that the technique of working stone by slowly pecking out the outline of a preconceived image was far more sophisticated than the final, simple outline or bas-relief would indicate. G. Bosinski and G. Fischer studied more than 500 incised slates found on the floor of a

Magdalenian camp overlooking the Rhine, in West Germany, and found hundreds of accumulated female images in the "buttocks" style, a large number of which had been overmarked as though in ritual, while the stones themselves were heavily overengraved like the stones from La Marche. M. Lorblanchet employed microscopic and chemical means, and A. Marshack ultraviolet, infrared, and fluorescence, to study the paints in the caves and to determine the modes of use and reuse of animal images and signs. The Abbé Glory spent more than a decade tracing all the incised lines in one intricately overengraved chamber at Lascaux, documenting in "the unknown Lascaux" a complexity of signs, symbols, "macaronis," and animal images, which indicated that the famous paintings represented only a small part of the cave's original use and importance.

The complexity of the Ice Age symbol systems may be one measure of the complexity of the Late Paleolithic cultures. Modern societies also use many types of image, symbol, and sign to mark the relevant categories and aspects of their cultures and to maintain the network of relations and activities that form the cultural tapestry. The first widespread and complex body of image and symbol found in the archaeological record indicates that these modes and capacities were present in the prehistoric Ice Age cultures, long before the beginnings of agriculture and civilization.

Precursors and Termination of Ice Age Art
The nearly 25,000-year development of image and symbol during the European Upper Paleolithic was a unique regional phenomenon that occurred under special geographic, climatic, and ecological conditions. When the climate warmed, the ice melted, and forests spread across Europe into what were once open grazing areas, the late Ice Age cultures and their "art" disintegrated. New hunting-gathering ways of life appeared. The Franco-Cantabrian "sanctuary" caves were abandoned. Realistic animal art, the high

point of Magdalenian creativity, virtually disappeared, although some rock painting continued to be made in the hills of Spain and engraved rock art began to be made in the subarctic, which had earlier been covered by the ice sheets. The Upper Paleolithic female images ceased being made. Representational art largely disappeared, although the mode of making and accumulating geometric signs and motifs, begun in the late Ice Age, continued and developed; it became the dominant "Mesolithic" style.

The Ice Age cultural phenomenon raises a host of questions. Was the European development due to the arrival on the continent of anatomically modern and evolutionarily more advanced and competent forms of humanity? Probably not, since different types of anatomically modern humans in other parts of the world during this period did not develop the same symbolic and cultural complexity. In the Middle East, where modern humans also displaced the Neanderthals, no tradition of animal art, female imagery, or personal decoration arose during this period. There is, however, the rare evidence for a crude beginning of painted animal art in South Africa and of geometric "macaroni" marking in caves of Australia, clearly made by different types of modern humans. Perhaps of greater significance is the slowly accumulating evidence for forms of symboling in the earlier Mousterian period of the Neanderthals, suggesting that many of the traditions that later effloresced in the European late Ice Age had their incipient beginnings in the earlier period.

It has long been known that the Neanderthals in Europe and Asia buried their dead, occasionally with symbolic grave goods—e.g. flowers at Shanidar (Iraq); tools, animal bones, and marked stones at La Ferrassie (France). These burials gave rise to the theory that the Neanderthals had arrived at an incipient "religious" awareness of death and an afterlife. It was widely believed, however, that the Neanderthals did not manufacture symbolic images or make personal decorations and that they therefore had no sense of "self" and lacked social complexity. It was even suggested that the Neanderthals had no capacity for language and that language began at the same time as Ice Age art. This assumed that other modern humans of this period, who did not develop comparable artistic traditions, may not yet have had language. It is therefore significant that there is accumulating evidence for different forms of symbolic manufacture in the Mousterian period of the Neanderthals.

At the Neanderthal site of La Quina (France) two pendant beads were found early in the century, a reindeer phalanx with a hole bored through and a fox canine with a hole that had begun to be bored

when it started to split. When these were excavated, they were considered to be "impossible" for the Mousterian period and were not discussed again until Marshack republished them more than a half-century later. Two pendant beads with holes intentionally bored through at the top, a wolf vertebra and a wolf foot bone, have been excavated from the earlier Micoquian period at the German site of Bocksteinschmiede, in Lonetal. Carved bone points for hunting large game also have been excavated from this period in Germany. Related to this capacity for working bone, at the early Mousterian site of Tata (Hungary) a nonutilitarian oval plaque had been carefully carved and beveled from a section of mammoth tooth; it had then been colored with red ocher and was handled or used, perhaps ritually, for a considerable period as evidenced by the hand polish along its edges.

These scattered early data became important when a Neanderthal skull was found around 1980 in a Chatelperronian level, ca. 34,000–32,000 B.P., at the French site of Saint-Césaire. Some years earlier A. Leroi-Gourhan had excavated pendant beads from a Chatelperronian level at the site of Arcy-sur-Cure and had termed them the earliest known examples of personal decoration made by anatomically modern man. The possibility now exists that the pendant beads were made and worn by Neanderthals.

The problem of the position of the Neanderthals in human evolution and of the Neanderthal capacity for symboling and even for human language is at present in heated debate. If, as now seems possible, the Upper Paleolithic "revolution" in art and symbol represented a historical and cultural regional development, rather than a major evolutionary and genetically determined event, then the complex reasons for the "sudden" rise, the long development, and the sudden disappearance of Upper Paleolithic art and symbol must be explained by reference to a host of temporal, regional, historical, and social cultural processes.

See also AURIGNACIAN; EUROPE; HOMO SAPIENS; LATE PALEOLITHIC; MAGDALENIAN; MOUSTERIAN; NEANDERTHALS; PALEOLITHIC CALENDAR; UPPER PALEOLITHIC. [A.M.]

Further Readings

Leroi-Gourhan, A. (1965) Treasures of Prehistoric Art. New York: Abrams.

Leroi-Gourhan, A. (1982) The Dawn of European Art: An Introduction to Paleolithic Cave Painting. Cambridge: Cambridge University Press.

Marshack, A. (1972) The Roots of Civilization. New York: McGraw-Hill.

Marshack, A. (1977) The meander as a system: the analysis and recognition of iconographic units in Upper Paleolithic compositions. In P. Ucko (ed.): Form in Indigenous Art: Schematization in the Art of Aboriginal and Prehistoric Europe. London: Duckworth, pp. 286–317.

Marshack, A. (1979) Upper Paleolithic symbol systems of the Russian Plain: cognitive and comparative analysis of complex ritual marking. Curr. Anthropol. 20:271–311.

Ucko, P., and Rosenfeld, A. (1967) Paleolithic Cave Art. London: Weidenfeld and Nicholson.

PALEOLITHIC LIFEWAYS

An important part of prehistoric investigation is the attempt to reconstruct the lifeways of early hominids. Some types of prehistoric behavior tend to leave evidence that is highly visible in the record, whereas others leave little or no direct evidence behind. Nonetheless, a primary goal of the prehistorian is ultimately to be able to make generalizations about hominid modes of life through time and space, including subsistence patterns, social organization, technology, and cultural norms and beliefs. Here, we first consider the methods employed to reconstruct Stone Age lifeways and then use these approaches to outline the major stages of Paleolithic adaptation through time.

Methods

Reconstructing Paleolithic lifestyles involves reconnaissance, survey, and meticulous excavation of Stone Age localities, followed by detailed identification and analysis of prehistoric remains. Such archaeological research aims to document patterns of technology, subsistence, and social behavior and to explain change or stasis in the prehistoric record. This reconstruction can be a subjective, imperfect science, since, as noted above, many aspects of hominid behavior leave few traces behind. Modern analogues, such as ethnographic, ethological, taphonomic, and geological studies as well as experimentation, can add valuable insights, but they must be used with caution. Researchers should be aware that concepts of ancient hominid lifeways have changed radically and often during the last two centuries. Theoretical perspectives and methodological innovations have brought about a new kind of rigor, sometimes referred to as the "New Archaeology." This approach to the study of prehistory attempts to construct formalized explanatory models about the past, which are designed to be tested by excavated archaeological evidence as well as evidence not yet discovered.

Dating　Chronological placement of sites is critical in understanding changes in Paleolithic lifestyles through time. Relative dating techniques, such as stratigraphic superimposition, biostratigraphy, and artifact seriation, are often useful when one is trying to correlate one site or regional sequence with another. Chronometric techniques, such as radiocarbon, potassium-argon, and fission-track dating, have proved fairly reliable for dating suitable materials from Paleolithic sites.

Environmental Reconstruction　Reconstruction of paleoenvironments helps prehistorians understand the geographic and ecological contexts in which fossil hominids are found. It can also augment our understanding of how early hominids adapted to new and varied environmental conditions through time.

Evidence for the flora of an area comes from fossil pollen, plant phytoliths, carbonized (burned) plant remains, leaf impressions in sediment, calcified root systems, and waterlogged or desiccated plant materials. Since many prehistoric species of plants have modern counterparts, it is often possible to predict reliably the types of climates and conditions that would have allowed such communities of flora to thrive, considering such variables as temperature, rainfall, sunlight, and soil chemistry.

Faunal remains, such as fossilized bones and teeth, mollusk shells, insect carapaces (rare in Paleolithic contexts), and footprints, can also yield valuable environmental clues, as many fossil taxa have similar modern descendants or near-relatives presumed to live under similar conditions. The faunal composition of a prehistoric assemblage may therefore yield clues to ground cover, rainfall, vegetation type, and proximity to water.

The sediments themselves may also contain environmental indicators. Oxygen isotopes may show how arid or wet an area was; soil formation may suggest how stable a landscape was and how much precipitation it received; and certain types of mineral alteration may indicate climatic conditions.

Subsistence　Reconstruction of the mode of procurement and range of foodstuffs for early hominid groups is based on both prehistoric evidence and patterns observed in modern animal species. Evidence of the types of foods that hominids consumed can come in a variety of forms. Plant foods, thought to be the staple for most hunter-gatherer groups, can be preserved as carbonized vegetable matter or pollen grains. In practice, however, it is often difficult to prove that pollen evidence necessarily represents the types of plants consumed by prehistoric human populations, since it could also represent the local and airborne background pollen in the vicinity of a Paleolithic site.

Other, sometimes subtle, forms of evidence are now being studied for indications of early human diet and subsistence. Among these are hominid tooth wear (macroscopic and microscopic polish and damage on teeth can indicate that materials had been chewed); microwear evidence on stone tools (microscopically detected damage and polish on stone-artifact edges can indicate the materials worked, for instance, cutting soft plants or slicing meat); trace-element analysis of prehistoric hominid remains (isotope proportions among common elements like carbon or nitrogen can indicate aspects of diet, such as proportion of grasses in the diet or degree of carnivory); coprolite analysis (analysis of remains in fossilized hominid feces can reveal microscopic or trace-element evidence of materials consumed); paleopathology (osteological trauma can indicate dietary deficiencies or abnormalities—e.g. dental hypoplasia); and artwork (pictorial representations in Upper Paleolithic artwork show some of the animals prominent in the minds of the hominids, whether primary prey or not).

Technology   The Paleolithic technologies permitted hominids to adapt to a wide range of environmental conditions. Reconstructions of prehistoric technological systems are based primarily on artifact representation and contextual associations, experimentation, use-wear studies, and ethnographic analogies.

Evidence for prehistoric technology is normally restricted to nonperishable materials: such substances as wood, hide, and vegetable fiber are preserved only in exceptional conditions, such as dry caves or waterlogged, anaerobic sediments. Artifacts made out of stone, however, are durable and can be found in most situations. Bone preservation is variable, with alkaline sediments tending to be conducive to mineralization.

By far the most numerous types of technology found in the Paleolithic record are stone artifacts, including percussors, cores, débitage (flakes and fragments), and retouched pieces. Careful examination of such materials, combined with replicative experiments and refitting studies, can often be instructive in documenting which stages of stone reduction actually occurred at a prehistoric site. Use-wear studies on raw materials can also provide important information on the functional modes of artifacts. Bone tools tend to be rare until the Late Paleolithic, when a great diversity of artifact types can be seen for the first time.

Other types of Paleolithic technology that may leave behind recognizable features are architectural structures (e.g. hut or tent foundations, postholes) and fire hearths.

Social Organization   Getting a good grasp on early forms of hominid social organization is a tempting but difficult task for the Paleolithic archaeologist. Among the fundamental properties of social groups are the size of groups that operate together in some

realm of life (e.g. regular mating relationships, foraging, territorial displays); the nature of relationships between males and females (their longevity, the investment of the male in the care and feeding of his young, matings of the female with plural males versus monogamy or exogamy—preferred mating outside of the family group (i.e. the operation of an incest taboo); and the type of group fissioning and fusing that might occur seasonally or for special activities. We need to know a number of these aspects of prehistoric social organization in order to understand the ancestry and evolution of modern human societies and to appreciate what might be basic biological or social norms in our lineage with a long period of development.

It is, however, extremely difficult to find any enduring evidence throughout most of the prehistoric record that will yield clues about social organization. We rely largely upon analogy with other primates and with hunter-gatherer groups to understand the full range of variation in the past. Group size was probably not large in the Paleolithic, as the subsistence demands of foraging human and nonhuman primates restrict the effective foraging group to a certain range, usually not much more than 25–50 individuals, far fewer when resources are sparse or seasonally restricted. Most primates and human groups appear to have some sort of exogamous rule in operation or a prescription to marry or mate outside of the immediate or perceived family group. Many researchers believe that there may be an ancient biological basis for the human taboo against incest.

Male-female relationships are also difficult to define in prehistory. Nonhuman primates exhibit a range of mating and socialization patterns between males and females, from fairly long-term monogamous arrangements to more seasonally promiscuous behavior. In the latter cases more dominant males tend to have better access to receptive females, but females in estrus tend to mate with multiple males. Thus it is difficult to compare directly the complex marriage relationships among human groups with primate mating behavior per se.

Human groups as a rule have some form of marriage, with a network of social responsibilities connected to this bond, and it is thought that this tendency to form long-term male-female bonds has considerable prehistoric depth. This bonding is intrinsically connected to the development of the human family concept, with both parents, and often their relations, involved in duties and benefits regarding the offspring. It is difficult, however, to determine when this behavior pattern began. The first real evidence is perhaps among the Neanderthals, since we find males, females, and children buried in the same general area, a pattern resembling a "family plot."

Primate groups also appear to have a sense of territory that is under their proprietary interest. This tends to be defended by the group against incursions from other groups, even of the same species, although defensive behavior in such instances generally involves threat displays rather than physical violence. By analogy it is thought that prehistoric human groups also tended to have a group-defended territory, but direct evidence is not yet available. It is only by relatively late in prehistory that we see definitive evidence for warfare or injuries inflicted by other humans.

Ritual and Symbolism   The use of symbols—arbitrary sounds or images representing other objects or ideas—is a characteristic of all modern human groups. Symbols are conveyed in many forms, such as language, art, music, dance, and oral traditions. This symbolic behavior is sometimes called *nonutilitarian*, because it is often not directly related to immediate subsistence needs; nonetheless, it is an integral part of every modern human society and helps to integrate individuals into the cultural beliefs and rules of their social group.

How far back such symbolic behavior can be traced is not clear. Language, music, dance, and oral traditions leave little direct evidence in the prehistoric record; other forms, such as art and rituals (e.g. burials), may have more prehistoric visibility. If one assumes that earlier (preanatomically modern) hominids possessed less sophisticated language abilities than modern humans, then the means of expressing and communicating ideas may have been different from those found in modern societies. The use of pigment for coloration, symmetry and finesse of stone artifacts, collection of unusual or exotic items, burial patterns and art styles have all been cited as evidence of such symbolic behavior.

(*See also* AGGREGATION-DISPERSAL; ARCHAEOLOGICAL SITES; BOW AND ARROW; CLOTHING; DIET; ECONOMY, PREHISTORIC; EXOTICS; FIRE; GEOCHRONOMETRY; HUNTER-GATHERERS; LITHIC USE-WEAR; MUSICAL INSTRUMENTS; PALEOBOTANY; PALEOLITHIC IMAGE; PALEOMAGNETISM; PRIMATE SOCIETIES; RITUAL; SITE TYPES; SPEAR; STONE-TOOL MAKING; STRATIGRAPHY; TAPHONOMY.)

Cultural-Historical Overview

Homo habilis *and* Homo erectus (*ca. 2–1 m.y.*)
The Oldowan industrial complex, associated with the first known flaked stone tools, can be traced back to at least 2.5 m.y. in East Africa and begins to be complemented by the large bifaces associated with the Acheulean period ca. 1.5 m.y. ago. Hominids contemporaneous with these industries are *Homo*

habilis and early *Homo erectus*, as well as *Australopithecus boisei, A. "aethiopicus,"* and *A. robustus* (in South Africa). Most sites appear to be associated with tropical or subtropical grasslands and woodlands. Hominid tool makers produced simple flaked and battered stone artifacts, including cores made on cobbles or blocks and a range of casually retouched flakes. Simple tools of organic materials, such as bone, horn, or wood, are also quite likely.

Little is known of territory size and land-use patterns, but the fact that both *Homo* and *Australopithecus* remains are sometimes found at the same localities suggests that at least two subsistence modes were in operation at this time. Most anthropologists assume that the larger-brained genus *Homo* was the principal tool maker, but this cannot be presently demonstrated with certainty.

Oldowan hominids probably foraged for a variety of foodstuffs, of which vegetable foods like berries, fruits, legumes, seeds, roots, corms, and tubers contributed the bulk of the diet. Animal bones of taxa weighing an average of several hundred kg. that are found at some Oldowan sites show indications of stone-tool cutmarks and probable hammerstone fracture. It is not clear how these bones were procured (scavenging or hunting) or how nutrients were processed from these animal remains. Nonetheless, the recurrent association of such animal bones and flaked-stone artifacts in anomalous concentrations suggests that the processing of animal carcasses was a habitual, and perhaps frequent, behavioral pattern. There is no clear evidence for symbolic behavior during this time.

Later Homo erectus/*Archaic* Homo sapiens (*ca. 1–0.2 m.y.*)   Of the numerous middle Pleistocene Paleolithic sites throughout the Old World few have the type of preservation that provides detailed information about hominid behavior. Many of these sites are geologically disturbed, found in high-energy fluvial regimes, suggesting that proximity to water was a major factor in site location.

Hominids identified as classic *Homo erectus* are known from the earlier part of this time period (e.g. the Sangiran, Zhoukoudian, Lantian, and Tighenif materials). Between 500 and 200 k.y. ago, however, many of the hominid fossils, such as those at Arago, Steinheim, Petralona, Saldanha, and perhaps Bodo, appear to have more sapient features, including an expanded braincase, and are here designated as archaic *Homo sapiens*.

Many sites, especially in Africa, the Near East, and western Europe, are characterized by the large bifacial forms, such as handaxes and cleavers, that are the hallmark of the Acheulean industry. These artifacts, especially in Africa, are sometimes found in

Reconstruction of a late *Homo erectus* occupation site.

astonishing numbers. Other artifact forms include a wide range of Mode I (Oldowan-like) cores and flakes, retouched flakes, and battered spheroids. The technological skill in producing bifaces and smaller flake tools seems generally to increase with time in many areas. Some middle Pleistocene sites, especially in eastern Asia, are characterized by nonhandaxe industries (Mode I). The reason for this technological dichotomy on either side of "Movius' line" is not well understood.

Although no direct evidence for clothing has been found during this time period, microwear polishes on stone tools from sites like Clacton and Hoxne (England) suggest that hide working was an impórtant activity, perhaps with skins scraped so as to be worked into supple material for simple garments.

Simple structural features, such as rock features and postholes, have been noted at several sites, including Terra Amata and Lazaret. These have been interpreted as huts or tents that were probably cov-

ered with branches and/or hides.

Evidence for fire comes from such sites as Zhoukoudian (China), Vértesszöllös (Hungary), Terra Amata (France), Kalambo Falls (Zambia), and Cave of Hearths (South Africa). Although some of these claims are disputed, it seems that at sites like Terra Amata clear hearth structures, ringed with stones, indicate human control of combustible materials. As early hominids spread into more temperate zones, fire would have been a more important innovation, especially in the winter.

Numerous bones of a wide variety of animals are characteristic of many middle Pleistocene sites, and at some occurrences, such as Torralba and Ambrona, the remains of large mammals are associated with stone tools. How much of these faunal materials are the result of hunting, scavenging, or incidental association is highly controversial.

No burials are known from this period, and claims for symbolic behavior have rested primarily on such evidence as pieces of red ocher found at some sites and the collection of unusual objects like rock crystals. The technological finesse involved in making large bifaces in the later Acheulean does suggest a strong sense of style, symmetry, and perhaps aesthetics. Although no representational art has been found in this period, a few sites, such as Bilzingsleben (Germany) and Pech de l'Azé (France) yielded bones with curious striations that do not appear to be utilitarian.

Neanderthal and Contemporaneous Hominid Populations (ca. 200-35 k.y.)   Beginning between 200 and 100 k.y. ago, and lasting until ca. 40-30 k.y. ago, new types of technologies emerged in many parts of the Old World. These are characterized by much less emphasis on the large bifacial tools of the Acheulean and more on recurrent types of flake tool (e.g. points, scrapers, denticulates) that were often made on flakes struck from prepared cores. Associated hominids in Europe, the Near East, and North Africa are almost exclusively Neanderthals, and later archaic *Homo sapiens* populations are known before 100 k.y. in Asia and eastern Africa, but in sub-Saharan Africa, at sites like Klasies River Mouth Cave (and Border Cave?) it appears that anatomically modern humans were associated with Middle Stone Age technologies well before 50 k.y. ago.

The diet of these Middle Paleolithic people probably varied greatly geographically: in western Europe, for example, common faunal remains include such animals as reindeer, horse, bison, cave bear, rhinoceros, deer, and mammoth; in South Africa such forms as Cape buffalo, *Pelorovis* (giant sheep), and eland are numerous. Although there is debate about the relative contribution of hunting and scavenging as a procurement mode for these animals, the high percentage of artifacts that appear to be hafted spear points suggests that at least smaller mammals were hunted with regularity.

The presence of Neanderthal burials in the prehistoric record, sometimes accompanied by what appear to be "grave goods," suggests that communication skills and symbolic behavior may have been more complex than among earlier hominid groups and that a concept of an afterlife may have been a cultural norm. Interestingly, there is little evidence for artwork at this time, aside from a few engraved, bored, or artificially shaped pieces, as well as ocher from some localities.

Homo sapiens sapiens (ca. 40-10 k.y.)   The Late Paleolithic hunter-gatherers of the later part of the last glaciation were anatomically modern humans, often exhibiting a much more·sophisticated technological repertoire than earlier Paleolithic populations.

Reconstruction of a Neanderthal activity area.

Reconstruction of an Upper Paleolithic campsite.

Blades tend to supersede flakes as the primary blank form for a wide range of implements, including end-scrapers, backed blades, burins, and *perçoirs*. Bone, antler, and ivory became more important during this time period and were worked into a wide range of implements including points, needles, and harpoons. The evidence of needles strongly implies sewn or stitched clothing.

Architectural features are more common during this period as well. Besides the occupation of caves and rock shelters open-air Late Paleolithic sites have been found in western Europe with stone or posthole patterns that suggest hut, tent, or teepee structures. In the Ukraine mammoth bones were widely used for building material as well as probable site furniture and fuel.

Hunters tended to concentrate on certain types of game animals, such as reindeer in southwestern France and red deer in northern Spain. Fish and shellfish also appear to have been important food-stuffs for the first time in many areas. Many archaeol-

ogists suspect that the organizational skills of these later Upper Paleolithic hunter-gatherers were much more sophisticated than those of earlier hominids, an important development being the predetermined scheduling of subsistence activities to coincide with the seasonal abundance of different resources.

In the Americas Paleoindian hunters were adept at bringing down mammoth and bison, as kill sites testify. In sub-Saharan Africa and much of the rest of the Old World Late Paleolithic people hunted large game like Cape buffalo, antelope, and hartebeest. The shift toward microlithic industries in many places in the late Pleistocene and early Holocene suggests the development of efficient archery technology.

Symbolic behavior flourished during this time period; evidence includes such art forms as mobiliary carvings, engravings, and occasional fired-clay figurines, monochrome and polychrome paintings on cave walls, and bas-relief carvings on cave and rock-shelter walls. A profusion of objects that appear to be elements of personal ornamentation also emerge at this time, as well as the continued use of ocher and other pigments. Burials appear to be more common than during Neanderthal times and are sometimes heavily endowed with grave goods, presumably for the afterlife.

The past 35 k.y. have seen little profound biological change in the human lineage, yet the pace of technological and subsistence innovation has increased at a tremendous rate with accumulated culture and perhaps better communications systems. The development of farming communities, pottery, metallurgy, and civilizations have all occurred in the last 10 k.y., to the point where human populations all over the world are changing their environments, sometimes to their own detriment, at an ever-accelerating pace.

See also ACHEULEAN; AFRICA; AMERICAS; ARCHAIC HOMO SAPIENS; ASIA (EASTERN); AUSTRALOPITHECUS; EARLY PALEOLITHIC; EUROPE; HOMO; HOMO ERECTUS; HOMO HABILIS; HOMO SAPIENS; LATE PALEOLITHIC; MIDDLE PALEOLITHIC; MOUSTERIAN; NEANDERTHALS; OLDOWAN; UPPER PALEOLITHIC. [N.T., K.S.]

Further Readings

Bordes, F. (1968) The Old Stone Age. New York: McGraw-Hill.

Campbell, B.G. (1987) Humankind Emerging, 5th ed. Boston: Little, Brown.

Coles, J.M., and Higgs, E.S. (1969) The Archaeology of Early Man. London: Faber and Faber.

Harris, J.W.K., and Yellen, J., eds. (1987) Papers dedicated to J. Desmond Clark. J. Hum. Evol. 15(8).

Lewin, R. (1984) Human Evolution: An Illustrated Introduction. New York: Freeman.

Pfeiffer, J. (1985) The Emergence of Humankind, 4th ed. New York: Harper and Row.

Wymer, J. (1982) The Palaeolithic Age. New York: St. Martin's.

PALEOMAGNETISM

History of the magnetic field of the earth. Most rocks contain sufficient iron-oxide minerals to make them slightly or strongly magnetic, and if the magnetism of these rocks was acquired when the rock formed then they may preserve a record of the orientation of the rock with respect to the earth's magnetic field at that time. Two principal uses have been made of paleomagnetic data in the study of hominid paleontology. The first is chronological and is based on the fact that the polarity of the global magnetic field has reversed many times at highly irregular intervals. The second is geographical and is based on the fact that the orientation and inclination of the field lines of the earth's magnetic field remain relatively fixed with respect to the poles of rotation while large parts of the outer part of the earth (the lithosphere) have

moved. This permits reconstruction of the latitudinal, if not longitudinal, position of landmasses at various times and also their rotation, if any, from their present orientation.

The earth's magnetic field has both horizontal and vertical components. If a balanced magnetized needle is left free to rotate about a vertical axis, one end seeks the north magnetic pole, revealing the horizontal component. If a balanced needle is magnetized and left free to rotate about a horizontal axis, it does not in general remain horizontal but fixes itself at a definite angle of inclination dependent on its latitude. If the declination and inclination of the field are mapped at a large number of points, the actual field is found to have a complex form. At the north magnetic pole the dip is vertically downward; at the magnetic equator the inclination is zero; and at the south magnetic pole the dip is vertically upward (in the convention of positive and negative magnetic moment). The magnetic equator is only approximately circular, and the magnetic poles are only approximately 180° apart. The actual magnetic field constantly changes in time, but it can be reasonably estimated by imagining a stationary dipole magnet situated at the earth's center. The calculated magnetic field produced by such a theoretical dipole is called the geomagnetic field. At any particular time the geomagnetic poles do not coincide with the actual magnetic pole, but, averaged over a long time period, the geomagnetic poles do coincide with the rotational poles. The long-term average of the earth's magnetic field is called the axial geocentric dipole field. The position of paleomagnetic poles is computed with respect to this model field. During periods when the magnetic field was reversed, the signs of the inclinations are reversed, so that at the north magnetic pole the dip direction is vertically upward, and for the south pole it is downward.

When igneous rocks cool from high temperatures in the earth's magnetic field, they acquire magnetization parallel to that of the field existing at that time. This is referred to as thermoremanent magnetization (TRM). Sedimentary rocks acquire magnetization as small magnetized particles settle through a water column and are aligned by the earth's field. This is detrital remanent magnetization (DRM). Again the magnetization direction is in approximate accord with the earth's field. In reddened sediments much of the magnetism is due to the presence of hematite, which acquires magnetism as it grows at low temperature. This is chemical remanent magnetization (CRM). Rocks also acquire magnetism at low temperatures (isothermal remanent magnetization; IRM) in the presence of large fields, such as those associated with lightning strikes, or in low magnetic fields over longer periods of time (viscous remanent magnetization; VRM).

If viscous effects for a sample are large, the sample is not suitable for paleomagnetic work. It is often possible to remove the effects of VRM or IRM (or "clean" the sample) by heating, or by subjecting the sample to alternating-frequency current, to recover the primary magnetization of a sample. The magnetization measured before any cleaning is the *natural remanent magnetization* (NRM).

The timing of reversals of geomagnetic polarity is reasonably well known from the Jurassic to the present. It is especially well known for the last 10 m.y. and can be used to refine the chronology at hominid fossil sites. The magnetic field is usually in one of two states—normal or reversed. Indeterminate directions are sometimes recorded but are not common. There is no discernible difference between the present normal period and any that occurred in the past. Consequently an initial estimate of the age of a rock sequence must be made before the polarity zonation can yield additional chronological information. This estimate may be based on radiometric dates or on paleontological age. If a stratigraphic section is extremely thick, and there is reason to believe that the rate of sedimentation was more or less constant, enough magnetozones may be encountered that their relative positions will allow a fit to the polarity-reversal scale with only rudimentary initial knowledge of the age. Because of the discontinuous nature of deposition in many continental settings where hominid fossils occur most frequently, care must be taken to establish that the sections studied represent more or less continuous deposition. Even so, short magnetozones may escape notice. In addition certain lithologies are more susceptible to remagnetization by viscous processes, and spurious magnetozones may be encountered. Such magnetozones have no chronological significance because they arise from effects other than field reversal and may cause erroneous inferences to be drawn.

The position of landmasses at various times in the past has been determined by paleomagnetic studies on the continents and by study of linear magnetic anomalies on the ocean floor. Times of contact between continents are established, as well as times of fragmentation, with obvious import for possible routes of primate dispersal. The paleolatitude, which emerges from remanent inclination analysis, must be considered when making paleoclimatic reconstructions. Also, marked changes in oceanic circulation are clearly related to changing continental configurations as documented by seafloor anomaly patterns. These circulatory changes are linked to other regional, and even global, climatic change.

See also GEOCHRONOMETRY; PLATE TECTONICS; STRATIGRAPHY. [F.H.B.]

Further Readings

Cox, A. (1973) Plate Tectonics and Geomagnetic Reversals. San Francisco: Freeman.

McElhinny, M.W. (1973) Paleomagnetism and Plate Tectonics. Cambridge: Cambridge University Press.

Strangway, D.W. (1970) History of the Earth's Magnetic Field. New York: McGraw-Hill.

PALEONTOLOGIC DATING *see* BIOCHRONOLOGY

PALEONTOLOGY

Study of ancient life by means of fossils. The field is conventionally divided into micropaleontology (concerned with fossil microorganisms), paleobotany (fossil plants, including spores and pollen), and paleozoology (fossil animals), which in turn includes invertebrate and vertebrate paleontology. Paleoanthropology lies at the interface of vertebrate paleontology, physical anthropology, and archaeology. Paleontology also embraces two parallel traditions: stratigraphic paleontology, which emphasizes the geological context of fossils and their applications in dating and correlating rocks, and paleobiology, which seeks to reconstruct the evolutionary history and life processes of the organisms represented by the fossils. Aspects of both traditions combine in the relatively new discipline of taphonomy, which studies the processes that lead to burial and fossilization of organic remains. Paleobiology has always owed much to neontology (the study of living organisms), especially to comparative anatomy and systematics. In certain cases even the methods of biochemistry and molecular biology can be applied to fossil remains. The comparison of cladograms and phylogenies derived from paleontology and from biochemical and molecular-genetic studies is also a currently active and fruitful field of research. Ultimately the chief importance of paleontology to evolutionary biology is that it provides the only direct record of evolution and phylogeny and the only means of discovering and studying large-scale patterns and processes of evolution.

See also ARCHAEOLOGY; EVOLUTION; MOLECULAR ANTHROPOLOGY; PALEOANTHROPOLOGY; PALEOBIOLOGY; PALEOBOTANY; PHYLOGENY; STRATIGRAPHY; SYSTEMATICS; TAPHONOMY. [D.P.D., R.L.B.]

PALEOPATHOLOGY

Study of disease in prehistory. In modern human populations environmental insults to a healthy state are often related to a person's way of life. For example, children attending schools in large numbers are more likely to contract infectious diseases, while farmers are particularly subject to fungal infection from spores in the soil. Extrapolating from contemporary and historical patterns of health and disease, and working with archaeological information. Paleopathologists can provide information about past lifeways and help measure adaptive success.

To achieve these goals paleopathologists must place the occurrence and frequency of disease in biocultural context. That is, they must interpret information on skeletal diseases in light of the archaeological, ecological, and demographic data available. Abnormally low bone density, for example, can be a measure of nutritional stress. When observed in adolescent and young adult females, however, it signals some association with reproduction, especially if other individuals in the population show no loss of bone and if faunal and floral remains suggest a relatively complete diet.

Biocultural considerations are also important in the initial diagnosis of disease and abnormalities in skeletal material, which often involves an epidemiological perspective to rule out competing diagnoses. This approach considers the type of change observed in the skeleton, where in the body disease is found, what segment of the population shows the pathology (age/sex profile), and what kind of structure and environmental context characterize that population. Skeletal evidence for tuberculosis, for example, can be easily confused with a fungal infection: both conditions tend to cause resorption of vertebral bodies. A soil-borne fungal infection, however, might affect young adults who work close to the soil more than any other age segment, while tuberculosis would threaten all age groups under urban conditions but probably the immature and the elderly most of all.

In addition to specific disease conditions (possible syphilis, leprosy, and tuberculosis are frequently studied in prehistoric populations) other nonspecific indicators of health stress are apparent in the skeleton. Some of these signs of ill health are the product of disruptions to growth processes, such as the so-called Harris lines and enamel hypoplasias, found in long bones and teeth, respectively. Harris lines show up as bands of dense bone in radiographs, because cells at a growth plate stop proliferating and "run in place" causing denser bone to occur at that site than would be expected. When growth resumes, these lines of growth arrest become visible. Such punctuations in bone deposition can also be observed in histological sections of bone. Similar disruptions during tooth formation show up as areas of the tooth crown that are malformed and susceptible to cavities (hypoplasias). Episodes of Harris lines and enamel hypoplasias provide some information

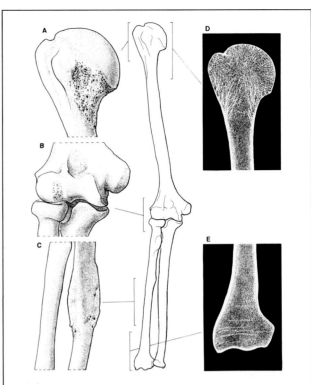

The field of paleopathology includes not only the study of obvious abnormalities, but also the analysis of normal variation that is related to the health status of a population. A) Infections are often distributed through the bloodstream, particularly affecting bone that is richly vascularized. In growing individuals metaphyses may be affected; in older persons muscle insertions may be common sites of infection. B) Osteoarthritis (OA) occurs commonly in older individuals, but is often localized to areas of joints that are stressed by habitual activities. "Atlatl elbow" refers to a pattern of OA observed in Amerindian groups that used throwing weapons. C) Fractures and other traumas can occur anywhere in the skeleton. Compression fractures on the front of the skull and midforearm breaks may signal interindividual conflict, while breaks near the wrist or ankle are more commonly the result of falls or accidents. D) All human populations show loss of bone with age. In radiographs bone loss can be seen as thin cortical bone or as spongy bone composed of sparse coarse trabeculae. When such loss occurs earlier in the life cycle than might normally be expected, it is considered to be evidence of poor health. E) Harris lines, or lines of growth arrest, occur when growth halts and then resumes. When observed in radiographs, they have traditionally been interpreted as evidence of poor health, due perhaps to episodic stress such as might occur with seasonal patterns of food availability. There is some indication, however, that they may instead signal that individuals were healthy and could recover from such stressful episodes.

about when in the life cycle environmental stresses had the most impact in a prehistoric population but are most useful when analyzed in conjunction with other possible indicators of stress, including degree of asymmetry and sexual dimorphism, overall body size, and periostitis.

Of all the environmental contexts that can affect health, diet or availability of essential nutrients may be the most significant. Many of the above signs of ill health, including the occurrence of specific infectious diseases, may be caused or exacerbated by nutrition in some way. The study of paleonutrition has therefore become an important focus within paleopathology. New techniques are available to quantify the biochemical composition of bones and evaluate the probable diet of an individual in prehistory. These focus on whether trace minerals, such as strontium, are present in high concentrations, as one would expect from a vegetarian diet of strontium-containing foods, and on whether carbon isotopes present in domesticated plants, such as maize, indicate dependence on such plants. These techniques are currently under intensive reevaluation.

In several parts of the world, such as the mountains of Peru and the deserts of Egypt, environmental conditions as well as treatment of the dead have favored preservation of soft and hard tissues. The study of mummies can yield even more detailed information than is available from skeletal studies. A tuberculosis bacterium cyst was discovered in the lung of an Incan mummy, for example, offering proof of the existence of pre-Columbian tuberculosis that can stand up under the scrutiny even of contemporary diagnosticians.

See also ARCHAEOLOGY; BONE BIOLOGY; FORENSIC ANTHROPOLOGY; SKELETON. [C.J.D.]

Further Readings

Brothwell, D.R. (1981) Digging Up Bones. Ithaca, N.Y.: Cornell University Press.

Cohen, M.N., and Armelagos, G.J., eds. (1984) Paleopathology at the Origins of Agriculture. New York: Academic.

Ortner, D.J., and Putschar, W.G.J. (1981) Identification of Pathological Conditions in Human Skeletal Remains. Washington, D.C.: Smithsonian Contributions to Anthropology, 28.

Steinbock, R.T. (1976) Paleopathological Diagnosis and Interpretation. Springfield, Ill.: Thomas.

PALIKAO *see* TIGHENIF

PAN *see* APE; HOMININAE

PAPIO *see* CERCOPITHECINAE

PAPIONINI *see* CERCOPITHECINAE

PARACATARRHINI *see* CATARRHINI; PARAPITHECIDAE

PARACOLOBUS *see* COLOBINAE

PARADAPIS *see* ADAPIDAE

PARADOLICHOPITHECUS *see* CERCOPITHECINAE

PARANTHROPUS

Genus name employed by some paleoanthropologists in reference to the "robust" australopithecine fossils from the South African sites of Kromdraai and Swartkrans (*Paranthropus robustus*) and to the "hyper-robust" australopithecine fossils from Plio-Pleistocene sites in eastern Africa (*Paranthropus boisei*).

The name *Paranthropus*, which means literally "beside man" or "next to man," was coined by R. Broom in 1938, when he described the first australopithecine specimen from the site of Kromdraai as belonging to the taxon *Paranthropus robustus*. Subsequently discovered australopithecine remains from Kromdraai and the site of Swartkrans were referred to *Paranthropus* by Broom, who considered that they were so distinct from the australopithecine fossils from Taung, Sterkfontein, and Makapansgat as to warrant their separation as a separate subfamily, the Paranthropinae. In 1959 a massively built australopithecine cranium from Bed I of Olduvai Gorge was attributed by L.S.B. Leakey to a novel taxon, *Zinjanthropus boisei*. J.T. Robinson was quick to recognize that this specimen had close affinities to the South African forms from Kromdraai and Swartkrans and proposed that *Zinjanthropus* was a junior synonym of *Paranthropus*. Robinson maintained that *Paranthropus* and *Australopithecus* (the "gracile" forms from Taung, Sterkfontein, and Makapansgat) represented separate phyletic lines of evolution, that they occupied different adaptive zones rather than different aspects of the same adaptive zone, and that therefore their generic separation was fully justified.

Subsequent studies by several workers, like P.V. Tobias and M.H. Wolpoff, in which all australopithecines were viewed as comprising a single evolutionary grade of organization, questioned the generic distinctiveness of *Paranthropus*. These "grade"-orientated, phenetic studies influenced opinion such that at present most students of (and all textbooks on) hominid evolution regard *Paranthropus* as a junior synonym of *Australopithecus*. Indeed, some workers have even argued that all australopithecine fossils simply represent size and/or temporal variants within the range of variation of a single anagenetic species lineage.

Despite the overwhelming scholastic influence of

this "grade" paradigm upon anthropologists a strong body of evidence has accumulated indicating that the *Paranthropus* specimens possess a host of derived morphological specializations that probably reflect significant functional differences between them and other early hominid taxa. These characteristic craniodental characters are almost certainly related to trophic (i.e. dietary) parameters, but because a number of workers have argued that these morphological features could have evolved from an *Australopithecus africanus* or an *A. africanus*-like ancestor there appears to have been a general reluctance to recognize that the "robust" and "hyper-robust" forms warrant separate generic status.

Even if strictly cladistic questions of sister-group relationships are put aside for the moment, there is every reason to admit *Paranthropus* as a valid genus, for it is almost certain that the unique specializations that these specimens share are testament to their having been members of a monophyletic group. That is, the *Paranthropus* specimens display so many craniodental features distinguishing them from representatives of other hominid taxa that there is good reason to believe that they constitute a unique and specialized evolutionary lineage. Thus J.T. Robinson and, more recently, R. J. Clarke, for example, have argued that the question of the ancestry of *Paranthropus* does not necessarily bear upon the question of its generic distinctiveness, because it comprises a group of highly specialized hominids. They have argued that the amount of difference between *Paranthropus* and other hominid taxa is "of considerably greater than specific value," as judged by modern mammalian taxonomic standards, and that therefore *Paranthropus* should be accorded separate generic status.

Along these same lines both Robinson and Clarke have argued that since the morphological differences between *Paranthropus* and *Australopithecus* are notably greater than those separating *Australopithecus* and *Homo*, *Paranthropus* had probably been separate from *Australopithecus* for a longer time than had *Homo*. As Clarke stated: ". . . if it is valid to place *Homo habilis* in a genus distinct from *Australopithecus*, it is far more valid to separate *Paranthropus* from *Australopithecus*." Indeed, Robinson has espoused the opinion that *Australopithecus* is a junior synonym of *Homo* inasmuch as they form part of the same evolutionary lineage, while *Paranthropus* retains its generic identity because it forms a separate evolutionary lineage.

Robinson's view was adopted by T.R. Olson, who has argued on purely cladistic grounds that the *Homo* and *Paranthropus* lineages were separate evolutionary entities, already recognizable by mid-Pliocene times in the Hadar and Laetoli hominid samples. Olson's argument is that the specimens comprising the hypodigm of *Australopithecus afarensis* are actually recognizable as belonging to the separate *Homo* and *Paranthropus* lineages, and that since *Australopithecus africanus* is a phylogenetic ancestor of *Homo* the genus name *Australopithecus* should be regarded as a junior synonym of *Homo*. Thus Olson has proposed that some of the Hadar and Laetoli fossils belong to the genus *Homo*, while others belong to the genus *Paranthropus*.

The question of the phylogenetic derivation of *Paranthropus* has recently been brought into stark light by A.C. Walker's discovery of a nearly complete, albeit nearly edentulous, cranium from the Pliocene sediments (ca. 2.5 m.y) on the western side of Lake Turkana. This specimen, which shows several characters that apparently attest to its "paranthropine" affinities, has been interpreted by Walker and several of his colleagues as representing an early specimen of *Paranthropus* (=*Australopithecus*) *boisei*. They have argued that this specimen reveals that *P.* (or *A.*) *boisei* evolved from *A. afarensis*, while the South African *P.* (or *A.*) *robustus* evolved independently from *A. africanus*. Should this unlikely phylogenetic scheme prove true, it would mean that not all of the "robust" forms could be assigned to the genus *Paranthropus*. The generic name *Paranthropus* could still be considered as valid in reference to the South African forms, as they represent a significant, specialized departure from the *Homo* (including *A. africanus*) lineage. While

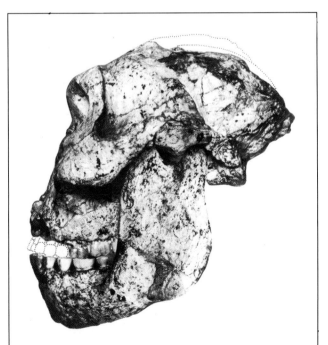

Composite skull of *Paranthropus* from Swartkrans. (From Tattersall, 1970.)

the generic name *Paranthropus* could still retain its validity under this scheme, however, there can be no doubt that in this case the genus name *Zinjanthropus* would have to be applied to the new hominid cranium from the western side of Lake Turkana and to the "hyper-robust" specimens from Tanzania, Kenya, and Ethiopia that have been accorded recognition as *Paranthropus* (or *A.*) *boisei*. In other words, two distinct genera of "robust" and "hyper-robust" australopithecines would have to be recognized.

It is nevertheless much more economical to interpret this new fossil cranium as belonging to the *Paranthropus* clade and to conclude that both *P. boisei* and *P. robustus* are more closely related to one another and to the taxon represented by this new fossil than to any other hominid species. Should this arrangement be accepted, there can be little doubt about the necessity to use the generic name *Paranthropus*. While this is similar to the arrangement proposed by Olson, it differs in that it does not necessarily recognize "paranthropine" elements in the Hadar and Laetoli hominid samples. Rather, these fossils, which appear to represent a single species group and which do not possess any recognizable "paranthropine" synapomorphies, will likely have to be assigned a new taxonomic designation.

Regardless of the interpretation of this new fossil find in relation to hominid phylogeny, there can be little doubt that the "robust" and "hyper-robust" australopithecines are so distinctive in comparison with other Plio-Pleistocene hominid taxa as to warrant separate generic status. These fossils share an extensive suite of unique cranial and dental features that must surely attest to their common ancestry and that are probably related to trophic specializations involving the generation and distribution of powerful masticatory forces.

See also **AUSTRALOPITHECUS; AUSTRALOPITHECUS BOISEI; AUSTRALOPITHECUS ROBUSTUS**. [F.E.G.]

Further Readings

Clarke, R.J. (1985) *Australopithecus* and early *Homo* in southern Africa. In E. Delson (ed.): Ancestors: The Hard Evidence. New York: Liss, pp. 171–177.

Olson, T.R. (1981) Basicranial morphology of the extant hominoids and Pliocene hominids: the new material from the Hadar Formation, Ethiopia, and its significance in early human evolution and taxonomy. In C.B. Stringer (ed.): Aspects of Human Evolution. London: Taylor and Francis, pp. 99–128.

Rak, Y. (1983) The Australopithecine Face. New York: Academic.

Robinson, J.T. (1954) The genera and species of the Australopithecinae. Am. J. Phys. Anthropol. *12*:181–200.

Tobias, P.V. (1967) The cranium and maxillary dentition of *Australopithecus (Zinjanthropus) boisei*. In L.S.B. Leakey (ed.): Olduvai Gorge, Vol. 2. Cambridge: Cambridge University Press.

Walker, A.C., Leakey, R.E.F., Harris, J.M., and Brown, F.H. (1986) 2.5-Myr *Australopithecus boisei* from west of Lake Turkana, Kenya. Nature 322:517–522.

PARAPAPIO *see* CERCOPITHECINAE

PARAPHYLY *see* MONOPHYLY

PARAPITHECIDAE

Family of African Primates that includes the oldest, and most primitive monkeys. As such they are the key to understanding the origins of the anthropoid primates: the group that includes New and Old World monkeys, apes, and humans. Parapithecids are found only in rocks of Oligocene age in the Fayum Province (Egypt), in an area of badlands at the eastern edge of the Sahara Desert. As currently understood, Parapithecidae includes the following genera and species: *Apidium phiomense*, *A. moustafai*, *Parapithecus fraasi*, *Simonsius grangeri*, and *Qatrania wingi*.

History of Study

The first recovered parapithecid was *Apidium phiomense*, a name approximately translating into "little sacred bull of the Fayum." A single jaw of a young *A. phiomense* was found by the professional collector R. Markgraf early in 1907 and described by H.F. Osborn. Osborn suspected that it had primate affinities or that it was a hoofed mammal—hence the name. Later in the same year Markgraf collected a more complete, adult lower jaw of a second kind of monkey for the Stuttgart Museum. This find was described by M. Schlosser in 1910 and 1911 as *Parapithecus fraasi*, meaning "next-to-an-ape," and he erected the family name Parapithecidae for it. No other specimens of *Apidium* or *Parapithecus* were recognized or recovered until 1961.

These two specimens were difficult to relate to modern primates and remained of uncertain evolutionary relationship throughout the 50 years that followed their description. Osborn could not decide whether *Apidium* might be an odd sort of pig or a primate, while others considered it a possible archaic ungulate, a monkey, or an ancestor of the extinct Italian primate *Oreopithecus*. *Parapithecus* was never questioned as a primate, but its systematic position was widely debated partly because of damage to the specimen at the front of the jaw with possible loss of teeth and tooth sockets. This damage led to misunderstanding of the numbers and kinds of its teeth, information that would have been useful in judging its affinities. Opinions about its closest relatives thus ranged from tarsiers to monkeys, apes, or even humans.

No record has survived of the precise stratigraphic levels from which Markgraf recovered *Apidium phiomense* or *Parapithecus fraasi*. That both come from upper levels of the Jebel Qatrani Formation in the Fayum was clarified only by the collection of more specimens in the past 25 years.

Many new finds from the Fayum badlands have been made since 1961. It is now clear that parapithecids are anthropoids, although to which anthropoid group they belong is open to interpretation. E.L. Simons described two new species of parapithecids, the first in 1962, *Apidium moustafai*. In 1974 he named a second, *Parapithecus grangeri*. P.D. Gingerich in 1981 recognized *P. grangeri* to be a distinct genus he named *Simonsius*. Simons demonstrated that all these species are closely related and assigned them to Parapithecidae. In 1981 another new kind of parapithecid primate, *Qatrania*, described by Simons and R.F. Kay, was recovered from the oldest level of the Jebel Qatrani Formation.

Age of the Parapithecids

All parapithecid fossils come from the Jebel Qatrani Formation, which conformably overlies the marine and fluvial Qasr el Sagha Formation of late Eocene age (ca. 37 m.y.). The top of the Jebel Qatrani Formation was eroded and then capped by volcanic flows variously dated at 25, 27, and, by a recent study, 31 m.y. This would bracket the Fayum fauna and its parapithecids as being early Oligocene in age. Faunal comparisons with Europe are of limited value for determining the age of these sediments more precisely, because most Fayum genera are endemic. The few genera that are shared between Europe and the Fayum, however, are all known from the early Oligocene of Europe, in agreement with the geochronologic evidence. Not all parapithecid species were contemporaries. *Qatrania* is the oldest, from near the bottom of the Jebel Qatrani Formation, and could be nearer 35 m.y. old. *Apidium moustafai* comes from a middle stratigraphic level in the formation; the other species are from slightly higher in the stratigraphic section.

Parapithecid Habitat and Adaptations

From all that can be learned concerning their anatomy and habitat, it is clear that parapithecids were monkeylike animals that resembled living squirrel monkeys from South and Central America in size, appearance, and probably habits. Parapithecid fossils come from continental sediments deposited by rivers, lakes, and streams in an area of low topographic relief. The Fayum region during the Oligocene, as evinced by sedimentological evidence, associated paleofloras, and vertebrate remains, had seasonal rainfall and was humid, subtropical to tropical, and densely forested (along the major streams at least). It is probable that there were more open savannas in interstream areas.

From the size of the teeth and skeletal elements parapithecids were much smaller than any living African monkeys and closer in size to the smaller living New World monkeys. *Qatrania*, the smallest, was as small as a marmoset, ca. 300 gm. *Apidium* was larger, between 700 and 1,300 gm. *Simonsius* was the largest, probably weighing up to 1,800 gm., the size of *Cebus*, the capucin monkey.

Not all the parapithecids are well known anatomically. What we know of their locomotion is based principally on study of bones of *Apidium*. To judge from the structure of its limbs and pelvis *Apidium* was an agile, saltatory quadruped and highly arboreal. Indirect evidence suggests *Simonsius grangeri* may have spent more time on the ground. This animal has very high-crowned cheek teeth, a feature common in living ground-dwelling Old World monkeys. (Grit in food found on the ground subjects the cheek teeth to greater wear; higher molar crowns are selectively advantageous for resisting such wear.)

Apidium, *Parapithecus*, and *Qatrania* species have low, rounded cheek-tooth cusps resembling the teeth of living fruit-eating monkeys and apes. Cheek-tooth enamel of *Apidium* was relatively quite thick. Thick

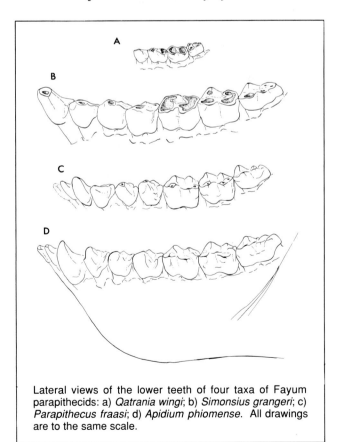

Lateral views of the lower teeth of four taxa of Fayum parapithecids: a) *Qatrania wingi*; b) *Simonsius grangeri*; c) *Parapithecus fraasi*; d) *Apidium phiomense*. All drawings are to the same scale.

enamel suggests that *Apidium* species may have eaten hard nuts or seeds. *Simonsius grangeri* has cheek teeth with sharper cutting edges; these imply a greater leaf component in its diet, judged by analogy with the structure of cheek teeth among living leaf-eating mammals.

Apidium had projecting canines and small, vertically implanted lower incisors set in a lower jaw fused at the midline in front. Thus this early group was already essentially anthropoidlike in using its incisors and canines for incision or separation of a bite of food. This differs from living strepsirhines, which have lower canines and incisors positioned in a comb for use mainly in fur grooming or bark scraping, not in incision. *Simonsius* is strikingly specialized by having lost its lower incisors. The projecting, robust, blunt lower canines of this animal touch one another in the symphyseal midline. Such a dental design would have served as a powerful puncturing device, although the functional details are unclear since the upper front teeth of *Simonsius* are still unknown. This dental specialization is unknown in any other primate. *Parapithecus fraasi* may have begun this specialization with the loss of permanent incisors and retention of just a single deciduous lower incisor as an adult. It is just as likely, however, that this species had two lower incisors in each jaw half, thereby resembling *Apidium*. The only known specimen of *Parapithecus fraasi* has symphyseal damage and may have lost one incisor from each side of the jaw post mortem.

The relatively small size of the eye sockets of parapithecids place them among daytime active (diurnal) mammals, as are the living anthropoids, but distinct from many prosimians with relatively large eyes (and eye sockets) and nocturnal habits. Probably the closest living ecological parallels to the parapithecid primates are found among South American monkeys.

Anthropoid Status of Parapithecidae

Many cranial and skeletal parts are known for *Apidium* and some for *Simonsius*. These show that parapithecids had reached the anthropoid or "monkey" grade of organization. Parapithecids are more monkeylike than all primates of the previous Eocene epoch (the geological period ca. 54-35 m.y. ago). They resemble anthropoids (apes, humans, and Old and New World monkeys), and not Eocene primates or modern Madagascar lemurs, in having reduced olfactory lobes of the brain, an anthropoid configuration in bony-ear structure (although the ectotympanic is not tubular as in all extant catarrhines), a bony partition between the eye socket and the space behind it that houses the jaw muscles (postorbital closure), closely packed cheek teeth, spatulate inci-

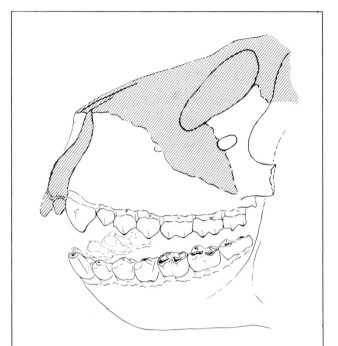

Reconstruction of the face and mandible of *Simonsius grangeri* in lateral view. Anatomical features of note include postorbital closure and symphyseal fusion, indicating anthropoid status. Also, the orbits were small, indicating diurnal habits.

sors (except *Simonsius*), and projecting canines. This advanced combination of characteristics has led all authorities to accept their status as the oldest undoubted anthropoids.

A more difficult and unresolved question concerns parapithecid relationships within Anthropoidea. Opinion is divided as to whether parapithecids are more closely related to the Old World (catarrhine) or New World (platyrrhine) branch of anthropoids, or are an entirely separate early branch.

On current evidence the least likely placement of the Parapithecidae would be as the sister group of living Old World monkeys, the Cercopithecidae. Although there are a few similarities between the molars and foot bones of cercopithecids and some parapithecids, the balance of evidence suggests that these similarities are caused by evolutionary parallelism. Otherwise many unusual anatomical characteristics of living Old World monkeys and apes, but not of parapithecids, must have evolved in parallel. Such a list would include independent loss of the front premolars, shortening of the face, separate ossification of a tubelike extension of the bony ring (ectotympanic) that supports the eardrum, and features of the limb bones.

A few paleontologists suggest that parapithecids are in or near the ancestry of New World monkeys. This is not as farfetched as would seem from the present wide oceanic separation of Africa and South

America. In the Oligocene the continents were closer together and island chains may have intervened between them. Such a view gains support from the adaptive similarity between parapithecids and living small Neotropical monkeys. Parapithecids also show many anatomical resemblances to platyrrhines not seen in modern catarrhines (human, apes, or Old World monkeys). For example, the tympanic bone of the ear is ringlike, resembling platyrrhines, rather than tubular as in catarrhines. What is important, however, is that most of these similarities seem to be holdovers from the last common ancestor of both these groups and do not indicate ancestral-descendant relationships. Primitive features held in common do not indicate a special genetic relationship. On the other hand parapithecids have no special or advanced similarities with platyrrhines that would place them exclusively in the line of platyrrhine ancestry.

The likeliest hypothesis is that the parapithecids are an early side-branch of anthropoid evolution. In other words, early Anthropoidea differentiated into two stocks, one leading to both platyrrhines and catarrhines and the other to parapithecids. This would explain the many persistently primitive features of skeleton, face, and dentition of parapithecids lost in the lineage leading to living Old and New World anthropoids. The conclusion that parapithecids are a group of primitive anthropoids in Africa 10 m.y. before the first record of platyrrhines lends support to the hypothesis of an African origin for that South American group.

See also ANTHROPOIDEA; CATARRHINI; FAYUM; OLIGOCENE; PLATYRRHINI; PROPLIOPITHECIDAE; TEETH. [R.F.K.]

Further Readings

Fleagle, J.G., and Kay, R.F. (1988) The phylogenetic position of the Parapithecidae. J. Hum. Evol. *16*:483–531.

Fleagle, J.G., and Simons, E.L. (1979) Anatomy of the bony pelvis in parapithecid primates. Folia Primatol. *31*:176–186.

Simons, E.L. (1986) *Parapithecus grangeri* of the African Oligocene: an archaic catarrhine without lower incisors. J. Hum. Evol. *15*:205–213.

Simons, E.L., and Kay, R.F. (1983) *Qatrania*, a new basal anthropoid primate from the Fayum Oligocene of Egypt. Nature *304*:624–626.

Szalay, F.S., and Delson, E. (1979) Evolutionary History of the Primates. New York: Academic.

PARAPITHECOIDEA *see* PARAPITHECIDAE

PARAPITHECUS *see* PARAPITHECIDAE

PARAUSTRALOPITHECUS *see* AUSTRALOPITHECUS

PAROMOMYIDAE

Family grouping that unites some of the most ancient and in many ways most primitive archaic primates. Only a few of these tiny primates were in the size range of the common brown rat; most were smaller. Although some of the included species have such advanced characters as reduced dental formulae and new dental specializations, and probably possessed other unknown unique features, the last common ancestor of the paromomyids, classifiable in this family, was probably the first, most primitive, primate—the "protoprimate."

The four recognized groups within the Paromomyidae cannot be unequivocally related to one another within the family. They are recognized as four tribes, awaiting new evidence and understanding, after which they may be united in two or more subfamilies. The four tribes are the Purgatoriini, the Paromomyini, the Micromomyini, and the Navajoviini. Members of this assemblage have been, at various times in the past, referred to the Microsyopidae, which some paleontologists still believe to be primates.

The tribe Purgatoriini is based on the genus *Purgatorius* from the early Paleocene and doubtfully also from the Cretaceous. The dentition is relatively well known for *Purgatorius unio*, dentally the most primitive primate. In this animal the trigonids of the lower teeth are still tall and prominent, in spite of the characteristically primate widening of the back part of the lower molars, the talonid. The early Paleocene *Purgatorius*, along with an equally ancient, still undescribed, plesiadapid from the famous Purgatory Hill locality, hint at the important dietary beginnings of the Primates. Although the full eutherian dental formula appears to have been present in *Purgatorius* (three incisors, canine, four premolars, and three molars in each half of the jaws), the wide talonids suggest the evolution of extensive crushing function in addition to the ancient cutting ability of the trigonids. A mixed diet of insects and fruit was likely the diet of the first arboreal archontans and primates.

The tribe Paromomyini is a much more varied assemblage of species, divided into the subtribes Palaechthonina and Paromomyina. Palaechthoninans (*Palaechthon*, *Plesiolestes*, and *Palenochtha*) are not far removed from *Purgatorius* in morphology, and probably in lifestyle, but they have lost one of the incisors (probably the third pair) and slightly enlarged the central incisors to form a kind of spoon or scoop presumably useful for small animals that may have been exploiting the rich and widespread tropical and subtropical forests of the Paleocene. A crushed skull of *Palaechthon* is the earliest indication of some of the proportions of the facial portion to the

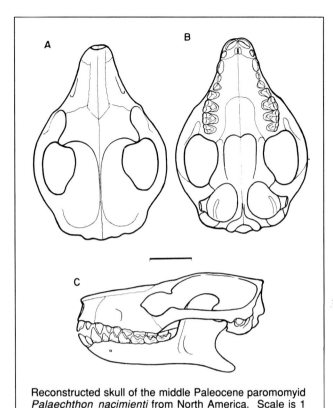

Reconstructed skull of the middle Paleocene paromomyid *Palaechthon nacimienti* from North America. Scale is 1 cm.

neural one in an early primate. As in the much bigger *Plesiadapis*, the smaller and older paromomyid also shows opossumlike proportions of its braincase to the rest of the cranium.

Paromomyinans (*Paromomys, Ignacius,* and *Phenacolemur*; the latter including the concepts *Elwynella* and *Arcius*, which are based on valid species but are judged not to be generically distinguishable from *Phenacolemur*) represent a distinct radiation of the archaic primates that managed to survive well into the late Eocene of North America. They emphasize their central pairs of incisors to an extreme (although they never became evergrowing or rodentlike) and reduce the teeth between these and their last premolars. The square and relatively flat molars, with their trigonids reduced almost to the talonid level, strongly suggest a considerable fruit component in their diet. They might have occupied a range of ecological niches not dissimilar to the burramyid and phalangerid phalangeriform marsupials of Australia and New Guinea.

The tribe Micromomyini (*Micromomys* and *Tinimomys*) contains the smallest known primates, smaller than the living mouse lemur. These astonishing early offshoots of the ancestral primate stock enlarged their fourth lower premolar into tall slicing devices and also had enlarged lower incisors. The sharp and prominent antemolar dentition is emphasized to such a degree at the expense of the molars

that it seems certain that micromomyinans, at least *Micromomys*, were thoroughly insectivorous, like some of the small galagos.

The tribe Navajoviini (*Navajovius* and *Berruvius*) consists of small, relatively nondescript (as far as the teeth are concerned) primates that occur in the late Paleocene and early Eocene. Both the North American *Navajovius* and the European *Berruvius* possess enlarged central incisors and molars that are assumed to have facilitated a primarily insectivorous diet. The exact affinities of the micromomyinans are not known. Their closest ties are probably with the more primitive palaechthoninans, and not with microsyopids as several workers have suggested.

See also PLESIADAPIFORMES. [F.S.S.]

Further Readings

Szalay, F.S., and Delson, E. (1979) Evolutionary History of the Primates. New York: Academic.

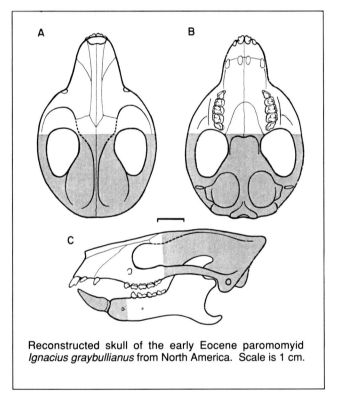

Reconstructed skull of the early Eocene paromomyid *Ignacius graybullianus* from North America. Scale is 1 cm.

PAROMOMYIFORMES *see* PLESIADAPIFORMES

PAROMOMYOIDEA

Superfamily of the archaic primate suborder Plesiadapiformes, of which Plesiadapoidea is the other member. Usually two family-group taxa, Paromomyidae and Picrodontidae, are included in the superfamily Paromomyoidea. This is not the most satisfactory arrangement, because various members of the group are only minimally known. This superfamily in fact represents only a convenient grouping of those archaic primates that are not admissible into the more clearly diagnosable Plesiadapoidea.

See also **PLESIADAPIFORMES.** [F.S.S.]

PAROMOMYS *see* PAROMOMYIDAE

PAŞALAR *see* NEAR EAST; PONGINAE

PASTORALISM *see* HUNTER-GATHERERS; NEOLITHIC

PATAGONIA

Southern South America including both Argentina and Chile. This region is famous for the rich Mesozoic and Cenozoic fossil sites first explored by the Ameghino brothers near the turn of the century. Its eastern portion is now a dry, steppelike grassland lashed by high winds coming off of the South Atlantic, but warm, moist forests existed there during parts of the Tertiary. Fossil ceboid monkeys come from Colhuehuapian early Miocene (21–19 m.y.) sites (Gaiman, Sacanana) and a series of Santacrucian late early Miocene (18–15 m.y.) sites (Pinturas, Rio Gallegos, Monte Leon, Monte Observacion). This fauna does not overlap with that from La Venta (Colombia) taxonomically, probably due to both temporal and ecological factors.

See also **CEBINAE; LA VENTA; PITHECIINAE.** [A.L.R.]

PATAUD, ABRI *see* ABRI PATAUD

PAUWELS' LAW *see* LAWS

PAVLOV

Complex of Late Paleolithic open-air sites (Pavlov I and II) at the foot of the Pavlov Hills, ca. 3 km. to the southeast of Dolní Věstonice in Moravia (Czechoslovakia). These sites have yielded a huge inventory of stone and bone tools, portable art, and fragments of fired clay. Assemblages from the site were used to define the Pavlov industry, which researchers interpret as a regional variant of the Eastern Gravettian technocomplex. Features at Pavlov include remains of round, oval, and oblong surface and semisubterranean dwellings as well as a burial of an adult male. The occupations are dated to ca. 25,000 B.P.

See also **DOLNÍ VĚSTONICE; PŘEDMOSTI.** [O.S.]

PEBBLE TOOL *see* STONE-TOOL MAKING

PECH DE L'AZÉ

The skull and mandible of a Neanderthal child were excavated from this cave in France in 1909, but they were not published in detail for many years after. The child may have been only ca. two years old at death, which has led to much discussion about its development and the presence or absence of Neanderthal characters. The face and cranial vault already show some Neanderthal features, and brain volume was probably large by the standards of modern two-year-olds (ca. 1,150 ml.).

See also **NEANDERTHALS.** [C.B.S.]

PEKING MAN *see* HOMO ERECTUS; ZHOUKOUDIAN

PELYCODUS *see* NOTHARCTIDAE

PENINJ

Northern Tanzanian stratified sequence of early Pleistocene age, ca. 1.3 m.y. by K-Ar and paleomagnetic dating. Located 50 mi. northeast of Olduvai near the western shore of Lake Natron, this early Acheulean site was discovered in 1959 and was studied by G. Isaac. In 1964 K. Kimeu discovered a nearly complete mandible of *Australopithecus boisei.* Isaac and M. Taieb returned to the site in the late 1970s to reassess the site but found no further hominids.

[T.D.W.]

PERÇOIR *see* AWL

PERICONODON *see* ADAPIDAE

PÉRIGORD

Medieval province of southwestern France centering on the Dordogne River and its tributaries (e.g. the Isle and the Vézère). This region of limestone plateaus, caves, and narrow, cliff-lined valleys is encompassed today in large part by the modern *département* of the Dordogne, and is known for one of the greatest concentrations of Paleolithic paintings, engravings, and occupation sites of any area in the world, concentrated within 50 km. of the village of Les-Eyzies-de-Tayac. The earliest systematic excavation of Paleolithic sites took place here, leading to the designation of many as type sites of Paleolithic industries,

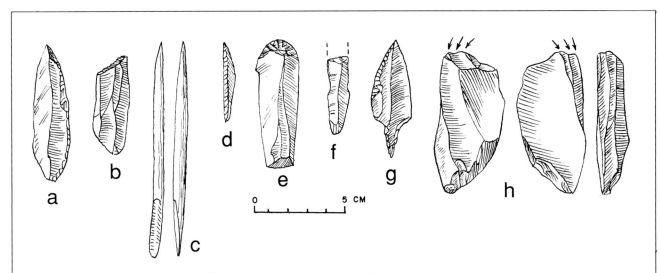

Tools of various stages of the French Perigordian. a) Chatelperron point (Perigordian I); b) obliquely truncated blade (Perigordian I); c) beveled-base bone point (Perigordian VI); d) microgravette point (Perigordian VI); e) end-scraper (Perigordian VI); f) Noailles burin (Perigordian Vc); g) Font Robert point (Perigordian Va); h) Raysse burin (three views, Perigordian Vc). For a gravette point (Perigordian IV) see GRAVETTIAN.

such as La Micoque, La Madeleine, La Gravette, and Le Moustier.

See also Abri Pataud; Aurignacian; Bordes, François; Cro-Magnon; Early Paleolithic; Gravettian; La Chaise; La Ferrassie; Laugerie Sites; Le Moustier; Magdalenian; Micoquian; Middle Paleolithic; Mousterian; Paleolithic Image; Pech de l'Azé; Perigordian; Peyrony, Denis; Regourdou; Solutrean; Tayacian; Upper Paleolithic. [A.S.B.]

PERIGORDIAN

Early Upper Paleolithic industrial complex of central and southwestern France (with brief extensions to northeastern Spain and the Paris basin), 34–32 k.y. and 28–21 k.y., named after the Périgord region at its geographical center. In 1933 D. Peyrony distinguished early Upper Paleolithic industries with stone points created by abrupt retouch or backing, then known as "lower" and "upper" Aurignacian, from the Aurignacian proper, or "middle" Aurignacian, with its bone points, thick, carinate scrapers and burins created by lamellar retouch. Like Peyrony's redefined Aurignacian the Perigordian consisted of five stages and represented a "parallel phylum" to the Aurignacian, with the two "phyla" interpreted as the lithic signatures of two different ethnic groups who coexisted in the same area for ca. 15 k.y.

On the basis of assemblages from the Dordogne sites of La Gravette, La Ferrassie, and Laugerie Haute Peyrony defined his five stages as follows: Perigordian I, levels with large, relatively broad backed points or knives known as Châtelperron points (La Ferrassie E); Perigordian II, with small semiabruptly retouched bladelets known as Dufour bladelets (La Ferrassie E'); Perigordian III, with truncated blades and small backed "Gravette" points and bladelets (Laugerie Haute, base of sequence); Perigordian IV, with leaf-shaped points (*flèchettes*) and large Gravette points (La Gravette); and Perigordian V, in three successive facies represented at La Ferrassie Levels J, K, and L, respectively: Va, with tanged leaf-shaped "Font-Robert" points, Vb with truncated blade segments, and Vc with diminutive multiple-truncation burins ("Noailles" burins) and flat-faced ("Raysse") burins.

This scheme has undergone several revisions. The original Perigordian II and its "type fossil," the Dufour bladelet, have been relegated to the Aurignacian on the basis of such assemblages as Les Vachons (Charente). The Perigordian III, which was the only Perigordian originally recognized at Laugerie Haute, was found stratified *above* the Perigordian Vc at the Abri Pataud just across the Vézère River and was redesignated Perigordian VI. F. Bordes argued that the Protomagdalenian of Laugerie Haute should be relabeled "Perigordian VII." Finally, the "type fossils" of the Perigordian Va, b, and c were found in differing combinations and stratigraphic order at Le Flageolet (Dordogne), which suggested that these differences are not the signatures of different ethnic groups or stages of cultural evolution. As a result of these changes, which have largely eliminated the Middle Perigordian phases of Peyrony's scheme, the bulk of the Aurignacian now occupies a hiatus between the Lower Perigordian (or Chatelperronian) and the Upper (IV, V, and VI), with a minimal period of chronological overlap at each end. The "parallel phyla" concept has become hard to sustain.

Although the technique of creating points through backing is widespread in Europe from 28 to 20 k.y., other specific hallmarks of Perigordian industries are lacking outside the core area, so that backed-point industries in eastern France and other countries are generally referred to as "Gravettian." Châtelperron-like assemblages, however, are found in Spain (Cueva Morin), and industries comparable with the Perigordian V in Italy. Some authors have thus suggested that one or both of these industries, which have few or no "Gravettes," be removed from the Perigordian technocomplex and designated separately as Chatelperronian and Noaillian.

Upper Perigordian industries are associated with cold but fluctuating conditions. Faunal remains are dominated by reindeer, with horse and red deer increasing in warmer intervals and at the extreme south of the area. Trade networks are reflected in widespread use of nonlocal flint and in the occurrence of marine shells and ivory, up to 400 km. from probable sources. Bone tools, although not common, are carefully shaped and well polished and several female (or "Venus") figurines are associated with Perigordian industries at Pataud, Tursac, Laussel, Lespugue, and Brassempouy. Animal outlines were engraved on stone slabs and on utilitarian objects, and a few decorated caves and rock shelters have been attributed to Perigordian contexts: outlines of mutilated hands from Gargas, carved salmon bas-relief from Poisson, and simple engraved animal outlines at Pair-non-Pair. Living sites often contain complex arrangements of hearths, slabs, and postholes, suggesting elaborate structures or ordering of space.

See also ABRI PATAUD; AURIGNACIAN; BREUIL, HENRI; CUEVA MORIN; GRAVETTIAN; HOMO SAPIENS; JEWELRY; LA FERRASSIE; LATE PALEOLITHIC; LAUGERIE SITES; PALEOLITHIC IMAGE; PALEOLITHIC LIFEWAYS; PEYRONY, DENIS; PROTOMAGDALENIAN; STONE-TOOL MAKING; UPPER PALEOLITHIC. [A.S.B.]

Further Readings

Gamble, C. (1986) The Palaeolithic Settlement of Europe. Cambridge: Cambridge University Press.

Laville, H., Rigaud, J.-P., and Sackett, J R. (1980) Rock Shelters of the Périgord. New York: Academic.

Wymer, J. (1982) The Palaeolithic Age. New York: St. Martin's.

PERIOD *see* TIME SCALE

PERMAFROST *see* GLACIATION; PLEISTOCENE

PERODICTICUS *see* LORISIDAE

PETRALONA

Village in northeastern Greece, where in 1960 a human skull encrusted in stalagmite was found deep in a nearby cave. It has been claimed that a whole skeleton was originally present, but this is unlikely. Because the original find spot was not studied carefully at the time of the discovery, many uncertainties about the associations and age of the skull remain to be resolved. Absolute dating by uranium series and thermoluminescence suggests that the skull may be as young as 200 k.y. or more than 350 k.y. old. Study of fossil mammals found elsewhere in the cave supports the more ancient age estimates, but claims for an antiquity of more than 700 k.y. are unlikely. The skull itself shows an interesting combination of features found in *Homo erectus* and such later hominids as the Neanderthals. Brain volume was probably ca. 1,230 ml., and the skull is long, low, and extraordinarily broad across the base. Skull thickness is very great, particularly in the region of the occipital torus, yet the supraorbital torus and inflated cheek bones contain enormous sinuses (air spaces), larger even than those of Neanderthals. Browridge shape and nasal form are reminiscent of those of Neanderthals, but the upper and middle face are broader and flatter, as in other middle Pleistocene fossils. The parietal region is expanded, as in other archaic *Homo sapiens* fossils, and it is with this group that the specimen is generally classified. Within Europe the Petralona fossil can be grouped with those from Arago, Vértesszöllös, and Bilzingsleben as showing a number of *erectus*-like features, yet these specimens may also lie near the origin of the Neanderthal lineage.

See also ARCHAIC HOMO SAPIENS. [C.B.S.]

PETROLEMUR

Middle-late Paleocene primate from southern China. This poorly known, enigmatic genus is known from a maxilla fragment and a juvenile mandibular fragment, each with five teeth. Although the samples are somewhat stratigraphically separated, the inferred occlusal relationships strongly suggest that the two specimens are congeneric. *Petrolemur*, although better referable to the primates than to any other known order of mammals, is difficult to place within the known taxonomic framework for the order. It may represent a hitherto unknown group of archaic primates that flourished during the Paleogene of Asia.

[F.S.S.]

PEYRONY, DENIS (1869-1954)

French prehistorian who excavated a number of major Middle and Upper Paleolithic sites in southwestern France, including La Ferrassie, Laugerie Haute, and Le Moustier. Like his predecessors Breuil and Mortillet, Peyrony was concerned primarily with characterizing Paleolithic assemblages and placing them in relative chronologic sequence and did so by the use of a fossil index (the presence of specific tool type considered diagnostic for a specific time period). Peyrony's delimitation of two contemporaneous Upper Paleolithic traditions, the Aurignacian and the Perigordian, challenged previously held assumptions that tool-making traditions evolved unilineally.

See also AURIGNACIAN; LA FERRASSIE; LAUGERIE SITES; LE MOUSTIER; PERIGORDIAN; UPPER PALEOLITHIC. [O.S.]

PFUPIAN *see* WILTON

PHANER *see* CHEIROGALEIDAE

PHARYNX *see* SPEECH (ORIGINS OF)

PHENACOLEMUR *see* PAROMOMYIDAE

PHENETICS

Study concerned with the similarity of organisms based on their phenotypic characteristics. In numerical taxonomy this similarity is represented by a numerical index, and organisms are classified together based on overall similarity. This is in contrast to cladistics, which is concerned with relationship in terms of recency of common descent.

See also CLADISTICS; NUMERICAL TAXONOMY; QUANTITATIVE METHODS. [L.F.M.]

PHENOTYPE

Outward characteristics of an individual, usually the product of a complex interaction between the genetic constitution and the environment. Natural selection operates among phenotypes and therefore affects the genetic structure of a population only indirectly.

See also GENETICS; GENOTYPE. [J.M.]

PHYLETIC EVOLUTION *see* EVOLUTION

PHYLETIC GRADUALISM *see* EVOLUTION

PHYLOGENY

Evolutionary history of one or (more generally) a series of interrelated species: the course of ancestry and descent interlinking a series of species through time. A *phylum* in this context is simply an evolutionary lineage, not restricted to any particular rank in the Linnaean hierarchy. A series of species descended from a common ancestral species is said to be a *monophyletic taxon*, a *clade*, or simply a *lineage*.

Phylogeny as Evolutionary History

As Darwin pointed out in 1859, the process of "descent with modification"—his characterization of evolution—necessarily results in a pattern of nested resemblances interlinking all life forms descended from a single common ancestor. When modifications occur within a lineage, they will be passed along to descendant organisms and ultimately to descendant species. These same novelties will be absent in collateral lineages. More closely related lineages will therefore tend to share a greater number of evolutionary novelties, reflecting a relatively more recent point of common ancestry. This observation has two interrelated consequences: 1) Darwin concluded that the notion of phylogenetic ancestry and descent explains why there is a nested pattern of resemblance linking all forms of life, a pattern previously recognized in early attempts to classify organisms. Put another way, the nested pattern of resemblance becomes the main prediction yielded by the conjecture that life has a single, unified phylogenetic history: if life has evolved, then there must be a single complexly internested pattern of resemblance linking all living creatures, past, present, and future. 2) Conversely, if there has been a phylogenetic history of life, that history can be reconstructed using standard procedures and principles of genealogical analysis developed both within and outside biological science. (For modern principles of phylogenetic—genealogical—reconstruction *see* CLADISTICS.)

The daily experiences of systematists and paleontologists since before the appearance of Darwin's *On the Origin of Species* in 1859 have abundantly verified the notion that life has had a unified phylogenetic history. The oldest fossils yet discovered are ca. 3.5 billion years old (from sediments in Australia), only 0.5 billion years younger than the oldest known rocks. The gross sequence of life forms in the fossil record agrees with the spectrum of primitive-to-derived forms extant in the modern biota: the earliest fossils are of bacteria, which are small simple organisms lacking the complexities of cellular anatomy characteristic of all other forms of life (save viruses, which are obligate parasites). Single-celled eukaryotic (i.e. with complex nuclei encased in membranes, and intracellular organelles) organisms first appear in the fossil record ca. 1.3 billion years ago. All multicellular organisms—plants, animals, and fungi—were derived from single-celled eukaryotes. Multicelled organisms (animals) first appear in the late Precambrian, ca. 700 m.y. ago. The first great evolutionary radiation (*see* ADAPTIVE RADIATION) of animal life occurred at the base of the Cambrian Period, some 570 m.y. ago. Fungi and true vascular (land) plants appeared in the late Silurian, ca. 400 m.y. ago.

The conventional classification of the major taxonomic entities does not accord well with the actual phylogeny—genealogical affinities—of the taxa. Whereas it is conventional to recognize five kingdoms—Prokaryota, Protista, Fungi, Plantae, and Animalia—there is a basic dichotomy between Prokaryota and Eukaryota. Eukaryota is presumably a monophyletic group, marked by features of cellular anatomy that appear to be evolutionary novelties shared by all descendants of a common ancestor. Prokaryota, on the other hand, are all those organisms (bacteria) lacking the advanced features that define Eukaryota; thus eukaryotes are predictably, and certainly, more closely related to some lineages of bacteria than to others. Recent work on bacterial anatomy and physiology has only confirmed the great heterogeneity of this group.

Likewise, the Protista are all eukaryotes lacking multicellularity; it has been known for over a century that some forms of single-celled life are more plant-like and others more animal-like. That classifications may be based on lines of genealogical descent is no guarantee that traditionally accepted taxa in classifications do in fact reflect the phylogenetic affinities of their constituent organisms.

Phylogenetic Patterns

There are some generalized patterns commonly exhibited by phylogenetic lineages through time. Typically a lineage begins as a single species (perforce) producing a series of descendant species: thus the standing diversity (total number of species) at any one point in time typically increases within a clade. If there is a regular increase up to a point, followed by a regular, gradual decrease in species diversity up to the point of extinction, a graphic depiction of species diversity within a clade resembles a spindle; in general such clade-diversity graphs are all called "spindle" diagrams. While the variation in spindle shapes is potentially limitless—so much so that simple classification and generalization of characteristic phylogenetic histories shared by a number of unrelated clades is both unrealistic and naïve—there are at least four identifiable components to phylogenetic patterns.

Adaptive radiations: These are typically rapid (in geologic time) expansions of species (and underlying phenotypic) diversity within a clade. Although clades may undergo a more gentle, progressive ex-

pansion in species diversity, adaptive radiations are common, often occurring at or near the beginning of a lineage. For example, the Devonian radiation within both the lungfishes and the coelacanth fishes produced by far the greatest amount of species and morphological diversity within each of the groups; following the Devonian, diversity in both groups has remained very low consistently up to the present day.

Because adaptive radiations so often occur in the early phases of a lineage's phylogenetic history it has long been postulated that adoption of a particular body plan (*Bauplan*) in an ancestral species confers the opportunity for radiation into a variety of ecological niches: the radiation is a consequence of the presence of a particular morphological complexion of the ancestor. But it seems more likely that lineages are especially well delineated if there is rapid diversification, for whatever reason, particularly early in its history; an early radiation establishes the lineage both in nature and, later, in the minds of systematists and paleontologists. Had the lungfish or the coelacanths not diversified, the probabilities are great that the lineages would not have persisted as they have, nor be recognized as major branches on the phylogenetic tree of vertebrate life.

Diversity reduction (in extreme form including extinction, the ultimate fate of all species and higher taxa) is of course the converse of adaptive radiation and diversity expansion in general. The phenomena are related by the simple equation $D = S-E$, i.e. species diversity is a reflection of speciation rate (S) less extinction rate (E). Much of contemporary macroevolutionary theory is devoted to analysis of the controls of speciation and extinction rates within lineages.

Steady-state: When neither speciation nor extinction rate exceeds the other for any great length of time, and when both rates are moderate, clade diversity remains roughly constant, the norm for a great number of clades through much of their phylogenetic histories. Such patterns are typically ended by periods of extinction that involve many other clades as well: mass extinctions are cross-genealogical ecological events. During periods of "steady-state," although new species continue to appear, generally little in the way of major anatomical change accrues within the lineage—arguably the case for the placental-mammal clade from the Oligocene on, with the possible exception of the hominoid subclade.

Living fossils: Modern lungfish and coelacanths are considered "living fossils." Although applied to a variety of not strictly comparable cases, this term most often means that living species bear a close anatomical resemblance to early members of the lineage and that the lineage is sufficiently old for there to have been a substantial amount of evolutionary change in other, closely related lineages. Both coelacanths and lungfish belong to the (clade) Class Osteichthyes (bony fishes); most numerous among bony fishes today are the teleosts, actinopterygian fish great in diversity and substantially changed from the primitive condition of actinopterygians of the Devonian. Although lungfish and coelacanths experienced adaptive radiations in their early history, for the vast bulk of their phylogenetic time species diversity was very low. Both speciation and extinction rates were low, which agrees with data on many lineages of "living fossils" suggesting that component organisms are generally broad-niched "ecological generalists." Ecological-niche theory has been a fruitful source of explanation for variation of characteristic rates of speciation and species extinction. Most species evolving in "adaptive radiations" seem, in contrast, to be ecological specialists, with concomitantly higher rates of both speciation and extinction.

Trends: Some lineages display a concerted, directional change in morphology of component organisms. For example, comparison of brain size in *Homo sapiens* with that of extant apes implies an increase in brain size in the phylogeny of our species. The fossil record of the past 4 m.y. or so confirms that brain size in our lineage has indeed increased progressively. Yet interpretation of such patterns in terms of the underlying evolutionary mechanisms (causal pathways) that has produced them remains an item of serious debate in evolutionary biology.

Laboratory experiments, where environmental conditions can be controlled and natural selection simulated, provide ample evidence that directional, generation-by-generation change in gene frequency and corresponding phenotypic expression can indeed proceed in a linear, directional manner, at least up to a point and for a limited number of generations, depending in part upon the nature of the available underlying variation. Darwin and virtually all succeeding evolutionary biologists applied the model of generation-by-generation adaptive change under the control of natural selection to large-scale patterns of phylogenetic change, especially linear trends, which also involve modifications of adaptations, albeit on a scale considerably larger, in terms of amount of change and of time involved, than that encountered in laboratory circumstances.

Yet the fossil record of most species, including those displaying phylogenetic trends between species within a lineage through time, indicates that the individual species involved tend not to undergo substantial change through time, especially in those very features shown to be involved in a long-term evolutionary trend. Except for examples involving size

increase (or, more rarely, decrease) through time, the anatomical properties of component organisms remain remarkably stable in most species throughout the greater bulk of a species' history.

The solution to the apparent enigma of trends lies in the recognition that the actual *process* of phylogenesis involves speciation as well as the adaptive modification of phenotypic properties of organisms via natural selection. Phylogeny is a sequence of successive speciations and concomitant extinctions. Anatomical change in evolution, to the extent that it is deterministic, is under the control of natural selection. But the context for adaptive change seems, at least to some degree, in turn to be under the control of the speciation process. According to the theory of punctuated equilibria, for example, most adaptive change occurs in conjunction with speciation (defined as the origin of a descendant from an ancestral reproductive community).

If species are real entities, with births (speciation), histories, and deaths (extinction), then the possibility arises that species themselves can be "sorted," in a manner analogous, if not wholly comparable, with natural selection. Differential success of species, where some species produce descendants at a faster rate, or descendants that are less prone to extinction than others, will bias the distribution of species— hence of phenotypes of constituent organisms within species—during the history of a lineage. The issue of species selection in macroevolution in general, and in the development of phylogenetic trends in particular, remains controversial. But patterns of phylogenetic history lie at the heart of testing rival theories of the evolutionary process.

See also ADAPTIVE RADIATION; CLADISTICS; CLASSIFICATION; EVOLUTION; SPECIATION; SPECIES; TAXONOMY. [N.E.]

Further Readings

Eldredge, N., and Cracraft, J. (1980) Phylogenetic Patterns and the Evolutionary Process. New York: Columbia University Press.

Simpson, G.G. (1953) The Major Features of Evolution. New York: Columbia University Press.

Simpson, G.G. (1961) Principles of Animal Taxonomy. New York: Columbia University Press.

Wiley, E.O. (1981) Phylogenetics. New York: Wiley.

PHYSICAL ANTHROPOLOGY

Study of humans as biological organisms, in terms of both their evolutionary history and their anatomical and physiological function—in contrast to *cultural anthropology*, the study of humans as social beings. In practice physical anthropology also embraces the study of the origins, evolution, systematics, behavior, and ecology of our closest living relatives, the pri-

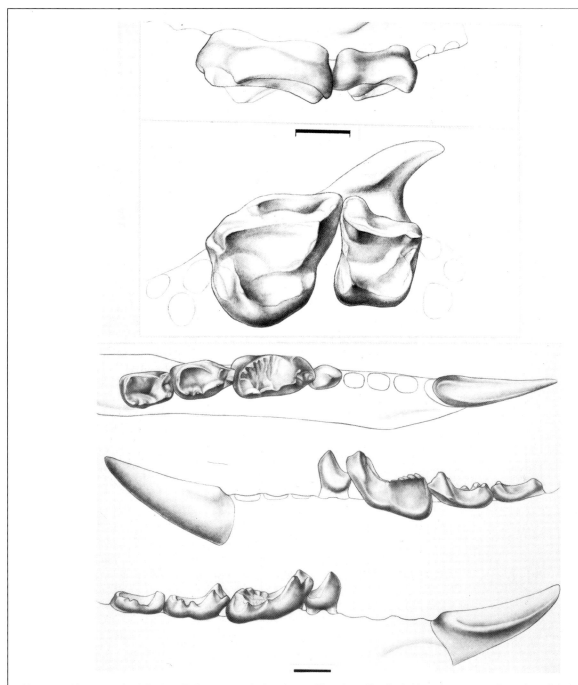

Upper and lower teeth of the late Paleocene archaic primate *Picrodus silberlingi*. Note the extreme flattening of the upper molars and the tremendously enlarged talonid and drastically reduced trigonid on the first lower molar. Scales are 1 mm.

mates. The field thus consists of a patchwork of disciplines employing different methodologies, which are united by their ultimate focus on a single theme: humanity and its biological context. Major aspects of physical anthropology include the study of human evolution; human adaptation, variation, and genetics; human demography; forensic anthropology and paleopathology; and primate ecology, behavior, and evolution. These diverse areas of study are ultimately united in the broadest interpretation of the first: how modern humans, in all their diversity, came to be.

See also ANTHROPOLOGY; FORENSIC ANTHROPOLOGY; PALEOANTHROPOLOGY; PALEOPATHOLOGY; PRIMATE SOCIETIES. [I.T.]

PICK *see* STONE-TOOL MAKING

PICRODONTIDAE

Tiny plesiadapiforms of the Paleocene of North America that are dentally among the most advanced (most changed from a primate common ancestor) of all Tertiary primates. There are two known genera: *Picrodus* (including *Draconodus*) and *Zanycteris*. The latter is known by a crushed skull, but most of our knowledge of these primates is based on teeth and mandibles. The central incisors were enlarged as in many archaic primates, and the antemolar dentition between the large incisors and the premolars was relatively unimportant compared with the large and highly modified molars. The first upper and lower molars are unusually enlarged compared with the most posterior ones, and they are modified in a telling manner. The crowns of the teeth are expanded and the enamel is heavily wrinkled on the molars. Emphasis is clearly on surface area, and the foods mashed were not particularly abrasive, judged from the low crowns of these molars. There are bats today that display molar characters convergently resembling picrodontids. These bats are nectar- and pollen-feeding forms, with a diet rich in energy and protein but easy on the teeth. It is almost certain that picrodontids (without any connotations of flying adaptations) were feeding on pollen, nectar, and possibly tree exudates like gums and maybe some nontoxic resins.

Picrodontids supply us with valuable evidence on just how widely plant foods were exploited by early primates and how exacting the adaptations of particular Paleocene primates were to the resources of the tropical and subtropical forests of the world.

See also PAROMOMYIDAE; PLESIADAPIFORMES. [F.S.S.]

PICRODUS *see* PAROMOMYIDAE

PIETERSBURG

South African Middle Stone Age industry (probable age 130–40 k.y.) with blade technology in addition to discoidal and Levallois cores, named after surface sites near Pietersburg, northern Transvaal, but best known from Cave of Hearths. Relatively few pieces have secondary retouch, but these include backed knives and side- and end-scrapers. Regional variants or related industries include the Orangian (Orange Free State) and Mossel Bay (Cape Province), as well as the Stillbay and other Middle Stone Age industries of southern Africa.

See also APOLLO-11; BORDER CAVE; CAVE OF HEARTHS; FLORISBAD; HOWIESON'S POORT; LEVALLOIS; MIDDLE STONE AGE; ORANGIAN; ROSE COTTAGE; STILLBAY; STONE-TOOL MAKING. [A.S.B.]

PILIOCOLOBUS *see* COLOBINAE

PILTDOWN

Between 1912 and 1915 an unsuspecting scientific community was led to believe that the remains of an early fossil hominid had successively been recovered from a gravel bed located in Piltdown, a small village nestled in the Weald of Sussex (England). Essentially these remains consisted of nine cranial fragments and a portion of a right mandibular ramus, plus a number of archaeological artifacts and a miscellaneous collection of mammalian fossils. Not until 40 years later were these remains declared to be bogus, the elements of an elaborate hoax.

Both J.S. Weiner (1915–1982) and K.P. Oakley (1911–1981), who played an integral role in the exposure of the Piltdown forgery in 1953, strongly suspected that Charles Dawson (1846–1916), a Sussex country solicitor and amateur archaeologist, was the perpetrator of the fraud. According to the story Dawson recounted to the Geological Society of London on December 18, 1912, his interest in the gravel deposit at Piltdown had been aroused when he found a fragment of a human cranium (ca. 1910) tossed up by laborers excavating a gravel pit located at the estate of Barkham Manor. Subsequently, in 1911, he is supposed to have picked up another and larger fragment of the same skull; impressed by the skull's general thickness, he took these two fragments to his friend A.S. Woodward (1864–1944), Keeper of Palaeontology at the British Museum (Natural History). Woodward, too, was excited by the find, and during the summer of 1912 the two men worked feverishly at Piltdown, occasionally assisted by such trusted associates as Pierre Teilhard de Chardin (1881–1955), excavating and sifting through the earth previously removed from the gravel pit. Their labors yielded a further seven fragments of the skull, which when fitted together made up the greater part of the left side of a human braincase. They also found the right half of a seemingly apelike jaw with two molar teeth, plus an assortment of fossil animal bones and "eoliths" (supposed primitive stone tools). Woodward was convinced that the skullcap and jaw were associated and felt justified in creating a new genus and species to describe the remains: *Eoanthropus dawsoni*, "Dawson's dawn man." It appeared to Woodward and his followers that

"*Eoanthropus*" was a feasible alternative to "*Pithecanthropus*" of Java, then known only from scanty remains, as the ancestral form of modern humans. Furthermore, the mammalian fossil fauna recovered from the site had been carefully selected and planted by the forgers at the gravel pit to indicate that "*Eoanthropus*" had roamed the Sussex countryside during either the late Pliocene or early Pleistocene.

From the time of the discovery's announcement, however, a number of scientists refused to accept the association of the cranium and jaw as belonging to the same taxon, let alone the same individual. According to these critics the jaw was that of a fossil anthropoid ape that had come by chance to be associated with human fossil remains in the deposit. In 1915 G.S. Miller (1869–1956), then Curator of Mammals at the U.S. National Museum of Natural History in Washington, concluded from his study of the Piltdown casts that the jaw was actually that of a fossil chimpanzee. This and similar arguments, however, were dismissed by Woodward and his supporters as most improbable, given the fact that no fossil apes later than the early Pliocene had been found in England or Europe.

Woodward's support of the monistic interpretation had been based on the apparent close association of the cranial and mandibular remains in the gravel, along with the evidence presented by the molar teeth, which were worn flat in a manner quite uncharacteristic of ape dentitions but commonly encountered among the most "primitive" extant human groups. In accordance with the notion that the Piltdown remains represented an early hominid, Woodward assigned the reconstructed skull the relatively small cranial capacity of 1,070 ml. Likewise, from his examination of the endocranial cast of *Eoanthropus*, the anatomist G.E. Smith (1871–1937) found evidence of primitive features, declaring it to be "the most primitive and most simian human brain so far recorded." But because the original skull used in the forgery had been broken in such a way as to preclude an accurate reconstruction anatomists like A. Keith (1866–1950) of the Royal College of Surgeons were able to argue for an alternative assembly and to raise the cranial capacity upward to ca. 1,400 ml.—close to the approximate average of modern *Homo sapiens*. Woodward's general reconstruction, however, was subsequently "vindicated" by Teilhard de Chardin's fortuitous find of a canine tooth at the Piltdown gravel pit in 1913. Later, in 1917, the dualistic theory suffered a further setback when Woodward announced, shortly after the death of Dawson, the discovery of Piltdown II. These remains, consisting of two cranial fragments and a molar tooth and a fragment of a lower molar of a species of fossil rhinoceros, had reportedly been found by Dawson in 1915 in the Piltdown neighborhood.

During the 1920s and 1930s more fossils of *Pithecanthropus* and *Australopithecus* (an even more primitive hominid) were discovered in Southeast Asia and Africa, respectively, progressively isolating "*Eoanthropus*" in the evolutionary sequence. In the light of these discoveries the Piltdown remains were subjected to increasing scientific scrutiny, and in 1953 it was finally demonstrated that the cranium and jaw contained different amounts of fluorine and other elements—indicating that the cranium was older than the jaw (later shown to be that of an orangutan). In 1959 carbon-14 dating confirmed this conclusion. Also, chemical analysis revealed that both the human and animal remains had been deliberately stained and that the human molar teeth had undergone artificial abrasion. The removal of the Piltdown anomaly assisted in the clarification of the modern interpretation of the hominid fossil record.

Since the demonstration that the Piltdown fossils were fraudulent, interest in the specimen has rested in the identity of the forger or forgers. The case against Dawson has since been contested by R. Miller, who regards Elliot Smith as the culprit. Others, such as J.B. Halstead, contend it was the geologist W.J. Sollas (1859–1930), while Stephen J. Gould has suggested that it was Teilhard de Chardin. More recently a contentious case against the author Arthur Conan Doyle (1849–1936) has been made by J.H. Winslow and A. Meyer, followed by an attempt by P. Costello to muster circumstantial evidence to implicate the Sussex chemist Samuel Woodhead. But without exception the cases brought against these suspects have rested exclusively on suspicion rather than on evidence.

See also CLARK, W.E. LE GROS; KEITH, ARTHUR; OAKLEY, KENNETH PAGE; SMITH, GRAFTON ELLIOT; TEILHARD DE CHARDIN, PIERRE; WOODWARD, ARTHUR SMITH. [F.S.]

Further Readings

Costello, P. (1985) The Piltdown hoax reconsidered. Antiquity 59:167–171.

Gould, S.J. (1980) The Piltdown controversy. Nat. Hist. 89(8):8–28.

Halstead, L.B. (1978) New light on the Piltdown hoax. Nature 276:11–13.

Millar, R. (1972) The Piltdown Men. New York: Ballantine.

Weiner, J.S. (1955) The Piltdown Forgery. London: Oxford University Press.

Winslow, J., and Meyer, A. (1983) The perpetrator at Piltdown. Science 83(4):32–43.

PINJOR *see* SIWALIKS

PITHECANTHROPUS *see* HOMO
ERECTUS

PITHECIA *see* PITHECIINAE

PITHECIINAE

Subfamily of platyrrhine atelid monkeys including the Pitheciini tribe of sakis ·(*Pithecia*) and uakaris (*Chiropotes, Cacajao*), the Aotini tribe of nocturnal owl (*Aotus*) and diurnal titi monkeys (*Callicebus*), and their fossil allies. Older classifications tended to employ two or three subfamilies for the five genera, giving the impression that they were distantly related and adaptively heterogeneous. Thus the realization that pitheciines are monophyletic as well as taxonomically diverse establishes them as a major facet of the platyrrhine radiation and one that has no ecological counterpart among the Old World primates.

Pitheciines are frugivorous and the pitheciins particularly prefer hard-shelled fruits or those with hard seeds. The more derived sakis and uakaris have unusually modified dentitions, with tall, narrow incisors; large, laterally splayed canines; flat-crowned, crenulate cheek teeth; and very robust jaws, enabling them to pry open and harvest seeds with well-protected pods, while aotins exhibit various primitive aspects of this pattern. Hard-fruit- and seed-eating specializations allow uakaris to exploit vast "black water" areas of Amazonia that are inhospitable to many other primates. There the poor soils selected for a flora having a low diversity of tree species with adaptations to resist predation by frugivores. This posed problems that "garden variety" frugivores have been unable to solve.

Fossil pitheciines are known from Patagonia and Colombia. The Colhuehuapian (21–20 m.y.) *Tremacebus harringtoni* and the Santacrucian (18–16 m.y.) species of *Homunculus* are aotins. The former, clearly allied with *Aotus*, was probably crepuscular and/or nocturnal. The latter may be one of the most primi-

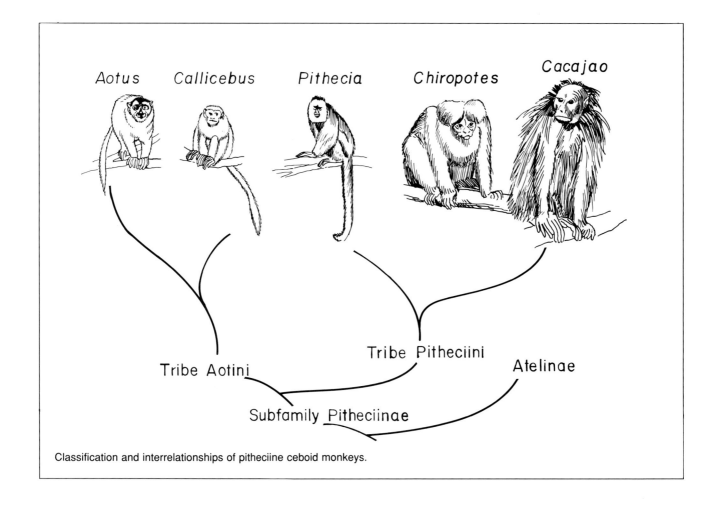

Classification and interrelationships of pitheciine ceboid monkeys.

tive members of the pitheciine subfamily. *Soriacebus ameghinorum*, also from the Santacrucian, is a primitive form belonging to the pitheciin tribe. From La Venta (16–14 m.y.) *Cebupithecia sarmientoi* is more closely related to the derived living saki-uakaris, while *Mohanamico hershkovitzi* is a more primitive member of the pitheciine subfamily. One of the most recent discoveries of pitheciines at La Venta is the presence in the fauna of a modern genus, *Aotus*. *Aotus dindensis* appears to have been crepuscular-nocturnal, like the living owl monkey. It represents the earliest record of a modern primate in the Neogene fossil record, and suggests a long history of relatively little change within the evolution of the genus *Aotus*.

See also DIET; LA VENTA; PATAGONIA. [A.L.R.]

Further Readings

Kinzey, W.G. (1986) New World primate field studies: what's in it for anthropology. Ann. Rev. Anthropol. *15*:121–148.

Rosenberger, A.L. (1981) Systematics: the higher taxa. In A.F. Coimbra-Filho and R.A. Mittermeier (eds.): Ecology and Behavior of Neotropical Primates. Rio de Janeiro: Academia Brasiliera de Ciências.

Szalay, F.S., and Delson, E. (1979) Evolutionary History of the Primates. New York: Academic.

PLANO

Terminal phase of the Paleoindian Tradition. Plano culture artifacts overlie the Clovis and Folsom levels at Blackwater Draw (New Mexico). Distributed for the most part on the High Plains of western America, the assemblage consists primarily of a series of long, unfluted lanceolate points with parallel to oblique pressure flaking; they are generally associated with the remains of extinct *Bison antiquus*. The complex dates between 10,000 and 7,000 B.P. and is best known from such sites as Agate Basin (Nebraska) and Hell Gap (Wyoming).

See also AMERICAS; PALEOINDIAN. [L.S.A.P., D.H.T.]

PLATE TECTONICS

Plate-tectonic theory developed rapidly during the early 1960s, as new data from geophysics and deep-sea geology confirmed the mechanism for "continental drift." The shape of the Atlantic Ocean provoked speculations about drift as soon as the first good maps appeared in the 1600s. Studies by Snider-Pellegrini, Taylor, Baker, Suess, Wegener, and DuToit between 1880 and 1925 developed evidence for the separation of a supercontinent, Pangea, into southern (Gondwana) and northern (Laurasia) parts by the formation of the equatorial Tethys Sea, and their

further breakup by the north-south opening of the Atlantic and Indian oceans. The first plausible mechanism to account for this motion came in parallel studies of ocean-floor geomagnetism and the first motion of earthquakes in the crustal shear planes, led by an astonishing generation of young scientists working under E. Bullard at Cambridge University. These studies conclusively proved that the ocean floor itself is a dynamic system, as A. Holmes and F.A. Vening-Meinesz had each proposed in the 1930s.

The earth's crust is presently divided into seven major and about as many minor plates, all moving independently and some carrying continents as passive freight. The motion of each plate is away from a *spreading center*—linear volcanic ridges, mostly in mid-ocean, in which ocean crust is formed—and towards a *subduction zone*, in which the cooled oceanic crust sinks down into the subcrust, where it is gradually reheated and absorbed. The deep ocean trenches are formed where plates override one another in the subduction zones, while the great laterally moving faults like the San Andreas accommodate sideways motion within and between plates.

The basic source of the tremendous energy of plate tectonics, which creates mountain ranges and oceans, is simply subcrustal heat. The spreading centers are swollen upward by the thermal expansion of the crust over zones of abnormal heat rising in "plumes," or convection cells in the subcrust, a process first envisaged by H.H. Hess in the 1930s. New crust is formed by the injection of fresh basaltic magma within the spreading centers, but the ocean crust is not so much pushed aside by these lava intrusions as it is pulled away by gravity, allowing the lava to well up through rifts and partings. The crust slides off the heated dome or ridge under its own weight, cooling and shrinking as it moves. The heat that drives this system appears to be a combination of primordial heat-of-compaction still dissipating from the core, and radioactive heat, mostly from the decay of potassium-40 in the mantle. The friction vulcanism associated with the shearing motion of plates against one another in subduction zones—in particular the "Ring of Fire" surrounding the Pacific basin—is reconversion of gravitational-kinetic energy to thermal energy.

Continents play a major role in plate tectonics and appear to control the location of both spreading centers and subduction zones. It is generally agreed that new oceans begin under continents, in the form of rift valleys. The continental mass is a blanket of dry, thermally opaque material that blocks subcrustal heat flow. At some point the trapped heat will lead to active updoming, with rifting along the stretched-apart crest. As the upper crust thins and heat flow increases in the zone of weakness, the doming "rips" laterally to adjacent domes. The segments of the resulting rift valley can be seen to change course at each domal node, with a "failed" third arm often extending from the obtuse angle (as one example, the shallow Nyanza Rift Valley of western Kenya, which extends to Lake Victoria from the Mau-Aberdares apex). Under the force of gravity the process feeds on itself; the flanks of the dome slide away, and eventually the relatively hot basaltic core of the ridge is exposed, several thousand feet below sea level. This process has been much studied in the East African Rift System, where the Red Sea and Gulf of Aden segments have evolved into a true ocean separating Arabia from Africa during the last 35 m.y.

Subduction zones operate only where oceanic crust is being consumed. The granitic continents cannot be drawn down into the basaltic subcrust, being far too buoyant, and thus they act to block subduction when brought into the trough. Subduction may continue, either by "flipping" (where the opposing plate margin, if it is oceanic, begins to descend under the continent-bearing plate) or, more commonly, by "jumping" rearward to a new subduction zone behind the jammed-up continent. This has the effect of transferring the continent to the opposing plate. The result is that a large percent of the total length of the world's subduction zones are located adjacent to, and are inclined beneath, continental margins; also, it is inevitable that the motion of continent-bearing plates (the plates of the Pacific Ocean basin have always been wholly oceanic) will eventually join the continents together in subduction zones. The Alps, Carpathians, Taurides, Elburz, Tien Shan, and Himalayas mark former subduction zones in which most of the former Tethys ocean has now disappeared. The continuing northward motion of the Afro-Arabian plate is now closing the Mediterranean remnant in a subduction zone extending from Sicily through Mesopotamia and Iran.

As the Mesopotamian juncture neared in the mid-Cenozoic, the previously isolated catarrhine fauna of Africa was exposed to periodic invasions of Eurasian mammals during low sea-level stands (i.e. in the late Eocene and more notably during the possibly multiple exchanges of the Oligocene "Grande Coupure"). But even as the juncture zone grew more permanent in the early Miocene, plate motion opened a new barrier in the expanding and deepening Red Sea basin. Passage across the northern end, in the Suez isthmus, was not established until the Pliocene, and Miocene exchange was only possible through the bottleneck of the Bab el Mandab isthmus (now sub-

merged) at the southern end. The early Miocene exchange brought dogs and hyenas into Africa and allowed the northward and eastward expansion of apes, elephants, and antelopes, among other African groups. More importantly, the redirection of global ocean circulation as continents shifted, and especially the gradual isolation and cooling of the polar regions, resulted in the expansion during the later Cenozoic of seasonally variable habitats at the expense of more equable conditions, culminating in the Pleistocene ice ages. In this regard plate tectonics has been a basic factor in human evolution.

The rate of plate spreading varies from place to place but (as a rule of thumb) is about as rapid as the growth of fingernails: ca. 3 cm./yr. From this it can be easily calculated that the two sides of the North Atlantic Ocean, about 8,000 km. apart, have been moving away from one another at this rate for 250 m.y. (i.e. since the late Triassic). Interestingly, calculations show that crust of this age has cooled to a density that is no longer buoyant with respect to the subcrust, and in actual fact there is no ocean floor anywhere that is older than Triassic. This has suggested a plate-tectonic megacycle, called the Wilson Cycle after J. Tuzo Wilson, in which worldwide continental dispersal (as heat builds up under the supercontinent of the previous cycle) is followed by coalescence into a new supercontinent (as rift-oceans cool and collapse). The Caribbean volcanic arc is the first sign that the over-age North Atlantic Ocean has begun to "collapse" (i.e. to develop subduction zones along the Atlantic coastlines).

See also CENOZOIC; KENYA; PALEOMAGNETISM; RIFT VALLEY; SEA-LEVEL CHANGE. [J.A.V.C.]

Further Readings

Condie, K.C. (1982) Plate Tectonics and Crustal Evolution, 2nd ed. London: Pergamon.

Schopf, T.J.M. (1980) Paleoceanography. Cambridge, Mass.: Harvard University Press.

West, R.M., ed. (1977) Paleontology and plate tectonics with special reference to the history of the Atlantic Ocean. Milwaukee Public Museum, Special Publications in Geology and Paleontology 2.

PLATYCHOEROPS *see* PLESIADAPIDAE

PLATYRRHINI

Infraorder of New World anthropoid primates also known as the Ceboidea. The scope of the platyrrhine adaptive radiation is remarkable. This has encouraged generations of primatologists to use the group as a natural laboratory of living analogues to examine morphological, behavioral, and ecological trends thought to have been important in the evolution of hominids. For example, brachiation and "antiprono-grade" locomotor behaviors have counterparts among both the apes and the ateline New World monkeys. In fact the anatomical similarities of upper-body shape shared by atelines and hominoids now support the theory that a type of arboreal climbing, rather than brachiation, preadapted protohominids to terrestrial bipedality. Similarly, the presence of hard-fruit masticatory adaptations in capuchin monkeys is serving as a dietary model for extinct hominoids with bunodont, thick-enameled cheek teeth. And the convergent evolution of fission-fusion social systems in spider monkeys and chimpanzees may shed light on the human condition, where ordered social flexibility is a prevalent theme. Most recently the role of platyrrhines as instructive analogues has grown into a new and perhaps more pertinent dimension, as paleontologists have recognized that they share many structural similarities with the earliest members of the catarrhine radiation, the Fayum Oligocene primates, which may have behaved more like some of the modern New World monkeys than any of the apes or Old World monkeys.

Their significance for broader questions notwithstanding, platyrrhines have been less intensively studied for their own sake than have Old World forms, although there are signs that the New World

represents the new frontier for the field of primatology in the coming decades. What they have to offer scientists is one of the order's most puzzling success stories. Where platyrrhines came from is hotly debated: from Africa across a narrower Atlantic Ocean or from Central America, evolving out of a still undiscovered ancestral anthropoid stock that lived in the shadows of the more successful North American radiations of nonanthropoids? Why does platyrrhine phylogeny seem to have unfolded as a single but highly diversified radiation, unlike the multi-stemmed catarrhine bush? Why do long-lived lineages seem to have dominated the macroevolutionary process, and why did terrestriality never emerge as a basic adaptive alternative to arboreality: all these are issues that have hardly yet been addressed.

Physically the platyrrhines display an impressive array of body sizes, ranging from the 100-gm. pygmy marmoset, *Cebuella pygmaea*, to the 10-kg. woolly spider monkey, *Brachyteles arachnoides*. Their dietary spectrum includes exudativores, insectivores, moderate carnivores, and both soft-fruit and hard-fruit specialists, as well as folivores. Locomotor habits are equally diverse, including scansorialists, leapers, quadrupeds, climbers, and acrobatic armswingers. These patterns tend to be phylogenetically distributed, and they indicate the ways in which the mod-

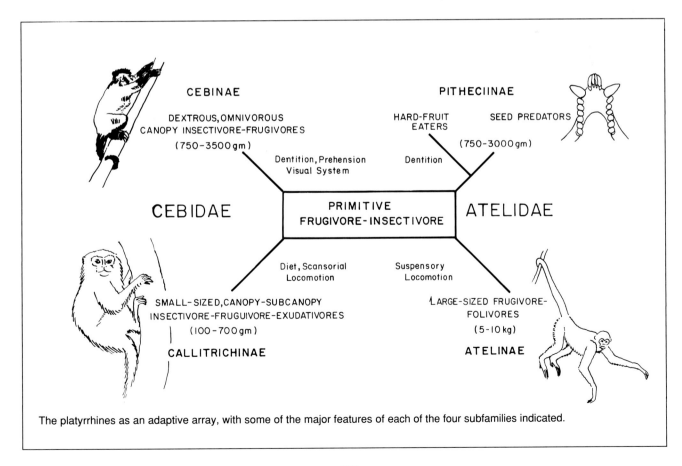

The platyrrhines as an adaptive array, with some of the major features of each of the four subfamilies indicated.

ern species have partitioned local habitats to allow for the coexistence of more than a dozen sympatric species in the lush communities around Amazonia. For example, the smaller callitrichines may be insectivorous and gumivorous scansorialists, while the larger, more agile atelines are more folivorous and frugivorous. The middle-sized, leaping pitheciines may concentrate on harder fruits and, secondarily, upon insects, while the same-sized, quadrupedal cebines dwell on concealed insects and forage for softer fruits when they are in season.

Because their fossil record is so poor, much of the interpretation and debate concerning the evolution of the platyrrhines has emerged from studies of the living species. The general outlines of the phylogenetic relationships of the living platyrrhines indicate that there are two major cladistic divisions, each with a pair of major subdivisions. These can be ranked at the levels of family (Cebidae, Atelidae) and subfamily (Cebinae, Callitrichinae; Atelinae, Pitheciinae), respectively. All of the fossil forms, except perhaps for the earliest one, *Branisella boliviana*, can be accommodated by this classification, although it has been commonplace to recognize many more higher taxa both for the living and the fossil forms. Opinions, however, are not unanimous on the interrelationships of the modern genera and groups. Serological studies in particular have been unable to resolve cladistic affinities at high taxonomic levels and tend to suggest some patterns of relationships at low taxonomic levels that are difficult to reconcile with comparative anatomy.

The key to understanding platyrrhine history relates to the role of the marmosets and the pitheciines within the adaptive radiation. The marmosets convergently exhibit features that resemble primitive mammalian patterns, such as small body size, clawed digits, and unconvoluted brains, yet they are bona fide anthropoids. While the primitiveness or derivedness of these features has been a matter of debate for decades, the other important question—to which modern forms are marmosets most closely related?—had been virtually ignored until recently, because it was thought to be imponderable without fossil evidence. The new neontological approaches, however, have indicated that the most likely answer to this question is that callitrichines are related to the cebines, *Cebus* and *Saimiri*.

The three genera of saki and uakari monkeys, in contrast, have taken a back seat to almost all of the other platyrrhines, perhaps because they are largely concentrated in the nearly impenetrable Amazon region, about which we know little. Yet current thinking is that these forms represent a clade of a larger adaptive radiation of pitheciine stock. It is also noteworthy that pitheciines have no adaptive counterpart among the Old World monkeys: they are a group of selective hard-fruit eaters. In a phylogenetic and paleontologic perspective the pitheciines are highly successful, comprising a monophyletic group of five living genera, as many as five fossil genera (*Homunculus*, *Tremacebus*, *Soriacebus*, *Cebupithecia*, *Mohanamico*), and a sixth bathyphyletic modern genus (*Aotus dindensis*). Thus they appear to have played an

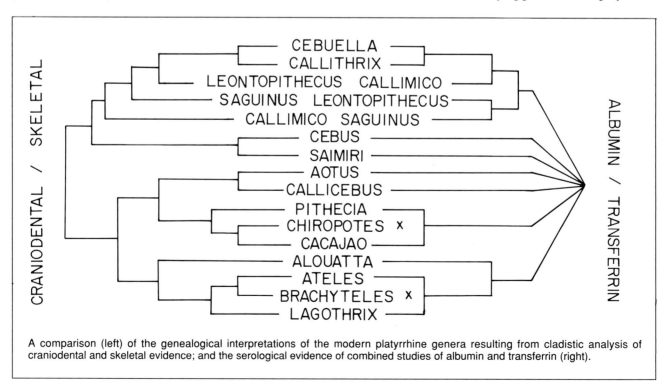

A comparison (left) of the genealogical interpretations of the modern platyrrhine genera resulting from cladistic analysis of craniodental and skeletal evidence; and the serological evidence of combined studies of albumin and transferrin (right).

important, enduring role in the ecological community of platyrrhines. Both of these issues are likely to remain at the forefront as the fossil record of platyrrhine evolution improves during the next decades.

See also ANTHROPOIDEA; ATELIDAE; ATELINAE; CALLITRICHINAE; CEBIDAE; CEBINAE; CEBOIDEA; PITHECIINAE. [A.L.R.]

Further Readings

Hershkovitz, P. (1977) Living New World Monkeys (Platyrrhini), Vol. 1. Chicago: University of Chicago Press.

Rosenberger, A.L. (1986) Platyrrhines, catarrhines and the anthropoid transition. In B.A. Wood, L. Martin, and P. Andrews (eds.): Major Topics in Primate and Human Evolution. Cambridge: Cambridge University Press.

PLEISTOCENE

Final epoch of the Cenozoic Era, characterized by a highly unstable global climate, with relatively rapid shifts between intervals with conditions much like the present and intervals of continental glaciation. For this reason the Pleistocene is informally known as the "Ice Ages." The final part of the Pleistocene, following the most recent glacial episode, has often been regarded as a separate chronostratigraphic unit (e.g. "Present Era," "Holocene Epoch"), but except for the level of human activity it is not distinct from other nonglacial intervals of the Pleistocene. In this book the "Holocene" is not separated from the late Pleistocene. It should also be noted that the term *Quaternary* originated in the eighteenth century to mean "unconsolidated deposits" as one of the four types of rock (the others being *Primary* for granites and lavas, *Secondary* for metamorphic rocks, and *Tertiary* for consolidated strata). Quaternary is now often used to mean an era coincident with the Pleistocene (plus Holocene), in schemes in which Tertiary is used for the rest of the Cenozoic. *Paleogene* and *Neogene* are used in this book for subdivisions of the Cenozoic Era, with Miocene, Pliocene, and Pleistocene grouped as the epochs of the Neogene sub-era.

All epochs are defined and subdivided on the basis of distinct stratigraphic breaks, which are most often generated by eustatic sea-level changes. These are arguably related to ice-volume and thus climate change, but in the Pleistocene the climatic effects are so marked as to make stratigraphic subdivisions seem to be explicitly "climatostratigraphic." Although the difference is more apparent than real, the tendency has been to appeal to scenarios of climate history rather than stratigraphic data in discussing Pleistocene history. Thus the terms *glacial*, for periods of ice advance and lowered average sea level and temperatures, and *interglacial*, for periods of climate more or less like the present, respectively, refer primarily to past climates but are often used in describing Pleistocene stratigraphic units as well.

The Pleistocene (from the Greek, "most recent") epoch was defined by Charles Lyell explicitly in terms of marine biostratigraphy. In the first edition of *Elements of Geology* (1833) he noted that the fossils in beds he assigned to "younger Pliocene" were markedly different from those of the older (standard) Pliocene. In a subsequent edition (1839) Lyell renamed the younger beds as Pleistocene. The difference in fossils was subsequently explained as the result of a change to glacial conditions, but only after Louis Agassiz demonstrated that continental glaciations had repeatedly invaded the northern hemisphere during this interval. The "golden spike" which defines the base of the Pleistocene is presently located in a sea-cliff section at Vrica, in the Italian province of Calabria. The defining level is placed in accordance with modern interpretations of Lyell's original discussion of the geology of Italy and its fossils. This is the level of the first appearance in the Italian strata of "cold guests"—mollusks that today live no farther south than the North Sea and the Baltic. The migration of these northern visitors into the Mediterranean reflects the onset of glacial climate intervals, whose intensity significantly exceeded that of any preceding cold-climate interval in the Cenozoic. The Vrica definition is presently correlated to deep-sea deposits at the top of the Olduvai paleomagnetic chron, with an age of ca. 1.6 m.y.

Until the 1960s the sequence of glacials and interglacials was reconstructed from geological evidence in formerly glaciated areas. Four glacials (Nebraskan, Kansan, Illinoisian, Wisconsinian) and three interglacials (Afton, Yarmouth, and Sangamon) (see table) were identified in North America from the sequences of moraines and tills, which are the landforms and deposits left behind by the melted Laurentide continental ice sheet. The interglacial stages are identified from the soils and water-laid sediments separating the tills and proving the temporary absence of glaciers at the type localities in Illinois and Iowa.

In northwestern Europe the moraines and tills of the Fennoscandian continental glacier define the four glacial stages, while the interglacials are marked by marine transgressions and pollen-bearing strata testifying to the presence of mixed deciduous forests.

The widely used Alpine System of Penck and Brückner (1909) recognized four glacials represented by the river terraces and associated moraines and three interglacials represented by steps separating one terrace level from the next. This volume follows the practice of most stratigraphers in using Menap, Elster, Saale, and Weichsel in place of the Alpine stages.

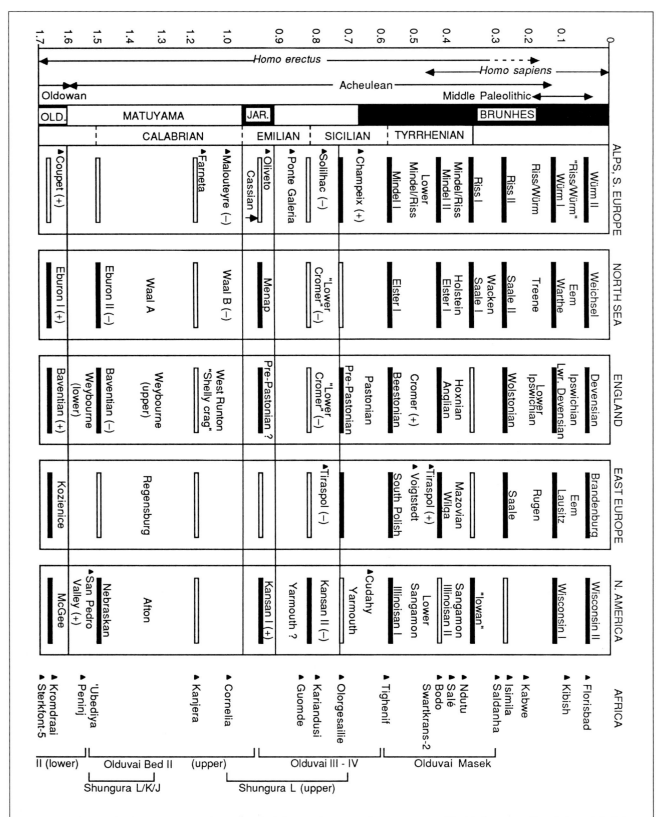

Pleistocene time scale. Bars represent the major glacials seen in oxygen isotope curves; filled-in bars are climatic lows (glacials or pluvials), which have been identified and dated in the various land sequences. Many climate swings are confused with one another, or obscured, because their effects are superimposed. (+) and (−) indicate paleomagnetic polarity measurements where known, corresponding to normal (black) and reversed (white) intervals on the paleomagnetic time scale. Important mammal fossil levels are indicated by filled triangles.

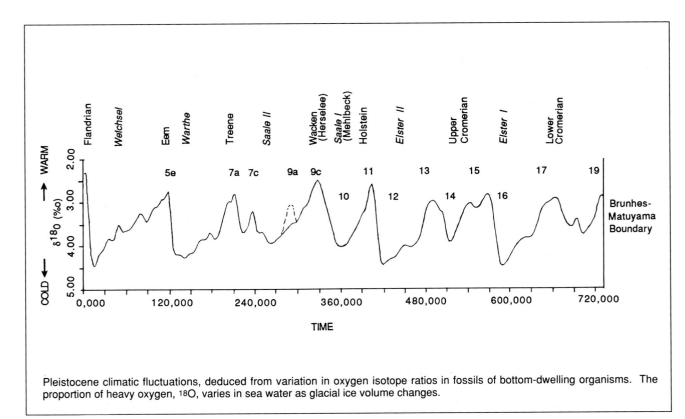

Pleistocene climatic fluctuations, deduced from variation in oxygen isotope ratios in fossils of bottom-dwelling organisms. The proportion of heavy oxygen, ^{18}O, varies in sea water as glacial ice volume changes.

In mountainous areas moraines are usually used to define local Pleistocene stratigraphies, such as those describing the fluctuations of the Cordilleran ice sheet or the Rocky Mountain glaciers. The Pinedale and Bull Lake glacials in western North America are based on such evidence.

Modern Subdivisions

The calcareous sediments on the floor of the deep oceans provide the most complete record of global climate known to date. In most places the sediments accumulate without interruption and at rates that are much less variable than in continental deposits. The ratio of oxygen isotopes ^{18}O and ^{16}O in the shells of bottom-dwelling foraminifera is the best currently known indicator of past climates, since it is controlled predominantly by the volume of land-based glacier ice. The changing composition of flora and fauna and the presence of ice-rafted rock detritus provide additional information on climate. Deep-sea sediments are dated by radiocarbon, by paleomagnetic reversals, and by tuning the climatic signal to astronomic chronology. Oxygen-isotope stratigraphy is used to subdivide deep-sea sediments into alternating stages of relatively high and relatively low oxygen-isotope ratios. The boundaries are drawn at the levels of fastest change. The even-numbered units enriched in ^{18}O indicate cold intervals and the odd-numbered units represent warm episodes with a decreased volume of land-based ice. The boundaries

separating pronounced isotopic maxima from succeeding pronounced minima are called *terminations*. Two consecutive terminations delimit a *glacial cycle*, labeled with capital letters in order of increasing age. The last termination is coeval with the last deglaciation and the next to last with the onset of the last interglacial. The last two completed glacial cycles (B and C) lasted ca. 115 k.y. each. The resolution of ^{18}O stratigraphy is limited by the delay in ocean mixing by selective dissolution and most importantly by burrowing seafloor fauna. As a result the precision of the method decreases with age.

The most complete and detailed records of Pleistocene climates on land come from the sequences of loess, which is calcareous (limey), wind-blown silt. Thick deposits are found in China, Europe, and North America in front of the formerly glaciated areas. Embedded fossils point to harsh and cold continental climate during the time of loess deposition and to mild and wet conditions during the formation of intervening soils.

The best-subdivided loess sequences are in central Europe, where they fill sheltered depressions on top of river-laid terrace gravels, making it possible to date the episodes of river downcutting and terrace aggradation relative to the loess sequence. In this way the Alpine glacial stages were correlated with the loess sequences and through them with the oxygen-isotope record (see table). It was found that the type Würm corresponds to two glacial cycles of the deep-sea record (stages 5b-2) and that the Riss corresponds to three cycles (stages 10-6). In contrast the episodes of river downcutting representing the interglacials Riss/Würm, Mindel/Riss, and Günz/Mindel were relatively short and probably related to episodes of increased rate of crustal movements.

In China beds of loess (glacially produced dust) and interglacial soils cover the North China plains and give evidence for alternating glaciations and warmer intervals in the late Cenozoic. The oldest layers date to ca. 2.5 m.y., equivalent to the mid-Pliocene cold-climate cycle found in deep-sea cores and also coincident with the earliest ice-rafted pebbles and clay, indicating floating ice, in the North Atlantic. Four major loess formations are recognized, from oldest to youngest: Wucheng, Lower Lishi, Upper Lishi, and Malan. Individual loess layers are indicated by the prefix "L" and the interglacial soil horizons by the letter "S." The well-developed soil level S5 is a prominent marker bed, and the loess units L1, L2, L5, L6, L9, and L15 are exceptionally thick.

The loess sequences in China, the paleoclimatic interpretations of dated fossils and sediments in North America and Europe, and the oxygen-isotope records of the deep-sea cores agree that a pronounced deterioration of world climate was seen at ca. 2.5 m.y., followed by a series of minor warm and cold alternations. An increase in the intensity of glaciations began ca. 1.6 m.y. (the present date for the beginning of the Pleistocene), and a further shift to even more pronounced and lasting glaciations began at ca. 0.9 m.y. This level of climate deterioration is sometimes considered as the onset of the "classical Pleistocene," since it is the age of the earliest evidence for continental glaciation (Günz or Menap) in Europe. However, this is the time of the second (Kansan) glaciation in North America, where conditions were more severe and where the ice sheets at each stage in the Pleistocene were twice as large as those of the northern Eurasian lowlands.

Early Pleistocene   According to interpretations of the oxygen-isotope curves, the first (mid-Pliocene) drop in global climate resulted in a buildup of continental ice, mostly in Antarctica and to a lesser extent in Greenland, the Arctic Archipelago, and Iceland; as noted, floating ice appeared in the North Atlantic, so glaciers from the ice caps probably advanced to sea level for the first time. Although this unprecedented deterioration of climate must have been a shock to the animals and plants of the later Cenozoic, including the African and Asian hominoid faunas, it reached only present-day levels. The succeeding late Pliocene climates were much milder than today, and the ice caps all but disappeared in the northern hemisphere. The climate first deteriorated to a new "ice age" level at 1.6 m.y., the level now identified with the beginning of the Pleistocene.

Apart from evidence in marine sediments and in the Chinese loess sequences, little is known of the climates of the early Pleistocene. Northern trees began to invade the lowlands of northern Europe ca. 2.5 m.y. ago, with the mid-Pliocene cooling. This event is documented in pollen found in the clays of the Pretiglian stage, in the sediments of the lower Rhine basin of Holland, Belgium, and northern Germany.

The climatic deterioration of the Pleistocene led to marked changes in the mammal fauna, including a notable trend to gigantism in the large animals of northern regions as an adaptation to cold. Even earlier, however, the mid-Pliocene "cold snap" at ca. 2.5 m.y. led to a wave of extinctions in temperate-region faunas. For many years this change, at the beginning of the classical Villafranchian mammal age of Europe and the Tatrot stage in the Siwaliks, was assumed by vertebrate paleontologists and anthropologists to mark the beginning of the Pleistocene, and even today this "definition" has its advocates. In Eurasia this great transition was marked by the "E-L-E" datum, so-called because of the initial appearance of elephants (*Elephas*, now *Mammuthus*, or "*Archidiskodon*"), bovines (*Leptobos*), and true horses (*Equus*). Compared with the mid-Pliocene revolution, the effect of first Pleistocene glaciation was less conspicuous, although it may have been coincident with the transition between Pliocene *Homo habillis* and Pleistocene *Homo erectus* in Africa. The end of the Villafranchian, during the great Elster glacial period at ca. 0.9 m.y., came with a second revolution in north-temperate mammal faunas, which ushered in the typical glacial-climate associations, followed (apparently) by emigration of *Homo erectus* into southern and eastern Eurasia.

Middle Pleistocene   Most stratigraphers have understood this period to be equivalent to the interval from the beginning of the "classical" Pleistocene, at ca. 0.9 m.y., to the end of the next-to-last glacial (Riss or Saale in Europe, Wisconsinian I in North America), at ca. 127 k.y. Some have advocated that the last paleomagnetic reversal, the beginning of the present "normal" polarity of the Brunhes chron at 0.72 m.y., be used as the criterion for the middle Pleistocene, but this is inconsistent with the requirement that all epochs, including the Pleistocene, be defined in fossiliferous marine sediments. The Emilian stage of the Italian sequence shows the return of "cold guests" during the Menap (Günz) glacial, and has been proposed as the location of a middle Pleistocene boundary section. It should be noted that the Jaramillo subchron in the later Matuyama falls very close to this level and is almost as convenient for global correlation as is the base of the Brunhes.

The correlation of classical middle Pleistocene subdivisions with the deep-sea record is tentative due to the absence of effective dating methods for strata of this age. From the paleoanthropological point of view the most important European horizon is the Holstein interglacial, which is generally correlated with the Hoxnian beds of England and the Steinheim beds of southern Germany, which have yielded skeletal remains of later "archaic *Homo sapiens*" and also archaeological material. Steinheim is also the type locality of the Steinheimian mammal fauna, which is characterized by many European species of large mammals (mammoths, mastodons, elephants, rhinos, hippos, lions, cave bears) that became extinct during the late Pleistocene.

The marine deposits of the Holsteinian, *sensu stricto*, have been found to represent a warm maximum only ca. 15 k.y. long, which is correlated with some certainty to oxygen-isotope stage 11, dated in marine sequences at 400 k.y. This climatic optimum, the warmest of the Pleistocene, is followed by the Warthe glacial advance. A later warm interval, not recognized in the Alpine "classical" sequence, has been differentiated as the Wacken interglacial, equivalent to isotope stage 9c. The Drenthe glacial advance at the beginning of the true Saale glacial at ca. 250 k.y. is followed by distinct warm-climate peaks, the Treene and/or Ohe, equivalent to oxygen-isotope stages 7a and 7, dated to 230 k.y.

Late Pleistocene   The late Pleistocene comprises the last interglacial, the last glacial, and the present ("Holocene") interglacial. The chronology of this period is relatively well known from radiocarbon dating of pollen-bearing lake beds, uranium-thorium dating of emerged coral reefs, back-counting of varved (annually laminated) glacial lake beds, and cores drilled into the ice caps of Greenland and Antarctica. The late Pleistocene begins with the very marked warm-climate interval, which in the North Sea basin is called the Eem interglacial. This correlates to peak 5e of the oxygen-isotope record and is dated to ca. 127 k.y. Studies of carbon dioxide levels indicate that the Eemian interglacial climates, which lasted for ca. 10–12 k.y., were warmer, at their maximum, than those of the present day. During the early part of the Last Glacial, between ca. 115 and 75 k.y., at least two major cold maxima in northern Europe alternate with warmer intervals attributed to the Amersfoort, Brorup, and Odderade interstadials. Studies of marine sediments of this age in the deep sea indicate that the main difference between the shorter, less extreme interstadial oscillations during a glacial advance and the longer, warmer interglacial conditions is that during the interstadials the temperature of the deep-ocean waters remains essentially unchanged, whereas they warm up by 2–3 degrees C during interglacials. Reforestation patterns reflected in the pollen found in ancient lake beds, also distinguish between the climates of interstadials and those of interglacials.

The climate between ca. 75 and 14 k.y., following the Odderade interstadial, was predominantly cold and dry, with an environment that has been called "polar desert." This interval, termed the Pleniglacial, was nevertheless interrupted by several ameliorations, or interstadials, during the middle (60–23 k.y.), which have been recognized worldwide. The last of these, the Denekamp between ca. 30 and 23 k.y., is particularly conspicuous and is known elsewhere by such terms as Würm2/3, Farmdale, Plum Point, Stillfried B, Paudorf, Mologeshekskaia, and Gota-Alvi.

The end of polar-desert conditions and the waning of Weischel glaciation began ca. 13.5 k.y. ago, in a succession of warming events and readvances called the Late Glacial phase. This transitional period consists of the Bølling interstadial, Older Dryas cool phase, Allerød warm phase, and Younger Dryas cool phase, as recognized in Denmark. The Older Dryas pollen-zone reflects the vegetation of northern Europe as glaciers began to melt, while the Younger Dryas pollen-zone, which dates from 11–10 k.y., marks conditions close to the present. Even at this time, however, moraines in the Herdla and Ra mountains of Norway; Sweden; and Finland (Salpausselka moraines) demonstrate that the Weichsel ice sheet had not yet fully melted.

If we consider the post-Weichsel as the final part of the Pleistocene, the world is now in the Flandrian interglacial. Following extremely mild conditions of the "thermal optimum" between 9 and 4 k.y., the later Flandrian was marked by a minor readvance of mountain glaciers. This has been called the "Little Ice Age," but even during this interval there were warmer oscillations, such as the period of classical times when Hannibal crossed Alpine passes now closed by glaciers and Vikings founded settlements in Greenland and Labrador.

In archaeological terms the most conspicuous transition of the later Pleistocene in Europe is the one between the Middle and Late Paleolithic. This appears to be contemporaneous with the transition between archaic and modern humans as far as the fossil record demonstrates and is interpreted to fall between 35 and 30 k.y. in Europe. In Africa these events seem to be significantly older, probably at ca. 50 k.y. but in some interpretations as old as 90 k.y.

Probably the most detailed succession of human artifacts, which at the same time contain various indicators of past climate, comes from the caves and rock shelters in the Périgord, of southwestern France. This sequence is well dated by radiocarbon; the changes in climate are interpreted from the changing shape and size of limestone fragments that make up the bulk of the cave sediments, as well as from pollen grains and animal bones found in the occupation levels.

Archaeological Subdivisions Archaeologists first classified Pleistocene strata according to embedded stone artifacts, using the terms Early, Middle, and Late Paleolithic. Later the Alpine stages of Penck and Brückner came into wide use by archaeologists, who attempted to refine and subdivide this system for their own use. In the interval of the Riss and Würm, particularly, multiple subdivisions based on climatic oscillations resulted in frequent miscorrelations from one area to another because local conditions, usually conditions of preservation, prevented the record of climate change in any given region from being complete.

One consequence among others is that the W1/2 interstadial (i.e. the warm-climate interval between Würm-1 and Würm-2 advances) in French cave sites does not correlate to the W1/2 interstadial in Austria and bears no relationship to the concept upon which Penck and Brückner described their Würm stage in the sequence of Alpine Terraces.

Pleistocene in Africa The earliest Pleistocene levels in Africa are reversed-polarity sediments laid down after the end of the Olduvai subchron. At Olduvai Gorge itself this level occurs in the middle part of Bed II. These beds correlate both radiometrically and paleomagnetically with the Okote Member at Koobi Fora (Kenya), Omo Shungura members J-K-L (southern Ethiopia), and lower Melka Kontouré (eastern Ethiopia). In all of these sequences this level coincides with the earliest occurrence of Acheulean bifaces and cores, together with a brief continuation of Oldowan-style artifacts (at Olduvai and Melka Kontouré). Fossil remains are rare in comparison, but as far as the evidence allows the base of the Pleistocene in Africa is also in the transition zone between the youngest known *Homo habilis* and the oldest known *Homo erectus*. A comparison of the mammal fossils suggests that Swartkrans (Member 1) and Sterkfontein (Member 5) in South Africa and the 'Ubeidiya site in Israel also belong to this time, but confirmative dating is lacking.

No well-defined climate change has been identified at the base of the Pleistocene in Africa, but glacial deposits on Mount Kenya, Kilimanjaro, and the Ruwenzoris extend thousands of meters downslope from the present glacier limits and indicate that Pleistocene climate changes also affected the tropics. The lakes of the Rift Valley, many of which have no outlets, show signs of "pluvial" expansion during the Pleistocene. In the American west similar changes in level of the great desert lakes of the have been dated to coincide with periods of glacial advance, and this is probably also the timing of the African pluvials, at least in a general way. However, the dating and correlation of the pluvial periods is at present highly controversial. Changes in sea level on the North African coast, due to Pleistocene glacial oscillations, have been related to continental stratigraphy. Fossiliferous beds with late *Homo erectus* remains and tools at Thomas Quarry and Tighenif, and at Salé near Rabat, are dated to the end of the "Günz-Mindel" interglacial in this way.

See also AFRICA; EUROPE; GEOCHRONOMETRY; GLACIATION; HOMO; PALEOLITHIC; PALEOMAGNETISM; SEA-LEVEL CHANGE. [J.A.V.C., G.K.]

Further Readings

Bowen, D.Q. (1978) Quaternary Geology. Oxford: Pergamon.

Berggren, W.A., and Van Couvering, J.A. (1981) Quaternary. In Treatise on Invertebrate Paleontology, Part A, Introduction: A505–543. Boulder, Colo.: Geological Society of America.

Butzer, K.W., and Isaacs, G.L., eds. (1975) After the Australopithecines. Hawthorne, N.Y.: Mouton.

Denton, G.H., and Hughes, T.J., eds. (1981) The Last Great Ice Sheets. New York: Wiley.

Sarnthein, M., Stremme, H.E., and Mangini, A. (1986) The Holstein Interglaciation: time-stratigraphic position and correlation to stable-isotope stratigraphy of deep-sea sediments. Quatern. Res. 26(3):283–298.

PLESIADAPIDAE

Most successful archaic primate family in number of recognized paleospecies and of individuals within these taxa. Plesiadapids are known from the early Paleocene of North America and from the middle Paleocene to early Eocene in both Europe and North America. Species of the genus *Plesiadapis* are some of the most common Paleocene mammals, and they have been used as stratigraphic horizon markers (similar to the concept of index fossils) to date sedimentary rocks.

There are five recognized genera of Plesiadapidae. The oldest, unnamed, is from the Puercan Paleocene of North America; *Pronothodectes* occurs in the Torrejonian middle Paleocene of North America; *Plesiadapis* (including *Nannodectes*) and *Chiromyoides* are known from the late Paleocene to early Eocene of both North America and Europe; and the youngest genus, *Platychoerops*, is known from the European early Eocene.

The undescribed oldest genus of the family is

known from molar and a few premolar teeth, and in these features it is remarkably similar to the ancient paromomyid *Purgatorius*. The younger and only slightly more advanced species of *Pronothodectes* (two species are known) display characters clearly antecedent to the three younger and more advanced genera. Although the central incisors are enlarged, a lateral pair is still retained, in addition to the canine and the second premolar. The premolars are upright and shortened, and the talonid on the third lower molars is characteristically expanded. The molars display the diagnostic ancestral features of the plesiadapids in having the upper-molar protocones more central on the lingual side of the tooth than in other archaic primates, and correlated with this are the more vertical and less procumbent lower-molar trigonids.

The widespread genus *Plesiadapis* contains at least 15 paleospecies, but these are all retained in the same genus because morphologically they form a relatively undifferentiated group. In contrast to the probably ancestral *Pronothodectes* members of *Plesiadapis* lose the lateral lower incisor but retain the upper one. The upper and lower incisors are highly characteristic not only of this genus but also of all of the other described ones. The robust and enlarged lower central incisors together form a broad-based shovel or scoop with a continuous marginal edge around them. This is most similar to what is seen in some marsupial phalangers and is not rodentlike. The enlarged central upper incisors have three distinct cusps on their outer edges and a more posterior (distal) one to stop the action of the lower incisors against it. These mittenlike upper incisors are as robust as the more simply constructed lower ones.

Chiromyoides is much more poorly known, even though five alleged species have been described, based on incisor structure. This genus is a superrobust version of the smaller species of *Plesiadapis*, and its rarity may be due in no small measure to an ecological niche that may not have allowed great population densities. The mandible and muzzle are considerably shortened and deepened, and the enlarged incisors also suggest a greater loading of forces on the feeding mechanism. The lower incisors, as well as the anterior cusp of the upper central incisors, have diagnostically sharp transverse cutting edges anteriorly.

A wood-gnawing and grub-hunting lifestyle, such as is seen in the lemuriform aye-aye and some marsupial phalangers, may be the best living equivalent for this genus. Like *Chiromyoides*, *Platychoerops*, the youngest and largest plesiadapid, evolved from a stock of *Plesiadapis*. It had well-crenulated upper molars surrounded by broad cingula (ledges), suggesting

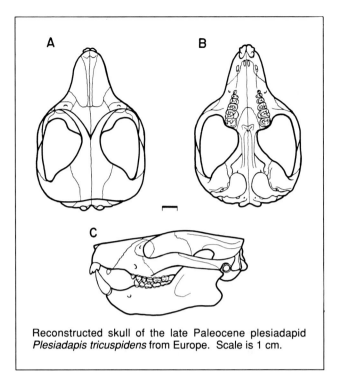

Reconstructed skull of the late Paleocene plesiadapid *Plesiadapis tricuspidens* from Europe. Scale is 1 cm.

a fully herbivorous diet, like that of the many species of *Plesiadapis*.

Most of our knowledge of plesiadapid cranial and postcranial anatomy derives from a few well-preserved cranial specimens from Europe and rare postcranial remains from both sides of the Atlantic. All archaic mammals, including the archaic primates, had a relatively larger head to body size than modern lemurs possess. In spite of this large head the brain was relatively small compared with the size of the skull or body, and *Plesiadapis* had a facial skull to neural skull proportion similar to that displayed by the living Virginia opossum. Yet, compared with similar-sized contemporary nonprimates like the ancient ungulate ancestors the arctocyonids, known plesiadapids had larger brains relative to their body size. The general shape of the skull was not unlike the broad and shallow skull of living marsupial phalangers, such as the genera *Trichosurus* and *Phalanger*. The skull of *Plesiadapis* unequivocally shows one of the diagnostic primate characteristics, an encasing of the middle-ear cavity by the petrosal, the same bone that houses the inner ear. Yet unlike euprimates this and other archaic primates lack the postorbital bar, characteristic not only of the primitive euprimates but also of other more evolved groups of placental mammals.

The postcranial remains, like the cranium, display a tantalizing mixture of archaic mammalian features intermixed with diagnostic primate attributes and probably unique plesiadapid characters. Some important distinctions about the levels of homology are difficult to sort out, because the archaic primates are relatively poorly known. The ability of the lower arm to rotate freely on the upper one and the nature of the upper and lower ankle-joint articulations leave no doubt that plesiadapids, or at least the nominal genus, were capable of performing activities found today in arboreal mammals. The very deep and laterally compressed terminal phalanges, which completely predict the shape of the claw in living mammals, indicate a claw structure like those found today

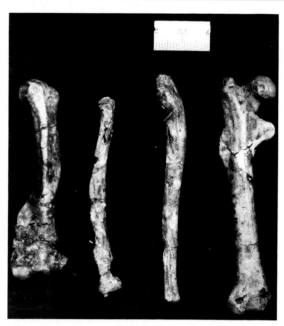

Representative long bones of the European *Plesiadapis tricuspidens.* From left to right: humerus, radius, ulna, and femur. Note the cylindrical capitulum on the distal end of the humerus and the forward bent olecranon process of the ulna, both features being often associated with mechanics necessary for arboreality. Scale is 2 cm.

in some of the most arboreal of clawed mammals, the colugos and tree-roosting fruit bats. Although plesiadapids were probably arboreal, the structure of the knee, as seen from the groove for the kneecap (patella) on the femur, indicates that they were relatively slower moving than the rapidly jumping, graspleaping, early representatives of euprimates (adapids and omomyids) or modern lemurids.

It thus appears that the Plesiadapidae were not only primarily herbivorous but were also arboreal, although many species probably pursued survival strategies as mixed as any in the somewhat similar living mammal families. We may think of these ancient primates as having occupied niches not entirely dissimilar to the arboreal phalangeroid marsupials and the living subtropical tree squirrels, the Sciuridae.

See also PLESIADAPIFORMES. [F.S.S.]

Further Readings

Szalay, F.S., and Delson, E. (1979) Evolutionary History of the Primates. New York: Academic.

PLESIADAPIFORMES

Taxonomic concept published by Simons in 1972 to encompass the archaic primate families that occur mostly in the Paleocene. Originally erected as an infraorder, it is regarded as a suborder in this encyclopedia. The semiorder Paromomyiformes, an equivalent concept, is used by students who regard the Primates as being divisible into two monophyletic branches, the second semiorder being the Euprimates. The archaic primates, the plesiadapiforms, although fully arboreally adapted like their archontan relatives the tree shrews and dermopterans, were quite distinct from the modern euprimates. The facial and neural halves of the skull had proportions similar to what we see in a Virginia opossum today. Not only were they similar to opossums, at least superficially, in their degree of neural development, but they probably did not differ significantly from them in terms of locomotion. Despite the archaic proportion of their skulls they could be distinguished from nonprimates by a complex of derived features. Among the most important of these characters are a special groove on the heel bone for a flexor tendon of the digits, features of the molar teeth, and the developmental derivation of the auditory bulla (the chamber that houses the middle-ear ossicles) from the petrosal bone.

The Plesiadapiformes represent the first known major radiation of the primates, and they, along with the other archontans, composed the first wave of placental mammals that we know to have invaded the arboreal milieu.

See also ARCHONTA; EUPRIMATES; MICROSYOPIDAE. [F.S.S.]

PLESIADAPIS   see   PLESIADAPIDAE

PLESIADAPOIDEA

Superfamily of the archaic primate suborder Plesiadapiformes. The three families united under this superfamily (Plesiadapidae, Carpolestidae, and Saxonellidae) almost certainly shared a common ancestor after the separation of that lineage from paromomyoids. Although Plesiadapoidea is monophyletic (its hypothetically acceptable last common ancestor is included in the group), and also probably holophyletic (it includes all known descendants of the common ancestor), the relationships among the three included families are not yet resolved.

The plesiadapoid common ancestor was a primate not far removed from the last common ancestor of all primates. It had, in each half of the upper and lower jaws, two incisors, a canine, three premolars, and three molars. Its cheek-tooth morphology was probably not very different from the middle Paleocene plesiadapid genus *Pronothodectes*. The central incisors, as in all known plesiadapoids, were characteristically enlarged and the upper central incisors were three-pronged and somewhat mittenlike. This last characteristic, however, may have been a retention from a paromomyid ancestry and therefore may not be an acceptable plesiadapoid diagnostic feature by itself. Plesiadapoids persisted into the early Eocene in both North America and Europe.

See also CARPOLESTIDAE; PLESIADAPIDAE; PLESIADAPIFORMES; SAXONELLIDAE. [F.S.S.]

PLESIANTHROPUS *see*
AUSTRALOPITHECUS AFRICANUS

PLESIOLESTES *see* PAROMOMYIDAE

PLESIOMORPHIC *see* CLADISTICS

PLIOCENE

Youngest epoch of the Tertiary Period, occupying the interval between 5.3 and 1.6 m.y. in the late Cenozoic. The term, meaning "most recent time," was proposed by Charles Lyell in 1833 for the epoch in which nearly all the fossils of marine mollusks and echinoderms were of still-living species. Lyell initially included all strata between the Miocene and the present in the Pliocene, dividing it into an "older Pliocene" and a "younger Pliocene," but subsequently renamed the "younger Pliocene" as the Pleistocene. In geological history the boundaries of the Pliocene are marked by two great events, the Messinian salinity crisis at its beginning and the first glacial episode of the Pleistocene at its end.

In England, northern Belgium (Flanders), and northern Italy the strata specifically assigned to the Pliocene in Lyell's original definition are everywhere separated from the Miocene by a gap in deposition, which is evidenced by an erosional unconformity (gullied and eroded Miocene beds covered by Pliocene beds). Modern research shows that in the North Sea basin the unconformity developed as the result of a sharp drop in global sea level. This drop in sea level, and the resultant erosional hiatus, helps to identify the Miocene–Pliocene boundary around the world. In the Mediterranean basin, however, the sea-

level decline had far more drastic consequences, cutting off the connection of the Mediterranean Sea to the world ocean. Prior to this time the Mediterranean and the Atlantic were connected through two shallow straits, one in Morocco and the other at the head of what is now the Guadalquivir River basin in southern Spain. With the supply of ocean water trickling to a halt, the Mediterranean first grew very concentrated and then evaporated, leaving an enormous salt-floored basin over 2,000 km. long and up to 5 km. deep. Deposits laid down during this period of increasing salinity and final evaporation are correlated with the Messinian Stage, the final stage of the Miocene.

The larger tributary river systems (Rhône, Po, and Nile) excavated prodigious canyons down to the floor of the Messinian desert during the final million years of the Miocene. These canyons, which were twice as deep as the Grand Canyon and are now almost completely filled, can be traced in the subsurface inland from the present river mouths for hundreds of kilometers, to Aswan in the case of the Nile and to the Italian lakes (the upper headwaters of the canyon) in the case of the Po.

The base of the Pliocene is defined in a Mediterranean outcrop that dramatically displays evidence for one of the most extraordinary events in geological history. At Capo Rosello, near Realmonte in the Agrigento district of southern Sicily, grey and black evaporite beds laid down on the floor of the desiccated Mediterranean are exposed at the foot of the beach cliff. These are directly overlain, in a knife-sharp contact, by chalk-white microfossil oozes that formed at the bottom of an ocean several kilometers in depth. The transition, at which the "golden spike" marking the base of the Pliocene is placed, records the catastrophic flooding of the basin when rising sea level overtopped and eventually broke through a former isthmus at Gibraltar. This titanic waterfall from the Atlantic gouged out the present straits to a depth of more than 200 m., probably in a few days' time.

All around the Mediterranean the sudden return of the ocean created backups and ponding in the coastal drainages, and initiated a regional episode of rapid burial and land-animal fossilization in satellite basins. In some, like the Wadi Natrun and Sahabi basins in northern Africa, fossiliferous sediments rest on salt beds that formed as the satellite basins were abandoned by the sinking Mediterranean. In the satellite basins of southern Spain fossil beds with African fauna are overlain by gypsum evaporites, overlain in turn by fossil beds with European fauna, reflecting the shifting biogeographical boundaries between Africa and Europe as the Guadalquivir straits closed and the Gibraltar straits opened. The macaques of Gibraltar, however, appear to be Pleistocene migrants, not Pliocene refugees.

In standard marine sequences the Pliocene consists of two stages typified in Italy, the Zanclean and the Piacenzian. Earlier literature refers to the Astian stage, but this term has been abandoned.

"Hipparion Datum" and False Pliocene

In the later nineteenth century German and Austrian geologists mistakenly correlated the Messinian evaporitic sequence in Italy to similar-looking evaporite beds in central Europe (e.g. the famous salt mines of Krakow), which were, as we now know, of middle Miocene age. This mistake was not detected for over 100 years, because the fossil shells from the Mediterranean region could not be directly compared with those of more northern regions, or those of the New World, and age-correlations were very imprecise. As a result most stratigraphers accepted the conclusion that the nonmarine "Pontian" Stage, which overlies the central European salt beds, was of early Pliocene age. The "Pontian" is characterized by abundant remains of the three-toed horse *Hipparion*, an immigrant from North America. Using the "Hipparion datum" as a guide, workers subsequently adopted the central European concept of the Pliocene throughout Asia (including the Siwaliks sequence) and back to the New World homeland of the hipparionines. In this view the Pliocene began ca. 12–10 m.y. ago, when *Hipparion* appeared in the geological record. Although French and Italian geologists had long argued that Lyell's definition involved much younger beds, they were proved right only as the result of deep-sea drilling in the Mediterranean.

Pliocene Climate and Fauna

The Pliocene saw climate changes of greater intensity and shorter duration than the Miocene, as the world gradually shifted toward Pleistocene conditions. The end-Miocene sea-level decline was a response to sudden growth of the Antarctic ice sheet and sharply lowered winter temperatures, which were followed by a warming trend and global transgression as the Antarctic ice again retreated. The early Pliocene warming trend reached a climax ca. 3.5 m.y. ago, attaining conditions more equable than any that have occurred since that time. Later, at ca. 2.5 m.y., global climate cooled to a new low, with renewed expansion of the Antarctic ice and a permanent northward shift of the austral polar front. The late Pliocene cold cycle was marked by the first appearance of ice-rafted debris in deep-sea deposits of the North Atlantic, indicating that the Greenland and other boreal polar ice sheets extended to sea level for the first time, and by the earliest traces of mountain glaciation in the western United States and Canada. In Europe this markedly colder climate is reflected in the paleobotanical-paleoclimatogical phase known as the Pretiglian, with its geomorphological equivalent in the earliest (Biber) terraces of the Danube-Rhine basin.

The 2.5-m.y. late Pliocene cooling event, because of its unprecedented severity, has been taken by some marine and continental stratigraphers as the logical beginning of the Pleistocene. This is based on a climatic concept of the Pleistocene, however, which was not advocated until long after Lyell defined the epoch on the basis of its fossil content. Most workers have come to accept the argument that the Pleistocene, like all other epochs, must therefore follow a stratigraphical definition in marine sediments. To complicate the matter, however, the formal proposal made in 1948 by the International Geological Congress to recognize the base of the Pleistocene (i.e. the top of the Pliocene) as being equivalent to the base of the Calabrian Stage in Italy also recommended (at the insistence of L.S.B. Leakey) that the base of the Villafranchian mammal age be taken as the boundary equivalent in continental sequences. The transition to typical Villafranchian mammal faunas in Eurasia is marked by the first appearance of forms adapted to highly seasonal, drought- and fire-resistant grasslands, such as the prairie elephants or mammoths, true bovines (cattle, bison, buffalo), and true one-toed equines. This has been called the "E-L-E" datum, for "*Elephas-Leptobos-Equus.*" Unhappily, however, the Villafranchian modernization of the Cenozoic fauna took place as a result of the climate change at 2.5 m.y. The supposed equivalence of Calabrian and Villafranchian, based on nothing more than similar lithology as the result of cold climate, is now known to be a million years in error according to radiometric dating.

The later Pliocene, between 2.2 and 1.6 m.y., was a time of moderate climates with relatively mild winters, interspersed with periodic swings to more severe conditions. In continental faunal history this was the middle Villafranchian in Europe, and the "Plio-" part of the famous Plio-Pleistocene sequences of East Africa, at Hadar, Laetoli, and the Lake Turkana basin.

Pliocene Evolution

By the beginning of the Pliocene the dryopithecines and pliopithecines of Europe and the sivapithecines of southern Eurasia had already become extinct. The intensification of ocean cooling in the late Miocene, and the resulting increase in severity of seasonal changes and expansion of the Afro-Arabian arid zone, had isolated the remaining extra-African hominoids—*Gigantopithecus*, hylobatids, and orangutans—in Southeast Asia, even as some of the more drought- and cold-tolerant cercopithecoids continued to adapt to the deteriorating conditions of the temperate lands.

In Africa the Pliocene began with *Australopithecus*, recognized from scanty remains at Kanapoi and Chemeron, as the only known survivor of a diverse assemblage of middle Miocene hominoids. Ancestral pongids may also have been present in Africa, although arguments from molecular biochronology suggest that they may not have differentiated from a common ancestor with the hominids before the early Pliocene. By the later Pliocene *afarensis* and *aethiopicus* (and perhaps an ancestral "robust" form) were distinct in East Africa and *africanus* was present in South Africa. From 2 m.y. ago to the beginning of the Pleistocene hominoids further diversified with the evolution of the fully "robust" australopithecines and *Homo habilis*.

See also CENOZOIC; "GOLDEN SPIKE"; KENYA; MIOCENE; PLEISTOCENE. [J.A.V.C., R.L.B.]

Further Readings

Berggren, W.A., Kent, D.V., and Van Couvering, J.A. (1985) Neogene, Part 2. in N.J. Snelling (ed.): The chronology of the Geological Record. Geological Society Memoir No. 10:211–260. London: Blackwoods.

Haq, B.U., Hardenbol, J., and, Vail P.R. (1987) A chronology of fluctuating sea-levels since the Triassic. Science 235:1156–1165.

Russell, D.E., and Savage, D.E. (1983) Mammalian Paleofaunas of the World. Reading, Mass.: Addison-Wesley.

PLIOPITHECIDAE

In the past there has been a much greater diversity of small apelike primates than exists now. These small creatures were distinguished by their generally primitive morphology, which made them look like some of the living apes, but they were not in fact apes at all and it would be incorrect to classify them as such. The most common of these primates belongs to a genus named *Pliopithecus*, found in many sites in central and southern Europe during the Miocene period; together with a number of other closely related genera this was probably the dominant primate in the Miocene woodlands of southern Europe. It was an animal the size of present-day gibbons, but it had no special relationship with these lesser apes.

The first specimen of *Pliopithecus* to be described came from Sansan in southern France. It was referred to as *Pithecus antiquus* by de Blainville in 1840, but this ambiguous generic name was altered to *Pliopithecus* by another French worker in 1849. Jaws and teeth were found from this prolific site, and their association with a rich mammalian fauna has enabled paleoecologists to reconstruct the habitat

there as a diverse and rich, probably subtropical, woodland. The age of Sansan is difficult to determine, since no radiometric dates are available, but comparison of the fauna with faunas from other, better-dated sites shows it to have been middle Miocene in age, probably ca. 14 m.y.

Many additional specimens of *Pliopithecus* have been collected over the years. Another site in France of similar age to Sansan is La Grive-Saint-Alban; Manthelan is slightly older. A number of slightly younger sites are known from Germany and Austria, the latter including Göriach, from which many jaws have come, and the youngest record of this genus is from Terrassa, near Barcelona (Spain). Many of the specimens from these sites were given separate names, but even though they span a range of from ca. 16 m.y. until at least 11–10 m.y. there is no good reason against putting them all into the single species *P. antiquus*.

Although known from many sites, *Pliopithecus* specimens were restricted to the jaws and teeth until important discoveries were made in Czechoslovakia at the site called Neudorf an der March, just over the border from Austria. The specimens are now kept jointly in Vienna and Basel. Three partial skeletons were found, one of them fairly complete, together with some isolated bones; thus nearly all parts of the skeleton are represented. They were described by Helmuth Zapfe, who assigned them to a new species and subgenus of *Pliopithecus* named *Epipliopithecus vindobonensis*. There are differences between this material and the type material of *Pliopithecus antiquus*, mainly in its retention of what have been interpreted as retained primitive characters. It most resembles the earliest known specimens from western Europe, particularly in its elongated molars, relatively narrow with well-developed cingula, and these similarities accord with the early age of the site, being equivalent to the earliest of the *Pliopithecus* sites.

The skull of "*Epipliopithecus*" shows it to have been a generalized primitive catarrhine primate. The skull is quite gracile, with no special adaptations for absorbing chewing stresses, and its diet can therefore be assumed to have consisted mainly of soft, easily-broken-down food, such as fruit. Its geographic range extended well into central Europe, where some degree of seasonality in the climate would have been inevitable, even in the warmer Miocene, and it apparently occupied much of the subcontinent. *Pliopithecus* is known from as far north as Przeworno (Poland), nearly at 51° and as far south as northern Spain, at 41°. Its postcranial adaptations show it to have been a quadrupedal arboreal climber, and it was probably an active animal both in the trees and on the ground. It is not certain whether it had a tail or

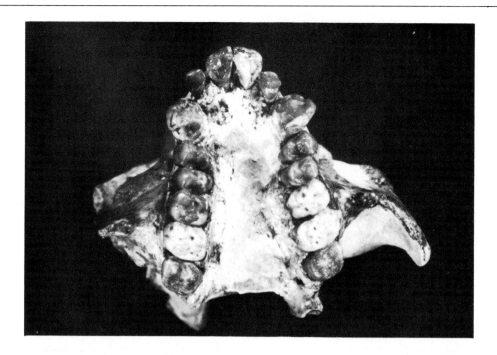

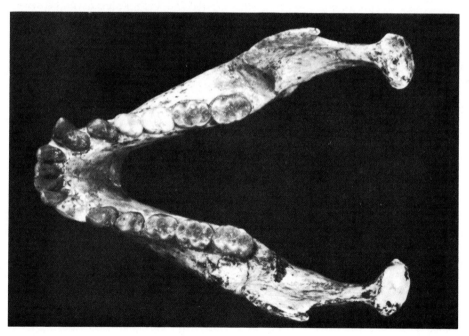

Upper and lower jaws of the skull of *"Epipliopithecus vindobonensis"* from middle Miocene deposits in Czechoslovakia, upper jaw above and lower jaw below.

not, but the indications are that it probably did.

More recent discoveries in Hungary of a remarkable type of pliopithecid have resulted in the identification of a whole range of new forms. The Hungarian species was originally named *Pliopithecus hernyaki* by Kretzoi, but he has since named a new genus for this form, *Anapithecus*. This distinction certainly appears justified, since it was much bigger than *Pliopithecus* and its teeth were very similar to those of lemurs. Its incisors and premolars seem to establish its relationship with the catarrhine primates, but its lower molars share many of the primitive characters seen in the teeth of certain lemurs, with development of the paraconid and broad, low, and waisted talonid regions of the lower molars. In some of these characters it resembles some of the original specimens first described from Sansan, but a reassessment of this latter material has shown it also to be distinct from the type material of *Pliopithecus antiquus*. It has since been renamed *Crouzelia auscitanensis*, and additional material and a second species described from La Grive-Saint-Alban. Adaptively these forms bear some resemblance to *Pliopithecus*, and their environments can also be inferred to have been similar.

Brief mention can be made of a number of incorrectly referred specimens of pliopithecid. *Pliopithecus posthumus* from Mongolia is probably not primate at all. "*Kansupithecus*" from the middle Miocene of China has been called a pliopithecid, apparently on the basis of size, but since other catarrhines of similar age and size are now known from that region (*Dionysopithecus*) it is more realistic to assign this edentulous mandible to that genus. *Laccopithecus robustus* from Lufeng (China) has been recently described from relatively complete material, and it may be related to gibbon ancestry or prove to be a pliopithecid, but the material is too poorly known at present to permit any firm conclusions.

See also APE; CATARRHINI; DIET; LEMUR; LOCOMOTION; MIOCENE; SPECIES; TAIL. [P.A.]

Further Readings

Andrews, P. (1985) Family group systematics and evolution among catarrhine primates. In E. Delson (ed.): Ancestors: The Hard Evidence. New York: Liss, pp. 14–22.

Harrison, T. (1987) The phylogenetic relationships of the early catarrhine primates: a review of the current evidence. J. Hum. Evol. 16:41–79.

PLIOPITHECOIDEA

Superfamily comprising two groups of primate: the Pliopithecidae and the Propliopithecidae, both of them long extinct. Represented in the fossil record of Africa and Eurasia, they are known from Oligocene and Miocene deposits spanning an age range of 35–10 m.y. ago.

The species included in this group are all small, and in most respects they lack distinguishing characters. They can be recognized as catarrhines by their loss of second premolars, but in most other characters they retain what is interpreted as the ancestral (primitive) catarrhine condition. In some cases, as in the morphology of their ear and the structure of the elbow joint, they retain a condition similar to that of many prosimians.

Its many primitive characters and the absence of any living representatives of this superfamily make it a difficult group to define. It is probably not a monophyletic group at all (i.e. it is probably not descended from a single common ancestor), but it is a convenient way of describing a group that has many similarities in morphology.

See also CATARRHINI; MIOCENE; OLIGOCENE; PLIOPITHECIDAE; PROPLIOPITHECIDAE; PROSIMIAN; SUPERFAMILY. [P.A.]

PLIOPITHECUS *see* PLIOPITHECIDAE

PLUVIALS

Pluvials (literally "rains") are subdivisions of the Pleistocene in subtropical and tropical areas, where intervals of relatively cold, wet climate reflect high-latitude glacials. In the 1930s, East African archeology was dated according to four pluvials based on former levels of Lake Victoria: Kageran, Kamasian, Kanjeran, and Gamblian, from oldest to youngest. These were later abandoned as unreliable, but recent work indicates that ancient lake levels in Africa can in fact be tied to global climate history.

See also GLACIATION; PLEISTOCENE. [J.A.V.C.]

Further Readings

McCall, G.J.H., Baker, B.H., and Walsh, J. (1967) Late Tertiary and Quaternary sediments of the Kenya Rift Valley. In W.W. Bishop and J.D. Clark (eds.): Background to Evolution in Africa. Chicago: Chicago University Press, pp. 191–220.

PODZOL *see* GLACIATION; PLEISTOCENE

POLYHEDRON *see* STONE-TOOL MAKING

POLYMORPHIC *see* GENETICS

POLYPHYLY *see* MONOPHYLY

POLYTYPIC

Because humans live in groups, the variation found among individuals can be analytically divided into two kinds: *polymorphic* and *polytypic*. The variation that exists within any group is polymorphic variation; the variation that exists among groups is polytypic variation. While polytypic variation is often more superficially obvious, approximately five times as much genetic variation is found within any human population as between populations.

See also POPULATION; RACE (HUMAN). [J.M.]

PONDAUNG

Range of hills with outcrops of stratified deposits of later Eocene age (ca. 44–40 m.y.) located near Mogaung (Burma), ca. 400 km. north of Mandalay. The Pondaung Formation has yielded fragmentary jaws and teeth of two possible early anthropoid primates,

Pondaungia and *Amphipithecus*. The former is considered an ancient catarrhine in this volume, but some workers think it a "lower" primate. *Amphipithecus* is more doubtful, and it is here discussed as a possible adapiform, although other authors group it closely with *Pondaungia*. The Pondaung sites were north of the Tethys seaway in the Eocene, but it is possible that mammals known there might have dispersed westward toward Europe and North Africa by the Oligocene; other connecting taxa (not primates) are known in Nepal and Turkey.

See also AMPHIPITHECUS; ANTHROPOIDEA; CATARRHINI; PALEOBIOGEOGRAPHY; PONDAUNGIA. [E.D.]

PONDAUNGIA

Poorly known genus of primate from the later Eocene (ca. 44–40 m.y.) Pondaung Formation of Burma, often considered the earliest catarrhine. *Pondaungia cotteri* was described by G.E. Pilgrim in 1927 on the basis of two partial lower jaws and two upper molars in a fragment of maxilla. The fossils had been chemically weathered before collection, so that the tooth surfaces were badly damaged. Some workers rejected them as primate, others considered them to be adapids, and still others placed them with catarrhines on the basis of superficial similarity to Fayum *Propliopithecus* and because of their geographic position. New collections made in the late 1970s included additional partial jaws that confirmed the primate nature of this animal, but uncertainty remains as to its precise affinity. The presence of a small paraconid near the metaconid on lower molars is a conservative feature typical of adapids and some other "lower" primates, while the deep and thick mandible, talonid of nearly equal height and breadth to trigonid, and midline distal hypoconulid are catarrhinelike features. The worn upper molars appear to have a well-developed hypocone surrounded by a small cingulum, as in anthropoids. Interpreting the majority of these features as derived characters shared with catarrhines results in the probable placement of *Pondaungia* as the oldest known Old World anthropoid.

See also AMPHIPITHECUS; ANTHROPOIDEA; CATARRHINI; PONDAUNG; PRIMATES. [E.D.]

Further Readings

Szalay, F.S., and Delson, E. (1979) Evolutionary History of the Primates. New York: Academic.

PONGINAE

Subdivision of Hominidae containing the orangutan and a number of fossil species. The orangutan is one of the three great apes, and formerly it was included with the chimpanzees and gorilla in a separate family, the Pongidae. Most authorities now believe, however, that the orangutan is more distantly related to humans than are chimpanzees and gorillas, and this is recognized by putting the former into its own subfamily and abandoning the concept of a great-ape clade. The family that combines all three great apes with humans is here called Hominidae.

Within Hominidae the pongines are the most specialized group. In a great many characters the African apes and humans retain the ancestral hominoid condition from which the orangutan has diverged, and this makes it easy to identify fossil orangutans, for they share at least some of the pongine specializations. It is less easy to identify hominine fossils because of the lack of hominine specializations.

The main characters by which the pongines differ from other hominoids include the following: the skull has an expanded and flattened zygomatic region, and together with a long upper face and great alveolar prognathism (projection of the lower face) this gives the face a distinctly concave shape when seen in side view. The lateral expansion of the lower face resulting from the large zygomatics contrasts with a much narrower upper face, which has relatively narrow orbits and a short distance between the orbits.

The browridges are not developed in the orangutan; this may be an ancestral hominoid character, since browridges are not present on any of the early fossil hominoids like *Proconsul*, but there is some indication that it may be a hominid specialization: prominent browridges are present on the African apes and fossil humans and on such early members of the hominid clade as *Dryopithecus*; if it is a hominid character, the lack of browridges on the orangutan would have to be seen as a reversion on its part to the ancestral condition and therefore as a derived character of the orangutan clade.

The premaxilla in the orangutan is rotated upward relative to the maxilla, so that the alveolar end (where the incisors are emplaced) forms a nearly horizontal shelf projecting in front of the nose; this is responsible for the alveolar prognathism and in part for the concave shape of the face, and it has also produced several changes in the morphology of the floor of the nose. The posterior end of the premaxilla is shifted posteriorly against the maxilla, and because of the rotation the two bones overlap; this results in the elimination of the incisive fossa, producing a smooth nasal floor, and in the great reduction in size of the incisive canals that carry the blood vessels and nerves between the nose and the mouth.

The dentition in orangutans is mainly noted for the thickened enamel on the molar teeth and the extreme degree of enamel wrinkling on the occlusal surfaces of the teeth. The enamel surfaces of the molar crowns are almost flat, as are the dentine surfaces beneath the enamel, and this seems to be related to the wrinkling of the crowns, since these crenulations take the place of enamel/dentine ridges formed during tooth wear. Finally, the lateral incisors are small relative to the central incisors.

These characters of the skull and dentition are unique to the orangutan. The African apes and humans are different from the orangutan but resemble

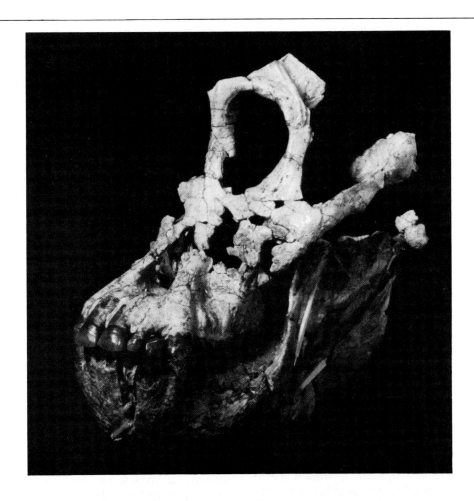

The face and jaws of *Sivapithecus indicus* from late Miocene deposits in Pakistan. This is the most complete fossil known for this genus, and it shows many of the characteristics of the orangutan face. Below it is compared in side view with a chimpanzee skull (left) and an orang skull (right).

the gibbons and monkeys and so must be said to retain the ancestral catarrhine condition. The recent discovery that a number of fossils also share the orangutan condition has led to a reassessment of the relationships of these fossils. Most of the specimens at present attributed to the genera *Sivapithecus* and (if separable from it) *Ramapithecus* can be shown to share some or most of these characters, particularly those of the nose and face, a finding made possible by the recovery of new and more complete fossil material from Turkey and Pakistan. The most complete specimen has been described by D. Pilbeam from Miocene deposits in Pakistan, and this adult individual of *Sivapithecus* has most of the face and jaws preserved. A less complete specimen from Turkey had been described a few years earlier, and while some of these characters of the face and palate were indicated by this specimen it required the more complete discovery from Pakistan to confirm the significance of these characters.

These two specimens thus confirmed the existence of the orangutan lineage during this part of the Miocene. This gave a date of 10.5–8 m.y. for the occurrence of this lineage, but more fragmentary fossils from earlier deposits in Pakistan pushed back the date of origin of the lineage to nearly 12 m.y. These specimens could be shown to have some aspects of the nasal and premaxillary morphology shown above to be characteristic of the orangutan. Earlier still is the large collection of isolated teeth from Paşalar (Turkey) dated by faunal comparisons to ca. 13 m.y. ago. It has been difficult to determine the affinities of this collection because of the lack of more complete jaws, but two characters of the dentition may indicate orangutan affinities. These are the flat dentine surface of the molars beneath the relatively flat thickened enamel of these teeth, and the disparity in size of the lateral and central incisors. If these characters are indicative of relationship, the origin of the orangutan clade must be taken as being at least 13 m.y. ago. This date is fully compatible with the divergence dates for the orangutan suggested by the molecular clock.

See also **Ape**; **Catarrhini**; **Dryopithecus**; **Hominidae**; **Miocene**; **Proconsul**. [P.A.]

Further Readings

Andrews, P., and Tekkaya, I. (1980) A revision of the Turkish Miocene hominoid *Sivapithecus meteai*. Palaeontol. 23:85–95.

Ciochon, R.L., and Corruccini, R.S. (1983) New Interpretations of Ape and Human Ancestry. New York: Plenum.

Patterson, C. (1987) Molecules and Morphology in Evolution: Conflict or Compromise. Cambridge: Cambridge University Press.

Szalay, F.S., and Delson, E. (1979) Evolutionary History of the Primates. New York: Academic.

PONGO *see* APE; PONGINAE

PONTIAN *see* MIOCENE

PONTNEWYDD

Cave in North Wales, where recent excavations have produced fragmentary Neanderthal-like fossils dating from more than 200 k.y. ago. Handaxe tools have been recovered from the same middle Pleistocene levels at the site. The most significant feature of the Pontnewydd teeth is the presence of Neanderthal-like taurodontism in the molars, where the tooth roots are undivided and the pulp cavity is enlarged.

See also **Archaic Homo sapiens**; **Neanderthals**. [C.B.S.]

POPULATION

Interbreeding group of organisms (also called a *deme*). Collectively the genotypes of the individuals in a population, or their gametes, constitute the gene pool of that population. Changes in the gene pool constitute microevolution. These changes may or may not affect the reproductive coherence of the population, thereby causing speciation and macroevolution.

See also **Genetics**; **Race (Human)**. [J.M.]

POSTGLACIAL *see* HOLOCENE

POTASSIUM-ARGON DATING *see* GEOCHRONOMETRY

PRAEANTHROPUS *see* AUSTRALOPITHECUS; AUSTRALOPITHECUS AFARENSIS

PREADAPTATION

Existing structure, item of behavior, or physiological process modified via natural selection to perform a new function. Preadaptations are often cited as intermediate stages in the development of complex adaptations—e.g. the evolution of flight in birds through stages of gliding and parachuting from heights.

See also **Adaptation**; **Evolution**. [N.E.]

PRE-AURIGNACIAN

Pre–Late Paleolithic blade industry from the Levant, defined at Jabrud, Shelter I, in the Anti-Lebanon Mountains of Syria. Also known from Ksar 'Akil (Lebanon) and possibly from Tabūn (Israel) and Haua

Fteah (Libya), the industry is characterized by true blade cores, burins, and end-scrapers including carinate forms that suggest "Aurignacian" affinities, in contrast to the similar Amudian. The pre-Aurignacian is followed at most sites by an Early Paleolithic industry without handaxes, the Jabrudian, and then by several levels of Levalloiso-Mousterian, suggesting an age well in excess of 60,000 B.P. The appearance and subsequent disappearance of a blade industry contemporary with or preceding the Mousterian have sometimes been seen as evidence for a Near Eastern origin or at least early presence of modern *Homo sapiens*.

See also AMUD; AMUDIAN; AURIGNACIAN; HAUA FTEAH; JABRUD; LATE PALEOLITHIC; MIDDLE PALEOLITHIC; STONE-TOOL MAKING; TABŪN. [A.S.B.]

PRE-BOREAL *see* GLACIATION; PLEISTOCENE

PŘEDMOSTI

Late Paleolithic open-air site or complex of sites covering a few square kilometers, excavated at the beginning of this century near the city of Přerov in Moravia (Czechoslovakia). It remains unclear today if these finds came from a single or a multilayered site or if they belonged to a single or to multiple sites. Remains uncovered included over 1,000 mammoths as well as a 4-by-2.5-m. oval mass grave of articulated and disarticulated human remains belonging to 29 predominantly subadult individuals. Lithic and bone assemblages from Předmosti have been assigned to a number of Late Paleolithic industries, including the Aurignacian, Szeletian, and Pavlovian. The one radiocarbon date for Předmosti indicates occupation at 26,000 B.P.

See also DOLNI VĚSTONICE; EUROPE; PAVLOV. [O.S.]

PREHISTORIC ARCHAEOLOGY *see* ARCHAEOLOGY

PREHISTORIC ECONOMY *see* ECONOMY, PREHISTORIC

PREHISTORY

Study of human cultures before writing. In Europe a distinction is often made between *prehistory*, the study of the vestiges of past cultures in their geological context up to the origins of agriculture, and *archaeology*, the study of Neolithic and later societies where historical and art-historical skills are used more than geological ones. Also in Europe the study of cultures that lacked written records but existed on the fringes of literate societies is called *protohistory*. Only in the Western Hemisphere, where native American societies at the time of European contact often represented a direct continuum with the prehistoric past, is the study of the prehistory integrally tied to anthropology, or ethnology.

Because prehistorians are almost entirely dependent on archaeological evidence to reconstruct the past, they must be able to extract the maximum amount of information from recovered objects and their geological, geographical, and environmental context. Increasingly prehistorians must collaborate with physicists, chemists, botanists, zoologists, geologists, and geographers in order to reconstruct the ages of sites, the functions of objects, the sources of raw materials, the environmental setting of sites, and other pieces of the past. In addition to a familiarity with these disciplines prehistorians must be able to draw on a knowledge of the ethnographic record.

See also ARCHAEOLOGY; ETHNOARCHAEOLOGY; GEOCHRONOMETRY; PALEOBOTANY; PALEOENVIRONMENTS; RAW MATERIALS. [A.S.B.]

Further Readings

Daniel, G. (1964) The Idea of Prehistory. London: Pelican.

Daniel, G. (1967) The Origins and Growth of Archaeology. New York: Crowell.

Thomas, D.H. (1979) Archaeology. New York: Holt, Rinehart and Winston.

PRENEANDERTHAL

Evolutionary scheme postulating that early and relatively unspecialized ("generalized") Neanderthals could have been the common ancestors of both "classic" Neanderthals and modern humans. Such workers as Sergi, Breitinger, Howell, and Le Gros Clark were adherents of this scheme in the 1950s and 1960s. European specimens like Steinheim, Swanscombe, and Ehringsdorf were seen as representative of the preneanderthal group, and in Southwest Asia the Tabūn and Skhūl fossils from Mount Carmel (Israel) were believed to occupy a comparable position. The model has lost favor recently, as opinions have become polarized about the phylogenetic position of the Neanderthals. Workers now tend to see either late Neanderthals themselves as direct ancestors or no members of the Neanderthal lineage as ancestors. In addition the dating and interpretation of the Mount Carmel material has considerably altered in recent years.

See also NEANDERTHALS; SKHŪL; TABŪN. [C.B.S.]

PREPARED-CORE

Technique of stone-tool manufacture in which the core is preformed to a shape suitable for the manufacture of a flake or flakes with a specific form. As stone technologies became more complex, the preparation of stone became more deliberate and refined: cores were skillfully "prepared," or flaked to a predetermined shape that would yield flakes or blades of a predictable size and shape.

The earliest examples of prepared cores are the so-called Levallois cores (and cruder, less standardized prepared cores often called "proto-Levallois") of the Acheulean and Mousterian periods, in which a large flake was typically removed from one face of a bifacially worked (often disk-shaped) core form. Well-known examples of such early prepared-cores include the Acheulean "Victoria West" industries of the Vaal River Valley in southern Africa with their circular and more pointed *hendebech* ("hen's-beak") cores from which oval-shaped flakes were detached. From the middle Pleistocene site of Kapthurin in the Baringo area of Kenya both Levallois cores and simple blade cores were recovered.

The classic Levallois, or "tortoise," cores of the later Acheulean and Mousterian/Middle Stone Age of the Old World, producing symmetrical oval flakes, are characterized by radial preparation of their dorsal

surface and careful preparation (faceting) of the striking platform to achieve the ideal edge angle and contour to detach a relatively large, sharp flake. Such flakes ideally have a sharp, acute edge around most of their circumference, except for the platform, since due to the core preparation the flake intersects the domed, upper surface of the core. This contrasts with the contemporaneous "discoidal core" technique, in which several flakes were struck from a bifacial, disk-shaped core, usually without elaborate platform preparation.

In northern Africa, at such sites as Tabelbala and Tachengit (Algeria), some Acheulean assemblages display an unusual prepared-core technique in which cleaverlike flakes were detached from large cores (Tachengit technique). And at some Acheulean sites in Africa a large flake was detached from a boulder, and subsequently another large flake detached from the first flake, producing a flake blank with a bulb of percussion on *both* faces, the so-called Kombewa or "Janus" flakes.

A sophisticated example of the prepared-core technique is evident in the production of Levallois points, in which intersecting scars on the core predetermined the shape of the final flake, a sharp point that was probably hafted to a spear. Such points are characteristic of the Middle Paleolithic. The blade cores of the Late Paleolithic and later periods are generally prepared to a cylindrical or prismatic shape for the production of a series of long, parallel-sided blades and also often involved careful preparation of striking platforms to maintain correct edge angles.

See also ACHEULEAN; BLADE; CLEAVER; CORE; FLAKE; LEVALLOIS; MIDDLE PALEOLITHIC; MIDDLE STONE AGE; MOUSTERIAN; PALEOLITHIC; STONE-TOOL MAKING. [N.T., K.S.]

Further Readings

Bordaz, J. (1970) Tools of the Old and New Stone Age. Garden City, N.Y.: Natural History Press.

Bordes, F. (1970) The Old Stone Age. New York: McGraw-Hill.

Clark, J.D. (1970) The Prehistory of Africa. London: Thames and Hudson.

Isaac, G.L. (1982) The earliest archaeological traces. In J.D. Clark (ed.): The Cambridge History of Africa, Vol. 1: From the Earliest Times to c. 500 BC. Cambridge: Cambridge University Press, pp. 157–247.

Three examples of prepared-core technique: a) Levallois tortoise core (left) and the Levallois flake; b) a Levallois point core (left) and the flake produced; c) a blade core.

PRESAPIENS

Term most clearly associated with the evolutionary scheme favored by the French paleoanthropologists Boule and Vallois. In their view the European fossil hominid sequence recorded the separate evolution of the Neanderthal and modern human lineages, with Swanscombe and, later, Fontéchevade representing ancient members of the "presapiens" lineage leading to modern humans.

See also BOULE, PIERRE MARCELLIN; FONTÉCHEVADE; SWANSCOMBE; VALLOIS, HENRI VICTOR. [C.B.S.]

PRESBYTIS *see* COLOBINAE

PRESSURE FLAKING *see* STONE-TOOL MAKING

PŘEZLETICE

Open-air locality with four superimposed strata of middle Pleistocene paleosols, lacustrine marls, and sands situated some 20 km. northeast of Prague (Czechoslovakia). At the time of deposition this locality was on the shores of a lake close to the mouth of a small river. Numerous diverse animal remains from these strata are assigned to the Biharian complex. Archaeological inventories, including stone tools made of quartz and lydite, bone tools, worked bone, flecks of wood charcoal, and burned stone and bone fragments, were predominantly not *in situ*. The lithic assemblage, which includes both large and small tools and consists of some 335 pieces, has been assigned to the Přezletician industry, a local variant of the proto-Acheulean. Faunal and floral remains indicate occupation during the Cromerian interglacial. A tooth fragment originally identified as human has been reassessed as nonprimate.

See also ACHEULEAN; EARLY PALEOLITHIC; EUROPE; STRANSKÁ SKÁLA. [O.S.]

PRIMATE ECOLOGY

Study of interactions between primates and their environments. The natural environments of the great majority of living primates are the wooded regions of the tropics and subtropics, in Central and South America, Africa (including Madagascar), and Asia. The largest number of primate species occurs in rain forests, vegetation that grows close to the equator in regions where annual rainfall is at least 1,500 mm. and where no more than four consecutive months have less than 100 mm. of rain. Tropical rain forest is dominated by tall broad-leaved trees, many of them evergreens, whose trunks and branches form a nearly continuous network above the ground. Tying many of the tree crowns together are woody-stemmed lianas, the typical climbing plants of the rain forest. The diversity of species of plants and animals in tropical rain forest is greater than in any other terrestrial environment, and in some West African areas as many as 15 primate species (including prosimians, cercopithecid monkeys, and great apes) may co-occur.

Away from the equator, where rainfall is lower and dry seasons more prolonged, tropical deciduous forests and savanna woodlands occur. These are also important primate habitats, but in most cases the number of species that live in them is much lower than in rain forest. Here trees are generally smaller, are spaced farther apart, and frequently shed their foliage during dry periods. Continuous overhead pathways are rare, and primates, such as baboons (*Papio* spp.), typically spend considerable periods of time on the ground. In savanna habitats water is in relatively short supply, and its availability often affects the distribution of primates. In areas of low rainfall in the tropics primates are usually absent, and with the exception of humans and some macaques few species of living primate have a significant part of their distribution within the temperate zone.

Since research on nonhuman primates is often undertaken either implicitly or explicitly to gain insights on human evolution and behavior, primate ecology has tended to concentrate on questions different from those pursued in the mainstream of ecological science. Although some primate ecologists have come from a biological background, many have been trained as anthropologists, psychologists, or anatomists, and this has led to a concentration on such topics as social and locomotor behavior. Primate ecology has also been influenced by the location of many study populations, remote from the temperate areas where the discipline of ecology (and many ecologists) have grown up. Not only has this tended to put primate ecology beyond the immediate view of the majority of ecologists, it has also limited the appeal of the subject to a relatively small number of people willing and able to work under unusual conditions. Remoteness from civilization and the nature of the animals have also limited the kinds of study techniques that can be used. Forest primates in particular are hard to capture without injury, and many field studies have therefore relied entirely on observational techniques. The most important piece of equipment in such field studies is a pair of binoculars.

The first scientific field studies of primates began in the late 1920s and early 1930s, sponsored by R.M. Yerkes, professor of psychobiology at Yale University. In 1931 one of Yerkes's research fellows, C.R. Carpenter, initiated studies on the population of howler monkeys (*Alouatta palliata*) on Barro Colorado Island in the Panama Canal, studies that have continued, with some interruptions, to the present day. A major surge in field studies began in the late 1950s, and in the next 25 years at least one population of most species came under scrutiny.

Although some progress has been made in under-

Some primates, such as this female black lemur (above), rarely leave the trees; others, such as this group of savanna baboons, (below), range widely on the ground.

standing the dynamics of wild primate populations, on the structure and functioning of primate communities, and on foraging strategies (issues in the mainstream of ecology), most attention has focused on the ecological determinants of social organization. The evidence accumulated to date suggests that the distribution and abundance of food and the kinds and densities of predators are the environmental factors that have the most significant influence on the organization of primate societies.

Field studies have led to an awareness that nonhuman primates are of interest not only because of their close relationship to *Homo sapiens* but also because they are a significant component of many of the ecosystems they inhabit. When not subjected to heavy pressure by human hunters, they are among the most numerous mammals in some tropical forests, particularly in Africa, where they can achieve a biomass (weight per unit area) approaching that of savanna ungulates. As medium- to large-sized consumers that are adept at arboreal life, have a broad range of more or less omnivorous diets, and are typically both long-lived and social (with low reproductive rates), primates occupy a special set of ecological niches and influence the functioning of rainforest ecosystems in many ways.

Responding over millions of years to the pressures imposed by primates and other animals feeding upon them, some rain-forest trees and lianas have evolved flowers that may be pollinated by primates. Others have evolved fruits that attract primates; after digesting the pulp of these fruits, primates may unwittingly drop the seeds undamaged at opportune germination sites. Many plants have evolved mechanical and chemical defenses against animal depredations, and foraging primates must cope with this array of defenses as they search for food. Primate ecologists have only recently begun to unravel these complex systems of interaction between rain-forest primates and their food supply. Along with other fascinating problems presented by the rain-forest ecosystems, these interactions may never be fully understood if present rates of forest destruction continue. The rapidity with which expanding human populations and consumer economies are destroying tropical forests and their primate populations is leading many primate ecologists to become increasingly involved in conservation efforts.

See also Diet; Population; Primate Societies. [J.F.O.]

Further Readings

Clutton-Brock, T.H., ed. (1977) Primate Ecology: Studies of Feeding and Ranging Behaviour in Lemurs, Monkeys and Apes. London: Academic.

Jolly, A. (1985) The Evolution of Primate Behavior, 2nd ed. New York: Macmillan.
Richard, A.F. (1985) Primates in Nature. New York: Freeman.
Richards, P.W. (1952) The Tropical Rain Forest. Cambridge: Cambridge University Press.
Terborgh, J. (1983) Five New World Primates: A Study in Comparative Ecology. Princeton, N.J.: Princeton University Press.

PRIMATE SOCIETIES

Primates, including humans, are social animals. When encountered in the wild, most primates are not alone. Instead, they are frequently in close proximity to other members of the same species. If one follows such a group for some time, it usually becomes apparent that it is not a transient phenomenon. Rather, it is a relatively stable, cooperative structure, whose members know each other well, have most of their nonaggressive social interactions with each other, and usually move in a synchronized fashion within the same limited geographical area (their home range). Members of one social group often behave aggressively toward members of another.

Although a primate social group typically contains individuals of both sexes and all ages, the actual size and composition of groups vary tremendously. Groups of monogamous primates, such as gibbons (*Hylobates*) and owl monkeys (*Aotus*), consist of a mated pair of adults together with a small number of immature offspring. Many forest-living monkeys in Africa and Asia live in so-called harem (or one-male) groups, which contain only a single fully adult male, several females (often three to eight, but sometimes more), and the females' immature offspring; gorillas (*Gorilla gorilla*) also typically live in small harems. Groups of many species of baboon (*Papio*) and macaque (*Macaca*) are often large; groups of 30–40 are common, with several adult males and many females; occasionally baboon groups number over 100 individuals. Similar large multimale groups occur in some rain-forest primates, such as the squirrel monkeys (*Saimiri*) of Central and South America and the red colobus monkeys (*Procolobus badius*) of Africa.

While primate societies normally consist of one or other of these broad categories of social group, some do not. Chimpanzees (*Pan troglodytes*) and spider monkeys (*Ateles*) live in loosely coherent communities in which individuals may spend much time on their own or with just small subsets of their social network. Members of the community, however, do share a common home range and are familiar with each other. Gelada baboons (*Theropithecus gelada*) of the high-altitude grasslands of Ethiopia are organized into harem groups, but these groups share their range with many others, forming a band whose

Grooming is an important component of the social behavior of these Mayotte lemurs (above); the dominant male of a group of Mauritian long-tailed macaques threatens an intruder (below). (Photographs by Ian Tattersall.)

size and structure, they also vary in the patterns of interaction that occur between individuals and in the patterns of migration in and out of groups. Social interactions, which involve communicative acts, are generally classed as *affiliative* (friendly or cooperative) or *agonistic* (competitive). Any one communicative act may involve a combination of visual signals, sounds, smells, or touch. Smell (olfactory communication) is used especially by lorises and lemurs, while loud long-range calls are particularly important in the signal repertoire of rain-forest monkeys and apes, which live in an environment whose vegetation interferes with long-range visual communication. Many affiliative interactions involve touch, of which grooming, in which one animal cleans the coat of another with its hands or mouth, is especially important.

In many primate societies males leave the group in which they are born, while females stay in their natal group. Affiliative interactions, leading to the formation of close social bonds, are particularly common between animals that have grown up together. As a result many primate groups have a social core of closely bonded female relatives. In these "female-bonded" primates males will often compete with each other for the opportunity of mating with the females. In harem groups this may lead to aggressive takeovers of whole groups by males migrating in from outside. These males may attack young infants. In a few "non–female-bonded" groups, especially those of chimpanzees and red colobus monkeys, females transfer out of their natal groups as they mature, and most social cooperation occurs between bonded males.

In multimale groups (and especially in baboons and macaques) competition typically takes the form of dominance interactions, in which animals displace or give way to others (without overt aggression) on the basis of the outcome of previous interactions. Such dominance relationships, found in both males and females, have considerable stability and allow group members to be ranked in a linear hierarchy.

One of the major goals of those studying primate societies has been to explain these patterns of variation. Available evidence strongly suggests that much of the variation is the result of different phylogenetic inheritances (e.g. the size, structure, and functional features of a galago versus those of a gorilla) interacting with a range of different environments. In any one environment two of the most crucial sets of variables affecting social organization are the distribution and abundance of food and the risk of predation. Thus a small-bodied forest-living nocturnal galago is not a conspicuous target for a predator, and by moving around with other galagos it may not be able to reduce significantly its risk of being preyed

members often feed together. Individuals of the orangutan (*Pongo pygmaeus*) and of several species of small, nocturnal lorises and lemurs typically move and feed on their own yet belong to a local network of familiar individuals. Although galagos in such a network may forage on their own, they often share a sleeping nest with other individuals.

Not only do primate social groups vary greatly in

upon. On the other hand insects (one of its main foods) are thinly scattered through its environment and searching for them in the company of other galagos would probably result in frequent competition over the same items. By contrast day-active squirrel monkeys in the forests of Amazonia are obvious targets for visually hunting eagles, while one of their preferred foods (ripe figs) occurs in large aggregations when giant trees are in fruit. By moving about in large groups, squirrel monkeys may reduce their risk of predation without significantly lowering their feeding efficiency.

Some recent analyses show close relationships between feeding efficiency and group size in wild primates, probably because food typically occurs in discrete clumps in which only a limited number of individuals can feed at one time without undue competition. Body size and mode of locomotion also influence the number of individuals that can efficiently move and feed as a unit. Obviously the food requirements of a single gorilla militate against large numbers of gorillas traveling together. However, the gorilla's staple food, the succulent stems and foliage of low-growing plants, occurs in denser patches than do the ripe tree fruits on which the closely related chimpanzee feeds. One tree crown can provide adequate food for far fewer chimpanzees (adult female weight 40 kg.) than squirrel monkeys (adult female weight 0.6 kg.), and this probably explains the fission-fusion nature of chimpanzee society.

Finally, the number of adult males in a group seems to be a compromise between the disadvantages in any one situation of male-male competition for breeding females and the advantages of male cooperation in warding off predators or competing primates (including competing males).

See also PRIMATE ECOLOGY; SEXUAL DIMORPHISM; SOCIOBIOLOGY. [J.F.O.]

Further Readings

Hinde, R.A., ed. (1983) Primate Social Relationships: An Integrated Approach. Oxford: Blackwell.

Jolly, A. (1985) The Evolution of Primate Behavior, 2nd ed. New York: Macmillan.

Kummer, H. (1971) Primate Societies: Group Techniques of Ecological Adaptation. Chicago: Aldine-Atherton.

Smuts, B.B., Cheney, D.L., Seyfarth, R.M., Wrangham, R.W., and Struhsaker, T.T., eds. (1987) Primate Societies. Chicago: University of Chicago Press.

Snowdon, C.T., Brown, C.H., and Petersen, M.R., eds. (1982) Primate Communication. Cambridge: Cambridge University Press.

PRIMATES

Order of mammals to which human beings and some 200 other living species belong. Classification of the group is not entirely settled: for example, all currently accepted classifications divide the living primates into two major groups (suborders), but zoologists differ as to whether *Tarsius*, the tarsier, should be classified with the "lower" primates (lemurs, lorises, bushbabies) in the suborder Prosimii, or with the "higher" primates (New and Old World monkeys, apes, humans) in the suborder Haplorhini. In the classification adopted for this encyclopedia the latter arrangement is provisionally preferred.

As in the case of any other natural group what essentially unites the primates is their common phylogenetic origin: all primates are descended from a single ancestor. Since evolution involves change, and Primates (spelled with a capital P and pronounced "pri-MAY-tees" only when used as a proper noun) has diversified considerably from that ancestor, we would not expect that this common origin would necessarily be reflected in the possession of a suite of diagnostic features by all members of the order. This turns out to be the case, at least in features that are observable in the fossil record, and it is probably for this reason that, following W.E. Le Gros Clark, recent students of Primates have generally characterized the order on the basis of several "progressive" evolutionary trends. Among these are the dominance of the visual over the olfactory sense, with the associated reduction of the olfactory apparatus and elaboration of stereoscopic vision; the improvement of grasping and manipulative capacities; and the tendency to enlarge the higher centers of the brain. Among those primates extant today the "lower" primates more closely resemble forms that evolved early in the history of the order, while the "higher" primates belong to groups more lately evolved.

"Trends," however, are of little use in providing a morphological definition of Primates with which the attributes of potential members of the order might be compared. Thus R.D. Martin has recently reinvestigated this problem, finding that a number of universal or near-universal features do indeed demarcate living primates from all other placental mammals. Unfortunately near-universality is more generally the rule than universality, and such features cannot be used in a rigid morphological definition, even (or especially) when such definition is based, as it must be, on an aggregation of animals already defined as Primates. Moreover, characteristics that do indeed definitively demarcate primates from other placentals, such as the possession of a brain that constitutes a significantly larger proportion of body weight at all stages of gestation, are impossible to apply to the fossil record, which is where the questions actually lie; for following the expulsion in the 1970s of the tree shrews from Primates there has been no doubt about which members of the living fauna belong to Primates and which do not.

There is similarly no question about which typical Eocene and later fossil forms are to be allocated to Primates, since by this epoch "primates of modern aspect" are present in the fossil record, and their aspect is modern enough to allay any doubts as to their phylogenetic affinities. The earliest primates, however, do pose a problem, and opinions have varied about whether the primates of the Paleocene epoch (ca. 64–54 m.y. ago) should indeed be admitted to the order. This is because these forms are both adaptively different from, and have no direct evolutionary links with, any living representatives of the order; to express this they are placed in their own primate suborder, Plesiadapiformes. The plesiadapiforms are recognized as primates because of resemblances to later members of the order in their chewing teeth and locomotor anatomy; these serve quite convincingly to demonstrate the common origin of the two groups, which probably took place toward the end of the Cretaceous period, sometime over 65–70 m.y. ago. Found in both the Old and the New Worlds, the plesiadapiforms retained clawed hands and feet, possessed large, specialized front teeth, and were probably arboreal in habit (see CARPOLESTIDAE; EUPRIMATES; PALEOCENE; PAROMOMYIDAE; PAROMO- MYOIDEA; PICRODONTIDAE; PLESIADAPIDAE; PLESIADAPI- FORMES; PLESIADAPOIDEA; SAXONELLIDAE).

No known plesiadapiform is a satisfactory candidate for the ancestry of the fossil "primates of modern aspect" typical of the Eocene epoch (54–36 m.y.). These later primates are grouped broadly into "lemurlike" forms, usually classified in the superfamily Adapoidea (see ADAPIDAE; ADAPIFORMES; EOCENE; NOTHARCTIDAE), and into "tarsierlike" forms, generally classed as omomyids (see ANAPTOMORPHINAE; EOCENE; MICROCHOERINAE; OMOMYIDAE; OMOMYINAE), although this elementary division may ultimately prove to be oversimplified. Eocene primates from both the New World and the Old World already exhibit the "trends" noted above that mark modern primates as a whole. These arboreal creatures possessed grasping hands and feet in which sharp claws were replaced by flat nails backing sensitive pads; the face was reduced in response to a deemphasis of the sense of smell; the eyes were completely ringed by bone and faced forward, producing wide overlap of the visual fields (hence stereoscopic vision) and suggesting a primary reliance on the sense of vision; and the brain was enlarged relative to body size when compared with other mammals of the time.

It is possible that the origins of some modern "lower" primates may be traced back to or through certain Eocene primate genera known in the fossil record. In any event it is widely accepted that the antecedents of the living primates are to be sought somewhere within the Eocene primate radiation, even where the details of this ancestry remain unclear. In North America the descendants of the Eocene primates gradually disappeared following the close of the epoch, while virtually all fossil "lower" primates from later epochs in Africa and Asia are quite closely related to the modern primates of those areas (see GALAGIDAE; SIVALADAPIDAE), except for Afrotarsius from the Fayum and possibly for a fragmentary strepsirhine recently found there.

The bulk of living strepsirhine primates, known as the lemurs, survive in Madagascar. Since the recent arrival of humans in that island many of the Malagasy primates have become extinct, notably the large-bodied climber-hanger Palaeopropithecus, the koalalike but huge Megaladapis, and the baboonlike Archaeolemur (see ARCHAEOLEMURIDAE; MEGALADAPIDAE; PALAEOPROPITHECIDAE). Extant Malagasy primates are grouped into five families (see CHEIROGALEIDAE; DAUBENTONIIDAE; INDRIIDAE; LEMURIDAE; MEGALADA- PIDAE). Other living strepsirhines include the lorises of Asia and Africa (see LORISIDAE) and the bushbabies of Africa (see GALAGIDAE). All extant strepsirhines possess dental scrapers or tooth combs (see LEMURIFORMES; TEETH), and all retain the primitive mammalian external nose, with a moist, naked rhinarium and associated structures. Additionally, all are united by possessing a "toilet claw" on the second digit of the foot (see LEMURIFORMES; STREPSIRHINI). All strepsirhines possess grasping extremities, although their manual dexterity is generally inferior to that of the "higher" primates, in comparison with which their brains also tend to be relatively small.

Anthropoidea

The "higher," or anthropoid, primates today are the dominant forms in all areas other than Madagascar. Their ultimate ancestry is obscure, but most researchers agree that it probably can be traced back toward the omomyid group of Eocene species. Of the living primates tarsiers are commonly regarded as closest to anthropoids in details of nasal structure and placentation, the partial rear closure of the orbit, and the bony ear. In turn some omomyids share dental, cranial, and postcranial structures with tarsiers, and some of the less extreme forms preserve incisor teeth that foreshadow the pattern characteristic of ancestral anthropoids. Opinion varies more widely on the paleogeographic wanderings of early anthropoids, with two main views current: 1) a broadly protoanthropoid stock of omomyids was distributed in western North America and eastern Asia (where a later Paleocene species has recently been recognized), which diverged by the early Eocene into two southward-expanding lineages: one entered South America to evolve into the platyrrhine New World monkeys, while the other spread across Eurasia into Africa as the ancestral catarrhines; or 2) a Eurasian protoanthropoid stock entered Africa by the early Oligocene, where it divided into early catarrhines and a platyrrhine ancestor that rafted or "island-hopped" across the South Atlantic to reach the Neotropics. Each hypothesis has both morphological and paleogeographical problems to answer before one can be firmly accepted as more likely, but there is broad agreement on the monophyly of Anthropoidea if not on the date or place of divergence of the two infraordinal clades (*see* ANTHROPOIDEA; CATARRHINI; PALEOBIOGEOGRAPHY; PLATE TECTONICS; PLATYRRHINI).

The platyrrhines include two major divisions in most classifications, but not all researchers agree on the contents of these groups. Here, two families are accepted: the generally small-bodied Cebidae with a lightly built masticatory system, and the mainly medium- to large-sized Atelidae, with more robust jaws and teeth. Early members of both families are known by ca. 20 m.y. ago, and most fossils can be closely linked to living genera. This pattern of *bathyphyly*, the long extension of evolutionary lineages, is a characteristic of the platyrrhines in strong opposition to the more "bushy" pattern of successive radiations seen in the catarrhines (*see* ATELIDAE; ATELINAE; CALLITRICHINAE; CEBIDAE; CEBINAE; MONKEY; PITHECIINAE).

Living catarrhines are readily divided into the Cercopithecoidea (Old World monkeys) and Hominoidea (lesser apes, great apes, and humans), but that distinction is not so easy to trace back into the past. Cercopithecoid monkeys are characterized by a bilophodont dentition and general skeletal adaptation to quadrupedal life on or near the ground, while hominoids share less derived teeth, a trend to larger brain and body size, and a complex of postcranial features emphasizing forelimb flexibility and suspension.

The earliest Old World anthropoid is probably the later Eocene Burmese *Pondaungia*, but its inclusion within the Catarrhini is questionable. More definite are the Oligocene (ca. 33–31 m.y.) primates from the Fayum deposits of northern Egypt. The family Parapithecidae includes species that share few features in common with living catarrhines (but have a number of derived characters of their own) and may be considered archaic members of this infraorder, little changed from its common ancestor. The contemporaneous propliopithecids have reduced the number of their premolar teeth to the two seen in living catarrhines and have a more "modern" postcranial

skeleton but still retain a conservative auditory region. It seems likely that they were similar to the common ancestors of the cercopithecoids and hominoids, although some authors continue to place them in the latter taxon (*see* FAYUM; OLIGOCENE; PARAPITHECIDAE; PROPLIOPITHECIDAE; PONDAUNGIA).

Three main higher-primate groups existed in the Miocene: the conservative pliopithecids of Europe (and probably Asia and Africa), in many ways similar to the earlier propliopithecids; hominoids, first seen by 23 m.y.; and early cercopithecoids, known after ca. 19–16 m.y. The last group apparently diverged from a "dentally hominoid" arboreal ancestor as a partially ground-dwelling lineage with a diet including more leaves and seeds than the mainly frugivorous hominoids. Although not common in the early or middle Miocene, Old World monkeys spread into Eurasia in the late Miocene and possibly replaced most hominoids there as the climate deteriorated and forests shrank. The Colobinae retained conservative catarrhine facial proportions but adapted to a diet concentrating on leaves by increasing tooth relief and sharpness and developing a sacculated stomach for better digestion of cellulose. Most living species are arboreal, but two Pliocene lineages became highly terrestrial. Cercopithecines retained mainly conservative teeth and an eclectic diet but often developed elongated faces and, in a variety of lineages, a high degree of terrestriality. The enigmatic Miocene Oreopithecidae of Africa and Europe may be an early offshoot of either the Cercopithecoidea or the Hominoidea (*see* CERCOPITHECIDAE; CERCOPITHECINAE; CERCOPITHECOIDEA; COLOBINAE; MIOCENE; OREOPITHECIDAE; PLIOCENE; PLIOPITHECIDAE; VICTORIAPITHECINAE).

The third main group of Miocene catarrhines included the earliest members of the Hominoidea, especially the species of *Proconsul*, but perhaps also such other genera as *Micropithecus* and *Afropithecus*. Known from 23–14 m.y., *Proconsul* was a quadrupedal frugivore that apparently shared a number of derived postcranial features with later apes. The classification of the Hominoidea varies widely among authors, but here three families are recognized, one for these early African forms; a second (Hylobatidae) for the gibbons and relatives, whose ancestry is not clear; and a third (Hominidae) for the great apes, humans, and extinct relatives. Hominids (and pliopithecids) were able to enter Eurasia from Africa (probably via Arabia and the Near East) ca. 16 m.y., after which two main lineages can be recognized until 8 m.y. The more conservative *Dryopithecus* was found mainly in Europe (but also rarely in Asia), while a more derived lineage apparently related to the living orangutan was represented in eastern Europe, Turkey, Indopakistan, and China. The last group is commonly assigned to the genus *Sivapithecus*, but some members were previously separated as *Ramapithecus*, and today several other genera (e.g. *Graecopithecus*) are often recognized. *Gigantopithecus* was a very large member of this clade known from a few 7-m.y. specimens in Indopakistan and many more from 1-m.y. sites in China. Fossil hylobatids are also known from the latter time period onward, but it has not yet been possible to identify any older fossil as gibbonlike, because the living forms are characterized by generally conservative crania and dentition but also by a highly derived hominoid postcranium linked to their ricochetal brachiating adaptation. Middle and later Miocene African hominids are also rare, although *Kenyapithecus* may be a member of this clade. The relationships among living hominids have not been unequivocally determined from comparative morphology, but in combination with molecular studies (especially immunology and DNA hybridization and sequencing) one phylogeny has emerged as widely acceptable. Hylobatids are seen as strongly distinct from the hominids, implying a rather ancient divergence, although dates provided by "molecular clock" hypotheses are questionable. *Pongo*, the orangutan, is distinct from the African apes and humans; the subfamily Ponginae is here recognized for the orang and its fossil relatives, as opposed to the Homininae. Views differ as to which was the first lineage to diverge among the hominines, with most molecular data placing chimpanzee closest to humans, but morphologists seeing little difference between chimpanzee and gorilla (*see* AFRICA; BARINGO; HOMINIDAE; HOMININAE; HYLOBATIDAE; MOLECULAR ANTHROPOLOGY; NEAR EAST; PONGINAE; SIWALIKS).

Human evolution took place mainly in Africa in the Pliocene and early Pleistocene. Species of *Australopithecus*, the first known bipedal hominine, range from ca. 4 to 1 m.y. At least two lineages are discernable, the "robust" species that flourished between 2.5 and 1.5 m.y. and went extinct soon after and a more conservative lineage (probably including *A. africanus* between 3 and 2 m.y.) that is near the ancestry of *Homo*. All *Australopithecus* species had large cheek teeth for their body size (means estimated at ca. 50-65 kg.) and were omnivores that probably concentrated on vegetable foods. Their brains were large compared with those of great apes of similar body size, but at 400-530 ml. they fell within the size range of living ape brains.

Significant brain-size increase is apparently evident for *Homo habilis*, the first species placed in the same genus as living humans, and also probably the first stone-tool maker. *Homo habilis* is known between 2 and 1.6 m.y. in eastern and southern Africa,

but as Oldowan tools have been found as early as 2.4 m.y. it may extend to that age as well. The earliest *Homo erectus* fossils, at ca. 1.8 m.y., were apparently contemporaneous with *Homo habilis*, but they differed in a larger brain and body size, a probable link to the Acheulean stone industry, and an ability to hunt, rather than just scavenge, larger game animals. *Homo erectus* probably spread into Eurasia by ca. 1 m.y. and evolved into what is commonly termed early (or archaic) *Homo sapiens* by ca. 500 k.y. in Europe or Africa. In turn this species diversified into various regional sublineages (such as the Neanderthals in Europe and the Near East or the Rhodesians in sub-Saharan Africa), most of which developed Middle Paleolithic technologies. Eventually anatomically modern humans evolved, probably in Africa, perhaps as long ago as ca. 120 k.y., developed a variety of Late Paleolithic tool kits, diverged into major geographic groups ("races"), and spread across the world displacing the other varieties by ca. 30 k.y.

See also AUSTRALOPITHECUS; BRAIN; HOMO; PALEOLITHIC. [E.D., I.T.]

Further Readings

Napier, J.R., and Napier, P.H. (1985) Natural History of the Primates. Cambridge, Mass.: M.I.T. Press.

Szalay, F.S., and Delson, E. (1979) Evolutionary History of the Primates. New York: Academic.

Wood, B.A., Martin, L., and Andrews, P. (1985) Major Topics in Primate and Human Evolution. Cambridge: Cambridge University Press.

PRIMITIVE *see* CLADISTICS

PRIORITY

Where different Linnaean names have been applied over the years to the same taxon, the valid name, the one that must be used to refer to that taxon, is the available name that has priority (i.e. that which was published first). To be available a name must have been published in accordance with the requirements of the *International Code of Zoological Nomenclature*. In the context of animal nomenclature, then, priority is seniority as determined by the date of a name's publication.

See also CLASSIFICATION; NOMENCLATURE; SYNONYM(Y). [I.T.]

PROCOLOBUS *see* COLOBINAE

PROCONSUL

The early Miocene of East Africa saw the earliest known radiation of hominoid primates. A number of closely related species and genera, of which *Proconsul* is the best known, produced the highest diversity of hominoids ever achieved at one place and time in the course of their history. Three species are usually assigned to the genus *Proconsul*, from such sites as Rusinga and Songhor (Kenya). Originally described as subgenera, but now generally considered separate genera, are *Rangwapithecus*, with now only one species, and the closely related *Nyanzapithecus*, with two. These are from the same sites as *Proconsul*; from a site in northern Kenya comes yet another genus, *Afropithecus*, which again is closely related. They may be placed in the family Proconsulidae.

These species range in body size from smaller than gibbons to the size of female gorillas. They thus span the size range of living apes. They were generalized arboreal primates, eating mainly fruit and living in tropical woodlands and forests with equable and nonseasonal climates. Some of the larger species may have been partly terrestrial, and some varied their diet with more leaves, but they lacked the extremes of adaptation seen in the living monkeys and apes. They survived in Africa until the middle Miocene, giving way to apes that had thickened dental enamel.

See also APE; HOMINOIDEA; MIOCENE; RUSINGA; SONGHOR. [P.A.]

PROCYNOCEPHALUS *see* CERCOPITHECINAE

PROGALAGO *see* GALAGIDAE

PROHYLOBATES *see* VICTORIAPITHECINAE

PRONOTHODECTES *see* PLESIADAPIDAE

PRONYCTICEBUS *see* ADAPIDAE

PROPITHECUS *see* INDRIIDAE

PROPLIOPITHECIDAE

The earliest known catarrhine primates come from Oligocene deposits in the Egyptian Fayum. The first specimen was found by a professional collector, Richard Markgraf, but more recent and much more extensive collections have been made by E. L. Simons. The primates have been given a number of names in the past, including *Aegyptopithecus zeuxis*, *Propliopithecus haeckeli*, *Moeripithecus markgrafi*, and *Aeolopithecus chirobates*, but they should now be recognized as two closely related species of a single genus, *Propliopithecus*, namely *P. haeckeli* and *P. zeuxis*.

These two fossil primates are known only from the Jebel Qatrani Formation in Egypt. The deposits making up this formation are divided into a number of quarries, and *Propliopithecus* is known from quarry V at 165 m. above the base of the formation to quarry M at 249 m. above the base. Another 100 m. higher is a basalt that has been radiometrically dated as 31 ± 1 m.y., and since the time of formation of the sediments was probably quite long the age range of this fossil genus was of the order 35–32 m.y. This gives a fairly precise age estimate for these important fossils, one that is considerably older than any other known catarrhine.

The two species of *Propliopithecus* range from smaller than most extant catarrhines to animals the size of gibbons. They have skulls with rather projecting, doglike faces, long slashing canine teeth, and molars with broad crowns and low rounded cusps. Brain size is small, and there is a marked constriction between the face and the braincase (postorbital constriction). There is no development of the auditory tube of the external ear, a character present in all other catarrhine primates. The molars have cingula developed, apparently thin enamel on the surfaces of the crowns, and overall are very apelike, which has led many authorities to include the group with the apes. It is now thought that all of these features are those that characterize the ancestral catarrhine condition; they were present in the common ancestor of all catarrhines and therefore cannot be said to be diagnostic of any one group within the Catarrhini.

The postcranial morphology of *Propliopithecus* is more distinctive. The arm bones are relatively stoutly built. The distal articular surface of the humerus indicates a stable elbow joint, with full extension of the arm not possible. This is also indicated by the morphology of the proximal ulna, which has a primitively long olecranon process. The fingers and toes are strongly developed and adapted for powerful grasping, and overall the postcranial morphology suggests quadrupedal climbing as the principal method of locomotion. In this it would have been like present-day howler monkeys of the tropical forest of South America. Some of these characters are probably primitive for the catarrhines, and this is particularly true of the retention of such characters as the entepicondylar foramen on the humerus; but taken all together, and in conjunction with the relative robusticity of the limb bones, this morphology is probably quite derived compared with the ancestral catarrhine morphotype.

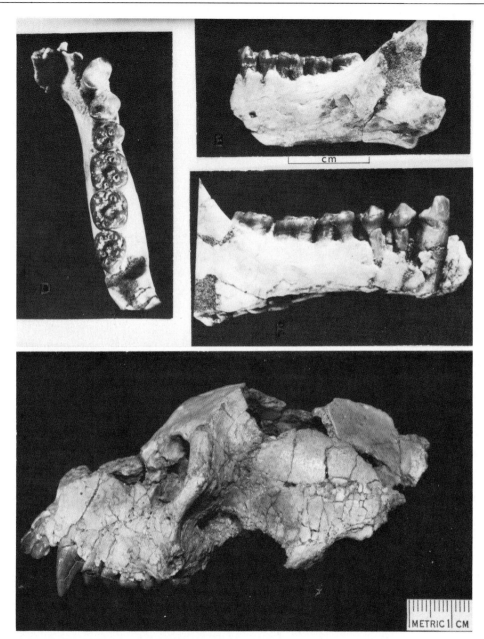

Above: three views of the type specimen of *Propliopithecus haeckeli*, left and right mandibular bodies. On the left, occlusal view of the right mandible; on the right, buccal views of the left mandible (above) and the right mandible. Below: lateral view of the first-discovered (and still most complete) cranium of *Propliopithecus zeuxis*. Subsequent finds have shown that the face in this specimen appears abnormally long.

The evidence from the postcranial skeleton is in contrast to the morphology of the skull and teeth just described. It is a good illustration of mosaic evolution, whereby some parts of the body evolve more rapidly and in a different way than do other parts. Just because *Propliopithecus* is the earliest known catarrhine, and is primitive in some respects, it cannot be assumed that it is somehow primitive in all respects or that it is itself "primitive." It shares some characters uniquely with other catarrhine primates (e.g. the loss of the second premolar), and this is sufficient to indicate its place as a member of the Catarrhini; but in other respects it lacks key catarrhine adaptations, as in the ear. It must therefore be recognized as a relatively primitive catarrhine, preceding the split between the two living superfamilies with which it shares no uniquely derived characters.

The adaptation of the skull and teeth of *Propliopithecus* indicate that it lived on a diet of relatively soft food. It has neither the cutting edges to its teeth nor the strong musculature needed to cut up or crush tough or hard food, and it appears therefore that it must have had a diet consisting largely of fruit. Such a diet is consistent with the postcranial evidence, which shows it to have been a slow and rather heavy-limbed climber in trees, which is where most fruit is found.

It is also consistent with the evidence available on the paleoenvironment in which *Propliopithecus* lived. Evidence from the sediments of the Jebel Qatrani Formation show them to have been laid down in low-lying lagoonal environments where the climate was probably hot and humid. The vegetation is known from the fossilized trunks of large tropical trees that are also commonly found in the deposits, and these show that the area surrounding the site was covered with tropical forests containing many large trees. These would probably have grown in a wet, hot climate without marked division into seasons. Still more information is available from looking at the other animals that are found in the same deposits as *Propliopithecus*. A large and varied mammalian fauna is present, and although it is composed of animals very different from most living today it is clear from the numbers of species, and from their adaptations, that the fauna as a whole indicates tropical forest.

Putting all this together, we see the *Propliopithecus* species as small and monkeylike; they were adapted for climbing and lived in trees; they ate the fruit that grew on the trees; the trees were part of a lowland tropical forest growing close to the sea in a hot and humid climate, almost certainly not highly seasonal. This is a picture of a type of catarrhine primate that is the sister group to the living monkeys and apes and that is claimed by some authorities to be ancestral to all living monkeys and apes.

See also APE; CATARRHINI; DIET; FAYUM; HAECKEL, ERNST HEINRICH; LOCOMOTION; MIOCENE; SPECIES. [P.A.]

Further Readings

Andrews, P. (1985) Family group systematics and evolution among catarrhine primates. In E. Delson (ed.): Ancestors: The Hard Evidence. New York: Liss, pp. 14–22.

Fleagle, J.G. (1986) The fossil record of early catarrhine evolution. In B.A. Wood, L. Martin, and P. Andrews (eds.): Major Topics in Primate and Human Evolution. Cambridge: Cambridge University Press, pp. 130–149.

Kay, R.F., Fleagle, J.G., and Simons, E.L. (1981) A revision of the Oligocene apes of the Fayum Province, Egypt. Am. J. Phys. Anthropol. 55:293–322.

Szalay, F.S., and Delson, E. (1979) Evolutionary History of the Primates. New York: Academic.

PROPLIOPITHECUS *see* PROPLIOPITHECIDAE

PROSIMIAN

Member of the lower primates, including the lemurs, lorises, galagos, tarsiers, their extinct relatives, and all early primates. The Prosimii is a formal taxonomic grouping of primates, originally based upon the four modern groups mentioned but later extended to include the early fossils. Its use reflects the hypothesis that these animals are all part of a natural group and thus are each other's closest relatives, especially as contrasted with the Anthropoidea or higher primates. Most current researchers do not accept that hypothesis, instead considering that the living tarsiers (and their extinct relatives) are the sister taxon of the anthropoids (forming the haplorhine group), while the living tooth-combed prosimians (Lemuroidea and Lorisoidea) are a distinct clade, the Strepsirhini. The extinct, early Cenozoic Adapidae are probably also strepsirhines. Together these two large groups comprise the Euprimates, as opposed to the archaic Paleogene Plesiadapiformes. Thus combining the plesiadapiforms, strepsirhines, and tarsiiforms in the single taxon Prosimii appears "unnatural" to many current workers and is not followed here. Nonetheless, many authors desire to have a formal term that contrasts this assemblage to the anthropoids, and the concept of prosimian is therefore found in many textbooks and some research papers.

See also ADAPIDAE; ANTHROPOIDEA; EUPRIMATES; HAPLORHINI; HIGHER PRIMATES; LOWER PRIMATES; PLESIADAPIFORMES; PRIMATES; SCALA NATURAE; STREPSIRHINI; TARSIIDAE. [E.D., I.T.]

PROTOADAPIS *see* ADAPIDAE

PROTOMAGDALENIAN

Upper Paleolithic industry dated ca. 22–21 k.y. B.P., defined by D. Peyrony on the basis of a level underlying the Solutrean at Laugerie Haute (France). Backed-bladelet technology and other aspects of the assemblage foreshadow the Magadalenian and represent a significant shift from the preceding backed-point technology of the Perigordian. The industry has also been referred to as "Perigordian VII" by de Sonneville-Bordes, due to the general use of backing technique and to the position of the industry in the sequence directly overlying the Perigordian VI (previously Perigordian "III") at both Laugerie Haute and Abri Pataud.

See also ABRI PATAUD; LAUGERIE SITES; MAGDALENIAN; PERIGORDIAN; PEYRONY, DENIS; STONE-TOOL MAKING; UPPER PALEOLITHIC. [A.S.B.]

PROTOSOLUTREAN

The earliest Solutrean-related industry, dated ca. 20 k.y. ago and found only at two sites in southwestern France: Laugerie Haute and Badegoule. It is characterized by unifacial points and the use of pressure-flaking.

See also LAUGERIE SITES; SOLUTREAN; STONE-TOOL MAKING; UPPER PALEOLITHIC. [A.S.B.]

PSEUDOLORIS *see* MICROCHOERINAE

PSYCHOZOA

A semitaxonomic term, of kingdom rank, employed by B. Rensch to reflect the great distinctions of humans from other animals. This concept has been used, rarely, by European authors, although it is in essence antievolutionary in denying the position of *Homo* as merely one member of one order of the Kingdom Animalia.

[E.D., I.T.]

PTERION *see* SKULL

PUC(H)ANGAN *see* HOMO ERECTUS; SANGIRAN DOME

PUERCAN *see* PALEOCENE; TIME SCALE

PUMICE *see* GEOCHRONOMETRY

PUNCTUATED EQUILIBRIUM *see* EVOLUTION

PURGATORIUS *see* PAROMOMYIDAE

PYGATHRIX *see* COLOBINAE

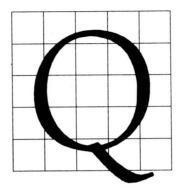

QAFZEH

Excavations at the Israeli cave of Jebel Qafzeh over a period of more than 50 years have produced a large sample of anatomically modern hominids associated with Upper and Middle Paleolithic (Levalloiso-Mousterian) industries. The Mousterian-associated sample of adults and children represent the oldest hominids of modern morphology found in Eurasia; they are newly dated at 92 k.y. One burial of a child is unquestionably associated with grave goods, but in other respects the inferred behavior of the early Qaf-zeh hominids seems little different from that of Neanderthals. The robust but modern morphology of the Mousterian-associated hominids from Qafzeh and the similar sample from Skhūl is considered by some workers to represent the ancestral morphology that gave rise to the European Cro-Magnons.

See also ARCHAIC MODERNS. [C.B.S.]

QATRANIA *see* PARAPITHECIDAE

QUADRUMANA *see* PRIMATES

QUADRUPEDALISM *see* LOCOMOTION

QUANTITATIVE METHODS

In biology these include numerical and mathematical descriptions or modeling of natural phenomena, as well as descriptive and inferential statistics. Relations between observed quantities can frequently be described in mathematical terms. Examples include the equation for geometric increase of a population through time or the change in size of an individual during growth, both as functions of time.

Mathematical Modeling

Mathematical modeling is used extensively in population ecology for modeling exchange of energy and resources in communities. In population genetics the change in gene frequencies due to natural selection, mutation, migration, and the influence of population size can be incorporated into a mathematical model.

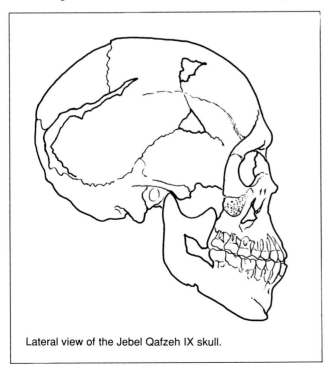

Lateral view of the Jebel Qafzeh IX skull.

The model relating metabolic rate to body mass for warm-blooded vertebrates can be represented as a simple exponential equation. One starts with basic biological principles involving metabolic rate as a function of heat loss from body surface area in relation to mass and deduces a model. The derived exponential equation describes the observed relation between calories consumed per unit time (metabolic rate) and body weight or mass and is descriptive and predictive for individual organisms and for mean tendencies of different taxa.

There are basically two types of mathematical models used in biology: *deterministic* and *stochastic*. In deterministic models equations relating the variables in the model are used to compute results or draw graphs that tell exactly how much one variable changes as others change. For example, a simple equation can generate the shapes of most species of snails by choosing specific constants for each species in the equation for a logarithmic spiral.

The word "stochastic" is synonymous with probabilistic. In stochastic models exact predictions cannot be made. Variables in the model have random components that lead to probability distributions for the variables of interest. Realistic models for population growth and population genetics for small populations are of this type. The population genetic phenomenon called *random drift* is based on a stochastic model that describes chance changes in frequency of genes from generation to generation as a consequence of the chance association of gametes in random mating populations. When the population is very small, all the offspring may descend from just a few individuals who may not be typical.

For some deterministic models linear algebra is a powerful tool. For example, the rate of increase in a population can be determined from the mortality rate and fecundity for each age group assumed to be constant from generation to generation. The methods of differential and integral calculus, including numerical integration, are required for other types of models. These methods frequently require the use of a computer for the extensive calculations involved.

Only the simplest stochastic models can be solved mathematically without the use of simulation or Monte Carlo techniques requiring repeated "runs" of the model on a high-speed computer. The phenomenon is simulated by specifying each parameter or feature and then randomly sampling possible values that may arise, using a random-number generator. Many repeated experiments are required to produce a distribution of results, in the form of a probability distribution. Some of the models used in evolutionary theory for speciation and proliferation of taxa are of this form.

Statistics

Statistics are among the most widely used of quantitative methods. Data are collected as measurements on a continuous scale (e.g. length, weight, angle, pH), meristic counts (number of teeth, digits, cusps), or frequencies of nominal variables (color, race, health, class, preference in a questionnaire).

Measurement data and counts may be summarized in terms of *descriptive statistics* that measure the average tendency (mean, median) or variation (standard deviation, coefficient of variation). Correlation coefficients are used to measure linear association of variables two at a time. Regression analysis is used to predict the value of one variable from others (what should the weight be of a male who is 49 years of age?). Frequencies are summarized by tabulations or converted to percentages and proportions. These descriptive statistics may be calculated for small samples (usually fewer than 30 observations), large samples, or even vast amounts of data, (such as the results of a national census).

Most research studies that employ measurements or counts report such descriptive statistics in the form of tables or graphs. Numerical taxonomy methods employ descriptive statistics to describe the numerical similarities or differences among taxa based on numerically coded characters. A computation rule, or algorithm, is used to find patterns of relationship among taxa based on the similarities or differences; these are then summarized in the form of a dendrogram, or treelike diagram.

Statistical inference is concerned with drawing conclusions about phenomena or populations based on experimental data or relatively small samples of observations drawn at random from populations of interest. We would like to make inferences about the larger body of data or the population sampled, using only the data at hand. One of the commonest statistics used in inference is the *standard error*. We can compute a standard error for just about any statistic calculated from data taken at random from the population of interest. The standard error tells us how variable the statistic will be in repeated samples; thus large samples have on the average smaller standard errors than small ones drawn from the same population. The standard error of the mean, for example, decreases inversely with the square root of sample size. Standard errors are frequently reported with a statistic and given with a plus or minus sign after the value of the statistic.

A *confidence interval* gives us the range of values that is likely to contain the true value of the parameter we are trying to estimate, along with the probability that intervals produced in the same way will contain the true value. Recording blood types for a random sample of people gives us an estimate of the blood-type frequencies for the population we have sampled. Confidence intervals for the frequencies will tell us how close we may be to the true values and the probabilities that the intervals will contain the true frequencies. The length of a confidence interval is frequently a simple function of sample size and frequently decreases roughly as the reciprocal of the square root of sample size (like the standard error of the mean). It takes a sample four times as large to halve the length of the interval. We may use general statistical results of this type in our design of statistical studies.

Descriptive statistics and confidence intervals are examples of estimates of unknown quantities. If we are interested in hypotheses about our experiments or about nature, we can formulate them as statistical hypotheses. For example, the statement that "the population that we have sampled is not evolving" may be translated into a statistical hypothesis about the gene frequencies through time in a large random-mating population where there is no effective selection, migration, or mutation. The statistical hypothesis would be "gene frequency is constant through time." We would test the hypothesis by observing gene frequencies through time and see if the differences we observe are due to chance or to evolution having occurred.

The statement that "the skull lengths are the same in two populations we are studying" is a hypothesis about a measurable quantity in populations of animals. A more specific statistical hypothesis might be "the mean skull length in population A is the same as the mean skull length in population B." This hypothesis is called the *hypothesis tested* or the *null hypothesis*. The alternative hypothesis is that the mean skull lengths are different. A test of a statistical hypothesis is a mathematically rigorous way of evaluating our hypothesis based on data collected from samples drawn at random from the populations. We will reject the hypothesis tested if the observed difference is large enough. Large enough is larger than would have occurred by chance if the populations were in fact not different. We must choose this probability of rejecting the true hypothesis tested before we do the test. If we do this, we can deduce the properties of our test (i.e. its power of finding differences when they exist). Another name for the chance or probability of rejecting our true null hypothesis is *significance level*. One test for continuous variables, and appropriate for our data on mean skull lengths, would be Student's *t* test if certain assumptions about the distribution of the weights in the samples were valid and our samples had been drawn at random from the two populations.

The *analysis of variance* is used to test similarly formulated hypotheses about the equality of two or more means and is a powerful tool for analyzing sources of variation due to experimental manipulation in the laboratory or the effects of geography and time in natural populations.

Chi-square tests are used to test for independence of variables in count data and to compare frequencies or proportions in such data over various populations sampled. For example, if our null hypothesis is that the sex-ratio is the same over several populations, then a chi-square test would be appropriate. Chi-square and *t* tables are widely available for looking up values of the test statistic corresponding to our prechosen significance level.

Data collected about objects or phenomena usually consist of many observations on each object or experimental unit. Thus on a single skull we might measure length, width, height, and any of a number of dimensions of interest. Collection-locality information might include, for each place, latitude and longitude, temperature, altitude, and a multitude of other features of that place at a given time. The majority of data collected are therefore multivariate in nature. Traditionally, however, the majority of statistical analyses look at variables one at a time and are known as *univariate statistical methods*. A *t* test, or an analysis of variance, are examples of univariate techniques.

Multivariate statistics, methods that look at many variables simultaneously, are being used more and more. The computations required are long and tedious but are made easier with the use of modern desktop or mainframe computers. Their interpretation, however, is more difficult. But the world is multivariate, and multivariate inferences are required and will become more common.

Some of the multivariate techniques commonly used are *multiple regression, principal-components analysis, factor analysis,* and *discriminant analysis*. Each method begins with many variables being observed for each individual or experiment. Multiple regression is concerned with predicting one or more variables from a whole suite of measured quantities. We may estimate brain volume as a function of a number of linear skull measures and also have a measure of how well our prediction does. Various stepwise procedures are available in computer programs for selecting an optimal subset of predictors in an orderly way. The presence of redundancy in the set of predictors, or *collinearity*, is reflected in high values of correlations among some of the predictor variables.

Principal-components analysis is a widely used data-reduction technique that depends on the presence of correlation among the measured variables. It is usually possible to find a relatively few indices or linear combinations of our original variables that summarize most of the information contained in all our measured variables, so that a plot of two of the most informative linear combinations (called *principal components*) will give us a one- or a very few two-dimensional diagrams that will show much of the structure of our multivariate data. We may be able to see trends associated with variables not in the analysis, or clusters of observations that help us to understand our data or formulate hypotheses about groups not yet recognized as distinct. Analysis of residuals not explained by the principal components can be informative about unique variables, or about cases not well expressed by the principal components.

Factor analysis, a multivariate method originally developed by psychologists, summarizes many measures in the form of a few common factors that explain all of the information shared by the variables. Thus a large battery of intelligence tests administered to a number of subjects may be measuring general intelligence, mathematical ability, and language ability (the factors of the mind), although these factors cannot be measured directly. Factor analysis is widely used in the social sciences and is becoming more popular among biologists and geologists. Factor analysis may be used as a model-building and hypothesis-testing procedure, while principal-components analysis is exploratory, looking for not-easily-discerned pattern and structure in multivariate data.

Multivariate analysis of variance is a generalization of analysis of variance. It is concerned with any or all differences in a set of measured variables in an experimental or field condition. Do the skulls in populations A, B, and C differ in any measured dimension? If so, in which dimensions and how much do they differ? Can the observed differences by summarized by overall size changes in all variables or are the differences also in terms of shape differences? If the populations do differ, we can use an index based on a combination of the characters to assign unknowns to the correct population and also to measure the probability of error of assignment. For example, we can assign a newly discovered fossil to one of a group of known populations or decide that it does not belong to any of them. This methodology, closely allied to multivariate analysis of variance, is

discriminant analysis. Very similar techniques in engineering and operations research are called *pattern recognition*.

Plotting the results of our analysis of among population differences, taking into consideration the variation and correlation within populations, is akin to principal-components analysis. We may have designated the groups or clusters beforehand, however, and want to see their relationships and differences. This method is called *canonical variates analysis*. Various descriptive measures of difference, called *distance statistics*, use all of the variables in the study and can be used to summarize relationships.

The exploratory multivariate techniques like principal components and multivariate distances are descriptive methods. Factor analysis may be used descriptively or inferentially. Models may be generated or specified and tested. Multivariate analysis of variance is an inferential technique. Cluster analysis and numerical taxonomy are descriptive multivariate methods.

Statistical Assumptions

All statistical tests require that we can properly make assumptions about our data so that we may use the test correctly and so that our chosen significance level will be what we say it is. The most important assumption is random sampling. Without random sampling we can only present descriptive statistics for our data at hand and not make inferences about the sampled populations we are interested in. A sample is random if the probability of each observation being in the sample is known. In the most common form, *simple random sampling*, the probability is the same for all individuals entering the sample. More restrictive assumptions are required for tests like the *t* test, where we must also know if variability is similar in the two populations sampled and that it follows the normal, well-known bell-shaped curve. There are statistical procedures that require fewer assumptions that are called *distribution free* or *nonparametric* tests. These, however, are usually not associated with easily interpretable descriptive statistics.

See also ALLOMETRY; MORPHOMETRICS; MULTIVARIATE ANALYSIS; NUMERICAL TAXONOMY. [L.F.M.]

QUINA MOUSTERIAN *see* MOUSTERIAN

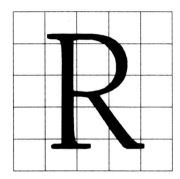

RACE (HUMAN)

Arbitrarily defined and geographically localized division of humans. It is equivalent to the zoological subspecies. Races have traditionally been designated on the basis of phenotypic characters, such as hair or eyes. More recently anthropologists have tried to designate races on the basis of the frequencies of alleles found within each race.

Because the criteria used to define races are arbitrary, anthropologists have not agreed on how many races exist or what they are. For example, while most may agree that the aboriginal populations of Asia, Africa, and Europe constitute the equivalents of subspecies, there is no consensus about the aboriginals of North America and Polynesia or the Ainu of Japan.

While races do indeed differ biologically from one another, such differences are small and often represent localized physiological adaptations. Further, the fact that races can and do interbreed makes their boundaries ambiguous and their historical existence ephemeral. It has never been adequately demonstrated that races differ intrinsically in intelligence or that any behavioral differences among them have a genetic basis.

See also POLYTYPIC; POPULATION; SUBSPECIES. [J.M.]

Further Readings

Molnar, S. (1983) Human Variation: Races, Types, and Ethnic Groups. Englewood Cliffs, N.J.: Prentice-Hall.

RACE, SKELETAL   *see*   FORENSIC ANTHROPOLOGY

RACEMIZATION DATING   *see* GEOCHRONOMETRY

RACLOIR   *see*   SCRAPER; STONE-TOOL MAKING

RADIOCARBON DATING   *see* GEOCHRONOMETRY

RADIOMETRIC DATING

Measurement of the time elapsed since closure of a particular geochemical or biochemical system, as determined by analysis of the radioactive atoms and (in most cases) their daughter products contained within a sample. The time of closure may represent rapid cooling from high temperatures, as in volcanic rocks; cooling consequent on uplift of a portion of the earth's crust, as in metamorphic rocks; incorporation in crystals or precipitation by absorption on surfaces, as in deep-sea sediments; or cessation of carbon exchange consequent on death (the basis for radiocarbon dating). Stratigraphic judgment is often required to relate the dated material to the age of a particular fossil.

See also GEOCHRONOMETRY. [F.H.B.]

RAIN FOREST   *see*   PRIMATE ECOLOGY

RAMAPITHECUS   *see*   PONGINAE

RANCHOLABREAN   *see*   TIME SCALE

RANGWAPITHECUS   *see* OREOPITHECIDAE

RANK *see* CLASSIFICATION; NOMENCLATURE

RAVIN DE LA PLUIE *see* EUROPE; PONGINAE

RAW MATERIALS

Natural substances utilized in human technology. A wide variety of materials found in nature were used for technological ends in prehistoric times, in either modified or unmodified form. These include stone, wood, bone, horn, and hide. The role of such materials was governed by their availability, the functional requirements of the tools, and prevailing cultural norms regarding artifact manufacture.

Groups of Raw Materials

Stone One of the most important materials for tool use and the one yielding the earliest archaeological evidence was stone. Rocks can be used or fashioned to serve in many activities, such as hammering, cutting, scraping, chopping, grinding, engraving, and perforating. Stone tools could have been used for animal butchery and the working of wood, hide, and, later, bone and antler.

During most of the Paleolithic the predominant mode of working stone into tools was *flaking* (also called *chipping*), generally through direct or indirect percussion but also, by late in the period, through pressure. Not all stone sources are suitable for flaking, and the properties of a particular stone affect the manufacturing process. The flaking qualities, size, and shape of a given raw material influence the methods and techniques used to make an artifact as well as its resultant form. In most circumstances the finer-grained the material (e.g. flint) and the more *isotropic* its structure (fracturing equally well in any direction with no preferential cleavage planes), the easier it is to control. Stone with superior flaking qualities often results in end products with a more standardized range of variation and an apparently higher degree of workmanship than those manufactured from coarser, nonisotropic stones.

The types of stone often used for tools include:

1) SEDIMENTARY ROCKS, such as
   a) *Cryptocrystalline* or *microcrystalline silicas*, including flints, cherts, jaspers, agates, chalcedonies
   b) *Opal*, an amorphous quartz
   c) *Vein quartz*, a coarser-grained quartz, normally from geothermal veins in rocks
   d) *Silicified wood*, which often retains some of the preferential grain of the original wood
   e) *Silcretes*, or silicified sediments
   f) *Silicified limestones*

2) METAMORPHIC ROCKS, such as
   a) *Quartzite*, in most cases metamorphosed sandstones
   b) *Indurated shale*, or shale subjected to high temperature and metamorphosed into a more homogeneous substance

3) IGNEOUS ROCKS, such as
   a) *Obsidian*, a superchilled volcanic lava (volcanic glass)
   b) *Volcanic lavas*, including basalts, trachytes, andesites, nephelinites, rhyolytes, and phonolites
   c) *Ignimbrites*, rocks formed from hot ash-flows ("welded tuffs")
   d) *Quartz crystal*.

The apparent sophistication in stone-artifact assemblages results from a combination of factors: the nature of the local, or imported, lithic materials, the functional requirements of the tools, the technological and functional norms of the social group, and the skill and motivation of the toolmaker. For example, at sites where raw-material sources are primarily small, poor-quality rocks artifacts may be made in a casual way. This appears to be the case at Early Stone Age sites in the Omo Valley (Ethiopia), where small pebbles of quartz were apparently smashed into sharp fragments.

Even the typological distinction between the "Developed Oldowan" and early "Acheulean" at Olduvai Gorge has been interpreted by some as being primarily a function of raw-material use. The poorly made bifaces of the Developed Oldowan are made predominantly of a quartz/quartzite from which it is relatively hard to produce large flakes; those of the Acheulean tend to be made of more easily worked lava from which the large flakes suitable for more finely worked Acheulean bifaces could be derived. In addition experiments by Jones have shown that the superior flaking qualities and cutting efficiency of certain Olduvai raw materials, basalt and trachyandesite, may require less trimming and so yield a cruder, less "sophisticated"-looking end product than does the phonolite also common at Olduvai. Phonolite handaxes may appear more refined in terms of their relative thinness and number of flake scars, even when produced by the same experimental archaeologist, simply because the ones made in basalt and trachyandesite require less fashioning to produce functionally similar results.

The casual ("chopper-chopping tool") industries

of China and Southeast Asia, contemporaneous with Acheulean industries of much of the rest of the Old World but almost devoid of characteristic Acheulean handaxes and cleavers, may in part be a function of raw-material selection. H.L. Movius originally suggested that such Asian traditions were culturally separated from Acheulean groups to the west ("Movius' line" being drawn between the western and eastern traditions). However, Pope, among others, has suggested that the use of sharp strips of bamboo in many parts of Asia may have put less of a premium upon well-made stone cutting implements, so that these lithic assemblages seem cruder than their western counterparts.

Wood   Next to stone, wood was almost certainly the most common raw material used in prehistory. The size, hardness, and ease of shaping would have had a profound effect on the types of artifacts that were made of wood. Normally woods are easier to work in a relatively fresh rather than a seasoned condition. After the discovery of the controlled use of fire, charring and scraping would have been another efficient way of shaping wood into desired tools.

Bone, Antler, and Ivory   Hard, durable parts of animal remains were made into a wide variety of forms, especially beginning in the Upper Paleolithic. Antler is best worked when first soaked in water to soften it. Tools of these materials include percussors (soft hammers and punches), projectile points and harpoons, needles, and handles for hafted tools. Pieces of antler can be removed from a larger rack by the "groove and splinter" technique, where a burin or flake outlines a desired planform on the outer surface of the antler, incising down to the spongy interior, at which point the piece can be pried or levered off. These materials can be worked with stone tools (scraped, sawed, incised, or ground).

Materials for Specific Activities

Containers   Humans are the only animals to make use of unmodified or modified materials as containers in which to carry other substances, such as foodstuffs, water, or material culture. It is likely that this extends well back in the prehistoric record. Materials used for containers might have included tree bark, large leaves, slabs of thin rock, hides (naturally desiccated or cured by human technology), eggshells, tortoise or turtle shells, skulls, horns, and wooden bowls. A pointed shaft of wood could also have functioned as a sort of spit for carrying small carcasses or larger pieces of meat. As material culture advanced, basketry and ultimately pottery were also common materials for containers.

Weapons and Hunting   Of offensive or defensive weapons the simplest could have been missiles of stone or wood and clubs of wood or bone. Simple spears could have been made of sharpened wood (with or without the use of fire) or (with the use of a projectile point) of stone, bone, antler, horn, or ivory. As technology became more complex, such weaponry as wooden or antler spear throwers and bows and arrows could have appeared. Lighter projected spears or arrows might have featured feather fletching to impart spin and stability to the shaft. There might have been slings of hide or vegetable material, and controlled fires and nets could have also been used in hunting, as well as snares, traps, and, after domestication, the dog.

Processing Plant Foods   Interestingly, recent and modern hunter-gatherers do not normally use cutting tools in processing plant foods. Tools include stone or wooden hammers for cracking hard-shelled nuts and fruits or pounding vegetable remains, or wooden digging sticks for harvesting underground vegetation, such as roots, tubers, and rhizomes. A variety of containers help in the collection of these foodstuffs. It is likely that early tool-using hominids employed similar technologies. In late Pleistocene and Holocene times, as more attention was probably paid to seed resources, the emergence of technologies for harvesting and processing these foods can be seen in the form of stone sickle blades, bone and antler sickle hafts, and grinding stones. Ground-stone axes and adzes become prevalent in many areas, particularly in regions of deforestation.

Fishing   During the later Pleistocene and the Holocene fish and shellfish become more common as food. Materials for harvesting such resources could have included stone tools to remove shellfish from rocks, prying implements in a range of raw materials to open shellfish, and spears to catch fish. More sophisticated forms of fishing could have used vegetable and stone traps and weirs, net fishing with vegetable nets and stone weights, and line fishing with the use of hooks or gorges of such materials as bone, antler, and shell.

Fire Production   The principal combustible materials from which fire can be produced are wood, other types of vegetation (dried leaves, grasses, bark, fruits, seeds), bones, and dung. The artificial production of fire generally involves creating intensive friction between harder pieces of combustible material (twigs or branches) through prolonged twirling or rolling, and the subsequent ignition of dried tinder, in the form of vegetation or dung, to produce flames.

Binding   By the Middle Paleolithic there are indications that hafting of projectile points and perhaps other tools was becoming common. It is likely that either cordage was employed to tie or lash things together or an adhesive mastic was being used.

Cordage could have been made of such materials as skin thongs, sinew, and rolled or braided vegetation. Adhesives or mastics could have been vegetable gums and resins or in some areas naturally occurring pitch.

Structures   Since the construction of simple structures in the form of sleeping nests is a common feature of the great apes, even early hominid populations probably exploited a range of materials for shelters. During the course of human evolution these may have included wooden branches, poles, or large bones for the framework; stones for anchoring; and bark, branches, grass, leaves, mud, or hides for wall construction. Bedding materials may have included soft vegetation, hides, or feathers.

Clothing   When clothing first became a necessity or a cultural norm, such materials as worked hides or beaten vegetation would most likely have been used. Probably by late Pleistocene times true woven cloth made from plant fibers also emerged.

See also ASIA (EASTERN); CLOTHING; DOMESTICATION; FIRE; OLDOWAN; STONE-TOOL MAKING. [N.T., K.S.]

Further Readings

Bordaz, J. (1970) Tools of the Old and New Stone Age. Garden City, N.Y.: Natural History Press.

Hodges, H. (1976) Artifacts: An Introduction to Early Materials and Technology. London: Baker.

Jones, P.R. (1979) Effects of raw materials on biface manufacture. Science 204:835–836.

Leakey, L.S.B. (1967) Working stone, bone, and wood. In C. Singer, E.J. Holmyard, and A.R. Hall (eds.): A History of Technology, Vol. 1. Oxford: Clarendon, pp. 128–143.

Leroi-Gourhan, A. (1969) Primitive societies. In A. Daumas (ed.): A History of Technology and Invention: Progress Through the Ages, Vol. 1. New York: Crown, pp. 18–58.

Merrick, H.V. (1976) Recent archaeological research in the Plio-Pleistocene deposits of the lower Omo Valley, southwestern Ethiopia. In G.L. Isaac and E.R. McCown (eds.): Human Origins: Louis Leakey and the East African Evidence. Menlo Park, Calif: Benjamin, pp. 461–482.

Movius, H.L. (1948) The Lower Palaeolithic cultures of Southern and Eastern Asia. Trans. Am. Philosoph. Soc. 38:329–426.

Pope, G.G., and Cronin, J.E. (1984) The Asian Hominidae. J. Hum. Evol. 13:377–396.

Spier, R.F.G. (1970) From the Hand of Man: Primitive and Preindustrial Technologies. Boston: Houghton Mifflin.

Stiles, D. (1979) Early Acheulean and Developed Oldowan. Curr. Anthropol. 20:126–129.

RECENT *see* HOLOCENE

RECK, HANS (1886–1937)

German volcanologist and paleontologist. In 1909, after receiving his doctorate in geology from Berlin University, Reck remained on at the Geological and Paleontological Institute as an assistant to his mentor W. von Branca. Between 1912 and the outbreak of World War I Reck conducted three overlapping expeditions to Africa: to the dinosaur site Tendaguru (now Tanzania) in 1912–1913, under the auspices of the Institute; to the German colonies in 1913, sent by the Prussian Academy of Sciences; and to Olduvai Gorge in 1913, on behalf of the universities of Berlin and Munich. The primary aim of this latter expedition was to study volcanic formations in the Rift Valley, which provided Reck with an opportunity for the first rigorous search for Pleistocene human and animal remains in East Africa. During his three months at Olduvai Reck identified the four main beds, which he labeled I to IV. It was in Bed II that he reportedly found the remains of the "Oldoway" human skeleton, which he believed represented the first prehistoric human remains to be found in sub-Saharan Africa. It was later shown, however, that the skeleton was an intrusive burial of modern age, with a radiocarbon date of only 15 k.y. Although Reck retained an interest in African paleoanthropology, after World War I volcanologic studies constituted his major scientific activity. In 1931, however, he made a brief visit to Olduvai in the company of L.S.B. Leakey, who subsequently extended Reck's pioneering work at the Gorge with spectacular results. In 1933 Reck wrote a popular book on Olduvai and in 1936 published with L. Kohl-Larsen a survey of the animal and human remains found by the latter in the Lake Njarasa region.

See also OLDUVAI. [F.S.]

REGOURDOU

Cave near Montignac, Dordogne, in southwestern France, yielding archaeological and human remains, dated to ca. 80 k.y. (Weichsel I) on faunal and sedimentological grounds. This site contained the skeleton of a young adult male Neanderthal at one end of a large stone-lined pit, divided by a wall of stone slabs. The other half of the pit contained the carefully arranged bones of a single brown bear (*U. arctos*). Associated faunal elements, flint tools of Quina Mousterian type, and stone structures suggest elaborate burial practices. The site, located close to the painted cave of Lascaux, was discovered by R. Constant and excavated by E. Bonifay in 1957–1961.

See also MIDDLE PALEOLITHIC; MOUSTERIAN; NEANDERTHALS; RITUALS. [A.S.B.]

RELIGION *see* RITUAL

RETOUCH

Removal of flakes from a piece of stone. Sometimes the term *primary retouch* refers to the initial, roughing-out stages of stone reduction, while *secondary retouch* designates the more refined reduction of stone material, as in the case of bifacial thinning or the shaping of flake tools. Some archaeologists restrict the term to refer to the formation of flake tools.

See also FLAKE; STONE-TOOL MAKING. [N.T., K.S.]

RETOUCHED PIECE *see* CORE; STONE-TOOL MAKING

REUNION *see* PALEOMAGNETISM

RHINOCOLOBUS *see* COLOBINAE

RHINOPITHECUS *see* COLOBINAE

RHODESIENSIS *see* ARCHAIC HOMO SAPIENS

RIFT VALLEY

Rift valleys form when the continental crust is subjected to tension. The East African Rift Valley system, one of the best-known examples, was produced by fracturing of the African crustal plate. The system extends southward from Lebanon and the Red Sea for a distance of 3,000 km. to the Zambesi River basin.

The East African Rift Valley of Ethiopia, Kenya, Uganda, and Tanzania has provided ideal conditions for the accumulation, preservation, and recovery of archaeological and paleontological remains. As Cenozoic rifting proceeded in eastern Africa, a series of elongate basins formed and disappeared. Lakes, ponds, and swamps in the rapidly subsiding basins trapped the sediments that rivers brought to them. Primates, including hominid species, left skeletal and cultural remains among the bones of thousands of other animals that lived and died in the basins, which became embedded in the sediments left by the ancient lakes and rivers. Because volcanic activity is closely associated with rifting the fossil-bearing levels in many places were sandwiched between volcanic-ash horizons or lava flows, which can be used to obtain radiometric dates. Continuing tectonic activity has promoted renewed erosion on modern rift-valley landscapes, exposing the ancient remains. The East African Rift Valley has therefore become a focus of the search for early hominids and traces of their activities. Hominid sites are densely concentrated along the north-to-south strip that corresponds to the rift valley, because the valley itself provides the rare circumstances so necessary for the location and study of paleontological and archaeological sites.

See also AFRICA; KENYA; PLATE TECTONICS; STRATIGRAPHY. [T.D.W.]

Further Readings

Bishop, W.W., ed. (1978) Geological Background to Fossil Man. Edinburgh: Scottish Academic Press.

RIPPLE MARKS *see* FLAKE; STONE-TOOL MAKING

RISS *see* GLACIATION; PLEISTOCENE

RITUAL

Ritual acts can be defined as beliefs in action. Evidence for ritual behaviors is of special interest for the study of human evolution, because they imply the existence of a belief system shared by a group of people, and belief systems, or ideologies, play an integral role in human cultural systems today.

To ethnographers rituals are institutionalized patterns of behavior that both express and reinforce group beliefs. Rituals involve the manipulation of symbols, often represented by special material objects, such as clothing, decoration, or artifacts. They take place at a set time and place and consist of behavioral acts that have become highly formalized and stereotyped. Religious rituals can take many forms and serve many ecological, ideological, psychological, and sociopolitical functions. Some rituals, such as baptismal or marriage ceremonies in our own culture, are individual-oriented and mark a person's transition from one recognized social state into another. Other rituals, such as Thanksgiving or Christmas celebrations, are group-oriented and express a relationship between a group of believers and the object or objects of their beliefs.

Evidence for prehistoric belief systems is notoriously difficult if not impossible to obtain directly. While a fairly direct relationship exists between a group's subsistence practices and the material remains that this behavior leaves behind at archaeological sites (e.g. remains of food prey, hunting and butchering tools), material evidence for past ideologies is far scarcer and more ambiguous. Evidence for rituals, which is archaeologically more accessible, can thus serve as an indirect indicator of the existence of belief systems in the past.

In general the archaeological record of hominids before the advent of archaic *Homo sapiens* ca. 400 k.y. ago contains few if any remains not associated with utilitarian behavior. With the appearance of this species, however, we begin to get increasing evidence for some sorts of ritual behavior.

Some scholars have argued that rituals or cults existed not only among archaic *Homo sapiens* but even among *Homo erectus* groups. Specifically the discovery of highly fragmented and charred *Homo erectus* remains belonging to a number of individuals and often bearing cutmarks and skinning marks at such sites as Zhoukoudian (China), has been used to argue for the existence of ritual cannibalism. Similar ideological explanations have been offered to account for over 500 charred and splintered bones belonging to over 50 Neanderthals of both sexes at the Krapina Cave (Yugoslavia). A recent study has even suggested that, rather than ritual cannibalism, data from Krapina suggest the practice of defleshing the deceased and secondary reburial of their bones. Similarly ambiguous explanations have been offered to account for cutmarks and skinning marks and artificially made enlargements of areas around the foramen magnum found on the crania of various premodern *Homo sapiens*, including the Bodo, Petralona, and Monte Circeo (Neanderthal) skulls.

The discovery of disjointed and apparently sorted skeletal remains of cave bears at such cave sites as Drachenloch (Switzerland) and Regourdou (France), in what appeared to have been artificially made cairns or under large stone slabs, have been used to argue for the existence of bear cults among the Neanderthals. A recent reexamination of the evidence, however, now suggests that most of these skeletal remains probably resulted from repeated deaths of bears in caves during hibernation and not from hominid ritual practices.

Our strongest evidence for the earliest ritual behavior comes from the way that archaic *Homo sapiens* disposed of their dead. Numerous intentional burials of Neanderthals are known from many parts of the Old World. Individuals of both sexes and of various ages were repeatedly buried with grave goods in either artificially dug graves or under earth mounds. At Le Moustier in southwestern France, for example, an adolescent male was liberally sprinkled with red ocher, given grave goods, and buried in a flexed position ca. 40 k.y. ago. The nearby cave site of La Ferrassie, dated to ca. 70–50 k.y., contained shallow pits and low mounds with burials of eight Neanderthals: adult male, adult female, four small children, one newborn infant, and one foetus. At the Teshik-Tash Cave in Uzbekistan (Soviet Central Asia) at least six pairs of mountain-goat horns were placed

vertically around the grave of a Neanderthal youth who was buried perhaps as much as 100 k.y. ago. Finally, researchers have argued that pollen remains of flowering plants found in the fill over a burial of an aged Neanderthal man at Shanidar (Iraq) indicate that flowers played a part in burial ceremonies ca. 60 k.y. ago.

The existence of this formalized and stereotypical way of disposing of the dead, one that certainly entailed a much greater investment of labor than needed to be expended, strongly implies ritual behavior and suggests that belief systems played a significant part in cultural practices of hominids who preceded anatomically modern humans. The advent of fully modern people brought with it, however, a veritable explosion in ritual and ideological behavior. The archaeological record of these Late Paleolithic people contains multiple evidence for this in the forms of burials, musical instruments, cave and portable art, and of architectural elaboration in cave and open-air sites.

See also BODO; DRACHENLOCH; HOMO SAPIENS; KRAPINA; LA FERRASSIE; LATE PALEOLITHIC; LE MOUSTIER; MUSICAL INSTRUMENTS; NEANDERTHALS; PALEOLITHIC IMAGE; SHANIDAR; ZHOUKOUDIAN. [O.S.]

Further Readings

Harrold, F.B. (1980) A comparative analysis of Eurasian Paleolithic burials. World Archaeol. *12*:196–211.

Pfeiffer, J.E. (1982) The Creative Explosion. New York: Harper and Row.

Pfeiffer, J.E. (1985) The Emergence of Humankind, 4th ed. New York: Harper and Row.

ROBIACIAN *see* EOCENE; TIME SCALE

ROBINSON, JOHN TALBOT (b. 1923)

South African paleontologist. Between 1947 and 1951 Robinson was R. Broom's assistant at the Transvaal Museum, Pretoria, and as a consequence was intimately connected with the discovery and interpretation of the australopithecines and other skeletal material recovered from Swartkrans and other sites, such as Makapansgat and Sterkfontein. After Broom's death in 1951 Robinson remained in Pretoria and continued to work at the Swartkrans site. According to Robinson the morphological dichotomy of the early fossil hominids from South Africa was correlated with behavioral and ecological differences, an idea that became known as the *dietary hypothesis*. The gracile (omnivorous) australopithecines were considered to be in the ancestry of *Homo*, whereas the robust (herbivorous) forms were viewed as divergent and overspecialized hominids that eventually became extinct. In 1963 Robinson accepted a position at the University of Wisconsin, where in 1972 he produced a major synthesis on the australopithecine postcranial skeleton. From this study Robinson deduced that these hominids were more arboreal than had hitherto been suspected.

See also AUSTRALOPITHECUS; BROOM, ROBERT. [F.S.]

ROBUSTUS, AUSTRALOPITHECUS *see* AUSTRALOPITHECUS ROBUSTUS; PARANTHROPUS

ROCK SHELTER *see* ARCHAEOLOGICAL SITES

ROGACHEV, ALEKSANDR NIKOLAEVICH (1912–1984)

Russian archaeologist who for many years headed archaeological research at the Kostenki-Borschevo Late Paleolithic sites. His work there revealed that the classic French sequences for Paleolithic stone-tool industries, widely adopted by European archaeologists, were not suitable for analysis of Russian data. This led Soviet archaeologists to recognize local synchronic as well as diachronic Paleolithic industries (cultures).

See also BORDES, FRANÇOIS; KOSTENKI; PEYRONY, DENIS. [O.S.]

ROMANELLIAN

Late Pleistocene Epipaleolithic industry, equivalent to the final stage of the Epigravettian and extending from southern Italy to the Mediterranean coast of France and the Rhône Valley between 12,000 and 10,500 B.P. Named after the type site of the Grotta Romanelli near Lecce (Puglia) in southern Italy, the industry is characterized by short, round end-scrapers, microgravette points, unifacial points, Azilian points with curved backs, microburins, and rare geometric microliths. Faunal remains suggest a greater diversity of resources than in the earlier phases of the Paleolithic, together with reliance on smaller species, such as rabbits and snails. At the Grotta Romanelli itself the Romanellian is associated with a series of nine or more human burials.

See also ECONOMY, PREHISTORIC; EPIGRAVETTIAN; EPIPALEOLITHIC; EUROPE; MESOLITHIC; STONE-TOOL MAKING; UPPER PALEOLITHIC. [A.S.B.]

ROMER'S RULER *see* RULES

ROSE COTTAGE

Cave site near Ladybrand, Orange Free State (South Africa), with a long archaeological sequence ranging from Howieson's Poort at or near bedrock (age ca. 90 k.y.), with a possible Middle Stone Age level below, to a series of Wilton levels dated as late as A.D. 850. As at Klasies River Mouth the Howieson's Poort level appears to be overlain by a flake-dominated Middle Stone Age industry (MSA 3 of Volman) lacking microliths, with possible affinities to the Orangian industry, which is otherwise limited to open-air occurrences. Most interesting is a "pre-Wilton" level with utilized microblades and microblade cores, which may represent one of the earliest contexts for this technology in southern Africa, ca. 25,000 B.P. or slightly younger based on a radiocarbon age of 25,640 B.P. for the top of the underlying sand.

See also HOWIESON'S POORT; KLASIES; LATER STONE AGE; MIDDLE STONE AGE; ORANGIAN; SECOND INTERMEDIATE; STONE-TOOL MAKING; WILTON. [A.S.B.]

ROUX' LAW *see* LAWS

RUDABANYA *see* DRYOPITHECUS; EUROPE

RUDOLF *see* EAST TURKANA; KENYA

RULES

In ecology and evolutionary biology there are several generalizations that are dignified by the title of "rules" but that are at best rules-of-thumb. Perhaps the best known of these are Bergmann's and Allen's rules. These state that members of a particular mammal group living in cold regions tend to be larger-bodied (Bergmann's), and to have shorter limbs, ears, and other protruding body parts (Allen's), than those from warmer ones. The physiological basis for both these generalizations lies in the relationship between body volume and surface area and in the necessity of shedding heat (by maximizing surface area relative to volume) in warmer climates and conserving it (by the reverse) in cooler ones. Other rules include Gloger's (melanins—skin and pelage pigments—tend to increase in warmer and more humid parts of a species' range), and Romer's (new adaptations often come about as responses to existing—not new—conditions). The main point to bear in mind about "rules" of this kind is that, despite their name, they do not represent laws that nature obeys but are simply observations about patterns that tend to recur in nature.

[I.T.]

RUSCINIAN *see* TIME SCALE

RUSINGA

Western Kenyan stratified sequence of early Miocene age; main fossil beds 17.8 m.y. by K-Ar dating of included tuffs, upper (Kulu) beds ca. 17 m.y. by interpolation. Most fossils in the 300-m.-thick sequence of volcano-detrital sediments exposed on Rusinga, a 4-by-12-km. island at the mouth of the Winam (Nyanza) Gulf of Lake Victoria, come from the lower Hiwegi Formation. The four principal collecting areas are Hiwegi Hill (R1, R3), Kaswanga Point (R5), Kiahera (R106-107), and "Whitworth's Pot-hole" on Gumba Hill (R114). Sites at Nyamsingula (R4, R6) in the overlying Kulu Formation are highly prolific, and a Hiwegi-like fauna is found in the underlying Kiahera and Wayando Formations. Discovered by the geologist E.J. Wayland in 1928, the fossil beds of Rusinga yielded tens of thousands of vertebrate fossils with over 50 mammal species, large and small, together with spectacularly preserved invertebrate and plant remains, to parties headed by L.S.B. and M.D. Leakey between 1931 and 1952. Major finds included the first complete skull of a proconsul in 1947 and the first articulated prehuman limbs in 1948. Recent discoveries include hundreds of proconsul remains in the natural catacomb of "Whitworth's Pot-hole" and also the virtually complete skeletons of what may be a family group of proconsuls at Kaswanga Point.

Rusinga is part of the Kisingiri volcano-detrital complex, and its fossil beds correlate with those of the nearby island of Mfwangano and also at Karungu, on the far side of the Rangwa vent on the adjacent mainland. In these latter areas the lower part of the sequence, below the Hiwegi level, is the most fossiliferous. A causeway now connects Rusinga Island to the mainland, and several important sites including Kaswanga Point have been scheduled for agricultural reclamation. Rusinga is the type site of *Proconsul nyanzae* and *Nyanzapithecus vancouveringi*; numerous remains attributed to *Proconsul africanus* (or female *P. nyanzae*), *Limnopithecus legetet*, and *Dendropithecus macinnesi*, as well as abundant prosimians, have been collected.

See also KENYA; KORU; LEAKEY, LOUIS;
LEAKEY, MARY; SONGHOR. [J.A.V.C.]

Further Readings

Andrews, P.J. (1978) A revision of the Miocene Hominoidea of East Africa. Br. Mus. (Nat. Hist.), Geol. Ser. 30:85-225.

Drake, R.E., Van Couvering, J.A., Pickford, M.H., and Curtis, G.H. (in press) New chronology for the early Miocene mammalian faunas of Kisingiri, western Kenya. London Geol. Soc. J.

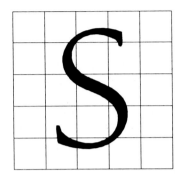

SAALE *see* GLACIATION; PLEISTOCENE

SACANANA *see* PITHECIINAE

SACCOPASTORE

Terrace deposit of the Aniense River on the outskirts of Rome (Italy), where two early Neanderthal skulls were found in 1929 and 1935. The terrace also contained fossil vertebrates, mollusks, and pollen attributable to the last interglacial (ca. 120 k.y. ago) and a few stone tools. The skulls probably represent a male and a female, and it is interesting to note that the supposed female specimen shows the more marked Neanderthal characteristics, although both have relatively small cranial capacities.

See also **NEANDERTHALS**. [C.B.S.]

SAGAIE

Bone or antler points characteristic of the Upper Paleolithic, especially the Magdalenian period. These sturdy projectile points are normally pointed at one

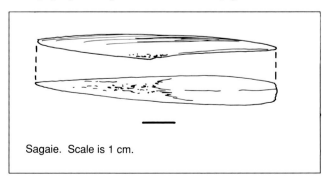

Sagaie. Scale is 1 cm.

or both ends, and are round or oval in cross-section. Some have beveled bases. Very early examples of bone points are also known from the Mousterian of eastern Europe.

See also **MAGDALENIAN**; **MOUSTERIAN**; **SPEAR**; **UPPER PALEOLITHIC**. [N.T., K.S.]

SAGUINUS *see* CALLITRICHINAE

SAHABI

Stratified exposure in northeastern Libya, of Mio-Pliocene age. In the 1930s Italian geologists found mammal fossils at several localities in the Wadi es-Sahabi, ca. 90 km. south of Ajdabiyan. Expeditions directed by N.T. Boaz between 1975 and 1981 greatly increased the collection, including the cercopithecoids *Macaca* and *Libypithecus*. This work also showed that the main fossil beds rest on Messinian evaporites deposited in the Terminal Miocene desiccation of the Mediterranean and on this evidence are restricted to the earliest Pliocene.

See also **LOTHAGAM**; **SEA-LEVEL CHANGE**. [D.P.D., R.L.B.]

SAHUL *see* AUSTRALIA

SAIMIRI *see* CEBINAE

SAINT-CÉSAIRE

Until the discovery of a Neanderthal partial skeleton at the rock shelter near Saint-Césaire (France) in 1979 the nature of the population responsible for the

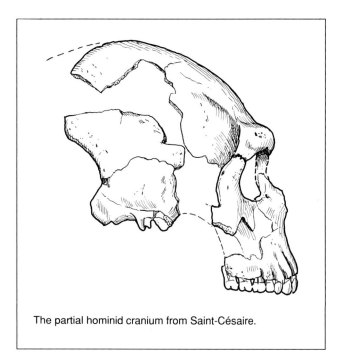

The partial hominid cranium from Saint-Césaire.

manufacture of the early Upper Paleolithic Chatelperronian industry remained an enigma. While
this industry appeared to represent a local development of the earlier Mousterian of Acheulean Tradition, only the Neanderthal-like teeth from Arcy-sur-
Cure and the modern-looking (but apparently
wrongly associated) skeleton from Combe Capelle
provided clues as to the nature of its makers. The
Saint-Césaire skeleton, however, is undoubtedly that
of a Neanderthal, and as it was recovered from the
higher of two Chatelperronian levels at the site it is
assumed to represent a contemporaneous human
population probably dating from less than 35 k.y.
ago. Furthermore, a second more fragmentary Neanderthal is also present in the same levels. The main
cranial parts consist of the right side of the front of a
skull with the face and right half of the mandible.
The form of the frontal bone, brows, face, and jaws
are Neanderthal, although the nose and teeth are
relatively small. The postcranial skeleton is fragmentary but Neanderthal-like in its robusticity.

See also **NEANDERTHALS**. [C.B.S.]

ST. ESTÈVE *see* L'ESCALE

ST. GAUDENS

Surface site in the Aquitaine basin, southern France.
The meager fauna is generally attributed to a middle
Miocene level, at ca. 13-12 m.y., but this is uncertain
due to the limited evidence of the fauna and inadequate stratigraphic control. The site is best known for
remains of *Dryopithecus fontani*.

See also **EUROPE; MIOCENE**. [R.L.B., D.P.D.]

SALDANHA

The middle Pleistocene site of Elandsfontein, also
known as Saldanha, near Hopefield (South Africa),
has produced extensive faunal remains and Acheulean artifacts. A partial human cranium lacking the
face and base was discovered there in 1953, and a
mandible and skull fragment that may be associated
were found a considerable distance away. The Saldanha skull resembles the Broken Hill cranium in its
general shape, although it is somewhat less robust,
with a smaller supraorbital torus and an endocranial
capacity of ca. 1,225 ml. It may represent a female
individual of the same kind of population, although
the Elandsfontein specimen may be more ancient,
on the order of 300 k.y. Some workers believe that
this specimen may represent part of an evolving
southern African lineage of hominids that gave rise
to modern humans through such evolutionary intermediates as the Florisbad specimen.

See also **ARCHAIC HOMO SAPIENS**. [C.B.S.]

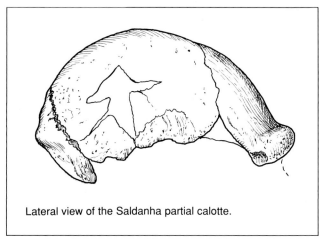

Lateral view of the Saldanha partial calotte.

SALÉ

Partial skull found in a Moroccan quarry in 1971. It
probably approximates the Thomas Quarries and
Sidi Abderrahman specimens in age, with a possible
antiquity of ca. 400 k.y. The skull is small, with a
cranial capacity of only ca. 900 ml., but the vault is
long, low, and relatively thick-walled. Muscle markings are only slightly marked, suggesting derivation
from a female individual. While most of these characters suggest assignment of the Salé skull to *Homo
erectus*, there are also some more "advanced" characters that are found in *Homo sapiens* specimens. These
include the basicranial proportions, an expanded
parietal region, and a rounded occipital region with
minimal development of an occipital torus. The occipital, however, is quite abnormal in its proportions,
suggesting the presence of pathology. Because of its
mosaic characteristics the classification of the Salé
skull is not generally agreed upon. Some workers

regard it as an evolved *Homo erectus* specimen, while others believe it represents an archaic *Homo sapiens*.

See also ARCHAIC HOMO SAPIENS; HOMO ERECTUS. [C.B.S.]

SALVAGE ARCHAEOLOGY *see* ARCHAEOLOGY

SAMBUNGMACHAN

Fossil-collecting locality in central Java: surface excavation dated at ?1–?0.2 m.y., based on lithostratigraphic correlation. A relatively complete hominid cranium was discovered in 1973 on the nearby Solo River. Although the provenance of the cranium is known, there is no substantial agreement about its age. Estimates range from late Pleistocene to early middle Pleistocene. The specimen seems "advanced" in its relatively large cranial capacity (1,035 ml.), but there is disagreement as to whether it should be classified with the Ngandong hominids or with the presumably earlier *Homo erectus* specimens from Trinil and Sangiran.

See also HOMO ERECTUS; INDONESIA; KOENIGSWALD, G.H.R. VON; SANGIRAN DOME; TRINIL. [G.G.P.]

Further Readings

Sartono, S. (1979) The stratigraphy of the Sambungmachan site, central Java. Mod. Quat. Res. Southeast Asia 5:83–88.

SAMBURU

Recently discovered late Miocene site in the Namurungule Formation, Samburu Hills, north of Lake Baringo in the Kenya Rift Valley. A single maxilla of an unnamed hominoid the size of a female gorilla has been found there.

See also APE; MIOCENE. [P.A.]

SAMPLING TECHNIQUES *see* ARCHAEOLOGY

SANDIA

Paleoindian projectile points, considered by some to be the earliest form in North America, first found at Sandia Cave and subsequently at the Lucy site (New Mexico). Sandia points are lanceolate with contracting or square concave bases, partial to full fluting, and a distinctive unilateral shoulder. Dating is based strictly on geological contexts, the Sandia type apparently underlying and coincident with Clovis points (ca. 12,000–10,000 B.P.).

See also AMERICAS; CLOVIS; PALEOINDIAN. [L.S.A.P., D.H.T.]

SANGAMON *see* GLACIATION; PLEISTOCENE

SANGIRAN DOME

Stratified sequence in central Java, dated at ca. 0.3–?0.2 m.y. on stratigraphic, radiometric, and paleomagnetic evidence. The Sangiran dome, an anticlinal fold in Neogene and Quaternary sediments ca. 10 km. north of Surakarta, has yielded numerous early hominid fossils mostly assigned to *Homo erectus*. The exposed portion of the dome is ca. 6 km. long and 3 km. wide. Four principal formations have been recognized since work by Dutch geologists began in the later part of the nineteenth century. At the base the Kalibeng Formation is composed of Pliocene marine clays, sandstones, limestones, and volcanic tuffs. Unconformably overlying the Kalibeng are more than 85 m. of the Pucangan (Putjangan) Formation, composed of black clays, sands, and volcanic layers. Conformably overlying the Pucangan Formation are the fluvial sediments of the Kabuh Formation, with an important marker-bed, the Grenzbank, which consists of up to 2 m. of well-consolidated calcareous sands, gravels, and silts. Recent work indicates that many if not most of the hominids and other vertebrate fossils derive from just below or just above the Grenzbank. Above the Grenzbank the upper 70 m. of the Kabuh Formation is made up of gravels, silts, sands, and clays, with volcanic tuffs intercalated throughout the sequence. The Kabuh is overlain unconformably by more than 50 m. of gravel, silts, sand, volcanic breccias, and tuffs, assigned to the Notopuro Formation.

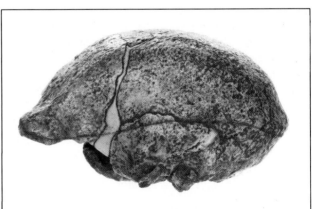

Lateral view of the Sangiran "Pithecanthropus II" calotte discovered by G.H.R. von Koenigswald in 1937. Photograph of cast. (From Tattersall, 1970.)

Because of the hominid discoveries in the Sangiran area many attempts have been made to date the sequence. Paleomagnetic studies have been contradictory and equivocal, as have indications of a single datable tektite horizon. Most of the recent radiometric and biostratigraphic studies indicate that the age of the earliest hominids from Sangiran has been overestimated and that the oldest hominids may be no older than 1.3 m.y. No firm consensus, however, has yet emerged.

See also Asia (Eastern); Homo erectus; Indonesia; Trinil. [G.G.P.]

Further Readings

Itihara, M., Sudijono, Kadar, D., Shabasaki, T., Kumai, H., Yoshikawa, S., Aziz, F., Soeraldi, T., Wikarno, Kadar, A.P., Hasibuan, F., and Kagemori, Y. (1985) Geology and Stratigraphy of the Sangiran Area. Indonesia: Geologic Research and Development Centre Special Publication, 4, pp. 11–45.

Pope, G.G. (1985) Taxonomy, dating, and paleoenvironment: the paleoecology of the early Far Eastern hominids. Mod. Quat. Res. Southeast Asia 9:65–81.

SANGOAN

Earliest stage, on stratigraphic grounds, of the Middle and Later Stone Age core-axe industries of central Africa. The Sangoan was named by Wayland for surface material found at Sango Bay (Uganda), on the west side of Lake Victoria, as well as from an *in situ* gravel deposit at Nsongezi, just to the north of the lake. The Sangoan is characterized by bifaces, particularly almond-shaped and cordiform types; prepared cores, polyhedrons, rostrocarinates, core-axes, and scrapers; and Sangoan picks. Extending throughout central Africa, from the Limpopo and Orange Rivers north to the Sahel, and east into Tanzania and Uganda, the industry is also associated at many sites, such as Kalambo Falls, with a small-tool component of scrapers, especially concave, notched, and denticulate forms, and other tools. The presence of concave scrapers, picks, and core-axes, together with the woodland or forest environment suggested at many sites, implies a connection with a woodland adaptation, possibly involving woodworking tools. Its probable age is later middle Pleistocene, although sites of probable early late Pleistocene age may be known from Zaire and Rwanda.

See also Early Stone Age; First Intermediate; Kalambo Falls; Middle Stone Age; Stone-Tool Making. [A.S.B.]

SAPIENS   *see*   HOMO SAPIENS

SAUVETERRIAN

Second stage in the classic Mesolithic/Epipaleolithic sequence of inland France, ca. 9500–7500 B.P., characterized by diminutive tools, especially biconvex points on microblades, retouched on both sides. The type site is the Abri Martinet at Sauveterre-la-

Lémance (Lot-et-Garonne), in the southern Périgord. Microblade industries from other areas including eastern Europe, although dissimilar in other ways, are sometimes referred to this industry.

See also Azilian; Epipaleolithic; Mesolithic; Stone-Tool Making; Tardenoisian. [A.S.B.]

SAXONELLA   *see*   SAXONELLIDAE

SAXONELLIDAE

Rare family of primates from the late Paleocene of Europe and North America, based on the single genus *Saxonella*. Although unique in enlarging its lower third premolar, this genus no doubt is derived from an ancestor that would be recognized as plesiadapid. Like several plesiadapiforms (e.g. *Phenacolemur*) the very long enlarged incisor is the only lower tooth anterior to the characteristically enlarged third premolar. The somewhat trenchant specialization of this tooth, which occurs independently in both multituberculates and marsupials, as well as in carpolestid primates (which enlarge the fourth premolar), is called *plagiaulacoidy*. The edge of such a lower tooth usually works against a flatter upper one, although in such marsupials as kangaroos and some phalangers its upper occlusal counterpart is equally bladelike, with a serrated edge. *Saxonella* shared with other plesiadapoids the mittenlike enlarged upper incisors that must have provided an excellent grip on whatever the animal held in its mouth. A tiny distal end of a humerus from the same European fissure where the teeth occur, and associated by size, strongly suggests that this animal was fully arboreal.

An interesting aspect of saxonellid distribution is the fact that so far no picrodontids or carpolestids are known in Europe, even though the equally small saxonellids and the larger plesiadapids occur on both sides of the incipient North Atlantic.

[F.S.S.]

SCALA NATURAE

Preevolutionary doctrine claiming that the diversity of the organic world was divinely arranged as a qualitative continuum, ranging from lower to higher and more "perfect" forms of life. Gradistic classification, which groups taxa according to their hierarchical position within a series of ranks meant to reflect levels of adaptive progress, is a derivative of the principle. T.H. Huxley applied these concepts in one of the earliest successful attempts to place human origins in an evolutionary perspective.

See also Anthropoidea; Cladistics; Classification; Grade; Huxley, Thomas Henry. [A.L.R.]

SCAVENGING *see* PALEOLITHIC LIFEWAYS

SCHWALBE, GUSTAV (1844–1917)

German anatomist and paleoanthropologist. Between 1899 and 1905, while professor of anatomy at the University of Strasbourg, Schwalbe undertook a detailed study of the fossil hominid record and concluded that the European Neanderthals were sufficiently different from modern *Homo sapiens* to warrant the rank of a distinct species (*Homo "primigenius"*). He also proposed two possible arrangements for the then-known fossil hominids: the pithecanthropines (i.e. Dubois's *Pithecanthropus erectus* = *H. erectus*), the Neanderthals, and the anatomically modern fossils of *Homo sapiens*. In the first arrangement, now known as the Unilineal (or Neanderthal) hypothesis, the Neanderthals are portrayed as an intermediary line between the pithecanthropines and modern humans, while the second depicts the Neanderthals and pithecanthropines as specialized offshoots from the human lineage. This latter proposal formed the basis of the "presapiens" theory that attracted considerable support during the first half of the twentieth century.

[F.S.]

SCIUROCHEIRUS *see* GALAGIDAE

SCRAPER

Term used traditionally in prehistoric archaeology to describe pieces of stone, usually flakes or blades, with retouch along one or more sides or ends. Found throughout the Paleolithic, side-scrapers (*racloirs*) are quite common in the Middle Paleolithic or Mouster-

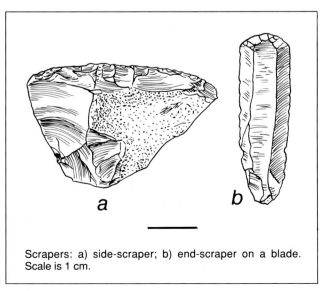

Scrapers: a) side-scraper; b) end-scraper on a blade. Scale is 1 cm.

ian period, while end-scrapers (*grattoirs*) are typical of the Upper Paleolithic. Many of these scraper forms could have been used for such activities as hide scraping or woodworking, while more acute-edged versions could also have served as knives.

See also FLAKE; MIDDLE PALEOLITHIC; MOUSTERIAN; RETOUCH; STONE-TOOL MAKING; UPPER PALEOLITHIC. [N.T., K.S.]

SCULPTURE *see* PALEOLITHIC IMAGE

SEAFLOOR SPREADING *see* PLATE TECTONICS

SEA-LEVEL CHANGE

Major changes in worldwide mean sea level, or *eustasy*, are an important factor in earth history and in hominoid evolution. Historical accounts of sudden changes in sea level, however, refer to local changes in elevation and not to eustatic changes.

Changes in Coastline Elevation

Spreading and cooling of ocean basins involve constant, slow subsidence along continental margins. Most river deltas and coastal plains, therefore, are steadily sinking by a centimeter or more per year. The fables of Atlantis may have been drawn from accounts of drowned coastal landscapes, complete with roads and buildings, which are locally preserved from sedimentation in the clear Mediterranean waters. On the other hand the Mesopotamian flood myths, including the biblical version, are based on the experience of life in a deltaic region drained by large muddy rivers, where natural levees grow ever higher as a result of slow subsidence but eventually fail catastrophically. In other areas of the world surveys show that "young" mountain ranges and plateaus are being constantly uplifted by tectonic and volcanic forces. Distorted ancient beach levels testify to such movements along geologically active coastlines, as in southern California and Chile.

Changing load can also affect local elevation, because the earth's crust slowly adjusts to redistributed weight by the process known as isostasy. In areas like Scandinavia and Hudson's Bay the entire region is slowly rising or "rebounding" in response to the melting away of the Pleistocene ice sheets ca. 12 k.y. ago. Other factors, such as changes in the local gravitational field due to slow shifts of mass in the earth's deep interior, may also have an effect. However, close monitoring of mean sea level by the Greenwich Observatory, the U.S. Coast and Geodetic Survey, and other agencies concerned with maintaining accurate elevation data has shown that the mean sea level has varied by only a centimeter or so since technically competent observations began, early in the 1800s, and there is no evidence that earlier historical sea levels were much different.

Evidence for Changes in Mean Sea Level

Has this always been the case? The thick sequences of marine beds found in coastal basins of Europe (such as the North German Plain, the London-Paris basin, the Gironde, Rhône, and Po valleys, and the lower Danube basin), represent a history of deposition for over 100 m.y. The sciences of stratigraphy and paleontology began as a study of these deposits. It was long ago found that these sequences included levels where the deposition of the beds had been interrupted by lengthy and widespread periods of erosion, which left very widely developed *unconformities* between the planed-off beds beneath and the beds deposited afterward. In the nineteenth century these regional unconformities were used as boundaries to divide the strata of Europe into *stages* and *series* (and the equivalent *ages* and *epochs*), which are now fundamental units in the geological time scales.

Almost from the beginning stratigraphers such as Déperet, Suess, and Grabau saw this as evidence for worldwide cycles of *transgression*, or rising sea level with consequent deposition, alternating with *regression* and erosion on the coastal plains. However, the effort to modernize the geological sciences during the early and middle twentieth century brought an atmosphere of rigorous skepticism. At first the absence of any techniques capable of dating or correlating stages over wide areas led most geologists to deny worldwide sea-level changes and to take the more conservative view that the major erosional unconformities did not extend beyond limited areas and were due to local subsidence and erosion only, as described above. The idea that mean sea level itself could change significantly was ridiculed, not for lack of plausibility but for lack of proof.

In the 1960s improved techniques began to support the concept of global sea-level change, at about the same time that continental drift began to emerge from disrepute. Newly refined time scales, based on the worldwide correlation of planktonic (free-floating) microfossils and on K-Ar radiometric dating, revealed that transgressions and regressions in different areas were generally synchronous. Work in California and New Zealand, where marine deposits show particularly clear evidence for climate change, also indicated that regressions were cold and transgressions were warm. Evidence mounted rapidly, and in the mid 1970s a group of stratigraphers and geophysicists at Exxon Production Research produced a global record of transgressions and regres-

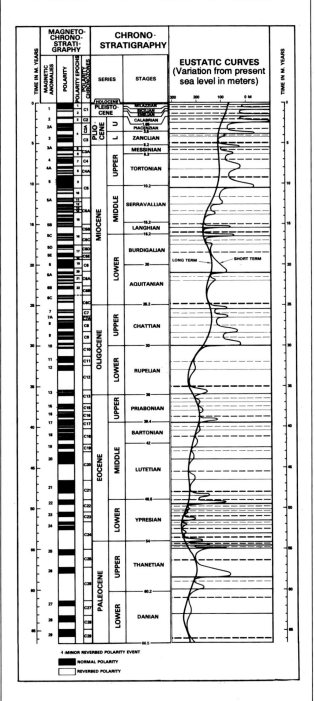

Cenozoic sea-level changes (Vail Curve). The long-term curve shows an average of high sea-level stands and probably reflects changes in the volume of the world ocean basins. The short-term curve shows variations down to 1 m.y. long, probably due to glacio-eustatic changes, but omits very short term variations (Milankovitch cycles). Sharp declines of 50 m. or more led to net regression on subsiding continental shelves and were the most opportune times for inter-regional migration of mammal faunas. (Courtesy of B.U. Haq.)

sions over the past 300 m.y. This analysis, quickly dubbed the *Vail Curve* after P. Vail, the group leader, was based on data gathered by the company in its worldwide search for oil. It showed beyond reasonable doubt that many of the major erosional unconformities found in continental-shelf sequences were of the same age worldwide and must have been caused by real changes in mean sea level.

Mechanisms of Sea-Level Change

According to present understanding, global mean sea level can be changed by more than one mechanism. The most rapid major changes are caused by variations in the volume of water in the ocean, but changes in the shape of the ocean basins affect sea level as well.

Glacio-Eustatic Change   The amount of water presently held in the world's ice caps is enormous, amounting to ca. 30 million cubic km. Roughly 80 percent of the world's ice is piled up on the Antarctic continent, where it reaches up to 8 km. in thickness, and virtually all the rest is on Greenland. It is calculated that if all the ice in these masses were to melt, world mean sea level would rise by 70 m. (220 ft.). As far as we know (see below) this has not happened since the Pliocene. However, estimates of glacial ice volume during the last ice age suggest that an additional 40–45 million cubic km. were withdrawn from the seas when the Pleistocene glaciations were at a maximum. This would have lowered sea level by as much as 110–130 m. (340–400 ft.). This is the general depth of the shelf break at the outer edge of the world's continental shelves, which suggests that the shelves (in their present form) are themselves glacial features.

Geological evidence shows that an ice cap has been present on Antarctica at least since the Eocene, that it expanded greatly in the Oligocene, and that it began to reach down to sea level in the Miocene. In the Pliocene glacial ice caps began to build up during cold-climate cycles in Greenland, Iceland, and the northern Rockies, and also in the Andes, Patagonia, and the Falklands. Finally, in the Pleistocene the cold-climate cycles produced huge but unstable continental ice caps on the Hudson Bay, Scandinavian, and Siberian lowlands. Each advance, and partial retreat, in the stepwise development of the world's ice caps is clearly seen on the Vail Curve. Many other, very similar swings in sea level are indicated in the early Cenozoic, and even in the Mesozoic, and it has been questioned whether these can all be due to ice-volume changes. No other mechanism is known, however, that could affect sea level so rapidly and profoundly.

Tectono-Eustatic Changes   Changes in the average global rate of sea-floor spreading, or plate tectonics, affect ocean-basin volume on a grander but slower scale. This is because the great submarine ridges that mark the spreading centers, such as the Mid-Atlantic Ridge, owe their elevation (up to 3 km. above average sea-floor depths) to the fact that their crustal rocks are newly formed and thus relatively hot and expanded. As the oceanic crust moves away from the spreading center, it gradually cools and shrinks, with a consequent decline in elevation. Thus a significant increase in spreading rates would create relatively wider ridges of hot, expanded rock, and a slowdown of spreading rates would have the opposite effect of reducing the size of the midocean ridges. Such spreading-rate changes would therefore change the capacity of the ocean basins and the displacement of the ocean water. Calculations based on known spreading rates indicate that this effect could act to change sea level by several hundred meters, but only over a period of 50 m.y. or more. Time-scale studies suggest that in fact the rate of seafloor spreading may have slowed down since the mid-Cretacous, when seas were at least 300 m. higher than today.

It is also true that the overall length of spreading centers can change. Spreading ocean basins are at a minimum when the continents are coalesced into one, as in the Ordovician and Permian Pangaeas, and these were times of maximum eustatic lowering. In the middle Cretaceous, on the other hand, the number of separate continents was greater than today, and eustatic levels were also at their highest; it has been speculated that this was largely or wholly because of the greater total length of spreading ridges dividing the continents.

Mountain building, an effect of plate-tectonic motion, should change in intensity as spreading rates change. Higher rates of mountain uplift result in higher rates of erosion and an increase in the amount of detritus displacing water in the oceans. Ocean-volume changes created in this way are, however, relatively small compared with glacio-eustatic or tectono-eustatic changes.

Thermo-Eustatic Changes   Warm water is more expanded than cold water. It has been found that the average temperature of the oceans changed by 1–2 degrees C in response to the climate variations of the Pleistocene. Although lagging somewhat behind the immediate effects of ice buildup and melting, the thermal contraction and expansion of the ocean emphasize glacio-eustatic changes in mean sea level.

Sea-Level Change and Hominoid Evolution

Hominoids originated as part of an isolated primate fauna in Miocene Afro-arabia, separated from the outside world by ocean barriers. Comparison of the Vail curve and the fossil record of Africa and South

America, however, shows that some of the major glacio-eustatic regressions may have been the cause of brief periods of intercontinental migration. It should be remembered that sea-level declines of the rapidity and magnitude indicated in the Vail curve will tend to expose any evolving land bridge in the foredeep between two moving continents. It is probably safe to say that all initiations of intercontinental migration (in the Cenozoic at least) will be found to be coincident with the downswing in a eustatic lowering event, because this is the time when rates of sea-level lowering are most likely to exceed rates of subsidence on continental shelves, and shorelines will recede to their maximum exposure.

The late Eocene/early Oligocene Fayum fauna of Egypt includes Eurasian mammals, such as genera of creodont carnivores, which appear to have arrived sometime during the later Eocene and before the "Grande Coupure." Communication was incomplete and apparently brief; the most likely cause is a late Eocene regression, at ca. 40 m.y. on the Vail curve. The impact of these immigrants on the African primate fauna may have been significant, but evidence has lately come to light that mammalian carnivores may already have entered Africa from Eurasia in the late Paleocene.

In the middle Oligocene, ca. 32 m.y. ago, Cenozoic sea levels reached their lowest point. With the recent redating of earliest anthropoids in South America to the later Oligocene some now think that the ancestral platyrrhines may have been able to cross the Atlantic from Africa via exposed sections of a transverse ridge during this great regression. African rodents, cichlid fishes, boas, and various insects also dispersed into South America at about this same time, which strengthens the possibility of a trans-Atlantic crossing. The mid-Oligocene regression may also have been one of several Oligocene regressions that allowed a whole host of mammal groups to enter Africa. These are groups that arrived in Europe during the early Oligocene "Grande Coupure" and that are found widely diversified in East Africa by the beginning of the Miocene. Included are the ancestors of modern African hedgehogs, rats, gerbils, squirrels, mole-rats, otters, weasels, dogs, cats, rhinos, pigs, hippos, giraffes, and antelopes; it can safely be assumed that this mass immigration revolutionized the African mammal fauna and resulted in major ecological pressures on the (unknown) Oligocene hominoids that gave rise to the new anthropoid groups of the early Miocene.

The emigration of hominoids to Eurasia may also have been triggered by falling sea level. Pliopithecids, first known from ca. 16 m.y., may have been in the first wave of African mammals to enter Europe via the

Zagros land bridge. This bridge began to develop where the Mesopotamian shoulder of Afro-Arabia encountered Iran and Anatolia and may have been exposed for the first time by the major sea-level drop during the later Burdigalian (later Orleanian, MN-4b) at ca. 17 m.y. The entry of dryopithecines and siva-pithecines into Europe and southern Asia (possibly by different routes, judging from their distribution) was delayed until ca. 14 m.y. coincident with the sharp drop in sea level recorded for the later middle Miocene (Serravallian). This is equivalent to the mid-Astaracian of Europe and the upper Chinji levels of the Siwaliks. Oreopithecids are known only from later Miocene levels in Tuscany but may also have found their way to the isolated Appenine landmass at this time.

Dating indicates that colonization of Europe and eastern Asia by advanced *Homo erectus*, and of the New World by *Homo sapiens*, also took place when glacial expansion lowered world sea level during the Elster (0.6 and 0.45 m.y.) and later Weichsel (c. 20 k.y.) sea level minima, respectively.

Pleistocene Sea Levels and Archaeology

Ancient beach lines above the level of the modern Mediterranean have long been related by geologists to the interglacial melting of the ice sheets, and are used extensively by archaeologists to define subdivisions of the Pleistocene. The standard subdivisions, as defined by Déperet in the early 1900s, are (from oldest to youngest) the Sicilian (about 90–100 meters above sea level); Milazzian (50–60 m. a.s.l.); Tyrhenian (30 m. a.s.l.) and Monastirian (20 m. a.s.l.).

Present usage differs considerably from the classical model and also includes regressional (i.e., cold-climate, glacial) stages during which sea level dropped by 100 meters or more from the interglacial levels. The Milazzian and Monastirian are no longer used, because of evidence that they are based on local elevation changes rather than eustatic changes,

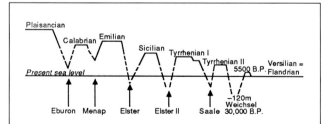

Mediterranean terrace levels, in order of age. The successively older terraces (identified by fossil shells on their surfaces) indicate a general decline of sea level through the Pleistocene as ice caps steadily increase in size. The gaps between terrace levels are periods of erosion that correspond to the major glacial intervals.

and the Tyrrhenian has been divided into several substages. The relationship of some of the older beach levels to interglacial melting is also complicated by the fact that they include levels dominated by cold-water molluscan fossils.

The most widely accepted interpretation of Mediterranean sea-level stages, published by K. W. Butzer in 1964, is as follows:

ITALY	elev. a.s.l.	MOROCCO	elev. a.s.l.	CLIMATE	approx. age (*)
Versilian	+2	Mellahian	+2	Warm	5 k.y.
Pontinian	−100	Soltanian		Cold	20 k.y.
Tyrrhen.III	+2	Ouljian	+5	Warm	60–80 k.y.
		Presoltanian		Cold	90–110 k.y.
Tyrrhen.II	+2–10	Pre-Ouljian	+5–10	V. warm	120 k.y.
Nomentanan	−200?	Tensiftian		Cold	0.2 m.y
		Kebibatan		Warm	?0.23 m.y.
Tyrrhenian	+25–30	Anfatian	+25–35	Warm	0.3 m.y.
Flaminian		Amirian		Cold	0.45 m.y.
Sicilian II	+50–60	Maarifian	+55–60	Warm	
Cassian		Saletian		Cold	0.9 m.y.
Sicilian	+100–110	Messaoudian	+90–100	Warm	
Emilian		Regregian		Warm	c. 1.0 m.y.
Calabrian		Upp. Moghrebian		Cold	c. 1.5. m.y.

(*) Ages modified by later workers

The Pontinian regression is named for the Po Valley where it is widely evidenced in boreholes, characteristically associated with cold-water mollusks presently living in the Baltic; some archaeologists use the term "Gravettian" for cultures of this age. A sea-level decline of the indicated magnitude was inadequate to expose a land bridge to Africa at Gibraltar or between Sicily and Tunisia, or to connect Crete or Cyprus to the mainland. However, Corsica and Sardinia were joined at this time in a single large island, and England and France were connected via the Dover lowlands, in which the Thames and the Seine came together to drain into the North Sea. As noted, this was also the probable occasion for the immigration of humans into the New World, since the previous opportunity (pre-Soltanian regression) seems to be much too old.

Tyrrhenian-II beaches are the most widespread of the Mediterranean levels, and are characterized by mollusks that today range as far south as Senegal. By recent dating of uranium-thorium ratios in corals found on these beaches, and by the magnitude of the warming event, we may be confident that this level is the last interglacial maximum (Eemian), seen in oxygen-isotope curves as level 5e.

There is some evidence that the long interval of mixed but mostly cold-climate conditions, which produced the erosional landscape of the Nomentanan, included a regression of as much as 200 m. below sea level. The equivalent levels in North Africa, the Tensiftian, have yielded hominid remains at

Rabat dated between 0.3–0.2 m.y. The Tyrrhenian-I warm-climate interval is represented in beach deposits with subtropical mollusks and extensive red soils, which may correlate to post-Mindel soils in the Alps and the Holsteinian of the Rhine delta. Flaminian regression is therefore regarded as correlative to the Elsterian (Mindel) glacial episode(s), at ca. 0.6–0.45 m.y., and the equivalent Amirian deposits in Morocco contain "advanced *Homo erectus*" dated to about this age at Thomas Quarries and Tighenif (Ternifine).

Major changes in both the mammal and the marine fauna, with many extinctions and intercontinental migrations, mark both the Cassian (i.e. end-Villafranchian) and Calabrian (mid-Villafranchian) cold-climate intervals. Although most of the studied deposits of this age occur above sea level, this is probably due to local tectonism; the faunal revolutions suggest glacio-eustatic regression with the uncovering of land bridges, together with severe environmental stress. The Cassian regression is generally correlated to the Menapian (Günz) glacial episode in Europe, and the Calabrian to the Eburonian (upper Donau) cold-climate sediments.

Coral Reefs and Sea Levels

Charles Darwin was the first to observe that coral reefs, as ever-growing communities, would maintain themselves at sea level despite changes in elevation. The abandoned reef structures are conspicuous and geologically durable formations and are the best dated markers we have of sea-level fluctuations over the later Pleistocene time. On the one hand corals preserve the oxygen- and carbon-isotope ratios of the seas in which they lived, and can be directly related to the history of global temperature and atmospheric changes. On the other hand they are very suitable for radiometric dating by the uranium-thorium method, which is reliable to ca. 150 k.y. and which can be extrapolated with less certainty to the middle Pleistocene.

Rising seacoasts in geologically active areas, particularly in Barbados and the Huon Peninsula of New Guinea, have been analyzed because they preserve both high-stand and low-stand reefs. Supporting data have come from the Ryukyu Islands, Indonesia, and Haiti and from drilling records on islands in Micronesia. By measuring the rate at which the reef-bearing coastlines are being uplifted and the age of reef corals at each level, the relative motion of the mean sea level can be determined, rather than just the high and low elevations. These coral-reef studies produce sea-level curves closely matching those obtained from oxygen-isotope records that reflect the variations in the amount of fresh water trapped in ice.

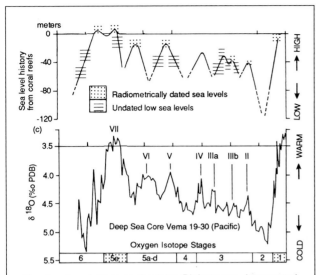

Sea-level variations in the later Pleistocene, interpreted from coral reef lines on the rising coast of the Huon Peninsula, New Guinea. Sea-level variations (above) are coincident with fluctuations in ice volume, seen (below) as variations of oxygen isotopes in successive layers of deep sea mud. (After Aharon and Chappell, 1986, Palaeogeogr., Palaeoclimatol., Palaeoecol., 56: 364. Redrawn by permission of Elsevier Scientific Publications, B.V.)

See also CENOZOIC; GLACIATION; PLEISTOCENE; RADIOMETRIC DATING; TIME SCALE. [J.A.V.C., G.K.]

Further Readings

Denton, G.H., and Hughes, T.J., eds. (1981) The Last Great Ice Sheets. New York: Wiley.

Haq, B.U., Hardenbol, J., and Vail, P.R. (1987) Chronology of fluctuating sea levels since the Triassic. Science 234:1156–1167.

Wilgus, C., et al. (1987) Sea level change—an integrated approach. Soc. Econ. Paleontol. Mineral., Tulsa, Okla., Spec. Paper.

SECOND INTERMEDIATE

Term proposed at the third Pan-African Congress in 1955 to refer to industries transitional between Middle Stone Age flake industries (e.g. Stillbay) and Later Stone Age industries with backed microliths. The term is no longer in use, since more careful stratigraphic work, especially at the type site of the most characteristic industry, the Magosian, has cast doubt upon its existence as a cultural evolutionary stage.

See also FIRST INTERMEDIATE; LATER STONE AGE; MAGOSIAN; MIDDLE STONE AGE; STILLBAY. [A.S.B.]

SEDENTISM *see* HUNTER-GATHERERS; NEOLITHIC

SEDIMENTATION RATES *see* TIME SCALE

SEMIBRACHIATION *see* LOCOMOTION

SEMIORDER

Category in the classificatory hierarchy that falls between the order and suborder. This rank has been introduced recently to express the fundamental distinction within Primates between the "modern" Euprimates and the "archaic" Paromomyiformes.

See also CLASSIFICATION; EUPRIMATES.. [I.T.]

SEMITERRESTRIAL *see* LOCOMOTION

SEMNOPITHECUS *see* COLOBINAE

SENGA-5

Late Pliocene or early Pleistocene open-air site in the Lusso (Kaiso) beds of the Semliki Valley (Albertine Rift Valley), in eastern Zaire. The site, excavated by J.W.K. Harris, has yielded numerous small quartz and a few quartzite flakes, simple pebble cores, and abundant remains of savanna mammals, tortoises, and fish in association with fossil wood and coprolites. Sediments and molluskan fauna suggest deposition on an ancient beach. Its suggested age, based on faunal correlations with the eastern (Gregory) Rift Valley, is between 2.3 and 1.9 m.y.

See also AFRICA; EARLY PALEOLITHIC; EARLY STONE AGE; OLDOWAN; OLDUVAI; OMO; PALEOLITHIC LIFEWAYS; STONE-TOOL MAKING. [A.S.B.]

SERIATION *see* ARCHAEOLOGY

SERIES *see* TIME SCALE

SERRAVALLIAN *see* MIOCENE; TIME SCALE

SEX, SKELETAL *see* FORENSIC ANTHROPOLOGY; SEXUAL DIMORPHISM

SEXUAL DIMORPHISM

Intersexual differences in physical form. Many primates, like the majority of mammals, exhibit sexual differences in morphology, physiology, and behavior. Some aspects of sexual dimorphism result directly from differences in the male and female sex hormones. Examples include the external genitalia and secondary sexual characteristics established at puberty (in humans, female breasts, male beard, and

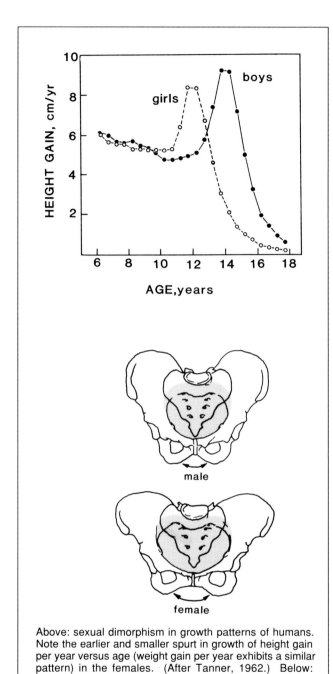

Above: sexual dimorphism in growth patterns of humans. Note the earlier and smaller spurt in growth of height gain per year versus age (weight gain per year exhibits a similar pattern) in the females. (After Tanner, 1962.) Below: anterosuperior views of human male and female pelves, illustrating the greater subpubic angle (arrows) and larger and differently shaped bony birth canal (shaded area) in females. (After Basmajian, Primary Anatomy, © The Williams & Wilkins Co., Baltimore, 1982.)

dimorphism. Although the differences in form between the sexes are usually described and analyzed at the adult stage, it is important to understand that these differences are merely the endpoints of sexually differentiated patterns of growth. Analysis of the ontogenetic bases of different patterns of sexual dimorphism can lead to insights into the ecological and social correlates of dimorphism.

Primate Dimorphism

The distribution of patterns of sexual dimorphism varies in interesting ways among the primates. In terms of overall body size the haplorhines (tarsiers, monkeys, apes, and humans) are generally dimorphic, while the strepsirhines (lemurs and lorises) are not. Some of the strepsirhines, however, are sexually dichromatic (having different coat colors). Among the haplorhines most species exhibit a moderate degree of dimorphism in overall size, with adult females being 75–90 percent of male weight. The most dimorphic primate species include the gorillas and orangutans among the apes, as well as the patas monkeys, mandrills, proboscis monkeys, and open-country baboons—here females are roughly half the size of adult males. The lesser apes (gibbons and siamangs) and various New World monkeys (marmosets, tamarins, titi monkeys) are among the higher primates that exhibit little or no dimorphism in size. In a few primates, notably some marmosets and the spider monkeys, females may be larger than males in overall size. Canine teeth also exhibit sexual dimorphism in most higher primates, largely paralleling in degree the overall differences in weight, although there are a number of exceptions to this generalization.

The primates reveal other interesting examples of sexual dimorphism. For instance, orangutan males sport prominent cheek pads and enlarged laryngeal air sacs, giving them a characteristic facial appearance (see figure). Male mandrills have brightly colored faces and external genitalia, while male hamadryas baboons differ from females in the enlarged cape of hair about their shoulders. Cases where males exhibit exaggerated versions of features also present in females include the prominent fleshy nose of the proboscis monkey and the specialized hyoid apparatus used by the howler monkey to communicate with conspecifics.

Sexual Dimorphism in Humans

Modern humans, with the majority of higher primates, exhibit a moderate degree of sexual dimorphism in body weight (see figure), although we are clearly an aberrant species in combining this size dimorphism with an almost total lack of canine tooth dimorphism. Within our wide-ranging species we

shape differences in the bony pelvis related to enlargement of the birth canal—see figure). Other shape differences between the sexes in primates are related to the generally larger overall body size of males and thus result from *allometry*, or differential growth. The relatively smaller brains, relatively larger faces (see figure), and differing limb proportions of males compared with females in many primates are examples of such allometric components of sexual

also see varying degrees of dimorphism. It is difficult to trace patterns of sexual dimorphism reliably in the fragmentary fossil record, but the available evidence suggests marked differences in overall size between the sexes in the apes of the Miocene (5–23.5 m.y. ago) as well as in the earliest hominids from which the lineage leading to modern *Homo* emerged. In the earliest australopithecines females may have been only three-quarters to one half (or less) the size of males, depending on the part of the body examined and the potential error of the estimates derived. Canine size and dimorphism were reduced early in hominid evolution, a change of undoubted behavioral significance, as Charles Darwin noted long ago.

Factors Influencing Sexual Dimorphism

A number of factors appear to be responsible for the variation in sexual dimorphism observed among primates. One important component is Darwin's notion of *sexual selection*, which is based on 1) competition among members of the sex that is more plentiful or in which some individuals are disproportionately successful at mating, and 2) choice of the more successful individuals in this competition by members of the opposite sex. Primatologists have generally viewed males as competing for access to, or choice by, females. Larger male body size, canine size, and such ornamental features as the cheek pads of male orangutans or the silvery pelage of fully mature male gorillas are believed to have evolved either for direct use in competitive interactions or as signals to females of the size and fitness of the male. A number of

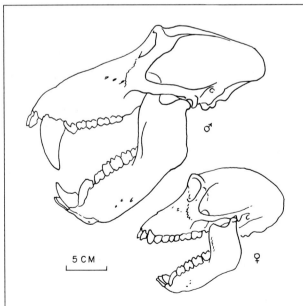

Skulls of male and female mandrill monkeys, illustrating the marked differences in size and shape between the sexes. Note particularly the extreme dimorphism in the canine teeth and the bony snout. (After Schultz, 1969.)

the bases of this argument, particularly the degree of male-male competition and variance in male reproductive success, are currently being examined in laboratory and field studies. It gains some support, however, from the empirical observation that sexual dimorphism among primates is *generally* strongest in polygynous, unimale, multifemale groups like hamadryas baboons and gorillas, and absent or weakest in monogamous, one-male, one-female groups like the lesser apes. This general relationship is also not without exception. For example, strongly dimorphic DeBrazza's monkeys (*Cercopithecus neglectus*) and patas monkeys (*Erythrocebus patas*) apparently do not exhibit strongly polygynous mating systems.

The need for males to protect females and their offspring from predators is another possible determinant of the degree of sexual dimorphism. The large canine and body size of males is seen as advantageous in defense and interspecific encounters, and the fact that terrestrial primates are often strongly dimorphic is cited as evidence of this purported relationship.

Another important influence on sexual dimorphism is the overall size of the species. For reasons not well understood the degree of dimorphism tends to increase with body size, so that the most dimorphic taxa in a given group are also generally the largest-bodied. Examples include the gorilla among the apes and the baboons among the Old World monkeys, although a few cases do not follow this general prediction.

Recently primatologists have begun to investigate the role of sex differences in niche utilization, feeding behavior, and other bioenergetic factors as influences on size dimorphism. The focus here is often on the possible advantages of smaller size in females, such as early reproduction, reduced energy requirements (particularly during pregnancy and lactation), and reduced feeding competition with males. Among humans there appears to be a relationship between the degree of weight dimorphism and protein availability.

Future research will likely clarify these and other factors, but clearly sexual dimorphism in primates is a complex phenomenon manifested in various ways and influenced by multiple causes.

See also ONTOGENY; PRIMATE ECOLOGY; PRIMATE SOCIETIES. [B.T.S.]

Further Readings

Campbell, B.G., ed. (1972) Sexual Selection and Descent of Man, 1871–1971. Chicago: Aldine.

Clutton-Brock, T.H., Harvey, P.H., and Rudder, B. (1977) Sexual dimorphism, socionomic sex ratio and body weight in primates. Nature 269:797–800.

Fedigan, L.M. (1982) Primate Paradigms: Sex Roles and Social Bonds. Montreal: Eden.

Frayer, D.W., and Wolpoff, M.H. (1985) Sexual dimorphism. Ann. Rev. Anthropol. *14*:429-473.

Leutenegger, W.E. (1982) Scaling of sexual dimorphism in body weight and canine size in primates. Folia Primatol. *37*:163-176.

Ralls, K. (1977) Sexual dimorphism in mammals: avian models and unanswered questions. Amer. Nat. *111*:917-938.

SHANIDAR

Huge cave in Iraq where the remains of nine Neanderthal adults and children were excavated from 1957 to 1961. The most important remains are a partial adult skeleton showing clear signs of disabling injury and disease (Shanidar 1), an adult partial skeleton supposedly buried with flowers (Shanidar 4), and a very large and robust partial skull (Shanidar 5). This informative sample of Neanderthals probably lived in Iraq more than 50 k.y. ago.

See also NEANDERTHALS. [C.B.S.]

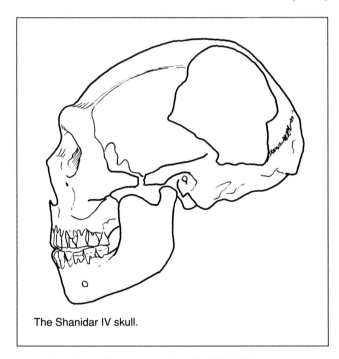

The Shanidar IV skull.

SHOSHONIUS *see* OMOMYINAE

SHUNGURA *see* OMO

SHUNGURAN *see* TIME SCALE

SIAMANG *see* APE; HYLOBATIDAE

SICILIAN *see* PLEISTOCENE; SEA-LEVEL CHANGE

SIDE-SCRAPER *see* SCRAPER; STONE-TOOL MAKING

SIDI ABDERRAHMAN *see* HOMO ERECTUS

SIDI HAKOMA *see* HADAR

SIMIAS *see* COLOBINAE

SIMIIFORMES *see* ANTHROPOIDEA

SIMIOLUS *see* CATARRHINI

SIMONSIA *see* ADAPIDAE

SIMONSIUS *see* PARAPITHECIDAE

SIMOPITHECUS *see* CERCOPITHECINAE

SIMPSON, GEORGE GAYLORD (1902-1984)

American paleontologist who held major appointments at the American Museum of Natural History (1927-1959), Columbia University (1945-1959), and Harvard University (1959-1970). While making numerous contributions to vertebrate paleontology (especially of the mammals), Simpson' also made original and important contributions to the evolutionary synthesis that began to emerge during the decade following the publication of Dobzhansky's milestone work *Genetics and the Origin of Species* in 1937. Simpson's book, *Tempo and Mode in Evolution* (1944), supplemented by *Major Features of Evolution* (1953), embodies a perspective that was an integral feature of the modern evolutionary synthesis.

[F.S.]

SINANTHROPUS *see* HOMO ERECTUS

SINOADAPIS *see* SIVALADAPIDAE

SISTER TAXON *see* CLADISTICS

SITE SURVEYING *see* ARCHAEOLOGY

SITE TYPES

Variety and distinctions of residential and special-purpose occupation localities seen in the archaeological record of hunting and gathering peoples. Ethnographic research among hunter-gatherers indicates that group size and subsistence activity are important aspects of settlement and are closely related to environmental conditions. Work on land-use patterns and group size of coresident units among these groups has revealed a number of cross-cultural regularities of significance to prehistoric archaeology. First, all ethnographically known hunter-gatherers are mobile in their subsistence pursuits. This mobility, however, can occur both on the level of a few individuals and on the level of the group. A given group thus uses a number of site types over a season, a year, or a lifetime.

Reasons for Variability

The organization of subsistence pursuits among hunter-gatherers varies greatly in the extent to which the whole group is moved to the food resources. On the one hand foragers constantly move the whole group to position it optimally in relation to the available resources. Logistically organized groups, those in which specialized procurement parties harvest specific resources and bring them back to the larger social group, constitute the other extreme of this scale. In this second case the social group as a whole moves far less frequently. The existence of these different strategies of positioning groups *vis à vis* resources implies that we can anticipate finding very different occupation and settlement records for areas occupied by groups of hunter-gatherers in the past.

Another significant feature found among many hunter-gatherers is a pattern of group aggregation and dispersal, in which a large number of people living together during one season break up into smaller coresiding units during other seasons. This feature suggests that we can anticipate finding different sizes of residential settlements or camps for a given group of hunter-gatherers.

While sites used by hunter-gatherers vary along parameters that include the organization of subsistence behavior; the season, nature, and duration of occupation; and group composition and size, two broad classes of site types can be distinguished for these groups: *residential camps* and *special-purpose camps*.

Residential Camps

These are sites where a group of people spend some time and sleep overnight. The nature of overnight stays, however, differs between foraging and logistically organized hunter-gatherers. The former exploit their regions using group-mobility strategies, and it is the whole group that occupies residential sites, or *base camps*. Logistically organized groups send out food-procurement parties that exploit resources within a particular region. These task groups may occupy overnight camps away from the residential camp of the whole group.

Base camps, occupied by large and diverse social units comprising individuals of all ages and of both sexes, for lengths of time exceeding a week or more, are locales where the widest variety of activities takes place. These include the construction of shelters, tool and clothing manufacture and repair, food preparation and consumption, and other routines generally involving whole coresidential groups. Furthermore, because all ages and both sexes reside at these sites, age- and gender-specific behavior takes place here as well.

Since base camps are occupied by large social groups for relatively lengthy periods of time, archaeological correlates of base camps in a given region are found in large sites with thick cultural layers. Living floors at these sites have the widest array of features, such as dwellings, hearths, work areas, and storage facilities. Tool and implement assemblages contain a wide variety of items associated with diverse activities and may include a small number of nonutilitarian objects, such as jewelry and pieces of portable art.

Organic remains resulting from subsistence activities at these sites show both greater abundance and greater diversity than at other site types. Finally, since residence at base camps is not year-round but restricted to one or two seasons, remains of food debris at these sites can be used both to estimate the time of the year that they were inhabited and to offer clues about the size of the coresidential units.

Overnight stops are most often occupied by small groups of same-sex individuals in the course of their forays to procure food or resources for a larger coresidential unit. Thus a group of hunters may stay overnight while hunting, or a trading party on an exchange expedition to a distant group may have to make temporary overnight camps during their trip. We can expect that people at such camps will cook and eat some food, and possibly repair or resharpen some tools, but also that the extent and variety of these activities will be far more limited than found at base camps.

Archaeological signatures at these types of sites include small size, thin cultural layers, and total absence or ephemeral presence of such features as shelters and hearths. Inventories of tools and implements are small and fairly uniform in composition. The amount and nature of organic remains reflect both the briefness of stays and the size of the group .

Daily life at the Pincevent Magdalenian base camp in the Paris basin. (After Jelinek, 1986.)

Special-Purpose Camps

These sites, variously termed *camps* or *locations* in the ethnographic and archaeological literature, are occupied for specific and finite purposes—e.g. lithic workshops, hunting and collecting camps, lookout spots for monitoring the movements of game animals, processing stations, ritual or ceremonial locales, and aggregation sites.

Lithic workshops are usually found near the outcrops of good-quality lithic materials and are the locations where small groups of tool makers come to obtain the necessary raw materials for making tools. Activities performed here include the quarrying of the rock itself and the shaping of the nodules into cores or in some cases into flakes and blades.

Since good quarry sites are repeatedly used over long periods of time, archaeological profiles generally do not show the same discrete spatial limits that other types of occupations exhibit. The scatter of lithic debris around quarries will be thick, extend over a large area, and be a product of numerous visits. These areas lack any features and have assemblages poor in cores but rich in unretouched cortical and waste flakes.

Occasionally, however, tool makers may use discrete spots at distances from a few to a few hundred meters from the quarried outcrop for reducing the nodules into appropriate preforms. These sites, like their equivalents near the quarry, lack such features as hearths or dwelling structures and have tool assemblages clearly related to the initial stages of lithic production. There are few or no food remains and no evidence for exploitation of any resources other than lithic. Since the task force visiting this location consists of only a handful of people, and since they spend a relatively short period of time obtaining the raw materials, the area with the lithic scatter is small and without any appreciable depth.

Hunting and collecting camps are occupied for short periods of time by a small group of people engaged in specific food-procurement tasks. They include locations for harvesting vegetable resources, spots for fishing and shellfish collecting, and kill sites where prey is dispatched. These camps range from spots where a single animal is killed or a few tubers dug up to mass kill sites where whole herds of animals are harvested by a large group of hunters.

Although varying from a few square meters to large areas, all of these sites generally exhibit short-term occupation by groups smaller than those found at the base camps in the region. They lack such features as dwellings, storage pits, and sizable hearths with thick ash deposits. Tool inventories at these sites are limited in number, homogeneous in kind, and associated with activities related to initial procurement and processing of specific food resources. Some resharpening of tools used in these activities may also take place here. Fewer organic remains are found at these sites than at base camps and consist of just the one or two species being harvested.

Kill sites, especially those where mass harvesting took place, may contain sizable amounts of skeletal remains. The composition of these remains, however is quite different from those found at base camps, containing a high percentage of parts with low nutritional value, such as skulls, vertebrae, and lower-limb extremities.

Lookout spots: Groups of hunters among both foragers and logistically organized hunter-gatherers may pause briefly during the hunt at specific spots to survey their prey, rest, snack, and resharpen their hunting implements. If such natural blinds as large rocks or thick bushes are present in the area, they will use them to conceal themselves from their prey. If natural barriers are absent, the hunters may build artificial blinds out of boulders or branches. These activities generate yet another type of special-purpose site in the archaeological record, one with some sort of a natural or human-made blind, a thin cultural layer with sparse remains of food debris, and possibly some lithic debris produced by tool resharpening.

Processing camps: Hunting or collecting task groups usually reduce their catches or harvests to easily transported parts of high food value. This processing is done adjacent to the kill or harvest site and generates remains that differ from those at the kill, fishing, or collection spot itself. While such processing camps are more common for logistically organized groups, similar sites can occasionally be generated by foragers as well. This will occur when unusually large numbers of animals are killed in one spot or an especially large species is taken. On such occasions one of the hunters may go back to the base camp to summon the rest of the group to help process the meat and bring it back to camp.

In the ethnographic present these processing locations are adjacent to the kill or harvest ones, but the limited size of most archaeological excavations may uncover only shell middens or areas of primary or secondary butchering rather than the kill site itself. Remains found at these locales usually do not contain the tools used to take down the prey (arrows, spears, harpoons) but only implements used to cut, skin, butcher, and perhaps fillet it. Thus the range of tools is much narrower than at base camps and similar in homogeneity, although not in tool types, to those at kill sites. The composition of the organic remains closely parallels that of kill or harvesting sites—only one or two species are represented. Since the processing of meat or fish may also involve drying or smoking it, such features as shallow hearths or smoke pits as well as various forms of drying racks may also be found at such locations. Overall, however, whatever features or inventories are discovered, they are all clearly related to a finite set of activities associated with processing of particular resources.

Ritual or ceremonial sites: Both foragers and logistically organized hunter-gatherers often have special locations for ritual or ceremonial purposes. These may include caves or rock shelters with sacred paintings, in- or above-ground cemeteries, and sacred sections of the regional landscape. While many rituals and ceremonies are conducted at the base camps themselves, when locations away from residential sites are used for these purposes the sacred activities generate material remains that differ significantly from those found at other types of sites.

Archaeological profiles of sites used for ritual or ceremonial purposes differ widely depending on the types of ceremonies performed there and on the size of the group engaged in these activities. The most easily identifiable are cemeteries with in-ground interments. Other special-purpose ceremonial sites contain both material features and inventories that have numerous nonutilitarian components. Such locations have a minimum of remains clearly identified with subsistence- and maintenance-related activities, such as the manufacture or repair of tools or clothing. Although some evidence for food preparation and consumption can be expected at these sites, both the materials and methods used in these activities may differ significantly from those found at residential base camps in the same region.

Aggregation sites: Some hunter-gatherers, especially foragers who live in small coresidential groups and who use extensive seasonal mobility in their subsistence pursuits, join other like-sized groups during particular seasons at large residential base camps. Activities that take place during these short periods of large gatherings include the expected subsistence-related component of food procurement and preparation, tool manufacture and repair, and shelter construction and use. In addition large gatherings of this kind also serve as special-purpose locales for finding mates, for exchanging information and goods, and for performing sacred rituals and ceremonies.

Archaeological identification of aggregation sites is a difficult task, because they exhibit many similarities to base camps in the same region. Aggregation sites will, however, be generally much larger in size and contain more dwelling remains and hearths, but due to the brevity of their occupation they have relatively thin cultural layers. Inventories at these sites may include tool groups much like those at base camps but also have significantly more objects like jewelry, engravings, portable art, exotics, or musical instruments, which are not related to everyday subsistence and maintenance activities but to the sphere of social and ritual interaction.

See also Aggregation-Dispersal; Archaeological Sites; Exotics; Hunter-Gatherers; Jewelry; Middle Stone Age; Musical Instruments; Paleolithic Image; Ritual. [O.S.]

Further Readings

Binford, L.R. (1980) Willow smoke and dog's tails; hunter-gatherer settlement systems and archaeological site formation. Am. Antiquity 45:4-20.

Butzer, K.W. (1982) Archaeology as Human Ecology. Cambridge: Cambridge University Press.

Jochim, M.A. (1981) Strategies for Survival: Cultural Behavior in an Ecological Context. New York: Academic.

Kelly, R.L. (1983) Hunter-gatherer mobility strategies. J. Anthropol. Res. 39:277-306.

Price, T.D. (1978) Mesolithic settlement systems in the Netherlands. In P.A. Mellars (ed.): The Early Postglacial Settlement of Northern Europe. London: Duckworth, pp. 81-113.

Soffer, O. (1985) The Upper Paleolithic of the Central Russian Plain. Orlando, Fla.: Academic.

SIVALADAPIDAE

One of three families often classified in the infraorder Adapiformes and superfamily Adapoidea. This taxon subsumes two mid-late Miocene genera from Indopakistan that have recently been considered related to adapids. Both of these genera have been known for decades, but only recently have fairly complete jaws with teeth of one, *Sivaladapis*, been forthcoming. In a review of the material J.H. Schwartz pointed out that *Sivaladapis* does not bear the distinctive dental features of an adapid. Rather, this primate, although resembling in some aspects of molar morphology the extant *Hapalemur*, shares with the North American notharctid *Smilodectes* such derived features as inwardly arcing cristids obliquae on M_{1-2}, thick buccal cingulids, and stout para- and hypocristids. The other "sivaladapid," *Indraloris*, is known from fewer specimens, but referred molars bear one of the unmistakable stamps of identity of the extant lorisid *Loris*: a well-developed protostylid, one of the dental features that distinguishes this from virtually all other primates. Given the apparent lack of affinity between *Indraloris* and *Sivaladapis*, it would seem that Sivaladapidae is an unnecessary taxon.

See also Adapidae; Lorisidae; Lorisoidea; Notharctidae. [J.H.S.]

Further Readings

Gingerich, P.D., and Sahni, A. (1984) Dentition of *Sivaladapis nagrii* (Adapidae) from the late Miocene of India. Int. J. Primatol. 5:63-79.

Schwartz, J.H. (1986) Primate systematics and a classification of the order. In D.R. Swindler (ed.): Comparative Primate Biology, Vol. I: Systematics, Evolution and Anatomy. New York: Liss, pp. 1-41.

SIVALADAPIS *see* SIVALADAPIDAE

SIVAPITHECUS *see* HOMINIDAE; HOMINOIDEA; NEAR EAST; PONGINAE

SIWALIKS

Neogene rocks classified as the Siwalik Group are exposed in a huge arc of extensive outcrops south of the Himalayas across the northern part of the Indopakistan subcontinent. They range from the Indus River in the west eastward to the Brahmaputra, a distance of over 2,500 km. Named for the Siwalik Hills near Hardwar in northern India, they form a vast and important fossiliferous region containing many separate sites, ranging in time from over 18 m.y. to younger than 1 m.y. and providing what is probably the best succession of mammalian evolution in the world. The fauna includes large hominoids formerly attributed to several genera, of which *Sivapithecus*, *Gigantopithecus*, and perhaps *Ramapithecus* are still current. Fossils have been collected from the Siwaliks intermittently since the early 1800s. But since 1973 a joint project of Yale, then subsequently Harvard University, with the Geological Survey of Pakistan, working in the Potwar Plateau south of Rawalpindi (Pakistan), has enormously expanded the faunal sample and has clarified many contextual matters involving geological and paleoenvironmental issues. The following account focuses mainly on this region, where the bulk of the fauna has been found.

Siwalik Stratigraphy

The Siwalik Group of rocks is divided into four formations: the Soan, Dhok Pathan, Nagri, and Chinji. The Chinji Formation is the oldest, overlying the Kamlial Formation, which is also fossiliferous. The Soan Formation includes the Tatrot and Pinjor units. All of these formations have their type sections in the Potwar Plateau, and all are lithostratigraphic units; however, the names have their origin in a classification by G. Pilgrim produced in the 1930s, which was essentially based on faunal criteria. Much confusion has resulted over the years from confounding the separate concepts and implications of faunal units, time units, and rock units under the same terminology. This problem was not helped by the difficulty until recently of accurately dating the succession. In the virtual absence of any volcanic rocks calibration of the sequence has now been achieved by paleomagnetic means. In the Potwar Plateau there are over 7,000 m. of sediments ranging from the Miocene to the Pleistocene, from over 18 m.y. in age to less than 1 m.y. The boundaries of the formations have been shown to be time-transgressive.

The sediments are the end result of the collision of the plate forming the Indopakistan subcontinent with the rest of Asia, leading to the uplift of the Himalayas. Subsequent erosion of the rising range produced considerable quantities of sediments deposited to the south by large and small river systems. Hence the fossils are preserved in a variety of fluviatile sedimentary situations, but particularly in abandoned flood-plain channels.

The environment may have been characterized by braided and meandering stream channels, and a variety of vegetation types may have covered the drainage basin, including forest, woodland, and grassland.

Siwalik Hominoids

Nearly 200 fossil specimens of large hominoids have been collected from the Potwar area alone. Other significant collections come from near Ramnagar (Kashmir) and from the Hari Talyangar region north of Delhi (India). Smaller hominoids are also known. The large hominoids belong principally to the genus *Sivapithecus*, including *Ramapithecus*, which many now believe to be the same taxon. Rarer specimens attributed to *Gigantopithecus* are also known. One large element of interest in these specimens originally revolved about the belief that some were hominids, more or less directly involved in our own ancestry. Recent work has produced many new hominoid specimens, including a very complete skull of *Sivapithecus*, and also a number of postcranials. It is now no longer thought tenable that these hominoids

are ancestral to humans: they seem clearly to be more closely allied to the modern orangutan. They remain, however, important in building up a picture of what ancestral hominoids were like and in understanding the causes of their evolution.

Small hominoids are known back to 16.1 m.y., but large hominoid specimens first appear at 11.8 m.y. They become extinct in the region at 7.4 m.y. in the Potwar, but may extend to 7.2 m.y. at Hari Talyangar. This coincides with a major faunal change in the Siwaliks, possibly related to climate. It is interesting that cercopithecoids first appear in the Siwaliks shortly after the disappearance of hominoids from the record. In India *Gigantopithecus* also occurs after this time. It is dated there at 6.3 m.y. An earlier significant faunal turnover occurred at ca. 9.5 m.y., involving the arrival of equids. This event, however, apparently did not affect the hominoids to any great extent. Although they occur throughout the sequence, hominoid specimens are concentrated at three horizons: at ca. 11.8 m.y., at 8.1 m.y., and, at Hari Talyangar, at 7.6–7.2 m.y.

The great interest of the Siwalik region, and of the Potwar sequence in particular, lies in its ability to provide information about mammalian faunal change in one region over a long time period. The fact that hominoids are part of this fauna adds to its value. In conjunction with work elsewhere periods of successive isolation and connection with other parts of the world can be demonstrated and their effects on the fauna closely documented. The Siwaliks also present the best opportunity available for investigating the possible interactions of climatic events and mammalian evolution through the Neogene.

See also HOMINIDAE; HOMINOIDEA; INDIA; MIOCENE; PAKISTAN; PALEOMAGNETISM; PLATE TECTONICS; PLEISTOCENE; PLIOCENE. [A.H.]

Further Readings

Badgley, C., and Behrensmeyer, A.K. (1980) Paleoecology of middle Siwalik sediments and faunas, northern Pakistan. Palaeogeo., Palaeoclimatol., Palaeoecol. 30:133–155.

Barry, J.C. (1986) A review of the chronology of Siwalik hominoids. In J.G. Else and P.C. Lee (eds.): Primate Evolution. Cambridge: University of Cambridge Press, pp. 93–105.

Barry, J.C., Johnson, N.M., Raza, S.M., and Jacobs, L.J. (1985) Mammalian faunal change in the Neogene of southern Asia and its relation to global climatic and tectonic events. Geology 13:95–130.

SKELETON

The human skeleton, like that of most primates, is relatively generalized by mammalian standards. Most primates have a primitive limb structure with one bone in the upper (or proximal) part of the limb (humerus and femur), a pair in the lower (distal) part (radius/ulna and tibia/fibula), and five digits on their hands and feet. Primates have retained many bones from our vertebrate ancestors that other mammals have lost—e.g. the clavicle, a bone that has been lost in the evolutionary history of most ungulates and many carnivores. Likewise, many mammals have reduced the number of digits on their hands and feet and reduced or coalesced the bones of their forearm and leg. In the number of separate skeletal elements and the configuration of their limbs primates are more similar to the primitive mammalian skeletal morphology than are many other living mammals.

The part of a primate's skeleton that lies behind the skull, or *postcranial skeleton*, serves several functions, such as providing support and protection for the organs of the trunk. However, its primary functions and those that seem to account best for the major differences in skeletal shape, are its functions with respect to locomotion. In this capacity the postcranial skeleton provides both a structural support and a series of attachments and levers to aid in movement.

Primate skeletons can be divided into three parts: axial skeleton (backbone and ribs), forelimb, and hindlimb.

Axial Skeleton

The backbone is made up of individual bones called vertebrae and is divided into four regions. The cervical, or neck, region contains seven vertebrae in humans, as in almost all mammals. The first two vertebrae, the atlas and the axis, are specialized in shape and serve as a support and pivot for the skull. The other cervical vertebrae are concerned with movements of the neck.

The second region of the backbone is the thorax. Humans have 12 thoracic vertebrae, while other primates have between 9 and 13, each of which is attached to a rib. Most of the rotational movements of the trunk involve movements between thoracic vertebrae. The ribs are connected anteriorly with the sternum to enclose the thoracic cage, within which lie the heart and lungs. On the outside the thorax is covered by the muscles of the upper limb. Primates exhibit considerable variability in the shape of the thorax. In quadrupedal species the thorax tends to be relatively deep dorsoventrally and narrow from side to side. In suspensory apes and in humans the thorax is broad, so that the scapula lies on the back.

The thoracic vertebrae are followed by the lumbar vertebrae. Humans have five lumbar vertebrae, but in other primates the number ranges between four and seven. Those species with long flexible backbones for leaping or running tend to have more lumbar vertebrae, while climbing and suspensory species have fewer vertebrae and hence a short, stiff backbone.

No ribs are attached to the lumbar vertebrae, but they have very large transverse processes for the attachment of the large muscles that extend the back. Most of the flexion and extension of the back takes place in the lumbar region. In most primates the thoracic and lumbar vertebrae form a gentle curve with a dorsal convexity (*kyphosis*). The human backbone is unusual in that the thoracic region has a dorsal convexity while the lumbar region has a ventral convexity (*lordosis*). This extra curvature is related to our bipedal posture.

The next region of the backbone is the sacrum, a single bone composed of several fused vertebrae. The

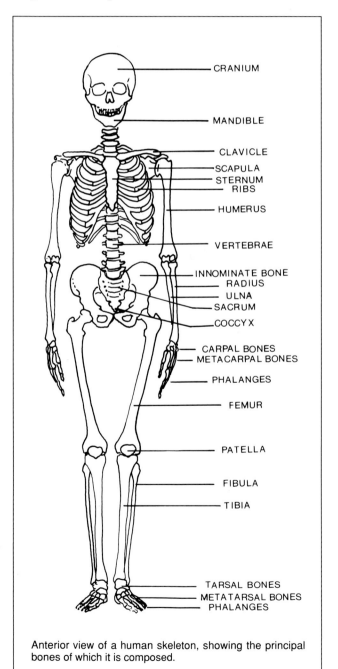

Anterior view of a human skeleton, showing the principal bones of which it is composed.

pelvis, or hip bone, is attached to the sacrum on either side while the tail joins it distally. Humans have five sacral vertebrae; other primates have between three and seven. Primates with a tail generally have fewer sacral vertebrae, while tailless species have more.

The last region of the spine is the caudal region, or tail. In humans and apes this consists of three or four tiny bones all fused together, called the coccyx. In other primates the caudal region forms a long tail made up of as many as 30 vertebrae.

The Forelimb

The primate upper limb is divided into four regions, most of which contain several bones. The most proximal part, nearest the trunk, is the shoulder girdle composed of two bones: the clavicle anteriorly and the scapula posteriorly. The small S-shaped clavicle is attached to the sternum anteriorly and to the scapula posteriorly. It provides the only bony connection between the upper limb and the trunk.

The flat, triangular scapula is attached to the sternum via the clavicle and is attached to the thoracic wall only by several broad muscles. The scapula varies considerably in shape among living primates. In suspensory species this bone tends to be relatively long and narrow with the glenoid cavity facing cranially. In quadrupedal species it tends to be broad with a laterally (or ventrally) facing glenoid. The human scapula is most similar to that of an orangutan.

The scapula articulates with the single bone of the upper arm, the humerus, by a very mobile ball-and-socket joint between the glenoid cavity of the scapula and the head of the humerus. Most of the large propulsive muscles of the upper limb originate on the chest wall or the scapula and insert on the humerus; the muscles responsible for flexing and extending the elbow originate on the humerus (or just above on the scapula) and insert on the forearm bones. The human humerus is very similar to that of extant great apes in having a head that faces medially rather than posteriorly and in the distinctive distal articulation with a rounded capitulum and a spool-shaped trochlea.

Two forearm bones articulate with the humerus: the radius on the lateral or thumb side and the ulna on the medial side. The elbow joint is a complex region with the articulation of three bones. The articulation between the ulna and the humerus is a hinge joint and functions as a simple lever system with the humerus. Humans resemble apes and other suspensory primates in having a very small olecranon process on the proximal end of the ulna. In quadrupedal primates and most other mammals the olecranon process is long so as to provide a powerful lever for extension of the elbow during quadrupedal walking and running.

The radius forms a more complex joint, since this rodlike bone rotates about the ulna. This movement of the radius and ulna is called *pronation* when the hand faces down and *supination* when the hand faces up. The muscles responsible for movements at the wrist and for flexion and extension of the fingers originate on the distal end of the humerus and on the two forearm bones.

Distally the radius and the ulna articulate with the bones of the wrist. The radius forms the larger joint, and in some primates (lorises, humans, and apes) the ulna does not even contact the wrist bones.

Primate hands are divided into three regions: wrist, metacarpals, and phalanges. The wrist, or carpus, is a complicated region. In most primates it consists of nine separate bones aligned in two rows. In humans and in African apes two of these have fused so that there are only eight bones. The proximal row articulates with the radius, and the distal row articulates with the metacarpals of the hand. Between the two rows of bones is a composite joint, the midcarpal joint, with considerable mobility in flexion, extension, and rotation.

The five rodlike metacarpals form the skeleton of the palm and articulate distally with the phalanges or finger bones of each digit. The joints at the base of most of the metacarpals are formed by two flat surfaces offering little mobility; however, the joint at the base of the first digit—the pollex, or thumb—is more elaborate in many species and shows special modifications associated with the requirements of manipulation and grasping. The joints between the metacarpal and the proximal phalanx of each finger allow mainly flexion and extension with a small amount of side-to-side movement (*abduction* and *adduction*) for spreading the fingers apart. There are three phalanges (proximal, middle, and distal) for each finger except the thumb, which has only two (proximal and distal). The joints between the phalanges are pure flexion and extension joints.

While all primate hands have approximately the same numbers of bones, the relative proportions of their hand elements can vary greatly in conjunction with particular locomotor needs. In arboreal species the digits, and especially the phalanges, are relatively longer than in terrestrial species. Many arboreal primates have greatly reduced or even lost the pollex (thumb), while lorises have reduced the index finger for enhanced grasping abilities between the pollex and the more lateral digits. In suspensory primates the digits are especially long. Species that rely on manipulative abilities for grasping insects, seeds, or other items tend to have a pollex and index finger that are more similar in length. Humans show a large number of detailed modifications of hand structure in association with the hand's almost exclusive use as an organ of manipulation rather than as part of the locomotor system.

The Hindlimb

The primate hindlimb can be divided into four major regions: pelvic girdle, thigh, leg, and foot. These regions are comparable with the shoulder girdle, arm, forearm, and hand of the forelimb.

The primate pelvic girdle is made up of three separate bones on each side (the ilium, ischium, and pubis) that fuse to form a single rigid structure, called the innominate bone. In contrast with the pectoral girdle, which is quite mobile and loosely connected to the trunk, the pelvic girdle is firmly attached to the backbone through a nearly immobile joint between the sacrum and the paired ilia. The primate pelvis, like that of all mammals, serves many roles. Forming the bottom of the abdominopelvic cavity, the internal part supports and protects the pelvic viscera, including the female reproductive organs, the bladder, and the lower part of the digestive tract. The bony pelvis also forms the birth canal through which the newborn must pass. In conjunction with this requirement most female primates (including women) have a bony pelvis relatively wider than in males of the same species. Finally, the pelvis plays a major role in locomotion. It is the bony link between the trunk and the hindlimb bones, and it is the origin for many large hindlimb muscles that move the lower limb.

The ilium is the largest of the three bones forming the bony pelvis. A long, relatively flat bone in most primates, it lies alongside the vertebral column and is completely covered with large hip muscles, primarily those responsible for flexing, abducting, and rotating the hip joint. The rodlike ischium lies posterior to the ilium, and most of the muscles responsible for extending the hip joint and flexing the knee arise from its most posterior surface, the ischial tuberosity. This tuberosity also forms our sitting bone. The pubis lies anterior to the other two bones and gives rise to many of the muscles that adduct the hip joint. The ischium and pubis join together inferiorly to form the ischiopubic ramus and completely surround the obturator foramen. The relative sizes and shapes of these three bones vary considerably among primate species in conjunction with different locomotor habits. The human pelvis is unique among all mammals in having a very short, broad ilium and a short, dorsally oriented ischium, associated with our bipedal locomotion.

The part of the bony pelvis that articulates with the head of the femur is called the acetabulum, and it lies at the junction of the three bones. The hip joint is a ball-and-socket joint that allows mobility in many directions.

The single bone of the thigh is the femur. The prominent features of this long bone are a round head that articulates with the pelvis, the greater tuberosity where many hip extensors and abductors insert, the shaft, and the distal condyles, which articulate with the tibia to form the knee joint. Most of the surface of the femur is covered by the quadriceps muscles responsible for extension of the knee. Attached to the tendon of this set of muscles is the third bone of the knee, the small patella. The human femur is unique among primates in having a large rounded head and a short femoral neck. The lateral condyle is larger than the medial one, and the shaft of the femur is angled medially so that the knee joint lies medial to the hip joint. This adaptation places our center of gravity closer to the midline and aids in balance during bipedal gait.

Two bones make up the lower leg, the tibia medially and the fibula laterally. The tibia is larger and participates in the knee joint; distally it forms the main articulation with the ankle. The fibula is a slender splintlike bone that articulates with the tibia both above and below and also forms the lateral side of the ankle joint. Arising from the surfaces of the tibia and fibula (and also from the distal-most part of the femur) are the large muscles responsible for movements at the ankle and those that flex and extend the toes during grasping or walking and running.

Like the hand the primate foot is made up of three parts: tarsus, metatarsus, and phalanges. The most proximal two tarsal bones are those that form the ankle: the talus above and the calcaneus below. The head of the talus articulates with the navicular bone. The navicular articulates with three small cuneiform bones, which in turn articulate with the first three metatarsals. The body of the talus sits roughly on the center of the calcaneus, the largest of the tarsal bones. The tuberosity of the calcaneus extends well posterior to the rest of the ankle and forms the heel process. The achilles tendon from the calf muscle attaches here, and this process acts as a lever for the entire foot. Anteriorly the calcaneus articulates with the cuboid, which in turn articulates with the metatarsals of digits IV and V.

In nonhuman primates the digits of the foot resemble those of the hand. Each of the lateral four digits has a long metatarsal followed by three phalanges. The shorter first digit, the hallux, is opposable like the thumb, or pollex, and has a mobile joint at its base for grasping. Primate feet show considerable differences from species to species in the relative proportion of different pedal elements, associated with different locomotor abilities. Arboreal species tend to have longer, more curved phalanges and

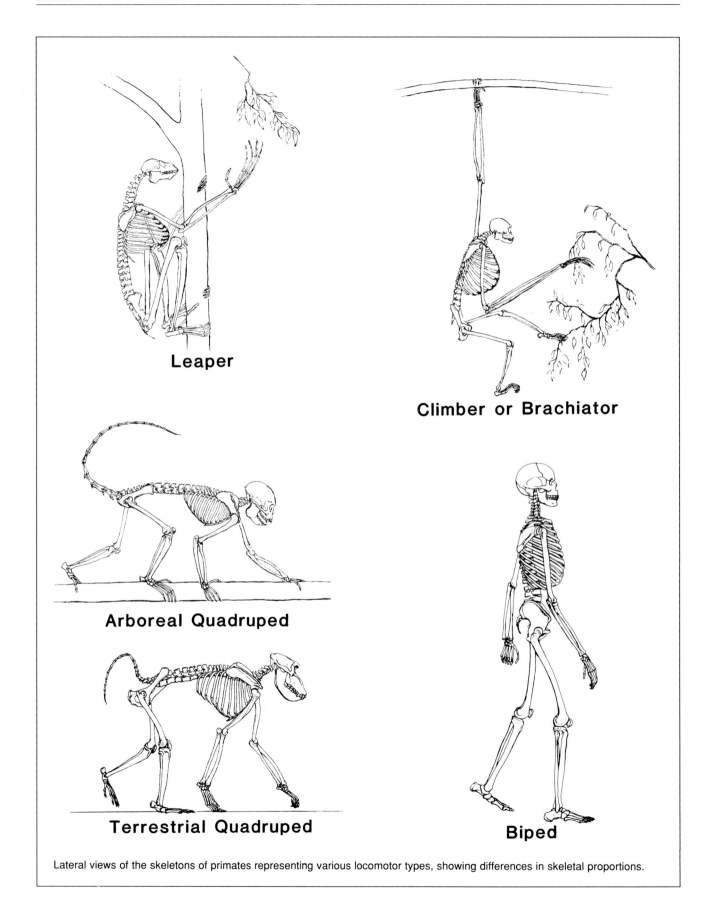

Leaper

Climber or Brachiator

Arboreal Quadruped

Terrestrial Quadruped

Biped

Lateral views of the skeletons of primates representing various locomotor types, showing differences in skeletal proportions.

usually a more opposable hallux, whereas terrestrial species have shorter digits.

Human feet are unique in their lack of an opposable hallux. Rather, all five digits are aligned side by side. In addition we have relatively short phalanges, and the tarsals form a set of bony arches that make the human foot a more effective lever during bipedal locomotion.

Skeletal Proportions

Primates vary considerably in their overall body proportions, in association with differences in their locomotor habits. Leaping primates are generally characterized by relatively longer hindlimbs than forelimbs and a long flexible trunk, especially in the lumbar region. Arboreal quadrupeds usually have a relatively long trunk and a long tail and forelimbs and hindlimbs that are more similar in length but short relative to trunk length or body size, as adaptations for balance. Terrestrial quadrupeds also have forelimbs and hindlimbs that are similar in length, but their limbs tend to be relatively longer relative to body size, since balance is not a problem on the ground. Suspensory primates usually have relatively long limbs and long hands and feet to permit them to suspend their body from a wide range of supports. They usually have a short, relatively rigid trunk.

See also BONE BIOLOGY; FORENSIC ANTHROPOLOGY; LOCOMOTION; MUSCULATURE; SKULL; TAIL. [J.G.F.]

Further Readings

Bass, W.M. (1971) Human Osteology. Columbia: Missouri Archaeological Society.

Clark, W.E. Le Gros (1959) The Antecedents of Man. Edinburgh: Edinburgh University Press.

Shipman, P., Walker, A., and Bichell, D. (1985) The Human Skeleton. Cambridge, Mass.: Harvard University Press.

SKHŪL

During excavations at the Mughâret es-Skhūl cave site on Mount Carmel (Israel), between 1929 and 1934, a number of adult and child partial skeletons were discovered. Many of the skeletons appear to have been intentionally buried, one even clasping the jaw of a pig. All were in levels associated with Levalloiso-Mousterian artifacts, but the dating of the site remains uncertain at present. Initial work suggested that the remains dated from the earlier late Pleistocene, but more recent studies using faunal and archaeological correlations suggest that the site dates from the later Mousterian, perhaps 40 k.y. ago. Ten individuals (seven adults and three children) are probably represented, and the material includes three reasonably complete adult skulls and some well-preserved long bones from the adults and children. Originally interpreted with the Tabūn remains

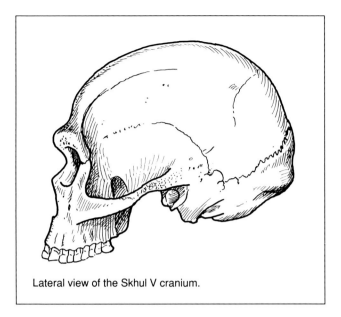

Lateral view of the Skhul V cranium.

as a "Neanderthal" population in the process of evolution into an early modern type, and later interpreted as possible hybrids between Neanderthal and modern populations, the Skhūl material is now generally regarded as representing one of the robust early modern populations of western Asia that still retain some archaic features from nonmodern ancestors. Some workers consider that these specimens, together with those from Qafzeh, may represent the ancestors of the European "Cro-Magnon" populations.

See also ARCHAIC MODERNS. [C.B.S.]

SKULL

The primate skull may be divided into two major components based on developmental and functional criteria: the neurocranium and splanchnocranium, or viscerocranium. The neurocranium houses the brain and is made up of two parts distinguishable by the type of bone formation underlying each. The membranous neurocranium, so called because the bones develop via intramembranous ossification, forms the calvarium and comprises the frontal bone, parietal bones, the squamous (or "flat") portions of the temporal bones, and the squamous portion of the occipital bone. The chondrocranium or basicranium develops from cartilage and comprises the ethmoid and sphenoid bones, as well as the petrous and mastoid regions of the temporal bones and part of the occipital bone. The basicranium serves as the floor of the neurocranium (and is therefore pierced by many nerves and blood vessels), and it also acts as a structural interface between the splanchnocranium and the neurocranium.

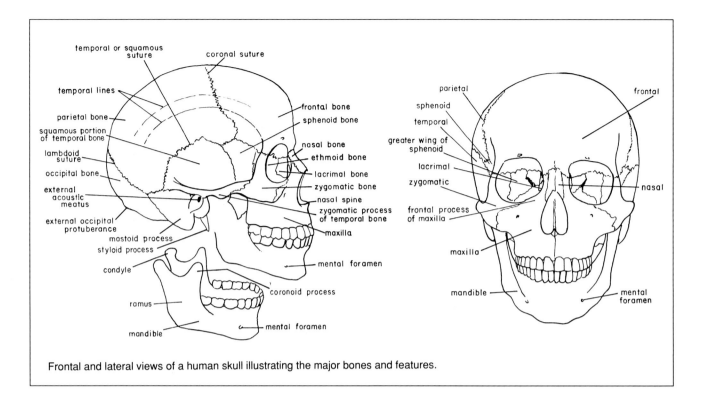

Frontal and lateral views of a human skull illustrating the major bones and features.

The splanchnocranium constitutes the rest of the skull, primarily the jaws and facial bones. The terms splanchnocranium or viscerocranium reflect the derivation of these bones from the embryonic "visceral" or branchial arches, which in primitive vertebrates line the wall of the digestive tract and support the gills. These bones develop via both membranous and endochondral ossification, and in the adult human state represent the paired nasal, lacrimal, zygomatic, and palatine bones, the single vomer and mandible, plus the two maxillae and two inferior nasal conchae.

Since primate skulls are often described or measured, a system of "landmarks," or defined points, has been developed to facilitate the process. Some of the most important landmarks are shown in the figure on the facing page.

The primary functions of the skull are to gather and break down food for nourishment and to support and protect the brain and the soft tissues associated with the special senses of hearing, sight, and smell.

Primate Diversity in Skull Form and Function
The rich diversity of skull form evidenced by our order is best illustrated by consideration of the functional specializations of the soft tissues associated with the various skeletal regions. For example, the skull of modern humans is dominated by the dramatically enlarged neurocranium, which houses our most salient morphological specialization, ca. 1,500 ml. of grey matter. Because our enormous cranial vaults are combined with relatively small faces, teeth, and chewing muscles, human skulls lack the marked bony ridges or protuberances, such as the sagittal crest or supraorbital torus, often seen in other primates. In other cases relatively large braincases and small facial skulls are related to the small overall body size of a species, as in the South American squirrel monkey (*Saimiri*) or the African talapoin monkey (*Miopithecus*), both of which may be dwarfed forms derived from larger ancestors. The basis for such shape changes is the differential, or *allometric*, growth of the facial skeleton relative to the neural skeleton, so that shifts in body size during ontogeny or among adults of closely related series result in a disproportionate change in facial size relative to overall skull size.

The orbits house the eyes and associated soft tissues and are particularly well developed in nocturnal species, such as the South American owl monkey (*Aotus*). Orbital hypertrophy reaches an extreme in the tarsier (*Tarsius*), where the weight of a single eyeball may exceed that of the brain, and the huge orbital cones envelop the facial skeleton. In general, however, the eyes exhibit a growth pattern similar to the brain, and thus the orbits usually decrease in *relative* size during ontogeny and among larger adults of a series varying in body size (compare the skulls of

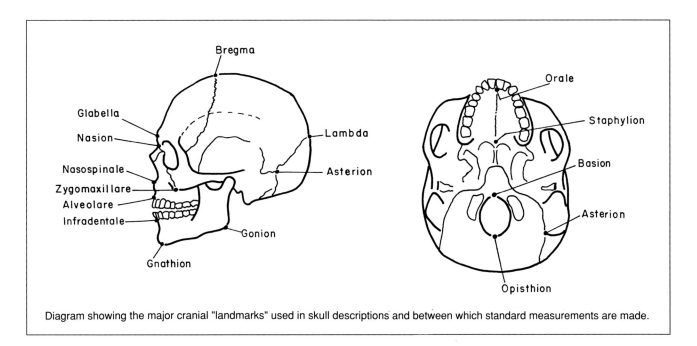

Diagram showing the major cranial "landmarks" used in skull descriptions and between which standard measurements are made.

the two small species on the left in the first figure with those of the large species on the right).

The degree of development of the bony midface, or "snout," is influenced by numerous factors. The strepsirhine primates generally rely more on olfactory stimuli in their social and feeding behavior than do the haplorhines and also exhibit relatively larger faces that protrude in front of the neurocranium rather than being more recessed under the skull vault. The nasal fossae in these primates are filled with bony turbinals that are covered by olfactory and respiratory epithelium. Certain extant haplorhines,

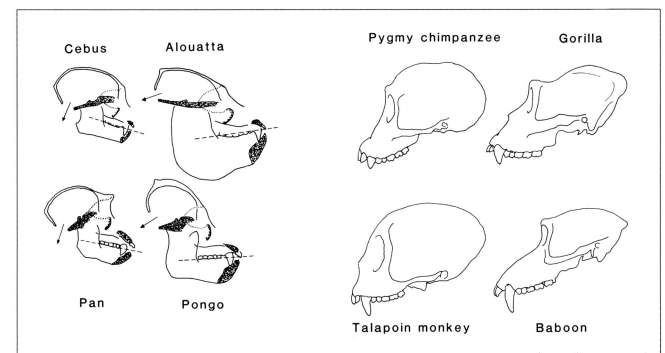

Left: differences in the positioning of the face relative to the skull base and cranial vault in howler monkeys (*Alouatta*) and orangutans (*Pongo*). The upward or dorsal deflection of the face may be related to enlargement of structures associated with vocalization. Right: a comparison of skull shape in two pairs of closely related forms differing markedly in overall body size. Above: female pygmy chimpanzee (ca. 40 kg.) and male gorilla (ca. 160 kg.); below: male talapoin monkey (ca. 1.2 kg.) and male baboon (ca. 25 kg.). Note the relatively enlarged faces and small braincases in the larger forms, resulting from differential growth in these regions as size increases.

such as howler monkeys, baboons, and gorillas, also have secondarily enlarged faces, due primarily to the effects of large body size and the positively allometric increase in the splanchnocranium and canine teeth (see figure).

Structures related to the production of sound may also affect skull form. In the howler monkey (*Alouatta*) the face is flexed upward or dorsally on an elongated and flattened skullbase, allowing for the suspension of an enlarged hyoid bone as part of a resonating chamber used to boom signals to conspecifics. The orangutan (*Pongo*) also exhibits a dorsally deflected splanchnocranium, perhaps related to the enlarged laryngeal sac, which functions as a resonating structure, especially in males. In *Homo* a secondary flexion or bending of the skull appears to be related to a restructuring of the pharyngeal and laryngeal region, yielding an enlarged supralaryngeal tract vital to the production of the complex and subtle sounds comprising human speech.

The dentition affects the size and shape of the splanchnocranium and also indirectly of the neurocranium, via related soft tissues, such as the chewing muscles, and bony support structures, such as the mandible and portions of the facial region. Larger teeth basically require a larger, more heavily buttressed maxillary and mandibular framework. An interesting example is seen in the intriguing and bizarre aye-aye (*Daubentonia*) from Madagascar. Here a deep and strongly flexed, beaklike face is related to the procumbent and continuously growing incisors that aye-ayes use to pry under tree bark for grubs and insects.

The chewing muscles, along with the teeth, the bony jaws, and other stress-bearing regions of the skull, comprise a functional unit that affects skull form in an important and reasonably predictable fashion. The mechanical task of this unit is primarily to break down ingested food by repetitive opening and closing of the jaws. The masticatory muscles, primarily the masseter, temporalis, and medial and lateral pterygoids, perform this function. The degree of force produced at the bite point can be roughly determined by taking a ratio of the *lever* (or power) *arm* of muscular effort, the distance from the jaw joint to the average line of action of the muscle, to the *load* (or resistance) *arm*, which is the distance from the jaw joint to the bite point. If one assumes a constant force input (i.e. muscles of the same size and power), a higher lever/load ratio reflects a mechanical situation capable of producing greater forces. Increased mechanical efficiency is often produced by moving forward the insertion of the masseter muscle and thus increasing the length of the lever arm, or by decreasing the length of the load arm, accomplished

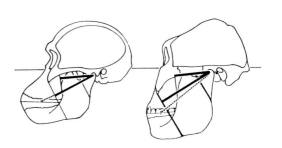

Illustration of cranial biomechanics using the early hominids *Australopithecus africanus* (left) and *A. boisei*. The heavy solid lines represent lever or power arms for the chewing muscles temporalis (shorter) and masseter. The dashed line represents the load or resistance arm to the molar teeth. Note the higher ratio of lever arm to load arm in *A. boisei*, providing increased mechanical efficiency and greater forces during chewing with the back teeth. (After DuBrul.)

through shortening of the lower face or by tucking the palate underneath the upper face.

Within the hominids the "robust" australopithecines (*Australopithecus robustus* and *boisei*) in particular exhibit aspects of this configuration. These basic principles of cranial biomechanics also help us make sense of the differences in skull form between the two subfamilies of Old World monkeys: the folivorous, or leaf-eating, colobines with their short faces and deep jaws have higher ratios of lever/load arms compared with the frugivorous, or fruit-eating, cercopithecines with their long and prognathic faces.

Current Research and Prospects

A number of relatively new approaches and techniques in the study of primate and mammalian skull form have yielded promising results, and much additional research will be completed in these areas in the future. Experimental approaches to masticatory biomechanics have involved cineradiographic filming of jaw and tooth movement, electromyographic determination of muscle activity, measurement of *in vivo* bone strain in various portions of the face, and investigation of the histochemical properties of the chewing muscles. The integration of such information with results of studies of comparative anatomy and biomechanical modeling has resulted in significant advances in our understanding of skull function.

Another important area of work involves the genetic and developmental factors controlling skull growth and form, since it is changes in these controls that result in evolutionary transformations of the skull. Recent studies in quantitative genetics, developmental abnormalities, and experimental approaches to intrinsic (e.g. developing tissue interactions) and extrinsic (e.g. hormonal) growth controls have provided new insights here. Finally, advances in evolutionary theory and the discovery of new fossil skulls of extinct primates also combine to provide important new information. Primatologists synthesize data from these and other fields in their continuing attempt to understand the form, function, and phylogeny of the skull of humans and non-human primates.

Evolution of Primate Skull Form

Our knowledge of cranial anatomy in the earliest primates is based largely on fossil remains of two Paleocene forms, *Palaechthon nacimiento* from North America and *Plesiadapis tricuspidens* from western Europe. These examples illustrate that the first primates were more similar to their mammalian contemporaries than to their later primate descendants or to any primates alive today. The skulls of these Paleocene primates generally resemble those of living tree shrews, with a long snout projecting in front of the relatively small braincase. Such a skull is designed to accommodate a large masticatory apparatus, with a long dental arcade and well-developed chewing muscles anchored to the skull vault, the zygomatic arches, and the lower jaw. The long face also reflects an acute sense of smell, whereas the eye sockets are relatively small, less frontated, and without the supportive postorbital bar characteristic of later primates. This combination of features has been used by some to argue that the earliest primates were nocturnal animals.

The fossil evidence indicates that plesiadapiforms had an ossified auditory bulla, a bony shell-like casing that envelops the chamber of the middle ear and its ossicles from below. This bullar capsule is formed by the petrosal bone, a derived homology that unites all the primates as a monophyletic group. Other mammals have analogously evolved ossified bullae by incorporating different cranial elements into a

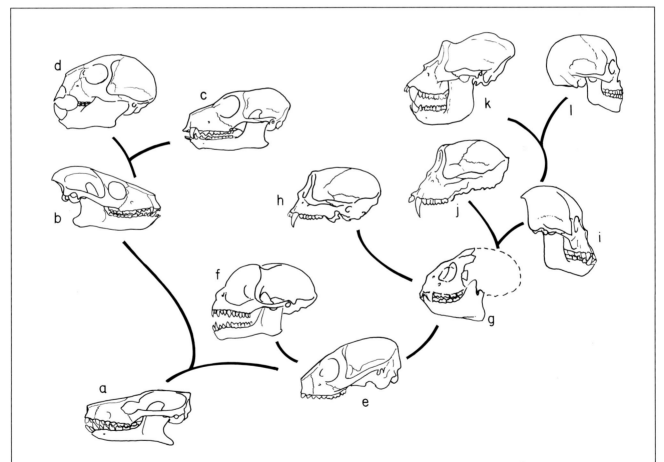

An array of skulls of extant and extinct primates, depicting the general evolutionary directions taken by some of the major taxonomic groups as well as some striking specializations. The diagrammatic linkages among these skulls reflect phylogenetic ties, but they do not represent the actual anatomical transformations among the species shown here. Several skulls are generalized, primitive designs indicative of ancestral patterns of important groups, as identified in parentheses: a) *Plesiolestes* (all primates); b) *Notharctus*; c) *Lemur* (lemurs and lorises); d) *Daubentonia*; e) *Rooneyia* (Tarsiiforms and haplorhines); g) *Apidium* (anthropoids); h) *Cebus*; i) *Proconsul* (hominoids); j) *Macaca*; k) *Gorilla*; l) *Homo sapiens*.

middle-ear covering, such as the ectotympanic bone, whose primary function is to provide a collar for the tympanic membrane. Some mammals lack an ossified bulla entirely but encase the ear region with membrane or cartilage. The evolution of a bony auditory bulla may be related to the development of a hearing mechanism sensitive to low-frequency sounds.

The second major radiation of primates occurred during the Eocene period and produced a new type of cranial organization. Eocene adapids, such as *Notharctus*, and omomyids, as exemplified by *Rooneyia*, are characterized by a reduced snout, relatively larger brains, more frontally directed orbits, and a postorbital bar developed from processes of the frontal and zygomatic bones. The postorbital bar stabilizes the zygomatic arches by solidly fusing them to the braincase, providing a lateral truss that resists the twisting generated during unilateral mastication in a face that is shorter and with more frontated orbits than found in Paleocene primates.

The early omomyids were perhaps the first primates to adopt a diurnal activity pattern. Their skulls reflect this change from a dominance of the olfactory/tactile sense and corresponding enlargement of the portions of the brain associated with the sense of smell, the primitive primate pattern that characterized the plesiadapiforms and that persists among many extant strepsirhines. One of the important skeletal features reflecting this change in omomyids is the loss of the deep posterior recess of the nasal cavity that forms part of the separation of the eye sockets in most mammals. In the modern haplorhines this space is occupied by the medial walls of the orbits, which have become frontated and closely spaced, enhancing the capacity for steroscopic vision. An orbital septum, or bony plate enclosing the posterolateral portion of the orbital space, is an important novel development in this group.

Anthropoids mark another adaptive transition in the evolution of the primate skull that is documented by such Oligocene forms as *Apidium*. In addition to a larger braincase their faces are proportionately shorter and more vertical, the mandibular symphysis and frontal bones are rigidly fused early in life, and a greatly modified zygomatic bone extends laterally around the orbital fossa to form a postorbital partition that in its detailed construction is unique among the mammals. One explanation of this suite of features is that they signify a more active, forceful use of the incisor teeth in harvesting foods, powered by masseter and temporalis muscles of larger size and strength. With a fused mandibular symphysis, large loads can be carried by the solidly rooted, large, spatulate incisors that are typical of anthropoids, and

power generated by muscles on either side of the head can be added together to increase the force of molar biting. Possibly to balance these forces and protect orbital contents from injury, the zygomatic bones have expanded in size and become firmly joined to the skull. The effect of this is to produce the postorbital plate, or septum, and reinforce the junction between the facial skull and the neurocranium. This basic anthropoid groundplan of skull form served as a foundation for marked diversification during Oligocene, Miocene, and Plio-Pleistocene times, yielding a broad array of extinct and extant monkeys, apes, and hominids.

The evolution of skull form in our own lineage has been the subject of intense interest and debate since the discovery of the Taung infant, formally named *Australopithecus africanus*, by R.A. Dart in the 1920s. This skull exhibited a counterintuitive mosaic of features, considering that common preconceptions, fueled by the fraudulent Piltdown skull, predicted that early hominids would have large, humanlike brains combined with primitive, apelike faces and teeth. Discovery of the Taung infant was followed by even more impressive fossil remains from South Africa, and beginning in the late 1950s the sediments of East Africa have yielded an unprecedented series of well-preserved skulls of humans and our close relatives. Combined with additional material from Asian and European sites, these African fossils permit us to sketch a fairly detailed, if ever-changing, scenario of human evolution over the past several million years based on craniodental remains.

Although specific phylogenetic connections are difficult to determine, particularly in the period 3.5–2 m.y. ago, we can discern two primary groups of hominids, and these are placed in the closely related but divergent genera *Australopithecus* and *Homo*. The australopiths are characterized, particularly in later and larger forms, by massive chewing teeth, well-developed sagittal crests, and large heavily buttressed faces adapted to generating great chewing forces and withstanding the resultant bony stresses. Relative brain size exhibits no apparent increase through time within this group, although the australopiths are more highly encephalized than the great apes. Authorities have interpreted the most salient aspects of skull form in the australopiths as evidence of an increasing specialization on some type of hard-food items, such as roots and nuts, perhaps a dietary adaptation related to exploitation of drier and more open-country environments. It has never been clearly demonstrated that these specialized herbivorous hominids used any of the primitive stone tools found in eastern and southern Africa in the early Pleistocene, and they disappear from the fossil record at

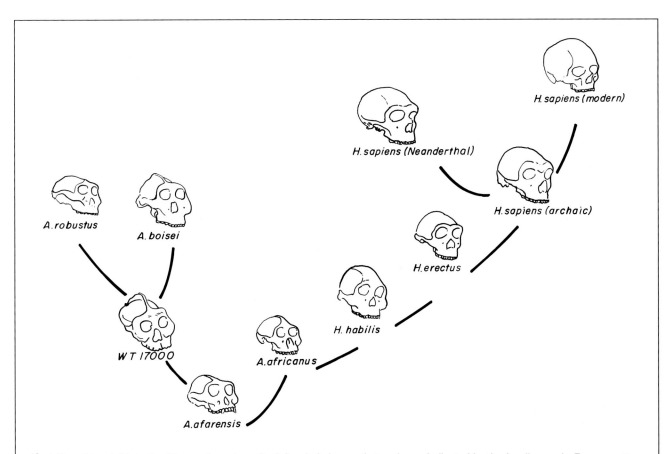

Evolution of hominid skulls. Two or three broadly defined phylogenetic trends are indicated by the fossil record. From a pattern similar to that of *Australopithecus afarensis* increasingly large masticatory muscles and chewing teeth produced the strongly buttressed, deep faces of the *A. robustus/A. boisei* lineage, which became extinct. A general decrease in tooth size, musculature, and face size, coupled with a dramatic increase in size of the braincase, marked the *A. africanus/Homo sapiens* lineage, although the intervening details of phylogenetic and morphologic evolution are unresolved. The development of large browridges, low-slung heads, and keeled vaults, for example, may have been a specialization of an *erectus/neanderthalensis* line.

ca. 1 m.y. ago.

A second lineage of early hominids, in all likelihood derived from a primitive early australopith like *Australopithecus afarensis*, exhibited quite different skull morphology and general adaptations. In this group the chewing teeth and associated masticatory apparatus became smaller and more gracile, while the brain literally exploded in an evolutionary sense, undergoing a three- to fourfold increase in overall size in a 3-m.y. period. Skulls of the genus *Homo* combine a large and rounded cranial vault devoid of sagittal cresting with a smaller and orthognathic (flatter) face. The evidence of skull form and the archaeological record clearly suggest that by ca. 2 m.y. ago our own genus had embarked on what would be a most successful evolutionary pathway, one characterized by behavioral flexibility and an adaptation to the natural environment based on culture.

Some interesting elaborations on this basic *Homo* pattern are seen in the well-known Neanderthal crania: the faces are enlarged and protruded in the nasal region and dominated by a heavy supraorbital torus or browridge. Some have interpreted this morphology as evidence of cold adaptation in glacially isolated hominids, while others have suggested a link to use of an enlarged anterior dentition as part of a cultural tool kit.

In any case a plentiful fossil record has revealed some haunting reflections that clearly inform us of the evolutionary pathways that culminated in our own species, *Homo sapiens*. Only time will tell whether this aberrant and highly encephalized species will avoid the fate of our closest cousins.

See also ALLOMETRY; BONE BIOLOGY; DWARFISM; GIGANTISM; MORPHOLOGY; ONTOGENY; SEXUAL DIMORPHISM; SKELETON; TEETH.. [B.T.S., A.L.R.]

Further Readings

Anderson, J.E. (1983) Grant's Atlas of Anatomy, 8th ed. Baltimore: Williams and Wilkins.

Biegert, J. (1963) The evaluation of characteristics of the skull, hands, and feet for taxonomy. In S.L. Washburn (ed.): Classification and Human Evolution. New York: Viking Fund Publ. Anthrop. no. 37, pp. 116-145.

deBeer, G.R. (1985) The Development of the Vertebrate Skull. Chicago: University of Chicago Press.

Enlow, D.H. (1982) Handbook of Facial Growth, 2nd ed. Philadelphia: Saunders.

Moore, W.J. (1981) The Mammalian Skull. Cambridge: Cambridge University Press.

Moss, M.L., and Young, R.W. (1960) A functional approach to craniology. Am. J. Phys. Anthropol. *18*:281-292.

Rak, Y. (1983) The Australopithecine Face. New York: Academic.

Szalay, F.S., and Delson, E. (1979) Evolutionary History of the Primates. New York: Academic.

Weidenreich, F. (1941) The brain and its role in the phylogenetic transformation of the human skull. Trans. Am. Phil. Soc. *31*:321-442.

Zingeser, M.R., ed. (1973) Craniofacial biology of primates, Symp. 4th Intl. Congr. Primatol., Vol. 3. Basel: Karger.

SMILODECTES *see* NOTHARCTIDAE

SMITH, [SIR] GRAFTON ELLIOT (1871-1937)

British (b. Australia) neuroanatomist and anthropologist. On receiving his doctorate of medicine in 1896 from the Medical School of the University of Sydney, Smith moved to England to continue his studies at Cambridge University. In 1900 he received the chair of anatomy at the Government School of Medicine in Cairo, where he remained until 1909, when he accepted the anatomy chair at Manchester University. Between 1919 and 1937 he served as first director of the newly established Institute of Anatomy and Embryology at University College in London. Smith's interests were wide-ranging. His most enduring contributions were in the area of comparative neuroanatomy, particularly as it pertains to primate evolution. Emerging from these studies was the notion that primate evolution involved an increasing elaboration of those areas concerned with sight, hearing, and touch and a corresponding decrease in the olfactory centers. Smith also brought his neuroanatomical expertise to bear on human paleontology and conducted a number of endocranial studies, including that of the celebrated Piltdown skull. Although his endorsement and interpretation of the Piltdown remains identify him as an early supporter of the "presapiens" thesis, in later years Smith softened his antagonistic views on the evolutionary significance of the Neanderthals. Smith was also a vigorous advocate of an extreme form of diffusionism that claimed Egypt as the cradle of civilization.

[F.S.]

SMITHFIELD

Later Stone Age Holocene industry of the southern African interior, named after nineteenth-century surface collections from near Smithfield, Orange Free State (South Africa). The industry is characterized by an abundance of end-, side-, and hollow scrapers; rarity or absence of backed microliths; and frequent association with ceramics and iron trade items. Faunal remains suggest a continuing dependence on hunting and gathering, although occasional herding of small stock may have been practiced. Its relationship to the Wilton industry remains unclear, as both are found in the interior up to historic times, although the Smithfield is much less widespread and also overlies the Wilton at several sites.

See also HUNTER-GATHERERS; LATER STONE AGE;
MAN-LAND RELATIONSHIPS; STONE-TOOL MAKING;
WILTON. [A.S.B.]

SOAN

Paleolithic artifacts of uncertain age and affinity from the Indus and Soan river valleys in the Punjab of India. In 1936 Helmut De Terra referred assemblages of "chopper-chopping tools" to the "Soan Culture." Soan artifacts include large and small flakes and large multifaceted cores and blades. Early Soan assemblages supposedly contain bipolar flakes and largely unifacially flaked massive "choppers." The late Soan includes choppers, scrapers, and flakes struck from prepared cores. Although localities with good stratigraphic successions are rare, some workers (especially the earlier ones) believed that the morphology of Soan artifacts converges on those produced with Levallois technology. The actual affinities and typological range of this supposedly distinct archaeological entity remain highly uncertain. Soan assemblages, however, do seem to be distinct from Acheulean-like industries also present in India. The actual temporal range of these artifacts can only be estimated as broadly representative of the middle Pleistocene.

See also ASIA (EASTERN); CHOPPER-CHOPPING TOOLS.
[G.G.P.]

SOCIOBIOLOGY

Although the term *sociobiology* had been used before, it became widespread only after 1975, when E.O. Wilson's *Sociobiology: The New Synthesis* was published. Wilson's book, in which he defined sociobiology as "the systematic study of all social behavior," has stimulated intense debate and a great deal of research.

An outgrowth of ethology, sociobiology has been heavily influenced by population genetics and evolutionary ecology. It has yet to become the preferred term to describe *all* studies of social behavior. Rather, it is most frequently used to describe studies on the genetics and evolution of social behavior and societies. A society, according to Wilson, is "a group of individuals belonging to the same species and organized in a cooperative manner." Although Wilson introduced this definition in his 1971 book *The Insect Societies*, the definition applies equally well to other organisms, including primates, where the most common unit of society is generally referred to as a *social group*, or *troop*.

A key concept in sociobiology is that social behavior does have a significant genetic component and that the societies resulting from social behaviors are therefore able to evolve under selection. As Wilson has argued, a simple behavioral difference between two animals (which may have a genetic basis) can result in a significant difference in their patterns of interaction with other individuals. An example would be variation in tolerance of the close proximity of other particular classes of individual, such as adult males. Multiplied through a series of the interindividual interactions that build social relationships, such small differences can create very different societal structures. If the original difference has some genetic basis and leads to a difference in individual reproductive success, then societal structure becomes subject to natural selection.

In addition to the concept that societies and their structure are adaptive in an evolutionary sense another important tenet of sociobiology is that kin selection will operate to reinforce sociality. The theory underlying kin selection (a theory first clearly expounded by the population geneticist W.D. Hamilton) is that the apparently self-sacrificing altruistic acts that are often observed in social animals may not be self-sacrificing in an evolutionary sense. If these acts are directed toward close kin sharing many genes with the altruist, they will tend to increase the representation of the altruist's genes in the next generation (and therefore its "inclusive fitness"). Efforts to promote the survival of one's own offspring are an obvious example of such kin selection, or nepotism, but the same principle can apply to brothers, sisters, and other relatives. Although the significance of such selection in the evolution of insect societies (in many of which all females inherit identical sets of genes from their fathers) is well established, its significance in vertebrate societies is less clear. It has yet to be adequately demonstrated, for instance, that kin selection (other than assistance to immediate offspring) has played a major role in the evolution of most primate societies.

An extension of kin-selection theory is group selection, a theory associated particularly with the writings of V.C. Wynne-Edwards. This theory (more properly called *intergroup selection*) holds that many

apparently altruistic behaviors in social animals have evolved because they have tended to increase the long-term reproductive success of one distinct group in relation to another. This requires that social groups be both relatively isolated from one another genetically and potentially subject to extinction. It has been pointed out that extensive between-group migration, such as occurs in many primate societies, would tend to nullify the effects of such selection, especially in the presence of individuals with any genetically based tendencies to antisocial "selfish" acts. While much social behavior seems readily explicable in an evolutionary sense in terms of the reproductive advantages it brings to individuals, intergroup selection cannot yet be totally dismissed as a potentially significant factor in social evolution.

From an early stage Wilson included human societies within the purview of sociobiology. This has brought sociobiologists into conflict with social scientists studying *Homo sapiens*; these scientists do not traditionally view human society from a Darwinian perspective but rather emphasize the roles of learning and culture as determinants of human behavior. While the large brain of modern humans provides tremendous learning abilities (making "nurture" a particularly significant determining factor in human behavior), there is abundant evidence that this learning is built upon a genetic substrate (our "nature") similar to that found in many other primate and nonprimate animals. Among the main goals of human sociobiology, then, are the better understanding of the interactions between nature and nurture in the development of human social behavior and the better understanding of the evolutionary basis of those aspects of human social behavior that do have a genetic underpinning. It is not one of the goals of human sociobiology to prescribe how people should behave; it is therefore a mistake to equate sociobiology with Social Darwinism, which is not a branch of science but a political philosophy.

See also ANTHROPOLOGY; EVOLUTION; GENETICS; PRIMATE SOCIETIES. [J.F.O.]

Further Readings

Barash, D.P. (1982) Sociobiology and Behavior, 2nd ed. New York: Elsevier.

Chagnon, N.A., and Irons, W., eds. (1979) Evolutionary Biology and Human Social Behavior: An Anthropological Perspective. North Scituate, Mass.: Duxbury.

Clutton-Brock, T.H., and Harvey, P.H., eds. (1978) Readings in Sociobiology. Reading, Pa.: Freeman.

Gray, J.P. (1985) Primate Sociobiology. New Haven, Conn.: HRAF.

Wilson, E.O. (1971) The Insect Societies. Cambridge, Mass.: Harvard University Press.

Wilson, E.O. (1975) Sociobiology: The New Synthesis. Cambridge, Mass.: Harvard University Press.

Wilson, E.O. (1978) On Human Nature. Cambridge, Mass.: Harvard University Press.

SOFT HAMMER see STONE-TOOL MAKING

SOIL see GLACIATION; PLEISTOCENE

SOLEILHAC

Possible early open-air archaeological site in the commune of Blanzac, Haute Loire, in central France, ca. 1–0.8 m.y. old. Located on the paleolakeshore of a volcanic crater, the fauna is just post-Villafranchian or early middle Pleistocene (*Elephas meridionalis, Equus caballus* and *E. stenonis, Cervus praemegaceros*), and the site has reversed polarity. Soleilhac yielded a small number of crude stone pieces resembling scrapers, denticulates, choppers, and a protohandaxe in association with an arrangement of basalt blocks measuring 6 m. by 1.5 m., possibly representing the oldest artificial structure in Europe.

See also EARLY PALEOLITHIC; EUROPE; MAN-LAND RELATIONSHIPS; STONE-TOOL MAKING. [A.S.B.]

SOLIFLUCTION see GLACIATION; PLEISTOCENE

SOLO see NGANDONG

SOLOENSIS see HOMO ERECTUS

SOLUTRÉ

Open-air archaeological site in the Ardèche region of eastern France, dated to the late Pleistocene by faunal and archaeological correlation, and radiocarbon ages greater than 30,400 to ca. 17,000 B.P. It was chosen in 1869 as the type site of the Solutrean industry. Located at the base of a cliff and recently reexcavated by J. Combier, Solutré contains archaeological industries identified as Mousterian, Lower Perigordian, Aurignacian, Upper Perigordian, Solutrean, and Magdalenian. Although considerably affected by cryoturbation and slumping, the Upper Paleolithic levels also contain faunal remains of horse, reindeer, and bovids, whose spatial associations (e.g. partial articulation and sorting of skeletal parts), suggest repeated use as an ambush site or butchering station.

See also ARCHAEOLOGICAL SITES; ECONOMY, PREHISTORIC; EUROPE; LAUGERIE SITES; MAN-LAND RELATIONSHIPS; MOUSTERIAN; SITE TYPES; SOLUTREAN; UPPER PALEOLITHIC. [A.S.B.]

SOLUTREAN

Later Upper Paleolithic industrial complex of France and Spain, ca. 21,000–18,000 B.P. (17,000 B.P. in Cantabrian Spain), named after the open-air site of Solutré (Saône-et-Loire) in eastern France. The Solutrean is characterized by several forms of thin, leaf-shaped points, shaped by distinctive flat, highly invasive unifacial and bifacial retouch. Superficial resemblances between these points and leaf-shaped Mousterian points, the abundance of flakes, and the relative paucity of Solutrean bone working led to a placement of the Solutrean "stage" *between* the Mousterian and the Aurignacian by Mortillet in 1881. In 1912 Breuil published a correct sequence for the French Upper Paleolithic, with a three-stage Solutrean phase (lower, middle, and upper; or I, II, and III) between the Aurignacian and the Magdalenian. A fourth stage, Protosolutrean, was added subsequently to distinguish the basal Solutrean at Laugerie Haute, with its generalized use of flat retouch without specialized point types, from the later stages.

Breuil's three stages were themselves distinguished by different forms of pressure-flaked stone points based on the Laugerie-Haute sequence: from the unifacial point (Solutrean I, or lower); to the classic laurel-leaf point (Solutrean II or middle); and the narrower willow-leaf and shouldered points (Solutrean III or upper), sometimes used to divide the Solutrean III into two successive stages, upper and final, respectively. Antler hafts or sleeves are also present at some sites, suggesting improvements in hunting technology. Although worked bone is rarer in the Solutrean than in the preceding early Upper Paleolithic industries, eyed needles are characteristic of the final stages.

In Spain, where the point types corresponding to Protosolutrean and Solutrean I are absent, the *earliest* Solutrean industries at 21,700–19,000 B.P. are characterized by bifacially worked leaf-shaped points, while the final stages exhibit shouldered points, hollow-base laurel-leaf points, and bifacial barbed and tanged arrowheads. Important sites include Parpalló in Valencia and La Riera in Cantabria. Backed bladelets and burins are also more common in the later Spanish industries than in southwestern France during the final Solutrean. Another variant of the Solutrean, with shouldered points throughout together with laurel-leaf points in the "middle" Solutrean, is recognized in Languedoc (Grotte de la Salpetrière, Gard). The Solutrean is absent in northern France and in Provence.

The Solutrean is the dominant industrial type of western Europe during the last glacial maximum, when northwestern and central Europe were apparently abandoned. The density of sites and increasing

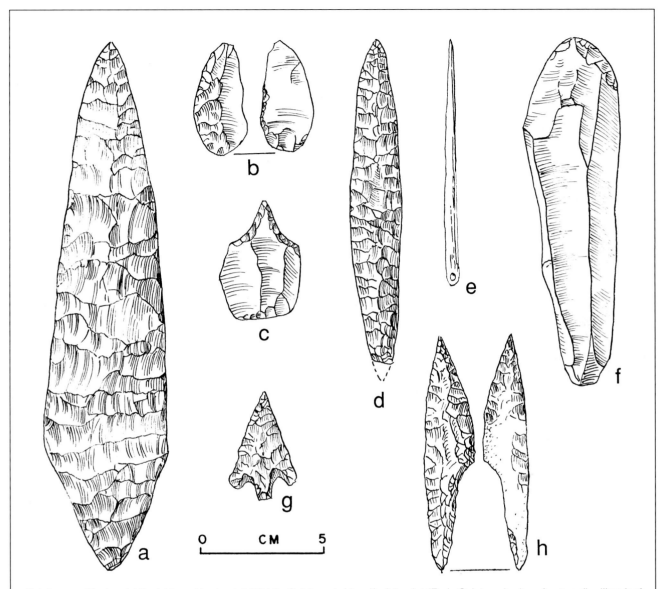

Solutrean artifacts: a) bifacial laurel-leaf point (Middle Solutrean); b) unifacial point (Early Solutrean); c) perforator; d) willow-leaf point (Later Solutrean); e) eyed bone needle; f) end-scraper; g) tanged and notched point (Spanish Solutrean); h) shouldered point (Final Solutrean).

elaboration of engraved, sculpted, and painted blocks and cave and rock-shelter walls, as well as the possibly ceremonial nature of the largest and thinnest stone points, may reflect social intensification due either to crowding or to more scheduling of resource-use within defined territories. The faunal remains from French sites are dominated by reindeer, with some later assemblages reflecting local increases in exploitation of ibex and horse. In Spanish Solutrean sites ibex, red deer, and horse are the most common mammalian species, and resource intensification is reflected in large numbers of mollusk shells. Human remains from several sites are morphologically similar to those from Combe Capelle.

Solutrean images are distinctive in the widespread use of large bas-reliefs of animals (Roc-de-Sers, Charente, and Fourneau-du-Diable, Dordogne), and of painted and engraved plaques (Laugerie Haute, Parpalló).

See also AURIGNACIAN; BOW AND ARROW; ECONOMY, PREHISTORIC; HOMO SAPIENS; HUNTER-GATHERERS; JEWELRY; LATE PALEOLITHIC; LAUGERIE SITES; MOUSTERIAN; PALEOLITHIC IMAGE; PALEOLITHIC LIFEWAYS; PERIGORDIAN; PROTOMAGDALENIAN; PROTOSOLUTREAN; SOLUTRÉ; STONE-TOOL MAKING; UPPER PALEOLITHIC. [A.S.B]

Further Readings

Gamble, C. (1986) The Palaeolithic Settlement of Europe. Cambridge: Cambridge University Press.

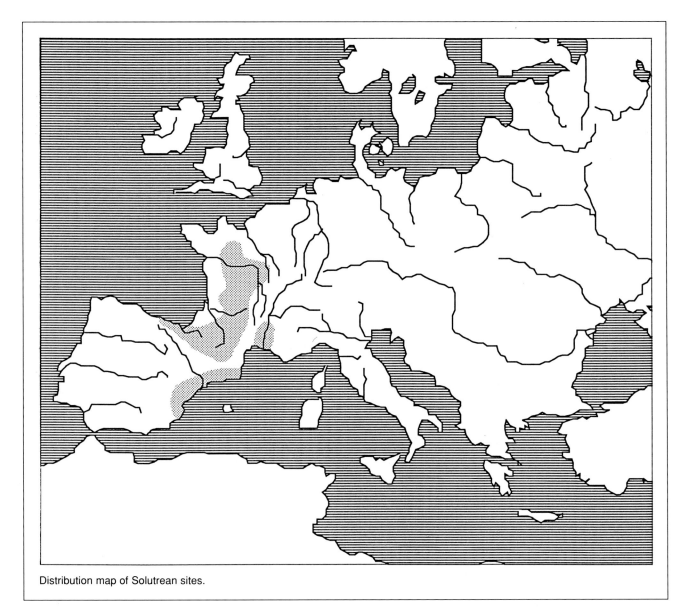

Distribution map of Solutrean sites.

Smith, P.E.L. (1964) The Solutrean culture. Sci. Am. 211(2): 86-94.

Wymer, J. (1982) The Palaeolithic Age. New York: St. Martin's.

SONDU *see* MABOKO

SONGHOR

Western Kenyan stratified site of early Miocene age, ca. 20 m.y. by K-Ar dating of interbedded biotite tuffs. First collected by L.S.B. Leakey in 1952, Songhor is a small but rich locality in red and brown clayey silts that lap against the granite of Songhor Hill, at the foot of Timboroa (Tinderet) volcano. Fossiliferous Songhor beds have also been traced eastward into the upper Mtetei Valley and southward to the Chamtwara beds above the Koru and Legetet Formations. Songhor is notable for its diversity of fossil primates, including prosimians, and is the type site of *Proconsul major, Rangwapithecus gordoni, Limnopithecus evansi,* and *Micropithecus songhorensis.* Other hominoids include *Proconsul africanus, Limnopithecus legetet, Micropithecus clarki,* and *Dendropithecus macinnesi.*

See also KENYA; KORU; LEAKEY, LOUIS; RUSINGA. [J.A.V.C.]

Further Readings

Harrison, T.E. (1981) New finds of small fossil apes from the Miocene locality of Koru in Kenya. J. Hum. Evol. 10:129-137.

Pickford, M.H., and Andrews, P.J. (1981) The Tinderet Miocene sequence in Kenya. J. Hum. Evol. 10:13-33.

SOUTH AFRICA

Country occupying the southern tip of the African continent. The oldest primate fossils that are known from South Africa consist of cercopithecid teeth from the early Pliocene deposits (ca. 5 m.y.) of E Quarry at Langebaanweg, near Cape Town. The fossiliferous cave deposits of Taung, near Kimberley in the Cape Province, and of Sterkfontein, Makapansgat, Kromdraai, Swartkrans, and Bolt's Farm in the Transvaal Province have yielded an abundance of cercopithecid fossils of later Pliocene and early Pleistocene age. With the exception of Bolt's Farm these sites have also yielded numerous specimens of *Australopithecus africanus* and *Paranthropus robustus* (the latter being referred to commonly as *Australopithecus robustus*). Several specimens probably attributable to *Homo habilis* together with a number of Early Stone Age artifacts have been recovered from Member 5 of Sterkfontein, while Paleolithic artifacts and specimens of *Homo* cf. *erectus* have been found in various stratigraphic units at Swartkrans. An "archaic" *Homo sapiens* calotte of middle Pleistocene age is known from the site of Elandsfontein (Hopefield), near Cape Town. This specimen is morphologically similar to the cranium from Kabwe (formerly "Broken Hill"), Zambia. The site of Florisbad, near Bloemfontein in the Orange Free State, has produced an incomplete cranium of late middle Pleistocene age (ca. 150–100 k.y.) that is morphologically similar to the Ngaloba and Omo II crania from Tanzania and Ethiopia. A few fragmentary human fossils in association with Paleolithic artifacts are known from the Cave of Hearths, close to the Makapansgat Limeworks. These fossils also likely date to the late middle Pleistocene. The site of Klasies River Mouth, situated along the Cape Coast, has yielded incomplete human fossils from Middle Stone Age layers that are dated by geological inference to between ca. 120 and 95 k.y. These specimens are morphometrically within the range of modern human anatomical variation. The remains of four individuals from the site of Border Cave, which have been attributed to a Middle Stone Age context of between ca. 110 and 85 k.y., are completely modern in appearance. The stratigraphic-archaeological context and the age of the Border Cave specimens are matters of some dispute. Nevertheless, the evidence from Border Cave for the presence of anatomically modern humans in the late middle to early late Pleistocene of southern Africa gains some support from the more securely provenanced fossils from Klasies River Mouth.

See also ARCHAIC HOMO SAPIENS; AUSTRALOPITHECUS; AUSTRALOPITHECUS AFRICANUS; AUSTRALOPITHECUS ROBUSTUS; BORDER CAVE; BRECCIA CAVE FORMATION; BROOM, ROBERT; CAVE OF HEARTHS; DART, RAYMOND ARTHUR; FLORISBAD; HOMO ERECTUS; HOMO HABILIS; HOWIESON'S POORT; KLASIES; KROMDRAAI; MAKAPANSGAT; PIETERSBURG; SMITHFIELD; STERKFONTEIN; STILLBAY; SWARTKRANS; TAUNG; WILTON. [F.E.G.]

Further Readings

Klein, R.G. (1983) The Stone Age prehistory of southern Africa. Ann. Rev. Anthropol. *12*:25–48.

Phillipson, D.W. (1977) The Later Prehistory of Eastern and Southern Africa. London: Heinemann.

Sampson, C.G. (1974) The Stone Age Archaeology of Southern Africa. New York: Academic.

SPARNACIAN *see* EOCENE; TIME SCALE

SPEAR

The earliest hunting or defensive weapons probably consisted of hand-held clubs or simple thrown missiles. The invention of a throwing or thrusting spear would have been a major innovation during the course of human evolution, emphasizing penetration and bloodletting rather than merely trauma from a blunt object.

Since the first spears were probably made from wood or horn, it is unlikely that very early forms of such artifacts would be preserved in the prehistoric record except under unusual conditions. The earliest examples of spears yet recovered come from the middle Pleistocene site (ca. 300,000 B.P.) of Clacton-on-Sea (England)—the tip of a yew spear—and the early late Pleistocene site (ca. 120,000 B.P.) of Lehringen (Germany)—a charred scraped wooden point associated with an elephant carcass.

During the Middle Paleolithic over much of the Old World a range of unifacially and sometimes bifacially flaked pointed stone-artifact forms occur that are usually assumed to be projectile points for spears, as are some specialized prepared-flake types (i.e. Levallois points). Such points are presumed to have been mounted on long, probably wooden, shafts. In North Africa Aterian Middle Stone Age assemblages include tanged pointed forms that strongly suggest hafting to a shaft. In the eastern European Middle Paleolithic are seen the first bone artifacts that appear to be probable spear points. Such hafted stone or bone projectiles could have involved the use of sinew, vegetable fiber, gum or resin mastic, or bitumen to help secure the point to a shaft. A Neanderthal male from the cave of Shanidar (Iraq) had a slightly healed cut on a rib that has been interpreted as a possible spear wound.

The Late Paleolithic industries of the Old World, as well as Paleoindian sites of the Americas, have a range of artifact forms that have been interpreted as spear points, including such lithic examples as Chatelperron points, Gravette points, Solutrean laurel- and willow-leaf points, and New World Clovis points. Bone points are common from the Aurigna-

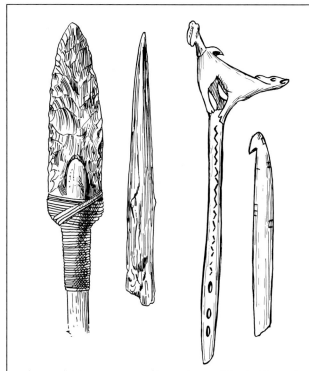

Left to right: reconstruction of possible hafting of Paleoindian Clovis point as a spear (point ca. 10 cm. long); broken tip of late Early Paleolithic fire-hardened wooden spear from Clacton (England) (ca. 40 cm.); two bone spear throwers, one engraved, from French Upper Paleolithic sites (shorter one ca. 18 cm. long).

cian onward, and the Magdalenian harpoons were almost certainly part of a composite spear. Barbed antler artifacts interpreted as spear throwers (the Aztec word *atlatl* is sometimes used) are known from the Magdalenian; these tools can increase the velocity of a propelled spear, in turn increasing maximum distance of a throw as well as deeper penetration into an animal. Such artifact types as the Solutrean *pointe à cran* and the Paleoindian Folsom and Cumberland points may have been atlatl dart points.

Spear technology appears to be represented in Upper Paleolithic cave art, for example at Niaux, Font de Gaume, and most notably Lascaux (France). At each of these sites animals (and, in a few cases, humans) appear to be shown with spears embedded in the bodies; at Lascaux, in the same scene as a wounded bison, is an object that some prehistorians have interpreted as a bird-effigy spear thrower.

With the advent of archery during the last 10 k.y. the spear became in many places a secondary hunting weapon, although still important in many modern hunter-gatherer technologies, including Australian and Tasmanian aborigines, Pacific islanders, Arctic Eskimos, the !Kung "bushmen," and American Indians. The use of the spear or lance in military combat became obsolete only at the turn of this century.

See also CLACTONIAN; MIDDLE PALEOLITHIC; PALEOINDIAN; PALEOLITHIC IMAGE; PALEOLITHIC LIFEWAYS; STONE-TOOL MAKING; UPPER PALEOLITHIC. [N.T.]

Further Readings

Oakley, K.P., Andrews, P., Keeley, L.H., and Clark, J.D. (1977) A reappraisal of the Clacton spear point. Proceed. Prehistoric Soc. 42:13–30.

SPEAR THROWER *see* SPEAR

SPECIALIZED *see* CLADISTICS

SPECIATION

Formation of descendant from ancestral species. The process of species formation depends upon conceptions of what species are. Thus, if species are arbitrarily delineated segments of an evolving lineage of interbreeding organisms, new species are seen to arise by a process of phyletic evolution of the phenotypic properties of organisms within the lineage. Such phyletic transformation would include primarily the transformation of adaptations through natural selection and the random changes engendered by genetic drift.

However, if the conception of species followed is some version of the *biological species concept*, the process of speciation is seen to involve primarily the origin of a descendant reproductive community from an ancestral species. Anatomical differences between ancestor and descendant species, involving aspects of organismic phenotypes not involved directly in reproduction, are seen as ancillary and consequential rather than as direct causes of speciation. The prime question is always "how did a single reproductive community become divided into two (or more) reproductive communities?"

Isolating Mechanisms

The geneticist T. Dobzhansky in 1937 coined the term *isolating mechanisms* for those causative agents that might play a role in either initiating or maintaining genetic isolation between two reproductive communities. Dobzhansky believed that natural selection was involved in the development of reproductive isolation, as the formation of hybrids between two incompletely separated protospecies would diminish the capacity of either species to adapt closely to the exigencies of their niches (or *adaptive peaks*). By the 1950s Dobzhansky's classification of isolating mechanisms had taken on the form still accepted today. Dobzhansky saw a fundamental dichotomy in isolating mechanisms. Organisms that are prevented from interbreeding by *geographic isolation*—i.e. organisms living in separate places (*allopatry*)—never meet and thus cannot mate. He reserved the term *reproductive isolation* for instances where organisms live in the same area (*sympatry*) but cannot or do not interbreed for a host of biological reasons, including lack of mutual attraction, mechanical inability, ecological isolation, and various degrees of incompatibility, where hybrids are not viable. The latter case is the strongest: reproductive isolation is held to be complete when, if organisms attempt to mate, they cannot produce viable offspring.

Dobzhansky referred to these factors as *mechanisms* because of his conviction that reproductive isolation is adaptively advantageous to species. The preferred view now is that geographic and biologic factors impeding reproduction among closely related organisms are a consequence of the ecological, distributional, and evolutionary histories of their species and populations. The question, though, remains: how is reproductive isolation typically developed?

In the 1930s and 40s Dobzhansky, and especially the biologist E. Mayr, favored the view that remains paramount in theories of speciation today: in most instances reproductive isolation begins in geographic isolation. New species arise from old only when the ancestral species becomes fragmented, with gaps in spatial distribution preventing the free exchange of genes between populations that once experienced some "gene flow." This is the essence of geographic, or allopatric, speciation.

Once geographic barriers have isolated portions of a species from one another, *if* sufficient evolutionary modification occurs in one or more populations such that reproduction is hindered or impossible should the populations once again come in contact, *speciation* is said to have occurred. Note that while many species are fragmented into fairly isolated populations speciation is by no means an inevitable consequence. The usual fate is local extinction of isolated populations or their merger back with other populations of the species, long before speciation can occur. Moreover, isolation of a population in itself does not guarantee the sort of evolutionary diversification required to lead to reproductive isolation when and if sympatry is reestablished.

There are several varieties, or modes, of allopatric speciation. Perhaps the simplest case involves climatic or other physical environmental change, disrupting a formerly continuous distribution. When the Isthmus of Panama emerged some 3 m.y. ago, communication between elements of the marine fauna of the Caribbean and Pacific was cut off. Another situation involves relatively small populations near the periphery of a species' range; already adapted to the environmental extremes tolerated by members of a species, the organisms of the small, isolated populations may undergo fairly rapid adaptive change. Speciation in such circumstances may take place as rapidly as a few hundreds, or thousands, of years. The *founder principle* is an extreme situation of allopatric speciation, where a single breeding pair, or gravid female, successfully colonizes an outlying region, founds a new population, and perhaps leads to the evolution of a new species.

Sympatric speciation—where reproductive isolation is developed without a period of geographic isolation—has been repeatedly invoked, especially for instances of parasites adapted to particular host species. Most such examples are readily interpreted as microallopatric—i.e. there is indeed physical separation between diverging populations. Nonetheless, theoretical models continue to emerge that suggest that speciation may be sympatric in some taxa.

Rates of Speciation

Rates of speciation tend to vary systematically between lineages—i.e. some lineages display greater characteristic rates of appearance of new species than others, often including their closest relatives. Moreover, rate of speciation tends to be postively correlated with rate of extinction. It has been suggested that ecological parameters may govern both speciation and extinction. In particular, ecological generalists (*eurytopes*, referring to organisms' abilities to tolerate a spectrum of environmental conditions or to draw upon a range of resources) appear more resistant to extinction but less likely to give rise to new species, than ecological specialists (*stenotopes*, more narrowly adapted organisms).

See also EVOLUTION; SPECIES. [N.E.]

Further Readings

Bush, G.L. (1975) Modes of animal speciation. Ann. Rev. Ecol. Syst. 6:339–364.

Eldredge, N. (1985) Time Frames. New York: Simon and Schuster.

Mayr, E. (1963) Animal Species and Evolution. Cambridge, Mass.: Harvard University Press.

SPECIES

Latin word meaning "kind," denoting its original sense in biological usage: species are different kinds of organisms. Early attempts to classify organisms, first formalized by Linnaeus into the system still in use today, recognized species as the lowest-ranked category of a series of hierarchically arrayed collections of organisms. Each species is included in a genus, in turn included in a family, and so on. Human beings are members of the genus *Homo*, species *sapiens*. The latinized name for any species is always accompanied by its generic designation: thus our species name is *Homo sapiens*. Species names are always written italicized.

The notion of different kinds of organisms has

long been associated with the recognition that "like begets like"—i.e. that species are associations of organisms that choose reproductive mates among themselves and do not, or cannot, mate successfully with organisms from other associations. Thus two ideas are bound up in most considerations of the nature of species: the notion of species as reproductive communities and the idea that organisms within a species resemble each other (as a rule) more closely than they resemble organisms within other species. Some concepts of species emphasize anatomical similarity as the major attribute of species, while others, including the *biological species concept* (currently the dominant view in biology) see species primarily as communities of reproductively interacting organisms.

Biologists have long debated the "reality" of species—i.e. are species actual entities or are they simply arbitrarily designated clusters of similar organisms? Pre-Darwinian thought saw species as immutable, fixed entities, as collections of organisms that had been "breeding true" since their initial creation some thousands of years before. Philosopher William Whewell summarized this attitude succinctly as late as 1837, when he wrote: "Species have a real existence in nature, and a transition from one to another does not exist."

It is clear that Darwin and many biologists subsequent to the publication of *On the Origin of Species* in 1859 saw the notion of evolution as antithetical to the concept of species as articulated, for example, by Whewell. Species fixity was discarded, and along with it the pre-Darwinian conviction that species are "real" entities in nature. However real and discrete species may seem at any moment, most evolutionary biologists since Darwin have seen species as evolving lineages of sexually reproducing organisms; through time the properties of the organisms are modified by evolution, and species are thought thereby to evolve by imperceptibly gradual degrees into descendants by direct transformation.

Biological Species Concept

A number of biologists have remarked that Darwin did not discuss the origin of species in his epochal book of the same title. (Having effectively discarded the concept of species, Darwin was concerned instead to establish the notion that life has had a complex history and that such history could be understood through a theory of the origin, maintenance, and modification of adaptations through natural selection.) With the advent in the 1930s of the "Modern Synthesis" (where the maturing science of genetics was integrated with Darwinian principles) evolutionists began to confront species as "real" enti-

ties. Theodosius Dobzhansky and subsequently Ernst Mayr developed the *biological species concept*, which remains the basis of all modern evolutionary definitions. Mayr's short version of the definition is: "Species are groups of actually or potentially interbreeding natural populations, which are reproductively isolated from other such groups." A more recent definition accepts the core of the biological species concept, while generalizing it and stressing that new species arise from old and also referring to the close similarities usually found among organisms within species: "A species is a diagnosable cluster of organisms within which there is a parental pattern of ancestry and descent, beyond which there is not, and which exhibits a pattern of phylogenetic ancestry and descent among units of like kind" (based on Eldredge and Cracraft, 1980).

In 1942 Mayr wrote that to justify a theory of the "origin of species"—i.e. any of the available models of "speciation"—one must suppose that species actually exist. Yet the biological species concept is widely acknowledged, even by its proponents, to pertain to but a single instant in time; through time the old Darwinian view is maintained, and species are considered to become transformed gradually into descendant species. More recently work in paleontology, notably the theory of punctuated equilibria, coinciding with analyses by Ghiselin and Hull, have supported the notion that species are indeed "real" entities in the fullest sense. Species are lineages of reproducing organisms that may—or, as is perhaps more common, may not—become substantially modified through time; they have births (speciation), histories, and deaths (extinction). And from time to time they may give rise to offspring (descendant species). The implications of this view for evolutionary theory are great. If species are real entities in this sense, the history of life cannot be reduced simply to a Darwinian story of origin and modifications of organic adaptations. And we must consider the differential survival and "reproductive success" of species as well as organisms when we consider the dynamics of the evolutionary process.

Many specialized concepts of species continue to appear in the literature. For example, *chronospecies* are arbitrarily delineated segments of evolving lineages, while *morphospecies* are recognized solely by the perceived similarity among organisms. Most of these extraneous concepts, which are not in wide use, are ably summarized by Cain. Arguments persist whether asexual organisms form true species; the definition of Eldredge and Cracraft was intended to encompass asexual organisms, but it appears that the biological species concept is best suited to sexually reproducing organisms.

See also CLASSIFICATION; EVOLUTION; PHYLOGENY; SPECIATION; SUBSPECIES; SYSTEMATICS; TAXONOMY. [N.E.]

Further Readings

Cain, A.J. (1960) Animal Species and Their Evolution. New York: Harper.

Eldredge, N. (1985) Unfinished Synthesis. New York: Oxford University Press.

Eldredge, N., and Cracraft, J. (1980) Phylogenetic Patterns and the Evolutionary Process. New York: Columbia University Press.

Mayr, E. (1942) Systematics and the Origin of Species. New York: Columbia University Press.

Mayr, E. (1963) Animal Species and Evolution. Cambridge, Mass.: Harvard University Press.

SPEECH (ORIGINS OF)

One of the most distinctive features of humankind is our unparalleled capability for communication. This is due in large part to our ability for speech. While many definitions of speech have been offered by those in diverse fields, here "speech" will refer to that unique form of rapid, verbal-vocal communication universally used by living humans.

Many components of human anatomy and physiology must interact to produce speech, but two basic human systems must be present: 1) a brain and associated nervous system sufficiently sophisticated to absorb, integrate, and direct the transmission of information; and 2) a peripheral anatomical system, what we generally term the *vocal tract*, which is capable of producing rapid, articulated sounds. The task in the study of human evolution is to determine when in our history a sufficiently developed brain and vocal tract first appeared that were capable of producing human speech.

Speech and the Brain

A traditional means of exploring when speech may have evolved uses endocasts—artificial or natural casts formed over time within braincases—as a vehicle to examine brain evolution and thus gain insight into the development of speech. Workers who have used this approach, often referred to as *paleoneurology*, have been particularly interested in charting the development of specific areas of the brain that often relate to speech production or general "language" capabilities. Of special concern has been the region of the inferior frontal gyrus of the dominant cerebral hemisphere known as Broca's motor speech area. This region was first suggested as being intimately related to speech production in 1861 by the French anthropologist Paul Broca. He came to this conclusion after noting a significant loss of tissue in the area of the frontal lobe upon the autopsy of an individual who lacked the ability to utter more than a few meaningless sounds. Paleoanthropologists who followed Broca have often spent considerable time trying to assess the appearance of Broca's area in fossil endocasts and thus gain some insight into the speech abilities of these early hominids. For example, the presence of endocast markings that may represent this region have been cited by some to suggest the possibility of nascent speech abilities in early members of *Homo*, such as the East African hominid KNM-ER 1470, dated at over 1.8 m.y. ago.

While data from paleoneurology have provided valuable information, there have been limitations to their use in charting the evolution of speech. For example, precisely locating speech centers in the brain appears to be more complicated than originally thought by Broca. Further, considerable debate exists among endocast experts themselves as to what markings are present and what they may mean. Finally, paleoneurology cannot tell us much about the inner workings of the brain and as a result can provide only limited evidence as to the origins of hominid speech.

Evolution of the Vocal Tract

Another approach has emerged within the last decade to address the question of when speech evolved. Rather than focus on the brain this approach has concentrated upon reconstructing the anatomy of our ancestors' vocal tract: the larynx ("voice-box"), pharynx, tongue, and associated structures. The ability to do this has been based upon data from both comparative anatomy and the fossil record. For example, studies on living mammals have shown that the position of the larynx in the neck is of prime importance in determining the way an animal can vocalize, as well as how it breathes and swallows. In almost all mammals the larynx is positioned very high in the neck. This high position severely limits the space (part of the pharynx) above the larynx responsible for the major modification of sounds produced inside the larynx at the vocal folds (cords). As a result the vocal repertoire of most mammals is very limited. Interestingly, human newborns and infants, until approximately one and a half to two years of age, also have a larynx positioned high in the neck. Baby humans accordingly show a limited repertoire in the variety of sounds they produce. After the first years of life, however, humans undergo a dramatic change in the anatomy of their vocal tract, with the larynx descending to a much lower position in the neck than that found in any other mammal. This lowered position significantly enlarges the portion of the pharynx above the larynx responsible for modifying sounds. In essence the low position of the larynx provides us with the anatomy necessary to make the varied sounds of human speech.

How to reconstruct the soft-tissue structures of our ancestors' vocal tract has until recently been a problem for those investigating the evolution of speech. Such structures as the larynx, comprising cartilages and membranes, are not preserved in the fossil record. Fortunately one portion of the vocal tract region that is preserved is its *roof*, the bottom of the skull or *basicranium*. Studies of this region in living mammals have shown that the shape of the basicranium is related to the position of the larynx in the neck. Knowledge of basicranial anatomy can thus tell us quite a bit about the location, and thus function, of an animal's vocal tract.

Discerning the relationships between the basicranium and vocal-tract structures in living mammals has enabled researchers to analyze the shape of fossil hominid basicrania and reconstruct the position of the larynx and related structures. Studies have shown, for example, that the australopithecines exhibit basicrania similar in many important aspects to those of the living apes. In view of these basicranial similarities it is likely that the vocal tracts of the australopithecines were also similar to those of the extant apes, with a larynx positioned high in the neck. Due to this position it is likely that the australopithecines had restrictions upon the types of sounds they could make, probably being incapable of producing a number of the universal vowel sounds found in human speech patterns. While it is still not fully clear when change toward the human condition began, preliminary studies have shown that the basicrania, and by extension vocal tracts, of some members of *Homo erectus* were already moving in the human direction. It was, however, not until the arrival of early *Homo sapiens*, some 400–300 k.y. ago, that we find skulls with basicrania that indicate the presence of a vocal tract similar to our own. It was at this time that modern vocal tracts appeared and our ancestors began to produce fully articulate speech.

See also AUSTRALOPITHECUS; BRAIN; HOMO ERECTUS; HOMO HABILIS. [J.L.]

Further Readings

de Grolier, E., ed. (1983) Glossogenetics: The Origin and Evolution of Language. Paris: Harwood Academic.

Harnad, S.R., Steklis, H.D., and Lancaster, J., eds. (1976) Origins and Evolution of Language and Speech. Annals Vol. 280. New York: New York Academy of Sciences.

Laitman, J.T. (1984) The anatomy of human speech. Nat. Hist. 93:20–27.

Lieberman, P. (1984) The Biology and Evolution of Language. Cambridge, Mass.: Harvard University Press.

SPHEROID   *see*   STONE-TOOL MAKING

SPIRIT CAVE   *see*   ASIA (EASTERN)

SPLIT-BASE BONE POINT

Diagnostic artifact form of the Aurignacian period of the Upper Paleolithic, ca. 34,000–28,000 B.P. These points are exemplary of a gradual shift away from stone for spear projectile points and are a precursor of the rich bone and antler technologies of later Paleolithic technologies.

See also AURIGNACIAN; PALEOLITHIC; SPEAR; UPPER PALEOLITHIC. [N.T., K.S.]

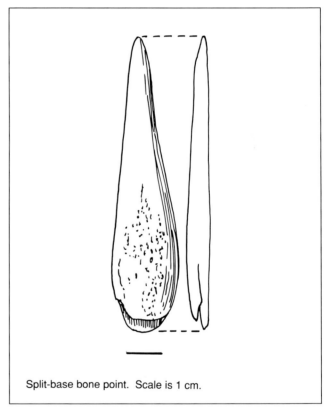

Split-base bone point. Scale is 1 cm.

SPY

Cave in Belgium, important as a site that in the last century produced confirmatory evidence for the existence of Neanderthals during the European Paleolithic. Two partial Neanderthal skulls and a partial skeleton were recovered in association with artifacts and extinct fauna in 1886. The two skulls show considerable variation, which may be attributed partly to sexual dimorphism.

See also NEANDERTHALS. [C.B.S.]

STADIAL   *see*   GLACIATION; PLEISTOCENE

STAGE   *see*   BIOCHRONOLOGY; TIME SCALE

STAR CARR

Mesolithic "Maglemosian" open-air site in Yorkshire (England), excavated in the 1950s by J.G.D. Clark and dated to ca. 9500 B.P. by radiocarbon, contemporary with the youngest Creswellian sites. A wet site with excellent organic preservation, Star Carr yielded remains of a brush pile or platform, in or at the edge of a former lake, possibly representing a dump rather than a prehistoric campsite, in association with barbed antler spearheads, bone awls and scrapers, and a large series of antler "frontlets," variously interpreted as ritual objects, hunting disguises, or a raw material cache. A wooden paddle and a roll of birch bark suggested the presence and/or construction of boats. The stone industry included flint axes and geometric microliths, such as angular backed bladelets approaching trapezes, probably relating to arrow manufacture. The associated fauna is dominated by red-deer remains, possibly representing repeated winter hunting episodes, but includes the earliest European evidence for the domesticated dog. In contrast to other Magelmosian sites fish remains were not recovered. The excavation and interpretation of the site reflect the economic approach to prehistory pioneered by its excavator.

See also Bow and Arrow; Domestication; Economy, Prehistoric; Mesolithic; Raw Materials; Ritual; Site Types; Stone-Tool Making. [A.S.B.]

STAROSEL'E *see* HOMO SAPIENS; NEANDERTHALS

STASIPATRY *see* SPECIATION

STASIS *see* ADAPTATION; EVOLUTION

STATES *see* COMPLEX SOCIETIES

STEGODON-AILUROPODA FAUNA

This fauna represents evidence for a biogeographic province of fossil mammals in tropical and subtropical East and Southeast Asia during the Pleistocene. Fossil assemblages from this area are usually characterized by *Stegodon* (an extinct proboscidean), *Ailuropoda* (giant panda), *Tapirus* (Malaysian tapir), *Pongo* (orangutan), and other mammals characteristic of a warm and humid climatic regime. These faunal assemblages, known primarily from Southeast Asia and southern China, are distinguished from the temperate northern Chinese faunas chiefly by the absence of cold-adapted forms. The *Stegodon-Ailuropoda*

Fauna has been subdivided into an early Pleistocene *Gigantopithecus* Fauna, which includes taxa with small body size, and the middle-to-late Pleistocene "Sino-Malayan Fauna" of Java, which includes taxa of relatively large body size. The validity of this division is still being debated.

See also Asia (Eastern); Gigantopithecus. [G.G.P.]

STEINHEIM

Skull found in a quarry near Stuttgart (West Germany) in 1933. It is a nearly complete cranium but is distorted. Cranial capacity is small (less than 1,200 ml.) and the cranial walls are thin, but the supraorbital torus is strongly developed. The occipital is evenly curved, and in its present state of preservation the position of maximum breadth of the skull is fairly high. The damaged face is small, relatively broad, and flat, with a large nasal opening and delicate cheek bones with an apparent canine fossa. Early on similarities were recognized between the Steinheim and Swanscombe fossils, although they were placed on separate lineages in Boule and Vallois's "presapiens" scheme. Many workers now regard the Steinheim skull as an early member of the Neanderthal lineage, citing its nasal form, occipital-torus morphology, and suprainiac fossa. The specimen is of middle Pleistocene antiquity, perhaps comparable with that of Swanscombe; both are often dated to the northern European Holsteinian interglacial.

See also Archaic Homo sapiens; Neanderthals. [C.B.S.]

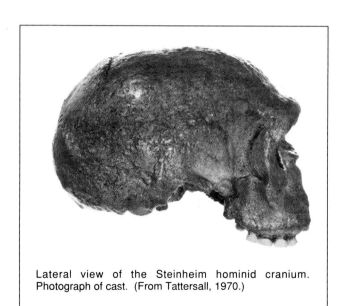

Lateral view of the Steinheim hominid cranium. Photograph of cast. (From Tattersall, 1970.)

STEINHEIMIAN *see* TIME SCALE

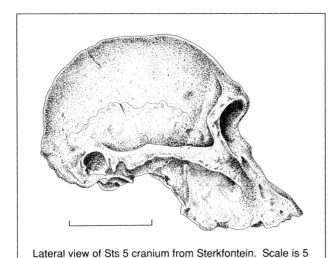

Lateral view of Sts 5 cranium from Sterkfontein. Scale is 5 cm. (From Eldredge and Tattersall, 1982.)

STERKFONTEIN

South African cave breccia deposit in dolomitic lime-stone located south of the Bloubank River ca. 9.6 km. north-northwest of the town of Krugersdorp, Transvaal Province, at 26°03′ S and 27°42′ E. The site was initially quarried for lime in the 1890s, and fossil bones from these deposits were sent to the British Museum (Natural History) in 1895. The first hominid specimen was recovered by R. Broom in 1936.

The site comprises six sedimentary (breccia) members. Field operations by R. Broom (1936–1939), Broom and J.T. Robinson (1947–1949), Robinson and C.K. Brain (1956–1958), and P.V. Tobias and A.R. Hughes (1966–present) have resulted in the recovery of over 300 hominid specimens, all of which derive from Members 4 and 5. The vast majority of hominid fossils come from Member 4, and these are attributable to *Australopithecus africanus*. No artifactual material is known from Member 4. Paleolithic artifacts were first discovered in 1956 by C.K. Brain in Member 5 of what was initially referred to as the "Extension Site." Subsequent work has yielded Early Stone Age artifacts as well as hominid specimens, probably attributable to *Homo habilis*, from Member 5. The faunal remains from Member 4 suggest an age of ca. 2.5 m.y. and the presence of comparatively wetter and more bush-covered conditions than during the accumulation of Member 5. The faunal age of Member 5 is somewhat less secure, with an estimated age of 1.5 m.y.

See also AUSTRALOPITHECUS; AUSTRALOPITHECUS AFRICANUS; BRECCIA CAVE FORMATION; BROOM, ROBERT; HOMO HABILIS. [F.E.G.]

Further Readings

Clarke, R.J. (1985) *Australopithecus* and early *Homo* in southern Africa. In E. Delson (ed.): Ancestors: The Hard Evidence. New York: Liss, pp. 171–177.

STILLBAY

African Middle Stone Age flake industry, originally included as the "eastern variant" (as opposed to the variant localized around Cape Town itself) of the South African Later Stone Age. Named for surface collections at Still Bay on the southeastern Cape Peninsula (South Africa), the Stillbay is characterized by faceted striking platforms, discoidal and Levallois technology, and bifacial or unifacial leaf-shaped or triangular points, often thinned at the base for hafting. Although the exact definition or integrity of the industry is ambiguous, due to the lack of context for the type collections, the term was extended to other Middle Stone Age industries, such as the Bambata, and (by L.S.B. Leakey) to cover industries with faceted striking platforms in East Africa. One of the best *in situ* occurrences of a Stillbay-like industry is at Skildergat, near Cape Town, where the Fish Hoek cranium may be associated with this industry or represent an intrusion from an overlying Howieson's Poort horizon.

See also APOLLO-11; BAMBATA; CAVE OF HEARTHS; FLORISBAD; HOWIESON'S POORT; LEAKEY, LOUIS; LEVALLOIS; MIDDLE PALEOLITHIC; MIDDLE STONE AGE; ORANGIAN; PIETERSBURG; ROSE COTTAGE; STONE-TOOL MAKING. [A.S.B.]

STIRTONIA *see* ATELINAE

STOCKIA *see* OMOMYINAE

STONE AGE *see* PALEOLITHIC

STONE-TOOL MAKING

The emergence of a flaked-stone technology during the course of hominid evolution marks a radical behavioral departure from the rest of the animal world and constitutes the first definitive evidence in the prehistoric record of a simple cultural tradition, or one based upon learning. Although other animals (such as the Egyptian vulture, the California sea otter, and Darwin's Galapagos finch) may use simple unmodified tools, or even manufacture and use simple tools (as in the termiting and nut-cracking behavior of wild chimpanzees), a fundamental aspect of human adaptation is a strong reliance upon technology for survival and adaptation. Archaeological evidence shows a geometric increase in the sophistication and complexity of hominid stone technology over time since its earliest beginnings 3–2 m.y. ago.

Stone is the principal material found in nature that is both very hard and able to produce superb working edges when fractured. A wide range of tasks can be executed with even a simple stone technology, including animal butchery (hide slitting, disarticulation, meat cutting, bone breaking), woodworking (chopping, scraping, sawing), hide scraping, plant cutting, and bone and antler working. Although other perishable materials, such as wood, bone, horn, and shell, were probably used early in the evolution of hominid technology, tools made of stone are relatively indestructible and so provide the longest and most detailed record of prehistoric tool manufacture. Stone tools supplemented biology as a means of adapting to the environment during the course of human evolution, and the study of their manufacture and potential uses reveals important information about the evolution of human culture.

Antiquity of Stone Tools

Archaeological evidence indicates that a flaked-stone technology is one of a suite of biological and behavioral changes in early hominid ancestors involving a selection for greater intelligence and possibly marking the emergence of the genus *Homo* between 3 and 2 m.y. ago in Africa. Before the advent of a flaked-stone technology hominids could have possessed a relatively rich technology that would have left little or no visibility in the prehistoric record. Missiles, clubs, nut-cracking hammers and anvils, stick probes, and simple bark or shell containers may have been used by early *Australopithecus*.

The oldest known archaeological sites bearing definite flaked-stone artifacts (Oldowan industry) include those found in Member F from the Omo Valley (Ethiopia), dated to ca. 2.4 m.y. ago, and possibly the archaeological sites from the Gona region of Hadar (Ethiopia), and Senga-5 (Zaire), perhaps between 2.6 and 2 m.y. old. Other sites believed to be at least 1.5 m.y. old include those in Member E at Omo; Koobi Fora (Kenya), in and above the KBS tuff; Olduvai Gorge (Tanzania), Beds I and II; and Peninj, west of Lake Natron (Tanzania). The stone artifacts from the South African caves of Swartkrans and Sterkfontein (Member 5) may be in this time range as well.

Raw Materials for Stone Tools

The typical types of rock from which flaked-stone artifacts are produced are relatively fine-grained and hard and tend to fracture easily in any direction (i.e. are *isotropic*). Commonly used rock types are flint or chert, quartzite, quartz, and various volcanic rocks, including obsidian or volcanic glass. Some materials, such as many flints or cherts, can be more easily worked after heat treatment (a controlled heating that alters crystal structure), a practice that may have begun in Late Paleolithic times.

The different types of raw materials vary widely in their overall geographic distributions and in the size, shape, quantity, and quality of material found at any one location. They may be found in *primary* geological context (at their site of origin or formation), such as a lava flow, quartz vein, quartzite layer, or flint nodule seam, or they may be in *secondary* (redeposited) context, such as cobbles in river gravels or rocks forming the pavement of desert surfaces.

Both the cultural rules regarding artifact design and the intended use of a tool influence what types of tools are found in the prehistoric record. Cultural norms and functional requirements for tools aside, the size, shape, quality, and flaking characteristics of the stone material also can strongly affect what sort of artifact may be made. More sophisticated, delicately flaked artifacts can generally be made in fine-grained materials like high-quality cherts and flints than are usually made in coarser-grained rocks. The relative abundance or scarcity of stone suitable for flaking affects the quantities and sizes of artifacts left behind at archaeological sites, so that artifacts made in rock available locally often tend to be larger and to be found in greater numbers than artifacts made in stones transported over greater distances.

In general there is increasing selectivity in use of stone materials over time in the Paleolithic. Later Stone Age peoples tended to concentrate more on finer-grained, higher-quality rock sources, often quite localized in distribution and transported some distance to the archaeological site, than did hominids in the earlier phases of the Paleolithic, who appear to have exploited available rock sources in a more opportunistic fashion.

Principles of Stone Fracture

The type of fracture or mechanical failure of rocks observed in stone-tool manufacture is often called *conchoidal fracture*, named after the shell- or conch-like ripples or swirls generally evident in the artifacts manufactured in finer-grained materials. In stone-tool manufacture a force is applied to the stone sufficient to break it in a controlled fashion. The stone usually fractures in alignment with its crystalline structure, and thus noncrystalline or finer-grained materials, especially isotropic materials with no preferential cleavage planes (such as obsidian or flint), tend to produce a smoother, more predictable fracture.

The stone is deliberately fractured (or *flaked*) either through a sharp, percussive blow (*direct* or *indirect percussion flaking*) or through the application of a compressive force (*pressure flaking*). The parent piece of rock is the *core*, and the spalls so removed are *flakes*.

The key to producing fracture in stone by flaking

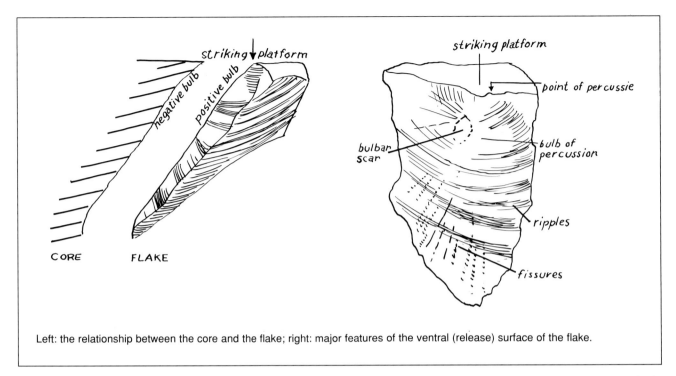

Left: the relationship between the core and the flake; right: major features of the ventral (release) surface of the flake.

is to find core edges with acute angles (less than 90°). Thus, in manufacturing tools from rounded pieces of rock, such as stream cobbles, those with pronounced overhangs or with flattened edges tend to be easier to flake than are more spherical pieces. When a hammer strikes the core obliquely and with sufficient force near one of these edges, a flake is detached, producing an associated scar (*flake scar*) on the core.

Characteristics of flakes include, on the ventral, or *release*, surface (the face detached from the inside of the core), a striking platform (*butt*) at the top of the flake, a bulb of percussion (*semicone*), a bulbar scar (*éraillure*), ripples or waves, and fissures (hackle marks); and on the dorsal, or outer, surface of the flake (representing the surface of the core), a cortex (weathered surface of the core) and/or scars of previous flakes removed from the core. Cores and retouched pieces exhibit the negative features of flake release, particularly a negative (concave) bulb of percussion and the conchoidal ripples or waves of percussion.

Although some natural processes (e.g. high-energy fluviatile or glacial forces) can produce percussion flaking on pieces of stone, they do not exhibit the controlled, patterned removal of flakes characteristic of even the earliest stone industries. Early hominids clearly had a sound intuitive sense of geometry when flaking rock and expertly exploited acute angles on cores.

Procedures and Techniques of Stone-Tool Manufacture

Numerous techniques of working stone are known ethnographically and experimentally. They include the following.

Hard-Hammer Percussion   Striking a core with a stone hammer to induce flaking—one of the most common techniques of flaking, used from the Early Paleolithic onward. The flakes tend to have large striking platforms and prominent bulbs of percussion. Cores characteristically have deep flake scars and prominent ridges between flakes.

Anvil (Block-on-Block) Technique   Striking a core against a stationary anvil to produce flakes. This percussion technique is sometimes used in flaking very large cores. The features on flakes and cores are similar to hard-hammer percussion.

Soft-Hammer Technique   A percussion technique involving flaking a core with a hammer that is softer than the core itself, such as a softer stone or wood, antler, or bone. This technique usually produces flakes with relatively small platforms, diffuse bulbs of percussion, and flatter release surfaces. There is often a prominent "lipping" at the intersection of the platform and the release (ventral) surface. Cores tend to have relatively shallow flake scars and subtle ridges between flake scars. This technique is particularly effective in the thinning of bifaces (e.g. handaxes or projectile points). Often striking platforms are faceted with numerous flake scars, which is an indication of preparing the core by steepening and regularizing the edge with a hammer or abrader.

Bipolar Technique   A percussion technique involving setting a core on an anvil and hitting the core from above with a hammerstone. This technique is

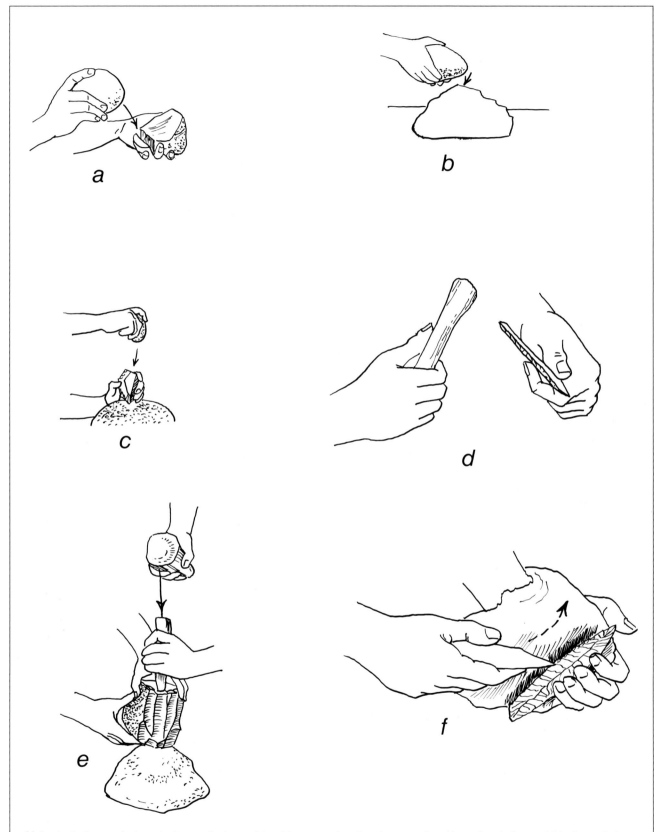

Major techniques of stone-tool manufacture: a) hard-hammer, free-hand percussion; b) anvil technique; c) bipolar technique; d) soft-hammer percussion; e) indirect percussion or punch technique; f) pressure flaking.

often used for very small or intractable, hard-to-flake raw materials. Flakes tend to have thin or punctiform platforms and very flat release surfaces with little bulb of percussion. Cores tend to be barrel-shaped in planform and thin, with flakes removed from both ends.

Indirect Percussion (Punch Technique)　Often used for blade production, this technique consists of setting a punch (or indirect percussor) on the core and detaching blades by hitting the punch with a hammer. Blades tend to have small striking platforms and diffuse bulbs of percussion and are slightly curved in side view.

Pressure Technique　Flakes can also be detached from a core or retouched piece through compressive force or through exertion of pressure on the stone with a pointed tool (such as a piece of antler or bone). This technique, first observed in the prehistoric record during the Late Paleolithic, allows a stone worker to carry out controlled and meticulous flaking and was often used to finish finely made projectile points that had been shaped initially through percussion flaking. Flakes tend to be quite small and thin, often breaking when pressed off the core, with a small platform and diffuse bulb of percussion, although it is also possible to produce more prominent, deep scars on a piece by pressure flaking. Pressure-flaked artifacts tend to exhibit shallow, regular flake scars. In Mesoamerica a pressure technique may have also been used for the removal of obsidian blades from prismatic cores.

Grinding and Polishing　Smoothing and shaping a rock (sometimes previously flaked into a rough shape) by grinding it against another rock. Such forms as axes and adzes were manufactured by this technique. Sometimes abrasive sand and water were used in the grinding process. This technique is often associated with Neolithic farming communities in the Near East, Europe, and North Africa, but it can be found also among some hunter-gatherer communities, as in parts of Australia.

Prehistoric Information from Stone Technology

The study of stone technology does not simply entail observing the techniques or procedures of artifact manufacture; ideally it considers a complex series of prehistoric actions that surround the creation of a set of tools at an archaeological site. It is useful to view stone technology as a *system*, from procurement of raw material, tool manufacture, transport of tools and raw materials, tool use, resharpening and reshaping of tools, and artifact discard or loss, through to the final incorporation of stone tools within the archaeological record. Within each major component of this system there are some basic questions that can yield important information about prehistoric behavior.

Acquisition of raw materials　What is the range of raw-material types exploited by prehistoric peoples? Are the sources *primary* (e.g. rock outcrop) or *secondary* (e.g. river gravel, surface erosion)? Is there evidence for selectivity in the acquisition of raw materials? Are certain materials used for some artifact forms and not others?

Transport of raw materials　Can distances from rock sources to prehistoric sites be measured? Transport of materials can occur at any stage of lithic reduction; for example, after a handaxe is roughed out at a quarry site, it may be transported and the final shaping of the artifact carried out at another locality. Transport of stone artifacts in a finished form is a major clue to the degree of *curation* (keeping things for future use) of artifacts by hominid groups.

Manufacture of raw materials　What techniques and strategies were employed by prehistoric peoples in stone-artifact manufacture? A flowchart can be devised to explain the reduction of an unmodified piece of stone into deliberate end products and waste products. Can various stages of stone-artifact manufacture be recognized from unfinished tools at an archaeological site, or by the types of débitage (flakes and fragments) being removed from cores and retouched pieces? Can tools of manufacture (e.g. percussors, anvils, pressure flakers) be recognized at prehistoric sites? Can we talk about stylistic norms or "mental templates" of artifact design among the tool makers? Are there other clues regarding the strength, skill, cognition, foresight, or preferential handedness of the tool makers?

Use of stone artifacts　Is there contextual evidence to suggest how stone tools were used at a prehistoric site (e.g. cutmarks and points of percussion on bone; tool marks on wood, bone, or antler objects; organic residues on stone artifacts; or characteristic edge damage and microwear polishes on stone artifacts)? What was the adaptive significance of specific artifact forms?

Rejuvenation or reuse of stone artifacts　Is there evidence of resharpening, reuse, repairing, or rehafting of tools?

Patterns of disposal　Is there evidence to suggest *why* stone artifacts ended up at a specific place? Were they discarded, lost, cached for future use, left as grave goods?

Postbehavioral effects　How altered is the spatial distribution of these artifact forms from the original patterning on the landscape at the time of hominid occupation or site abandonment? Has there been any geological sorting of materials (e.g. fluvial winnowing of lighter materials)? Is there evidence of admixture of archaeological materials from different levels? Does the physical or chemical alteration of stone artifacts give clues to their mode of burial and diagenetic changes?

Major Stages of Stone Technology in Prehistory

Prehistorians often divide up the Stone Age of the Old World (Africa, Europe, and parts of Asia) into technological stages:

Paleolithic ("Old Stone Age")

The Paleolithic is generally divided up into three main stages according to the technological practices and major artifact types present:

A) Early (or "Lower") Paleolithic (in sub-Saharan Africa called the "Early Stone Age"). This stage is often divided into:

  1) Oldowan or Mode I technology, characterized by simple core forms—e.g. choppers, polyhedrons, discoids—associated débitage, and often casually retouched flakes (scrapers and awls). Hard-hammer percussion, bipolar technique, and anvil technique were employed. This stage has sometimes been called "Pre-Chellean" in Europe.

  2) Acheulean or Mode II technology, characterized by large bifacial forms, especially hand-axes or cleavers, a range of simpler core forms, and retouched flakes. Hard-hammer percussion, anvil technique, and, in later Acheulean industries, soft-hammer percussion were employed. These technologies were formerly referred to as "Chellean" in Europe, and the cruder bifacial forms sometimes assigned to the "Abbevillian."

B) Middle Paleolithic or Mode III technology (in sub-Saharan Africa referred to as the "Middle Stone Age" and in Europe the Mousterian), usually characterized by a range of well-made side-scraper forms and unifacial points and use of prepared-core techniques of tool making, especially the Levallois method. Hard-hammer and soft-hammer percussion were typically employed. The presence of apparent projectile points as well as tanged artifacts of the Aterian (a North African variant of the Mousterian) suggest that hafting with cordage or mastic was practiced during this stage.

C) Late Paleolithic or Mode IV technology (termed the "Upper" Paleolithic in much of Europe and often in northern Africa and the Near East; rare in sub-Saharan Africa, but found in both "Middle" and "Later Stone Age" assemblages), characterized by blade industries, often associated with such artifact forms as end-scrapers, burins, and awls. Bifacially worked points may be present, as well as a range of bone- and antler-tool forms. Hard, soft, and indirect percussion were typically employed, as well as some pressure flaking. Spear throwers are known from this period, and some small projectile points also suggest the possible use of bows and arrows.

Mesolithic

This is designated as Mode V technology (in sub-Saharan Africa this technological stage is found among the microlithic technologies of the "Later Stone Age"). It is characterized by microlithic tools, particularly such geometric forms as triangles, trapezoids, and crescents, which were used to form composite tools. These technologies are often associated with the use of bows and arrows. In some areas, such as temperate Europe, flaked-stone axes were used, sometimes attached to antler sleeves, which in turn would be hafted to a wooden handle. Hard, soft, and indirect percussion were typically employed, the "groove and snap" method of producing blanks for geometric microliths, and pressure flaking.

Neolithic

This stage, designated as Mode VI technology, is characterized by ground-stone tools, such as axes and adzes, and is usually associated with pottery. A wide range of flaked-stone tools was still employed, often with an associated blade technology. Hard, soft, and indirect percussion were used, as well as pressure flaking and grinding/polishing. Grinding stones for cereal processing, known from some Mesolithic sites, become more plentiful in early farming communities.

This system of classification of the major developmental stages of stone-tool making works reasonably well in western Europe but not necessarily elsewhere. For example, the later stone industries of the Americas constitute sophisticated traditions often centering on the manufacture of bifacial points as well as unifacial scrapers, which do not fit well into this classification scheme.

Thus in many geographical regions independent

terminologies have been developed to subdivide industrial or economic stages of indigenous prehistoric inhabitants. In Southeast Asia and Australia there are prehistoric technologies with ground-stone axes that would not normally be termed Neolithic, since these peoples in other regards are very different economically and technologically from the early farmers of the Near East, Europe, and Africa. It is also important to note that these technological stages did not develop at precisely the same rate in different geographic areas. For example, blade technologies appeared earlier in Southwest Asia than in western Europe.

Stone Tools as Cultural Markers

Stone artifacts can often serve as important cultural markers for certain chronological periods, technological stages, or regional styles during the Stone Age. Some tools, such as certain types of projectile points, may be restricted in time and space and therefore indicative of particular cultural systems, while others, such as side-scrapers, may represent forms found widely in different temporal or geographical contexts.

Role of Tools in Human Evolution

Some scientists, anthropologist Sherwood Washburn and the sociobiologist E.O. Wilson, have emphasized the interplay between learned behavior, such as technology, and genetic evolution, forming a feedback system that accelerated both biological evolution and cultural innovation (through a "bio-cultural feedback system" or "gene-culture co-evolution").

From ca. 2.5 m.y. ago to relatively recent times stone tools provided a technological means to a wide range of functional and adaptive ends for our human ancestors. It is certain that tools have played an extremely important role in human evolution, particularly within the past 3–2 m.y. Tools have constituted a vital part of our cultural adaptation to the environment, an adaptation based upon intelligent technological innovations designed to meet the requirements of the situations and environments faced by our ancestors. Prehistoric evidence of stone-tool making serves as the most continuous, lasting record of this human adaptation.

> *See also* ACHEULEAN; ARCHAEOLOGY; BIPOLAR TECHNIQUE; CORE; EARLY PALEOLITHIC; FLAKE; LATE PALEOLITHIC; LITHIC USE-WEAR; MESOLITHIC; MIDDLE PALEOLITHIC; NEOLITHIC; OLDOWAN; PALEOLITHIC; PREPARED-CORE; RAW MATERIALS; RETOUCH; SOCIOBIOLOGY; UPPER PALEOLITHIC. [N.T., K.S.]

Further Readings

Bordaz, J. (1970) Tools of the Old and New Stone Age. Garden City, N.Y.: Natural History Press.

Bordes, F. (1970) The Old Stone Age. New York: McGraw-Hill.

Hodges, H. (1976) Artifacts: An Introduction to Early Materials and Technology. London: Baker.

Leakey, L.S.B. (1967) Working stone, bone, and wood. In C. Singer, E.J. Holmyard, and A.R. Hall (eds.): A History of Technology, Vol. 1. Oxford: Clarendon, pp. 128–143.

Oakley, K.P. (1976) Man the Toolmaker. Chicago: University of Chicago Press.

Spier, R.F.G. (1970) From the Hand of Man: Primitive and Preindustrial Technologies. Boston: Houghton Mifflin.

Swanson, E., ed. (1976) Lithic Technology. The Hague: Mouton.

STORAGE

Food is preserved for consumption at a later time most commonly by salting, pickling, drying, or freezing. Ethnographic data on hunter-gatherers indicate two disparate subsistence behaviors. Groups found in lower latitudes generally consume immediately what can be harvested from nature. Groups in higher latitudes, where the availability and abundance of foods is more seasonally restricted, are prone to storing foods in large quantity during periods of their peak abundance and using these stores during the resource-lean months. These differences in subsistence behavior have significant impact on the settlement systems, coresident group sizes, and economic and sociopolitical relationships of ethnographically known hunter-gatherers. Because of this, evidence for food storage is of special interest to prehistoric archaeologists.

Unequivocal evidence for storage economies is first documented during the Late Paleolithic. Numerous in-ground storage pits measuring 1–2 m. in diameter and up to 1 m. in depth are repeatedly found in Late Paleolithic sites on the East European plain (e.g. Dobranichevka, Eliseevichi, Mezhirich, Mezin, Radomyshl', Suponevo, Yudinovo) dating between 26,000 and 12,000 B.P. Their contents indicate that late Pleistocene groups first stored meat supplies during the late summer or early fall and reused the pits after consuming the stored resources to store the bones themselves for use as fuel and raw materials for the manufacture of tools, implements, and jewelry.

> *See also* ECONOMY, PREHISTORIC; LATE PALEOLITHIC; MEZHIRICH; SITE TYPES. [O.S.]

Further Readings

Soffer, O. (1985) The Upper Paleolithic of the Central Russian Plain. Orlando, Fla.: Academic.

Testart, A. (1982) The significance of food storage among hunter-gatherers: residence patterns, population densities, and social inequalities. Curr. Anthropol. 23:523–537.

STRANSKÁ SKÁLA

Jurassic limestone hill on the outskirts of Brno (Czechoslovakia), with three localities yielding middle Pleistocene paleoanthropological materials. Paleosols inside two small caves, as well as the downslope scree outside the caves, contained remains of both large mammals and microfauna assigned to the Biharian complex. The cave deposits also contained ca. 40 artifacts, predominantly of hornstone and limestone, consisting of simple flakes, cores, choppers, and hammerstones. These materials are considered Cromerian in age and probably reflect occupation during the "Günz-Mindel" interglacial. Recent excavations both upslope and downslope from the cave and talus have revealed Late Paleolithic occupations.

See also ACHEULEAN; EUROPE; PŘEZLETICE. [O.S.]

STRATIGRAPHY

Much of the history of the earth and of life on it is read from the study of the temporal and spatial relations of stratified rocks. Sedimentary rocks are of prime interest, but stratigraphic principles may also be applied to layered volcanic rocks and to metamorphic rocks that have not been so transformed that their original sedimentary (or igneous) character is obliterated.

The practice of stratigraphy rests on three great principles: *superposition*, which states that in an undisturbed vertical section rocks high in the section are younger than those below; *original horizontality*, which states that strata are horizontal or nearly so when they are deposited; and *original lateral continuity*, which states that strata are continuous over their area of deposition until they reach the margins of the basin in which they were deposited or disappear by thinning to zero.

Rock strata may be classified by any of their properties (e.g. lithology, fossil content), or by inferred attributes, such as the time or environment of origin. In general the classification units formed on the basis of one feature do not coincide with those based on another. A different set of units is thus needed for each sort of classification that is used. The three most common categories of classification are those based on lithology, fossil content, and age, which give rise to the three main branches of stratigraphy: *lithostratigraphy*, *biostratigraphy*, and *chronostratigraphy*. Other bases of classification (e.g. magnetostratigraphy, isotope stratigraphy) are certainly in use and rely on many of the conventions and definitions relating to these principal three. Lithostratigraphic and biostratigraphic units determined for one area are always of limited extent, and only chronostratigraphic units are recognizable, at least in principle, worldwide. Each of the stratigraphic categories has its own peculiar terminology such that the names of units do not overlap, in general, from one kind of classification to another. Any interval of sedimentary rock (a chronostratigraphic unit) represents a certain

interval of geologic time (a geochronologic unit), but geochronologic units are intangible while rock units are material. To keep this difference clear each geochronologic unit has a precisely corresponding chronostratigraphic unit. Thus a geologic Period corresponds to a System, an Epoch to a Series, and so on.

A vital point in stratigraphy is the distinction between strata and time. In writing or speaking of strata, or features of the strata, such as biostratigraphic zones, it is important to use the modifiers "lower" and "upper" in referring to position or stratigraphic orientation. In discussing chronostratigraphic units, including chronozones, and in all references to age rather than stratigraphic position, the appropriate modifiers are "early" and "late." Unfortunately there seem to be no words that would distinguish "middle" position from "middle" time, although "medial" is sometimes forced into use as a time term. With these distinctions in mind it is logically impossible to speak of a "Lower Pleistocene age," a "Late Tortonian formation," or a "Lower Pliocene climate change." It is correct, of course, to refer to the Early Pleistocene age of Lower Pleistocene rocks or to a formation belonging to the Upper Tortonian Stage laid down during the Late Tortonian Age. The capitalization of the modifiers is, strictly speaking, always improper because "Upper Pleistocene Substage" and comparable subdivisions are not formal units. As a matter of taste, however, many stratigraphers capitalize "Late," "Lower," and so forth when they mean an exact and complete subdivision of a rock or time unit, and use lower case when the meaning is intentionally meant to be vague or simply comparative.

The rock record of the passage of geologic time is far from complete. It is broken by myriad discontinuities of varying length: *diastems* (short) and *unconformities* (long). Evidence for the missing interval of record is also a part of stratigraphy and may be of much importance when a study (such as hominid paleontology) requires knowledge of even brief gaps in the record.

Lithostratigraphy

Every stratigraphic unit is composed of rock, but only lithostratigraphic units are based on the type of rock. These units are bodies of rock strata that are defined by some degree of observable lithologic homogeneity. Inferred features, such as time or mode of origin, play no part. Insofar as fossils or other special characteristics (e.g. remanent magnetization) are treated as part of the lithology, they may be used for recognition of a lithostratigraphic unit but do not form the basis for definition.

Formations are the basic units of lithostratigraphy. A formation is a body of strata, not necessarily uniform, but clearly distinct and mappable over a wide area. Larger units composed of two or more formations are called *groups*, and subdivisions of formations are called *members*, but a formation need not be divided into members. A *bed* is the smallest formal lithostratigraphic unit and represents a lithologic stratum distinct from layers above and below. The term *beds* also refers to formations or members in some cases (e.g. Olduvai Beds I, II, etc.).

For each named lithostratigraphic unit a particular sequence of strata is designated as its type section, or *stratotype*. In this way the description of the unit is linked to a particular body of rock that can be revisited to determine what was meant when the unit was defined. It is akin to the type specimen of a species in biology. Lithostratigraphic units are identified elsewhere by their lithology and relative stratigraphic position, although in other sections they may differ in thickness and internal detail. The boundaries of lithostratigraphic units are drawn, insofar as possible, at sharp breaks in lithology. Where contacts are gradational, the boundary may be arbitrarily placed at an easily recognized level.

Lithostratigraphic unit names consist of two parts, the name of a local geographic feature near which the unit is typically exposed, and the term for its rank (formation, member, etc.), or else with the name of the dominant rock type of which the unit is composed (e.g. Hadar Formation, Turkana Grits, Kabarnet Trachyte).

A lithostratigraphic unit extends laterally from the type sections as far as its characteristic lithology remains substantially unchanged. If marker beds have been used for the definition of lithologic units, their extension does not justify extension of the lithostratigraphic units unless the character of the section between them has remained the same.

Biostratigraphy

Differences in fossil content of rock strata form the basis for biostratigraphic classification. These differences may be variations in any feature of the fossil content of the rocks—presence or absence, the complete assemblage of fossils, the morphology or evolutionary stage of particular fossils, the frequency or abundance of fossils, and so on. Provided they are based on directly observable features in the strata, they are valid, but they are of different kinds.

Any kind of a biostratigraphic unit is a *biozone*, but several terms are used to clarify the kind of biozone that is meant. An *assemblage-zone* is a group of strata characterized by the assemblage of all forms present, or of the presence of forms of certain specified kinds. The *range-zone* of a species consists of the strata between the lowest and highest occurrence of the fossil remains of that species in a given area. In general only part of the range-zone of a species is represented at any one locality, because species neither appear nor disappear everywhere at precisely the same time. Consequently the range-zone must be inferred from regional studies; new finds may extend a range-zone upward or downward. *Concurrent-range-zones* are the coincident parts of the range zones of two or more specified taxa, which are selected for their possible temporal significance. *Acme-zones* are groups of strata defined on the basis of the abundance of specified taxa regardless of their association or range.

Like lithostratigraphic units some biostratigraphic units may have a designated type section, but for others this is not possible. A range-zone, for example, is defined as a body of strata that contain a certain taxon. As such it has both horizontal and vertical extent. Therefore it is not possible to define a range zone by reference to a single section. Biostratigraphic correlation is established by showing that geographically separated bodies of strata contain the same diagnostic biologic features as does the type section. Biozone units are named by combining the name of one or more appropriate fossils with the name of the kind of zone being defined.

Chronostratigraphy

Rocks formed during a specified interval of time are time-stratigraphic, or chronostratigraphic, units. The objectives of chronostratigraphy are to determine the age relations of strata in local sections and to establish a hierarchy of named units of regional and global applicability. The conventional terms, with their geochronologic equivalents, are as follows.

Time-stratigraphic (Eonothem)	*Geochronologic* Eon
Erathem	Era
System	Period
Series	Epoch
Stage	Age
Chronozone	Chron

Time-stratigraphic units are independent of rock types or thickness. They can be recognized by rock type only in the type section where they are defined.

There is more conceptual difficulty with time-stratigraphic units than with any other sort. This arises because the only record of the passage of geologic time is that contained in the rocks themselves. If we wish to define a specific interval of time (with regard to rocks), we must first specify an interval of rock and then define the time interval as being that over which the interval of rocks was deposited. To extend this time interval to other localities it must be correlated from the type locality, and this is generally done by biostratigraphic means. Hence some would argue that in practice the distinction between time correlation and biostratigraphic correlation breaks down and that maintaining two sets of terms is sophistry. Few workers would deny that biostratigraphic units may closely correspond to chronostratigraphic units or deny the enormous practical contribution of biostratigraphy to chronostratigraphy, but most would offer a host of reasons why the boundaries of a biostratigraphic unit differ temporally from place to place. Conceptually at least, the two sorts of classification are different, one objective and observable but limited in the geographical extent over which it may be applied, the other interpretative but pervasive. In a few instances where marker beds that closely approximate an instant in time are preserved (e.g. volcanic-ash falls in marine settings, the iridium anomaly at the end of the Cretaceous period), the correspondence, or lack thereof, between bio- and chronostratigraphic units can be fruitfully investigated.

The discovery of various dating methods based on radioactive decay has, in a sense, made the distinction between chrono- and biostratigraphic units clearer. Radiometric dates are measures of time, and if a body of rocks is dated it is placed in time regardless of its fossil content, but the age itself does not place it in any particular biostratigraphic unit. Rather, the time significance of biostratigraphic units is learned in this way. Radiometric dating is not a cure-all for determining chronostratigraphic placement, because many rock sequences are not amenable to dating. Furthermore, the error associated with an age determination is a fraction or percentage of the age, which remains roughly constant. Thus the real uncertainty, expressed in years, becomes larger for older rocks. On the other hand there is no reason to believe that the pace of evolution has changed over the course of time. Therefore the error associated with biostratigraphic correlation may be larger than errors on radiometric ages for young rocks but less for older rock sequences.

Correlation

The word *correlation* is used in several different senses that obscure its meaning. In general it means that equivalency of one sort or another has been shown to exist between strata in two geographically separated sections. To some workers correlation means that time-equivalency has been demonstrated and that other kinds of equivalency (lithologic, biostratigraphic) should not be called correlation. To preclude ambiguity one should state, or attempt to determine, what sort of correlation is being discussed: the following discussion deals only with time-correlation.

Only a few types of strata are formed in geologic instants (e.g. volcanic-ash layers and their altered equivalents, varves, some turbidites, geochemical anomalies, and perhaps geomagnetic polarity reversals); where these occur, they are extremely useful. Physical continuity of most lithostratigraphic units does not imply that all strata belonging to the unit were deposited at the same time, particularly if the unit is of great geographic extent. Nonetheless, physical continuity does suggest that the strata were deposited continuously and over only some part of geologic time much smaller than its totality. Biostratigraphic criteria give firmer evidence for correlation, because the biologic process of evolution occurs, in many groups of organisms, at a more rapid pace than the geological process of deposition in many cases. Biological transitions also require some amount of time, however, and therefore time correlations based solely on biostratigraphic evidence are also subject to error, but the errors are generally smaller than those based on lithologic criteria. Radiometric criteria of correlation may have errors that are larger or smaller than biostratigraphic errors, depending on the age of the strata under study.

Even in ideal cases where such key beds as volcanic-ash layers are used for correlation from one section to another, correlation is not always straightforward. Many volcanic-ash layers look similar in the field, but the presumption that two ash layers are correlative should be tested by studying their lithologic, mineralogic, and chemical characteristics. In some cases one volcanic ash may be very similar in all characteristics to another that is known to be different. Therefore any correlation of volcanic-ash layers should be in agreement with biostratigraphic evidence. Geochemical anomalies, such as the iridium anomaly at the end of the Cretaceous, may also be produced in geological instants and thus be useful in refining biostratigraphic correlations. Note, however, that it is biostratigraphic data that confine the intervals of strata to be sampled, making the problem of locating such anomalies a practical one.

Paleomagnetic polarity is a feature that should be characteristic of all strata deposited during particular time intervals, because the magnetic field of the earth is a global phenomenon. Chronostratigraphic correlation should therefore be possible by correlating boundaries between normal and reversed magnetozones. In practice the situation is more difficult, because magnetic transitions are not distinct from one another, falling into only two classes—reversed below to normal above, and vice versa. This means that there must be a strong presumption of the identity of a particular transition derived from other data (litho- or biostratigraphic) before correlation is possible. Once established, paleomagnetic correlation can be used to investigate the extent to which other correlations are time-transgressive. Another feature of magnetostratigraphic correlations that must be kept constantly in mind is that the ages assigned to transitions have an inherent uncertainty arising from the time required for transition to complete itself (on the order of 5 k.y.), from the poor fidelity of magnetic recording of some rock types, from errors associated with radiometric ages on which the temporal placement of some boundaries is made, and from errors in the models of sea-floor spreading rates on which the placement of other boundaries is made.

Sedimentary Facies

Lateral relationships between strata are of great importance, particularly in the reconstruction of ancient landscapes. Sands may be deposited along the shoreline of a lake at the same time that finer sediments are being deposited farther offshore and gravels are being laid down in stream channels. As a result rock types change as the strata within a defined unit are traced laterally; these lithologic features are called *sedimentary facies*. In treating facies it is imperative to maintain time correlation laterally along a unit, because the objective of studying changes in facies is to document lateral variations in coexisting environments, preferably over a short time interval. The term *facies* has also been applied to the rocks deposited in particular sedimentary environments irrespective of their lateral relationships, but such units are properly termed *lithotopes*. Facies, then, are all of the primary characteristics of the strata in a specified interval, both lithologic and biologic, that reflect the environmental conditions under which the strata were formed.

Depositional environments are not fixed in geographic position but change position as time passes for many reasons. Thus the shoreline of a lake advances and retreats as its water budget changes or as subsidence in the lake basin waxes or wanes. As the position of the shoreline changes, so too do the kinds of sediments being deposited at a particular spot. The characteristic sediments of laterally adjacent environments are deposited in vertical succession. This relationship is known as Walther's Law. The vertical succession of facies in a section of conformable strata therefore reflects the lateral sequence of environments.

Factors that control the distribution of sedimentary environments that give rise to stratigraphic facies are manifold. Some of the more important are the amount of sediment supplied to an area of deposition, the climate in the immediate region and also in the source area of the sediments, tectonic movements, changes in base level (for whatever reason), changes in the kind or degree of biological activity, and chemical changes in water bodies associated with the site of deposition. Not all of these factors are independent, and a change in one will induce a change in another. Any particular change recorded within the sediments may not be easily attributable to one particular cause. Climatic changes and tectonic movements are completely or largely insensitive to changes in the other factors but may induce large changes in them. Thus climate and tectonics may be viewed as more basic controlling factors than the others.

See also BIOCHRONOLOGY; GEOCHRONOMETRY; "GOLDEN SPIKE"; PALEOBIOGEOGRAPHY; PALEOMAGNETISM. [F.H.B.]

Further Readings

Ager, D.V. (1981) The Nature of the Stratigraphical Record. New York: Halsted/Wiley.

Dunbar, C.O., and Rodgers, J. (1957) Principles of Stratigraphy. New York: Wiley.

Eicher, D.L. (1976) Geologic Time. Englewood Cliffs, N.J.: Prentice-Hall.

Hedberg, H.D., ed. (1976) International Stratigraphic Guide. New York: Wiley.

STRATOPHENETICS

Term coined by P.D. Gingerich in 1976 for a technique of phylogeny reconstruction involving three steps: 1) Stratigraphic organization of all fossil samples. This includes determining the number of biological species represented in each sample; arranging in chronological sequence all samples within a given stratigraphic column; and correlating separate columns to yield a composite column with all species in proper temporal order. 2) Phenetic linking of similar species populations in adjacent stratigraphic intervals to form a branching pattern of lineages. Lineages showing significant change through time are then divided arbitrarily into paleontological chronospecies. 3) Testing of the resulting phyletic hypothesis, by collection of additional fossils and by judgment of whether the density and continuity of the fossil record is sufficient to render the hypothesis significantly more plausible than alternative hypotheses. This judgment involves considerations of paleogeography and functional interpretations of morphology as well as of morphology itself.

This stratophenetic method was originally applied by Gingerich to the Paleocene Plesiadapidae of western North America. The best subsequent examples of stratophenetic analyses have likewise been provided by Gingerich and his co-workers in studies of other Paleocene and Eocene mammal groups from the same region. The results of these studies have also been interpreted by their authors as strong evidence for the dominance of phyletic gradualism as opposed to punctuated equilibrium in mammalian evolution.

Gingerich regarded the stratophenetic method as a codification of the traditional method of phyletic inference rather than as a novel approach. He introduced the term *stratophenetics* principally to distinguish this method from cladistics, which he regarded as "a narrower comparative method . . . sometimes based purely on morphology with little regard for time." Therefore the most salient feature of the stratophenetic approach was conceived to be its reliance on stratigraphic superposition to indicate the temporal ordering of fossil forms and to provide a time dimension that cladistic analysis explicitly ignored. Gingerich acknowledged that his method required a relatively dense and continuous fossil record to provide accurate results. On the other hand he emphasized that it made use of all evidence in the fossil record—temporal, geographic, and morphological— in contrast to cladistics, which used only morphology. Gingerich argued that cladistic analysis could best be used in evaluating competing hypotheses considered equally likely on stratophenetic grounds.

The stratophenetic method has been criticized on a number of grounds. Due to the nature of the samples—teeth—most stratophenetic analyses have been based on single characters, usually measures of tooth size. Character-state polarity has received little attention in this frankly phenetic approach; definition of chronospecies has often been based on scant morphological evidence and small sample sizes; linkage of species into lineages has been thought to be too subjective; and evolutionary change within restricted sedimentary basins has been too hastily inferred in preference to considering immigration of species as an alternative. Just as cladists condemn "evolutionary" systematics in general for inextricably commingling data on cladistic relationships with data on morphological distance, they condemn stratophenetics for intertwining systematics and biostratigraphy, potentially in a circular fashion. The interpretations of stratophenetic analyses as supporting phyletic gradualism rather than punctuated equilibrium have also been contested.

As usual in such epistemological disputes some truth is to be found on all sides. The power of cladistic analysis is now well recognized, even by most "evolutionary" systematists, and it seems fair to say that the problem of character-state polarity must be taken into account in any systematic study, whatever the philosophy of the investigator. On the other hand, however, stratigraphic superposition, when used with due caution, is as valid and valuable as any of the other clues to character-state polarity, all of which are admitted to hold pitfalls for the unwary. And it remains undeniable that paleontology alone gives access to the actual record of evolution. Numer-

ical taxonomists as well as cladists have justly emphasized the necessity of examining multiple characters. In like fashion the proponents of stratophenetics have once again underlined the need to focus all available lines of evidence on systematic problems. This insistence on the relevance of non-morphological, and especially stratigraphic, data to phyletic reconstruction may be the chief contribution of the stratophenetic viewpoint, transcending differences of opinion on how best to avoid circularity in research design.

See also CLADISTICS; EVOLUTIONARY SYSTEMATICS; PHYLOGENY. [D.P.D., R.L.B.]

Further Readings

Gingerich, P.D. (1976) Cranial anatomy and evolution of Early Tertiary Plesiadapidae (Mammalia, Primates). University of Michigan Papers on Paleontology 15, pp. 1-140.

Gingerich, P.D. (1979) Stratophenetic approach to phylogeny reconstruction in vertebrate paleontology. In J. Cracraft and N. Eldredge (eds.): Phylogenetic Analysis and Paleontology. New York: Columbia University Press, pp. 41-77.

Gingerich, P.D. (1984) Primate evolution: evidence from the fossil record, comparative morphology, and molecular biology. Yrbk. Phys. Anthropol. 27:57-72.

STREPSIRHINI

Subgroup within the order Primates, typically recognized as a suborder. Loosely referred to as the "lower" primates, Strepsirhini includes the living lemurs of Madagascar, the lorises of sub-Saharan Africa and Southeast Asia, and the bushbabies, also of sub-Saharan Africa, as well as fossil and subfossil taxa thought to be either ancestral to, or extinct sisters of, the living forms. Here the suborder Strepsirhini is subdivided into the infraorders Adapiformes and Lemuriformes. Adapiformes comprises three families of Eocene taxa, subsumed under the superfamily Adapoidea; one of these families, Adapidae, has traditionally been viewed as the group from which modern strepsirhines evolved. The infraorder Lemuriformes includes the extant lemurs and indriids of Madagascar and various subfossil relatives (distributed within the superfamilies Lemuroidea and Indrioidea) as well as the mouse and dwarf lemurs of Madagascar (family Cheirogaleidae), the lorises (family Lorisidae), and the bushbabies (family Galagidae), which together constitute the superfamily Lorisoidea.

History of Classification of Strepsirhini

Lemurs and lorises—the "lower" primates—were first grouped together in 1811 by the German systematist Carl Illiger as "Prosimii." Illiger kept a third "lower" primate, the tarsier, in its own group, Macrotarsi (a name that refers to the elongated tarsal bones of *Tarsius*), but in 1883 the British comparative anatomist William Henry Flower pulled together lemurs,

Strepsirhine primates (clockwise from lower right): ruffed lemur, *Varecia variegata* (representing the family Lemuridae); smallest of living primates, the mouse lemur, *Microcebus murinus* (family Cheirogaleidae); slow-climbing African potto, *Perodicticus potto* (family Lorisidae); and small, long-legged African bushbaby, *Galago senegalensis* (family Galagidae). All are characterized by the development of a grooming claw on the second digit of the foot (most visible in the illustration in the larger animals). *Varecia, Propithecus,* and *Microcebus* are today found on the island of Madagascar. Of the five, *Microcebus, Perodicticus,* and *Galago* are nocturnal. The figures are drawn roughly to scale. (Drawing courtesy of J. Anderton.)

lorises, and the tarsier as a single group of primates, distinguished from St. George Mivart's suborder of "higher" primates, Anthropoidea, proposed in 1864. Flower called his suborder of "lower" primates Lemuroidea, but Illiger's Prosimii eventually became the accepted taxonomic referent for this group.

In 1918 the British comparative anatomist R.I. Pocock argued that *Tarsius* had closer evolutionary ties to anthropoid primates than to lemurs and lo-

rises because of similarities between the former taxa in the configuration of the lateral margin of the nostril. *Haplorhinism* is a condition among mammals in which the nostril is rounded aborally and is not discontinuous, or "slit," as is the case in "strepsirhinism." Anthropoid primates as a group are typically haplorhine and, according to Pocock, so is *Tarsius*: he united these in the suborder Haplorhini. Lemurs and lorises had nostrils that bore slits laterally: Strepsirhini, created by the French comparative anatomist Étienne Geoffroy in 1812, was resuscitated as a suborder to receive these primates.

However, the notions of Strepsirhini and Haplorhini as groups to replace the suborders Prosimii and Anthropoidea did not receive much support until the 1950s, when W.C.O. Hill published the first volumes of his monumental and influential treatise *Primates, Comparative Anatomy and Taxonomy*. Volume I was entitled *Strepsirhini*, while Volume II, which dealt with *Tarsius*, began the series on Haplorhini. This work emphasized the features that are today typically associated with Haplorhini: haplorhine primates were further distinguished from strepsirhines by having a fused rather than divided upper lip and by lacking a moist, naked rhinarium that otherwise would proceed from the nasal region, through the split upper lip, to the membrane of the oral cavity. During the 1970s studies on placental and fetal membranes, the bony and soft tissue anatomy of the ear region, and the structure of the retina supposedly demonstrated the dissociation of *Tarsius* from the lemurs and lorises and the reality of the groups Strepsirhini and Haplorhini. In 1980, however, the German primate anatomist H.O. Hofer pointed out that *Tarsius* and even some marmosets (New World anthropoid primates) are "strepsirhine"—i.e. the nostrils are not consistently aborally rounded—so that Pocock's original case for disbanding Prosimii and Anthropoidea was unfounded; Hofer also questioned the homology of the fused and "dry" internarial region of the upper lip of *Tarsius* and anthropoids, since this condition is found in other mammals, such as horses and ungulates.

Defining Strepsirhini

Since strepsirhinism is a condition common to many mammals—not just to lemurs and lorises but to rodents, lagomorphs, carnivores, insectivores, bats, elephants, and tree shrews—the possession of such a configuration of the external nares (and even upper lip) by any of these groups does not distinguish it from the others. Thus being strepsirhine, while descriptively accurate, does not set apart a strepsirhine primate from any other strepsirhine mammal. But, as J.H. Schwartz and I. Tattersall have pointed out, one morphological feature does distinguish lemuroids, indrioids, and lorisoids as a group: they all possess a compressed, spikelike "grooming" claw on the second pedal digit. To this distinctive characteristic we might add a second: the development of the anterior lower teeth (either six or four, depending on the specific taxon) into somewhat elongate and slender teeth whose crowns are tilted procumbently; this set of specialized teeth is usually referred to as a tooth comb. With the exception of *Daubentonia* (the aye-aye) all extant primates that possess a grooming claw also develop a tooth comb. If, indeed, these two features do unite as an evolutionary group lemuroids, indrioids, and lorisoids, and if the aye-aye is related to a specific group of lemurs, then we must conclude that this primate "lost" the tooth comb.

On the basis of extant taxa a group of primates we might call Strepsirhini can be defined on the basis of its universal possession of a grooming claw and, secondarily, on the development of a tooth comb. Associating fossil taxa with extant strepsirhine primates is, however, problematic—if we wish to state that any is a member of the larger group to which specific lemurs and lorises belong. The only Eocene primate for which a grooming claw is known is itself only known from damaged postcranial remains. Thus we can suggest that this was a strepsirhine primate, but, without associated teeth or skull or taxonomically identifiable bones, the broader identity of which Eocene group or groups may have had a grooming claw remains unknown. Of the Eocene taxa only among Adapidae is there a hint that the short crowns of the lower incisors are inclined forward into a miniature tooth comb, analogous to the diminished tooth combs of various subfossil lemurs. But lest we think that, at least for the extant taxa, we can remain secure in the unquestionable security of the subordinal divisions Strepsirhini and Haplorhini, we must not forget that *Tarsius* possesses a grooming claw on its second pedal digit and that, even though it lacks a tooth comb, it can be compared quite favorably in dental and postcranial morphology with extant lorisoids, especially galagids and cheirogaleids.

See also ADAPIFORMES; ANTHROPOIDEA; LEMURIFORMES; PROSIMIAN. [J.H.S.]

Further Readings

Hill, W.C.O. (1953) Primates, Comparative Anatomy and Taxonomy, Vol. I: Strepsirhini. Edinburgh: Edinburgh University Press.

Hill, W.C.O. (1955) Primates, Comparative Anatomy and Taxonomy, Vol. II: Haplorhini: *Tarsius*. Edinburgh: Edinburgh University Press.

Schwartz, J.H. (1984) What is a tarsier? In N. Eldredge and S.M. Stanley (eds.): Living Fossils. New York: Springer-Verlag, pp. 38–49.

Schwartz, J.H. (1986) Primate systematics and a classification of the order. In D.R. Swindler (ed.): Comparative Primate Biology, Vol. I: Systematics, Evolution and Anatomy. New York: Liss, pp. 1–41.

Schwartz, J.H., and Tattersall, I. (1985) Evolutionary relationships of living lemurs and lorises (Mammalia, Primates) and their potential affinities with European Eocene Adapidae. Anthropol. Pap. Am. Mus. Nat. Hist. 60:1–100.

STRIKING PLATFORM *see* FLAKE; STONE-TOOL MAKING

SUBFAMILY

Category of the classificatory hierarchy that falls immediately below the family. The *International Code of Zoological Nomenclature* requires that subfamily names end in the suffix "-inae."

See also CLASSIFICATION; NOMENCLATURE. [I.T.]

SUBFOSSIL *see* FOSSIL

SUBGENUS

Category of the classificatory hierarchy that lies between the genus and the species and that is used to group species within genera. The subgenus name is formed by placing a third latinized and italicized name in parentheses between the genus and specific name as, for example, in *Hapalemur (Prolemur) simus*. The use of subgeneric designations is relatively rare in primate systematics.

See also CLASSIFICATION; GENUS; NOMENCLATURE; SPECIES. [I.T.]

SUBORDER

Rank of the classificatory hierarchy lying immediately below the order and above the infraorder.

See also CLASSIFICATION. [I.T.]

SUBSPECIES

Units of classification within the species. Many species are *polytypic*, containing a number of recognizable variants in different geographical areas, and it is frequently useful to recognize these by formal names. A subspecies is named by adding a third latinized, italicized term at the end of the binomen denoting the species concerned, producing a "trinomen." In this way we arrive at subspecies names, such as *Lemur fulvus rufus*, which designates a geographically discrete and readily recognizable variant of the species *Lemur fulvus*, a widely distributed inhabitant of Madagascar. In the human family *Homo erectus pekinensis* is a subspecies name widely used to designate the "Peking man" variant of *Homo erectus*, although it should be noted that in general subspecies of the same species in the living biota do not differ anatomically enough to be readily recognizable on the basis of the parts that are preserved in the fossil record.

While living subspecies are distinct and recognizable to the eye, however, they do not have a discrete identity in the way that species do. Conspecific subspecies owe their separate existences to accidents of geographical separation and remain genetically compatible. When given the opportunity to interbreed, as when contact is reestablished, they will merge with one another. While any subspecies is a potential new species, speciation requires a genetic event that subspecies by definition have not undergone.

See also CLASSIFICATION; NOMENCLATURE; SPECIATION; SPECIES; SYSTEMATICS. [I.T.]

SUBTRIBE

Category of the classificatory hierarchy that may be used between the genus and the tribe.

See also CLASSIFICATION. [I.T.]

SUNDALAND *see* AUSTRALIA; INDONESIA; PALEOBIOGEOGRAPHY

SUNGIR

Late Paleolithic open-air site at the outskirts of the city of Vladimir (U.S.S.R.), dated to 24,000 B.P. Archaeological remains include three burials with extremely rich grave goods. The skeletons of a 55-to-65-year-old male, a seven-to-nine-year-old girl, and a nine-to-13-year-old boy were each covered with ca. 3,000 cut and drilled ivory beads (originally sewn onto their clothing) and with numerous pendants and necklaces of shell and animal teeth. Inventories found with the two juveniles, who were buried head to head in a joint grave, included numerous bone implements and ivory spears, including two that measured over 2 m. in length. Lithic inventories from Sungir are assigned to the Streletskaya industry.

See also EUROPE; KOSTENKI; LATE PALEOLITHIC; MEZHIRICH. [O.S.]

SUPERFAMILY

Highest of the family-group categories of the classificatory hierarchy, falling immediately below the hyporder (or below the infraorder in earlier classification schemes) and above the family. The *International Code of Zoological Nomenclature* recommends that all superfamily names end in the suffix "-oidea."

See also CLASSIFICATION; NOMENCLATURE. [I.T.]

SUTURE *see* SKULL

SWANSCOMBE

Three parts of the rear of a human skull associated with flint handaxes were discovered in a gravel pit at Swanscombe, near the River Thames (England). In 1935 an occipital bone was discovered in the upper Middle Gravels, followed by the associated left parietal a year later and the right parietal in 1955. The bones are thick by modern standards, but the occipital torus is only slightly developed, as are the muscle

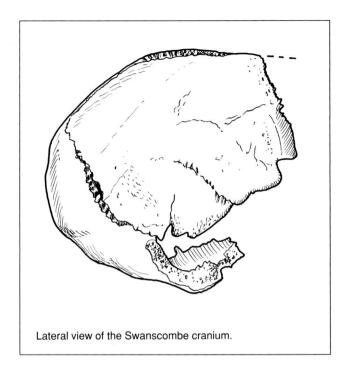

Lateral view of the Swanscombe cranium.

insertions, leading to the suggestion that the skull belonged to a female. The brain size of the Swanscombe woman was probably ca. 1,325 ml., and the overall cranial shape is rather modern, without the characteristic occipital angulation and torus development found in archaic hominids or the bulging occipital plane found in many Neanderthals. Parietal curvature is rather flattened, however, with a short midsagittal length, while the occipital bone is broad, as in many archaic hominids. Three features in particular point to Neanderthal affinities. These are the gracile and double-arched occipital torus surmounted by a central depression (the suprainiac fossa) and the suggestion at the occipital margins that there was a developed occipitomastoid crest. It seems likely that the Swanscombe woman was a member of an early Neanderthal population that lived in Europe over 200 k.y. ago. Related fossils may include those from Pontnewydd (Wales), Biache (France), and Steinheim (West Germany).

See also ARCHAIC HOMO SAPIENS; NEANDERTHALS. [C.B.S.]

SWARTKRANS

South African cave breccia deposit of early Pleistocene age, from 1.7 to 1 m.y. by faunal correlation. Swartkrans lies north of the Bloubank River some 2 km. northwest of the site of Sterkfontein, in the Transvaal Province. Fossil bones were recovered from the site during lime-mining operations in the 1930s, and the first hominid specimen was discovered by R. Broom and J.T. Robinson in 1948. This specimen was described in 1949 by Broom, who attributed it to a novel species of the "robust" australopithecine genus *Paranthropus*, namely *P. crassidens*. Work by Broom and Robinson (1948–1949) and Robinson (1951–1953), and extensive excavations by C.K. Brain (1965–present) have resulted in the recovery of the remains of well over 100 individuals of *Paranthropus* (commonly referred to as *Australopithecus robustus*) from this site. In 1949 Robinson discovered a fossil mandible of *Homo*, which Broom and he assigned to *Telanthropus capensis*. Subsequent work by Broom, Robinson, and Brain has produced the remains of some six individuals of *Homo*, which most workers regard as *Homo* cf. *erectus*. These *Homo* fossils derive from the same breccias as the *Paranthropus* remains; thus Swartkrans provided the first conclusive evidence for the contemporaneity of *Homo* and "robust" australopithecines, since confirmed in the Lake Turkana sequence of East Africa.

Two sedimentary members were recognized and formally named by K. Butzer in 1976, and until recently it was thought that the *Paranthropus* fossils came from the earlier Member 1 breccia, while the *Homo* remains derived from both Members 1 and 2. Excavations by Brain, however, have resulted in the subdivision of the Member 2 breccia into four separate units: Brown (Member 2), Early Stone Age (Member 3), Middle Stone Age (Member 4), and "*Antidorcas bondi*" (Member 5) units. *Paranthropus* and *Homo* fossils, in addition to Paleolithic artifacts, are known from Member 1 and the Brown unit, while indications of fire as well as several *Paranthropus* teeth have been recovered from the Early Stone Age unit. Faunal elements from Swartkrans indicate that these breccia deposits span a considerable period of time, with periods of breccia accumulation interrupted by erosional cycles.

See also AUSTRALOPITHECUS ROBUSTUS; BRECCIA CAVE FORMATION; BROOM, ROBERT; PARANTHROPUS. [F.E.G.]

Further Readings

Brain, C.K. (1981) The Hunters or the Hunted? An Introduction to African Cave Taphonomy. Chicago: University of Chicago Press.

Brain, C.K. (1985) Cultural and taphonomic comparisons of hominids from Swartkrans and Sterkfontein. In E. Delson (ed.): Ancestors: The Hard Evidence. New York: Liss, pp. 72–75.

SYMPATRY *see* SPECIATION

SYMPHALANGUS *see* APE; HYLOBATIDAE

SYMPLESIOMORPHIC *see* CLADISTICS

SYNAPOMORPHIC *see* CLADISTICS; HOMOLOGY

SYNONYM(Y)

Synonyms are different Linnaean names applied to the same taxon. The valid name for any animal taxon, the one that must be used for it, is the oldest name applied to it that conforms to the requirements of the *International Code of Zoological Nomenclature*. The valid name is the *senior* synonym; all others subsequently applied to the same taxon are known as *junior* synonyms and are not used in reference to the animal in question. When two forms formerly thought to have been distinct are discovered to be in fact the same, they are placed in synonymy, and the senior synonym becomes the valid name for the inclusive taxon.

See also CLASSIFICATION; NOMENCLATURE; PRIORITY; TAXON; TAXONOMY. [I.T.]

SYSTEMATICS

Study of the diversity of life and of the relationships among taxa, living and fossil, at the various levels of the taxonomic hierarchy. The late paleontologist G.G. Simpson pointed out that systematics is at once the most elementary and the most inclusive component of zoology: the most elementary because any discussion of living things is dependent on some degree of systematization having been carried out, and most inclusive because information gained from virtually every branch of biology can eventually contribute to the solution of systematic problems.

The primary goal of zoological systematists is to order the diversity of animal life into sets based on the relationships between the myriad kinds of animal. Early systematists arranged organisms into groups on the basis of the common similarities they saw among them, and the system of classification of living things introduced by the systematist Linnaeus in the mid-eighteenth century reflected his perception that a hierarchy exists in nature, a hierarchy reflected in the way that organisms seem naturally to fall into ever more inclusive sets. Human beings, for example, group naturally with the other higher primates at one level, with Primates as a whole at another, with all mammals at a yet higher level, and so on. Hence the various ranks of Linnaeus's classificatory scheme—species, genera, families, orders—become ever more inclusive as one ascends the hierarchy of his classificatory system: genera belong to families, families to orders, orders to phyla.

Following the advent of evolutionary thought in the mid-nineteenth century, the basis for this natural nesting of groups of organisms became apparent: the hierarchy of similarities among organisms results from varying propinquity of descent. Closely related organisms share many similarities because they inherited them from a recent common ancestor; more distantly related forms share fewer similarities because more evolutionary change has taken place in their respective lineages since a remoter common ancestry.

All modern systematists agree on the evolutionary basis for the order seen in nature. There is much disagreement, however, on how best to proceed in uncovering and classifying this order. Over the years many schools of thought have emerged both on how best to reconstruct the relationships among the various components of the living world and on how to classify them. Some systematists favor quantitative methods, others qualitative; some group organisms on the basis of general similarity, while others insist that only certain kinds of resemblance are of value in reconstructing evolutionary relationships.

At present, despite the misleading similarity in the names involved, the most important division between opposing schools of systematic thought is that between the *evolutionary systematists* and the *phylogenetic systematists*. Both seek to order organisms into natural groups on the basis of shared "homologous" similarities, those inherited from a common ancestor. The phylogenetic systematists, however, insist that only "derived" homologous states, those representing unique "evolutionary novelties" acquired and passed along by the common ancestor, may be used in forming natural groups. In other words, in reconstructing evolutionary histories they reject the use of "primitive" similarities inherited from a remote common ancestor that also gave rise to descendants not belonging to the monophyletic group immediately under consideration. Phylogenetic schemes and classifications put forth by evolutionary systematists, on the other hand, tend to depend on overall resemblance between organisms rather than on inferred strict branching sequences in phylogeny. Since new characters tend to accumulate more rapidly in some lineages than in others, application of the two approaches can on occasion produce strikingly different phylogenies and classifications. Purely phenetic phylogenies produced by numerical taxonomists and others can be different yet, and differ among themselves.

See also CLADISTICS; CLASSIFICATION; EVOLUTION; EVOLUTIONARY SYSTEMATICS; MONOPHYLY; NUMERICAL TAXONOMY; PHYLOGENY; STRATOPHENETICS; TAXONOMY. [I.T.]

Further Readings

Eldredge, N., and Cracraft, J. (1980) Phylogenetic Patterns and the Evolutionary Process. New York: Columbia University Press.

Mayr, E. (1969) Principles of Systematic Zoology. New York: McGraw-Hill.

Simpson, G.G. (1961) Principles of Animal Taxonomy. New York: Columbia University Press.

SZELETIAN

Early Upper Paleolithic industry, dating to ca. 30,000 B.P., that is widely distributed in central Europe. It contains diagnostic bifacially worked leaf points and occasional split-base bone points. This industry is named after the Szeleta Cave in the Bükk Mountains in northeastern Hungary, where it was first identified.

See also **AURIGNACIAN; EUROPE; ISTALLÖSKÖ; SOLUTREAN.** [O.S.]

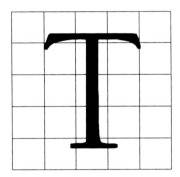

TABARIN *see* BARINGO

TABELBALA *see* PREPARED-CORE

TABŪN

Cave on Mount Carmel (Israel), originally excavated between 1929 and 1934 by the same team that investigated the nearby site of Skhūl. A Levalloiso-Mousterian industry was recovered from levels C and D at the site, which also produced two hominid fossils, a skeleton of a female (Tabūn 1), and a mandible, probably of a male (Tabūn 2). As with Skhūl the

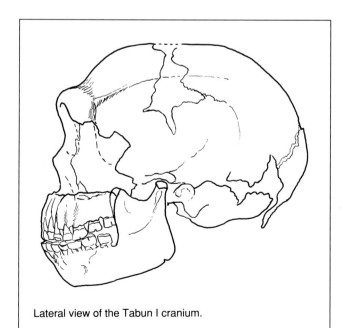

Lateral view of the Tabun I cranium.

material was originally dated to the early late Pleistocene, but recent research at the site suggests a possible age of ca. 50 k.y. for level C. Tabūn 1 is the reasonably complete skeleton of an adult female with a relatively small skull (capacity ca. 1,300 ml.) and body. Brow development is strong, and although the occipital region is rather rounded the specimen is clearly of Neanderthal type. The skeleton was the first one in which the unusual pubic-bone morphology characteristic of Neanderthals was recognized. The separate mandible of Tabūn 2 is large, but it displays a slight chin and only small retromolar spaces. Its status and classification are less clear than those of Tabūn 1.

See also NEANDERTHALS. [C.B.S.]

TABUNIAN

Early Paleolithic Tayacian-like industry without handaxes at Tabūn, Mount Carmel (Israel), comparable with the Jabrudian.

See also EARLY PALEOLITHIC; JABRUDIAN;
STONE-TOOL MAKING; TABŪN; TAYACIAN. [A.S.B.]

TACHENGIT *see* PREPARED-CORE

TAIL

Humans and apes lack an external tail, but most other primates have them, and there is no doubt that our early ancestors possessed a tail prior to ca. 20 m.y. ago. The lowest part of our vertebral column, the coccyx, is the bony remnant of the tail of our ancestors, and the muscles that support our pelvic organs from below are modified versions of the same muscles that move the tail in other primates.

Most primates that are arboreal quadrupeds or leapers have a long tail. This appendage appears to serve primarily as an organ for maintaining balance during walking, running, and leaping in trees. In several of the larger New World monkeys the tail is prehensile and is used as a "fifth limb" to grasp branches and food. In many of these species this fifth limb lacks fur on the ventral surface. Rather, the skin has dermatoglyphics similar to the fingerprints found on the grasping surfaces of the hands and feet. More terrestrial species often have relatively shorter tails. Loss of the tail in suspensory primates, including the ape and human lineage, seems to be the result of two factors. Suspensory species do not need this organ for balance; and because they frequently adopt upright postures they can further benefit from rearrangement of the tail structures to support the pelvis from below.

See also L*OCOMOTION*; S*KELETON*. [J.G.F.]

Further Readings

Wilson, D.R. (1972) Tail reduction in *Macaca*. In R.H. Tuttle (ed.): The Functional and Evolutionary Biology of Primates. Chicago: Aldine-Atherton, pp. 241–261.

TANZANIA

Country situated just south of the equator, on the eastern coast of Africa. A long history of paleoanthropological research in Tanzania has yielded some of the most important data bearing on human evolution.

Olduvai Gorge, Tanzania's most famous fossil locality, lies at the edge of the Serengeti Plains. Discovered and first worked by H. Reck and other German scientists and subsequently studied for many years by L.S.B. and M.D. Leakey, Olduvai has provided a wealth of archaeological and paleontological resources in a well-documented geological context that spans the last 2 m.y.

Some 50 km. to the south, at Laetoli, even older rocks crop out. These Pliocene deposits have yielded many mammalian remains, including hominids. More important, however, was the discovery during the 1970s of hominid footprints in a volcanic-ash layer. Hominid crania have been found associated with Middle Stone Age implements at Laetoli and along the shores of nearby Lake Eyasi. Deposits to the west side of Lake Natron, at Peninj, have yielded important archaeological evidence and a hominid mandible. At Lake Ndutu, near Olduvai, an early hominid cranium was found with other archaeological remains.

Because research has concentrated in the northern areas of Tanzania, comparatively little work has been done farther to the south along the rift valley,

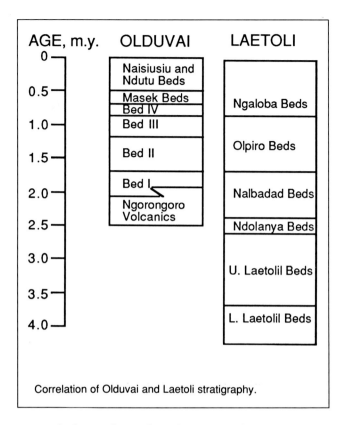

Correlation of Olduvai and Laetoli stratigraphy.

particularly in the Rukwa basin. As these areas are searched, Tanzania will contribute additional discoveries to the record of human evolution.

See also A*FRICA*; L*AETOLI*; O*LDUVAI* G*ORGE*. [T.D.W.]

Further Readings

Reader, J. (1981) Missing Links. Boston: Little, Brown.

TAPHONOMY

Subject dealing with the processes affecting animals from their deaths to their possible fossilization. It began essentially as an ancillary field to paleoecology. Devised by the Russian geologist Efremov in 1940 to encompass studies in what he referred to as the "transition of animal remains from the biosphere into the lithosphere," the word derives from the Greek *taphos*, "burial," and *nomos*, "law."

Taphonomy is a response to two facts: fossils are not living animals and fossil assemblages are not living animal communities. Fossils are just the remains of animals, usually some pieces of the hard parts buried in sediments. In the case of vertebrates we face the problem of what piles of broken bones actually mean in biological terms. To answer this question, and to reconstruct the paleoecology of these creatures with any confidence, we must assess the degree to which fossil assemblages constitute representative samples of the communities of animals from which they were derived.

Taphonomy encompasses a number of other concerns, some of which were already in existence when the word was invented. German scientists in the 1920s had coined a few relevant terms, such as *biostratonomy* (the study of the embedding of fossils in sediments) and *aktuopaläontologie* (investigations into the remains of modern animals in the contemporary environment). These latter studies were directed toward discovering and understanding fossil analogues. This is really no more than a branch of actualism, or Lyell's uniformitarianism, the idea that the present is the key to the past.

Most of this early work concerned animals in the marine environment, but in the early 1960s Olson reintroduced the word *taphonomy* into western usage in his consideration of late Permian terrestrial vertebrates of the United States and U.S.S.R. He stressed its importance and the need to keep it distinct from paleoecology, although the two subjects were closely related.

The science of taphonomy has developed along fairly independent lines around the world and has focused on slightly different subjects: the aims to which such work was directed depended mostly on the paleontological interests of the investigator. Much research in taphonomy has been carried out with a particular problem in mind, often of a paleoecological nature, beginning as a reaction to some other concern. The intention has often been to rectify preservational bias in an assemblage so as to reveal matters of paleoecological interest or to allow the assumptions and limitations of paleoecological conjecture to be more clearly stated. Taphonomy is sometimes described as the study and evaluation of *information loss*. Others, however, see it as *information gain*, for the state of fossil material may provide unique data about the agents that have caused such preservational bias. Often the agent of modification or collection can be of as much paleoecological interest as the fossil remains themselves.

This positive approach has led to investigations that are less disparate and more united in their aims. Such work has generated much basic information that has permitted the formulation of more general rules and principles that find wider application. Consequently the relevance of taphonomy to matters other than paleoecology is also becoming realized. In a more recent and broader formulation, as the study of ways in which preservation affects the fossil record, it has important implications for biostratigraphy and evolutionary questions.

Subject Matter of Taphonomy

Efremov regarded taphonomy as the transition of animals from the biosphere to the lithosphere. This description, although accurate, is operationally diffi-

cult, because there are so many ways in which animals can become fossils.

A more direct, and perhaps more objective, approach to the practice of taphonomy is to enumerate and then explain the differences between fossil collections and living communities of animals. Most questions about sites and assemblages can then be framed and possibly answered in terms of these differences. For vertebrates, the most relevant organisms for hominid sites, they include the following: the animals are dead; there are usually no soft parts preserved; the skeletons are often disarticulated; bones are often concentrated together; bones are mostly damaged; parts of the skeleton occur in proportions different from their occurrence in life; remains are buried in sediment or other rock; bones are sometimes preferentially oriented within the rock; bones are altered chemically.

The list illustrates some of the scope of taphonomy. These distinctions all apply to individual animals. The question of how whole communities are represented in the fossil record also involves the association of different species and their numbers or relative proportions, or the numbers of individuals of different age or sex groups within each species.

There are two complementary lines of approach for tackling these issues. One, which could be referred to as *paleotaphonomy*, examines the content and context of fossil or archaeological sites in greater detail than has been usual. Another, *neotaphonomy*, concentrates on the modern environment and applies its results to fossil situations by analogy. This latter work can be in the form of observations of modern situations where bones naturally accumulate, such as a hyena den, preferably in an environment where the modern animals are reasonably well known. This permits the relation between the modern bone assemblage and the community from which it is derived to be more easily understood. Alternatively the work may be more experimental in nature, perhaps in laboratory situations, studying the effect on bones of a limited and controlled range of specific processes. For example, experiments have been performed with flume tanks, or artificial stream tables, to investigate the effects of moving water on different kinds of bones.

The resolution of taphonomical studies extends from highly detailed work on specific fossil sites, from microstratigraphy or the analysis of microscopic scratches on bone, to matters on a much larger scale. Some environments, for example, are much more likely to preserve bone than are others. Fossils may have been more likely to be preserved at particular times in the past than during others. Such factors as these directly pertain to large-scale issues of paleobiogeography and evolution.

Taphonomy and Hominids

These factors clearly affect the nature of the hominid fossil record. On a global scale taphonomical considerations influence the distribution of sites available for the preservation of hominids. East Africa is famous for fossil sites, due mainly to the existence of the Rift Valley that transects it. Here a combination of geological circumstances has produced conditions highly favorable to the accumulation and preservation of bone. Obviously this circumstance has an impact on interpretations of the distribution of hominids on a world scale. To a certain extent the absence of fossil hominids from elsewhere in Africa may reflect taphonomical rather than paleobiological factors.

Taphonomical factors have their effects on the distribution of hominids in time as well, and this in turn affects not only paleoecological inference but also how we see evolution as having taken place. If so many circumstances conspire to influence the preservation of a fossil, how can we know how closely the first and last occurrences of a particular species in the fossil record represent its biological origination and extinction? Taphonomy helps answer such questions of time resolution that are essential for understanding the mode of evolution, such as discriminating between punctuated or gradualistic models. Taphonomy is also vital to questions of the influence of external forcing factors on evolution. It may provide insight into the question of whether events of speciation and climate that appear contemporaneous in the fossil record are truly synchronous.

On a finer scale paleoanthropology is an obvious case where taphonomy makes a contribution, exposing the workings of factors that control and modify bone assemblages. Paleoanthropologists and archaeologists are interested in the behavior of humans and human ancestors, and they are often concerned with collections of bone that may represent the food debris of hominids. At the same time exaggerated claims have often been made about bone assemblages thought to have been produced by humans, and here taphonomy has the valuable role of critically examining these claims.

The condition of bone assemblages accumulated by hominids potentially provides details of hominid behavior, such as food selectivity, butchery practices, or domestication. Since the late 1960s a good deal of taphonomical work, mainly in Africa, has specifically aimed at understanding hominid sites and behavior.

Taphonomy can help solve some fundamental anthropological problems, such as the identification of sites as having been produced by hominids; the recognition of bone tools; the determination if early hominids were hunters or scavengers; the description of butchery practices; the identification of human-inflicted violence on human remains; the description of the meat component of the diet; the identification of domestication.

These issues are often interrelated. The first of them, the identification of sites as having been produced by hominids, is fundamental. It applies particularly, but not exclusively, to early hominid localities: how is hominid involvement in a site to be recognized? This question has arisen a number of times since the beginning of the last century, and rudimentary taphonomical work concerning it has been carried out since then. A classic recent example relates to South African cave sites where australopithecines have been found. Were the bones associated with the early hominids collected by them or were they, along with the hominids, the food remains of carnivores? The solution involved some of the earliest serious taphonomical work on hominids, carried out by C.K. Brain among others.

Normally for an occurrence to be regarded as a site bones must be present in some quantity. The problem of the objective differences between a fossil collection and a living community initially relates to the concentration of remains: what processes result in bones becoming accumulated together? Not only hominids but other carnivores, such as hyenas and leopards, collect bones, and a good deal of taphonomical work has studied such animals, distinguishing their collections from others. Flowing water also concentrates bones, prompting research on the effect of moving water on different parts of the skeleton. In practice the question of bone-collecting agency leads to a close study of some of the other objective differences, notably damage to bones and the differential representation of skeletal parts. These factors, such as carnivores and moving water, leave their imprint on bone collections, but how do their effects differ from those of hominids?

Two of the notable features of the South African cave collections were the markedly different proportions in which parts of the skeleton were represented and the fact that the remains were broken in consistently repeated ways. R.A. Dart suggested, plausibly at the time, that the bones were the deliberately selected and modified tools and weapons of the hominids. Taphonomical work has since shown that the different proportions can be explained by such factors as the relative robusticity of different bones, their specific gravity, and the time of epiphysis fusion. The anomaly does not require human intervention. These factors also explain the characteristic patterns of damage, and nowadays, with increasing knowledge of bone breakage by nonhuman agencies, researchers are generally much more critical of claims concerning bone tools.

A more recent example of this issue concerns the peopling of the New World. The earliest putative evidence for the arrival of humans in North America takes the form of bones claimed to show the effects of human working, some of them alleged to be artifacts. Taphonomical work on bone damage assists in discriminating between human agencies and other factors potentially responsible for creating these bone objects. In neither of these cases, the South African cave sites and the North American occurrences, have damaged bones been found with stone tools. Association of bones with artifacts has traditionally been axiomatic in affirming hominid involvement at a site, but recently even this criterion has come into question, some regarding certain associations as fortuitous. This objection has resulted in increased subtlety in taphonomical analysis, which has, for example, established microscopic distinctions between scratch marks produced by humans using stone tools and marks made by teeth of other carnivores. In turn this endeavor has led to attempts to discriminate between scavenging and hunting behavior on the part of early hominids.

Inferences concerning the butchery practices of early humans here come into play, and the matter is a more explicit object of inquiry in other contexts. Part of the process of butchery is the dismemberment of carcasses. It is interesting to discover the ways in which skeletons fall apart under natural conditions and to compare this information with sequences of disarticulation deduced from archaeological sites. It appears that, like damage to bones, it is the nature of the skeleton that fundamentally controls sequences of dismemberment rather than the idiosyncrasies of any external agent. Consequently human butchery practices are sometimes less distinctive than has been supposed.

Evidence of breakage and damage to human bones has been called upon to answer questions regarding human violence to other humans. Apparently unusual fractures on human specimens have frequently been attributed to violent or cannibalistic behavior. Rarely were they considered in the context of other possible causes. Taphonomy has demonstrated the need for caution in such assertions, refining the analysis of human remains in this respect.

Other anthropological issues rely upon the ability to answer questions regarding the numbers, or at least relative proportions, of different species in an assemblage or paleocommunity. These questions are particularly difficult to answer, because they require far more information about relative taxonomic and skeletal preservation if our reconstructions are to be treated with any confidence. Among these problems is the perennial one of estimating the relative amount of different meat food items at an archaeological site and what this means in terms of diet. Many of the obvious questions, such as how much meat of each particular species is consumed, and how often, are hard to answer. Taphonomical work is helpful primarily by being critical of rash suggestions but also by providing positive information about the time interval represented by the accumulation of bones at particular sites.

Inferences about animal domestication and hunting also sometimes depend upon an estimation of the relative proportions of different age groups in a bone assemblage, and here again taphonomical factors are important. It is essential to be able to assess the relative survivorship of skeletons from animals of different individual age.

Taphonomy Today

These brief examples show the relevance of taphonomy to important paleoanthropological issues. Most of our information about past hominids comes from fossil sites, and it is vital to understand the nature of our data if we are to use them properly. This is really what taphonomy is about. It began by assimilating to its subject matter activities that many scientists already were performing. Is it simply, as someone once insisted, just a matter of doing paleoecology properly? Partly, but not entirely. By drawing together relevant information from a variety of fields it focused attention on an area that was not being examined adequately. Interpretation of bone assemblages associated with hominids was anthropocentric, with little concern for the many other nonhuman processes involved in the formation of such accumulations. In addition a large number of studies with an explicitly taphonomical orientation have produced a formidable body of information regarding the nature and dynamics of such processes. Workers are coming to see this information as being applicable to much broader problems that rely on the interpretation of the fossil and archaeological records, involving not just paleoecology but global paleobiogeography and the mode and tempo of evolution. Present-day taphonomical work is decreasingly a reaction to narrow problems at particular sites, although this remains valuable, and is increasingly designed to formulate rules, almost the laws Efromov hoped for, that are of much more general applicability.

See also ETHNOARCHAEOLOGY; FOSSIL. [A.H.]

Further Readings

Behrensmeyer, A.K., and Hill, A. (1980) Fossils in the Making. Chicago: University of Chicago Press.

Behrensmeyer, A.K., and Kidwell, S.M. (1985) Taphonomy's contribution to paleobiology. Paleobiol. *11*:105–119.

Brain, C.K. (1981) The Hunters or the Hunted? An Introduction to African Cave Taphonomy. Chicago: University of Chicago Press.

Hill, A. (1978) Taphonomical background to fossil man. In W.W. Bishop (ed.): Geological Background to Fossil Man. London: Geological Society of London, pp. 87–101.

Shipman, P. (1981) The Life History of a Fossil. Cambridge, Mass.: Harvard University Press.

TARDENOISIAN

Third stage in the classic Mesolithic/Epipaleolithic sequence of inland France, ca. 8000–6000 B.P. or possibly later, named after the type site of Fère-en-Tardenois. It is distinguished from earlier industries by the presence of geometric microliths, microburin technique, scalene triangles, trapezoids, and points with concave bases. The term is sometimes used to describe industries with geometric microliths from other regions, such as eastern Europe, as well as to distinguish northern French sites (Tardenoisian) from southern ones (Sauveterrian).

See also AZILIAN; BOW AND ARROW; EPIPALEOLITHIC; MESOLITHIC; SAUVETERRIAN; STONE-TOOL MAKING. [A.S.B.]

TARSIER see OMOMYIDAE; TARSIIDAE; TARSIIFORMES

TARSIIDAE

Family of tarsiiform haplorhine primates including only the living tarsier. No other primate presents as many radical anatomical specializations as the tarsiers, a group of four living species all assigned to the genus *Tarsius*. And no other primate, except for humans and australopiths, has stimulated as much controversy. The tarsier's remarkable morphology is associated with an unusual nocturnal, predatory lifestyle, making the genus sufficiently divergent overall to warrant a taxonomic placement in its own family. Such a claim is reserved here for only one other living primate, the Malagasy aye-aye, *Daubentonia*, although many would obviously also rank *Homo* and its fossil allies in a unique family.

Tarsiers occur in the Philippines and on some islands of the Malay archipelago, including Borneo, Sumatra, Sulawesi, and other minor islands in the chain. How long they have been isolated there, cut off from continental Asia, is unknown. It is unlikely, however, that their peculiarities have a remote Ter-

tiary origin. Rather, they probably evolved fairly recently and rapidly, perhaps partially in response to their relict distribution.

Once it became clear that these phantomlike, long-legged mammals were not related to jerboas (Rodentia) or opossums (Marsupialia), as some early naturalists believed, tarsiers became the focus of a lively systematic debate. This continues unabated more than a century later. The discussion involves objective issues, such as the tarsier's correct genealogical position within the order Primates, as well as the subjective concerns and disagreements over the philosophies of classification and the methods of paleobiological reconstruction. The scope and intensity of this dispute is a reflection of the problem: morphologically aberrant taxa are difficult to comprehend evolutionarily, and at stake is the very basic picture of primate evolution during the Cenozoic. The two predominant views regarding classification are that tarsiids should be placed either with the lemur-loris "prosimian" group or, alternatively, with the anthropoids. Advocates of the latter view assign tarsiers and anthropoids to a larger taxonomic group, the "haplorhines" and place the lemurs and lorises in the "strepsirhines." This position presumes that tarsiers are the closest living relatives of the anthropoids, a point that is almost unanimously accepted by specialists. History, however, shows a preference for their classification in Prosimii, and many still adhere to this, both to preserve consistency and because some feel that classifications need not mirror phylogeny so exactly. Some would argue further that tarsiers represent a "prosimian grade" of evolutionary progress equivalent to that of lemurs and lorises. Another relatively recent view, now essentially discarded, is that tarsiers are the only surviving descendants of the Paleocene group Plesiadapiformes. That view has been expressed in classifications that dichotomize "plesitarsiformes" and "simiolemuriformes" as phylogenetic sister groups.

Tarsiers are nocturnal, saltatory predators. Their most striking functional adaptations are thus evident in the visual and auditory systems, the dentition and the locomotor skeleton. Relative to body size, tarsiers have the largest eyes of any living mammal; consequently the greatly enlarged eye sockets dominate the morphology of the skull. A bony flangelike rim surrounds the perimeter of the orbit, serving as an ocular collar. Each eyeball alone exceeds the mass of the brain. Its receptor cells are all of the rod type, sensitive to low levels of light. Color-sensitive cones are absent. As in owls and some deep-sea fish the eyes are also somewhat "tubular" in shape rather than spherical, and they are forwardly aligned to provide a

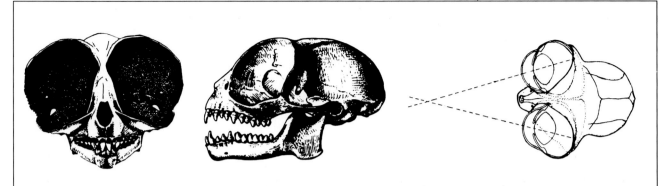

Frontal, lateral, and dorsal views of the tarsier skull with the eyeballs and optical axes shown in the latter.

high degree of binocularity. Therefore, however large the eye socket, a tarsier's eye is larger still. More than half of it protrudes beyond the bone underneath the lid, so that the animal's face bears an unusually soft, rounded appearance. Because the eyes are too large to be moved efficiently by their extrinsic muscles, the whole skull is delicately balanced on the spine to facilitate accurate head-scanning maneuvers, including the capacity to swivel the head around more than 180°.

Why are tarsier eyes so much larger than those of other nocturnal primates? In part because, as haplorhines, tarsiers lack a tapetum lucidum. This is an accessory cell layer common in nocturnal strepsirhines and other mammals. Lying adjacent to the retina, it provides indirect stimulation of the photoreceptor cells by reflecting light back toward them, thus making the most of twilight and moonlight. The absence of a tapetum in tarsiers is compensated by an increase in eyeball size, and like the presence of a central foveal spot on its retina, this also serves as a phylogenetic marker indicating close affinities with anthropoids, which have a similar derived pattern.

In addition to having very large external ears for collecting sound tarsiers have an unusually enlarged middle ear. Unlike most other primates their auditory bulla is partitioned into two discrete cavities. The eardrum opens into the external ear via a long bony tube, which also acts as a sound filter of some sort. These evolutionary novelties are still imperfectly understood, but observing the animals in the wild leaves no doubt that tarsiers use hearing first and vision second in locating and capturing prey.

The vertical-clinging-and-leaping locomotor style of tarsiers involves many muscular and osseous specializations of the postcranial skeleton. Most of these are strikingly developed in the hindlimb, whose elements are all very much elongated. The forelimb: hindlimb ratio, for example, yields an intermembral index of only 56, the hindlimb being nearly twice the

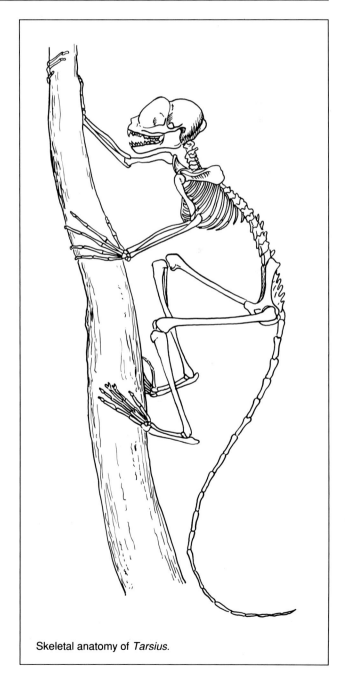

Skeletal anatomy of *Tarsius*.

length of the forelimb. The anatomy of the lower leg is also unique among living primates. The fibula is reduced to a sliver of bone up near the knee, while its lower two-thirds is completely fused to the tibia. This results in a tight hinge joint for the upper ankle, so that rotation of the talus upon the tibiofibula is stabilized in the flexion-extension plane. Fusion also strengthens the bone against bending, which may be considerable at the beginning of a leap. Tarsier hands and feet are very large, giving the animal energetically efficient, passive purchase while waiting silently for food to arrive. The proximal part of the tail is also built to bend against a vertical trunk and serve as a third base of support behind the pelvis. Perhaps most impressive of all is the exceptionally elongated leverage system of the foot, especially the calcaneum and navicular bones of the tarsus, which inspired the animal's taxonomic name.

The origins of tarsiids are still unclear. The family Omomyidae includes a number of forms that show important resemblances to the modern tarsiers. They were widely distributed in North America and Eurasia during the Eocene and survived up until the early Miocene. Many of the omomyids were probably diurnal, a feature of their haplorhine heritage. Among them are species known informally as "necrolemurs," a reference to a morphological pattern exemplified in the genus *Necrolemur*. It and its European allies have been classified recently as either microchoerine omomyids or tarsiids. They may, however, represent the ancestral tarsier stock. Some foreshadow derived, tarsierlike anatomical adaptations, including elongated tarsals, partially fused tibiofibulae, and large orbits. The recently discovered *Afrotarsius*, from the Egyptian Oligocene, may also turn out to be a member of the tarsiid group, in or near the ancestry of one of the most unusual members of the Primate order.

See also AFROTARSIUS; ANTHROPOIDEA; HAPLORHINI; LOCOMOTION; LOWER PRIMATES; MICROCHOERINAE; OMOMYIDAE; PRIMATES; STREPSIRHINI; TARSIIFORMES. [A.L.R.]

Further Readings

Cartmill, M., and Kay, R.F. (1978) Craniodental morphology, tarsier affinities, and primate suborders. In D.J. Chivers and K.A. Joysey (eds.): Recent Advances in Primatology, Vol. 3: Evolution. London: Academic, pp. 205–214.

Gingerich, P.D. (1978) Phylogeny reconstruction and the phylogenetic position of *Tarsius*. In Chivers and Joysey, pp. 249–255.

Niemitz, C. (1984) Biology of the Tarsiers. Stuttgart: Gustav Fischer.

Rosenberger, A.L. (1985) In favor of the necrolemur-tarsier hypothesis. Folia Primatol. 45:179–194.

Simons, E.L. (1972) Primate Evolution: An Introduction to Man's Place in Nature. New York: Macmillan.

Szalay, F.S., and Delson, E. (1979) Evolutionary History of the Primates. New York: Academic.

Lateral view of the right lower and upper toothrows of *Tarsius syrichta*, top. Below, oblique views of the right toothrows of the same specimen.

TARSIIFORMES

The three (possibly four) living species of *Tarsius*, and the Oligocene *Afrotarsius*, constitute the family Tarsiidae. *Tarsius*, however, is merely the barely surviving representative of a remarkably varied and widespread radiation of haplorhine primates that evolved sometime in the Paleocene from lemur-like strepsirhine primates, an unknown representative of the family Adapidae (in a broad sense). Currently the fossil tarsiiforms that are not tarsiids are grouped in the family Omomyidae.

The fossil animals treated under the Omomyidae and its subfamilies share a number of significant similarities with the living tarsiers. These shared derived features suggest that the taxonomic concept Haplorhini (which includes the tarsiiforms and anthropoids) is a valid one. The following shared derived features of the osteology of the living haplorhines are also present in representative omomyids; and it is likely that these were some of the diagnostic haplorhine features in contrast to the strepsirhine ancestor of that protohaplorhine.

The ancestral haplorhine had a shortened skull, and the olfactory process of its brain was above the midline septum of the facial skull. This interorbital septum was formed from the orbitosphenoid bone, which separated the eyes from each other. The carotid artery, which at least partly nourishes the brain in most primates, entered the skull on the medial side of the middle-ear cavity (encased by the auditory bulla), and one of its branches inside the bulla, the promontory artery, was enlarged compared with the stapedial artery, which passed through the stapes (the stirrup bone). This last character complex suggests an early increase of fresh blood supply to the brain, which suggests either an increase in visual acuity or brain enlargement, or both. The olfactory lobe was relatively reduced compared with contemporary strepsirhines, and the temporal lobe was relatively enlarged. These last features, although of "soft" anatomy, can be deduced from endocranial casts. Added to these cranial characters, a number of subtle, but important and telling, modifications in the postcranium of the known omomyids suggest representative ancestral conditions for the living haplorhines.

There is strong temptation for primatologists to consider living tarsiers as "typical" of the once greatly diversified, widespread, and undoubtedly locally abundant fossil tarsiiforms of the Eocene and Oligocene. The study of tarsier morphology and behavior reveals that these relict living species have a complex and unique history and that their characteristics reflect a series of unique adaptations that probably did not occur at the same time.

The rat-sized living tarsiers are carnivorous, taking every conceivable prey they can handle, from snakes to birds. Yet it is certain, judging from the dental and gnathic (jaw) adaptations of the fossil tarsiiforms, that in addition to the insectivory and carnivory emphasized in some species many either were primarily frugivorous or were sap feeders, or specialized on tough seeds; some were even probably leaf eaters. Such diverse feeding strategies probably demanded social and locomotor strategies quite distinct from what we observe in the living tarsiers.

The enormously enlarged eyes of living tarsiers necessitated many correlated changes that render them unique among other tarsiiforms. Yet the need for such large eyes in the nocturnal tarsiers is intimately tied to the loss early in haplorhine history of the primitive mammalian tapetum lucidum behind the retina. Nocturnality may not have been the rule among Paleogene tarsiiforms. On the other hand the early tarsiiforms, like tarsiers, were probably different in some important ways from contemporary lemur-like strepsirhines. In spite of their probable "prosimian," or primitive euprimate, similarities to their non-haplorhine relatives (such as a soft woolly pelage and

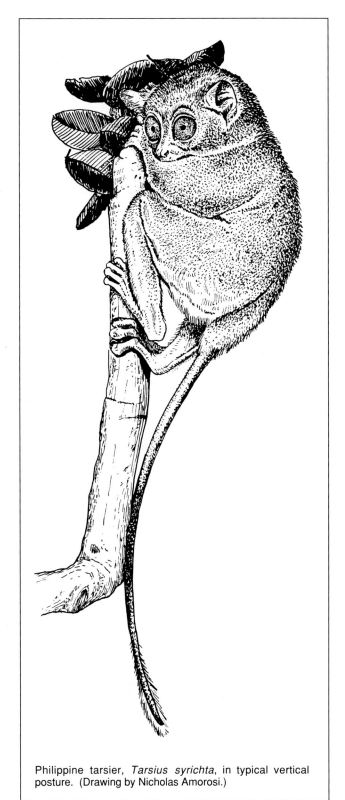

Philippine tarsier, *Tarsius syrichta*, in typical vertical posture. (Drawing by Nicholas Amorosi.)

large or expandable membranous external ears), the omomyid tarsiiforms, many of them probably diurnal (active during the day), not only had shortened muzzles but also probably had an upper lip that was not cleft and that therefore allowed a greater range of facial expressions than we see in strepsirhines today. As suggested by the reduced olfactory bulb, and an admittedly assumed haplorhine nose and lip condition, the stage among the earliest tarsiiforms, omomyids (in a broad sense), was set for the evolution of primarily visual displays and communication in which an active face was increasingly favored by selection during the social interactions of these animals.

The jumping ability of living tarsiers is phenomenal: they are capable of up to 1,500 leaps per night, averaging ca. 1,000. Yet what we can deduce from the poorly known postcranial remains of Paleogene tarsiiforms suggests that the early and more primitive members of the group were not as committed to vertical clinging and bipedal graspleaping as are living tarsiers. Most omomyids were probably rather like the other early euprimates: fast-moving, primarily quadrupedal graspleapers.

What caused the disappearance of a once so widespread and successful radiation of haplorhine primates? In addition to the climatic deterioration of the Tertiary the primates that possessed the best biological adaptations to diurnal living were the very forms that had evolved from the early tarsiiforms. The diurnal anthropoid primates came to dominate the forests, capable of competing even with the fruit-eating birds, and it is perhaps no accident that the only tarsiiforms that escaped the brutal competition were species of the genus *Tarsius*, the ancestor of which had turned nocturnal to survive.

See also ANTHROPOIDEA; HAPLORHINI; OMOMYIDAE; PRIMATES; TARSIIFORMES. [F.S.S.]

Further Readings

Hill, W.C.O. (1955) Primates, Comparative Anatomy and Taxonomy, Vol. VII: Haplorhini: Tarsioidea. Edinburgh: Edinburgh University Press.

Szalay, F.S., and Delson, E. (1979) Evolutionary History of the Primates. New York: Academic.

TARSIUS *see* OMOMYIDAE; TARSIIDAE; TARSIIFORMES

TATA

Mousterian site in Hungary of probable early Weichselian age (?110–70 k.y.), excavated by L. Vertés, among others. The industry is distinguished by the use of Levallois technology, small size, numerous side-scrapers, and bifacial retouch on small points and handaxes. Finely ground pigments were recovered from Tata in an early Mousterian context, together with a carved mammoth tooth and other incised bone objects. These represent some of the earliest carved and incised objects known.

See also CLACTONIAN; EUROPE; LEVALLOIS; MIDDLE PALEOLITHIC; MOUSTERIAN; PALEOLITHIC IMAGE; STONE-TOOL MAKING. [A.S.B.]

TATROT *see* SIWALIKS

TAUNG

South African cave breccia probably of late Pliocene age, ca. 2 m.y. Taung is the type locality of *Australopithecus africanus*. The Taung hominid skull was discovered at the Buxton Limeworks there in November 1924, having been blasted from a breccia-filled solution chamber in the Thabaseek limestone tufa, the oldest of five tufa carapaces that fan out from the Precambrian dolomites of the Gaap (or Kaap) Escarpment at Buxton. The cave from which the skull was reported to have been taken was completely obliterated by mining operations that continued to cut into the tufa for a number of years after the discovery of the hominid specimen. The now-abandoned Buxton Limeworks is located 9.6 km. southwest of the town of Taung and ca. 130 km. north of Kimberley in the Cape Province. The discovery site of the hominid skull was probably located at 27°32′ S and 24°45′ E.

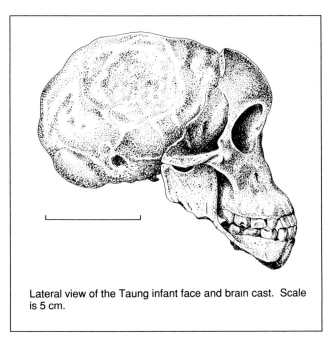

Lateral view of the Taung infant face and brain cast. Scale is 5 cm.

The hominid skull was described in 1925 by R.A. Dart, who attributed it to the novel taxon *Australopithecus africanus*. The cave from which it reportedly came, known as the *Australopithecus* Cave, was only one of several fossiliferous cave deposits (e.g. Hrdlička's Cave, Spier's Cave) that were exposed in the immediate vicinity during the course of mining the tufa bodies in the Buxton Quarry. No artifactual material was recovered from the *Australopithecus* Cave.

The geochronological age of the Taung hominid site is a matter of dispute. Much of the so-called "Taung Fauna" probably derives from breccia deposits other than the *Australopithecus* Cave itself; thus many of the earlier faunal age estimates may not pertain directly to the hominid specimen. An ill-founded attempt at geomorphological dating in the early 1970s suggested an age of less than 870 k.y. for the hominid, which prompted speculation that the skull may be that of a "robust" australopithecine. Preliminary thermoluminescence analyses of calcite from the outer Thabaseek tufa have suggested an age in the vicinity of 1 m.y. but may not date the tufa itself. Analyses of the cercopithecid fauna that derives from the *Australopithecus* Cave indicates an age of ca. 2 m.y., and the hominid specimen itself is morphologically more similar to those from Sterkfontein and Makapansgat than to the younger "robust" australopithecine fossils from Kromdraai and Swartkrans.

See also AUSTRALOPITHECUS; AUSTRALOPITHECUS AFRICANUS; BRECCIA CAVE FORMATION; DART, RAYMOND ARTHUR; KROMDRAAI; MAKAPANSGAT; STERKFONTEIN; SWARTKRANS. [F.E.G.]

Further Readings

Delson, E. (1984) Cercopithecid biochronology of the African Plio-Pleistocene: correlation among eastern and southern hominid-bearing localities. Cour. Forsch. Inst. Senckenberg 69:199–218.

Peabody, F.E. (1954) Travertines and cave deposits of the Kaap Escarpment of South Africa, and the type locality of *Australopithecus africanus*. Bull. Geol. Soc. Am. 65:671–706.

Vogel, J.C. (1985) Further attempts at dating the Taung tufas. In P.V. Tobias (ed.): Hominid Evolution. New York: Liss, pp. 189–194.

TAUTAVEL *see* ARAGO

TAXA *see* TAXON

TAXON

Category of organisms at any level of the classificatory hierarchy (plural *taxa*). A kingdom, an order, a family, a genus: all are taxa. Informally taxa above the level of the genus are known as *higher taxa*.

See also CLASSIFICATION; NOMENCLATURE; SYSTEMATICS; TAXONOMY. [I.T.]

TAXONOMY

Theory and practice of classifying organisms. This has two separate aspects, in both of which theory and practice are intertwined: first, the process of classifying organisms, which can be done on the basis of various criteria of which the most important is phylogeny; and second, the naming of the units recognized in the classification, which is governed by rules laid down in the *International Code of Zoological Nomenclature*. Thus, while the naming of taxonomic units is an objective process that must follow established procedures, the recognition of these units and their incorporation into the classificatory hierarchy is less clear-cut, the bases of any classification depending on the intentions of the classifier.

See also CLASSIFICATION; NOMENCLATURE; SYSTEMATICS. [I.T.]

TAYACIAN

Early Paleolithic flake industry found in Europe and possibly in the Near East during the later middle Pleistocene, ca. 0.45-0.15 m.y. (late Elster to Saale glacial stages). Lacking or poor in handaxes and Levallois technology, the industry is characterized by large numbers of small, often crude flakes, denticulates, core-choppers, crude scrapers, and points, especially the *pointe de Tayac*. The type site, as defined by Breuil, is La Micoque, near Les-Eyzies-de-Tayac (Dordogne) in southwestern France, where some "Tayacian" levels are also referred to as "pre-Mousterian." Other important sites with a similar industry include Arago, Ehringsdorf, Tabūn, and Jabrud.

See also ARAGO; BREUIL, HENRI; CLACTONIAN; EARLY PALEOLITHIC; EHRINGSDORF; EUROPE; JABRUD; JABRUDIAN; TABUNIAN. [A.S.B.]

TCHADANTHROPUS *see* HOMO; YAYO

TECHNOLOGY

System by which raw materials, including food items, are extracted and transformed for human use, or, more specifically, the set of behaviors or procedures carried out on a raw material, leading to its transformation. Succeeding stages of the Paleolithic (and later cultures) may be characterized in terms of the increasingly sophisticated technology used in the production of stone tools.

See also MESOLITHIC; NEOLITHIC; PALEOLITHIC; STONE-TOOL MAKING. [A.S.B.]

TEETH

Organs that assist in the acquisition and mechanical breakdown of food and in several nondigestive functions, such as defense and display. Teeth have long been a subject of interest to comparative anatomists.

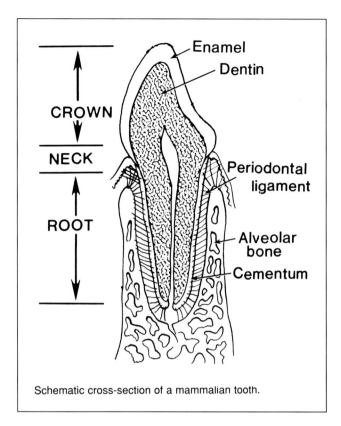

CROWN

NECK

ROOT

Enamel

Dentin

Periodontal ligament

Alveolar bone

Cementum

Schematic cross-section of a mammalian tooth.

First, because of their complexity and evolutionarily conservative character teeth are important for determining evolutionary relationships among primates. Second, dental structure, when understood in functional and adaptive terms, is important for assessing dietary preferences and social structure of living primates. Moreover, because teeth are composed in large part of inorganic calcium salts they are commonly preserved in the fossil record, so it has been possible using dental anatomy to trace evolutionary changes in many primate groups and to reconstruct phylogenetic and adaptive patterns of extinct primates.

The mammalian tooth has a *crown, neck,* and *root.* In cross-section the tooth is composed of a column of *dentin* containing a *pulp cavity* with nerves and vessels. Covering the dentin of the root is a thin layer of *cementum.* The root is suspended in its bony crypt, or *alveolus,* by the *periodontal ligament,* which takes its origin from the alveolar surface and inserts into the cementum. On the crown the dentin is covered by a hard, crystalline layer of *enamel.*

To fully appreciate the dental anatomy of primates it is useful to consider that of their reptilian and mammalian forebears. Several major advances distinguish mammalian dentitions from those of reptiles. The most obvious of these is *heterodonty.* The reptilian ancestors of mammals had simple conical teeth from the front to the back of the jaw. Mammals exhibit regionally differentiated tooth groups that

serve special functions. From front to back on each side of the upper and lower jaw in the primitive mammalian dentition is a series of simple nibbling teeth, *incisors,* followed by a projecting and pointed *canine* used for grasping and stabbing purposes. Behind the canines is a series of increasingly complicated cheek teeth, or postcanines, the *premolars* and *molars,* used for separating a bite of food and chewing it to increase its surface area to speed the digestive processes after swallowing. All of the lower teeth are embedded in the mandible; the upper incisors are in the premaxilla, the other upper teeth in the maxilla.

To simplify reference, the major tooth types are referred to by their initial letters, thus: M, molars; P, premolars; C, canine; I, incisors. In the sequence within tooth types the teeth are referred to by numbers—e.g. M1, first molar; P2, second premolar. Upper and lower teeth are distinguished by super- and subscripts, respectively—e.g. M^2, second upper molar, I_1, first lower incisor. Note that numbering is based on homology, not position; thus the premolars of humans are known as P3 and P4, even though there are only two of them, since the anterior premolars present in remote ancestors have been lost.

Accompanying the development of heterodonty in the mammalian dentition was a change in the way teeth were replaced. Typically in reptiles the tooth at each position (*locus*) in the jaw is replaced a number of times, and the total number of teeth increases with the continued growth of the animal throughout life. In mammals the tooth at each locus is replaced only once, at most, and the total number of tooth loci is strictly limited. Thus mammals have a set of "baby," or deciduous, teeth and a complement of adult, or permanent, teeth.

The structure of mammalian cheek teeth has departed far from that of reptiles. The earliest mammals, like *Kuehneotherium,* had upper and lower cheek teeth with a single cone (*cusp*), in front of and behind which were single small cusps. As in reptiles the upper and lower teeth alternated in the jaws so that each lower tooth fit between, and internal to, two upper teeth. This primitive arrangement became modified by the increasing size of the accessory cusps, their "rotation" with respect to the principal cusp to form reversed triangles, and the addition of sharp crests between the cusps. The triangles of the upper teeth had the principal cusp located internally, whereas the principal cusp of the lower molar was external to the accessory cusps. As the molar teeth came together during mastication, the lower triangular teeth fit into the embrasures between the reversed upper triangular teeth. In this way food interposed between the teeth was not only punctured between the cusps but the crests joining the cusps moved

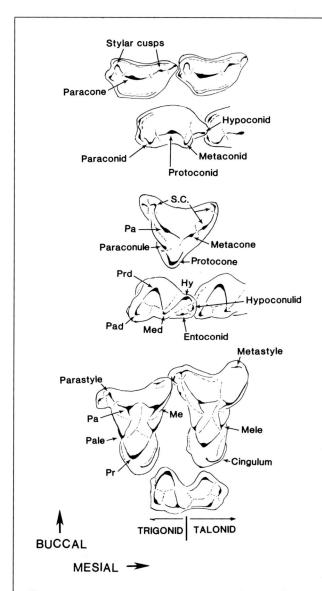

Three stages in the evolution of the tribosphenic molar. Top: *Kuehneotherium* from the later Triassic; middle: *Aegialodon*, early Cretaceous (upper tooth reconstructed); bottom: *Kennalestes*, Cretaceous (Santonian). For each taxon upper-left teeth are at the top and lower-right teeth at the bottom. Tooth cusps are identified in full as they first appear and in abbreviated form thereafter. (Abbreviations: end, entoconid; hy, hypoconid; hyd, hypoconulid; me, metacone; med, metaconid; mele, metaconule; mes, metastyle; pa, paracone; pad, paraconid; pale, paraconule; pas, parastyle; pr, protocone; prd, protoconid; s.c., stylar cusps.) (Redrawn after Crompton, 1971; Crompton and Kielan-Jaworoska, 1978.)

across one another, producing a shearing action to cut the food. A further modification was the addition of a small "heel" onto the back of the lower cheek teeth that served initially as a "stop" to prevent food particles from being driven onto the gums. As this surface expanded, it served as a platform for crushing food against the upper principal cusp. The modi-

fications just described served as the basis for the *tribosphenic molar* of therian mammals. This molar pattern underlies and was ancestral to the first primates.

Basic Characters of Eutherian Dental Structure

As judged from the study of Cretaceous eutherian mammals and living dentally primitive eutherians, the adult ancestors of primates had three incisors, one canine, four premolars, and three molars on each side of the mouth in upper and lower jaws. This configuration may be expressed as a *dental formula* of 3.1.4.3/3.1.4.3. The incisors and canines had a deciduous precursor; the first premolar (the one closest to the canine) apparently did not, but the second through fourth premolars had deciduous precursors. Permanent molars lacked deciduous counterparts. Thus the primitive eutherian *deciduous* dental formula was 3.1.3/3.1.3.

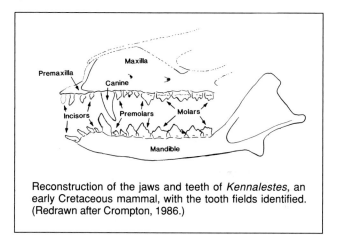

Reconstruction of the jaws and teeth of *Kennalestes*, an early Cretaceous mammal, with the tooth fields identified. (Redrawn after Crompton, 1986.)

The eutherian ancestor of primates had small, cylindrical to slightly spatulate incisors with blunt tips. The canines were larger than the incisors, slightly curved, and projected above the plane of the incisors and premolars. The upper canine was the first tooth behind the premaxilla/maxilla suture. The premolars changed in shape from front to back. The first was a cone, compressed laterally. The second and third premolars showed an increased complexity by the addition of cusps and crests. The fourth of the series may have been a complex molarlike tooth.

The three upper molars of the generalized eutherian ancestors of primates had three principal cusps arranged in a triangle, the *trigone*. The *protocone* was the sole lingual cusp. (According to anatomical convention the side of each tooth closest to the front of the tooth arcade is its *mesial* side; the side farthest from the front of the jaw is its *distal* side. The tongue side of a tooth is the *lingual* side, and that closest the cheek is the *buccal* side.) There were two buccal cusps, the *paracone* mesially and the *metacone* distally. A pair of sharp, curved crests led buccally away from the protocone defining a small central trigone basin. Between the protocone and paracone was a *paraconule*, while between the protocone and metacone was a *metaconule*. Protoconule and metaconule also each had a pair of crests running buccally from them to either side of the buccal cusps.

Buccal to the paracone and metacone was a wide region called the *stylar shelf*, strongly developed in primitive eutherian mammals. The significant development of this region may be accounted for by the large size of the crests running mesiobuccally from the paracone and distobuccally from the metacone. The ends of those crests were supported by small cusps called the *parastyle* and *metastyle*, respectively. The cusps of the upper and lower teeth served as puncturing devices in the initial stages of mastication. The crests were important during the precise cutting-up of food before swallowing.

Lastly, mention should be made of the molar *cingulum*, a raised rim at the edges of the crowns. Upper molars of early mammals had a well-developed cingulum on the buccal margins of the stylar shelf and on the mesial and distal margins as well. The triangular shape of the molars of early mammals leaves a space or embrasure lingually between the protocones of adjacent molars into which the principal lingual cusp of the lower molars, the protoconid, fits (see below). The role of the cingulum was apparently to deflect away from the gums any food particles driven upward by the movement of the protoconid into this space. Incidental contact occurred, and wear was produced between the protoconid and the distolingual cingulum of the upper molars. Repeatedly in mammalian evolution a small cusp raised fortuitously along this cingulum has been selectively enlarged as a *hypocone*.

Mesially the lower molars of the generalized eutherian ancestors of primates had a triangular arrangement of cusps called the *trigonid*. The trigonid had a single cusp buccally, the *protoconid*, with two lingual cusps, the *paraconid* mesially and the *metaconid* distally. Trigonid cusps were tall and pointed. A pair of sharp curved crests led lingually away from the protoconid toward the paraconid and metaconid.

Behind the trigonid of each lower molar was a heel-like projection, the *talonid*. The talonid was primitively lowered well below the level of, and much narrower than, the trigonid. Centrally the talonid was hollowed out as a basin enclosed by a raised rim of three cusps with their connecting crests. A buccally situated cusp, the *hypoconid*, supported short crests running mesially to the base of the trigonid and distally to the back of the tooth. Lingually was an

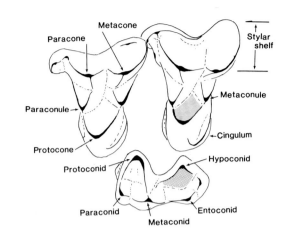

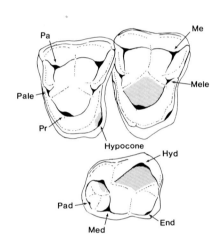

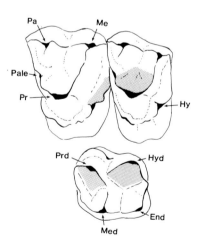

Upper and lower molars. Top: *Kennalestes*, a Cretaceous mammal; middle: *Omomys carteri*, a middle Eocene primate; and bottom: *Saimiri sciureus*, a living monkey. Various features mentioned in the text are indicated. Crushing surfaces of the protocone and hypocone (if present) are indicated by stippling. (*Kennalestes* redrawn after Crompton and Kielan-Jaworoska, 1978.)

entoconid with crests running up to the *metaconid* and toward a distal cusp, the *hypoconulid*.

The triangle formed by the talonid cusps was reversed from that of the upper-molar trigone, and the trigonid cusps were fitted into the embrasures between the upper cheek teeth. In the case of the first lower molar (M_1) the space was between the upper fourth premolar and first molar (P^4 and M^1); M_2 fit between M^1 and M^2; and so forth. The talonid basin was fitted over the protocone when the teeth were fully occluded.

Chewing Behavior in Mammals

The mechanisms by which the teeth are used to bring food into the mouth, called *ingestion*, is accomplished with the incisor teeth assisted by the canines and premolars when more force is required to separate a bite of food. Once the food is in the mouth, *mastication* is the process by which it is broken up by the premolars and molars and mixed with lubricating and digestive juices before swallowing. The complex structure of the molars is best understood by reference to the masticatory process in living primitive mammals, such as the American opossum. In the beginning stages of mastication large particles of food are punctured and crushed between the projecting and pointed cusps of the molars. After the food is sufficiently softened and divided, the masticatory process becomes more regular. The lower jaw is shifted to the side where chewing is to occur. The teeth are brought into position so that the lower and upper outer crests are vertically aligned and in contact. Guided by the structural fit between the molars, the lower teeth are moved upward and lingually in the *power stroke*. This movement is terminated when the talonid basin and protocone contact in *centric occlusion*. Then the teeth are dropped out of occlusion as the jaws are opened in preparation for another masticatory cycle. In the masticatory process of structurally primitive mammals chewing occurs on only one side of the jaw at a time, with only incidental contact occurring between the teeth on the opposite side of the jaw.

Precise fitting together of the cusps and crests occurs during the power stroke only after the food is first thoroughly punctured and crushed. After puncture-crushing the principal action is one of shearing, with the crests of the teeth being moved past one another. Several distinctive features of the molar crests of primitive mammals, like *Kennalestes* of the Cretaceous, may be understood with reference to movements in the power stroke. In these forms the protoconid and its associated concavely curved crests moved upward and lingually into an embrasure between triangular upper molars. At first proto-

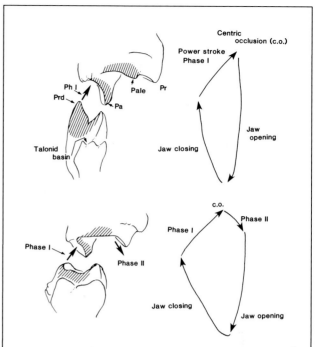

Jaw movement during chewing. Top: Cretaceous mammal *Kennalestes*; bottom: living platyrrhine *Saimiri*. Each tooth pair is arranged to show how a lower molar protoconid and its crest (viewed from the back) moves, first, across the crest leading from the upper-molar paracone and, second, across the crest leading from the paraconule (viewed from the front). This movement is Phase I of the power stroke and terminates when the protocone fits into the talonid basin. In *Kennalestes*, or in living primitive mammals like the American opossum, the jaws are opened from the point of centric occlusion. In *Saimiri* and other primates a second phase (Phase II) begins at centric occlusion. In Phase II the protocone is dragged across the talonid basin before the jaws are opened. The path of the chewing cycle in *Kennalestes* and *Saimiri* viewed from back to front is illustrated on the right. (*Kennalestes* redrawn after Crompton and Kielan-Jaworoska, 1978.)

conid crests engaged reciprocally curved upper-molar crests running mesially from the paracone and distally from the metacone; any food trapped between them was sheared. As the protoconid crests moved farther upward and lingually, they engaged a second set of concavely curved crests running from the paraconule and metaconule. Thus each lower-molar crest moved in sequence past a pair of upper-molar crests. This sequence of shearing events is called *en echelon* shearing. Emphasis was placed in early mammals on en echelon shearing crests associated with the triangular-shaped embrasures between the upper teeth and the mesial and distal sides of the protoconid. Other en echelon shearing blades were also utilized by the hypoconid as it moved upward and lingually into the trigone basin, but these were not as important.

At the apex of the upward and lingual movement

of the lower teeth the talonid basin closed against the protocone in centric occlusion. In primitive mammals the jaws were then moved apart in preparation for the next chewing cycle. Thus the interaction of the teeth to break down the food occurred up to and including centric occlusion, Phase I, with the emphasis on en echelon embrasure shearing. Such crushing as was to be found occurred between the protocone and talonid basin as centric occlusion was reached. There was little or no Phase II grinding of the flat surfaces of the talonid across the protocone after centric occlusion.

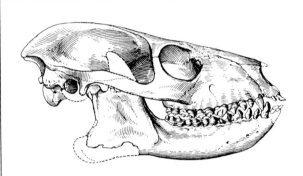

Lateral view of the skull of *Notharctus*, an Eocene primate, illustrating slightly spatulate incisors, projecting canines, and the presence of four premolars and three molars. (From Gregory, 1920.)

Dentition of the Earliest Primates of Modern Aspect

The appearance of the teeth of the first primates of modern aspect, as exemplified by *Notharctus* from the middle Eocene, is in marked contrast with the condition of primitive eutherians. The incisors of primitive primates were reduced to two on each side above and below and became somewhat more spatulate. Canines remained large and projecting. Early forms had four premolars, but the number was soon reduced to three. Changes in molar structure were conditioned by the appearance of and gradually expanded importance of Phase II of the power stroke of mastication. In early primates, such as *Omomys*, more of a premium was placed on the crushing surfaces of the talonid basin and protocone. Following centric occlusion, rather than breaking off occlusal contact as was done in early mammals, the expanded crushing surface of the talonid was dragged across the protocone in a grinding action. As Phase II crushing was enhanced, the importance of en echelon embrasure shearing declined. One cusp importantly associated with embrasure shearing, the paraconid, was greatly reduced or lost. The stylar shelf was reduced in size and importance as the

embrasure-shearing crests leading mesially and distally from the paracone and metacone, respectively, became smaller. Also, the second series of shearing crests associated with the paraconule and metaconule was deemphasized for similar reasons. There was an increased importance of crests associated with the talonid basin and its crests and the protocone and its crests.

General Tendencies in Primate Evolution

The dentitions of living primates have departed widely from the primitive primate condition. The following summarizes a few of the specializations of the living forms.

Incisors and canines: Incisors of primates have become adapted for a variety of tasks, such as ingestion and grooming. Primitively the paired incisors on each side of the jaw acted in concert with spatulate upper incisors for grasping and manipulating food items to position them for being cut away powerfully by the canines and cheek teeth. Many kinds of early primates reduced the number of incisors and modified them into stabbing, gouging, or piercing teeth. Such structures apparently were useful for extramasticatory uses, ranging from killing or subduing prey to tearing bark from food trees to promote the flow of nutritious gum. The living strepsirhine primates have modified their lower incisors and canines to form a comb for grooming fur. Some strepsirhine species have further modified the tooth comb for the purposes of prying up bark or scraping gum. The incisors of anthropoids are more spatulate and are used for powerfully separating a bite of food for mastication.

Canines: Whereas in lemurs the lower canine became part of the tooth comb, primitive projecting canines are retained in most living anthropoids, where they have many uses, including the powerful prying open of tough food. In many anthropoids the canines of males are much larger than those of females. Canine sexual dimorphism is best accounted for by sexual selection as well as the role of males in protecting the social unit from predation.

Premolars: Repeatedly in primate evolution the premolars have been reduced in number and the premolar battery broadened and shortened. Only occasionally, among some Eocene forms, are four premolars found. More commonly the number has been reduced to three or even two, as among the Old World monkeys and apes. A striking development among lemurs is the enlargement of the lower mesial premolar, P_2, into a caninelike tooth in association with the incorporation of the lower canine into the tooth comb. Among anthropoids the front premolar, P_2 or P_3, is modified at the front for shearing against the upper canine. In some Old World monkeys this development has reached an extreme where the mesial surface of this lower premolar is elongate and its enamel migrates onto the root, forming a "hone" for sharpening the upper canine.

Molars: Many of the changes of the occlusal patterns have been importantly mediated by selection for specialized diets. This being so, and since so many of the dietary specializations of primates (e.g. for leaf eating and fruit eating) have occurred in parallel in a number of independent lineages, there are a number of recurring themes in primate molar evolution. For example, there has been the tendency for a reduction in the height of the trigonid and a reduction of the crests running from the protocone, with an accompanying loss of the paraconid. Accompanying the lower molar changes are a reduction of the importance of the stylar cusps and crests and loss of the paraconule and metaconule and their crests. These changes are a reflection of a move away from the system of en echelon embrasure shearing, where the protoconid and its crests are moved into the embrasures between the upper teeth. An increase in the importance of Phase II crushing and grinding may have been the driving force behind these changes. As the talonid basin (and its principal cusp, the hypoconid) and protocone expanded, and with the appearance of the hypocone and expanded trigonid crushing/grinding surfaces, there was little space available for embrasure shearing. The emphasis has shifted to shearing crests that surround the crushing surfaces, such as those associated with the protocone and hypocone. Thus there has not always been a move away from shearing as such. Rather, there was a shift from embrasure shearing to shearing between crests on the edges of the talonid basin and protocone.

Trends in Relation to Social and Dietary Selection

Teeth have become adapted for many specialized tasks in primates. Some of these are best understood as nondietary adaptations, while others have to do primarily with the diet. Most nondietary specializations are restricted to the incisors and canines. A good example is the strepsirhine tooth comb, with which the animal grooms its fur. Especially among anthropoid primates there is a strong correlation between social structure and sexual dimorphism in the canines. Males and females of monogamous or polyandrous anthropoids tend to have similar-sized canines, whereas the canines of polygnous species tend to be quite dimorphic. In extreme cases the canines of males can be more than 25 percent larger than those of females. Another factor influencing canine dimorphism is terrestriality. Primates that

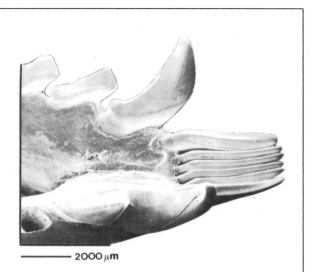

The lower teeth of a prosimian showing a tooth comb consisting on each side of the mandible of two incisors and a canine. (Photograph courtesy of K. Rose.)

spend more time foraging on the ground tend to be more dimorphic than their arboreal close relatives.

Primates eat many kinds of plants and animal foods, but each species tends to specialize on just a few. A part of this dietary specialization is modification in the structure of the teeth. Many primates are insect eaters, and this was the diet of the most primitive primates of the Paleocene and Eocene. The front teeth of living insectivorous primates have structural designs that are often more a reflection of nonfeeding adaptations than strictly of dietary habits. For example, insect-eating strepsirhines have tooth combs that are essentially the same as their more frugivorous close relatives. In contrast the cheek teeth of all insect-eating primates are quite distinctive and stereotyped. The molars of insect eaters have sharply pointed cusps and well-developed, trenchant shearing crests. These structures assist in puncturing the tough chitinous exoskeletons of insects and in cutting up the insects to enhance the digestion of the chitin.

Primates have become adapted to a variety of plant diets. These adaptations can be fully appreciated only when the complex interplay of biomechanics and structural/historical factors is understood. For example, adaptations of the front teeth for gum eating differ greatly in living strepsirhines and anthropoids, because the former began the adaptive process with a fully developed tooth comb, whereas the latter started with spatulate incisors and projecting lower canines. Gum-eating strepsirhines have relatively elongate tooth combs to improve their ability to gouge bark and scrape gum. The same sort of adaptation has been achieved in some small gum-eating

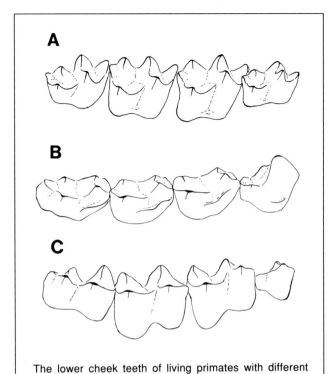

The lower cheek teeth of living primates with different diets: a) insectivorous *Galago senegalensis*; b) frugivorous *Cheirogaleus medius*; c) folivorous *Propithecus verreauxi*. Note that the insectivorous and folivorous taxa have sharper cusps and longer cutting crests than do the frugivorous species.

marmosets by lateral compression, strengthening, and enlargement of typically anthropoid spatulate incisors.

Anthropoids have evolved several other specializations of the front teeth for eating plant foods. Those that eat primarily fruits have enlarged incisors for husking and scraping, whereas those that eat mostly leaves requiring little incisal preparation have comparatively small incisors. The canines of seed-eating anthropoids are enlarged and tusklike.

There are a number of adaptive changes in the cheek teeth of fruit- and leaf-eating primates. Primates that eat fruit or gum have flattened, rounded tooth cusps with an emphasis on crushing and grinding surfaces, but little shearing. In species adapted for eating seeds the molars resemble those of fruit eaters, but the enamel is much thicker to resist the greater forces engendered when seeds are broken. Species that specialize in eating leaves, or other plant parts containing structural carbohydrates, resemble insectivorous species in having strongly developed, trenchant cutting edges on the molars but tend to differ in that they often do not have sharply pointed cusps for puncturing.

See also DIET; SKULL. [R.F.K.]

Further Readings

Crompton, A.W., and Kielan-Jaworowska, Z. (1970) Molar structure and occlusion in Cretaceous therian mammals. In P.M. Butler and K.A. Joysey (eds.): Development, Function and Evolution of Teeth. London: Academic, pp. 249–288.

Hiiemae, K.M., and Kay, R.F. (1972) Trends in the evolution of primate mastication. Nature 240:486–487.

Kay, R.F. (1975) The functional adaptations of primate molar teeth. Am. J. Phys. Anthropol. 43:195–216.

Kay, R.F., and Covert, H.H. (1984) Anatomy of behavior of extinct primates. In D. Chivers, B.A. Wood, and A. Bilsborough (eds.): Food Acquisition and Processing in Primates. New York: Plenum, pp. 467–508.

Kay, R.F., and Hylander, W. (1978) The dental structure of mammalian folivores with special reference to Primates and Phalangeroidea (Marsupialia). In G.G. Montgomery (ed.): The Biology of Arboreal Folivores. Washington, D.C.: Smithsonian Institution Press, pp. 173–191.

TEILHARD DE CHARDIN, PIERRE (1881–1955)

French paleontologist and philosopher. Just as Teilhard's philosophical texts are a curious blending of science and religion, so was his career. As a young student of theology at Ore Place, Hastings in Sussex, England, (1908–1912, 1913), Teilhard assisted in the diggings at Piltdown (1912) and is credited with discovering the canine tooth (1913) that vindicated Smith Woodward's reconstruction. Later, during the late 1920s and early 1930s, he was involved in the early excavations of *Sinanthropus pekinensis* at Zhoukoudian, near Beijing. While in China Teilhard also made some important contributions to paleoprimatology, as well as the fundamental observation of the strong separation between southern and northern Pleistocene faunas on the plains of China, which are not attributable to geographical barriers (such as mountain ranges), unlike such differences throughout the rest of Eurasia. Also while in China he completed the manuscript for *Le Phenomène humaine*, a meditative outgrowth of his scientific researches. In 1946 Teilhard, frustrated in his desire to publish his philosophical works and to teach at the Collège de France, moved to the United States. He spent the last five years of his life living in New York City, where he was associated with the Wenner-Gren Foundation for Anthropological Research.

See also PILTDOWN. [F.S.]

TEILHARDINA *see* ANAPTOMORPHINAE

TELANTHROPUS *see* HOMO ERECTUS

TELL *see* ARCHAEOLOGICAL SITES

TENSIFTIAN *see* PLEISTOCENE; SEA-LEVEL CHANGE

TERNAN *see* FORT TERNAN

TERNIFINE *see* TIGHENIF

TERRESTRIALITY *see* LOCOMOTION

TERTIARY

First, and principal, period of the Cenozoic, including, in order of ascending age, the Paleocene, Eocene, Oligocene, Miocene, and Pliocene epochs. The term was coined by G. Arduino in seventeenth-century studies of the geology in the northern Apennines (Italy), in which he divided the strata into *Primary* (igneous), *Secondary* (metamorphic), *Tertiary* (consolidated strata), and *Quaternary* (unconsolidated strata). The first two terms have long been abandoned, and a growing number of geologists are in favor of replacing the latter two as well, by subdividing the Cenozoic into two approximately equal periods, Paleogene and Neogene. Primates first appear in the fossil record just prior to the Tertiary; the Anthropoidea, which originated in Africa during the Eocene, underwent an explosive radiation in the southern hemisphere during the middle Tertiary.

See also Cenozoic; Neogene; Time Scale. [J.A.V.C., R.L.B.]

TESHIK-TASH

Cave in Soviet Uzbekistan, where in 1938–1939 the partial skeleton of a Neanderthal boy aged ca. nine years was found. The child was apparently buried within an arrangement of goat skulls. The cranium and mandible are particularly well preserved and show clear Neanderthal features in the face, mandible, and cranial vault. The brain size of the child was already large (ca. 1,500 ml.). The antiquity of the specimen is uncertain, although it is often attributed to the last glaciation, but it is especially significant in indicating the eastern extent of Neanderthals during the late Pleistocene.

See also Neanderthals. [C.B.S.]

TETONIUS *see* ANAPTOMORPHINAE

THAILAND

Country of ca. 500,000 sq. km. in the center of mainland Southeast Asia. A variety of Paleolithic assemblages have been reported over the last 50 years. Radiometric dates from the Lampang Province in northern Thailand indicate that Paleolithic artifacts recovered there are older than 0.7 m.y. Two localities, Mae Tha and Ban Don Mun, have yielded unifacially and bifacially worked quartzite cobbles that stratigraphically underlie basalts of reversed polarity. Another locality, Kao Pah Nam, has yielded artifacts and a hearth in association with fauna in a paleo-rock shelter. The locality remains undated, but the mammalian fauna strongly suggests a middle Pleistocene age. Most Paleolithic assemblages from Thailand have been attributed to the Hoabinhian, which, at least locally, seems to have given rise to Neolithic cultures. One such well-known locality is Spirit Cave, where evidence for late Pleistocene plant use has been recovered.

See also Asia (Eastern); Hoabinhian. [G.G.P.]

Further Readings

Pope, G.G., Barr, S., Macdonald, A., and Nakabanlang, S. (1986) Earliest radiometrically dated artifacts from Southeast Asia. Curr. Anthropol. 27:275–279.

Pope, G.G., Frayer, D.W., Liangchareon, M., Kulasing, P., and Nakabanlang, S. (1981) Paleoanthropological investigations of the Thai-American Expedition in northern Thailand (1978–1980): an interim report. Asian Perspective 21:147–163.

THANETIAN *see* PALEOCENE; TIME SCALE

THERMOLUMINESCENCE DATING *see* GEOCHRONOMETRY

THEROPITHECUS *see* CERCOPITHECINAE

THOMAS QUARRIES

Three quarries near Casablanca (Morocco) have produced Pleistocene faunal material, and hominid specimens were found at the Thomas 1 quarry in 1969 (a mandible) and Thomas 3 quarry in 1972 (cranial fragments). The sites are of approximately the same middle Pleistocene age, and they in turn approximate the age of the finds from Salé and Sidi Abderrahman. The Thomas 1 mandible is similar to those from Tighenif (ex-Ternifine), especially mandible 3, but is robust with large teeth, although the third molar is reduced in size. The Thomas 3 cranial fragments have not yet been studied in detail, but they include frontal, facial, and dental parts of a small individual, probably comparable with the Salé specimen in size. The associated teeth, like those of Salé, are large and heavily worn, yet the associated face is delicately built.

See also **Archaic Homo sapiens; Homo erectus**. [C.B.S.]

TIFFANIAN see PALEOCENE; TIME SCALE

TIGHENIF

Open-air site of early middle Pleistocene age (ca. 0.7–0.5 m.y.) in Algeria, previously known as Ternifine or Palikao. It is known for three mandibles and a parietal fragment attributed to *Homo erectus* and for tool assemblages of Acheulean handaxes and flaked pebbles, associated with abundant faunal remains. The artifact and fossil horizons are now submerged under lake waters.

See also **Acheulean; Homo erectus**. [R.P.]

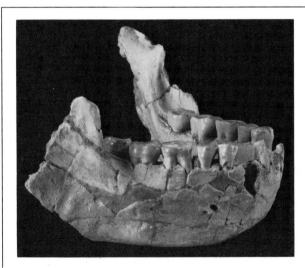

Homo erectus mandible from Tighenif.

TIGLIAN see GLACIATION; PLEISTOCENE

TILL see GLACIATION; PLEISTOCENE

TIME SCALE [see TIME CHART, p. xxxv]

The concept of a geological time scale, consisting of dates (in years) assigned to chronostratigraphic boundaries, is the basic formality of prehistory. The establishment of a realistic, if crudely calibrated, time scale through uniformitarian reasoning was the great triumph of Victorian geology, giving explanatory power to earth history and underpinning the Darwinian revolution in biology. In modern geology developing and refining the time scale continue to be major objectives. Radiometric analyses are the most

widely used calibration tool, but rates in other natural systems (e.g. deep-sea sedimentation; biomolecular differentiation) have been used to interpolate ages for the time scale.

The antiquity of geological strata has been an issue since Hutton, Playfair, and Lyell first raised the possibility that earth history was measured in millions of years, simply in order to account for the building up of the geological succession by observed processes of deposition. The idea that the past extended immeasurably farther back than the beginning of written history or legend has been disconcerting to anthropocentric views, and the geological time scale has repeatedly emerged as a key issue in creationist controversy. To this end "creation science" keeps pace with geology, with recent explanations of radiometric dating, geomagnetic polarity reversals, and seafloor spreading that have as their only test that they agree with a scripturally based time scale of ca. 6 k.y., which was first proposed in rejection of Lyell's views.

Within the scientific community the nineteenth century saw two fundamentally different models of earth history, each with its own implicit and very different time scale. In what may be seen as an overreaction to existing "catastrophist" ideas, which accommodated the brevity of the scriptural scenario, the uniformitarian school of geologists envisaged a steady-state world of ever-repeating cycles, and cycles within cycles, "without a vestige of a beginning, nor any prospect of an end." The timing of the cycles, the youngest of which Lyell recognized as the epochs of the Tertiary, could not be measured except by rough estimates of depositional rates. A time scale without years, published in 1893 by H.S. Williams, calibrated the Phanerozoic (the eon of conspicuously fossil-bearing strata) with a reasonable degree of accuracy in terms of the *chrone*, a unit equivalent to the duration of the Eocene. In the same paper Williams also introduced the term *geochronology*.

On the other hand physicists exploring the laws of thermodynamics showed that energy in any system was available only because of its initial irregular distribution, and through entropy the system would eventually reach a universal average, the "heat death." William Thompson (Lord Kelvin), working from flawed assumptions, calculated that the sun and its planets were following a path of entropy only 100 m.y. in duration, with the solid earth dating from not more than 20 m.y. ago. Although most geologists came to see this as a more realistic way to look at the past, attempts to fit all of earth history into this time frame were not satisfactory.

The reconciliation of these two views followed Becquerel's discovery of radioactivity, which in itself accounted for most of the heat Thompson thought came from a recently molten state, and which later provided the basis for radioactive dating. The progressive cooling of the solid Earth, when viewed as a process begun ca. 4.5 billion years ago, provides all the time needed for the lengthy evolution of atmosphere and continents. It also accommodates the development of the metazoan fossil record over the last 600 m.y., under conditions that were essentially no different from today, as the uniformitarian observations demanded.

Cenozoic Time Scale

A geological time scale for the Cenozoic, covering the period of greatest interest to human evolution, began to take shape only in the 1950s, with the development of the K-Ar and carbon-14 methods, followed by perfection of the uranium fission-track method in the 1960s. In the 1970s refinements of the K-Ar method made it possible to obtain reasonably accurate dates on volcanics as young as the early Pleistocene, while the use of the mass spectrometer doubled the range of the carbon-14 method. At present the effective upper limit of the K-Ar method and the lower limit of carbon-14 leave an interval between ca. 300 and 50 k.y., roughly equivalent to the time of the Neanderthals, in which there are few accepted dates.

Most radiometric techniques, including K-Ar and fission-track, measure the age of a mineral from the time it crystallizes. Some potassium-bearing and uranium-bearing minerals form in sedimentary environments, but for the most part such low-temperature minerals are easily recrystallized and give unreliable dates; the potash mineral glauconite, which forms on the seafloor under restricted conditions, is an arguable exception. The most reliable dating comes from "hard" (i.e. relatively stable) minerals, formed in igneous environments and rapidly transferred to the stratigraphic sequence in lava flows or ashfalls. It is not common to find good fossil beds or magnetostratigraphic sequences in direct association with contemporaneous and datable volcanic deposits, although the attention given to such instances, as in East Africa, may make it seem otherwise. Overshadowing the problems of accuracy in analysis and stratigraphic placement, however, the most difficult task in constructing the time scale is the correlation of dated material to chronostratigraphic boundary levels.

At the present time the generally accepted time scale is based on a series of critically evaluated "hard dates" on high-temperature volcanic minerals, mainly mica and potash feldspar for K-Ar and zircon and apatite for fission-track, and whole lavas, selected on the basis of superior analytical quality and stratigraphical relevance. Most of these "best dates" are from continental deposits, since most datable minerals, glauconite and zircon excepted, are much more susceptible to decomposition in the marine environment. To synthesize the dating in a global framework, however, the preferred dates are all correlated to the standard global deep-sea planktonic microfossil zonations, where they can best be integrated with magnetostratigraphy and stable isotope stratigraphy. The dated levels, as might be expected, seldom coincide exactly on magnetostratigraphic and biostratigraphic boundaries, and interpolations from the selected calibration points are based on estimations of sedimentation rate in the stratigraphic context.

The weakest link in the correlation chain that connects the dated levels to the global time scale is the relationship of the deep-sea stratigraphy to the stage and epoch boundaries. The latter are typified in shallow-marine deposits with abundant shelly macrofossils, pace Lyell, in which substantial parts of the section may be condensed or missing, and in which micropaleontological and magnetostratigraphic data are difficult to interpret. To take one well-known example, until recently all time scales showed the base of the Pliocene at ca. 12–10 m.y., not because the definition of the Pliocene was in doubt but because it had been egregiously miscorrelated from the type areas in Italy and Flanders to the Vienna basin. This level was then correlated from Denmark to Florida according to the first appearance of the equid Hipparion in western Europe and was firmly, and quite accurately, dated with the advent of K-Ar technique both in southern Germany and in North America. The initial correlation error, made by Hans Suess in the late nineteenth century, went undetected until 1970 despite the fact that the actual boundary was only half as old, at 5.3 m.y., and despite the fact that marine fossils, if not deep-water planktonic microfaunas, are abundant both in the Italian Pliocene type section and in the Vienna basin. The Plio-Pleistocene boundary, often given in earlier time scales with values between 3.5 and 1.8 m.y., has also been a problem to correlate to the base of the Calabrian Stage as specified by international agreement. The current value of 1.6 m.y., however, has gained consensus support, partly because it is referred to a section that exposes relatively deep-water sediments, with a clearly developed microbiostratigraphy.

An alternative philosophy of time-scale calibration, considered by its proponents to be "objective" rather than "subjective," includes dates on glauconites in averaging all published ages that have been applied to marine chronostratigraphic boundaries.

The "objective" time scales differ by a few percentage points at some levels (e.g. at the Eocene-Oligocene boundary) compared with the "hard" or "subjective" scale, as summarized here. The variance may be due as much to differences in biostratigraphic or magnetostratigraphic correlation as to real differences in calibration, but the subject has aroused much controversy.

Molecular time scales for particular phylogenies, which are independent of stratigraphy and therefore biological and not geological despite their time scope, have also been developed. These assume invariant and irreversible rates of differentiation in complex proteins, such as RNA, hemoglobin, and immune-system enzymes. Under these assumptions the amount of difference between any two living species, in terms of their mutual difference from a third species, is a function of the time since they became genetically distinct. Quantification of this difference in years has proven difficult, with estimates of the human–great-ape split ranging from 8 to 3 m.y. ago. The basic tenet of invariant rates has also been questioned on theoretical grounds.

See also BIOCHRONOLOGY; CENOZOIC; GEOCHRONOMETRY; MOLECULAR CLOCK; PALEOMAGNETISM. [J.A.V.C.]

Further Readings

Berggren, W.A., Kent, D.V., Flynn, J.J., and Van Couvering, J.A. (1985) Cenozoic geochronology. Geol. Soc. Amer. Bull. 96:1407–1418.

Haq, B.U., Hardenbol, J., and Vail, P.R. (1987) A chronology of fluctuating sea-levels since the Triassic. Science 235:1156–1165.

Odin, G.S., ed. (1985) Numerical Dating in Stratigraphy, Part 1. New York: Wiley.

TINDERET   *see*   FORT TERNAN; KENYA

TINDERETIAN   *see*   TIME SCALE

TINGTSUN   *see*   DINGCUN

TINIMOMYS   *see*   PAROMOMYIDAE

TJONGERIAN   *see*   UPPER PALEOLITHIC

TLAPACOYA

Archaeological site in the Basin of Mexico, generally thought to be important in establishing a firm association between artifacts and bones of extinct animals. Although evidence for human use of the site is scanty, radiocarbon dates of 20,000 B.P. derive from a hearthlike depression and a fallen tree immediately beneath which a bifacial blade was found. Andesite implements and a chalcedony scraper uncovered at this site have also been attributed to this early period.

See also AMERICAS; PALEOINDIAN. [L.S.A.P., D.H.T.]

TOOL MAKING   *see* STONE-TOOL MAKING

TOOTH WEAR   *see*   TEETH

TORRALBA   *see*   AMBRONA

TORRE IN PIETRA

Open-air archaeological site located 24 km. northwest of Rome (Italy), dated to the later middle Pleistocene by fauna (*Equus caballus, Elephas antiquus, Bos primigenius, Rhinoceros mercki, Cervus elaphus*) and K-Ar. The archaeological horizon at the base of fluviatile sands and gravels is underlain by a tuff dated to 0.43 m.y. Excavated by A. Blanc, the lithic industry at this site is referable to the Acheulean.

See also ACHEULEAN; EUROPE. [A.S.B.]

TORREJONIAN   *see*   PALEOCENE; TIME SCALE

TORTOISE CORE   *see* STONE-TOOL MAKING

TORTONIAN   *see*   MIOCENE; TIME SCALE

TORUS, SUPRAORBITAL   *see*   SKULL

TRACHYPITHECUS   *see*   COLOBINAE

TRANSFERRIN   *see*   IMMUNOLOGICAL DISTANCE; MOLECULAR ANTHROPOLOGY

TRANSFORMATION SERIES

Set of states of the same character in different members of a group of organisms that is believed to represent a morphocline from primitive to derived.

See also CLADISTICS; CLINE; EVOLUTIONARY MORPHOLOGY; EVOLUTIONARY SYSTEMATICS; MORPHOCLINE. [I.T.]

TREENE *see* GLACIATION; PLEISTOCENE

TREE SHREWS

The tree shrews comprise an order, Scandentia, of small mammals that are widespread throughout the forested areas of both insular and mainland Southeast Asia. The best-known tree-shrew genus is *Tupaia*, the common tree shrew, which is represented by numerous species; but even this is poorly studied, and little indeed is known about the other five treeshrew genera in their native habitats.

The tree shrews are of particular interest to primatologists because for many years these mammals were considered to be the "most primitive" of the primates. Various authors pointed particularly to certain aspects of their brain and basicranial anatomy, as well as to their possession of a postorbital bar (a bony strut defining the lateral edge of the orbit that is also characteristic of all living primates), to justify the inclusion of the tree shrews in Primates; today, however, it is clear that this relationship cannot be substantiated. In some ways *Tupaia* probably does resemble the earliest primates, for instance in being a clawed, moderately small-bodied, opportunistic frugivore that lives in solitary-ranging pairs. But in general these are primitive eutherian mammal traits and not characteristically primate ones. Scandentia possibly forms part of a major group, Archonta, to which bats, colugos, primates, and maybe elephant shrews also belong; but this remains to be firmly demonstrated.

See also ARCHONTA; PRIMATES. [I.T.]

Further Readings

Luckett, W.P., ed. (1980) Comparative Biology and Relationships of Tree Shrews. New York: Plenum.

Tattersall, I. (1984) The tree-shrew, *Tupaia*: a "living model" of the ancestral primate? In N. Eldredge and S. Stanley (eds.): Living Fossils. New York: Springer-Verlag.

TREMACEBUS *see* PITHECIINAE

TRIBE

Category of the classificatory hierarchy that lies below the subfamily and above the genus. Subtribes may, however, be interposed between the tribe and the genus. The *International Code of Zoological Nomenclature* recommends that the suffix "-ini" be used to terminate tribe names.

See also CLASSIFICATION; NOMENCLATURE. [I.T.]

TRINIL

Fossil-collecting area in central Java; dated to the

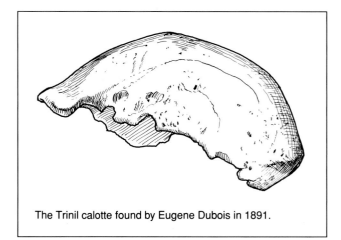

The Trinil calotte found by Eugene Dubois in 1891.

middle Pleistocene by lithostratigraphic correlation. Trinil is the name of a village on the Solo River in east-central Java, close to where E. Dubois unearthed the first evidence of *Homo erectus* in 1891. The evidence consisted of a molar, skullcap, and femur that Dubois christened "*Pithecanthropus erectus.*" Dubois's original find was initially the subject of much controversy. Not only did his contemporaries question the specimens' status as a hominid ancestor, but they also criticized his association of the femur with the skullcap. Decades later Dubois modified his own position and considered that the specimen represented some form of giant "gibbonoid" primate that was nonetheless ancestral to modern humans.

Today paleoanthropologists are unanimous in recognizing these specimens as *Homo erectus*. They were excavated from a gravel bed that has been correlated with the lower portion of the Kabuh Formation, whose Trinil Fauna is usually considered to span the middle Pleistocene. However, controversy about the absolute and relative age of the locality and fauna continues today. Some workers feel that the Trinil Fauna actually predates the reputedly early Pleistocene Djetis Fauna. Others feel that they are the same age (i.e. early middle Pleistocene). Presently the only thing that virtually all workers agree on is that both the fauna and the hominid(s) were transported prior to deposition. Subsequent excavations, some on a massive scale, have failed to unearth more hominid finds from Trinil.

See also ASIA (EASTERN); DJETIS; INDONESIA; SANGIRAN DOME. [G.G.P.]

TRINOMEN *see* SUBSPECIES

TROGOLEMUR *see* ANAPTOMORPHINAE

TROPICAL FOREST *see* PRIMATE ECOLOGY

TSHITOLIAN

Central African Later Stone Age industry named after Bene Tshitolo, a Luba group occupying the plateau north of Bibange in Kasai Occidentale Province (Zaire). The Tshitolian is characterized by blade and discoidal core technology; arrowheads with tangs, shanks, or wings; microlithic elements, especially *tranchet* arrowheads, trapezes, and segments, together with a continuation and refinement of such Lupemban forms as lanceolate and bifacial foliate points, biconvex core-axes, core and flake scrapers, and choppers. The industry is often associated with evidence of intensive grain and tuber exploitation or possibly cultivation in the form of pottery, bored stones, and grindstones. Radiocarbon ages range from ca. 13,000 to 2000 B.P., and the distribution is restricted to forest and forest-savanna mosaics in and around the eastern Congo basin, with possible extensions into the savanna areas of Rwanda and Burundi.

See also LATER STONE AGE; LUPEMBAN; MESOLITHIC; NEOLITHIC; STONE-TOOL MAKING. [A.S.B.]

TUFF *see* GEOCHRONOMETRY

TUGENIAN *see* TIME SCALE

TUPAIA *see* TREE SHREWS

TUPAIIDAE *see* TREE SHREWS

TURKANAPITHECUS

Fossil hominoid from Kalodirr, in northern Kenya, dated to ca. 17 m.y. ago. *Turkanapithecus kalakolensis* is represented by a partial skull, an upper jaw, and some postcranial elements. Its relationships are unknown at present.

See also HOMINOIDEA; MURUAROT. [P.A.]

TUROLIAN *see* TIME SCALE

TURSAC INTERSTADIAL *see* GLACIATION; PLEISTOCENE

TYPE SPECIES *see* GENUS; NOMENCLATURE

TYPE SPECIMEN *see* NOMENCLATURE

TYPICAL MOUSTERIAN *see* MOUSTERIAN

TYRRHENIAN *see* PLEISTOCENE; SEA-LEVEL CHANGE

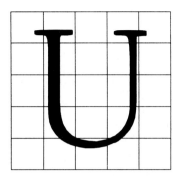

U.S.S.R.

Largest nation in the modern world, with a maximum dimension of ca. 11,000 km. (east-west) and an area of ca. 14 million sq. km., spanning two continents: Europe and Asia. Few fossil primates are known, but ?*Dryopithecus* inhabited the Caucasus (Georgia) in the middle Miocene, and cercopithecids are known from the late Miocene, late Pliocene, and late Pleistocene. The earliest unequivocal evidence for human occupation comes from the southernmost Caucasian and Central Asian regions of the Soviet Union. Numerous localities with predominantly pebble-chopper tools and flakes are known from Central and East Asia. The most secure lithic evidence comes from the stratified site Karatan I, found in a 90-m. loess deposit in Tadzhikistan. Materials from this site have been thermoluminescence-dated to ca. 200,000 B.P. Industries with handaxes have been found in numerous localities in western Asia and the Caucasus. The least ambiguous data on hominid occupation here come from the stratified Azych, Kudaro I and III, and Tsona cave sites in the Caucasus. Faunal and pollen data indicate that these upland sites were first occupied during a warm interglacial period, possibly the one preceding the Okskoye (=?Elster) glaciation. While the lowest layer at Azych contains chopper-chopping tools in association with a Tiraspol fauna, the lowest deposits at Tsona and Kudaro contain handaxe industries that at the Kudaro sites are associated with hearths. Data for early human occupation of the European U.S.S.R. are more ambiguous and come from a number of localities (e.g. Korolevo, Luka-Vrublevetskaya, Mikhailovka) with heavily weathered stone handaxes and unmodified flakes. While their dating is uncertain, none is considered much older than the penultimate glaciation.

The dating and distribution of these early sites and localities suggest that the Soviet Union was occupied first during the middle Pleistocene and that it was possibly populated from disparate areas including the Indian subcontinent, the Near East, and central and western Europe. Neanderthals are known from the Teshik-Tash Cave in Uzbekistan and from the caves of Kiik Koba and Staroselye in Crimea. Late Paleolithic sites, some with structures, burials, and portable art, include Dyuktai, Malta, Mezhirich, Molodova, Kostenki, and Sungir.

See also Asia (Eastern); Dryopithecus; Dyuktai; Early Paleolithic; Europe; Kostenki; Malta; Mezhirich; Middle Paleolithic; Molodova; Neanderthals. [O.S.]

Further Readings

Klein, R.G. (1973) Ice-age Hunters of the Ukraine. Chicago: University of Chicago Press.
Soffer, O. (1985) The Upper Paleolithic of the Central Russian Plain. Orlando, Fla.: Academic.
Wymer, J. (1982) The Palaeolithic Age. New York: St. Martin's.

'UBEIDIYA

An open-air archaeological site in fluvial deposits, probably of early middle Pleistocene age, in the Jordan Rift (Israel). Tool assemblages are characterized by choppers and small tools, rarely handaxes. Claims of a Pliocene fauna suggest mixing of older fossils into the artifact levels.

See also Early Paleolithic; Near East. [R.P.]

UGANDA

Nation in East Africa, ca. 240,000 sq. km. in size. Two isolated Miocene volcano-detrital complexes in the Kavirondo country of eastern Uganda have yielded important fossil primates. At Napak the type of *Micropithecus clarki* is associated with *Proconsul major*, *P. africanus*, *Dendropithecus macinnesi*, and *Limnopithecus legetet*. Napak is closely comparable with Koru and Songhor in western Kenya, both in its abundant mammal fauna and in its K-Ar dates of ca. 19 m.y. The somewhat younger Moroto volcanic complex has yielded a famous and nearly complete mandible of a giant proconsul, formerly placed in *P. major*, which was pieced together over the years from fragments collected by schoolboy expeditions.

Other fossil sites in Uganda have no significant hominoid material. Bukwa, on the west flank of Elgon near the Kenyan border, has an important early Miocene fauna like that of Rusinga, last excavated in the 1960s. Sites in the Albert Rift of western Uganda and neighboring parts of Zaire, Rwanda, and Burundi, mainly in the Kazinga Channel between Lake Albert and Lake Edward (Lake Mobutu), have yielded very small and scrappy early and middle Miocene collections. Abundant Mio-Pliocene fossils occur on the Uganda side of Lake Albert in shallow gullies near the village of Kaiso, excavated mainly by W.W. Bishop in the 1950s. Both the paleontology and the stratigraphic relationships at Kaiso are very similar to Kanam (Kenya). Rich sites of roughly the same age have recently been reported on the Zaire side of the lake.

Uganda is the type area of the Sangoan (Middle Stone Age) culture, with numerous sites in the Lake Victoria, Lake Kyoga, and Lake Albert terraces, and in the Kazinga Channel.

See also **AFRICA**; **BISHOP, WILLIAM W.**; **KENYA**. [J.A.V.C.]

Further Readings

Bishop, W.W. (1964) The later Tertiary in East Africa: volcanics, sediments, and faunal inventory. In W.W. Bishop and J.D. Clark (eds.): Background to Evolution in Africa. Chicago: University of Chicago Press, pp. 31-56.

UINTAN *see* EOCENE; TIME SCALE

UINTANIUS *see* OMOMYINAE

ULAZZIAN *see* MOUSTERIAN; UPPER PALEOLITHIC

UPPER CAVE *see* ZHOUKOUDIAN

UPPER PALEOLITHIC

Stage of European Paleolithic development charac-

terized by the development of blade and burin technology, proficient hunting of large game (possibly to extinction in some cases), and sophisticated working of organic materials (bone, antler, horn, ivory, tooth, shell), as well as a proliferation of "jewelry" and of carved/painted/incised images on stone, organic materials, and cave and rock-shelter walls.

Geographical and Chronological Extent
Since later Pleistocene archaeological developments in northwestern and sub-Saharan Africa, India, China, Southeast Asia, Australia, and the New World are substantially different from those in Europe, the Near East, and northeastern Africa, the term "Upper Paleolithic" is often reserved for the blade and burin technologies of the latter regions. In this volume Late Paleolithic is employed for late late Pleistocene industries on a worldwide basis as a broader term, including the Upper Paleolithic, mainly of Europe. Also referred to as "Mode IV" (J.G.D. Clark) or "Leptolithic," Upper Paleolithic industries replaced flake and prepared-core industries, such as the Mousterian, at ca. 35,000 B.P. and were themselves replaced by microlithic technologies between 20,000 and 10,000 B.P. The Upper Paleolithic thus occurred during the maximum cold phases of the last glacial.

In most of Africa outside the northeast a sustained

Very large Upper Paleolithic prismatic blade cores from Upper Perigordian of Rabier (France). (Photograph © Eric Delson.) For tool types, see articles on specific industries.

Late Pleistocene climate and cultural sequences in major Upper Paleolithic sites in southwestern France, ca. 37–11 k.y. (Modified after Laville et al., 1980.) The sequence of Aurignacian phases and the coexistence of Aurignacian and Chatelperronian (=Lower Perigordian) was first based on studies at La Ferrassie, then substantiated at Abri Pataud and Roc de Combe. Laugerie Haute provides the most complete sequence from final Perigordian through middle Magdalenian, overlapping Abri Pataud below and matching La Madeleine (type locality of the Magdalenian) above. Most of these sites have been dated by radiocarbon, and correlation among them has also been proposed by Laville et al. on the basis of interpretation of local environmental indicators, as summarized at the left.

blade and burin technological state is absent from cultural sequences, although blade technology itself appears sporadically within prepared-core and flake sequences (Mode III, Middle Stone Age) at a much earlier date than in Europe. Painted images, decorative objects, bone working, and sophisticated hunting appear in Africa at an age comparable with that of the early Upper Paleolithic, but also in a Mode III (flake technology) context. A widespread shift to Mode V (microlithic) technology accompanied by the more intensive exploitation of small-scale resources begins in Africa by 20,000 B.P., well before the comparable shift to Mode V technologies in most European regions. Culture histories in southern and eastern Asia, the Pacific, and the New World appear equally divergent from the European pattern. It is thus inappropriate to extend the European-based Upper Paleolithic designation beyond the limits of Europe and adjacent regions, exclusive of northwestern Africa. The significant exception is Siberia, where true Upper Paleolithic technologies (although in combination with flake tools), economic adaptations, and symbolic behavior were widespread after 20,000 B.P.

Divisions of the Upper Paleolithic

The classic division of the Upper Paleolithic into Aurignacian, Perigordian, Solutrean, and Magdalenian industries is based on the earliest explorations of sites of this age in southwestern France. The first definition of the Upper Paleolithic by Lartet and Christy was paleontological; the "cave bear and mammoth" and "reindeer" ages were based on the dominant animals in the faunal remains from many western European Upper Paleolithic sites. Prior to the reindeer age the Aurignacian of Aurignac, Le Moustier, and Abri Lartet was recognized as a transitional industry succeeding the Mousterian at the end of the "cave bear and mammoth age," followed by the Solutrean and Magdalenian of Solutré, La Madeleine, and the Laugerie sites during the "reindeer age."

Subsequent chronologies based on tool typologies rather than stratigraphy were developed by de Mortillet from 1867 to 1910. In these schemes the Aurignacian (incorporating the Perigordian), characterized by elaborate bone tools, was seen as an early stage of the Magdalenian and disappeared as a separate entity by 1881; the Solutrean, with its bifacially worked leaf-shaped points on flakes, was placed between the Mousterian and Aurignacian/Magdalenian. The importance of stratigraphy in determining the relative chronology of Upper Paleolithic subdivisions, and the restoration of the Aurignacian to its appropriate place at the beginning of the Upper Paleolithic, were not established until Breuil's work at the beginning of this century. Basing his conclusions

on the work of Peyrony and others, Breuil also defined three stages within each of three Upper Paleolithic industries: Aurignacian, Solutrean, and Magdalenian. The "lower" and "upper" Aurignacian corresponded to the Chatelperronian and Upper Perigordian, respectively, while the "middle" Aurignacian incorporated the type industry from Aurignac.

In 1933 Peyrony introduced refinements to Breuil's scheme, the most important of which was the separation of the Perigordian (=Breuil's lower and upper Aurignacian) from the Aurignacian *sensu stricto*, and the development of five parallel stages for each tradition or "phylum." The Perigordian was distinguished by the use of backing (abrupt retouch) along one side of a blade to create a point; the Aurignacian was characterized by a series of bone-point forms. Implicit in this scheme was a model of two distinct cultural units, who shared the same terrain in southwestern France over a long period of time (ca. 15 k.y.) but who did not "interbreed" or adopt each other's technology, except in limited instances, represented by the so-called "second-group" Perigordian industries (Perigordian II, Vc) with traces of Aurignacian "admixture." Additionally the "Protomagdalenian" and "Protosolutrean" industries, prior to the Solutrean proper, were defined from Laugerie Haute.

While the subdivisions of the four (or five, if Chatelperronian is separated from Perigordian) recognized Upper Paleolithic industries became more elaborated, it gradually became apparent, through statistical approaches (e.g. de Sonneville-Bordes's 92-type list) and further excavation, that the sequence of the Dordogne did not even apply to eastern France, let alone to other regions of Europe and the Near East. In southern Europe, the Near East, and northeastern Africa small-tool industries (Mode V) become increasingly dominant after 20,000 B.P.; in northern and eastern Europe final Paleolithic industries reflect a greater level of economic specialization and cultural elaboration than in the west. Recently various authors (e.g. Gamble) have proposed the division of the Upper Paleolithic into two major periods: early (EUP) and late (LUP), with a break occurring almost everywhere around the time of the glacial maximum, ca. 20,000–18,000 B.P.

Early Upper Paleolithic Industries of Europe

The earliest blade industry in Europe, from Bacho Kiro (Bulgaria), may date to ca. 40,000 B.P. In several areas the first Upper Paleolithic industries, dated to 35–33 k.y. ago, share many characteristics with the preceding Mousterian industries of the same region. Over half of some Chatelperronian (Perigordian I) assemblages consists of flake tools of Mousterian affinities, and the only skeletal remains identified with this industry to date are those of a Neanderthal (Saint-Césaire). From southern Italy an industry with similar backed knives or points in an assemblage with many flake tools (date ca. 31,000 B.P.) is known as the Uluzzian, from the type site of Uluzzo, near Lecce.

In Hungary and Czechoslovakia leaf-shaped points, similar to those found in later Mousterian (or "Altmühlian") sites of southern Germany, characterize an early Upper Paleolithic industry with both blade tools and Levallois technology, known as the Szeletian; a similar industry, the Jermanovician, is described from Poland. All of these early Upper Paleolithic transitional industries have yielded bone and other organic materials, worked into points, awls, and beads or pendants. The early Upper Paleolithic level at Kent's Cavern (England) also contained leaf-shaped points, although they are unlike the examples from central Europe.

The Aurignacian, known from most European countries south of the North European plain (except the U.S.S.R.), is the most widespread industry of the European Upper Paleolithic. However, some of the apparent similarities between different regions may in fact be due to a common level of technological development rather than to "stylistic" patterns across a common cultural group. It is characterized by blade technology, a range of bone points from split-base to solid forms, a proliferation of "jewelry" in ivory, bone, stone, and shell, carved and incised bone and antler, heavy invasive marginal retouch, and thick scrapers and burins (gouges) created by lamellar removals. Initial overlap with the Chatelperronian is demonstrated by interstratification at two sites, and with the Szeletian by differential locations of assemblage types in the landscape. The earliest dated Aurignacian sites (ca. 34,000 B.P.) are in southern Germany, in association with numerous carved figurines (Vogelherd, Geissenklösterle), and in southern France (Abri Pataud): The "richest" sites both in density and in elaboration of boneworking and carving are located in areas dominated by large gregarious herbivores (horse, mammoth, reindeer). In the Mediterranean region Aurignacian sites are rare or absent, although some of them (e.g. Vindija) are associated with humans supposedly intermediate in morphology between Neanderthals and *Homo sapiens sapiens*.

Upper Perigordian industries characterized by narrow backed points (gravettes) and associated with certain types of bone points, perforated teeth, and female figurines in stone and ivory are known from southwestern France; industries with related specific stone-tool types, termed either Perigordian or Gravettian, occur in Germany, Belgium, Spain, and

Italy. To the east and north a similar group of industries, but with a variety of different point types, known as the Eastern Gravettian (including Pavlovian, and at the early Kostenki sites), occur from Poland to Russia and south to Romania, Yugoslavia, and Greece. As in the Aurignacian the development of carvings (figurines), decorative items, elaborate group burials (Předmosti, Sungir), and site complexity is greatest in the areas associated with large herbivores, such as eastern Europe, with little boneworking or personal ornamentation in association with Mediterranean sites (with the significant exception of the Grimaldi Caves).

Late Upper Paleolithic Industries of Europe
The Weichselian glacial maximum (20,000–18,000 B.P.) was marked by the abandonment of many areas of northern Europe and by the intensification of adaptations in southern Europe in the context of Solutrean industries, characterized by bifacial and unifacial leaf-shaped points and a profusion of carved and engraved images. As the climate began to moderate, regionally diverse and elaborate industries developed in Europe. In Switzerland, France, Spain, Belgium, and Germany Magdalenian industries with highly developed bone and antler technology, including barbed harpoons, backed microblades, and in the latest sites geometric microliths, were widespread between ca. 17 and 12 k.y. Most of the painted caves in France and Cantabrian Spain are associated with this industrial group and probably reflect large-scale regional interactions among bands of hunters.

On the North European plain a group of industries characterized by backed knives (*Federmesser*) and tanged points reflect specialized reindeer hunting and are locally known as Hamburgian (Germany), Tjongerian (Low Countries), and Creswellian (England). In eastern Europe and the Russian Plain a variety of assemblage types with backed points (evolved Gravettian) and other tools, such as truncation burins and geometric microliths, are associated with a proliferation of carved ivory ornaments, mammoth-bone "huts" of varying dimensions, and considerable evidence for long-distance trade and possibly social stratification.

In southeastern and Mediterranean Europe, on the other hand, the backed-point (Gravettian) tradition continues in the form of much smaller tools ("Epigravettian"), with limited evidence of elaboration in images, decorative elements, or carved bone and antler, with the significant exception of the Pyrenees region of Spain (especially Parpalló). Long-distance trade is evident, however, in the importation of obsidian from Melos to the Greek mainland (Franchthi

Cave), and sites in northwestern Greece suggest seasonal movement and scheduling of resource use.

Near East and Northeastern Africa

The Upper Paleolithic of the Near East and northeastern Africa does not follow the classic western European sequence, except in the general resemblance of some of the industries (e.g. Antelian) to the widespread Aurignacian of Europe. Additionally, the earliest blade industries in both the Near East and North Africa (Amudian, pre-Aurignacian) occur in the midst of or prior to a Middle Paleolithic sequence (Haua Fteah, Jabrud, Tabūn). Following the Middle Paleolithic in the Levant a six-stage sequence is often recognized, based on the Mount Carmel sites, and demonstrates a slow development from flake-blade industries with triangular leaf-shaped points and many Mousterian forms (Emiran, Stage 1 = Lower Antelian) to evolved microlithic ones (Kebaran, Stage 6). The intervening stages are known variously as Antelian 2 through 5, Aurignacian (= Antelian 3, 4 = Upper Antelian), and Athlitian (= Antelian 5). As in southeastern Europe the final industries are microlithic and continue into the Mesolithic without a sharp break.

In eastern North Africa (e.g. Haua Fteah) an early blade industry, the Dabban, at ca. 40,000 B.P. is succeeded by a backed-microblade (Mode V) industry, the eastern Oranian, at ca. 18,000–16,000 B.P. The sequence in the Nile Valley is more complicated and reflects overlapping influences from the blade-using cultures of the Near East and Cyrenaica, and the flake and Late Stone Age industries of sub-Saharan Africa. In Ethiopia and Kenya industries based on blades (Hargesian, Eburran) appear toward the end of the late Pleistocene but are not accompanied by the evidence of elaborate painting, carving, and bone-working characteristic of European Upper Paleolithic sites. Grindstones used both for food processing (tubers, wild grains) and for pigment grinding are common at many African sites, however.

Upper Paleolithic Adaptations

Major innovations of Upper Paleolithic people signify an increasing ability to exploit cold environments. These included improved technologies, especially bone and antler working, but also the invention of the spear thrower, harpoon, bow and arrow, fish weir, calendar or other notation of time or seasonal change, eyed needle for tailored clothing, controlled

Part of the Upper Paleolithic shelter of Laugerie-Haute, where a long sequence from Perigordian through Magdalenian industries is preserved. (Photograph © Eric Delson.)

high-temperature-hearth and ceramic technology (Dolni Věstonice), boats (Melian obsidian on Greek mainland), stone lamps (Lascaux), and other items especially important in a culture dependent on animal protein for long periods of the year. Evidence of long-distance trade, large-scale ritual sites, and possible social stratification indicates the development of social mechanisms to reduce risk in unpredictable environments. The greater density of remains and the faunal dominance of particular sites by single species may indicate increased scheduling of resource use, as well as a greater amount of mass-processing and storage against hard times (logistical behavior).

See also ABRI PATAUD; AGGREGATION-DISPERSAL; AMUD; AMUDIAN; ARCHAIC MODERNS; ASIA (EASTERN); ATHLITIAN; AURIGNAC; AURIGNACIAN; AWL; BACHO KIRO; BADEGOULIAN; BARADOSTIAN; BATON DE COMMANDEMENT; BLADE; BOW AND ARROW; BURIN; CHATELPERRONIAN; CLOTHING; CRESWELLIAN; CRO-MAGNON; CUEVA MORIN; DABBAN; DIET; DOLNI VĚSTONICE; DOMESTICATION; ECONOMY, PREHISTORIC; EMIRAN; EPIGRAVETTIAN; EPIPALEOLITHIC; EUROPE; EXOTICS; FIRE; FLAKE-BLADE; GRAVETTIAN; HAMBURGIAN; HARPOON; HAUA FTEAH; HOLOCENE; *Homo sapiens*, HOWIESON'S POORT; HUNTER-GATHERERS; IBERO-MAURUSIAN; ISTALLÖSKÖ; JEWELRY; KEBARA; KEBARAN; KOSTENKI; LA FERRASSIE; LASCAUX; LATE PALEOLITHIC; LATER STONE AGE; LAUGERIE SITES; LE MOUSTIER; LEVALLOIS; MAGDALENIAN; MALTA; MAN-LAND RELATIONSHIPS; MESOLITHIC; MEZHIRICH; MIDDLE PALEOLITHIC; MOLODOVA; MOUSTERIAN; MUSICAL INSTRUMENTS; NEANDERTHALS; NEAR EAST; PALEOLITHIC; PALEOLITHIC CALENDAR; PALEOLITHIC IMAGE; PALEOLITHIC LIFEWAYS; PAVLOV; PERIGORDIAN; PLEISTOCENE; PRE-AURIGNACIAN; PŘEDMOSTI; PROTOMAGDALENIAN; PROTOSOLUTREAN; RAW MATERIALS; RITUAL; ROMANELLIAN; SAGAIE; SAINT-CÉSAIRE; SKHŪL; SOLUTRÉ; SOLUTREAN; SPLIT-BASE BONE POINT; STONE-TOOL MAKING; SUNGIR; SZELETIAN; TABŪN. [A.S.B.]

Further Readings

Gamble, G. (1986) The Palaeolithic Settlement of Europe. Cambridge: Cambridge University Press.

Klein, R.G. (1969) Man and Culture in the Late Pleistocene: A Case Study. New York: Chandler.

Laville, H., Rigaud, J.-P., and Sackett, J.R. (1980) Rock Shelters of the Périgord. New York: Academic.

Soffer, O. (1985) The Upper Paleolithic of the Central Russian Plain. Orlando, Fla.: Academic.

Wymer, J. (1982) The Palaeolithic Age. New York; St. Martin's.

URANIUM-SERIES DATING *see* GEOCHRONOMETRY

URANIUM-THORIUM DATING *see* GEOCHRONOMETRY

USE-WEAR, LITHIC *see* LITHIC USE-WEAR

USNO *see* OMO

UTAHIA *see* OMOMYINAE

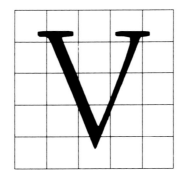

VAIL CURVE *see* SEA-LEVEL CHANGE

VALID *see* CLASSIFICATION;
NOMENCLATURE

VALLESIAN *see* TIME SCALE

VALLOIS, HENRI VICTOR (b. 1889)

French anatomist and paleoanthropologist. Following his mentor, M. Boule, at the Muséum National d'Histoire Naturelle in Paris, Vallois became the leading proponent during the 1940s and 50s of the "presapiens theory," whereby Neanderthals were seen as not ancestral to modern *Homo sapiens*. According to this viewpoint modern humans are derivatives of a separate lineage. Vallois considered the specimens of Piltdown (prior to exposure of forgery in 1953), Fontéchevade, and Swanscombe to be evidence of a European "presapiens" lineage. More recent analyses, however, have shown that these specimens are not significantly different from other contemporaneous hominids.

See also BOULE, MARCELLIN; HOMO SAPIENS;
NEANDERTHALS. [F.S.]

VALLONNET

Early archaeological and faunal site in a cave near Nice at Roquebrune-Cap-Martin, in southeastern France. The combination of an early middle Pleistocene (early Biharian) fauna, "cold" pollen, and normal magnetic polarity suggests association with the "Günz" glaciation and the Jaramillo subchron, age ca.

0.95–0.9 m.y. To date this could be the oldest archaeological site in Europe, with a simple industry of "pebble tools" and small unmodified flakes.

See also EARLY PALEOLITHIC; EUROPE; FRANCE;
STONE-TOOL MAKING. [A.S.B.]

VARECIA *see* LEMURIDAE

VARIATION *see* EVOLUTION

VARVES *see* GLACIATION;
PLEISTOCENE

VELIKA PECINA

Cave in Yugoslavia that produced a frontal bone in association with early Upper Paleolithic (Aurignacian) artifacts in 1961. This adult frontal bone has a modern form of supraorbital torus and is important as one of the oldest absolutely dated modern specimens in Europe, since the succeeding stratigraphic level has been dated at ca. 34 k.y. by radiocarbon.

See also HOMO SAPIENS. [C.B.S.]

VENUS FIGURINES *see* PALEOLITHIC
IMAGE

VÉRTESSZÖLLÖS

Travertine site near Budapest (Hungary) that produced two hominid specimens between 1964 and 1965. The site is generally dated to a temperate stage within the "Mindel" glaciation of continental Europe, and absolute uranium series dates originally suggested an age of more than 300 k.y. Recent dating attempts, however, suggest an age of only ca. 200 k.y. for the hominid levels. The hominid specimens comprise some teeth of a child (Vértesszöllös 1) and the occipital bone of an adult (Vértesszöllös 2). The affinities and classification of the latter specimen have been the subject of much dispute. Although thick and fairly angulated, with a centrally developed occipital torus, the specimen is also large, with a long and curved occipital plane. The cranial capacity of the whole skull was probably more than 1,300 ml., which has led to suggestions that it is an archaic *Homo sapiens* fossil; but other workers, pointing to its age, thickness, and shape, prefer to classify it as *Homo erectus*. The specimen may well derive from a population similar to that represented at Petralona (Greece).

See also ARCHAIC HOMO SAPIENS; HOMO ERECTUS. [C.B.S.]

VERTICAL CLINGING AND LEAPING *see* LOCOMOTION

VICARIANCE *see* PALEOBIOGEOGRAPHY

VICTORIAPITHECINAE

Subfamily of Cercopithecidae that includes the two earliest genera of Old World monkey, *Victoriapithecus* and *Prohylobates*. The oldest known cercopithecid fossils are probably an upper molar and unpublished canine and elbow fragments from Napak (Uganda), dated to ca. 19 m.y. ago. About 15 jaws and isolated teeth have recently been described from the Kenyan locality of Buluk, dated to 17 m.y., and two teeth were recovered from deposits at Loperot of probably similar age. In North Africa Wadi Moghara (Egypt) yielded three partial lower jaws named *Prohylobates tandyi*, and a single mandible fragment was described from near Gebel Zelten (Libya) and named *P. simonsi*; both of these localities are probably ca. 16 m.y. old. However, it is from the early middle Miocene (ca. 15 m.y. ago) sites on Maboko Island and nearby Nyakach on Lake Victoria (Kenya) that these early monkeys are best known, from over 500 specimens including both teeth and fragmentary postcrania.

Victoriapithecines share an apparently derived mandibular symphysis structure, as well as several features that are probably conservative among cercopithecids or eucatarrhines, such as P_4 long axis slightly oblique to molar row, variably present small hypoconulid on M_{1-2}, and incompletely bilophodont upper molars with persistent crista obliqua (un-

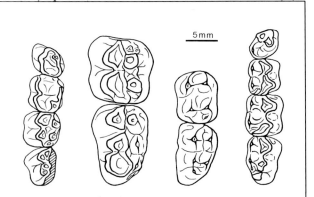

Lower dentition of victoriapithecine cercopithecids, all ca. 16–15 m.y. old, from left to right: *Prohylobates tandyi*, Wadi Moghara (Egypt); *P. simonsi*, Gebel Zelten area (Libya); two jaws of *Victoriapithecus macinnesi*, Maboko Island (Kenya) (to illustrate variation).

known in *Prohylobates*). Molar crown relief is low, the trigonids short, flare moderately developed, and lower-molar bilophodonty (nearly) complete. Several authors have suggested a morphological dichotomy in known postcranial elements, especially of the elbow, indicating one arboreal and one semiterrestrial form (species?), but that has not been supported dentally. Either one species is extremely rare, or the two morphs document sexual or great individual variation. It was previously suggested that the Maboko sample included two species that documented the divergence between cercopithecines and colobines, but that view has been abandoned because the present large sample indicates only a single species. Instead it appears that Victoriapithecinae represents the sister taxon of all later cercopithecids, which share several derived characters that their common ancestor must have evolved after separating from the victoriapithecines.

See also AFRICA; CATARRHINI; CERCOPITHECIDAE; CERCOPITHECINAE; COLOBINAE; KENYA; UGANDA. [E.D.]

Further Readings

Benefit, B., and Pickford, M. (1986) Miocene fossil cercopithecoids from Kenya. Am. J. Phys. Anthropol. 69:441–464.

Delson, E. (1979) *Prohylobates* (Primates) from the early Miocene of Libya: a new species and its implications for cercopithecid origins. Geobios 12:725–733.

Leakey, M.G. (1985) Early Miocene cercopithecids from Buluk, northern Kenya. Folia Primatol. 44:1–14.

Strasser, E., and Delson, E. (1987) Cladistic analysis of cercopithecid relationships. J. Hum. Evol. 16:81–99.

Szalay, F.S., and Delson, E. (1979) Evolutionary History of the Primates. New York: Academic.

VICTORIAPITHECUS *see* VICTORIAPITHECINAE

VICTORIA WEST *see* LEVALLOIS; PREPARED-CORE

VILLAFRANCHIAN *see* TIME SCALE

VILLAGE *see* ARCHAEOLOGICAL SITES; NEOLITHIC

VILLANYIAN *see* TIME SCALE

VINDIJA

Cave in Yugoslavia that during recent excavations has produced a number of fragmentary late Pleistocene fossil hominids from a sequence containing Mousterian and Upper Paleolithic tools. The earlier specimens are Neanderthal-like and the later specimens anatomically modern in morphology. Specimens in an intermediate stratigraphic position, however, are claimed to show a transitional morphology and to be associated with an Aurignacian industry. In any case the specimens in question are very fragmentary, and the archaeological associations need to be clarified by further work.

See also NEANDERTHALS. [C.B.S.]

VINDOBONIAN *see* MIOCENE

VIRCHOW, RUDOLPH (1821–1902)

German pathologist, anthropologist, and statesman. On receiving the M.D. degree from Friedrich Wilhelm Institute of the University of Berlin in 1843, Virchow conducted research into pathological histology. In 1847 he assisted in the founding of the journal *Archiv für Pathologische Anatomie und Physiologie und Klinische Medizin*. In the same year he was appointed lecturer in pathological anatomy at the University of Berlin. Nine years later, largely in recognition of his pioneering contributions to pathology, public health, and sanitary reforms, he was made full professor. In addition to his academic and medical activities Virchow was a political activist and was a member of the Prussian National Assembly and the German Reichstag, where he vigorously opposed the policies of Bismarck. As a scientist Virchow was a cautious empiricist. He considered that Darwin's theory of natural selection lacked sufficient inductive demonstration and persuaded many of his colleagues that the Feldhofer (Neanderthal) skull was merely a pathological specimen. In the late 1860s Virchow played an active role in founding the German Anthropological Society and the Berlin Society for Anthropology, Ethnology, and Prehistory, of which, from 1869 until his death, he was president and editor of the organization's journal, *Zeitschrift für Ethnologie*.

[F.S.]

VOICE BOX *see* SPEECH (ORIGINS OF)

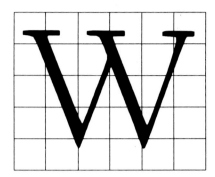

WADI MOGHARA *see* AFRICA; VICTORIAPITHECINAE

WADI MUGHARA *see* SKHŪL; TABŪN

WALLACE, ALFRED RUSSEL (1823-1913)

British naturalist. During his early career Wallace undertook two important collecting expeditions, the first to the jungles of the Amazon (1848-1852) and then to the Malay Archipelago (1854-1862). It was during this latter expedition that he independently formulated a theory of natural selection, which he communicated to Darwin in 1857. In the following year his paper, and extracts from Darwin's letters and manuscripts, were presented under a joint title to the Linnaean Society (London), announcing the theory of evolution by natural selection. With regard to human evolution Wallace, believing in a spiritual purpose behind consciousness, argued that the genus *Homo* had been shielded from the action of natural selection. Wallace also founded the science of evolutionary zoogeography.

See also **DARWIN, CHARLES; EVOLUTION; NATURAL SELECTION.** [F.S.]

WARTHE *see* GLACIATION; PLEISTOCENE

WASATCHIAN *see* EOCENE; TIME SCALE

WASHAKIUS *see* OMOMYINAE

WASHBURN, SHERWOOD L. (b. 1911)

American physical anthropologist. On completing his doctoral thesis (under the direction of E.A. Hooton) at Harvard in 1939, Washburn began his professional career at Columbia University. After World War II he went to the University of Chicago (1947), where he remained until 1958, when he received an appointment at the University of California, Berkeley. Washburn's writings on the "new physical anthropology" during the 1950s and early 1960s did much to heighten anthropological consciousness of changes occurring in evolutionary biology at that time. He also played a major role in determining the theoretical and methodological orientation of primate behavioral research in America during the 1960s. In this same period he advanced an early version of the "knuckle-walking" hypothesis, proposing that the progression from brachiation to bipedalism had involved an intermediate stage similar to modern pongids.

[F.S.]

WEICHSEL *see* GLACIATION; PLEISTOCENE

WEIDENREICH, FRANZ (1873-1948)

German anatomist and paleoanthropologist. After receiving his M.D. degree from the University of Strasbourg in 1899, Weidenreich was appointed professor of anatomy there in 1904. While at Strasbourg his interest in primate evolution was enhanced by his association with G. Schwalbe. After World War I

Weidenreich held several academic appointments at German universities, first at Heidelberg (1919–1927) and then in Frankfurt (1928–1933), before he was obliged to leave Germany because of his Jewish ancestry. Following a short stint at the University of Chicago, he was appointed to succeed Davidson Black at the Peking Union Medical College in 1935. It was here that Weidenreich undertook a protracted study of the fossil hominid ("*Sinanthropus*") materials discovered at Zhoukoudian. His descriptions and interpretations of this material form an imposing series of monographs published in *Palaeontologia Sinica* between 1936 and 1943. With the outbreak of World War II Weidenreich returned to the United States, where until his death he worked at the American Museum of Natural History in New York City.

See also HOMO ERECTUS; ZHOUKOUDIAN. [F.S.]

WEST TURKANA

Informal name referring to fossiliferous Plio-Pleistocene (0.7–4 m.y.) strata exposed west of the northern part of Lake Turkana in northern Kenya, between 3°30′ and 4°20′ N latitude. The total outcrop area is ca. 200 km., mostly in a strip between 5 and 10 km. wide immediately west of the lake. The stratigraphy has not been formally described, but the strata have been correlated with the Koobi Fora Formation east of the lake and with the Shungura Formation north of the lake in southern Ethiopia by analysis of volcanic-ash layers within the sediments. The oldest strata are exposed in the southern half of the area and consist of poorly fossiliferous diatomites, claystones, and sandstones near 4 m.y. in age, which correspond to the lowest part of the Koobi Fora Formation. These are overlain by fossiliferous fluvial and lacustrine deposits mainly between 1 and 4 m.y. old. These younger sediments, for instance at Kaitio, correlate with the main fossiliferous parts of the Koobi Fora and Shungura Formations.

Facies changes are marked and occur over short lateral distances. Basin-margin deposits are represented by volcanic-pebble conglomerates of alluvial fans with associated poorly sorted siltstones, by high-energy beach sands and conglomerates, and by cryptalgal stromatolites. Basinal deposits are represented by laminated claystones and by sandstones and siltstones deposited in fluvial channels and on floodplains.

The mammalian fauna is rich and diverse. Important hominid fossils from the region include the *Homo erectus* skeleton from Nariokotome, ca. 1.6 m.y. old, and the *Australopithecus boisei* skull from Lomekwi, nearly 2.5 m.y. in age.

See also AUSTRALOPITHECUS; EAST TURKANA; NARIOKOTOME; STRATIGRAPHY. [F.H.B.]

Further Readings

Brown, F.H., Harris, J.M., Leakey, R.E., and Walker, A. (1985) Early *Homo erectus* skeleton from west Lake Turkana, Kenya. Nature *316*:788–792.

Harris, J.M., and Brown, F.H. (1985) New hominid locality west of Lake Turkana, Kenya. Nat. Geo. Res. *1*:289–297.

Walker, A., Leakey, R.E., Harris, J.M., and Brown, F.H. (1986) 2.5-Myr *Australopithecus boisei* from west of Lake Turkana, Kenya. Nature *322*:517–522.

WHITE SANDS *see* OMO

WICKER'S FARM *see* FORT TERNAN

WILLANDRA LAKES *see* AUSTRALIA

WILLENDORF *see* PALEOLITHIC IMAGE

WILTON

Later Stone Age industry of southern Africa, named after the Wilton rock shelter west of Howieson's Poort in the Cape Province (South Africa) and characterized by a microblade technology yielding small convex scrapers, backed bladelets, backed points, and segments. Also associated with the industry are ostrich-eggshell beads and fragments of containers, bone awls and arrow linkshafts, pierced marine shells, rock paintings, and, in the later stages, ceramics and iron beads. Faunal remains indicate widespread use of marine and other small-scale resources, as well as effective big-game hunting. The industry is widely distributed in both coastal and interior sites, and comparable microlithic industries with backed segments from central and East Africa have also been referred to this industry. In southern Africa the Wilton industry begins ca. 9000 B.P. and continues to the historic present in some areas, although microblade technology may be present as early as 25,000 B.P. at Rose Cottage Cave. Microlithic industries are widespread at 18,000 B.P. or earlier in eastern central Africa at the sites of Matupi (Zaire), Kalemba (Zambia—Nachikufan industry), Kisese (Tanzania), Lukenya Hill (Kenya), and Uganda (Buvuma Island). During the Holocene, industries similar to the Wilton include the Zambian Wilton, and the Pfupian and Matopan of Zimbabwe.

See also BOW AND ARROW; ECONOMY, PREHISTORIC; HUNTER-GATHERERS; LATER STONE AGE; MESOLITHIC; ROSE COTTAGE; SMITHFIELD; STONE-TOOL MAKING. [A.S.B.]

WISCONSIN *see* GLACIATION; PLEISTOCENE

WOLF'S LAW *see* LAWS

WOODWARD [SIR] ARTHUR SMITH (1864-1944)

British paleontologist. While an undergraduate at Owen's College (now Manchester University) Woodward came under the influence of the geologist William Boyd Dawkins (1837-1929), who encouraged him to apply for a position in the Department of Geology (later Palaeontology) at the British Museum (Natural History) in 1882. During the next few years Woodward spent his days cataloguing the museum's collection of fossil fishes, and his evenings attending classes at the University of London to complete his scientific education. Although he matriculated with honors in 1887, what prompted Woodward's promotion to Assistant Keeper in 1892 was the appearance of the first volumes of his *Catalogue of the Fossil Fishes in the British Museum*, which is considered "not only as a monument of meticulous accuracy, of intense research, but also as the source of many other ichthyological publications." Equally important was his introductory textbook *Outlines of Vertebrate Palaeontology*, which had a great influence in its time on students of paleontology and zoology. By 1900 Woodward was regarded as a world authority on fossil fish. In recognition of this he was made Keeper in 1901, the same year he was elected a Fellow of the Royal Society. From 1912 onward, however, Woodward's attention was diverted from work for which he was better qualified by his involvement in the interpretation of the remains recovered from a gravel pit at Piltdown, Sussex (England), which were later shown to have been an elaborate hoax. From all indications Woodward was not involved in the fabrication of this deception; indeed, on retiring from the museum in 1923, he continued to work at the site in a fruitless effort to gather further evidence. He received his knighthood in 1924.

See also PILTDOWN. [F.S.]

WRIGHT, SEWALL (b. 1889)

American geneticist. After receiving his doctorate at Harvard University in 1915, Wright worked as a geneticist for the U.S. Department of Agriculture (1915-1925) and then at the University of Chicago (1926-1954) and the University of Wisconsin (1955-1960). He is regarded as one of the founders of population genetics. He also developed a mathematical theory of evolution and formulas for evaluating the statistical consequences of various mating systems, noting that natural selection among individuals operates largely on the separate average gene effects. His genetic models, and particularly his "adaptive landscape" notion, are accepted as crucial to subsequent advances in evolutionary biological methodology.

See also EVOLUTION. [F.S.]

WÜRM *see* GLACIATION; PLEISTOCENE

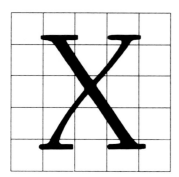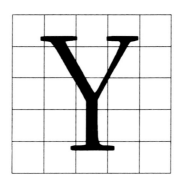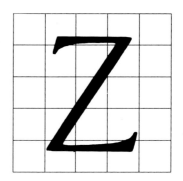

XENOTHRIX *see* PITHECIINAE

XIHOUDOU

Archaeological site in southern Shanxi Province (China) that has yielded artifacts, traces of fire, and a disputably early fauna. Some Chinese workers regard it as the earliest evidence of hominid activity in China. However, the fauna, which supposedly dates to a time equivalent with the Villafranchian in Europe, contains elements that probably have been redeposited and mixed with younger elements. Both fossils and artifacts appear to be rolled and abraded. Thus it is likely that the entire assemblage is "time-transgressive." The artifacts may date to the early middle Pleistocene.

See also ASIA (EASTERN); CHINA. [G.G.P.]

YABROUD *see* JABRUD

YABRUD *see* JABRUD

YABRUDIAN *see* JABRUDIAN

YARMOUTH *see* GLACIATION; PLEISTOCENE

YASSIOREN *see* NEAR EAST; PONGINAE

YAYO

Open-air site in Chad, of early Pleistocene age based on fauna; also known as Koro-Toro. A partial hominid cranium found at Yayo, consisting of the front of the braincase and face, is usually attributed to early *Homo* but was said to possess characteristics of both *Australopithecus* and *Homo*. The Yayo hominid was originally named "*Tchadanthropus uxoris*" by Y. Coppens.

See also AFRICA; HOMO. [R.P.]

YERKES, R. *see* PRIMATE ECOLOGY

YETI

Legendary "abominable snowman" of the Himalayas, roughly equivalent to the "Bigfoot" of North America. One suggestion is that the extinct hominoid *Gigantopithecus* still survives in the Himalayan snows; but apart from the inherent improbability of such scenarios there is no convincing proof either from Asia or North America of the continuing existence of a large hominoid unknown to science.

[I.T.]

YINGKOU *see* JINNIU SHAN

YUANMOU

Stratified exposure in Yunnan Province (China), from the middle Pleistocene, dated to between ca. 0.5 and 0.6 m.y. by paleomagnetic and faunal correlation. The fluviolacustrine beds at Yuanmou have yielded many mammalian fossils, including two hominid upper medial incisors. Artifacts and wood-ash are also known from Yuanmou. On the basis of paleomagnetic and biostratigraphic studies the teeth, belonging to the same individual, were originally thought to date to ca. 1.7 m.y. ago. Reexamination of the Yuanmou paleomagnetic correlations and bio-stratigraphy, however, suggests the much younger age. There is also some question as to whether the Yuanmou incisors were found *in situ*. In any case even the early description of the incisors recognized a strong affinity to Zhoukoudian *Homo erectus* front teeth, which are also "shovel shaped."

In 1987 numerous new isolated teeth were recovered from early Pleistocene and Pliocene horizons low in the Yuanmou sequence.

See also ASIA; CHINA; HOMO ERECTUS; ZHOUKOUDIAN. [G.G.P.]

ZAMBIAN WILTON   *see*   WILTON

ZANYCTERIS   *see*   PICRODONTIDAE

ZELTEN   *see*   AFRICA; VICTORIAPITHECINAE

ZHOUKOUDIAN (CHOU-K'OU-TIEN)

Stratified cave and fissure deposits near Beijing (China), dated from Pliocene to late Pleistocene on paleomagnetic, radiometric, and mainly faunal evidence. Locality 1 at Zhoukoudian is a karst cave site ca. 45 km. southwest of Beijing. Since 1927 work by Chinese and Western researchers has resulted in the recovery of more than 40 *Homo erectus* individuals and roughly 100,000 artifacts from over 40 m. of deposits at the Locality 1 infilling. Artifacts have also been recovered from Localities 3, 4, 13, 15, and the much younger "Upper Cave," while other localities have yielded faunal remains as old as mid-Pliocene.

The sequence at Locality 1 has been divided into 17 layers from top to bottom. Layers 1 to 13 have yielded evidence of hominid activity in the form of artifacts, hominid fossils, and/or ash deposits. All of these layers (except possibly 13) are of normal polarity, and thus the entire hominid-bearing portion of the locality has been assigned to the Brunhes Chron. Several kinds of radiometric evidence, including uranium-series, fission-track, and thermoluminescence dating, indicate that the hominid-bearing Locality 1 sequence can be securely dated between 0.46 and 0.23 m.y. ago. Recently it has been suggested that Locality 1 stratigraphy is composed largely of post-depositional strata that do not relate to the occupational history of the site. Furthermore, it has been

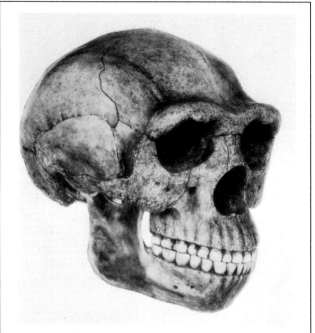

Reconstruction by F. Weidenreich of a hominid cranium from Zhoukoudian.

suggested that the evidence for fire is chemical in origin or too thick in places to be the result of fires maintained by hominids. Carnivores have also been hypothesized to be the main taphonomic agents responsible for the accumulation at Zhoukoudian. These ideas, however, are viewed as speculative and ill-founded by Asian specialists familiar with the locality. In fact a comparison of the stratigraphic sequence and paleoclimatological evidence (palynological, biostratigraphic, and chemical data) indicate that hominids were consistently present at the site during relatively moist and warm periods.

In any event it is clear that the numerous quartz flakes that occur throughout layers 1–13 are hominid artifacts that attest to the continuous or intermittent use of the site. Incised bones are also present at Locality 1, but in spite of suggestions put forward nearly 50 years ago there is little evidence for a bone-tool industry. Similarly, evidence for cannibalism is equivocal at best, and carnivores and rodents undoubtedly played some role in the modification of bone at the site. Burnt hackberry seeds and numerous specimens of large deer may also represent components of the diet of *Homo erectus*, but their presence at Zhoukoudian might be due at least in part to nonhominid agencies.

Another locality at Zhoukoudian, the Upper Cave, has yielded three fossils of *Homo sapiens sapiens*. F. Weidenreich originally perceived three "racial types" in these individuals: Esquimoid, Mongoloid, and Polynesian. Few modern workers support this interpretation, preferring instead to recognize the Upper Cave specimens as indicative of the range of variability in prehistoric northern Chinese populations. Carbon-14 dates obtained for the Upper Cave deposits suggest a maximum age of between 11 and 18 k.y.

Chinese researchers continue to excavate periodically at Zhoukoudian, and a few new specimens of *Homo erectus*, some of which fit on to casts of the prewar specimens, have been recovered as a result of post-1949 excavations. The original specimens disappeared while in the care of American marines captured at the beginning of World War II when the Japanese invaded Beijing. Despite subsequent intensive efforts the whereabouts of these fossils remain a mystery. Fortunately Weidenreich provided detailed descriptions in a series of monographs and made excellent casts prior to the disappearance of the original materials.

See also ASIA (EASTERN); CHINA; HOMO ERECTUS. [G.G.P.]

Further Readings

Binford, L., and Ho, C.K. (1985) Taphonomy at a distance: Zhoukoudian the cave home of Beijing Man? Curr. Anthropol. 26:413–443.

Wu, R., and Dong, X.R. (1985) Homo erectus in China. In R. Wu and J.W. Olsen (eds.): Paleoanthropology and Paleolithic Archaeology in the People's Republic of China. New York: Academic, pp. 79–88.

Wu, R., and Lin, S. (1983) Peking Man. Sci. Amer. 248(3):86–94.

ZINJANTHROPUS *see* AUSTRALOPITHECUS BOISEI; PARANTHROPUS

ZONE *see* BIOCHRONOLOGY

ZOOARCHAEOLOGY *see* DOMESTICATION

ZOOGEOGRAPHY *see* PALEOBIOGEOGRAPHY

ZUTTIYEH

The cave site of Mugharet-el-Zuttiyeh (Israel) was excavated between 1925 and 1926 and produced the first nonmodern fossil hominid recovered in western Asia. The frontal bone and part of the upper face of the Zuttiyeh hominid was derived from the Jabrudian level of the site, which is believed to date from the late middle Pleistocene. The specimen therefore clearly antedates Neanderthals, such as those from Tabūn, Amud, and Kebara. The Zuttiyeh specimen must have had a relatively small cranial capacity, and the supraorbital torus is quite straight and strongly developed laterally. The upper face is flat, in contrast to that of the later Neanderthals, and this has led to debate about the affinities of the specimen. Some workers believe that the Zuttiyeh fossil represents a primitive ancestral Neanderthal, in which midfacial projection had not yet evolved, while others believe that it may be more closely related to the ancestry of the modern people represented at the sites of Qafzeh and Skhūl.

See also ARCHAIC HOMO SAPIENS; ARCHAIC MODERNS; JABRUDIAN NEANDERTHALS. [C.B.S.]